WORLDMARK ENCYCLOPEDIA

of Cultures and Daily Life

WORLDMARK
ENCYCLOPEDIA
of Cultures and Daily Life

Volume 2 – Americas

Timothy L. Gall, Editor

GALE

Detroit • New York • Toronto • London

Worldmark Encyclopedia of Cultures and Daily Life
was produced by Eastword Publications Development, Inc., Cleveland , Ohio

Gale Research Staff:

Allison K. McNeill, *Project Editor*

Andrea K. Henderson, *Contributing Editor*; with assistance from the Cultures & Customs Team

Lawrence W. Baker, *Managing Editor*; Leah Knight, *Acquisitions Editor*

Michelle DiMercurio, *Art Director*; Cynthia Baldwin, *Product Design Manager*

Randy Bassett, *Image Database Supervisor*; Robert Duncan, *Imaging Specialist*; Maria L. Franklin, *Permissions Specialist*

Shanna P. Heilveil, *Production Assistant*; Evi Seoud, *Assistant Production Manager*; Mary Beth Trimper, *Production Director*

Cover Images:

Africa—High school girls, Botswana *(Jason Laure)*; Woman in traditional dress, Eritrea *(Cory Langley)*;
  Men in traditional dress, Kenya *(David Johnson)*

Americas—Group of boys, Bahamas *(Cory Langley)*; Men in kilts, Scottish Americans *(A. McNeill)*; Women dancing,
  Bolivia *(David Johnson)*

Asia—Group of girls, Philippines *(Susan D. Rock)*; Man making shoes, Pakistan *(Cory Langley)*; Women and children,
  Bangladesh *(Cory Langley)*

Europe—Boy with cow, Albania *(Cory Langley)*; Woman on bench, Lithuania *(Cory Langley)*; Cheese porters,
  Netherlands *(Susan D. Rock)*

Library of Congress Cataloging-in-Publication Data

Worldmark Encyclopedia of Cultures and Daily Life.
  p. cm.
Includes bibliographical references and indexes.
Contents: v.1. Africa—v.2. Americas—v.3. Asia and Oceania—v.4. Europe
Summary: Provides information on approximately 500 cultures of the world, covering twenty different areas of daily life including
clothing, food, language, and religion.
ISBN 0-7876-0553-0 (v.1: alk. paper).—ISBN 0-7876-0554-9 (v.2: alk. paper).—ISBN 0-7876-0555-7 (v.3: alk. paper).—ISBN
0-7876-0556-5 (v.4: alk. paper)
  1. Ethnology–Encyclopedias, Juvenile. 2. Manners and customs–Encyclopedias, Juvenile. [1. Ethnology–Encyclopedias.
2. Manners and customs–Encyclopedias.] I. Gale Research. II. Title.
GN333.W67   1997
305.8'003–dc21   97-3278
                                                                                                                                    CIP

∞™ The paper used in this publication meets the minimum requirements of American National Standard for Information
Sciences—Permanence Paper for Printed Library Materials, ANSI Z39.478-1984.

Printed in the United States of America

10 9 8 7 6 5 4 3 2

TABLE OF CONTENTS

Editor: Timothy L. Gall

Senior Editor: Daniel M. Lucas

Associate Editor: Susan Bevan Gall

Copy Editors: Deborah Baron, Janet Fenn, Mary Anne Klasen, Patricia M. Mote, Deborah Ring, Kathy Soltis, Rosalie Wieder

Typesetting and Graphics: Brian Rajewski

Data Input: Janis K. Long, Maggie Lyall, Cheryl Montagna, Tajana G. Roehl, Karen Seyboldt, Kira Silverbird

Proofreaders: Deborah Baron, Janet Fenn

Editorial Assistants: Katie Baron, Jennifer A. Spencer, Daniel K. Updegraft

ADVISORS

CATHY BOND. Librarian, Conestoga Senior High School, Berwyn, Pennsylvania.

MARION CANNON. Librarian, Winter Park High School, Winter Park, Florida.

KELLY JONS. Librarian, Shaker Heights High School, Shaker Heights, Ohio.

JOHN RANAHAN. High School Teacher, International School, Manila, Philippines.

NANCY NIEMAN. Middle School Teacher, Delta Middle School, Muncie, Indiana.

VOLUME INTRODUCTIONS

RHOADS MURPHEY. Emeritus Professor of History, University of Michigan.

JAMES L. NEWMAN. Professor, Department of Geography, Maxwell School of Citizenship and Public Affairs, Syracuse University.

ARNOLD STRICKON. Professor Emeritus, Department of Anthropology, University of Wisconsin.

ROGER WILLIAMS WESCOTT. Emeritus Professor of Anthropology and Linguistics, Drew University.

CONTRIBUTORS AND REVIEWERS

ANDREW J. ABALAHIN. Doctoral candidate, Department of History, Cornell University.

JAMAL ABDULLAH. Doctoral candidate, Department of City and Regional Planning, Cornell University.

SANA ABED-KOTOB. Book Review Editor, Middle East Journal, Middle East Institute.

MAMOUD ABOUD. Charge d'Affaires, a.i., Embassy of the Federal and Islamic Republic of the Comoros.

JUDY ALLEN. Editor, Choctaw Nation of Oklahoma.

HIS EXCELLENCY DENIS G. ANTOINE. Ambassador to the United States, Embassy of Grenada.

LESLEY ANN ASHBAUGH. Instructor, Sociology, Seattle University.

HASHEM ATALLAH. Translator, Editor, Teacher; Fairfax, Virginia.

HECTOR AZEVES. Cultural Attaché, Embassy of Uruguay.

VICTORIA J. BAKER. Associate Professor of Anthropology, Anthropology (Collegium of Comparative Cultures), Eckerd College.

POLINE BALA. Doctoral candidate, Asian Studies, Cornell University.

MARJORIE MANDELSTAM BALZER. Research Professor; Coordinator, Social, Regional, and Ethnic Studies Sociology, and Center for Eurasian, Russian, and East European Studies.

JOSHUA BARKER. Doctoral candidate, Department of Anthropology, Cornell University.

IGOR BARSEGIAN. Department of Sociology, George Washington University.

IRAJ BASHIRI. Professor of Central Asian Studies, Department of Slavic and Central Asian Languages and Literatures, University of Minnesota.

DAN F. BAUER. Department of Anthropology, Lafayette College.

JOYCE BEAR. Historic Preservation Officer, Muscogee Nation of Oklahoma.

SVETLANA BELAIA. Byelorussian-American Cultural Center, Strongsville, Ohio.

HIS EXCELLENCY DR. COURTNEY BLACKMAN. Ambassador to the United States, Embassy of Barbados.

BETTY BLAIR. Executive Editor, Azerbaijan International.

ARVIDS BLODNIEKS. Director, Latvian Institute, American Latvian Association in the USA.

ARASH BORMANSHINOV. University of Maryland, College Park.

HARRIET I. BRADY. Cultural Anthropologist (Pyramid Lake Paiute Tribe), Native Studies Program, Pyramid Lake High School.

MARTIN BROKENLEG. Professor of Sociology, Department of Sociology, Augustana College.

REV. RAYMOND A. BUCKO, S.J. Assistant Professor of Anthropology, LeMoyne College.

JOHN W. BURTON. Department of Anthropology, Connecticut College.

DINEANE BUTTRAM. University of North Carolina-Chapel Hill.

RICARDO CABALLERO. Counselor, Embassy of Paraguay.

CHRISTINA CARPADIS. Researcher/Writer, Cleveland, Ohio.

SALVADOR GARCIA CASTANEDA. Department of Spanish and Portuguese, The Ohio State University.

SUSANA CAVALLO. Graduate Program Director and Professor of Spanish, Department of Modern Languages and Literatures, Loyola University, Chicago.

BRIAN P. CAZA. Doctoral candidate, Political Science, University of Chicago.

VAN CHRISTO. President and Executive Director, Frosina Foundation, Boston.

YURI A. CHUMAKOV. Graduate Student, Department of Sociology, University of Notre Dame.

J. COLARUSSO. Professor of Anthropology, McMaster University.

FRANCESCA COLECCHIA. Modern Language Department, Duquesne University.

DIANNE K. DAEG DE MOTT. Researcher/Writer, Tucson, Arizona.

MICHAEL DE JONGH. Professor, Department of Anthropology, University of South Africa.

GEORGI DERLUGUIAN. Senior Fellow, Ph.D., U. S. Institute of Peace.

CHRISTINE DRAKE. Department of Political Science and Geography, Old Dominion University.

ARTURO DUARTE. Guatemalan Mission to the OAS.

CALEB DUBE. Department of Anthropology, Northwestern University.

BRIAN DU TOIT. Professor, Department of Anthropology, University of Florida.

LEAH ERMARTH. Worldspace Foundation, Washington, DC.

NANCY J. FAIRLEY. Associate Professor of Anthropology, Department of Anthropology/Sociology, Davidson College.

GREGORY A. FINNEGAN, Ph.D. Tozzer Library, Harvard University.

ALLEN J. FRANK, Ph.D.

DAVID P. GAMBLE. Professor Emeritus, Department of Anthropology, San Francisco State University.

FREDERICK GAMST. Professor, Department of Anthropology, University of Massachusetts, Harbor Campus.

PAULA GARB. Associate Director of Global Peace and Conflict Studies and Adjunct Professor of Social Ecology, University of California, Irvine.

HAROLD GASKI. Associate Professor of Sami Literature, School of Languages and Literature, University of Tromsø.

STEPHEN J. GENDZIER.

FLORENCE GERDEL.

ANTHONY P. GLASCOCK. Professor of Anthropology; Department of Anthropology, Psychology, and Sociology; Drexel University.

LUIS GONZALEZ. Researcher/Writer, River Edge, New Jersey.

JENNIFER GRAHAM. Researcher/Writer, Sydney, Australia.

MARIE-CÉCILE GROELSEMA. Doctoral candidate, Comparative Literature, Indiana University.

ROBERT GROELSEMA. MPIA and doctoral candidate, Political Science, Indiana University.

MARIA GROSZ-NGATÉ. Visiting Assistant Professor, Department of Anthropology, Northwestern University.

ELLEN GRUENBAUM. Professor, School of Social Sciences, California State University, Fresno.

N. THOMAS HAKANSSON. University of Kentucky.

ROBERT HALASZ. Researcher/Writer, New York, New York.

MARC HANREZ. Professor, Department of French and Italian, University of Wisconsin-Madison.

ANWAR UL HAQ. Central Asian Studies Department, Indiana University.

LIAM HARTE. Department of Philosophy, Loyola University, Chicago.

FR. VASILE HATEGAN. Author, *Romanian Culture in America*.

BRUCE HEILMAN. Doctoral candidate, Department of Political Science, Indiana University.

JIM HENRY. Researcher/Writer, Cleveland, Ohio.

BARRY HEWLETT. Department of Anthropology, Washington State University.

SUSAN F. HIRSCH. Department of Anthropology, Wesleyan University.

MARIDA HOLLOS. Department of Anthropology, Brown University.

HALYNA HOLUBEC. Researcher/Writer, Cleveland, Ohio.

YVONNE HOOSAVA. Legal Researcher and Cultural Preservation Officer, Hopi Tribal Council.

HUIQIN HUANG, Ph.D. Center for East Asia Studies, University of Montreal.

ASAFA JALATA. Assistant Professor of Sociology and African and African American Studies, Department of Sociology, The University of Tennessee, Knoxville.

STEPHEN F. JONES. Russian Department, Mount Holyoke College.

THOMAS JOVANOVSKI, Ph.D. Lorain County Community College.

A. KEN JULES. Minister Plenipotentiary and Deputy Head of Mission, Embassy of St. Kitts and Nevis.

GENEROSA KAGARUKI-KAKOTI. Economist, Department of Urban and Rural Planning, College of Lands and Architectural Studies, Dar es Salaam, Tanzania.

EZEKIEL KALIPENI. Department of Geography, University of Illinois at Urbana-Champaign.

DON KAVANAUGH. Program Director, Lake of the Woods Ojibwa Cultural Centre.

SUSAN M. KENYON. Associate Professor of Anthropology, Department of History and Anthropology, Butler University.

WELILE KHUZWAYO. Department of Anthropology, University of South Africa.

PHILIP L. KILBRIDE. Professor of Anthropology, Mary Hale Chase Chair in the Social Sciences, Department of Anthropology, Bryn Mawr College.

RICHARD O. KISIARA. Doctoral candidate, Department of Anthropology, Washington University in St. Louis.

KAREN KNOWLES. Permanent Mission of Antigua and Barbuda to the United Nations.

IGOR KRUPNIK. Research Anthropologist, Department of Anthropology, Smithsonian Institution.

LEELO LASS. Secretary, Embassy of Estonia.

ROBERT LAUNAY. Professor, Department of Anthropology, Northwestern University.

CHARLES LEBLANC. Professor and Director, Center for East Asia Studies, University of Montreal.

RONALD LEE. Author, *Goddam Gypsy, An Autobiographical Novel*.

PHILIP E. LEIS. Professor and Chair, Department of Anthropology, Brown University.

MARIA JUKIC LESKUR. Croatian Consulate, Cleveland, Ohio.

RICHARD A. LOBBAN, JR. Professor of Anthropology and African Studies, Department of Anthropology, Rhode Island College.

DERYCK O. LODRICK. Visiting Scholar, Center for South Asian Studies, University of California, Berkeley.

NEIL LURSSEN. Intro Communications Inc.

GREGORIO C. MARTIN. Modern Language Department, Duquesne University.

HOWARD J. MARTIN. Independent scholar.

HEITOR MARTINS. Professor, Department of Spanish and Portuguese, Indiana University.

ADELINE MASQUELIER. Assistant Professor, Department of Anthropology, Tulane University.

DOLINA MILLAR.

EDITH MIRANTE. Project Maje, Portland, Oregon.

ROBERT W. MONTGOMERY, Ph.D. Indiana University.

THOMAS D. MORIN. Associate Professor of Hispanic Studies, Department of Modern and Classical Literatures and Languages, University of Rhode Island.

CHARLES MORRILL. Doctoral candidate, Indiana University.

CAROL A. MORTLAND. Crate's Point, The Dalles, Oregon.

FRANCIS A. MOYER. Director, North Carolina Japan Center, North Carolina State University.

MARIE C. MOYER.

NYAGA MWANIKI. Assistant Professor, Department of Anthropology and Sociology, Western Carolina University.

KENNETH NILSON. Celtic Studies Department, Harvard University.

JANE E. ORMROD. Graduate Student, History, University of Chicago.

JUANITA PAHDOPONY. Carl Perkins Program Director, Comanche Tribe of Oklahoma.

TINO PALOTTA. Syracuse University.

ROHAYATI PASENG.

PATRICIA PITCHON. Researcher/Writer, London, England.

STEPHANIE PLATZ. Program Officer, Program on Peace and International Cooperation, The John D. and Catherine T. MacArthur Foundation.

MIHAELA POIATA. Graduate Student, School of Journalism and Mass Communication, University of North Carolina at Chapel Hill.

LEOPOLDINA PRUT-PREGELJ. Author, *Historical Dictionary of Slovenia.*

J. RACKAUSKAS. Director, Lithuanian Research and Studies Center, Chicago.

J. RAKOVICH. Byelorussian-American Cultural Center, Strongsville, Ohio.

HANTA V. RALAY. Promotions, Inc., Montgomery Village, Maryland.

SUSAN J. RASMUSSEN. Associate Professor, Department of Anthropology, University of Houston.

RONALD REMINICK. Department of Anthropology, Cleveland State University.

BRUCE D. ROBERTS. Assistant Professor of Anthropology, Department of Anthropology and Sociology, University of Southern Mississippi.

LAUREL L. ROSE. Philosophy Department, Carnegie-Mellon University.

ROBERT ROTENBERG. Professor of Anthropology, International Studies Program, DePaul University.

CAROLINE SAHLEY, Ph.D. Researcher/Writer, Cleveland, Ohio.

VERONICA SALLES-REESE. Associate Professor, Department of Spanish and Portuguese, Georgetown University.

MAIRA SARYBAEVA. Kazakh-American Studies Center, University of Kentucky.

DEBRA L. SCHINDLER. Institute of Arctic Studies, Dartmouth College.

KYOKO SELDEN, Ph.D. Researcher/Writer, Ithaca, New York.

ENAYATULLAH SHAHRANI. Central Asian Studies Department, Indiana University.

ROBERT SHANAFELT. Adjunct Lecturer, Department of Anthropology, The Florida State University.

TUULIKKI SINKS. Teaching Specialist for Finnish, Department of German, Scandinavian, and Dutch, University of Minnesota.

JAN SJÅVIK. Associate Professor, Scandinavian Studies, University of Washington.

MAGDA SOBALVARRO. Press and Cultural Affairs Director, Embassy of Nicaragua.

MICHAEL STAINTON. Researcher, Joint Center for Asia Pacific Studies, York University.

RIANA STEYN. Department of Anthropology, University of South Africa.

PAUL STOLLER. Professor, Department of Anthropology, West Chester University.

CRAIG STRASHOFER. Researcher/Writer, Cleveland, Ohio.

SANDRA B. STRAUBHAAR. Assistant Professor, Nordic Studies, Department of Germanic and Slavic Languages, Brigham Young University.

VUM SON SUANTAK. Author, *Zo History.*

MURAT TAISHIBAEV. Kazakh-American Studies Center, University of Kentucky.

CHRISTOPHER C. TAYLOR. Associate Professor, Anthropology Department, University of Alabama, Birmingham.

EDDIE TSO. Office of Language and Culture, Navajo Division of Education.

DAVID TYSON. Foreign Broadcast Information Service, Washington, D.C.

NICOLAAS G. W. UNLANDT. Assistant Professor of French, Department of French and Italian, Brigham Young University.

GORDON URQUHART. Professor, Department of Economics and Business, Cornell College.

CHRISTOPHER J. VAN VUUREN. Professor, Department of Anthropology, University of South Africa.

DALIA VENTURA-ALCALAY. Journalist, London, England.

CATHERINE VEREECKE. Assistant Director, Center for African Studies, University of Florida.

GREGORY T. WALKER. Associate Director, Office of International Affairs, Duquesne University.

GERHARD WEISS. Department of German, Scandinavian, and Dutch, University of Minnesota.

PATSY WEST. Director, The Seminole/Miccosukee Photographic Archive.

WALTER WHIPPLE. Associate Professor of Polish, Germanic and Slavic Languages, Brigham Young University.

ROSALIE WIEDER. Researcher/Writer, Cleveland, Ohio.

JEFFREY WILLIAMS. Professor, Department of Anthropology, Cleveland State University.

GUANG-HONG YU. Associate Research Fellow, Institute of Ethnology, Academia Sinica.

RUSSELL ZANCA. Department of Anthropology, College of Liberal Arts and Sciences, University of Illinois at Urbana-Champaign.

COUNTRY INDEX

This index lists the culture groups profiled in the four volumes of this encyclopedia by the countries in which they reside. Culture groups are followed by the continental volume (in *italics*) in which each appears, along with the volume number and the first page of the article.

PREFACE

The *Worldmark Encyclopedia of Cultures and Daily Life* contains articles exploring the ways of life of over 500 culture groups worldwide. Arranged in four volumes by geographic regions—*Africa, Americas, Asia & Oceania,* and *Europe*—the volumes of this encyclopedia parallel the organization of its sister set, the *Worldmark Encyclopedia of the Nations.* Whereas the primary purpose of *Nations* is to provide information on the world's nation states, this encyclopedia focuses on the traditions, living conditions, and personalities of many of the world's culture groups. Entries emphasize how people live today, rather than how they lived in the past.

Defining groups for inclusion was not an easy task. Cultural identity can be shaped by such factors as geography, nationality, ethnicity, race, language, and religion. Many people, in fact, legitimately belong in two or more classifications, each as valid as the other. For example, the citizens of the United States all share traits that make them distinctly American. However, few would deny the need for separate articles on Native Americans or African Americans. Even the category Native American denies the individuality of separate tribes like the Navajo and Paiute. Consequently, this encyclopedia contains an article on the Americans as well as separate articles on the Native Americans and the Navajo. Closely related articles such as these are cross-referenced to each other to help provide a more complete picture of the group being profiled. Included in this encyclopedia are articles on groups as large as the Han of China, with over one billion members, and as small as the Jews of Cochin, with only a few dozen members. Unfortunately, although the vast majority of the world's peoples are represented in this encyclopedia, time and space constraints prevented many important groups from being included in this first edition. The editors look forward to including many more culture groups in future editions of this work.

Over 160 contributors and reviewers participated in the creation of this encyclopedia. Drawn from universities, consulates, and the press, their in-depth knowledge and first hand experience of the profiled groups added significantly to the content of the articles. A complete listing of the contributors and reviewers together with their affiliations appears in the front of each volume.

ORGANIZATION

Each volume begins with an introduction that traces the cultural developments of the region from prehistoric times to the present. Following the introduction are articles devoted to the peoples of the region. Within each volume the articles are arranged alphabetically. A comprehensive table cross referencing the articles by country follows the table of contents to each volume.

The individual articles are of two types. The vast majority follow a standard 20-heading outline explained in more detail below. This structure allows for easy comparison of the articles and enhances the accessibility of the information. A smaller number do not follow the 20-heading format, but rather present simply an overview of the group. This structure is used when the primary purpose of an article is to supplement a fully rubriced article appearing elsewhere in the set.

Whenever appropriate, articles begin with the **pronunciation** of the group's name, a listing of **alternate names** by which the group is known, the group's **location** in the world, its **population**, the **languages** spoken, the **religions** practiced, and a listing of **related articles** in the four volumes of this encyclopedia. Most articles are illustrated with a map showing the primary location of the group and photographs of the people being profiled. The twenty standard headings by which most articles are organized are presented below.

INTRODUCTION: A description of the group's historical origins provides a useful background for understanding its contemporary affairs. Information relating to migration helps explain how the group arrived at its present location. Political conditions and governmental structure(s) that typically affect members of the profiled ethnic group are also discussed.

LOCATION AND HOMELAND: The population size of the group is listed. This information may include official census data from various countries and/or estimates. Information on the size of a group's population located outside the traditional homeland may also be included, especially for certain groups with large diaspora populations. A description of the homeland includes information on location, topography, and climate.

LANGUAGE: Each article lists the name(s) of the primary language(s) spoken by members. Descriptions of linguistic origins, grammar, and similarities to other languages may also be included. Examples of common words, phrases, and proverbs are listed for many of the profiled groups, and some include examples of common personal names and forms of address.

FOLKLORE: Common themes, settings, and characters in the profiled group's traditional oral and/or literary mythology are highlighted. Many entries include a short excerpt or synopsis of one of the group's most noteworthy myths, fables, or legends. Some entries describe the accomplishments of famous heroes and heroines or other prominent historical figures.

RELIGION: The origins of traditional religious beliefs are profiled. Contemporary religious beliefs, customs, and practices are also discussed. Some groups may be closely associated with one particular faith (especially if religious and ethnic identification are interlinked), while others may have members of diverse faiths.

MAJOR HOLIDAYS: Celebrations and commemorations typically recognized by the group's members are described. These holidays commonly fall into two categories: secular and religious. Secular holidays often include an independence day and/or other days of observance recognizing important dates in history that affected the group as a whole. Religious holidays are typically the same as those honored by other peoples of the same faith. Some secular and religious holidays are linked to the lunar cycle or to the change of seasons. Some articles describe unique customs practiced by members of the group on certain holidays.

RITES OF PASSAGE: Formal and informal episodic events that mark an individual's procession through the stages of life are profiled. These events typically involve rituals, ceremonies, observances, and procedures associated with birth, childhood, the coming of age, adulthood, and death.

INTERPERSONAL RELATIONS: Information on greetings, body language, gestures, visiting customs, and dating practices is included. The extent of formality to which members of a certain ethnic group treat others is also addressed, as some groups may adhere to customs governing interpersonal relationships more/less strictly than others.

LIVING CONDITIONS: General health conditions typical of the group's members are cited. Such information includes life expectancy, the prevalence of various diseases, and access to medical care. Information on urbanization, housing, and access to utilities is also included. Transportation methods typically utilized by the group's members are also discussed.

FAMILY LIFE: The size and composition of the family unit is profiled. Gender roles common to the group are also discussed, including the division of rights and responsibilities relegated to male and female group members. The roles that children, adults, and the elderly have within the group as a whole may also be addressed.

CLOTHING: Many entries include descriptive information (size, shape, color, fabric, etc.) regarding traditional clothing (or a national costume), and indicate the frequency of its use in contemporary life. A description of clothing typically worn in the present is also provided, especially if traditional clothing is no longer the usual form of dress. Distinctions between formal, informal, and work clothes are made in many articles, along with clothing differences between men, women, and children.

FOOD: Descriptions of items commonly consumed by members of the group are listed. The frequency and occasion for meals is also described, as are any unique customs regarding eating and drinking, special utensils and furniture, and the role of food and beverages in ritual ceremonies. Many entries include a sample recipe for a favorite dish.

EDUCATION: The structure of formal education in the country or countries of residence is discussed, including information on primary, secondary, and higher education. For some groups, the role of informal education is also highlighted. Some articles may include information regarding the relevance and importance of education among the group as a whole, along with parental expectations for children.

CULTURAL HERITAGE: Since many groups express their sense of identity through art, music, literature, and dance, a description of prominent styles is included. Some articles also cite the contributions of famous individual artists, writers, and musicians.

WORK: The type of labor that typically engages members of the profiled group is discussed. For some groups, the formal wage economy is the primary source of earnings, but for other groups, informal agriculture or trade may be the usual way to earn a living. Working conditions are also highlighted.

SPORTS: Popular sports that children and adults play are listed, as are typical spectator sports. Some articles include a description and/or rules to a unique type of sport or game.

ENTERTAINMENT AND RECREATION: Listed activities that people enjoy in their spare time may include carrying out either structured pastimes (such as public musical and dance performances) or informal get-togethers (such as meeting for conversation). The role of popular culture, movies, theater, and television in everyday life is also discussed.

FOLK ARTS, CRAFTS, AND HOBBIES: Entries describe arts and crafts commonly fabricated according to traditional methods, materials, and style. Such objects may often have a functional utility for everyday tasks.

SOCIAL PROBLEMS: Internal and external issues that confront members of the profiled group are described. Such concerns often deal with fundamental problems like war, famine, disease, and poverty. A lack of human rights, civil rights, and political freedom may also adversely affect a group as a whole. Other problems may include crime, unemployment, substance abuse, and domestic violence.

BIBLIOGRAPHY: References cited include works used to compile the article, as well as benchmark publications often recognized as authoritative by scholars. Citations for materials published in foreign languages are frequently listed when there are few existing sources available in English.

A glossary of terms and a comprehensive index appears at the end of each volume.

ACKNOWLEDGMENTS

The editors express appreciation to the members of the Gale Research staff who were involved in a number of ways at various stages of development of the *Worldmark Encyclopedia of Cultures and Daily Life:* Christine Nasso, Barbara Beach, and Leah Knight, who helped the initial concept of the work take form; and Larry Baker and Allison McNeill, who supported the editorial development of the profiles. Allison McNeill and Andrea Kovacs Henderson selected the photo illustrations. Marybeth Trimper, Evi Seoud, and Shanna Heilveil oversaw the printing and binding process.

In addition, the editors acknowledge with warm gratitude the contributions of the staff of Eastword Publications—Debby Baron, Dan Lucas, Brian Rajewski, Kira Silverbird, Maggie Lyall, Karen Seyboldt, Tajana G. Roehl, Janet Fenn, and Cheryl Montagna—who managed interactions with contributors; edited, organized, reviewed, and indexed the articles; and turned the manuscripts into the illustrated typeset pages of these four volumes.

SUGGESTIONS ARE WELCOME: The first edition of a work the size and scope of *Worldmark Encyclopedia of Cultures and Daily Life* is a daunting undertaking; we appreciate any suggestions that will enhance future editions. Please send comments to:

Editor
*Worldmark Encyclopedia
of Cultures and Daily Life*
Gale Research
835 Penobscot Bldg.
Detroit, MI 48226
(313) 961-2242

INTRODUCTION

by
Arnold Strickon

THE STUDY OF THE ANCIENT

The ancestors of modern humans evolved in Africa. They migrated into the Eurasian land mass as pre-modern species. The last of the continental land masses occupied by human beings were those of the Western Hemisphere. The people who first occupied the land mass of the New World were full members of our species, modern Homo sapiens. The question of the antiquity of human beings in the New World is still being hotly debated among interested scientists. As this is being written, scientists postulate that it was between 12,000 and 15,000 years ago that humans first set foot in the New World. This is according to the most widely accepted and presently available evidence. Scientists call these earliest settlers of the New World "Paleoindians." They are the ancestral population of the Americas.

The terms *Indian* and *Native American* are widely used and misused. In this "Introduction," the terms *Indian* and *American Indian, Inuit, Eskimo, Aleut* and *Hawaiian* are used to refer to people of those specific ethnic backgrounds. The term *Native American* is used to refer in general to all the descendants of the original settlers of the New World, whatever their specific ethnic background.

There was, of course, no one to record the arrival of the first humans. Our knowledge of it derives from the efforts of scientists from a wide range of fields. Archeologists study ancient tools and other artifacts made or modified by human effort and left behind by people who have generally left no written historical record. Paleoanthropologists study ancient human remains and paleontologists study ancient animal remains of all kinds. Anthropologists study the culture, the way of life, arts, and technology of peoples—living or historical. Linguists study the languages of a people. In addition, botanists, geologists, zoologists, and even chemists and physicists contribute their expertise to efforts to understand the first Americans, focusing their special knowledge and techniques upon the physical remains left behind by the Paleoindians in ancient campsites scattered from Alaska to Chile.

Living populations contribute data to this effort as well. Linguists compare the similarities and differences among Native American languages and make inferences about the history of these languages and the people who spoke them. Geneticists compare marker genes and genetic frequencies among geographically far-flung populations and make inferences about historical connections among them.

Scientists from these diverse fields collect and analyze clues to help us learn when and where the first pioneers entered the New World and settled. The task is made more difficult because the first settlers were foragers—people who subsisted by hunting, fishing, and gathering wild, edible plants. Foragers live in small, widely scattered groups that are almost always on the move. Thus, what they leave behind is spread over a wide geographic area. Physical belongings are not likely to be preserved from generation to generation, leaving little for future archeologists to study.

Most European settlers of the New World believed until well into the nineteenth century that God had created the world only a few thousand years earlier. By the mid- to late-nineteenth century, however, thinking about the age of the earth, and of the creatures who lived upon it was undergoing radical change. The work of Sir Charles Lyell (1798–1875), the founder of modern geology, and Charles Darwin (1809–82), creator of the theory of evolution, expanded the time stage on which history played from thousands to millions of years.

By the end of the nineteenth century most scientists agreed that modern humans—in the Old World and the New—had evolved from forms different from the historic human species, Homo sapiens. Investigators found pre-sapiens (that is non-modern and extinct) human remains in most parts of the Old World, but none in the New. This led scientists to postulate that the New World was occupied relatively recently, after the appearance of modern forms of humanity some 40,000 years ago. Darwin had pointed out that the anthropoid (man-like) or great apes, such as gorillas and chimpanzees, had no representatives living in the New World. In fact, no fossil remains of great apes have ever been found anywhere in the New World.

THE PLEISTOCENE: THE GLACIAL EPOCH

The emergence of Homo sapiens occurred 1.6 million years ago during the Pleistocene epoch when gigantic glaciers covered much of the planet. In the northern hemisphere these glaciers isolated habitable portions of the New World from regions of the Old World inhabited by humans. This seemed to support the idea that the earliest modern human populations could not have occupied the New World earlier than 8,000 year ago, when the last glaciers "withdrew." From the end of the nineteenth century until the 1920s and early 1930s, this was the accepted time period for the human settlement of the New World. Both professional and amateur archeologists claimed to have discovered sites containing ancient remains dating to an earlier period; in these cases, the evidence was dubious, the excavation and record-keeping badly done, and therefore, the case not proved.

FIRST EVIDENCE OF THE PALEOINDIANS

In 1926, while excavating a site in central New Mexico near the town of Folsom, scientists uncovered the bones of a giant buffalo that had been extinct since the Pleistocene. Imbedded in one of its ribs was a finely chipped stone projectile point, about five centimeters (two inches) long, with a central channel running most of its length. There could be no doubt that it was made by the hands of a human being, and that it was stuck into the living bone of an animal that had been extinct for thousands of years. Archeologists discovered other sites containing "Folsom Points" elsewhere in the southwestern and western US, and in the western provinces of Canada in the years that followed. Archeologists generally believe that these artifacts are 8,000 to 9,000 years old.

Shortly after the discovery of the Folsom artifacts, scientists unearthed another, even earlier and more significant, projectile point at Clovis in eastern New Mexico. The initial discovery was followed by the excavation of many more Clovis sites, where more characteristic artifacts and projectile points with the distinctive Clovis design were found. Since then, excavations containing Clovis-related artifacts have been made all over North America, including some as far south as central Mexico. In addition, scientists working in South America have found assemblages of artifacts similar to those found at Clovis. Clovis artifacts have been discovered in association with the remains of animals such as mammoths and relatives of the llama and horse—all of which had long been extinct in the New World by the time the Europeans arrived. (In fact, one noted archeologist has suggested that it may have been the hunting by the Paleoindians that drove many of the large Pleistocene mammals to extinction.) The association of these assemblages with long-extinct game animals is a powerful indication that modern human beings were in the New World 12,000 to 14,000 years ago. There have even been claims for earlier dates for New World sites: students of the Monte Verde excavations in southern Chile have assigned dates as early as 30,000 years ago to that location, and a few archeologists have made similar claims for sites in the Amazon River basin in Brazil. As of the late 1990s, findings from the sites alleged to predate Clovis are being subjected to further study before gaining widespread acceptance.

When Did Humans Come to the Americas?

For a period of 100,000 years or more, gigantic continental glaciers alternately covered and uncovered many parts of what are now Earth's temperate zones. During periods of extreme cold, snow and ice in these areas failed to melt, causing the glaciers to expand in thickness and extent. By locking up huge amounts of water as ice, these periods of glacial expansion also led to a drop in sea levels all over the world. Within the glacial period, referred to as the Pleistocene epoch by geologists, there were times when rising temperatures caused melting, reducing the size of the glaciers. When this occurred, sea levels rose once again.

This rising and falling of the sea was crucial for the population of the New World by people from the Old World. An arm of the sea (now known as the Bering Straits) separated the New World from adjacent parts of Asia. For foraging people, especially for those who lived 100,000 years ago, such a stretch of open ocean was indeed an unbreachable obstacle. About 50,000 years ago there was a period of glacial expansion and growth that caused a fall in sea level of some 200 feet. This was sufficient to open a land bridge between Siberia and North America. There is no evidence that Homo sapiens, even if such a population existed in northern Asia at this time, found their way across the land bridge to the New World. Some 45,000 years ago, the weather warmed, the glaciers retreated, and the sea level rose once again. This warm period created a barrier between the Old World and the New World that was to last for 20,000 years. The last glaciation took place between 25,000 and 15,000 years BP (before the present). It led to a fall in sea

level, lowering the surface of the Bering Straits about 10 meters (300 feet) and once again creating an isthmus (land bridge) between Asia and North America. This time, there was human settlement in northeast Asia. It is around this time—between 12,000 and 14,000 years ago—that the earliest Paleoindians appear in the archaeological record. These first settlers did not necessarily realize they were going to a New World—they were following the large game that they hunted. As their hunting grounds slowly shifted eastward across the land bridge, the occupation of the Americas commenced.

Who Were They?

It is highly probable that the process of migration across the isthmus between the continents lasted for a long time, perhaps as long as the land bridge remained passable. It is unlikely, however, that all the migrants came from any single linguistic, cultural, or social group. In fact, there is every reason to suppose the opposite. Some linguists have suggested that America was originally peopled by three distinctive linguistic populations that came in three waves within a few thousand years of each other. Recent work in historical linguistics classifies all languages spoken by Native Americans (not counting the Hawaiians) as belonging to one of three ancestral language families: Amerind, Eskimo-Aleut, or Na-Dene. Some linguists believe that Amerind speakers were the first group to come to what are now the Americas. Most languages spoken by American Indians appear to be descended from that language. The second of the ancestral languages, Eskimo-Aleut, is still spoken by the groups in the Arctic and sub-Arctic regions of Alaska and Canada. A number of American Indian languages originated from the third of the ancestral languages, Na-Dene. The most common of these are the Athabaskan tongues, which include languages spoken in the northwestern quarter of North America and Navajo and Apache spoken in the American Southwest. This linguistic view of the first settlers in the New World is supported by comparative genetics.

In the beginning, the Paleoindian population was small. A modest population increase of 1 percent per year over a period of 12,000 to 15,000 years resulted in a very large population. Conservative estimates place the New World population in 1492 at about 12 million people, while other estimates are as much as three or four times greater. As their numbers grew and became more geographically dispersed, the simple hunters and gatherers that had begun the human occupation of the New World developed a wide variety of Native American cultures. We cannot here trace the archaeological record to see how and by what processes these simple societies were transformed. We must, rather, be content to describe this complexity in the broadest and most general of terms.

CLASSIFICATION OF NATIVE AMERICANS

Why and how are cultures classified? Every culture, every society—like every person—is unique. Yet for some purposes it is useful to classify people into larger abstract entities called categories or classifications, such as spouse, parent, or member of a political party. In considering the larger category, much of the uniqueness of each individual is overlooked. So it is with cultures. Every culture, in all its detail, is unique, but it may be useful to classify cultures along lines of resemblance. One way of doing this is along lines of similarities of artifacts, art styles, and other regularities that can be observed. Cultures that are geographically adjacent to each other are classified as "culture areas." Similarities of economy and major political institutions are classified as "culture types." In either case these terms permit us to stress the similarities among otherwise distinctive societies and cultures.

Classification by Culture Area

A culture area is a region where people of differing social and political groups practice roughly similar life styles, art forms, technologies, subsistence practices, and philosophical and religious beliefs. In the New World, culture areas generally coincided with natural ecological regions. The various people in these societies need not be of a similar race or even speak the same language. They do not constitute a single political entity, and may fight quite bloody wars among themselves. Thus, Europe may be viewed as a culture area, and North Africa as another.

The culture area does not exist in nature, but rather in the mind of the historian or anthropologist. Not all people who live within the geographical confines of a culture area necessarily follow the way of life typical of that area. A culture area that includes village-dwelling farmers may also contain hunters and gatherers, or fishers. It may also contain people marked by philosophical and religious beliefs, artistic traditions, quite different from those of the larger number people who typify the culture area.

Museum curators originally developed the idea of the culture area in the first decades of the twentieth century as a way of organizing museum exhibits. It has since grown to represent a useful tool for describing the way of life or culture of large areas of the world.

Classification by Culture Type

Another way to classify cultures and societies is by *social* or *culture type*, where the emphasis is placed on social, political, demographic, or economic characteristics, or some combination of these. A culture type may cut across a culture area classification. Thus one might speak of "industrial states" as a culture type that would include societies in different "culture areas" such as Europe and Asia. The culture type is an idea or construct that serves the analyst of the group—not necessarily the people who comprise it. As with the culture area, the purpose of the culture type is to permit us to generalize and speak of broad similarities among societies.

NATIVE AMERICA AT THE CONQUEST

The European conquest of the native peoples of the New World was not one event, but a process that continued for hundreds of years, and continues today.

In Native America, culture areas and culture types intersect in an interesting way. The cultures of pre-conquest North and South America are quite distinctive. Art styles, beliefs, details of village and extra-village political arrangements, and family and kinship institutions tend to differ; there were also differences in the subsistence crops grown and species of game animals hunted. In spite of these differences, anthropologists identified several social and political culture types that were the same on both continents, and observed an approximate parallel between culture areas and culture types. Major culture categories are described in the sections that follow.

The Southeast and the Circum-Caribbean

The first major Spanish settlement in the New World was on the island of Hispaniola in the Caribbean Sea, where the modern nations of Haiti and the Dominican Republic are located. Relatively large and complex societies based upon productive agriculture existed on many of the neighboring Caribbean islands, in parts of Central America, in northern South America, and in what is now the southeastern United States. In its northern reaches the subsistence base of these societies rested upon corn (maize); in the southern continent and the Caribbean islands, upon corn or manioc. The people of both areas lived in rather large villages; populations of over 1000 were not unusual. Shared political and religious institutions often linked a number of villages into larger political units called confederacies or chiefdoms. These societies had part-time chiefs and priesthoods with restricted powers over the members of the confederacy except in times of crisis. It was people of this type who had created the great palisaded villages and temple mounds in Cohokia in southern Illinois, the largest archeological remains in the United States. Succumbing more to Spanish diseases than to Spanish military might, these societies in the Caribbean were rapidly destroyed and their people almost exterminated. In parts of Central America and on the South American mainland some survived by withdrawing inland, especially to the rainforests of the Amazon River basin. Here, reduced in numbers and simplified in culture content and political organization, some survived.

In North America the chiefdoms or confederacies of the southeast fared somewhat better, with many surviving in place until early in the nineteenth century. Ultimately, however, Americans, hungry for more land, forced the southeastern Indians to relocate. The United States government resettled Indians on reservations far from their ancestral homes. In the Florida Everglades—territory particularly well-suited for defense and guerrilla warfare—the Seminole managed to survive for a time without suffering military defeat, but the United States ultimately subdued even them.

The cultures of the Southeastern United States—the Choctow and Seminole for example—are presented in detail in this volume. The Cuna Indians, also described in this volume, lived in eastern Panama and are the descendants of this type of Indian society. Their current society is far less complex than was that of their ancestors before the coming of the Europeans.

The State Societies of Meso-America and the Andes

The Spanish came into contact with the people of the Caribbean islands first. Soon, however, tales of immense wealth on the mainland enthralled and hypnotized them, drawing them to explore there. What they found—the great state societies of Meso-America (the region from central Mexico south through Guatemala and Belize) and the Andes—was even more spectacular than the tales had led them to believe.

The aboriginal state societies of Meso-America and the Andes were the central jewels of Spain's New World empire for 300 years, although there were differences between the two regions. To many observers, the art and monumental architecture of Meso-America appear more interesting and sophisticated than that of the Andean civilizations. However, the Inca empire in the Andes practiced bureaucratic controls and central administrative complexity that were far more advanced, in the eyes of modern observers, than the organizational practices of their counterparts in Meso-America.

When the Spanish found these state societies, they already had long histories of expansion. Again, there were differences in the way the societies implemented their expansion practices. The Aztecs of the Valley of Mexico expressed domination of their neighbors by demanding tribute payments from those they defeated rather than by direct political incorporation or military occupation. The Inca empire of South America, on the other hand, had expanded by military force by defeating neighboring states and then incorporating them. Once that was accomplished, the defeated aristocracy was incorporated into the Inca state. The Inca sometimes resettled the population of the defeated group in a foreign region, where the defeated people would be surrounded by a population loyal to (or sufficiently cowed by) the victorious Inca. Then, the territory evacuated by the defeated people would be repopulated by a people loyal to the Inca state.

The state societies of the New World were characterized by social stratification. There was an upper class of royalty and aristocrats, and a middle class of artisans, artists, bureaucrats, architects, and engineers. The society rested upon the labors of the largest part of the population, the agricultural peasants. The peasants produced the crops and other products that provided the economic foundation of the empire.

The state conscripted peasants to serve in the army and on a wide variety of construction projects desired by the rulers. The projects included roads, walled cities, temples, storehouses, and huge irrigation systems. The peasants accomplished great feats of engineering without metal tools and without the use of the wheel. In the Andes, there was no knowledge of written language, although in Meso-America, however, there was. The Indians of Meso-American also developed a calendar system that was more accurate than the one used by the Europeans who conquered them.

Initially, gold and silver attracted the Spanish to the New World states. The real wealth of these states for the Spanish, however, lay in their massive population of peasant farmers, as it had been for the Incas and Aztecs before them. The peasants lived in agricultural villages where they farmed to provide food for themselves and the rest of society. The peasants were assessed part of the food they grew as taxes to support the state and priesthood. In the Inca empire, peasants provided two-thirds of the goods they produced for this purpose.

The Inca state designed, built, and maintained the irrigation system that most of the peasants required to grow their crops. The government also maintained roads, storehouses, and reserve food supplies in case of emergencies or local crop failure. The priesthood dealt with the complex spiritual world of the Inca people. The Inca state was a vast, complex, and centralized political system. Initiative flowed from the top down, and obedience and wealth flowed from the bottom up.

The states of central and southern Mexico lacked the centralized character of their Andean counterparts, however, but they too, showed the characteristics of a complex state—hierarchy of social class and well-developed religious, trade, and military institutions.

When the Spanish conquered the New World states, they intertwined their own institutions with those of the pre-conquest state, thus asserting control over the agricultural peasants. Contact with the Spanish came at a high cost for Indian societies. Millions died from exposure to previously unknown European diseases ranging from the common cold to smallpox. These plagues disrupted families and destroyed age-old patterns of community life. Despite massive drops in population from disease, villages still had to send workers to labor in the mines, construction projects, and plantations of the Spanish.

The Spanish justified their conquest of the New World by citing the obligation to bring Christianity to the Indians. As part of this effort, the Spanish destroyed every symbol and structure of the Indian religions. If the symbols were made of precious metals that could be melted down and shipped as gold or silver ingots to Spain, so much the better. The Spanish attempted to convert massive numbers of Indians to Christianity in great ceremonies carried out in Spanish and Latin. For those Indians forced to participate, such a "conversion" could have had scant meaning. Over time, the Indians did become Catholic, but they did not completely forget their old religious beliefs. Many of the old pagan beliefs were transformed and incorporated into the folk Catholicism that the Indians still practice in many parts of modern Meso-America and the Andes.

There was resistance and rebellion by some Indians against the Spanish, but none was successful in the long run. However, the culture and languages of the ordinary people of the New World states did not completely disappear, as demonstrated by the articles in this volume on the Guatemalans, Mayan, Peruvians, Ecuadorians, Bolivians, Quechua, and Aymara.

The pre-conquest populations had been so large that, in spite of the high mortality following conquest, enough people remained to provide the foundation for the human population of these colonies. In the modern homelands of the pre-Columbian states, the majority of the population are descendants of *both* Indian *and* Spanish ancestors.

It is not only genetically that the Indians left their mark. Millions of people of Mexico and Guatemala speak Nahuatl, the language of the Aztecs, or various dialects of Maya. The linguistic situation is similar in the Andean countries, where millions speak Quechua and Aymara. In Mexico, about ten percent of the people do not speak Spanish as their primary language; in Ecuador and Peru, that figure rises to twenty-five percent; and in Bolivia, those who do not speak Spanish as their household language rises to fifty percent. In all of these cases the vast majority of are speakers of Quechua, Aymara, Nahuatl, or Maya.

Village Farmers

The people known as village farmers largely inhabited the forested land of the hemisphere, including the northeast, southwest, and the Amazon River Basin. In what is now the United States, this included the forested lands east of the Mississippi River, where the people were primarily growers of corn, beans, and squash—which they planted together and called "the three sisters." Their diet was supplemented with animal proteins from hunting and fishing.

European Americans subjugated most of these village farmers east of the Mississippi River by the early nineteenth century. They displaced these people from their home territories and resettled them on reservations, often in the Indian Territory (present-day Oklahoma and parts of Kansas and Nebraska). The Indian Territory was far—and ecologically different—from their original homelands. Here their traditional ways of life were put under immense pressure. The US government and private groups subjected the Indians to growing pressure to use European farming methods and to surrender their traditional family institutions. Missionaries sought for them to surrender traditional religious beliefs. The government took their children away to educate them in boarding schools that attempted, above all else, to strip the children of their cultural heritage.

The conquerors incorporated whole communities and states into their empires in Mexico and the Andes. Among village farmers the possibility existed for escape. People of the village farmer type had fewer material goods to slow them down or hold them back, and there were other areas—unsettled or less densely settled—to which they could escape. However, escape only delayed for a short time—a few generations at best—some kind of incorporation into the conquering empires or the nations that replaced them.

In South America, village farmers were found primarily in the basins of the Amazon and Orinoco Rivers, where they grew corn or manioc as their chief subsistence crop. Manioc or cassava is a plant whose large tuber—sometimes weighing as much as 20 kilograms (40 pounds)—resembles a massive yam. The Indians (and present-day Brazilians) use the tuber to produce flour and starch for cooking. Manioc remains a major food source in Brazil and Latin America. Manioc comes in two varieties, sweet and bitter. The bitter variety is more widely used and contains large amounts of prussic acid, a poison. The grower must remove the poison through a complex processing procedure involving grating and pressing before the manioc can be safely consumed.

Kinship, age, and gender provided the hierarchy that ordered daily life among village farmers. All aspects of life—household structure, economics and trade, religious life and rituals, warfare and defense, and intergroup relations—were largely organized by these same three characteristics. Work tasks were assigned on the basis of age and sex and not always in the ways we would expect today. Women, for example, did most of the farming. Each household produced most of its needs, but people depended upon their kinsmen-neighbors to help them in times of crisis. Thus, everyone is society contributed according to their place in the hierarchy. There were no professional priests, armies, artisans or artists, traders, or, for that matter, people who did nothing but farm or hunt.

There were no social classes among the village farmers. All in the community lived at essentially the same economic level. If economic conditions improved, they improved for all; conversely, if conditions worsened, they worsened for all. However, some people had more influence than others. Some were better farmers, weavers, hunters, or warriors than others. The powers of leaders, however, were governed by the constraints of age, gender, and kinship. No one member can force another to do something. For example, a man may have chosen not to join in an attack against another community, and his relatives and neighbors could not physically coerce or punish him for so choosing. However, such a decision could not be made lightly and was not without repercussions. The request would have come from the members of his community, all of whom were kinsmen. Every member of the community knew that one day, he or she would need help from those same kinsmen. Thus, it was difficult to refuse to give assistance when called upon.

Even the residential arrangements differ from what is typical in modern Western cultures. Groups of people—often a group of brothers and their wives and children or a group of sisters and their husbands and children—resided together in a single large structure. (A couple never lived alone with their children in a separate home.) Within the extended family structure, each couple and their children had their own sleeping places and campfire, but all were within plain sight and hearing of each other. Home was not a place of privacy.

In many groups in the Amazon River basin—Yanomamo, Xavante, and Tenetehara, among others—men did not live in the same residence as their wives and children. Instead, they resided with adult males and older boys of the community in a Men's House. Women and children lived in group dwellings of their own. A man, his wife (or wives), and children still constituted a family, which represented a significant social and economic unit.

As the conquerors discovered new groups during their explorations, they incorporated whole communities and states into their empires. For the people of the Amazon and Orinoco basins, this process continued into the twentieth century. Even as of the late 1990s, new, previously unknown or barely known, groups of Indians are discovered in Brazil and Venezuela. However, the rate of discovery of new groups is declining, as fewer and fewer of them retain their independence. There are fewer deep forests to which they might escape. When these Indians experience first exposure to European viruses, it was just as deadly in the late 1990s as it was in 1496. A number of Indian groups are attempting to organize themselves into alliances for political opposition to European expansion into the little remaining territory.

Village Farmers and Pastoralists of the American Southwest
In many ways, the cultural conditions for the people of the American Southwest are different. The first dimension of this difference is environmental. The Northeast and Southeast culture areas are found in humid, temperate forests. The Southwestern culture area is the high, arid deserts of what is now New Mexico, Arizona, Colorado, and Utah. Within this region are two different types of societies that came to share much in the way of cultural content.

The first of these Southwest societies are the *Pueblo* (after the Spanish word for "village") people. The modern Pueblo people includes groups such as the Hopi described in greater detail later in this volume. These groups are traditionally growers of corns, beans, and squash. Their villages consist of adobe "apartment houses" several stories high. Their founders located them atop high, flat plateaus, called *mesas* or tables. The Pueblo people have left behind a long archaeological record in the region. Their ancestors had also lived in great multi-storied pueblos, but until several hundred years before the Spanish arrived these were not located on the mesa tops. They moved to these easily defensible locations due to the appearance at that time of hunting people and raiders from the north—ancestors of the Apache and Navaho—speakers of Athapaskan languages.

After the Spanish arrived, the Apache and Navaho learned how to herd sheep. They also learned agriculture and weaving from the Pueblos, but this did not dampen their raiding proclivities. The raids were now against the Spanish, and later, the Americans, as well as the Pueblos.

Although the Spanish occupied the Southwest relatively early in the conquest, an Indian revolt drove them out in 1680. The stark, dry country and lack of significant plunder helped preserve the independence of both the farmers and the hunters until the period of the US Civil War (1860s). By this time an increasing European population in the Southwest led the US government to bring the Hopi, Zuni, and Navaho under its control. The Apache fought on for a few years more. In 1886, the last of the remaining independent Apache leaders, Geronimo, succumbed to American soldiers.

The US government placed the Indians of the Southwest on reservations. Unlike many of the eastern Indian groups, those of the Southwest ultimately stayed in their traditional territories. The reservations, however, were much smaller than the Indians' pre-reservation territories. Within the territory of the United States, the Indians of the Southwest have probably managed to retain a larger proportion of their pre-European cultures than any other groups located between Alaska and the Rio Grande River.

Foraging People

Although foraging peoples are often found living among agricultural peoples, there are culture areas populated largely by foragers—peoples living by hunting, gathering, fishing, or some combination of the three—only. Foragers generally live in highly mobile groups, and in North America these groups varied widely in terms of population size and density. There were even large degrees of variation in social complexity and technological sophistication, reflecting differences in historical experience and habitat.

Buffalo Hunters and Guanaco Hunters

The open grasslands of the Great Plains of western North America and of the Pampas of southeastern South America supported herds of large herbivorous grazing animals before the arrival of the Europeans. In North America, these grazers were the buffalo *(Bison)* that roamed in huge herds numbering in the thousands or perhaps tens of thousands. The large grazing herbivore of the Pampas was the guanaco; the wild relative of its better known domesticated cousins, camel and llama. These animals lived in relatively small herds of perhaps fifty animals or less.

Prior to the arrival of the Spanish, small groups of Indians hunted on the grasslands of North and South America, where hunting large herding game on foot was difficult. Hunters attempted to wage as stealthy an attack as possible, since the herd would bolt as soon as the animals sensed a threat. Thus, the herd would quickly be out of range of the hunters' simple weapons. The number of animals the hunters could hope to kill was therefore quite limited. A group of hunters, with careful planning, could improve their results by inciting a herd to stampede off a cliff. However, even when such a massive kill was successful, the means of preserving meat, chiefly drying (jerking), limited the amount of meat that the hunters could preserve for later use. Thus, hunting conditions dictated that the groups of hunters be quite small—about 100 people. Their social organization and technology were simple, based upon kinship and neighborly cooperation.

Things changed drastically on both continents after the arrival of the Spanish and their domesticated horses. The Indians of the Plains and Pampas soon acquired horses, and learned—or taught themselves—how to ride. The impact of this development was dramatic. For many scholars, the emergence of the Great Plains and Pampas as distinctive culture areas dates from the introduction of the horse. It was now possible for the hunters to keep up with fleeing herds, hunting as they went. The Great Plains of North America could now support larger populations. Groups of over 1,000 people could remain together for long periods. The Indians' demand for horses led to trade with and raids against the Spanish, and later Argentines, Mexicans, Americans, and other Indians. The larger populations, the trade, and warfare led to the appearance of some temporary, more complex, societal institutions that governed these activities to some degree. It was a complexity rarely found among hunting and gathering people. The way of life that the Plains could now support was so attractive that many previously agricultural groups abandoned or curtailed their past way of life and became hunters of the buffalo.

Similar developments occurred at the northern edge of the Pampas in what is now northern Argentina and adjacent parts of Paraguay and Brazil. In the Pampas, the Indians also became more efficient hunters of guanaco from horseback, but the guanaco lived in small herds. Thus, improvements in hunting of guanaco did not result in the dramatic increases in the size of the hunters' groups that had occurred among the Plains Indians of North America.

In North America, these mounted warriors and hunters of buffalo generated a culture that became, in the eyes of most non-Indians, the stereotypic Indian culture. The icons of this culture—teepees, warfare, horses, feathered headdress, and all the rest of what is seen in film and on television—*is* Indian culture to people around the world. Even today, these icons are over-represented whenever Indian culture is described, thereby fostering a distorted view that all Native Americans were like these hunters.

European expansion had helped create the Pampas and Plains cultures, and improved transportation and agricultural technology helped end it. Railroads, thoroughbred cattle, refrigerated ships and railroad cars, barbed wire, windmill-driven pumps, steel moldboard plows, and mechanical reapers made it possible for European farmers to make massive use of the American Plains, and Latin American Pampas. By warfare or treaty, the Argentines and Americans drove the Indians out of the great grasslands by the end of the nineteenth century. The colorful, dramatic, and romantic cultures that had emerged on the Pampas and the Plains in the early years of the eighteenth century barely lasted two centuries.

Other Foragers of the New World

In South America, the simple cultures of the pre-horse Pampas extended as far south as Tierra del Fuego at the very tip of the continent. In the northern reaches of the western United States and Canada were a variety of hunters and gatherers, their societies reflecting the habitats they exploited, the game and plants they sought, and the size of the population they could sustain. Furthest north were the Aleuts and Inuit (or Eskimos). The Tlingit, Kwakiutl, Nootka, and Haida and similar peoples inhabited the temperate rain forest of the Northwest Coast—from Vancouver Island to central Alaska. Outsiders knew them best as carvers of totem poles, but their talents and abilities extended far beyond those. The people of these cultures exploited rich fisheries, including massive salmon runs in their rivers and streams. They mastered sophisticated food preservation techniques, hunted mammals on land and sea, and collected a rich harvest of wild plants. They supported very large populations—perhaps 10,000 people—though not in a single community. They lived in fixed villages of impressive wooden plank buildings, and were governed by complex systems of social organization that differentiated social rank based upon kinship, rather than by specialized political institutions.

The Paleoindians who had arrived in the New World some 8000 years before the first European settlement evolved into a wide variety of distinctive societies and cultures. They did not—and do not—constitute one single society. They did not recognize a common identity any more than Europeans, Asians, or Africans did. The patterns of Native American culture molded and channeled what was to happen to the next wave of settlers to arrive in the New World.

The first known European settlers in the New World—Vikings from Iceland and/or Greenland—arrived and settled briefly in northern Newfoundland in the second half of the tenth century. These settlements did not long survive, however; the first effective, sustained European presence in the New World began with the Spanish in the last years of the fifteenth century.

CHARTER SOCIETIES AND CULTURES

Canadians refer to "charter societies and cultures" when describing the cultures that first traveled from Europe to what is now Canada. These were the people who provided the basic culture—laws, customs, and institutions—that influenced development in Canada from the time of their arrival until the present day. It was the charter societies that made the first contact with the Native Americans, and to which the Native Americans had to respond. For Canada, there were two charter societies—England and France. Later immigrants to Canada adjusted to the preexisting society and culture of English or French Canada, not the other way around.

The concept of the charter society remains useful in studying the New World, where four major charter societies—the major European conquerors and colonizers—and five significant charter cultures have been identified. Britain left its indelible mark on the social and cultural development in Canada, in much of what is now the United States, and on a number of Caribbean islands, including Jamaica and Barbados. France also played a major role in parts of Canada; to a lesser degree in the lower Mississippi River valley in the United States; and in several islands in the Caribbean, most notably in Martinique and the part of Hispaniola now known as Haiti. The third charter society for the New World was Portugal, which colonized the great eastern bulge of South America, notably Brazil. Finally, Spain, which colonized much of the New World, left its cultural imprint from California, in North America, to Tierra del Fuego, at the far southern tip of South America, and all over the Caribbean, especially in Cuba, Puerto Rico, and the part of Hispanola now known as the Dominican Republic. The fifth charter culture, unlike the other four, was brought by slaves who were brought by colonizers and conquerors.

Plantation Societies

The societies created in the New World by the European conquerors were not uniform. Most obviously, they differed by areas settled by the charter societies. However, even settlements by the same colonizing power differed from area to area. For example, English colonies in New England and the Caribbean islands differed greatly from each other. Differences were most

dramatic between colonies that were located in different ecological and environmental regions. Colonies of different colonizing powers might show some similarities if they inhabited similar settings and were involved in similar economic undertakings. The most striking pattern of similarity between colonies of different charter societies is illustrated by plantation societies, built upon the production of valuable tropical or semi-tropical crops, especially sugar. These crops, for large-scale export, were grown on landed estates that depended for the most part upon massive numbers of slave laborers. The plantation society was the point of insertion of the charter culture of the African slaves brought to the New World by the colonizers. Unlike the other charter societies, the Africans were not supported by the institution of state power. African culture was carried in the minds of those Africans who survived the horrors of the shipment from Africa. The culture survived despite the attempts by slave masters to expunge anything that remained of the slaves' former way of life. In some areas—part of the United States, the Caribbean, and Brazil, for example—the number of slaves was so great that they represented the majority in the population of the region and imposed their cultural mark upon the later cultures of the area.

Still other colonies saw few, if any, slaves. The colonizers' decision to introduce slaves was neither random nor routine. It reflected the habitat and ecology of the region, the economic goals of the European colonizers, and the type of Native American society that had inhabited the region before the arrival of the Europeans. Prior to the arrival of the Europeans, village agriculturalists tended to inhabit those regions that were to become the regions of plantation societies.

The native peoples of the Caribbean islands were largely wiped out by disease and the violence of the conquest. In Brazil, however, there was a large, thinly inhabited back country that served as a place of refuge for many Indian populations. There were massive displacements ever deeper into the Amazon and Orinoco River basins of coastal and other Indian societies accessible to the Europeans. They were not safe there forever. In later centuries the lure of gold, diamonds, rubber, and other commodities drew the Europeans and their heirs ever deeper into regions that had once provided safe refuge to the Indians. This process continues even in the late 1990s.

These same tropical and semi-tropical areas held great potential value for the Europeans as a place to grow sugar crops. Sugar was only in its early stages of becoming a common commodity in European marketplaces. Sugar could be easily shipped over long distances as brown sugar, or in an even more condensed form as molasses. Molasses was the most profitable of all, since it could be converted into rum. Sugar could best be grown in tropical conditions, but it required great amounts of intensive labor. The colonizers hoped to use the Indians for this purpose, but the Indians managed to escape. Elsewhere, on the Atlantic island colony of Madeira, the Portuguese had already solved the labor problem on sugar plantations by importing slaves from Africa. This solution was introduced to the Americas on the sugar plantations on the northeast coast of Brazil, where enslaved Africans were imported to work. From there, this pattern of sugar plantation agriculture spread over much of the rest of the tropical and semi-tropical New World.

The trade in African slaves continued for some three hundred years after the conquest. The enslaved Africans who survived shipment to the New World did not come from a single society or culture in Africa. In Brazil, on the northern coasts of South America, in the Caribbean, and the southeast United States, the Africans left their indelible stamp. Their presence shaped religious practice and concepts, family life and organization, music, and folklore. They influenced not only the plantation regions, but the greater nations of which these later became a part as well.

Plantation America was not the only system to grow out of economic opportunity and a unique labor force. Similarly, the variables of economic potential for the colonizers interacting with Native American cultural and demographic patterns produced two other important social and cultural New World patterns, known as Indo-America and Euro-America.

Indo-America

The Europeans found much of value in the New World. The regions of the pre-conquest New World were largely temperate or semi-tropical. Although generally not suited to sugar production, they did have the potential to support a wide variety of European crops and animals. Of even greater importance to the Europeans were the gold and silver that could be found there. For the Spanish, most important of all were the large, dense, and highly organized populations of agricultural peasants that the Spanish Empire gained by the conquest. These peasants were accustomed to laboring to produce crops for their own subsistence and for their masters as well. The Spanish destroyed the ancient aristocracies and bureaucracies, but they retained or modified the structures of command. They simply replaced the former rulers with their own leaders to control the mass of surviving Indians. In these densely populated regions, there was no need to import African slaves or European peasants, workers, and farmers. The Indian peasantry remained the source of Spanish wealth and power as they had been for the Aztecs and Incas before them.

The Spanish attempted to maintain a sharp separation between Spanish and Indian. As always with such attempts, it was doomed to failure, and mating between Spanish and Indians began almost immediately. Most of the children of these unions were rejected by both the Spanish and Indian communities. In time in contemporary Mexico, Guatemala, Ecuador, Peru, and Bolivia, however, the descendants of people of mixed ancestry became the majority or plurality. Despite the great numbers of people of mixed ancestry, political power remained in the hands of people of European background until the early years of the twentieth century. This situation only changed beginning with the early years of the twentieth century. By the late nineteenth century, political and economic differences had developed between the still largely white upper class and the largely mixed-race, urban, middle- and working-classes in these nations. These differences were of social class within a more all-encompassing national culture.

As previously noted, about ten percent of the population of Mexico does not speak Spanish as their primary language; in Ecuador and Peru, the proportion rises to twenty-five percent, while in Bolivia it reaches about fifty percent. The vast majority of these speakers are American Indian. Largely in rural areas within these nations, there are still communities that maintain modified Indian culture and speak the local Indian language. These cultures are not unchanged from those of their 16th century ancestors. Rather, they have been much buffeted

by the non-Indian world, and in some places and times, have risen in rebellion and revolution. They show a continuity with the past in many cultural practices, including language, the form of the Catholicism they practice, arts, lore, diet, and sometimes family organization. The Indian way of life is not totally shared by the other people of equivalent social and economic position in their homeland.

It should not be assumed that these Indian communities are in some way more "Indian" in a genetic sense. The people of these communities—like the rest of the nation in which they live—show a great deal of admixture of European genes. What defines a community as Indian is its culture, not primarily the physical appearance of its members. In the nations of Indo-America a person's "racial" identity is a function of his or her cultural affiliation, not physical appearance.

Euro-America

In North America, Euro-America extends roughly from northern Mexico north to the southern edges of the Arctic slopes. In South America, Euro-America extends roughly from southern Brazil, through Uruguay, Chile, and Argentina south to Tierra del Fuego. The habitat in South America did not offer the opportunity and potential for growing high-profit crops like sugar, and thus, there was no economic rationale to import slaves on a massive scale. Although great wealth lay buried beneath the land, it was not until the nineteenth century that this potential was appreciated and the technology developed to exploit it. The population of Indians who inhabited these regions was relatively small in number and relatively mobile. There were no great central states under which they were organized, and because of their small number, they offered no great potential as a labor force to the Europeans.

In North America, the colonists and their European masters lusted after furs, which the Indians would collect and trade, with little immediate or obvious negative impact upon their culture. In the long run, however, the European impact was just as profound upon these people as it had been upon the agricultural Indians who lived further south. These temperate colonies offered a variety of economic benefits to the European empires. These, however, were not as valuable as those colonies that lay in less temperate areas.

The European populations of Euro-America were small in the beginning. The crops, timber, fish, and livestock they produced were essentially similar to those produced in Europe. In southern Brazil and Uruguay, in Argentina and Chile, in the English colonies north of Virginia, and in the French colonies of eastern Canada, the inhabitants created European societies. These were not perfect and complete copies of their European homelands, however, since the class structure was incomplete—few aristocrats settled in these lands. Not all European regions sent immigrants to the New World. A middle class of free farmers, artisans, and merchants was over-represented, especially in North American. These isolated bits of Europe, sitting on the edge of vast forests, prairies, and plains, were to be the lure and haven for the third round of population transfer from the Old World to the New World.

IMMIGRANT SOCIETIES

The Industrial Revolution that began quietly in Europe in the eighteenth century has continued to enhance in power and impact until the present. It initiated and stimulated a wave of demographic change probably unmatched in prior history. The economic, political, social, and cultural changes that it inaugurated worked together to set Europe, and later the rest of the world, on the move. By the middle of the nineteenth century, a tidal wave of migration began to flow. This flow of humanity occurred both within and between the nations of Europe and between Europe and the Americas. The flow within Europe was primarily a rural-to-urban migration, with large numbers of people from farms and small towns being drawn to the growing industrial cities. To a large degree, this was also true of the population movements between Europe and the Americas. People left peasant farming communities and moved to industrial and commercial cities. In this case, however, the cities were in another hemisphere half a world away. Many also came to the Americas seeking land, which was in short supply and expensive in Europe, but was available and relatively inexpensive in many parts of Euro-America.

The potential host societies in the Americas sought immigrants during this period, and in fact, competed for them. These societies were driven by their expanding economies and apparently unquenchable need for inexpensive labor.

North Americans think of the goal of the immigrant waves of the nineteenth and early twentieth centuries as directed primarily at the United States and, to a lesser degree, towards Canada. In truth, however, the immigrants were drawn to countries all over the Americas. The greatest number went to those nations in Euro-America: the United States and Canada, southern Brazil, Uruguay, Chile, and Argentina. Smaller numbers of European immigrants settled in other parts of the Americas as well. In the nineteenth and early twentieth centuries, far fewer immigrants came to the Americas from Asia and Africa, but by the mid-twentieth century, these numbers would grow. In the second half of the twentieth century the impact of industrialization, war, and revolution increased the flow of emigrants and refugees from Asia. Also, discriminatory laws against Asians in many host countries were softened, and the gates to Asian immigration were thus opened a bit wider.

The world in which new immigrants arrived had been shaped by the various charter societies for several hundred years. The assumption on the part of the host populations was that the newcomers would learn the ways of the host country, give up their "foreign ways," and in time, become indistinguishable from everyone else. In the United States, this was expressed through the metaphor of "the melting pot." In some ways, this metaphor was accurate, but in others it was not.

Acculturation, Assimilation, and Ethnicity

Social scientists distinguish between acculturation and assimilation, two social and cultural processes. Acculturation refers to the process by which a group—usually socially and politically subordinate—learns the culture, language, dress, rules, and laws, of another—usually dominant—group. Assimilation refers to the process by which one group loses its identity through total absorption into another group. Acculturation without assimilation is common. Assimilation without acculturation is rare at best, and may even be impossible.

Many variables contribute to the process of acculturation and assimilation for an immigrant group, family, or individual. For generations of immigrants who came from the Old World as adults, acculturation occurs rather slowly because they are already trained in and accustomed to another culture. The first generation born in the new circumstances faces a complex problem. In their home environment, they learn aspects of their parents' native culture; in the outside world—at school, for example—they are exposed to the host culture. The grandchildren of the original immigrants (the second generation born in the new environment) will usually be exposed to relatively little of the grandparents' native culture. After two generations, all other things being equal, it will usually be difficult, if not impossible, to identify any highly visible cultural differences between the descendants of the immigrants and those of the host population.

All things, however, are not always equal. A Norwegian family, as an example, that settled in a place where there were no other Norwegian immigrants would have to learn the ways of the hosts quickly in order to live their everyday lives. The children, and certainly the grandchildren, of such a family would probably have few opportunities to even think of themselves as "Norwegians" or "Norwegian-Americans."

If, on the other hand, that same family had settled in a community with many other Norwegian immigrants, they would face a different situation. They would have people with whom they could continue to practice at least some aspects of Norwegian culture. They could attend and support Norwegian-oriented institutions like churches, parochial or after-hours schools, colleges and universities, hospitals, newspapers, magazines, and social clubs. In a case such as this, two levels of acculturation might be observed. At the level of everyday life—on the job, in the street, in the public school—the people in such an immigrant-based community would appear no different than anyone else. At another level, they would practice a rich culture of Norwegian origin. They might, in appropriate circumstances, think and speak of themselves as "Norwegian-Americans." Such a community could celebrate Norwegian Independence Day (17 May) as a holiday that mixes together Norwegian and American culture, symbols, and themes. The Norwegian immigrant family that settled among non-Norwegians and thus lost a sense of Norwegian identity would be considered assimilated. The Norwegian family that settled with other Norwegians to create a Norwegian-American community must be considered less assimilated. Both, however, are acculturated.

The process of assimilation is far more complex than the process of acculturation. Many factors affect the process of adaptation to a new way of life in a new culture. Examples include the nature of the diplomatic, political, and military relationship between the host and the homeland of the immigrant group; and racial categories and stereotypes held by both immigrant group and host nation, as well as the laws and customs relating to such issues in the host country. There are also important social and cultural differences among immigrants from a single country that influence acculturation and assimilation. Late nineteenth century Italian immigrants, for example, were different in almost every way from those who arrived late in the twentieth century. The older charter populations in the New World did not always welcome those who came later. Levels of education, wealth, social class, religion, and other factors had major effects on immigrants. Very often the later immigrants were discriminated against—even to the point of physical attacks—due to racial, religious, social, economic, and other fears and prejudicial attitudes that the older populations had learned from their own ancestors. Most North Americans can easily understand the process of the loss or preservation of "national identity" by immigrant populations—perhaps having experienced it within recent generations in their own families. However, much the same process was at work all over the Americas, for not only immigrants from the Old World to the New, but also for those immigrating between countries of the Americas. Huge flows of population—black, white, and brown—flowed from rural to urban locations within the nations of the Americas and between them.

The effects of these processes of acculturation and assimilation, conquest and colonization, have left the New World a mosaic of cultures and societies. None is homogeneous. All reflect a mix of identities and loyalties, social classes, races, and religions that is constantly changing and never stable. It is this complex set of psychological, social, and cultural processes that defines ethnicity in the New World.

Thus, generalizing about ethnicity is complicated at best. The reader will encounter the many groups that populate the nations of the Americas in this volume. It is more important to be alert to and aware of this complexity. The writers' attempts to inform is unavoidably subject to some distortion. This volume provides a place to begin learning about the people of the Americas. It also leads the reader on, to sources for further study in the process of discovering the people and cultures of the Americas.

AFRICAN AMERICANS

ALTERNATE NAMES: Blacks
LOCATION: United States
POPULATION: 33 million (half of whom live in the Southern states)
LANGUAGE: English (sometimes with Black English variants)
RELIGION: National Baptist Convention; Church of God in Christ (Pentecostal); Roman Catholicism; Nation of Islam; African Methodist Episcopal Church; African Orthodox Church; Judaism; Rastafarianism
RELATED ARTICLES: Vol. 2: Americans

¹ INTRODUCTION

Unlike other immigrants to the United States, the ancestors of today's African Americans did not come to America of their own free will. Beginning in 1619, they were captured and forcibly brought from their West African homelands to serve as slaves, mostly on Southern plantations. The inhuman conditions aboard the ships on which they traveled killed many Africans before they reached the New World. When the thirteen British colonies declared and ultimately won their independence from Britain in the 18th century, the institution of slavery was retained, although largely confined to the Southern states. During the Civil War, President Lincoln signed the Emancipation Proclamation, freeing the Southern slaves; the Thirteenth Amendment to the Constitution, passed in December 1865, abolished all slavery in the United States. At the close of the Civil War, African Americans accounted for 14% of the US population.

The newly freed slaves made progress during Reconstruction, especially in education, but the end of this period, in 1877, brought a new era of repression marked by lynchings and other forms of persecution, in which the recently formed Ku Klux Klan played a prominent role. In 1909 the National Association for the Advancement of Colored People (NAACP) was formed. The following two decades saw the migration of about 1.6 million Southern blacks to Northern cities in search of newly available industrial jobs. Weathering the hardships of the Depression, blacks continued their northward migration through the years of Franklin Roosevelt's New Deal policies and World War II.

During the Civil Rights Movement of the 1950s and 1960s, the country's most egregious forms of racism were eliminated, as blacks joined forces to demand their legal and human rights through civil disobedience and other forms of protest and social activism. The 1954 Supreme Court ruling in *Brown v. Board of Education* declared school segregation illegal. Progress was also made in the area of voting rights, as well as the desegregation of public facilities, especially in the South. In 1963, the Reverend Martin Luther King, Jr., delivered his famous "I Have a Dream" speech at the Lincoln Memorial. The 1960s also saw the growth of the black nationalist movement, whose leadership was assumed by the Black Panthers following the assassination of Black Muslim leader Malcolm X.

By the 1970s, African Americans had been elected as mayors of several major cities, and affirmative action programs had created new opportunities in employment and education. However, many of these programs were weakened or eliminated during the presidency of Ronald Reagan in the 1980s. Still, African-American achievement in American society has been remarkable in the past decade. In the 1990s, the country's continuing racial tensions were brought to the forefront of national attention by events including the riots in Los Angeles in response to the court's decision in the Rodney King case and the 1995 acquittal in the O. J. Simpson murder trial.

² LOCATION AND HOMELAND

According to the United States Census Bureau, there were an estimated 33 million African Americans in the US in 1995, a population larger than that of most African nations and one that represents 13% of the total US population. Some 53% of blacks in the United States live in Southern states. The ten states with the largest black populations in 1990 were New York, California, Texas, Florida, Georgia, Illinois, North Carolina, Louisiana, Michigan, and Maryland. As of the same year, 83% of blacks lived in metropolitan areas, although only 57% lived in central cities.

³ LANGUAGE

African Americans speak English, although some blacks, either in addition to or instead of Standard American English, speak a variant known as Black English Vernacular (BEV), or Black English. In the late 1990s, the term ebonics was coined by linguists to refer to the grammar of Black English. The grammar and syntax of Black English are traceable to West African and Niger-Congo languages. They include the frequent omission of forms of the verb "to be" ("He nice" instead of "He is nice"); the use of "be" in place of "is" ("He be home today"); the absence of endings from third person singular verbs ("She know"); absence of the possessive*s* when possession is signified by word order ("That John house"); replacement of a final "th" sound in a word by an "f" sound ("I going wif you"); and replacement of indefinite pronouns such as "anyone" by negative pronouns when verbs are negated ("He don't like nobody"). Black English Vernacular has introduced African words such as *goober* (peanut), *tote* (carry), *juke* (juke box), and *okay* into the English language, as well as produced original terms later incorporated widely into general informal or conversational use, such as *jive*, *hip*, and *jazz*. In other cases, Standard English terms have been given new meanings, as in the case of *cat, rap, bad,* and *awesome*.

In late 1996, Black English Vernacular, newly labeled Ebonics, was the subject of nationwide debate when the Oakland, California, school board passed a resolution declaring it a separate language distinct from standard English in order to institute programs aimed at educating teachers in this dialect and inculcating respect for its African linguistic roots.

⁴ FOLKLORE

African Americans have a folklore tradition that dates back to the period of black slavery. Early forms of African-American folklore include animal-trickster tales, spirituals, and folk beliefs, such as the belief in conjurers, figures similar to African medicine men who, by using spells and charms, could either heal or cause injury. Folk traditions were also passed down through the generations by proverbs, sermons, prayers, and a variety of folktales.

Modern African-American folklore includes the "dozens," insult matches favored especially by young men and generally including disparaging remarks about each other's mothers. Another popular type of folklore consists of rumors about organized anti-black conspiracies. Today these rumors take the form of "urban legends" that are in widespread circulation in the black community but virtually unknown to other ethnic communities. Examples include the assertions that the Ku Klux Klan tampers with Church's fried chicken in ways that cause sterility among black men; that American scientists deliberately created the AIDS virus and then attempted to test it by infecting African populations with it; and that twenty-eight African Americans were killed in the course of interferon research at the Centers for Disease Control in Atlanta.

5 RELIGION

The National Baptist Convention of the U.S.A., Inc., with over 7.5 million members in 1990, is the largest black religious denomination, followed by the Church of God in Christ, a Pentecostal sect (1990 membership of over 5.5 million). Roman Catholicism (with a black membership of two million in 1990) and the Nation of Islam both claim large black followings as well. Other religious affiliations include the African Methodist Episcopal Church, the African Orthodox Church, Judaism, and Rastafarianism.

6 MAJOR HOLIDAYS

African Americans observe the national holidays of the United States and the religious holidays of the faiths to which they belong. Dates with special significance for African Americans are the birthdays of the Reverend Martin Luther King, Jr., on January 15 and of Malcolm X on May 19, and Juneteenth, which commemorates the date on which black slaves in Texas learned that they were free—June 19, 1865. The joyous holiday of Kwanzaa, the festival of first fruits, is celebrated from December 26 to January 1. Each day of this holiday, inaugurated by the philosopher Maulana Karenga in 1966, is devoted to and named for a particular virtue.

7 RITES OF PASSAGE

African Americans with active religious involvement mark major life events such as birth, marriage, and death within their respective religious traditions. "Jumping the broom" is a time-honored custom at African-American weddings. The African Americans of Louisiana's New Orleans Creole community are known for their jazz funerals. Observers within the black community have decried the lack of coming-of-age rituals for young black men, and some groups, including the Urban League and PUSH (People United to Save Humanity) have begun to develop rite-of-passage programs that focus on responsibility, values, character, and discipline. (PUSH also offers such programs for young women.) Increasing numbers of parents are also adopting African-based rites of passage for children, which are called *mfundalai,* or Changing Season rites.

8 INTERPERSONAL RELATIONS

Common greetings in Black English Vernacular include "Word up," "Yo," and "Look out." A common nonverbal greeting consists of slapping another person's outstretched palm. When done above the head it is called a "high five"; at knee level it is

a "low five." The women's version of this greeting consists of sliding one's forefinger across the forefinger of the other woman. Expressions of farewell include "See you later," "Word to the Mother" (referring to the motherland of Africa), and "Stay black." "Man" is commonly used in informal situations as a form of address for men; black women often address each other as "girlfriend." Many young African Americans still observe the West African custom of addressing their elders as "Aunt" or "Uncle." Like people from many Asian and Latin American cultures, African Americans, especially those from the South, often avoid eye contact as a sign of respect.

9 LIVING CONDITIONS

Average life expectancy for African Americans of both sexes was 70.3 years in 1990, compared with 33 years in 1900 (and compared with 75.4 years in 1990 for Americans of all races). African Americans have a disproportionately high incidence of heart disease, diabetes, high blood pressure, cancer, AIDS, obesity, and asthma. The health of low-income blacks in particular is affected by a lack of affordable high-quality medical care and the health insurance that could pay for it. The rate of Sudden Infant Death Syndrome (SIDS) for black infants is as much as twice as high as for whites, a fact attributed to the lower quality of prenatal care many black mothers receive.

Limited in their choice of housing by income and racial discrimination, the great majority of African Americans lived in substandard housing until the middle of the 20th century. Between 1950 and 1970 the proportion of blacks living in substandard dwellings dropped from 73% to 23%. In 1991, 12% of black dwellings had moderate physical problems, while nearly 5% had severe problems. In the same year, 42% of blacks owned their own homes, compared with 64% of the total population and 67% of whites. Of all black householders, including renters, 86% had telephones in 1991, 58% had clothes washers, and 42% had clothes dryers. In 1992, 53% of the nation's public housing was occupied by blacks.

In 1991, roughly 51% of African Americans owned one car, truck, or van; 19% owned more than one; and 29% owned no motor vehicles.

10 FAMILY LIFE

African-American family life offers many variations on the nuclear-family model, including single-parent families (usually headed by women); "blended" families that include a couple's children with previous partners as well as any children they may have together; adults, who live together, with or without children; and extended families, which have long played an especially important role in the lives of African Americans. In addition to grandparents, extended families may include aunts, uncles, cousins, and other relatives, who may join the nuclear family either temporarily or long-term. One prominent social trend has been a decrease in the number of married African-American couples, which has been associated with a variety of factors, including a demographic shortage of black men (83 men aged 15 and older for every 100 women); increased opportunities for black women in the labor market; imprisonment of large numbers of black men; unemployment and low earnings among black men; and rising rates of intermarriage.

11 CLOTHING

African Americans wear clothing similar to that worn by other Americans. Certain fashions among inner-city youth, such as baggy, loose-fitting pants and baseball caps worn backwards, have caught on among young men of other ethnic and racial groups.

12 FOOD

Traditional African-American food, commonly known as "soul food," originated with the mingling of the West African culinary heritage of black slaves with the cooking styles and available foods of the American South. In particular, the African custom of using all edible parts of both plants and animals was of great importance to the sustenance of blacks, who had to make do with scraps and leftovers. This practice has been especially evident in the preparation of pork, which has long been the most common meat eaten by African Americans, who traditionally used virtually all parts of the animal, including the hocks, snout, ears, feet, and tail—everything, it was said, "but the oink." Other dietary staples of African-American diet have included chicken, corn, both white and sweet potatoes, okra, and a variety of greens. Barbecues are popular among African Americans, who take great pride in their sauce recipes. Depending on geographical region, fish has also been a staple of the African-American diet, and fish sandwiches with hot sauce on white bread are a current favorite in black communities. Popular desserts, including pralines and shortening bread, are often sweetened with molasses; and watermelon, which was brought to the New World from Africa, is still a favorite food.

13 EDUCATION

Education has been a strong concern of those seeking to improve the lives of African Americans, especially those in inner-city neighborhoods. In 1991, the high school dropout rate for black 19- and 20-year-olds was 16.9%. Recent studies found that as many as 40% of black men were functionally illiterate, and that young black prison inmates far outnumbered young black college students. Cities including Baltimore, Detroit, and Milwaukee have experimented with Afrocentric and multicultural curricula and other programs geared toward the cultural background and educational needs of African-American youth. Among the oldest black colleges in the nation are Wilberforce University, Fisk University, Talladega College, Morehouse College, Howard University, and Tougaloo College.

14 CULTURAL HERITAGE

The most famous period in African-American literature was the Harlem Renaissance between the two World Wars, when writers including Langston Hughes, Countee Cullen, and Zora Neale Hurston exposed racial injustice in works that reflected their personal experience. Classics of black literature in the years following this period included Richard Wright's *Native Son*, Ralph Ellison's *Invisible Man*, and James Baldwin's *The Fire Next Time*. The Black Aesthetic Movement of the 1960s and 1970s reflected developments of the civil rights and black nationalist movements, as well as African Americans' growing awareness of their African cultural roots. Since the 1970s, many black women writers have risen to prominence, including Nobel laureate Toni Morrison, former US Poet Laureate Rita Dove, Maya Angelou, Alice Walker, and Gloria Naylor.

Important genres of African-American music include spirituals, gospel, rhythm and blues ("R&B"), ragtime, jazz, soul, Motown, funk, and, most recently, rap music. Some of the greatest names of the jazz tradition include trumpeter Louis Armstrong, vocalist Ella Fitzgerald, bandleaders Duke Ellington and Dizzy Gillespie, saxophonist Charlie Parker, and trumpeter Miles Davis.

Prominent African-American visual artists in the 20th century have included Romare Bearden, Benford Delaney, Jacob Douglas, Aaron Douglas, Horace Pippin, Clementine Hunter, Keith Haring, and Jean-Michel Basquiat.

15 WORK

For the past two decades, the unemployment rate of blacks has been twice that of whites; in the 1980s this ratio rose to two and one half. In 1993, the unemployment rate for black men over the age of 16 was 13.8%; for women the figure was 12%. (The rate for single black men was 21.9%.) Blacks—especially black men—are disproportionately employed in low-paid blue-collar jobs. In 1991, 22% of blacks (and over 30% of black men) were employed as operators, fabricators, and laborers, as compared with 13.2% of whites. In contrast, only 18% of blacks were employed in professional and managerial jobs, compared with 31% of whites.

16 SPORTS

Many disadvantaged black youths dream of a professional sports career—especially in basketball—as a way out of the urban ghetto, a dream most poignantly portrayed in the 1994 documentary film *Hoop Dreams*, which chronicles the lives of two talented inner-city teens over several years. Although the chances of making it as a professional athlete are slim, sports scholarships give many young blacks, such as those described in the film, educational opportunities that can provide solid, if less spectacular, forms of upward mobility.

Within the field of professional sports, current issues include the hiring of blacks in coaching and front-office positions. In addition to the accomplishments of great African-American athletes in basketball, baseball, boxing, and football, black athletes have more recently made pioneering achievements in what had been all-white sports, tennis and golf. Arthur Ashe became the first black American to garner the Wimbledon and US Open championships, and in 1997 21-year-old Tiger Woods became the first athlete of black ancestry to win the Masters' Tournament.

17 ENTERTAINMENT AND RECREATION

African Americans enjoy many of the same types of leisure-time activities as other Americans, including television, movies, concerts, dancing, family gatherings, and both participatory and spectator sports. The Black Entertainment Television cable network, with some 25 million subscribers in the early 1990s, broadcasts music videos, black collegiate sports, public affairs programs, and reruns of popular programs such as *The Cosby Show*. Dance clubs, at which music is provided by disk jockeys, create a sense of community for many young people, with popular dance styles including hip-hop, lofting, and house.

[18] FOLK ART, CRAFTS, AND HOBBIES

Traditional forms of African-American folk art include basket weaving, pottery, wood-carving, quilting, and the making of musical instruments. Prominent characteristics of black folk art include a pervasive religious theme; the frequent appearance of bird, serpent, and other animal imagery; the use of significant figures in African-American history, both white and black, including Abraham Lincoln and Dr. Martin Luther King, Jr.; and a talent for transforming scrap objects into works of art.

[19] SOCIAL PROBLEMS

Social problems faced by African Americans include the lack of good jobs, high unemployment, gang violence, the sale and use of crack cocaine in inner-city areas, reductions in social spending by governments at all levels, and tensions with recently arrived Asian and Hispanic immigrants. In 1991, 45.6% of all African-American children in the United States lived below the poverty level.

[20] BIBLIOGRAPHY

Bates, Karen Grigsby, and Karen Elyse Hudson. *Basic Black: Home Training for Modern Times.* New York: Doubleday, 1996.

Billingsley, Andrew. *Climbing Jacob's Ladder: The Enduring Legacy of African-American Families.* New York: Simon & Schuster, 1992.

Franklin, John Hope, and Alfred A. Moss, Jr. *From Slavery to Freedom: A History of African Americans.* 7th ed. New York: Knopf, 1994.

Harris, Jessica B. *The Welcome Table: African-American Heritage Cooking.* New York: Simon & Schuster, 1995.

Kelley, Robin D. G. *Into the Fire: African Americans Since 1970.* The Young Oxford History of African Americans. New York: Oxford University Press, 1996.

Medearis, Angela Shelf. *A Kwanzaa Celebration: Festive Recipes and Homemade Gifts from an African-American Kitchen.* New York: Dutton, 1995.

Rose, Tricia. *Black Noise: Rap Music and Black Culture in Contemporary America.* Middletown, CT: Wesleyan University Press, 1994.

AFRICAN BRAZILIANS

LOCATION: Brazil
POPULATION: About 16 million
LANGUAGE: Portuguese with some African terms
RELIGION: Afro-Brazilian sects such as Condomble; spiritualist sects
RELATED ARTICLES: Vol. 2: Brazilians

[1] INTRODUCTION

Brazilians of African origin comprise nearly 10% of the total population of Brazil. As in the US, their arrival can be traced back to the slave trade of the mid-1500s. It is estimated that nearly 4 million or more slaves were shipped to Brazil from various African countries. This is vastly higher than the number of slaves that were imported into the US, which has been estimated at approximately 600,000. It is not surprising, therefore, that Afro-Brazilian culture is an important part of Brazilian society. Afro-Brazilian cooking customs and religion, for example, are practiced not only by Blacks, but also by Brazilians of all races and ethnic backgrounds.

Brazilian law prohibits discrimination on the basis of race. Little overt tension or racial violence exists in Brazil, as it does in many countries around the world, including the US. However, subtle racial discrimination continues to exist, and Afro-Brazilians have limited access to higher education and economic opportunities. As a whole, Afro-Brazilians are a socioeconomically disadvantaged group in society.

[2] LOCATION AND HOMELAND

Brazil is an ethnically diverse country. The population of 162,661,214 persons is primarily composed of indigenous Indians, mainly Amazonian tribes; Portuguese and other European immigrants; and Afro-Brazilians (about 16,000,000). More recent immigration in the 19th and 20th centuries has added Arabs and Japanese to the mix. These ethnic groups have intermixed. As a result, the percentage of the population that considers itself to be Black in the national census has been in dramatic decline, while the number of those who consider themselves Brown has increased. This has been called the "bleaching" of Brazil.

The northeastern state of Bahia can be considered the heart of Afro-Brazilian culture. Both sugar and cacao were produced in the northeast region and Bahia became the port of arrival for many slaves. Afro-Brazilians reside throughout the country, however, with large concentrations in the major cities of Rio de Janeiro and Sao Paulo.

[3] LANGUAGE

The official language of Brazil is Portuguese. Afro-Brazilians originating from many different African countries and ethnic groups learned Portuguese as a way of communicating both with colonial Brazilians and with each other. Some words of African origin have been incorporated into everyday language (i.e., *samba*). This can be seen most clearly in the area of Afro-Brazilian religion, which retained the original African names of deities, ceremonies, and dances.

⁴ FOLKLORE

One of the most revered historical figures is Zumbi, a rebel slave leader in the region of Palmares. Many Afro-Brazilians celebrate 20 November, the date on which Zumbi jumped off a cliff to avoid being captured by government forces. The heroic actions of Zumbi have made him a legendary figure to Afro-Brazilians.

⁵ RELIGION

Afro-Brazilian religious sects are becoming increasingly popular with Blacks and Whites alike in Brazil. There are a variety of religious groupings that continue to follow traditional African religious practices. The first is *Condomble,* a religion practiced by slaves from the Yoruba tribe. Based largely in the state of Bahia, Condomble followers worship many different gods and goddesses of nature, such as Iemanja, the goddess of the sea. Condomble services are characterized by pulsating drums and rhythmic music that encourages followers to reach a trancelike state. These ceremonies are conducted not on Sunday mornings, but late at night. It has been estimated that over 1,000 Condomble temples exist in the city of Salvador, Bahia.

Other spiritualist sects, such as *Umbanda,* combine African and non-African religious influences. In these religions, it is common for the services to be led by a female priestess. Umbanda is becoming widespread in Brazil's major cities. Followers of Umbanda invite spirits into their bodies as part of the services. When they are "possessed," they traditionally light a cigar. Umbanda services account for the majority of cigar sales in Brazil.

⁶ MAJOR HOLIDAYS

Bahia is the center of Afro-Brazilian culture and it is there that its festivals are most celebrated. On 2 February, residents of Salvador celebrate the *Condomble* goddess of the sea, Iemanja. Gifts and offerings are made to Iemanja and are floated out to sea in small handmade sailboats. These offerings are usually sent by fishermen's wives, in the hope that the goddess will protect the fishermen and ensure calm waters. Condomble rhythmic music accompanies the ceremonial events.

Another Afro-Brazilian festival is held in the city of Cachoeira. An Afro-Brazilian religious society holds an annual festival to celebrate the liberation of slaves in Brazil. Dancing, music, and prayer act to remind Afro-Brazilians of the suffering of their slave ancestors. Afro-Brazilians also celebrate Carnival (*see* **Brazilians**).

⁷ RITES OF PASSAGE

Major life transitions, such as birth, puberty, and death, are marked by ceremonies appropriate to each Afro-Brazilian's religious tradition.

⁸ INTERPERSONAL RELATIONS

It is difficult to distinguish Afro-Brazilian customs from those of Brazilian society as a whole. Afro-Brazilian mannerisms, traditions, rituals, and music have been incorporated into wider Brazilian culture.

Afro-Brazilians are an outgoing and gregarious people. They speak animatedly and use a variety of hand gestures to add emphasis to what they are saying. Afro-Brazilians are also accustomed to close personal contact. Women will often walk down the street hand in hand, and male friends will greet each other with a hug.

Music has been incorporated into many aspects of Afro-Brazilian life. Samba clubs that rehearse for Carnival are an important form of social organization. In addition, music is incorporated into their traditional sports, *capoeira* (a martial art), and into religious services. Most Afro-Brazilians are deeply religious and these beliefs pervade every aspect of their lives. It is common, for example, for food and candles to be left on street corners as offerings to spirits.

In January in Bahia, colorful ribbons are sold that are believed to be good luck. These ribbons must be received as gifts and should never be bought for oneself. These ribbons are tied with multiple knots around the wrist. The wearer makes a wish with each knot tied. The ribbons are then worn continuously until they fall off from daily wear. Only then are the wishes granted.

⁹ LIVING CONDITIONS

Many Afro-Brazilians live in poverty in the urban slums that surround the major cities of Sao Paulo and Rio de Janeiro. Many of these slums, called *favelas,* are on steep hillsides. The earlier settlers can be found at the base of the hill, which is more accessible. These areas are likely to have electricity and running water. Further up the hillside are newer, less accessible communities. Pathways between houses are narrow and cramped. Often large families will live in a single-room dwelling. The lack of running water and accumulation of sewage in these densely concentrated areas create many health problems for residents. Gastrointestinal and infectious diseases are widespread. Clinics and health care, when they exist in the favelas, are overcrowded and poorly equipped.

The favelas surrounding Rio de Janeiro are also at risk of flooding. Heavy rain will carry garbage down the hillsides and can create landslides that wash away flimsy housing.

¹⁰ FAMILY LIFE

In Brazil, there are different types of socially accepted marriages. Unions between couples can be religious, civil, or common-law. Civil marriage are those recognized by the state, and most couples undergo a civil wedding followed by a religious ceremony.

Long-term relationships between couples that live together are common and socially accepted in Brazil. This practice, known as *amasiado,* is common among Afro-Brazilians. Official forms of marriage are perceived to be unnecessary. As with other types of marriage, some couples ultimately separate while others may last a lifetime. Couples in amasiado are accepted as married by the community and may have children without fear of being shunned.

The extended family provides an additional source of mutual assistance and support. Godparentage is taken very seriously and entails many responsibilities. Family loyalty takes first priority, and relatives offer both economic and moral support to family members in need.

¹¹ CLOTHING

Regional differences in dress in Brazil are pronounced. In the largely Afro-Brazilian regions of Bahia, Black women dress in clothing inspired by 18th century attire. Colorful, full-length skirts are worn with delicately embroidered white blouses, which are sometimes worn off the shoulder. Women in Bahia, known as *Baianas,* also wear scarves or turbans wrapped tightly around their heads.

Brightly colored beads are worn by both men and women. These beads have religious symbolic meaning. The color of the beads worn reflects the individual's *orixa,* or African *Condomble* god.

12 FOOD

Afro-Brazilian food combines African, Portuguese, and indigenous ingredients and cooking traditions. African peppers and spices are now grown in the tropical northeastern state of Bahia and are used widely in Afro-Brazilian cooking. *Dende* oil, for example, is extracted from an African palm now grown in Brazil. Dende is used to make *moqueca,* a spicy mix of sautéed shrimp, tomato, and coconut milk.

The most distinctive Afro-Brazilian dish is *feijoada,* also considered to be the national dish of Brazil. Feijoada is a black bean and pork stew, traditionally cooked in African-style earthenware pots. The dish was created by Brazilian slaves. They were given the discarded pieces of pork, such as the tail, snout, and feet, which they stewed slowly with spices and beans. This dish was so tasty that it was soon copied by the slave owners. Feijoada is now usually made with prime cuts of pork and beef and is a Saturday lunch time favorite.

13 EDUCATION

Brazil has a serious problem of illiteracy. Approximately 20% of the Brazilian population does not know how to read or write, while many others have only a rudimentary ability to read. Although the proportion of children that attend school has increased since the 1960s, the quality of the education they receive is poor. Not surprisingly, the schools in the poorer neighborhoods where many Afro-Brazilians live have limited resources. Classes are extremely crowded and there is often a shortage of books. A larger proportion of Afro-Brazilian children, moreover, fail to attend school. Many children, particularly in both rural and urban areas, begin work at a young age to help the family make ends meet. The low level of education most Afro-Brazilian children receive makes it difficult for them to find employment as young adults.

14 CULTURAL HERITAGE

Most of the slaves brought over from Africa were illiterate, and slave owners preferred to keep it that way. As a result, an oral tradition of storytelling and history became very important in Afro-Brazilian culture. Many family histories, stories, and myths continue to be passed down through successive generations. Afro-Brazilian themes have also become an important aspect of Brazilian culture. Jorge de Lima is a poet who was widely read in the 1960s. He drew from African-style verses and wrote about the plight of Africans in Brazil.

Afro-Brazilian cultural heritage can be more readily seen in the powerful influence it has had on Brazilian music generally. Brazil's varied music traditions draw heavily from traditional African instruments, rhythm, and dance. Samba music, now popular around the world, is a direct descendant of African music. A more pure form of Afro-Brazilian music is performed by *afoxes,* dance groups that perform to music of the *Condom-*

ble religion. Using drums and percussion, these dance groups have increased in popularity in recent years. The African influence continues to shape Brazil's music and culture.

15 WORK

Brazil is a vast country and common types of work vary from region to region. In the northeast regions, cattle-raising and ranching are important economic activities. In the southeast, sugarcane, cotton, and coffee are also grown and exported. This diverse agricultural sector provides employment as field hands for many Afro-Brazilians. This work, however, pays poorly and is very laborious. In addition, many field workers are separated from their families to find employment at harvest time.

Brazil also has an impressive industrial and manufacturing sector. Autos, shoes, textiles, and electronic equipment are all made in Brazil, providing steady employment for many people. The manufacturing sector, however, does not generate enough employment for the millions of urban slum dwellers. Many *favela* (slum) residents work as self-employed street vendors or develop small-scale enterprises in their own homes. Many women, for example, work as seamstresses or hairstylists from their homes.

16 SPORTS

Perhaps the most famous soccer player in the world is an Afro-Brazilian, Edson Arantes do Nascimento. Better known as Pele, he continues to be a global personality. He rose from a low-income family in the state of Sao Paulo, and had limited formal education. Pele led the Brazil national team to World Cup championships in 1958, 1962, and 1970. Brazil was the first country to win the World Cup three times.

A more distinctive Afro-Brazilian "sport" is *capoeira.* This form of Angolan martial art is now more of a dance than an actual form of fighting. Brought over by slaves from Angola, this form of foot-fighting was banned by slave owners. In order to disguise this practice, slaves transformed foot-fighting into a rhythmic gymnastic/dance form. Accompanied by music, capoeira dancers gracefully use arm and leg motions, designed to barely miss the opponent. Well-aimed high kicks skim over the head of the other fighter.

17 ENTERTAINMENT AND RECREATION

Most entertainment revolves around music and dancing. Preparations for Carnival, for example, can begin up to six months in advance of the festival. Samba schools are popular in the *favelas (slums)* and provide an outlet and form of recreation for many Afro-Brazilian youths.

The other central form of recreation for Afro-Brazilian youths is practicing the national sport—soccer. Brazil is probably the country most enthusiastic about soccer in the world. Both in urban and rural areas, playing soccer is the preferred after-school activity.

18 FOLK ART, CRAFTS, AND HOBBIES

Afro-Brazilians produce a wide variety of arts and crafts. In Bahia, the African tradition of cooking in ceramic pots is still followed, and functional clay pots can be found in many markets. Intricately handcarved rosewood and handmade lace are art forms passed down through successive generations. Banana leaf fibers are sometime used in place of thread for lacemaking.

Many Afro-Brazilian arts and crafts are closely linked to African religious traditions. Many objects used in *Condomble* rituals are produced by skilled goldsmiths in Bahia. Charms and other forms of jewelry traditionally worn around the waists of slave women in Brazil are still popular.

The state of Bahia is also home to a growing number of painters. Numerous galleries have been set up in Salvador, Bahia, to market the paintings of talented local artists. Many of these paintings deal with themes relating to Afro-Brazilian life and culture.

19 SOCIAL PROBLEMS

Drug trafficking and related violence are serious problems that are on the rise in urban slums, or *favelas*. Organized gangs operate in the favelas, selling drugs and engaging in other types of crime. In part, this is the result of high unemployment among youths. Teenagers in the favelas are unlikely to have completed their formal education, and their employment prospects are bleak. The lure of easy money by selling drugs has drawn many young people into this dangerous activity. Conflicts between competing gangs often lead to violence and many deaths. Other forms of violent crime are also becoming widespread in the favelas.

20 BIBLIOGRAPHY

Birnbaum's South America 1994. New York: HarperCollins, 1995.

Devine, Elizabeth, and Nancy L. Briganti. *The Travelers' Guide to Latin American Customs and Manners.* New York: St. Martins Press, 1988.

Page, Joseph A. *The Brazilians.* New York: Addison Wesley, 1995.

Reynolds, Edward. *Stand the Storm: A History of the Atlantic Slave Trade.* London: Allison and Busby, 1985.

Rojas-Lombardi, Felipe. *The Art of South American Cooking.* New York: HarperCollins, 1991.

Smith, T. Lynn. *Brazil: People and Institutions.* Baton Rouge, LA: Louisiana State University Press, 1963.

Taylor, Edwin. *Insight Guides: Brazil.* Boston: Houghton Mifflin Company, 1995.

Weel, Thomas E. *Area Handbook for Brazil.* Washington, D.C.: American University, 1975.

—by C. Sahley

ALEUTS

ALTERNATE NAMES: Unangan
LOCATION: Aleutian Islands; Alaska
POPULATION: 10,000
LANGUAGE: English; Aleut
RELIGION: Based on animism

1 INTRODUCTION

About 1,100 miles southwest of mainland Alaska lie the Aleutian Islands. They are home to a people known as the Aleuts, who also inhabit the Pribilof Islands and parts of western Alaska proper. No one knows the meaning of the word "Aleut," which was first bestowed upon the islanders by Russian fur traders. Among themselves, the Aleuts are known as *unangan*, which means, "the people." Racially and ethnically, the Aleuts are close relatives of the Inuit, or Eskimo. Nonetheless, they have developed their own unique culture and language.

Contact between the Aleuts and the outside world was first established around 1750, when Russian fur traders entered the area in search of fox, fur seals, and sea otters. They forced most of the Aleut men to hunt sea otters and other animals for their pelts and, by the latter part of the century, relocated some Aleuts to the Pribilof Islands to serve as forced labor in harvesting the pelts of the northern fur seal. The Aleut population suffered a steady decline over the next 100 years as a result of illness and maltreatment at the hands of the outsiders. By 1867, when the United States purchased Alaska, only about 3,000 Aleuts still lived on the islands, and an outbreak of tuberculosis at the close of the century reduced this small population still further.

In 1913 the Aleutian Islands were designated a National Wildlife Refuge by the US Department of the Interior, which banned the hunting of sea lions and prohibited most other hunting without a special license. Between the two world wars, most Aleuts left their villages to relocate to the Alaska coast, where they worked in salmon canneries. The US Navy removed the remaining villagers during World War II and destroyed many villages to prevent possible Japanese access to them. After the war, a naval base was built on Adak Island. The Aleut League was formed in 1967 to lobby for expanded economic assistance from the federal government, but it had little success. The 1971 Alaska Native Claims Settlement Act provided each Aleut village with title to some land within the Aleutian Islands and created the Aleut Corporation, which was also given ownership of certain lands. Today most Aleuts live in mainland Alaska rather than the islands, where government jobs provide virtually the only employment.

2 LOCATION AND HOMELAND

The Aleutian Islands are located at approximately the same latitude as the British Isles, that is, about 800 miles south of the Arctic Circle. The entire Aleutian chain consists of over 150 small islands of volcanic origin and is typically divided into four sub-groups: the Near Islands, the Fox Islands, the Rat Islands, and the Andreanof Islands.

The climate of the Aleutian Islands is harsh and forbidding. In the summer the weather is generally wet, cool, and cloudy, while winter brings cold temperatures, bitter winds, and heavy

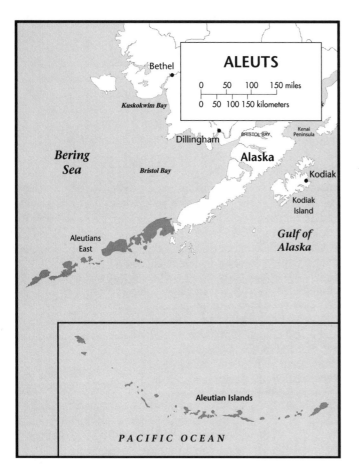

precipitation. Most of the time, the islands are covered with a thick layer of fog, and heavy rainstorms are frequent occurrences. These barren, wet, and windswept islands provide little support for trees or long-rooted vegetation, which cannot grow on the mountainsides, cliffs, reefs, and rocky soil. Thus, the Aleuts have always established their settlements near the seashore, depending for their sustenance on the enormous local populations of fish, sea mammals, and birds, the seasonal migrations of which lead them to feed in Aleutian waters at certain times of the year. The islands are also used as breeding grounds for sea mammals such as sea lions and fur otters.

The Aleut population was once estimated at between 12,000 and 25,000 individuals. At the time of the 1990 US census, it stood at roughly 10,000 people, of whom only some 1,500 lived on the Aleutian Islands, with the rest residing on the Alaskan mainland and elsewhere. There are some thirteen native villages remaining, most of them in the eastern Aleutians and the Pribilof Islands.

³ LANGUAGE

The language of the Aleuts originated from the same remote ancestor as that of the Inuit, from which both probably separated more than 2,000 years ago. Today they form two quite distinct and independent branches. Modern speakers of Aleut and Inuit cannot understand one another at all. The Aleutian language is spoken nowhere else in the world but on the Aleutian Islands and their immediate environs. The total number of speakers of Aleut is about the same as the total number of surviving Aleuts, that is, somewhere around 10,000.

⁴ FOLKLORE

The Aleuts have a strong storytelling tradition. Reflecting the communal nature of Aleut folktales, storytellers typically begin their narratives with the clause "This is the work of my country." As a method of discipline, parents often tell their children cautionary tales peopled by dangerous characters called "outside men." The Aleuts also have a tradition of folk medicine, including a knowledge of herbs, that has been passed down through the generations. They traditionally believed that all running water, especially sea water, was sacred and practiced sea bathing even in the winter.

⁵ RELIGION

The early Russian fur traders who first came in contact with the Aleuts also first exposed them to Christianity, particularly the Russian Orthodox variety. The first Russian missionaries arrived in Aleut territory by the late 18th century, and Russian Orthodoxy had largely replaced the precontact Aleut religion by the mid-1800s. Today most Aleuts belong to the Russian Orthodox church, and many have been trained as priests.

Like those of most hunting and gathering cultures, the traditional religion of the Aleuts was based on animism, which imparts spirits or souls to all the animals and objects in the landscape, together with the belief that these spiritualized animals and objects could be influenced by prayer or sacrifice. According to Aleut belief, human beings possessed several souls, or spiritual essences, one of the most important of which was the name. A common belief among Aleuts is that a dead person's soul will occupy the body of a newborn infant if the child is given the same name as the deceased.

The belief that the environment can be influenced, either for good or ill, by human intervention led to the development of a whole constellation of customs and taboos intended to ensure prosperity and prevent disaster. Many such customs and taboos were designed to placate and mollify the souls of the polar bears, whales, walrus, and seals that are the Aleuts' chief prey. By way of example, one might note the widespread custom by which it was considered proper for a hunter's wife to offer a dead seal a drink of water when it was brought to the entranceway of the dwelling. This token of hospitality was believed to relieve the animal's soul of any resentment it might feel toward having been killed. In some areas, especially western Alaska, complex annual ceremonies of thanksgiving are performed to honor the souls of seals and whales that have given their lives for the sake of the Aleut hunters and their families.

The most important human figure in Aleut religious belief was the shaman, who served many vital roles within Aleut society. The Aleut shaman was either male or female and functioned as priest, doctor, and counselor to his or her people. In times of crisis, the shaman provided a course of action for the group to follow. In times of sickness, the shaman healed and cured. In times of deprivation, the shaman located the source of the problem, usually some member of the social group who had been guilty of breaking a taboo and thus angering the souls of the animals.

⁶ MAJOR HOLIDAYS

In addition to the national holidays of the United States, most Aleuts celebrate the holidays of the Russian Orthodox calendar.

⁷RITES OF PASSAGE

Aleuts observe major life events such as births, weddings, and funerals within the Russian Orthodox religious tradition. In the traditional Aleut religion, commoners and slaves were cremated when they died, but young children and members of the elite were mummified. After removal of the internal organs, the body was washed in a stream, oiled, wrapped in furs, and suspended in a dry cave.

⁸INTERPERSONAL RELATIONS

The indigenous population of the Aleutian Islands was traditionally organized into small, relatively stable settlements scattered here and there throughout the island chain. Within each social group, a formal hierarchy was maintained. Each settlement, called a deme, was composed of an extended kin group and dominated by a chief. A higher chief was chosen by election from among the *deme* chiefs to govern a larger group of villages or an entire island. The village leader's responsibilities included watching over village hunting grounds, settling disputes among village members, determining the appropriate punishment for criminals, organizing the group's activities, and leading the village warriors in the warfare that frequently broke out among villages, usually as a result of insults, raids, or murders committed by members of other villages. In return for his leadership efforts, the deme chief received a share of all catches made by the hunters of the village.

Social status was determined according to wealth, and traditional Aleut society was divided into three distinct classes—the upper class, the common or working class, and slaves. Since they lived in permanent settlements all year round, the Aleut were able to accumulate commodities such as furs, shells, and slaves, and those who possessed much personal property were highly regarded. Aleuts shared food and possessions according to three principles: duty to relatives, repayment of a loan of supplies or equipment, and generosity toward the less fortunate. Through this system of mutual obligations, the Aleut protected the welfare of every village member.

⁹LIVING CONDITIONS

The Aleut had a sophisticated level of precontact medical knowledge, much of it gained from their awareness of the anatomical similarities between humans and the marine mammals that populated their environment. Some of their knowledge came from autopsies of these sea mammals. Their medical treatments included bloodletting and a form of acupuncture, as well as various spiritual measures. Today modern medical care is available to a limited extent to Aleut villagers, although they must travel to cities for certain services.

The traditional Aleut house (called a *barabara*) was a gigantic structure built on a rectangular frame made of whalebone or driftwood logs. The house was sunk three or four feet into the ground to provide added insulation. As a result, the entranceway was in the roof, as was another opening designed to allow light to enter the dwelling. The roof itself consisted of rafters of crisscrossing logs or other pieces of available wood, covered with sod and dried grass. The houses of the Aleut were similar to the sod dwellings of the Inuit in consisting of a single room. In many cases, however, that single room was very large, housing as many as 150 individuals from 40 or 50 different families. The family units within a single house divided the space into stall- or cubicle-like living areas that lined the walls of the common area. By the beginning of the 20th century, nearly all Aleuts lived in conventional above-ground dwellings that housed a single nuclear family. For transportation, the Aleut most often relied on skin-covered boats, usually using them to skim the waves in search of aquatic mammals to hunt.

¹⁰FAMILY LIFE

Unlike many aboriginal cultures, traditional Aleut society was not based on the tribal unit. Instead, the basic social unit was the extended family, consisting of a man and wife and their unmarried children, along with their married sons and their nuclear families. In the normal course of events, several such family units joined forces to hunt and provide one another with mutual protection and support. Such a group of families was named by adding the suffix *miut*, or "people of," to the name of the geographic region they inhabited. The leader of the group was typically the oldest male still physically able to participate in the hunt. Such a group leader was called upon to resolve quarrels within the group or among his own group and others.

¹¹CLOTHING

For the Aleut, life often depended on one single piece of clothing, the parka, or outer jacket, made of fur and bird skins. As opposed to the traditional Inuit parka, the Aleut parka did not have a hood. Rather, it had a high collar protecting the neck and stretched clear to the ankles for all-over protection from the elements. In keeping with the somewhat milder temperatures of the islands, the Aleut parka was often worn with nothing underneath, and many Aleuts traditionally spent much of their time barefoot. Special to the Aleut was a unique type of headgear—either a hat or a visor, shaped somewhat like an inverted garden trowel, made of wood, and brightly decorated with animal motifs and abstract designs. Some examples of Aleut head wear are elaborately adorned with ornamental objects including shells, beads, feathers, sea lion whiskers, and carved ivory figurines. The level of ornamentation of the headgear signaled the status of an Aleut. Only the wealthiest hunters earned the right to wear the most beautiful hats, as well as hats that covered the entire head.

Today most Aleuts wear modern, Western-style clothing.

¹²FOOD

The Aleut did not normally store food, since the damp climate made it difficult to maintain most foodstuffs in an edible state. And with most animal resources readily available on a year-round basis, there was little motivation to develop effective means of food preservation. As a rule, the traditional Aleut diet was characterized by greater variety than that of the Inuit. Meat was provided by marine mammals, such as sea otters, sea lions and harbor seals. Other food resources included marine invertebrates (such as sea urchins, mussels, and clams) and fish (including halibut, cod, and several different species of salmon). The typical Aleut meal combined fish and sea mammal meat with edible plants like cow parsnip, wild parsnip, kelp, and other greens, although plant foods played a relatively small role in the Aleut diet. The Aleut also had at hand many kinds of edible berries, including blueberries, blackberries, cranberries, and salmonberries.

[13] EDUCATION

The curriculum of today's Aleut schools is similar to that of other schools around the world. Children are taught math, history, spelling, reading, and the use of computers. Aleut teachers are also concerned that the students learn something about their culture and old traditions. Most Aleut villages have high schools, but relatively few villagers attend college.

[14] CULTURAL HERITAGE

Ritual dances were part of the Aleut cultural and religious tradition, although early missionaries banned dancing because they considered it sinful. At wintertime feasts celebrating the tribe's ancestors, wooden masks with pictures of spirits and ancestors were worn by dancers. When dancing, Aleut men wore special gloves decorated with puffin beaks that rattled with the movements of the dancers. Special dances were done to ensure the success of the whale hunt.

[15] WORK

Traditionally, the Aleut survived by harvesting sea lions, whales, and fish in their skin-covered boats as well as by foraging on land for birds' eggs and plants. Today many Aleut have entered the modern work force. Even those who live on the islands and still hunt, fish, and gather their traditional foods participate at least to some degree in the modern cash economy. Many travel from their villages to work at seasonal construction and fishing jobs.

[16] SPORTS

Aleut men traditionally engaged in contests of strength such as wrestling, plus a variety of throwing and catching games.

[17] ENTERTAINMENT AND RECREATION

Traditional recreational games of the Aleut include a form of chess played on a board with 56 squares instead of the customary 64 and a nonstandard distribution of pieces at the beginning of the game. Cat's cradle is another traditional favorite. Today's Aleut enjoy many of the same modern recreational pursuits as other Americans.

[18] FOLK ART, CRAFTS, AND HOBBIES

Traditionally, the Aleut have excelled at weaving dune grasses to make baskets, sleeping mats, and other necessary household items. They have also devoted much time and effort to the creation of their elaborate headgear. Nearly the only craft that is still practiced is the weaving of grass baskets.

[19] SOCIAL PROBLEMS

Today, like many other Native American peoples, the Aleuts suffer from declining population and the destruction of their culture. The rate of unemployment is high, and alcoholism is a major problem.

[20] BIBLIOGRAPHY

Laughlin, William S. *Aleuts, Survivors of the Bering Land Bridge.* New York: Holt, Rinehart, and Winston, 1980.

Marquis, Arnold. *A Guide to America's Indians:* University of Oklahoma Press, 1974.

Oliver, Ethel Ross. *Journal of an Aleutian Year.* Seattle: University of Washington Press, 1988.

Osborne, Kevin. *The Peoples of the Arctic.* Chelsea House, 1990.

Ray, Dorothy Jean. *Aleut and Eskimo Art: Tradition and Innovation in Southern Alaska.* Seattle: University of Washington Press, 1981.

Villoldo, Alberto. *Skeleton Woman.* New York: Simon and Schuster, 1995.

AMAHUACAS

LOCATION: Peru (Amazon river basin area)
LANGUAGE: Panoan
RELIGION: Indigenous religion based on spirits, with possible Christian influences

¹ INTRODUCTION

The Amahuacas are an Amerindian tribe who live in the Peruvian part of the great Amazon river basin area, which extends through Brazil to parts of Bolivia, Colombia, Ecuador, Venezuela, and Peru. The Amazon River and its mighty tributaries (17 of which are over 1,600 km or 1,000 mi long) drain about 40% of South America, including the largest area of tropical rain forest in the world.

The first expedition of Spanish conquerors into this region was led by Vicente Yánez Pinzón, who discovered the mouth of the Amazon and ascended it for about 80 km (50 mi) in AD 1500. This was a section of the river subsequently referred to as the Río Marañón. Subsequently, the Spanish explorer and conqueror Francisco de Orellana embarked on the first descent of the river from the Andes to the Atlantic Ocean in 1541.

Battles with Amerindian tribes occurred from the 16th century onwards and have continued in one form or another even until today: a variety of scattered tribes, including the Amahuacas, continue to try to defend their land rights and their way of life. The comparative remoteness of many areas allowed for the establishment of small settlements, missions, and trading posts, as well as some river ports established early on (such as Pucallpa on the Ucayali river, one of the longest tributaries of the Amazon), but prevented the total conquest of this vast area. Even 30 or 40 years ago, large areas of the eastern lowlands and jungles of Peru, known as the *montaña,* where the Amahuacas and other groups live, were largely unexplored.

Even before the arrival of the Spaniards, the many tribes scattered in this part of the Peruvian Amazon basin area and along the Ucayali River were engaged in a complex relationship with each other, which included trade on the one hand and raids on the other.

² LOCATION AND HOMELAND

The Amahuacas of eastern Peru are part of a group of tribes classified together as Panoans and located generally in the Ucayali Valley. Some of the stronger and more aggressive tribes such as the Chama Indians lived along the shores of the Ucayali River itself. They went on raids and took slaves from neighboring tribes who also spoke the same or closely related languages.

These continual raids compelled the Amahuacas to seek a less exposed position. They feared some of their more powerful neighbors because if they were captured during raids they would be taken to work as slaves for them. Together with some other tribes, they kept to the headwaters of some of the tributaries. In the case of the Amahuacas, they settled mainly along the headwaters of the Ucayali, the Juruá, and the Puruá rivers.

This is a hot, humid region which has an immensely rich plant and animal life. Jungle life usually conjures up images of unpleasant mosquitoes and dangerous snakes, but in the Amazon basin area only about 1 in 25 varieties of snakes is poison-

ous. A great variety of tall trees form a thick canopy so high up they seem to reach for the sky, in all shades of green, with the occasional brilliant burst of flowers. Manatees and turtles swim in the rivers, along with hundreds of species of fish. Fireflies light up the darkness in flashes of gold or green or red. Flocks of parakeets splash their color against the sky, and hundreds of different butterflies add bright touches of turquoise, yellow, orange, red, and black in gorgeous patterns. In the evening the cicadas beat their wings in noisy concert before the hush that precedes nightfall, when the nocturnal animals begin their secretive forays.

³ LANGUAGE

The Amahuacas speak a language that forms part of what is known as Panoan, and which is also spoken by neighboring tribes such as the Chamas, Remos, Cashibos, Nianaguas, Ruanaguas, and others. The language features suffixes "-gua" and "-hua," both of which mean "people."

⁴ FOLKLORE

The Amahuacas, along with many Amerindian tribes of the area, have creation stories of how the world came to be, how they as a people came to be, and also stories in which animals play a prominent part. Long centuries of observation led to an appreciation of the skills and strengths of many different animals, who play roles that are sometimes of symbolic importance in stories. There are extended family formations where the affiliation to a particular animal (sometimes called a "totem") is not only a symbol of identity but also a focal point for the contemplation of that particular animal's strengths and qualities.

Early explorers, adventurers, and traders differed greatly in their capacity to appreciate the various Amerindian cultures. The Amahuacas and others were sporadically visited by Christian missionaries from the 17th century onwards, but many missions failed over the centuries. However, this type of contact with White people, even if it did not succeed in Christianizing many groups in this area, did influence some of their myths, legends, and stories. The individual variations of each group have meant that Christian concepts have been incorporated in widely different ways, even by groups living in the same vicinity.

⁵ RELIGION

The Amahuacas believe that every living thing has a spirit, be it a rock, a tree, a bird, a jaguar, a body of water, or a person. There is a widespread belief among people of the Amazon that there are also some evil river spirits, although in some interpretations they are thought to correspond more closely to ghosts. The Amahuacas have shamans who are seen as mediators between this world and the spirit world.

Amahuacas share a belief, widespread among the Amerindian tribes of the Amazon basin, that illness is not a natural event. Rather, it is often attributed to the harmful influence of either another person or a being from the spirit world. It is thought that illness is caused by an actual attack by one of these agents, and it is believed that a thorn or a similar sharp object which is harmful enters the person and causes the illness. It is therefore important for the shaman to manufacture his own magic thorns or similar sharp objects, which he can then direct

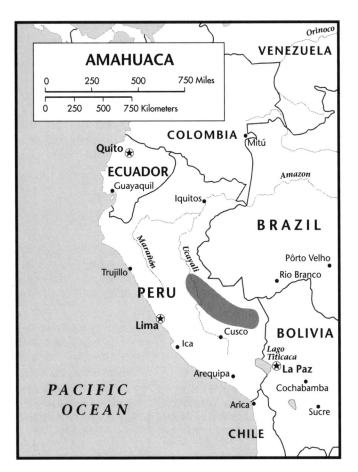

AMAHUACA

0   250   500   750 Miles

0   250   500   750 Kilometers

at the offending person or entity. Shamans are seen not only as protectors for the group, both from evil spirits and from illness, but also as people who can cause harm if the occasion calls for this type of action. The Amahuaca who is preparing himself to be a shaman has to imbibe a special drug, called *cayapí,* and then he has to isolate himself in the forest and receive his magic thorns from a magician there.

Catholic missions have not been successful among many tribes in this area, including the Amahuacas. The Amahuacas were not only hostile to some of the raiding tribes, especially the Piros, the Cashibos, and the Shipibos, who at various times enslaved them, but also to White people. It was reported in the 19th century that slaves were in some cases kept to work for the capturing tribe and in other cases were sold to White people.

Nevertheless, one of the Amahuaca beliefs (about what happens to human souls after death) is superficially similar to Catholic belief, and it may be that even the few attempts to Christianize the Amahuacas on the part of missionaries left faint traces. The Amahuacas believe that a soul after death usually goes to a heaven or paradise, but some go to a type of underworld. This may be an adaptation of the Christian concepts of heaven and hell. However, where the Amahuaca beliefs differ is in the vision of what heaven offers. The soul continues to live in some respects as it did when on earth. If it is in heaven, it can get married and it consumes food. If it goes to a lower or netherworld, it lives with a spirit called Tjaxo.

6 MAJOR HOLIDAYS

The Amahuacas are very isolated from mainstream Peruvian culture and do not participate in the holidays, whether religious or secular, of the majority of Peru's inhabitants.

7 RITES OF PASSAGE

When an Amahuaca baby is going to be born, the mother retires to a secluded place and is usually assisted by a few other women during childbirth. After the baby is born, the afterbirth and the umbilical cord are buried in the earth.

Some tribes along the Ucayali River have special rites when a girl reaches puberty. The Chama customs include an elaborate festival where a group of teenage girls, having reached puberty, are gathered together during the full moon at night, while the adults of the tribe celebrate the girls' fertility by dancing and singing all night. Some other tribes isolate the girls for a few days to mark the transition from childhood to adulthood. Among the Amahuacas, no special ceremonies are reported.

There have been cases where a girl is betrothed or promised in marriage while she is still a child, but in the majority of cases if a girl wishes to marry, the girl's father has to give his permission. In some cases a man has several wives.

There is great variation in burial ceremonies, and some of these have changed over time. At different times, all of these have been practiced in the Ucayali River region: cremation, burial in a funerary urn, burial in a canoe, burial underneath the floor of the house, and burial in the earth outside of the house.

Travelers to the Ucayali reported that the Amahuacas at one time cremated the body of the dead person and then consumed the ashes. This was done by mixing the ashes with *masato* and drinking them. In more recent history, the Amahuacas continued to cremate the body but no longer consumed the ashes. Infants are buried in urns. The personal effects of the deceased are burned, and sometimes the house is either burned or abandoned. The small fields where the dead person grew his or her crops are then passed on to relatives.

8 INTERPERSONAL RELATIONS

Greetings respect social norms, which include the positions occupied by the various members of the family and the extended family.

It would be difficult to approach an Amahuaca casually, since this tribe has long been suspicious of strangers, quite often for very good reason. The rubber boom that swept the region in the 19th century decimated at least 90% of the Amerindian population: the Indians died from diseases to which they had never been exposed before, from brutal working conditions when they were forced to work as slaves, from starvation, and from armed conflict.

Girls and boys are allowed to have sexual relations once they have reached puberty.

9 LIVING CONDITIONS

For those unused to living in the tropical lowlands, life in the Ucayali river region can be very hard. It is remarkable that the Amahuacas and others adapted and survived, perhaps for hundreds if not thousands of years, in what is perceived by many as a hostile environment, where nature is fierce rather than benign. Some jungle ants not only sting but also bite; there are also scorpions and spiders, some of which are poisonous, as well as several poisonous snakes. In some rivers, the boa constrictor and the cayman pose dangers. Jaguars are hunted but also greatly feared.

The Amahuacas use a number of medicinal plants, including the leaves of a plant known as *Dracontium longpipes* used for snake bites, and also seek help in case of illness from their shamans. Many of the medicinal herbs of this area are not generally known to outsiders.

The Amahuacas lead a simple, sustainable lifestyle, but the strategies for survival require a considerable number of skills. The pattern of agriculture in this area includes the slash-and-burn method, which means that when the land is exhausted after a few years, it becomes necessary to move on to another part of the forest to grow crops, often in clearings on the shores of a river. This requires a type of house which is light, and methods through which a house can be quickly rebuilt elsewhere.

The Amahuacas build rectangular huts with sticks and cane. Often the chonta palm is used for thatching roofs. Some 19th-century travelers thought that the Amahuacas and some other tribes probably moved about a great deal, because they reported that they saw them living in boats. It is now appreciated that proper care and conservation, in an environmental sense, of this large jungle area with its many rivers and tributaries does in fact require small settlements scattered over a large area, and mobility to allow the land to lie fallow for a time while other small areas are cultivated. This conservation strategy, which evolved over thousands of years, is now in danger of being overturned by colonists from outside the area, landowners hungry for more land, prospectors, and others.

The Amahuacas use balsa rafts for river transport and undertake land-based hunting expeditions on foot, although on the Ucayali River itself other tribes use dugout canoes.

10 FAMILY LIFE

The role of women is important among the Amahuacas in the sense that their society is matrilineal. When a couple get married, they go to live with the bride's family. The extended family unit can consist of a man with several wives, but it is usual for the man to work with and for his wife's father. The Amahuacas do not live close together in large villages, but rather in extended family households over a scattered area. A household can consist of the head of the household as leader of the unit, his wife, his married daughters, and his unmarried sons.

The women do much of the productive and often heavy work, including farming and transporting goods, as well as cooking and preparing drinks such as *masato*. They also make pottery and weave. Most Amerindians in this area grow cotton for weaving, and *urucú* or *genipa* for body paint.

The Amahuacas keep guinea pigs as pets.

11 CLOTHING

Amahuaca women wear a cotton skirt. Clothing for important or ceremonial occasions may include, for the man, a garment known as the *cushma*. These garments sometimes have painted panels. The designs are often geometric and the colors include black and red. They are woven of bark or cotton.

Amahuacas tattoo the face in a permanent form of ornamentation, which is usually carried out in childhood. The tattoo is made by using a thorn and soot from the copal tree. They also blacken their teeth. The dark color is obtained by chewing a species of pepper.

Although little clothing is worn, a great variety of ornaments are used, including beaded necklaces, headbands, arm bands, anklets, bracelets, and rings.

12 FOOD

A wide range of food is available in this region, including wild fruits and berries, wild honey, fish (including catfish), and game such as water hogs, deer, tapir, peccaries, monkeys, agutis, some water snakes and caymans, and some species of water fowl, as well as parrots. The Amahuacas are skilled hunters and use bows and arrows. The arrows have four different types of tips. They also grow and use certain types of poison for fish. Food is sometimes cooked over open fires. The Amahuacas grow corn and cassava or manioc, and they use stone grinders to prepare some of the food. They also make their own clay cooking pots and a few wooden utensils, as well as sieves and graters.

13 EDUCATION

The education of boys includes the teaching of all the necessary survival skills, especially hunting and fishing, as well as house-building and boat-building and the making of weapons such as bows and arrows. Girls are taught cooking, farming, pottery, and weaving skills.

The Amahuacas do not use a written language. They transmit their sense of identity and their explanations about the world orally, through chants and stories. Officially, therefore, they are considered "illiterate."

14 CULTURAL HERITAGE

Music and dance form an important part of life for most Amerindian tribes of the Ucayali region. Musical instruments include gourds, rattles, flutes, and drums. These are played on ceremonial occasions.

The Amahuacas pass on to their children the sense of who they are, how they came to be, how the world came to be, and so on through stories which are transmitted orally.

15 WORK

Collecting wild plants and berries is an activity that men, women, and children can perform. Hunting and fishing is a man's job among the Amahuacas. Women often till the soil and transport goods, as well as look after young children, cook, weave, and make pottery and ornaments.

16 SPORTS

It has been noted by a variety of travelers that games are often very individual affairs among the Amerindian tribes of the Ucayali. There are miniature bows and arrows as well as dolls made for young children, and other miniature toys, but these are played with individually and these efforts do not develop into team games or sports. Children also play with corn-leaf balls, but team-based ball games are not played. Sometimes children enjoy wrestling. There are no adult sports.

[17] ENTERTAINMENT AND RECREATION

Most Indian groups of the Ucayali, including the Amahuacas, enjoy occasions for feasting. Typically, a successful hunt can provide an occasion, or the arrival of visitors from tribes the Amahuacas consider friendly, or a special ceremonial event. Drinking bouts are quite frequent. Fermented drinks are made from corn, sugarcane, and other plants.

[18] FOLK ART, CRAFTS, AND HOBBIES

Pleasingly shaped and simple pottery in everyday use is made by Amahuaca women. They also weave cotton for simple garments, and these are sometimes decorated with panels in various colors. Dyes are prepared from *genipa* and *urucú*.

The Amahuacas sleep in hammocks in their huts, and weaving a strong yet resilient hammock out of *fique* or hemp requires real skill. Baskets and various types of bags for carrying are also woven. Some pipes are made for smoking tobacco, which is not in general use. Among the Amahuacas it is often the shaman who uses tobacco ceremonially in various rituals to protect a person or a group from illness or enemies.

Ornaments and jewelry are made, including earrings and beaded necklaces.

[19] SOCIAL PROBLEMS

The Amahuacas have resisted incursions for a very long time, but there has been a significant change that could shatter the Amerindian communities of eastern Peru. A US oil company signed a contract early in 1996 with the Peruvian state oil company. It is thought that this is the most biologically diverse region on the planet. There are about 19 Amerindian tribes in this area, probably including Amahuaca settlements between the upper Piedras River and the Cujar River, which is a tributary of the Purús river. There are also some tribes that have possibly never been contacted before.

Oil prospecting requires detonating underground explosives at particular set intervals and analyzing the shock waves to assess oil deposits. Wildlife will be severely disturbed in the area, which will threaten the food supply of the Amerindian communities. It will also be difficult, if not impossible, to maintain the roving, seminomadic pattern that is an essential part of the way of life for Amahuacas and others. The Amahuacas range over long distances and their lifestyle, which plays a part in the conservation of the important resource which is the Amazon basin, may not survive this type of onslaught.

[20] BIBLIOGRAPHY

Jaulin, Robert, ed. *El Etnocidio a través de las Américas.* Mexico: Siglo XXI Editores S. A., 1976.

Personal communication and June 1996 bulletin, Survival International, London.

Steward, Julian Haynes, ed. *A Handbook of South American Indians.* New York: Cooper Square, 1963.

—by P. Pitchon

AMERICAN IMMIGRANTS

LOCATION: United States
RELATED ARTICLES: Vol. 2: Americans

[1] INTRODUCTION

Virtually all Americans are immigrants or descendants of immigrants. As far as we know, the very first immigrants to America migrated from Asia to the North American continent somewhere between 15,000 and 40,000 years ago. The descendants of these first immigrants are now known as Native North Americans, Native Americans, American Indians, or First Nations people.

The majority of African Americans are not considered to be descended from immigrants because their ancestors were brought to America against their will. Another group of early colonists who were not truly immigrants were some 50,000 English criminals exported to America by the British government. They also did not freely choose to immigrate to America, but once in the New World, they settled down to a new life and became productive citizens.

European explorers arrived on the North American continent in the 15th century and continued to explore its lands throughout the 16th century. By the 17th century, England, France, Spain, and the Netherlands had all established American colonies. The Dutch (Netherlands) were conquered by the English in the late 17th century and withdrew from America, leaving the English, French, and Spanish to fight for control of the continent. The Europeans pushed the Native North Americans westward as they expanded their territories, eventually confining the original North American inhabitants to small reservations on undesirable land.

The 13 English colonies revolted against the crown in 1775 and declared independence from England in 1776. By 1783, the colonists had won the American Revolutionary War and established themselves as the United States of America. The US Constitution contained no laws on immigration. In 1790, the US government did legislate the process for becoming a naturalized US citizen, however, restricting this privilege to any "free white person" who had resided in the US for at least two years. In 1810, US president Thomas Jefferson increased the residency requirement to five years, where it has remained ever since.

Because the original 13 states were former English colonies, the language, religion, architecture, customs, and legal, economic, and governmental systems of those English colonists became the standard for the United States. For the next 200 years, all immigrants were expected to be assimilated to the English norm. Only in the 1980s and 1990s has the expectation begun to shift away from assimilation towards multiculturalism in the US. The basic structure of US society is still based on the English standard, however.

The original English Puritans were fiercely Protestant, committed to a strong work ethic, and violently opposed to any extravagance. They had come seeking freedom from religious persecution but then refused that same freedom to others in their colonies. Other colonists, however, such as William Penn, promoted religious freedom for all, and a number of Catholics and Jews began to settle in America as well. In the 18th century, Scottish and Scotch-Irish (Protestant), Welsh (Protestant), French Huguenot (Protestant), and German (Protestant, Catholic, and Jewish) immigrants arrived in the US. Most came to escape religious, economic, and/or political oppression. France and Spain also continued to control parts of North America, and French and Spanish immigrants (nearly all Catholic) settled in those areas.

The rate of immigration rose sharply after the invention of the steamboat in 1819, which cut the length of an ocean crossing from two or more months to one or two weeks. Those who had resisted the notion of traveling for months in miserable conditions over dangerous seas on a sailing ship were much more inclined to take a one- or two-week trip on a heavy steamship. Most ship captains also required that passengers supply their own food, and more people could afford to buy one or two weeks' worth of meals than two or more months' worth. Conditions on the new steamships were still overcrowded and unsanitary, and many immigrants continued to become seriously ill or even die en route. But overall, the risks were fewer and the costs much less, and the number of immigrants increased rapidly.

A population boom throughout Europe in the late 18th and 19th centuries, caused by better living conditions and medical care, had also created pressure to emigrate. Most European countries did not have enough land to support all the new people, nor were there enough jobs in the pre-industrial cities to support landless peasants. Therefore, people were forced to look elsewhere for means of support. The US was expanding rapidly and needed workers and homesteaders. Those immigrants who wished to continue farming took advantage of all the free or cheap land available in the US, especially when the Homestead Act went into effect in 1862 (giving parcels of land at little or no cost to anyone who agreed to work it for at least five years). Others who wanted to get off the farm took one of the plentiful jobs available in mining, railroad and canal construction, lumbering, smithing, and other skilled and unskilled labor necessary for expansion.

Immigrants who came to the US before 1880 are considered to be in the "first wave" of immigration. First-wave immigrants are also called "old immigrants." Up until the 1880s, the US had an open-door policy allowing almost anyone to enter the US. Certain restrictions were applied in the mid-1800s to those with communicable diseases and to indigents with no resources, and no skills to acquire those resources. However, few were turned away, and the US population grew in its multinational character.

"Old immigrants" were primarily Irish, German, Scandinavian, Canadian, and Chinese. Many were single young men who hoped to save up enough money to return home in better circumstances. Some did in fact return to their homelands, but the majority ended up settling permanently in the US. These young men then encouraged their relatives and friends to join them in America, setting off a chain migration. The friends and relatives settled near the original immigrants, creating ethnic neighborhoods or farming communities. "Chinatowns," "Germantowns," and Irish parishes sprang up across the US. Some of them still exist today.

About two-thirds of all US immigrants by the mid-1800s came through New York City. In 1855, the city opened Castle Garden, a reception center for immigrants where they could stay while being processed. Castle Garden was replaced in 1892 by Ellis Island, which remained in service until 1943. Millions of immigrants to America passed through Ellis Island in its 51 years of functional existence. Recently, Ellis Island was renovated and reopened as a museum of US immigration history.

The period of 1880–1920, the second wave of US immigration, is referred to as the "Great Migration" because so many immigrants entered the US during those four decades. In contrast to the first-wave, or "old immigrants," these second-wave "new immigrants" came mostly from southern and eastern Europe, and Japan. Southern and eastern Europeans looked quite different from the old immigrants. While the old immigrants were generally fair-skinned Anglo-Saxons, the new immigrants were darker-skinned Slavic and Mediterranean peoples. Most old immigrants had spoken English or another Germanic language upon arrival in the US, but the new immigrants spoke languages that sounded completely foreign to the old immigrant population. Many more Jews came during the Great Migration, along with Eastern Orthodox and Italian Catholics.

The influx of Japanese to the West added to the anti-Asian sentiments already developing in response to the Chinese presence there. Filipinos "imported" to work on the sugar plantations of Hawaii and in the agricultural industry of the West Coast further increased the perceived Asian threat to European Americans. In 1882, the US government passed the Chinese Exclusion Act, the first serious restriction on immigration and the only one to target a single ethnic group in US history. The act was extended in 1892 for another 10 years and was then extended indefinitely in 1902. The Chinese Exclusion Acts were not repealed until 1943 when China became a US ally in the war against the Japanese in World War II (1939–45).

The Great Migration of 1880–1920 brought 27 million immigrants through Ellis Island. In 1907, Congress passed legislation barring immigrants with physical or mental disabilities that would prevent them from working, immigrants with tuberculosis, and unaccompanied minors (children without adult supervision). Only about 1% of all immigrants were rejected. Once the US reached its western border and the rate of expansion began to slow down, US residents began to feel pressured by all the new arrivals. In 1921, therefore, the US Congress passed the first generally applied immigration act, limiting new immigrants to 3% of the total population from each ethnicity or nationality already living in the US. This was an attempt to keep the ethnic makeup of the US predominantly Anglo-Saxon.

The Johnson-Reed Immigration Act of 1924 limited immigration even further, setting stricter quotas for all nationalities. The Oriental Exclusion Act of the same year prohibited any Asians from immigrating. In 1929, the stock market crashed, and the US economy descended into the Great Depression. Jobs were scarce, and there was no longer much to offer new immigrants. In response, Congress enacted the first complete national origins quota system, establishing a total limit of 150,000 immigrants from the Eastern Hemisphere, divided up according to percentages of the current US population. Great Britain was allowed nearly half the total allowance. Great Britain, Ireland, and Germany combined comprised two-thirds of the total. Italy, which had been sending the largest number of immigrants of any country just prior to enactment of the quota system, was now allowed only 6,000 immigrants per year.

Because the restrictions pertained only to nations of the Eastern Hemisphere, there was no limit on the number of Mexicans who could immigrate to the US. Mexican workers leapt at the chance to fill the gaps left by European and Asian laborers who could no longer immigrate. However, there were not many jobs available during the Depression years of the 1930s. The US even began a "repatriation program" to remove Mexican Americans back to Mexico. With the onset of World War II in 1939, however, American men left their jobs to fight in the war, and the US suddenly suffered a labor shortage. Those same Mexicans who had been repatriated a few years before were now hired as *braceros*, contract workers with temporary visas.

World War II also brought other immigrants to the shores of America. In 1946, Congress passed the War Brides Act, allowing the immigration of foreign women (and men) who had married or become engaged to US military personnel while they were stationed overseas. Many British women in particular became US residents through this act. The Displaced Persons Act of 1948 opened the doors to US immigration a little bit wider, allowing refugees from wartorn Europe to move to America. Many Jews who had been excluded by earlier immigration acts were now able to escape Nazi terrorism through the Displaced Persons Act. The Chinese Exclusion Acts were also repealed, as mentioned above.

A new quota system was introduced in 1952 by the McCarran-Walter Act. The new system still favored northern and western Europeans, however. Not until 1965 did Congress loosen the restrictions on southern and eastern European immigration, as well as immigration from other continents. The Immigration and Nationality Act of 1965 removed the quota system and instead allowed immigration on a first-come, first-served basis, with preferences given to those who had close family members already in the US, and those with "desirable" job skills. Total annual limits were placed on immigration from the Western Hemisphere (120,000) and elsewhere (170,000), with a maximum of 20,000 allowed from any one country. In 1978, the act was revised to a single global limit of 290,000, with no distinctions between hemispheres.

Post-World War II immigrants are considered to be the "third wave." The third wave of US immigration is characterized by an easing of restrictions and a rise in the numbers of immigrants from Asia, Latin America, and the Caribbean. The 21 countries with the highest rates of immigration today are Canada, Mexico, Costa Rica, El Salvador, Guatemala, Honduras, Nicaragua, Colombia, Ecuador, Peru, the Dominican Republic, Haiti, Jamaica, Nigeria, India, Iran, Korea, the Philippines, Thailand, Greece, and Italy. The fastest-growing segment of the US population is now Hispanic Americans from Latin America.

Between 1975 and 1988, some 900,000 refugees from Vietnam, Cambodia, and Laos also entered the US. Because of the need to assist refugees from Indochina and other parts of the world, the US passed the Refugee Act of 1980, setting a special quota of 50,000 for refugees and allowing the US president to accept more as well, if necessary. The general limit for total immigration to the US was also raised from 290,000 to 320,000.

A "refugee" is defined as one who is homeless due to racial, religious, political, or social persecution. Economic oppression is not considered valid for refugee status. This distinction and the way it is used to exclude certain people from immigrating to the US has become quite controversial in recent years. Immigration limits and the refusal by the US government to grant certain people refugee status leads many of those who are excluded to enter the US by "illegal" means. The number of "illegal" immigrants—the preferred term among the Hispanic community is "undocumented migrants"—has risen sharply in the latter half of the 20th century. Mexicans have crossed the US border without proper documentation since the late 1800s, but they are now being joined by Central Americans, Haitians, and Dominicans.

In an effort to reduce the number of undocumented migrants, the US government passed the Immigration Reform and Control Act of 1986, granting amnesty to undocumented migrants who arrived in the US before 1982 and could prove at least five years' residency. Immigration offices were unprepared for the hordes of people who applied for amnesty. Those who met the requirements were automatically given a "green card," or legal immigrant status. With legal status, they could now sponsor their relatives to immigrate. So many chose to do so that the US government had to create a new quota category in 1990 to accommodate relatives of recent amnesty recipients.

The 1986 Immigration Reform and Control Act also imposed stiff penalties on employers who knowingly hire "illegal aliens." Unfortunately, this did little to stem the flow of undocumented migrants but did make their situation once in the US much worse than before. A number of employers stopped hiring undocumented migrants, forcing them to go even further underground to find work. Consequently, they became even more vulnerable to exploitation. Many employers, however, discovered that even with the fines they could still save money by hiring undocumented migrants because they could pay them much less than the minimum wage required by law.

Undocumented migrants contribute a great deal of money to the US economy through paying taxes (which almost all do on a regular basis) and spending their money. They also help keep prices down by saving employers wage costs. Very few undocumented migrants make use of government services (such as welfare or food stamps), and what it costs to educate their children is much less than what they give back to the economy. Undocumented migrants also create jobs by starting new businesses and by spending their money at other businesses, enabling those businesses to hire more workers. Despite these realities, however, many established Americans blame much of the economy's ills on undocumented migrants, claiming they take jobs away from "legal" Americans and drain the economy though the use of public services. In fact, neither is true. As long as both the US economy and the migrants benefit from the arrangement, as they now do, undocumented migration to the US will continue.

In the 1980s and 1990s, the movement in America has been away from assimilation to the Anglo-Saxon norm and toward multiculturalism. Cities with large Hispanic populations have become de facto bilingual, and many schools now offer bilingual education. Ethnic groceries make it possible for newcomers to continue to eat the traditional foods of their former homelands. Multicultural education and ethnic and racial pride are gaining force across America. Racism and prejudice are still widespread realities, however. A nation made up of individuals from many different racial, ethnic, and cultural backgrounds was a unique experiment when it began in the 18th century. Whether or not Americans can continue to create themselves out of such disparate elements in healthy and harmonious ways remains to be seen.

² LOCATION AND HOMELAND

Groups of immigrants from the same country or ethnic background tend to settle together, at least in the early days of their immigration. Because most immigrants entered the US by way of New York City, many simply settled there or in the surrounding areas. New York City itself is home to large concentrations of Irish, Chinese, Italian, Jewish, Greek, Indo-Chinese, Dominican, Puerto Rican, Hungarian, Russian, and Ukranian Americans, among others. Members of these groups are also spread across the Northeast (Boston is home to many Irish and Jewish Americans, in particular). Franco-Americans live in the northern sections of the Northeast, near the Canadian border.

California and the West Coast are very popular among Asian, Central American, and Mexican Americans. Cuban and Haitian Americans, as well as some US Central Americans, on the other hand, prefer Miami, Florida. Filipinos and Japanese are heavily concentrated in both California and Hawaii, those being common ports of entry for Pacific immigrants. Texas is another popular destination for both Mexican and Vietnamese Americans. There is also a fairly large German American population in Texas.

For the most part, however, German Americans chose the farmlands of the Midwest and Dakotas, as did Scandinavian Americans. A special group of German immigrants, called the Amish, also settled in the Midwest, as well as the Mid-Atlantic region. They set up their distinctive farming communities on the fertile soil of such states as Pennsylvania, Ohio, Indiana, and Illinois.

Immigrants who were not interested in farming headed for the industrial cities of the Northeast, Mid-Atlantic, and Midwest regions of the US. Chicago drew Italian, Jewish, Slavic, Polish, Greek, Hungarian, and Irish Americans. Hungarian Americans, along with Slavic, Polish, and Ukrainian Americans, also settled in cities such as Detroit, Pittsburgh, Philadelphia, Buffalo, and Cleveland. Arab Americans continue to flock to the Detroit, Michigan, area where they were originally drawn by jobs at the Henry Ford Motor Company. Many still work in the automotive industry.

Scotch-Irish immigrants in the 18th century tended to settle in Pennsylvania, while those from Scotland preferred the South, especially North Carolina. Louisiana, with its French flavor, drew both Cajuns from Canada, and French plantation owners from Haiti. Bordering on Mexico, and having once been Mexican territory, Arizona and New Mexico are natural destinations for Mexican Americans.

Between 1820, when immigration records first began to be kept, and 1991, the largest number of immigrants came from Germany (7,094,000, or 12.1%). Italy was next (5,403,000, or 9.2%), followed by Great Britain (5,136,000, or 8.7%), Ireland (4,730,000, or 8.0%), and Austria-Hungary (4,329,000, or 7.3%). Almost half (45.3%) of all US immigrants throughout much of US history, therefore, have been from those five European nations. German Americans are now the largest ethnic group in America, followed (in descending order) by Irish, English, African, Italian, Mexican, French, Polish, Native

North American, Dutch, Scotch-Irish, Jewish, Scottish, and Swedish Americans.

Although they have recently made up the majority of US immigrants, Asian, Caribbean, and Latin Americans comprise only 17.1% of total US immigration from 1820 to 1991. According to 1988 figures, today's immigrants prefer to settle in California (30%), New York (17%), Florida (10%), Texas (7%), New Jersey (5%), and Illinois (4%). Almost three-fourths (73%) of all new immigrants currently settle in these six states.

³ LANGUAGE

In general, US immigrants are expected to learn English, and most work hard to do so. Foreign-born immigrants who do not speak English are at a great disadvantage in the English-dominated society of the US. Language barriers severely limit employment opportunities and make life in general much more difficult. American-born children of first-generation immigrants grow up speaking English at school and with their friends, however, so they develop a natural fluency. This can create tension in the family as children become more capable in many ways than their parents. Parents may also resent the fact that their children lose fluency in the language of the parents' homeland. Communication and cultural conflicts abound between first- and second-generation immigrants due to these language differences.

The recent influx of Spanish-speaking immigrants has led to de facto bilingualism in many major cities, including Miami, New York City, Los Angeles, and Chicago. Hispanic Americans promote bilingual education, at least in elementary school, to give their children a greater chance of succeeding. An anti-Hispanic backlash among some European Americans has spawned the "English Only" movement, which began in Miami in 1980 and spread quickly across the US. "English Only" proponents want to have English declared the official language of the US.

American English has incorporated many words from its immigrants' languages, however. "Cookie," "spook," and "waffle" come from the Dutch, while German Americans contributed "kindergarten," "gesundheit," "ouch," "delicatessen," and "blitz." Even Filipino Americans, though small in number, have given American English the words "yo yo" and "boondocks."

English has borrowed numerous words from the French, including "boulevard," "avenue," "laissez-faire," "coup" and "coup d'état" "potpourri," "r.s.v.p." (*répondez, s'il vous plaît*), "chic," and "déjà vu." French and Italian have given Americans many words for foods and cooking methods, such as "omelet," "mayonnaise," "hors d'oeuvres," "bouillon," "filet," "purée," "sauté," and "à la mode" from the French, and "pasta," "spaghetti," "ravioli," and the like from Italian.

Many US immigrants Americanize their names in order to blend in with mainstream society. This was particularly true for second-wave immigrants. German names like Schmidt became the common English name Smith. Lebanese Americans changed their names from Hassad and Ashshi to their English equivalents, Smith and Cook. Italian Americans simply removed the final letter or letters from their names to change Italian-sounding names like Rossi and Gilberti to the English Ross and Gilbert. Today's immigrants are more likely to retain their original names, although some Hispanics drop their mother's surname, keeping only their father's (as is customary in mainstream America), and some Asians reverse their names to follow the standard American given name-surname order.

4 FOLKLORE

Immigrants to the US bring with them the legends and folktales of their homelands. Some of those tales have made it into the general American culture. The German stories in the Grimm brothers' collection, as well as those by the French storyteller Charles Perrault and Danish master Hans Christian Andersen, are very well-known by nearly all second- and later-generation Americans. Persian tales from the *Arabian Nights* and English nursery rhymes from *Mother Goose* are also quite familiar to most Americans.

Poet Henry Wadsworth Longfellow immortalized two early American heroines. Longfellow's poem *The Courtship of Miles Standish* recounts the romance of Priscilla Mullins (Molines), a French Huguenot immigrant, and *Evangeline* tells the story of a young Cajun woman of that name. A real-life Cajun character who has since become legendary is pirate Jean Lafitte.

In recent years, increasing efforts are being made to record the folktales of various ethnic groups in America. Hmong legends have been collected by Charles Johnson in a book called *Myths, Legends, and Folktales from the Hmong of Laos*, published by Macalester College in 1985. Amy Tan and other Asian writers have begun telling the stories handed down to them by their parents and grandparents. Anthologies of Irish, Scottish, and other folklore are becoming widely available as well in libraries and bookstores across America.

5 RELIGION

The first English colonists in America were staunch Protestants and gave the US a definite Protestant character for much of its history. The early English Protestants were joined by Dutch, French (Huguenot), Scotch-Irish, Scandinavian, and German Protestants during the 18th and early 19th centuries. This union cemented the Protestant slant of the US. The Irish constituted the first major wave of Catholics in the US and came to dominate the American Catholic Church. Italian, some German, Polish, and Hispanic Catholics found Irish Catholicism rather unappealing when they arrived in the US and finally formed their own parishes.

The Greeks and Eastern Europeans brought another form of Christianity to America, known as the Orthodox Church. Small groups of Anabaptists, such as the Amish, Quakers, and Mennonites, created their own distinctive Protestant communities. American Jews gathered together and built synagogues, and Asian American Buddhists and Hindus constructed temples and ashrams. Eventually, enough Arabs immigrated to the US to establish Muslim mosques; the lack of mosques had discouraged Arab immigration for some time.

Clearly, the US is no longer a Protestant nation. Christianity is still the majority religion, but other religions are well represented. Mainstream Americans have recently shown an increasing interest in Asian philosophy and religion, such as Buddhism, Zen, yoga, and the martial arts.

6 MAJOR HOLIDAYS

Most US immigrants learn to celebrate major American holidays such as Memorial Day (the last Monday in May), Independence Day (4 July), Labor Day (the first Monday in September), and Thanksgiving (the last Thursday in November). They also celebrate whichever holidays are recognized in their particular religious faith. Many non-Christian Americans observe Christmas as well because it has become as much a secular, commercial holiday as a religious one in America.

Every ethnic group seems to have its own New Year's Day. The official American date for New Year's is 1 January, but for Jewish Americans, New Year's (or *Rosh Hashanah*) falls sometime in September or October; for Chinese and Vietnamese Americans, it occurs in late January or early February; the Cambodian American New Year is in mid-April; and Hmong Americans ring in the New Year in December.

French Cajun and Creole Americans hold a huge festival every year in New Orleans on *Mardi Gras* ("Fat Tuesday"), the day before the Christian observance of Lent begins on Ash Wednesday. Parades of costumed, masked figures, music and dancing, feasting, and general revelry draw thousands of visitors from across America. Irish Americans introduced St. Patrick's Day on 17 March, and Italian Americans made Columbus Day on 12 October into a national holiday.

Certain holiday traditions have also spread from specific ethnic groups into mainstream America. Blindfolded children of all backgrounds swing sticks at Hispanic *piñatas* (hollow, animal-shaped pottery or plaster containers that are filled with candy and gifts), and try to break them so the contents will spill out. The American name for Santa Claus comes from the Dutch word for St. Nicholas, *Sinterklaas*, but the character itself was brought to America by the Germans. German Americans also introduced the traditions of Christmas trees and New Year's Eve festivities.

7 RITES OF PASSAGE

Other than birth, marriage, and funeral rites, most American immigrants drift away from traditional rites of passage. As a society, America has few meaningful rituals to denote passage from one stage of life to the next. Academic graduations, the first job, getting a driver's license, reaching the legal drinking age, buying a house, and marriage are today's American rites of passage. Only Jews (and some Native North Americans) have managed to maintain their traditional rituals. Most Jewish boys and many Jewish girls go through a *bar* or *bat mitzvah* at the age of 13, the ritual age of adulthood.

8 INTERPERSONAL RELATIONS

Every immigrant group brings with it to the US its own customs of interpersonal relations. American-born children, however, quickly become "Americanized" and begin to lose their distinctive ethnic style of interaction. Certain tendencies may remain for generations, such as the Italian American flair for dramatics versus the German American somber stoicism.

Nearly every immigrant group soon establishes mutual assistance organizations, as well as social and cultural associations. These organizations and associations replace the support given by extended families and close-knit communities in the immigrants' homelands.

9 LIVING CONDITIONS

Newly arrived immigrants to the US often live in overcrowded slums until they are able to earn enough money to move to better neighborhoods. Those who do not speak English have an added barrier to success and must work extra hard to improve their circumstances. Even immigrants who have English language skills and upper-level educational and employment experience may still have to start working below their qualification level and find themselves with a much lower standard of living than that to which they were accustomed in their former homeland.

Refugees suffer from shock, injuries and illnesses sustained prior to and during immigration, post-traumatic stress disorder, and other stress-related diseases. Many of today's refugees from Indochina and Latin America have problems as severe as those found in survivors of Nazi concentration camps in World War II (1939–45).

Many immigrant groups continue to practice traditional folk remedies, such as teas or charms, to cure illness. First-generation immigrants from less industrialized countries are often hesitant to use modern Western medicine or go to Western doctors or hospitals. Mainstream Americans, on the other hand, are becoming increasingly interested in some of these folk remedies, creating an "alternative" medicine movement. Eastern medicine, brought to the US by Asian Americans, has gained many adherents throughout the US among Asian and non-Asian Americans alike.

10 FAMILY LIFE

Family structure is perhaps the element of immigrants' lives that undergoes the most change upon resettlement in America. Many immigrants come from cultures that center on extended families with clearly defined gender and generational roles. American society, on the other hand, is highly mobile (creating a focus on nuclear family units), youth-oriented, and much less gender-defined. Immigrant families are often torn apart by immigration or the need to travel once in the US to find work. Children quickly learn that American youth are independent and begin to resent their parents' control. Foreign-born parents are dismayed by their Americanized children's lack of respect and obedience. Foreign-born parents whose traditional culture involves arranged marriages are also distressed when their Americanized children want to go out on dates without chaperones and choose their own mates.

Many women are forced to work outside the home to help support the family, perhaps the first time they have ever done so. Men feel diminished because they are no longer the sole breadwinner, and they may feel their authority is threatened. Some women discover that they like having more freedom and begin to resist their traditionally defined roles. Some men who are frustrated by their inability to support their families and by their wives' new independence turn to drugs or alcohol to numb their feelings. They may also take out their frustrations on the women and children around them by becoming verbally or physically abusive. Domestic violence is a serious problem among some immigrant families.

The generation gap that always exists between parents and children, and even more so between grandparents and grandchildren, is intensified by the cultural differences between foreign-born parents and grandparents and American-born children. For some immigrants, a new conflict between men and women is introduced by the increased freedom for women in the US, and the necessity for women to work outside the home. Tensions lessen with each succeeding generation as the family becomes more Americanized. However, with the lessening of tensions comes a loss of traditional ethnic culture.

11 CLOTHING

Today's world is becoming increasingly westernized, and many recent US immigrants arrive in America with much the same clothing as mainstream Americans wear. Others, such as some Asian Indian women and Muslim Arabs, continue to wear their traditional clothing in the US. Separatist groups like the Amish and conservative Mennonites wear distinctive dress based on centuries-old styles. All ethnic groups have cultural festivals in which dancers or parade participants wear the traditional dress of their particular culture, but most US immigrants quickly adapt to American-style clothing for everyday use.

Certain elements of typical American dress were introduced by US immigrants. For example, the blue denim used to make blue jeans is probably based on a kind of Cajun cloth dyed with indigo. Tartan plaids and tweed woolens were brought to America by the Scottish and Scotch-Irish. Various immigrant groups have brought with them different types of hats now worn by all Americans, such as the English bowler or French beret.

12 FOOD

American food is a colorful blend of many different ethnic traditions, as well as indigenous foods such as squashes and turkey. The cuisine of some immigrant groups has become popular on its own, like Mexican, Italian, French, Chinese, Japanese, Asian Indian, Middle Eastern (Arab), Greek, and Cajun. Ethnic restaurants do a good business in most areas of the US. Newer immigrant groups are beginning to introduce their cuisines to the general American public; restaurants serving Cuban, Central American, Vietnamese, or Cambodian foods are gaining popularity.

Many immigrant groups have introduced specific foods that have become a part of mainstream American eating. Jewish Americans contributed bagels with lox, deli foods, kosher dill pickles, potato latkes, and chicken soup (as a cure for the common cold). From the Dutch came pancakes, waffles, coleslaw, doughnuts, and cookies, while the Germans brought beer, frankfurters, hamburgers, potato salad, bratwurst, liverwurst, and pretzels. Sauerkraut is credited to both Germans and Poles, and Poles and Russians share credit for vodka. Poles also gave America kielbasa, pierogis, Polish dill pickles, and Polish ham, and Russians taught Americans to eat chicken kiev, stroganoff, sour cream, borscht, and pumpernickel bread, as well as to drink tea with lemon. The Scottish can be thanked for Scotch whiskey.

13 EDUCATION

Almost without exception, immigrants to the US place a high value on education. A number of immigrants come to the US expressly to pursue higher education or to give their children a chance at a good education. A few immigrant groups dismissed higher education at first as unnecessary (such as Polish, Slavic, and Italian Americans), believing a steady job was more important than an academic degree. Later generations of these groups have become more interested in education after seeing the opportunities it makes available in the US. In particular, after World War II (1939–45), many soldiers took advantage of the

GI Bill to pay for higher education and advanced themselves to skilled labor or professional positions.

A number of immigrant groups founded ethnic schools, usually meeting on weekday afternoons or weekend mornings, to promote their traditional language and culture. Armenian, Russian, Ukrainian, Greek, Chinese, Japanese, and Korean Americans, among others, created these schools to teach their children traditional ethnic ways. Foreign-born parents for the most part want their children to become Americans, but they also fear the complete Americanization that makes their children strangers to them and to their ancestral language and traditions. Most children resent the extra time they must spend on ethnic school work when their other American friends are out playing or taking part in extracurricular activities. Some children, on the other hand, appreciate learning about their ethnic background and enjoy speaking their ancestral language.

The Roman Catholic parochial school system, which provides good-quality, inexpensive private education for many American children, was established by Irish Americans in the 1830s-1840s. German Americans introduced the concept of kindergarten and founded the first US kindergartens in the 1850s. They are also responsible for the inclusion of physical education in school curricula. Higher education for the deaf was developed in large part by the French American Gallaudet family, founders of what is now called Gallaudet College in Washington, D.C., the only liberal arts college for the deaf in the US. French Americans also founded the Julliard School of Music in New York City, the premier music school in America.

Other colleges and universities founded by US immigrant groups include St. Olaf College in Northfield, Minnesota, established in 1874 by Norwegian Americans; and Princeton University in Princeton, New Jersey, founded by Scottish Americans as a Presbyterian seminary in 1746.

14 CULTURAL HERITAGE

American arts culture, like American food, is a rich mixture of various ethnic elements contributed by the multitude of immigrants who make up America's population. Greek architecture with its massive columns stands alongside small Swedish log cabins and Haitian "shotgun" houses. Latin American surrealist fiction and poetry shares the shelf with books of Japanese haiku. The Japanese arts of *ikebana* (flower-arranging) and *origami* (paper-folding) are pursued by non-Japanese as well as Japanese Americans. One of the most enduring symbols of America, the Statue of Liberty, is a combination of French and Jewish talents. The statue was designed by French artist Frédéric-Auguste Bartholdi, and the poem on the base ("Give me your tired, your poor,/ Your huddled masses, yearning to breathe free . . . ") was written by Jewish American Emma Lazarus.

The Hollywood film industry was founded by two Hungarian Americans, Adolph Zukor and William Fox, and countless immigrant American actors and directors have made it a worldwide success. Italian Americans brought with them a love of opera, and in New York City in 1932, Italian immigrant Lorenzo Da Ponte founded the Italian Opera House, the first opera house in the US.

American music is a true festival of ethnicity. Cajun music, Zydeco, Latin salsa, Cuban rhythms, Mexican mariachi and Tex-Mex sounds, Polish and German polkas, Asian Indian ragas, and the drone of Scottish bagpipes are heard across the US. The rumba, mambo, Conga lines, and chachachá, very popular dances in mainstream America during the 1930s and 1940s, were introduced by Cuban immigrants. The now-common Christmas carol, "Carol of the Bells," was first brought to the US by the Ukrainians.

The structure of blues music, one of the most "American" forms of music, is based on Haitian folk songs sung by early Haitian immigrants to Louisiana in the 19th century. Haitian Americans also contributed certain drums and rhythms, as well as the banjo, to American music. Early American folk music consisted largely of old ballads from England, brought by the very first English settlers. Today's American folk music, as well as country and western, rock, funk, and other genres, is an inextricable blend of elements from nearly every immigrant group that has ever set foot on the shores of America.

15 WORK

America is built on the backs of its immigrants. All immigrant groups, from the very first to the most recent, documented and undocumented, have poured their energies into the American labor pool. Many immigrants begin in unskilled, menial labor positions because they lack the language and/or industrialized job skills to be employed at higher levels. Even those with advanced degrees and experience must often start out in jobs for which they are overqualified, until they gain the language skills and accreditation required in the US for higher-level positions.

During times of expansion and economic growth, the US has encouraged immigration in order to build its labor force. During the late 1800s, the US even advertised for immigrants in Western European countries. In contrast, when the economy is depressed, immigration is discouraged because of fears of job scarcity. Peoples of many less-industrialized countries continue to see America as a land of opportunity regardless of the current state of the US economy because even during a depression, the US still offers a great deal more in the way of economic advancement than do their homelands.

When the US chooses to restrict immigration during economic downturns, many underprivileged peoples choose to use "illegal" means of gaining entry to America. Undocumented migrants have always existed in US society; the agricultural industry of the West and Southwest was largely developed through undocumented migrant labor. Employers continue to hire undocumented workers because they do not have to pay them the legal minimum wage and can therefore save a great deal in wage costs. The employers' savings are passed on to the consumer in lower prices. Although the US government makes occasional attempts to stem the flow of undocumented migration, the US economy actually benefits from the migrants' labor, encouraging both sides (migrants and government) to continue playing their part in the game.

16 SPORTS

Many sports now popular in the US were introduced by immigrant groups. For example, both downhill and cross-country skiing were brought to America by the Norwegians, while the Scots brought golf and curling (a sort of shuffleboard on ice). The Italians taught Americans to play bocce (lawn bowling), and the Chinese, Japanese, and Koreans shared their various martial arts.

The US introduced the sport of baseball to other countries, and many players from those countries now add their skills to US teams. Cuban, Dominican, and Central American players, among others, are common in the US major leagues. Softball leagues and Little League teams are sponsored by many different US immigrant groups. Soccer, the most popular sport in the rest of the world, is becoming more popular in the US through the influence of a variety of immigrant groups. Sports, particularly baseball, can open the door for some immigrants who would otherwise have a difficult time being accepted for immigration to the US.

17 ENTERTAINMENT AND RECREATION

All immigrants to America bring with them their own forms of entertainment and recreation. Some of those entertainments make their way into the larger American culture. For example, the early English Puritans were very somber people who did not believe in frivolous activities. When the Germans arrived, however, they instilled a different sense of fun into American society. Rather than the strict observances of the Puritan sabbath on Sundays, German Americans spent the day resting and enjoying a break from their labors. Today's understanding in the US of weekends as a time of play descends from those original German Americans. German Americans also introduced the ever-popular Oktoberfest, and beer gardens, to the US.

Many US immigrant groups gather one or more times a year for cultural festivals that serve as ethnic pride and education events, as well as times for socializing. Among some traditional groups, the festivals are also an opportunity to meet potential marriage partners. Others simply enjoy eating their ethnic foods, wearing their traditional costumes, and listening and dancing to traditional ethnic music. On an everyday basis, most US immigrants quickly adopt American forms of entertainment and recreation, such as watching television or going to movies.

18 FOLK ART, CRAFTS, AND HOBBIES

Examples of ethnic folk arts can be found at the various cultural festivals held across the US each year. Certain ethnic crafts, such as painted Ukrainian Easter eggs and Hmong *paj ntaub* (an intricate form of needlework, also known as *pa ndau*), have become more widely popular in America. Some Amish crafts are considered valuable collectors' items in the US.

Mexican and Central American folk arts are gaining popularity among the general American public today. Hispanic American murals grace the walls of many buildings in major US cities, and shops selling *santos* (homemade religious figurines) or other Latin American crafts are frequented by Hispanic and non-Hispanic Americans alike. The new trend towards multiculturalism and ethnic pride in the US is creating a wider market for folk arts and crafts of all ethnic groups in America today.

19 SOCIAL PROBLEMS

The Ku Klux Klan, a violent white supremacist group, was founded in the 19th century by Scotch-Irish Americans. This was not the beginning of racism in America, however. Racism has always been a serious problem in American society, as has religious discrimination, ethnic hostility, and cultural prejudice.

The Puritan settlers of the 1600s came to the New World to escape religious persecution in England but then proceeded to persecute non-Puritans who dared to settle near them in America. Anti-Asian legislation was passed in California as early as the 1850s, and the Chinese Exclusion Act, barring any further Chinese immigration to the US, was passed a short time later in 1882.

Anti-German hysteria during World Wars I (1914–18) and II (1939–45) was so extreme that music by Beethoven was banned from symphony concert programs, sauerkraut was renamed "liberty cabbage," and even dachshunds (meaning "German hounds") were dubbed "liberty hounds." Hungarian Americans also met with suspicion during the wars, as Hungary was allied with Germany. All American ethnic groups were driven to hide their ethnicity and prove themselves "good Americans" during the war years.

One of the most blatant and grievous examples of racial hostility in the US was the internment of Japanese Americans in detention camps during World War II (1939–45). Americans whose only crime was their ethnic background were forced from their homes and imprisoned for the duration of the war with Japan. Anti-Asian violence continues to be a problem today, particularly with the recent influx of large numbers of Indo-Chinese refugees into many US cities.

Although the American consciousness is beginning to shift towards multiculturalism and ethnic pride today, racism and cultural conflicts still plague the US. Current immigration policies, though made more inclusive by reforms in the 1960s, continue to provoke accusations of racism, as white Cubans are welcomed while black Haitians and Dominicans are denied entry. Mixed-race Mexicans and Central Americans are also refused refugee status. In 1986, only 3% of Salvadoran refugees were granted asylum by the US government, as opposed to 90% of Polish refugees. US investments in foreign countries and influence over their governments play a large part in refugee status decisions as well. However, racism cannot be denied.

The great experiment of a nation created out of many racial, ethnic, and cultural elements continues in America. New immigrants arrive daily to add their ingredients to the mix, and American society takes on a slightly different flavor with each one. The US is faced with many decisions today about who and how many to allow through its doors, and tomorrow will surely bring others. The choices that are made will determine the future shape of America.

20 BIBLIOGRAPHY

Gonzales, Juan L., Jr. *Racial and Ethnic Groups in America*, 2nd ed. Dubuque, IA: Kendall/Hunt Publishing, 1993.

Reimers, David M. *A Land of Immigrants*. New York: Chelsea House, 1996.

US Bureau of the Census. *Detailed Ancestry Groups for States*. 1990 Census of Population Supplementary Reports, CP-S-1-2. Washington, DC, October 1992.

—by D. K. Daeg de Mott

AMERICANS

LOCATION: United States
POPULATION: 260 million
LANGUAGE: English; Spanish and other minority languages
RELIGION: Christianity (Roman Catholic, Protestant [Baptist, Methodist, Lutheran, Presbyterian]); Judaism; Islam
RELATED ARTICLES: Vol. 2: African Americans; American Immigrants; Native North Americans

¹ INTRODUCTION

The United States of America, with a population of 260 million, is a nation of immigrants. The very first Americans are thought to be prehistoric Asian peoples who first arrived on the North American continent sometime before 10,000 BC. From these first settlers evolved the cultures of the North American Indian tribes. When the European explorers first came to North America in the 1500s, an estimated two million people were living in the land that was to become the United States. The Europeans had advanced industrial, military, communications, transportation, and construction technologies that enabled them to dominate the native peoples. Successive waves of European immigrants ultimately led to a policy of forcibly resettling the tribes to make way for the new settlers. In the process, thousands of native people were killed or died when driven from their homes. By 1890, according to the official census count, there were only 248,253 native peoples remaining in the United States. Still, many tribal societies survived warfare with white settlers and retained their cultures. Their survival, however, has been on the fringes of North American society. Today, less than 1% of the population of the United States consists of these first Americans.

Another people subjected to the domination of the early European Americans were the African slaves who were forcibly brought by businessmen to America to work the plantations in the South during the 18th and 19th centuries. By the outbreak of the Civil War in 1861, the slave population of the United States had reached a figure of 4,000,000 persons. Although slavery was abolished in the 1860s, discrimination against blacks remained institutionalized until the major social legislation of the 1960s. Even in the late 1990s, racism is one of America's enduring social problems. As of 1996, approximately 13% of the population of the United States can trace its ancestors back to these African peoples.

Ultimately, the Native Americans, African Americans, the European settlers, and the successive waves of immigrants that followed worked together to build one of the most powerful nations on Earth. Americans excel or lead in almost all areas of human endeavor.

European immigration to the United States peaked between 1880 and 1920 when over 20 million Europeans came to America. In 1900, 96% of all immigrants to the United States came from Europe, especially from Germany, Ireland, and Italy. In many cases these immigrants were fleeing starvation, poverty, and war. America offered hope and opportunity. For them, America was a great "melting pot" where people from many different lands came together and melted into a new American society. People from throughout Europe left the languages and customs of their native lands behind and began the process of being assimilated into American society. After three or four generations in the new land, their descendants felt as American as the descendants of the original colonists. Unfortunately, the Europeans were reluctant to welcome non-Europeans into this "melting pot." Still, Americans held a deep belief in the principles of equal rights and equal opportunities. These principles, embedded in the nation's constitution and enforced by law, ultimately opened the door to full participation in American society to all Americans. Some would argue, however, that the door has not been opened very wide. Consequently, minority groups in America continue to struggle to assert their rights as American citizens.

In the 1990s, the American immigrant is more likely to be Asian (38% of all immigrants) or Hispanic (48%) rather than European (9.6%). Demographers predict this immigration pattern will continue. They estimate that by the year 2050 over 20% of the population will claim Hispanic origin (up from 10% in 1990) while another 11% will be Asian (3% in 1990). By then, only 53% of the population will be of European origin, as opposed to 76% today. Census categories, however, can be confusing and sometimes misleading. Whereas the terms Asian and Black are terms that define a *race* of peoples, the term Hispanic defines a geographic location (people from the Caribbean, Mexico, and Central and South America). Consequently, a person of Hispanic origin can be of any race. Many Hispanics are black while others trace their ancestors to the European countries of Portugal and Spain. There are even small percentages of Hispanics with Japanese, Chinese, or Filipino ancestry.

Now that the non-European groups are becoming a stronger force in American culture, the "melting pot" paradigm is fading. Today, most academics term America a multicultural society that is more like a "salad bowl" than a "melting pot." The well-known political scientist Sammual Huntington observed that President William Clinton is the first American president to stress diversity instead of unity as a national goal.

² LOCATION AND HOMELAND

The land Americans came to call their own is located in the Western Hemisphere on the continent of North America. The United States is the fourth-largest country in the world with a total area of 9,372,607 sq km (3,618,773 sq mi). The northeastern coast, known as New England, is rocky, but along the rest of the eastern seaboard, the Atlantic Coastal Plain rises gradually from the shoreline and merges with the Gulf Coastal Plain in Georgia. To the west is a plateau, bounded by the Appalachian Mountains. This plateau extends from southeast Maine into central Alabama. Between the Appalachians and the Rocky Mountains, more than 1,600 km (1,000 mi) to the west, lies the vast interior plain of the United States. The Rockies and the ranges to the west—the Sierra Nevada, the Coast, and Cascade ranges—are parts of a larger mountain system that extends through the western part of Central and South America. Between the Rockies and the Pacific Ranges lies a group of vast plateaus containing most of the nation's desert areas, known as the Great Basin. The coastal plains along the Pacific Ocean are narrow, and in many places, the mountains plunge directly into the sea. Separated from the continental United States by Canada, the state of Alaska occupies the extreme northwest portion of North America. The state of Hawaii consists of a group of Pacific islands formed by volcanoes rising sharply from the ocean floor.

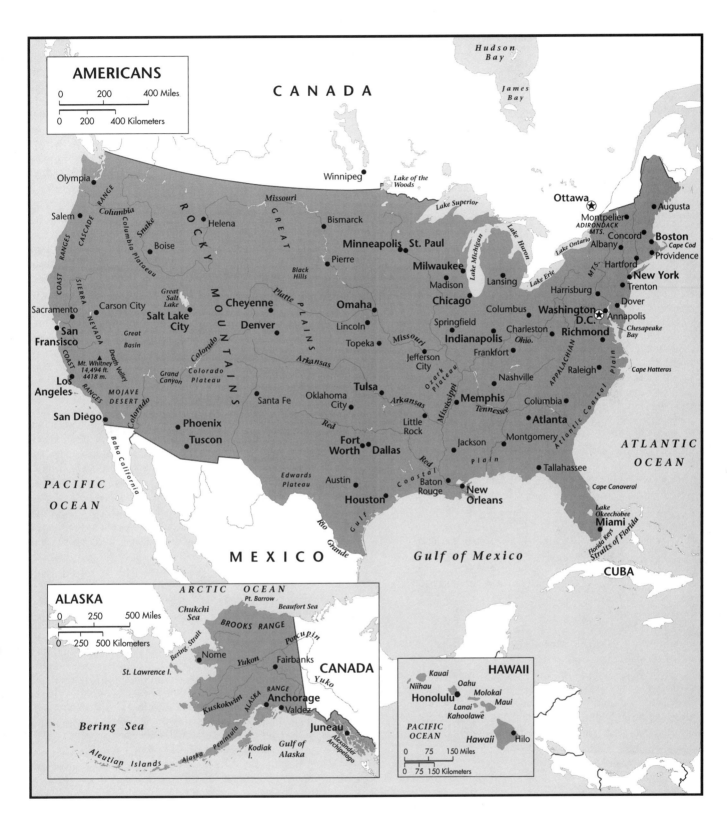

³LANGUAGE

The primary language of the United States is English, enriched by words borrowed from the languages of Indians and immigrants, predominantly European. Over 86% of all Americans speak only English while at home. Over 7% of the population speaks Spanish at home. The majority of Spanish speakers live in the Southwest, Florida, and eastern urban centers. Other languages spoken at home (each with less than 1% but more than

0.5% of the population) include French, German, Chinese, and Italian.

4 FOLKLORE

Characters associated with the taming of the American wilderness, especially cowboys and Indians, are featured prominently in American folklore. Among the best known of these mythical figures are John Henry, Paul Bunyon, and Pecos Bill. John Henry was a "steel-driving man" (someone who used a sledgehammer to drive spikes into railroad ties) who challenged a steam-driven hammer to a spike-driving contest. As the story goes, John Henry won the race but immediately died thereafter. Paul Bunyon was a woodsman who could fell a tree with a single swing of his ax. He rode a giant blue ox named Babe. Pecos Bill was a cowboy in the so-called "wild west." He could lasso a tornado and ride a mountain lion.

Americans are fascinated with outlaws. Among America's most famous outlaws are Billy the Kid and Al Capone. Born in 1859, Billy the Kid had a career of cattle rustling and murder. He was shot and killed in New Mexico by Sheriff Pat Garrett on 15 July 1881. In the 1920s, "Big Al" Capone was a gangster who dominated the Chicago crime scene. He engaged in gang warfare and bootlegging during America's Prohibition period when the sale of alcohol was prohibited. Although a ruthless killer, Al Capone was never convicted for any of his violent crimes; he went to jail for income tax evasion.

Since baseball is known as the national pastime, it is fitting that the story of baseball hero Babe Ruth has reached mythic proportions. The "Babe" is considered by many as the best player ever to have played the game. Some people have said that with the World Series, baseball's championship, on the line and his team, the New York Yankees, behind on the scoreboard, Babe pointed with his bat to the outfield bleachers and then promptly hit a home run right to the designated spot.

Americans have a deep belief that anyone can achieve wealth and success if he or she works hard enough and smart enough. Consequently, every American knows a "rags to riches" story of someone who has beaten the odds and gone from poverty to immense wealth.

5 RELIGION

Although all of the world's major religions have adherents in the United States, the US is primarily a Christian nation. Over 26% of the population is Roman Catholic, while another 63% are Protestant or non-denominational Christian. The largest Protestant denominations are the Baptists with 10% of the population, followed by the Methodists (8%), Lutherans (5%), and Presbyterians (3%). Almost 2% of the population is Jewish and 0.5% is Muslim. Only 1% of the population classifies itself as agnostic, while another 7.5% has no religion.

Although Americans observe the holidays and traditions of their respective faiths, no religious holiday has become as institutionalized as Christmas, the day Christians celebrate the birth of Jesus Christ. However, for many Americans, the Christmas holiday has become as much a secular holiday as a religious one. The custom of buying Christmas presents for family and friends has made Christmas an important season for many of America's retailers. Americans' willingness to spend money on Christmas gifts is an indicator of the overall health of the US economy. Consequently, the profits generated during the Christmas shopping period are watched closely by stock market investors on Wall Street and economic analysts in the government in Washington, D.C.

Although the US constitution mandates a strict separation between church and state, the relationship between these two spheres of society is often blurred. For example, American currency is inscribed with the words "In God we Trust" and many public offices, including most public schools, close for the important Christian holidays. In areas with a heavy Jewish population, the public schools close for the Jewish holidays as well. On the other hand, officially sanctioned prayers in public school are forbidden.

6 MAJOR HOLIDAYS

The most important non-religious holidays celebrated by Americans are Independence Day (the fourth of July) and Thanksgiving Day (the fourth Thursday in November). Independence day celebrates the signing of the United States' Declaration of Independence from England on 4 July 1776. On the fourth of July, many Americans have an outdoor picnic or barbecue. Many communities sponsor parades with high school marching bands, local dignitaries in antique cars, and firetrucks with their sirens blaring. At the end of the day, people gather at a local park to watch a display of fireworks.

Thanksgiving Day celebrates the Pilgrims' first harvest in the new world. When the Pilgrims arrived from England, they had little knowledge of how to survive in their new land. They were helped by the local native Americans who taught them how to plant corn. The harvest was successful, and the Pilgrims celebrated by inviting the local inhabitants to share in a meal of thanksgiving. Since then, Americans have set aside Thanksgiving Day as a day to give thanks for their good fortune. For children and adults, a traditional activity is watching the Thanksgiving Day Parade in New York City on television. The parade features giant helium-filled balloons made in the shapes of famous cartoon characters. These balloons, some nine or ten stories tall, float high among the New York skyscrapers and are dragged through the streets by teams of people holding long ropes. Thanksgiving day is one of the busiest travel days of the year with many Americans visiting family and friends. Another prominent feature of the day is the football games that are televised nationally. The highlight of the day is the Thanksgiving Day meal (see Food).

7 RITES OF PASSAGE

Apart from religious rituals and family occurrences like births, deaths, and marriages, rites of passage for all Americans include their first day at school and the day they graduate from high school. High school graduating classes have reunions every 5 or 10 years. Of particular importance are the 10-year and 20-year reunions. Of somewhat lesser significance, but heavily anticipated nonetheless, is the day a teenager receives his or her driver's license. Many teens take the written and skill tests required to earn a license to drive shortly after their sixteenth birthday. Sixteen is the minimum driving age in most states. Perhaps the most bittersweet rite of passage is a person's retirement from the workforce. This day is often marked by some celebration involving one's coworkers and close family members. A prominent individual with a long career at one company may be given a party at a local banquet hall. A lesser employee or one with few years at the same company may celebrate the event with a special lunch at a local restaurant. The traditional gift for someone retiring from the workforce is a gold watch.

8 INTERPERSONAL RELATIONS

Americans are generally regarded as friendly and outgoing. In formal business communications, men are referred to as Mr. and women as Ms. (Ms. came into popular use during the 1970s when women argued for equal treatment in the workplace.) In social correspondence, some women prefer Mrs. or Miss. This may be the case with older American women. Social etiquette is changing as the society struggles to become less racist and less sexist. In business settings, shaking hands with people upon first meeting them is appropriate. This is true when meeting either men or women. However, when a man is introduced to a woman, the man may prefer to wait for the woman to offer her hand first. Kissing another person on the cheek in a business setting is not appropriate unless you know the person very well. Often in a social setting, men and women who have met previously kiss each other on the cheek upon greeting. In business and social settings, addressing the newly met person by his or her first name is typical. Exceptions to this include: if Mr., Ms., or Mrs. was used in the introduction; if the new acquaintance is significantly older or has significantly greater stature; if the situation is formal in atmosphere. In these cases, Mr., Mrs., or Ms. should be used to avoid offending anyone. When meeting or talking with someone, Americans feel that looking the other person directly in the eyes is important. This is a sign of openness and trustworthiness, as is a firm handshake.

Young people begin dating in groups or under loose adult supervision at the ages of twelve or thirteen. However, dating begins in earnest when teenagers begin receiving their drivers' licenses at the age of 16. At this age, parents rarely chaperone their children. Using the family car for a first date is an extremely important occasion for any teenager. Traditionally, the boy was the one to ask the girl out on a date; customarily, the boy would pay for the date. These social norms, however, are fading. Dates are frequently scheduled for Friday or Saturday nights. A typical date might consist of a casual meal and a movie or concert. School dances and sporting events are also popular. Most parents set curfews for their children to be home by midnight.

American society values equality, so language should not be used in a derogatory, sexist, or racist manner. A sexist or racist remark made to a coworker is not only rude but also illegal. Although there is a wide disparity in income levels among Americans, Americans think of America as a classless society. Some people have said that the American president Abraham Lincoln treated his butler with the same respect he treated visiting heads of state. In a country where most Americans referred to the American president William Jefferson Clinton (elected in 1992) as "Bill," the average citizen feels his or her voice in political affairs is as important as that of the very wealthiest and most powerful of Americans.

9 LIVING CONDITIONS

Americans have one of the highest per capita incomes in the world. The average American household has income of over $31,000 per year. Almost 70% of American homes are single-unit structures. The median size of a single, detached one-family house is 1,700 square feet, about 20% of homes have more

than 2,500 square feet, and 14% have less than 1,000 square feet. The remaining homes are multiple dwelling units such as two- and four-family houses and large apartment buildings with more than 50 units. Sixty-four percent of American families own their own homes. Almost every American household has hot and cold running water, electricity, indoor plumbing, a refrigerator, a telephone, and a television. Almost 90% of American homes have toasters, 73% have automatic coffee makers, 87% have microwave ovens, and 76% have a clothes washer.

Not all Americans, however, share in this wealth. Although they represent less than 1% of the total population, a significant number of Americans are homeless. Estimates of the homeless population in the United States range from 50,000 to 3,000,000. Children account for almost 25% of the homeless population.

Automobiles are a very important part of American life. In many suburban communities pedestrians are an uncommon sight. Consequently, public transportation is not a primary form of transportation, and many housing developments no longer include sidewalks. Most Americans would find it hard to survive without an automobile for transportation. Everywhere in America are well-paved roads (including a multi-lane, high speed, interstate highway system that links every major and secondary city in the nation). Driving from east coast to west coast and from north to south is possible using these high-speed interstate highways.

America has been termed a consumer society. In fact, for many people, shopping is as much a pastime as a chore. In most American communities, shoppers are drawn to the local mall. The mall became a fixture in American society in the 1970s when developers began to gather hundreds of independent stores under one roof. These giant buildings, decorated inside with trees and fountains, are flanked by acres of parking lots. Inside, shoppers can go from store to store and be sheltered from the weather. The local mall took the place of the town square and quickly became a favorite meeting place for teenagers. The mall also changed the nature of the community by forcing the stores in the downtown area of the city out of business, thereby hastening the decay of America's urban centers. Another trend in American consumerism is the mail order catalog. Pioneered in the 1920s by Sears and Montgomery Ward, the mail order catalog made a comeback in the 1980s and now offers Americans at-home shopping for everything from fruit to sweaters to sofas.

10 FAMILY LIFE

Most Americans get married for the first time when they are in their twenties. However, almost 50% of first-time marriages end in divorce. American families consist of two or three children. For every 100 live births, there are 37 abortions. The issue of abortion is one of the most divisive ones in American politics. Even though legal since 1973, many Americans still see abortion as a morally tinged decision. When asked if a legal abortion should be available if a woman's health is at stake or if the fetus has a serious defect, over 80% of people surveyed in 1995 thought an abortion should be available. However, when the only circumstance is that the woman is not married or can't afford more children, less than 50% thought a legal abortion should be available. Almost 33% of all births in the United

States are to single mothers as opposed to 5% in 1950. Today, 27% of children live with one parent.

In the 1950s and 60s, the husband in the family typically went to work and the wife usually stayed home and managed the house and children. Women's roles in society were more strictly defined then, and opportunities outside of the home were limited. In the 1970s and 80s, however, economic pressures and the increasing desire of more women to pursue careers in the workforce resulted in both husband and wife working full-time jobs. However, the school day does not conform to the work day, and many children spend the hours before and after school in day care centers or alone at home until their parents return from work sometime after 5:00 pm, the typical end of the work day.

Increasing public tolerance of single-sex marriages as well as the high divorce rate and incidence of birth to unwed mothers is changing the definition of family in American society. The traditional notion that family members are primarily related by blood is being expanded to include bonds based more on emotional or economic factors. Extended and blended families, comprised of a husband and wife and their children and relatives from previous marriages, are altering the way Americans view the household family unit.

Mobility of Americans increasingly means that family members find themselves living many hundreds of miles away from their parents and siblings. When older adults are no longer able to live on their own, they typically move into a nursing home or assisted living facility rather than into the homes of their children.

11 CLOTHING

Conservative dress for a businessman typically consists of a western-style suit and a tie. Conservative dress for a businesswoman is a suit or dress in a subdued style—in muted colors and with modest tailoring. Less traditional businesswomen may prefer more fashionable styles, stronger colors, and more dramatic tailoring. Increasingly common among American businesses is the "dress-down" day. On this day, typically Fridays, all employees are encouraged to wear casual clothes. Men's and women's suits give way to casual slacks or skirts and sweaters. Formal footwear is replaced by running shoes or loafers. Many Americans who work in service industries or factories wear uniforms that are supplied by their employers.

When not at work, Americans prefer casual clothes, such as denim blue jeans, T-shirts, and sweatshirts. Increasingly, a baseball cap with team or other logo has become an important addition to the casual wardrobe. Casual clothing is often decorated with the logo of a sports team or the designer who designed the clothes. T-shirts almost always carry some advertisement or message. Casual footwear for Americans typically means some type of sports shoe: Tennis, basketball, walking, etc. These sports shoes can be very expensive and some, especially those endorsed by professional sports figures, are highly prized by some teenagers and young adults.

Children who attend private schools typically wear school uniforms. Children who attend public schools are free, within reason, to wear what they like to school. For many public school students, school clothes are the same as their play clothes. However, the increasingly outrageous fashions of school children sometimes disrupt the educational process. The behavioral problems associated with the way children dress in school led president Bill Clinton of the United States in 1996 to recommend that public schools introduce uniforms as a way to improve behavior and academic performance.

Young adults in their late teens and early twenties may have their bodies tattooed or pierced. Until the early 1990s, tattoos were socially taboo. Women did not usually have tattoos. Consequently, the decision to get a tattoo was an act of social defiance and independence. By the late 1990s, some young men and women, following the lead of fashion models and rock stars, found tattooing a socially acceptable practice. Accordingly, the decision to get a tattoo no longer has quite the same significance it did when fewer people engaged in the practice. Young adults in the 1990s find they have to go farther if they want to make a social (as well as fashion) statement with their bodies. This may explain the phenomenon of body piecing. Body piercing first gained widespread social acceptance in the 1960s and 70s when women began piercing their ear lobes and wearing pierced earrings. In the 1980s, having more than one hole pierced in each ear became fashionable for young women. At that time, young men took up the practice as well. However, unlike women, men have one ear pierced and wear a small earring. A minority of young Americans also pierce other parts of their bodies including their noses, eyebrows, navels, tongues, lips, and nipples. Whereas pierced ears are as common as the suit and tie, pierced noses and eyebrows still gain attention as unique fashion statements.

12 FOOD

The foods Americans eat are as diverse as the population. Regional specialties include clam chowder in the northeast seaboard, Tex-Mex with jalapeno peppers and tortillas along the border with Mexico, and spicy Cajun dishes in Louisiana. To say that all Americans favor a typical selection of food would be a gross oversimplification. However, certain foods are common throughout the United States and are familiar to almost all Americans.

For American children, a typical morning breakfast may consist of a bowl of cereal and cold milk and a glass of juice. Children's breakfast cereals, made out of wheat, rice, or corn, have brand names like "Fruit Loops," "Cheerios," and "Frosted Flakes." The more popular ones are heavily coated with sugar. Cereal boxes (some as large as 13 inches high, 8 inches wide, and 3 inches deep) are creatively decorated with games, contests, and advertisements. Oftentimes, children read the box as they eat their morning bowl of cereal. Older Americans may have a glass of orange or grapefruit juice, a cup of coffee, and toast and butter. Recently, bagels and cream cheese, always a favorite of New Yorkers, have become popular throughout the country. A more hearty breakfast for children and adults alike may consist of eggs, hash brown potatoes, and either ham, bacon, or sausage. Also popular are pancakes or waffles covered with butter and maple syrup.

At the mid-day meal, young American children rarely refuse peanut butter and jelly sandwiches. Adults and older children prefer sandwiches made with sliced meats (bologna sandwiches are popular with children), cheese, and lettuce. Soups are also widely consumed.

Dinner is the main meal of the day for most Americans. The conventional dinner meal consists of a portion of meat (chicken and pork are affordable and popular), a vegetable like broccoli, corn, peas, or green beans, and a salad made from fresh lettuce.

Increasingly, however, the busy schedules of Americans make it difficult for families to find the time not only to prepare the meal but also to sit down together to eat it. An alternative to the traditional home-made family meal may be a pre-prepared frozen dinner purchased at a grocery store. These meals can be quickly defrosted, warmed in a conventional or microwave oven, and ready for serving within ten minutes. Also popular are pizzas that are ordered from local pizza restaurants and delivered to the home hot and ready for serving.

The frantic pace of American life has led more and more Americans from the kitchen and into restaurants for many of their daily meals. Among the most popular restaurants are those that offer "fast foods," especially hamburgers and French fries. In a fast food restaurant, the customer orders his or her meal from a fairly restricted menu at a counter. The food is delivered wrapped in paper or cardboard and served on a tray. The food is then taken by the customer to tables provided for the customers' convenience. Upon finishing the meal, customers clean up after themselves. Most fast-food restaurants are equipped with a drive-through window. The customer drives his or her car up to a microphone and places the order. He then drives his car to a window in the side of the building where an attendant takes his money and gives him his food in a bag. Among the most popular of these fast food restaurants are McDonald's, Wendy's, Taco Bell, and Burger King.

Perhaps the most enduring traditional American meal is the annual Thanksgiving dinner. The traditional version of this meal consists of a whole roasted turkey stuffed with seasoned bread cubes and served with gravy. Children often ask for the legs of the bird, referred to as "drumsticks." Side dishes include mashed potatoes and gravy, corn, cranberries, a salad, and rolls. The meal is topped off with apple or pumpkin pie for dessert. In many parts of the country, a traditional feature of the Thanksgiving meal is the ceremonial breaking of the wishbone. Two people each hold an end of the wishbone and make a wish. They pull the wishbone apart, and whoever holds the larger end will have their wish granted.

13 EDUCATION

Most American children start their formal education at the age of 5, although many attend preschool or day care from an earlier age. The school year begins sometime near the beginning of September and ends in mid-June. Children do not attend school during the summer months of June, July, and August. This poses a dilemma for families where both parents work. Five-year-olds go to kindergarten where they learn socialization skills and receive instruction in arithmetic, reading, and writing. Although attended by most five-year-olds, kindergarten is not mandatory in all states; it is only a half-day program. After kindergarten, children attend elementary school (also referred to as primary or grade school) for grades one through six. In some school districts, primary schools end at grade four or five, after which the children attend what is known as middle school. Middle schools include grades six and seven, after which time the students attend junior high school. Junior high school goes until grade eight or nine. High school starts at grade 9 or 10 and goes to grade 12. The configuration of elementary, middle, junior, and high school is often a function of the number of students in a district and other nonacademic factors. Some districts have only elementary schools (1 through 8) and a high school (9 through 12). In most school districts, the school day lasts about six hours for elementary students and up to eight hours for high school students. Children attend school Monday through Friday.

A feature of many school districts is busing to achieve racial integration. Until the 1960s, many students were segregated by race for education. Some school districts directed resources to white schools and away from black schools. To correct the situation, the federal courts required offending districts to bus children to schools outside of their neighborhoods to achieve racial balance in the classrooms. When first instituted, busing resulted in "white flight" as whites moved out of cites affected by busing and into adjacent suburban neighborhoods insulated from the court orders. Some argue that this demographic trend resulted in even greater segregation and a general impoverishment of America's urban centers as the more wealthy white citizens moved away. Others argue that the remedy offered superior educational opportunities to black children and a more equal educational environment. Since the first court order in 1954, the issue of racial integration in American schools has torn at the fabric of American society. In the late 1990s, the racial makeup of schools and neighborhoods is still an underlying motivation in where many people choose to live.

Children are required by law to attend school until age 16, usually having completed 11 years of education. As of 1994, just under 20% of the US population age 25 and over does not have a high school diploma. Another 34% stop their formal education after receiving their high school diploma. About 17% go on to attend some college but do not receive a degree. Seven percent receive a degree from a technical college which offers a two-year program designed to prepare the student for a specific job. Fifteen percent of Americans graduate from a four-year college while another 7.5% go on to graduate from a professional or graduate school (another three to eight years depending on the discipline). As would be expected, the more highly educated Americans make the highest earnings in the workforce.

14 CULTURAL HERITAGE

It can be argued that Americans do not have a common cultural heritage. For many Americans, their cultural heritage is that of the homeland of their immigrant ancestors. However, some cultural forms, which are viewed by the rest of the world as typically American, have evolved. Among them are the numerous popular musical forms including the blues, gospel, jazz, rock and roll, and country and western. In the world's symphony halls, America is represented by many important composers including Virgil Thomson, Charles Ives, Aaron Copeland, and John Cage.

American poets of significance include Walt Whitman, Emily Dickinson, Wallace Stevens, Robert Frost, T.S. Elliott, John Ashbery, and James Merrill. Novelists also feature prominently in American culture. Colonial American life (1700s) has been captured in Nathaniel Hawthorne's *The Scarlet Letter* and life before the Civil War (1861–65) was chronicled in the works of Mark Twain, including *The Adventures of Huckleberry Finn*. The excesses of the 1920s inspired *The Great Gatsby* by F. Scott Fitzgerald, while the Great Depression (1929–40) that followed inspired *The Grapes of Wrath* by John Steinbeck. Works of contemporary authors like Norman Mailer, Truman Capote, and Thomas Pynchon continue to explore the human experience.

Perhaps America's most conspicuous contribution to world culture is the motion pictures that are synonymous with the city of Hollywood, California. Feature films like *Gone With the Wind, The Sound of Music,* and the *Wizard of Oz* are both embedded in the American psyche and distributed worldwide. Of similar significance are television programs. Throughout the world, people see America through the reflection of such popular programs as *Bonanza, Dallas,* and *Baywatch.*

15 WORK

The United States has an advanced industrialized economy offering almost any job conceivable. The typical American workweek lasts 40 hours. Although the workday could begin and end at any hour, most Americans work between the hours of 8 am and 5 pm. The lunch break typically starts between 11:30 am and 12:30 pm and lasts between 30 minutes and an hour. Businesses, however, do not close during the lunch break. By law, as of 1996, the minimum wage employers must pay employees is $4.20 per hour. After 40 hours, an employee is entitled to overtime pay. Though some workers are paid by the hour, many Americans receive a weekly salary. Instead of an hourly wage, these employees are paid a fixed sum and are not paid extra when their work week extends past 40 hours. Many companies offer their employees one or two weeks of paid vacation after one year on the job. The number of vacation days given to an employee typically increases with the number of years he or she has been on the job, but rarely exceeds four weeks. Americans begin to retire from the workforce at age 65, although many work well into their 70s.

In the 1950s, the American workplace was dominated by white men. Since then, federal laws banning discrimination on the basis of sex and race have opened the workplace to women and ethnic minorities. Consequently, the workplace is becoming more diverse. However, the leadership of many American companies is still composed predominantly of white males.

In the late 1990s, a phenomenon of immediate urgency in the American workplace was the practice of "downsizing." In order to stay competitive in the world economy, companies of all sizes were reducing the size of their workforces by laying off large numbers of employees. This was the case even with companies that were performing well and generating generous profits for their owners. Many of the employees who were downsized out of their jobs were the more highly-paid white-collar workers in their 40s and 50s. Through the decades of the 1950s, 60s, and 70s, workers felt that there was an unwritten understanding that if a worker was loyal to his or her employer and did a good job, he or she could expect to work at that company until retirement—at least as long as the company was profitable. In the 1990s, workers lost their jobs not because they were performing poorly, nor because the company was losing money, but because the company had changed its organizational structure and eliminated the workers' positions altogether. This "change in the rules" is changing employees' attitudes toward employers and is forcing them to be more self-reliant and self-centered. Savvy employees no longer see their employers in a paternal light, and company loyalty is no longer part of the employer/employee relationship.

Another challenge for the American economy is the scarcity of good paying jobs for lower-skilled workers. The manufacturing jobs of the 1950s and 60s paid good wages and offered good benefits to low-skilled workers, most of whom were sup-

ported by a powerful labor union. However, these jobs have increasingly been automated or shipped offshore to countries where nonunionized workers earn a fraction of their American counterparts. The jobs available to low-skilled workers offer much less.

These structural changes in the economy are increasing the income disparity between the rich and the poor in American society.

16 SPORTS

About 40% of all Americans play sports. Americans enjoy and participate in all sports. The primary sports played by school children include baseball, basketball, football (American style), ice hockey, and soccer. Although these more rigorous sports are abandoned by most Americans as they reach their mid-40s, interest in them remains strong and, except for soccer, they are the most popular spectator sports enjoyed by Americans. Older Americans who participate in competitive sports prefer golf, tennis, and bowling.

The most popular noncompetitive sport is walking for exercise, followed by swimming, bicycle riding, freshwater fishing, and camping.

17 ENTERTAINMENT AND RECREATION

Entertainment opportunities abound in the United States. Many Americans go to motion pictures, sporting events, and amusement parks. Perhaps the best known amusement park in the United States is Disney World in Orlando, Florida. This mammoth installation is a city unto itself. Americans also entertain themselves by going to a restaurant for dinner or by reading. Sporting events including games staged by the National Football League (NFL), major league baseball, and the National Basketball Association (NBA) are watched by millions both on TV and in giant stadiums and arenas, many holding 50,000 persons or more. The annual football championship game, the "Super Bowl," is always the most watched televised event of the year. In fact, "Super Bowl Sunday" is approaching the status of an American holiday.

Many Americans have hobbies like gardening, coin collecting, and model building. However, no entertainment medium is as widely experienced as television. The average American spends close to four hours a day watching television. This number is certainly higher for children. The most popular shows on television are half-hour-long situational comedies, referred to as "sit-coms." These shows are shown during "prime time," the most popular viewing period of the day, between 8 pm and 10 pm. Most popular shows during the daytime are soap operas where ongoing dramatic interpersonal situations are presented with story lines running for months or years. In many American households, the television is on whenever someone is in the house, even if no one is watching. In 1994, there were 814 television sets per 1,000 people, the highest ratio in the world. In England, there were only 434 sets per 1,000 people, and in China, 37.

America is becoming a nation of gamblers. Gambling, long considered a morally objectionable activity, is increasingly becoming a socially acceptable form of entertainment. Until the late 1970s, most forms of gambling were either illegal or highly restricted. Gambling's transition to respectability was aided by the institution of state-sponsored lotteries which are now used in 37 states as a means to generate revenues. In 1994, more Americans gambled than went to movies, theater, opera, and concerts combined. Americans spent six times as much money on gambling as on all spectator sports combined.

Popular children's toys include video games and bicycles. Action figures like GI Joe are popular with boys, while crafts and dolls are preferred by girls. Perhaps the most famous doll in America is "Barbie." Most American girls have at least one Barbie doll.

[18] FOLK ARTS, CRAFTS, AND HOBBIES

Typical American crafts include basketweaving, knitting, needlepoint, woodworking, pottery, glass blowing and weaving. If a visitor from another country set out to purchase a craft item essentially American, he or she may wish to shop for a patchwork quilt.

[19] SOCIAL PROBLEMS

American society struggles with many social problems chief of which are crime, alcohol and drug abuse, poverty, racism, sexism, and violence. The prevalence of sex and violence in American movies, television shows, and even popular songs on the radio has led the government to encourage the entertainment industry to establish a ratings system designed to help parents shelter their children from objectionable content. According to estimates, US citizens spend as much as $50 billion a year on illicit drugs. Surveys have shown that over one-third of the US population 12 years old or over—more than 77 million people—have used illicit drugs at some time in their lives. In 1992, 40% of high school seniors reported using illegal drugs.

By the age of 19 almost 70% of American girls and 80% of American boys have had sexual intercourse. Almost one in five 15-year olds is having intercourse. Although American teen sexual activity is similar to that in other developed countries, American girls are twice as likely to become pregnant: one out of ten teenage women in the United States becomes pregnant.

Nearly 900,000 persons were convicted of felony offenses in 1993. Operation of the justice system costs each citizen more than $360 per year, with a total of nearly $5 billion being spent annually. The number of persons under correctional supervision increased nearly 150% from 1980 to 1992.

[20] BIBLIOGRAPHY

Baer, Beverly, and Neil Walker, ed. *Almanac of Famous People.* 5th ed. Detroit: Gale Research, 1994.

Bloom, Harold. *The Western Canon: The Books and School of the Ages.* New York: Harcourt Brace, 1994.

Boy Scouts of America. *The Big Bear Cub Scout Book.* Irving, TX: Boy Scouts of America, 1984

Ewen, David. *The World of Twentieth Century Music.* Englewood Cliffs, NJ: Prentice-Hall, Inc., 1968.

Fabricant, Florence. "The Geography of Taste." *The New York Times Magazine,* 10 March 1996, 40–41.

Gall, Timothy L., and Daniel M. Lucas, ed. *Statistics on Alcohol, Drug and Tobacco Use.* Detroit: Gale Research, 1996.

Gall, Timothy L., and Daniel M. Lucas, ed. *Statistics on Weapons and Violence.* Detroit: Gale Research, 1996.

Hilt, Jack. "The Theory of Supermarkets." *The New York Times Magazine,* 10 March 1996, 56–61.

Nieporent, Drew. "Who Is the Best Restaurateur in America?" *The New York Times Magazine,* 10 March 1996, 42–74.

Price Waterhouse. *Doing Business in the United States.* New York: Price Waterhouse, 1994.

Rich, Frank. "Loving Las Vegas." *The New York Times,* 8 May 1996, Op-Ed section.

Schmittroth, Linda, ed. *Statistical Record of Women Worldwide.* Detroit: Gale Research, 1991.

Tilove, Jonathan. "America, Where Are You? New York or Mayberry?" *The Cleveland Plain Dealer,* 12 May 1996, Opinions & Ideas section.

UNESCO. *Statistical* Yearbook. Paris: United Nations Educational, Scientific and Cultural Organization, 1993.

U.S. Department of Commerce. *Statistical Abstract of the United States.* Washington, DC: Government Printing Office, 1995.

Usdansky, Margaret L. "Single Motherhood: Stereotypes vs. Statistics." *The New York Times,* 11 February 1996, Ideas and Trends section.

THE AMISH

ALTERNATE NAMES: Anabaptists
LOCATION: United States (majority in Ohio, Pennsylvania, and Indiana; Montana; Florida; Texas); Canada (Ontario)
POPULATION: 144,000
LANGUAGE: English (with outsiders); German dialect known as Pennsylvania Dutch [or Pennsylvania German] (with each other)
RELIGION: Amish (an Anabaptist Christian sect)

1 INTRODUCTION

The Amish are members of a Protestant religious sect distinguished by its commitment to the religious practices and attitudes pioneered by the breakaway Anabaptist movement in 16th-century Europe, and in particular by its rejection of many features of modern life in the Western world. In the late 17th century, followers of the Swiss cleric Jacob Ammann broke away from the Mennonites (as the Anabaptists of northern Europe were then known) to form their own church, whose members came to be called the Amish. To the basic Anabaptist doctrines of adult baptism and nonviolence, Ammann added the inclusion of ceremonial foot-washing in the communion service, the strict shunning of excommunicated church members, and the practice of dressing in plain clothing.

Responding to government persecution and economic hardship, the Amish, like other Anabaptist groups, began emigrating to other parts of the world, including America. They arrived in the United States in two stages. The first wave of Amish immigrants settled in Pennsylvania between 1727 and about 1790; the second migrated to Ohio, New York, Indiana, and Illinois between 1815 and 1865. The Amish who remained in Europe were eventually assimilated into Mennonite or mainstream Protestant congregations, leaving only those who had emigrated to preserve their religious tradition. In the New World, the Amish faced hardships, including pressure to fight in the American Revolution, but found the religious freedom they had sought. They have continued to practice their religion, succeeding at agricultural and, more recently, nonagricultural work while preserving their cultural roots across the generations.

Those communities that practice strict adherence to Amish precepts and customs are known as the Old Order Amish and are easily recognizable to outsiders by their somber, conservative clothing reminiscent of a previous century and by their use of horse-drawn buggies instead of automobiles. In their attempt to live lives of simplicity comparable to those of their ancestors, they also farm without tractors and make do at home without telephones, electricity, central heating, and other modern conveniences. Living in close-knit communities, they rely on each other and on their devotion to their religion to meet their needs and ensure the continuation of their way of life.

2 LOCATION AND HOMELAND

The Amish population in the United States is estimated at 144,000. Their three largest communities are located in Ohio and Pennsylvania and, together with Indiana, account for 70% of the total Amish population. Both Ohio and Pennsylvania have over 200 Amish church districts, and Indiana has more

than 100. The Amish also live in other parts of the country and can be found as far west as Montana and as far south as Florida and Texas. Altogether, they are found in more than 20 states in the US as well as in the Canadian province of Ontario.

3 LANGUAGE

The Amish speak English with outsiders and a German dialect among themselves. Their language is a combination of their native German and the English that they learned upon their arrival in North America. It is known as Pennsylvania Dutch. In this case, the word "Dutch" does not refer to the Netherlands, but rather comes from the German word *Deutsch*, which means "German." A sample of Pennsylvania Dutch words:

Mamm	Mother
Daat	Father
Grossdawdi	Grandfather
Grossmudder	Grandmother
redd-up	tidy up
outen	turn out, as in "outen the light"
strubbly	messy
dabbich	clumsy
rutchich	not well-behaved

4 FOLKLORE

The Amish do not believe in any non-Christian folktales, myths, or legends. However, many have retained a body of beliefs about folk healing, derived from both German and rural American traditions. Home remedies, including teas, tonics, salves, and poultices, are passed on from one family to another and between generations. In addition, some Amish subscribe to a somewhat controversial type of faith healing called sympathy "curing," or "powwowing," which relies on charms, amulets, and physical treatments. The following is a typical powwowing charm, said to cure a person who has worms. The following words are repeated silently while the healer circles the patient three times:

You are a little worm, not entirely grown.
You plague me in marrow and bone.
You may be white, black, or red,
In a quarter of an hour, you will be dead.

5 RELIGION

The Amish are Christians who believe in the direct influence of the Holy Spirit on the heart of the believer. For them, the Bible is of primary importance since they consider its text to be the direct word of God. They adhere to the Anabaptist tenets of nonviolence and adult baptism. Their congregations are headed by bishops, ministers, and deacons, all of whom the members choose by casting lots. Regarding church buildings as a sign of worldliness, the Amish hold their three-hour services in the homes of church members without adornments such as candles, flowers, or musical instruments. Minor offenses against church rules typically result in a rebuke or temporary ban, while serious infractions such as adultery or refusal to submit to church authority may result in excommunication and in "shunning" by the entire community.

⁶ MAJOR HOLIDAYS

The major Christian holidays that are important to the Amish include Christmas, Good Friday, Easter, Ascension Day, and Pentecost, although the manner and degree of observance vary from one community to another. Every wedding is a holiday in itself, involving not only the day on which the service actually occurs (always a Tuesday or Thursday) but also the day of communal preparation that precedes it. Christmas is the most important holiday, although Christmas trees and Santa Claus do not form part of the festivities (children may, however, receive modest presents, such as a simple toy or nuts and candy). The extended family holds a festive meal on Christmas Day. Good Friday is observed as a day of fasting. Some Amish observe Christmas and Easter for two days in the European manner. Thanksgiving is celebrated without all the festivities usually associated with it by non-Amish Americans. For the Amish, Thanksgiving is a quiet day for visiting friends and relatives.

⁷ RITES OF PASSAGE

The Amish have neither religious nor secular rituals surrounding birth. Baptism normally occurs in adulthood. Weddings are large public affairs in which the entire community participates; for this reason they are usually held at the end of the year, when the agricultural workload is light and everyone can be involved. There is a church ceremony followed by an elaborate communal meal. The couple's parents provide substantial gifts, such as farm equipment or livestock, to help the couple start out on their own. Guests bring household gifts.

Although death is treated with solemnity, it is accepted as a matter of course. The funerals usually takes place on the third day after death. The dead person is dressed in white and buried in a coffin made to traditional specifications by an Amish carpenter.

⁸ INTERPERSONAL RELATIONS

Many Amish people have the same family names—among a population of 144,000, there are only 126 surnames altogether. The most common names in Indiana and Ohio are Miller and Yoder; in Pennsylvania, they are Stoltzfus and King. Given the small number of surnames, it is common to find Amish persons who share exactly the same first and last names, a problem dealt with by the widespread use of nicknames within the Amish community.

The Amish believe in living life as simply and plainly as possible. They do not baptize their children, serve in the military, vote, fight, or recognize the authority of any worldly government. The Amish suspicion of government and authority is a holdover from the mistreatment they received long ago from the governments of their European homelands. As much as possible, the Amish reject worldly things and material goods. Within their church congregations, they strive to maintain strong discipline, as well as honesty and love for all, inspired by the example set by the earliest Christians. The Old Order Amish avoid modern technology in farming and manufacturing. They worship in private homes, and they continue to live as their ancestors have for generations.

⁹ LIVING CONDITIONS

Since the Amish practice of separation from the outside world rules out college attendance, there are no Amish physicians,

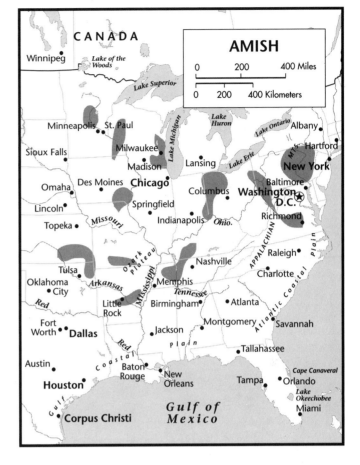

and the Amish must find doctors they trust outside their own communities. In choosing a doctor, they tend to value empathy and character over technical skill and scientific knowledge. In addition to licensed physicians, the Amish also consult with folk healers and other providers of alternative medicine, including chiropractors. Some Amish people resist preventive health care measures such as immunization.

Amish homes tend to be large and simple, with little decoration other than quilts and china. Furnishings must be spare enough to allow room for religious services, which rotate from one home to another instead of being held in a church. Area rugs are preferred over wall-to-wall carpeting, which is considered overly extravagant. In the winter, individual rooms are heated with a kerosene heater or wood stove rather than central heating. The use of electricity and other services provided by public utilities is forbidden.

The main means of transportation for the Amish is the horse-drawn buggy or wagon. They do not use motor vehicles, and most refuse even to ride bicycles, although Amish children are allowed to ride scooters.

¹⁰ FAMILY LIFE

The Amish are strongly committed to marrying within their own communities—and remaining married to their original partners—since the perpetuation of their way of life depends on producing new generations rather than increasing their numbers through conversion of people from outside their communities. The centrality of the family in Amish life can be seen in

The main means of transportation for the Amish is the horse-drawn buggy or wagon. They do not use motor vehicles, and most refuse even to ride bicycles, although Amish children are allowed to ride scooters. (Missouri Division of Tourism)

the fact that the Amish measure the population of their communities by the number of families rather than the number of individuals. Their families are large: seven is the average number of children in an Amish family, and one-fourth of the Amish have ten or more children.

The husband is the head of the household, but the husband and wife make important family decisions jointly. Husbands and wives do not display affection in public.

Strict obedience is expected of Amish children although attitudes toward children are generally loving and affectionate. Amish children begin helping their parents with farm work or other domestic chores at an early age. Older children are expected to help care for and set an example for their younger siblings.

An Amish person who is excommunicated by the church and shunned by the community is also shunned by his or her spouse and family.

11 CLOTHING

The Amish fasten all their clothing by means of old-fashioned hooks and eyes rather than buttons, zippers, or Velcro. Amish women wear long dresses with bonnets or white prayer caps, shawls, capes, or aprons. They never use makeup or perfume, nor do they wear jewelry of any kind, including wedding rings. Although they do not use patterned fabrics, their clothes can be colorful. Besides the neutral black, gray, and brown, dresses

may also be green, maroon, or purple, among other colors. The men normally wear ordinary work shirts with full-cut pants called "broadfalls." The broadfalls are so named because instead of having a zipper in front, they have a wide flap that folds down when necessary and is fastened up at the sides. Broadfalls are always held up by suspenders, never belts. Men and women wear boots, sneakers, or any other plain, comfortable footwear. In the summer, many go barefoot. Boys and men stay clean-shaven until they get married, at that time, they grow beards, but never mustaches.

12 FOOD

Amish meals are prepared in old-fashioned country kitchens, on a gas or wood stove, since the Amish do not use electricity. Meals tend to be plain and filling. Even so, the Amish do enjoy some unique and tasty dishes. Dandelion salad with bacon-fat dressing is a favorite. Another is *Snitz unKnepp*, dried apple slices cooked in sugar water with dumplings like doughnuts and served as a stew. Snitz pie is a pie made from dried apples. *Chow-chow* is an assortment of pickled vegetables. A tasty snack is cup cheese, a creamy smooth cheese that is best when spread on bread or crackers. Lebanon bologna is a type of cold sausage, and red beet eggs are pickled in beets and vinegar and sometimes eaten straight from the jar. In Amish families, the main meal is served in the evening during the part of the year when school is in session. When summer comes, the main meal is served at noon, with soup and sandwiches for supper.

13 EDUCATION

The Amish have their own schools, where children of all ages learn together in one-room schoolhouses with no restrooms and no hot water. Amish young people complete school only up to the eighth grade. After that, they are expected to become full-time workers on the family farms, although they sometimes continue their schooling one-half day each week, perfecting their skills in German, spelling, and arithmetic. The Amish do not believe it is necessary for their young people to attend high school or pursue an education at the college level. All anyone needs, they feel, is to be able to read a newspaper and calculate the finances of the farm. They do not value education for its own sake or feel that education makes one a better person. As for life skills, Amish boys learn farming from watching and helping their fathers, while Amish girls learn to be good home-makers by imitating their mothers. Teachers in Amish schools are not required to have attended college. Instead, young Amish people who have distinguished themselves as students simply remain in the school, assuming the role of teacher to the younger children.

14 CULTURAL HERITAGE

Although artistic expression does not play an important role in the plain and simple lifestyle of the Amish, they do enjoy singing religious songs—mostly slow, somber hymns sung *a cappella* as part of their religious services. There are also faster songs, sung mainly at weddings and in evening singing sessions held on Sunday nights. The Amish also entertain their young children with sing-alongs and nursery songs.

There are several Amish publications, including two newspapers, *Die Botschaft* ("The Message") and the *Budget,* which consists largely of news about the various Amish communities. There is also a magazine for Amish teachers, *Blackboard Bulletin,* a monthly called *The Diary: Of the Old Order Churches,* and a publication called *Family Life.*

15 WORK

Almost all Amish people are farmers, with farms small enough to be run by their families without the aid of mechanization, including tractors. More concerned with subsistence than with high profit margins, most Amish farmers raise livestock in modest numbers along with a variety of crops. Some of the Amish work in their communities as tradespeople, making, repairing, and providing the things needed on the farms. Today, an increasing number run nonfarm businesses. The Amish community in Pennsylvania's Lancaster County is home to over 1,000 such businesses, including furniture makers, construction contractors, and quilt shops. Relying on long hours and quality workmanship, Amish entrepreneurs are thriving, with a failure rate much lower than the average for small businesses.

Some Amish people run shops or restaurants that cater to non-Amish visitors, such as city dwellers out on a weekend drive in the country.

16 SPORTS

The Amish play as hard as they work. Although they do not participate in organized or professional sports, they often play games of softball or volleyball. In season, hunting is a popular pastime among Amish men, and Amish boys enjoy hiking. The country life of the Amish provides many opportunities for outdoor recreation. In the summer, everyone enjoys fishing, swimming, and all kinds of games; while in the winter, sledding and skating on frozen ponds provide plenty of excitement.

17 ENTERTAINMENT AND RECREATION

Amish children usually play with homemade rather than store-bought toys. Teenage girls enjoy playing clapping games called "botching," played by two people seated opposite each other in chairs. Families often spend leisure time attending weekly auctions and visiting relatives and other members of the community. In the fall, the many weddings that take place typically occupy much of a family's leisure time.

18 FOLK ART, CRAFTS, AND HOBBIES

The Amish are known for their quilts, which feature distinctive styles and sewing techniques. Quilt making is an important communal activity as well as a form of artistic expression. In addition, it has taken on increasing economic significance as Amish women have begun selling quilts to the general public in greater numbers. Amish quilts are also exhibited in museums and other public places, both in the United States and in other countries throughout the world. Photography and other types of representational art are forbidden among the Amish.

19 SOCIAL PROBLEMS

A problem for the Amish and similar groups is the struggle to maintain their traditional ways in the face of the temptations of the modern world that surrounds them. The Amish are very much in the world, if not of it, and they see quite clearly the advantages that modern technology can provide. An Amish farmer toiling behind a horse-drawn plow can look up and watch his neighbor do his plowing with a tractor in a fraction of the time. The contrast is even more evident to the young people. Like teenagers everywhere, many Amish young people engage in typical forms of mischief. Usually, though, they return to the old ways as they grow older. All in all, the Amish have been remarkably steadfast in maintaining their traditions.

20 BIBLIOGRAPHY

Ammon, Richard. *Growing Up Amish.* Atheneum, 1989.

Bender, Sue. *Plain and Simple: A Woman's Journey to the Amish.* New York: Harper & Row, 1989.

Hostetler, John A. *Amish Society.* 4th ed. Baltimore: Johns Hopkins University Press, 1993.

Kenna, Kathleen *A People Apart.* Boston: Houghton Mifflin, 1996.

Kraybill, Donald. *Old Order Amish: Their Enduring Way of Life.* Baltimore: Johns Hopkins University Press, 1993.

Nolt, Steven M. *A History of the Amish.* Intercourse, PA: Good Books, 1992.

Williams, Jean Kinney. *The Amish, The American Religious Experience.* New York: Franklin Watts, 1996.

Yoder, Doyle. *America's Amish Country.* Berlin, OH: America's Amish Country Publications, 1992.

ANTIGUANS AND BARBUDANS

PRONUNCIATION: An-TEE-gahns and Bar-BYEW-dahns
LOCATION: Antigua and Barbuda
POPULATION: 75,000
LANGUAGE: English; Creole dialect
RELIGION: Anglican Church; other Protestant groups; Roman
  Catholicism

¹ INTRODUCTION

The nation of Antigua and Barbuda (pronounced An-TEE-gah and Bar-BYEW-dah), located in the Leeward Islands, consists of two islands lying approximately 43 km (27 mi) apart and also encompasses a third, uninhabited island, Redonda. The country's main source of income is tourism, which employs most of the population, and its international airport serves as a base for travel throughout the region. Christopher Columbus sighted the island of Antigua in 1493 and gave it its original name, Santa María de la Antigua. The Carib Indians and the island's scarce water supply kept the Spanish, as well as the French, English, and Dutch, from colonizing it until 1632, when a group of British settlers from St. Kitts landed and managed to stay, establishing tobacco and ginger plantations. Except for a brief period of French rule in 1666, Antigua, joined shortly afterward by neighboring Barbuda, was to remain under uninterrupted British control for over 300 years.

In 1674, Sir Christopher Codrington introduced sugar plantations to Antigua, together with the large numbers of African slaves needed to work on them. Eleven years later, Codrington leased the island of Barbuda, primarily to supply Antigua with livestock and provisions. The Codrington family's lease of Barbuda continued for nearly 200 years; in 1860 Antigua and Barbuda were legally united under Great Britain.

As the sugar industry on Antigua grew, much of the land was deforested, exacerbating the island's water supply problems, which have continued to the present day. After the slaves were emancipated in 1834, their living conditions were little better than they had been under slavery and were in some instances worse, as they were now required to provide their own food and shelter out of their meager wages. There was little improvement in the situation of Antigua's Black laborers over the next century. The inhabitants of Barbuda, which had no plantations, continued their subsistence farming on small plots of land. In the 1930s, drought and economic depression worsened conditions on Antigua to the point of civil unrest, and a specially appointed British commission recommended the establishment of a trade union, which proceeded to win a series of labor victories for Antiguan workers.

Extending its influence to the political realm, the Antigua Trades and Labour Union (ATLU) formed the Antigua Labor Party (ALP) in 1946. Thanks largely to its efforts, Antigua and Barbuda achieved universal adult suffrage with no income or literacy requirements by 1951. The party's leader, Vere Cornwall Bird, rose to political prominence, becoming chief minister of the Antiguan Parliament in 1961. Full internal self-government for Antigua and Barbuda was granted by the British in 1967. Complete independence followed in 1981 (a seces-

sion movement on Barbuda was contained when that island was promised internal autonomy).

Except for the years between 1971 and 1976, the ALP has remained Antigua's ruling party from 1946 to the present. In the 1990s the government fended off multiple scandals, including allegations of smuggling Israeli arms to Colombian drug cartels, as well as misuse of public funds. Nevertheless, the Antigua and Barbuda public, as well as overseas investors, have retained confidence in the government and the country has achieved much international acclaim for its input and contributions to democracy, human rights, economic and social programs, and on issues relating to defense—particularly of the Americas. In 1994, Vere Cornwall Bird (Father of the Nation) resigned as prime minister and was succeeded by his son, Lester B. Bird.

The Barbudans express the marginalization of their society by both the British (formerly) and the majority on Antigua (presently) in the proverb, "Barbuda is behind God's back."

² LOCATION AND HOMELAND

Antigua and Barbuda—close to the midpoint of the Lesser Antilles—is located at the outer curve of the Leeward Islands, between the Atlantic Ocean and the Caribbean Sea. Antigua is 650 km (404 mi) southeast of Cuba. With an area of 281 sq km (108 sq mi), it is the second-largest of the Leeward Islands and about two-thirds the size of New York City. Its terrain is mostly low-lying, although Boggy Peak, located among volcanically formed hills in the west, rises to 399 m (1,309 ft). The interior is primarily scrub-covered with some forest cover.

Annual rainfall—averaging about 11 cm (4.3 in) per year—is lighter than that on most other islands in the West Indies, and there are no permanent rivers or streams on either Antigua or Barbuda, so water supply and conservation are of great concern to the nation's people. However, the country's dry climate, together with its abundant natural harbors and sandy beaches (said to number 365, one for each day of the year) have made it a prime location for tourism, and Antigua was one of the first sites in the Caribbean to attract foreign tourists as a vacation spot.

Barbuda lies about 50 km (31 mi) northeast of Antigua and is about half its size—176 sq km (68 sq mi). It is very flat—its highest elevation is 44.5 m (146 ft)—with sandy beaches and a large lagoon and mangrove swamp on its western side. The island, which was leased to a single British family for nearly 200 years, has only one village, Codrington. Much of the island is a scrub-covered wilderness covered with cactus and thornbush and roamed by a variety of undomesticated animals, including what may be the only deer on a Caribbean island. The uninhabited island of Redonda, which has been under the jurisdiction of Antigua since 1869, has an area of 2.6 sq km (1 sq mi). Phosphate mining was carried out on the island until 1914.

A 1991 census recorded the population of Antigua and Barbuda as just under 66,000, of which 1,200 lived on Barbuda. However, other estimates place the total population closer to 75,000 with 1,500 or more on Barbuda. St. John's, the country's capital and economic center, has an estimated population of between 35,000 and 40,000 people. Blacks descended from African slaves account for approximately 95% of the population, with the remainder of European, Asian, Arab, and mixed descent.

³ LANGUAGE

English is the official language of Antigua and Barbuda, but most inhabitants speak a Creole dialect that is based on standard English combined with African expressions and local slang. English pronunciation and grammar are also modified. One of the most noticeable differences is in the use of object pronouns in the subject of a sentence, as in "Her my friend" (which also omits the helping verb "is" that would be found in the standard English sentence, "She is my friend."). A similar construction is "Us alive" for "We are alive." Objective pronouns may also replace possessive pronouns, as in "You come me church," which also omits the preposition "to" of the standard English construction, "You come to my church."

⁴ FOLKLORE

Obeah, a collection of animistic beliefs and practices derived from Africa, has adherents in Antigua and Barbuda, although it has been declared illegal. Those who subscribe to it believe it can heal the sick, harm one's enemies, and even be used for such mundane purposes as "fixing" a court case. Its features include a belief in spirits (of which the best-known are *jumbies*) and the preparation of herbal potions. There is also a body of unrelated medicinal folklore that has been preserved on the islands, which includes such remedies as the use of a paste made from a plant known as the cancanberry bush to treat thrush, and the ingestion of maiden-blush tea for a variety of purposes.

⁵ RELIGION

The Anglican Church has the largest membership of any religion in Antigua and Barbuda, claiming about 45% of the population. Other Protestant groups, including the Baptist, Methodist, Pentecostal, Seventh-Day Adventist, Moravian, and Pilgrim Holiness churches, collectively account for about 42% of the population, and about 8% are Roman Catholic.

⁶ MAJOR HOLIDAYS

Public holidays in Antigua and Barbuda include New Year's Day (1 January), Labor Day (first Monday in May), CARICOM Day (3 July), Independence Day (1 November), Christmas (25 December) and Boxing Day (26 December), as well as Good Friday, Easter Monday, and Whit Monday, which occur on different dates each year.

The nation of Antigua and Barbuda is particularly known for its Carnival celebration, held in late July through the first Tuesday in August. Most of the festivities take place in the capital city of St. John's, including street parades led by revelers wearing elaborate glittering costumes, calypso and steel drum music, street dancing ("jump-up"), and contests. The climax of the festival is J'Ouvert on the first Monday in August, when thousands of celebrants pour into the streets at 4:00 AM in a frenzy of dancing accompanied by steel drum and brass bands. The island of Barbuda holds its own more modest Carnival celebration, Caribana, in June.

⁷ RITES OF PASSAGE

The religious confirmation of young men and women, performed at puberty, signals their acceptance into the Church by the general congregation. Other major life transitions, such as

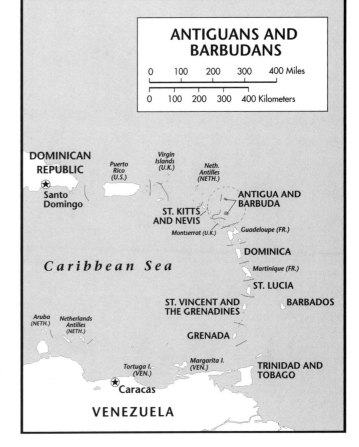

birth, marriage, and death, are also marked by religious ceremonies.

⁸ INTERPERSONAL RELATIONS

"Aunty" and "Uncle" are sometimes used as terms of respect in addressing one's elders, and a woman may be addressed by the word "Mistress" before her last name. A handshake is a customary greeting among business associates.

⁹ LIVING CONDITIONS

Most Antiguans and Barbudans live in houses constructed of concrete and wood, with at least two bedrooms, a living/dining room, a kitchen, and a bathroom. Most homes on both islands now have indoor plumbing and electricity.

The average life expectancy in Antigua and Barbuda is 73 years. In the late 1980s, gastroenteritis and dysentery, mostly due to poor sanitation, were the most common illnesses and causes of death, especially in children. Other causes of death include heart disease, cerebrovascular disease, cancer, and influenza. Hypertension is the most common medical condition on Barbuda, which has a 10-bed hospital. There is some malnutrition among the nation's children, some of whom are not immunized against common diseases.

Antigua and Barbuda has 1 physician for every 2,200 people, and one general hospital, the Holberton Hospital. In the early 1990s the hospital was often short of basic supplies, but since 1994 supplies and services have been readily available. Sewage treatment and waste disposal problems have been under better control since the mid-1990s.

Antiguan girl carrying water jug. Many children are raised by relatives other than their parents, and some grow up in a succession of different households. (AP/Wide World Photos)

Antigua has 240 km (149 mi) of roads, previously known for their absence of street signs and other markings, including village names and distance indicators. Today, many streets and roads are marked, and through the cooperative efforts of local business and community organizations, road signs and village markers are more commonplace.

In 1992, 17,000 motor vehicles were registered. There is a railway consisting of 78 km (48 mi) of narrow-gauge track. St. John's is the major port, and Vere Cornwall Bird International Airport, about 10 km (6 mi) northeast of St. John's, accommodates large jetliners, serving as a hub for tourist travel in the region.

10 FAMILY LIFE

Couples in Antigua and Barbuda, as in other parts of the English-speaking Caribbean, are united in three basic types of relationships: legal marriage, unmarried cohabitation, and "visiting unions," where the man and woman live apart and the woman raises the children. Many children are raised by relatives other than their parents, and some grow up in a succession of different households. Decisions about where a child will live are influenced by a variety of factors, including the parents' financial situation and employment patterns, educational opportunities, and the necessity of caring for the elderly. Inheritances are usually divided equally among legitimate and illegitimate children, and a 1987 law made it illegal to discriminate

against children born out of wedlock. The country's fertility rate in 1994 was 1.67 children for each woman. With the growth of the tourism industry, an increasing number of women have entered the labor force.

11 CLOTHING

The people of Antigua and Barbuda wear modern Western-style clothing. Colorful costumes are worn by many during the Carnival celebration in August.

In 1992, a national competition to select a national dress was held as a part of the islands' eleventh anniversary of independence. The winning design was submitted by native Antiguan Heather Doram. The costume, which has versions for men and women, is worn by many Antiguans and Barbudans on Independence Day, 1 November.

12 FOOD

The Creole cuisine of Antigua and Barbuda is similar to that of other West Indian nations and includes such staples as rice and peas, pumpkin soup, and pepperpot soup. Fish and shellfish are an important part of the national diet, and the regional species of spiny lobster is especially popular, as are crabs and conch. Fungi, a sort of cornmeal pudding made with boiled okra, is another staple on the islands, especially served with salt fish.

Breadfruit (originally introduced to the region from the East Indies) is another staple, and meat-filled pastries ("pasties") are sold by street vendors. The country's most distinctive fruit is the Antigua black pineapple, which is exceptionally sweet.

13 EDUCATION

Primary and secondary education is compulsory between the ages of 5 and 16, and pre-primary schooling is available from the age of 3. The educational system in Antigua and Barbuda is based on the British system, which has grade levels called "forms." Primary education is provided for five or six years, after which an examination is taken to pass on to the upper grades. Students then complete four or five years of secondary education.

There are 45 primary schools and 12 secondary schools. Although the nation has a literacy rate of 90%, there are serious deficiencies in the educational system, including a shortage of qualified teachers and inadequate facilities and supplies. Technical and teacher training is offered at the Antigua State College, and there is an offshore medical school, the University of Health Sciences, which was founded in 1982. In addition, the regional University of the West Indies has a continuing education facility in Antigua and Barbuda.

14 CULTURAL HERITAGE

The music of the Fife Band is an important part of the islands' musical heritage. The band is made up of a stringed guitar, drum, and fife (or flute).

The Museum of Antigua and Barbuda, in St. John's, is dedicated to preserving the islands' heritage by maintaining their archaeological relics and historic buildings.

Internationally acclaimed author Jamaica Kincaid was born and grew up on the island of Antigua and now resides in the United States. Her novels and short stories, including *At the Bottom of the River* (1983) and *Annie John* (1985), provide a vivid portrait of the Antiguan people and way of life based on images and memories from her youth. Kincaid has also been a staff writer for *The New Yorker* magazine since the 1970s, and her 1988 book-length essay, *A Small Place,* is a searing indictment of British colonialism, the tourist industry, and government corruption and neglect in post-colonial Antigua. Antiguan playwright Dorbrene "Fats" Omarde is known for dramas that address the social and political issues confronting his country.

¹⁵ WORK

The vast majority of people in Antigua and Barbuda are employed by the government. The figure for total employment in commerce or in service-sector jobs is 82% of the work force, while agriculture employs 11% and industry employs the remaining 7%. Since tourism-related jobs are, in many cases, seasonal, it is a common practice to have more than one source of income, which may include such part-time agricultural pursuits as keeping livestock or selling produce from "backyard farming" at the market. Fishing is an important source of income on Barbuda, as are government employment and tourism.

¹⁶ SPORTS

Cricket is the national sport of Antigua and Barbuda, and the country has produced some of the world's most outstanding players, including Viv Richards, Andy Roberts, Richie Richardson, and Curtley Adams, a fast bowler. Antiguan teams compete against teams from neighboring islands, and Antiguans play on the West Indies cricket team, which has been one of the world's best since the 1970s. Soccer is another popular sport.

¹⁷ ENTERTAINMENT AND RECREATION

The Caribbean's universal male pastime of dominoes is enjoyed in Antigua and Barbuda. A game called *warri* is also popular. Favorite types of music include calypso, reggae, and hymns.

Cricket is played recreationally, as are soccer, basketball, and netball.

¹⁸ FOLK ART, CRAFTS, AND HOBBIES

Antiguan artisans are known for the exceptional quality of their handthrown pottery. Striking items, both decorative and functional, are also crafted from handwoven sea cotton adorned by batiking and embroidery. Other handicrafts include woodcarving and basketry.

¹⁹ SOCIAL PROBLEMS

Antigua and Barbuda has serious environmental problems that threaten the nation's economy and the health of its residents. In the absence of a central sewage system, contamination by raw sewage and other forms of domestic waste poses a grave threat to the water supply in a country without permanent natural lakes or perennial rivers. In addition, the removal of sand for construction purposes threatens the nation's beaches, which are the basis of its tourist industry.

Inadequacies in the educational system have contributed to a shortage of skilled workers, and the tourist industry, while highly labor-intensive, creates work that is in most cases unskilled and low-paid. The government's abolition of personal income taxes and its reliance on foreign borrowing has left the country with a massive foreign debt.

²⁰ BIBLIOGRAPHY

Cameron, Sarah, and Ben Box, ed. *Caribbean Islands Handbook.* Chicago: Passport Books, 1995.

Carom, Robert. "Ancient Rights." *The New Yorker* (6 Feb 1989): 76–94.

———. *Caribbean Time Bomb: The United States' Complicity in the Corruption of Antigua.* New York: William Morrow, 1993.

Gall, Timothy, and Susan Gall, ed. *Worldmark Encyclopedia of the Nations.* 8th ed. Detroit: Gale Research, 1995.

Kincaid, Jamaica. "Alien Soil." *The New Yorker* (21 June 1993): 47–51.

———. *Annie John.* New York: Farrar Straus Giroux, 1983.

———. *A Small Place.* New York: Farrar Straus Giroux, 1988.

Lazarus-Black, Mindie. "Antiguans and Barbudans." In *Encyclopedia of World Cultures* (*Middle America and the Caribbean*). Boston: G. K. Hall, 1992.

———. *Legitimate Acts and Illegal Encounters: Law and Society in Antigua and Barbuda.* Washington, DC: Smithsonian Institution Press, 1994.

Luntta, Karl. *Caribbean Handbook.* Chico, CA: Moon Publications, 1995.

Meditz, Sandra W., and Dennis M. Hanratty. *Islands of the Commonwealth Caribbean: A Regional Study.* Washington, DC: US Government, 1989.

Nicholson, Desmond V. *Antigua, Barbuda, and Redonda: A Historical Sketch.* St. John's, Antigua: Museum of Antigua & Barbuda, 1992.

Schwab, David, ed. *Insight Guides. Caribbean: The Lesser Antilles.* Boston: Houghton Mifflin, 1996.

Smith, Keithlyn B., and Fernando C. Smith. To Shoot Hard Labour (The Life and Times of Samuel Smith, an Antiguan Workingman 1877–1982). London: Karia Press, 1986.

United States. Central Intelligence Agency. *World Fact Book.* Washington, DC: Government Printing Office, 1994.

Walton, Chelle Koster. *Caribbean Ways: A Cultural Guide.* Westwood, MA: Riverdale, 1993.

—reviewed by K. Knowles

ARAB AMERICANS

For more information on Arab history and culture, *see* **Vol. 1: Algerians, Egyptians, Libyans, Moroccans, Sudanese, Tunisians**; and **Vol. 3: Alawis, Bahrainis, Bedu, Druze, Emirians, Iraqis, Jordanians, Kuwaitis, Lebanese, Ma'dan, Maronites, Omanis, Palestinians, Qataris, Saudis, Syrians, Yazidis**, and **Yemenis**.

OVERVIEW

The first Arabs to immigrate in large numbers to the US were Lebanese Christians in the 1880s (*see* **Lebanese Americans**). Lebanese Muslims began to immigrate to America in the early 1900s and were joined by other Arabs, mostly Palestinians. Arab immigration to the US continued in a steady stream until 1924, when the US placed severe restrictions on the number of immigrants allowed in from each country. Arab countries were given extremely low quotas; for example, only 100 Syrians were allowed to enter the US each year. Arab immigrants continued to trickle in to America for the next few decades, but sizeable immigration did not resume until US immigration reforms were introduced in 1965, opening the doors to much greater numbers of Arabs. The humiliating defeat of Arab forces by Israel in the Six-Day War of 1967 triggered a sharp rise in Arab immigration to the US. Since 1970, over 10,000 Arabs each year have immigrated to America.

Early Arab immigrants were mostly poor, uneducated farmers hoping to earn money quickly and then return to their homelands. The majority were Christian. Many became traders or peddlers. Others took factory jobs, especially in the Detroit auto industry. Detroit and Dearborn, Michigan, continue to lure Arab immigrants today. Detroit is the number-one port of entry in the US for Arab immigrants, and three out of five immigrants to Detroit are Arab. The Detroit-Dearborn area currently boasts the largest Arab American population in the US.

Arab immigrants to the US since World War II (1939–45) differ in a number of ways from those who came before. The great majority (approximately 78%) are Muslim. They are mostly well-educated professionals, or students seeking higher education. Whereas earlier Arab immigrants tended to take up the life of the traveling salesperson (both men and women worked as peddlers), newer immigrants are more likely to settle down in large cities and work in their various professions. Lebanese immigrants dominated earlier waves, while recent waves have brought a majority of Palestinians.

When Palestine was partitioned into a Jewish state and an Arab state in 1947, and the nation of Israel was formed in 1948, hundreds of thousands of Palestinian Arabs were driven from their homes. Many decided to immigrate to the US, at least temporarily. Civil unrest and a lack of economic opportunities in their former homeland led a great number to decide to stay in America permanently.

The Egyptian Revolution in 1952 drove many wealthy Egyptians out of Egypt when their property was confiscated and their businesses nationalized. As a result, Arab countries suffered a severe "brain drain" with 90,915 Arabs immigrating to the US in the 1950s and 1960s, most of them (90%) professionals. In the past few decades, other Arabs, such as Yemenis, Iraqis, and North Africans, have also immigrated to the US in search of a better life than that available to them in their conflict-ridden homelands.

Getting an exact count of the Arab American population is impossible for a number of reasons. Immigration records are misleading because early Arab immigrants were often listed as "Turks" (since Lebanon was under the rule of the Ottoman Turkish Empire). More recent immigrants frequently come to the US from some other country than their homeland, as so many are displaced Palestinian refugees, and they are registered according to their last residence rather than as Palestinians. Some are still listed under vague categories such as "other Asian" or "other African." Self-reported statistics on the US Census are also incomplete because Arab Americans may fear revealing themselves as such due to anti-Arab sentiments in America. Others classify themselves in terms that are difficult to distinguish clearly as Arab.

An acceptable estimate of the current Arab American population is 2,500,000. About half are immigrants or descendants of immigrants from 1880–1940; the rest are post-World War II immigrants. Arab Americans live all across the US, though the largest population (over 200,000, of whom half are Lebanese Americans) is in the Detroit-Dearborn, Michigan, area. Boston, Chicago, New York City, and Los Angeles all have Arab American populations of more than 100,000. Almost 50,000 Arab Americans live in San Francisco, and the cities of Houston, Jacksonville (Florida), and Phoenix have Arab American populations of more than 20,000 each.

Christian Arab Americans have tended to become Americanized quite quickly. Many early immigrants Americanized their names in order to fit in with mainstream American society. More recent immigrants find less need to change their names in the new atmosphere of multiculturalism in the US. However, some still use Americanized names in public and reserve their Arabic names for family use. The Arabic language is an integral part of the Islamic religion, so Muslim Arab Americans retain at least some fluency in Arabic, even into the third and fourth generations. Christian Arab Americans are more likely to lose their fluency in Arabic as soon as the second generation.

Muslim Arabs hesitated to immigrate to the US in the early years of Arab immigration because America was a Christian nation, by and large. There were no mosques in America in the 19th and early 20th centuries. Although mosques have been built and Muslim communities have developed in several regions of the US, Muslim Arab Americans still find it difficult at times to follow some of their religious practices, such as praying facing Mecca five times a day or fasting during the month of Ramadan. However, Islam does provide alternate ways of meeting religious obligations, and many Muslim Arab Americans choose to give extra money to charity or spend time educating young Muslims in place of missed prayers or fasting. Second- and later-generation Muslim Arab Americans often leave their parents' religion as they become Americanized and/ or marry non-Arabs.

Because Druze religious leaders are not allowed to leave their homeland in the Middle East, Druze Arab Americans have never built a place of worship in the US. Many attend Christian churches instead, as Druze and Christians worship the same God.

Christian, Druze, and Muslim Arab Americans almost never intermarry, nor do Sunni and Shi'ite Muslim Arab Americans

or Maronite and Melkite Christian Arab Americans. Arab Americans do intermarry, however, with non-Arabs. Muslim Arab Americans discourage marrying non-Arabs, but some do, especially as later generations become less attached to their religious and cultural traditions.

Intermarriage with non-Arabs creates difficulties for both parties, however, particularly in the area of family relations. The extended Arab family, with its complex and close relationships, is quite foreign to Western Europeans who focus on the nuclear family unit. Non-Arab American spouses can become quite frustrated with the multitude of in-laws who drop in at any time without warning, call at all hours, help themselves to food from the kitchen, etc., all of which are expected in Arab culture. Arab Americans may not understand their non-Arab spouses' frustrations or lack of connection with their own extended families.

Arab culture also has great respect for the elderly, and aged parents and grandparents are always cared for at home. Nursing homes do not exist in Arab countries, and Arab Americans almost never make use of them in the US. This can be another source of tension between Arab and non-Arab American spouses, as most non-Arab Americans are not used to caring for aging relatives in their homes.

Family and food are central elements of Arab culture, and this remains true for Arab Americans. Both family and food are enjoyed by Arab Americans at picnic festivals known as *mahrajan*. Arab foods such as hummus, kibbe, fattoush salad, and baklava have become popular in mainstream American society today, thanks to the many Arab Americans who opened Middle Eastern restaurants in cities across the US.

Arab Americans also place a high value on education. Although the earliest immigrants were mostly uneducated and illiterate, they made sure that their children were given the best education available in America. Many of today's Arab immigrants are students seeking higher education. In general, Arab Americans do very well in school and work hard to obtain their degrees.

Perhaps most central to an Arab's heart is poetry, and Arab Americans have lost none of their love for this art. Lebanese American poet Kahlil Gibran became internationally known with the publication of his book of mystical verse, *The Prophet*. Written in English, *The Prophet* has since been translated into 20 languages. More than four million copies have been sold in the US alone.

Because early Arab immigrants to the US were mostly Christian and tended to scatter across the country in their work as traders, they met with little overt discrimination or prejudice from other Americans. They blended in with Christian mainstream America, and their small, scattered numbers did not pose an economic threat to established communities. Later Muslim Arab immigrants, however, stood out in sharp relief from mainstream America, with their exotic religious and cultural customs. They were also more likely to settle together in Muslim Arab American communities, presenting a more noticeable perceived threat to non-Arab Americans.

Since World War II, anti-Arab sentiment in the US has been on the rise. The US has consistently supported Israel in the Arab-Israeli conflict that began in 1947, although the US has also participated in efforts to bring peace to the warring factions. Jewish Americans, whose population is about twice that of Arab Americans, are quite vocal in their support of Israel. Such dissension creates a difficult situation for Arab Americans who are then seen as "the enemy." US politicians hesitate to accept any support from Arab Americans for fear of alienating Jewish American voters.

In general, Arab Americans are stereotyped in mainstream American culture as terrorists and/or greedy oil barons. With the heightening terrorist activity in the Middle East, the oil embargo of the 1970s and rising oil prices since then, the Iran-Iraq War of the 1980s, and the Gulf War of the 1990s, anti-Arab sentiment in the US has steadily increased. Arab Americans are often subject to discrimination, harassment, and even violence.

In the past few decades, Arab Americans have formed a number of organizations to address these problems and work towards legal, political, and educational solutions. In Washington, D.C., and Los Angeles, Jewish American and Arab American groups have joined together to begin establishing better relations between their peoples. Hopefully, these movements toward greater understanding and harmony will lead to a more peaceful existence for Arab Americans in the US.

BIBLIOGRAPHY

Ashabranner, Brent. *An Ancient Heritage: The Arab-American Minority.* New York: HarperCollins, 1991.

Mindel, Charles H., Robert W. Habenstein, and Roosevelt Wright, Jr., ed. *Ethnic Families in America: Patterns and Variations*, 3rd ed. New York: Elsevier, 1988.

Naff, Alixa. *The Arab Americans.* New York: Chelsea House, 1988.

—by D. K. Daeg de Mott

ARAUCANIANS

LOCATION: Chile; Argentina
POPULATION: About 800,000
LANGUAGE: Araucanian
RELIGION: Roman Catholicism mingled with indigenous religious beliefs

¹ INTRODUCTION

The Araucanian Indians lived in southern, central, and northern areas of Chile and, later, partly in what is today Argentina. They were divided into three main groups: the Picunche or northern people, the Mapuche in the central area, and the Huilliche or southern people. The Araucanians first fought the Inca invaders from Peru in the 15th century. The Incas, under their leader Tupac Yupanqui, extended their empire briefly in Chile as far south as the Santiago area, around what is today Chile's capital. Then Spanish conquerors who arrived from Peru invaded the lands of the Araucanians and other Amerindian groups, initially under Diego de Almagro, and then under Pedro de Valdivia, who founded the modern capital of Santiago.

The Araucanians established a reputation as fierce warriors who bravely defended their lands and their way of life, but the northern Picunche, who lived in the pleasant farming areas of Chile's Central Valley between the Aconcagua and Bío Bío rivers, were relatively peaceful and were easily overcome by the Incas, and were then subdued and assimilated by the Spaniards in the 17th century. The Mapuche and the Hulliche groups of Araucanians continued to resist the Spaniards for hundreds of years, answering to no central authority and choosing leaders only for the specific purpose of waging their wars of resistance.

² LOCATION AND HOMELAND

The main group of Araucanians that still remain in Chile today are the Mapuche, numbering some 800,000 people. Initially the Mapuche lived between the Itata and Toltén rivers, while the Huilliche or southern Araucanians lived between the Toltén and the island of Chiloé. The Mapuche finally lost their independence in the War of 1880–1882. After this defeat they were forced to settle further south on small reservations called *reducciones,* where about half of the Mapuche family groups still live today, many of them in the vicinity of towns such as Temuco, Villarica, Pucón, Valdivia, and Osorno, as well as in the southern island region of Chiloé. Some 400,000 Mapuche have had to migrate to the cities and now live the life of poor, urban workers.

In the 16th century some Mapuche crossed into Argentina, in the region of Patagonia. They resisted the Spanish colonizers until the 19th century. After Argentina gained its independence from Spain, the struggle against the Indians continued until 1879 when, during a cruel war led by General Julio Argentine Roca, the Mapuche's and other Amerindian's lands, such as those of the Tehuelche, were conquered and thousands of Indians were killed. Those that remained were forced to work on the ranches of the new owners, or in military forts, or as domestic servants. General Roca adopted a tough attitude to the hard fate of the Indians, and appeared to rejoice in the conquest of such a huge tract of land. Today, there are still a few Mapuche reservations in Argentina, particularly on the shores of Lake Rucachoroi and Lake Quillén. However, most Mapuche Araucanians today continue to live in Chile.

³ LANGUAGE

The Mapuche continue to speak the Araucanian language, as do the remaining Argentine Araucanians who are descended from the Chileans, and who crossed the border into Argentina during the long and troubled period of resistance against the Spanish settlers. Their language, which they call Mapudungu, also survives in many place names: *quen* means "place," as in the town of Vichiquen, while *che* means "people," and *mapu* means "land." Mapuche, therefore, translates as "people of the land." In times of war the Mapuche chose a leader who was called a *Toqui,* while in peacetime their leader was called the *Ulmen.* Choosing people to perform certain tasks because of their abilities was a strength of the Mapuche. Messengers, called *huerquenes,* were chosen because of their excellent memories.

⁴ FOLKLORE

Araucanian folklore survives today thanks to the continuing if impoverished existence of the Mapuche. They honor the memory of their greatest hero, the wartime leader or *Toqui* called Lautaro, who was chosen to do battle against the Spanish invaders. In common with many other Amerindian groups, they were astonished by the sight of Spanish riders on their swift horses. At first they thought the Spaniards were superhuman gods, and they perceived rider and horse as one entity. The young Mapuche leader Lautaro acquired important advantages with which to fight the Spaniards, because he had the opportunity to learn their language and their ways in the Spanish camps where his ability was recognized: he was trained as Pedro de Valdivia's page.

Lautaro escaped from the camps and developed original guerrilla tactics, and he trained his warriors to ride horses. During lengthy battles, his warriors would fight in waves for short periods of time, then other groups of warriors would replace them in other waves, so that none of his men would be too tired. He won all the southern territories for his people over four years of remarkable battles with the Spaniards, and Lautaro eventually killed the Spanish conqueror Pedro de Valdivia. Lautaro even reached the gates of Santiago, held by the Spaniards, but the night before he planned to storm Santiago, a Yanacona Indian who had once fought with the Spaniards and then with the Mapuche killed him while he was asleep in his tent. After this tragic loss, the Mapuche retreated to the south, where they continued their resistance for three centuries, right up to their decisive defeat in the 1880s.

There is an interesting Mapuche legend which relates to the southern islands of the Chiloé region. It begins with a battle between the evil serpent Cai Cai, who rises furiously from the sea to flood the earth, and her good twin Tren Tren, who slumbers in her fortress among mountain peaks. The Mapuche try unsuccessfully to wake Tren Tren. The evil serpent Cai Cai's friends, the pillars of Thunder, Wind, and Fire, pile up the clouds to make rain, thunder, and water. Finally, a little girl dances with her reflection in Tren Tren's eye and her laughter awakens Tren Tren, who also begins to laugh. Deeply insulted, the evil Cai Cai and her friends fall down the hill.

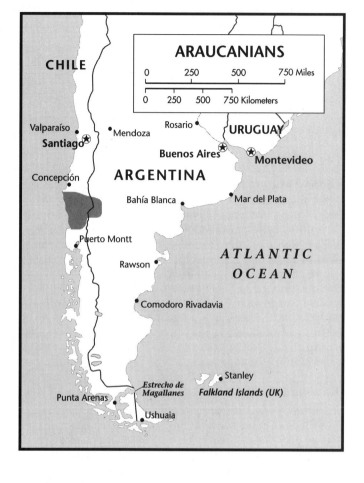

But Cai Cai is angry and shatters the earth, scattering islands all over the sea, and the water climbs higher and higher, trying to flood the mountain peaks where Tren Tren lives. But Tren Tren pushes and manages to raise the mountain up towards the sky and the sun, until the evil serpent Cai Cai and the Pillars of Thunder, Wind, and Fire fall from the peak into the deep chasm, where they are silenced.

⁵ RELIGION

The Mapuche believe in the forces of creation (*Ngenechen*) and destruction (*Wakufu*) and the ultimate balance between them. When the Spaniards arrived they were perceived as an expression of Wakufu. The zeal with which they finally drove the Mapuche from their lands and forced them to pay tribute to the Spanish crown, and the impoverishment and threat to the Mapuche culture which followed from their forced resettlement in overcrowded reservations at the hands of the newly independent Chileans, did nothing to make the Mapuche change their minds.

The Araucanians and many other Amerindian groups evolved variations of shamanistic beliefs practiced in Central Asia, from where their ancestors probably came. Reverence for nature, as well as the acknowledgment of forces of good and evil, are part of this belief system. Traditional prayer meetings called *machitunes* are held to invoke the help of the gods and goddesses for rain and good crops. Another type of meeting, called a *malón,* which is still regarded as important by Mapuche who uphold their religion, involves listening to dreams as well as prophecy.

Jesuit missions were established early on during the Spanish colonial period, even as far south as Chiloé, and Roman Catholicism has coexisted alongside the original religious beliefs of the Araucanians, in some cases mingling with them, especially since some Mapuche have more recently become city dwellers and are gradually growing away from some of their own customs and beliefs.

6 MAJOR HOLIDAYS

Mapuche who live in cities and have joined the urban poor celebrate the major Chilean national holidays together with the rest of the population, including Independence Day and the discovery of America on 12 October.

The Mapuche who live on reservations have maintained some of their own celebrations, which do not have a strictly secular character, since the Mapuche do not divide the material from the spiritual in a sharp way. One of the best-known festivals is the *nquillatún,* which lasts for three days and dedicates the lands and the harvest to the gods and goddesses, and which is still celebrated on the reservation of Huapi Island on Lake Ranco.

7 RITES OF PASSAGE

All major life events, such as birth, puberty, marriage, and death, are marked in special ceremonies among the Araucanians. Important members of the tribe such as chieftains, called *lonkos,* play special roles. There are religious connections to each event, and it is thought that important information is gathered from the gods and goddesses on all such special occasions by the women chosen to speak with them. In keeping with the Araucanian beliefs in good and evil, the women who deal with the forces of destruction are the called *kalku,* and those who deal with the forces of creation are the *machi.* Music accompanies the ceremonies, and there is a strong oral tradition that weaves poetry, the history of the people, legends, and religious beliefs into the celebrations.

Traditional Araucanian family celebrations are large, since each chieftain can have many wives and many children, and gatherings for major occasions such as a birth or a wedding will also include brothers, sisters, cousins, aunts, uncles, and grandparents.

8 INTERPERSONAL RELATIONS

There is a formal structure governing Araucanian society which is centered on the extended family. People are ranked according to age and relationship as well as special and socially recognized skills. There is, however, a contrast between this element and the fact that there is no single, central authority that governs them. The lack of a central authority, and the recognition of individual merit in appointing people to particular tasks and responsibilities within the Araucanian culture, has enabled the Araucanians, particularly the Mapuche, to develop a particularly independent spirit and a resilience which survives among many of them even today.

The formality of a greeting is well-regulated, but a stranger can only come into a traditional Mapuche environment with the utmost care: strangers who come with another Mapuche may be welcomed with elaborate feasting and great hospitality, but those who come alone could just as easily be met with hostility and silence.

9 LIVING CONDITIONS

The Mapuche have tried to preserve and defend their way of life for centuries, but their less-than-happy encounters with the Spaniards and their descendants have left them in a condition of poverty. Some Mapuche continue to live in a fairly traditional style, but many have migrated as poor workers to towns where they share the lot of other urban workers as *pobladores* in shantytowns with poor housing and health conditions. The hardiness of the Mapuche makes them especially prized workers in some demanding working environments where the weather and the terrain tax people heavily. Yet the Mapuche acquired a reputation early on for toughness and indifference to hardship.

This "indifference" noted by Europeans is revealing: it is quite possible that the traditional cultural standards of the Mapuche and the adverse circumstances of their more recent history demanded a stoic outlook, and that the ability to develop endurance was highly prized by the Mapuche themselves because it was, in part, a necessary survival tactic as well as a virtue. Their seeming indifference has been a victory of character over circumstance, rather than a curious lack of sensitivity.

The housing in shantytowns among other urban poor people is basic, and the shelters can be of adobe and bits of other materials. In remote country areas the traditional thatched roof huts known as *rucas* provide shelter. In towns the bus is the most common form of transport, but in more remote areas horses are still used, and in the southern Chiloé region boats are an important form of transport. The Mapuche share with other poor people of Chile the difficulties of access to health care. In some towns there are better facilities; in more remote areas, people often rely on traditional healers or herbal remedies.

10 FAMILY LIFE

The Mapuche group of Araucanians who still live on *reducciones* or reservations have tried to maintain the traditional family group structures, which include the extended family unit and a clan-like structure with a clan head or chief. The various Mapuche chiefs get together in the traditional way to arrive at important decisions by a process of lengthy discussion and consensus. This is an ancient process of decision-making which probably survives from a distant Central Asian past.

This collective spirit traditionally ensured that land was owned and worked by the group as a whole rather than by individual families. Power, whether in economic, social, or political terms, rested on the family, and at the head of the extended family stood the *lonko* or chief, with several wives and many children. The sense of family identity extended to grandparents, aunts and uncles, cousins, and relatives by marriage.

Although this sense of family identity survives psychologically, this type of social structure is gradually being undermined, as various efforts both to Christianize the Mapuche and to erode their freedom and their access to land takes its toll. Under the dictatorship of Augusto Pinochet in the 1970s, a land law was passed that further restricted the Mapuche Araucanians, and various efforts were made to further assimilate them and make them resemble the rest of society.

The role of women is important in a variety of ways. Very often women continue to maintain traditions even though their husbands and sons are engaged in struggles for work that bring them into contact with white society both politically and economically.

In some Mapuche settlements it is quite common to keep dogs not only as pets but also as guard dogs.

11 CLOTHING

Men in towns wear Western-style shirts and trousers; women are sometimes dressed more traditionally, with colorful aprons embroidered in abstract patterns; head scarves, sometimes decorated with gold coins; other types of jewelry such as long, heavy necklaces which include motifs such as crosses and coins; and gold earrings. Traditional skirts are long, and some forms of dress also include innovations, developed during colonial times, of Spanish elements such as elaborate, lace-edged collars.

Younger Mapuche girls often wear Western-style clothing such as sweaters and skirts, and boys wear shirts or sweaters and trousers.

12 FOOD

Traditional hunting and fishing, as well as some planting and harvesting of crops such as corn and various fruits, ensured a varied diet for the Araucanians. More-modern town dwellers adapt to the food that has developed over the centuries which includes elements of Spanish and other European cuisines, including corn turnovers or *empanadas* with fillings of hard-boiled egg, olives, raisins, and ground meat. The distinctive *curanto* oven allows meat and vegetables to steam for hours, wrapped in leaves, and some Mapuche who live on the island of Chiloé sometimes cook in this way.

Traditional feasting on special occasions can still last for several days. Utensils include clay pots.

13 EDUCATION

The Jesuits were active in early efforts to educate the Amerindians all over South America, and Chile was no exception. But struggles over land, and clashes caused by the expansion of Spanish conquests, also created dilemmas for the Araucanians, who did not want their way of life to disappear. Nevertheless, those who received an education in Western-style schools later developed organizations that helped them take part in Chile's political life. The Mapuche who lost their lands and had to emigrate to the towns to survive now try to offer their children opportunities to attend school. On the reservations many still try to preserve a traditional way of life. There have also been some efforts to develop a type of school that includes Spanish as well as important elements of traditional Araucanian culture.

14 CULTURAL HERITAGE

The music of the Araucanians includes special instruments such as whistles made out of wood, a type of flute called the *trutruca,* and various percussion instruments such as the *cultrun.* Music and dancing always accompanied important rituals. A type of poetic singing *(mapudungu)* in the Araucanian language included the reciting of legends, special invocations and prayers, and stories associated with the forces of life and death.

Special meetings include a type of tribal group dreaming and invocation as well as prophesying, called the *malón,* which are important elements of Araucanian culture.

15 WORK

The Mapuche who still live on reservations engage in some farming or fishing, as well as the production of handicrafts. A majority of Mapuche town dwellers live as urban workers. In their brave and remarkable struggle to preserve their culture and identity, they gradually developed in the 20th century a number of organizations to represent their interests. One of the most important modern Mapuche leaders was Manuel Aburto Manquilef. Following his lead, the Mapuche in towns affiliated themselves with larger trade union movements, especially the Workers' Federation of Chile during the 1930s. Some Mapuche joined political parties, and a few were elected to Chile's Congress.

Working conditions and opportunities for work were closely linked to the struggle for representation and preservation of their identity, as well as their part in union movements, which led to persecution during military rule in Chile during the 1970s and 1980s. Many Chilean workers and leaders of workers' movements, including Mapuche, were killed or simply disappeared.

Not all the Mapuche took the path of opposition and struggle. Some thought that silence, conciliation, or accommodation with the military regime would ensure better chances of survival.

Women often contribute to the family's earnings by taking part in markets and fairs to sell their wares. In what is today a more democratic country, many Mapuche continue to struggle both to improve their working conditions and to try to preserve their customs and identity.

16 SPORTS

Many of the younger Mapuche who are growing up in towns and are gradually changing their habits and lifestyle are enthusiastic soccer supporters. In more traditional settings, a lifestyle that has included both hunting and fishing combined both practical skills necessary for survival as well as the enjoyment of developing and mastering these skills. Some of the Mapuche who have lived either on the island of Chiloé or by the shores of other lakes are skilled boaters.

17 ENTERTAINMENT AND RECREATION

Mapuche who live in or near towns enjoy the many fiestas beloved of many Chileans. Some of these are religious feast days, and others are linked to agricultural events or special cultural events.

18 FOLK ART, CRAFTS, AND HOBBIES

The Mapuche are skilled weavers of cloth and baskets, jewelry-makers, and potters. Traditional crafts included tool-making for hunting and fishing, including spears and bows and arrows. They used wooden tools to farm potatoes and corn. They also thatched the straw roofs for their traditional houses known as *rucas,* an activity that still continues in some areas.

The descendants of the Mapuche who live on the island of Chiloé have blended with the original Chono Indian inhabitants and still maintain a distinctive culture, which includes the use of a special loom, which they use to weave sweaters and ponchos. Llama wool is used elsewhere, but on Chiloé sheep's wool is used, and the women prepare dyes made from herbs.

There are several important craft fairs in Chile which display Araucanian arts and crafts. One of these is an annual cultural fair in the town of Villarica on the Chilean mainland.

[19] SOCIAL PROBLEMS

The social problems of the Mapuche are related to economic hardship as well as to the struggle to preserve their traditions and identity. The situations of town dwellers and inhabitants of the *reducciones* or reservations differ in some important respects. Some of the Mapuche inhabitants of the reservations prefer to keep themselves aloof from the ways and customs of Europeans, even today, and try to teach their children the traditions and beliefs of the Araucanian culture. Other groups of Mapuche, who emigrated to the towns when they lost their lands, have been engaged in a struggle in which they joined trade unions as a way of fighting poverty by fighting for workers' rights generally. There is a growing awareness of their struggle in Chile today, and a more sympathetic attitude to their difficulties.

[20] BIBLIOGRAPHY

Galeano, Eduardo. *Memorias del Fuego.* Vols. 1, 2, and 3. Madrid: Siglo XXI Editores S. A., 1992.

Luna, Félix. *Soy Roca.* Buenos Aires: Editorial Sudamericana, 1990.

Perrotet, Tony, ed. *Chile.* Hong Kong: APA Publications (HK) Ltd, 1995.

—by P. Pitchon

ARGENTINES

LOCATION: Argentina
POPULATION: 32.3 million
LANGUAGE: Spanish (official); Italian; English; Quechua; other native languages
RELIGION: Roman Catholicism (official); evangelical Protestantism

[1] INTRODUCTION

Argentina derives its name from the Latin word for silver, *argentum,* and this is what drove the Spanish to explore the land during the 16th century. There was little silver to be found, however, but the fertile soil of the Pampas was to become the country's most valuable asset. It was during the late 1800s that Argentina found a wealthy outlet with the export of meat and grain to Europe. This lucrative trade increased until, by the early decades of the 20th century, Argentina had become one of the wealthiest nations in the world. However, soaring inflation and a damaging series of complex political conflicts in recent years have badly affected the economy.

Argentina has always attracted European immigrants. During the 19th century, waves of Europeans, such as Italians, Basques, Welsh, English, Ukrainians, and immigrants of other nationalities poured into Buenos Aires. In the 16th century, early European settlers discovered a wide range of Indians across the country, with different economic and social systems. There were large populations in the Andes, in the tropical and temperate forests there were seminomadic farmers, and nomadic hunters and gatherers lived in the Amazon and on the Patagonian steppes. But as the European settlers moved out across the country to claim the lands for their own, the Indian populations were ousted from their lands and virtually disappeared. A quasi-feudal system of land control was established in Argentina, similar to those of most other Latin American countries.

During the 1820s, a series of independence movements throughout South America combined to pry control of the continent away from the hands of Spain. Under the leadership of General José de San Martín and others, the United Provinces of the River Plate, Argentina's direct forerunner, declared independence in 1816. The Argentina Constitution was established in 1853.

During the 1970s and 1980s, the military government was embroiled in the Dirty War against "subversives," an infamous chapter of Argentina's history which saw the death of thousands of innocent victims. Paramilitary death squads, operating with the covert approval of the authorities, were responsible for many other victims. A familiar phrase used at this time referred to people "disappearing." What the phrase meant was that someone had been abducted, detained, tortured, and probably killed. All of this was carried out without any pretense of the administration of justice.

Eventually, a fast-declining economic situation and growing public resentment brought about huge demonstrations in the streets. In order to stay in power, General Leopoldi Galtieri decided to launch an invasion of the Falkland Islands in an attempt to distract public unrest. War with Britain followed, but Argentina's badly trained and demoralized army finally had to admit a humiliating defeat after 74 days. Argentina's military dictatorship was over, and within a year Raul Alfonsin of the Radical Civic Union was elected to the presidency.

In 1983 the country set up a federal system along the lines of the United States. Today there are at least 18 different parties represented in Congress. The most important are the Peronists, named after the late Juan Peron, a party identified with the trade unionists, and the Union Civica Radical of the former President Raul Alfonsin, which represents the middle classes.

2 LOCATION AND HOMELAND

Argentina is the world's eighth-largest country, only slightly smaller than India. It has a total area of about 2.8 million sq km (1.1 million sq mi), excluding the South Atlantic island and the Antarctic quadrant it claims as national territory. From Quiaca on the Bolivian border to Ushuaia in Tierra del Fuego, it is nearly 3,500 km (2,175 mi), about the same distance as from Havana, Cuba, to the Hudson Bay in Canada, or from the Sahara Desert to Scotland.

Approximately 80% of the population of 32.3 million people lives in urban areas. More than 33% live in Gran Buenos Aires, which includes the Capital Federal and its suburbs in the Buenos Aires province. The majority of people (85%) come from European stock, including about 400,000 Jews, the world's eighth-largest Jewish community. Approximately 15% of the population are Mestizo—people of mixed Indian and European blood.

The four main provinces are the Andes; the lowland North; the Pampas, home to the famous *gaucho,* the Argentine cowboy; and Patagonia. The Andes separate Argentina from Chile, while rivers form its borders with Uruguay, Brazil, and Paraguay. The country also shares a short border with Bolivia.

3 LANGUAGE

The official language of Argentina is Spanish, but a number of the European-descended communities still maintain their own languages, such as the Italians, who constitute the largest immigrant group. As a result, Italian is widely understood, as is English, another significant immigrant community. In the Chubut province, descendants of Welsh immigrants can be found, still preserving many Welsh customs and traditions. The Welsh language itself, however, has almost died out. Some 17 native languages still survive, though some are spoken by very few individuals. Quechua-speakers are numerous in the Andean Noroeste, while in the southern Andes there are at least 40,000 Mapuche-speaking Indians. In northeastern Argentina, there are about 15,000 Guarani-speakers, an equal number of Tobas, and about 10,000 Matacos.

4 FOLKLORE

Despite the fact that Argentina regards itself as extremely cultured and European, spiritualism and the worship of the dead play an important part in the lives of the people. One of its own famous novelists, Tomas Eloy Martinez, has commented that the country's national heroes, such as San Martin, are honored not on the anniversary of their birth but of their death, in the same way that saints' days are celebrated. Steady processions of pilgrims regularly visit the Recoleta and Chacarita cemeteries in Buenos Aires where personal prayers are said and ritual

offerings are left, especially at the tombs of Juan and Evita Peron and the tango singer Carlos Gardel.

During the 1800s, the *gaucho,* the Argentine cowboy, came to represent a free-spirited symbol for the country. He was seen as a rebel who took on authority in order to preserve his freedom. Legends about him grew, and he became the inspiration for many writers.

5 RELIGION

The official state religion is Roman Catholicism, but evangelical Protestant movements are making converts among traditional Catholic believers, as is happening elsewhere in South America. The Catholic religion also faces its own internal conflicts, particularly where popular beliefs differ from official doctrine—such as the example of the cult of Difunta Correa, based in the San Juan province. Despite a determined campaign by the church authorities to undermine her veneration, hundreds of thousands of Argentine Catholics continue to make annual pilgrimages and offerings.

6 MAJOR HOLIDAYS

All the main Christian festivals such as Easter and Christmas are celebrated throughout the country. There are also national celebrations of historical times and heroes such as the May Revolution of 1810; Independence Day on 9 July; Malvinas Day, on 10 June, which celebrates the establishment of the "Comandancia Politica y Militar de las Malvinas" in 1829; and Dia de San Martin, the anniversary of San Martin's death on 17 August.

7 RITES OF PASSAGE

Baptism, First Communion, and saints' days are major events, important to both individuals and families. Because of the strong Spanish and Italian heritage and the abiding influence of the Catholic Church, these occasions are used as important family get-togethers which serve to reinforce the family structures.

Younger people, however, are no longer getting married in church as a matter of course, and there is a growing trend toward divorce and remarriage. Civil marriages have become popular.

8 INTERPERSONAL RELATIONS

Argentines are extremely gregarious and eagerly invite visitors to participate in their activities.

One famous pastime is drinking *mate,* a Paraguayan tea made from holly leaves. This is more than a simple drink like tea or coffee. It is an elaborate ritual, shared among family, friends, and colleagues. For those taking part, the sharing of the tea-making process seems to be the whole point of the *mate* ritual. During the process, one person is responsible for filling a gourd almost to the top with the tea. Meanwhile, water is heated, but not boiled, in a kettle and then poured into the vessel. Everyone sips the liquid from a silver tube with a bulbous filter at its lower end that prevents the leaves from entering the tube.

Argentines are quite formal in public and are very aware of the proper civilities. Even when asking a stranger for directions in the street, one is expected to approach the person with a greeting such as *buenos dias* or *buenas tardes,* "good day" or "good afternoon."

9 LIVING CONDITIONS

The major cities in Argentina have a European look to them. The middle classes live in tall, modern apartment buildings, or in bungalows with small gardens. Since the 1930s, rural workers have flocked to the big cities and a number of slums have sprouted on the outskirts, where the workers live in shacks. Rural houses are often built of adobe, with earth floors and roofs of straw and mud.

10 FAMILY LIFE

The strong Catholic and Spanish heritage has meant that the role of the family plays a central part in Argentine life. There is still a strong belief in the nuclear family, which also extends to grandparents, uncles and aunts, and close relatives.

Much social life is family-centered, and occasions such as birthdays, First Communions, weddings, and funerals are of major importance. A favorite family get-together is the barbecue. Mealtimes are also regarded as important occasions for family cohesion and are often elaborate, time-consuming events.

11 CLOTHING

Most city-dwellers wear Western-style clothes, and many enthusiastically follow the fashions of Europe, particularly those of Italy.

In the rural areas, however, many workers on the *estancias* wear at least part of the *gaucho* costume—a wide-brimmed hat and loose trousers tucked into the boots. In the northwest, the Indians wear ponchos, colorful skirts, and bowler hats.

12 FOOD

Given the enormous cattle ranches of the Pampas, it is hardly surprising to find that the Argentine diet is very meat-oriented. At the same time, there is a surprising ethnic and regional variety to Argentine cooking. The huge Italian presence has resulted in a great popularity for pasta dishes such as spaghetti, lasagna, cannelloni, and ravioli. Beef, though, is the center of most meals. The most popular form is the *parrillada,* a mixed grill of steak and other cuts.

Some regions have very distinctive food. The Andean northwest offers very spicy dishes, and it is common to find Middle Eastern food in the Mendoza north.

13 EDUCATION

With a 94% literacy rate, Argentina is one of Latin America's most literate countries. From the age of 5 to the age of 12, education is free and compulsory, and the comprehensive secondary education system is based on the French model.

Universities are traditionally free and open, but the courses tend to be rigidly specialized. With so much higher education available, the system has turned out many people with professional qualifications, such as doctors and lawyers, not of all of whom can easily find work in Buenos Aires. Despite this, few of them are willing to move to the provinces.

14 CULTURAL HERITAGE

During the early 19th and 20th centuries, Buenos Aires readily adopted French trends in art, music, and particularly architecture, which can be seen in many of the turn-of-the-century buildings in the capital.

Argentine writers, much of whose work is available in English, have achieved international stature. They include Jorge Luis Borges, Julio Cortazar, Ernesto Sabato, Manuel Puig, Osvaldo Soriano, and Adolfo Bioy Casares.

In Buenos Aires, the Teatro Colon opera house is one of the finest of its kind in the world. Classical music and ballet, as well as modern dance, are staged here. The capital also has a lively theater circuit, as rich as any major city elsewhere in the world. Even in the provinces, live theater is an important part of cultural life.

15 WORK

Despite its abundant natural resources and its well- educated and cultured population, Argentina has failed to live up to its

The best-known and most-striking feature of Argentine popular culture is the tango, both as music and dance. It first became popular in 1880, when it emerged from working-class districts where it was frequently played in brothels. (Susan D. Rock)

potential. Earlier in the 20th century, Argentina was seen to be on a par with prosperous countries such as Canada and Australia. Yet it has not only patently failed to keep up with them, it has continually fallen behind them.

Its per capita GDP of nearly us$6,800 makes Argentina one of Latin America's wealthiest countries, but its economy is in a constant state of crisis with international debts amounting to $62 billion. Faced with such a huge foreign debt that is unlikely ever to be repaid, the living standards of the middle class are being eroded, while the working class and the poor are seriously suffering.

Like other Latin American countries, one of Argentina's fundamental problems lies in the poverty of its rural areas. Control of the richest agricultural lands of the Pampas are in the hands of a small number of wealthy families, while most rural people are reduced to scratching out a living on marginal lands or working as poorly paid workers on the big estates.

Corruption and inefficiency have plagued state enterprises, where workers frequently hold down a number of government jobs. A standing Argentine joke is to refer to these employees as *noquis,* named after the traditional potato pasta served in Argentine households on the 29th of each month—the implication being that these people appear on the job just before their monthly paychecks are due. Not surprisingly, such corruption has led to massive inflation rates, often exceeding 50% per month. Despite a determined government clean up of noqui

workers, which led to a drop in state employment from 1 million to 370,000 persons between 1990 and 1995, reform measures have hardly touched government departments in the provinces.

16 SPORTS

The country is soccer-crazed. Argentina won the World Cup, at home in 1978, and again in 1986. It has provided a number of internationally known players such as Diego Maradona and Daniel Passarella, who now coaches the national team. There are more first-division soccer teams in Buenos Aires than anywhere else in the world. Of the country's 20 teams, 8 are based in the capital, while 5 are in the nearby suburbs.

Several tennis players have also become world-famous, such as Guillermo Vilas and Gabriela Sabatini.

The game of basketball has also become a notable sport in Argentina, following the influx of many North American athletes who were unable to play professional basketball in America or Europe. In 1995, the Argentine national team defeated the US team for the gold medal in the Pan American Games in Mar del Plata.

17 ENTERTAINMENT AND RECREATION

The best-known and most-striking feature of Argentine popular culture is the tango, both as music and dance. It first became popular in 1880, when it emerged from working-class districts where it was frequently played in brothels. It was a blend of *gaucho* (cowboy) verse with Spanish and Italian music. Then came Carlos Gardel, the music's most famous exponent, who created the *tango cancion,* the "tango song," lifting it out of the brothels and the poor streets and into the smart salons of Buenos Aires.

For many Argentines, the tango song sums up the fears and anxieties of life. It can carry themes as diverse as love, jealousy, and betrayal to everyday subjects such as going to work or coping with one's neighbors. It is often full of sad nostalgia about a way of life that is fast disappearing.

Argentines are traditionally great cinema-goers, although outside Buenos Aires many cinemas have had to shut down with the arrival of the video cassette.

18 FOLK ART, CRAFTS, AND HOBBIES

In artisans' *ferias,* found throughout the country, the variety of handicrafts is extensive. *Mate* paraphernalia is widespread, and gourds and *bombilas* range from simple and inexpensive aluminum, often sold in street kiosks, to elaborate and expensive gold and silver found in jewelry stores. In the province of Salta, the distinctive *ponchos de Guemes* are produced.

19 SOCIAL PROBLEMS

Runaway inflation seems to have been halted by the government under Carlos Menem, which has reduced the public sector deficit by selling off inefficient state enterprises and curbing the powers of militant labor unions. The trouble is that continuing privatization has led to increasing unemployment, justified by the government as a necessary casualty of reform.

In 1995, official unemployment figures stood at 12.2%, and then rose to nearly 20% as the economy contracted in the aftermath of President Menem's election.

20 BIBLIOGRAPHY

Bernhardson, Wayne. *Argentina, Uruguay and Paraguay: A Lonely Planet Travel Survival Kit.* 2nd ed. Hawthorn, Australia: Lonely Planet Publications, 1996.

—by P. Pitchon, reviewed by T. Morin

ARMENIAN AMERICANS

For more information on Armenian history and culture, *see* **Vol. 4: Armenians**.

OVERVIEW

Few Armenians immigrated to the US before the late 1800s. The first massive wave of immigration began around 1890 as a result of massacres of Armenians by the Ottoman Turk sultan Abdul Hamid. In the decade from 1890 to 1900, over 12,000 Armenians refugees entered the US. Although the Turkish Empire forbade emigration for a few years (1899–1907), Armenian immigration to the US continued sporadically until the end of World War II (1939–45). A particularly large number came in 1915 after a second round of massacres by the Ottoman Turks (often referred to as the Genocide).

The second wave of Armenian immigration to the US began in the 1950s and continues today. Most of these second-wave Armenian Americans are from Iran, Lebanon, the former Soviet Union, and other countries of the Armenian Diaspora. They tend to be more educated, skilled, and worldly than first-wave immigrants (although first-wave Armenian Americans were much more highly skilled and educated than most other immigrants to the US at that time). Many recent Armenian immigrants arrived with some proficiency in the English language, and a few came complete with financial fortunes from their former homelands.

For the most part, Armenian Americans were too few in number and too scattered throughout the US to engender much discrimination. The one exception was Fresno, California, where a large Armenian American community suddenly developed in a fairly small area during the first wave of immigration. Fortunately, a long history of violent oppression had equipped the immigrants with the ability to avoid direct confrontations, and the racism never escalated to physical violence. The Armenians quickly were assimilated into American culture and were soon accepted as "Americans."

The exact Armenian American population today is uncertain. There are no official records of the number of Armenian immigrants because they were often mistakenly recorded as "Turks," "Arabs," or "Russians" in the early days, and recent immigrants have Lebanese, Iranian, or other passports. Armenian American population estimates run anywhere from 600,000 to 1,000,000. The 1990 US Census lists just over 300,000 persons reporting "Armenian" ancestry. About 40% of Armenian Americans are foreign born. Los Angeles, which has the fastest-growing Armenian American population, has a much higher percentage of foreign-born persons in its Armenian American community.

The Turkish Armenians of the first wave of immigration tended to settle in northeastern cities, particularly New York City, Providence (Rhode Island), Worcester (Massachusetts), and Boston. Russian Armenians have settled mostly in southern California, especially Los Angeles. Iranian Armenians have almost all settled in Los Angeles.

Some early Armenian immigrants later moved from the Northeast to the Midwest, settling in Chicago, Detroit, Racine (Wisconsin), and Waukegan (Illinois). About half of the Armenian American population today lives in the northeastern and mid-Atlantic states; one-third (33%) live in California; 14% are in the Midwest (mainly Wisconsin, Michigan, and Illinois); and the rest are in Texas and Florida.

The Armenian language is one focus of the dispute between traditional and progressive Armenian Americans. Traditionalists believe that fluency in Armenian is a requisite for a claim to Armenian ethnicity. Progressives (most of whom are not fluent in Armenian) feel that fluency is good but not necessary. The fact is that few second- or later-generation Armenian Americans speak, read, or write Armenian. By the 1960s, English was the official language of the Armenian American community, and even Armenian churches have modified their services to include portions in English. All-day and afternoon (or Saturday morning) schools exist throughout the Armenian American community to teach children the Armenian language, along with Armenian culture and history. Attendance at these schools is low and dwindling, however.

The Armenian Church was traditionally the center of Armenian life, and it has continued to play a crucial role in the lives of Armenian Americans, although its influence is rapidly declining among successive generations. Many Armenian Americans do not attend services on a regular basis, and a growing number are no longer even affiliated with the church.

The Armenian Church is said to have been founded in the first century AD by St. Thaddeus and St. Bartholomew, two of Jesus' original apostles. In AD 301, Armenia's King Tiridates III converted to Christianity, making the Armenian Christian Church the first national Christian church in the world. In the millennia following, the Armenian Church became divided into separate factions. These factions are represented in the US by the Eastern and Western Diocese of the Armenian Church of North America (EWDACNA), the original American diocese founded in 1892, allied with the Patriarchate in Armenia; the Eastern and Western Prelacy of the Armenian Apostolic Church of America (EWPAACA) allied with the Catholicate of Cilicia in Lebanon.

The EWPAACA was created in 1933 when members of the Tashnag (Armenian revolutionary) party murdered Archbishop Tourian in New York City during a Christmas Eve service. All Tashnag members were expelled from Armenian Apostolic churches and forced to begin their own. The Tashnag congregation remained independent until 1957, when they allied themselves with the Catholicate of Lebanon.

In recent years, there has been increasing talk in support of reuniting the two factions. A new leader, Karekin I, was elected in April 1995 as the worldwide head of the Armenian Apostolic Church. Karekin visited the US and Canada in early 1996, calling for reunification of the Armenian Church in America. Born in Syria, Karekin served as the primate of the Armenian Apostolic Church in America from 1974 to 1977, so he is familiar with the situation of the Armenian Church in the US, and he himself is familiar to Armenian Americans. A "unity commission" has been established to work towards unifying the two factions, both of whose headquarters are located in New York City.

Armenians have also become affiliated with other churches. In the US, 69% of Armenian Americans belong to the Armenian Apostolic Church, while 10% are Armenian Protestant (of various denominations), and 3% are Armenian Catholic. Some 13% of Armenian Americans belong to other non-Armenian churches, and 5% are not affiliated with any church. In 1992,

there were 115 Armenian churches and parishes in the US: 53 EWDACNA, 28 EWPAACA, 28 Armenian Protestant (of which 10 were in Los Angeles alone), and 6 Armenian Catholic. All Armenian American churches suffer from a severe shortage of adequately trained clergy.

With each succeeding generation, Armenian Americans become more "Americanized." Most young Armenian Americans today follow mainstream American customs around birth, weddings, funerals, etc. They celebrate mainstream American holidays, such as Thanksgiving and American Independence Day (4 July), as well as the major Christian holidays of Christmas and Easter. Some Armenian Americans may include elements of their Armenian heritage in these celebrations, performing Armenian folk dances and serving Armenian foods like rice pilaf and shishkebab.

Recent Armenian immigrants to the US maintain more of their traditional customs, but those customs vary according to the land of their birth. Armenians today are scattered among a number of countries in Europe and Asia, including Turkey, Iran, Lebanon, and the former Soviet Union. This is known as the Armenian Diaspora. Therefore, traditional "Armenian" customs are flavored by the cultures of Armenian Americans' various former homelands.

Overall, Armenian Americans have a high level of education. With each successive generation, more Armenian Americans attend college and universities and become professionals and executives. The average income for Armenian Americans is fairly high compared to other ethnic groups in America and continues to increase with subsequent generations. Many early Armenian immigrants became small business owners, and there is still a high rate of small business ownership among Armenian Americans today. But fewer children enter the family business as more go on for higher education and become doctors, lawyers, teachers, etc.

The best known Armenian Americans in the worlds of music and literature are singer-actress Cher (Sarkisian Bono Allman) and Pulitzer Prize-winning author William Saroyan. Other successful Armenian American actors include Arlene Francis (Arlene Kazanjian) and Mike Connors (Krekor Ohanian). Singer Kay Armen was well-known in the 1950s, and the Zildjian family has made world-famous cymbals for generations, beginning in Constantinople and continuing after the family immigrated to the US.

Celebrated Armenian Americans in the worlds of science, technology, and public life include Christopher Der Seropian, who developed in 1843 the black and green dyes used on all US currency today; Dr. Varazted Kazarijian (1879–1974), a world-renowned plastic surgeon; and George Deukmejian, elected governor of California in 1982, and reelected for a second term in 1986.

Football's Ara Parseghian and wrestler Robert Manoogian are among the important Armenian American figures in sports. Another is lesser-known Captain G. Harry Adalian, inventor of the high-speed Futurity Foto-Finish Camera that was installed at the finish line of race tracks beginning in 1936 to eliminate disputes over winners of horse races.

The biggest problem for Armenian Americans today is factionalism within the Armenian American community itself. Conflicts exist over everything from church factions to Armenian language proficiency to musical tastes (what is called "traditional" Armenian music in the US is considered "Turkified" by non-Turkish Armenian Americans). There is also disagreement over current immigration from former Soviet Armenia. Some Armenian Americans, including leaders in the community, feel that no one should leave the fledgling "free" Armenian republic. Those who do are seen as deserters and traitors. However, few if any Armenian Americans have moved back to Armenia to support the new nation.

The sudden influx of Soviet Armenians to America has also caused an increase in anti-Armenian discrimination. Their sheer numbers make them noticeable and threatening to others who are struggling to find employment and access to services. Soviet Armenians also often get into trouble in the US because they try to operate in old Soviet ways, which are not acceptable in America, such as bribing officials and playing the system. Well-established Armenian Americans resent being given a "bad name" by these new immigrants.

More and more Armenian Americans, however, are calling for reconciliation and unification among Armenian Americans on all fronts. They realize that until they learn to work together, they will never succeed in getting their special needs met in America.

BIBLIOGRAPHY

"Armenian Patriarch Bridges Church Division." *The Christian Century* 113, no. 6 (21 February 1996): 191–92.

Bakalian, Anny. *Armenian-Americans: From Being to Feeling Armenian.* New Brunswick, NJ: Transaction Publishers, 1993.

Bernardo, Stephanie. *The Ethnic Almanac.* Garden City, NY: Dolphin Books/Doubleday & Company, 1981.

Mooradian, Moorad. "The Armenian-Pacific American Equation." *The Armenian Reporter* 29, no. 13 (30 December 1995): 2ff.

—by D. K. Daeg de Mott

ASHÁNINKA

ALTERNATE NAMES: Campa (derogatory)
LOCATION: Peru; Brazil
POPULATION: 45,000
LANGUAGE: Asháninka; Spanish
RELIGION: Native mythical beliefs

1 INTRODUCTION

The Asháninka are an ethnic group of the Peruvian Amazon rain forest. They are also known in Peru and abroad by the name "Campa," which they consider derogatory because it derives from the Quechua *thampa,* which means ragged and dirty. *Asháninka* means "our fellows" or "our kinfolk." In 1595 an expedition led by Juan Vélez took along two Jesuit priests, Juan Font and Nicolás Mastrillo, in the first attempt by the Europeans to colonize the area. Franciscan and Dominican missionaries also joined in the efforts to establish settlements in the jungle. But in 1742 this first period of colonization came to a sudden end with a general Indian rebellion led by the legendary Juan Santos Atahualpa. The uprising lasted until 1752 and succeeded in expelling all missionaries and colonists from the area. The Asháninka and their neighbors controlled the area for over a century.

By the mid-19th century two simultaneous economic situations brought the missionaries back: the encroachment of agriculture from the Andes, and of the rubber-tapping industry from the Amazon. In 1847 a military garrison was set up, and from there recolonization by Franciscans and European, Chinese, and Japanese settlers began. Some 2 million hectares (5 million acres) of Asháninka territory, along with the main rivers, were granted to the British-owned Peruvian Corporation 44 years later. The Asháninka were then used as labor, and the appalling working conditions together with virus epidemics took a heavy toll on the communities. In the lower part of the territory, with the rubber boom came slavery, a trend that continued even after the rubber economy collapsed in 1915.

During the last decades of the 20th century, the Asháninka territory has been the site of conflicts between the Peruvian Army and rebel groups. Some Asháninka had a messianic leader, Guillermo Lobatón, whom they regarded as the Son of the Sun. He became the leader of the Movement of the Revolutionary Left, or MIR, inspired by the teachings of Fidel Castro. In 1965, many died in fighting between the military and the MIR. Only 14 years later, the Tupac Amarú Revolutionary Movement (MRTA) killed the Asháninka leader of the Pichi river, claiming he had helped the police take their own leader. Since the beginning of the 1980s, the Shining Path has entered their territory. Since then, guerrilla as well as army actions often result in Asháninka deaths.

2 LOCATION AND HOMELAND

The Asháninka, one of the largest ethnic groups of the Americas (their population numbers around 45,000 people), inhabit mainly the Central Forest in the Amazonian part of the eastern Andean foothills in Peru, but their communities stretch across the easternmost Peruvian Amazon and even as far as the State of Acre in Brazil. They inhabit an area of more than 103,600 sq km (40,000 sq mi). Their traditional heartland is the Gran Pajonal, a remote plateau of rolling terrain dissected by the gorges of rivers. On the slopes there are *pajonales* (grasslands), created in part by a long history of Ashāninka clearing and burning.

Difficult access to the region allowed the inhabitants to remain isolated from outside influences until relatively recently. The area is strategically important, being directly east of the Peruvian capital, Lima, and linked to it by roads that cross the Andes. The degree of integration with their neighbors varies according to the geographic situation. Close to the frontiers, the Ashāninka are more integrated with the settler society, living side by side with them. But in remote areas, they are often the only inhabitants of large territories.

³ LANGUAGE

The Ashāninka language belongs to the pre-Andean Arawak linguistic family, which is the largest language family in South America and includes several dialects. In the Central Peruvian forest there are some variations: in the south of their territory they speak Ashāninka, while in the north Ashéninka is spoken. Ashāninka, like all pre-Columbian Arawak languages, is of a highly verbal nature. When examining oral narratives it has been found that the ratio of verbs to nouns is about four to one. As to gender, it is straightforward for humans but when it comes to animals, gender depends on whether they were male or female when they were human, before they were transformed into animals, all in reference to legends.

Most of the population is monolinguistic until and if they go to school, where they learn Spanish. Children are given a provisional name when they start walking. Their official name is decided when they are seven years old.

⁴ FOLKLORE

Among the Ashāninka, history and nature are explained through myths and heroes. A great cliff in the Tambo river, for example, used to be a Spanish ship which Avireri, a powerful hero, transformed into a rock, its sailors becoming red ants. Other dangerous insects, like wasps, are also transformations of bad men. The moon itself used to be a man who ate other men, and as a punishment he was exiled to the sky. From there, he continues eating Ashāninka souls, which explains the phases of the moon. As to the origins of their neighbors, it is said that Avireri, the great mythological transformer, turned a murderous hawk and his wife into huge rocks, and they can be seen in the Ene river. Their feathers became canoes and each carried Piros, Matsiguenkas, Shipibos, and all the other Indian groups that live down the river.

A technological genius named Inka, according to another Ashāninka myth, was swept away by a great flood of the river Tambo and carried to Lima where the White people, the Wiracocha, captured him and are still forcing him to produce Western goods which really belong to them. Only the return of Inka will bring justice to the land.

⁵ RELIGION

The Ashāninka cosmovision is mainly mythical. There is not a figure of a creator but a hero, Avireri, who transformed humans into animals, plants, mountains, and rivers. Their universe is inhabited by the living forms that can be seen, and also by a host of invisible beings. Their spiritual universe is dualistic. Good spirits or *amatsénka,* "our fellow spirits," reside on the mountain ridges in their territory, along the rim of the known world, and on other levels in the universe. Among them are the Sun *(Pavá)* and the Moon *(Kashirí).* There are male and female spirits and they reproduce, albeit not through sex as their genitalia are diminutive and they are devoid of the passion of lust. The good spirits can assume the guise of several animals which have a power denied to humans, like a bird that can fly.

There are also evil spirits or *kamári,* a term used to refer to that which is repugnant, malevolent, or reprehensible. Some animals, like the deer, are demons and cannot be eaten. Nature is populated by bad spirits, like the Katsivoreri of Mironti, who can kill if encountered. Death is feared because the soul can return to earth as a bad spirit. The Ashāninka also traditionally believed in the existence of child wizards who had to be killed or buried alive, or even left to die of hunger. They personify the very real dangers of the jungle.

The Ashāninka have shamans or *sheripiári* who are intermediaries between the people and supernatural beings. Shamans use tobacco and some hallucinogens to enter trances that will allow them to communicate with the supernatural. Illness is cured with the help of steam baths, magical herbs, and sessions with the healer, who tries to send the disease back to the one who originated it. In the case of the plague and the flu, it is believed that they were brought by White human beings, blond with blue eyes, a mythical explanation that bears some resemblance to historical facts.

Throughout their history, the Ashāninka have had an apocalyptic vision of the world. They believe that this world is plagued by evil forces and people will be destroyed, and then there will be a new world with new people without sickness or death.

⁶ MAJOR HOLIDAYS

The Festival of the Moon is a celebration of the god Kashirí who, according to the legend, is the father of the Sun. Kashirí appeared to a young girl and introduced her and her people to manioc (cassava). He taught them how to grow it and prepare it, putting an end to years of a diet of earth. He made the young girl his wife, and in giving birth to the Sun she was burned to death. Kashirí began taking his nephews to the forest, where he slaughtered and ate them. When his brother-in-law threatened to kill him, he escaped by rising into the sky. Kashirí continues eating human souls and that explains why the moon gets fatter every month.

As some of the formal education available to the Ashāninka is provided by Christian missionaries and, in any event, because Peru is a fervently Catholic country, some Indians gradually lose their traditions in the process of acculturation and begin to celebrate national holidays.

⁷ RITES OF PASSAGE

The magical world of the Ashāninka includes a number of rites aimed at protecting the people. Prospective parents, for example, follow a diet during the pregnancy. They refrain from eating turtle meat, for fear that this would make their child slow-moving and slow-witted. Ashāninka children are born in the house and the umbilical cord is cauterized with burning coal.

The mother has to remain indoors for a week. The child is only named when it learns to walk, and at the age of seven it gets a new name.

When girls reach adolescence, they spend up to six months in isolation. During that time they spin thread. Afterwards they are welcomed back to daily life with a celebration that has been described as "orgiastic." Although after death a human soul can join the good spirits if the person was sufficiently good in his or her lifetime, the Asháninka consider it far more likely that the soul will become an evil ghost. In that case, it will revisit the settlement and attack those living there. That was the reason why, traditionally, the Asháninka would often abandon a settlement after someone died. If the deceased was believed to be a witch, the corpse was sometimes cremated so that the soul would be destroyed by the flames and would be prevented from joining the demons that taught it witchcraft.

8 INTERPERSONAL RELATIONS

The Aráwakan tribes were perceived by explorers as being hostile among themselves and towards the Whites. But inside the villages there is a real sense of community: many economic activities are carried out collectively, such as hunting and fishing, and the take is divided equally among the dwellers. There is also enough evidence of intertribal trade to suggest that it has always existed. Exchanging goods must have involved some degree of amicability and a recognition of the skills of others.

The Asháninka have been described as morose but open to and capable of change. Some Whites distinguish between "civilized campas" and "savages," and of the latter say they are rough and practice cannibalism on victims of war to assimilate their virile qualities. Nowadays, it is said that most Asháninka are friendly and carry out trade or work as day laborers in order to get metal tools.

9 LIVING CONDITIONS

Traditionally a native community would house between 300 and 400 people. There is a communal home surrounded by private dwellings of nuclear families which are related to the other families. They also erect observation platforms. There is a constant fire burning inside the houses, and woven or bark mats for sleeping. The houses have two walls made of tree trunks, palm leaf roofs, and floors raised 20 cm (8 in) from the ground, built with pona palm trunks. But, as we have already said, the Asháninka territory has been the scene of conflicts between the Peruvian Army and guerrillas, as well as of the illegal trade in coca. Nowadays, under the raised floor, the Asháninka build trenches where they keep provisions, anticipating attacks. The situation has affected the Asháninka living conditions badly. Many are now refugees, having been forced to abandon their homes and land to save their lives. Historically, the Asháninka would only leave their homes for three reasons: soil exhaustion, a death in the family, or pressure by colonizers.

In 1991 the world witnessed a degree of malnutrition among Asháninka refugees never before seen in the American continent. Epidemics, such as cholera and measles, are another cause of premature death, and gastric, respiratory, and skin diseases are a common denominator among communities. The violence in the region has also affected the mental health of the population. Transport to many of the remaining Asháninka communities is costly. Vast regions are only accessible by light

airplane as the roads cannot be used. The traditional means of transportation in the rivers is pointed balsa rafts held together with chonta nails and crossbeams.

10 FAMILY LIFE

There are few restrictions on marriage among the Asháninka, apart from the immediate family. It is possible to marry a cousin but not an uncle or aunt. To prevent pregnancy, some women eat chantini roots. Polygyny is practiced, and women used to be traded for goods from other tribes. According to early accounts, many Asháninka were not married, and widows and widowers did not get married again.

As social conditions have worsened, the typical way of life of the Asháninka has become almost impossible for many communities. The traditional family and community life that was closely linked with nature has had to be abandoned, as most men have had to devote themselves to defense duties. Nevertheless, in the midst of this crisis, women have taken up the role of community organizers. They have formed mother's clubs and crafts committees both to generate income and to feed their families and refugees. In many cases, women have replaced men on the communal farms, and it is they who cultivate the land.

11 CLOTHING

The Asháninka wear *chusmas,* a traditional garment made of a long piece of fabric with an opening in the middle for the head: from front to back for men, and from side to side for women. It is joined on the sides with vertical lines for men and horizontal lines for women. The chusmas are made of dyed wild cotton and ornamented with feathers and beads. Certain plants are sometimes used to perfume the fabrics. The Asháninka wore chusmas before they came in contact with White people, only then they were reserved for special occasions. On regular days, they would go virtually in the nude, though women often would wear an apron suspended from a string, covering their genitals. Accessories include nasal pendants and pins made of silver, pins for the lower lip, necklaces, feather headdresses, and arm and leg bands. They also groom their hair with a composite comb, paint their bodies with genipa, and blacken their teeth with Piperaeae.

12 FOOD

The list of Asháninka crops is long, and ingredients for meals are certainly varied. Crops include yucca, the staple regional vegetable, as well as yams, peanuts, sweet potatoes, bananas, pineapples, tuber beans, macaba, pumpkins, and peppers. Some communities have added potatoes, maize, and lima beans. To grind the food, they use a wooden plate and a stone. Women are in charge of the garden, and men hunt. The Asháninka also keep and eat chickens and their eggs, and they hunt tapirs, boars, and monkeys. To supplement their diet, they collect honey, a root called *mabe,* ants, and several palm fruits. They also fish. The meat is cooked over the fire using sticks, in the shape of a pyramid or a rectangle, to hold it. The smoke from the fire helps preserve the meat for a few days. The Asháninka season their dishes with salt and pepper. Out of necessity, the Asháninkas have begun to produce cash crops, like coffee.

13 EDUCATION

Education has been badly affected by the social unrest in the area. Since 1990, according to the Satipo Educational Services Unit, 71 rural schools have been closed and the same number of teachers are counted as "disappeared," as it is not known if they are dead, have joined the rebels, or are in hiding. Though many schools have been destroyed, some make do with improvised chairs and tables made of tree trunks, and blackboards donated by aid organizations.

14 CULTURAL HERITAGE

Music and songs are part of Asháninka ceremonies and rituals. Their voices, imitations of jungle animal sounds, and stamping of the feet are accompanied by various instruments which they make using available materials and decorate with indigenous paints in their particular style. Early accounts of what had been found among the Asháninka include lists of their numerous instruments: two-headed monkey-skin drums, five to eight-tube panpipes, bone flageolets, six-hole longitudinal flutes, two-hole transverse flutes, and musical bows.

15 WORK

Most Asháninka still live by fishing, hunting, and cultivating small plots of land. Early observers characterized the Asháninka as hunters rather than agriculturists because most males spent much of their working time hunting. Though meat is indeed the main source of protein and the frequent movement of the early settlements was related to the depletion of local game supplies, most of a family's food comes from cultivated plants. Through the slash-and-burn method they grow yucca, plantain, peanuts, sweet potatoes, and sugarcane. Colonization brought extensive coffee, cacao, rice, and coca plantations to some areas. They also grow medicinal herbs and *barbasco*, which is used for fishing. When possible, the Asháninka cultivate plots of land along the riverbanks, but in violent circumstances they move to the hilltops. Selling their produce provides some income. Asháninka communities are self-sufficient, and most economic activities are carried out collectively. The product is divided among the families. There is also a long tradition of trade between tribes.

16 SPORTS

The Asháninka, since before the arrival of the Europeans, made some objects that seem to indicate the practice of some kind of sport or games, such as humming tops, bull-roarers, and maize-leaf balls. In tune with their status as warriors, they also practiced wrestling. In modern times, those who live side-by-side with settlers take part in the spectator sport culture. Soccer is Peru's favorite sport, and it is played even in the most remote regions.

17 ENTERTAINMENT AND RECREATION

Contact with Western civilization has brought to some communities new forms of recreation. Radio and television have joined more traditional forms of entertainment such as storytelling, singing, and dancing. Actually, a number of Asháninka did more than watch: in Werner Herzog's film *Fitzcarraldo* (1982), the majority of extras were Asháninka men. In remote areas, where life continues to be quite similar to the past, the division between work or ceremonies and recreational time is not as sharp: there is a lot of work to do, but because many activities are carried out collectively, they also offer a chance for social intercourse.

18 FOLK ART, CRAFTS, AND HOBBIES

The Asháninka traditionally are a seminomadic tribe, and as such their material culture is minimal. But the few objects they possess are manufactured with great skill and are artistically decorated. One of their most characteristic designs is that of a heavy line outlined by one or two fine lines. Similar designs, consisting of complex angular, geometric patterns drawn in rectangular panels, adorn most objects, from pots and beadwork to musical instruments and clothes. The Asháninka make the fabric for their typical costume, the *chusma*. They use wild cotton and two different kinds of frames to weave: one for small bands, and a vertical loom for large pieces of cloth. With gynerium stalks, the Asháninka make twined telescope baskets. They also make sieves and mats. Some containers are made of calabashes. Their plates are made of clay and have red designs.

19 SOCIAL PROBLEMS

The Asháninka traditional way of life is a casualty of the war between the national army and guerrilla groups. The mountain area of the Asháninka's forest territory was the birthplace of the rebel Shining Path. The Asháninka and other Indian peoples of the region have tried to remain outside of the conflict between the national army and the guerrillas but have often been its victims. Many have been reduced to the status of refugees in their own land, and those who have been able to remain in their villages have seen their social structure severely affected by political violence. Furthermore, the coca that has been grown in the area for centuries and used since ancestral times for its medicinal qualities has been turned into cocaine in the hands of the Whites, a dangerous and profitable drug that attracts outsiders interested in the illegal trade. Asháninka peoples, together with other indigenous tribes from the region, have formed pressure groups and with the help of international organizations demand justice and defend their human rights. There is still a long way to go before they can also secure Indian rights and be free to conduct their own way of life.

20 BIBLIOGRAPHY

The Asháninka Disaster and Struggle. Soren Hvalkof. Indigenous Affairs. May/June 1994.

Documentos de Trabajo. Centro Amazónico de Antropologia Práctica—CAAP. Desplazadòs de la Selva Central. March 1993.

Enciclopedia Ilustrada del Perú. Peísa, 1988.

Lewington, Anna. *What Do We Know about the Amazonian Indians?* New York: P. Bedrick Books, 1993.

———. *Rainforest Amerindians.* Austin, TX: Raintree Steck-Vaughan Publishers, 1993.

Pullman, Geoffrey, K. *Handbook of Amazonian Languages.* Hawthorne, NY: Mouton de Gruyer, 1986.

South American Indians. Tribes of Peruvian and Ecuadorian Montana. 1963.

Steward, Julian Haynes, ed. *Handbook of South American Indi-ans*. New York: Cooper Square, 1963.

Voz Indigena Asháninka. Edición Especial de la Comisión de Emergencia Asháninka. October 1995.

—by D. Ventura-Alcalay, reviewed by V. Salles-Reese

ASIAN INDIAN AMERICANS

For more information on Asian Indian history and culture, *see* **Vol. 3: Indians**.

OVERVIEW

Asian Indian Americans began migrating to the US from India in small numbers during the 19th century. By 1900, the US Census counted 2,050 Asian Indians living in the US, mostly professional men, merchants, and travelers who settled along the east coast, particularly in New York. Asian Indian students also came to study at American colleges, mostly on the east coast, although a sizeable number attended universities in California by the time of World War I (1914–18).

Asian Indian nationalists, organizing a revolt against British rule in India in the 1800s and early 1900s, used the US as a base for their activities. The Ghadr ("Revolution") Party was organized by Asian Indian nationalist Har Dayal in 1913 with its headquarters in San Francisco. After 1905, Asian Indian laborers began immigrating in large numbers to Canada. When Canada began to regulate Asian Indian immigration, turning away several thousand applicants, many chose to enter the US instead. Though most were from an agricultural caste in India, the majority found work in the railroad and timber industries. Because almost all Asian Indian immigrants at this time were single males, they were willing to work long hours for low wages and soon became a threat to other potential employees. The same was true for those Asian Indians who had found their way to California where they were employed as migrant farm-workers. European American workers began to intimidate them, trying to force them off the job as they had earlier tried to intimidate Chinese and Japanese workers. The Asian Indians formed partnerships to protect themselves and saved money to buy their own land. By 1919, they owned 2,077 acres and leased 86,315 acres of land in California, producing rice, cotton, nuts, fruits, and potatoes.

European Americans formed the Asiatic Exclusion League in the early 1900s to persuade the US government to restrict Asian immigration. The government did indeed turn away some 3,453 Asian Indians between 1908 and 1920. At first, Asian Indians tried to fight back through legal means, filing suits in court and lobbying government officials. When these methods failed to achieve success, Asian Indians sought the help of radical Har Dayal and the Ghadr Party. When Dayal was arrested and deported after a demonstration, however, the movement fell apart and all but disappeared in America by 1917.

The Immigration Act of 1917 placed severe restrictions on Asian immigration to the US, and the Alien Land Law of 1920 prevented those of Asian ancestry from owning land. Some Asian Indians transferred the title of their land to European American friends so as not to lose it, while others were forced to become landless laborers once again. A number of Asian Indians married Mexican women and put their lands in their wives' names and the names of their American-born children. (Antimiscegenation laws prevented Asian Indians from marrying American women.) Between 1913 and 1946, 92% of Asian

Indians living in southern California were married to Mexican women (76% of those in central California, and 47% in northern California).

Asian Indian immigration to the US slowed down considerably from the 1920s through 1940s. By World War II (1939–45), the number of Asian Indians in the US had dwindled to 2,405. Only 4% were professionals, while 65% were in agriculture (15% farmers, 50% laborers). At the end of World War II, relations between India and the US improved, and Asian Indians were finally allowed to immigrate to the US, become US citizens, own property, and marry Americans.

At first, only a small number of Asian Indians took advantage of these new opportunities; about 6,000 Asian Indians immigrated to the US between 1947 and 1965. In the past few decades, however, Asian Indian immigration has increased rapidly, with 387,223 residing in the US by 1980, and 786,694 by 1990. While the total US population increased by only 9% between 1980 and 1990, the Asian Indian population rose by 95.2%. Asian Indians are now the fourth-largest group among Asian/Pacific Americans.

Many Asian Indian Americans are students who decided to change their status to "immigrant" once in the US. In the 1992–93 academic year, there were almost 36,000 Asian Indian students in the US. Because Asian Indian migration to the US in significant numbers is such a recent development, and because so many are young students, most Asian Indian Americans (over 75% in 1990) are foreign-born. Asian Indian families have not lived in the US long enough to have developed a large population of second- or third-generation American-born children.

Most Asian Indians continue to settle in California (22.8%) and New York (20.3%), with sizeable communities in New Jersey (11%) and Illinois (8.5%), especially Chicago (7.6%), as well. During recent decades, the number of Asian Indian women migrating to the US has just about equalled that of Asian Indian men. The overall median age of Asian Indian Americans in 1990 was 29.4 years. Less than 3% of Asian Indian Americans are over the age of 65, as compared to 13% of European Americans. Most Asian Americans are in the middle-adult taxpaying age range.

There are almost 2,000 languages and dialects spoken in India, with Hindi (spoken by 30% of the population), English, and 14 regional languages—including Bengali and Urdu—officially recognized by the constitution. Because most Asian Indian Americans are foreign-born, they speak their native languages, as well as English. Almost 78% of Asian Indian Americans speak a language other than English at home, but over 70% also speak English quite well. Only 2% speak no English at all.

Asian Indian religions have greatly influenced American life since the mid- to late 1900s, when Buddhist and Brahmanic philosophies birthed movements such as Theosophy (originating in 1875) in the US. The first Asian Indian religious leader to visit the US was Swami Vivekananda in 1893. He established the Vedanta Society to bring Hindu teachers to the US and spread the wisdom of the Vedas (Hindu scriptures). Many Hindu, Buddhist, Ayurvedic, and other Asian Indian philosophies have since made their way into American life. A recent Asian Indian religious teacher and healer to settle in the US is Deepak Chopra, author of many books, including *Quantum Healing: Exploring the Frontiers of Mind/Body Medicine*

(1989), and founder of the American Association of Ayurvedic Medicine.

Asian Indians celebrate many different holidays, depending on their religious and cultural backgrounds. Immigrants to the US bring their religious and cultural traditions with them, continuing to celebrate the holidays of their homeland. Some of the major holidays celebrated by various Asian Indian Americans are Baisakhi, the Hindu solar new year; Buddha Purnima, the birthday and day of enlightenment of Gautama Buddha; Dussehra and Durga Puja, the triumph of good over evil; Deepavali or Diwali, the festival of lights (also the financial new year); Gandhi Jayanti, the 2 October birthday of Mahatma Gandhi; Holi, a spring festival; Ramadan, Id'Ul'Fitr, Id-Uz-Zuha, and Muharram—Muslim holidays; American Independence Day on 4 July; Asian Indian Independence Day on 15 August; Janmashtami, the birthday of Lord Krishna; Mahavir Jayanti, the birthday of Vardhamana Mahavira; Onam, and Pongal or Sankranti, harvest festivals; and Republic Day on 26 January, marking the adoption of India's constitution in 1950.

Asian Indian Americans are more likely to be wealthy than members of any other American ethnic group, including European Americans. At least 44% of Asian Indian American households have a yearly income of $50,000 or more (compared to 26% of European American households). American-born Asian Indian Americans are less likely to be wealthy than their foreign-born counterparts: Only 27% have yearly incomes over $50,000, as opposed to 44.5% of foreign-born Asian Indian Americans. The wealthiest Asian Indian Americans live in New York, New Jersey, or Connecticut.

About half as many Asian Indian American families (7.2%) live below the poverty line as do other Asian American families (13.1%). Asian Indian Americans are also less poor than European Americans, of whom 7.8% live below the poverty line. Once again, however, American-born Asian Indian Americans are less wealthy than their foreign-born counterparts, with 12% living below the poverty line, as opposed to 7.1% of foreign-born Asian Indian Americans.

Very few Asian Indian Americans live alone. The vast majority live either in family households or with friends, fellow students, etc. Most live in nuclear family units of at least three persons (about 70%). Less than 10% live with extended family members. In 1990, some 65% of Asian Indian American males and 70% of females over the age of 15 were married. Divorce is rare (about 2%).

Many foreign-born Asian Indian American women wear traditional dress, which varies according to the region of India in which the women grew up. Most wear *sarees* (or *saris*), made from six yards of silk, cotton, or other lightweight fabric draped around the waist over a long petticoat, with the end gathered together over one shoulder. A close-fitting blouse of matching fabric and color is worn underneath. Styles of draping and decorating the saree vary from region to region in India.

Asian Indian American men have mostly adopted Western-style clothing, only wearing traditional dress on special occasions. Traditional Asian Indian clothing for men consists of a long robe called a *sherwani* worn over either tight-fitting pants called *churidars*, or looser, straighter pants. Sometimes a loose shirt called a *kurta* is worn instead of the robe, and a vest is often added. A *dhoti*, several yards of fabric draped around the legs to form loose trousers, is sometimes worn instead of other types of pants.

Asian Indian food has become very popular in the US in recent years. Most medium-sized and large cities have at least one Asian Indian restaurant, where dishes such as *dal* (lentil soup), *tandoori* chicken (coated with a yogurt sauce and baked in a special oven called a *tandoor*), and *chapatis* (flat bread) are served. The Asian Indian diet, based on rice and other grains, several kinds of beans, and vegetables, with lean meats such as fish and chicken, is very healthy and appeals to vegetarians and meat-eaters alike.

Asian Indian Americans place a high value on education and are generally high achievers. Almost 60% of Asian Indian Americans over the age of 25 are college graduates: 6% have doctorates, 8% have professional degrees, 19% have master's degrees, and 25% have bachelor's degrees. About 10% have had some college education but have not received a degree. Asian Indian Americans have a mean high school grade-point average of 3.80 (out of 4.0).

With their high grade-point averages and competitive scores on standardized tests and college entrance exams, Asian Indian Americans are eligible for acceptance at the best universities in the US. Some schools, such as California State University at San Francisco, Harvard, Yale, and Stanford, have a significant Asian Indian student population. Despite the high numbers of Asian Indian and Asian Indian American students, however, few universities have chairs for Asian Indian studies.

Traditional Asian Indian music is divided into two styles: Hindustani, which is popular in the north; and Karnatak, popular in the south. The predominant musical instruments are the *sitar* in the north and *veena* in the south, both of which resemble a guitar. Flutes, drums, and other instruments are also prevalent. Ravi Shankar (b.1920) is a well-known Asian Indian sitarist who established the Kinnara School of Music in Los Angeles in 1967. Shankar also collaborated with Asian Indian conductor Zubin Mehta (b.1936), former director and conductor of both the New York and Los Angeles Philharmonic Orchestras, to fuse Western and Eastern music and bring Asian Indian music to the attention of the West.

There are many successful Asian Indian American writers of both fiction and nonfiction, including Dhan Gopal Mukerji, one of the first Asian Americans to write books for children; Bharati Mukherjee, who won the National Book Critics Circle Award for her novel *The Middleman and Other Stories* (1988); and Ved Mehta, a journalist and staff writer for *The New Yorker* magazine.

A large percentage (almost 44% in 1990) of Asian Indian Americans are employed in professional and managerial positions, although their proportion is dropping as more nonprofessional Asian Indians migrate to the US. Through the extended family or ethnic network, Asian Indian Americans have virtually taken over the running of newsstands in New York City. Almost 30% of independent motels in the US are managed by Asian Indian Americans, mostly from the Patel family. A growing number of gas stations are owned by Asian Indian Americans, and Asian Indian Americans are second only to Hasidic Jews in the Diamond District of the jewelry trade.

Although Asian Indian Americans have been largely successful in their new home country, they have been (and continue to be) the victims of racial prejudice. "Glass ceilings" prevent them from attaining the highest executive positions in corporations, despite excellent academic and professional qualifications. Discrimination leads many European Americans and other non-Asian Indians to refuse to see an Asian Indian American doctor. Hate crimes cause injuries, death, and tremendous stress in Asian Indian American communities. In September 1987, for example, Asian Indian American doctor Kaushal Sharan was attacked near his home in Jersey City, New Jersey, by members of a racist gang who beat him unconscious. At that time, many anti-Asian Indian hate crimes were being perpetrated in Jersey City by gangs calling themselves the Dotbusters (referring to the red dot, or *bindi*, worn by East Indian women on their foreheads) and the Lost Boys.

BIBLIOGRAPHY

Bacon, Jean Leslie. *Life Lines: Community, Family, and Assimilation Among Asian Immigrants.* New York: Oxford University Press, 1996.

Fenton, John Y. *Transplanting Religious Traditions: Asian Indians in America.* New York: Praeger, 1968.

McClain, Charles, ed. *Asian Indians, Filipinos, Other Asian Communities, and the Law.* New York: Garland Publishing, 1994.

Motihar, Kamla. "Who Are the Asian Indian Americans?" In *The Asian American Almanac,* Susan Gall, ed. Detroit: Gale Research, 1995.

Saran, Parmatma. *The Asian Indian Experience in the United States.* Cambridge, Mass.: Schenkman Publishing Co., 1985.

———. *The New Ethnics: Asian Indians in the United States.* New York: Praeger, 1980.

—by D. K. Daeg de Mott

AYMARA

LOCATION: Bolivia; Peru; Chile
POPULATION: About 2 million (Bolivia); 500,000 (Peru); 20,000 (Chile)
LANGUAGE: Aymara; Spanish
RELIGION: Roman Catholicism combined with indigenous beliefs; Seventh Day Adventist

1 INTRODUCTION

The Aymara are more than an ethnic group. They constitute a linguistic unity among several ethnic groups, such as the Lupaca, Pacaje, Canchi, Uru, etc. They are found in the altiplano (high plains) of the Bolivian Andes. Bolivia has the highest proportion of indigenous peoples of any country in South America, and not surprisingly, it is the poorest country on the continent.

The Aymara appeared in the altiplano after the decline of the Tiahuanaco civilization (1580 BC–AD 1172), probably having migrated from the southern part of the continent. The Aymara resisted the invading Incas for over 100 years before succumbing to their rule in the late 15th century. The Aymara later joined forces with the Incas to fight and subdue other native tribes. While the Aymara retained their own language and many of their customs, the influence of the Incas on their religious and social traditions was pronounced. It is sometimes difficult for anthropologists today to determine whether a practice or custom has Inca or Aymara origins.

The Aymara faced great hardships under Spanish colonial rule. In 1570, the Viceroy decreed forced labor in the rich silver mines on the altiplano. Potosi was once the site of the richest silver mine in the world. Millions of Aymara laborers perished in the wretched conditions in the mines.

2 LOCATION AND HOMELAND

The Aymara live on high-altitude plains in the Bolivian Andes, on the Lake Titicaca plateau near the border with Peru. The altiplano is at an elevation of 3,000 m to 3,700 m (10,000–12,000 ft) above sea level, where weather conditions are cold and harsh, making agriculture difficult. An ethnic group closely related to the Aymara live among the Uru islands on Lake Titicaca. These communities live not on land but on islands that are made of floating reeds.

An estimated 2 million Aymara live in Bolivia, with 500,000 residing in Peru, and about 20,000 in Chile. It should be emphasized that the Aymara are not confined to a defined territory in the Andes. After almost five centuries of hybridization of the region, many live in the cities, participate fully in Western culture, go to urban schools (sometimes private ones), play a variety of sports (basketball, tennis, soccer, volleyball, cycling), and dress in Western-style clothes. Most of the ethnic and cultural characteristics pointed out here refer to isolated villages and to the rural regions where perhaps half of the Aymara live.

3 LANGUAGE

The Aymara language, originally called *jaqi aru* (the language of the people) is still the dominant language in the Bolivian Andes and in the southeastern parts of Peru. Aymara is an amazingly versatile language in which—through suffixes—a word can be concrete or abstract, noun or verb, and through which nuances can be incorporated into the language, something unknown to many modern languages. In the rural areas one finds that the Aymara language is predominant, while in the urban areas the Aymara are bilingual in Spanish and Aymara, and even trilingual in Spanish, Quechua, and Aymara in regions where Inca rule was prominent. The Aymara language is the second-most-prevalent indigenous language in the Americas, second only to the Quechua spoken by descendants of the Incas. Since colonial times, most Aymara Indians have Christian first names but preserve their Aymara last names, for example, Francisco Mamani ("falcon" in Aymara). Given the large numbers of Aymara-speaking people in Bolivia, there are several radio stations and a couple of television channels that transmit only in Aymara.

4 FOLKLORE

The Aymara share with other ethnic groups some of the Pan-Andean myths of origin. In one of them, the god Tunupa is a creator of the universe, but he is also the one that taught the people all his customs: how to develop agriculture, the songs they sang, how to weave, the languages each group had to speak, and the precepts to lead a moral life. Aymara mythology abounds in myths of origin such as the origin of the wind, of hail, of mountains, and of lakes.

5 RELIGION

The religious practices of most Amerindian groups are a unique fusion between their traditional, indigenous practices and the religion imposed by the colonizers. The Aymara are no exception. The Aymara, however, have had two cultures imposed on them: first by the Incas, and later by the Spanish. The Incas permitted the Aymara to maintain their language and all their customs, yet many of the religious practices of the Inca religion were adopted by the Aymara. Similarly, the Incas adopted the idols of the groups they vanquished and kept them in their temples. The similarity of these beliefs, which revered natural forces such as the sun, the moon, and thunder, made the new religion easy to assimilate.

Catholicism was introduced during the colonial period and has been adopted by the Aymara. The Aymara, for example, will attend Mass and celebrate baptisms, and they follow the Catholic calendar of important Christian events. The content of their many religious festivals, however, bears evidence of their traditional beliefs. The Aymara regularly make offerings to Mother Earth, in order to assure a productive harvest or to cure illnesses.

The Aymara believe in the power of spirits that reside in mountains, in the sky, or in natural forces, such as lightning. The most potent and sacred of their gods is Pachamama, the Earth Goddess who has the power to make the soil fertile and ensure a good crop.

Most recently, the Seventh-Day Adventists have made great inroads in Aymara communities, and the religion is attracting an increasing number of followers.

6 MAJOR HOLIDAYS

The Aymara, being mostly Bolivian, celebrate the same holidays as everybody else in the country: the civic holidays such

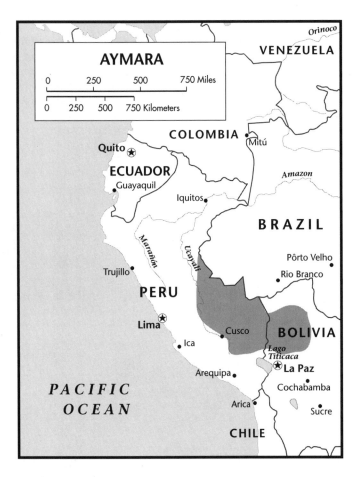

as Independence Day and the religious ones such as Christmas and Easter. One particular holiday is *Dia del Indio,* on 2 August, which commemorates their cultural heritage. The Aymara celebrate many holidays throughout the year. In every town, they celebrate the day of their patron saint on the liturgical Catholic calendar. These festivals last up to seven days and are celebrated with music, traditional dancing, and abundant consumption of alcohol. For each fiesta, a host is found. This person, known as the *preste,* is responsible for providing the food and drink for the community. To be a preste is an honor that Aymara seek, and they save for years in order to afford the expense.

The Aymara also celebrate Carnival. Carnival is a festival marking the beginning of Lent that is widely celebrated throughout South America. Dancing to drums and flutes accompanies a week-long celebration. Also important is the festival *Alacistas,* which features the God of Good Luck. Most households will have a ceramic figure of the Good Luck spirit, known as *Ekeko.* Purported to bring prosperity and grant wishes, the Ekeko doll is a round, plump figure, carrying miniature replicas of household goods, such as cooking utensils, bags of food, and money.

7 RITES OF PASSAGE

An Aymara child is gradually introduced to the social and cultural traditions of the community. Key stages in the development of a child are marked by traditions and rites of passage. A significant event in the life of an Aymara child is the first hair cut, known as *rutucha.* A baby's hair is allowed to grow until

the child is able to walk and talk. At approximately two years old, when it is unlikely that he or she will succumb to childhood diseases that are prevalent in the Andes, the head is shaved bare.

8 INTERPERSONAL RELATIONS

A dominant feature of the Aymara culture is reciprocity and the social obligation to help other members of the community. The exchange of labor and mutual aid play an essential role within an *ayllu* or community. Such exchanges are invoked at times when substantial amounts of labor are required that a single family cannot provide. An Aymara peasant might ask for help from a neighbor to build a house, dig an irrigation ditch, or harvest a field. In return, he or she is expected to reciprocate by donating the same number of days' labor to the neighbor.

9 LIVING CONDITIONS

Living conditions of the Aymara depend mainly on where they live and how much they have been integrated to the Western style of life. To generalize about their living conditions would be a gross mistake. Many Aymaras that reside in cities live in modern houses or apartments. There are also large numbers of poor Aymaras in the cities who have just one room. In rural areas, the construction of an Aymara house depends largely upon its location and the availability of materials. A typical Aymara house is a small oblong dwelling constructed of adobe, although near the lake reeds are the primary building material. Thatched roofs are made of reeds and grasses.

The high altitude makes life in the altiplano very difficult. The low level of oxygen in the air can leave one with *soroche* (altitude sickness), which causes headaches, fatigue, and nausea. Soroche is also potentially fatal. In order to adapt to life in the mountains, the Aymara have undergone clear physiological changes that enable them to cope in this environment. Most significantly, the Aymara and other mountain peoples have a greatly increased lung capacity relative to their body size. Expanded lung capacity enables them to increase their intake of air and, therefore, oxygen.

The use of coca leaves also ameliorates the effects of altitude sickness. Chewing coca leaves releases a mild alkaloid that combats fatigue and hunger. Coca leaves produce a mild medicinal effect and do not contain cocaine, which results only after major chemical processing of the leaves.

10 FAMILY LIFE

The central social unit of the Aymara is the extended family. Typically, a family will encompass parents, unmarried children, and grandparents in one house, or in a small cluster of houses. Large families are common, with many families having seven or eight children. Systems of reciprocity and mutual obligation are very strong within the extended family, and cousins, in-laws, and other relatives form a network of support and assistance. Relatives help with minding the children and harvesting, and they may provide loans in times of economic hardship.

There is a sharp division of labor within an Aymara household, but women's work is not necessarily considered inferior. Planting, in particular, is a task ascribed to women that is highly respected. Women in Aymara society also have inheritance rights. Property owned by females will be passed down from mother to daughter, ensuring that not all land and property goes to the sons, as it does in other cultures. This practice, however, has had some drawbacks, as parcels of land become so small through generations of inheritance divisions as to be agriculturally impractical.

Marriage is a long process which entails many steps. Getting married involves many stages and ceremonies, such as the inheritance feasts, a planting ritual, and the building of the house. Despite the lengthy marriage ritual, divorce is accepted and is relatively simple.

11 CLOTHING

Clothing styles vary greatly among the Aymara. Men in the cities wear regular Western clothes, and women wear their traditional *polleras* (ample skirts) made of fine materials, such as velvet and brocade. They wear shawls that are embroidered, and bowler hats (some of which are made in Italy). In the altiplano, the story is different. The strong cold winds that blow on the altiplano require warm woolen clothing. Demonstrating the clear influence of the colonial Spanish, women wear long homespun skirts and sweaters. Layers of skirts are used to provide some protection against the cold. For festivals or important occasions, women will wear as many as five or six skirts on top of each other. Traditional weaving techniques dating back to pre-Inca times are used to produce brightly colored shawls, which are also used to strap children to their backs or carry loads of goods. For headwear, the women wear distinctive *bowbin,* or bowler hats. Aymara men in the altiplano wear long cotton trousers and woolen caps with ear flaps. In many regions, men also wear ponchos. Both sexes may wear sandals or shoes, but many go barefoot despite the cold.

12 FOOD

In cities, the Aymara diet is varied with one distinctive characteristic: *aji,* a hot pepper used to season the dishes. In the countryside, potatoes and grains, such as quinoa, form the staple diet. Quinoa, which is becoming increasingly popular in health food stores in the US, is a nutritious, high-protein grain which has been grown in the Andes for centuries. The extremes of temperature that exist in the high Andes make it possible for potatoes and other tubers to be naturally freeze-dried and preserved. The cold air at night will freeze the moisture from the potato, while the sun during the day will melt and evaporate it. After a week lying out in the elements, the potatoes are pounded. The result is *chuño,* small, rock-hard pieces of potato that can be stored for years. Lengthy soaking in water will rehydrate them and prepare them for cooking.

Meats are also freeze-dried. A traditional dish is *olluco con charqui*—*olluco* is a small potato-like tuber, which is cooked with *charqui,* dried llama meat. Llamas are important for their wool and packing ability and are therefore consumed only rarely. Fish from Lake Titicaca or neighboring rivers is an important part of the diet in many communities.

Food is cooked in clay stoves into spicy stews or soups. Condiments include *aji,* other hot peppers, and peanut sauces. For festive occasions, guinea pig is eaten. Spicy guinea pig stew is the most desirable dish at a feast.

13 EDUCATION

In Bolivia, primary school education is mandatory until the age of 14. However, as in other developing countries, children of

Aymara women dancers in traditional dress in La Paz, Bolivia. (David Johnson)

subsistence peasants are less likely than their urban counterparts to complete their schooling. Most rural families rely on children to conduct many essential household chores. Children often have the responsibility of tending to a herd or taking care of younger siblings. Male children are more likely to complete school than are girls, who have greater household responsibilities, even at a very young age.

Despite this, Bolivian literacy rates are fairly high, estimated at 85% for males and 71% for females. Perhaps this is the result of the rural school program that was massively implemented after the agrarian reform of 1953. The state universities, being virtually free, educate many Aymara who achieve degrees in all the professions, including medicine, law, and engineering. There are also trade schools where Aymara electricians, carpenters, plumbers, and mechanics are trained.

14 CULTURAL HERITAGE

The Aymara have a rich musical tradition. Although a clear Spanish influence can be discerned, the Aymara's primary musical influences date as far back as their pre-Inca ancestors. Percussion and flutes are featured prominently at festivals and celebrations. Panpipes (*zampoñas*) and the *pututu* horn, made out of a hollowed-out cow's horn, are traditional instruments that are still widely played. Homemade violins and drums are also common.

Indigenous dances have also been passed down through the generations. Each festival has its particular traditional dances. Many dances feature large, brightly painted masks and costumes. Many dances symbolize and parody the Spanish colonizers. The "old man dance," for example, features a bent-over Spanish aristocrat with a broad top hat. In this satirical dance, the dancer imitates the gestures and mannerisms of old Spanish gentlemen to comic effect.

The Aymara have a very rich and long oral tradition. During colonial times many of their songs, poems, and stories were compiled by missionaries or Ladino Indians (Indians that had learned how to write). In the 20th century, many ethnographers and linguists have also transcribed their texts. Aymara literature has recently undergone a renaissance. Now there are many Aymara who write down their stories and legends. Many of them are published in bilingual (Spanish-Aymara) editions.

15 WORK

Many Aymara are subsistence farmers in a harsh, high-altitude environment. The high altitude, cold nights, and poor soil greatly limit the types of crops that are able to be sown. The Aymara follow traditional patterns of agricultural production, often still relying on pre-Columbian terraces, and following a careful pattern of crop rotation. The most important crop is the potato, which originated in the Andes. Also important is corn, quinoa (a grain), and barley. Many families own land at different altitudes, which enables them to grow a diverse range of crops.

Tractors or even oxen teams are rare in the high Andes. Traditional agricultural implements, such as the *taclla,* a foot plow, are still widely used. While the men do the plowing and digging, the sacred task of planting is reserved exclusively for women, as only they have the power to give life. This is also out of deference to *Pachamama,* the Earth Goddess.

The Aymara are also herders, deriving both wool and meat from herds of llamas, alpacas, and sheep. A family may also supplement their grazing herd with a couple of cows, frogs, or chickens. Many communities are beginning to diversify economically and produce off-farm income. The growing tourist trade has increased the demand for the luxurious wool of the alpaca, and sweaters are often knitted for the tourist trade, generating much-needed cash income. Some Aymara also work as laborers in silver or tin mines. These mines are dangerous and can cause health problems. However, they offer a scarce opportunity for cash income.

Many Aymara have entered politics since the reforms of 1952. They have founded a political party, Katarista, and they have senators and representatives in the Bolivian congress.

16 SPORTS

Although there are no sports that are strictly Aymara, soccer is the Bolivian national sport and many Aymara participate.

17 ENTERTAINMENT AND RECREATION

With the proliferation of mass media, the Aymara now enjoy their own TV shows, both as spectators and as performers. A kind of soap opera in Aymara is transmitted on the Aymara channel. There are musical groups that have made recordings that are avidly consumed by many Aymara. Urban Aymara are frequent moviegoers. One of the preferred activities is to dance in folklore festivals, for which they rehearse many months. Young people use these occasions to socialize among peers.

18 FOLK ART, CRAFTS, AND HOBBIES

The Aymara are skilled weavers, a tradition dating back to their pre-Inca origins. Many ethnologists believe that the textiles of the Andes are among the most highly developed and complex textile traditions in the world. The Aymara use a great many materials in their weaving, including cotton, as well as sheep, alpaca and llama wool. Additionally, the Aymara use totora reeds to make fishing boats, baskets, and related artifacts. Styles, patterns, and colors used in textile-weaving differ by region. Among the most sought-after textiles are those made in the town of Potolo. Potolo weavers emphasize zoomorphic designs which depict horses, llamas, and other animals.

19 SOCIAL PROBLEMS

The social problems faced by the Aymara stem from colonial times. European colonizers and their descendants have marginalized the Indians and exploited them constantly, putting them in the lower strata of the social scale. Beginning with the Spaniards, the Aymara culture (and, for that matter, of all Amerindians) has been stigmatized and forced to acculturate to the colonizers' imposed values and beliefs. In spite of all the efforts made during almost half a millennium to erase or extirpate their culture, however, the Aymara have preserved some of their indigenous traits, which unfortunately have maintained them on the fringes of a society sharply divided among classes. It has been only in the second half of the 20th century that there has been an openness to accept their heritage without derogatory connotations. After the MNR revolution of 1952 [see "Bolivians"], all Indians enjoy all the civil rights of every Bolivian. With their access to education, their participation in the life of the country is beginning to be more active, but there are still class and racial barriers to overcome before they can fully participate in the modern life of the country. Unfortunately, too many of the Aymara still remain in poverty in rural areas, forcing large numbers to migrate to the cities where life becomes even harder for them in many respects.

20 BIBLIOGRAPHY

Albo, Xavier, and Félix Layme. *Literatura Aymara: Antología.* La Paz, Bolivia: Hisbol, 1992.

Bouysse-Cassagne, Therese. *La identidad Aymara: Aproximación histórica.* La Paz, Bolivia: Hisbol, 1987.

Crowther, Geoff. *South American on a Shoestring.* Hawthorn, Australia: Lonely Planet Publications, 1994.

La Barre, Weston. *The Aymara Indians of the Lake Titicaca Plateau, Bolivia.* Memasha, WI: American Anthropological Association, 1948.

Moss, Joyce, and George Wilson. *Peoples of the World: Latin Americas.* Detroit: Gale Research, 1989.

Reader, John. *Man on Earth: A Celebration of Mankind.* New York: Harper & Row, 1988.

—by C. Sahley, reviewed by V. Salles-Reese

BAHAMIANS

LOCATION: Bahamas
POPULATION: 272,000
LANGUAGE: English; Bahamian dialect
RELIGION: Christianity

¹ INTRODUCTION

Although the islands of the Bahamas are actually located in the western Atlantic Ocean, they are often identified with the Caribbean. They were the first islands to be sighted by Christopher Columbus in 1492, and the explorer named them *baja mar* (literally, "low water" in Spanish) for the shallow sea that surrounds them. Since the Bahamas lacked the mineral wealth found on other islands in the region, the Spanish did not settle them but rather used the native population of Lucayans as slaves on Hispaniola and other islands. Within a quarter of a century, the islands were depopulated and remained so for over 100 years.

During the 17th century, the Bahamas became both a refuge for English settlers and a base for pirates, including the notorious Blackbeard. The first permanent English settlement was founded in 1649 on the island of Eleuthera by colonists from Bermuda, and more settlers followed, bringing African slaves with them. In the 1780s the islands received an influx of British loyalists—also with slaves—from the colonies following the defeat of the British in the American Revolution. By the end of the 18th century, the number of Blacks in the Bahamas was twice that of the European population.

Slavery was abolished in Britain and its possessions in 1833, but illegal slave traders used the Bahamas as a base to smuggle slaves into the southern United States. During the American Civil War, New Providence became a site of blockade-running and gunrunning for the Confederate States. In the following decades, the Bahamian economy languished, except for a temporary period of prosperity during the Prohibition era in the United States, when rumrunners operated on Nassau. With the introduction of commercial aviation in the 1930s, the islands' tourism industry began, and by the end of the following decade it had become their primary source of income.

A series of constitutional changes in the 1960s led to full national independence in 1973. In the 1960s new tax and finance restrictions in the United States led to the Bahamas' becoming an international center of finance. Today, tourism and banking, together with shipping registration, are the nation's most important economic sectors. Since 1986 total tourist arrivals—mostly from the United States—have topped 3 million per year, over half of which are cruise ship passengers.

² LOCATION AND HOMELAND

Located in the Atlantic Ocean off Florida's southeastern coast, the Bahamas is an archipelago consisting of approximately 700 islands, of which about 30 are inhabited, as well as over 2,000 reefs and cays. Their total land area of 13,934 sq km (5,380 sq mi, or slightly more than the combined area of New Jersey and Connecticut) is spread out over nearly 260,000 sq km (100,390 sq mi). The islands are bisected by the Tropic of Cancer, which passes between Great Exuma Island and Long Island. Besides the United States, the Bahamas' nearest neighbors include

Cuba to the southwest, and Haiti and the Turks and Caicos Islands to the southeast.

The two main islands of the Bahamas are New Providence, where the capital city of Nassau is located, and Grand Bahama, the site of Freeport, the nation's only other metropolitan area. The remaining, less-developed islands are generally called either the "Family Islands" or the "out islands." Among these are Bimini, Abaco, Eleuthera, the Exumas, Andros, Cat Island, Long Island, Rum Cay, and Crooked Island. The islands' terrain includes rocky cliffs, dense jungle swampland, pine forests, isolated coves, and sandy beaches. The highest point in the Bahamas, on Cat Island, is only 63 m (207 ft) above sea level.

The Bahamas has an estimated population of some 272,000 people, of whom about 65% live in cities and about 35% in rural areas. New Providence and Grand Bahama, the most densely populated islands, account for more than 75% of the Bahamian population. About 85% of Bahamians are of African descent, 8% are of mixed ancestry, and the remainder are White (mostly of British origin). Most White Bahamians live on New Providence, the Abacos, or Grand Bahama.

In the 1950s and 1960s—the era of the Civil Rights movement in the United States—race relations in the Bahamas began to change. Until then, economic opportunities for Blacks were severely limited, and they endured the overt racism of being barred from theaters, hotels, shops, and other public places. Thanks to a movement known as the Quiet Revolution, together with government policies that improved educational and job opportunities, the lot of Black Bahamians has improved and a new Black middle class has come into being on New Providence and Grand Bahama.

³ LANGUAGE

Standard English is the official language of the Bahamas, but most of the population speaks some version of an English-based Creole language called the Bahamian dialect. The language of the working class is the furthest from standard English, while that of Whites and middle-class Bahamians of African ancestry generally falls somewhere on a spectrum between the official language and the creolized version.

An example of the Bahamian dialect can be found in the following verse from the poem "Islan' Life" by poet and playwright Susan J. Wallace:

Islan' life ain' no fun less ya treat errybody
like ya brudder, ya sister, or ya frien'
Love ya neighbour, play ya part, jes' remember das de art,
For when ocean fen' ya in, all is kin.

⁴ FOLKLORE

The Bahamas is rich in myths and legends, especially those related to specific islands. Little Exuma Island is said to be haunted by a woman named Pretty Molly Bay, who is actually the source of two different legends. In one, she is a drowned slave who roams the beaches at night; in the other, she is a young White woman turned into a mermaid. There are stories about creatures called "chickcharnies"—three-toed sprites with red eyes—who hang upside down from trees on the island of Andros and are capable of turning a person's head around to face backwards. Bimini is traditionally associated with the Fountain of Youth, and North Bimini with the lost city of Atlantis.

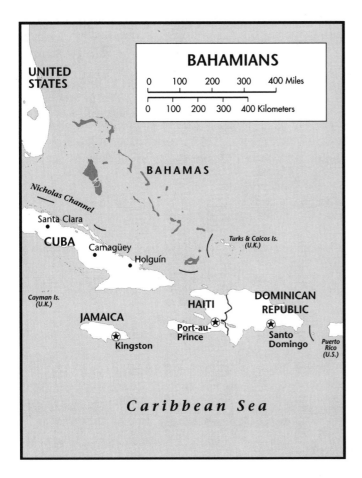

BAHAMIANS

0   100   200   300   400 Miles

0   100   200   300   400 Kilometers

UNITED STATES

BAHAMAS

Nicholas Channel

Santa Clara

CUBA
Camagüey
Holguín

Turks & Caicos Is.
(U.K.)

Cayman Is.
(U.K.)

JAMAICA

Kingston

HAITI
Port-au-Prince

DOMINICAN REPUBLIC

Santo Domingo

Puerto Rico
(U.S.)

Caribbean Sea

The 19th-century Haitian leader Henri Christophe, who committed suicide according to official accounts, is popularly thought to have escaped to Inagua Island in the Bahamas. The American playwright Eugene O'Neill based his play *The Emperor Jones* on this legend. The Bahamas' history as a base for pirate operations in the 17th and 18th centuries has spawned tales about buried treasure throughout the islands (treasure has actually been found on some sunken ships and on Cat Island).

⁵ RELIGION

Most Bahamians are Christian: Baptists account for about 33% of the population, while Roman Catholics and Anglicans account for about 20% each. It is not unusual for Bahamians to attend services at their own church and others as well. The influence of Christianity is reflected in the popularity of gospel music on the islands. On some of the islands, Christian beliefs are combined with the ancient African practice of *obeah*.

⁶ MAJOR HOLIDAYS

Public holidays in the Bahamas include the major holy days of the Christian calendar as well as Labor Day (the first Friday in June), Independence Day (10 July), Emancipation Day (the first Monday in August), and Discovery Day (12 October). The best-known celebration on the islands is Junkanoo, held on both Christmas and New Year's. Thought to be descended from the day off formerly given to slaves on Christmas, it is a boisterous, colorful event that shares much of its character with Carnival festivities in such Caribbean countries as Trinidad and Tobago. Costumed groups unified by specific themes compete

for prizes as they and masses of other revelers parade through the streets to the accompaniment of whistles and goatskin drums called *goombays*. Fringes of brightly colored crepe paper adorn masks and costumes alike.

⁷ RITES OF PASSAGE

Christian ceremonies such as baptism and confirmation mark the major passages from one stage to another in a Bahamian's life.

⁸ INTERPERSONAL RELATIONS

The Bahamas has a large urban population heavily influenced by the country's large tourism industry. The legal system is based on English common law.

⁹ LIVING CONDITIONS

Living conditions range from the modern urban bustle of Nassau (on New Providence) and Freeport (on Grand Bahama) to the rural existence on the Family Islands (also called the out islands), whose inhabitants have little or no exposure to tourists and live a simpler, more traditional life. Migration to the cities for better jobs has produced an urban housing shortage, especially in low-income areas. In the 1980s new housing did not keep pace with demand. A World Bank report described 40% of the islands' dwellings as being in average to poor condition. Most Family Islanders live near the shore in villages whose scattered houses are simple wooden structures, some without plumbing or electricity (according to the World Bank, two out of three households in the Family Islands did not have running water in 1986).

The Bahamians have made great progress in health care since the 1960s. Average life expectancy is 68 years for men and 75 years for women. In 1992 there was 1 physician for every 714 people. There is a system of clinics on the out islands (there were 107 clinics in 1992), and patients who need additional care are flown to Princess Margaret Hospital in Nassau. Most Bahamian doctors receive their training in the United States, Great Britain, or Canada. Bahamians in the out islands often use folk medicine, including herbal remedies, such as boiling parts of certain plants to produce medicinal teas.

Motorists in the Bahamas drive on the left side of the road, a legacy of the British presence on the islands. The more densely settled islands of New Providence and Grand Bahama have modern, paved roadways, but few Bahamians own their own cars. In 1991 the country had only 70,000 registered passenger vehicles, including buses, taxis, government-owned vehicles, and motor scooters (a very popular form of transport). More than half the registered vehicles were on the island of New Providence. Most of the Family Islands have only one or two roads, which run the length of the island, and boats are the preferred mode of transportation, since settlements are usually located near the coast. There are no railways on the Bahamas, but there are international airports at Nassau and Freeport.

¹⁰ FAMILY LIFE

Although the model family in the Bahamas is the two-parent nuclear family, the migration of adults to Nassau and Freeport has left many families in the out islands headed by grandparents, and there are also households headed by single parents. However, it is unusual for unmarried couples to live together. A

Many jobs are related to tourism, which, together with related employment, provides jobs for the majority of Bahamians. (Susan D. Rock)

they are a popular breakfast food. The traditional Bahamian breakfast is based on the diet of fishers who needed a hearty meal before spending the day at sea.

Chicken Souse

2 chickens	2 cups chicken broth
cut-up celery stalks	10 allspice berries
4 potatoes, chopped	1 bay leaf
2 onions, chopped	1 teaspoon dried thyme
2 Scotch Bonnet peppers	½ cup lime juice

Put both chickens in a large pot with enough water to cover, and bring the water to a boil. After cooking for two minutes, pour out the water and add enough fresh water to cover the chickens. The vegetables and all other remaining ingredients except the lime joice should be added when the water boils, and the mixture should be allowed to simmer for 10 minutes. Then add the lime juice and simmer for 10 more minutes. May be served hot immediately (after skimming off the fat), or served cold after refrigeration.

13 EDUCATION

Over 96% of adult Bahamians are literate. Education is mandatory between the ages of 5 and 14, but most students continue their schooling until at least the age of 16. The educational system is modeled on that of Great Britain, with secondary education referred to in terms of "forms" (12th grade is called "6th form") and exams required in order to attend college. Students must also take exams at the end of every school year in order to pass to the next grade. Before independence in 1973, students from the out islands traveled to Nassau for their secondary education, but in the years since then secondary schools have been started on many of these islands.

The government-run College of the Bahamas opened in 1974, and the Bahamas has also been home to a branch of the University of the West Indies since the 1960s. The Industrial Training Center offers programs in such fields as electrical installation, plumbing, and auto mechanics, and the Bahamas Hotel Training College prepares students to work for hotels, tourism organizations, and other tourism-related businesses. In addition, many Bahamians attend colleges and universities in North America and Great Britain.

14 CULTURAL HERITAGE

Susan Wallace, from the island of Grand Bahama, is the nation's best-known poet. She has also edited *Back Home,* an anthology of Bahamian literature. Playwright Winston Saunders, author of *You Can Bring a Horse to Water,* is the director of the Dundas Theatre, which stages plays by Bahamian and other authors. The meticulously groomed and disciplined Royal Bahamas Police Force Band, reflecting the British influence on Bahamian history and culture, performs at all major public events. Well-known artist Alton Lowe captures many facets of Bahamian life in his realistic paintings.

15 WORK

The government is the largest employer in the Bahamas. Many government jobs are related to tourism, which, together with related employment, provides jobs for the majority of Bahamians—estimated at 50% or more of the labor force. Agriculture

child's primary caretaker, generally either the mother or grandmother, is also the person in charge of discipline in the family. Adult children often give their mothers gifts or financial assistance. On the out islands men and women often do the same kinds of work, including farming and wage labor. According to a 1994 agricultural survey, 33% of the nation's farmers were women (and 50% of all agricultural workers were Haitians).

11 CLOTHING

Bahamians wear modern Western-style clothing. Colorful costumes of all kinds can be seen at the annual Junkanoo festivals in Nassau and other locations.

12 FOOD

Seafood is the mainstay of the Bahamian diet. The conch shellfish is a national favorite used in many dishes. Other popular fish and shellfish include grouper, snapper, crayfish (which Bahamians call "lobster"), and shark. Peas and rice, reflecting the islands' African heritage, is a dietary staple consisting of dried pigeon peas and rice prepared with thyme and other spices. Souses—dishes containing lightly pickled meats—also figure prominently in Bahamian cuisine. Developed in the days before refrigeration to preserve meats in the islands' tropical climate, they are made from various meats (including lamb tongue and mutton) or conch stewed in lime juice and spices. Served with cooked grits and johnny cake (a type of bread),

A Bahamian child's primary caretaker, generally either the mother or grandmother, is also the person in charge of discipline in the family. (Cory Langley)

and industry are much smaller contributors to the nation's economy and employ far fewer people. Subsistence farming and fishing have traditionally been the main occupations on the out islands, whose inhabitants also earn money producing crafts or through seasonal employment in resort areas. Due to the shortage of salaried jobs in these areas, many residents move to Nassau or Freeport to seek employment.

16 SPORTS

Softball is the most popular sport in the Bahamas, whose teams compete regularly in the World Softball Conference. Other favorite sports include basketball, volleyball, and track and field. Student athletes compete in intramural and interscholastic basketball and volleyball, and scholarships in these sports have helped many Bahamian young people attend universities in the United States. Water sports, including sailing, windsurfing, and fishing, are popular with Bahamians and tourists alike. Many islanders race in the Family Islands regatta, held every April and based in George Town, on the island of Exuma.

17 ENTERTAINMENT AND RECREATION

In addition to the indigenous Bahamian *goombay* (goatskin drum) music, calypso, soca, and reggae are also popular, as is gospel music, which is performed in concert halls and on out-

door stages as well as in churches. There is approximately one television for every four persons in the Bahamas. Programming includes American situation comedies, professional sports, British Broadcasting Corporation (BBC) programming, and British and Canadian educational broadcasting. Church programs are broadcast on Sundays. Radio programming includes calypso music, soft and hard rock, "oldies" music, and talk shows.

18 FOLK ART, CRAFTS, AND HOBBIES

Bahamian folk music is closely related to the African-based Junkanoo festival, where the popular goatskin drum called the *goombay* was originally heard. Today, *goombay* is also used to refer to the calypso-style music whose satirical lyrics it often accompanies. In the out islands, local bands playing the goombay, the guitar, and the saw entertain at weddings and dances. Folk dance in the Bahamas ranges from the European quadrille to the African-derived jump dance and the West Indian limbo.

Crafts including woodcarving, quilting, basketry, and shell-work that were once produced chiefly for use by their creators have become profitable commercial items for sale to the country's tourists. The straw work produced on the out islands is especially distinctive. Using palm fronds braided into long strips which are then sewn together, the island women make hats, baskets, purses, and other items, often decorating them with raffia paper and seashells.

[19] SOCIAL PROBLEMS

The Bahamas has not traditionally been a violent society, and in the past serious crimes such as homicide were rare. However in recent years, drug trafficking has caused a substantial increase in crime. In New Providence the use of "crack" cocaine has resulted in frequent armed robberies.

[20] BIBLIOGRAPHY

Boultbee, Paul G. *The Bahamas.* Santa Barbara, CA: Clio Press, 1989.

Cameron, Sarah, and Ben Box, ed. *Caribbean Islands Handbook.* Chicago: Passport Books, 1995.

Collingwood, Dean W., and Steve Dodge, ed. *Modern Bahamian Society.* Parkesburg, IA: Caribbean Books, 1989.

Craton, Michael, and Gail Saunders. *Islanders in the Stream: A History of the Bahamian People.* Athens, GA: University of Georgia Press, 1992.

Gall, Timothy, and Susan Gall, ed. *Worldmark Encyclopedia of the Nations.* 8th ed. Detroit: Gale Research, 1995.

Meditz, Sandra W., and Dennis M. Hanratty. *Islands of the Caribbean Commonwealth: A Regional Study.* Washington, DC: US Government, 1989.

Otterbein, Keith F., and Charlotte Swanson Otterbein. "Bahamians." In *Encyclopedia of World Cultures.* Boston: G. K. Hall, 1992.

McCulla, Patricia. *Bahamas.* New York: Chelsea House, 1988.

Robertiello, Jack. "Soused in Bahamian Tradition." *Americas* (Jan–Feb 1996): 58.

Walton, Chelle Koster. *Caribbean Ways: A Cultural Guide.* Westwood, MA: Riverdale, 1993.

—by R. Wieder

BARBADIANS

ALTERNATE NAMES: Bajans
LOCATION: Barbados
POPULATION: 264,400
LANGUAGE: English with West African dialect influences
RELIGION: Christianity: Anglican church (majority); Roman Catholicism; Methodism; Rastafarianism; other groups include Jehovah's Witnesses, Hindus, Muslims, Baha'is, Jews; Apostolic Spiritual Baptist is the island's only indigenous religion

[1] INTRODUCTION

Barbados is unique among the islands of the Caribbean in having been governed by only one colonial power, the British, and the resulting influence has given the country its nickname of "Little England." The Barbadians' name for themselves (Bajans—pronounced BAY-juns) is derived from "Barbajians," which is the way the British commonly pronounced Barbadians. Although previously settled by the Arawak and Carib Indians, the island was uninhabited when the British first landed there in 1625. Sugar-growing was introduced by the Dutch from Brazil shortly afterward, and African slaves were imported to work on the great sugar plantations. After the abolition of slavery in 1834, Black workers stayed on the plantations and life on the island changed very little. Economic and political power was maintained by a small minority of White landowners, and the fortunes of the territory were dictated by the alternating booms and slumps of the sugar trade.

Following an outbreak of rioting in 1937, the Barbados Progressive League, antecedent of today's Barbados Labor Party, was founded to promote social, economic, and political reform. Sir Grantley Adams emerged as its leader. A series of political reforms culminated in universal suffrage in 1950 and Grantley Adams became premier of a self-governing Barbados in 1953. Errol Barrow broke away from the Barbados Labor Party in 1954 to found the Democratic Labor Party and led Barbados into independence in 1966. In 1976 Errol Barrow was defeated by Tom Adams, the son of Sir Grantley Adams. In 1974 Barbados participated in the founding of CARICOM (the Caribbean Community and Common Market), and in 1994 the island was the site of the United Nations Global Conference on Sustainable Development of Small Island Developing States.

[2] LOCATION AND HOMELAND

Belonging to the Lesser Antilles, Barbados is the easternmost Caribbean island, with a total area of 430 sq km (166 sq mi). The terrain of the pear-shaped island consists of lowlands and terraced limestone plains separated by rolling hills that run parallel to the coasts. With a 1995 estimated population of 264,400 persons on an island about the size of San Antonio, Texas, Barbados is one of the world's most densely populated countries (606 people per sq km or 1,570 people per sq mi—five times the population density of India). However, in recent decades its population has been controlled by an effective family planning program; current population growth is 0.5% per year, compared with 2% to 3% for most developing nations.

About 70% of the population is Black, descended from West Africans brought to the island to work as slaves on sugar plantations. Another 20% are "Colored" (of mixed Black and White descent), and 4% are White, descendants of both wealthy plantation families and indentured servants from Scotland, Ireland, and Wales (called "redlegs" because many wore kilts that allowed their legs to become sunburned). Most people in Barbados have some admixture of European blood. The remaining 6% of Barbados' population are relatively recent immigrants, many from south Asia and the Middle East.

³ LANGUAGE

English is the official language of Barbados, but it is universally spoken in a dialect strongly influenced by the languages of West Africa. Many words, such as *duppy,* the term for ghost, are derived from African terms, and the African practice of duplicate words ("sow-pig," "bull-cows," "gate-doors") has also been imported into the language. Doubling is used for emphasis ("fast fast" instead of "very fast"), another typical African practice. The present tense of verbs is used to express actions in the past ("She cook dinner last night"). Actions in the present are expressed by the present participle ("He dancing to the music"), while the simple present tense (accompanied by "does") is reserved for habitual actions ("He does dance on Tuesdays").

Common words and expressions in Barbadian and their standard English equivalents are

BARBADIAN	STANDARD ENGLISH
again	now
all two	both
black lead	pencil
cool out	relax
duppy umbrella	mushroom
fingersmith	thief
jump up	dance
nyam or yam	eat
sand side	beach
t'ink	think
yuh	you
break fives	shake hands
tie-goat	married person
hag	bother

⁴ FOLKLORE

Barbados has a rich body of folklore that harks back to the African roots of most of its population. A number of folk beliefs center around ways to keep the ghost of a departed person—known as a *duppy*—from returning to haunt the living. These include sprinkling rum on the ground, walking into the house backwards, and hanging certain herbs from the windows and doorway. Other figures from Barbadian folklore include the *Conrad,* an avenging spirit thought to possess people, making them do and say strange things; the *heartmen,* who kill children and offer their hearts to the devil; and the *baccoo,* a tiny man who lives in bottles and can decide one's destiny.

Some examples of Barbadian proverbs are:

"One-smart dead at two-smart door" (No matter how smart you seem to be, there's always someone who can outwit you).

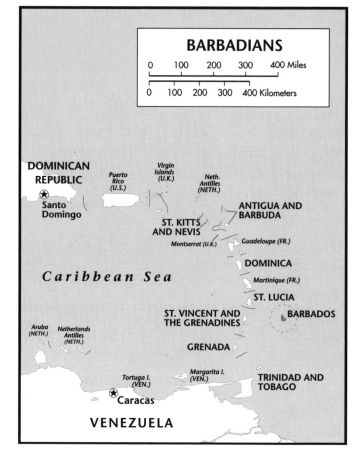

"Coconut don' grow upon pumpkin vine" (Children inherit their parents' characteristics—equivalent of US proverb, "The apple doesn't fall far from the tree").

"Coo-coo never done til de pot turn down" (equivalent to US proverb, "It's never over until it's over" or "It's not over until the fat lady sings").

⁵ RELIGION

Religion plays an important role in the lives of Barbadians. The school day usually begins with a prayer, small revivalist churches abound throughout the island, and there is a one-year waiting list for church choirs who want to perform on the popular Sunday afternoon television program, *Time to Sing,* which features a different group every week. Priests exert some influence over public policy and cultural life (one reason for the absence of casinos from the island), and a substantial amount of radio air time is devoted to religious programming.

The main religion is Christianity. The Anglican church has the most members, a legacy from the days of British rule. Other Christian denominations include Roman Catholic, Methodist, and Jehovah's Witness. Altogether, over 140 different sects and denominations are represented among the island's population. Other religious groups include Hindu, Muslim, and Baha'i. A small Jewish community descended from Sephardic Jews expelled from Spain worships at a synagogue that dates back to 1640. The Jewish synagogue, destroyed in the hurricane of 1830 and rebuilt in 1834, fell into disuse in the early 1900s and was only recently restored with the help of public and government donations. Rastafarianism, which originated in Jamaica, was introduced to Barbados in 1975. After a rocky period when it was associated with rebellious youths and criminals attracted by its cocky image and dreadlocks, it has been accepted by Bajan society and includes among its ranks such well-known figures as actor Winston Farrell and calypso artist Ras Iley.

The Apostolic Spiritual Baptists (popularly known as "Tie-heads") occupy a special place in Barbados' religious spectrum, as the island's only indigenous religion. Fashioned after other West Indian revivalist religions, the sect, founded in 1957 by Bishop Granville Williams, combines Christian observance with the foot stomping, hand clapping, and dancing characteristic of African religious practices. Converts are baptized and then sequestered for 7 to 10 days in the "Mourning Ground," a special area of the church. Tie-heads, so-called because of the cloth turbans worn by both men and women, sport colorful gowns in colors symbolic of particular qualities.

6 MAJOR HOLIDAYS

In addition to the major holidays of the Christian calendar, Barbadian holidays include New Year's Day (1 January), May Day (1 May), CARICOM Day (first Monday in August), Independence Day (30 November), and United Nations Day (first Monday in October). The island's major celebration is the Crop Over festival, which takes place in July and early August. The Barbadian equivalent of Thanksgiving in the United States, it is derived from the traditional festival that marked the sugarcane harvest. Events include the ritual presentation of the Last Canes and the judging of costumed groups (called "bands") on Kadooment Day (1 August), the climax of the festival. The festivities include calypso music and abundant food.

7 RITES OF PASSAGE

Couples often engage in "visiting" relationships, in which the man visits the woman at her home, or common-law marriages, recognized after five years of cohabitation, both of which are similar in their rights and conditions to legal marriages. Major life events (birth, puberty, marriage, death, etc.) are marked by the religious ceremonies particular to each Bahamian's faith community.

8 INTERPERSONAL RELATIONS

Barbadians are known for their politeness and civility, a legacy both of British influence and of the island's high population density—living in close proximity to others imposes pressure to avoid censure and unpleasant confrontations. Describing his homeland, well-known Barbadian author John Wickham wrote, "The inability of people to remove themselves from one another has led to concern for public order, a compassion for others, and a compelling sense of a neighbor's rights and integrity."

9 LIVING CONDITIONS

The standard of living on Barbados is among the highest in the Caribbean. In 1995 its annual per capita income was US$7,000 (The Bahamas had the third-highest per capita income of an independent country in the new world—US$12,000.) The United Nations' 1993 Human Development Report rated the quality of life on Barbados—based on such factors as health,

education, and earning power—first among all developing nations worldwide for the third consecutive year. The island even came out ahead of such industrialized countries as Ireland, Italy, and Spain. Over 75% of Barbadians own their own homes, and 34% own cars. Approximately 94% of the households on Barbados have running water, 85% have televisions, the same percentage have refrigerators, and 68% have telephones. In Bridgetown, the nation's capital, conditions are crowded, but there are no shantytowns or squatter camps, and few people go homeless.

The traditional Barbadian wooden house, which can still be seen throughout the island, is called a "chattel" house. A single-story structure built from a single layer of planks, it boasts a unique feature—portability. It can be taken apart and moved to another location, traditionally when its owner is evicted by the landlord or saves enough money to buy his or her own plot of land elsewhere. The house is usually symmetrical, with a door in the center and windows to either side. The traditional roof of wooden shingles has given way to sheets of galvanized iron that create uncomfortably hot conditions within.

The newer type of house, and the one favored by Barbadians today, is the suburban "wall" house built of cement blocks and stucco, so-called because it is usually surrounded by a small cement wall. By economic necessity, the wall house, like its wooden predecessor, is often built in stages. Just as second and even third structures were often added to the chattel house ("two-roof house and shed"), the wall house may consist of cement block additions added to a wooden home, one room at a time.

The excellent health care system developed on Barbados in the postwar period has reduced the incidence of infectious disease and improved the overall health of the population significantly. It consists of a modern 600-bed hospital and a network of polyclinics and specialized hospitals throughout the island. Average life expectancy is 72.9 years for males and 77.2 for females. In the past 20 years, the infant mortality rate has declined from 45 deaths per 1,000 births to approximately 10 deaths (less than half that of New York's Harlem neighborhood). In addition to modern medicine, many Barbadians still rely on folk medicine and use home remedies either as a supplement or as an alternative to conventional treatment.

Barbados' small size and flat terrain have facilitated travel, and it is possible to get to any point on the island quickly and easily, a fact that has enabled many rural dwellers to commute to urban jobs. However, the traffic congestion accompanying Barbados' growing prosperity has strained the narrow, winding roads of Bridgetown, a city founded in 1628.

10 FAMILY LIFE

Many Barbadian households are based on arrangements other than that of a legally married couple living together with their children—this is a legacy of slavery, which often separated men from women and from their children, as well as the traditional shortage of males on the island due to emigration.

Since male commitment to women is often tenuous, a woman's economic survival is closely connected to her children. When they are young, child support from their father is an important—and sometimes even the sole—source of income. As the children grow older, they begin to help out with chores and finances, and they are a woman's main source of support in

Educational opportunities on Barbados have expanded greatly since World War II, and the country boasts a literacy rate of between 95% and 100%, the highest in the Caribbean. (Barbados Tourism Authority)

old age. Grandmothers play an important role in child-rearing, often taking care of the children so that the mother can work.

Having gained increased power since the 1960s due to better educational and job opportunities, women have been freed from some of their traditional dependence on childbearing and have become more empowered in their domestic relationships with men. Today, common-law marriages are legally recognized after five years, and each partner is entitled to half the joint property.

11 CLOTHING

Barbadians wear modern Western-style clothing in casual, business, and formal situations. Colorful and inventive costumes may be seen at festivals, especially the Crop Over celebration in July and August. Members of the Apostolic Spiritual Baptist sect (popularly known as "Tie-heads") are known for their turbans—worn by both men and women—and their colorful gowns.

12 FOOD

Generations of Barbadian cooks have triumphed over the island's limited selection of produce—as well as the Barbadian's traditionally limited budget—to create a rich culinary tradition that draws on West African, English, Spanish, French, and other types of cuisine. *Cou-cou,* one of the most popular

national dishes, is a cornmeal and okra pudding related to the African *foo-foo.* It is typically served with gravy and salt cod, another dietary staple. Another favorite food is flying fish, a locally abundant species. These fish are served fried, steamed, or baked using a special Barbadian seasoning that combines onion, garlic, pepper, thyme, paprika, lime juice, and other flavors.

Rice served with any of a variety of peas (including green, blackeye, cow, and gunga) is another dietary staple. The variety of ways pork is used to supplement the islanders' diet has inspired the claim that the only part of a pig Barbadians can't use for some dish is its hair. The most famous pork dish is pudding and souse. A black pudding made from sweet potatoes and pig's blood, stuffed into cleaned pig's intestines and boiled, is sliced and served with "souse," made from cooked pig meat pickled in lime juice and hot peppers and served with onions, cucumbers, and peppers.

Popular beverages include coconut water, lemonade with fresh limes, and drinks made from such fruits as mangoes, guavas, gooseberries, tamarinds, and passion fruit. *Mauby* is a beverage made from the bark of a tree. *Falernum* is an indigenous liqueur made from lime juice, sugar, rum, and water, flavored with almond extract. A favorite dessert is coconut bread, which may be prepared using the following recipe:

Coconut Bread

6 oz brown sugar	2 tsp almond extract
6 oz shortening	¼ lb raisins or mixed fruit
1 large egg	1 cup milk
3 cups grated coconut	1¼ lbs flour
1 tsp powdered cinnamon	½ tsp salt
1 tsp powdered nutmeg	3 tsp baking powder

Combine shortening and sugar. After beating the egg, add it in and mix thoroughly. Next, mix in the spices, almond extract, fruit or raisins, grated coconut, and milk. After sifting, mix in the dry ingredients and pour the dough into two greased loaf pans—a 1-lb pan and a 2-lb pan. Preheat oven to 350°F and bake loaves for one hour, or until browned. Cool on racks before serving.

13 EDUCATION

Educational opportunities on Barbados have expanded greatly since World War II, and the country boasts a literacy rate of between 95% and 100%, the highest in the Caribbean. One of the strongest values typically imparted by the Barbadian family is the importance of academic achievement, and 85% of young people between the ages of 11 and 17 are enrolled in school. Attendance is legally required between the ages of 5 and 16, and all education is free, including college.

Students are tracked into classes based on standardized test scores, so many travel great distances to schools located far from their homes. Thousands of children can be seen at bus terminals throughout the country every day on their way to or from school. However, new zoning was introduced in the 1990s to ameliorate the situation.

Thanks to movements aimed at giving recognition to the Barbadians' African heritage, children are now exposed to African folklore and music in the schools. A branch of the University of the West Indies was opened on Barbados in 1963, and other institutions of higher learning include Barbados

Community College, the Samuel Jackman Prescod Polytechnic, the Codrington College Seminary, Barbados Institute of Management and Productivity, and Erdiston Teachers Training College.

14 CULTURAL HERITAGE

Although Barbados has a long oral storytelling tradition, written literature by Barbadians received its first real debut in the 1940s and 1950s in a Barbadian literary magazine called *Bim,* which was the first showcase of works by a number of Caribbean writers destined for future fame, including Derek Wolcott, the 1992 Nobel laureate in literature, who was born in St. Lucia but has spent a large portion of his time in Trinidad. Well-known Barbadian writers include essayist John Wickham, novelist George Lamming (best known for *In the Castle of My Skin*), and poet Edward Kamau Braithwaite, winner of the 1994 Neustadt International Prize for Literature and a professor of Comparative Literature at New York University.

Barbados has a flourishing community of artists producing paintings, murals, sculptures, and crafts, many of which reflect strong African influences. The arts on Barbados have been supported since the mid-1950s by the Barbados National Arts Council, and tourism has provided many local artists, especially musicians, with patrons.

15 WORK

Most Barbadians belong to a large middle class that includes both skilled blue-collar workers and white-collar professional and managerial employees. The labor force contains an equal number of men and women. About 40% of employment on Barbados is in service-sector jobs (about 20% in government), while commerce accounts for about 14%; manufacturing, 10%; construction, 9%; agriculture, 3.5%; and other sectors account for the rest. Unemployment in 1995 stood at 16.4%.

16 SPORTS

Cricket is by far the most popular sport on Barbados—some have called it a "national religion." When the nation gained its independence in 1966, it immediately challenged the rest of the world to a cricket match. Most of Barbados' national heroes are cricket stars, such as Sir Everton Weekes, Sir Clyde Walcott, Sir Frank Worrell, and Sir Garfield Sobers, recognized as the greatest all-around cricketeer of all time. The effigy of Sir Frank Worrell adorns the island's five-dollar currency note. Other popular sports include horse-racing, soccer, hockey, rugby, volleyball, and softball. The local game of road tennis, played with a homemade wooden paddle and a long piece of wood for a "net," is a cross between ping-pong and lawn tennis.

17 ENTERTAINMENT AND RECREATION

The traditional locale where Barbadian men spend their leisure time is the rum shop, which combines the functions of grocery store, bar, and domino parlor. The island has one rum shop for every 150 adults. Women have traditionally gravitated toward the local church as a social center. Dance, music, and theater are all popular pursuits, and about 80% of Barbadian households now have television sets.

18 FOLK ART, CRAFTS, AND HOBBIES

In additional to the popular calypso, reggae, and steel band music that reflects the influence of neighboring Trinidad and Jamaica, Barbados has its own indigenous musical tradition, the *tuk* band, which provides the backbeat for all major celebrations on the island. Composed of pennywhistles, snare drums, and bass drums, it is reminiscent of a British military band, but with a distinctly African flair.

Barbadian crafts include pottery, mahogany items, and jewelry. The Barbados Investment and Development Corporation (BIDC) supports the preservation of the island's handicrafts by running numerous shops where local craftspeople sell their wares, as well as offering workshops for beginners and experts alike.

19 SOCIAL PROBLEMS

Some observers have seen a connection between the growth of tourism on Barbados and the rise of such problems as crime, drug use, and prostitution. In addition, tourism has contributed to water pollution and damage to the island's coral reefs, as well as overly rapid development of the coastline. A more traditional indigenous problem is family violence, which has decreased dramatically within the span of a single generation as women have become empowered by increased educational and employment opportunities, and their economic dependence on men has decreased.

20 BIBLIOGRAPHY

Beckles, Hilary. *A History of Barbados: From Amerindian Settlement to Nation-State.* New York: Cambridge University Press, 1990.

Brathwaite, Farley, ed. *The Elderly in Barbados.* Bridgetown: Carib Research and Publications, 1986.

Dann, Graham. *The Quality of Life in Barbados.* London: Macmillan, 1984.

Gmelch, George. *Double Passage: The Live of Caribbean Migrants Abroad and Back Home.* Ann Arbor: University of Michigan Press, 1992.

Handwerker, W. Penn. "Barbadians." In *Encyclopedia of World Cultures (Middle America and the Caribbean).* Boston: G. K. Hall, 1992.

Meditz, Sandra W., and Dennis M. Hanratty. *Islands of the Caribbean Commonwealth: A Regional Study.* Washington, DC: US Government, 1989.

Pariser, Harry S. *Adventure Guide to Barbados.* Edison, NJ: Hunter Publishing, 1995.

Potter, Robert B. *Barbados.* Santa Barbara, CA: Clio Press, 1987.

Walton, Chelle Koster. *Caribbean Ways: A Cultural Guide.* Westwood, MA: Riverdale, 1993.

Wilder, Rachel, ed. *Insight Guides: Barbados.* Boston: Houghton Mifflin, 1995.

—reviewed by C. N. Blackman

BELIZEANS

LOCATION: Belize
POPULATION: Over 200,000
LANGUAGE: English; Spanish; local Creole
RELIGION: Roman Catholicism (62%); various Protestant denominations (30%); evangelical groups such as Pentecostals, Jehovah's Witnesses, and Seventh-Day Adventists; Mennonites; Mormons; Baha'is

¹ INTRODUCTION

Mayan Indians built several major centers within what is now Belize in the 1st millennium AD. At 42 m (138 ft), the Sky Palace pyramid at Caracol is still the nation's tallest handbuilt structure. Probably at least 400,000 people inhabited the Belize area around AD 900—twice as many as today. Mayan civilization had collapsed by the time Spanish expeditions reached the area in the 16th century, and diseases like smallpox and yellow fever took a heavy toll on the remaining population.

While the Spanish were able, at times, to control the western part of present-day Belize, English buccaneers used the eastern, Caribbean side as a base for their raids and for cutting logwood, which was used in the production of a dye needed by the woolen industry. Mahogany later supplanted logwood as the major export. British settlers forcibly brought in slaves from Africa to do the work. Before slavery ended in 1838, two other groups had made their presence: free Creoles of mixed African and European blood, and Garifuna, descendants of Africans and Carib Indians. Soon after, more Maya began fleeing into the colony to escape a war in the Yucatan and forced labor in Guatemala. Even so, the colony of British Honduras, established in 1862, had only 37,000 inhabitants in 1901.

British Honduras became the independent Republic of Belize in 1981. Mexico and Guatemala had inherited Spain's claim to the territory, but Mexico dropped its claim in 1893. Guatemala never formally renounced its claim but established full diplomatic relations with Belize in 1991.

² LOCATION AND HOMELAND

Belize is a little larger than the US state of Massachusetts. It is bordered on the north by Mexico, on the west and south by Guatemala, and on the east by the Caribbean Sea. It is flat and swampy along the coast and mostly level in the north. The southern part has mountains reaching a high point of 1,177 m (3,861 ft). Belize's climate is warm and humid. There are 17 rivers. The longest barrier reef in the Americas (about 290 km or 180 mi) runs parallel to its coastline.

More thinly settled than anywhere else in Central America, Belize had a population of only slightly more than 200,000 in the mid-1990s. Creoles, of mixed African and European ancestry, had been the largest group, but the 1991 census showed that they accounted for only 30% of the population. Mestizos, of Indian and European descent, came to 44%. Another 15% were Mayan Indians. The Garifuna, or Black Caribs, descended from escaped African slaves and Carib Indians from St. Vincent and Dominica, came to 7%. There were also East Indians (descended from immigrants from present-day India), Arabs, Chinese, and about 6,000 Mennonites from Mexico and Canada.

About 40,000 Mestizos were recent immigrants who either fled fighting in Guatemala and El Salvador during the 1980s or came to Belize seeking work or land to farm. As many as 65,000 Belizeans were living in the United States in the late 1980s. Most of them were Creole or Garifuna.

³ LANGUAGE

English is the only official language in Belize and the only language of instruction in the public schools. The 1991 census found that at least 80% of the population could speak some English or Belizean Creole, which is a dialect of English difficult for outsiders to understand. For 33% to 50% of the population, English or Creole was the first language, but many of these people could not speak standard English well. Spanish was spoken by about 60% of the people and was the first language of 33% to 50% of the population. Smaller numbers spoke Mayan languages or Garifuna as their first language, and the Mennonites spoke Low German as their language. Perhaps 33% of the population can speak two or even three languages.

⁴ FOLKLORE

Belizean folklore is a combination of European, African, and Maya beliefs. Creoles speak of a phantom pirate ship seen at night, its rigging lit by flickering lanterns. It is credited with luring sailors to destruction on the treacherous coastal coral reef. "Greasy Man" lives in abandoned houses, and "Ashi de Pompi" resides in the ashes of burnt houses. They come out at night to frighten people. *Sisimito* or *Sisemite* are great hairy creatures that carry women off to mate. They are impossible to track because they can reverse the position of their feet to heelfirst, making it appear that they are walking in the opposite direction.

Of Mayan origin is a belief in four-fingered "little people" of the jungle, the *duende*. When encountered in the jungle they must be given a four-fingered salute, hiding the thumb. The duende can cause disease, but placing gourds of food for them in a doorway will prevent an epidemic. They can capture people and drive them mad, but they can also grant wishes and confer the gift of mastering a musical instrument instantly. Xtabay is a lovely maiden who leads men astray in the forest. Also of Mayan origin is the belief that Saturdays and Mondays are lucky, while Tuesdays and Fridays are unlucky.

Many Creoles and Garifuna believe in *obeah,* or witchcraft. Great harm can be caused by a black doll made from a stocking stuffed with feathers from a dark fowl and buried under the victim's doorstep. Shoes are frequently crossed at bedtime to keep evil spirits from occupying them during the night. A certain species of black butterfly is said to bring early death or at least bad luck to its beholder. To ward off the evil eye, the Garifuna paint an indigo cross on the forehead of an infant.

⁵ RELIGION

In 1993, 62% of the Belizean people were Roman Catholic, while 30% belonged to various Protestant denominations, including the Anglicans (12%) and Methodists (6%). Evangelical groups like Pentecostals, Jehovah's Witnesses, and Seventh-Day Adventists have been gaining on the mainstream Protestant denominations. Other religious groups include Mennonites, Mormons, and Baha'is.

⁶MAJOR HOLIDAYS

St. George's Caye Day, on 10 September, originally celebrated a British victory over the Spanish. It now commemorates local heroes and is celebrated with parades, patriotic speeches, and a pageant. Independence Day is celebrated on 21 September. Both days are occasions in Belize City for street parades, floats, and block parties. The birthday of Queen Elizabeth II, 21 April, is also a national holiday, as is Commonwealth Day, 24 May, and Columbus Day, 12 October. Garifuna Settlement Day is on 19 November, commemorating the day in 1832 on which a large number of their community reached Belize from Honduras in dugout canoes. The Garifuna also hold a New Year's celebration, called Yancanú, from 25 December through 6 January. It is named for a Jamaican folk hero, "John Canoe."

San José Succotz has fiestas on 19 March and 3 May. In the south there are traditional fiestas in San Antonio around 17 January and in San Pedro towards the end of June. These fiestas resemble their counterparts in Guatemala.

⁷RITES OF PASSAGE

Mestizo and Maya customs are similar to those of their counterparts in Guatemala and Mexico's Yucatan Peninsula. Garifuna infants are baptized at the first opportunity. They have already been bathed ritually on their ninth day of age in water steeped with various herbs and leaves. Godfathers are more important than godmothers. Young children are generally indulged, but some are sent to live with another family, usually of a higher economic and social position, in order to obtain an education. Sometimes the Catholic Church acts as the caretaker for such children.

A death in the Creole community is observed with an evening wake in the home of the deceased. Guests bring gifts and take refreshments while praying, singing, dancing, and playing games. Burial is usually the next day. A second wake is held nine days later. Although Catholic, the Garifuna also have a deep belief in the power of the *gudiba*, deceased ancestors, who are honored.

⁸INTERPERSONAL RELATIONS

Greetings, gestures, body language, visiting customs, and dating among Mestizos and Maya are similar to the customs observed by their counterparts in Guatemala and the Yucatan. Creoles carry Old-World courtesy to the point of being reluctant to declare a negative; thus "maybe" or "possibly" usually means "no." Young people often meet at public dances, but Creole or "Spanish" (Mestizo or Maya) girls are rarely allowed to attend unless there is a special occasion.

⁹LIVING CONDITIONS

In dollar terms, the national income per person of Belizeans is among the highest in Central America, but the cost of living is also high because so many goods must be imported into this small nation. In the early 1990s, about 60% of all children under three years of age suffered some form of malnutrition. Poor sanitation in rural areas contributed to a high incidence of intestinal parasites, especially among children. Malaria remained the leading health problem, and dengue fever, also carried by mosquitoes, staged a comeback in the 1980s. There were fewer than 100 physicians in Belize in the late 1980s.

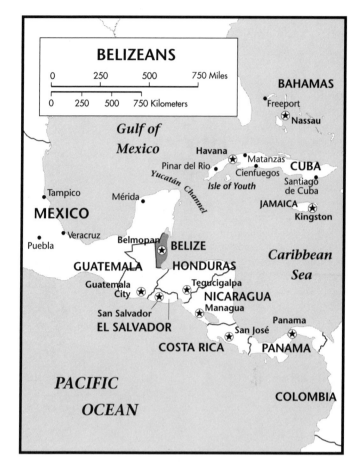

The 1980 census found that 70% of Belizean houses were made of wood, 12% of concrete, and 7% of adobe. Creoles generally live in white painted clapboard bungalows, often on stilts and with corrugated-iron roofs. Outside the towns, most Garifuna live in two-room oblong frame houses with palm thatch or iron roofs and leveled mud floors. The kitchen is a separate building of similar construction. Yucatecan Maya mostly live in huts of plastered limestone or palmetto trunks with steep thatched roofs, while the Kekchí Maya have houses of rough-hewn planks topped with palm thatch. In Belize City, elite families live in oceanfront neighborhoods.

¹⁰FAMILY LIFE

For many ethnic groups and for the lower class generally, a formal marriage ceremony is not necessary, but wider kinship ties are in place, including close links to grandparents, aunts and uncles, and nephews and nieces. Marriage between members of different groups has been widespread. The average number of births per Belizean woman who had completed her childbearing years, as measured in 1991, was 4.5 children. Many lower-class households in Belize City are headed by single parents, usually women.

¹¹CLOTHING

The business dress for men is a short-sleeved cotton or poplin shirt and trousers of tropical-weight material. Ties are seldom worn. Women generally wear simple cotton dresses.

The average number of births per Belizean woman who had completed her childbearing years, as measured in 1991, was 4.5 children. (Mary A. Dempsey)

12 FOOD

The midday meal is the main one; Creoles call dinner "tea." For Mestizos and Mayans, the diet is much like that of Guatemala, with corn tortillas and beans as the staple foods. In the interior, wild-game dishes like roast armadillo and roast paca have a Yucatecan flavor. Among Creoles, rice and red kidney beans are the staples, often accompanied by fried bananas or plantains. The Creoles and Garifuna consume lots of fish, usually boiling or stewing it in coconut milk or frying it in coconut oil. The Garifuna also make fiery-hot cassava fritters from a gruel prepared by cooking and crushing cassava in coconut milk. Another Garifuna dish is *hudut,* a stew composed of pounded plantains, fish, and coconut milk. *Nanche* is a sweet liqueur made from crabou fruit. Many Belizeans mix the local rums with condensed milk.

13 EDUCATION

Belize has, by Central American standards, an enviable educational record. More than 90% of all adults can read and write. Education is free and compulsory between the ages of 6 and 14. In 1992, 96% of all primary-school-age children were in school. However, only 36% of secondary-school-age children were in school. A joint partnership of government and churches manages the school system. The University College of Belize was established in the 1980s. Other institutions of higher learn-

ing are Belize Teachers' College, Belize School of Nursing, and Belize College of Agriculture.

14 CULTURAL HERITAGE

Among Mestizos, marimba music is popular. A marimba ensemble is made up of half a dozen men playing two large wooden marimbas, which resemble xylophones, perhaps supported by a double bass and a drum kit. The nation's top marimba group in the early 1990s was Alma Belicena. Mexican-style mariachi music is also heard.

Brukdown is the name given to Creole music played by guitar, banjo, accordion, steel drums, and the jawbone of an ass. It is accompanied by lyrics that often express social satire. Calypso is sometimes heard but has largely been displaced by reggae. *Cungo* is an offshoot of reggae. In the 1980s, Garifuna players made "punta rock" the rage throughout the nation. Its instrumentation includes maracas, drums, and turtle shells. Merengue, salsa, punk, and rap are also popular.

The Yancanu festival of the Garifuna begins with the blowing of a conch shell at midnight on Christmas Eve. Anywhere from 6 to 12 dancers—usually men only—perform in bright long-sleeved shirts, kiltlike skirts, and knee-length stockings, also wearing masks. Strings of seashells make rustling noises as they dance and sing, accompanied by a group of four drummers who keep time with the palm of the hand. Among Creoles, the *punta* is a wake dance in which a couple occupies the center of a ring formed by hand-clapping and chanting onlookers, accompanied by the beat of a drum. Maya dances are still performed at fiestas held in the south and west of the country.

Among Belizean painters are Manuel Carrero and Manuel Villamer, and among sculptors, George Gabb and Frank Lizama. Writers include Zee Edgell, Zoila Ellis, Felicia Hernandez, Sharon Matola, Yasser Musa, Kiren Shoman, and Simone Waight.

15 WORK

Although there is a serious labor shortage, the unemployment rate was about 15% in the early 1990s, and the rate was over 40% for youths who had dropped out of school. Many Creoles seek higher-paying work abroad and send remittances home to their families. Garifuna men often venture from their communities for seasonal work, then return to their villages. The labor shortage has been eased by large numbers of migrants from Central America. In 1994 the minimum wage was $1.12 an hour, but only $0.87 for domestic workers. The normal work week, by law, was no more than six days and 45 hours.

Women experience an unemployment rate 2½ times higher than men. Jobs available to women typically have low status and wages, and few women are in top managerial positions. The law mandates equal pay for equal work, but women often are underpaid for work similar to that performed by men.

16 SPORTS

Soccer is the most popular sport, closely followed by basketball. Baseball and softball are also played. There are a number of horse-racing meets around New Year's, and bicycle races are held. Other sports include polo and boxing.

17 ENTERTAINMENT AND RECREATION

Among Creoles, all national celebrations are accompanied by open-air dancing, called "jump-up." Almost all villages, particularly those along the Caribbean coast, have their own discos, playing Afro-Caribbean music. There are only two or three cinemas, which mainly show films imported directly from the United States. Dish antennas now receive and rebroadcast more than 50 television channels via satellite signals, offering fare such as CNN News from Atlanta, Cubs baseball games from Chicago, and Spanish-language *telenovelas* (soap operas) from Venezuela.

18 FOLK ART, CRAFTS, AND HOBBIES

Souvenirs like straw baskets and carvings in wood, slate, and stone can be found at the National Handicrafts Center in Belize City. Jewelry is made from black coral.

19 SOCIAL PROBLEMS

The migration of "Spanish" from Hispanic Central America into Belize is a cause of social tension in what has been until recently a prevalently English-speaking Creole society. A "brain-drain" of educated Creoles taking up residence in the United States has exacerbated the situation. Petty crime is rife in Belize City, and youth gangs have established a foothold there. Imported crack and powdered cocaine can now be found, in addition to a plentiful supply of marijuana. About half the rural population does not have access to pure water. The barrier reef and its marine life are threatened by water pollution, coral removal, and spearfishing.

20 BIBLIOGRAPHY

Setzekorn, William D. *Formerly British Honduras: A Profile of the New Nation of Belize*. Rev. ed. Athens, Ohio: Ohio University Press, 1981.

Taylor, Douglas MacRae. *The Black Carib of British Honduras*. New York: Wenner-Gren Foundation for Anthropological Research, 1951.

Whatmore, Mark, and Peter Eltringham. *Guatemala & Belize: The Rough Guide*. 2nd ed. London: Rough Guides, 1993.

—by R. Halasz

BOLIVIANS

LOCATION: Bolivia
POPULATION: 7 million
LANGUAGE: Spanish; Quechua; Aymara
RELIGION: Roman Catholicism; Protestantism

1 INTRODUCTION

There is evidence that the highlands of Bolivia and some of its jungle areas have been inhabited for thousands of years, well before the arrival of Spanish conquerors in the 15th century. Early Amerindian settlers may have been nomadic hunters at first, while later they established agricultural communities. Evidence of this early period, which lasted until about 1400 BC, includes several ceremonial sites. From this time until about 400 BC, an Amerindian culture known as Chavín developed in parts of Bolivia as well as Peru. It was followed by the Tiahuanaco culture, which lasted until about AD 900. An important site was the ceremonial center of Tiahuanaco on the shores of Lake Titicaca in the highlands of the Bolivian Andes. This civilization was prosperous and highly developed, with excellent road and lake transport systems, irrigation systems, and dramatically beautiful building techniques for its settlements and ceremonial sites. Subsequently, Aymara Indians (probably from the region of Coquimbo in Chile) invaded and settled in Bolivia, and finally the mighty Peruvian Incas extended their empire into the present Bolivian territory at the end of the 15th century.

In the 1530s, Spanish conquerors who had initially begun to explore Peru also extended their forays into Bolivia, which they called Alto Peru. Among these men were Diego de Almagro and Francisco Pizarro. During the Spanish colonial period, Bolivia was part of the Viceroyalty of Peru. The town of La Plata, in the Charcas region, was founded in 1538 and was the seat of the Audiencia de Charcas (the most important legal body of Colonial Alto Peru). The city of La Paz, which is Bolivia's political capital today, was founded by Alonso de Mendoza in 1548. General Antonio José de Sucre, who fought with Simón Bolívar, gained Bolivian independence from Spain in 1825 and established the República of Bolívar in honor of the liberator. The new republic was formed with a senate and a house of representatives.

Bolivia has been a mining country. First, it was famous for its silver mines in Potosí, which provided great riches to the Spanish Crown during the 16th and 17th centuries. Subsequently, it was one of the first providers of tin for the world market. Pitiful conditions for miners led to the establishment of a radical workers' party, the National Revolutionary Movement (MNR), which came to power under President Victor Paz Estenssoro in the 1950s, during whose presidency Bolivia nationalized the mines and underwent agricultural, industrial, and social reforms.

Bolivia was later plagued by a number of military dictatorships, and then by disastrous economic conditions under left-wing president Siles Zuazo. Paz Estenssoro, also a left-wing politician, restored economic stability. In the last two decades Bolivia has achieved political and economic stability. Democratic elections in 1989 brought to power the Revolutionary Left (MIR) candidate, Paz Zamora, and in 1993 Gonzalo

Sánchez de Lozada was elected. Mining, cattle- and sheep-herding, and agriculture are important economic activities, but in recent years the illegal production of coca paste made from coca leaves, which goes into the manufacture of cocaine, has become a major problem and an illegal money-spinner for local drug barons. The government has been running a crop substitution program to persuade peasant farmers to plant other types of crops so that they can earn their livelihood in a more constructive way.

2 LOCATION AND HOMELAND

Bolivia is a landlocked South American country of almost 7 million people, of whom over 50% are Amerindian, speaking mainly Quechua and Aymara as well as Spanish. The remainder are descendants of Spaniards, Mestizos (part Amerindian, part Spanish), and a few other Amerindian groups, some in the rain forest area of the Amazon river basin. Bolivia shares a border to the north and east with Brazil, to the west with Peru, to the southeast with Chile, to the south with Argentina, and to the southeast with Paraguay.

Bolivia has a very diverse climate and territory. In the western part of the country, the Andean Cordillera extends from north to south with some of the highest peaks in South America. The center of the country consists of fertile valleys, and the lowlands extend towards the east to the Amazon rain forest.

3 LANGUAGE

The official language of Bolivia is Spanish, although many Amerindians, as well as others, speak either Quechua, the language spoken originally by the Incas, or Aymara, a language spoken by Amerindians prior to the arrival of the Incas. Most Amerindians speak Spanish as well, although a few peasants in isolated parts of the country do not speak any Spanish.

Spanish names of saints are very popular, as are Catholic names such as Jesús, José and, for girls, María. Many Quechua- and Aymara-speaking people have Amerindian last names and Spanish first names.

4 FOLKLORE

A myth of the early Incas and other Amerindians was that a White, bearded teacher, or the Creator God called Viracocha, had come to teach the Indians and would return. When the Spanish conquerors arrived in the 16th century, the Incas, who by then had extended their empire into Bolivia, mistook the White Spanish conquerors for Viracocha and, perhaps, companions of his. This belief was very widespread and existed even as far away as Mexico, where the Aztecs called this figure Quetzalcoatl, and it contributed to the Spaniards' easy entry into the major Amerindian cities. The Spanish exploited these myths for their own benefit.

5 RELIGION

Most Bolivians are Roman Catholic. However, among the Aymara- and Quechua-speaking Amerindian groups, certain beliefs and rituals remain that stem from local religions which pre-date the Spanish conquest. The respect for nature is embodied in the belief in Mother Earth, known as Pachamama.

Among the Aymara, there is a household god known as Ekeko, a god of prosperity who also presides over matchmaking prior to marriage and helps people without homes. An important fes-

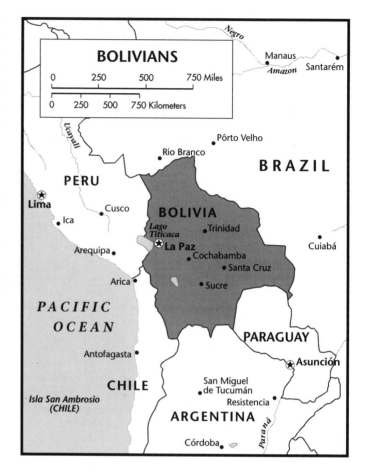

tival in La Paz, Bolivia's mountain capital, called the Alasitas, is principally in honor of Ekeko. The artisans sell miniatures of everything imaginable, and people buy them believing that the things they represent will be plentiful in their homes. *Ekeko* means "dwarf," and he is generally a benevolent god.

6 MAJOR HOLIDAYS

Bolivians, in common with many other Latin Americans, celebrate the main Catholic holidays such as Easter and Christmas, as well as Corpus Christi. They also celebrate Labor Day and their Independence Day on 6 August.

A major festival celebrated in March is Pookhyái, celebrated in the Andean town of Tarabuco in the department of Sucre. It was here that the famous heroine Juana Azurduy made her mark, leading her people against the Spanish in the Battle of Jambati on 12 March 1816, liberating the town. *Pookhyái* is a Quechua word meaning "entertainment," and during the festivities dozens of groups in local costume dance and sing, and the whole town, together with thousands of visitors, takes part in a special Quechua Mass and procession. It is a joyful celebration during which Bolivians give thanks for their freedom as a nation.

Carnival is celebrated throughout Bolivia the week before Lent, and the best-known celebration is the colorful *Entrada* in the town of Oruro. The *Diablada*, one of the most representative dances, has elaborate costumes and masks of the devil. Choreographed as a battle between good and evil, the dancers celebrate the triumph of good, in the person of the Archangel

Young Bolivian woman with llama at Lake Titicaca, Bolivia. Families keep a close watch on their daughters' friends and social contacts. (Anne Kalosh)

Michael, over evil, in the person of Lucifer and his devils. Other groups reenact the Conquest, where the Spanish conquerors such as Francisco Pizarro fight with the Incas. The feasting and dancing last for several days.

⁷ RITES OF PASSAGE
Most children in Bolivia receive the Catholic sacraments of baptism at birth, First Communion at the age of seven, and confirmation at puberty. These ceremonies are regarded as important events by many Bolivian families.

During the teenage years, Bolivian boys and girls are still expected to maintain close ties with their families. The poverty of many Bolivians means that young people work, often from a young age, to supplement the family income.

Many Bolivians marry in church, but they have to have a civil marriage as well. When a person dies, the full religious rites of the Catholic Church are often followed. A priest will often attend a dying person, who may wish to offer a final confession. Among many Indian communities, Catholic and Indian beliefs coexist.

⁸ INTERPERSONAL RELATIONS
A formal greeting will include the words *"mucho gusto,"* which is the equivalent of the English "pleased to meet you."

There is also an informal greeting, *"Qué tal?"* which means, "How are you?" But Bolivians do not stop there. It is also considered polite to inquire about the welfare of other family members, and the greetings can become quite elaborate.

Men shake hands, but it is customary among urban men and women to greet each other with a kiss.

Visits are considered an important form of social communication and can take a number of forms: many religious festivals and important family events are occasions for reunions of family and friends. When people visit, it is customary to offer a small cup of black coffee. A pre-Columbian drink that still exists in the Andean region is *chicha.* Made from fermented corn, it is consumed by people in towns and villages.

Bolivian society is divided by marked classes which do not mix easily. In some small cities they are still very traditional when it comes to dating. Families keep a close watch on their daughters' friends and social contacts. In many places, girls are not expected to date boys who are unknown to their parents. The parents will inquire about the boy's family or may already know his family. A girl is not expected to date boys outside an approved social circle. Many people marry when they are still quite young, and the custom of having a *novio* or steady boyfriend in a serious relationship is seen as appropriate for a girl.

⁹ LIVING CONDITIONS
Bolivia is one of the poorest countries of the Americas, and the people's health suffers accordingly. A serious disease called *chagas,* carried by the bite of the vinchuca beetle, which is particularly prevalent in the rural lowlands, has no known cure and eventually affects the heart. One estimate suggests that as many as a quarter of Bolivians are affected by this disease, although precise figures are not obtainable.

Many Bolivians, particularly in some of the Indian communities in rural areas, live outside of the cash economy altogether. They lead a sustainable, simple lifestyle. In the major cities, such as La Paz, which is the capital, or Cochabamba or Sucre—the legal capital, a more modern lifestyle prevails that is similar to that in major towns in other parts of Latin America.

Housing in the countryside often involves simple huts of adobe with thatched roofs. In the towns and cities, brick and cement are used, and often red tiles are used for roofs in the traditional Spanish manner.

Many people who do not have access to a car use buses and trucks for local and intertown travel. Pack animals are used in the more-remote highland areas. Practically all towns are connected by extensive bus routes.

¹⁰ FAMILY LIFE
Women in one sense have a lower status than men in Bolivia, yet in another sense they are at the center of family life and are regarded as very important in their role as mother, wife, and member of the extended family unit. In the lower classes, women are the economic support of the families. Since colonial times, Indian women have taken part in the commercial activities in the country.

Although the trend is changing, families have traditionally been quite large in Bolivia: six or seven children is not uncommon. Families do not consist only of a father, a mother, and their children, but include many relatives such as grandparents, aunts, uncles, and cousins. The traditional extended family is the main social support system in Bolivia.

11 CLOTHING

In the cities, men wear trousers and shirts, or suits, and women wear skirts and blouses or dresses. Bolivian Indian women wear voluminous skirts, shawls, and bowler-shaped hats. This manner of dressing is a hybrid form, since it derives from old Spanish fashion. Men in the countryside often wear *ponchos,* which are derived from the Spanish cape, particularly in the cooler climate of the Andean highlands, where they are woven from wool and serve to keep out the cold mountain winds. In the countryside many Indians maintain their traditional, distinctive ethnic clothing.

12 FOOD

The bedrock of the Bolivian diet in the Andean highlands or altiplano is the potato, and many poorer people in this region eat a mainly carbohydrate-based diet. Main meals in the major towns include some meat, but there is also rice, quite often served with potatoes as well as some salad or vegetables. Visitors to Bolivia do not necessarily share the preference for plain and filling food. Instead they enjoy, as many Bolivians do, some of the tasty snacks.

One of these is the turnover or *empanada,* which varies from country to country in Latin America. The flour used to make the turnovers is made from wheat. Empanadas, which are shaped like half moons and are often fluted at the edges, are fried or sometimes baked. The imaginative aspects relate to the wide variety of fillings, which include chicken, cheese, and beef. A typical midmorning Bolivian snack is the *salteña,* a spicy round chicken, meat, or vegetable pie stuffed with olives, onions, hard-boiled eggs, and other ingredients.

In La Paz, the Bolivian capital, pieces of beef heart are grilled on skewers. These are known as *anticuchos.* A hot, peppery sauce called *llajua* is often served with meats. In the lowlands and the Amazon region, exotic meats such as alligator, armadillo, and agouti are also eaten, while fine salmon trout from Lake Titicaca is a delicacy.

13 EDUCATION

Primary education is available in principle to all Bolivian children, but it did not really reach the villages until the reforms instituted by the Revolutionary National Movement (MNR) under Victor Paz Estenssoro in the 1950s. Since then, secondary education has also become more accessible. Most Bolivian cities, including La Paz, Cochabamba, and Sucre, have universities, some of which have been in existence for hundreds of years. The largest universities are state-funded and are virtually free. There are also many private universities. The educational reform taking place presently is modernizing the curriculum and requirements from elementary through university levels.

14 CULTURAL HERITAGE

Traditional music in the Bolivian Andes features flutes such as the *quena* and the panpipe, as well as stringed instruments derived from the Spanish guitar called *charangos.* To the untutored Western ear, this music can sound mournful, but attention rewards the listener, who marvels at the skill of the musicians and the range of tones and rhythms often suggestive of majestic mountain heights and the freedom of magnificent birds wheeling joyfully in the sky. Mountain dancing is often demure and suggests a mixture of Amerindian and Spanish courtly influences, whereas in the lowlands and in the Tarija region the music of warmer climates is more exuberant.

Bolivia has many fine churches that date from Spanish colonial times. Among painters who excelled in religious themes is Holguín, whose paintings of the birth of Christ and the birth of the Virgin Mary are displayed in the town of Sucre in the exquisite Church of La Merced, built in 1581.

Among Bolivian writers, one of the best known is Alcides Arguedas, who died in 1946. He was also a sociologist and a diplomat and served for a time as Bolivia's Minister for Agriculture. He dealt with major aspects of Bolivian Indian life, and his novels include *Raza de Bronce* (which translates as "The Bronze Race"), *Vida Criolla, Pisagua,* and *Wata-wara.* Another important modern writer is Augusto Céspedes, who examined the lives of the immensely wealthy Bolivian tin barons in a novel called *El Metal del Diablo* (which means "The Devil's Metal"). Bolivia has produced several excellent poets, among them Ricardo Jaimes Freire at the beginning of the 20th century. Julio de la Vega is exuberant in his *Poemario de exaltaciones.* Jaime Saenz was the first to use superrealism. Oscar Cerruto is a major Bolivian poet, and among current poets one of the best is Pedro Shimose, the son of Japanese immigrants to Bolivia. The essayist Fernando Diez de Medina is also worth mentioning.

The poetry and songs of the Quechua language constitute a significant tradition for Quechua-speakers in Bolivia and Peru alike. In this language are included hymns, prayers, songs of love and war, satirical pieces, epic poems, plays, stories, and songs of mourning. A vivid example of the latter, which actually formed part of the mourning rituals upon the death of the last Inca king, Atahualpa, who was murdered by the Spaniards. can be found in the poem *El Llanto de las Nustas:*

Among Bolivian Indians, who form a significant part of Bolivia's population, it is no exaggeration to say that their history has been one of suffering and loss.

15 WORK

In rural areas, many Bolivians work as farmers on small landholdings. Miners have a long tradition in Bolivia, beginning with the silver mines of the Potosí region during Spanish colonial times and continuing with the tin mines. When there was an international tin crisis in the 1980s, thousands of tin miners were left destitute and, to avoid starvation, many made their way to the lowlands to grow coca leaves for the illegal cocaine industry. The Bolivian government has embarked on a crop substitution program, encouraging other crops, some of which can be exported. Since so many depend for their livelihood on farming, the government has had to adopt a gradual approach to this ongoing problem, which essentially has its roots in drug consumption in developed countries.

In the towns many people are employed in casual labor, as street vendors and hawkers, in the construction industry, as domestic servants, or as plumbers, electricians, or carpenters. There is also a professional middle class; the traditional professions such as law and medicine are still popular, but there are also increasing numbers of engineers and technicians of various types.

16 SPORTS

All kinds of modern sports are played by Bolivian youth. There are interschool athletic competitions, as well as professional basketball, volleyball, and soccer teams. Probably the most popular sport is soccer, and major towns have stadiums filled with enthusiastic crowds during matches. One of the best-known stadiums is the Hernando Siles in La Paz.

17 ENTERTAINMENT AND RECREATION

As in many other Latin American countries, there are many cinemas in Bolivia and people enjoy going to the movies. There are also theaters in most of the main towns. One of the major theaters is the Teatro Municipal in La Paz, where enthusiasts can see both classical and modern plays as well as dance performances and musical events.

In the town of Santa Cruz, there are modern and popular discos to which many young people enjoy going. There are also good discos in La Paz, Cochabamba, and Sucre.

One of the most enjoyable events in Bolivia is Carnival, celebrated everywhere but with interesting variations related to local costumes, dancing, and music.

18 FOLK ART, CRAFTS, AND HOBBIES

One of Bolivia's major crafts is weaving. Most young girls in rural areas learn to weave and spin, and it is thought that this ancient craft has been in existence in Bolivia for thousands of years. Patterns and colors vary according to region; quite often the patterns are either geometric or zoomorphic (depicting animals), while occasionally they show aspects of domestic life. Alpaca and llama wool were used traditionally, but sheep's wool is also used today.

Garments woven in the traditional way include warm and practical ponchos as well colorful hats with long ear-coverings, useful in cold mountain weather, known as *chullos*.

Many interesting musical instruments are made in Bolivia, including the armadillo-backed *charango*—a type of guitar—as well as native violins and a wide variety of woodwind instruments.

19 SOCIAL PROBLEMS

The serious social problems in Bolivia relate to the continuing poverty of so many of its inhabitants. Despite many efforts to eradicate coca production, hundreds of thousands of people are employed in its growth and distribution. Many peasant farmers who are often desperately poor have attempted to grow other types of crops. The crop substitution programs instigated by the Bolivian government offer replacement crops such as coffee and bananas, which are certainly not competitive products and which make earning a decent livelihood difficult for many people.

20 BIBLIOGRAPHY

Jaulin, Robert. *El etnocidio a través de las Américas*. Mexico: Siglo XXI Editores, 1976.

Swaney, Deanna, and Robert Strauss. *Bolivia: A Travel Survival Kit*. 2nd ed. Hawthorn, Australia: Lonely Planet Publications, 1992.

Zalamea, Jorge. *La poesía ignorada y olvidada*. Bogotá: Ediciones La Nueva Prensa, 1965.

—by P. Pitchon

BRAZILIANS

LOCATION: Brazil
POPULATION: 162,661,214
LANGUAGE: Portuguese
RELIGION: Roman Catholicism; Protestantism; Afro-Brazilian religions; other indigenous beliefs

¹ INTRODUCTION

Brazil was colonized by the Portuguese. In colonial times, Brazil played an important role in the world economy, providing nearly 75% of the world's supply of coffee. After independence from Portugal, Brazil underwent a period of economic growth and relative prosperity. A rubber boom led this period of economic growth, which was also fueled by sugar and gold. Brazil has since developed a significant industrial sector and is currently the world's tenth-largest economy. However, serious problems of poverty and inequality remain. This elusive economic development gave rise to the saying, "Brazil is the land of the future—and always will be."

² LOCATION AND HOMELAND

Brazil is a large country, with a landmass equal to that of the continental United States. However, most of Brazil remains sparsely populated. Nearly one-third of Brazil's landmass is taken up by the Amazon basin. Most of the lowland areas in the north and west of Brazil remain populated only by native Amazonian tribes. Major indigenous tribes include the Yanomamo, Xavantae, and the Cayapo. The Amazon rain forest in Brazil is under threat as a result of extensive logging and deforestation. Many indigenous tribes are facing cultural extinction.

The majority of Brazil's population of 162,661,214 people live in the densely populated south and southeast regions, where the major cities of Sao Paulo, Rio de Janeiro, and Belo Hortzante are located. Brazil is an ethnically diverse country. Its population comprises European migrants, descendants of African slaves, and a variety of indigenous ethnic groups. Although Afro-Brazilians play an important cultural role, problems of racial discrimination exist. While Blacks have the same legal rights as Whites, most Blacks live in poverty in the *favelas* or urban slums of Brazil.

³ LANGUAGE

The official language of Brazil is Portuguese. In pre-colonial times, many different indigenous languages were spoken throughout Brazil. At that time the *lingua franca* (the language used by different groups to communicate with each other) was Tupi. Today, Portuguese is the dominant language, but there remain more than 200 tribal groups that speak indigenous languages and dialects.

⁴ FOLKLORE

Each of the various ethnic groups in Brazil has its own tradition of folktales and myths (see **African Brazilians**; **Kayapos**; **Tenetehara**; **Xavante**).

⁵ RELIGION

The beliefs of many Brazilians reflect elements from African, European, and indigenous religions. A wide range of religious traditions and practices coexist in Brazil, from the European religions of Catholicism and Protestantism, to the multitude of spiritual sects of African origin such as *umbanda*.

While many Brazilians claim to be Roman Catholic, these beliefs are often infused by traditional practices. Offerings and gifts are made to saints and protective spirits for favors in this life. Self-sacrifice plays an important role in convincing saints to grant requests. Fervent believers, for example, may crawl on their knees to sites of spiritual significance to demonstrate their faith.

After Catholicism, Afro-Brazilian religions are the most important in Brazilian society. *Umbanda,* for example, is one of the most rapidly growing sects. Attracting both African and non-African Brazilians, Umbanda sects use music, dancing, and sometimes alcohol to reach a trance state that enables believers to communicate with spirits. Also significant is *Condomble* of African origin. Condomble priestesses also seek to communicate with African spirits. Their ceremonies sometimes include the sacrifice of goats and chickens.

⁶ MAJOR HOLIDAYS

Carnival in Brazil is one of the world's most famous festivals. Celebrated for the five days preceding Ash Wednesday (in February), Carnival virtually brings the country to a halt as Brazilians take off work to join street festivals, dance contests, and other festive activities. The major Carnival parade takes place in Rio de Janeiro, with elaborate costumes and floats that are the result of many months' preparation. During Carnival, dance balls and samba contests are held. The festivities last well into the morning hours. While other Latin American countries also celebrate Carnival, only in Brazil is it done on such a grand scale.

⁷ RITES OF PASSAGE

Major life transitions (such as birth, marriage, and death) are marked by ceremonies appropriate to each Brazilian's religious tradition.

⁸ INTERPERSONAL RELATIONS

Brazilians speak animatedly and use a variety of hand gestures for emphasis. For example, when a Brazilian speaker moves his or her fingers under the chin, this means "I don't know." Placing the thumb between the index and middle fingers is a sign of good luck.

Brazilians are accustomed to late-night dinners and parties. Many restaurants in the major cities do not open for dinner until 8:00 or 9:00 pm. The people make up for lost sleep during the afternoon *siesta*. Stores and many businesses close for three or four hours during lunch, and many Brazilians go home and have lunch and a short nap before returning to work.

Not surprisingly, Brazilians are also heavy coffee drinkers. In many city plazas, there are roving street vendors selling sweet espresso to passersby.

⁹ LIVING CONDITIONS

Brazil is a land of contrasts. Its cities combine modern skyscrapers, suburban houses, and impoverished slums. Known as

BRAZILIANS

0   250   500   750 Miles

0   250   500   750 Kilometers

favelas, Brazil's urban slums have been estimated to be home to as many as 25 million people. The inhabitants of the favelas, which are built on hillsides surrounding the major cities, live in desperate poverty. Many of the older houses or shacks in the favelas now have electricity and running water. However, poor sanitation causes serious health problems. There is no garbage collection or sewer access in the favelas. A life of crime is often the only alternative for unemployed youth with no economic opportunities.

In contrast, the upper and middle classes that live relatively near the favelas have a high standard of living. Brazil's major cities are very modern, with large shopping malls, restaurants, and superhighways. There are many luxury high-rise apartment buildings and large houses with all of the amenities one would expect in the United States. Most of the middle- and upper-class families have servants to assist with housework.

There is a diverse range of housing and living conditions in rural areas. The type of housing depends largely on the weather. Adobe, stone, and wood are all used as housing material. In the Amazon, reeds and palm are used to construct houses.

¹⁰ FAMILY LIFE

A family in Brazil generally consists of parents and 5 to 7 children, although some families continue to have as many as 15 children. Both the nuclear and extended families play an important social role. Most socializing (drinking, dining, gambling, etc.) is conducted with members of the extended family. Godparents remain extremely important in rural areas, but their importance may be declining in urban areas. Godparents of a higher economic class are often chosen, as they have the financial means to take care of the child if a problem arises.

Gender differences are clearly marked in Brazilian society, and sexism is an ingrained feature of the culture. Limited educational opportunities, especially for lower-class women, keep females tied to traditional roles. Few middle- and upper-class women work outside the home, although in recent times this number has begun to increase. It is a common custom for middle- and upper-class women to have social "teas" at 4:00 or 5:00 in the afternoon, before returning home for dinner with their husbands.

Female beauty is highly valued, and Brazilian society can be considered to be very flirtatious. It is common for young women to wear short skirts or shorts in an attempt to attract the attention of men. This, however, probably serves to perpetuate machismo among Brazilian men.

Marital infidelity is a serious social problem in Brazil. It is very common for men to take a mistress on a long-term or permanent basis. While this behavior is not completely sanctioned in Brazilian society, it is widespread and is tolerated.

11 CLOTHING

Brazilian dress in urban areas is very modern. Young people wear jeans and skirts, although among women short skirts and dresses are also very common. Business attire is very similar to that worn in the United States, with men wearing suits and ties.

Dress varies more widely outside of urban areas. In the south plains regions near the border with Argentina, the *gaucho* (cowboy) style is still worn. This includes ponchos, wide straw hats, baggy pants known as *bombachas,* and boots. In the Amazon, native Amerindians wear face paint and traditional tunics. In the predominantly Afro-Brazilian region of Bahia, women wear bright, colorful skirts and head scarves.

12 FOOD

Brazilian food reflects the many cultural groups that have settled there. Combining cooking styles and ingredients from the rain forest and the Portuguese and African cultures, Brazil's cuisine is a unique melting pot of influences. The African influences are particularly pronounced in the southeastern region of Bahia, where spicy seafood dishes may be flavored with peanuts, coconut, lime, or other tropical ingredients.

In Brazil it is a longstanding tradition to have *feijoada* for lunch on Saturday afternoons. Considered the national dish, *feijoada* is a stew of black beans with different types of pork—such as sausage, bacon, and salt pork—and an occasional piece of dried beef. A good feijoada, it is claimed, will have a minimum of five cuts of pork. This dish was common among the slaves in Brazil who used discarded cuts of pork, such as the snout, tail, and feet. These cuts are still often used. Feijoada is often accompanied by rice and/or vegetables such as collards or kale.

13 EDUCATION

Brazilian children are required to attend school for a minimum of eight years. In reality, however, a large percentage of the population fail to receive an adequate education. The national literacy rate is 83% for men and 80% for women, although these rates are much lower in some regions. Attendance at the secondary level is low. Brazilian schools are generally underfinanced and overcrowded. In order to cope with the large num-

Man from the Amazon Ayuca region of Brazil. Nearly one-third of Brazil's landmass is taken up by the Amazon basin, and most of northern Brazil remains sparsely populated. (PhotoEdit)

ber of students, children attend classes either in the evening or in the morning.

There are a growing number of universities and technical schools. These higher-level institutions of education, however, tend to be filled by middle- and upper-class students. Places are limited, and entrance exams are very difficult.

14 CULTURAL HERITAGE

Brazil has a wide variety of folk and modern music. Samba is perhaps the most popular and well-known internationally. Samba, however, is but one of Brazil's many rhythms and musical traditions. In the northeast, Portuguese guitar introduced during colonial times is still popular. African dances and percussion endure in Afro-Brazilian culture and are used in religious ceremonies. African influences are strongly felt in modern music as well.

Brazil has been the birthplace of musical forms that have become popular worldwide. In the 1950s, for example, a fusion of American jazz and samba rhythms known as Bossa Nova made international stars of singers such as Sergio Mendes. More recently, the *Lambada* topped the charts in the United States and Europe. The *Lambada* is in fact a version of *carimbo,* a musical tradition of the northern regions with strong Caribbean influences.

A street in Alter do Chão, a remote town along the Amazon River in northern Brazil. The majority of Brazilians, however, live in the densely populated south and southeast regions of Brazil, where the major cities combine modern skyscrapers, suburban houses, and impoverished slums. (Susan D. Rock)

¹⁵ WORK

Brazil's economy is diverse. It has both an extensive raw material and agricultural sector as well as heavy industry and manufacturing. Brazil continues to be the largest coffee exporter in the world, and also produces sugar, soybeans, and corn for the export market. Many people in the northeast work in the sugar plantations and mills, while coffee laborers are found in the south. In addition, harvesting rubber, timber, and nuts provides a way of life for many inhabitants of the Amazon regions.

Of all the South American countries, Brazil has been the most successful in exporting its manufactured products. Brazilian shoes, for example, are now found in stores around the world. Automobiles and steel products are also major exports. While these industries provide formal employment for many, a significant proportion of urban Brazilians rely on small-scale, informal economic activities to survive. Women, for example, might become seamstresses or street vendors. A great many young women from the *favelas* (urban slums) find employment as servants in middle-class homes.

¹⁶ SPORTS

While soccer is popular throughout Latin America, in Brazil it is close to a national obsession. The city of Sao Paulo, for example, has three soccer stadiums which hold matches nearly three times a week. The stadium in Rio de Janeiro is also spec-

tacular. It seats 200,000 people and is the largest stadium in the world. Brazil has won more World Cups than any other country, and its most famous soccer player, Pele, is still a popular and highly regarded figure. It has been suggested that he might run for the presidency.

Volleyball is also very popular. The Brazilian women's volleyball team won the gold medal at the Barcelona Olympics in 1988, defeating Peru in overtime.

¹⁷ ENTERTAINMENT AND RECREATION

In Rio de Janeiro and other seaside cities, the primary form of recreation is the beach. Brazil is the nation with the largest coastline in the world, and this is reflected in Brazilians' love for the beach and sunbathing. People from all social and economic backgrounds flock to the beaches in the summer.

Samba schools are an important source of recreation in the *favelas* (urban slums). More of a community or neighborhood club, samba schools work virtually all year long to prepare for the Carnival festivities. They teach dancing, create costumes, and write songs for the annual Carnival song competition.

Televised soap operas are extremely popular with Brazilians of all social classes. *Telenovelas,* as they are called, are broadcast in the evenings and attract a huge following. These soap operas are not permanently ongoing, but last from a few months up to a year. Brazilian soap operas are so popular that they are successfully exported to other Latin American countries.

18 FOLK ART, CRAFTS, AND HOBBIES

A rich tradition of folk art and handicrafts arises from different regions in Brazil. In the mining region of Minas Gerais, goldsmithing and jewelry are the local art forms. Gemstones such as diamonds, opals, sapphires, and rubies are produced in Brazil. A popular piece of jewelry throughout Brazil is the *figa*. The *figa* is a pendant of a hand with the thumb between the first and index fingers—the symbol of good luck. In areas where ranching predominates, leather goods are made from cattle- and goatskins. Shoes, handbags, and wallets of high quality are also crafted in these regions. In Amazon regions, woven straw baskets, weapons, textiles, and beads are produced by Amerindians.

A unique traditional art form originates from the San Francisco River. This river, once believed to house evil spirits, led 19th-century boaters to carve fierce-looking figureheads, called *carrancas,* on their boats. These carvings of beasts that are half-human and half-animal were thought to provide protection from spirits and ward off bad luck. While most boaters no longer believe in these superstitions, many boaters still carry carrancas.

19 SOCIAL PROBLEMS

A serious social problem in Brazil is the number of homeless children that live on the streets. It has been estimated that as many as 8 to 12 million street children live in desperate poverty. Street children, as young as seven and eight years old, have often been abandoned by parents who are too poor to be able to provide for them. Street children live a dangerous life. Drug abuse and glue-sniffing are serious problems among street children. They are forced to resort to stealing, pickpocketing, and prostitution to survive. Although children have full protection under the law, thousands of street children have been murdered by Brazilian police. Many "death squads" were hired by shop owners who believed that the immense problem of street children could only be solved by eliminating them. In response, many community groups, and the children themselves, have organized to raise awareness of children's rights.

20 BIBLIOGRAPHY

Birnbaum. *Birnbaum's South America 1994*. New York: HarperCollins, 1995.

Devine, Elizabeth, and Nancy L. Braganti. *The Traveler's Guide to Latin American Customs and Manners.* New York: St. Martins Press, 1988.

Rojas-Lombardi, Felipe. *The Traveler's Guide to Latin American Customs and Manners.* New York: St. Martins Press, 1991.

Taylor, Edwin. *Insight Guides: Brazil.* Boston: Houghton Mifflin Company, 1995.

Weel, Thomas E. *Area Handbook for Brazil.* Washington, D.C.: American University: 1975.

—by P. Pitchon

CAJUNS

ALTERNATE NAMES: Acadians; (*Cajuns* is the shortened form)
LOCATION: United States (Louisiana; Texas)
POPULATION: 500,000
LANGUAGE: Cajun French; English
RELIGION: Roman Catholicism, often mixed with old folk beliefs, pagan superstitions, and African spiritual practices
RELATED ARTICLES: Vol. 2: Americans

1 INTRODUCTION

The history of the Cajun people is a tale of persecution, displacement, and the struggle to find a permanent homeland. Cajuns are the descendants of exiles from the early French colony of Acadia in Canada, an area that today comprises Nova Scotia and New Brunswick. ("Cajun" is a shortened form of the word "Acadian.") In 1713, after 150 years of control by France, the area was ceded to the British, who demanded that its French settlers swear allegiance to Britain and renounce their Catholicism. After steadfastly refusing to comply with these demands, the Acadians were driven into forced exile by British soldiers in 1755. Some fled to France or other parts of Canada, others to the Eastern Seaboard of the United States, and still others to the West Indies. Eventually a number of Acadians made their way to Louisiana, which already had a strong French presence although it was then under Spanish rule. In 1765, led by Bernard Andry, a Acadian community was established in the bayous of southern Louisiana, an area that came to be known as Acadiana.

Settled in a land very different from the one they had left, with exposure to varied ethnic groups including Spaniards, Native Americans, and Black Creoles, the Cajuns developed a distinctive culture of their own, living a rural lifestyle and relying on farming, fishing, and cattle raising for subsistence. They lived in relative isolation until the 20th century, when improved transportation and communication as well as compulsory education began to break down the barriers between their communities and the mainstream culture. Recent decades have been marked by concern over the preservation of Cajun ethnicity in the face of increasing cultural assimilation, with a particular focal point being the survival of the Cajun language. Meanwhile, certain aspects of Cajun culture have gained recognition and popularity among the general US population, notably Cajun food and music.

2 LOCATION AND HOMELAND

By 1790, about 4,000 Acadians occupied the wetlands along the banks of the Mississippi River near New Orleans. This area is full of swamps and bayous, which helped provide a safe haven for the persecuted French settlers. As their numbers grew, the Acadians moved west to settle on the Louisiana prairies. A few continued west into the wide open spaces of Texas, where they became cowboys and cattle ranchers. Today, the total number of Cajuns in the United States is estimated to be over 500,000. Modern-day Cajuns do not reject the ways of the larger society, but they do strive to maintain many of the cultural and occupational traditions of their ancestors.

³ LANGUAGE

When the Cajuns first settled in Louisiana, they spoke French. Over time, their language changed as words from German, Spanish, English, and various Indian languages were added to the original French of colonial times to form what is today known as Cajun French, an oral language that does not appear in any written form. In addition to words from other languages, Cajun French is distinguished from standard French by its simplified grammar and use of some archaic forms of pronunciation retained from the 17th century. Today, Cajun French is in decline, and English is spoken in many Cajun homes as well as in public places, although often with a French accent. It is not unusual to find younger Cajuns who speak only English, while older Cajuns tend to speak Cajun French among themselves.

⁴ FOLKLORE

The most important Cajun folk figure is the heroine of Henry Wadsworth Longfellow's poem, "Evangeline." The poem tells the story of how the Acadians were driven out of Canada and wandered for years before reaching their new home in Louisiana. In the poem, Evangeline is separated from her lover, who finally gives her up for dead and marries someone else. When Evangeline reappears and discovers what has happened, she kills herself. Another famous Cajun folk figure is Jean Lafitte, a Cajun adventurer who became both a notorious pirate and a prominent political figure and entered the realm of legend.

⁵ RELIGION

Most Cajuns are members of the Roman Catholic Church. However, since their arrival in Louisiana, their Catholic beliefs have become mixed with a host of other influences, from old folk beliefs and pagan superstitions dating back to the culture of pre-Christian Europe to African spiritual practices transmitted to them by African slaves and their descendants who migrated to Louisiana from the West Indies during the 1800s.

⁶ MAJOR HOLIDAYS

Cajuns celebrate all the major religious holidays that are celebrated by Christians the world over. But for Cajuns, the most important by far is Mardi Gras, a time of celebration which precedes Lent. Cajun Mardi Gras is a much more purposeful celebration than the enormous New Orleans street party that most people associate with the festival. During Cajun Mardi Gras, masked riders go from house to house within the Cajun community urging those inside to come out, join in the fun, and make a contribution of food and drink to the community celebration. This tradition is a time of fun and fellowship for Cajuns, but, more important, it is a way of ensuring that all those in the community have enough food to last until the end of summer, when the new crops can be harvested. The demand that each household contribute to the celebration is actually a way of checking to make sure that every household has enough food to allow it to give some away. Any household that is unable to contribute to the Mardi Gras is likely to be in need of some assistance from the group.

⁷ RITES OF PASSAGE

Major life events, including birth, marriage, and death, are marked by rituals within the Roman Catholic Church.

⁸ INTERPERSONAL RELATIONS

The Cajuns are an extremely close-knit group and have maintained their unity and their culture by emphasizing loyalty and cooperation. When a member of the community is in need, others give freely, knowing that their goodwill and generosity will be returned if necessary. Traditional Cajun houses are built with a hallway at the front entrance, bounded at one end by a door leading outside, and at the other by a door leading into the house. The outer door is always left unlocked so that anyone needing a place to spend the night can enter and sleep in the hallway without disturbing those inside. In a tradition known as the *boucherie*, neighboring families each bring one animal to the local butcher to be slaughtered. Over several weeks, all the animals are butchered and the meat is shared out equally. The butcher, who does not contribute an animal, receives an equal share in return for his work.

⁹ LIVING CONDITIONS

Most Cajuns today have access to modern health-care facilities, but this was not always so. Isolated in the swamps, bayous and backwoods, they traditionally relied on folk healers, usually women with a knowledge of the medicinal effects of plants and herbs. The folk healers, whose wisdom has not been entirely lost, are simultaneously feared and admired, since they have the power to harm as well as to heal with their special knowledge.

Traditional Cajun architecture consists of daubed or half-timbered houses with gable roofs, mud chimneys, and outside stairways leading to attics. Spaces between the timbers are filled with a mixture of mud, Spanish moss, and ground clam shells called *bousillage*. This mixture, held together by the lime that is extracted from the clam shells, is strong and fire-resistant, which makes it an excellent material for use in construction. The timbers themselves are often of cypress, a wood that is plentiful; strong and hard; resistant to rot, warping, and insects; and difficult to burn. Cajun landholdings are often surrounded by the characteristic *pieux*, a unique type of rail-and-post fence. Many old Cajun houses are still occupied today, modernized with plumbing, electricity, and corrugated metal roofing.

Cajuns use the meandering waterways of the Mississippi delta as routes of transportation, and the traditional means of getting about is a small boat known as a *pirogue*. Often a pole is used to push the pirogue along although today most are equipped with outboard motors. Swamp boats, which skim the shallow waters and are powered by a large fan mounted at the rear, are also used by many contemporary Cajun bayou dwellers.

¹⁰ FAMILY LIFE

The distinguishing characteristic of the Cajun family is its extended network, created through intermarriage, that links each family to all the others in the immediate community—forming, as it were, one single family. In such a network, no one is left out, and institutions such as mental hospitals and retirement homes have never developed, since the aged and the infirm have always been cared for by the community at large. Since marriage is so vital to the unity of the group, Cajun courtships tend to be short, and most Cajuns marry at an early age. Even so, a Cajun young women is always free to turn down an offer of marriage. Sometimes she does this by sending the suitor a paper-doll cutout of a young man as a symbol of rejection. By the same token, a Cajun father can speed up the marriage process by painting the top of his chimney with whitewash as a sign that there is a girl of marriageable age in the house.

When a wedding does take place, the wedding feast is invariably held outdoors. The entire community joins in the festivities and gives gifts to the newlyweds. In one tradition, called "flocking the bride," the women from neighboring families each give the new bride one chicken to start her own flock.

When older people get married, or when people whose spouses have died get married for a second time, it is the occasion of a special celebration called a "charivari." When the older newlyweds return home from their modest, and often secret, wedding ceremony, the neighbors arrive at their house, banging on pots and pans and making a racket outside the house. The noise continues until the secretive newlyweds finally give in and invite the neighbors to come into the house for dancing, feasting, and merrymaking.

When a Cajun child is born, the women in the family begin making towels, blankets, bedspreads, mattresses stuffed with Spanish moss, and other household necessities. These are then saved to be used as a dowry, or wedding gift, when the time comes for the child to get married.

11 CLOTHING

Cajuns today generally wear ordinary clothing, sturdy and no-nonsense, which is best suited for their outdoor lifestyle. One type of fabric that they traditionally weave is usually dyed blue with dye from the indigo plant. This material may have been the origin of the modern denim used to make blue jeans.

12 FOOD

Cajun cooking is spicy and exotic, and increasingly popular among non-Cajuns. The predominant dish is gumbo, in which just about all available food is cooked together in one large pot, heavily flavored with herbs and spices. Bouillabaisse is a traditional French soup made of fish in a tomato broth, while *boulette* is a spicy shrimp croquette. In jambalaya, rice and other foods are cooked together in a spicy mixture. Much of the Cajun diet is made up of seafood and animals that are to be found in the waters and woods of the swamps and bayous. These include the shrimp, oyster, crab, turtle, frog (only the legs are eaten), quail, squirrel, pigeon, rabbit, muskrat, squid, and crayfish—called "crawfish" by the Cajuns (fried crawfish are sometimes called "Cajun popcorn").

Jambalaya

1 frying chicken cut into 8 pieces
4 tbsp. flour
4 tbsp. oil
1 medium onion, chopped
2 cloves garlic
½ bell pepper, chopped
4 oz. sausage or cubed ham
1 one-pound can tomatoes
1 tsp. Tabasco or cayenne pepper
2 cups rice
2 cups water

Coat chicken with flour and brown in oil. Remove from

pan and use drippings to sauté onion, garlic, and pepper. Combine all ingredients and cook on stove top in covered pot for 25 minutes or until rice is tender. (Can also be prepared in an electric frying pan).

13 EDUCATION

Living isolated lives deep in the Louisiana backwoods, many Cajuns in the past received little or no formal education. Today, Cajuns attend public schools, and they make the same choices concerning higher education that might be made by similar rural people all over the United States. Some choose to stay at home, work at traditional jobs, and carry on the traditional culture, while others choose to go on to college, often leaving the Cajun community to assimilate themselves into the larger society.

14 CULTURAL HERITAGE

There is no specifically Cajun literature, for Cajun French is exclusively a spoken language. The most important Cajun contribution to American cultural life is Cajun music, which preserves much of the archaic folk tradition of the original French Acadians. The basic instruments on which Cajun music is played are the accordion and the fiddle. It is earthy, exciting music, and sometimes very sad. Among the best known Cajun musicians are Dewey Balfa, Dennis McGee, Zachary Richard, and the group Beausoleil, led by Michael Doucet.

15 WORK

Traditionally, the Cajuns are a self-sufficient people who fish, hunt, trap, and farm to provide for themselves and their families. Out of the waters of the swamps and bayous they gather fish, shrimp, clams, oysters, and crawfish. They trap and hunt fur-bearing animals such as muskrat, squirrel, and rabbit. Some gather Spanish moss. Farmers raise cotton, corn, or sugarcane. Prairie Cajuns operate cattle ranches and plant rice. In fact, one-fourth of all rice grown in the US comes from the Louisiana prairie lands. Today, harvesting shrimp and oysters has grown into a major industry. Exploratory drilling for oil in the wetlands and adjacent offshore areas has provided the Cajuns with another source of employment.

16 SPORTS

Cajuns enjoy all the sports that are popular among the general population of the United States, but they also enjoy more unusual pastimes such as cockfights and crawfish races. Probably the best-known Cajun athlete is New York Yankees pitcher Ron Guidry, who won the Cy Young award for his performance in the 1978 baseball season.

17 ENTERTAINMENT AND RECREATION

The favorite form of recreation for Cajuns is a get-together involving singing, dancing, and food. The *fais-dodo* is a big Saturday night dance party attended by the entire community, young and old alike. Annual festivals are also popular. One of the biggest is Lagniappe on the Bayou, which is held in the town of Chauvin every year. Others include the New Iberia Sugar Festival, and the Annual Cajun Rice Festival and Parade.

18 FOLK ART, CRAFTS, AND HOBBIES

Cajun folk artists are best known for their skill in weaving just about anything. The favored material is a special kind of brown cotton grown only in Cajun country, which is used to make blankets and clothing. But Cajun weavers can also make baskets and other objects out of palmetto leaves, corn husks, pine needles, and split oak bark. Handmade Cajun chairs are famous, as are the wide variety of items Cajun craftspeople fashion from Spanish moss, which grows on trees everywhere in the swamps and bayous.

19 SOCIAL PROBLEMS

The biggest threat to the Cajun way of life is damage to the environment as a result of the increasing presence of the oil industry in the area. Offshore oil rigs often spill oil into the water, and the maze of undersea pipelines changes the migration patterns of the sea creatures that the Cajuns depend upon so heavily for their sustenance. Cajuns also feel pressured by the rise in the number of sportsmen entering the swamps and bayous, who are often granted licenses to hunt and fish in areas which Cajuns have traditionally considered to be their own.

see also Acadia, Evangeline, New Brunswick, Nova Scotia, Louisiana, Zydeco

20 BIBLIOGRAPHY

Conrad, Glenn R., ed. The Cajuns: Essays on Their History and Culture. Lafayette, LA: Center for Louisiana Studies, University of Southwestern Louisiana, 1983.

Dormon, James H. The People Called Cajuns. Lafayette, LA: Center for Louisiana Studies, University of Southwestern Louisiana, 1983.

Gould, Philip. Cajun Music and Zydeco. Baton Rouge: Louisiana State University Press, 1992.

Gutierrez, C. Paige. Cajun Foodways. University Press of Mississippi, 1992.

Hoyt-Goldsmith, Diane. Mardi Gras: A Cajun Country Celebration. New York: Holiday House, 1995.

Kunz, Virginia. The French in America. Lerner Publications, 1966.

Rushton, William Faulkner. The Cajuns: From Acadia to Louisiana. New York: Farrar Straus & Giroux, 1979.

CAMBODIAN AMERICANS

For more information on Cambodian history and culture, see **Vol. 3: Khmer**.

OVERVIEW

Cambodians did not begin migrating to the US in large numbers until 1979. After the Vietnam War, which also ravaged Cambodia, and the takeover of Cambodia by the brutal Khmer Rouge regime, refugees began fleeing the country, seeking asylum in Thailand. When American journalists sent filmed reports of starving Cambodian refugees back to the US and other countries in the West, Americans and Europeans responded by opening their doors to these immigrants.

Most Cambodians arrived in the US in the early 1980s. Voluntary resettlement agencies, many affiliated with churches, were set up to assist the refugees in finding sponsors to help them adjust to life in the US. Over 34,000 Cambodians immigrated to the US in 1980 and 1981. From 1982 to 1984, more than 36,000 entered the US. The influx of refugees began to dwindle after that, with less than 20,000 entering in 1985 and 1986, and less than 12,000 from 1987 to 1990. Improvements in the political situation in Cambodia in the early 1990s reduced the number of emigrants significantly.

Some 150,000 Cambodian Americans were counted by the 1990 US Census, but this figure may be low because many Cambodian Americans may not have responded to the census, being so new to the country and its ways. Nearly half (70,000) of all Cambodian Americans live in California, particularly in Long Beach (17,000). Los Angeles also has a large Cambodian American population (4,250), although the second-largest Cambodian American population in California is in Stockton (10,000). Massachusetts also hosts a large number of Cambodian Americans (14,000), about half of whom live in the city of Lowell. Other states with large Cambodian American populations are Texas (6,000), Pennsylvania (5,500, mostly in Philadelphia), Virginia (4,000), New York (4,000, the majority in New York City), Minnesota (4,000), and Illinois (3,000).

Because they are such newcomers to the US, Cambodian Americans remain largely unacculturated to American society. Only about 20% of foreign-born Cambodian Americans had become naturalized US citizens by the early 1990s. As a recent refugee population, Cambodian Americans are also very young (only the young are willing and/or able to tear themselves away from their homes and venture out on a very risky journey). The median age of those with Cambodian ancestry in the US, according to the 1990 Census, was 19.4 years, as opposed to 34.1 years for other US residents. Almost half of the total Cambodian American population in 1990 was under the age of 18, about 42% of them born in the US.

The Cambodian language, also called Khmer, is related to Vietnamese and other Southeast Asian languages. The Cambodian alphabet is based on that of ancient India, which is quite different from the Roman alphabet used to write English. Therefore, Cambodians have to learn not only a new language but also a new alphabet upon arriving in the US. Because Cambodian Americans are such recent arrivals to this country, their general level of proficiency in English is still quite low, though most are making rapid progress in their English-language skills. Typical greetings in Cambodian (spelled phonetically) are *Jum-ree-up soouh* ("Good Day") and *Sohm lee-uh haee* ("Goodbye").

Proverbs are an integral part of Cambodian education, and Cambodian Americans continue to revere these expressions of folk wisdom, such as "The new rice stalk stands erect; the old stalk, full of grain, leans over," and "Losing money is better than wasting words." Anyone can see the sound advice in "Don't let an angry man wash your dishes; don't let a hungry man guard your rice." Cambodian Americans find special guidance in the proverb, "Travel on a river by following its bends; live in a country by following its customs."

Nearly all Cambodian Americans are Buddhist, the traditional religion of Cambodia. Buddhism is divided into the "Northern School," or Mahayana Buddhism, and the "Southern School," or Theravada Buddhism. Cambodians follow the Southern School, which preaches the importance of becoming a monk and reaching Nirvana (eternal bliss) through one's own efforts, rather than with the help of Bodhisattvas (enlightened beings), as is encouraged by the Northern School. This teaching, combined with the law of Karma (or *Kam* in the Cambodian language), which states that good deeds cause the soul to be reincarnated as a higher self, tends to make Cambodians diligent, responsible workers.

Some Cambodian Americans have converted to Christianity, but the majority continue to practice their traditional Buddhism. Whereas in 1979 there were only 3 Cambodian temples in the US, by 1990 there were more than 50. Most Buddhist temples in the US are in houses or apartments, but there are a few traditional temples with attached monasteries, such as the large complex in Maryland.

Weddings, a traditional rite of passage, are still celebrated in traditional ways by most Cambodian Americans. Although weddings in Cambodia are usually arranged by the parents, young Cambodian Americans more commonly choose their own partners. The bride wears an elaborately decorated brocade dress called a *kben*, along with many bracelets, anklets, and necklaces. Grooms sometimes still wear the traditional baggy pants and jacket, but many have shifted to Western-style suits and tuxedos. The wedding ceremony consists of a procession, a feast with much toasting of the new couple, rituals performed by a Buddhist monk, and gifts (often money) to the couple from the guests.

The most important Cambodian holiday is the New Year, or *Chaul Chnam*, and it is still celebrated by most Cambodian American communities. Usually occurring in mid-April, Chaul Chnam lasts for three days. Buddhists go to the temple and pray, meditate, and make plans for the coming year. Many Cambodian Americans also play a traditional New Year's game called *bos chhoung*, in which young men and women stand facing each other, about five feet apart. One young man throws a rolled-up scarf to a woman in whom he is interested. She tries to catch it, and if she misses, she must sing and dance for him. If she catches it, she throws it back to him. If he misses it, he must sing and dance for her.

Most Cambodian Americans are poor, having arrived in the US as refugees so recently. Lack of language skills and cultural understanding creates high unemployment and low income. Some 42% of Cambodian American families were living below the poverty level in 1990, according to the US Census, and 51% relied on public assistance to survive. Cambodian Americans suffer from the typical health problems associated with poverty (anemia and vitamin deficiency diseases related to malnutrition, reduced immunities, etc.) as well as mental and physical health problems specific to refugees from a wartorn country (depression, insomnia, post-traumatic stress syndrome, and the like). A recent study showed that in over 80% of Cambodian American households in California, at least one family member was under a physician's care.

Traditional Cambodian healing techniques are still practiced by Cambodian Americans. Traditional healers, known as *krou Khmer*, use massage, herbal medicines, and "coining" (*koh khchal*), where a coin dipped in kerosene is pressed against the body at strategic points to relieve pain.

Families are extremely important to Cambodian Americans. So many lost family members to the wars in Cambodia that remaining and future family members are cherished. Cambodian American families tend to be large, and children are treated with tremendous affection. A high proportion of Cambodian American families are headed by single mothers, not because of divorce but because the fathers were killed in the Cambodian wars.

Women are generally granted a lower status than men in Cambodia, but their opinions are still respected. Only men may become Buddhist monks, and education is usually reserved for males. Though the ideal woman in Cambodia is an obedient domestic manager, young Cambodian American women are beginning to venture beyond that role and become well-educated professionals, sometimes making significant financial contributions to their families.

Many Cambodian Americans lack formal education. Over 50% of Cambodian American men have no more than a sixth grade education, according to the 1990 US Census, and 90% have not graduated from high school. Cambodian American women have even less schooling, with 66% at a sixth grade level or less and 95% without a high school diploma. Even those Cambodian Americans who were highly educated in Cambodia before coming to the US find that their educations are irrelevant to the American work world, and their lack of English language skills handicaps them further. Foreign-born Cambodian Americans with elite backgrounds in Cambodia often end up working as janitors or other menial laborers in the US.

Young Cambodian Americans are beginning to do quite well in school, however, and are generally dedicated students. Only 6% of Cambodian Americans between the ages of 16 and 19 are high school dropouts, as opposed to 10% of European Americans and 14% of African Americans between 16 and 19 years old.

Traditional Cambodian literature is based on models from India and consists largely of poetry, proverbs, and fables. European literary forms, such as the novel, did not become popular in Cambodia until the 1970s. Since the takeover of Cambodia by the Khmer Rouge, many intellectuals have been killed, and almost no literature has been produced.

Cambodian Americans have mostly used literature as a way to tell of the atrocities of the wars in Cambodia. Autobiography is the most prevalent Cambodian American literary form. Many Cambodian American writers have coauthors to help tell their stories in English, but others have become proficient enough in

English to write their stories by themselves. One of these independent authors is Someth May, whose autobiography *Cambodian Witness: The Autobiography of Someth May* was published in 1986.

Most Cambodian Americans were farmers in Cambodia, but when they came to the US, they settled in cities. Lacking the job and language skills necessary to find employment, many have remained unemployed. Those who do find jobs usually work in low-paying service and menial labor occupations. The unemployment rate for Cambodian Americans drops significantly with each year they reside in the US, however. Of those who arrived between 1987 and 1990, almost 17% are unemployed. Only 12% of those who arrived in 1985 and 1986, however, are unemployed, and even fewer (11%) of those who arrived between 1982 and 1984 are unemployed. The rate continues to drop, falling to 9% of those who arrived in 1980 and 1981, and 7% of those who arrived before 1980. Clearly, Cambodian Americans have the determination to succeed and the will and ability to obtain the skills necessary to be productive members of the American labor force.

Poverty, unemployment, language barriers, and cultural dislocation all cause serious difficulties for Cambodian Americans, particularly those who have only recently arrived in the US. Racial discrimination also affects Cambodian Americans, as it does other racial minorities. The generation gap between foreign-born Cambodian Americans and their American-born children (or children who were so young when they came to the US that they have no memories of Cambodia) creates tension in Cambodian American families and communities as well. Young Cambodian Americans often discard their Cambodian first names and take on English ones to blend in better with their American peers. Some young Cambodians in tough urban settings have been forced to form gangs for self-protection.

Cambodian Americans also suffer from a stereotype that has developed because of differing cultural values. In Cambodia, courtesy and indirectness are highly valued, causing them to appear passive in the more aggressive American society. Cambodian Americans are far from passive, however, as their survival in the face of great odds proves.

BIBLIOGRAPHY

Bankston, Carl L., III. "Who Are the Cambodian Americans?" In *The Asian American Almanac*, Susan Gall, ed. Detroit: Gale Research, 1995.

Haines, David W. *Refugees as Immigrants: Cambodians, Laotions, and Vietnamese in America*. Totowa, N. J.: Rowman & Littlefield, 1989.

—by D. K. Daeg de Mott

CANADIANS

LOCATION: Canada
POPULATION: 27.3 million (1991)
LANGUAGE: English and French (both official); Italian; German; Chinese; Spanish
RELIGION: Roman Catholicism, Protestantism (majority); Judaism; Buddhism; Sikhism; Hinduism; Bahaism; traditional religions of native groups
RELATED ARTICLES: Vol. 2: French Canadians, Native North Americans

¹ INTRODUCTION

Canada is the world's second largest country, surpassed in area only by Russia. It is also one of the least densely populated, with most of its population concentrated in a strip 180 miles (290 kilometers) wide along its border with the United States, and vast uninhabited or sparsely populated expanses to the north. The name "Canada" is derived from *kanata*, a Huron-Iroquois term for "village" or "settlement." Amerindian and Inuit peoples first migrated to present-day Canada from Asia across the Bering Straits around 10,000 BC. The native population is thought to have numbered between 10 and 12 million at the time the British and French were establishing their first settlements in the area.

The colonial rivalry between England and France for control of Canada began in the 15th century. In 1497 John Cabot landed on the shores of Newfoundland at the head of an English expedition. Some 40 years later, Jacques Cartier claimed the Gaspé Peninsula for the French and discovered the St. Lawrence River. By the late 17th century, France and Britain were rivals for the region's rich fish and fur trade. Their North American hostilities, reinforced by wars in Europe, were ended by the Treaty of Paris in 1763, giving the British control over what had formerly been New France.

The 19th century saw the creation of the Dominion of Canadian by the British North America Act of 1867. By 1949, with the addition of Newfoundland, the Dominion had grown to include 10 provinces. Since World War II, Canada has played an active role in world affairs as an influential member of the British Commonwealth, a founding member of the United Nations, and a member of the North Atlantic Treaty Organization (NATO). Domestically, a historic development has been the growth of the French Canadian separatist movement since the 1960s, leading to the establishment of French as Quebec's official language in 1974 and the elevation of the separatist Parti Quebecois to power in Quebec in the elections of 1976. Political independence for Quebec, while thus far defeated at the polls, has remained a contentious issue for both the province and the country as a whole.

In 1992, Canada signed the North American Free Trade Agreement (NAFTA), joining with the United States and Mexico to create a common economic market. The agreement went into effect in 1994.

² LOCATION AND HOMELAND

Canada is a vast country characterized by great geographical variety. Covering about two-fifths of the North American continent, it has an area of 3,849,650 square miles (9,970,594 square

kilometers), of which about 90% is land and the rest is fresh water. Canada also has the world's longest coastline, totaling nearly 151,600 miles (243,924 kilometers). The country's dominant topographical feature is the Canadian Shield, a rocky area of forests, lakes, and wilderness that surrounds Hudson Bay and covers roughly half of Canada, separating the eastern and western parts of the country.

The Atlantic provinces, to the east of the Shield, include two islands: Newfoundland and Prince Edward Island. The Great Lakes-St. Lawrence lowlands south and southeast of the Canadian Shield are home to the largest portion of Canada's population and contain the major cities of Toronto and Montreal, as well as the nation's capital, Ottawa. The farmlands and ranching areas of the Western Plains lie west of the Canadian Shield and east of the Rocky Mountains. Still farther west lies the Western Cordillera (mountain range), which includes the Rockies. Canada's western coast is lined with deep fjords and inlets. The northernmost part of Canada includes the tundra that lies north of the tree line and the country's Arctic islands, of which the largest, Baffin Island, covers an area greater than California.

Although Canada is 10% larger than the United States (including Alaska), it has only about 10% as many people—just under 27.3 million, according to the 1991 census. Many areas of the country are sparsely settled, while nearly two-thirds of all Canadians are concentrated within 100 miles (160.9 kilometers) of the US border. Three-fourths are urban dwellers. Toronto is the most populous metropolitan area, with around 3.9 million persons in 1991, followed by Montreal, with approximately 3.2 million. Canadians of British descent are the country's largest ethnic group, accounting for roughly 45% of the population. French Canadians account for around 30% (80% in Quebec), and smaller percentages (from 1 to 3%) are represented by a variety of other European groups, including Germans, Italians, and Ukrainians. Canada also has a growing Asian community.

Canada's native peoples represent only about 2% of the population. As of 1991, there were around 365,000 Amerindians in Canada, belonging to 604 tribes and living on over 2,000 reserves. Métis (people of mixed European and Amerindian descent) numbered 75,000, and the Inuit (Eskimos) numbered 30,000, living mostly in the Northwest Territories.

³LANGUAGE

Both English and French are Canada's official languages. Speakers of both languages have the right to publicly funded primary and secondary education in their own language. Although Canada is generally considered a bilingual country, only 16% of the population is actually bilingual. About 61% speak English only and 24% French only (82% in Quebec). Other languages spoken as a mother tongue are (in order of importance) Italian, German, Chinese, and Spanish.

In the Prairies, the most common nonofficial language is German; in central Canada, Italian; in British Columbia, Chinese; in the Northwest Territories, Inuktitut; in the Yukon, the Athapaskan languages of the Déné family; and in the Atlantic region, Micmac. Canada's native peoples speak between 50 and 60 different languages belonging to 11 distinct linguistic families.

⁴FOLKLORE

Canada's folklore tradition is generally divided into four main strains: native, French Canadian, Anglo-Canadian, and other ethnic groups (such as the Ukrainians of the prairie, Manitoba's Icelanders, or the Yiddish-speaking Jews of Montreal). The native tradition includes creation and hero myths, such as the Raven and Thunderbird cycles of the West Coast and the Nanabozo stories of the Algonquian peoples.

The oral tradition of the French Canadians was strengthened by colonial laws against the establishment of presses and by the scarcity of French schools, both of which made it important for French Canadians to transmit their culture orally across the generations. Popular characters in French Canadian folklore include a hero figure named Ti-Jean (short for *petit Jean* or Little John) and a hunter named Dalbec. Jokes and anecdotes—including "Newfie" jokes about Newfoundlanders—are popular forms of folklore among Anglo-Canadians.

⁵RELIGION

Approximately 90% of Canadians are Christians, divided about equally between Catholics and Protestant groups including the United Church of Canada and the Anglican, Presbyterian, Baptist, and Lutheran churches. Other religions include Judaism, Buddhism, Sikhism, Hinduism, the Baha'i faith, and the traditional religions of native groups. Roman Catholics are in the majority in Quebec and New Brunswick, while the other provinces are predominantly Protestant.

⁶MAJOR HOLIDAYS

Canada's most important national holiday is Canada Day (formerly Dominion Day), on 1 July, commemorating the establishment of the Dominion of Canada in 1867. Canadians celebrate their nation's "birthday", in much the same way their neighbors in the US celebrate the Fourth of July: with patriotic ceremonies, picnics, and fireworks. The holiday marking the beginning of summer in Canada is Victoria Day, the Monday preceding May 25 (called Dollard Day by residents of Quebec, who prefer to remember a 17th-century French war hero on that date rather than Britain's Queen Victoria). Canada's Labour Day, like that of the US, occurs at the end of summer (the first Monday in September). Other legal holidays include New Year's Day, the major holidays of the Christian calendar, and a

Thanksgiving holiday similar to that of the US but held on the second Monday in October.

⁷RITES OF PASSAGE

Canadians mark births, marriages, and deaths in ways similar to most western nations.

⁸INTERPERSONAL RELATIONS

Canadian's reputation for courtesy, tolerance, and cooperation is reflected in the traditional designation of their country as the "peaceable kingdom."

⁹LIVING CONDITIONS

In 1992 and 1994, Canada ranked first among 160 nations in the United Nations Human Development Report's quality-of-life index, based on life expectancy, education, and income. Two out of every three Canadians own their own homes. Single homes are the most common type of dwelling although the current trend is toward greater numbers of multifamily structures. One in seven Canadian homes is heated by wood.

As a group, Canadians enjoy excellent health. Canada has one of the world's lowest infant mortality rates—1 out of 100 live births, significantly better than that of the United States. Life expectancy is 74 years for men and 80 years for women. The Canadian national health plan—which has been a focus of attention in the US debate about the future of its own health-care system—covers at least three-quarters of all the nation's health-care expenses. A 1995 survey found that middle-aged Canadians' risk of stroke and heart disease had increased since 1970 due to higher cholesterol levels, high blood pressure, and lack of regular exercise. Stress and lack of time due to job demands were cited as reasons for bad health habits on the part of the nation's aging "baby boomers."

Due to Canada's vast geographical expanse and scattered settlement patterns, the development of an adequate transportation system has been crucial to its development and survival as a nation. After the United States, Canada has the world's highest per capita use of motor transportation. Private automobiles are used for four-fifths of urban travel, and there is one passenger car for every two persons. Canada's severe winters make road maintenance an ongoing and expensive task. The government-owned Canadian Railways (CNR) and privately owned Canadian Pacific provide important all-weather transportation over great distances in large volume. Water transportation is heavily used for both domestic and international shipping, and international air service is provided by government-owned Air Canada and Canadian Airlines.

¹⁰FAMILY LIFE

Nuclear families are the norm throughout Canada. The multigenerational extended family, which represented 7% of all households in 1951, now accounts for fewer than 1%. The Canadian birthrate has declined rapidly from an average of 3.2 children per family in 1971 to 1.7 in the late 1980s. Fewer women now are marrying in their teens, and many are waiting longer before having their first child. The average age at marriage the is mid-twenties for men and the early twenties for women. In most families, women complete their childbearing within a relatively short time, with children separated from each other by only a few years. The majority of married couples share similar ethnic, religious, and educational backgrounds.

Liberalized divorce laws, a variety of social changes, and a decline in religious belief have resulted in a growing divorce rate. Currently, close to half of all Canadian marriages (4 out of 10) end in divorce.

Women made up 45% of the labor force in 1992, compared to 31% in 1966. However, they earned only two-thirds as much as men. In 1990, the average income for full-time employment was $22,799 for women, compared with $34,921 for men.

11 CLOTHING

Canadians wear modern, Western-style clothing. They may wear the traditional costumes of their ethnic groups (Eastern European, Asian, Middle Eastern, and so forth) on special occasions. In the western provinces, American-style cowboy gear is worn for special occasions and festivals, such as the Calgary Exhibition and Stampede in Alberta.

12 FOOD

Different foods are found in the different regions of Canada. "Brewis" (cod) is a favorite in Newfoundland, and the Maritime provinces are known for their seafood, including clams, oysters, salmon, lobster, cod, mackerel, and herring. Clambakes are especially popular on Prince Edward Island. In New Brunswick, the unusually shaped ostrich fern sprout, known as the fiddlehead, is considered a delicacy. Quebec has a distinctive French-Canadian cuisine. Popular dishes include the *tourtière*, a meat pie, and *ragoût de boulettes et de pattes do cochon*, a stew made from meatballs and pigs' feet. Quebec is also known for its maple syrup, and families enjoy traveling to one of the province's many sugar shacks to sample this local product in candies, cookies, and other foods—even in ham and eggs.

Ontario has a wide variety of produce and cheeses; two of the province's favorite dishes are roast pheasant and pumpkin pie. Big, hearty meals are the rule in the rugged Prairie provinces of Manitoba, Saskatchewan, and Alberta. Alberta is known for the quality of its grain-fed beef, and wild rice is a delicacy in Manitoba. Moose meat and fresh lake fish, including Arctic grayling and char, are widely eaten in the Northwest Territories.

13 EDUCATION

Nearly the entire adult population of Canada is literate. Education is administered by each province individually, although in all cases it is compulsory from the age of 6 or 7 to 15 or 16. In spite of some individual differences, the various educational systems are basically similar in all provinces except Quebec, which has two parallel systems, one of which is specifically for French-speaking, Catholic students. Most higher education is government-funded. Canada's best-known universities are the University of Toronto and McGill University in Montreal. The oldest is Laval University in Quebec. Canada's 69 degree-granting institutions also include community and regional colleges, as well as colleges of applied arts and technology.

14 CULTURAL HERITAGE

Well-known Canadian authors of the past have included Lucy Maud Montgomery, author of *Anne of Green Gables*, and short-story writer Stephen Leacock. Margaret Atwood, Robertson Davies, Mordecai Richler, and Margaret Laurence are among the best-known modern writers.

Internationally acclaimed classical musicians have included pianist Glenn Gould and vocal artists Jon Vickers and Maureen Forrester. Well-known popular performers include Joni Mitchell, Neil Young, and Gordon Lightfoot.

Prestigious theatrical events include the Stratford Festival and Shaw Festival, both held every year in Ontario, and the Festival Lennoxville in Quebec.

15 WORK

In 1992, 73% of all civilian employees were employed in service-sector jobs, 27.7% in industry, and only 3.5% in agriculture. In 1990 the average income for full-time employment among Canadians 15 years and older was $30, 274. About one-third of Canada's labor force is unionized.

Like their neighbors in the United States, Canadian workers are increasingly finding themselves working harder for the same pay, as jobs become more competitive and less secure. Longer hours and greater pressure on the job have produced higher levels of dissatisfaction in the workplace, which in turn have led to increased absenteeism, job burnout, and associated family problems. While the 1995 unemployment rate of 9.5% represents a decrease compared to the double-digit unemployment experienced by Canada in recent years, many workers were angered by the fact that corporate profits reached record highs in the same year.

16 SPORTS

Ice hockey is Canada's national sport, and its stars are worshiped as national heroes. Professional games draw thousands of fans on Saturday nights, and youngsters often rise as early as 4:00 or 5:00 am on weekends to play on little-league teams that can book space at ice rinks only in off-hours. Other popular winter sports include skiing, ice-skating, snowshoeing, and tobogganing. Favorite summer sports include baseball, volleyball, and soccer. Canadians often perform calisthenics during the seventh-inning stretch of professional games, led from the dugout roof by fitness-minded fans. Among Canada's traditional sports, lacrosse was originated by the native population before the arrival of Europeans, and curling was adopted from the Scots.

17 ENTERTAINMENT AND RECREATION

Canadians today enjoy more leisure time than ever before and spend it in a variety of sporting and other recreational activities. Like their US counterparts, Canadian families spend much of their evening time watching television. Many are regular newspaper readers. Their scenic native land provides many Canadians with recreation in the form of vacation trips, on which they spend some $6 billion a year. Many own weekend and vacation cottages on lakeshores or in wooded areas. If they choose, however, Canadians can also spend their entire vacation at the mall; the West Edmonton Mall—the world's largest shopping mall, with over 800 stores—boasts seven amusement parks, a large indoor ice rink, a 14-story-high roller coaster, several aquariums, and its own hotel.

¹⁸FOLK ART, CRAFTS, AND HOBBIES

Amerindian artists produce crafts, including jewelry, beaded moccasins, baskets, and leather goods, as well as stylized artwork that is displayed and sold in galleries and gift shops. The Inuit are known for their soapstone, ivory, and serpentine carvings as well as prints, paintings, drawings, and wall hangings, all in a distinctive native style. Their art shares certain common themes, including the group's traditional lifestyle and survival techniques, the animals native to its homelands, and the myths and spirits of its traditional religions.

¹⁹SOCIAL PROBLEMS

Canada has fewer violent crimes than many other societies. Its national homicide rate of about 600 a year is one-third the number typically recorded in New York City alone. Its cities are generally clean, efficiently run, and relatively free of such common urban problems as homelessness and illegal drug dealing. The global recession of the early 1990s threw Canada into an economic slump that included double-digit unemployment from 1991 through 1994. It has a large national debt and faces growing demands for decentralization from many of its regions. However, Canada's most serious problem is the threat that Quebec will secede and become a sovereign state, a move with grave political and economic implications for all Canadians.

²⁰BIBLIOGRAPHY

The Canadian Encyclopedia, 2nd ed., 4 vols. Edmonton: Hurtig, 1988.

Chacko, James. *Cultural Sovereignty: Myth or Reality.* Windsor, ON: University of Windsor Press, 1986.

Cunningham, Hilary. *Canada.* Insight Guides. Boston: Houghton Mifflin, 1992.

Driedger, Leo, ed. *Ethnic Canada: Identities and Inequalities.* Mississauga, ON: Capp Clark Pitman, 1987.

Gall, Timothy, and Susan Gall, ed. *Worldmark Encyclopedia of the Nations.* Detroit: Gale Research, 1995.

Giberson, Mark. "Work and Family in the '90s: A Fairy Tale Turned Nightmare." *Communication World.* March 1996: p.12.

"Just Getting Older, Not Better." *Maclean's.* February 5, 1996: p.7.

Kalman, Bobbie. *Canada: The Culture.* New York: Crabtree Publishing, 1993.

Kaplan, Susan B. "Northern Composure: Americans Could Learn Some Valuable Lessons in Civility from Our Canadian Neighbors." *Newsweek*, 12 February, 1996: 17.

Malcolm, Andrew. *The Land and People of Canada.* New York: HarperCollins, 1988.

Richler, Mordechai. *Oh Canada! Oh Quebec! Requiem for a Divided Country.* New York: Knopf, 1992.

Weihs, Jean. *Facts about Canada, Its Provinces, and Territories.* H. W. Wilson Co., 1995.

—by R. Wieder

CENTRAL AMERICANS IN THE US

For more information on Central American history and culture, *see* **Vol. 2: Belizeans**, **Costa Ricans**, **Salvadorans**, **Guatemalans**, **Hondurans**, **Nicaraguans**, and **Panamanians**.

OVERVIEW

The first officially recorded Central American immigrants entered the US in 1820. Central Americans continued to immigrate to the US in small numbers until the mid-20th century. Beginning in 1950, Central American immigration to the US increased steadily, with the greatest numbers occurring in the 1970s when several Central American countries erupted in civil war.

During the 1950s and 1960s, most Central American immigrants to the US were middle- and upper-middle-class Panamanians and Hondurans. Many were students pursuing higher education, while others were young professionals in search of advanced career opportunities. In the 1970s, however, the make-up of Central American immigrants changed dramatically. Most were from El Salvador and Nicaragua (where violent civil wars had erupted) and Guatemala (where a repressive military government was in control). The majority were uneducated, illiterate peasant farmers with few, if any, industrialized job skills. Unlike there predecessors, these immigrants were rejected as legal immigrants by the US and were refused refugee status. Those who chose to remain in the US without official sanction were classified as "illegal aliens." The preferred term in use today among the Hispanic American community, however, is *undocumented migrant*.

Because of strict US immigration policies, Central Americans resort to desperate measures to immigrate. Smugglers and "tour operators," sometimes called *coyotes*, profit from the situation by transporting refugees across the various borders between Central America and the US. Coyotes may provide false documents and visas for a very high price. For most Central Americans, illegal immigration to the US is extremely dangerous. In 1981, retired Arizona rancher Jim Corbett, a Quaker, founded the Sanctuary Movement by giving aid to Central American refugees crossing the US-Mexico border. A year later, Reverend John Fife and the congregation of the Southside Presbyterian Church in Tucson, Arizona, declared their church a "Sanctuary church," sheltering refugees and helping them resettle in the US. Since then, a number of other congregations have joined the movement.

Most Salvadoran and Guatemalan refugees settle in Los Angeles, California, sometimes called the "Central American capital of the US." In 1990, an estimated 350,000 Salvadorans and 110,000 Guatemalans lived in Los Angeles. There are also large populations of Salvadorans and Guatemalans in San Francisco, Houston, New York City, and Washington, D.C. Most Nicaraguans prefer to settle in Miami, Florida, however. New York City hosts many immigrants from various Central American countries, as does Los Angeles.

Determining the exact number of Central Americans living in the US is impossible because so many are undocumented migrants not included in official population counts. Estimates place the US Central American population at over one million. About half live in California. Los Angeles has the second-highest Salvadoran population in the world, exceeded only by San Salvador. In 1985, Salvadorans were the largest Central American group in the US, followed by Guatemalans, Hondurans, Nicaraguans, and small numbers of Panamanians, Belizeans, and Costa Ricans.

In Los Angeles, the majority of Central American immigrants live in the Pico-Union section, an overcrowded slum. Conditions there are hardly better than the Central American refugee camps from which some of the immigrants started their journey. As many as 20 people may share a one-room apartment where they sleep and eat in shifts. Landlords exploit the fears of undocumented migrants by charging exorbitant rents and threatening to turn the migrants in to the INS if they do not pay.

Employers also exploit undocumented Central Americans. Lack of documentation, along with a lack of language (the majority speak Spanish) and appropriate job skills, makes it very difficult for most US Central Americans to find employment. Those who are lucky enough to find jobs are often paid less than minimum wage and expected to work long hours in poor work environments. Fear of detection forces the workers to accept these unfair working conditions. Common employment for undocumented US Central Americans includes unskilled labor, low-level work in the service industry, migrant farm work for men; and domestic service or work in the garment industry for women. Most jobs are only part-time.

The majority of Central American immigrants of the past three decades suffer from serious physical and mental health problems caused by experiences in their homelands and the difficult journey to the US. Undocumented migrants are often afraid to go to the doctor or hospital, however, for fear of detection by the INS, so many of their ailments go untreated. A number turn to folk remedies prescribed by *sobadors* or *curanderos* (folk healers) or to drink *remedios* (herbal teas). Others may take advantage of clinics set up specifically for Central American immigrants in cities such as Los Angeles. US Central Americans have also banded together to form organizations to help each other. The largest of these is the Central American Refugee Center (CARE-CEN), which has branches nationwide.

Central Americans have traditionally turned to the family for support, but most US Central Americans' families have been torn apart by the violence in their former homelands and separation during immigration. Traditional male and female roles are also disrupted in the US because finding jobs is often easier for women than for men. In Central America, the man is the undisputed head of the household and chief breadwinner. Some Central American immigrant men who are frustrated and angry at their situation in the US turn to alcohol and drugs. Some take their frustrations out on the women and children around them, making domestic violence is an increasing problem among US Central Americans.

Prior to 1982, most undocumented US Central Americans were afraid to send their children to school for fear they would be detected by immigration authorities. In 1982, however, the US Supreme Court ruled that children of undocumented migrants are entitled to free public education. Since that time, parents have not had to show evidence of citizenship or legal immigrant status to enroll their children in school. More US Central American children, therefore, now attend school. How-

ever, most have had sporadic educations in their homelands and have a difficult time catching up to their age-appropriate grade level. Language barriers also create problems for US Central American students, many of whom speak only Spanish at home. Older students may also feel resentment towards being treated as children, having functioned as adults in Central America.

Despite the obstacles they face, US Central Americans have created a community in their new homeland. They have organized a number of soccer leagues, including the El Salvador Soccer League in Los Angeles, which has 19 teams. Many Central Americans play in major league US sports, especially baseball. Through education and consciousness-raising, US Central Americans have raised other Americans' awareness of conditions in Central America. Numerous films have been made in recent years concerning Central Americans, such as *Salvador*, *Under Fire*, and *El Norte*.

Many US Central Americans still hope to return to their homes in Central America, as soon as political situations improve. As the number of second-generation US Central Americans increases, however, the sense of permanent US residency increases.

BIBLIOGRAPHY

Bachelis, Faren. *The Central Americans*. New York: Chelsea House, 1990.

Jensen, Jeffry. *Hispanic Americans Struggle for Equality*. Vero Beach, FL: Rourke Corporation, 1992.

Novas, Himilce. *Everything You Need to Know about Latino History*. New York: Plume, 1994.

—by D. K. Daeg de Mott

CHILEANS

LOCATION: Chile
POPULATION: 12 million
LANGUAGE: Spanish
RELIGION: Roman Catholicism (official); some Protestantism; some indigenous religions

1 INTRODUCTION

Several Amerindian cultures such as the Atacameño, the Diaguita in the north, and the Araucanian further south thrived in Chile prior to the arrival in the 15th century of Inca invaders from Peru. The Incas extended their empire for a short time as far as Santiago, which is now Chile's capital city.

In 1520 the Portuguese explorer Fernando de Magallanes (or Ferdinand Magellan) sailed through the straits at the southern tip of Chile. In 1536, the Spaniard Diego de Almagro crossed into Chile from Peru, but it was Pedro de Valdivia who established the first Spanish settlement at Santiago in 1541. Spanish colonial rule lasted until the beginning of the 19th century, when conflicts with Spain led the Chilean military leader, Bernardo O'Higgins, to join forces with José de San Martín from Argentina to liberate the Chileans from Spanish rule. O'Higgins became the first ruler of the independent republic of Chile in 1818, and in further struggles this joint Andean army also fought the Spanish royalists as far as Peru.

Chile developed two main political parties, the Conservatives and the Liberals, and Chile's economy developed as a result of trade that flourished with European powers such as England in the 19th century, and the United States in the 20th century. First, there was a nitrate boom in the late 19th and early 20th centuries. Copper and silver mining became important sources of income, and farming developed. Initially wheat was an important crop, but gradually a variety of fruits and vegetables gained in importance as they found markets locally and abroad.

Today Chile is a democracy, with a senate and a house of representatives. In the 20th century Chile has experienced dramatic changes of government, including the socialist rule of Salvador Allende, who was freely elected in 1970, followed by a military take-over (during which Allende was assassinated) in 1973 by Augusto Pinochet. Pinochet's rule ended when Patricio Aylwin, leader of a coalition of 17 opposition parties, was elected president in 1989. Since Aylwin took office in March 1990, democratic rule has continued.

2 LOCATION AND HOMELAND

Chile's Pacific coastline is over 4,000 km (2,485 mi) long. The Andes mountains run the full length of this immensely long, narrow country, which borders Argentina to the east and Peru and Bolivia to the north. Chile has a varied climate, from the northern Atacama desert, through snow-clad Andean peaks, to farmlands where grapes provide excellent Chilean wine and other fruits such as peaches and cherries are grown for export, to grain and cattle country, as well as fishing zones further south where snow-covered volcanoes and lakes abound.

About a quarter of Chile's 12 million inhabitants are of European (mainly Spanish) descent, with a few of mixed German, Austrian, Swiss, Italian, or British and Irish ancestry. The remainder are mainly Mestizo (mixed Spanish and Indian ancestry). About 4 million people live in the capital, Santiago. Some 400,000 Mapuche Indians, a group of the Araucanians, still live in reservations or *reducciones*.

3 LANGUAGE

The official language of Chile is Spanish. Although Chile belongs to the so-called "southern cone" countries of South America, which include Argentina and Uruguay, their accent is quite distinct. To some, it might sound generally softer, with the "ch" sound almost like a "sh" sound, and an attractive, melodious lilt in the speech.

Chilean names derive from saints and apostles of the Catholic Church as well as from Roman and other Spanish names, and in some cases from names of Anglo-Saxon or German origin.

4 FOLKLORE

One of the important folk heroes of Chile is a Mapuche Indian called Lautaro, who learned Spanish and was at the service of the Spanish conqueror Pedro de Valdivia. He was chosen by his people to lead the resistance against the Spanish. Having learned the Spanish ways and arts of war, he proved a formidable opponent, teaching his people to ride horses and developing effective war tactics that gave Mapuches an advantage in known terrain. Lautaro was already at the gates of Santiago, the capital, when he was killed, and the Mapuches retreated southward where they continued to fight the Spanish and where even now, in various ways, many of them continue to resist assimilation.

Many myths and legends survive in Chilean folklore. Among these is one that comes from the islands of Chiloé in southern Chile. It is the tale of a lost city whose streets are paved with gold and silver. It is said that all who go there lose their memory, that a mist always hides it from sight, and that it will be seen only once, at the end of the world, so that all the nonbelievers will come to know of its existence. In this hidden city there is fabulous wealth. This legend sprang from the tales of explorers of Chile's forbidding southern Andes, some of whom brought back tales of wonderful treasures they had seen.

The War of the Pacific which Chile fought in 1879 against its neighbors Bolivia and Peru gave Chile its most famous military hero, Captain Arturo Prat Chacón, whose brave resistance aboard the battleship *Esmeralda* led to his death on 21 May. Most importantly, it earned large territories from Bolivia and Peru, leaving the former landlocked. This date has been a national holiday ever since.

5 RELIGION

The official religion of Chile is Roman Catholicism, and the majority of Chileans are Roman Catholic, although there is freedom of religion and some Protestant faiths are present in Chile. Many of the surviving Indians have also been converted to Catholicism. Some Mapuche Indians continue to practice their own religion. Their beliefs include worship of the creator Ngenechen and the destroyer Wakufu.

Among the religious festivals is the feast of San Sebastian in Yumbel, near the town of Chillán; the Fiesta de Cuasimodo during Easter in the outskirts of Santiago; and the religious festival of La Tirana near the northern city of Iquique, which

CHILEANS

0   250   500   750 Miles

0   250   500   750 Kilometers

includes dances representing good and evil forces in the form of maidens and devils. The latter developed out of a mixture of Catholic and Amerindian beliefs.

⁶ MAJOR HOLIDAYS

Aside from the main Catholic holidays such as Christmas, the Immaculate Conception on 8 December, Corpus Christi, and Easter, Chileans celebrate Labor Day on 1 May, as well as two Independence holidays: Independence Day on 18 September, and what the military has called "Liberation Day" on 11 September (although it is still a holiday, the country is split down the middle arguing if it should be considered one). Two dates commemorate the wars of the 19th century, 18 September, Independence Day; and 19 September, Day of the Glory of the Armed Forces, which is celebrated with a military parade. The discovery of America by Christopher Columbus is celebrated on 12 October.

⁷ RITES OF PASSAGE

Many Chilean Catholics consider baptism and First Communion important for the identity of a child as a Catholic. Civil marriage is often accompanied by a church ceremony which is considered more significant. In some very religious families, when a person dies, nine days of prayers according to Catholic custom are held in the home and attended by the person's family and close friends.

According to popular beliefs still adhered to in the countryside by some *campesinos* or peasants, and among city dwellers known as *pobladores* in poorer neighborhoods, the spirits of people who have died violently will continue to linger in the area where they died, and the living can appeal to them in their prayers, asking them to intercede on their behalf. Little shrines with flowers and candles, known as *animitas* (which means "little spirits") are often set up in the vicinity and sometimes become places of prayer and pilgrimage.

⁸ INTERPERSONAL RELATIONS

Chileans have a relaxed attitude towards time, and on social occasions in particular people are not expected to arrive on time, but rather up to an hour late. This approach is often misunderstood in cultures where the attitude is that "time is money." In Chile, this is occasionally true in some business or professional sectors where the sense of hurry and the virtues of efficiency imported from other cultures, such as the European or the North American, have been adopted. But in general, this flexibility also has its virtues, enabling people to enjoy themselves with a carefree attitude, and to accept the unexpected with greater ease.

One of the best types of gatherings is the typical Chilean *asado* or barbecue, which involves large quantities of meat, and large cuts, grilled on open charcoal fires in private yards and gardens or in parks or other public places during festivals. This is an occasion for family and friends to gather, and it is common in these gatherings for the generations to mingle easily: children, parents, and grandchildren, as well as other relatives and friends.

Formal greetings and introductions involve handshakes, but among friends, both women and men, the usual greeting is a kiss on the cheek.

⁹ LIVING CONDITIONS

About 40% of Chile's population are considered middle-class. A small group of upper-class people, perhaps 10% of the population, live in elegant houses in city neighborhoods such as Providencia, La Dehesa, or Vitacura in the capital, Santiago. This elite group continues to deploy strong economic, social, and political influence, and quite often a family in these conditions will have a summer home in the Valparaíso-Viña del Mar coastal resort area. It is also a landowning class, and many families of this type will also own a ranch. Presently, many of the rich are from the industrial class. The remainder of the population is divided between peasants or *campesinos* and poor city dwellers known as *pobladores,* who live in crowded shantytowns, particularly in Santiago, where housing is often a type of squatter's home made from every and any material at hand, such as zinc, bits of wood and brick, and any other available building material.

Unlike their middle-class counterparts, the pobladores do not own cars but rather use public transport, usually buses. In more remote areas of Chile there are fewer roads and in some areas, particularly in the south, the boat is an important means of transport. In the countryside, particularly in rural areas such as the Andes mountains, pack animals and horses are a means of transport for local people.

10 FAMILY LIFE

Until recently, most Chileans had large families, although modern urban lifestyles, particularly among the middle classes, have included a change in family size, with modern families tending to have two or three children. Even though many poor working women have to leave their children to go to work, and middle-class professional women employ servants (often the same women who have to leave their own children) to help them look after their own families, women everywhere in Chile are considered the pillars of family life and are expected to fulfill this role. In the past, maids became part of the family. Nowadays, they work 9:00–5:00 schedules and a great number make more than secretaries do.

This often means that women take up a larger share of chores as well as family duties in addition to work outside the home, since men are not as willing to share household responsibilities as in some European or North American environments. This is particularly true in poorer households, where the women have little extra help and often rely on the older children to look after younger ones.

11 CLOTHING

Modern, middle-class city dwellers dress in Western-style clothes. Men wear suits, and women in offices are expected to dress quite formally, with suits or dresses, although trousers are also accepted. Good grooming is expected of women, and this includes regular hairstyling and makeup. Given Chile's large middle class and lively cultural life, exceptions to this rule are found, for example, among those involved in the arts.

In the countryside, Chile's *huasos* or cowboys wear the *poncho,* a type of cloak, often with colorful stripes worn for festivities. Regular ponchos worn at other times are usually earth-colors. They also wear broad-rimmed straw hats in summer and felt hats in winter. They wear boots, and sometimes finely crafted spurs.

12 FOOD

A typical Chilean dish is *pastel de choclo* (baked corn paste). A much-loved soup, a hearty meal in itself, is *porotos granados* or white bean soup, which also includes pumpkin, peppers, and sweet corn. A delicious and popular snack is a type of turnover made of wheat flour, called *empanada.* Many Latin Americans have interesting variants of fillings for the empanada. In Chile the most typical empanada is baked, and it is called *empanada de pino,* which it means it is filled with minced meat, onions, a slice of hard-boiled egg, and an olive. Other empanadas are fried and filled with cheese. During popular street festivals, empanadas are often accompanied by fermented fruit juices, such as a thirst-quenching type of apple cider called *chicha de manzana.*

Avocados, called *palta* in Chile, are used in salads or mashed up as a topping for bread (usually eaten for the after-

noon snack called *onces*) or as an accompaniment to grilled meat. Native stews called *cazuelas* are made from beef, chicken, or fish and include potatoes, pumpkins, corn and green beans.

The range of climates produces an interesting selection of food in Chile, and in the south along the coast excellent varieties of shellfish are often eaten raw with lemon juice or prepared on open charcoal grills. In the more remote islands of Chiloé in southern Chile, stones are heated and placed in a hole to form a type of oven called a *curanto* where fish, beef, pork, and vegetables (most importantly potatoes) are wrapped in vegetable leaves and covered by sand, then steamed for hours for special occasions, such as communal house-building. The community helps build a new house and the owners "pay" back the favor with a *curanto.*

13 EDUCATION

Primary schooling has been free in Chile since 1860, and literacy rates have been improving steadily since then, with a current estimated 80% literacy rate. As in many other developing countries, education in Chile is highly valued, particularly as a means of escaping poverty and a life of hardship. The national University of Chile was founded in 1843, and since then increasing numbers of Chileans attend university, forming a rapidly growing middle class. The Catholic Church has also played an important role in developing education.

14 CULTURAL HERITAGE

Chile has a rich cultural heritage and a love of the arts which has given rise to numerous literary, theatrical, and musical activities. The national dance of Chile is the *cueca,* which involves rapid, emphatic steps reminiscent of the Spanish *zapateado (flamenco)* in which the feet tap the beat on the floor.

An important political and artistic protest movement arose during the 1960s, acquiring a special force and meaning later during the military dictatorship of Augusto Pinochet in the 1970s. Its most famous figure was Violeta Parra, whose passionate voice embodied the yearning of an entire people, and whose style blended folk, classical, and modern influences. Her children Isabel and Angel continued this creative movement, which became known as the New Song movement (*La Nueva Canción Chilena*). Other groups such as the Inti Illimani or the Quilapayún also blended folk traditions and instruments from other Latin American countries, and many exiled Chileans toured the world, sharing their music with young people everywhere.

Chile has a strong literary tradition and has the distinction of having produced two Nobel Prize winners, the poets Gabriela Mistral and Pablo Neruda. Their powerful poetry goes beyond the individual to sing about the condition of humankind. These poets not only conveyed an intensely personal and intimate voice in their work, but also genuine social concerns. An interesting and very modern playwright who also gave expression to the suffering in his country caused by the Pinochet dictatorship is Ariel Dorfman. The work of modern novelists such as José Donoso, Jorge Edwards, Antonio Skármeta, and Isabel Allende has been translated into various languages including English, and their work is becoming better known. Isabel Allende's work sometimes combines social and political awareness with a poetic, imaginative sensibility.

15 WORK

Chile has undergone a modern economic experiment which began during the 1980s and which has benefited some sectors of the economy. It has been particularly successful in growing crops, especially fruit and excellent wines, for export. Sectors involved in these activities have done well. Copper mining continues to be very important. But working conditions vary sharply according to social class, and the economic improvements have not been able to deal with many marginalized poor people, particularly the *pobladores* of the shantytowns, who have to make do with informal labor and odd jobs. This situation is repeated throughout Latin America, where many cannot find secure employment, and the economic solutions ignore the needs of many poor people.

16 SPORTS

The most popular sport is soccer, which is played and followed enthusiastically by many Chileans.

Horse-racing is a popular spectator sport in Santiago. Many Chileans in rural areas have a tradition of fine equestrianism, and the Chilean *huasos* or cowboys compete in unusual *medialunas* (corrals in the shape of a half moon), parts of which are heavily padded. The steers have to be driven against this padded section by two mounted huasos riding two horses; one drives the steer from behind and the other has to press the steer against the padded wall and bring the steer to a full stop. The technique is difficult and involves unusual movements that demand great agility. The Chilean horses, called *corraleros,* are short and stocky and well suited for the rodeo. It is not a violent sport and is popular only in the central valley and in the south of Chile.

Chile has fine beaches, and many people enjoy swimming in resorts such as Valparaíso and Viña del Mar. Boating and fishing in Chile's beautiful lakes are both popular, and there are several ski resorts near Santiago and in the south (Chillán has the longest ski run in South America), among which is the well-known resort of Portillo, visited by both Chileans and their Argentine neighbors.

17 ENTERTAINMENT AND RECREATION

Chilean town-dwellers enjoy movies, and there is a lively theatrical tradition. Santiago's Municipal Theater is a well-known venue, but there are many smaller venues for artists, playwrights and poets, actors, and singers to get together. Chileans are distinctive because they enjoy themselves not only as spectators but also as enthusiastic participants in a variety of activities that blend art and popular culture with recreation. In Santiago's main square, the Plaza de Armas, there is open-air evening entertainment with musicians, dancers, and comedians attracting people who are out for a stroll or a leisurely drink or snack. Young people often meet in the evening in cafés or bars, and they enjoy dancing. It is a sociable city where it is easy to meet people because the city center is relatively small. People also enjoy shopping, and some of the better neighborhoods such as Las Condes have elegant shopping districts and malls.

Chileans enjoy snacking and eating out, and one of the popular venues is the large Mercado Central, a lovely market which includes many small snack bars and informal eating places offering varieties of shellfish.

Chileans also enjoy trips to the seaside. Valparaíso and Viña del Mar are popular, but there are also beautiful beaches near smaller towns closer to the northern Atacama desert region and the towns of La Serena (the biggest tourist development in the last 10 years), Iquique, Antofagasta, and Arica. People also enjoy excursions further afield, to the rich farmlands of central Chile, to the lake district, and to the southern Andes, enjoying fishing, hiking, boating, white-water rafting, visits to farms, to ski resorts, or to thermal baths. Chile has over 2,000 volcanoes and a number of beautiful national parks, some of which, in the north, have geysers and, in the south, glaciers.

18 FOLK ART, CRAFTS, AND HOBBIES

In Chile, taking part in some kind of artistic activity is not left simply to professionals, because Chileans have a tradition of expressing themselves through a variety of artistic media where historical, social, and political concerns blend with purely artistic ones. Many people combine a career or various types of work with an artistic hobby, which can include playing musical instruments such as guitars, singing, painting, writing poetry, dancing, or acting. There are many musical groups or *peñas* in towns across Chile, playing a variety of music ranging from folk to *salsa* music from other Latin American countries as well as modern, Western-style pop music.

Weaving, basket-making, pottery, woodcarving, and jewelry-making are crafts that surviving Amerindian communities such as the Aymara in the north, close to the Bolivian border, or the Mapuches in the south continue to produce. Leatherworking began as a craft and has continued in a more modern, industrial setting. The town of Pomaire is famous for its pottery. It includes many potters who often make miniature figures that derive from storytelling or religious traditions, and the beautiful clay *pailas* or pots of varying sizes and shapes find their way into many Chilean gardens and kitchens.

A unique feature of Santiago is the large cluster of arts and crafts shops called Los Graneros del Alba (in the back of the church of Los Dominicos) where visitors can watch artisans in the process of making their wares. In a uniquely Chilean way, this is combined on weekends with music and dancing.

19 SOCIAL PROBLEMS

Chile's social problems relate directly to the poverty-stricken conditions not only of the surviving Amerindian groups, but also of city dwellers or *pobladores* who do not have enough work or can only find temporary work.

The gap between rich and poor continues to matter and is quite sharp in Chile. The wealthy landowners and industrialists possess not only most of the economic wealth but also the greater share of political and social influence. The growth of a significant and well-educated middle class does not of itself solve the problem of underemployed and undereducated poor people, although it is an important indicator of development. Chile's poor people are movingly described by the Uruguayan writer Eduardo Galeano as people who, because they are not consumers, do not exist. These are people who are "used and thrown away," and the fate of Chile, he says, is to scratch a living from the bowels of its mountains, in search of copper, unable to manufacture even a pin for export because pins from other countries will be cheaper. Meanwhile, continues Galeano, workers without work "rummage in the garbage" and see signs everywhere saying, "There are no vacancies. Do not insist."

[20] BIBLIOGRAPHY

Galeano, Eduardo. *Memorias del fuego: III. El siglo del viento.* Madrid: Siglo Veintiuno de España Editores S. A., 1993.

Perrotet, Tony, ed. *Insight Guides: Chile.* Hong Kong: APA Publications Ltd, 1995.

—by P. Pitchon, reviewed by V. Salles-Reese

CHINESE AMERICANS

For more information on Chinese history and culture, *see* **Vol. 3: China and Her National Minorities**; **Han**.

OVERVIEW

The first Chinese immigrant to the US arrived in 1820. For the following thirty years, few Chinese immigrated to America. When gold was discovered in California in 1848, however, many Chinese were drawn to what they called *Gum San*, the "Gold Mountain." The numbers of Chinese gold-seekers increased rapidly from 450 in 1850 to 2,716 in 1851 to 20,000 in 1852. After that, immigration slowed to an average of 4,000 Chinese per year for the next several years.

Most of these first Chinese Americans were men because a respectable Chinese woman could not leave her parents' or in-laws' home. Therefore, the early Chinese American community consisted of bachelor societies governed by a district association. "Chinatowns" developed all along the West Coast, where Chinese American men could find the goods and services they needed in their new American home, such as housing, traditional Chinese groceries and restaurants, laundries, and the like. Most Chinatowns also had gambling rooms, many had temples, and a few had theaters for traveling Chinese opera troupes.

Due to the dramatic lack of women in the early Chinese American community, prostitution was big business. Local societies, known as "tongs," ran the business, importing young Chinese women (or girls) to act as sexual slaves. "Tong wars" between rival societies made the US national news in the late 1800s.

As the number of Chinese Americans who were willing to work for low wages increased (discrimination prevented them from obtaining high-wage labor), other Americans began to feel threatened by what they termed the "Yellow Peril." Racist organizations initiated boycotts of Chinese American goods and services. Anti-Chinese gangs stormed Chinatowns and wreaked havoc, destroying homes and property and physically attacking Chinese American residents. Many Chinese Americans fled to larger Chinatowns for safety. By 1876, San Francisco's Chinatown housed over 30,000 people in an area of nine city blocks.

The California state government joined the anti-Chinese movement by passing discriminatory acts in the 1850s such as the foreign Miners Tax and Alien Poll Tax. In 1854, the state of California ruled that no person of Chinese descent could testify in court, thereby declaring open season on Chinese Americans. European Americans robbed, beat, and even killed Chinese Americans freely, without punishment, because the victims and other Chinese American witnesses could not testify against them.

By 1882, the US government decided the situation had gotten out of hand and passed the Chinese Exclusion Act, barring any more Chinese laborers from entering the US for the next decade. Other Chinese immigrants were only to be admitted under severe restrictions. Chinese immigrants were also denied US citizenship "hereafter," relegating them to permanent alien status.

The Asiatic Exclusion League was founded in 1886 to lobby the federal government for further restrictions. In 1892, the Geary Act extended the Chinese Exclusion Act for another 10 years, and in 1902, it was extended indefinitely. Not only was the number of new Chinese arrivals stemmed, but also previous Chinese immigrants decided to leave the increasingly oppressive US and return to China. The Chinese American population fell from 107,488 in 1890 to 71,531 in 1910.

In 1924, the final blow was delivered. The new Immigration Act passed that year barred any foreigners not eligible for US citizenship from entering the country. This prohibited all future Chinese immigration, including Chinese women married to men who were already US citizens. Chinese Americans in the US were faced with further discriminatory laws forbidding them to own land, have certain jobs, attend certain schools, or marry European American women.

The situation for Chinese Americans improved when China became an ally of the US during World War II (1939–45). On 17 December 1943, US Congress repealed the Chinese Exclusion Acts. Chinese immigration to the US was still limited to 105 persons per year, but it was a step in a more welcoming direction. The McCarran-Walter Act of 1952 removed race as a basis for immigration discrimination, and 10 years later US President John F. Kennedy signed legislation allowing over 15,000 refugees from Communist China to enter the US. Finally, the 1965 Immigration Act eliminated the national origins quota system for immigration entirely and enabled up to 20,000 Chinese to immigrate to the US each year.

The number of people who reported themselves as being of Chinese (or Cantonese) ancestry on the 1990 US Census totalled 1,530,265. Almost 70% are foreign-born. Most Chinese Americans live either in California (654,707) or New York (242,242), with sizeable populations also in Hawaii (96,293), Texas (55,598), Massachusetts (48,197), New Jersey (47,700), and Illinois (44,825). Washington State, Florida, Maryland, and Pennsylvania each host more than 25,000 Chinese Americans as well. The numbers of men and women immigrating from China to the US have been fairly equal in recent years.

The Chinese language is fundamentally different from English in both its spoken and written forms. Therefore, attaining English language proficiency is quite difficult for older foreign-born Chinese Americans. Most foreign-born Chinese Americans continue to speak Chinese at home, and almost three-fourths (72%) of those over the age of three do not speak English very well. American-born Chinese Americans, and those who came to the US as very young children, naturally grow up fluent in English. Many American-born Chinese American children attend Chinese language schools to maintain their connection with the language and culture of their heritage.

Early Chinese immigrants to the US retained much of their traditional culture, which includes customs, folklore, and religion, and passed it on to their descendants. Traditional Chinese religion is a mix of Buddhist, Confucian, and Taoist elements. Chinese American communities in the 1800s each had a temple, most of them Taoist. Some of those early temples remain in California, and another was rebuilt in San Jose in 1991. Homes and shops in early Chinese American communities also frequently had altars to various deities. Some restaurants, homes, and shops continue the tradition today. Some Chinese Americans have converted to Christianity, and churches of various denominations can be found in Chinatowns.

Along with American holidays, most Chinese Americans also celebrate traditional Chinese holidays such as the fall Moon Festival, Ching Ming (ritual visits to ancestors' graves) in the spring, and Chinese New Year. Chinese New Year celebrations—with parades, firecrackers, and long, elaborate dragon puppets carried by dozens of dancers—have become very popular among the rest of the American population as well. Many visitors to the gold-rush town of Marysville, California enjoy the annual "Bomb Day" festival held there. Early Chinese Americans built a temple there to the water god Bok Kai, and every year since the 1880s they have honored him with a parade, including a huge golden dragon, during the second month of the Chinese lunar calendar.

Although most Chinese Americans make use of Western medicine, they still turn to traditional Chinese remedies for minor ailments. Traditional Chinese health practices have also become more widely accepted by Americans in recent years. Chinese medicinal teas and soups are sold in health food stores, and acupuncturists treat Chinese and non-Chinese Americans alike. The Chinese martial art of tai chi chuan, a form of kung fu, is taught across the US as a way to improve physical, mental, emotional, and spiritual health. Other forms of kung fu are also popular in the US.

Although living conditions were often quite desperate for early Chinese Americans who were restricted to low-paying jobs and crowded into Chinatowns for safety from racial violence, most Chinese Americans now live in much better circumstances. The number of Chinatowns has dwindled as the need for them diminished. Networks of already established Chinese Americans help newcomers find housing and employment, and extended family groups provide other needed support.

The family is central to traditional Chinese culture, and many Chinese Americans still hold to Confucian values that emphasize respect for elders and a clear hierarchy of authority among extended family members. Family loyalty and unity is more important than individual dreams and achievements. All emotional and financial support is expected to be supplied by the family. This very closed and structured system creates tightly bonded families where divorce is rare and children remain enmeshed with their parents throughout life. Younger, American-born Chinese Americans sometimes find this family closeness stifling. It conflicts with the modern American values of independence and autonomy they have learned in school and from other American friends. But it can also serve as an anchor of stability in the ever-changing, often confusing, world of the industrialized US.

Food is almost as important as family to traditional Chinese. Many Chinese Americans continue to eat traditional foods prepared in traditional ways. Rituals and etiquette surrounding the preparation, serving, and consumption of food are passed on from one generation to the next. Today, Chinese restaurants are located in almost every city in the US, as well as in smaller towns and villages. There are even Chinese fast-food chains. Chinese food is now one of the most popular ethnic foods in America, and even non-Chinese Americans know how to use chopsticks. Fortune cookies, canned chop suey, and other "Chinese" foods are sold in mainstream supermarkets, and scores of

CHINESE AMERICANS

| 0 | 200 | 200 | 400 Miles |

| 0 | 200 | 200 | 400 Kilometers |

Chinese cookbooks are available in libraries and bookstores throughout the US.

Although Chinese Americans were barred from attending public schools up through the mid-1800s, they are now well integrated into the American educational system. Confucianism promotes education as the key to a successful life, and Chinese American parents continue to encourage their children to do well in school. Chinese American families place a high value on education and spend a large amount of their time, energy, and money on their children's schooling. Chinese American children who also attend Chinese language school put in many hours of study each night to keep up with the increased amount of homework.

Chinese Americans have shared much of their traditional culture, as well as their experience as immigrants, with the wider US public through their writings, music, and art. Well-known Chinese American writers include Maxine Hong Kingston (b.1940), Betty Bao Lord (b.1938), Amy Tan (b.1952), Gus Lee (b.1946), Gish Jen (b.1955), David Wong Louie (b.1954), playwrights C. Y. (Chin-Yang) Lee (b.1917), Frank Chin (b.1940), and David Henry Hwang (b.1957), and poets Nellie Wong (b.1934) and Alan Chong Lau (b.1948).

Until recently, Chinese Americans did not find much success in the American art world. Painter Yung Gee (1906–1963), an immigrant from Canton, was the only Chinese American in the modernist art scene in New York City in the 1920s. He was attacked several times in the streets by racist thugs when walking with his European American wife. Dong Kingman (b.1911)

became the first Chinese American artist to have his work shown and purchased by the Metropolitan Museum of Art in 1940. Today, however, there are many successful Chinese American artists. Maya Lin (b.1959), a sculptor and architect, is perhaps the best known. She designed the Vietnam War Memorial in Washington, D. C., and the Civil Rights Memorial in Montgomery, Alabama. Another famous Chinese American architect is I. M. Pei (b.1917), who has designed many buildings including the John F. Kennedy Memorial Library in Boston, Massachusetts, and the Rock and Roll Hall of Fame and Museum in Cleveland, Ohio.

Chinese American cellist Yo-Yo Ma (b.1955) is known worldwide. He has made over 50 recordings, won 8 Grammy awards, and has been given a number of honorary degrees from various universities, including an honorary doctorate from Yale University in New Haven, Connecticut. Herb Wong, a disc jockey for over 30 years in San Francisco, is also president of the Association of Jazz Educators. He encourages young Chinese Americans to express themselves creatively, especially in music.

Chinese American workers have made great contributions to American society. In the 1800s, they worked in factories and sweat shops, coal and quicksilver mines, and on farms in the West. Some 10,000-12,000 Chinese Americans blasted through mountains and laid track for the Transcontinental Railroad from 1865-69. However, they were still faced with discrimination in hiring and were legally forbidden to own land. Eventually, they set up laundries, restaurants, and gambling

Chinese American women doing morning tai chi exercises at Washington Square, San Francisco. (Alison Wright Photography)

establishments across the US, since these were the only businesses open to them.

In the Civil Rights Movement of the 1960s, however, new areas of employment were opened to Chinese Americans. Many were now able to pursue higher education and enter a variety of professions, while others were allowed to join trade unions and become skilled laborers. Some successful Chinese American professionals are Nobel Prize-winning physicists Chen Ning Yang (b.1922) and Tsung Dao Lee (b.1926); physicist Chien Shing Wu (b.1912), who received from Princeton in 1958 the first honorary doctorate in science ever given to a woman; electronics specialist An Wang (1920–1990), founder of Wang Laboratories; computer-industry entrepreneurs David Lam, David Lee, and Albert Yu; US senator Hiram Fong (b.1907); Elaine Chao (b.1952), former peace corps director and current president of the United Way of America; Lily Lee, who in 1983 became the first Chinese American woman mayor in the US; newsanchor Connie Chung (b.1946); actors Anna May Wong (1907–61), Bruce Lee (1940–73), Rosalind Chao, and B. D. Wong (b.1962); and film director Wayne Wang (b.1949).

In contrast to traditional Chinese culture, Chinese American women and men both work outside the home as wage earners, often at more than one job. Many Chinese Americans own family businesses where all members of the extended family, including children, work long hours. The traditional Chinese work ethic remains strong among both foreign-born and American-born Chinese Americans.

In their early history, Chinese Americans were almost completely unrepresented in American sports. Today, however, a growing number of young Chinese Americans are rising to the top of the sports world, particularly in tennis, track and field, gymnastics, and figure skating. In 1989, tennis-player Michael Chang (b.1972) became the youngest man ever to win the French Open. In 1984, Tiffany Chin placed fourth in women's figure skating at the Olympics, and Michelle Kwan (b.1980) won the silver medal in women's figure skating in the 1994 Goodwill Games. Both Chin and Kwan have skated in many World Championship and Olympic competitions.

Chinese Americans still enjoy traditional Chinese opera, performed by traveling companies in Chinatowns across the US. Chinese films, particularly Hong Kong action movies, are very popular among young Chinese Americans, as well as with non-Chinese American audiences. Bruce Lee became enormously successful as a martial artist and actor in many "kung fu" films. His son, Brandon Lee (1965–1993) followed in his father's footsteps but met an early death in 1993 when a prop gun accidentally went off during the filming of *The Crow*.

Despite their widespread success in today's American society, Chinese Americans still suffer from racial discrimination. One notorious example was the brutal murder in 1982 of Chinese American Vincent Chin by two unemployed European American auto workers in Detroit (who called him a "Jap" and blamed him for their lack of work). The auto workers were convicted only of manslaughter, fined $3,780 each, and sentenced to three years' probation.

BIBLIOGRAPHY

Bernardo, Stephanie. *The Ethnic Almanac*. Garden City, New York: Dolphin Books/Doubleday & Co., 1981.

Moy, Tina. *Chinese Americans*. New York: Marshall Cavendish, 1995.

US Bureau of the Census. *Detailed Ancestry Groups for States*. 1990 Census of Population Supplementary Reports, CP-S-1-2. Washington, DC, October 1992.

———. *The Foreign-Born Population in the United States*. 1990 CP-3-1. Washington, DC, July 1993.

Yu, Connie Young. "Who Are the Chinese Americans?" In *The Asian American Almanac*, Susan Gall and Irene Natividad, ed. Detroit: Gale Research, 1995.

—by D. K. Daeg de Mott

CHOCTAW

PRONUNCIATION: chok-taw

LOCATION: United States (Southeast Oklahoma; Mississippi; Louisiana)

POPULATION: 100,000 (Oklahoma)

LANGUAGE: English; Choctaw

RELIGION: Traditional Choctaw; Christianity

RELATED ARTICLES: Vol. 2: Native North Americans

¹ INTRODUCTION

The Choctaw, along with the Creek, Chickasaw, Cherokee, and Seminole nations, were called the "Five Civilized Tribes" by European Americans because they had organized systems of government and education, and many of their ways seemed to reflect European culture. The Choctaw had their first encounter with Europeans in the fall of 1540. The Spanish explorer Hernando de Soto was making his way west from Florida when he came upon a Choctaw village. Afraid that de Soto and his forces were going to take them prisoner, the Choctaw attacked. Their bows and arrows did little against the Spaniards' armor and guns. The Spaniards won the battle, and more than 1,500 Choctaw died. Fortunately, that was the Choctaw's last encounter with Europeans for more than 150 years.

Throughout the first half of the 18th century, the Choctaw sided with the French in their war with the British over control of the New World. Shifting alliances between the three Choctaw bands and the European forces in the area, however, caused a Choctaw civil war in 1748. One of the bands had decided to side with the British and the nearby Chickasaw tribe. The French helped their Choctaw allies defeat the British and the British-allied Choctaw. The treaty signed at the end of the war made it clear that the Choctaw were never again to ally themselves with the British. They held true to this in the American Revolutionary War (1775–83), when many Choctaws sided and even fought with the American colonists against Britain.

After the United States became an independent country, the Choctaw continued to be on good terms with the government. Often, in exchange for Choctaw land, the US government would agree to pay off Choctaw debts and frequently gave the chiefs gifts. For a large cession of land in 1805, the government agreed to pay the Choctaw an annuity of $3,000, which immensely helped the tribe, providing it with a stable income. The Choctaw sided with the Confederacy in the Civil War in 1861, greatly influenced by the fact that the states of Texas and Arkansas (bordering the tribal lands) seceded from the union. In addition, the commerce and business routes used by the Choctaws were within the states sympathizing with the south. The Union also withdrew its troops from the Choctaw Nation as war threatened. The US government stopped paying the annuity; the agents of the government were southern men. When the Confederacy approached the Choctaws, they were ready to join. After the war, the US government began paying the annuity again, but further Choctaw land cessions required by the government prevented the Choctaw from climbing out of their poverty.

² LOCATION AND HOMELAND

The Choctaw are originally from what is now the northwestern US, but after hearing good land was plentiful in the east, they emigrated to present-day Mississippi and Alabama. The climate there is very warm and humid, providing them with good farming conditions in the rich soils near the rivers. The land is home to abundant forests, filled with a great variety of wild game, fish, and berries for food.

Traditionally, there were two distinct Choctaw clans, designated by the Creator. Intermarriages between the two clans were forbidden, and Choctaws followed their mother's clan. Today most Choctaw do not know from which clan they are descended.

In 1820 the Choctaw and the US government signed a treaty at Doak's stand in which the Choctaw agreed to cede the remainder of their land in Mississippi to the US government. An article in the treaty promised a blanket, kettle, rifle gun, bullet molds and nippers, and ammunition sufficient for hunting and defense for one year. The Treaty of 1830, signed at Dancing Rabbit Creek, conveyed to the Choctaw Nation a tract of country west of the Mississippi River, in fee simple to them and their descendants. This treaty also gave them the right of self-governance. Of the nearly 20,000 Choctaw living in Mississippi at that time, about 14,000 moved west to Oklahoma. Many of those who stayed in Mississippi were cheated out of their land by a cruel Bureau of Indian Affairs (BIA) employee who refused them the right to register. The 6,000 Choctaw who had stayed in Mississippi consequently fell into harsh poverty, while their kinsmen in Oklahoma became prosperous. The Oklahoma Choctaw quickly rebuilt their tribal structure and began farming, soon producing a crop surplus which they sold to the US government. By 1855, a generation later, about 6,000 more Choctaw had moved to Oklahoma to escape the rough conditions in Mississippi. This left only some 2,000 in the Choctaw's ancestral homeland.

After the Civil War, however, the Choctaw's prosperity in Oklahoma began to change. The US government informed the Choctaw that European and African Americans would be allowed to live on Choctaw land. By 1890 there were 10,017 Choctaw, 28,345 European Americans, and 4,406 African Americans living on Choctaw land in Indian Territory. The Choctaw had become a minority in their own land.

When the General Allotment Act of 1887 was put into effect for the Choctaw in November 1907, the Oklahoma Choctaw lost their tribal designation and were forced to become Oklahoma citizens. While there are Choctaw communities in Oklahoma today, there is no Choctaw reservation. There is a Choctaw reservation in Mississippi. The total population of the Choctaw Nation of Oklahoma is over 100,000.

³ LANGUAGE

The Choctaw language is part of the Muskogan language family and is related to Creek, Chickasaw, Seminole, and Miccosukee. The word "Oklahoma" comes from the Choctaw language. When future Choctaw chief Choctaw Allen Wright was asked what he thought Indian Territory should be named if it were to be controlled under one common government, he replied *okla homma*, meaning "red people" in Choctaw.

The Choctaw have done a good job of preserving their language. In 1819 they requested the assistance of Christian missionaries in translating the Bible and some hymns into the

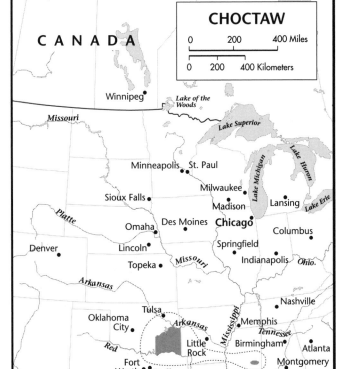

CHOCTAW

0   200   400 Miles

0   200   400 Kilometers

CANADA

ers, were often consulted by members of the tribe to give aid in their particular area of specialty.

The Choctaw believed that every person had two souls. After a person's body died, one soul stayed among the living Choctaw to frighten them. The other soul went to a good or a bad place, depending on how the deceased had lived his or her life. Most Choctaw's souls went to the good, sunny place. Only the souls of murderers were condemned to the dark place.

Perhaps the most remarkable characteristic of Choctaw religion is its promotion of complete peace and harmony among peoples. The Choctaw almost never attacked anyone throughout their history. They did, however, defend themselves, their loved ones, and their way of life to the death when attacked by others. Today, the majority of Choctaw are Christian.

6 MAJOR HOLIDAYS

Every summer since 1949, the Choctaw have hosted the Mississippi Choctaw's Indian Fair in Pearl River, Mississippi. The fair is held on the campus of the Choctaw Central High School and nearly 20,000 people—including both Native North Americans and non-Native North Americans—come every year. The four-day fair promotes tourism in the area and helps the Choctaw maintain their tribal heritage and customs. Another Choctaw festival is held at Tushka Homma, Oklahoma every Labor Day weekend. It is open to the public and free of charge. Between 80,000 and 100,000 visitors every year enjoy country music concerts in the amphitheater, handmade arts and crafts, sports and children's activities, Choctaw social dancing, stickball exhibitions, a quilt show, War Monument Memorial Services, rides, animal acts, and more. The Chief gives the annual State of the Nation address.

7 RITES OF PASSAGE

One of the most elaborate ceremonies the Choctaw traditionally performed was when someone died. The deceased person's corpse was wrapped in animal skins or tree bark and then placed on a platform high above the ground, where it was left until it decomposed. During that time, friends and relatives would come by and mourn. When the body had fully decomposed, the tribal official known as the "bone picker" (usually ornamented with body paint and tattoos) would scrape the remaining flesh from the bones with his long fingernails. Once the bones were cleaned, they were placed in a box and stored in the community bone house. After the bone-picker had finished his unsavory task, he would preside over a feast for family and friends of the deceased—with his unwashed bare hands. Once a year, all the bones that had been collected in the bone house during the past 12 months were buried together in a mound, and a communal funeral was held.

This death ritual was abandoned in the 19th century, however. European Americans and mixed-blood Choctaw did not approve of the ceremony, thinking it uncivilized. Consequently, beginning in the 19th century the Choctaw buried the corpse with many of the deceased's valued possessions to accompany his or her soul to the afterlife. Then, after a mourning period, a tribal feast was held. This custom was changed even further as more Choctaw converted to Christianity and Christian elements were added.

Choctaw language. In addition, missionaries worked with them to create a Choctaw dictionary, as well as a grammar and spelling book using the Roman alphabet. There are book/tape sets that offer instruction in the Choctaw language, available through the Choctaw Nation of Oklahoma. Many Choctaw today still communicate in their native language when English is not necessary.

4 FOLKLORE

The Choctaw often tell a story about how they ended up in Mississippi. They began in the northwest and, in their search for good farmland, moved in an easterly direction. Every night the chief stuck a pole in the ground, and every morning it was leaning east. So they continued east until one morning they woke up and the pole was sticking straight up. That was where they decided to stay. To celebrate and to thank the Great Spirit, they built a large mound at that spot: present-day Nanih Waiya, Mississippi, which means "leaning mound."

5 RELIGION

While the Choctaw did not believe in any one, highest being, they did believe that there were spirits everywhere and that all things had a soul. Their medicine men, or *alikchi*, were traditionally thought of as prophets. When the *alikchi* saw a good vision, it was considered a good omen for the upcoming battle or raid. A dark vision undoubtedly meant bad luck or even death. Other members of Choctaw society were also seen to have special powers. These healers or rainmakers, among oth-

8 INTERPERSONAL RELATIONS

Each of the three Choctaw bands was traditionally ruled by a district chief, or *miko*. The mikos were elected by the men of their district, and together the three mikos governed the entire Choctaw nation. Each village had their own council of elders, which had a chief to preside over the meetings. The Choctaw always elected their public officials and were always very democratic about it. Although women were not allowed to vote, they had a great deal of power in that clan membership was inherited through the mother and, therefore, women were at the head of the all-important clan. The eldest woman of each clan was highly respected by all in the community.

Increased contact with the British and French, and later with European Americans, significantly changed parts of Choctaw tribal structure and society. Many Choctaw women married British and French men, producing a large minority of Choctaw mixed-bloods, who later became fairly influential in the tribe. In addition, the tribe's judicial system was changed to be more like that of the United States. Traditionally, Choctaw who committed a crime were punished by the victim's family. But by the late 19th century, the Choctaw had instituted the "light horsemen," a group of sheriffs and judges that traveled from town to town, holding trials.

In the last 100 years the Choctaw have experienced many changes in their tribal structure. Since 1975 the Choctaw in Mississippi have had a tribal constitution stating that the tribal chief is to be elected by all tribe members every four years. The tribal council meets once every quarter and makes the laws for the Choctaw reservation in Mississippi. The state government legally has no power over those Choctaw living on the reservation. In Oklahoma, there is no reservation; it is considered "Indian Country." The Choctaw Nation of Oklahoma has its own constitution in place, with three branches of government: an executive branch, a legislative branch (with 12 council members), and a judicial branch. There is a Tribal Court at Tushka Homma, and the council also meets there monthly.

9 LIVING CONDITIONS

Traditionally, the Choctaw lived in wood-frame houses constructed by fastening wooden poles together with vines. For insulation, the walls were then packed with mud, and the outside was covered with cypress or pine bark. There was one door three or four feet tall, and two small holes were left in the ceiling to allow the smoke from the cooking fire to escape.

When the Choctaw nation split in two in the 1830s, both groups grew accustomed to living in very different ways. The Choctaw in Oklahoma, who received a $3,000 annuity from the US government, were much better off than the poverty-stricken, landless Mississippi Choctaw. At the beginning of the 20th century, however, their respective conditions began to reverse. In 1907, the General Allotment Act was put into effect for the Oklahoma Choctaw, and many of them were swindled out of their land. In 1918, the US government recognized the severe poverty of the Choctaw living in Mississippi and instituted programs to improve their living conditions.

Recently, efforts have been made to help the Choctaw further improve their housing. In 1965, the Choctaw Housing Authority (CHA) began building modern, sturdy homes for Choctaw living in Mississippi. A few years later, the CHA was established in Hugo, Oklahoma, to improve the standard of living among those of Choctaw descent living in Oklahoma.

10 FAMILY LIFE

Choctaw society is matrilineal (lineage is inherited through the mother). Children belong to their mother's clan. Traditionally, a mother raises her daughters while the mother's brothers, as the closest male relatives in her clan, raise her sons. Marriage between two people of the same clan is prohibited.

In the past, women were not allowed to speak their husband's name but would refer to him as "my children's father." They never dared look upon their son-in-law's face but would avert their eyes when he came into the room. This practice is not followed today.

11 CLOTHING

In the days before the Choctaw had contact with Europeans, Choctaw men wore a loincloth and a belt in the summer, and in the winter, they added leather moccasins, leggings, and shirts woven from feathers. Women commonly wore deerskin skirts and added moccasins and a deerskin shawl in the winter.

Today's Choctaw wear modern Western-style clothing for everyday purposes. Traditional clothing is sometimes worn for ceremonies and festivals.

12 FOOD

The Choctaw, along with the other peoples of the "Five Civilized Tribes," made many traditional dishes, such as the following:

Blue Grape Dumplings

½ gallon unsweetened grape juice
2 cups sugar
2 tablespoons shortening, melted
1 teaspoon baking powder
1 cup water
Flour

Bring grape juice to a rolling boil with the sugar.

Mix water, shortening, and baking powder. Add enough flour to make a stiff dough.

Roll out thin on a floured board and cut into small pieces.

Drop each piece one at a time into the boiling juice. Cook over high heat about 5 minutes, and then simmer for about 10 minutes, covered.

Remove from heat; let stand for 10 minutes, covered, before serving. May be served with cream or plain.

Wild Onions and Eggs

Wild onions, cut up (any amount you want)
1 cup water
1 cup shortening, melted
6 eggs

Cut up enough wild onions to fill a 6- to 10-inch skillet. Add water and shortening to onions.

Salt to taste, and fry until water is almost gone (15 to 20 minutes).

Break eggs on top of onion in skillet, and stir well. Fry until eggs are scrambled. Serve hot.

[recipes contributed by the Choctaw Nation of Oklahoma]

13 EDUCATION

In the 1810s, the Choctaws asked Cyrus Kingsbury, a Presbyterian missionary, to help them set up a school. With Kingsbury in charge, the first Choctaw school opened in 1818 in Elliot, Mississippi. The school was founded with the interest money from a large annuity the US government had promised to pay the Choctaws for their 1816 cession of three million acres of land. When they were relocated to Oklahoma, again they used their annuity funds to build good Choctaw schools. Because of their fairly high level of education (even compared with most European Americans who lived in Indian Territory in the second half of the century), the Choctaw became better off economically.

Although presently most Choctaw children attend public elementary schools, in 1968 Choctaw Central High School was built in Pearl River, Mississippi. There are currently a number of Choctaw- and government-run programs to increase the educational level of the Choctaw. On the Mississippi reservation, there are adult education programs to help strengthen the Choctaw's English reading and writing skills. The Oklahoma Choctaw Council has established nearly a dozen Headstart centers throughout southeastern Oklahoma. The Oklahoma Nation also runs a Higher Education Vocational Development Program, GED programs, job training, and other assistance programs. Near Hartshorne, Oklahoma, there is a boarding school operated by the Choctaw Nation, called Jones Academy. More than 90% of Choctaw teenagers attend high school, and 70% of the adult population has attained a high school diploma.

14 CULTURAL HERITAGE

Dancing used to be a very important part of the Choctaw culture, but over the years the traditional dances were not performed as frequently. In recent years, however, the younger generations have regained an interest in their traditional culture and are reviving the traditional dances. In Broken Bow, Oklahoma, the public school offers a Choctaw dance program. Students learn the dances of their ancestors and they often travel to perform at ceremonies and festivals.

15 WORK

Traditionally, the Choctaw farmed and hunted. Choctaw children (mostly boys) hunted with a blow gun, or an *uski thompa*. A hollow piece of swamp cane through which long, sharp darts were blown, it could kill an animal instantly. Other Choctaw boys hunted with rabbit sticks, which are similar to billy clubs. They would line up in groups of 8 to 10 boys, cross the field together to flush out the rabbits, and then beat them in the heads with their sticks.

After losing nearly all of their land to European American settlers when the General Allotment Act was put into effect at the turn of the century, many Choctaw went to work in the timber and mining industries.

In 1953 the US government instituted a number of vocational training programs in Mississippi to help prepare Choctaw for jobs in the mainstream industrialized job market. The Chata Development Company was created in 1969 by the Choctaw council to help find and create jobs for Choctaw in Mississippi. In 1977 the Chata Wire Harness Enterprise was established near Pearl River. This factory employs many Choctaw, making electrical parts for cars for the General Motors

(GM) company. The GM factory, built in 1973, is located in an industrial park that is also the home of many other industries, such as the Choctaw Greeting Enterprise of the American Greetings Corporation. Despite all these factory openings, however, unemployment on the Mississippi reservation is still at about 20%, well above the national average.

The Oklahoma Choctaw are doing well, though. They have opened bingo parlors in Durant, Pocola, Idabel, and Arrowhead, which has proven to be a very successful business, attracting many tourists. In addition, the Choctaw in Oklahoma run the Arrowhead Resort and Hotel in Canada, Oklahoma, and Travel Plazas in Hugo, Pocola, Idabel, and Durant. The tribe also owns a finishing plant, a trailer manufacturing plant, and tribally-owned and managed day care centers. Profits from all these businesses go to programs for Choctaw assistance.

16 SPORTS

A traditional Choctaw sport is *ishtaboli*, or "stick ball," which is similar to modern-day lacrosse. The small ball is made from deerskin or cowhide that is stitched together. The players use two sticks, or *kapucha*, at the same time. Kapucha are made from hickory wood and are about three feet long. A point is scored when the ball is scooped up in the net of the stick and thrown against the other team's goal post. Ishtaboli games used to be huge ordeals, typically lasting more than 12 hours (or until one team had scored 100 points), with 75–100 players per team. Traditionally, ishtaboli games were sometimes used to settle differences, but today the Choctaw play just for fun.

17 ENTERTAINMENT AND RECREATION

The Choctaw often held dances and feasts, frequently centered around an ishtaboli match. Before the match, the women would lay out some of their possessions and bet on which team would win. The players then performed a lengthy dance that lasted all night, before starting the game at dawn. When the game was over, the women who had bet on the winning team claimed their prizes, and there was a great celebration with a large feast. Another common way the Choctaw entertained themselves was with bow and arrow competitions, which they still hold at their annual festivals.

18 FOLK ART, CRAFTS, AND HOBBIES

Choctaw women have always been master basket-weavers, which is the Choctaw's most elaborate art. The women make the baskets by cutting sticks of cane from a swamp. They let the sticks dry, and then slice them into thin strips. Different colored strips are created with dyes made from wild berries and roots.

19 SOCIAL PROBLEMS

One of the biggest problems of the Choctaw tribe is their lack of unity. While the Choctaw in Mississippi are able to live together and function as a tribe on the reservation, they are separated from their kinfolk in Oklahoma. The Choctaw in Oklahoma, on the other hand, have no reservation and are consequently scattered throughout the state, making it difficult to maintain a sense of unity. However, they keep in touch with a monthly newspaper, *Bishinik,* which means "newsbird" in Choctaw.

In recent years, health has been a serious problem for the Choctaw as well. On the reservation in Mississippi, many die from tuberculosis and pneumonia. On the reservation, new health service programs teach the Choctaw how to help prevent such diseases by improving their nutrition. In Oklahoma, health clinics have been opened in Hugo, Broken Bow, McAlester, Poteau, and Durant, as well as a hospital in Talihina, to treat those of Choctaw descent. Social assistance programs include a Recover Center for drug and alcohol dependency problems, and Chi Hullo Li, a residential treatment center for women who suffer from addictions as well as abuse. The women in the program may have their children live with them if they wish.

More than a dozen sites in Oklahoma serve nutritious lunches, some five days a week. Other Oklahoma programs even offer such necessities as burial assistance.

[20] BIBLIOGRAPHY

Conklin, Paul. *Choctaw Boy*. New York: Dodd, Mead & Company, 1975.

Kimball, Yeffe, and Jean Anderson. *The Art of American Indian Cooking*. Garden City, New York: Doubleday & Co., 1965.

Lepthien, Emilie U. *The Choctaw*. Chicago: Children's Press, 1987.

McKee, Jesse O. *The Choctaw*. New York: Chelsea House, 1989.

Morrison, James D. *The Social History of the Choctaw Nation: 1865–1907*.

Reddy, Marlita A., ed. *Statistical Record of Native North Americans*, 2nd ed. Detroit: Gale Research, 1995.

—reviewed by J. Allen

COLOMBIANS

LOCATION: Colombia
POPULATION: 32 million
LANGUAGE: Spanish (official); various Amerindian languages
RELIGION: Roman Catholicism; native Amerindian religions

[1] INTRODUCTION

Colombia was settled by the Spanish in the 16th century. Initially, and up to the war of independence that freed Colombia from Spanish rule, it was known as the Viceroyalty of Nueva Granada. During Spanish colonial rule, many Amerindian tribes were subdued and heavily taxed by the Spanish Crown. Slaves were brought from Africa but were eventually freed during the period of struggle for independence. During an uprising in the capital, Bogotá, on 20 July 1810, the local inhabitants threw out their Spanish officials. This day is commemorated as Independence Day, although the struggles continued for several years. In the War of Independence, the Venezuelan-born leader Simón Bolívar played a key role, joining forces with the Colombian leader Francisco de Paula Santander. Colombia, Venezuela, and Ecuador together became the Republic of Gran Colombia, although each became an independent nation not long after.

Colombia has had several dictators in the 20th century. In the late 1950s President Lleras Camargo formed a government of national unity to end bitter years of political strife between members of the two main parties, the Liberals and the Conservatives. This led to the present phase of democratically elected presidents, which has continued to this day. More recently there have been fears that the democracy and independence of major institutions such as the judiciary and Congress are being compromised, thanks to power and money concentrated in the hands of drug traffickers, who also developed private armies in some instances. Equally, many judges as well as members of a vigorous press with a long and honorable tradition in Colombia have paid with their lives for attempts to expose the activities of powerful outlaws.

Various left-wing guerrilla factions have also fought army units for decades. An unusual feature of Colombian life is that political and social unrest coexist with able and fairly stable economic management.

[2] LOCATION AND HOMELAND

Colombia occupies the northwestern corner of South America and has both Pacific and Caribbean coastlines. The mighty Andes mountains cross into Colombia from the southern border with Ecuador and divide into three long ranges or *cordilleras* which run the length of the country. To the east, extensive plains run as far as the Orinoco River which borders Venezuela; to the south, thick jungle extends towards the Amazon River and the borders with Peru and Brazil. These contrasting features contribute to Colombia's natural beauty and variety, as well as to a climate ranging from cool, through temperate, to tropically hot.

The capital, Bogotá, is located on a high plateau over 2,400 m (8,000 ft) above sea level at the foot of the eastern range of the Andes.

Colombia has a variety of Amerindian tribes, scattered partly in the north in the desert peninsula of La Guajira and high up in the Caribbean coastal ranges of the Sierra Nevada de Santa Marta, as well as in the south, particularly in the Amazon region, with a few tribes in other areas such as the Tierradentro region.

Aside from the minority Amerindian population, about 20% of the population are white and about 5% are black. The majority are *mestizo* or of mixed Amerindian and white descent; there are people of African descent or mixed black African and white descent in the Caribbean and Pacific coastal areas.

³ LANGUAGE

Although the various Amerindian tribes continue to speak their own languages, Spanish is the official language of Colombia. The accent varies considerably according to the region, but it is generally recognized that the Spanish spoken in the capital, Bogotá, is remarkably clear.

People usually use both their father's and their mother's surnames, in that order, as in many other Latin American countries. The strong influence of the Catholic Church has made names like María very popular, usually in combination with another name, such as María Cristina, María Teresa, or María Elena. It is not unusual even for men to use the name María in combination with masculine names, such as José María, Pedro María, or even Jesus María. The names of the apostles are generally popular for boys.

Among poorer townsfolk there is a tradition of exotic names of famous warriors or unusual kings derived from ancient history, and it is not unusual to find people called Hannibal, Nebuchadnezzer, Mithridates, or Darius.

⁴ FOLKLORE

Amerindian, black African, and Spanish folk customs have combined with beliefs and practices from all three traditions to create a rich culture which expresses itself in a great variety of festivals, which occur throughout the year in Colombia.

Barranquilla, on Colombia's Caribbean coast, and other coastal towns along the Magdalena River celebrate a yearly Carnival which combines Spanish colonial, Amerindian, and black African influences, colorful costumes and masks, and flutes and African drums.

In colonial times, sedan-chairs were a form of transport which is remembered in the city of Medellín. The chairs are decorated with a fabulous array of flowers and paraded through the city streets.

The Feast of St. Francis is celebrated in the Chocó region in the Pacific. He was adopted as the patron saint of the miners in this mainly black, gold-mining region, and this festival links up with many other celebrations along the rivers where the statues of various saints are paraded in canoes and on rafts. There is also music, singing, and dancing. The miners of the Chocó gave St. Francis the affectionate Spanish nickname of *San Pacho,* and the festival is also known by this name.

⁵ RELIGION

Roman Catholicism is the religion of Colombia. Many Colombians have a strong faith, and the Church has played an important role in the life of Colombia. Even the main political parties developed in relation to attitudes towards the church, with the conservatives adopting more favorable attitudes of support, and the liberals adopting an anticlerical role. Women have played a significant role in maintaining a tradition of strong faith.

Some Amerindian groups have adopted Catholicism, but in remote areas they continue to practice their own beliefs, which include various forms of shamanism.

⁶ MAJOR HOLIDAYS

Colombia celebrates Independence Day on 20 July, the discovery of America on 12 October, and makes provision for the main Catholic holidays. It also marks Easter with major religious events such as the Holy Week procession in the town of Popayán, during which many statues of Jesus, the Virgin Mary, and saints such as St. John the Evangelist are paraded by groups of *cargueros* or carriers along the streets. Others walk alongside carrying lit candles called *alumbrantes.* It is considered a great honor to take part in the processions, which are solemn and have a very Spanish flavor. The people of Popayán are traditionalists who remember their Spanish origins with pride, and various members of the Order of Knights of the Holy Sepulcher of Jerusalem also take part in the procession, in formal dress and white capes.

⁷ RITES OF PASSAGE

All the main Catholic rituals that mark important phases in a person's life are observed by a majority of the population in Colombia. Among these are baptism and First Communion, as well as Catholic marriage and burial rites. Some practices have included a mixture of either Amerindian or black African customs. Even recently in some villages on the Caribbean coast, for example, it was not uncommon when a child died for the child to be "loaned" to neighboring villages so their inhabitants could also participate in the ceremonies.

⁸ INTERPERSONAL RELATIONS

Colombian customs vary according to region and social class in certain respects. For example, it is generally recognized that in coastal areas such as Barranquilla people are more informal, spontaneous, and easygoing, yet in the neighboring town of Cartagena, which has a strong historical sense and many colonial features, people are a bit more formal. The people of the capital, Bogotá, are generally considered more reserved, and it is still the custom there for close family members to address each other using the formal *usted* rather than the informal *tu.* They have also maintained an older, Spanish form of address, *Su merced,* which means "Your mercy"—which remains from colonial times in the 16th century.

Women usually greet each other with a kiss; men shake hands, but if they are friendly they shake hands and pat each other on the back several times as well.

It is considered essential to offer the visitor, whether on business or social occasions, a small cup of black coffee called a *tinto.* It is also considered rude to launch directly into a business discussion, or even a social one, without first inquiring after the person's welfare and that of his or her family.

⁹ LIVING CONDITIONS

Out of a population of 32 million, some 7 million Colombians live in the capital, Bogotá. Other major towns are Medellín, Cali, and Barranquilla. Living conditions vary greatly according to social class. All main towns have wealthy suburbs with tasteful, modern housing that includes houses and apartment blocks. In poorer areas there are often large shantytowns, and housing can vary from fairly solid constructions to basic shelters built with a variety of materials and corrugated metal roofs. There has been an increase in middle-class housing, but the construction boom has also included rising prices which have put even modest housing units beyond the reach of many. In mountain villages some houses can still be quite basic, with adobe walls and thatched roofs, although some village housing can include plastered walls and tiled roofs. In poorer areas along the Pacific and Caribbean coasts, especially in more remote villages, the hotter climate allows a type of housing that uses local cane, reeds, and palm branches. In such areas it is not unusual for people to use hammocks rather than beds.

Access to health care also varies greatly, and poor people rely on state hospitals, which usually are better equipped in major cities, as well as on nursing care often provided by religious nursing orders of nuns. In other instances, poor people appeal to native healers called *curanderos,* some of whom have genuine healing ability, although there are many charlatans. People with better financial resources have access to modern, well-equipped hospitals and health centers.

It is relatively expensive to run a car, so many people rely on public transport in the form of buses, and this form of transport also is used from one town to another. Because of the mountainous terrain, air transport developed early in Colombia, with even quite remote locations boasting an airstrip, whereas railways are much less developed. Colombians often joke about arriving "either by mule or air."

¹⁰ FAMILY LIFE

Close family ties and extended families are an important aspect of Colombian life. Colombians often have large families and often keep in touch through weddings, anniversaries, birthdays, baptisms, and other special occasions, with a family network that extends to second and third cousins. This network is more easily maintained in small to medium-sized towns. The population distribution of Colombia means that there are many towns of this type, in particular along the densely populated foothills of the three ranges of the Andes mountains which cross the country in a north–south direction.

The Church has also been influential in stressing the importance of close family ties. Family networks act as a vital support in the absence, for many, of welfare benefits which are much less developed than those in North America or Europe. Godparents or *padrinos* may also play a supportive role, sometimes helping with tuition or gifts to assist a family. Family members are also depended upon to provide jobs wherever possible.

In cases where the stresses of extreme poverty lead to the abandonment of children, who are left to fend for themselves on the street, schemes have been devised where foster mothers are appointed for a whole street and, with state help, provide daytime shelter and meals during the day. Despite these efforts, there are children who are absolutely destitute and have to fend for themselves.

The great variety of animals due to the range of climates means that Colombians will often keep as pets exotic animals such as monkeys and parrots, as well as the more usual cats and dogs, etc.

¹¹ CLOTHING

Clothing varies according to climate in Colombia. Although Western-style clothing is worn everywhere, men on the coast sometimes wear cotton shirts with colorful, bright patterns. In cooler areas of the Andes mountains, both men and women wear woolen *ruanas,* which evolved originally from Spanish capes. Middle- and upper-class women wear stylish versions of the ruana, which depart from the traditional brown shades of virgin wool and can be striped or plain, using a wide range of colors. Traditional peasant women in mountain areas wear voluminous fringed shawls called *pañolones.*

¹² FOOD

Colombia has a great variety of fruits and vegetables. The traditional stew, known as the *cocido* in Bogotá, can include 20 different kinds of vegetables as well as various types of potatoes. Another typical dish from Bogotá is the *ajiaco,* which includes a bright yellow potato known as *papa criolla* as well as chicken and corn, served with a slice of avocado and cream. A typical dessert is made with sweet, stewed figs called *brevas,* served with *arequipe,* which is milk cooked with sugar until it reaches the consistency of toffee.

On the coast a great variety of fish are served fried or sometimes grilled, often with rice flavored with coconut milk. A well-known Caribbean dish is *arroz con chipi-chipi,* or rice with tiny clams. In the Antioquia region and its capital,

Medellín, rice and red beans, served with cornmeal cakes known as *arepas,* and often with fried plantains, are part of the staple diet. In the eastern plains known as Los Llanos, which is mainly cattle country, whole roast calf is sometimes served, traditionally cooked on a spit over a fire and turned manually over and over for about four hours. In other rural areas, roast suckling pig or *lechona* is popular.

Poor people in cities sometimes have a more meager diet than in outlying areas where people can grow their own food. In some cases, the urban poor subsist on diets of bread and potatoes, to which they occasionally add other vegetables.

13 EDUCATION

Primary education is free in Colombia, but about 20% of children in cities and 40% in rural areas do not go to school at all. The birth rate remains fairly high, and about half of the population is under 20 years old, so demand for schooling exceeds what the government can provide.

Despite these difficulties, there have been significant improvements in some aspects of education, particularly the expansion of college and university education since the 1960s. There are over 20 universities, as well as technical and commercial institutes, and training schools that have helped Colombia improve the skills of factory workers.

Colombia also has a reputation for the quality of its schooling, which is considered high, even if it is not able to provide for all those who need it.

14 CULTURAL HERITAGE

Colombia has a rich musical heritage which blends Amerindian, African, and Spanish elements. In the Andes region, 12-string guitars called *tiples* are often used to sing the courtly and romantic *bambucos* which derive partly from Spanish and partly from Amerindian music. On the coast, the most famous music is the *cumbia;* the music is part of most festivals there and is played with flutes and drums. The women wear round-necked, lace-edged blouses and wide, flowery skirts. The men hold lit candles, and the dance itself is graceful, suggesting the swaying of palm trees.

Apart from a rich folk culture, the main cities, in particular Bogotá, have theaters, art galleries, bookshops, and many movie theaters, as well as symphony orchestras.

Colombia has produced excellent painters in the 20th century, including Fernando Botero. Some of his portraits of over-blown, self-important figures are satirical and have achieved international fame. There are many other Colombian painters, including Alejandro Obregón, whose bright, joyful colors recall the landscapes of his Caribbean homeland.

Colombia developed a strong romantic tradition which expressed itself in poetry during the 19th century. This tradition continued into the 20th century in the work of José Asunción Silva and many others. Other influences such as surrealism and existentialism also influenced the development of modern poetic styles. Thoroughly modern poets in this sense are Leon de Greiff and Jorge Zalamea Borda. A folk tradition that incorporates black African elements played a part in the development of other poets such as Porfirio Barba Jacob. Various other Spanish literary traditions, such as the picaresque, influenced some of the best-known poems of Rafael Pombo, who is loved by many children for his humorous depiction of an elegant and pompous frog in the poem *El Renacuajo Paseador (The Strolling Frog),* which most children learn at school.

Colombia's most famous novelist is Gabriel García Márquez, a Nobel Prize-winner. His imaginative novels have been translated into many languages. In his novel *One Hundred Years of Solitude,* the mental realities of people are contrasted with historical events and with time in such a way that a "fabulous" or mythical kind of time is convincingly created. His success encouraged a type of Latin American writing that gives free reign to the imagination. This school of writing has come to be known as "magical realism."

Colombians have a strong tradition of historical writing; among well-known modern historians are Rafael Núñez and Indalecio Liévano Aguirre, who wrote an interesting biography of Simón Bolívar the Liberator.

15 WORK

About 20% of the population are underemployed in Colombia, and people work as street vendors, in markets, on construction jobs, or in a variety of odd jobs. Poor women often find employment as servants. Skilled workers who work in manufacturing have better conditions and more secure employment. Small commercial traders and shopkeepers form an important part of the economy, and there is a growing class of graduates who find employment in trade, manufacturing, or finance. The traditional preference for careers in medicine or law is supplemented by new careers in various fields of engineering, and in communications and computers.

In rural areas people usually work in the fields, and in many parts of Colombia children add to the family income by working extra hours.

16 SPORTS

The most popular sport is soccer, but many other sports are played in Colombia. There are many sporting tournaments that include basketball, volleyball, golf, tennis, and swimming. In cattle-ranching areas there are rodeos. People in river or coastal areas enjoy boating and fishing. Cycling has developed as a competitive sport in which Colombians usually excel because they are used to training in difficult, mountainous terrain.

A game called *tejo* is played among the poorer town dwellers in the Andes region, and consists of trying to land a horseshoe over an upright stick fixed some distance away from the thrower. Much of the betting involved in this game includes whole crates of beer.

17 ENTERTAINMENT AND RECREATION

Popular culture in Colombia includes folk music and dancing, as well as enthusiastic participation in the many secular and religious *fiestas* around the country. Some towns, such as Manizales and Bogotá, have bullfighting seasons which draw large crowds, and it is not unusual for *aficionados* or amateurs to try their hand at bullfighting as well.

People also enjoy the movies, and festivals that revolve around beauty queen contests. Depending on the festival and the region, the winner is given titles such as the Queen of Coffee, or the Queen of Sugar, celebrating the importance of particular agricultural products that form part of Colombia's economy.

Another popular pastime is the *paseo* or outing, when a group of friends or family members leave the town or city to visit a place in the countryside. Some town-dwellers have land or a small farm or relatives in rural areas; wealthy people often have large ranches; others simply travel by bus with friends to outlying areas, choosing a small town or village with beautiful scenery or a few amenities such as a river or a good luncheon place where they can relax, have a picnic, and spend the day. Quite often people will take instruments such as guitars along as well.

[18] FOLK ART, CRAFTS, AND HOBBIES

Colombians are very fine craftspeople, known for beautiful woodwork and metalwork, as well as weaving. When the Spanish conquerors first arrived on the high mountain plateau where they later founded the capital city of Santa Fé de Bogotá, they were astonished at the skill in textile production of the Chibcha Indians, who had developed interesting techniques for dyeing and printing as well as weaving.

The Quimbaya Indians of northwestern Colombia were famous goldsmiths, and during the colonial period there were noted gold- and silversmiths. This tradition of metalworking continues among artisans and jewelry-makers today. Colombians made fine furniture during the colonial period, and woodworking and furniture-making are ongoing skills of many independent craftspersons who coexist with more sophisticated furniture manufacturers. Pottery has been made for centuries, both by the Amerindians and by subsequent *Mestizo* craftspeople.

A typical Colombian instrument is the *tiple* or 12-string guitar, which is still made in Colombia. On the coast, the tradition of drum-making that originated in Africa was brought to Colombia along with the slave trade and continues to this day. Craftspersons also make reed flutes and rattles. A number of Amerindian tribes weave beautiful bags called *mochilas* which are hung loosely over the shoulder and which city dwellers also find practical to use. Amerindian hammocks in various styles are also purchased, and town-dwellers in the tropical zones of Colombia often hang them up on their front porches or verandas.

[19] SOCIAL PROBLEMS

Severe social problems in Colombia are caused by the widely differing living standards between rich and poor. Colombians often have a caustic wit, as exemplified in the sharp verse attributed to the Colombian humorist Gabriel Ocampo Giraldo: "Here, thanks to a just sentence, lies a thief who was a beginner, who did not steal enough to prove his innocence!" There is ongoing conflict between army units and guerrilla armies. Problems continue with the activities of the drug traffickers, who often employ large numbers of people and resort to violence to settle scores with rivals. They have also used bribes to obstruct the course of justice, and some of them have become immensely wealthy. A continuing problem is kidnapping in order to obtain ransom money, a device often used by guerrilla armies or sometimes by drug traffickers who want to threaten people they think are interfering with their activities.

The atmosphere of insecurity has given rise to the increasing use of security guards to guard individual citizens who feel threatened, as well as to protect private homes and public buildings.

[20] BIBLIOGRAPHY

Antología del humor colombiano. Medellín: Ediciones A. A., Editorial Bedout, 1962.

Caballero, Enrique. *Historia económica de Colombia.* Bogotá: Banco de Bogotá, 1971.

de Friedemann, Nina S. *Fiestas.* Bogotá: Villegas Editores, 1995.

Olive de Coll, J. *La Resistencia Indígena Ante la Reconquista.* Mexico: Siglo XXI Editores, 1976.

Pombo, Rafael, *Los Mejores Versos.* Buenos Aires: Editorial Nuestra América, 1959.

—by P. Pitchon, reviewed by T. Morin

COMANCHES

LOCATION: United States (Oklahoma; Texas)
POPULATION: 10,000
LANGUAGE: English; Comanche
RELIGION: Native American Church
RELATED ARTICLES: Vol. 2: Native North Americans

¹ INTRODUCTION

Originally, the Comanches were part of the Shoshone tribe, who lived in the mountains of what is now northern Wyoming and Montana. Late in the 17th century, they broke into two bands, and those who would later be known as the Comanches moved south. In the Southern Plains, they met the Utes, who introduced them to Spanish traders. In this context, the Comanches assumed a new name, either "Koh-Mahts" or "Kwuma-ci," rather than their original "Nerm." The precise meaning of the Ute names are uncertain, but linguists think they mean "one who fights us all the time." The Spanish transformed the Ute words into "Comanche."

Once the Comanches had settled into their new home in the Southern Plains, they divided into five major groupings: the Penatekas, who lived the farthest south; the Nokohi of the east; the Kotsoteka of the north, and the Yamparika to their north; and the Quahadi of the west. The main enemies of the Comanches were the Pawnees, Osages, Arapaho, and Apaches. Although the five Comanche bands were independent of one another, they often came together to fight a common enemy (as was the case with many battles against the Apaches, who sought to gain land, horses, and captives).

There were two main European forces who interacted with the Comanches in the 18th century: the French and the Spanish. The French had purely economic interests in the land. They wanted a strong trading post and a steady source of income from the New World for the king. They had neither religious nor social interests in the area and were, therefore, able to maintain healthy relations with the Comanches. The French traded guns, ammunition, and metal goods such as knives and pots. When the French were defeated by the British in the French and Indian War of 1763, however, many French traders left the continent, and the Comanches lost valuable trading partners.

The Spanish, on the other hand, had very different goals. They were eager to convert the Comanches to Catholicism and desperately wanted Comanche land for the mineral wealth it possessed. Angered by the Spanish desire for dominance, the Comanches often raided Spanish pueblos in New Mexico and Texas. The Spanish had brought smallpox to the New World, however, and many Comanches died in a smallpox epidemic in 1780-1781. The tribe was greatly weakened, and they could no longer fight the Spanish. A few of the bands met with the Spanish governor of New Mexico, De Anza, and in 1786 they agreed to peace terms that promised trade and rest to both parties. Due to the autonomy of the different Comanche bands, the southernmost people continued raiding the Spanish pueblos in Texas, believing the treaty did not apply to them since they had not participated in the negotiations. The unstable treaty was maintained until Texas won its independence in 1836.

The Comanches and European American settlers suffered continuous conflict throughout the 19th century. The worst fighting occurred in Texas, where the Comanches had the largest land holdings, referred to as *Comancheria*. In the late 1830s, the Nation of Texas formed a special division of soldiers called the Texas Rangers. They were given the job of fighting the Comanches in Comancheria and keeping them out of the settlers' way.

In 1840 leaders of twelve Comanche bands went to the council house in San Antonio to try to reach an agreement with the Texas lawmakers, an agreement that would bring hostilities to an end. At this meeting, the Texans demanded that the Comanches return all European American captives. Because each Comanche band was autonomous, however, it was impossible for the Comanches to make this promise. Acting impulsively, the Texans took the Comanches hostage to better their bargaining position. The Comanches tried to escape, and all twelve of the leaders were killed in what has become the Council House Massacre—one of the most dramatic episodes in the Comanches' struggle to maintain their land. When Texas became a US state in 1845, the Comanches' hostility turned toward the US government. They resisted reservation life until the spring of 1875, when the government declared that any Comanche not living in so-called "Indian Territory" (present-day Oklahoma) would be shot on sight. This finally brought the Comanches to their knees, and they reluctantly became the last Native American tribe to submit to life on a reservation.

In the mid 1800s, at the height of their power and reign over the land, the Comanches numbered more than 20,000. Today only 10,000 remain, and of those, only half live in their native southwestern homelands.

² LOCATION AND HOMELAND

When the Comanches arrived on the Southern Plains at the start of the 18th century, they had to fight the Apache (their most challenging enemy) to obtain land. Comancheria, as the Spanish called the vast territory the Comanches ruled, incorporated over 24,000 square miles stretching from southeast Colorado to southwest Kansas, and from eastern New Mexico to central Oklahoma and Texas. The climate is mild, and the buffalo were plentiful throughout the year. With buffalo as a staple, the Comanches became a nomadic hunting people who followed the herds and settled along streams for water.

Territory was always important to the Comanches. They were a communal people, and when they were forced onto individual land plots by the General Allotment Act of 1887, they chose their property according to the old patterns of the Comancheria. The four remaining bands settled more or less where they had in the old days. The Penteka went to the south, the Quahadi lived in the west, the Nokomi went east, and the Yamparika took the northernmost property. The Comanche population, according to the Comanche Tribe's Enrollment Office in 1997, is 10,000. Only 50% live in their old homelands of Oklahoma and Texas.

³ LANGUAGE

The Comanche language belongs to the Uto-Aztecan family of Native North American languages. Because many of the Plains people spoke different languages, they developed a form of sign language to communicate with those from different tribes. In this sign language, the Comanches were often referred to by making a side-to-side, snake-like motion in the air with the finger moving backwards. The snake referred to the Shoshone, the Comanche's ancestors; *Shoshone* means "snake people." In this way, the Comanches were always connected to their ancestral heritage. While efforts are being made to preserve this sign language, not many Comanches understand it any more. The few who still understand are those born before 1926. Those born after 1926 were educated in Bureau of Indian Affairs (BIA) schools where indigenous and traditional languages were suppressed.

Today a federal grant is making possible a preschool total language immersion program for 3–4-year-olds in order to ensure the survival of the Comanche language. In addition, a Comanche Language Preservation Committee has been formed.

During World War II, Comanche Code-Talkers, an elite group of 17 young men fluent in the Comanche language, received special communications training from the United States army. They were employed to send critical messages in a special code that confused the enemy.

⁴ FOLKLORE

According to Comanche myth, the Comanches were created by the Great Spirit after it had destroyed another people in a great flood. The former people displeased the Great Spirit, and a fresh start was needed.

Several stories are told concerning the tribe's emigration south, in which they left the Shoshone people. The first states that two bands were camping together and two boys, one from each band, were playing. One boy accidentally kicked the other in the stomach, and he eventually died. His band was irate and would have attacked the other if an elder had not intervened. He told both groups that they were one people and should not fight amongst themselves. Both bands agreed but also understood that they could no longer live together. Thus, the Shoshone stayed in the north and the other, who later became the Comanches, moved south.

The second story also starts with a camping party. Men from both bands went on a hunting expedition. A bear was killed with two arrows, one shot by a man in one band, and one from the bow of a man in the other band. Unable to decide who had shot the fatal arrow, the quarreling bands decided to go their separate ways.

Other legends exist regarding the Comanches' migration. One story tells how the Comanches split from the more peaceful Shoshone and traveled down the "Snake River" to continue their warlike, political, and opinionated way of life. Other sources of the snake image may be rooted in legends about the Comanche settling in an area inhabited by many snakes, and how they were considered to be "as dangerous as snakes."

⁵ RELIGION

Compared to the other Plains Indian tribes, the Comanches held few ceremonies. The night before the men went into battle or on a raid, the War Dance was performed. The Comanches believed that to dance the War Dance during the day would bring bad luck to their side.

Unlike all other Plains tribes, the Comanches do not perform the Sun Dance. In 1874, however, a radical Comanche preacher, Ishatai, claimed to have communicated with the Great Spirit. He told the Comanches that the Great Spirit wanted them to perform the Sun Dance and that if they did, they would win the Spirit's favor and drive away the European Americans forever. With assistance from the neighboring Kiowas, the Comanches performed the Sun Dance in 1874. Afterwards, they set out with Kiowa and Cheyenne warriors to attack a European American trading post at Adobe Walls in the Texas panhandle. Although the Native North Americans greatly outnumbered the European Americans, their bows, arrows, and lances were hardly a match for the guns and rifles of the European American settlers. The Comanches lost the battle—and lost their faith in the Sun Dance, which was never performed again.

After being forced onto the reservation, many Comanches began practicing peyotism. In 1918 Comanches helped form the Native American Church, which combines ideas of Christianity with the sacramental use of peyote.

⁶ MAJOR HOLIDAYS

The Comanches were unique among the Plains peoples, as they did not hold annual gatherings or assemblies. In fact, the Comanches rarely congregated. Sometimes they hunted or fought together, but almost never did they gather for a formal intratribe meeting.

Today the Comanches hold an annual Comanche Homecoming in Walters, Oklahoma, during the third week in July. People from many different tribes come together for this huge powwow which celebrates the similarities of Native North American cultures. The Comanche Nation Fair is held yearly at Old Craterville Park, Ft. Sill, Oklahoma, the last weekend in September.

⁷ RITES OF PASSAGE

For the early years of a child's life, he or she is called a variety of nicknames. Later a formal name is given in a public ceremony. This new name is most often based on an important experience in the child's life.

⁸ INTERPERSONAL RELATIONS

The Comanches had an elaborate system of social dos and don'ts. For example, hospitality was sacred, and all invited guests were treated with the utmost respect. This is why the Comanches took such great offense when they were invited to talks with the US government and were later mocked or hurt. Equally important was the prohibition on stealing from friends and allies; to do so brought severe punishment—although strangers were fair game. Lying was once an important taboo; to call someone a liar, or *e-shop,* was the worst imaginable insult.

Each person belonged to a family hunting band; each band varied in size. Comanche social structure was quite loose, and people changed hunting bands as needed or desired. If a band leader made a decision that was unpopular, people either started a new band or organized a change in leadership. There was no central ruling government, which allowed each band full autonomy.

Within each band there were band councils comprised of adult males. Decisions had to be unanimous, which caused many divisions because Comanches would rather leave than create conflict. A band chief ran each council meeting as long as he retained the support and cooperation of the others. A respected elder acted as a peace chief and brought wisdom and fairness to the mix. Before each battle, raid, or hunt, a war chief was elected. This war chief held power only until the task was completed.

Unlike other Plains tribes, the Comanches were not organized into military societies. While they often joined together for battles, they always returned to their smaller, independent bands when the fighting was over. During the hunt, each man did his own killing, and there was rarely a limit placed on the number of buffaloes taken. This was due to the abundance of buffalo on the Southern Plains throughout the year.

9 LIVING CONDITIONS

Because they were a migratory hunting tribe, the Comanches lived in portable tipis. Tipis were made by stretching many buffalo hides sewn together across a cone-shaped frame of four wooden poles tied together at the top. The Comanches, as well as the Blackfeet and Shoshone, used a four-pole tipi construction; most Plains tribes in the same area used a three-pole construction, even today. The Comanches had very little furniture in their tipis. Large piles of buffalo-skin robes served as beds, seats, and tables. The opening of the tipi always faced the rising sun in the east.

During the summer months, the Comanches often slept outside in wooden framework shelters with flat roofs covered with leaves and branches. The shelters had no sides and thus allowed a breeze to circulate while offering shade during the daytime.

10 FAMILY LIFE

In traditional Comanche society, all children were highly valued, but boys were preferred. When they reached courtship age, boys and girls had to follow very strict courting rules. They were forbidden to show interest in each other while in camp, but they frequently arranged secret meetings outside of camp. When a boy decided that he wanted to marry a certain girl, he would give the girl's family a horse as a way to show that he would be able to provide for her. If his proposal was accepted, he would leave his tipi and live with his new wife in her family's tipi. Polygamy was common. Very often, the second and third wives would be sisters of the first wife. It was felt that sisters would get along with each other better and be less likely to quarrel. The first wife was always considered the boss, however. To avoid conflicts and disharmony, men never spoke directly to their mothers-in-law.

11 CLOTHING

Today Comanches wear Western-style clothing for everyday purposes. Traditional clothing is still worn for ceremonials, however.

Traditionally, the Comanches made nearly all their clothing from deer and buffalo skins. Because of the warm climate in which they lived, Comanche boys went naked until they were 8–10 years old, when they would start to wear a breechcloth. A breechcloth is a piece of animal hide passed between the legs then draped over a belt around the waist to hang down in front and back. Girls wore only a breechcloth until they were about 12 years old, when they would begin to wear women's clothing. Women's clothing emphasized modesty. Comanche women wore loose fitting deerskin dresses with long sleeves. They decorated the dresses with fringe, beads, and small pieces of metal

(after contact with Europeans, when metal began to be received in trade). Women also wore beaded moccasins made of buffalo skin. All Comanches used shampoo and soap made from yucca plant root.

Comanche men wore a breechcloth made of deerskin. In the summer, they went naked from the waist up. In the winter, they wore warm buffalo-skin robes and high leather boots that covered their legs. Men had pierced ears and long hair worn in two braids, decorated with strips of fur, leather, and feathers. Before battle, men painted their faces black. At other times, they would paint their faces in various colors and designs, none of which had any particular significance. Women often painted yellow or red lines around their eyes. They also painted the insides of their ears red and decorated their cheeks with orange or red triangles or circles. This was simply considered stylish and had no other deep significance.

After the US forced the Comanches to relocate to Indian Territory in present-day Oklahoma, the government provided them with clothing made of cheap materials in a one-size-fits-all design that was usually too large to fit anyone. Children were not provided with any clothing at all. The women would cut the government clothing down to size for the adults, then use the leftover fabric for children's clothes.

12 FOOD

The acquisition of horses (introduced to North America by the Spanish) in the 17th century made buffalo hunting much easier for the Comanches. With more meat available, the Comanches became a healthier, and eventually more numerous, tribe. They ate all edible parts of the buffalo, plus deer, antelope, and black bear meat. When other meat was extremely scarce, they would be forced to eat their horses to survive (dog and human meat were strictly forbidden).

Boiled meat called *söp* is made by boiling chunks of lean meat in water until tender. A staple food for the Comanches and other Plains tribes was *pemmican*. Traditionally made from buffalo meat mixed with berries and nuts, "glued" together with boiled buffalo fat, pemmican was extremely healthy and would last for years when stored in leather pouches called *parfleches*.

Modern Pemmican
(pie filling)

1 quart apple cider	2 teaspoon salt
2 cups seedless raisins	2 teaspoons cinnamon
1 cup dried currants	2 teaspoons ground ginger
3 apples, peeled, cored, and chopped	1 teaspoon ground cloves
1 cup chopped suet	1 teaspoon nutmeg
2 pounds ground venison	½ teaspoon allspice

Put the cider, raisins, currants, apples, and suet in a large saucepan. Cover and let simmer over low heat for two hours. Stir in the remaining ingredients, and let simmer uncovered for another two hours, stirring occasionally. Use as pie or pastry filling. Makes 2 quarts.

[Adapted from Kimball and Anderson, *The Art of American Indian Cooking* (Garden City, NY: Doubleday & Co.), 1965, p. 121.]

[13] EDUCATION

At the Bureau of Indian Affairs (BIA) schools in Indian Territory (present-day Oklahoma) in the late 19th and early 20th centuries, Comanche children were taught European American ways and values. At both boarding schools and day schools on the reservation, boys were taught vocational skills such as bookkeeping, while girls were taught how to iron, set a table, and address party invitations. Both boys and girls were taught to play croquet and baseball.

In 1935, when the US Congress passed the Oklahoma Indian Welfare Act, new schools funded by the US government but run by Native North Americans were opened, replacing the BIA schools. But Native-run schools were short-lived. They were closed after World War II (1941–1945) when the US government reduced its spending. Today there are a few Comanche schools in operation, but the majority of Comanche children attend public schools. In 1990, Comanche school-attendance rates were as follows:

AGE	PERCENT ATTENDING SCHOOL
3–4	26.9
5–14	88.0
15–17	95.4
18–19	38.8
20–24	25.3

Of those Comanche 25 years old or older in 1990, 6.6% had less than a 9th grade education; 74.2% (75.8% of men, 72.3% of women) had a high school diploma or higher; 45.4% had at least some college; and 14.2% (14.9% of men, 13.3% of women) had a Bachelor of Arts degree or higher.

[14] CULTURAL HERITAGE

In the past, "sweats" were a form of purification or cleansing, but they were not considered a ritual religious ceremony.

[15] WORK

Comanche work has changed dramatically since the days before the European invasion. When they were masters of the Comancheria, boys learned to ride horses and hunt at a very early age, and girls were taught to cook and tan hides. While men made weapons and hunted, women prepared the food, tanned hides, and made tipis and clothes. When forced to relocate to Indian Territory (present-day Oklahoma), the Comanches had to learn to farm. After the General Allotment Act of 1887 divided their lands into parcels too small to farm successfully, many Comanches found jobs off-reservation, working as herders or farmers for European Americans. These jobs usually paid very low wages.

Many Comanches lost their already marginal jobs during the Depression of the 1930s and fell into even deeper poverty. In 1935, as part of the New Deal, Congress passed the Oklahoma Indian Welfare Act, which allowed Native North Americans to form business-development groups. The Comanches helped reestablish the Comanche, Kiowa, Kiowa-Apache Business Council which had been disbanded in 1887 after the General Allotment Act. In 1966, however, the Comanches broke away and formed their own Comanche Business Council. The Comanche Business Council has since organized the operation of a meat-packing plant as well as a leather-tanning factory on Comanche lands in Oklahoma. Many Comanche men and women still must find work off-reservation, however. A number of young Comanches enlist in the US Armed Services, the modern expression of their traditional warrior identity.

[16] SPORTS

The Comanches traditionally played a sport called *shinny* which was very similar to modern-day lacrosse. They also played a sport similar to soccer.

[17] ENTERTAINMENT AND RECREATION

Traditionally, Comanche elders would tell stories around campfires at night to provide entertainment as well as education for the children.

Today Comanches enjoy the same forms of recreation as other Americans. A traditional pastime at tribal powwows is the hand-game, a gambling game for teams in which sticks are hidden in the hands of some team members and the opposing team must guess who the stick holders are.

[18] FOLK ART, CRAFTS, AND HOBBIES

Comanche crafts represented everyday life with toy versions of real people and objects, much like "playing house"—dolls in cradleboards, miniature tipis, and so on.

In their art, Comanches used certain symbols to represent healing and medicine; for example, a buffalo design on a shield would represent the strength of the buffalo.

[19] SOCIAL PROBLEMS

The Comanches suffer a great deal from racial discrimination in Oklahoma. A recent study showed that more Comanches are arrested than European Americans for similar offenses and that more force is used while arresting Comanches than while arresting European Americans.

[20] BIBLIOGRAPHY

Alter, Judy. *The Comanches.* New York: Franklin Watts, 1994.

Foster, Morris W. *Being Comanche: A Social History of an American Indian Community.* Tucson: University of Arizona Press, 1991.

Kimball, Yeffe, and Jean Anderson. *The Art of American Indian Cooking.* Garden City, New York: Doubleday & Company, 1965.

Lodge, Sally. *The Comanche.* Vero Beach, Florida: Rourke Publications, 1992.

Mooney, Martin J. *The Comanche Indians.* New York: Chelsea House, 1993.

Reddy, Marlita A., ed. *Statistical Record of Native North Americans,* 2nd ed. Detroit: Gale Research, 1995.

Rollins, Willard H. *The Comanche.* New York: Chelsea House, 1989.

—by D. K. Daeg de Mott, reviewed by J. Pahdopony

COSTA RICANS

ALTERNATE NAMES: Ticos
LOCATION: Costa Rica
POPULATION: 3.1 million
LANGUAGE: Spanish; English
RELIGION: Roman Catholicism (over 90%)

¹ INTRODUCTION

Christopher Columbus was the first European to arrive in what is now Costa Rica, in 1502, on his fourth and last voyage. It was probably named "rich coast" because of the gold ornaments worn by Indians, but it was never a source of great wealth for the Spanish. Indeed, when Central America freed itself from Spanish rule in 1821, the population of Costa Rica was under 70,000. San José became the capital of the Central American federation in 1823, and that of Costa Rica when it became an independent nation in 1838. During this period, coffee became an all-important export and source of national wealth; bananas, introduced in 1871, also became a major export crop. Political life was generally tranquil until 1948, when thousands died in a civil war. A new constitution then abolished the army, limited the power of the executive, and established a civil service. Since then, Costa Rica has held to a tradition of orderly, democratic rule.

² LOCATION AND HOMELAND

Costa Rica is about the size of the US state of West Virginia. It is bounded by Nicaragua on the north, Panama on the southeast, the Caribbean Sea to the east, and the Pacific Ocean to the south and west. Mountain ranges run northwest–southeast the length of the country, reaching as high as 3,810 m (12,500 ft) above sea level. Some of the mountains are volcanic. About half the population lives in the small, fertile, central plateau nestled in the highlands. The lowlands along the Pacific and Caribbean coasts are hot and generally rainy, swampy, and heavily forested.

Costa Rica had a population of about 3.1 million in the mid-1990s. About 95% of the population is either of European (generally Spanish) or mixed European and Indian ancestry. The remainder are of Indian, African, or Chinese descent. The number of refugees fleeing political strife in other Central American countries reached some 200,000 in the 1980s but fell to about half that number in the 1990s. Costa Ricans call themselves Ticos.

³ LANGUAGE

Spanish is the universal language. Vos is often used in place of tú as the singular familiar pronoun. Costa Rican Spanish is also influenced by Mexican television. There is a peasant country dialect but few regional variations. The 15,000 or so Indians belong to six linguistic groups. Some of the 50,000 or so Blacks—mostly descendants of Jamaican immigrants—use English as their principal language.

⁴ FOLKLORE

Indians see the world as created by God (Sibu) and controlled by good and evil spirits. A few sukias (shamans) are credited with curing illness, controlling the weather, and foretelling the future. Curanderismo (curing) with herbs and chants is also practiced by non-Indians. In Costa Rica these healers, also credited with concocting love potions and casting spells, are called brujas (witches); they are always female and at least 50 years old.

Catholic folklore is plentiful. As in all of Latin America, saints—including uncanonized "popular saints"—are prayed to as intermediaries before God, and statues and pictures of saints in the home are believed to confer good luck.

⁵ RELIGION

More than 90% of the population are baptized Roman Catholics. The constitution recognizes Catholicism as the national religion and provides for state support of the Church while permitting the free exercise of "other cults not opposed to universal morality or good customs." Only a Catholic marriage ceremony is recognized by the state without the need of a civil ceremony. Catholic doctrine is part of the public-school curriculum, and only a parental note excuses children from these lessons. However, in general Costa Ricans neither observe nor expect rigid conformity to the doctrines and rules of the Church.

⁶ MAJOR HOLIDAYS

Of Costa Rica's 15 public holidays, most are religious in character. Some businesses close for Holy Week (late March or early April), which is commemorated with religious processions. Christmas Eve (24 December) is celebrated with visiting, drinking, dancing, and gift-giving as well as Midnight Mass. The feast day of Our Lady of the Angeles, Costa Rica's patron saint, occurs on 2 August. On this day, La Negrita, a small black stone image of the Virgin said to have appeared to a poor Indian girl over 300 years ago, is carried in solemn procession from the Basilica in Cartago to the parish church of St. Nicholas. It is returned on the first Saturday in September.

Among secular holidays, the most important is Independence Day, on 15 September. This day is commemorated also in the other Central American countries that won their independence from Spain in 1821.

⁷ RITES OF PASSAGE

Parents of newborn children receive gifts from relatives and neighbors, and a man and woman—generally a married couple—are asked to serve as godparents, as in many other Latin American countries. The godparents traditionally take the infant to church to be baptized. A child's first birthday is also a great occasion. After entering school at age seven, boys and girls play apart. Working-class children may be expected to do chores or supplement the family income as early as age six. A middle- or upper-class girl's 15th birthday is a special occasion, marked by a party comparable to a debut. No fiesta or dance is complete without a "queen" and "princesses." No similar events exist for boys, but they enjoy much greater freedom and are steeped in the ways of machismo—assertive masculinity.

Most adult Costa Ricans let their birthdays pass unnoticed. A woman is considered well past her prime by age 40. Higher-status men, however, may celebrate their 50th birthday with a big party, and couples celebrate their silver and golden wedding anniversaries. Old women may spend much of their time in church, while old men gather in parks, cafes, or bars to talk.

Funerals are required by law to be held within 24 hours of death, and few corpses are embalmed. Whenever possible, a church ceremony is held, and mourners then proceed to the cemetery for the burial. If there is time, a wake may be held first, with the deceased placed in an open coffin in the family living room. A rosary and sometimes a Mass are held on the anniversary of the death for a decade or two. Widows sometimes wear black for the rest of their lives, although this practice is becoming obsolete.

8 INTERPERSONAL RELATIONS

Foreign visitors have described Costa Ricans as hospitable and gracious. Strangers are favored with a greeting in small towns. Acquaintances are greeted as *amigo* (friend) and given ritual shoulder-patting embraces. Yet this is misleading, for many Costa Ricans say they have no real friends other than relatives. They value privacy and rarely invite nonrelatives, except for friends from childhood and professional colleagues, to their homes. A great deal of socializing goes on outside the home, in clubs or bars, or at fiestas or other community diversions.

Dating is not common, and in rural areas and among more traditional urban families, girls under 18 must still be chaperoned at night. Movies, dances, and band concerts in the park are among the occasions where young people may get to know one another. If a boy and girl go out on a date even once, they are generally thought to be *novios* (boyfriend and girlfriend) who do not date anyone else.

9 LIVING CONDITIONS

Costa Rica enjoys, with Panama, the highest standard of living in Central America. Life expectancy is on a par with the United States, and infant mortality is the lowest in Latin America. Many Costa Ricans credit the social security system, which took over community hospitals, for improved health. However, protein-deficient malnutrition remains common among landless peasants, and there has been an increase in obesity, alcoholism, smoking, and narcotics use. Most Costa Ricans live in small wooden or cement-block houses, with floors of wood or tile and roofs of zinc or corrugated iron. The urban poor, however, generally live in overcrowded, usually rented, slum dwellings. Squatters' shanties can be found on the fringes of the cities. Buses, rather than automobiles, are the main form of public transportation. Both coasts are also linked by rail with the capital, and there are airplane landing strips throughout the country.

10 FAMILY LIFE

The extended family group is the basis of Costa Rican society. Brothers, uncles, and cousins are expected to help other family members in times of need. Much of social life consists of Sunday visits to kin and to their parties, christenings, weddings, and funerals. Several generations may live under the same roof. Desertion and abandonment of children by fathers is common among the poor. It is not uncommon for a grandmother, her daughters, and their children to live together without an adult male present. Family size has dropped sharply since 1960 because of birth control. Women form a growing proportion of the labor force, and sex discrimination in hiring and salary is

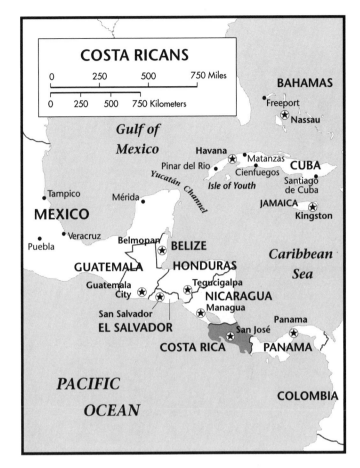

forbidden. Divorce, once seen as a disgrace, occurs more frequently than in the past, but separation and desertion remain far more common. Many women are also victims of domestic violence.

11 CLOTHING

Traditional women's costumes are based on a sheer, low-cut frilled, ruffled, or puffed white blouse and a flounced, flowered, full cotton skirt, which varies in color. A fringed, colored silk or cotton *rebozo* (shawl) is draped around the shoulders or over the head. A cross, medallion, or locket is usually suspended around the neck, and circular golden earrings are worn. Traditional men's costumes generally consist of dark trousers and a long-sleeved white shirt with a red knotted handkerchief at the neck and a colored sash around the waist. A straw Panama hat is also worn.

Clean, unwrinkled clothing is very important to urban working-class people, and many of them will skimp on food to buy stylish clothing. All but the poorest people dress up on Sundays and special occasions. Conversely, the upper and middle classes, more secure in their status, now dress more informally. Even top government ministers now doff their suit jackets on many occasions, confining themselves to sports shirts or short-sleeved shirts with neckties. Jeans and tee-shirts are everyday wear for young people of all classes. Girls wear school uniforms, and older girls are expected to wash and iron the blouses of their uniforms and to press the skirts daily.

A Costa Rican boy cleaning fish. In the Costa Rican diet, however, beef or pork is preferred to fish. (Cory Langley)

12 FOOD

The Costa Rican diet is based on rice, beans, tortillas or bread, fried plantains, and strong black coffee, sometimes prepared from home-grown berries, with lots of sugar. Vegetables and fruits, though available year-round, are not especially common. The midday meal is the main one.

Beef or pork is preferred to fish. *Olla de carne,* the traditional stew, is made with beef, potatoes, corn, plantains, squash, yucca, and other vegetables. Other popular entrees include *paella* and *zarzuelas* (spicy seafood stews). These dishes are derived from Spain but adapted to local ingredients. *Pozol,* a corn-based soup in Mexico and other Central American countries, is made with beans in Costa Rica. Rice, chayote (a pear-like fruit), and other ingredients may be added; in Guanacoste Province pozol is made with corn and a pig's head. *Gallopinto,* a popular peasant dish, is basically beans with an egg, although its name suggests chicken. *Chayotes rellenos* are chayotes parboiled in salted water, stuffed with cheese, eggs, butter, and bread crumbs, covered with butter and bread crumbs, and then baked.

13 EDUCATION

Costa Rica boasts the highest literacy rate in Central America. Elementary education is compulsory between the ages of 6 and 15. Even in the mid-1980s, however, 16% of the population had less than two years of schooling. The high-school dropout rate remains high, and many graduates enter college unable to read or write acceptably. Well-to-do parents usually send their children to private schools, where instruction is at a higher level.

The main institutions of higher learning are the University of Costa Rica, in a suburb of San José, and the National Autonomous University, in Heredia. Because of political pressure, almost all applicants are admitted, which has resulted in overcrowding and has hampered quality. Founded in 1976, the Autonomous University of Central America is a private institution organized into autonomous colleges on the British plan. The Institute of Technology is near Cartago; a San Carlos branch has a school of forestry and agriculture.

14 CULTURAL HERITAGE

Costa Rica has a national orchestra, opera house, and dance company. Alejandro Monastel is a classical composer who employs native folk themes. The marimba and guitar are popular instruments for folk dances. Among popular performers are Los Talolingas, who wrote "La Guaria Morada," regarded as the nation's "second national anthem." Lorenzo (Lencho) Salazar writes popular humorous songs. Some Indians retain their traditional dances and musical instruments, and the calypso is popular among Caribbean Blacks.

A government-subsidized House of the Artist has offered free lessons in painting and sculpture since 1951. The Museum of Costa Rican Art was founded in 1977. Francisco Amighetti and Richard Kliefoth are among the nation's painters and graphic artists.

Costa Rica's best writers have been chiefly essayists and poets, including Justo Facio, Roberto Brenes Mesén, and Joaquín García Monge. Social protest is represented by Carlos Luís Fallas and Alberto Cañas. Urban life is depicted by Alfonso Chase and Carmen Naranjo. Ricardo Fernández Guardia was a historian and short-story writer; Moises Vincenzi was a novelist and philosopher.

15 WORK

About three-quarters of all Costa Ricans are members of the working class. These include farm and domestic workers, gardeners, janitors, and vendors. Because of a widespread prejudice against manual labor, young people with middle-class aspirations prefer even poorly paid white-collar occupations, such as secretary or bank clerk. The work ethic and work hours in Costa Rica differ from those in the US. As in most Latin American societies, work is seen as a necessity but not an end in itself. The work week is often cut short on Friday afternoon, and there are many holidays.

16 SPORTS

Soccer is the national sport—or even national mania—of Costa Rica. It is played mostly by young working-class males who began kicking a ball around at age two. Even the smallest hamlet is likely to have at least one team. It is also by far the chief spectator sport. Bicycling also has many working-class participants and spectators. Boxing and wrestling also are popular spectator sports for men of the working class. Basketball, volleyball, and tennis are played chiefly by upper- and upper-middle-class boys, and tennis and golf by their fathers. Baseball is more popular along the Caribbean coast. Among other sports are horse-racing and automobile- and motorcycle-racing. Once popular, cockfighting is now illegal.

17 ENTERTAINMENT AND RECREATION

Films are extremely popular, but most moviegoers are under 25 years of age. Some films are banned by a censorship board, usually for reasons of sexual licentiousness. Transistor radios are played everywhere, with popular music predominating. Even the poorest homes are likely to have television sets. Favorite programs include cartoons and old movies from the United States, and Mexican *telenovelas* (soap operas). There are many other diversions and leisure-time activities, including sports, fiestas, dances, and games of chance. The national lottery, held each week, is a major event. There is a grand prize at Christmas.

18 FOLK ART, CRAFTS, AND HOBBIES

Because it has only a small Indian population, Costs Rica has little in the way of native arts and crafts. A symbol of the nation, although dating back only to about 1900, is the elaborately painted wooden oxcart, typically done in brightly colored geometric patterns or stylized motifs such as flowers. There are a number of folk-dancing groups, and many songs, dances, poems, and stories have Indian and African as well as Spanish roots.

19 SOCIAL PROBLEMS

Costa Rica's chief social problem is the poverty that grips perhaps one-third of its population. Most farmers have only tiny plots or none at all. The environment is threatened by slash-and-burn agriculture and the cutting of forests. Politically, Costa Rica has a large, expensive, and relatively unproductive bureaucracy. It has, however, maintained democracy and individual rights and freedoms, avoiding the armed conflicts and dictatorial rule that have gripped other Central American countries. There is no standing army. Crime-control is hampered by the lack of a career police force. Thousands of personnel are fired with each change in national administration; working in the bureaucracy does not guarantee continued employment.

20 BIBLIOGRAPHY

Biesanz, Richard, et al. *The Costa Ricans*. 2nd ed. Englewood Cliffs, NJ.: Prentice-Hall, 1987.

Lascaris, Constantino. *El costaricense*. San José: Editorial Universitaria Centroamericana, 1975.

—by R. Halasz, reviewed by T. D. Morin

CREEKS

ALTERNATE NAMES: Muskogee
LOCATION: United States (Oklahoma; Alabama; Georgia; Florida, California; Texas)
POPULATION: Approximately 44,000
LANGUAGE: English; Muskogee (Creek)
RELIGION: Traditional Creek; Muskogee (Creek) Protestant
RELATED ARTICLES: Vol. 2: Native North Americans

1 INTRODUCTION

In 1670, British traders began referring to part of the group of Native Americans of the Creek Confederation who lived along the Ocmulgee River (in what is today the state of Georgia) as the Ochesee Creek Indians. They made their homes and villages along many rivers and streams in the southeast United States, in what are today the states of Georgia, Alabama, part of South Carolina, part of Tennessee, and northern Florida. Although the Muskogee (Creek) people shared a common language, culture, and history, they did not consider themselves a nation. Instead, the Creek Confederation was more like an alliance between all the different Creek towns.

The first encounter between the Creeks and Europeans, with the Spanish explorer Hernando de Soto in the late 16th century, was brief but devastating. De Soto made captives of some of the natives, disciplining them cruelly. He burned some alive, cut off their hands, hanged, and beheaded them.

Not until the British began trading with the Creeks in the 17th century did the Europeans significantly influence the Creek Confederacy. In exchange for guns, ammunition, metal pots and pans, European clothing, and beads, the British wanted deer skins and Native American captives for the slave trade. To meet British demands and acquire European goods, the Creeks began overhunting deer, upsetting the balance of nature in the southeast and causing a serious decline in the deer population. They also began making slave raids on neighboring Native American tribes. These activities made them very unpopular among other tribes in the southeast.

Soon the French and Spanish began to compete with the British for control of the southeast. The Creeks, eager to remain on friendly terms with all the European powers, made informal agreements with all three and maintained profitable trade arrangements with each of them. They officially allied themselves with no one until the British began having conflicts with the American colonists. The Creeks then sided with the British and supported them throughout the American Revolutionary War (1775–83). When the colonists won and established the United States of America, the British-allied Creeks were naturally considered untrustworthy by the new government. Over the next few years, the Creeks lost large tracts of land to the US government.

A mixed-blood Creek by the name of Alexander McGillivray (1753–87) decided the Creeks would be more powerful and therefore less able to be coerced out of their lands if they were one unified nation. During the late 1700s, McGillivray worked with both the Spanish government officials in Florida and the US government to ensure autonomy for the Creeks. At the same time, he worked with the Creeks to unite them under one government. When McGillivray died at the age of 34 in 1787, the Creeks lost their motivation to unite and became more deeply divided than ever.

The Creeks became known to European Americans as one of the so-called "Five Civilized Tribes" because many of their ways reflected European customs and values. In 1796, US President George Washington sent Benjamin Hawkins, a former Senator from North Carolina, as the chief agent to the Indian tribes in the Southeast. Hawkins administered a "civilization" program that he believed would improve standard of living for the Creeks, Cherokees, Choctaws, Chickasaws, and Seminoles. The program attempted to impose white social, political, and economic values on the tribes and convert them from their traditional ways of life to the agricultural-industrial life of white European Americans. Geographically, there were two groups of Creeks: the Upper Creeks, and the Lower Creeks. Originally, geography was all that divided them. However, as contact with Europeans and European Americans increased, the Upper and Lower Creeks began to diverge more seriously. The Lower Creeks were eager to adopt the ways of Europeans and abandoned many of their Creek traditions. The Upper Creek, on the other hand, were much more wary of the Europeans and remained attached to their Creek way of life. The tension between the Upper and Lower Creeks reached its climax in 1813, when the Upper Creeks attacked a fort housing European Americans and full- and mixed-blood Lower Creeks. Throughout the following year, European Americans and Lower Creeks attacked Upper Creek settlements. In the end, the Lower Creeks, aided by the US government, won the Creek War. The Upper Creeks were forced to cede 25 million acres of their lands in Alabama and Georgia to the US government, without payment.

In 1824, a half-blooded Creek named William McIntosh decided to sell the rest of the Creeks' lands to the US government. He and his three aides made an offer to agents of the Bureau of Indian Affairs (BIA), at the time a section of the US War Department. When told of the offer, US President Monroe ordered the BIA agents not to accept it on the grounds that it was illegal and unethical because no Creeks but McIntosh and his aides were involved. The agents went against President Monroe's orders, however, and signed a treaty with McIntosh, giving him a large sum of money for lands that were not his to sell. In fact, the Creek Nation had passed a law stating that "no more land would be sold." As McIntosh signed the treaty, he was warned by another Creek named Opothle Yoholo that his life was in danger. Six months later, the recently formed Creek National Council (a governing body similar to that which McGillivray had promoted decades earlier) arrested and executed McIntosh and his aides. In 1826, the US signed a new treaty with the Creeks, nullifying the illegal treaty of 1824. This was the first and last time that the US government ever nullified a treaty.

The McIntosh faction and its followers moved to the west and settled along the Verdigris River in eastern Indian Territory (present-day Oklahoma) around 1828. Under the Indian Removal Act passed by US Congress in 1830, other members of the Five Civilized Tribes, including the Muskogee (Creek) who had not signed McIntosh's treaty, were forcibly removed from their southeastern homelands and relocated to Indian Territory in 1836 and 1837. On March 25–27, 1836, the Upper Creeks and Lower Creeks held their last general council in Alabama; hostilities broke out soon right before their emigration to Oklahoma. During the journey, made almost entirely on foot, an estimated 40% of the Creeks died, leaving only 14,000 to create a new life in Oklahoma. The removal of the Five Civilized Tribes is remembered as the "Trail of Tears" because of the tragic number of deaths it caused.

During the American Civil War (1861–65), some of the McIntosh-faction Creeks sided with the Confederate States, but many who came in the Indian removal tried to stay neutral. This caused old wounds to open between the Creek factions. At least four battles in the Civil War pitted Native Americans against each other. When the Confederates lost, the Creeks found themselves in a precarious position. Because some of the Creeks had fought with the Confederates, the whole Muskogee (Creek) nation was forced to cede a large amount of their land in Oklahoma to the victorious Union government. Although the Creeks were allowed to keep about 160 acres of land under the General Allotment Act of 1889, many individuals lost their land to unethical European Americans who tricked them into selling it when oil was discovered in Oklahoma at the turn of the 20th century.

In 1907, Oklahoma became a state, and the Creeks lost their official identity as a separate people. Lands in the former "Indian Territory" were not considered to be "reservations" by the US government, nor were the Native Americans who lived there officially recognized as tribal nations. Native Americans did not become citizens of the US until 1924. Creeks have struggled to survive on dwindling lands in a European-dominated culture to which they were poorly adapted. Finally, in 1970 the US government made it legal for Native Americans to elect their own chiefs and tribal governments. The Creeks elected Claude Cox as their Principal Chief in 1971. Bill Fife served as Principal Chief from 1991–94, and R. Perry Beaver was elected in 1994. They established a number of education and housing programs to improve the standard of living for the Creek people.

² LOCATION AND HOMELAND

The Creeks are descendants of a tribe belonging to the Mississippian Culture, a group of highly civilized Native Americans living in the southeast long before the Europeans arrived on the continent. Much of Mississippian culture was similar to that of the Aztecs in Mexico, leading scholars to conclude that a number of Aztecs migrated north and east thousands of years ago, introducing their customs and ways of life to the peoples they met along the way.

When Europeans first encountered the Creeks in the 17th century, the Creeks were split into two subgroups: the Upper Creeks, and the Lower Creeks. The Upper Creeks lived in Alabama along the Coosa, Tallapoosa, and Alabama Rivers, while the Lower Creeks made their homes along the Chattahoochee and Flint Rivers in Georgia. Rich, fertile river valleys and a long growing season made farming both easy and practical for the Creeks. Game animals abounded in the dense forests, and fish were plentiful in the many rivers and streams. In the 1830s, the Creeks were forcibly relocated to a plot of land in eastern Oklahoma, near both the Arkansas and Canadian rivers. The climate in Oklahoma is hot and dry, and the land is much less fertile than that of the southeastern US. Farming is much more difficult in Oklahoma than in the Creeks' former homelands.

According to the US Census, the total Creek population in 1990 was approximately 44,000. More than half live in Oklahoma. The only federally recognized group of Creeks remaining in the southeast is the "Poarch Band of Creek Indians," in Atmore, Alabama. There are some groups remaining in the southeast that claim to be Creeks but are not recognized by the Creek Nation.

³ LANGUAGE

The Creeks, like many other Southeastern tribes, speak Muskogee, or Creek, a member of the Muskogean family of Native North American languages. Scholars believe that the Creeks probably spoke more than six different languages up through the 1600s, when they were still a loosely connected confederation of towns.

Preservation of the Creek (or Muskogee) language began with the Reverend John Fleming, the first Presbyterian missionary to the Creeks in Oklahoma, in 1832. He created a written Creek alphabet and published a children's Creek reader, *Istusi in Naktsoka,* in the 1830s. Fleming later published other books in the Creek language and helped the Creeks translate Christian hymns and parts of the Bible into their native tongue. The first English and Muskogee dictionary was written by the Reverend R. M. Loughridge and Church Elder David M. Hodge (who acted as interpreter) in 1914.

⁴ FOLKLORE

According to traditional legend, the Creek people were born from the earth's navel, located somewhere within the Rocky Mountains. After a time, the earth became angry, opening up and trying to swallow them again. They left this land and began to travel toward the rising sun. Their journey led them to the southeastern region of the US, where they flourished and created a complex system of social structures to govern themselves.

Within the Creek Confederacy, there are many different clans. The Creek tell the story of how each clan got its name in this way: In the beginning, when This World was first created, it was covered by a thick fog. It was impossible to see anything. When the people went out in search of food, they often got lost. Therefore, each group of people came up with a call so that they could find each other. Because of these calls, the people learned there were other groups in This World in addition to themselves. Eventually, a great wind blew the fog away. The first group of people felt the wind and watched as it blew the fog away, and they named themselves the Wind Clan. They are considered the first clan. Every group thereafter named themselves according to the first animal they saw—and so the Deer, Bear, and Turtle Clans came to be.

⁵ RELIGION

The Creeks, like many other Southeastern tribes, are a highly religious and highly ceremonial people. Christianized Creeks refer to God as the "Master of Breath" (who created all life). The Traditional Ceremonial Creeks refer to the Creator as "The One Above." The Creeks widely and wisely used the healing power of plants. The juices from certain crushed plants provided them with morphine and salicylic acid, the substance from which aspirin is made. The Creeks also brewed teas that relieved indigestion and other stomach ailments from leaves, branches, and roots.

The Creeks' most important formal ceremony has long been the *posketv,* or Green Corn Ceremony. It takes place near the end of the summer and marks the ripening of the corn and the beginning of a new year. It is a time of forgiveness and purification for both the ceremonial grounds and the Creek people. Every element of the ceremony is in some way symbolic of the purification and cleansing taking place. One major element of the ceremony is the harvest of the New (Green) Corn, usually during July and August. No corn is eaten before then. The celebration of a single crop is not unusual considering its importance as the major food crop, producing even when other crops failed. During the four-day ceremony, there is much prayer, and the people fast. They abstain from eating not only the new corn but also all food. The men drink a tea brewed from holly leaves, which acts as a powerful emetic, causing them to vomit. They view this as a form of purification, readying them to accept the blessings of the new year. Participants in the ceremony are also expected to lay aside ill feelings, forgive wrongs done to them, and forget the conflicts of the previous year. Creek traditionally believe that all people should act with a pure heart and mind.

At the beginning of the Green Corn ceremony, all fires are extinguished. The central fire is then relit by the medicine man. From that central fire, then, all the cooking fires in the ceremonial grounds are rekindled, and the new year begins. (Each family has a camp where meals are prepared.) These traditions are carried on today by the Traditional Ceremonial people of the Creeks.

A large percentage of Creeks have been converted to Christianity, and there are many Muskogee (Creek) Protestant churches in the Muskogee (Creek) Nation. Services are conducted in both English and the Muskogee language.

⁶ MAJOR HOLIDAYS

Creeks on each of the 17 traditional ceremonial grounds within the Muskogee (Creek) Nation still hold the Green Corn Ceremony every summer. It is a time for worship and thanksgiving.

⁷ RITES OF PASSAGE

In the past, a boy was not traditionally considered a man until he performed a heroic act in battle or on a raid. Once he performed this act, he was given a title describing the feat. At the next Green Corn Ceremony, a naming ceremony was held in which all boys who had performed a brave deed during the previous year were recognized and officially given their new name.

⁸ INTERPERSONAL RELATIONS

The Creeks are a very democratic people among themselves. The Muskogee (Creek) Nation has a central government presided over by the elected Principal Chief and Second Chief. The Nation itself is divided into eight districts. The National Council has 26 representatives elected from these districts, and they make up the legislative branch of the government. The judicial branch consists of six Supreme Court judges and one district judge, who are all appointed by the Principal Chief.

Harmony and balance have traditionally been important concepts among the Creek. The Creek people attempted to balance work and play, religion and politics, and respect for nature.

9 LIVING CONDITIONS

The Creeks traditionally lived in villages called *italwas*. In the center of each village was a square where religious and political events took place. The square was surrounded by low buildings with open fronts and seats inside facing the square. During the warm summer months, meetings took place in these buildings. In the winter, public meetings were held in a town house called the *chakofa*, located in the central square. The chakofa was a large, circular structure with a cone-shaped roof. The sacred fire was kept in the chakofa.

The residential homes of the village families surrounded the square and the *chakofa*. Each family had a compound that consisted of a small chakofa; an open-sided, airy summer home; and two or three storage sheds. The small chakofas, which served as the Creeks' winter homes, were made by weaving young, flexible saplings between thick, sturdy wooden posts into a cylindrical shape. The walls were then covered with a grass and clay mixture that served as insulation, and the roof was made of cypress bark. Inside, the only items of furniture were sleeping platforms covered with mats made of deerskin and beaver fur.

Today Creeks live in modern, Western-style homes. The Creek Housing Authority provides low-cost housing for low-income families. These brick homes consist of three-bedrooms, one-and-a-half baths, and one-car garages and are constructed by Creeks. Thus, the housing authority provides jobs as well as housing.

10 FAMILY LIFE

The clan is the central unit of Creek society. Clans comprise all people who are descendants of the same ancestral clan grouping. Loyalty to one's clan traditionally came before anything else, and one's clan membership determined one's place in society. Clans are matrilineal (membership is inherited through the mother). Fathers are important within the family system, but in the clan, the mother's brother (the mother's nearest blood relation) functions as the primary disciplinarian and role model. Clan members consider membership in the clan to define "family"; for example, clan members of approximately the same age consider each other siblings, even if they have never met. Clan ties are strong and serve to unite and empower Creek people even today. The clan system influences marriage choices, personal friendships, and political and economic relations. Killing or eating one's own clan animal is traditionally considered a serious offense.

Marriages were often arranged by older women in the tribe, but the bride-to-be had the final say in the matter. When a young man wished to marry a young woman, he was prohibited from speaking directly to her. Instead, he went to her maternal female relatives to propose the idea. When both families had agreed that the match was a good one, the young woman made the final decision. To do this, the young woman set out a bowl of hot cereal for her suitor on a certain morning agreed upon in advance. The young man then had to request permission to eat the cereal. If the young woman consented, it meant that she agreed to marry him. If she refused his request, it stood as a rejection of his marriage proposal.

The actual wedding ceremony was simple. The man had to kill a deer, not only to provide his new wife with food and clothing but also to prove his merit as a provider. The woman, in turn, had to prove her worth as a domestic manager by pre-

paring corn or some other food and presenting it to her husband. The newlyweds then lived for a year in a house the husband had built for his wife. At the end of the year, the couple could divorce if they wished, as simply as they married. The wife kept all the domestic belongings, including the house.

Children were highly valued in Creek society. Like the house, the children belonged to the mother. The mother was directly involved in the raising of her daughters, while her brothers did most of the parenting of her sons. The children's father was responsible for the upbringing of his sisters' sons.

11 CLOTHING

Today's Creeks wear modern Western-style clothing for everyday purposes. Traditionally, the Creeks in the southeast wore very little clothing at all because the climate was so hot and humid. Early Muskogee people wore clothing made of woven plant material or animal skins, such as buckskin. In the colder winter months, the continual fire burning in the family chakofa kept it so warm inside that they rarely had to add any extra clothing, but animal skins and furs were used for warmth when they ventured outside.

In the 1600s, European fashion began to influence Creek clothing styles. Woven cloth was more comfortable and colorful than buckskin, and it became a popular trade item in the southeast. Because cloth came in so many colors and patterns, Creeks developed a more individualized style of dress, even using the traders' novelties such as bells, ribbons, beads, and pieces of mirror to decorate their clothing. Men began to wear ruffled cloth shirts with beaded sashes, and jackets with buckskin leggings. Women wore ruffled cloth dresses decorated with novelty trim, and pocketed aprons. Both men and women wore soft deerskin moccasins, often elaborately decorated with beadwork. During traditional ball games, Creek men wore only a breechcloth to make free movement easier. During the Green Corn Ceremony, women wore beautiful dresses covered with flowing ribbons during the Ribbon Dance.

Today, Creek women still wear their ribboned dresses during the Green Corn Ceremony. Men have adopted the common Western outfit of jeans, boots, and fitted shirts.

Creek men traditionally painted and tattooed their bodies. For men, tattoos revealed their war rank and tribal status in the community. Only women who were considered prostitutes tattooed their bodies.

12 FOOD

The Creeks traditionally supplied all of their food through communal efforts in farming, gathering, hunting, and fishing. The women did the farming and gathering, while the men and older boys hunted and fished. Even small children and the elderly tried to help in any way they could. Among the crops the women raised were squash, beans, and corn; they gathered wild nuts and berries. (A typical Creek recipe follows for dumplings made from wild grape juice.) Corn was by far their staple food. "Modern" corn, or maize, and wild seed crops were introduced to the southeast US from Mexico around AD 200. Bottle gourds and squash had been cultivated by the Muskogee people since approximately 1000 BC. Squash was important as a food source, and gourds were used to make cooking and eating utensils and masks. All food gathering and hunting followed a seasonal cycle.

The men supplemented the diet by catching fish in the many nearby rivers and streams in the spring and, mainly in the winter, by hunting the deer, bears, rabbits, and squirrels that abounded in the dense southern forests.

Grape Dumplings

2 quarts possum grapes

3 cups water

2 cups sugar

2 cups flour

2 teaspoons baking powder

2 tablespoons shortening

Grape juice: Boil grapes and strain the pulp, saving the juice. After adding sugar, set the juice aside to cool. (Frozen grape juice may be substituted for fresh juice.)

Dough: Sift together flour and baking powder, and cut in shortening. Add enough juice to form a soft dough and roll out into a ½-inch-thick sheet, then cut into strips. Boil the strips of dough in the remaining grape juice.

13 EDUCATION

After the Creeks were forcibly relocated to Indian Territory (present-day Oklahoma) in the 1830s, they established their own tribal schools there. Kendell College was a Muskogee (Creek) institution started in Muskogee, Oklahoma. It was later moved to Tulsa, Oklahoma, and became Tulsa University. Bacone College, which was transferred from the Cherokee Nation, is owned and operated by the American Baptist Association today. At one time, it was exclusively for Native American students, but it is now a multicultural junior college.

The Creeks were always strong supporters of education. They agreed to let Presbyterian missionaries set up boarding schools on their lands in Indian Territory, the first in Coweta Mission in 1843. Creek parents were eager for their children to learn English so that they could be successful in the world of the European American. Today almost 9% of the adult Creek population has a college degree, and more than 91% of all Creek children ages 3–17 are currently enrolled in public schools. The Muskogee Nation runs its own Head Start program.

14 CULTURAL HERITAGE

Two modern Creeks who have been successful in the worlds of literature and art are poet Joy Harjo (1951) and actor/artist Will Sampson (1934–87). Harjo draws on her Creek and Cherokee background to write compelling poetry about the importance of language, memory, and stories in shaping who we are as people. Sampson's first big break in acting came in 1975, when he was chosen to play the role of Jack Nicholson's mute Native American friend in *One Flew Over the Cuckoo's Nest*. Throughout his film career, Sampson insisted on portraying Native Americans honestly, making them multidimensional characters. He was a pioneer in expelling the traditional "savage" or "brave warrior" stereotyped image of Native Americans in Hollywood motion pictures.

Though he was best known as an actor, Will Sampson was also a highly successful visual artist. His paintings have been displayed at many museums nationwide, including the Smithsonian in Washington, D. C.

15 WORK

Since the 1970s, some Creek in Oklahoma have raised cattle with great success. The Creek Nation operates five bingo parlors, which provide a source of income for the Nation. Tulsa Bingo is the second-largest tourist attraction in the state of Oklahoma.

The Muskogee Nation plans to open a truck plaza and Burger King restaurant in Okmulgee, Oklahoma, in 1997, and has plans for another plaza in Muskogee, Oklahoma.

16 SPORTS

The Creeks, like many other southeastern tribes, were masters at a game called "stick ball." Similar to modern-day lacrosse, stick ball was a highly active and violent game. It served as a way to develop warrior skills, as well as providing fun and entertainment. To play the game, each of the members of two teams held two sticks. The players would pass a small ball made of animal hide back and forth down the length of the playing field, which was about the size of today's football fields. The aim was to throw the ball over the other team's goal at the end of the field and score a point. There were no other rules, and the games were often quite violent. Stick ball was sometimes called "the little brother of war." Rather than fighting, the Creeks would sometimes settle their differences with a game of stick ball.

Another popular Creek sport was "chunkey." Two men each had a long stick with a crook at one end. A flat, smooth stone disk was thrown down a bumpy (or "chunkey") field. The men each then attempted to throw their stick so that the disk would catch in the crook. Whoever threw his stick closest to the disk won. A difficult game of perception and timing, chunkey trained men in the art of throwing spears.

Today Creeks play football, basketball, tennis, golf, baseball, softball, and participate in track-and-field sports. Many young Creek men and women have attended college on athletic scholarships. R. Perry Beaver, principal chief in the late 1990s, is a retired high school football coach.

A well-known Creek athlete is baseball player Allie Reynolds, who pitched for the Cleveland Indians and the New York Yankees. He holds the World Series record at seven wins, two losses, and five saves.

17 ENTERTAINMENT AND RECREATION

Modern Creeks enjoy the same forms of recreation that other American citizens do.

Traditional Creek dances are considered sacred and are not used for entertainment.

18 FOLK ART, CRAFTS, AND HOBBIES

Long before the Europeans arrived on the North American continent, Creek women were highly skilled weavers and tailors. They used plant fibers and animal skins to make elaborately decorated clothing and containers. When the Creeks began trading with the Europeans, the women acquired glass beads, European cloth, and new ideas and patterns. By combining traditional Creek and European styles, Creek women greatly enhanced their already beautiful work. Today's Creek women supplement their income with the sale of their traditional arts and crafts.

[19] SOCIAL PROBLEMS

The Muskogee Nation has social problems similar to those of other Native American groups. The Nation has its own tribal counselors who deal with specific tribal problems as they occur.

[20] BIBLIOGRAPHY

Avery, Susan, and Linda Skinner. *Extraordinary American Indians*. Chicago: Children's Press, 1992.

Brown, Virginia Pounds, Laurella Owens, and Nathan H. Glick. *Southern Indian Myths and Legends*. Birmingham, AL: Beechwood Books, 1985.

Green, Michael D. *The Creeks*. New York: Chelsea House, 1990.

Gregory, Jack, and Rennard Strickland. *Creek and Seminole Spirit Tales: Tribal Folklore, Legend, and Myth*. Pensacola, FL: Indian Heritage Association, 1971.

Hahn, Elizabeth. *The Creek*. Vero Beach, Florida: Rourke Publications, 1992.

Heinrich, June Sark. "Native Americans: What Not to Teach," in *Unlearning Indian Stereotypes, A Teaching Unit for Elementary Teachers and Children's Librarians*. New York: The Racism and Sexism Resource Center for Educators, a division of The Council on Interracial Books for Children, 1977.

Hendrix, Janey B. *Changing Fashions of the Five Tribes*. Park Hill, OK: Cross Cultural Education Center, 1982.

Henri, Florette. *The Southern Indians and Benjamin Hawkins 1796–1816*. Norman, OK: University of Oklahoma Press, 1986.

Littlefield, Daniel F. *Alex Posey: Creek Poet, Journalist, and Humorist*. Lincoln: University of Nebraska Press, 1992.

Martin, Joel W. *Sacred Revolt: The Muskogee's Struggle for a New World*. Boston: Beacon Press, 1991.

Oliver, Louis Littlecoon. *Chasers of the Sun: Creek Indian Thoughts, Poems, and Stories*. Greenfield Center, NY: The Greenfield Review Press, 1990.

Reddy, Marlita A., ed. *Statistical Record of Native North Americans*, 2nd ed. Detroit: Gale Research, 1995.

Scordato, Ellen. *The Creek Indians*. New York: Chelsea House, 1993.

Swanton, John. *Early History of the Creek Indians and Their Neighbors*. Washington: Government Printing Office, 1922 (Smithsonian Institution, Bureau of Ethnology Bulletin #73).

———. *Myths and Legends of the Southeastern Indians*. AMS Press. (Originally published as Bulletin #88 of the Smithsonian Institution, Bureau of American Ethnology, 1929.)

Wright, J. Leitch, Jr. *Creeks and Seminoles: The Destruction and Regeneration of the Muscogulge People*. Lincoln: The University of Nebraska Press, 1987.

—by D. K. Daeg de Mott, reviewed by J. Bear

CREOLES OF LOUISIANA

LOCATION: United States (Louisiana; Texas)
LANGUAGE: Continental, or "old Louisiana," French; Cajun; French Creole (*Gombo* or *couri-veni);* English
RELIGION: Roman Catholicism; some local sects

[1] INTRODUCTION

There is no single definition for the word "Creole." It has been used to refer to people of mixed ancestry or African ancestry as well as people born in the Americas rather than Europe. Starting in the 16th century, it came into use in the Americas to distinguish between residents of European colonies who were born in Europe and those who were born in the colonies to European parents. In Louisiana, which was once a French possession, the word is used in two distinct ways. It was originally applied to the white descendants of early French or Spanish settlers in the area, who were known for their adherence to the ways and the language of their ancestors. Although this meaning is still in limited use, the word "Creole" is primarily used today to refer to persons of mixed African, French, and Spanish ancestry.

Blacks first arrived in Louisiana in the 18th century as slaves transported from the Caribbean and West Africa (primarily from the Senegal River basin). Due to the high ratio of blacks to whites in southern Louisiana and the liberal French and Spanish attitudes toward the intermingling of the races, black influence on the culture of the region was unusually strong, and New Orleans and the surrounding plantation region took on an African–West Indian character that was enhanced by the arrival of thousands of additional slaves and free blacks from Haiti at the turn of the 19th century. The relatively high degree of racial tolerance that prevailed in the region was evident in laws (including *Le Doce Noir* and *Las Siete Partidas*) governing master-slave relations that accorded various rights to slaves, including the right to gain their freedom under certain circumstances.

As a result of these laws and the attitudes that spawned them, a greater number of slaves were freed in southern Louisiana before the Civil War than in other parts of the South. Called *gens libres de couleur,* or "free people of color," these blacks worked in occupations ranging from laborer and craftsman to merchant and planter. The most privileged members of this group, many of them born to white plantation owners and black female slaves or freewomen, formed an elite population, some of whom owned slaves themselves. A number had their children educated in Europe (historical records document the presence of about two thousand foreign-educated blacks in Louisiana in 1866). However, they generally refused to admit the children of newly freed slaves to their own schools. In addition to occupation and financial status, racial heritage was an important aspect of social standing, and Creoles of color followed a practice, common among many blacks, of according a higher status to those with lighter skins. A variety of categories, such as *griffe, quadroon,* and *octoroon,* existed for classifying people of color according to their racial ancestry.

From the post–Civil War era to the civil rights movement, the Creoles were pressured to conform to rigid racial expectations that were often in conflict with the more fluid notion of race characteristic of their culture and background. The Jim Crow segregation that followed Reconstruction in the South created artificial boundaries between the Creoles and the French-speaking white Cajuns of their region. Traditionally, the two groups had regarded each other as allies, and each group had had a significant cultural impact on the other. The segregationist mentality pitted them against each other by making the Cajuns, often regarded as inferior by other whites, feel that their own social standing could be improved if the Creoles were pushed even farther down the social ladder. To escape from the pervasive racial discrimination of the Deep South, some Creoles migrated to Los Angeles and San Francisco after World War II. Following the civil rights victories of the 1950s and 1960s, Creoles have shown a renewed interest in preserving the special cultural heritage nurtured by the centuries-old intermingling of races and ethnic groups in the bayous of Louisiana.

2 LOCATION AND HOMELAND

The Creole community originated (and largely remains) in the bayous of southern Louisiana along the Gulf of Mexico. There is a particularly strong Creole presence in downtown New Orleans and in the inland bayou parishes of Bayou Teche, St. Martin, and St. Landry, as well as in the Lafayette, St. Landry, Evangeline, and Calcasieu parishes of the part of southwest Louisiana known as "Cajun Country" or "Acadiana." In the 20th century, Creoles from Louisiana have migrated to Texas, especially Beaumont, Port Arthur, and Houston, and to parts of the West Coast.

Modern census surveys do not include Creoles as a distinct demographic group; at one time, they were classified as FMC (free man of color) and *mulâtre* (mulatto). It is thought that approximately a third of the population in the French-speaking parishes (districts) of southern Louisiana is black. However, this figure does not account for the substantial number of English-speaking blacks, both in Louisiana and in Texas and California, who consider themselves part of the Creole community.

3 LANGUAGE

Historically, the French language was a major part of the Creole identity, setting the group apart from other southern blacks. However, in recent years, the use of French has declined, especially among people under forty. There are actually several different varieties of French spoken in southern Louisiana. The least common Continental, or "old Louisiana," French, which is closest to the French of the original colonial settlers. This language is still used by a small minority of Creoles in urban and upper-class rural areas, and it also survives in Catholic schools. Creoles in the Acadiana region of southwest Louisiana speak Cajun, the language of the descendants of the Acadians, French Canadians who migrated to the area in the 1760s after being expelled from their homeland by the British. Strictly an oral language, Cajun French is characterized by a simplified grammar and the use of some archaic terms. French Creole, the third language variant of French-speaking Creoles, is a pidgin language related to the pidgins of West Africa and the Caribbean. Its vocabulary is mostly French, and its pronunciation shows African influences, while its grammar is similar to those

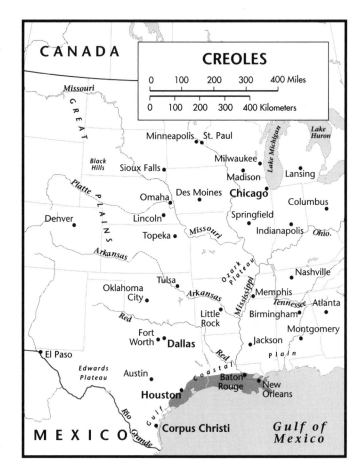

of other African-European Creole tongues. Often called *Gombo* or *couri-veni,* it is most common in the plantation region of southern Louisiana, where it is also the first language of some whites.

4 FOLKLORE

The mingling of Roman Catholicism with African religious influences in the lives of Creoles has resulted in a body of folk religion traditions that includes home altars and the placement of crosses made of blessed palms or magnolias over the doors of houses, as well as the practice of voodoo. The Creoles are also known for their belief in a variety of healers and spiritualists who make use of both prayers and charms. African religious traditions are also perpetuated by special churches whose services include spirit possession and ecstatic behavior, as well as prayers to ad hoc saints, including Martin Luther King, Jr., and Chief Blackhawk.

In the city of New Orleans, Creole Mardi Gras celebrations include special traditions handed down over the generations. The Zulu parade mocks white carnival festivities by displaying white stereotypes about blacks. Participants paint their faces black, wear grass skirts and wild, frizzy wigs, and carry spears. As they walk, they throw coconuts to the crowd. In contrast with the primarily middle- and upper-middle-class Zulu parade, the festivities of working-class Creoles feature a parade with a Native American theme whose participants dress up as Plains Indians and engage in call-and-response singing, drumming, and other traditional activities.

5 RELIGION

The majority of Creoles are Catholics, making up the largest per capita black Catholic population in the United States. Besides various local sects, the Josephite Fathers, based in Baltimore, are especially active in the Creole churches of Louisiana. The Catholic religion has played a major role in preserving the social and cultural unity of the Creoles.

6 MAJOR HOLIDAYS

The Creoles observe the national holidays of the United States and the holy days of the Christian calendar. For the Creoles, as for other residents of southern Louisiana, the major celebration of the year is Mardi Gras, the festive holiday observed just before Lent with costumed pageants, feasting, and other forms of merrymaking. All Saints' Day (*Toussaint*) on November 1 is observed as a special occasion for honoring the dead by cleaning and painting their tombs. Candlelight ceremonies may be held as well.

7 RITES OF PASSAGE

Major life events of the Creoles are celebrated within the Catholic Church. Perhaps the most distinctive rites of passage of Creole origin are the jazz funerals held in New Orleans, in which a jazz band follows the body to the cemetery, playing dirges on the way there and parade music on the way back.

8 INTERPERSONAL RELATIONS

Nicknames, often retained from childhood, are popular among the Creoles. Some, such as *Nene, Soso,* and *Guinee,* have African origins. Relationships with one's godfather and godmother (*parrain* and *marraine*) hold a special place in Creole culture, as they do in many of the Catholic countries of Europe. In New Orleans, Creole social life is closely associated with social clubs, benevolent societies, and church activities.

9 LIVING CONDITIONS

Like their Cajun neighbors, rural Creoles have access to modern medical care but also have a tradition of folk healing by practitioners called *traiteurs,* who are thought to have the power to both heal and harm using their familiarity with herbal medicine and other types of esoteric knowledge.

The traditional Creole cottage, both in New Orleans and in rural plantation areas, is constructed with half-timbering and mud-and-moss plastering called *bousillage.* Two rooms wide, with a central chimney and a continuous-pitch roof, it has porches, elevated construction, and louvered doors and windows that reveal a Caribbean influence. Other characteristic Creole dwellings include shotgun houses with their long corridor of single rooms, bungalows, and mobile homes. Creole houses are typically painted in bright primary and pastel colors.

In addition to modern forms of land transportation, the Creoles, like other residents of the Louisiana bayou, use various types of small boats to navigate the waters of the Mississippi delta.

10 FAMILY LIFE

Creoles usually marry in their teens and early twenties within the Catholic Church, although common-law marriages are also legal in Louisiana. Rural families may give a newly married couple some land to help them start out on their own. Especially in rural areas, families tend to be large, and members of the extended family usually live near each other. Elderly parents often join the households of their grown children, especially after they are widowed. Women are associated traditionally with domestic activities, and family life is closely tied to conservative values, including education, hard work, and participation in the religious life of the community. In contrast with this ethic is the fast street life of bars, dance halls, and social clubs often indulged in by groups of young men, who are still expected to settle down eventually and make a commitment to family life.

11 CLOTHING

For the most part, Creoles wear typical modern clothing similar to that of other Americans. However, for dances and other social occasions involving zydeco music, many Creoles favor Western-style cowboy clothing, including Stetson hats, vests, jeans, and cowboy boots. The single most popular item of dance hall clothing is the straw cowboy hat often worn by both men and women.

12 FOOD

Cajun and Creole cooking have influenced each other extensively over the years and have many similarities. However, the predominant influence in Cajun cooking is French, while Creole cooking also features elements of Spanish, African, Native American, Italian, and other traditions. In general, there is a stronger gourmet aspect to Creole cooking than to Cajun. Gumbo, a popular dish that is also a Cajun staple, is said to have been created by black slaves who worked for the early French and Spanish settlers in Louisiana (its name is derived from the African word for okra). It is a stew that can be made from a wide variety of vegetables and fish, meat, or chicken. A common Creole version is *gumbo z'herbes*, which contains seven different kinds of greens.

Other characteristic Creole dishes include jambalaya, made from rice, sausages, seafood, and spices; étouffé, a stew made with crayfish (locally called crawfish) or shrimp and served over rice; and *grillade*, thickly sliced round steak seared in oil and then braised. Popular ingredients in Creole food include andouille, a spicy country sausage served in gumbo and jambalaya or with red beans; crawfish (shellfish that resemble tiny lobsters and can be eaten either fried or boiled); filé (pronounced fee-LAY), a powder made from ground sassafras leaves and used to flavor and thicken gumbos; and roux, a gravy base made with flour and oil that is used in gumbo and a number of other dishes. Beignets, puffy fried squares of sourdough bread dusted with powdered sugar—are a popular breakfast staple, often accompanied by chicory coffee. Pralines, a brown-sugar candy containing pecans, are a favorite dessert and dessert ingredient, and they can be found in creations such as praline bread pudding, praline crepes, and a variety of desserts served with praline sauce.

13 EDUCATION

The free blacks who were the ancestors of many of today's Creoles placed a high value on education; those who could afford it even sent their children abroad to be educated in Europe. Creoles today take advantage of the educational opportunities available to all Americans, attending both public and Catholic institutions.

14 CULTURAL HERITAGE

The Creoles of New Orleans have played a central role in its legendary jazz tradition, from such figures as Sidney Bechet and Jelly Roll Morton to today's Marsalis family. The Cajun-influenced Creole music of southwestern Louisiana is called zydeco, a word said to be derived from *les haricots* (the snapbeans) and traditionally associated with the phrase *les haricots sont pas salés* ("the snapbeans are not salty"), which refers to hard times when there is no salted meat available. (This phrase is also the title of a famous zydeco tune.) Zydeco has drawn on several different ethnic traditions, deriving its language and melodies from Cajun folktunes; syncopated rhythms, improvisation, and blues patterns from African and Caribbean music; singing and drumming styles from the Native Americans; optional use of the guitar from the Spanish; and the accordion from the Germans. Its main instruments are the violin and accordion, with a rhythm section that includes the *frottoir*, a washboard of corrugated metal (strummed with beer bottle caps or other objects) that is either freestanding or made with a sort of collar so that it can be worn like a bib while it is played. Zydeco music, in great demand as dance music, serves as a unifying force for the Creole community, which gathers in crowded dance halls and church social halls for evenings of lively dancing to this music, which is played in strenuous four-hour sets. Zydeco also has a tradition of commercial recordings that dates back to the 1950s.

15 WORK

Traditionally, Creoles in rural areas raised sugarcane, rice, and other crops while those in New Orleans and other urban areas worked as craftspeople, artisans, or merchants. Today Creoles work in many different fields, including the professions, the service sector, construction, and the oil industry.

16 SPORTS

Cajuns enjoy the mainstream American sports, such as softball and volleyball, as well as outdoor activities including swimming, fishing, and horseback riding.

17 ENTERTAINMENT AND RECREATION

Focal points of Creole social life include Mardi Gras crews (groups that plan organized participation in the annual Mardi Gras festivities), knights of Peter Klaver (a black Catholic men's society), and social clubs. Dancing to zydeco music is a popular pastime, practiced in church social halls and in roadside dance halls that hold hundreds of people. Dance enthusiasts also enjoy "trail rides," social outings involving groups of people (both men and women) who ride horses to a series of dance events, stopping to dance and visit at every stop along the way, with beer and home-cooked food awaiting them at the last stop. Sometimes musicians or a disc jockey playing recorded music even rides alongside them on a flatbed truck.

18 FOLK ART, CRAFTS, AND HOBBIES

Creole artisans are known for their carpentry and wrought-iron work.

19 SOCIAL PROBLEMS

Like other African Americans, the Creoles have faced racial discrimination, and many have experienced poverty. For a time, the French culture of the Creoles, like that of the Cajuns, was threatened by laws that banned French from classrooms and even from the schoolyard altogether. Today, Creoles display pride in their unique culture and try to ensure its preservation through events and organizations such as the Louisiana Zydeco Festival and Creole Inc., a group devoted to promoting recognition of the Creole heritage and lifestyle.

20 BIBLIOGRAPHY

Brasseaux, Carl A. *Creoles of Color in the Bayou Country.* Jackson, MS: University Press of Mississippi, 1994.

Dormon, James H., ed. *Creoles of Color of the Gulf South.* Knoxville, TN: University of Tennessee Press, 1996.

Gould, Philip. *Cajun Music and Zydeco.* Baton Rouge: Louisiana State University Press, 1992.

Haskins, James. *The Creoles of Color of New Orleans.* New York: Crowell, 1975.

Spitzer, Nicholas R. "Black Creoles of Louisiana." *Encyclopedia of World Cultures.* Boston: G. K. Hall, 1992.

———. *Zydeco: Creole Music and Culture in Rural Louisiana.* El Cerrito, CA: Flower Films, 1984.

—by R. Wieder

CUBAN AMERICANS

For more information on Cuban history and culture, *see* **Vol. 2: Cubans**.

OVERVIEW

Prior to 1958, only about 40,000 Cubans had immigrated to the US. Most of them lived in south Florida. These early Cuban Americans were responsible for the development of the US cigar industry. In 1958, members of the Fulgencia Batista government of Cuba became aware that the government was about to fall to Fidel Castro's forces, and some 3,000 fled to the US. When Castro did in fact take over the government in 1959, the first major wave of Cuban immigration to the US began. All told, somewhere between 215,000 and 280,000 Cubans immigrated to the US in 1958–1962. Most were white, middle-aged, well-educated, and fairly wealthy. When Castro announced that his government would be run on Marxist-Leninist principles and began nationalizing Cuban farming and industry, wealthy landowners and business people escaped to America.

The Cuban Missile Crisis in 1962 severely curtailed Cuban immigration to the US for the next three years. About 74,000 Cubans managed to enter the US through clandestine means in 1962–1965, but the next major wave of immigration did not begin until Castro opened Cuban borders in late 1965. Castro then allowed the US to organize so-called "Freedom Flights" to airlift Cubans who wished to immigrate to the US. Two flights per day from Cuba to Miami, Florida, from late 1965 to April 1973 brought a total of up to 340,000 or more Cubans to America. The majority continued to be white, well-educated people from the middle-class, but a number of working class Cubans also joined the exodus.

Castro closed Cuba's borders again in May 1973, and no Cubans were allowed to emigrate for the next seven years. In May 1980, however, Castro decided to permit Cubans to be boat-lifted to the US from the Cuban port of Mariel. These "Marielitos," as they came to be called, were quite different from previous waves of Cuban immigrants. As opposed to the predominantly white, middle- and upper-class, well-educated family immigration of the past, 85% of the Marielitos were men, 65.6% were single, 40% were black, and 86.2% were blue-collar workers.

At the time it was reported that Castro had emptied Cuba's prisons and mental institutions and unloaded all the "undesirables" onto the US. Estimates are that 16% of the Marielitos were ex-convicts, 4% of which were hard-core criminals. US police arrested active criminals and sent them to US prisons. A number ended up in the Atlanta Federal Penitentiary, where they staged a rebellion in which they took more than 100 hostages in 1987 when told they were to be sent back to Cuba. Cuban American Catholic Auxiliary Bishop Agustin Román, who had been expelled from Cuba in 1961, convinced the prisoners to release the hostages, and the rebellion was quieted.

The most recent wave of Cuban immigration began in the 1990s, when the Soviet Union collapsed and Soviet aid to Cuba was cut off. The Cuban economy and government began to falter, and many Cubans decided to flee the potential disaster and look for better opportunities in the US. Even Fidel Castro's daughter immigrated to America in December 1993. Huge numbers of Cuban refugees crossed the waters between Cuba and Florida on homemade rafts, called *balsas*, made of large inner tubes. These newest immigrants are referred to as *balseros*, after their common mode of transportation. This sudden influx of Cuban immigrants has created stress among Cuban and non-Cuban Americans alike in southern Florida, and the *balseros* continue to come.

By far the largest Cuban American community is in the Miami, Florida, area. Early Cuban immigrants believed their stay would be temporary, assuming that Castro's regime would not last. Therefore, they chose to live as near to Cuba as possible to facilitate their return. Miami, Florida, is only about 150 miles from Cuba. When Castro maintained his rule and more Cubans fled to the US, they naturally settled among their compatriots, thereby creating a vibrant Cuban American community in Miami. Also attractive to Cuban immigrants were the US government assistance programs available in the Miami area. The first program was established in 1959.

Cuban Americans are the third-largest Hispanic American group (after Mexicans and Puerto Ricans), excepting perhaps Dominican Americans if "illegal" immigrants are counted. The total Cuban American population in 1990, according to the US Census, was 1,069,000. By 1993, the estimated population of Cuban Americans had risen to 1,120,000. Up to 60% of all Cuban Americans live in the Miami, Florida, area. One section of Miami that has a large concentration of Cuban Americans has come to be called "Little Havana." The entire population of Florida is 58.5% Cuban American, making it the most-Cuban state in the US, as of 1993. The second-largest Cuban American community is in Union City, New Jersey, and New Jersey was the second-most-Cuban state in 1993, with Cuban Americans making up 10.1% of the total state population. The third-most-Cuban state in the US in 1993 was New York (9.6%), followed by California (7.6%)

Cuban Americans have been slow to be assimilated into mainstream American culture for two reasons: throughout Cuban immigration to the US, many immigrants have believed their stay in America was only temporary and that they would soon be returning to Cuba; and the Cuban American community, especially in Miami, Florida, is so strong and tightly knit that the majority of Cuban Americans never have to interact with non-Cuban Americans. Most first-generation Cuban Americans continue to speak Spanish at home and among friends. Many Cuban Americans who work in Cuban American-owned businesses also speak Spanish in the workplace. This means that some Cuban Americans never have to speak English at all.

Due to the large concentration of Spanish-speakers in the Miami, Florida, area, the city has become de facto bilingual, with all signs and public information printed in both English and Spanish. In 1973, Dade County (where Miami is located) commissioners passed an ordinance declaring the county officially bilingual. Only seven years later, however, in 1980, an anti-Cuban American backlash prompted a referendum (that passed easily) reversing the 1973 ordinance and declaring English as the only official language of Dade County. The "antibilingual referendum" spurred an English Only movement in other regions of the US with large Spanish-speaking populations. Some proponents of English Only want English to be declared the official language of the US on a national level.

Children marching in Calle Ocho Parade in Miami, Florida. The Cuban American community, especially in Miami, is so strong and tightly knit that the majority of Cuban Americans never have to interact with non-Cuban Americans. (Steven Ferry)

Despite the 1980 English Only referendum, however, the use of Spanish has continued to grow in Dade County and elsewhere.

The great majority of Cuban Americans are Catholic. Since Fidel Castro outlawed the practice of religion in Cuba in 1961, many Cubans have become nonpracticing Catholics. Immigrants to the US, however, found the US Catholic Church very supportive in their relocation efforts, and many Cuban Americans have become active churchgoers once again. There are also a number of Protestant Cuban Americans, as well as 7,000–10,000 Cuban American Jews. Cuban American Jews formed the Cuban Hebrew Circle in 1961 as a means of social, cultural, and religious support. The Afro-Cuban religion Santería also claims some adherents among Cuban Americans.

Baptism and First Communion are especially important rites of passage for Catholic Cuban Americans, as are the holidays of *La Noche Buena* (Christmas Eve) on 24 December; *El Dia de los Tres Reyes Magos* (Three Kings' Day, or Epiphany) on 6 January; and *La Semana Santa* (Holy Week), Palm Sunday, and Good Friday before Easter. A parade is held each year in Miami on Three Kings' Day. Other important Cuban American festivals include the Feast of Our Lady of Charity, the patron saint of Cuba, on 8 September; the Feast of Santa Barbara on 4 December; and All Saints' Day on 1 November.

Cuban Americans are much better off economically than other Hispanic Americans. This is due partly to the fact that most of the earlier Cuban immigrants were from the middle and upper classes in Cuba and had the education, skills, and financial resources to be successful in the industrialized US. Also, the average age of Cuban Americans is significantly older than that of other Hispanic American groups, giving them added wisdom and experience to apply to life in America. Cuban Americans also have the highest level of education among Hispanic Americans: 63% are high school graduates, and 20% have graduated from college.

Cuban Americans are still not as well off as the average American citizen, however. In 1987, the average income for a Cuban American family was $27,294, as compared to an average of $30,853 for the total US population; and 13.8% of Cuban Americans lived below the poverty line, as compared to 10.6% of the total US population. Educationally, Cuban Americans also lag behind the total US population. The median years of education for Cuban Americans in 1991 was 12.4, whereas the median number of years for all Americans was 12.7.

Although Cuban Americans have only been in the US in large numbers for a few decades, they have made a significant impact on mainstream American culture. As early as the 1930s, Cuban dances such as the rumba, mambo, and chachachá were becoming very popular among the general US population, as were conga dance lines. Cuban music, which is a blend of Spanish, African, and Creole rhythms, is a central element of Cuban American gatherings. In Miami, Latin salsa music combined with American pop music to produce a unique form of music called Miami Sound. The foremost promoter of Miami Sound is Cuban American Gloria Estefan, with her band, the Miami Sound Machine. Estefan also helped launch the career of Afro-Cuban American singer Jon Secada.

Two other Cuban American musicians and bandleaders who became well-known and well-loved in America were Xavier Cugat and Desi Arnaz. Desi Arnaz went on to become an actor on the *I Love Lucy* show with his wife, Lucille Ball. Their children, Desi Arnaz, Jr. and Lucie Arnaz, also became entertainers. Another successful Cuban American actor is Andy Garcia. Other Cuban Americans in the arts include ballet dancer Fernando Bujones and writers Cristina Garcia and Oscar Hijuelos. In 1990, Hijuelos became the first Hispanic writer to win the Pulitzer Prize.

Cuban Americans have begun to make their mark in politics and public office, particularly in the state of Florida. Xavier Suarez was elected mayor of Miami in 1985. He was the first Cuban American to fill that post. Earlier, in 1979, Margarita Esquiroz became the first Hispanic woman to be appointed a judge in Florida. Cuban Americans finally broke through to the federal level in 1989 when Ileana Ros-Lehtinen was elected to US Congress from Florida. Four years later, in 1993, Lincoln Diaz-Balart became the second Cuban American to be elected to US Congress.

Sports have long been an avenue of success for Cuban Americans. Swimmer Pablo Morales won a gold medal at the 1992 Summer Olympics. Alberto Salazar won both the New York and Boston Marathons in 1982 and was selected for two Olympic marathon teams. The sport with the most representation by Cuban Americans by far, however, is baseball. Among the many Cuban American major league stars are René Arocha, José Canseco, Mike Cuellar, Martín Dihigo, Miguel Angel Gonzales, Orestes Minnie Miñoso, Tony Oliva, Rafael Palmeiro, Tony Perez and his son Eduardo, José Tartabull and his son Danny, and Luis Tiant. Preston Gomez was the first Hispanic manager in the major leagues.

Because Cuban Americans who came during the first two waves of immigration were mostly white, middle- and upper-class professionals, they had fewer difficulties adapting to life in the US than did other Hispanic Americans. Later Cuban immigrants (the Marielitos and balseros), however, the majority of whom are black, lower-class, blue-collar or unskilled workers, have met with discrimination and rejection from both mainstream Americans and the established Cuban American community.

Largely, the influx of Marielitos and balseros has set off racist paranoia among white, non-Hispanic Americans and has led to the English Only movement and other forms of prejudice against all Cuban and other Hispanic Americans. Established Cuban Americans indulge in their own racism and classism, shutting out the new Cuban immigrants and forcing them to become marginalized. Tensions in the Cuban American community itself, as well as tensions between Cuban and non-Cuban Americans, continue to increase as more and more refugees flock to the US from Cuba. Miami, Florida, is a particular hotbed, as most Cuban immigrants still choose to settle there.

BIBLIOGRAPHY

Cockcroft, James D. *Latinos in the Making of the United States*. New York: Franklin Watts, 1995.

Galván, Raúl. *Cuban Americans*. New York: Marshall Cavendish, 1995.

Jensen, Jeffry. *Hispanic Americans Struggle for Equality*. Vero Beach, FL: Rourke Corporation, 1992.

Marvis, Barbara J. *Contemporary American Success Stories: Famous People of Hispanic Heritage*, vols. II and III. N.p.: Mitchell Lane, 1996.

—by D. K. Daeg de Mott

CUBANS

LOCATION: Cuba
POPULATION: 11 million
LANGUAGE: Spanish
RELIGION: Forbidden by Communism, but Roman Catholicism and Santeria are practiced clandestinely

¹ INTRODUCTION

Cuba was discovered and claimed for Spain by Columbus during his first voyage to the New World in 1492. The island's indigenous population of Arawaks, who had displaced the Ciboneys from most of the island, staged their last significant uprising against the Spanish in the mid-1500s. In the late 1700s, African slaves were brought to Cuba as were Asian indentured laborers in the mid 1800s. Despite several revolutionary movements and a brief period of occupation by the English, Cuba remained a Spanish colony through the late 1800s. Most notable among the rebellions was the Ten Years War which began in 1868. The rebels, known as Mambises, fought mostly with machetes for lack of guns. On 24 February 1895, Jose Marti, Cuba's patriarch, led the War of Independence. Key military figures in the revolution included Antonio Maceo (known as the "Bronze Titan"), Maximo Gomez, and Calixto Garcia. In 1898, the US intervened in the Cuban war and Spain relinquished Cuba's sovereignty to the US under the Treaty of Paris. On 20 May 1902, the United States ended its military occupation of Cuba, formally inaugurating the Cuban republic. The US and Cuba maintained close ties, with the Cubans leasing Guantanamo Bay to the Americans under the Platt Amendment.

Governments in Cuba during the early and mid-1900s were often plagued with corruption and were short lived, for the most part, with the US stepping in from time to time. Despite an unsettled political climate, Cuba's natural beauty made it a haven for people from all over the world, and a popular vacation spot for Americans. In the 1940s and 1950s, vice and corruption were widespread in Havana, with the government establishing alliances with members of organized crime from the US.

On 26 July 1953, Fidel Castro began his revolutionary movement with an attack on the army barracks at Moncada. In 1959, Castro's guerrilla movement successfully overthrew the existing government of Fulgencio Batista. Batista supporters were jailed and executed. Castro passed an agrarian reform act (which limited private land ownership), confiscated all foreign-owned investments, and established what would be a long-standing relationship with the Soviet Union. While the peasant class made some quick gains, middle and upper class citizens were stripped of most of their possessions. Over the next few years, approximately 1 million Cubans left home, most fleeing to the US.

In January of 1961, the US established an economic blockade of Cuba, halting the import of American goods to the island, and persuading a number of nations also to cease trade with Castro. In April, CIA-trained Cuban exiles staged the Bay of Pigs invasion, a failed attempt to topple the Castro regime. Later that year, Castro proclaimed Cuba a socialist country and declared, "I am a Marxist-Leninist and shall be until the day I die." The following year, the Cuban Missile Crisis (when the US discovered Soviet missiles in Cuba) was, perhaps, the most tense period of the Cold War. The crisis ended when the Soviets agreed to remove the missiles and, in exchange, the US promised never to invade Cuba.

In the 1970s, Cuba made some social and economic strides. Schools and low-rent housing units were built, countryside roads were paved, and health care improved for many. At the same time, however, the government became more controlling and oppressive. By the end of the 1970s, the economy began to slip and, aggravated by political oppression, life on the island became intolerable for many. Since then, numerous Cubans have sought to exile themselves from the island, most notably during the Mariel Boatlift of 1980 when more than 125,000 Cubans made their way to Florida.

Today, Cuba remains the only communist government in the Western hemisphere. After the collapse of the Soviet Union in the early 1990s, an already struggling Cuban economy took a turn for the worse. Facing civil unrest in the wake of an all-but-collapsed economy, the Cuban government has been forced to dabble in capitalism and reverse its position on tourism. Farmers' markets were legalized in 1994 and Castro has opened the doors to foreign investors. Nonetheless, political and economic unrest continues and since 1994 tens of thousands have left Cuba, risking their lives in makeshift rafts in an effort to flee.

² LOCATION AND HOMELAND

A country of approximately 11 million people, Cuba is the largest island in the Antilles archipelago in the Caribbean Sea. It is located approximately 145 km (90 mi) south of Florida and is situated at the key approaches to the Atlantic Ocean, the Gulf of Mexico, and the Caribbean Sea. Columbus described Cuba as "The most lovely that eyes have seen." The island's topography is very diverse. Approximately 35% of the total land mass is made up of three extensive mountain systems: the Sierra Maestra (where Castro formulated his guerrilla-style revolution), the Guamuhaya, and the Guaniguanico. Two extensive plains account for 65% of the entire island surface and house almost 95% of the total population. There are nearly 200 rivers, most of which are short, narrow, and shallow. The combination of trade winds, the warm waters of the Gulf Stream, and sea breezes give Cuba a moderate and stable climate. Annual average temperature varies only by about 6°C (10°F); the average winter low is 21°C (70°F) and the average summer high is 27°C (81°F). The island has extensive arable land, accounting for more than half of the island. Other areas are used for cultivating sugar (Cuba's key export), rice, coffee, cocoa, and plantains. Nickel is the principal mineral on the island, and Cuba is the fourth-largest exporter of nickel in the world.

Cuba is home to a number of rare birds and animals, many found nowhere else. The island's Bee hummingbird is the world's smallest bird, measuring just 5 cm (2 in).

Cuba is not lacking in beaches, with more than 100 in total. The most famous is Varadero, considered one of the finest in the world. The island, like many of its neighbors in the Caribbean, is subject to hurricanes. More than 150 such storms have been recorded since the days of Columbus. Cuba has also experienced a number of earthquakes (about 200 since the 16th century), mostly along the southeast coast.

In the late 1800s, Cuba was organized into 6 provinces: Pinar del Rio, Havana, Matanzas, Santa Clara, Puerto Principe

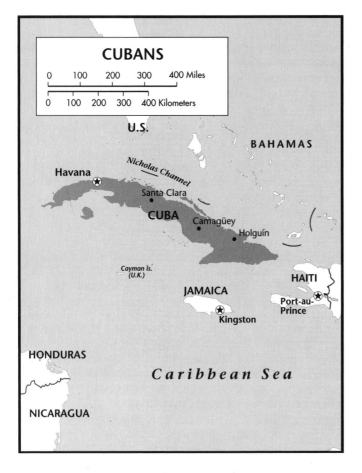

CUBANS

0   100   200   300   400 Miles

0   100   200   300   400 Kilometers

U.S.

BAHAMAS

Nicholas Channel

Havana ★

Santa Clara

CUBA

Camagüey

Holguín

Cayman Is. (U.K.)

JAMAICA

HAITI

Port-au-Prince ★

Kingston ★

HONDURAS

Caribbean Sea

NICARAGUA

of Latin America. Marti wrote of the US, "I have lived within the monster and I know its entrails." Marti, being of frail physique, was killed in his first day of battle. For exiles and island-dwellers alike, Marti embodies all that it means to be Cuban.

Fidel Castro is without question a modern-day icon of legendary proportions. He stands for all that is the Revolution, and for this he is revered by some and despised by others. However, none can dispute Castro's ability for delivering long and dramatic speeches. Perhaps the most famous of his discourses was a five-hour marathon at his trial following the Moncada attack where he uttered the famous line, "Condemn me if you will. History will absolve me."

Ernesto "Che" Guevara's image, on murals, billboards, and the like, can be found throughout Cuba. Guevara, a key figure in Castro's revolution, has been elevated to a stature usually reserved in other cultures for martyrs and saints. Cuban schoolchildren begin their day by reciting the patriotic slogan, "Pioneers of communism, we shall be like Che." Guevara, a medical doctor from Argentina, joined Castro and a band of other revolutionaries on board a used yacht named *Granma* by its original owner, after his grandmother (*Granma* later became the name of one of the 14 provinces and of the state-run newspaper). The yacht, which left from Mexico, made its way to Cuba, only to be captured by Batista. Guevara, Castro, and Castro's younger brother, Raul, headed for the hills, the Sierra Maestra, and from there staged the revolution that culminated with the overthrow of a fleeing Batista on 1 January 1959. After serving as president of the National Bank of Cuba, "Che" resigned his post in 1965 and went to Bolivia to join the revolutionary movement in that country. He was killed by the Bolivian army in 1967. Castro declared a three-day period of national mourning, and to this day the government sponsors campaigns with themes of "Let's Be Like Che."

5 RELIGION

As a communist country, religious affiliation is deemed antirevolutionary in Cuba. Nonetheless, many Cubans maintain a Catholic tradition, although they tend to do so covertly for fear of persecution. Much more openly practiced, Santeria is an African-based religion introduced into Cuba by the slaves. Worshippers would disguise their gods in the images of the Christian saints so as not to be accused of heresy. Our Lady of Charity, for instance, is Ochun. The rough equivalent of a priest or spiritualist in Santeria is known as a *babalao*. When someone is initiated into Santeria, they dress all in white for one year. A small group of Jews live in Cuba and celebrate holidays such as Passover to the best of their ability, given the economic restrictions.

6 MAJOR HOLIDAYS

Major holidays in Cuba mark significant points in the revolution (1 January and 26 July). May Day (a communist holiday worldwide) is celebrated, as is 10 October, marking the declaration of war against Spain in 1868. Catholics honor Three Kings Day on 6 January, Epiphany.

7 RITES OF PASSAGE

Young girls in Cuba sometimes celebrate *los quince* (literally, "the 15"), the Latin American version of a sweet 16 party, but one year earlier. At los quince, often celebrated with great pag-

(later known as Camaguey), and Santiago de Cuba. In 1976 the island was reorganized into 14 provinces: Pinar del Rio, Havana, the city of Havana, Matanzas, Cienfuegos, Villa Clara, Sancti .Spiritus, Ciego de Avila, Camaguey, Las Tunas, Holguin, Granma, Santiago, and Guantanamo.

Cuba's population consists mostly of whites, blacks and mulattos (a mix of white and black). Additionally, there is a small Asian population on the island. Very few Cubans can trace their ancestry to the indigenous populations.

3 LANGUAGE

Cubans speak Spanish. Their names are composed of three parts: first (given) name, father's surname, and mother's maiden name; for example, Jose Garcia Fernandez.

4 FOLKLORE

One of the better-known pieces of Cuban folklore is El Bizarron, the story of a man who outsmarts the devil. However, most of Cuba's heroes come not from folklore but from real life. Jose Marti is Cuba's undisputed national hero. Marti was the mastermind behind the War of Independence and is noted for his inspiring prose and poetry. The verses of his most famous poem, "The White Rose," have been put to music in what is Cuba's most moving song, "La Guantanamera."

Marti, who was born in 1853, lived in exile in New York City for a period of about 15 years beginning in 1881. Originally enamored with the US and its freedoms, Marti soon became disenchanted with the US and its threat of annexation

food, clothes, liquor, medicine, cigarettes, and gas. *Paladares* are illegal private restaurants.

In ironic contrast to the living conditions of the locals, tourists in Cuba enjoy the best of accommodations, food, and drink. For the tourist, nothing is lacking.

10 FAMILY LIFE

Both tradition and economic necessity dictate the structure of the extended family in Cuba. More often than not, one or more of the grandparents live with a married couple and their children. For the same reasons, children tend to live at home until married.

Machismo is alive and well in Cuba. While women are expected to work outside the home, they are also expected to do the cooking, cleaning, and the like.

11 CLOTHING

The *guayabera,* an embroidered man's shirt, is considered a traditional, elegant article of clothing and is still worn today in both formal and informal settings. For everyday purposes, however, people tend to wear casual attire. As in so many parts of the world, blue jeans from the US are a hot commodity.

12 FOOD

Like so many other aspects of Cuban culture, traditional Cuban cuisine is rich in both Spanish and African influences. Pork, the meat of choice in a traditional meal, is almost always accompanied by rice and beans. When the white rice and the black beans are cooked together, they are called *arroz congri* (literally, "rice with gray"). White rice and kidney beans make *moros y cristianos* ("Moors and Christians"). Plantains, which when green are fried up as *tostones* or *mariquitas* (also used as a derogatory term for gays), and when ripe as *maduros,* round out the meal. *Yuca* (cassava), *malanga* (taro), and *boniato* (sweet potato) are also common elements of a traditional meal. *La raspita,* the scrapings from the bottom of a pot of rice, would never make its way onto the plate during an elegant meal but is often enjoyed by the cook in the privacy of the kitchen or is shared in a small informal gathering. Typical fruits include avocados, mangoes, guavas, mammees, and papayas. Traditional beverages include *guarapo* (sugarcane juice) and rum.

Bleak economic conditions have made the traditional meal a thing of the past. The ration under the Special Period consists of a piece of bread per person per day, three eggs per week, and a portion of fish or chicken per month. A family of four gets one small bottle of cooking oil four times a year, and milk is available only for children under the age of eight. These items are often hard to come by, as are staples such as rice and beans. Many Cubans haven't had beef or pork in years. A piece of beef on the black market can cost as much as a month's wages.

13 EDUCATION

In 1961 the government initiated a campaign to wipe out illiteracy. Education is both free and mandatory, and today Cuba has one of the highest literacy rates in all of Latin America (94%). Shortages have dictated that textbooks be shared and workbooks be erased and passed along to the next class.

Higher education is also free, but admission is affected by one's political affiliations. Scientific and technical areas are

In Cuba, handmade cigars are as much a craft as they are an export item. (Cory Langley)

eantry not unlike a wedding, the young lady will usually wear an extravagant gown made especially for the occasion.

8 INTERPERSONAL RELATIONS

Cubans are known for their warmth, friendliness, sense of humor, wit, and resilience. Cubans greet each other with a handshake and by saying *hola* ("hello"). Like other Latins, Cubans have very expressive body language—wrinkling one's nose, for instance, means "What?" Commiserating in difficult times is as much a pastime as are sports or television. Traditionally, when young girls dated, they brought along a *chaperona* (chaperone); this has recently gone out of fashion.

9 LIVING CONDITIONS

Ever since the collapse of the Soviet Union in 1991, Cuba has been going through what it calls the "Special Period"—a mandatory belt-tightening way of life. Under the Special Period, energy consumption is drastically reduced, oxen are put to work in the fields, people get around on bicycles, and food rations are slashed to a minimum survival level. Once recognized as one of the best in the Third World, the health care system in Cuba today is such that patients must bring their own bedsheets to the hospital, and surgeons are given one bar of soap per month with which to wash their hands. Black marketeers, known as *macetas,* illegally buy and sell goods such as

Tourism jobs are highly sought after because of their access to dollars and foreign goods. Here a street vendor prepares to sell flowers to tourists visiting Havana. (Cory Langley)

emphasized. The University of Havana, founded in 1728, is the leading institution of higher education on the island.

14 CULTURAL HERITAGE

Music is, perhaps, the single most important aspect of Cuba's popular culture. Cuban music is a combination of Spanish and African influences. Typical styles of music include charanga, son, rumba, mambo, cha-cha-cha, and danzon. From a blend of these rhythms evolved "Salsa" (literally, "sauce"). Celia Cruz, now exiled in the US, is known throughout the world as the Queen of Salsa. Cruz began her career in Havana in the late 1940s with the group Sonora Matanzera. Other world-renowned Cuban artists include Beny More, Arsenio Rodriguez, and Israel "Cachao" Lopez. Notable postrevolutionary performers include the groups Los Van Van, Irakere, NG, Dan Den, and Yumuri Y Sus Hermanos. In addition to traditional music, teenagers are also known to enjoy rock and roll—of both the US and homegrown varieties.

In Cuba, ballet is to the fine arts as baseball is to sports—it reigns supreme. The Cuban National Ballet Company has performed the world over. Its founder, leader, and star, Alicia Alonso, is considered one of the best dancers of all times. Cuba's film industry, which saw a period of growth under government control and sponsorship in the early days of the Revolution, has declined in recent years. One film, produced in the 1990s, *Fresa y Chocolate* (Strawberry & Chocolate) won sev-

eral international awards and was nominated for an academy award. The film tells of a young, straight militant who (although reluctant at first) befriends a gay intellectual.

Several Cuban writers and poets, including Jose Marti and Alejo Carpentier, have left their mark upon Latin American literature. A recent and notable example is Herberto Padilla who wrote an award-winning collection of poems, *Out of the Game,* about the myths of revolutionary society. While receiving critical acclaim worldwide, Padilla's work was banned in Cuba and Padilla was arrested.

Painters and sculptors prior to the Revolution demonstrated European influences, while postrevolutionary artists like Manuel Mendive and others have incorporated Afro-Cuban mythology and folklore into their work. Other artists have produced abstract works, and many have produced works with themes of protest. Under Castro's policy set forth in 1962, which states, "Within the Revolution, everything; outside the Revolution, nothing," artists who disagree with the Revolution and its ideals are silenced. The more outspoken ones are sentenced to labor camps.

15 WORK

The labor force in Cuba is divided almost evenly among services, agriculture, trade, manufacturing and mining, and utilities. Tourism jobs are highly sought after because of their access to dollars and foreign goods. Many teachers, doctors, and engineers have left their professions to work in more lucrative jobs as waiters or bellhops.

16 SPORTS

Sports are a very important part of Cuban life and identity. "Sports is a right of the people," reads a banner inside the arena in the athletic complex in Havana. Castro, himself an athlete and enthusiast, was once offered a contract to pitch on a baseball team in the US. Outstanding young Cuban athletes at the age of eight or nine are selected to attend an EIDE, a boarding school where they take academic courses and play different sports. The next step, at age 15 for those who excel, is to attend an ESPA, a school for athletic improvement and perfection. The top 1,000 athletes end up at a CEAR, a center for high-yield training.

Cuba has been referred to as the "best little sports machine in the world," consistently turning out champion Olympic athletes. In 1992, Cuba won more Olympic medals per capita than any other country. Cubans excel in baseball, boxing, track and field, and volleyball. Unlike the millionaire athletes of the US, top athletes in Cuba, albeit heroes of society, make about 300–600 pesos ($8–16) a month, which is two to four times the average Cuban's salary.

17 ENTERTAINMENT AND RECREATION

State-run television operates anywhere from 6 to 12 hours a day, with mostly sports programming and some recent American movies. Other programming includes *novelas* (short-run soap operas) from Latin America. However, one will rarely find a young Cuban just sitting at home watching TV. Young Cubans, when they are not partaking in sports, will be involved with one or another of many government programs. The Young Communists Union, for instance, operates numerous computer instruction centers. Older Cubans can be found playing dominoes or chess, or sitting at Copelia, the ice cream parlor featured in the film *Fresa y Chocolate,* or simply strolling El Malecon, the boulevard that runs along the waterfront in Havana.

18 FOLK ART, CRAFTS, AND HOBBIES

Handmade cigars are as much a craft as they are an export item. Considered the finest in the world, more than 3 million are produced (one at a time) each year. An experienced worker can make a cigar from start to finish in just two minutes.

19 SOCIAL PROBLEMS

Cuba is often cited as a violator of human rights. Government control is strong. Members of neighborhood watch groups, Committees for the Defense of the Revolution, watch their neighbors and report on all nonconformist behavior to the government. In addition, special brigades of paramilitary agents have been formed to crack down on protesters.

Tourism has brought about what is being called "tourism apartheid" where the locals are not allowed into the resorts unless they are accompanied by foreigners. Additionally, prostitution is on the rise.

While blacks have made demonstrable strides in Cuba, only a handful are in the upper echelons of government. Gays and lesbians are openly discriminated against. They are banned from the Communist Party, and AIDS victims are quarantined.

20 BIBLIOGRAPHY

Oppenheimer, Andres. *Castro's Final Hour.* New York: Simon & Schuster,1992.

Perez, Louis A., Jr. *Cuba: Between Reform and Revolution.* New York: Oxford University Press, 1988.

Perrottet, Tony, and Joann Biondi, ed. *Insight Guides: Cuba.* Boston: Houghton Mifflin, 1995.

Suchlicki, Jaime. *Cuba from Columbus to Castro.* New York: Charles Scribner's Sons, 1974.

—by L. Gonzales, reviewed by G. C. Martin

CUNAS

ALTERNATE NAMES: Cuna-Cueva
LOCATION: San Blas Islands (or Mulatas Archipelago), along the Gulf of Darien from Panama to the Colombian border
LANGUAGE: Cuna (Chibchan group of languages)
RELIGION: Indigenous spirit-based beliefs

1 INTRODUCTION

What is now Panama was inhabited by the Cuna Indians when the Spanish began exploring the Panamanian coastline early in the 16th century. (It is believed that the Amerindian peoples, including the Cuna Indians or Cunas, are descended from Central Asians who migrated across the Bering Straits some 20,000 years ago and gradually moved southwards.) The first Spanish explorer was Rodrigo de Bastidas in 1501, followed by Christopher Columbus on his fourth voyage to America in 1502, and Diego de Nicuesa in 1509. None of them was successful in establishing a colony, partly because of the hostility of the Amerindians who lived there, although Martín Fernández de Enciso succeeded in founding the settlement of Santa María along the western shores of the Gulf of Darién.

Panama was part of Colombia until it became an independent nation in 1903. Today the Cunas live inhabit an area that includes part of Panama and part of Colombia.

2 LOCATION AND HOMELAND

The Cuna Indians inhabit 30 or 40 islands in an archipelago of some 400 islands strung along the Gulf of Darien from Panama to the Colombian border. Some Cunas also live on Colombia's Pacific coast near the Panamanian border. The dwellers of the archipelago, sometimes referred to as the San Blas Islands or the Mulatas Archipelago, also farm along the shores of the Panamanian coastline proper, which is very close to the islands. The hinterland is jungle and has very few roads. The comparative inaccessibility of the Cuna settlements has helped them preserve their way of life.

3 LANGUAGE

The language of the Cunas is classified as belonging to the Chibcha group of languages. The people who inhabited the great plateaus of the Andean highlands in central parts of Colombia were known as Chibchas and are now extinct, but their descendants mixed with the Spanish and form a significant part of the *mestizo* (mixed) population of Colombia. The language of the Cunas is part of the Pacific-Chibchan group of languages.

Names are sacred and naming ceremonies take place when girls and boys become teenagers. These ceremonies have an unusual feature: there is a special chanting of all available names. The parents of a child listen attentively, and when they hear a name they like they interrupt the ceremony and the choice of the name is made immediately.

Many Cunas also have Spanish names, and because the US has been prominent in the Panama Canal Zone, some have also taken English names.

4 FOLKLORE

Among the first and most memorable of the Cuna to be discovered by Spanish explorers were the small population of albinos (estimated to be less than one percent of the total population), most of whom lived on one island. The albinos were somewhat of an outcast group in the Cuna society, and many folktales grew up around them. For example, here is a Cuna legend reflecting the historic Cuna practice of Sun worship, which is no longer carried out today:

Inhabiting the fertile Darien region since time immemorial, the Cunas, descendents of the Sun, were blessed by the gods with a beautiful homeland, including magical lakes, rushing rivers, luxuriant jungles filled with exotic fauna and flora, and mountains where gold was stored.

Once upon a time, the Sun wanted to reward the tribe's shaman, called the *nele,* for his wisdom, goodness, and generosity. Appearing before the *nele* one afternoon at the hour of the sacrifice, the Sun offered to grant him anything he desired. Although the shaman's humility at first prevented him from making a request, the Sun repeated hi offer. The shaman, who was old and did not have long to live, resolved to ask for something that would benefit the entire tribe after he was gone.

He asked the Sun to send his own son to the Cunas, to serve as their leader. Although this was a difficult request, the Sun agreed, and after three days two beautiful blond children—a boy and a girl—appeared in the sky at dawn, surrounded by golden light, and came down to earth. The people were overjoyed and gave thanks to the Sun for this miraculous occurrence. The children were raised in a golden palace with lavish gardens, and, when grown, they were married in a festive ceremony.

Eventually, however, they were unfaithful, both to each other and to their divine origins. As punishment, the Sun turned them from divine beings into mere mortals, condemned to suffer like other human beings. However, from their first union have come the albinos, who, with their blue eyes and nearly white hair, are still considered children of the Sun. It is said that they cannot bear the light of day. The rest of the Cunas, believed to be descended from the subsequent unions of the two original children of the Sun, still consider themselves to be descendents of a god.

Although the albinos comprise a small percentage of the Cuna population, their existence caused early explorers to label the Cuna the "white Indians."

5 RELIGION

The Cunas have a close connection with nature and see themselves as a part of it. Every living thing has a spirit counterpart—animals, men, bodies of water, rocks, trees, and plants. The Cuna believe that what is taken from nature must be replaced in some way.

Becoming a shaman is regarded as an important vocation. Shamans may be men or women, and they perform three types of functions: curing illness in individuals, believed to be caused in most cases by the loss of one's soul; curing villages of epidemic illness; and establishing rapport with spirits, leading to the ability to predict the future. The shaman who serves the latter function is typically born into the role, but receives training, usually requiring a period of jungle isolation.

6 MAJOR HOLIDAYS

Most Cunas are Panamanian or Colombian citizens. Many continue to resist assimilation and do not celebrate their respective country's major national holidays. However, some Cunas have allowed and even encouraged their young people to go to the town of Colón at the mouth of the Panama Canal and receive a Western-style education. After education, most return to the islands. These Cunas speak Spanish, and in a few cases some have even learned English. While living among non-Cuna people, Cunas take part in the celebration of national holidays. These include Independence Day, celebrated in both Panama (5 November) and Colombia (20 July).

7 RITES OF PASSAGE

Women give birth in a special hut set aside for this purpose that men are not permitted to enter. If a girl is born, there is a joyous response on the father's part, because he is then allowed to leave the matrilineal household of his wife's family and set up his home independently with his wife and daughter. If a son is born, the father has to remain in his father-in-law's home. A father is not permitted full authority over his sons in the beginning. The father-in-law has that privilege and duty, until he considers that the young father has learned his parenting skills adequately.

The Cunas are fond of their children, and although respect for elders is expected, they are not harsh in the upbringing of young children. Parents decide on a husband for their daughter when she is young. As she approaches adulthood, parents cut their daughter's hair, and there is a special celebration in honor of this occasion.

When a person dies, he or she is wrapped in a hammock and buried in a lonely place in the jungle on the mainland. The husband or wife chants a song of praise and lamentation.

8 INTERPERSONAL RELATIONS

The Cunas respect the different positions that family members hold, and greet each other accordingly. Greeting are different when the Cunas are working or are engaged in trade. On these occasions, the men are in the background and the women are the dominant partners, and they can be very forward and even fierce. When entertaining visitors, the men stay in the background. The women play a more forthright role.

Modern Cuna women appear to have no difficulty in being assertive. This tends to confirm the view of the traditionally powerful position of Cuna women, and reinforces the matrilineal foundation of Cuna culture.

9 LIVING CONDITIONS

The Spaniards who first visited the gulf of Darien and the Panamanian coast found the conditions very difficult. The Cunas fiercely resisted the encroachment of Europeans.

The houses of the Cunas are quite long and can accommodate extended family units. The thatched roofs are made out of palm fronds, and the walls out of bamboo or cane. The houses

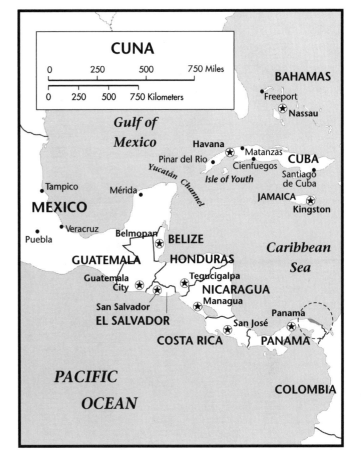

of some villages are very close together, with very little space between one and another.

The Cuna are excellent sailors. They use canoes known as *cayucas* made from a single, hollowed-out tree trunk, usually that of a large tree. The canoes are often fitted out with sails and are well-suited for navigating the waters of the Darien between the Panamanian coast and the islands. In the forests beyond the coast, the men go on hunting expeditions on foot.

10 FAMILY LIFE

Extended family units and clans are held together by the female line. Many aspects of Cuna family life indicate a matriarchal society in which women play a leading role.

Among the Cunas, women own almost everything. A man cannot trade or sell any article without first seeking his wife's permission. On the other hand, if she wants to sell the perfumed berry beads she has made into necklaces, or garments she has made, it is her right and she does not have to obtain permission from anyone else.

The Cunas keep dogs as pets.

11 CLOTHING

The Cunas are famous for their techniques in preparing layer upon layer of cloth, cutting out patterns, and sewing pieces on top of each other in colorful geometric patterns and lively col-

A Cuna woman on the beach with a parrot in Panama. Cuna women wear long, narrow skirts which are tightly wrapped around them. They use ankle bands as well as arm bands of many beaded strands. (Jack Grove. PhotoEdit)

ors including red, yellow, and black. They prepare blouses for women using this technique, and these are widely admired in both Colombia and Panama. The women also wear long, narrow skirts that are tightly wrapped around them. They use ankle bands as well as arm bands of many beaded strands. The men wear dark trousers, bright shirts, and straw hats. In many areas, Cunas wear these traditional articles of handcrafted clothing and jewelry to complement a Western-style wardrobe.

The Cunas have golden-brown skin, almond-shaped eyes, high cheekbones, and shiny, straight black hair. Women wear striking earrings that are large, thin gold disks, rather like flaming suns.

12 FOOD

The Cunas grow yams, corn, and sugarcane in jungle clearings along the coastline. Their diet also includes a variety of fruits such as plantains, bananas, and mangoes. They also drink *chicha,* a fermented drink prepared from sugarcane mixed with plantains, corn, and water. In Cuna family homes there are big jars where the *chicha* is stored. A refreshing drink, called *coco de agua,* is provided by the green coconut.

The Cunas also eat fish and a species of iguana. They stew sea turtle and eat rice boiled in coconut milk. Their traditional hunting weapons were spears and blow guns.

13 EDUCATION

The men teach their sons both hunting and fishing skills as well as how to sew their own simple garments, which include a loose-fitting shirt and trousers. The women teach their daughters how to prepare and cook food, some basic farming skills, and the elaborate sewing techniques to make their beautiful blouses, known as *molas.*

Some Cuna men have received a Western-style education on the Panamanian mainland. Generally, the Cunas expect the young men who have been educated to return to their island and mainland settlements.

14 CULTURAL HERITAGE

Music and dance are important for the Cuna. They preserve their strong cultural identity by passing down to their children accounts of their background, history, and values through stories, myths, and legends.

15 WORK

Work is divided in very specific ways among the Cunas. The men hunt and fish and also make their own clothes. The women make their own distinctive clothes; they cook, weave, sew, and make hammocks. The women are also work as sailors and traders. For many years, visitors have been able to sail to the San Blas region from the Panamanian town of Colón.

Cuna women sail in their canoes to meet tourist and trading boats to sell their goods. They are accompanied by men who do not participate in the actual trading.

The coconut palm is important in this region, and was once used as a form of currency. For the modern Cuna, it provides fibers for making clothing, brooms, threads for sewing and weaving, lamp wicks, rope, and hammocks. It provides sweet coconut water for drinking and coconut milk for cooking. The coconut palm is a source of fuel, and dishes are made from coconut shells.

16 SPORTS

Cunas are skillful sailors and fishers, but do not consider these activities sports in the Western sense. They engage in these activities for their livelihood.

17 ENTERTAINMENT AND RECREATION

Important occasions are celebrated with feasts, and it is considered appropriate to mark these occasions with generous amounts of food and drink.

18 FOLK ART, CRAFTS, AND HOBBIES

The Cunas are noted for their skills with textiles. They decorate cloth with bright geometric patterns, dye it in a variety of colors, and cut and sew several layers to make the women's blouses, known as *molas*. The molas are prized in Colombia and Panama. They have found their way into exhibitions of Amerindian art. *Molas* may also be framed and hung as works of art, or used to make cushions. These practices are generally found outside the Cuna communities. The Cunas also make beaded necklaces and woodcarvings.

19 SOCIAL PROBLEMS

The Cunas have tried to defend their way of life for centuries, and have energetically resisted assimilation. In the 1920s, the Panamanian government decided that the Cunas were too autonomous and sent a contingent of officers to police the islands of San Blas and the surrounding coastal area in the Gulf of Darien. At that time, the jungles that stretched inland from the coast did not have a single road. The police officers were all killed by the Cunas.

Since that disastrous interaction, a more peaceful climate of coexistence has generally prevailed. There is now a Panamanian governor for the archipelago. The governor's residence is in El Porvenir, a small, clean, whitewashed town on the mainland. A few markets have been established there, where the Cuna women sell their wares to visitors. Visitors may only come to El Porvenir for the day.

On the Pacific coast of Colombian mainland near the Panamanian border where some Cunas live, there are real worries that policies to develop Colombia's Pacific coast may threaten the way of life of the Cunas there.

20 BIBLIOGRAPHY

Cobb, Charles E., Jr. "Panama: Ever at the Crossroads." *National Geographic Magazine* (April 1986).

Feeney, Corinne B. *Arch-Isolationists, the San Blas Indians.* February 1941.

Los descendientes del Sol y otras Leyendas de América. Barcelona: Editorial Labor S.A., 1986.

Marden, Luis. "The Land that Links the Americas." *National Geographic Magazine* (November 1941).

—by P. Pitchon

DAKOTA AND LAKOTA

ALTERNATE NAMES: Sioux
LOCATION: United States (North and South Dakota, Minnesota, Nebraska, Montana); Canada (Alberta, Saskatchewan, Manitoba)
POPULATION: 103,000
LANGUAGE: English; Dakota Sioux
RELIGION: Traditional
RELATED ARTICLES: Vol. 2: Native North Americans

¹ INTRODUCTION

The term Sioux (a French form of *Nadowi-is-iw*, "little adders," a name given them by their enemies, the Chippewa) has been used for a large group of bands and tribes who spread historically from Minnesota to the prairies of the Dakotas and as far as Montana. Speaking a common language with dialectical variations, these peoples today, as in the past, refer to themselves as Dakota in the east, Nakota in the central region, and Lakota in the west. In all three regional dialects, this term means "allies" and it was extended to affiliated tribes such as the Cheyenne and Arapahoe, both Algonkian speakers who fought alongside them in war. The unity of the Allies is symbolically expressed in the term *oceti sakowin*—the Seven Fireplaces. The easternmost Dakota groups are the *Mdewak'ant'unwan* ("Spirit lake village"), *Wahpek'ute* ("Leaf shooters") *Sisit'unwan* ("Fish scale village"—although the meaning of this term is debated), and *Wahpet'unwan* ("Leaf village"). These four groups are collectively referred to as the Santee (*Isan t'i*—"Knife dwellers"—refering to the name of a lake). The central groups also call themselves Dakota which sometimes was pronounced Nakota. These are the *Yankton* ("End dwellers") and the *Yanktonais* ("Little End Dwellers"). These two groups are classed together as Yankton or "Middle" Sioux. The westernmost groups, known collectively as the Teton Sioux (*Titunwan*, or "Prairie dwellers") form the third division. They subdivided themselves historically into seven further fireplaces: *Oglala* ("Scatters their own"), *Sicangu* ("Burned thighs"), *Mnikowoju* or *Miniconjou* ("Planters by water") *Oohenunpa* ("Two kettles"—literally, "Two boilings"), *Itazipco* or *Icazipo* ("Without Bows"), *Sihasapa* ("Black Feet"), and *Hunkpapa* ("Campers at the opening of the circle"). Today these people use their own language for self-ascription, the Tetons calling themselves the Lakota and the others using Dakota. In 19th-century literature, these groups were collectively called Sioux or Dakota (and thus the Dakota Territory, which is, in fact, occupied in the west by the Lakota and the east by the Dakota).

The Allies originally kept their own historical records in the form of winter counts. These pictographic documents highlight each "winter" or year with its most significant event. By their reckoning, the Allies have hunted and gathered on this continent since their emergence into this world, and in any case since long before the coming of Europeans. Items of European culture such as horses, cloth and later guns were initially acquired through trade with other Indians and later directly with Europeans through the fur trade (late 1700s until about 1851). Early contact resulted in widespread epidemics of European diseases that ravaged native populations.

The first written mention of the "Naduesiu" by Europeans was by Jean Nicolet in 1639, with the first recorded contact between the Dakota and the explorers Radisson and Grosselier in 1660. The first fur trading post was established on the Mississippi in 1683. The Dakota territory was "claimed" by the King of France in 1689 and later "purchased" by the young nation of the United States in 1803 (the Louisiana Purchase). Louis and Clark visited the Dakota territory in 1804, and the first treaty with the Eastern Allies was signed with Zebulon Pike, ceding two parcels of Dakota land on the Mississippi river for American forts. The Dakota allied with the British in the War of 1812. Fort Snelling, the first military outpost in the country of the Dakota, was built on one of these parcels in 1819. Fort La Framboise (later renamed Ft. Pierre) was built in 1917.

The first large-scale outbreak of hostilities between the military forces of the United States and the western Lakota took place in 1854 when a Lakota was jailed for the killing of a cow owned by a Mormon settler. Known as the Mormon Cow incident, Lieutenant Grattan and 29 of his men were killed in retaliation, and this sparked the Sioux War of 1855. A peace treaty was signed with the Lakota in 1856 and the Lakota who had killed the cow was released.

As the 19th century went on, the Eastern Dakota were increasingly pressed by settlers wanting their land. The United States government habitually delayed meeting its treaty obligations and did nothing to discourage encroachment of settlers into Dakota territory. In an attempt to maintain their land and resources, Inkpaduta killed 40 settlers and took four captives in 1857, but a year later the Yanktons ceded their eastern lands, retaining only a small parcel on the east bank of the Missouri River. Further pressure from settlers and continued delays in the government's treaty payments resulted in the Minnesota Dakota conflict of 1862. During this conflict some Dakota fled to Canada and the west. By 1864 the remaining Santee were removed from their homelands to Nebraska.

When gold was discovered in Montana in 1863, settlers traveled to the gold fields by way of the Bozeman trail, disrupting game ecology. and splitting the great buffalo herd in two. Hostilities continued with the unceasing expansion of whites through and to the territory of the Lakota. The first Fort Laramie Treaty was signed with the Lakota in 1851, but when the US Army failed to fulfill its obligation to keep settlers off of Lakota land, hostilities erupted, most notably resulting in the death of Captain Fetterman and 80 of his men in the Wagon Box Fight in 1866. In 1868 the Red Cloud War ended with the signing of the second Fort Laramie Treaty. The United States abandoned the forts along the Bozeman Trail which was closed to white migration, and the Lakota agreed to allow a railroad to pass through their country. This treaty also established the domain of the Lakota: the lands to the west of the Missouri River in the present state of South Dakota and parts of its border states as well as hunting rights in lands contiguous to the territory.

Once again whites abrogated their treaty agreements when gold was discovered during the Custer expedition to the Black Hills in 1874. The United States attempted to acquire the territory legally in 1875 and, when that effort failed, set up a commission in August of 1876, which fraudulently declared the territory was legally ceded according to the terms of the Fort Laramie Treaty. On 31 January, 1876 the United States military announced that all Native Americans must leave their hunting territories and report to reservations. General George Armstrong Custer and the 7th Cavalry went out to round up the Lakota who would not follow this order. Custer's command was crushed in the Battle of the Little Big Horn on 26 June, 1876, but only a year later, the Oglala under Crazy Horse came in to Fort Robinson. Crazy Horse was murdered on 5 September while in custody at the Fort. By 1878 the Tetons were all on reservations except for Sitting Bull and his supporters, who had fled to Canada. Homesick and missing their relatives, Sitting Bull and the majority of his people returned to their territory in 1881, taking up residence on the reservation.

The United States hoped to assimilate the Native Americans, making them independent landowners and dissolving both religious and civil authority. U. S. President Ulysses S. Grant instituted the Grant Peace Policy 1869, whereby each reservation was allocated to a single Christian denomination to administer and proselytize (this policy was rescinded in 1882). Land allotment to individuals under the Dawes Act sought to dissolve the vast land holdings of the natives and sell the "excess" lands to white settlers. The first attempt to parcel out the Great Sioux Nation territory was in 1888 and the second, in 1889, when the government managed to acquire the ¾ signatures necessary to cede land.

By the late 1880s the status of the Allies had been so drastically reduced that spiritual remedy was sought. The Ghost Dance, begun by the visions of a Paiute Indian named Wovoka (Captain Jack) in Utah, spread throughout the Plains in the late 1880s. This faith taught that through prayer and dancing the earth would roll up and be renewed. The ancestors and the buffalo would return and the Europeans would disappear. Some Lakota also claimed that sacred shirts would protect them from the bullets of the whites. The Ghost Dance movement gained strength in-1889, a year of drought and famine. The killing of Sitting Bull by Tribal Police on 15 December, 1890, further disheartened the people. The Indian Agent at Pine Ridge panicked over this situation and called in troops which violated an understanding he had with the Lakota. At the same time, Chief Big Foot and his Miniconjou and Hunkpapa followers traveled down from the Cheyenne River agency to Pine Ridge to meet with Red Cloud and receive horses from him. They were arrested to the west of Pine Ridge and brought to Wounded Knee Creek. While the Lakota were being disarmed, a shot was heard, and the soldiers began shooting into the encampment, massacring 368 men, women and children.

The Lakota and Dakota struggled against great odds to preserve their cultural life. In the 1880s some Santee returned to Minnesota and small reservations were granted. In 1905, the first individual allotments were made on the Pine Ridge agency itself. All Native Americans were granted citizenship in 1924. Allotments continued until the United States reversed the policy of forced cultural assimilation and destruction of traditional cultural and political institutions through the Indian Reorganization Act, which allowed Indian tribes to constitute themselves as legal entities and again own and control land communally. The IRA was a mixed blessing; while it gave the tribes some autonomy, it also imposed governmental structures (tribal councils) that derived from American civil government rather than from traditional forms of authority.

The Lakota and Dakota continued to struggle for their legal, cultural, religious, and territorial rights, working through extended family governance as well as other traditional forms of social organization. The United States set up the Indian Claims Commission in 1946 to settle outstanding treaty claims on the part of Native peoples. Although the Supreme Court has recognized the illegality of the seizure of the Black Hills by the United States government, the Lakota and Dakota people involved in the suit refuse to accept the monetary settlement prescribed by the Federal government and continue to press for a return of the federally controlled regions of the Black Hills to their rightful owners. In the 1970s, Indian groups became more visible as contemporary peoples as they protested their political and cultural plights, particularly with the occupation of Wounded Knee by the American Indian Movement (AIM) (27 February–8 May, 1973), which brought world attention to Native issues. Legislation such as the Indian Self-Determination and Educational Assistance Act (1975), the Indian Child Welfare Act (1978), and the Native American Grave Protection and Repatriation Act (1990) helped bolster Indian rights in the judicial and governmental arenas. Contemporary concerns of the Lakota and Dakota people include tribal sovereignty, religious rights in general as well as protection of religious rituals from exploitation, return of the Black Hills, jobs, language retention and revival, cultural and political autonomy.

² LOCATION AND HOMELAND

Some Lakota claim that their people inhabited the Black Hills since the beginning of time. Others hold that the Allies emerged from a cave or from under a lake to inhabit the upper world. Anthropologists and archaeologists, who believe the inhabitants of this continent migrated from Asia across the Bering Strait, place origin of the Dakota people in the southeastern United States. At earliest European contact, the Dakota and Lakota occupied the woodlands of a territory centered in what is now known as Minnesota. By the late 1700s the Lakota spread westward to Montana and Wyoming and were successful on the plains as warriors as well as horsemen and hunters. They fought prolonged wars with the Crows, Pawnees, Shoshones, Omahas and Kiowas, who blocked their westward migrations.

Today Lakota and Dakota live on a number of reservations: in South Dakota—the Lake Traverse, Standing Rock, Crow Creek, Lower Brule, Yankton, Flandreau, Pine Ridge, and Rosebud Reservations; in Nebraska, the Santee Reservation; in Montana, the Fort Peck Reservation; and in North Dakota, the Fort Totten Reservation. There are also Dakota and Lakota in present day Canada in Alberta, Saskatchewan, and Manitoba. As many as 85% of Native Americans live in urban areas, so it should be no surprise that there are many Lakotas and Dakotas in off-reservation cities such as Pierre, Rapid City, Scotts Bluff, Denver, Chicago, Los Angeles and Minneapolis-St. Paul. According to the 1990 United States Census, there are 103,255 Sioux people, making them the fourth largest native group in the United States. Two of the ten largest reservations in the United States are Lakota: Pine Ridge (11,200 persons), which is ranked second, and Rosebud (8,000), which is ranked sixth.

³ LANGUAGE

Lakota and Dakota are still spoken today and are commonly used during religious ceremonies and traditional social events. Great pains are taken today to preserve and expand the number of speakers of these dialects. Lakota, Dakota and Nakota are mutually intelligible dialectical variants of one of many languages of the Siouan family. Formal study and recording of Dakota by Euro-Americans was first carried out by the Pond brothers and Stephen Returns Riggs, all of whom were Protestant missionaries. Fr. Eugene Buechel, S.J., continued this work among the Lakota, building on a dictionary first started by the Pond brothers and published by Riggs. Native Dakota scholar Ella Deloria and Lakota scholar George Bushotter also worked on the language, recording native stories in their original dialects.

⁴ FOLKLORE

The Dakota and Lakota have a tradition of oral literature that continues into the present. Many stories are shared among the different groups of the seven fireplaces, and some stories have been picked up from the many surrounding cultures. The ability to tell stories well is honored. Many Dakota stories were recorded in Dakota by Stephen Riggs and Ella Deloria. Dakota stories in English were also written by Charles Eastman. Lakota stories were recorded in the native language by George Bushotter and Eugene Buechel, S.J. Dr. James Walker recorded many stories narrated by George Sword, including stories of the creation of the word and the behaviors of the spirits.

Stories of the trickster Iktomi provide moral lessons by showing how NOT to behave. There are also many versions of the story of how the White Buffalo Calf Woman brought the Sacred Pipe to the Lakota. Magical, handsome heroes come to save the people, and still other stories tell of war and peace, love and conflict, and every other human occurrence. Many stories are very funny and are told both to entertain and instruct.

⁵ RELIGION

The religion of the Dakota teaches various ways to gain assistance from spiritual powers in order to live this life well. Sweat lodge rituals are used to purify an individual for contact with the divine. Individuals pray, make sacrifices and endure suffering to make themselves pitiful so that the spirits would come to their assistance. The Dakota also adopted the *mdewiwin* ritual from the nearby Ojibway, with several levels of initiation into a healing lodge that helps individuals and the community through life.

The famous Lakota spiritual leader Black Elk described Lakota religion as consisting of seven rites: *Wanagi Yuhapi*, the keeping of the soul; *Inipi*, the rite of purification (sweat lodge); *Hanbleceyapi*, the rite of crying for a vision; *Wiwanyag Wacipi*, the sun dance; *Hunkapi*, the making of relatives; *Isnati Awcial-owan*, preparing for womanhood, and *Tapa Wanka Yap*, the throwing of the ball. There are also a variety of healing ceremonies called *lowanpi* "sings" or *yuwipi,* a sing in which the spiritual leader is tied and later unbound in the darkness by the spirits. Lakota and Dakota continue to rely upon a variety of healers who used both prayers and various medicines to help their patients. Smudging and praying and offering food for the departed spirits are also important religious practices, as are acts of generosity and hospitality.

In the 19th century some Dakota and Lakota became Christian. Traditional spiritual leaders like George Sword and Black Elk also became Christian leaders. While some individuals held exclusive allegiance to one or the other belief, others participated and still participate in both religious forms. Both the government and the missionaries initially attempted to suppress traditional religious beliefs. Today both groups have a deeper respect for traditional religion. Some Dakota and Lakota follow what are called the traditional ways, while others belong to one Christian denomination or other, and some, as in the past, pray in both groups. The majority of Lakota and Dakota today hold that all religions seek to contact the same God and see prayer as a way to unify the people. There is controversy over non-Lakota or Dakota conducting traditional ceremonies. For example, charging admission for such things as sweat lodges is disrespectful.

Some Lakota and Dakota belong to the Native American Church, a group that combines Christian and traditional beliefs with the use of peyote as a sacrament that brings wisdom to those who use it. Native American Church congregations vary, based in how much Christianity and tradition they incorporate into their ceremonies. Individuals from other tribes often visit to participate in all-night prayer services.

⁶ MAJOR HOLIDAYS

In the past different groups came together for the annual Sun Dance, although the Lakota and Dakota were so far-ranging by the end of the 19th century that it is unlikely they were all ever able to meet as a single body. Buffalo hunts were sometimes occasions for summer gatherings as were trade fairs with other tribes. Trade with fur traders and at Army forts were also important social occasions. With the official ban on religious ceremonies, traditional religion went underground, and people substituted American civil and religious holidays for their own annual religious and economic gatherings. Thus the 4th of July, Thanksgiving, Christmas, Easter, Veterans Day, and other holidays became important on the reservations. The public Sun Dance was revived on Pine Ridge in 1961 and has become centrally important. Today, there are many Sun Dances in a single season. Powwows are important secular as well as religious events put on by different communities as well as reservations, often with prizes for dancers and singers. Most of these gatherings occur in the summer. The Sisseton Wahpeton Wacipi (*wacipi* means dance) is the oldest continuously celebrated event in the state of South Dakota. Many of the summer powwows are open to whomever wishes to attend in a respectful manner.

⁷ RITES OF PASSAGE

Dakota and Lakota children were and some continue to be treated ceremonially at birth with traditional naming and ear piercing. Names have never been static, for as individuals achieve social recognition or are healed of a serious illness or are adopted by other extended families, new names are granted. Girls underwent a "sing" and were instructed in arts and manners proper to women when they reached their first menses. Boys would undertake vision quests, although individuals could do this at any time when they needed spiritual aid. Marriage was not ceremonialized in the past. Individual males could be initiated into various societies of curers, dreamers, and healers, and women had special associations for their various arts such as quill work. Leadership also conferred a different status on an individual, although in the past leadership was situational and transitory. For the Dakota, entrance into the *Mdewiwin* "Medicine Lodge" was accomplished through a series of ordeals and rites of passage to convey new status.

The most important and extended rite of passage was for the dead. In the past, there would be a long period of mourning during which those close to the deceased would show their sorrow through self-mutilation, such as cutting one's hair. In some instances, the soul would be ceremonially kept in a special bundle by a designated keeper for a period of a year and then released.

Dakota and Lakota rites of passage are very much alive today. There has been a revival of the girl's puberty ritual and many individuals participate in the rites of passage mentioned above. These rites are all public and are accompanied by large feasts and give-aways (a distribution of gifts) to honor those undergoing the rituals. Young boys are taken out on vision quests. Boys and girls will be given a new name after a great achievement such as finishing a military tour of duty. Graduations from high school and college are marked in a traditional way by tying on an eagle feather (for men) or eagle down plume (for women), and giving the graduate a star quilt. There are also prayers and handshakes to mark these sacred events. Both Christians and Traditional people honor the dead with prayers, honoring songs, large feasts and giveaways, both at the time of death and to mark the one-year anniversary of the death. Food is also placed out to feed the spirit of the deceased.

8 INTERPERSONAL RELATIONS

The basis of Dakota and Lakota life is kinship. Those related by birth and marriage are counted as kin, as are other human beings sometimes formally included through the *hunka* (adoption) ceremony. The extended family remains the focal social unit. Indeed, kinship is projected to the entire universe. Thus Lakotas end their prayers with the phrase *mitakuye oyas'in* "for all my relatives."

Dakota and Lakota society was once based in small roving bands organized by leaders according to needs. This leadership would be extended over larger groups at times of communal hunts and in warfare. Individual freedom was and continues to be highly prized. If a person was not content with how things were done, he or she was free to form another group. The smallest social group was the *tiyospaye* "residential group or band" and consisted in cooperating families and individuals who attached themselves to that group. A number of these bands would comprise an *oyate* "people" such as the Sicangu or Oglala.

The coming of the Europeans modified group structures, and a split arose between those who wanted to adopt white ways quickly and those who did not. The native governance of the Dakota and Lakotas became more centralized and stable to deal with the European incursion into the territory and lives of these people.

In contemporary Lakota and Dakota life, personal freedom remains essential, but this is balanced by obligations to one's extended family and tribe. So, too, many Dakota and Lakota enter the United States military services and are respected for that; one is expected to sacrifice for the people and to be generous and kind to everyone, but especially to the poor and elderly.

The Lakotas describe themselves as *ikcey wicasa*, ordinary people, and no one is supposed to be boastful. Even important governmental or religious leaders are expected to act humbly. Dakotas and Lakotas are wonderfully humorous and enjoy teasing one another as well as making self-deprecating remarks.

Individuals are expected to excel but never to separate themselves from the group.

Dakotas and Lakotas today frequently perform the *hunka* (adoption) ceremony to increase the size of their families. Both Lakotas and Dakotas, as well as outsiders who have grown close to certain families, will be honored in this way. Special songs are sung and a name is given to the adopted, sometimes the name of a deceased relative whom the adopted one resembles in some way. The relationship of a *kola* (Lakota) or *koda* (Dakota) is also vital and represents a deep bond of friendship existing between two individuals.

9 LIVING CONDITIONS

Before the coming of the Europeans, the Dakota and Lakota were mobile peoples. The Dakota who lived in the woodlands had bark houses supported by poles in the summer and skin tents called tipis (*tipi* means "they dwell." Lakotas generally use the word *tiobleca* for these dwellings) in the winter. These dwellings were comfortable and warm. In winter they were surrounded by wooden windbreaks for added protection from the elements. As the western Lakota moved onto the prairie, they used tipis almost exclusively. With the advent of horses, dwellings could be larger and were carried further than when the Lakota depended on human and canine transport. In the east and west, life could be difficult with frostbite, snow blindness, and starvation, as well as attacks from enemies or wild animals.

During the reservation period, Lakotas and Dakotas adopted European-style log cabins, and today they have wooden frame houses. Originally, the Lakota settled according to families along creek bottoms, but the government wanted to centralize construction of new dwellings in housing developments. This caused further social disruption. Agency towns tended to hold the largest concentration of people since jobs with the government, schools, and missions were more available there.

In the 1950s the United States government sponsored a relocation program to help people find employment in the cities and to become more assimilated. Many people left the reservation but eventually returned. Today the Dakota and Lakota continue to be a highly mobile people; some live far from the reservations but return to renew family bonds. While some of the dwellings look poor, the mark of a prosperous Lakota or Dakota is not money or lavish surroundings but good relationships with one's family.

10 FAMILY LIFE

Lakota and Dakota people stress individual freedom, so each person is expected to make decisions for himself or herself. Children, too, are respected in this way and treated as adults, being allowed to make their own decisions and learn from their mistakes. In the past, prosperous men might marry a woman and her sisters and form a household. Extended families continue to be very important, and there were strong kinship obligations in terms of respect and mutual assistance. There was no marriage ceremony, but marriages were sometimes arranged and often sealed with a ritual exchange of property, such as the groom bringing horses to his bride's parents. Once married, one was expected to avoid direct contact with one's in-laws. Children have always been honored as especially sacred beings.

Grandparents have an especially close relationship with their grandchildren. Anyone related to a child who is two generations away is considered a grandparent (rather than a great aunt or great uncle as in Euro-American society).

Women's roles in traditional Dakota and Lakota society included gathering food, cooking, and making clothes and tipi covers. Women have traditionally been treated with respect and dignity. Today, women as well as men are active in family and tribal affairs, serving as educators and political leaders. Women are healers and also have important roles in the Sun Dance and in Native American church services.

11 CLOTHING

Before the trade for European-manufactured cloth, Dakotas and Lakotas used tanned and dressed animal skins, such as deer and buffalo, to protect themselves from the weather as well as to indicate their social status. There is a great seasonal variation in the weather of Dakota and Lakota territory. In the harsh winters moccasins and leggings were used to protect feet and legs. Mittens and gloves protected hands from frostbite. Early Europeans and Euro-Americans frequently commented on the careful ornamentation and good taste exhibited in native dress. Face paint as well as hair style were done with care by both men and women. There was ordinary clothing for daily life and special dress for social events.

Today Dakota and Lakota wear contemporary clothing for everyday purposes. Some men wear cowboy boots and broad brimmed hats. Women wear dresses or pants. For powwows, men and women will wear beautiful dance costumes decorated with intricate beadwork. Women wear leggings, moccasins, buckskin dresses, and shawls. Men wear brechclouts, moccasins, leggings with bells, and different types of headdresses. Individuals wear everyday clothing for most prayer ceremonies, traditional or Christian, but special dress for those dancing the Sun Dance. Men sometimes wear ribbon shirts for special occasions, while women sometimes wear ribbon dresses. Indian-style clothing is having a significant effect on the fashions of non-Indians, as styles are borrowed back and forth.

12 FOOD

The buffalo served as the staple food for the Dakota and Lakota in their pre-reservation days, but they also ate deer and other game, as well as wild fruits and plants, ducks and geese, and less often, fish. The Dakota harvested wild rice and grew some corn. The Lakota traded for corn and other produce. Eating was not only for nutrition but also a social event. This is also true today. When someone is to be honored, the family of that person will feed whoever comes for the ceremony. Food is freely shared and special attention is paid to the poor and the elderly. Early Euro-American observers consistently remarked on and benefited from the generosity of the Lakota and Dakota peoples.

At religious and social rituals today, the food served is a mixture of traditional and contemporary items. Dakotas and Lakotas still serve dried corn, *timpsila* (prairie turnips), *wasna* (pounded dried meat, berries, and fat), *wojapi* (berry pudding), tripe, boiled beef or buffalo and soups when they are available. Fried bread, although made with flour introduced by Euro-Americans, is considered part of traditional fare. This food may be supplemented with fried chicken, soda crackers, store-bought bread, fruit cocktail, potato salad, beans, pies, and cake. Food is distributed by the providers, and it is always abundant. Those attending feasts bring their own dishes and plenty of

containers to carry back food they cannot finish. This extra is called *wateca,* and the mark of a good feed is the over-abundance of food which will be used for days thereafter.

Venison and Wild Rice Stew

½ pound shoulder of venison, cut into 2-inch cubes
2 teaspoons salt
1/8 teaspoon black pepper
2 quarts water
1½ cups wild rice, washed in cold water
2 onions, peeled and quartered

Place the venison, water, and onions in a large kettle, bring to a boil, then turn down the heat and let simmer uncovered for 3 hours until the venison is tender. Add the salt, pepper, and rice. Cover and let simmer another 20 minutes. Stir, then let simmer uncovered for another 20 minutes, or until the rice is tender and most of the liquid is absorbed. Makes 6–8 servings.

(Adapted from Kimball and Anderson, *The Art of American Indian Cooking.* Garden City, New York: Doubleday & Co., 1965, p. 102.)

13 EDUCATION

Dakota and Lakota children learned from observation and imitation without coercion. They learned from the people around them the practical skills they needed to survive and the artistic and religious dimensions of life to enhance their existence. With the coming of the reservation system, the government and churches insisted that the children enter formal schooling. While the Dakota and Lakota were interested in learning European ways, they had already adopted much of this foreign technology. They wanted their children to learn how to deal effectively with the outside world, but they were not in favor of the loss of their own culture that these schools caused. Boarding schools deliberately sought to separate children from their native culture and language, considered both as inferior. Children did learn well in these schools and acquired skills that were helpful to them but at a high psychological and cultural cost. Most damaging was the fact that children were not parented; they were raised for long periods of time in institutions and thus never learned effective parenting skills themselves.

Today there are few boarding schools, and education is largely in the hands of the tribes and reservation communities. Mission schools also have local community school boards to advise them. There are Bureau of Indian Affairs schools on the reservations as well as contract schools (government schools run by the local community) and mission schools. Dakotas and Lakotas off the reservation attend public or private schools, and local Indian centers set up cultural educational programs. Schools stress education in the local culture and language as well as western education.

In addition to primary and secondary schools, there are a large number of colleges on the reservations chartered and administered by the tribes. Some of these colleges are Oglala Lakota College (Pine Ridge Reservation), Sinte Gleska University (Rosebud Reservation), Sitting Bull College (Standing Rock Reservation), Sisseton Wahpeton College (Lake Traverse Reservation), Fort Peck College (Fort Peck Reservation), Little

Hoop College (Fort Totten College), and Nebraska Indian College (Santee Reservation).

Today, nearly 70% of Dakotas and Lakota over the age of 25 have at least a high school diploma, and 40% have attended college, though less than 9% have managed to attain a Bachelor of Arts degree or higher.

14 CULTURAL HERITAGE

In literature Charles Eastman is known for his many works on Dakota life and belief as well as his eye-witness account of the tragedy of Wounded Knee. George Bushotter worked with the Bureau of American Ethnology to record linguistic and cultural data about his people, the Lakota. Luther Standing Bear told of his life during the reservation and boarding school periods. Dakota Ella Deloria was an accomplished linguist who worked with Franz Boas and also wrote a novel called *Water Lilly* about the life of the Lakota at the time of contact from the perspective of women. Vine Deloria, Jr. is a lawyer, educator, and author. He brought the situation of the contemporary native people to the consciousness of larger American society through such books as *Custer Died for Your Sins* and *God is Red*. Lakotas such as Oscar Howe, Arthur Amiotte, and Martin Red Bear have excelled in the visual arts. Kevin Locke is an internationally known traditional flute player. Matthew and Nellie Two Bulls are well known for their traditional singing as well as their composition of songs. There are several well-known singing groups that travel around the country. Billy Mills won Olympic gold medals for running. Tim Giago is the Lakota publisher of *Indian Country Today*, a national native newspaper.

15 WORK

In the past, men and women had separate spheres of work. Men hunted and acted as warriors. Women dressed skins and cared for children and gathered wild fruits and roots and ran the household. All worked together when moving the camp. Certain individuals acted as healers and spiritual leaders in addition to their every day roles. Dakotas and Lakotas excelled in many things but never tried to separate themselves from the group. One's first duty was always to care for one's family.

Today, unemployment is very high on the reservation due to the marginality of the land and its remoteness from urban and industrial centers. Some Dakota and Lakota work in tribal government or with the federal government. Some are religious leaders, both traditional and Christian. Others are community or district leaders. Some work as educators, educational administrators, doctors, drug and alcohol counselors, and nurses. Some work as ranchers or farmers. Some Dakota and Lakota go off to cities to find employment because of the lack of opportunity on the reservations, but the tribes work hard to bring employment to the reservation that will be culturally appropriate for the people.

16 SPORTS

The Dakota were very fond of a ball game similar to lacrosse. Different bands or villages would oppose one another in these games that were religious in character. It was a game that tested both physical endurance as well as tempers. Women also played a ball game that entailed knocking a ball with clubs on a surface of ice. Foot races as well as target shooting with bow and arrow were popular. Lakotas were known for their fondness of horse racing.

Dakotas and Lakotas also play and excel at Euro-American sports such as basketball, football, and track and field events. High school sports are followed with particular relish on the reservation, especially basketball. Many also follow national sports from couches as do other Americans. Rodeo is also a sport in which many Lakota and Dakota participate successfully.

17 ENTERTAINMENT AND RECREATION

Children slid down hills on pieces of bark or using barrel staves. On the prairie they used the ribs of buffalos. Sometimes the boys would "surf" down the hills while standing erect on their sleds. Young men and boys also played at snow skates, glancing sticks off an ice surface so that they traveled great distances.

Dakotas and Lakotas are traditionally fond of gambling and often bet on ball games. Other betting games involve guessing. One game required the person on the opposite team to guess where an object (a pit or sometimes a bullet) was hidden in a series of four moccasins or mittens. These guessing games were quite lively and were accompanied by singing and drumming, physical movement in rhythm with the music, and psyching out the opposite team. Women gambled using plum stones in a dish which were tossed to reveal certain patterns which individuals would bet on. Betting never interfered with daily life, and individuals had a detachment in losing objects. No one was deprived of food or livelihood in these exchanges.

Today, Dakotas and Lakotas have revived traditional guessing games. A hand game in which one guesses the position of two marked sticks out of four is played to the accompaniment of singing and drumming. Money may change hands.

Children today ride bikes and horses, go to movies, play on swings and monkey bars, watch television, and play music. They dance both traditional style and like their Euro-American neighbors. Adults attend dances or movies and watch their favorite sports or movies on television.

18 FOLK ART, CRAFTS, HOBBIES

Dakota and Lakota have a long tradition of artistry. Daily utensils and containers were decorated with paints and dew claws (parts of a deer's foot). Women used dyed, plaited porcupine quills to decorate household objects, moccasins, and clothing. Hides were also tanned by women and painted by men. Women originally learned quilting from missionaries and favor the star quilt design. Women are expert at sewing, and groups of women can turn out a beautiful finished star quilt in an evening if required for a ceremony or religious event. Some women design beautiful ribbon shirts. European trade goods allowed artistic creativity to be expressed in new media. Glass beads replaced porcupine quills, and ledger books and paper replaced hides for artistic expression. Quilting and beadwork continue the fine artistic achievements of the past. It is not uncommon to see pens, salt shakers, and even sneakers decorated with beadwork. Some families continue to do quillwork, and both men and women make silver jewelry and other crafts. Dakotas and Lakotas engage in the fine arts as well as musical and dramatic performances. Today both men and women excel at the decorative arts and create their own costumes for traditional dancing.

[19] SOCIAL PROBLEMS

The incursion of whites into the territories of the Dakota and Lakota caused widespread social and economic disruption. The buffalo herd was hunted to near extinction, and bands were restricted to smaller and smaller territories which were economically marginal. The Dakota were finally exiled from their own territories after the Minnesota-Dakota Conflict. The government and churches also disrupted cultural and leadership patterns in an attempt to weaken the resolve of these groups and assimilate them into American society. Economically, the reservations continue to be marginal and depressed. Much of the crime on the reservations can be linked to the use of alcohol. Dakotas and Lakotas have higher rates of suicide (particularly among the youth), alcoholism, diabetes, fetal alcohol syndrome, heart disease, and other maladies than do the neighboring white populations. More and more, the people themselves are looking at developing culturally appropriate solutions to these problems, and a new generation of leaders is arising.

[20] BIBLIOGRAPHY

1990 Census Profile: Race and Hispanic Origin. US Department of Commerce, Economics and Statistics Administration, Bureau of the Census, Number 2, June 1991.

Brown, Joseph. *The Sacred Pipe*. Norman: University of Oklahoma Press, 1954.

Buechel, Eugene. *Lakota-English Dictionary*. Paul Manhart, ed., Pine Ridge, SD: Holy Rosary Mission, 1970.

Buechel, Eugene. *Lakota Tales and Texts*. Paul Manhart, ed., Pine Ridge, SD: Red Cloud Indian School. 1978.

Demallie, Raymond. "The Sioux in Dakota and Montana Territories." In *Vestiges of a Proud Nation*. Burlington, VT: Robert Hull Fleming Museum.

DeMallie, Raymond and Douglas Parks, ed. *Sioux Indian Religion*, Norman: University of Oklahoma Press, 1987.

Doll, Don *Vision Quest: Men, Women, and Sacred Sites of the Sioux Nation. New York:* Crown Publishers, Inc.

Erdoes, Richard. *Native Americans: The Sioux*. New York: Sterling Publishing, 1982.

Howard, James. *The Canadian Sioux*. Lincoln: University of Nebraska Press, 1984.

Meyer, Roy. *History of the Santee Sioux: United States Indian Policy on Trial*. Lincoln: University of Nebraska Press, 1993.

Neihardt, John. *Black Elk Speaks*. Ed. John Neihardt. Lincoln: University of Nebraska Press, 1971.

Pond, Samuel. *The Dakotas or Sioux in Minnesota as They Were in 1834*. St. Paul: Minnesota Historical Society Press, 1986.

Riggs, Steven Return. "A Grammar and Dictionary of Dakota." Smithsonian Contributions to Knowledge, 4. Washington, DC: Government Printing Office, 1852.

Riggs, Steven Return. *Dakota-English Dictionary*. J. Dorsey, ed. Contributions to North American Ethnology, 7. Washington, D.C.: Government Printing Office, 1890.

Riggs, Steven Return. James Owen Dorsey, ed. *Dakota Grammar, Texts and Ethnography*. Contributions to North American Ethnology, vol. 9, pp. 1-232. Washington, DC: Government Printing Office 1893.

Videos

Dakota Conflict, KTCA Public Television, Minneapolis-St. Paul. 1993. (1 hour video).

Dakota Exile, KTCA Public Television, Minneapolis-St. Paul 1995 (1 hour video).

Dakota Encounters: The Travels of Joseph Nicollet Among the Dakota. First Light Productions, 1995. (13.5 minutes video).

—by R. A Bucko and M. Brokenleg

DOMINICAN AMERICANS

For more information on Dominican history and culture, *see* **Vol. 2: Dominicans**.

OVERVIEW

Dominicans have been immigrating to the US in small numbers since the early 20th century, but mass migration did not begin until the end of Generalissimo Trujillo's oppressive reign in the Dominican Republic in 1961. Trujillo had tightly restricted emigration while in power, so few Dominicans were able to leave the country. After Trujillo was assassinated in 1961, however, thousands of Dominicans fled to Puerto Rico and the US. Political instability and disastrous economic conditions, along with human rights abuses, continue to drive huge numbers of Dominicans from their homeland.

Some emigrants go the "legal" route by applying for visas at the American consulate in Santo Domingo, the capital city of the Dominican Republic. Long lines of applicants form every day, with dozens turned away before they even reach the door. Of the 300–350 who make it into the consulate each day to apply for a visa, about 70% are rejected. Most return the next day to try again. The American consulate in Santo Domingo is reported to be the second-busiest consulate in the world.

Dominicans already living "legally" in the US can sponsor family members to immigrate. Most documented Dominican immigrants today are relatives of established Dominican Americans. "Legal" Dominican immigration to the US is largely a chain migration, begun by an individual who is then followed by up to 80 or more relatives. The Dominican government supports emigration because it relieves some of the pressure on the Dominican economy, both by reducing the population and through the money that Dominican Americans send back to their families in the Dominican Republic. The Dominican economy receives about $600 million to $800 million a year this way. Without these contributions from emigrants, the Dominican economy would suffer.

Acquiring a visa, especially if there are no sponsors, takes a long time, and there are no guarantees that a visa will ever be granted. The US refuses to grant "refugee" status to Dominicans because the US supports the Dominican government and cannot admit that its citizens require asylum. Therefore, many Dominicans choose to use "illegal" means of entry into the US. Middle-class Dominicans who can prove steady employment in the Dominican Republic can get temporary tourist visas to the US. They then overstay their visit and become instead "illegal aliens," or undocumented migrants (the preferred term in the Hispanic American community). About 10,000 of the 30,000 tourist visas issued to Dominicans each year are abused this way.

Those Dominicans who cannot get tourist visas take more desperate measures. They pay smugglers to ferry them across the Mona Passage between the Dominican Republic and Puerto Rico. The Mona Passage is 70 miles of rough, shark-infested water. Most of the smuggler's boats are much too small to make the crossing safely. Hundreds of Dominicans die each year when boats capsize. At least 6,500 Dominicans are known to have died while making the crossing in the 1980s, and unknown numbers of others were probably also lost at sea. Despite the dangers, however, thousands of Dominicans continue to risk their lives each year to make it to the US. In the 1980s, an estimated 40,000–50,000 Dominicans succeeded in crossing the Mona Passage to Puerto Rico. Most of them then continued on to the US.

Puerto Rico is a common first stop for undocumented Dominican migrants for two reasons: it is close to the Dominican Republic; and it is a US Commonwealth, meaning that Puerto Ricans are US citizens and can move without restrictions between the US and Puerto Rico. Undocumented Dominican migrants make their way to Puerto Rico, where the US Border Patrol is less vigilant than at mainland US borders, and establish themselves with new Puerto Rican identities. As Puerto Ricans, they are then able to enter the US without question.

Puerto Ricans resent the presence of so many undocumented Dominicans, but stopping the flow of migration is difficult. Smugglers come up with increasingly clever ways of eluding border police, and modern technology makes creating convincing false documents easier. Border police arrested and deported nearly 15,000 undocumented Dominican migrants from Puerto Rico in 1990, but that is only a fraction of those who actually crossed the border.

In an attempt to reduce the numbers of "illegal aliens" in the US, Congress granted amnesty in 1986 to all undocumented migrants who could show that they had been living in the US for at least five years. Hordes of people applied for amnesty, many of them Dominicans. Those who were granted amnesty were automatically given green cards, making them "legal" immigrants. Newly documented immigrants then rushed to sponsor their family members to immigrate. The US government had to create a new immigration quota category in 1990 to accommodate all the relatives of those who were granted amnesty. A significant number of Dominicans helped fill this new quota.

The great majority of Dominicans settle in New York City, particularly in the Washington Heights district. Of the more than 1,000,000 Dominicans in the US and Puerto Rico today, some 700,000 live in New York City, with 150,000 of them in Washington Heights. In recent years, more immigrants have come to New York City from the Dominican Republic than from anywhere else in the world. New York City is not the only destination for Dominican immigrants, however. Close to 300,000 live in Puerto Rico but hope to save up enough money to move on to the US. In the late 1980s, Dominican immigrants also began settling in Miami, Florida. Smaller numbers of Dominicans now choose to reside in Chicago, Boston and other Massachusetts cities, Providence (Rhode Island), and various cities in New Jersey as well.

About half of the estimated 1,000,000 Dominican Americans are undocumented migrants. Accordingly, the 1990 US Census counted only 505,690 Dominican Americans, of whom 347,858 were foreign-born. Nearly 67% (337,867) lived in New York. Census figures show Dominican Americans as the fourth-largest Hispanic group in the US, after Mexican, Puerto Rican, and Cuban Americans. When undocumented migrants are included, however, the Dominican American population most likely exceeds that of Cuban Americans.

Dominican Americans are Spanish-speaking Catholics. The family is central to Dominican life, and traditional families include a wide range of extended relatives. These extended families provide a tremendous amount of support, both emotional and financial, to their members. That support is sorely missed by Dominican Americans, whose families have typically been torn apart by immigration. Dominican Americans are forced to rely on fractured families, many of which (over 40%) are headed by women alone. To replace the help normally provided by extended families, Dominican Americans have established organizations and associations to assist each other. There are also a great number of Dominican American cultural, recreational, and social clubs.

Although Dominicans have only been in the US for a short time, they have managed to contribute to mainstream American society in a variety of ways. Uniquely Dominican restaurants called *fondas* have become popular in both New York City and Miami. *Fondas* are constructed like diners, but the tables have tablecloths and flowers on them like a more formal restaurant. They serve "Spanish and American" food to appeal to a wide range of customers. Young Dominican Americans have revitalized the New York City public school system, which had been dying due to the migration of other residents to the suburbs. Between 1990 and 1993, some 23,000 Dominican American students entered the New York City public school system.

Merengue music, a blend of Spanish and African elements, was developed in the Dominican Republic and is a constant presence in Dominican American communities. It has become popular among other Hispanic Americans as well and is beginning to spread to a wider, mainstream American audience.

Dominican Americans own about 9,000 small businesses in New York City, including 70% of the *bodegas* (Hispanic grocery stores) and 90% of the independent "gypsy" cabs. A significant number of "buckeyes," those who hand-roll cigars, are also Dominican American. Most Dominican Americans are relegated to blue-collar jobs, however, because of a lack of language skills, job skills, or legal immigrant documentation. Some 80% of Dominican Americans work in factories or in the service industry (hotels, restaurants, fast food establishments, etc.). About 40% of Dominican American women work in less than ideal conditions in the garment industry. Only 13% of Dominican American men and less than 3% of Dominican American women are professionals.

Perhaps the best-known arena for Dominican American contributions to American society is sports, especially baseball. Baseball is extremely popular in the Dominican Republic, and major league teams in the US regularly recruit Dominican players. In 1990, there were 26 Dominican players in the US major leagues. Every US major league team has at least one Dominican player today.

Most Dominican baseball players return to the Dominican Republic in the US off-season to play in the Dominican league, giving them year-round training and experience. Dominican Americans also sponsor numerous Little League and other amateur teams. Well-known early Dominican players (in the late 1950s and early 1960s) in the US major leagues include Ozzie Virgil, Juan Marichal, and the brothers Felipe, Matty, and Jesus Alou. Some of the more recent Dominican players are Pedro Guerrero, Rafael Santana, Julio Franco, George Bell, Joaquín Andújar, Tony Fernandez, Alfredo Griffin, Mario Soto, and José Uribe.

Undocumented Dominican Americans suffer the same problems as other undocumented migrants in the US: poverty, unemployment, and exploitation. Most employers will not hire undocumented migrants, and those who do pay them less than minimum wage and force them to work long hours without a break in miserable working conditions. The workers cannot complain because the employer might turn them in to immigration officials.

Because of the difficulties in finding decent employment, some undocumented Dominican migrants turn to drug-dealing to support themselves. Unfortunately, because the Washington Heights neighborhood of New York City had already developed a reputation as a center of illegal drug activity before Dominican immigrants began to settle there, the Dominicans inherited the reputation whether or not they were involved in the activities themselves. Many non-Dominican Americans believe the stereotype that "all Dominican Americans are drug-dealers." Innocent Dominican Americans are subjected to searches, harassment, and even brutality by local police. In 1992, Dominican Americans in Washington Heights rioted after a European American police officer shot and killed a Dominican American youth. The court determined that the shooting was justified, but many Dominican Americans felt otherwise.

Tensions also exist between Dominican and Puerto Rican Americans. Longstanding ill-feeling between Puerto Ricans and Dominicans persists among those in the US. Also, because Puerto Ricans are US citizens, they are allowed to vote. Those Dominican Americans who are undocumented migrants—half the Dominican American population—are not allowed to vote. Therefore, Dominican Americans must rely on others to represent their interests in the public sphere. The majority of Hispanic American politicians and voters in New York City, where most Dominican Americans live, are Puerto Rican. Dominican Americans generally feel that they are not being adequately represented by Puerto Rican Americans, and they resent Puerto Rican Americans for this. Puerto Rican Americans resent Dominican Americans for threatening their established presence as the Hispanic majority in New York City. Until more Dominicans are able to become "legal" US residents, these tensions will likely continue.

BIBLIOGRAPHY

Bandon, Alexandra. *Dominican Americans*. Parsippany, NJ: New Discovery Books, 1995.

Dwyer, Christopher. *The Dominican Americans*. New York: Chelsea House, 1991.

US Bureau of the Census. *Detailed Ancestry Groups for States*. 1990 Census of Population Supplementary Reports, CP-S-1-2. Washington, DC, October 1992.

———. *The Foreign-Born Population in the United States*. 1990 CP-3-1. Washington, DC, July 1993.

—by D. K. Daeg de Mott

DOMINICANS (DOMINICA)

PRONUNCIATION: dah-men-EEK-uhns
LOCATION: Dominica
POPULATION: 72,000–82,000
LANGUAGE: English; kwéyòl (French-based dialect)
RELIGION: Roman Catholicism; small groups of Anglicans, Methodists, Pentecostals, Baptists, and Seventh-Day Adventists, Baha'is, and Rastafarians

¹ INTRODUCTION

Dominica (pronounced dah-men-EEK-uh) is the most mountainous island in the Lesser Antilles. Historically, its rugged terrain delayed foreign settlement, and more recently it has slowed the pace of modernization on the island. Today, Dominica—popularly referred to as "the nature island of the Caribbean"—remains among the world's few locations with virtually untouched tropical rain forests. The island is also home to the Lesser Antilles' largest enclave of the Amerindians from whom the Caribbean takes its name—the Caribs, most of whom live on a reserve on its northeast coast.

The Caribs inhabited the island, which they called *Waitikubuli,* when it was sighted by Christopher Columbus on a Sunday *(dies dominica)* in 1493. The Spanish did not attempt to colonize Dominica, which was the object of a political tug-of-war between the French and British throughout the 17th and 18th centuries, with both nations simultaneously attempting to subdue the Caribs as well. In 1805 the French finally gave up all claims to Dominica, which remained a British colony until it gained its independence in 1978. However, due to the lengthy French presence on the island as well as the proximity of the French islands of Guadeloupe and Martinique, the cultural influence of the French endured.

By 1834, when the British empire emancipated its slaves, Africans brought to labor on the island's coffee and sugar plantations made up a majority of the population. In 1902 the once-powerful Caribs, reduced to dire circumstances, sought better land and increased recognition from the British and were granted 3,700 acres in the northeast of the island, where they still live on what is known today as Carib Territory. In spite of economic progress under the direction of colonial administrator Henry Hesketh Bell between 1899 and 1905, Dominica remained relatively poor and undeveloped during the first half of the 20th century, its fragile economy vulnerable to the disruptions of worldwide depression and war.

By the 1950s, however, British government assistance, agricultural expansion, and exploitation of the island's abundant hydroelectric resources inaugurated a period of development and relative prosperity. In 1951 universal adult suffrage was granted by the British government, followed by a new constitution in 1960 and complete internal autonomy by 1967. The independent Commonwealth of Dominica came into being on 3 November 1978. In 1980 Dame Mary Eugenia Charles, head of the Democratic Freedom Party, became the first female head of government in the Caribbean. Reelected in 1985 and 1990, Dame Charles retired in 1995 at the age of 76.

² LOCATION AND HOMELAND

Although usually regarded as the northernmost of the British-speaking Windward Islands, Dominica is actually at the mid-point of the Lesser Antilles and could also be grouped with the Leeward Islands. Facing the Atlantic Ocean to the east and the Caribbean Sea to the west, it is nearly equidistant from Guadeloupe to the north and Martinique to the south. Dominica's area of 750 sq km (290 sq mi) is slightly more than four times the size of Washington, DC. Rainfall on Dominica is extremely heavy, and much of the land is covered by dense and largely unexploited rain forests containing rare wildlife species. Hundreds of rivers and streams flow into gorges, forming natural pools and crater lakes. One of the island's most unusual natural features is the volcanically bubbling Boiling Lake, the second-largest lake of its kind in the world. An egg will supposedly boil within three minutes in its 92°C (198°F) waters.

A central mountain ridge runs from Cape Melville in the north to the island's southern cliffs. Its highest point, Morne Diablotins, rises to 1,448 m (4,747 ft), the second-highest mountain in the Lesser Antilles. Surrounding the mountains are several national parks, most notably the Morne Trois Pitons National Park in the southern part of the island. One geographical feature that has been of great consequence to Dominica is its location just west of the chief point of origin of the hurricane belt. Hurricanes David and Frederick in 1979 caused more than 40 deaths and 2,500 injuries, leaving two-thirds of the population homeless and causing extensive crop damage.

Estimates of Dominica's population vary from 72,000 to around 82,000. About one-third of the country's residents live in the capital city of Roseau and the surrounding area. With a population density of about 37 people per sq km (95 people per sq mi), Dominica is one of the most sparsely populated countries in the Caribbean region. The majority of Dominicans are of African or mixed descent, with smaller minorities of Carib or European ancestry. The Carib population numbers approximately 3,400, most of whom live on a 3,700-acre reserve in the northeast called the Carib Territory. Bataka is the largest of its eight hamlets, and other settlements include Sinecou and Salybia.

The Caribs, whose language is no longer spoken, are striving to preserve the remaining vestiges of their culture, which has been eroded by intermarriage and the introduction of Western religion and customs to the island. They do not celebrate the nation's November 3rd independence day because it also commemorates the date in 1493 when Columbus first sighted the island, an event that ultimately led to their political, economic, and cultural decline. Most of Dominica's remaining Caribs are of mixed ancestry—full-blooded Caribs are said to number 50 or fewer.

³ LANGUAGE

While English is the official language of Dominica, most of the population also speaks a French-based patois, or dialect, called *kwéyòl* (derived from the word "Creole"). While kwéyòl is a distinctive language unique to Dominica, it has elements in common with the dialects spoken on St. Lucia and other islands with French-influenced cultures. Kwéyòl is a source of pride among Dominicans and is increasingly being used in print. A kwéyòl dictionary was published in 1991. *Cocoy,* a type of pidgin English, is spoken in the villages of Marigot and Wesley in

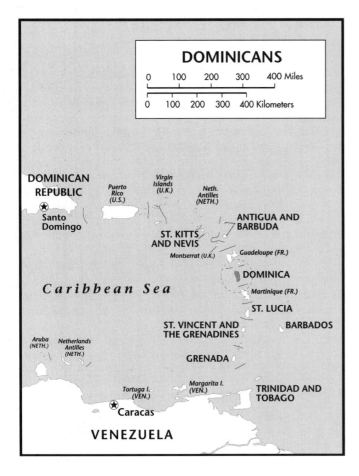

DOMINICANS

0   100   200   300   400 Miles

0   100   200   300   400 Kilometers

DOMINICAN
REPUBLIC
★
Santo
Domingo

Puerto
Rico
(U.S.)

Virgin
Islands
(U.K.)

Neth.
Antilles
(NETH.)

ANTIGUA AND
BARBUDA

ST. KITTS
AND NEVIS

Montserrat (U.K.)   Guadeloupe (FR.)

Caribbean Sea

DOMINICA

Martinique (FR.)

ST. LUCIA

ST. VINCENT AND
THE GRENADINES   BARBADOS

Aruba
(NETH.)   Netherlands
Antilles
(NETH.)

GRENADA

Tortuga I.
(VEN.)   Margarita I.
(VEN.)   TRINIDAD AND
TOBAGO

★
Caracas

VENEZUELA

crawled onto the island from its original home at the bottom of the sea. Looking at the Master Boa is supposed to be fatal unless a person has abstained from both food and sex for a certain number of days beforehand.

Many Dominicans believe in *obeah,* a collection of quasi-religious beliefs and practices derived from Africa. Obeah is believed to have the power both to heal the sick and harm one's enemies, and its practices include the use of herbal potions.

Flying witches called *suquiyas* are the subjects of a number of Dominican proverbs.

5 RELIGION

The historical French influence on Dominica left the island's population predominantly Roman Catholic. About 80% of Dominicans belong to the Catholic Church. Smaller groups belong to the Anglican, Methodist, Pentecostal, Baptist, and Seventh-Day Adventist churches, and the Baha'i and Rastafarian religions are represented as well. The Caribs' religious practices combine features of Christianity—such as belief in Jesus, the saints, heaven, and hell—with the nature worship inherited from their ancestors.

6 MAJOR HOLIDAYS

Dominica's public holidays are New Year's Day (1 January), Carnival (14–15 February), Good Friday and Easter Monday (late March or early April), May Day (1 May), Whit Monday, August Monday (1 August), National Day—also called Independence Day (3 November), Community Service Day (4 November), and Christmas Day and Boxing Day (25 and 26 December). The main religious holidays are Christmas and Easter. *Tou Saintes* (All Saints' Day) is celebrated on 1 November. The country's largest festival is Carnival, which occurs on the two days preceding Ash Wednesday and is marked by masquerades, calypso contests, feasting, street dancing ("jump ups"), and parties. In keeping with the history of Carnival as an "anything goes" affair, slander and libel laws are suspended for the duration of the festivities.

Independence Day on 3 November commemorates the date in 1978 when Dominica became an independent nation with speeches, parades, and calypso music. On Creole Day, usually the Friday before Independence Day, Dominicans celebrate and display their Creole heritage by wearing traditional costumes; conducting all business in *kwéyòl,* their native dialect; eating distinctly Dominican dishes such as *crapaud* (frogs' legs); and listening and dancing to Dominican folk music.

7 RITES OF PASSAGE

Major life transitions, such as birth, marriage, and death, are marked by religious ceremonies according to each Dominican's faith community.

8 INTERPERSONAL RELATIONS

Dominicans are known for being more reserved than some of their neighbors in the Caribbean, and they place a high value on good manners. A common greeting is *"Cakafete,"* the equivalent of "How are you?"

9 LIVING CONDITIONS

Dominica is one of the poorest nations in the Caribbean. Many Dominicans live in single-story wooden houses with corrugated

northeastern Dominica, which were originally settled by freed slaves from Antigua.

KWÉYÒL (PRONOUNS)	STANDARD ENGLISH
mwen/mon	I
ou	you (singular)
I	he/she/it
nou	we
zò	you (plural)
yo	they

SIMPLE SENTENCES:

Sa ki non'w?	What is your name?
Non mwen sé Paul.	My name is Paul
Bon jou, Misyé.	Good day, sir
Bonn apwé midi.	Good afternoon
Bon swé.	Good night
Mon swèf.	I am thirsty
Mon fen.	I am hungry
Mon pa fen.	I am not hungry
Jodi sé yon bèl jou.	Today is a beautiful day
Lapli ka tonbé.	It is raining
Byenvini.	Welcome

4 FOLKLORE

According to a Carib legend, a giant boa constrictor called the Master Boa has lived for centuries in a hole on Morne Diablotin. The Escalier Tête-Chien (Master Boa's Staircase), a basalt formation near Sineku, is said to be the spot where the snake

Political rally in the Carib Territory, Dominica. The majority of Dominicans are of African or mixed descent, with smaller minorities of Carib or European ancestry. The Carib population numbers approximately 3,400, most of whom live on a 3,700-acre reserve in the northeast called the Carib Territory. (AP/Wide World Photos)

iron roofs, typically protected from the island's heavy rainfall by wide overhangs and an absence of porches. Average life expectancy is 74 years for males and 80 years for females, and the infant mortality rate is 9.9 deaths per 1,000 live births. Health care is provided at local clinics, 12 health centers, and the 136-bed Princess Margaret Hospital in Roseau. There are also hospital facilities at Portsmouth, Marigot, and Grand Bay.

Dominica has about 700 km (435 mi) of roads, of which 370 km (230 mi) are paved and much of the rest is blacktopped. In spite of the relatively good condition of the roads following major improvements in 1986, travel can be tortuous on these narrow, winding mountain thoroughfares: it commonly takes up to 40 minutes to travel the 10 km (6 mi) from the capital city of Roseau to the nearby fishing village of Scott's Head. Roseau is the country's main port. There are plans for the construction of a new international airport to encourage expansion of the tourist industry.

¹⁰ FAMILY LIFE

In addition to formal marriages, Dominicans also enter into common-law relationships (living together—with or without children—without being married) and "visiting unions," where the man and woman live apart (essentially, female-headed households).

¹¹ CLOTHING

The Dominicans wear modern Western-style clothing. However, on Creole Day and other special occasions women still wear the traditional national costume: the brightly colored *jupe* (a skirt with lace petticoats), *la wobe douilette* (a wide blouse), and a madras hat called *tete case*.

¹² FOOD

Dominican cuisine combines French, English, and African influences. Dietary staples include fish, yams, and other vegetables. The *ti-ti-ri* is a tiny whitefish found in Dominican rivers and served fried with garlic and lime. The most distinctive local food in Dominica is probably mountain chicken, which is not actually chicken but rather the legs of the *crapaud,* a local species of frog. Other regional favorites include crab backs (stuffed crabshells), *boija,* a coconut-cornmeal bread, and *funchi,* a cornmeal-and-okra pudding. Cassava bread is a staple among the Carib population. One popular beverage is a seamoss drink—made from vanilla, algae, and milk, and resembling a vanilla milkshake—which is also a favorite in Grenada. Another local drink, *Bwa bande* (brewed from the bark of the tree of the same name), is reputed to enhance male sexual potency.

13 EDUCATION

The adult literacy rate in Dominica is approximately 95%. Historically, the Catholic Church has played an important role in education. Widespread access to public education was not attained until the 1960s. By the 1980s, all but 2 of the nation's 66 primary schools were government-operated, and the secondary schools (which currently number 10) were equally divided between the government and the church. Before the 1960s, few students received a secondary education because rural areas had no secondary schools, and the island's mountainous terrain and precarious roads prohibited traveling to cities or towns to attend school.

Primary and secondary education is based on the British system of grade levels called "forms." Children attend school from age 5 to 15, at which point they are in the third form (equivalent to eighth grade in the US). As of the late 1980s, there were no laws making school attendance mandatory. While family circumstances make it necessary for a number of school-age young people to work part- or full-time, families and communities place a strong emphasis on academic achievement as one of the few means of social and economic advancement available on the island.

Most students end their secondary schooling in the fifth form (equivalent to tenth grade), except for a relative few who continue their studies in order to qualify for admission to a university. Dominica has a teacher training college, a nursing school, and a technical college, and the University of the West Indies also offers programs on the island. Many qualified Dominican students have been unable to attend college for financial reasons. The United States, Great Britain, Canada, and France have offered assistance by making scholarships and other forms of financial aid available to Dominican students.

14 CULTURAL HERITAGE

Dominican-born novelist Jean Rhys (1894–1979) is mostly associated with Europe, where she spent much of her life. However, West Indian speech patterns figure in several of her short stories, Caribbean scenes appear in her 1934 novel, *Voyage in the Dark,* and her last work, *Wide Sargasso Sea* (1966), is set in the Caribbean. Phyllis Shand Allfrey was a poet and novelist who returned to Dominica in the 1950s after being educated in the United States and England. In addition to writing *The Orchid House,* her only completed novel, she was an editor of two Dominican newspapers and served as a cabinet minister in the short-lived West Indian Federation of the late 1950s and early 1960s. *The Orchard House* was adapted for film by British television in 1990. Lennox Honychurch, author of *The Dominica Story: A History of the Island* and *Our Island Culture,* is a well-known contemporary Dominican historian, folklorist, and painter.

Alwin Bully, co-author of *Speak Brother Speak,* is a well-known Dominican playwright and founding member of the Peoples' Action Theatre. He has also written radio plays and musicals. Dominica also has a School of Dance and a professional dance troupe, the Waitukubuli Dance Company, whose name is based on the island's original Carib name. The Carib Territory is home to several notable visual artists, including Faustulus Frederick and Jacob Frederick.

15 WORK

The Dominican labor force totals about 25,000 people, of whom an estimated 40% are employed in agriculture (including food processing), while industry and commerce employ 32%, and the rest work in other sectors of the economy. The standard work day is eight hours long. Officially unemployment is at 10%, but the actual figure is thought to be closer to 15%, and a number of Dominicans have sought work on St. Thomas and other nearby islands.

Per capita income on Dominica is the lowest of any country in the Antilles. Earnings are low for workers in agriculture and commerce alike. The distribution of land on the island favors the operators of large estates, which are located on deep soil near the coast, rather than small farmers, who often have to contend with erosion-prone plots on the steep terrain of the island's interior. (They traditionally call these small plots "gardens.")

16 SPORTS

The nation's most popular sports are cricket and soccer (called "football"). Major cricket games draw thousands of fans, and the game is especially popular in the Carib Territory. Other favorites include volleyball, basketball, and squash.

17 ENTERTAINMENT AND RECREATION

Dominican men, like their counterparts in other parts of the Caribbean, enjoy whiling away their leisure hours playing dominoes in one of the many rum shops on the island. Popular music on the island embraces a number of styles—reggae, Zouk, Cadance, and others.

18 FOLK ART, CRAFTS, AND HOBBIES

Traditional Dominican dances include the Quadrille, Jing-ping, Heel-and-Toe, and Bélé. The typical "Jing-ping" band consists of an accordion, a bass instrument called a "boom-boom," and a percussion instrument called a "shak-shak." The Carib Territory has 16 craft shops that turn out intricately woven and colorfully dyed straw hats, baskets, and other woven goods. The Caribs are also known for their carved canoes. Other crafts on Dominica include mats woven from a special grass called *vertivert.*

19 SOCIAL PROBLEMS

Dominica's already sparse water supply is further threatened by pollution from agricultural chemicals, untreated sewage, and industrial waste. Dominica has been used by international drug traffickers as a transshipment point for narcotics.

20 BIBLIOGRAPHY

Baker, Patrick. *Centring the Periphery: Chaos, Order, and the Ethnohistory of Dominica.* Montreal: McGill-Queen's University Press, 1994.

———. "Ethnogenesis: The Case of the Dominica Caribs." *América Indígena* 48, no. 2 (1988): 377–401.

Booth, Robert. "Dominica, Difficult Paradise." *National Geographic* (June 1990): 100–120.

Cameron, Sarah, and Ben Box, ed. *Caribbean Islands Handbook.* Chicago: Passport Books, 1995.

Gall, Timothy, and Susan Gall, ed. *Worldmark Encyclopedia of the Nations.* 8th ed. Detroit: Gale Research, 1995.

Honychurch, Lennox. *The Dominica Story: A History of the Island.* Roseau, Dominica: Dominica Institute, 1984.

————. *Our Island Culture.* Roseau, Dominica: Dominican National Cultural Council, 1988.

Luntta, Karl. *Caribbean Handbook.* Chico, CA: Moon Publications, 1995.

Meditz, Sandra W., and Dennis M. Hanratty. *Islands of the Commonwealth Caribbean: A Regional Study.* Washington, DC: US Government, 1989.

Myers, Robert A. *Dominica.* Santa Barbara, CA: Clio Press, 1987.

Schwab, David, ed. *Insight Guides. Caribbean: The Lesser Antilles.* Boston: Houghton Mifflin, 1996.

Stuart, Stephanie. "Dominican Patwa: Mother Tongue or Cultural Relic?" *International Journal of the Sociology of Language*102 (1993): 57–72.

United States. Central Intelligence Agency. *World Fact Book.* Washington, DC: Government Printing Office, 1994.

Walton, Chelle Koster. *Caribbean Ways: A Cultural Guide.* Westwood, MA: Riverdale, 1993.

—by R. Wieder

DOMINICANS (DOMINICAN REPUBLIC)

LOCATION: Dominican Republic; United States (primarily New York City)
POPULATION: 7.8 million in the Dominican Republic; 0.5–1 million or more in New York City
LANGUAGE: Spanish
RELIGION: Roman Catholicism; Evangelical Protestantism; Voodoo

1 INTRODUCTION

The Dominican Republic occupies the eastern two-thirds of the island of Hispaniola, which it shares with the nation of Haiti. Hispaniola was sighted by Christopher Columbus in 1492, and four years later his brother, Bartolome, founded Santo Domingo, the present-day capital of the Dominican Republic and the oldest city in the Western Hemisphere. Due to its strategic location in relation to other trading ports in the Caribbean, the Dominican Republic came under the rule of a succession of foreign powers, including France and Haiti as well as Spain.

Under the leadership of national hero Juan Pablo Duarte, independence was declared in 1844, but the government remained unstable, with power passing into the hands of a series of dictators. In addition, the nation reverted to Spanish rule for four years between 1861 and 1865. The United States occupied the Dominican Republic from 1916 to 1924, and in 1930 the 30-year rule of Rafael Trujillo—direct and through hand-picked surrogates—began. Although Trujillo expanded industry and introduced economic reforms, his regime ruthlessly suppressed human rights, engaging in blackmail, torture, and murder to ensure its hold on power.

Trujillo was assassinated in 1961, and writer Juan Bosch came to power briefly before being ousted in a 1963 military coup. After a period of instability that included US military intervention in 1965, former Trujillo appointee Joaquin Balaguer was elected president, an office he has held for most of the time since then, although democratic elections have been held every four years, and other candidates were elected in 1978 and 1982. Balaguer was reelected most recently in 1994. Despite some instability (including a planned military coup that was averted in 1978 with pressure from the United States) and periodic election-related violence and fraud allegations, the country has essentially been governed democratically since the 1960s.

2 LOCATION AND HOMELAND

With an area of approximately 48,741 sq km (18,819 sq mi), the Dominican Republic is about the same size as Vermont and New Hampshire combined. It is bounded on the north by the Atlantic Ocean, on the south by the Caribbean Sea, and on the east by the Mona Passage, which separates it from Puerto Rico. The country is very diverse geographically, with terrain ranging from semiarid desert to fertile farmlands and mountain peaks. Both the highest and lowest points in the Caribbean region are found in the Dominican Republic.

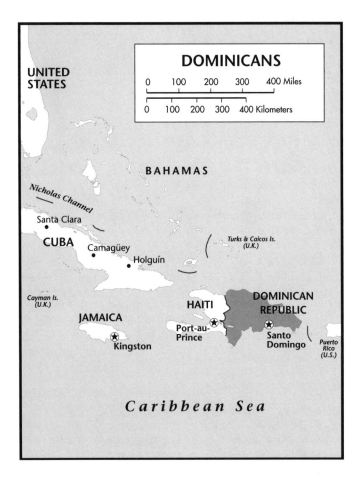

About three-fifths of the country's terrain is covered by four mountain ranges. The largest is the Cordillera Central, which runs through the center of the Dominican Republic from east to west and extends into Haiti. It contains the Caribbean's highest peaks, Pico Duarte (3,175 m or 10,417 ft) and Pico la Pelona (3,168 m or 10,393 ft). The Cordillera Septentrional runs from east to west in the northern part of the country, and two lower ranges, the Sierra Neiba and Sierra de Bahoruco, stretch across the country's southwestern region.

The fertile Valle de Cibao, containing the Dominican Republic's richest agricultural land, stretches from east to west between the two northern mountain ranges, covering about 5,180 sq km (2,000 sq mi), or some 10% of the country's terrain. In contrast, the area between the two southern mountain ranges, called the Cul-de-Sac, is the country's most barren and is home to only 10% of the population. It is the lowest terrain in the Dominican Republic and also in the West Indies as a whole. The other major low-lying region is the Caribbean coastal plain in the north. The country's four major rivers are the Yaque del Norte, the Yaque del Sur, the Yuma, and the Artibonito.

About 7.8 million people live in the Dominican Republic, 60% in the cities and 40% in rural areas. The capital city of Santo Domingo has a population of 2.1 million. The 20th century has been marked by massive rural-to-urban migration: the population of Santo Domingo approximately doubled every 10 years between 1920 and 1970. The second- and third-largest cities, Santiago and La Romana, also experienced dramatic growth, especially in the 1960s and 1970s.

International emigration is also a fact of life in the Dominican Republic, and about one in seven Dominicans now lives abroad. New York City has the highest concentration of Dominicans—between 0.5 million and 1 million or more—of any city in the world except Santo Domingo. Florida and New Jersey also have substantial populations of Dominican immigrants. Some Dominicans emigrate because they are unemployed or are seeking better-paying jobs. Others leave in order to pursue an education or to join relatives already in the US. The money sent home by these *dominicanos ausentes* (absent Dominicans), totaling about $500 million annually, is an important factor in their homeland's economy.

About 70% of the country's population is classified as Mulatto (of mixed Black and White ancestry), 16% as White, and 11% as Black. However, these broad classifications actually encompass a more complex range of racial distinctions. *Blanco* (white) refers to Whites and persons of mixed White and Amerindian descent (Mestizos); *Indio claro* (tan) refers to Mulattos, including those with Amerindian ancestry; *Indio oscuro* (dark Indian) describes anyone who is mostly Black with some White or Amerindian ancestry; and *Negro* (which is not a derogatory term in the Dominican Republic) is reserved for persons who are 100% African.

³ LANGUAGE

Spanish is the official and universally spoken language of the Dominican Republic. While the Spanish of the Dominicans is considered relatively close to "classical" Castilian Spanish when compared to that of other Latin American countries, it has a distinctive accent and incorporates numerous local idioms as well as many African and Taino (Amerindian) words and expressions. Some English is spoken in the capital city of Santo Domingo.

⁴ FOLKLORE

Combining Catholic beliefs with African customs, *formularios* and *oraciones* are special incantations intended to attract good luck or avoid the evil eye. Many Dominicans also have a quasi-magical belief in the powers of the saints, expressed in *santos* (saints) cults. Images of one or two saints are kept in the house, and goods are offered to them in exchange for carrying out the wishes of the worshipper. On the "Night of the Saints" *(Noche Vela)*, the saints are believed to be called to earth.

⁵ RELIGION

The importance of religion in the Dominican Republic is reflected in the cross and bible at the center of the nation's coat of arms. A significant portion of the money that Dominican emigrants send back home is sent to their churches. While some 93% of the population is Roman Catholic, many do not attend church regularly, and, as in a number of other Catholic countries, the women are generally more observant than the men. Religious customs among observant Catholics include *rosarios*, processions organized to pray for intercession from a patron saint or the Virgin.

Evangelical Protestantism has become increasingly popular in recent years. Its embrace of family values, including strictures against alcohol, prostitution, and wife-beating, have made it especially attractive to low-income Dominicans, who traditionally have had unstable family structures. Followers of spirit worship and Voodoo (introduced into the country by Haitian immigrants) are thought to number about 60,000.

6 MAJOR HOLIDAYS

Many holidays in the Dominican Republic are religious in nature. In addition to Christmas and Good Friday, they include the Day of Our Lady of Altagracia (21 January), Corpus Christi (17 June), and the Feast of Our Lady of Mercy (24 September). Secular holidays include Día de Duarte, commemorating the birthday of national hero Juan Pablo Duarte (26 January), Independence Day (27 February), Labor Day (1 May), and Dominican Restoration Day (16 August). Every town also holds a festival in honor of its patron saint, combining religious observance with such secular activities as dancing, drinking, and gambling. The Dominican Independence Day (27 February), which falls around the beginning of Lent, is the occasion for a boisterous Carnival celebration which draws over half a million people annually to festivities in Santo Domingo.

7 RITES OF PASSAGE

Major life transitions, such as birth, marriage, and death, are marked by religious ceremonies appropriate to each Dominican's faith community.

8 INTERPERSONAL RELATIONS

When addressing each other, Dominicans use the formal pronoun *usted* instead of the familiar form *tu,* unless the relationship is a very close one.

Compadrazgo, a relationship resembling that of godparents in the United States, is an important part of the social fabric of the Dominican Republic. The *compadre* (literally, "co-parent") is chosen when a child is baptized, and the special relationship that ensues—with both the child and his or her parents—is a way of strengthening the bond between friends or even reinforcing other types of relationships, such as that between an employee and employer. Exploiting this dynamic, the country's long-time dictator Rafael Trujillo held mass baptisms where he became the compadre to thousands of peasant children in order to ensure their parents' loyalty.

9 LIVING CONDITIONS

Traditional rural dwellings are made of wood with roofs of thatch or corrugated tin and are often painted in bright colors. To keep the farmhouse cool, cooking is usually done in a separate structure with slotted sides that release smoke and heat. In the 35 years since the end of the Trujillo regime, which prohibited emigration within the country, rural-to-urban migration has created a severe urban housing shortage, and slums and squatter settlements have sprung up in the capital city of Santo Domingo.

The Dominican Republic's infant mortality rate in 1993 was 49 deaths per 1,000 births, and average life expectancy was 69 years. Hospitals and medical personnel are concentrated in Santo Domingo and Santiago, the two largest cities, with a lower quality of health care in rural areas. Health programs are offered through the nation's public welfare department (covering between 70% and 80% of the population) and the social security department (covering 5% of the population, or 13% of the work force). However, the country's economic troubles have resulted in shortages of doctors and nurses, medication, and surgical supplies. Public health care has been described as inadequate, with long treatment delays, and many who can afford it consult private physicians.

There are modern roads in the cities of the Dominican Republic, and a major highway connects Santo Domingo and Santiago. However, few Dominicans own their own cars—most of the nation's passenger cars are driven by either the very wealthy or by tourists. In rural areas, many roads are unpaved. The nation's railways are used mainly for transporting sugarcane.

10 FAMILY LIFE

Traditionally, the extended-family household with a dominant father-figure has been the norm among the middle and upper classes. In contrast, low-income people have less stable family ties, and many of their households consist of either a couple (with or without children) living together in a common-law marriage, or a female-headed household with an absentee father. While women still consider a man the head of the household, they have been able to exert increased authority within the family as they have won greater educational and employment opportunities and an increased measure of control over the number of children they bear.

11 CLOTHING

People in the Dominican Republic wear modern Western-style clothing.

12 FOOD

The popular Caribbean dish of rice and beans *(arroz con habichuelas)* is a staple in the Dominican Republic, where it is nicknamed "the flag" *(la bandera)* and served with stewed beef. Another favorite dish is *sancocho,* a meat, plantain, and vegetable stew. Plantains, common throughout the Caribbean area, are especially popular in the Dominican Republic. Ripe fried plantains are called *amarillas,* green fried ones are *patacon pisao,* and they become *tostones* when fried and mashed. Popular snack foods include *chicarrons* (pieces of fried pork) and *empanadillas* (tangy meat tarts). Puddings—including sweet rice, corn, and banana pudding—are a popular dessert.

Banana Pudding

6 overripe bananas, peeled and mashed
1 cup sugar
3 tablespoons melted butter or margarine
3 egg whites, beaten to stiff peaks
1 cup orange juice
2 tablespoons sweetened shredded coconut for garnish

Preheat oven to 325°F. Combine bananas, melted butter or margarine, orange juice, and sugar with mixing spoon or electric mixer. Carefully fold in stiffly beaten egg whites and transfer mixture to buttered or nonstick casserole or baking pan. Bake for about 40 minutes or until puffy and golden brown. Remove from oven and sprinkle top with shredded coconut.

13 EDUCATION

The estimated literacy rate of the Dominican Republic was 83% in 1990. Students must attend school for eight years, but many leave earlier to help support their families. Additional

Agriculture has traditionally been the main source of employment in the Dominican Republic, but today a growing number of Dominicans work in service-related jobs, especially in the tourism industry. Most Dominican farmers are sharecroppers or tenant farmers. (AP/Wide World Photos)

barriers to education include a shortage of teachers, especially in rural areas, and a lack of adequate facilities. Institutions of higher learning include the Autonomous University of Santo Domingo and four private universities.

14 CULTURAL HERITAGE

Historically, the Henriquez-Ureña family has been at the center of the Dominican Republic's literary heritage. Salomé Ureña de Henriquez was a respected 19th-century poet who also established the country's first higher education facility for women, the Instituto de Señoritas. In the 20th century, the critic Pedro Henriquez-Ureña was also deeply involved in education. Many consider Gaston Fernando Delingue, who wrote in the late 19th and early 20th centuries, to be the Dominican national poet. The country's best-known writer internationally is undoubtedly novelist, essayist, and short-story writer Juan Bosch, who served briefly as president following the assassination of Rafael Trujillo. The Dominican Republic has a National Symphony Orchestra, and a National School of Fine Arts, located in Santo Domingo.

15 WORK

Agriculture has traditionally been the main source of employment in the Dominican Republic, but today a growing number of Dominicans work in service-related jobs, especially in the tourism industry. Most Dominican farmers are sharecroppers or tenant farmers, and those who do own their own farms generally have fewer than 2 hectares (5 acres) and grow only enough food to feed their families. The country suffers from an extremely high rate of unemployment—an estimated 30% of the work force was unemployed in 1992—which has led to widespread emigration. Race has traditionally dominated Dominicans' employment options, with higher-status jobs in business, government, and the professionals held by lighter-skinned persons. In general, the wages of female workers are lower than those of their male counterparts, their unemployment rate is higher, and many are denied full employment benefits.

16 SPORTS

The Dominican Republic's national sport is baseball, and thousand of fans attend the major games, which are usually held at one of Santo Domingo's stadiums. The United States currently has more Dominicans on its major and minor league baseball teams than players from any other Latin American country or any single state in the US. The town of San Pedro de Macorís in particular has produced more professional players—including Juan Samuel of the Philadelphia Phillies and Joaquín Andujar of the Oakland A's—than any other locality in the world. Unlike the baseball season in the United

States, the season in the Dominican Republic runs from October to February. Other popular Dominican sports include horse-racing and cockfighting.

17 ENTERTAINMENT AND RECREATION

Dance is a national passion in the Dominican Republic. Even the smallest towns have a dance hall, and there are annual *merengue* festivals in Santo Domingo, Puerto Plata, and Sosúa. Since the 1970s, local dance rhythms have been influenced by US disco, the steps have become less formal, and the music has gotten faster. Salsa music is also very popular. The major cities, especially Santo Domingo, have an active night life, with numerous nightclubs and gambling casinos, where patrons may (legally) play blackjack, craps, and roulette.

18 FOLK ART, CRAFTS, AND HOBBIES

Dominican folk music reflects Spanish, African, and Amerindian influences. A native percussion instrument, the *güira*, is a legacy of the Taino people who were among the island's original inhabitants. Together with the *maracas* and the *palitos* (also in the percussion family), and the guitar, it is used to accompany Dominican folk songs called *decimas*, which are usually romantic in nature. Other popular folk instruments include the *balsié* (accordion) and *pandero* (tambourine). The national dance of the Dominican Republic is the *merengue,* which features a stiff-legged step that is something like a limp. Other folk dances include the *yuca,* the *sarambo,* the *zapateo,* and the *fandango.*

Local crafts include mahogany woodcarvings, woven goods, pottery, handmade rocking chairs (which have been popular ever since one was given to President John F. Kennedy as a gift), ceramics, macramé, and handknit clothing. Dominicans also produce hand-crafted amber jewelry as well as jewelry made with *larimar,* also known as Dominican Turquoise, a light-blue stone unique to the region.

19 SOCIAL PROBLEMS

The Dominican Republic suffers from serious economic and social problems, including a 30% unemployment rate, with an additional 20% of the work force underemployed. Migration from rural to urban areas has created a housing shortage and a rise in urban crime. In Santo Domingo, the capital, much housing is substandard and the water quality is poor. In the 1980s international drug traffickers attempted to use the Dominican Republic as a transshipment point for illegal substances, resulting in a rise in narcotics-related crimes.

20 BIBLIOGRAPHY

Creed, Alexander. *Dominican Republic.* New York: Chelsea House, 1987.

Ferguson, James. *The Dominican Republic: Beyond the Lighthouse.* London: Latin America Bureau, 1992.

Gall, Timothy, and Susan Gall, ed. *Worldmark Encyclopedia of the Nations.* 8th ed. Detroit: Gale Research, 1995.

Georges, Eugenia. *The Making of a Transnational Community: Migration, Development, and Cultural Change in the Dominican Republic.* New York: Columbia University Press, 1990.

Grasmuck, Sherri, and Patricia R. Pesser. *Between Two Islands: Dominican International Migration.* Berkeley: University of California Press, 1991.

Haggerty, Richard A. *Dominican Republic and Haiti: Country Studies.* Washington, DC: US Government, 1991.

Pariser, Harry S. *Adventure Guide to the Dominican Republic.* Edison, NJ: Hunter Publishing, 1995.

Safa, Helen I. *The Myth of the Male Breadwinner: Women and Industrialization in the Caribbean.* Boulder, CO: Westview Press, 1995.

Walton, Chelle Koster. *Caribbean Ways: A Cultural Guide.* Westwood, MA: Riverdale, 1993.

Whiteford, Linda, and Kenneth J. Goodman. "Dominicans." In *Encyclopedia of World Cultures (Middle America and the Caribbean).* Boston: G. K. Hall, 1992.

Wiarda, Howard J., and Michael J. Kryzanek. *The Dominican Republic: A Caribbean Crucible.* 2nd ed. Boulder, CO: Westview Press, 1992.

—by R. Wieder

DUTCH AMERICANS

For more information on Dutch history and culture, *see* **Vol. 4: Netherlanders**.

OVERVIEW

The first Dutch in America came with the Dutch West India Company to pursue the fur trade. The company established the New Netherland colony along the Hudson River in the early 1620s, and the first settlers arrived in 1624. By 1664, when the English seized the colony and renamed it New York, the Dutch population had grown to 7,000. It was almost 200 years, however, before Dutch migration to the US began in earnest.

Between 1847 and 1913, there were four major waves of Dutch immigration to the US. The first wave lasted from 1847 to 1857 and consisted largely of Catholics and Seceders (a conservative Dutch Reformed sect) searching for greater religious freedom. After the American Civil War ended in 1865, a second wave of Dutch immigrants flocked to the US. Most were farm laborers drawn by offers of free or cheap land in the Midwest. The US wanted to expand its territory westward and recruited immigrants through programs such as the 1862 Homestead Act, which gave away parcels of land for free to those who agreed to farm it for a certain number of years. Available land was dwindling in the Netherlands, and industrialization was slow to occur, so there were fewer and fewer opportunities for landless peasants. The US offered a chance to become a landowner, and many jumped at that chance.

The third wave from 1880 to 1893 was prompted by an agricultural crisis in the Netherlands. Bad weather and overworked land caused low crop yields for several years in a row, beginning in 1878. This time, even farm owners chose to leave their homes and search for better opportunities elsewhere, particularly in the American Midwest and West where land was still available at fairly cheap rates.

The fourth major wave of Dutch immigration to the US occurred in 1903–1913, spurred by an economic slump in the Netherlands. This time the immigrants were mostly urban and settled in major industrial centers in America, such as New York City and Chicago. Some craftspeople and merchants had also immigrated with the farmers of the previous three waves, escaping high taxes and fees in the Netherlands, but the majority of Dutch immigrants to the US from 1847 to 1913 were farming families.

In the years immediately following World War II (1939–45), another wave of Dutch immigrants came to the US to escape the war torn conditions in their homeland. About 80,000 Dutch entered the US during this last major wave of immigration. Some were Jews who had survived the Holocaust.

Although the earliest Dutch settlers lived in what became New York State, along the Hudson River, subsequent immigrants moved west and settled at first almost entirely within a 50-mile radius of the southern shoreline of Lake Michigan. Later, they spread throughout the US. Most Dutch Americans immigrated in entire family units and settled with others from the same province of the Netherlands. After immigrants of the first wave (1847–1857) established themselves in the US, a pattern of chain migration began where relatives and friends of the original immigrants followed them to America. These new-

comers settled near their kin, creating tightly knit rural communities, or urban neighborhoods in later years, of Dutch Americans. Surrounded by compatriots, they were slow to assimilate and remained quite "Dutch" for a number of generations.

Of the 6,241,246 Dutch Americans in 1990 (according to the US Census), 34% still lived in the Midwest. A significant number continue to live in the Hudson River area of New York State, as well. The city of Renssalaer, New York, was founded by Dutch *patroon* Kiliaen van Renssalaer in the 1600s. Patroons were wealthy Dutch who were allowed to create an estate in the New Netherland colony if they attracted at least 50 more settlers to the New World. Renssalaer is the only patroonship that survived. Several other towns and cities in New York State, including Albany, the state capital, were founded by the Dutch. The New York City neighborhood of Harlem, originally established by New Netherland governor Peter Stuyvesant in 1658 as a farming community, was called Nieuw Haarlem.

California now has the most Dutch Americans (593,748), followed by Michigan (561,484), New York (370,608), Pennsylvania (355,007), and Texas (325,130). The most-Dutch states in the US today are Iowa, where Dutch Americans make up 6.3% of the total population; and Michigan, which is 6.0% Dutch American. Pella, Iowa, and Holland, Michigan, were both founded by Dutch immigrants and remain largely Dutch American communities.

Dutch Americans are divided into four major linguistic groups: Hollanders (the majority), who speak Dutch; Frisians, who speak Frisian, a language related to but distinct from Dutch; Flemish-speaking peoples from what is now Belgium (the Flemish language is almost identical to Dutch), and Dutch-speaking Germans from Hanover and Ost Friesland. Some Dutch words that have been adopted into common American usage are "cookie," "waffle," "spook," and perhaps "Yankee" (which may have been a Dutch nickname for Dutch sailors). The American name for "Santa Claus" also comes from the Dutch: *Sinterklaas* is their word for St. Nicholas.

Dutch Americans maintained their ethnic languages longer than many other ethnic groups due to their clannishness and the conservative nature of the Dutch Reformed Church, to which most Dutch Americans belong. The Dutch Reformed Church is a Protestant Calvinist denomination that has been in existence for hundreds of years. The first Dutch Reformed church in America was founded in 1628 in the New Netherland colony, making Dutch Reformed one of the oldest denominations in the US. The Christian Reformed Church was established in 1857 in Michigan, after a split in the Dutch Reformed church there.

The Dutch Reformed Church has a history of schisms and separations. The first major wave of Dutch immigration to the US was made up partly of Seceders, members of a conservative sect that had split off from the parent church in the early 1800s. In the late 1800s and early 1900s, a small number of Doleantie secessionists, also known as Kuyperians, immigrated to the US and joined the Christian Reformed Church, quickly becoming its leaders. Today's Dutch Reformed Church in the US is still split into two branches: the original Reformed Church in America, founded in 1628, and the Christian Reformed Church, founded in 1857.

Dutch Protestants strongly resisted Americanization, especially in their church life. The original settlers of New Netherland intended to create a Dutch colony and therefore zealously guarded and promoted their Dutch identity. The Dutch Reformed Church believed that the Dutch way was the true way and made every effort to keep the Church in America pure. Once the English took over New Netherland and renamed it New York, those Dutch who remained struggled to determine their identity in the now-English colony. As English became the official and common language of New York, second and later generations of Dutch Americans lost their fluency in Dutch. By 1762 the Dutch Reformed Church conceded to Americanization and began holding some services in English to maintain its membership. By the end of the American Revolutionary War (1775–83), all Dutch Reformed Church services were in English.

Later Dutch immigrants to the US came with the intention of making America their new home and were therefore more interested in adapting to American ways. The Dutch Reformed Church took on a new spirit of assimilation, searching for a way to remain faithful to its Dutch traditions while at the same time being true to its American setting. As a fairly strict, conservative Church (in both of its American branches), the Dutch Reformed Church continues to struggle to find a balance between tradition and modernization.

Dutch Catholics who immigrated to America assimilated much more quickly into mainstream American life. This was due largely to the multicultural aspect of Catholic parishes in the US. Also, Dutch Catholics tended to be wealthier and more urban than Dutch Protestants (who were mostly farmers), so they had the resources to establish themselves quickly in industrialized US society. Dutch Catholic, and later Jewish, immigrants came to the US in noticeable numbers, but by far the majority of Dutch Americans were and are members of the Dutch Reformed Church.

Dutch Americans have made tremendous contributions to American culture, from the colonial era when they founded towns and cities that still exist today, to the very Declaration of Independence, which owes much of its spirit and wording to the Dutch declaration of independence from Spain 200 years earlier. Pancakes, waffles, doughnuts, cookies, coleslaw, and pretzels (though pretzels are also credited to German Americans) were introduced by the Dutch. Rutgers University in New Brunswick, New Jersey, was founded in 1766 (as Rutgers College, in Paterson, New Jersey) by Dutch Americans, as was Hope College, which in 1866 grew out of Hope Academy, established in 1851 in Holland, Michigan, by the Dutch American founders of that city.

Famous Dutch Americans include film director Cecil B. DeMille, artist Willem de Kooning, poet Mark Van Doren and his brother, writer Carl Van Doren, and singer/songwriter Bruce Springsteen (who is half-Italian American, half-Dutch American). Walter Percy Chrysler, who introduced the Chrysler automobile and became a leading automobile manufacturer, was Dutch American, as was educator Clarence Dykstra. Len Dykstra is a well-known Dutch American baseball player.

No fewer than three US presidents claimed Dutch ancestry: Martin Van Buren (president from 1836–1840), Theodore Roosevelt (1901–1908), and Franklin Delano Roosevelt (1932–1945). The Roosevelts traced their heritage back to Klaes Martensen van Roosevelt, who immigrated to the US in 1644. It is clear that the US would not be what it is today were it not for the Dutch. Although Dutch Americans are a relatively small group in the total US population, they have played an enormous role in the history and development of America.

BIBLIOGRAPHY

Olsen, Victoria. *The Dutch Americans*. New York: Chelsea House, 1989.

Rose, Peter G., trans. and ed. *The Sensible Cook: Dutch Foodways in the Old and the New World*. Syracuse, New York: Syracuse University Press, 1989.

Swierenga, Robert P., ed. *The Dutch in America: Immigration, Settlement, and Cultural Change*. New Brunswick, NJ: Rutgers University Press, 1985.

US Bureau of the Census. *Detailed Ancestry Groups for States*. 1990 Census of Population Supplementary Reports, CP-S-1-2. Washington, DC, October 1992.

—by D. K. Daeg de Mott

ECUADORANS

LOCATION: Ecuador
POPULATION: 11,466,291
LANGUAGE: Spanish; Quechua
RELIGION: Roman Catholicism; some Pentecostal and Protestant churches

¹ INTRODUCTION

Ecuador, as its name suggests, straddles the equator in South America. Located north of present-day Peru, Ecuador once formed part of the Inca Empire. The Ecuadoran city of Quito, moreover, acted as a secondary capital of the empire. The Incas had built an extensive footpath system that linked Cusco, the capital of the Inca empire in Peru, to Quito, over 1,600 km (1,000 mi) away.

During colonial times, Ecuador continued to be ruled from Peru, this time by the Spanish Viceroyalty in Lima. In 1822, Ecuador was led to independence by General Antonio José de Sucre, a lieutenant of famed liberator Simón Bolívar. Independence, however, did not lead to political stability. The 19th century was a time of intense political struggle between pro- and anti-Church factions. Ecuador succumbed to military rule in the late 1800s, and again in the 1960s and 1970s. Ecuador has experienced democratic rule since 1979.

² LOCATION AND HOMELAND

Ecuador encompasses many geographical regions and therefore has a rich diversity of plants and animals. Ecuador has three broad geographic areas: the coast, the sierra (mountains), and the jungle lowlands. These varied geographical regions and climatic conditions have created many habitats that allow a rich diversity of wildlife and flora to thrive. Off the Pacific coast of Ecuador, furthermore, are the renowned Galápagos Islands. The Galápagos Islands, which are classified as a protected area by the Ecuadoran government, are scarcely populated by humans. Instead, they are home to sea lions, penguins, flamingos, iguanas, giant tortoises, and a great many other animals. It is said that Darwin found the inspiration for his theory of evolution when he visited the Galápagos in 1835. The Galápagos Islands are now a popular destination for ecological tours.

Ecuador has a human population of 11,466,291 people.

³ LANGUAGE

The official language of Ecuador is Spanish. A significant proportion of its Andean population, however, speaks the ancient Inca language of Quechua and a variety of related dialects. Although mainly an Andean language, the Quechua language also spread into the lowland jungle areas at the time of the Spanish conquest as a result of migration and the influence of Quechua-speaking missionaries.

A variety of indigenous tribes exist in the Ecuadoran Amazon. These native peoples have their own languages that are unrelated to Quechua. These groups include the Jivaro and the Waoroni.

⁴ FOLKLORE

A number of folk beliefs are common among rural dwellers, combining Catholic tradition and indigenous lore, as well as vestiges of medieval Spanish custom. The "in-between" hours of dawn, dusk, noon, and midnight are feared as times when supernatural forces can enter and depart the human world. Many rural folk fear the *huacaisiqui*, which are spirits of abandoned or aborted babies, thought to steal the souls of living infants. A character specific to the Sierra region is the *duende*, a large-eyed sprite with a hat who preys on children. The blacks of Esmeraldas have inherited the folklore of their ancestors, including the figure of the *tunda*, an evil water spirit who takes the shape of a woman with a club foot.

⁵ RELIGION

Ecuador is predominantly a Roman Catholic country. Catholicism was introduced by the Spanish at the time of the conquest. The question of the role of the Church in state and society was one that generated significant political conflict in Ecuador. After independence from the Spanish, political struggle occurred between the pro-Church conservatives and the liberals who believed in a more limited Church role. This political struggle ended with a constitution that ensures a separation of Church and State.

In the late 1960s, the Church in Ecuador and elsewhere in Latin America began to defend the poor and argue for social change. The "theology of liberation," as it was called, found religious justification for social change and political reform. Many bishops and priests spoke out against the government in defense of the rural poor.

The influence of the Roman Catholic Church in rural society seems to be in decline. In the 1980s, Pentecostal and Protestant churches have begun to expand their influence in the countryside.

⁶ MAJOR HOLIDAYS

Christmas in many towns in Ecuador is celebrated with a colorful parade. In the town of Cuenca, reputed to have the most festive parade, townspeople decorate and dress up their donkeys and cars for the procession. On New Year's, the festivities include fireworks and the burning of effigies, made by stuffing old clothes. Many Ecuadorans take this opportunity to mock current political figures. These dummies are nicknamed *viejos* or "old ones" and symbolize the passing year.

Carnaval, or Carnival, a major festival preceding Lent, is celebrated with much festivity. During the hot summer month of February, Ecuadorans celebrate Carnival by throwing buckets of water at each other. Even fully clothed passersby are at risk. Sometimes pranksters will add dye or ink to the water to stain clothing. In some towns, throwing water has been banned, but this practice is hard to repress. It is virtually impossible to avoid getting wet during Carnival, and most Ecuadorans accept it with good humor.

⁷ RITES OF PASSAGE

Most Ecuadorans are Roman Catholic and therefore mark major life transitions, such as birth, marriage, and death, with Catholic ceremonies. Protestant, Pentecostal, and Amerindian Ecuadorans celebrate rites of passage with ceremonies appropriate to their particular traditions.

8 INTERPERSONAL RELATIONS

In Ecuador, it is customary for most activity in cities to close down between 1:00 and 3:00 PM for the afternoon siesta. During this time, many offices and stores are closed. This custom, which exists in many Latin American countries, arose as a way to avoid working during the intense afternoon heat. Most people go home for an extended lunch and even a nap. They return to work in the late afternoon when it is cooler and work until the early evening.

In Ecuador, one is expected to kiss the cheek of anyone to whom one is introduced, except in a business context where it is more appropriate to use a handshake. Female friends will kiss each other on the cheek, while male friends will often greet each other with a full embrace. This practice is very common in most Latin American countries.

9 LIVING CONDITIONS

The major cities of Ecuador, Quito, and Guayaquil are modern cities, with modern offices and contemporary apartment buildings. The style of housing in these two cities, however, varies as a result of their histories and locations. Quito, in the dry Andean highlands, is characterized by beautiful colonial architecture. The city remains relatively small as a result of its isolated, high-altitude location. Guayaquil, in contrast, is a more modern, bustling port city of over 2 million people. Guayaquil's busy economy has attracted huge waves of migration from the Andean region. Nearly a third of Guayaquil's population live in large sprawling shantytowns with limited electricity and running water. The poor housing and limited availability of clean water create unsanitary conditions that can cause serious health problems. Infectious diseases are, therefore, a problem for many poorer Ecuadorans.

Middle-class homes and apartments in the major cities, however, have modern amenities and conveniences. These cities are densely populated, and few homes have large yards such as those found in the US. In most middle-class neighborhoods, in fact, houses are all connected side by side and, in this way, form a city block.

In rural highland areas, most small-scale farmers live in small one-room houses with thatched or tiled roofs. Most often, these homes have been built by the families themselves, with assistance from family and friends. In the jungle areas, housing structures are made of locally available materials, such as bamboo and palm leaves.

The people of the jungle regions face many critical health problems. Parasites and river blindness are problems caused by contaminated water supplies. Malaria also remains a problem in humid jungle areas that attract mosquitoes.

10 FAMILY LIFE

An Ecuadoran household typically consists of a nuclear family; that is, a husband, a wife, and their children. It is also common for grandparents or other members of the extended family to join the household. The role of women differs greatly in middle-class urban areas from that in rural village life. In Andean communities, women play an important role in the economic activities of the household. In addition to helping plant gardens and tend animals, many women are involved in petty trading. While there is a clear division between male and female roles

in rural areas, both make important contributions to the household income.

In middle- and upper-class households, in contrast, women are less likely to work outside the home. Commonly, women in these social classes devote themselves to managing the household and rearing children. These patterns, however, are beginning to change. There are a growing number of middle- and upper-class women who continue their education and find jobs outside of the home.

11 CLOTHING

Clothing worn in the urban areas of Ecuador is very Western. Men wear trousers and a pressed shirt, or a suit to work. Women wear both pants and skirts. Although jeans and tee-shirts are becoming the clothing of choice for Ecuadoran youth, the use of shorts is still rare.

Clothing outside of the major cities, however, is diverse. Perhaps the most distinctive dress in the Andean region is worn by the Otavalo Indians. The Otavalo are considered a subgroup of the Quechuas, as they speak the Quechua language. Otavalo men are distinctive for their long, black braids and their identical black and white outfits. Otavalo men dress impeccably in white short trousers, white buttoned shirts, and solid black ponchos. They also wear stiff felt hats and sandals. Otavalo women wear delicately embroidered white blouses.

The role of Ecuadoran women differs greatly in middle-class urban areas from that in rural village life. (Susan D. Rock)

12 FOOD

Ecuador is an Andean country, and its population has relied on the potato as a staple crop since pre-Inca times. Over 100 different types of potatoes are still grown throughout the Andes. A traditional Andean specialty is *locro,* a dish of corn and potatoes, topped with a spicy cheese sauce. Seafood also forms an important part of the diet in coastal areas. A common snack item, popular throughout Ecuador, is *empanadas*—little pastries filled with meat, onions, eggs, and olives. Empanadas are sold in bakeries or by street vendors and can be considered the Ecuadoran equivalent of fast food.

Bananas are also an important part of the diet. Some varieties of bananas, such as plantains, are a nonsweet, starchy vegetable like a potato. They need to be cooked and are used in stews or are served grilled. Grilled bananas are often sold by street vendors.

Coffee is also grown in the Andean highlands. Coffee in Ecuador is served in a very concentrated form, called *esencia.* Esencia is a very dark, thick coffee that is served in a little container alongside a pot of hot water. Each person serves a small amount of coffee into his or her cup, then dilutes it with hot water. Even diluted, this coffee is very strong!

13 EDUCATION

In Ecuador, education is compulsory until age 14. In practice, however, there is a serious problem with illiteracy, and a high proportion of students drop out of school. This problem is most severe in rural areas. For many rural families, children can play an important role by working on the landholding. It is difficult for many families to survive without this labor, and many children receive only minimal formal schooling.

14 CULTURAL HERITAGE

Much of Ecuador's musical tradition has Andean roots. Precolonial instruments and musical styles are still popular in Ecuador. Flutelike instruments include the *quena,* an instrument used throughout the Andean countries. However, regional variations do exist. While most panpipes played in Peru or Bolivia comprise two rows of bamboo, the traditional Ecuadoran *rondador* has only one row. Other important wind instruments include the *pinkullo* and *pifano*. The Andean culture has also been influenced by its colonial past. Brass instruments are very popular in the Andes, and many village festivals and parades feature brass bands. String instruments were also introduced by the Spanish and adapted by the Andean peoples.

The coastal tradition draws more from Caribbean and Spanish influences. Colombian *cumbia* and *salsa* music are popular with young people in urban areas. American rock music is also played on the radio and in urban clubs and discos.

Ecuador also has a strong literary tradition. Its most well-known writer is Jorge Icaza, who wrote a moving book about the plight of the Ecuadoran Amerindians. His most famous book, *The Villagers,* describes a brutal takeover of indigenous land. This book raised awareness of the exploitation of indigenous peoples in the Andes by landowners. Although it was written in 1934, it is still widely read in Ecuador today.

15 WORK

Work and lifestyles in Ecuador vary dramatically from region to region. In the mountains, most people are small-scale subsistence farmers. Many male youths find employment as field workers on sugarcane or banana plantations. This work is difficult and laborious, and pays extremely poorly.

Ecuador also has a fair-sized manufacturing industry. Food processing, which includes activities such as flour milling and sugar refining, are important to the economy. However, much of the urban population makes a living not from employment, but by creating a small-scale enterprise. Home "cottage" industries include dressmaking, carpentry, and shoemaking, among others. Street vending also provides an economic alternative for many women in both the *sierra* and the urban slums.

Ecuador is also an oil-rich country. In the 1970s, an economic boom was sparked by the extraction of oil, and hundreds of thousands of jobs were created by the growing oil industry. In the 1980s, however, the boom ended with Ecuador's growing debt and declining oil prices. Ecuador still produces oil, but its reserves appear limited.

16 SPORTS

Spectator sports are popular in Ecuador. Soccer, as elsewhere in Latin America, is a national pastime. Bullfighting, a sport introduced by the Spanish, is also popular. Famous bullfighters (known as *matadors*) from Spain or other South American countries come to Ecuador and attract huge crowds. In some rural villages, a nonviolent version of bullfighting provides entertainment at some *fiestas*. Local men are invited to jump into a pen with a young bull calf to try their skills as matadors. Another blood sport that is prevalent throughout Ecuador is cockfighting. This entails tying a knife to the foot of a rooster (or cock) and having it fight another rooster. These fights usually end up in the death of one of the roosters.

Ecuadorans are also fond of playing different types of paddle ball. One type of paddle ball uses a heavy 1-kg (2-lb) ball and appropriately large paddles with spikes. A variation of this game uses a much smaller ball, which is hit with the hand rather than with a paddle. Standard racquetball is also played, although membership in clubs with courts can be prohibitively expensive.

17 ENTERTAINMENT AND RECREATION

The principal form of entertainment in the Andes is the regular festivals or *fiestas* that exist to mark the agricultural or religious calendar. These fiestas often last for days and involve music, dancing, and the consumption of alcoholic beverages such as *chicha*, brewed from corn.

In urban areas, many Ecuadorans go to *penas* on weekends for a special night out. *Penas* are clubs that feature traditional

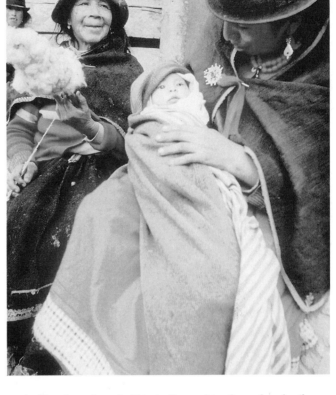

An Ecuadoran household typically consists of a nuclear family; that is, a husband, a wife, and their children. It is also common for grandparents or other members of the extended family to join the household. (Susan D. Rock)

music and folklore shows. This is often a family outing, even though these shows often go on until the early morning. When teenagers or young adults go out on their own, they are more likely to go to a club or disco that plays American rock and dance music. However, these clubs only exist in the major urban areas.

18 FOLK ART, CRAFTS, AND HOBBIES

Panama hats actually originated in Ecuador. These woven straw hats were made in the city of Cuenca. They were produced for export to California gold-rushers and were also sold in large quantities to workers building the Panama Canal, thus giving rise to the name. Panama hats became a huge export item for Ecuador in the early to mid-1900s. While Panama hats are still made in Ecuador, they are no longer in great demand overseas. A good Panama hat, it is claimed, can be folded up and passed through a napkin ring, and it will then reshape itself perfectly for use.

Ecuadorans produce a wide variety of handcrafted goods, ranging from woven textiles, to woodcarvings, to ceramic goods. The market at Otovalo, Ecuador, is sometimes claimed to be the most extensive and varied market in all of South America. This market was established in pre-Inca times as a major market where goods from the mountains could be exchanged for goods from the lowland jungle areas. Today, the Otovalo market continues to be an outlet for handwoven, vegetable-dyed textiles and tapestries made by the Otovalo Indians.

¹⁹ SOCIAL PROBLEMS

Machismo is a serious problem in Ecuador, as it is in other Latin American countries. It is common for men to feel that they should have unquestioned control over their wives, daughters, or girlfriends. Many Latin American men, in addition, believe in different standards of acceptable male and female sexual behavior. It is common for married men to have one or more long-term mistresses, while their wives are expected to be faithful and monogamous. Improvements in the education of women are beginning to make some impact on this behavior, as women increasingly are demanding greater respect. However, these beliefs are deeply ingrained in the culture and are difficult to change.

²⁰ BIBLIOGRAPHY

Box, Ben. *The South American Handbook.* New York: Prentice Hall General Reference, 1992.

Hanratty, Dennis, ed. *Ecuador, a Country Study.* Washington, D.C.: Federal Research Division, Library of Congress, 1991.

Perrotet, Tony, ed. *Insight Guides: Ecuador.* Boston: Houghton Mifflin Company, 1993.

Rachowiecki, Rob. *Ecuador and the Galapagos: A Travel Survival Kit.* Oakland, CA: Lonely Planet Publications, 1992.

Rathbone, John Paul. *Cadogan Guides: Ecuador, the Galapagos and Colombia.* London: Cadogan Books, 1991.

—by C. Sahley, reviewed by T. Morin

ENGLISH AMERICANS

For more information on English history and culture, *see* **Vol. 4: English.**

OVERVIEW

The original 13 American colonies, which became the United States, were founded by the English beginning in 1607. The land had been claimed for England long before, in 1497, by Italian sea captain John Cabot and his son, Sebastian. The Cabots were sailing under the commission of English king Henry VII and explored the east coast of North America from what is now Newfoundland to South Carolina. The English neither sponsored nor conducted any further North American exploration for the next 80 years.

Hard times for the peasant class in England from the late 1550s through the 1600s prompted many to look for new opportunities. The tyrannical reign of King James I (r.1603–1625), who levied heavy taxes, refused to call Parliament, and otherwise abused his powers, also drove many English out of the country. King Charles I, who followed King James I, was even more tyrannical. Thus it was that the 13 English colonies were founded in America.

The first colony did not survive. Established in 1587 with funding from Sir Walter Raleigh, the so-called "Lost Colony" on Roanoke Island lasted for only a short time. The sea captain who transported the 150 colonists (25 of them women and children) was supposed to take them to Chesapeake Bay but instead left them on Roanoke Island and promptly abandoned them. When supplies began running low, the colony leader, John White, found passage back to England to request aid but was detained for three or four years by the authorities there. When White was finally able to return to the colony in 1591, it was deserted. Only the word "Croatan," the name of a nearby Native North American tribe, was found, carved on the trunk of a tree. Some suspect the colonists were killed by the Croatans or other Native North Americans. Others believe the Native North Americans may have been friendly and the colonists joined their community. No one may ever know the true fate of the Lost Colony.

Jamestown, founded in 1607 by the London Company, became the first successful English colony in North America. The second successful colony, Plymouth, was established in 1620 by a group of Puritans (Anglican reformers) who called themselves "Pilgrims." The Pilgrims came to North America on a ship called *Mayflower.* Ten years later, a larger group of Puritans founded Massachusetts Bay Colony. Whereas Jamestown was founded purely for economic gain, Plymouth and Massachusetts Bay were created as religious havens for members of a persecuted sect. Likewise, Maryland was later established as a haven for Catholics and Pennsylvania for Quakers, both of whom were not welcomed in England. Georgia was originally intended as a debtors' colony, where those who had been imprisoned for unpaid debts in England could find a new start. But the English government refused to transport many debtors, so the idea never took form.

By 1733, all 13 colonies were established, including New York which had been seized from the Dutch (under whom it had been known as New Amsterdam) in 1664. Though the initial numbers of settlers were fairly small, immigration increased steadily throughout the colonial period. Some 14,000 colonists settled in Virginia between 1607 and 1624, and Maryland had a population of 8,000 by 1657. The population of Massachusetts Bay Colony grew from 2,000 to 16,000 in just 13 years (1630–1643), and Georgia's population similarly increased from a mere 100 in 1733 to as many as 9,000 in 1760. Between the years of 1717 and 1760, the number of settlers in North Carolina jumped from 9,000 to 93,000, and in South Carolina in the same period, from 19,000 to 100,000.

Overall, the total population of the 13 original colonies went from 220,000 in 1690 to 1,500,000 in 1760, then soared to 2,750,000 by 1790. Between 80% and 85% of the population was English. English customs, clothing, architecture, language, literature, law, and religion dominated in the colonies and shaped early US culture. Although persons of English descent are now only the third-largest ethnic group in the US (after German and Irish), English culture still predominates in America.

Once the Revolutionary War (1775–83) began, English immigration to America virtually ceased until about 1790. Then, a shortage of land in England led a number of farmers to take advantage of the new lands being cleared in the US. Beginning in the late 1790s, thousands of textile workers also began flocking to the US from England, settling in the mill towns of New England and New Jersey. Immigration was brought to a halt again when England and France went to war in 1803, and all ships were commandeered for military use. When the war ended in 1815, English immigration to the US resumed with force, bringing 750,000 English to the shores of America between 1815 and 1860. Most settled in the north.

The American Civil War (1861–65) once again halted immigration, but as soon as the war ended, the largest wave of English immigration to the US began. A series of crop failures in England, plus a tremendous increase in opportunities available in America because of industrialization and westward expansion, created a high motivation for immigration. From 1865 to 1895, some 2,300,000 English moved to the US. Some took industrial jobs in the East, while others became farmers or ranchers in the Midwest and West.

One interesting group of English immigrants to the US were the gentlemen ranchers who set up huge cattle operations in the West in the late 19th century. Most were young aristocrats who had been educated at Eton or Harrow or one of the other elite schools in England. They played tennis and chess, drank tea, and rode with the cowboys during round-up time. Scottish and Irish aristocrats also established cattle ranches, though most of them took the enterprise more seriously than did the English. For the most part, the English gentlemen were drawn to the romance of the "Wild West," and once real life took over and the free range became overcrowded, harsh winters killed off the cattle, and Native North Americans put up a fight for their dwindling lands, the gentlemen packed up and moved back to England. They did leave behind new cattle breeds to blend with the American stock, and some great stories of the "English cowboys."

Since the late 18th century, most English immigration to the US has been made up of individuals and individual families. There has been no great chain migration of entire communities and no development of "Englishtowns" in the US. Immigration from England to America has steadily dropped off during the

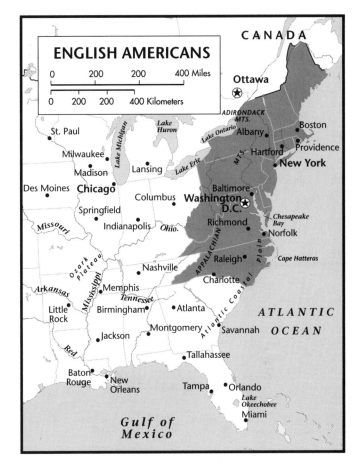

20th century. One exception to that trend were the 70,000 English war brides who came to the US in the 1940s. "War brides" were English women who met American servicemen stationed in England during World War II and either married them in England or became engaged to them, marrying them later in the US. English war brides were the largest group of female immigrants to the US in the 1940s. Because there were so many of them, the US Army and federal government facilitated their immigration. Congress passed the War Brides Act of 1945 and the Alien Fiancées and Fiancés Act of 1946 to allow qualified women (and men) to immigrate. The US Army set up embarkation camps in England to process applicants, then provided free overseas transportation on army ships. The war brides comprised the last significant wave of English immigration so far in US history.

In the 1990 US Census, a total of 32,651,788 persons reported having English ancestry. Another 1,119,154 persons claimed "British" ancestry, but this could also include Welsh, Scottish, and even Irish ancestors. Less than 1% of English Americans are foreign born (many of whom are likely to be war brides). Because English Americans have lived in the US since before it became the US and currently make up at least 13% of the total US population, they are one of the standards to which other immigrants assimilate.

Today, English Americans live in every state of the Union. The top five states in terms of numbers of English Americans are California (3,645,975), Texas (2,023,901), Florida (1,845,667), New York (1,566,019), and Ohio (1,449,303). In terms of percentage of population, the most-English states are Utah (43%), Maine (30%), Idaho (29%), Vermont (26%), and New Hampshire (24%). Wyoming, where most of the 19th-century gentlemen ranchers congregated, is sixth (22%), followed by Oregon (20%).

English place names pepper the map of the US. A few examples are Plymouth, Salem, Marblehead, Boston, Albany, New York, New Jersey, Virginia, Maryland, Pennsylvania, Maine, Delaware, and Cape Cod. English surnames are also common in America, such as Williams, Davies, Thomas, Evans, Charles, Morgan, James, Scott, Rivers, Hill, Brooks, Ford, Woods, Young, Black, Brown, Longfellow, Little, Armstrong, Taylor, Wainwright, Carpenter, Miller, Cartwright, Bishop, Masters, Bailey, and Smith (the most common surname in America).

The official church of England is, and has been for some time, the Anglican Church. Anglican immigrants to the US created the Episcopal Church in America. Other early English immigrants were Puritan, Quaker, or members of other Anabaptist sects, who established American denominations including American Friends (Quaker), Congregationalist, Unitarian, and American Baptist. Puritan Pilgrims in New England were the first Americans to celebrate Thanksgiving, joining with friendly neighboring Native North American peoples to give thanks for the fruits of the harvest.

English Americans Roger Williams, Increase Mather and his son, Cotton, and Jonathan Edwards were all important colonial religious leaders and writers. Colonial English American artists of note include Benjamin West and Charles Willson Peale. The 19th century saw a flowering of English American literature, with contributions by such writers as Nathaniel Hawthorne, Ralph Waldo Emerson, Oliver Wendell Holmes, Edgar Allan Poe, Walt Whitman, Emily Dickinson, Samuel Clemens (better known as Mark Twain), and three men who were also part French: Henry Wadsworth Longfellow, Henry David Thoreau, and John Greenleaf Whittier. Later English American writers include T. S. Eliot, William Faulkner, and Tennessee Williams.

So many English Americans have contributed to American culture in the 20th century it would be impossible to list even a representative sample. A few of the best-known are film director Alfred Hitchcock, architect Frank Lloyd Wright, and actors and entertainers Vanessa Redgrave, Cary Grant, Bob Hope and Will Rogers (who is half Cherokee).

The majority of colonial and Revolutionary leaders were English Americans, among them Benjamin Franklin, Daniel Webster, Samuel Adams, James Otis, George Washington, and John Adams. Forces on both sides of the American Civil War (1861–65) were led by English Americans: Union general Ulysses S. Grant, and Confederate general Robert E. Lee. Besides George Washington, John Adams, and Ulysses S. Grant, a number of other English Americans have served as US president, including James Madison, John Quincy Adams, William Henry Harrison, John Tyler, Zachary Taylor, Millard Fillmore, Franklin Pierce, Abraham Lincoln, Andrew Johnson, James A. Garfield, Grover Cleveland, Benjamin Harrison, William H. Taft, Warren G. Harding, Calvin Coolidge, Harry S. Truman, and Lyndon B. Johnson.

US history is replete with English Americans who have made significant contributions, such as polar explorer Admiral E. Byrd; naval officer Commodore Matthew C. Perry; Army general George C. Marshall, author of the Marshall Plan; and inventors Eli Whitney, Samuel F. Morse, Isaac M. Singer, Tho-mas A. Edison, and Wilbur and Orville Wright. Samuel Slater founded the American textile industry; Colonel Edwin L. Drake founded the American oil industry; Clara Barton founded the American Red Cross; Dr. William Janes Mayo and his brother, Charles Horace, founded the Mayo Clinic in Rochester, Minnesota; and Marshall Field founded the famous department store of the same name. Railroad tycoon James J. Hill, historian Charles A. Beard, and humanitarian Jane Addams were also English Americans.

The list could go on and on. Although English immigration to the US has been minimal in the 20th century, the English were among the founders of the US and so had a tremendous impact on American life. Descendants of those early settlers continue to create an English American backdrop to US culture, despite the fact that they are now only the third largest ethnic group in America.

BIBLIOGRAPHY

Cates, Edwin H. *The English in America*. Minneapolis: Lerner Publications, 1966.

Erickson, Charlotte. *Leaving England: Essays on British Emigration in the Nineteenth Century*. Ithaca: Cornell University Press, 1994.

US Bureau of the Census. *Detailed Ancestry Groups for States*. 1990 Census of Population Supplementary Reports, CP-S-1-2. Washington, DC, October 1992.

———. *The Foreign-Born Population in the United States*. 1990 CP-3-1. Washington, DC, July 1993.

Virden, Jenel. *Good-bye, Piccadilly: British War Brides in America*. Urbana/Chicago: University of Illinois Press, 1996.

Woods, Lawrence M. *British Gentlemen in the Wild West: The Era of the Intensely English Cowboy*. New York: The Free Press, 1989.

—by D. K. Daeg de Mott

FILIPINO AMERICANS

For more information on Filipino history and culture, *see* **Vol. 3: Filipinos**.

OVERVIEW

The first Filipinos, people from the Philippines, to set foot in what is now the US were crew members of the Spanish galleon, *Nuestra Señora de Esperanza* (Our Lady of Hope), which landed on the shore of present-day California on 18 October 1587. Filipinos were conscripted to work on Spanish ships in the Manila Galleon Trade between Mexico and the Philippines from 1565 to 1815. To escape the harsh treatment inflicted on them by their Spanish officers, many Filipinos jumped ship in New Orleans beginning around 1765 and settled there. By 1833, a significant Filipino community had developed in the fishing village of St. Malo in the Mississippi River delta area.

St. Malo was destroyed by a hurricane in 1893, and the survivors founded Manila Village, south of New Orleans. Forty years later, in 1933, Manila Village had a Filipino population of 1,500. The Manila Village Filipinos developed the process of sun drying shrimp to market outside Louisiana. Eventually, this first wave of Filipino immigrants moved on to the present-day states of California, Texas, and New Mexico.

In 1903, after the US had defeated Spain in the Spanish-American War of 1898, the US annexed the Philippines, which had been a Spanish colony for nearly 400 years. When the Filipinos revolted against American occupation, American forces crushed them, killing an estimated one million Filipinos. The Filipinos then became the only Asians ever colonized by the US. As colonists, they were free to immigrate to the US, and many did. This is considered the second wave of Filipino immigration.

Many Filipino students also came to the US during this second wave, which lasted from about 1906 to 1934. The US government gave scholarships, or "pensions," to young Filipinos (male and female) to study at American universities. These students were called *pensionados*. Pensionados were expected to return to the Philippines when they had finished their studies, but many stayed in the US.

Filipino laborers were also "imported" during the early 1900s to provide cheap labor on the US west coast, particularly in the agricultural industry, although some found work in salmon canning factories. Most of the laborers were young single men, between the ages of 16 and 22, with little formal education. Without family attachments, they were prime candidates for seasonal migrant work. As physically small people (in general), they were considered ideal for "stoop" labor—planting, and picking things that are close to the ground—a very demanding job. The young Filipinos were so eager for employment that they were willing to take jobs that were too harsh for others to consider.

Filipinos were then recruited for the Hawaiian sugar industry, when Japanese immigration was restricted. Between 1907 and 1929, Hawaiian employers imported 71,594 Filipino workers. About 15,000 of them later moved to California. Many stayed in Hawaii, however, eventually making up a significant percentage (18% by 1930) of Hawaii's resident population.

US immigration laws in the 1920s prevented any Asians except Filipinos from immigrating to the US. Therefore, Filipinos were in great demand as low-wage workers on the west coast. From 1920 to 1929, 51,875 Filipinos arrived in California, along with the 15,000 who moved there from Hawaii. Filipinos also found their way to the Alaskan salmon canneries, quickly becoming the largest immigrant group employed there. By 1930, the Filipino population on the US mainland had reached 45,200. Thousands more were in Hawaii and Alaska. European Americans began to feel threatened by the Filipino presence, and the US government decided to restrict any further Filipino immigration after 1934.

Those Filipinos already residing in the US were subjected to brutal attacks and harsh laws restricting their access to government aid. Working at such low-wage, seasonal jobs, many found the winters particularly difficult. Antimiscegenation laws prevented Filipino men from marrying European American women, leaving them with little opportunity for family development, as Filipino men outnumbered Filipino women in the US by 15 to 1 at that time.

The Third Wave of Filipino immigration occurred after World War II, lasting from 1945 to 1965. This wave was made up of military personnel and their families, students, and exchange workers. Foreign-born Filipinos became eligible for US citizenship during this time, making life in the US much easier for Filipino immigrants.

The 1965 Immigration Reform Act, which lifted discriminatory restrictions on all Asian immigration, opened up the Fourth Wave of Filipino migration to the US. In the first two decades after the passage of the Act, 668,870 Filipino immigrants arrived in the US. From 1960 to 1980, the Filipino population in the US more than quadrupled from 176,130 to 781,894. Filipinos continue to flow into the US in this Fourth Wave, many of them well-educated professionals and highly skilled workers, creating what is known as a "brain drain" in the Philippines.

According to the US Census, the Filipino American population was 1,406,770 in 1990. At 19% of all Asians in the US, Filipino Americans are the second-largest group among Asian/Pacific Americans (Chinese Americans are the largest). About two-thirds of Filipino Americans in 1990 were foreign-born, and three-fourths lived in the West (52% in California and Hawaii). Other US states with significant Filipino American populations are Illinois, New York, New Jersey, and Washington. Southern states also host large numbers of Filipino Americans. Although early Filipino immigrants tended to settle in rural agricultural areas, today's Filipino Americans, generally better educated than earlier immigrants, are choosing large urban centers and suburbs as their homes.

Filipinos speak more than 70 dialects, most of which belong to eight major language groups. The most common of these groups are Tagalog, Visayan, and Ilocano. About two-thirds of Filipino Americans speak a dialect from one of these three groups, with the majority speaking forms of Tagalog. In California, Tagalog is the third most spoken foreign language, after Spanish and Chinese. A few Filipino words have become standard in English usage, such as *yo-yo* and *boondocks*.

Many Filipinos speak English before arriving in the US, due to their years as a US colony in the early 20th century. Filipino Americans have the highest rate of English language proficiency of any Asian/Pacific American group. Despite these

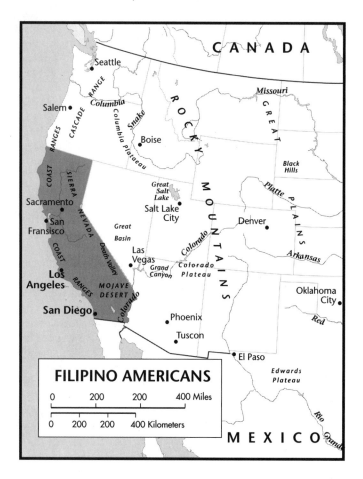

FILIPINO AMERICANS

| 0 | 200 | 200 | 400 Miles |

| 0 | 200 | 200 | 400 Kilometers |

The number of Filipino women migrating to the US has increased to the point where Filipino American women now outnumber Filipino American men (100 women for every 86 men).

This fact, combined with the repeal of antimiscegenation laws and the shift from single male to family migration, has led to a sharp rise in the number of Filipino American family households. Because of their traditional cultural and religious (Roman Catholic) values, most Filipino Americans have large families; in 1990, the average Filipino American family consisted of 4.0 persons, as compared to 3.2 persons for all US families. Filipino Americans have a much higher birth rate than any other ethnic group in the US, excepting Mexican Americans.

Over three-fourths (78%) of Filipino American families are headed by a married couple. Some 15% are headed by a woman alone, and 6% by a man alone. Though extended family groups are traditional in the Philippines, Filipino Americans generally live in nuclear family units. This lack of available support can prove difficult for those used to turning to other family members for help. Also, because children usually attend public schools, they are exposed to European American culture and values without the balancing force of an extended Filipino community at home. Filipino American parents struggle to keep Filipino traditions alive in their Americanized children.

In keeping with the fact that many Filipinos came to the US as students, Filipino Americans place a high value on education. In 1990, almost 83% of Filipino Americans 25 years old or older were high school graduates, compared to 78% of all Asian/Pacific Americans and 75% of the total US population. Of the same age group, nearly 39% were college graduates, just slightly above the 38% rate for all Asian/Pacific Americans, but well above the total US population rate of 20%. In contrast to any other Asian/Pacific American group or the total US population, more Filipino American women than men are college graduates.

Despite their high levels of education, however, Filipino Americans educated outside of the US often find it difficult to obtain employment in the US that is in keeping with their educational qualifications. Strict licensing requirements for certain occupations in the US (such as doctors, lawyers, dentists, and pharmacists) prevent some Filipino Americans from practicing their professions in the US, even though they may have been fully qualified, practicing professionals in the Philippines.

The rich cultural heritage of Filipinos and Filipino Americans is only recently being made available to the wider public. There are many successful Filipino American writers, including Jessica Tarahata Hagedorn (b.1949), Jose Garcia Villa (b.1914), and Carlos Bulosan (1913–1956). Bulosan's autobiography, *American Is in the Heart* (1946), has been named one of the 50 most important American books ever published.

A currently successful Filipino American singer/actress is Tia Carrere (b.1969), who had lead roles in the 1992 films *Wayne's World* and *Rising Sun*. A well-known Filipino American ballet dancer is Maniya Barredo (b.1951), who was the first Filipina to give a solo dance concert in the US at Carnegie Hall in May 1972. Barredo served as the prima ballerina of the Atlanta Ballet and became its dance coach in 1983.

Filipino Americans had the highest rate of participation (over 75%) in the American workforce in 1990 of all US citizens. Both Filipino American men and women have higher

promising statistics, however, foreign-born Filipino Americans still experience language barriers. Some 40% of foreign-born Filipino Americans speak a native Filipino language at home, making it difficult to become truly fluent in English.

Most Filipino Americans are Roman Catholic, the predominant religion of the Philippines, dating to 400 years as a Spanish colony before the US took over in 1903. A few Filipino Americans are Protestant, and there is a minority Muslim population. Rites of passage celebrations center around Christian (or Muslim) traditions.

Along with Christian or Muslim religious holidays, Filipino Americans continue to celebrate Philippine Independence Day on 12 June with parades, cultural fairs, folk dances, and traditional foods. Rizal Day on 30 December commemorates the martyrdom of Jose Rizal, a Philippine national hero. Philippine–American Friendship Day is added to the American Independence Day celebration on 4 July.

Although early Filipino immigrants to the US worked at low-paying, seasonal jobs and therefore lived in poor, often harsh conditions, later waves of Filipino immigration have brought well-educated, highly skilled Filipinos who have been fairly successful in the American work world. The majority of Filipino Americans now have comparable incomes to the rest of the US population and enjoy a moderate to high standard of living. Foreign-born Filipino Americans in 1990 had a higher average standard of living than American-born Filipino Americans because of the higher education and skill levels of recent Filipino immigrants.

rates of participation in the labor force than those of the general US population. Over half of employed Filipino Americans work at white-collar jobs, while the rest work in service, labor, or agricultural (farming, fishing, forestry) occupations.

The medical profession has a particularly high number of Filipino American workers. Nearly every hospital in New York and New Jersey has Filipino American doctors and nurses on staff. Filipino Americans are also well represented in government and military posts, particularly in the US Navy.

Filipino Americans have largely overcome their bleak beginnings in the US, transforming themselves from a population of uneducated seasonal laborers to one of the more successful ethnic groups in America. Racial prejudice still afflicts these moderately dark-skinned people, and the legacy of discrimination and exclusion from the rest of American society still shows its scars. For the most part, however, as the US approaches the 21st century, Filipino Americans are creating better and better futures for themselves in America.

BIBLIOGRAPHY

Cordova, Fred. *Filipinos, Forgotten Asian Americans: A Pictorial Essay, 1763–circa 1963.* Text editor, Albert A. Acena. Dubuque, Iowa: Kendall/Hunt Publishing Co., 1983.

Espiritu, Yen Le. *Filipino American Lives.* Philadelphia: Temple University Press, 1995.

Mangiafico, Luciano. *Contemporary American Immigrants: Patterns of Filipino, Korean, and Chinese Settlement in the United States.* New York: Praeger, 1988.

McClain, Charles, ed. *Asian Indians, Filipinos, Other Asian Communities, and the Law.* New York: Garland Publishing, 1994.

Melegrito, Jonathan. "Who Are the Filipino Americans?" In *The Asian American Almanac,* Susan Gall, ed. Detroit: Gale Research, 1995.

Melendy, Howard Brett. *Asians in America: Filipinos, Koreans, and East Indians.* New York: Hippocrene, 1981.

Root, Maria P. P., ed. *Filipino Americans: Transformation and Identity.* Thousand Oaks, Cal.: Sage Publications, 1987.

—by D. K. Daeg de Mott

FRENCH AMERICANS

For more information on French history and culture, see **Vol 4: French**.

OVERVIEW

The French first arrived on the North American continent in 1523 when Italian explorer Giovanni da Verrazano, sailing under the auspices of the king of France, Francis I, came with his French crew in search of the Northwest Passage. Verrazano was unsuccessful, as was Jacques Cartier, who followed him in 1534. However, Cartier also came with the intention of claiming lands for France and bringing back riches. Cartier sailed up the St. Lawrence River and claimed the surrounding lands as "New France." By the early 1700s, New France had expanded to include all of the territory between what is now northeastern Canada through the American Midwest, south to New Orleans. Virtually all of North America from the Appalachian Mountains to the Missouri River was claimed by France.

Most of France's early dealings with North America involved the fur trade. French fur traders established alliances with many Native North American tribal groups, who supplied them with furs, guides, and transportation in return for European goods (see **Native North Americans**). French explorer and cartographer Samuel de Champlain arrived in 1603 and mapped much of the Northeast, including Lake Champlain, to which he gave his name. Champlain also founded Quebec and Port Royal (now called Annapolis Royal), the first permanent French settlements in North America.

French Jesuit missionaries began to arrive in the 17th century as well, establishing missions along the St. Lawrence River and around the Great Lakes. Other French explorers and traders also came to ply their trades in the 17th and 18th centuries, extending French territory further and further inland. René-Robert Cavelier, Sieur de La Salle traveled down the Mississippi River (thinking it might be the Northwest Passage) and claimed the territory of Louisiana for France, naming it after then-king Louis XIV. The French founded a number of cities during the 17th and 18th centuries that still exist today, including New Rochelle (1688), Detroit (1701), New Orleans (1718), and St. Louis (1764).

The struggle between the British and French for control of North America finally came to a head in 1754, and what is now known as the French and Indian War began. It ended nine years later, in 1763, with the defeat of the French. All of New France was turned over to Britain, except for New Orleans, which the French then ceded to Spain. Most French settlers simply adapted to the change in government, though when the American colonists revolted against British rule a few years later, the French saw their chance to get back at their conquerors and stood with the colonists in support of independence.

Many French immigrants to America in the 16th–18th centuries were Huguenots, French Calvinist Protestants who were fleeing persecution in Catholic France. Most Huguenots were middle-class merchants, skilled laborers, craftspeople, and business entrepreneurs who contributed a great deal to the early development of the American colonies. Priscilla Mullins (Molines), a French Huguenot, came to America on the *Mayflower* in 1620 and later married John Alden. Her descendants include John Quincy Adams and Henry Wadsworth Longfellow, who immortalized Priscilla in his poem *The Courtship of Miles Standish*. Many other significant early American figures were descendants of Huguenots, including Paul Revere, Frances Marion (the "Old Swamp Fox"), John Jay, and Alexander Hamilton.

During the 1790s, a number of French aristocrats fled to the US to escape persecution or even death in the French Revolution. At the same time, a revolution in the French colony of St. Dominque in the Caribbean drove out the French aristocrats there, most of whom also came to the US. A shift in French politics in 1815 then led French Bonapartists to flee to the US. Between the 1790s and 1850s, some 10,000–25,000 French immigrated to America.

French immigration has never been substantial. The largest wave occurred in 1841–1850, when 77,262 French immigrants entered the US. For the most part, conditions in France were and are good enough that few French citizens wish to leave. Those who do immigrate tend to adapt quickly to their new surroundings, assimilating completely into mainstream American culture. The only communities that have remained distinctly French are Quebec, in Canada, and New Orleans, Louisiana, where Acadians from northeastern Canada relocated and became known as Cajuns (see **Cajuns**). The state of Louisiana continues to base its legal system on the Code Napoléon (a code of laws written by Napoleon Bonaparte), the only state to do so; other states use English Common Law. There is also a somewhat less distinct French culture in New England, made up of immigrants from Quebec, who call themselves Franco-Americans.

The most-French states in the US are Vermont (23.5%), New Hampshire (18.4%), Maine (18.1%), Rhode Island (13.3%), and Louisiana (12.9%). For the most part, however, French Americans are well distributed throughout the US. The top five states in terms of numbers of French Americans are California (1,036,230), Michigan (652,472), Massachusetts (634,870), New York (625,590), and Texas (571,273). Louisiana is sixth, with 550,513 French Americans, followed by Florida (508,322), Ohio (360,184), Illinois (355,678), and Missouri (268,143). French immigration since the mid-19th century has been slight, so most French Americans are at least second-generation, if not third-, fourth-, or later-generation. The percentage of foreign-born French Americans is just slightly over 1% of the total French American population of 10,326,936, according to the 1990 US Census.

Because the French have been in America for so long, they have contributed a great deal to American culture. French place-names abound, including New Orleans, St. Louis, Detroit, New Rochelles, Cadillac, Vincennes, Eau Claire, Duluth, Sault Ste. Marie, Boise, and numerous others. Many French words have become common in American usage, such as boulevard, avenue, laissez-faire, coup, potpourri, r.s.v.p. (*répondez, s'il vous plaît*, or "respond, please"), chic, déjà vu, à la carte, and cuisine. In the realm of cuisine, Americans have adopted not only a number of French foods, but also their names and terms for their preparation: omelet, mayonnaise, hors d'oeuvres, bouillon, consommé, café au lait, canapé, croissant, éclair, vinaigrette, salade nicoise, hollandaise, parfait, coq au vin, filet, julienne, purée, à la mode, à la king, and au gratin, to name just a few.

Although many early French immigrants were Huguenots, most French Americans are Catholic. They celebrate traditional Christian rites of passage and holidays. The Cajun community in New Orleans is known for its Mardi Gras ("Fat Tuesday") festivities in February, occurring the day before Ash Wednesday, which marks the beginning of Lent. In Lowell, Massachusetts, the Franco-American community takes special notice of the Feast of St. John the Baptist on 24 June with a week-long festival, which has been held each year since 1970.

Most French immigrants to America were fairly well educated and they continued to value education highly in their new home. Girard College in Philadelphia and the Julliard School of Music in New York City were both founded by French Americans. The Gallaudet family made significant contributions to education for deaf persons. Thomas Hopkins Gallaudet founded the Hartford School for the Deaf in Connecticut and taught with sign language rather than the mouth movements commonly used at the time. His sons also served the deaf community: Thomas, Jr., established a church where deaf persons could worship; and Edward served as the president of Columbia Institution for the Deaf and the Dumb and the Blind in Washington, D. C., which was later renamed Gallaudet College in honor of Thomas, Sr.

Fanueil Hall in Boston, Massachusetts, was given to the city by Peter (Pierre) Fanueil, a second-generation French American merchant. Perhaps the most famous French contribution to American culture is the Statue of Liberty, designed by French sculptor Frédéric-Auguste Bartholdi. The statue was presented to the US by France in 1884 to commemorate the French-American alliance begun in the American Revolutionary War (1775–83) and continuing through the French Revolution (1789–93) and beyond. The site chosen for the statue was Bedloe's Island in New York Harbor, where Huguenot immigrant Isaac Bedloe had pastured his cows in the 1650s. The island was renamed Liberty Island.

There have been many successful French American writers, among them Henry David Thoreau (part French, part Scottish), Henry Wadsworth Longfellow, Edna St. Vincent Millay, John Greenleaf Whittier, Kate Chopin, Will Durant, Stephen Vincent Bené, Anaïs Nin, Paul Theroux, and Jack Kerouac (born Jean-Louis Lebris de Kerouac). French American visual artists include John James Audubon and John LaFarge (sometimes called the "father of mural painting in America").

Composer Darius Milhaud and orchestral conductor Pierre Monteux are just two of the numerous French American musicians who have added their talents to US society. On stage and screen, French Americans include actors Claudette Colbert, Charles Boyer, Nanette and Shelly Fabares, and Robert Goulet, among others. French American film director Jean Renoir is the son of the famous French Impressionist painter Pierre-Auguste Renoir.

Four US presidents so far have claimed French ancestry: John Tyler, James Garfield, Theodore Roosevelt, and Franklin Delano Roosevelt (the Roosevelts were also part Dutch). The French American La Follette family of Wisconsin spawned three generations of governors and senators, serving from 1901 into the 1930s. Jacqueline Lee Bouvier Kennedy served as the first lady of the US from 1960 to 1963 and maintained a high profile in American culture for the rest of her life. The first woman ever to deliver the keynote speech at the Republican National Convention was French American Anne Legendre

Armstrong in 1972. Armstrong later served as the US ambassador to Great Britain in 1976–1977.

French Americans have also made significant contributions to the business, science, and intellectual worlds of US society. Pierre Samuel du Pont de Nemours and his son Eleuthère Irenée du Pont de Nemours, founders of the Du Pont chemical manufacturing company, developed nylon, dacron, and teflon. Dr. Edward Trudeau established the world's first sanitarium for tuberculosis sufferers at Saranac Lake, New York, in 1884. More recently, feminist scholar Ti-Grace Atkinson has helped open new doors in Americans' and others' thinking.

Joan Benoit Samuelson, a French American, won the gold medal in the Olympic Women's Marathon in 1984, the first year it was included in the Olympic Games. French Americans Ron Guidry, James Barrett, Lou Boudreau, Jesse Burkett, and Leo Durocher have all made their mark in baseball, as has quarterback Bobby Hebert in football. Hockey is perhaps the favorite sport among French Americans and has seen many French American stars, including Mario Lemieux, Jean Beliveau, Jacques Plante, and Maurice "Rocket" Richard.

French Americans have always adapted well to American life and assimilated easily into mainstream culture. They have met with little serious discrimination and are generally well respected by other Americans. With the long-standing alliance between France and the US, dating back to the American Revolutionary War, Americans view the French as friends and therefore welcome them into their country.

BIBLIOGRAPHY

Kunz, Virginia Brainard. *The French in America*. Minneapolis: Lerner Publications, 1990.

Stone, Amy. *French Americans*. New York: Marshall Cavendish, 1995.

US Bureau of the Census. *Detailed Ancestry Groups for States*. 1990 Census of Population Supplementary Reports, CP-S-1-2. Washington, DC, October 1992.

———. *The Foreign-Born Population in the United States*. 1990 CP-3-1. Washington, DC, July 1993.

—by D. K. Daeg de Mot

FRENCH CANADIANS

ALTERNATE NAMES: Cajuns (in the US)
LOCATION: Canada (mainly Quebec); United States (mainly Louisiana and New England)
POPULATION: 6.5 million in Canada; 2–5 million in the US
LANGUAGE: French
RELIGION: Roman Catholicism
RELATED ARTICLES: Vol. 2: Canadians; Vol 4: French.

[1] INTRODUCTION

French Canadians are descendants of Canada's colonial-era French settlers. Most live in the province of Quebec, where they account for a majority of the population. French Canadians can also be found in other parts of Canada—notably in the Maritime provinces—as well as in the United States. The past 35 years have seen a strong resurgence of the French Canadians' sense of cultural identity. With this has come a political separatist movement with far-reaching implications not only for Quebec, but for all of Canada and the United States as well.

The French presence in Canada began in 1534, when the explorer Jacques Cartier claimed the Gaspé Peninsula for France; the following year, Cartier discovered the St. Lawrence River. Permanent settlement did not start until the beginning of the 17th century, when Samuel de Champlain founded Quebec City in 1608. With the discovery of the Great Lakes, the fur trade flourished and missionaries began to arrive. The French eventually carved out an enormous territory stretching east to the Maritime provinces, north to the Hudson Bay, west to the Great Lakes, and south to the Gulf of Mexico. Around 10,000 French settlers immigrated to the New World between 1608 and 1756.

By the late 17th century, France and Britain, already at war with each other in Europe, had become rivals for control of the region known as New France. After France's defeat in the French and Indian Wars which began in 1756, Britain won control of New France; and British rule was officially recognized by the Treaty of Paris in 1763. In the region of the present-day Maritime provinces, the Acadians (French Canadians from the northeast) had already come under British rule by 1713, and roughly 10,000 (out of a total population of about 13,000) were deported in 1755. Many eventually returned to their homeland, while others settled in Quebec and still others, who later became known as Cajuns, settled in Louisiana.

In spite of their British rulers' negative attitudes toward their language and culture, the French Canadians remained a distinct cultural group in Quebec and elsewhere. Contributing factors were the unifying influence of the Catholic Church, the strong tendency to marry within their own community, and the tradition of having large families. When the provinces of Quebec, Ontario, New Brunswick, and Nova Scotia joined to form the Dominion of Canada on July 1, 1867, French Canadians accounted for one-third of the new country's population.

In the 20th century, military service in the two world wars revealed the continuing cultural divisions in Canadian society. British Canadian soldiers mocked the broken English of their French counterparts, and the draft was viewed as an affront to the independent spirit of the French Canadians. After 1945, there were growing demands for political autonomy in Quebec, and, beginning in 1960, the province was swept by the "Quiet Revolution," a wave of political, educational, religious, and economic reform. The influence of the Catholic Church was greatly reduced, and a more modern and secularized French Canadian society emerged.

French was recognized as Quebec's official language in 1974, and the separatist Parti Québécois came to power in the province in 1976. A proposal for political independence from the rest of Canada was defeated at the polls in 1980, but French Canadian separatism has remained a contentious issue for both the province and the nation as a whole.

2 LOCATION AND HOMELAND

The 6.5 million French Canadians living in Canada represent about a quarter of the country's total population. The majority—5.1 million—live in Quebec, Canada's largest province. The French Canadians of the Maritime provinces—New Brunswick, Nova Scotia, and Prince Edward Island—are unified by their distinctive Acadian background and culture; they account for around 15% of the population in those provinces. There are also French Canadian communities in Ontario and the western provinces, with the greatest populations in Manitoba and Alberta. In addition, there were over 2 million persons of French Canadian descent in the United States as of the 1990 census (the actual number may be as high as 5 million). Most live in Louisiana, where they are known as Cajuns, or in New England.

3 LANGUAGE

French Canadians are the largest group of Francophones (French speakers) in North America. The majority of French Canadians are concentrated in Quebec, where they represent about 80% of that province's 6.89 million residents. About 15% of the population in the Maritime provinces (Nova Scotia, New Brunswick, and Prince Edward Island) speaks French, and there are Francophone areas in Manitoba and Ontario. Although French and English both have the status of official languages in Canada, the country is predominantly English-speaking, and Francophones are perennially concerned that their "French island" will be swallowed up in an "ocean of English." While Canada is generally considered a bilingual country, only 16% of the population is actually bilingual. About 61% speak English only and 24% French only.

The vocabulary and pronunciation of Canadian French differ from those of the language spoken in France. Québécois is based on an archaic form of French and contains many English expressions. Many terms are closer to the English than to the French form of the word. For example, "to marry" is *marier* instead of the French term, *épouser*. Similarly, "appointment" is *appointement* instead of *rendezvous*, and "ignore" is *ignorer* instead of *négliger*. Joual, a special dialect spoken in Montreal, shortens so many words by contracting and dropping syllables that it is incomprehensible to most outsiders. (For example, the phrase *Je ne suis capable* is shortened to a single syllable, pronounced "shway.")

The Acadians speak a distinctive form of French characterized by many archaic expressions preserved from the 17th-century dialects of western France. Acadian dialects differ from one region to another, and in Moncton, New Brunswick, contact with English speakers has produced a French-English called Chiac. Such hybrids are also generically known as

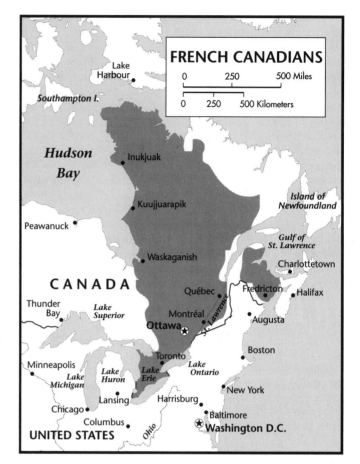

"franglais." The Canadian educational system promotes the use of modern, standard French in its French-language schools and discourages the use of both archaic expressions and the mingling of French and English.

4 FOLKLORE

The oral tradition of the French Canadians was strengthened by colonial laws against the establishment of presses and by the scarcity of French schools, both of which made it important for French Canadians to transmit their culture orally across the generations. Popular characters in French Canadian folklore include a hero figure named Ti-Jean (short for *petit* Jean, or Little John) and a hunter named Dalbec.

5 RELIGION

The majority of French Canadians are Roman Catholic. Until the 1960s, the church was central to French Canadian politics, education, health, family structure, and economic life. Since that time, however, the French Canadian community has become more secular. Church attendance has declined, and the influence of the Church on daily life has decreased. The Acadians traditionally combined Catholicism with a belief in the supernatural, including sorcery and spirits, but this phenomenon has been on the wane in recent decades.

6 MAJOR HOLIDAYS

French Canadians call Victoria Day, celebrated on the Monday preceding May 25, Dollard Day, preferring to remember a

17th-century French war hero on that date rather than Britain's Queen Victoria. The most important religious holidays for French Canadians are Christmas and Easter. Many—especially those in rural areas—still observe the traditional Christmas celebration, which includes a large midnight supper (*Réveillon*) of *tourtières* (meat pies), *ragaut* (stew), and other dishes, served after the family has returned from midnight mass on Christmas Eve. On St. Jean Baptiste Day (24 June), the Québécois celebrate their patron saint with parties, bonfires, and fireworks. The Acadians' patron saint is Our Lady of the Assumption, and Assumption Day (15 August) is their day of celebration.

7 RITES OF PASSAGE

Most French Canadians observe the major life cycle events, such as birth, marriage, and death, within the traditions of the Roman Catholic church. The government of Quebec, the home of Canada's largest French-speaking population, recognizes common-law marriage in cases where couples have lived together for two years.

8 INTERPERSONAL RELATIONS

Like their English-speaking neighbors, French Canadians are hospitable, friendly, and polite, and consider good manners important. It is common for men to open doors for women or give up a seat if a woman is standing. French Canadians use the common greeting of *Bonjour* (Good day) for "Hello" and *Au revoir* for "Good-bye." Adults use first names and informal forms of address (such as *tu* rather than *vous*) only with people they know well, such as close friends or relatives. Both men and women may exchange kisses on both cheeks in a European-style greeting. Close women friends often greet each other by embracing. The American "thumbs down" gesture is considered offensive. French Canadians consider it good manners to keep both hands above the table during a meal. Women rest their wrists against the table, while men lean on their forearms. Elbows, however, are only placed on the table after the meal is over. It is considered bad manners to eat on the street unless one is at a cafe or food stand.

9 LIVING CONDITIONS

Housing in Canada varies from one region to another, depending on the local availability of building materials. Two out of every three Canadians own their own homes. Single homes are the most common type of dwelling although the current trend is toward greater numbers of multifamily structures. The homes of the Acadians, like most of those in the Maritime provinces, are mostly built of wood.

Overall, Canadians enjoy excellent health. Canada has one of the world's lowest infant mortality rates—1 out of 100 live births, significantly better than that of the United States. Life expectancy is 74 years for men and 80 years for women. The Canadian national health plan—which has been a focus of attention in the US debate about the future of its own health care system—covers at least three-quarters of all the nation's health-care expenses. Acadians still retain some of their traditional belief in folk medicine, including herbal cures and consultation with traditional healers (who are believed to have the power to cure various illnesses or stop bleeding).

After the United States, Canada has the world's highest per capita use of motor transportation. Private automobiles are used for four-fifths of urban travel, and there is one passenger car for every two persons. Canada's severe winters make road maintenance an ongoing and expensive task. Motorists cope with sub-zero winter temperatures by plugging their cars into battery warmers overnight. The government-owned Canadian Railways (CNR) and privately owned Canadian Pacific provide rail transportation. Water transportation is heavily used for both domestic and international shipping, and international air service is provided by government-owned Air Canada and Canadian Airlines.

10 FAMILY LIFE

Until the 1960s, the family lives of French Canadians were heavily influenced by the Roman Catholic Church. Large families were the norm, because of strictures against birth control and also the desire to bolster the size of the French Canadian community. Today the average couple has only two children, and the French Canadian divorce rate is comparable to that among other groups in North America: roughly half of all newly married couples eventually divorce. The increased divorce rate has raised the number of single-parent families.

Traditionally, French Canadian women either performed agricultural labor or worked as teachers, nurses, or factory laborers. Since the 1970s, however, educational and employment opportunities for women have expanded, and women have entered the professions and other traditionally male area of the economy in increasing numbers. Quebec established an affirmative-action program for women in the early 1980s.

11 CLOTHING

French Canadians wear modern Western-style clothing. The traditional costume of the Acadians, which is still worn on special occasions, consists of white bonnets and blouses, black skirts, and white aprons for the women and white shirts, black vests, and knee-length black pants for the men. White stockings and black shoes are worn by both men and women.

12 FOOD

Quebec has a rich, distinctive French-Canadian cuisine. Popular dishes include the *tourtière*, a meat pie, and *ragoût de boulettes et de pattes do cochon*, a stew made from meatballs and pigs' feet. Other favorites also include French onion soup, pea soup, and *poutine*, a traditional dish made with French fries or grated potatoes. Quebec is also known for its maple syrup, and in early spring families enjoy traveling to one of the province's many sugar shacks for a "sugaring off," where local manufacturers sell samples of their products. In addition to candies, cookies, and other sweets, even foods such as ham and eggs are served, all cooked in maple syrup. Children enjoy eating *tourquettes*, a natural candy made by pouring boiling maple syrup onto fresh snow.

Tourtière

1½ to 2 pounds pork, ground or finely chopped
1 clove of garlic, crushed
1 medium onion, chopped
½ cup hot water
¼ teaspoon celery salt
¼ teaspoon ground cloves

salt and pepper to taste
double 9-inch pie crust, homemade or frozen

Mix the water, pork, and seasonings in a saucepan. Cook over a low flame for 20 to 25 minutes and then cool. (Optional: ¼ cup dry bread crumbs may be added at this point.) Cover the bottom of a 9-inch pie pan with bottom layer of pie dough, add pork filling, and cover with top layer of dough. Seal the crust by pinching the edges together. Preheat oven to 350°F and bake pie about 35 minutes, or until browned.

13 EDUCATION

Education in Canada is administered by each province individually, although in all cases school attendance is compulsory from the age of 6 or 7 to 15 or 16. Quebec has two parallel systems, one of which is specifically for French-speaking, Catholic students. The Acadian populations of New Brunswick, Nova Scotia, and Prince Edward Island are legally guaranteed access to French-language schools in predominantly French-speaking areas.

Most higher education in Canada is government-funded. Laval University in Quebec is Canada's oldest university, and McGill in Montreal is one of its most prestigious. The first francophone university outside Quebec, the University of Moncton in New Brunswick, was established in 1963.

14 CULTURAL HERITAGE

Canada has an extensive francophone communications network. The Canadian Broadcasting System's Radio Canada broadcasts French-language news programs, dramas, films, and sports events, as well as US programs dubbed into French. French Canadian radio stations must allot 75% of their programming to music by French recording artists. Folk and country music are especially popular with Acadians.

Leading contemporary French Canadian authors include playwright Michel Tremblay and short-story writer Mavis Gallant. Perhaps the most renowned French Canadian author of the 20th century was Gabrielle Roy, whose first novel, *The Tin Flute* (1945), drew a stark portrait that opened the eyes of many in Canada, France, and the United States to the plight of Quebec's urban poor.

15 WORK

In 1992, 73% of all civilian employees in Canada worked in service-sector jobs, 27.7% in industry, and only 3.5% in agriculture. In 1990 the average income for full-time employment among Canadians 15 years and older was $30,274. The unemployment rate in Quebec is higher than that in other provinces, and it reached 15% during the economic slump of the early 1990s.

Before the 1980s, management positions in Quebec tended to be dominated by English speakers. However, after the separatist Parti Québécois came to power in 1976, many English speakers left the province and those who remained became part of a new social order in which the socioeconomic gap between the two groups has narrowed substantially. Today there is a French Canadian bourgeoisie with interests in industry, financial institutions, and other economic strongholds. French Canadians work in the government as both managers and lower-level employees. They work in the professions and as small entrepre-

neurs. The emerging class of French entrepreneurs has traditionally favored businesses such as construction, in which they could overcome barriers posed by a lack of formal education or the need for extensive verbal contact with English-speaking clients. There is still a French-speaking working class in both unionized and nonunionized fields. Many Quebecois have performed hazardous and health-threatening work in the province's asbestos mines.

Before the 20th century, the French-speaking Acadians in the Maritime provinces participated in a subsistence economy that combined farming, fishing, and forestry. Today many engage in commercial farming and fishing; this has kept rural areas populated in spite of some migration to the cities.

16 SPORTS

Hockey, the Canadian national sport, is popular among French Canadians. Every team in the National Hockey League includes French Canadians, and Quebec has had two professional teams since 1972. The Montreal Canadiens—popularly known as the "Habitants" or "Habs"—have won the Stanley Cup, awarded to League champions, over 20 times. The exploits of Maurice Richard, the French Canadian hockey star of the 1940s and 1950s, are legendary. His suspension from the Canadiens before the 1955 Stanley Cup playoffs triggered rioting by fans that resulted in an estimated $100,000 worth of damage.

17 ENTERTAINMENT AND RECREATION

In addition to the French-language radio and television programming broadcast by the Canadian Broadcasting Corporation (CBC), Quebec also has a large audience for English-language television and radio programming and magazines. *Le Journal de Montréal* and *La Presse* are the most widely read French-language newspapers.

Like Canadians of all backgrounds, French Canadians enjoy the beautiful and varied scenery of their native land on vacation trips, one of Canada's most popular forms of recreation. Many families own small cottages in the woods or at a lake shore, which they visit on weekends and during vacations. Others prefer to travel to distant parts of the country for camping or other outdoor activities.

A time-honored pastime among French Canadian families in Quebec is the "sugaring off" ritual. Early in the spring, they head for the woods to tap maple trees for sap that is then boiled down in *cabines à sucre* ("sugar shacks") to make maple syrup and maple sugar.

18 FOLK ART, CRAFTS, AND HOBBIES

Traditional crafts among the Acadians include knitting and weaving, and colorful hooked rugs are a specialty.

19 SOCIAL PROBLEMS

The global recession of the early 1990s threw Canada into an economic slump that included double-digit unemployment from 1991 through 1994; this reached its highest level in Quebec, where unemployment was as high as 15%. French Canadians have historically occupied a lower socioeconomic position than Anglophones. Traditionally, they have not been as well educated and have suffered widespread discrimination by the English-speaking majority.

A major concern of French Canadians today is the preservation of their culture and language against the threat of assimilation into English-speaking North America, especially in light of Quebec's decreased birth rate and its large number of immigrants from many different cultures (most of them non-francophone). In both Quebec and the Maritimes, the drain of resources caused by emigration to other parts of Canada and to the United States is also a concern.

[20] BIBLIOGRAPHY

The Canadian Encyclopedia. 2nd ed. 4 vols. Edmonton: Hurtig, 1988.

Cunningham, Hilary. *Canada.* Insight Guides. Boston: Houghton Mifflin, 1992.

Gall, Timothy, and Susan Gall, ed. *Worldmark Encyclopedia of the Nations.* Detroit: Gale Research, 1995.

Kalman, Bobbie. *Canada: The Culture.* New York: Crabtree Publishing, 1993.

Labelle, Ronald. "Acadians." *Encyclopedia of World Cultures.* Boston: G. K. Hall, 1992.

Lemco, Jonathan. *Turmoil in the Peaceable Kingdom: The Quebec Sovereignty Movement and Its Implications for Canada and the United States.* Toronto: University of Toronto Press, 1994.

Malcolm, Andrew. *The Land and People of Canada.* New York: HarperCollins, 1988.

Pilon, Lise. "French Canadians." *Encyclopedia of World Cultures.* Boston: G. K. Hall, 1992.

Richler, Mordecai. *Oh Canada! Oh Quebec! Requiem for a Divided Country.* New York: Knopf, 1992.

Wartik, Nancy. *The French Canadians.* New York: Chelsea House, 1989.

Watkins, Mel, ed. *Canada.* Handbooks to the Modern World. New York: Facts on File, 1993.

Weihs, Jean. *Facts about Canada, Its Provinces, and Territories.* H. W. Wilson Co., 1995.

—by R. Wieder

FRENCH GUIANANS

LOCATION: French Guiana (French American Dependency)
POPULATION: 100,000
LANGUAGE: French; Amerindian languages; Taki-Taki
RELIGION: Roman Catholicism; traditional Amerindian beliefs

[1] INTRODUCTION

During the 17th century, explorers began to roam all over South America, enduring terrific hardships, feverishly searching for the famed Eldorado. *Eldorado* means "the golden one" and many Europeans thought they would find a city of gold. The French explorer Daniel de la Ravardiere was no exception, and traveling through previously unexplored territory in 1604 along the Cayenne River, he finally arrived at what is now Cayenne, the capital of French Guiana. Many hardships awaited the explorers and subsequent settlers. Eventually coffee, indigo, and sugarcane were cultivated. The Jesuits, famous in many parts of South America for their work with Amerindians, established several village colonies of Amerindians who had been living for centuries in the thickly forested interior of this tropical land.

In 1763 about 14,000 people disembarked at Kourou on the coast, lured by glittering promises that ended in disaster: some 11,000 people died of tropical fevers and 2,000 returned to France, shaken and disillusioned. After this catastrophe, Malouet, the French administrator, tried to reestablish the colony and by the end of the 18th century there were 1,300 Whites, 400 free Blacks and 10,500 Black slaves. Slavery was finally abolished in 1848, after many struggles and various attempts both to end it and to reintroduce it. While this was socially a progressive move, economically the plantation economy was ruined.

In 1852 French Guiana became a penal colony and the French sent many convicts there, particularly to the notorious Devil's Island. In 1855 gold was discovered, and in the ensuing gold rush, agriculture was neglected once again. Hindus who had arrived to work the land left for neighboring Brazil and Dutch Guiana.

As a penal colony French Guiana proved unproductive, and this type of status was formally abolished in 1940. Convicts who gained their freedom were not allowed to return to their country of origin but had to remain in French Guiana. With no serious attempt made to train them or to find them productive work, they became paupers, eking out a miserable existence as penniless beggars, occasionally managing to do casual work, until their deaths.

Nicol Smith, who visited the colony in the early 1940s, reported that convict labor still existed, and Smith even visited one of the large prison camps in the interior where convicts were engaged in timber logging. The governor of the time, Robert Chot, told Smith that not only were the convicts well-fed, but they were even allowed to fish and to hunt wild game such as deer, wild boar, and agouti on weekends! If this was the case, then it is quite possible that freed convicts fared worse in terms of a basic diet than when they were convicts. For many, however, freedom was preferable under any circumstances.

French Guiana ended its colonial status and became a department of France in 1964. It is governed by a prefect with

FRENCH GUIANANS

the help of an elected council and is represented in the French parliament by a deputy and a senator. French Guianans are, in effect, French citizens and, as such, have access to the European community.

2 LOCATION AND HOMELAND

French Guiana, with an area of 91,000 sq km (35,135 sq mi), is about the size of Ireland. It has an Atlantic coastline stretching 320 km (200 mi) along the north and northeast, a border with Brazil to the south, and a border with Suriname to the west. The Maroni River forms its western border with Suriname, and the Tumuc-Humuc mountains run along the southern border with Brazil. The southeastern part of the border with Brazil is formed by the Oyapock River.

French Guiana is very underpopulated for its size. Only about 100,000 people live there permanently, with about 40,000 living in the capital, Cayenne. Despite being sparsely populated, there is a colorful mixture of peoples in French Guiana. About 70% of the population, descended from a mix of French, Black and Asian Indian settlers, are known as Creoles. There are also settlements of people of Indochinese (Vietnamese) origin, since Vietnam was once a French colony. In the interior, there are several Amerindian tribes, including the Oyampi and the Palikour, who farm the tropical forests using traditional slash-and-burn methods and who still live according to their own traditions. The Gualibi Caribs live along the coast and have mingled with the Creoles. There are also black tribes-

people descended from runaway slaves, known as the Djuka, the Paramaka, and the Boni. They are descended from runaway slaves of African origin who were originally taken to the British West Indies and who escaped to the jungles of French Guiana, where access was difficult and the motivation of the locals to track them down was weak. In this way, after many hardships, they achieved their freedom and partially reverted to a lifestyle that differed from the hard life of a West Indian plantation slave, but was similar to the life their families once had in the African jungles.

3 LANGUAGE

The official language of French Guiana is French, but other languages are spoken, including a variety of Amerindian languages, while the Black tribespeople speak Taki-Taki, which is partly derived from English.

French Guiana is heavily influenced by the culture of mainland France in many ways, and girls and boys are usually given French names. Popular French boys' names such as Jean, Paul, Pierre, or Daniel are often combined, in the French manner, and become Jean Paul or Jean Pierre. Many girls have names that end in "-ette," a French diminutive that means "little": Yvette, Suzette, Jeanette. Often girls will have combined names that include "Marie" (Mary): Marie Claire, Marie José, Marie Christine, and Marie Therese. In countries with significant Catholic populations, the custom of naming a girl Maria or Marie, often used in combination with another name, is widespread and is found throughout South America. This custom is less widespread in Protestant countries because the emphasis on the Virgin Mary is not as strong as among Catholic populations.

4 FOLKLORE

Heroes vary according to the particular cultural mix, but for the historically conscious a very important figure was the abbess Mother Anne Marie Javouhey, the mother superior of St. Joseph of Cluny, who between 1827 and 1846 established a thriving colony for slaves who had been freed.

5 RELIGION

Most French Guianans are Roman Catholic, although in the tropical forests in the interior region, some Amerindian tribes follow their own spiritual and religious practices, which probably derive from Central Asia, including shamanic practices. There are also Black tribes descended from runaway slaves in the interior who have their own religious practices, and settlers from Vietnam, formerly the French colony called Indochina, who have their own religious customs. Although Buddhism was prevalent when Indochina was a colony of France, many Indochinese became Christian, and there were also tribal peoples living in more remote areas who were not Buddhist. There are also some Chinese settlers, and during the 19th century there were large numbers of Hindus who originally came from India to work in agriculture in the Guianas, particularly British Guiana and subsequently French Guiana. A number of Arabs, some of whom are Muslim, also made their way to French Guiana at a time when various countries in the Middle East were colonies of France.

Although French Guiana is mainly Catholic, it shares with some areas of the Caribbean an astonishingly varied cultural and religious background.

6 MAJOR HOLIDAYS

Major French holidays such as Bastille Day are celebrated, as are Labor Day and major Catholic holidays such as the Feast of the Assumption, Easter, and Christmas. Carnival is celebrated for the three days preceding Lent (in February) including Ash Wednesday.

7 RITES OF PASSAGE

Children are often baptized and also enjoy their First Communion, usually at the age of seven, when according to Catholic custom they receive a special name and are received into the Church. This is usually an important occasion for traditional Catholic families, and for the child it is often a memorable occasion.

Young people in French Guiana, particularly in the capital, Cayenne, are influenced by French culture as well as local customs that have developed out of their own colonial history. They enjoy dating and parties, just as young people do everywhere. Many couples marry in church.

When a person dies, a *novena* or cycle of prayers is said according to Catholic custom, and close relatives and friends are expected to visit.

8 INTERPERSONAL RELATIONS

A friendly and informal greeting in the French style is *"Salut!"* which means "Hello," whereas formal greetings would include the phrase *"Comment allez vous?"*

People in French Guiana generally enjoy social visits and festive occasions. Family occasions are important. Young people enjoy going out together, and a favorite occasion is an outing to a beach. There are good facilities for swimming just outside Cayenne, but these outings are more than sporting occasions; they are pleasant social occasions and a chance for young people or families to spend time together in a relaxed, informal manner.

9 LIVING CONDITIONS

The standard of living in French Guiana is relatively high, although the lifestyle of the Amerindians, who represent about 4% of the population, differs considerably from that of the majority Creole population.

The health of French Guianans has improved considerably over the years. In particular, the work of the Pasteur Institute has made significant gains in helping to control and reduce serious diseases such as yellow fever, malaria, and leprosy.

Heavily subsidized by the French government, the economy allows for more consumption than would otherwise be the case if French Guiana were to rely for significant income on its major exports alone.

Housing in the interior, particularly in Amerindian settlements, often consists of simple huts with thatched roofs. In Cayenne, many streets have houses built in individual and varied styles, painted in bright colors such as light blue or yellow. The brilliant tropical flowers of many small gardens add to the impression of gaiety so often found in warm climates.

In the interior, rivers are often navigable by canoe or motorboats for long stretches. In towns, people use buses and cars for transport.

10 FAMILY LIFE

Family life in French Guiana varies according to the customs of diverse settlers, but in general the family unit is close and family ties are considered very important. The Catholic faith prevalent among a majority of French Guianans also reinforces the importance of close-knit families. Families tended to be large in the past, but now many people have fewer children than in traditional families in many countries in Latin America, following a more modern trend.

11 CLOTHING

Western-style shirts and trousers for men, and blouses and skirts or cotton dresses for women, are often worn. One distinctive feature in Cayenne, the capital, is that many women are quite fashion-conscious and tend to follow French styles and tastes in dress, although there are local adaptations because French Guiana has a very warm climate.

12 FOOD

There are various types of food eaten in Cayenne because the mix of settlers, including some Chinese and, formerly, settlers from India, have all influenced the local cuisine. However, tasty fish and seafood dishes, including shrimp, are often eaten, sometimes seasoned with different spices and served with rice. The hot pepper known as cayenne, known and used in many parts of the world, takes its name from French Guiana's capital.

It is claimed that even when French Guiana was a notorious convict colony, the convicts ate comparatively well: their diet included meat and fish stews, pork, and shrimp.

13 EDUCATION

French Guiana has an 80% literacy rate. Primary schooling has been available to most people for some time, and secondary schools exist in Cayenne and some other smaller towns. Schooling is modeled on the educational system in France.

14 CULTURAL HERITAGE

Music and dance vary according to the diverse traditions of French Guiana. Black tribespeople who still live in the interior have percussion-based music and drumming, whereas some Amerindians produce quite different music where woodwind instruments have a central place. The capital, Cayenne, is Westernized to the extent that there are strong influences of more-modern music, including French ballads and pop and rock music.

15 WORK

French Guiana had a long tradition of cheap, convict-based labor, which did not bring prosperity to its inhabitants. The modern economy relies on the export of tropical hardwoods logged in Inini, the inland forested region of the country, and valuable seafoods such as shrimp. At one time gold was a major export in the mining sector, but people are now employed extracting bauxite, and diamond mining has also provided work. The fishing industry provides some employment.

A unique form of work in French Guiana is that provided by the modern space agencies located on the coast at Kourou. The European and French space agencies are both located there, and it was from Kourou that the *Ariane* rocket was fired in 1996. Unfortunately, this 10-year project failed when the *Ariane* rocket exploded in space, but millions of people around the world probably got their first look at Kourou and French Guiana's beautiful coast and starry skies on television during the rocket's launch. Work continues apace and brings in several thousand extra personnel to work in one of the most advanced industries in the world.

16 SPORTS

Water-based sports are popular with many in French Guiana and include boating, swimming, and fishing. Others enjoy soccer.

17 ENTERTAINMENT AND RECREATION

French Guianans, particularly in Cayenne, enjoy going to the movies, and watching television is also a popular pastime. Young people enjoy going to discos, and along Cayenne's main commercial areas there are now good shops with French imports, as well as cinemas, cafés, dance clubs, and nightclubs.

A favorite pastime is going to the beaches outside Cayenne for picnics and swimming, and families or groups of young people often spend the day there.

18 FOLK ART, CRAFTS, AND HOBBIES

Crafts and folk art in French Guiana derive from Black, Amerindian, and even Vietnamese artisans and include textiles, pottery, and woodcarvings. Some of the early Vietnamese (formerly called Indochinese) groups arrived in French Guiana as convicts and were later freed. Some of these, called the Hmong, live in separate villages; their carvings in wood and their weaving are particularly appreciated.

19 SOCIAL PROBLEMS

French Guiana is a land of astonishing contrasts, with tribes who live only with the basics needed for survival in the jungles of Inini on the one hand, and the most modern space technologies based in Kourou on the other, with a modern, French-oriented population of Creoles in Cayenne, and many smaller settlements along the coast as well as villages with diverse groups such as the Hmong Vietnamese.

Some people think that despite the legal status of French Guiana as simply another department of France, this is really a colony under a different name. Despite exports of minerals, seafood, and timber, French Guiana is not independent economically, but remains heavily dependent on French government subsidies for its relative prosperity. Were this situation to change, life could become very difficult for French Guianans. It is too soon to tell how the establishment of modern space agencies at Kourou will affect the local population socially and economically in the long run.

20 BIBLIOGRAPHY

Smith, Nicol. "Color Glows in the Guianas, French and Dutch." *National Geographic* (April 1943).

—by P. Pitchon

GARIFUNA

LOCATION: Eastern coasts of Belize, Guatemala, Honduras, and Nicaragua; United States; Caribbean islands
POPULATION: 200,000–500,000
LANGUAGE: Spanish; English; Garifuna
RELIGION: Catholicism, incorporating aspects of the traditional religion

1 INTRODUCTION

The Garifuna make their home along Central America's Caribbean coast in a territory that spreads across the borders of four different nations. They are descendants of the Caribs, an indigenous people of the Lesser Antilles. In the 17th and 18th centuries, Caribs on the island of St. Vincent intermarried with African slaves whom they captured in raids on European settlements or who escaped from their captors. According to some accounts, the resulting people, known as Black Caribs, formed a separate group distinct from other Caribs in the region, later called "Yellow" or "Red." However, other sources claim that the island people themselves recognized no such distinction and that these color designations were later applied solely by Europeans, who arbitrarily divided the native people into different groups based on skin color.

However the distinction came about, the Black Caribs, unsuccessful in their protracted resistance to British colonization of St. Vincent, were deported to the island of Roatan off the coast of Honduras in 1797. The deportees, who represented only about one-fourth of the former Black Carib population, managed to survive and reestablish their culture in an unfamiliar setting. They eventually migrated to the Central American mainland, where they settled mainly in the coastal lowlands of Honduras, Guatemala, Nicaragua, and Belize (then known as British Honduras).

Over the next two centuries, both their population and territory expanded significantly, and they formed a major part of the work force on the Central American coast for over 100 years. In 1823 additional Black Caribs migrated to Belize, forced out of Honduras by a civil war in that country. In spite of their relocation to new territories and their incorporation of other local Black populations, the Garifuna have maintained a distinct cultural identity, preserving both the language and many of the customs, beliefs, and rituals of their island ancestors.

2 LOCATION AND HOMELAND

The Garifuna live in a succession of villages and towns along the eastern coasts of Belize, Guatemala, Honduras, and Nicaragua. These Caribbean lowlands have a varied terrain that includes mangrove swamps, tropical rain forests, river valleys, coastal plains, and pine and palm savannas. Many Garifuna have emigrated to large cities in Central America and the United States. Those in the US live primarily in enclaves in New York, Chicago, Los Angeles, and other major cities. There are also small groups of Garifuna on the Caribbean islands of Trinidad, Dominica, and St. Vincent.

Due to their geographic dispersion, it is impossible to arrive at exact demographic figures for the Garifuna population (in addition, only Belize counts them as a distinct ethnic group). Their total numbers have been estimated at anywhere between

200,000 and 500,000. Some estimates place the Garifuna community in the United States alone at around 100,000.

³LANGUAGE

Spanish is the official language of the countries in which the Garifuna live, except for Belize and the US, where the official language is English. The native language of the Garifuna (called Garifuna or Garinagu) is derived from the Arawak and Carib languages of their island ancestors.

⁴FOLKLORE

Although it has long been illegal, *obeah,* the traditional witchcraft or voodoo of the Caribbean, is still practiced in secret by some Garifuna. Its rituals involve dances, drumming, and trances in which the dead are contacted, and it is generally used either to harm one's enemies or to ward off spells one fears from others. A characteristic object used in such spells is the *puchinga* doll made of cloth stuffed with black feathers and buried under the doorstep of the intended victim. Crosses are sometimes painted on children's foreheads to ward off the evil eye.

⁵RELIGION

The Garifuna practice a version of Catholicism that incorporates many aspects of their traditional religion, mingling a belief in saints with reverence toward *gubida,* the spirits of their ancestors, and faith in shamans or "spirit helpers" (called *buwiyes*). Their religious practices—which encompass dancing, singing, drumming, and alcohol—have long been considered suspect by established churches and surrounding communities, which have accused them of paganism and devil worship. Some buwiyes have served as Roman Catholic priests or nuns.

Among the most important traditional religious practices is the *dugu,* a ritual feast held to appease the gubida when they are thought to be angry at a living relative (which manifests itself most typically in an illness suffered by that person). A dugu lasts from two to four days and is attended by both friends and relatives of the affected person, who sometimes come all the way from the United States in order to attend. Lavish amounts of food are prepared—both traditional dishes that were favored by the gubida (such as cassava bread, pork and plantains) and foods that are currently popular (including rice and beans, cheddar cheese, and soda pop). The participants engage in ritual song and dance, led by a buwiye, who calls forth the gubida. After the contents of the feast, together with rum, have been ceremonially offered to the ancestral spirit, they are either thrown into the sea or buried underground.

⁶MAJOR HOLIDAYS

Many Garifuna ritual observances are held on the holy days of the Christian calendar, but some occur on the dates of secular holidays as well. Festivities generally include processions and street dancing, often in masks and costumes. John Canoe (*Yankunu*) dancers perform at Christmastime and receive money, drinks, or homemade candies for their efforts.

On 19 November, the Garifuna of Belize celebrate Settlement Day, commemorating the original establishment of a significant Garifuna presence in that country in 1823, when a number of their ancestors, forced out of Honduras, arrived there

to join the small band already settled at Stann Creek. In Dangriga, the center of Belize's Garifuna community, there is a ritual reenactment of the settlers' arrival by celebrants who row in from the ocean in dugout canoes. Their cargo duplicates that carried by their ancestors: rudimentary cooking utensils, drums, cassava roots, and banana tree saplings. When they land on the shore, they are joined by hundreds of spectators in a lively procession that winds through the streets of Dangriga to the Catholic church and ends with a special ceremony. Afterwards, the crowd continues the festivities by dancing and feasting on traditional Garifuna foods.

⁷RITES OF PASSAGE

Major life transitions (such as birth, puberty, and death) are marked by religious ceremonies that combine Catholic traditions with ancestral rites.

⁸INTERPERSONAL RELATIONS

Physical violence is rare among the Garifuna. Aggression is almost always sublimated in such practices as name-calling, cursing, gossip, and satirical songs, and an aggrieved person may even resort to the form of witchcraft known as *obeah* for revenge.

⁹LIVING CONDITIONS

Houses are typically either wooden or made of wattle and daub with thatch roofs. Wooden houses are raised several feet off the ground on posts and may have porches. Many villages still have no electricity, and in the towns, where it is more common, there are frequent power outages. Garbage is often thrown into the sea or disposed of in open ditches and streams; in some cases, it is tossed out the back door. Most houses have no sanitary facilities.

The growing consumption of "junk food," including many fried foods and foods high in refined sugar, has lowered the nutritional level of the Garifuna diet, and obesity has become common among the women. Protein deficiencies are widespread among preschoolers. The Garifuna use both modern medicine and folk remedies ("bush medicines") but retain their traditional belief that the most important determinant of health is the power wielded by the spirits of their ancestors.

¹⁰FAMILY LIFE

It is common for women to bear children without having established a permanent or legal relationship with the father, and legal marriage forms the basis of only a minority of households. Due to the centrality of women to family life, the Garifuna are generally considered a matrifocal society. In the past, households were often made up of three generations of women. Increasingly, however, only the oldest and youngest generations remain, as the adult population of working age emigrates in search of better employment opportunities, leaving the grandparents behind to rear the children. Since the 1960s, many women have emigrated to major cities in Central America or the United States, where they are employed in the textile industry or find work as maids.

Garifuna mothers do not display the same level of physical involvement with their children as do mothers in many comparable cultures, a fact that observers have correlated with a perceived tendency toward independence and individualism in the culture. Mothers wean children early, in some cases do not breast-feed at all, and easily leave them with caregivers for short or long periods of time. In keeping with the generally nonviolent nature of the Garifuna, children are raised with little or no corporal punishment. Fights among children themselves are frowned upon and firmly broken up by adults. The elderly commonly attempt to control the behavior of younger family members by threatening to withhold their inheritance. Domestic violence is also extremely rare among the Garifuna.

11 CLOTHING

Most Garifuna wear modern Western-style clothing. Even among the older women, very few still wear the traditional shell-trimmed ethnic costumes. However, the brightly colored full skirts that many wear, together with the kerchiefs worn on their heads, do give them a distinctive appearance compared to the younger women, who wear jeans, tee-shirts, and tight skirts that could be seen in virtually any locale. The men also wear jeans, and these days the traditional straw hats have been replaced by baseball caps. Young people's attire has been influenced by the emigration patterns of their parents and peers, and in the towns one may see some of them sporting the latest fashions from New York—a favorite emigration destination—paid for with remittances sent by relatives abroad.

12 FOOD

Dietary staples include rice, fish, green bananas, plantains, and coconut milk, which is used to prepare many dishes, such as *hudut,* where it is mixed with pounded boiled plantains. The green bananas are boiled and served as a starchy vegetable. "Boil-up," or *falmou,* is adapted from the spicy pepperpot of the Garifuna's island ancestors, and its milder present-day version consists of fish, tubers, and coconut milk. While manioc or cassava plays an especially prominent role in the diet of the Garifuna in Honduras, who eat it boiled as a vegetable, it is important throughout the culture as the basic ingredient of the flatbread called *areba.* This food and the customs surrounding its preparation have long been among the central unifying traditions of the Garifuna, whose very name is based on the term *karifuna,* which means "of the cassava clan."

Cassava roots were traditionally grated by hand on stone-studded wooden boards, a lengthy and tedious job formerly relieved by group singing and today often avoided altogether by the use of electric graters. The resulting pulp is then strained by hand in 2 m (6 ft) long bags made from woven leaves, which are hung from a tree and weighted at the bottom to squeeze out the starch and juices (which are poisonous). The white meal that remains is left to dry overnight, sifted, and made into the dry flatbread that still connects the Garifuna with their ancestors.

The most popular beverages are coffee and various "bush teas," sweetened by generous amounts of sugar. Common desserts include cakes and puddings made from sweet potatoes, rice, and bread scraps. An especially popular dessert is the candy called *tableta,* made with grated coconut, ginger root, and brown sugar. The ingredients are boiled until they stick together, poured into a greased pan to cool, and either cut up or broken into squares. Children may be seen selling this confection, which is a favorite among tourists, at bus stops and other public places. In recent years, "junk foods" high in fats and refined sugar have become popular with many Garifuna, and cooking styles for many dishes have changed from boiling and roasting to frying.

13 EDUCATION

School attendance is generally low beyond the primary grades. However, rudimentary levels of literacy are valued and most Garifuna do receive sufficient schooling to attain them. Most are also interested in improving their command of either Spanish (in Honduras and Guatemala) or English (in Belize). A higher level of educational achievement is common among the Garifuna of Belize, many of whom have excelled as schoolteachers.

14 CULTURAL HERITAGE

The Garifuna have a rich heritage with roots in both African and indigenous cultures. Their traditional music, which includes work songs, hymns, lullabies, ballads, and healing songs, is characterized by African-influenced call-and-response patterns and complex drum rhythms. A number of songs are typically sung as an accompaniment to daily tasks, such as the baking of cassava bread *(areba).*

The most characteristic Garifuna dance is the *punta,* which has its roots in African courtship dances. It is performed by couples, who compete for attention from spectators and fellow dancers with their fancy and flirtatious moves. The *paranda* is a slow dance performed only by women, who dance in a circle with a shuffling movement and traditional hand movements and sing as they dance. A sacred dance, the *abaimahani,* is performed at the *dugu,* a feast held for the spirit of a deceased ancestor. The dancers—all women—form a long line, linking little fingers, and sing special music for the occasion. The *Wanaragua* or *John Canoe* dance, typically performed at Christmastime, includes songs lamenting the absence of loved ones.

While maintaining the older cultural traditions, the Garifuna are also forging new ones of their own. Contemporary musicians have transformed the age-old music that accompanies the punta, creating the popular "punta rock." The paintings of internationally acclaimed artist Benjamin Nicholas depict aspects of Garifuna history and culture in bold, modern styles. A group of young Garifuna emigrés in Los Angeles created the Walagante Dance Group to perpetuate the traditional dances of their people.

15 WORK

The Garifuna have traditionally lived by fishing and small-scale subsistence farming. In the 20th century, the banana industry became a major employer, creating jobs both in the agricultural field itself and in the major ports that sprang up along the coast. Since World War II, many Garifuna have sought employment with the United States merchant marine. Currently, however, the largest segment of the work force consists of underemployed wage laborers, and many Garifuna have emigrated to other countries, especially the United States, in search of better employment opportunities.

In the towns, those Garifuna who still farm often travel 5 to 10 miles to their plots, leaving early in the morning by bus and returning late in the afternoon. The civil service, especially the teaching profession, has been a major employer of Garifuna in Belize. Many children of Garifuna emigrants to the United

States enter the professions—including medicine, engineering, and education—some returning home and others remaining abroad permanently.

16 SPORTS

Soccer is a popular sport among the Garifuna. Young people organize games on flat open areas in their towns or villages or on the beach.

17 ENTERTAINMENT AND RECREATION

Punta parties, named for the lively and sexually provocative traditional dance that is performed at them, are a favorite form of entertainment. Pop musicians have developed "punta rock," which combines the beat of traditional punta music with the electric guitar sounds of rock music and contemporary Garifuna lyrics. This music, which originated in Belize, is becoming popular throughout the Caribbean. In a reverse development, the Garifuna have adapted the popular West Indian reggae music in a form of their own called *cungo.*

Today, many Garifuna households in the larger towns have television sets. Television is also a preferred form of recreation among the Garifuna when they emigrate abroad, and a TV is one of the first purchases of Garifuna emigrants to the United States.

18 FOLK ART, CRAFTS, AND HOBBIES

So few of the Garifuna still practice the group's traditional crafts—including hat-making, drum-making, basket-weaving, and the carving of dugout canoes—that the National Garifuna Council of Belize held a workshop in 1987 to teach them to young people to help them preserve the heritage of their ancestors.

19 SOCIAL PROBLEMS

The lack of promising employment opportunities in their native regions has led many Garifuna to emigrate to other parts of Central America and to the United States, affecting the structure of both families and communities—it has been estimated that as many as 50% of the men are absent from the average Garifuna community at any given time. With growing numbers of women also emigrating, communities are essentially being depleted of an entire generation of working-age adults. The elderly and very young are left to survive together, often on remittances by absent family members, until the young people are old enough to emigrate as well.

In recent years there has been increased concern about alcoholism among the Garifuna. While alcohol consumption itself has risen—a fact that some have attributed to the social dislocations caused by unemployment and emigration—it is also the case that consumption levels formerly considered acceptable are now regarded as excessive. Marijuana use—mainly by young men—has become common among Garifuna living in towns.

20 BIBLIOGRAPHY

Gonzalez, Nancie. *Sojourners of the Caribbean: Ethnogenesis and Ethnohistory of the Garifuna.* Urbana, IL: University of Illinois Press, 1988.

———. "Garifuna." In *Encyclopedia of World Cultures.* Boston: G. K. Hall, 1992.

Gullick, C. J. *Myths of a Minority.* Assen: Van Gorcum Press, 1985.

Kerns, Virginia. *Women and the Ancestors: Black Carib Kinship and Ritual.* Urbana, IL: University of Illinois Press, 1983.

Mallan, Chicki. *Belize Handbook.* Chico, CA.: Moon Publications, 1995.

Olson, James S. *The Indians of Central and South America: An Ethnohistorical Dictionary.* New York: Greenwood Press, 1991.

Sletto, Jacqueline Wiora. "Ancestral Ties That Bind." *Americas* 43, no 1 (1991): 21–27.

Whitten, Norman E., Jr. "Ethnogenesis." In *Encyclopedia of Cultural Anthropology,* edited by David Levinson and Melvin Ember. New York: Holt and Co., 1996.

Wilk, Richard, and Mac Chapin. "Belize: Land Tenure and Ethnicity." *Cultural Survival Quarterly* 16, no 3 (1992): 41.

—by R. Wieder

GERMAN AMERICANS

For more information on German history and culture, *see* **Vol. 4: Germans**.

OVERVIEW

Germans began immigrating to America in colonial times. By 1776, the German population in America had reached about 225,000. The founding of Germantown, Pennsylvania, in 1683 is considered to be the birth of the real German presence in America. More and more families came to join the original 34 settlers, and by 1790 the Germantown population had grown as high as 3,000, or 556 families. Most of these early German settlers were farmers or craftspeople. German American farmers introduced diversified farming (planting a variety of crops), crop rotation, and the use of fertilizers (manure, red clover, and gypsum, or lime) to American farming.

Germany did not become a unified nation until 1871, so prior to that time, German-speaking immigrants were not "German" but rather hailed from various regions or small states. In the 1700s, most came from the southern and western areas of today's Germany, along the Rhine River. The majority were Protestants, such as Mennonites, Amish, Reformed, and other Anabaptist sects, fleeing religious persecution. Many settled in the religiously tolerant colony of Pennsylvania. German immigrants of the 1800s tended to come from northern and eastern regions, such as Prussia, Bavaria, and Saxony. They came not for religious but political freedom. Whether driven by religious or political motives, all German immigrants came to America looking for improved economic opportunities as well.

A small (4,000–10,000) but significant group of Germans came to the US in 1848, after the failure of a political revolution and social reform movement in Germany. The "forty-eighters," as they were called, were radical intellectuals who, as the leaders of the failed revolution, needed to escape the consequences of their failure. They were quite different from the farmers and craftspeople who had preceded them to America, and conflicts arose between the old immigrants, called the "Grays," and the new immigrants, known as the "Greens." However, the intellectuals' presence gave a new depth and vitality to the German American community and gave them a more powerful voice in national politics.

Most German Americans were against slavery and many fought with the Union Army in the American Civil War (1861–65). There were also a number of German American soldiers in the Confederate Army, but eventually the German American community fell in fairly solidly behind President Lincoln. The German American vote helped elect Lincoln, and they remained his staunch supporters. The German Americans were also instrumental in the labor union movement of the late 1880s. German American craftspeople had brought their guild system along with them to America. These craft guilds evolved into trade unions, giving rise to the general labor union movement.

Although Germans had been immigrating to the US in huge numbers since the 1830s (surpassed only by the Irish), they were eclipsed in the Great Migration of 1880–1920 by southern and eastern Europeans who began flocking to America. Compared to these new "foreigners," German Americans seemed to be members of the old, settled establishment. Until the outbreak of World War I, when anti-German hysteria erupted, German Americans became part of the status quo in the US. Their presence was so strong in some communities that new immigrants wondered if they had immigrated to America or to Germany!

All this changed, however, with the start of World War I. German Americans suddenly became the face of the enemy, and they were subjected to violent harassment. Anything remotely "German" was attacked and/or destroyed. Books were burned, street names changed, German businesses boycotted. Music by German composers, such as Beethoven, was removed from public performances. Even hamburgers, sauerkraut, and dachshunds were renamed "liberty burgers," "liberty cabbage," and "liberty hounds." German Americans were physically attacked, tarred and feathered, and even killed. Robert Paul Prager, a German-born coal miner, was lynched by a hyperpatriotic mob in 1918. Prager became the symbol of anti-German violence. On 5 April 1992, the first annual Prager Memorial Day was held in remembrance of all the victims of anti-German hysteria during World War I.

After World War I ended, thousands fled the resulting economic disaster in Germany. Between 1919 and 1933, some 430,000 Germans emigrated to the US. Many were Jewish (see **Jewish Americans**). As a result of the anti-German sentiment in the US, German Americans had gone underground, hiding their ethnicity and attempting to blend in as much as possible with mainstream American society. Many Americanized their names. German heritage festivals were suspended for a number of years. The new immigrants joined in the drive to be assimilated, losing their Germanness as quickly as possible.

When Hitler came to power in Germany, another surge of intellectuals, many of them Jewish, fled his regime and came to the US. A total of 130,000 Germans immigrated to the US between 1933 and 1945. German Americans already in the US did not support Hitler, either. Most were decisively anti-Nazi; the rest were indifferent. German Americans made up one-third of US armed forces during World War II. Anti-German sentiment began to wane in America with the German Americans' obvious show of support for the Allied cause.

It was not until recent decades, however, that German Americans began to reclaim their ethnic heritage. The new climate of multiculturalism and the demise of communist East Germany has lessened people's fear of German Americans. Cultural festivals have reemerged, and Oktoberfests are now popular among German and non-German Americans alike. German immigrants continue to come to America's shores. In 1980, the US Census showed that German Americans had surpassed British Americans as the largest ethnic group in America. Today, German Americans make up almost one-fourth (23.3%) of the total US population.

According to the US Census, 57,985,595 Americans claimed some German ancestry in 1990. Only a small percentage (less than 4%) are foreign-born. Most German Americans are, therefore, at least second- or third-generation. German Americans are both the largest ethnic group in America and the most widely dispersed. They are spread across the US, although the highest concentrations remain in the middle Atlantic and midwestern states of early German American settlement. Wisconsin and Minnesota have the highest percentages of German Americans in their total state populations. The

largest numbers of German Americans live in California (4,940,252), Pennsylvania (4,316,386), Ohio (4,070,387), Illinois (3,327,767), and Texas (2,951,726).

Because German Americans have been in the US for so long and are so numerous, they have made countless contributions to American culture. German words now in common usage in the US include *kindergarten*, *gesundheit*, *ouch*, *delicatessen*, *blitz*, *sauerkraut*, and *wiener*. Dozens of cities, towns, and streets are named after German people or places. Many of the Christmas traditions now seen as standard in America, such as Christmas trees (*Tannenbaum*) and Santa Claus (Kris Kringle), were introduced by German Americans, as were New Year's Eve festivities. Early German settlers also brought with them a much more relaxed attitude toward the Sabbath than that preached by the Puritans. German Americans transformed Sundays in America from days of rigid observances to days of rest and relaxation.

Food is extremely important to German Americans; they love to gather to eat and drink. Beer, a German specialty, has become one of the favorite beverages in America. Most American brewing companies, such as Pabst, Anheuser-Busch, and Schlitz, were founded by German Americans. The Heinz, Hershey, Kraft, and Fleischmann companies were also founded by German Americans. Other foods introduced by German Americans that are now common fare in American diets include frankfurters, hamburgers, sauerkraut (although some credit Polish Americans with this addition), potato salad, bratwurst, liverwurst, and pretzels.

Two German American women also gave us kindergarten. Caroline Louisa Frankenberg and Margarethe Meyer Schurz are both credited with opening the first kindergarten in the US in the 1850s. By the 1870s, kindergartens had become part of the public education system. German Americans also introduced physical education into the American school system.

So many German Americans have made significant contributions to American arts and letters that it would be impossible to list them all. Germans love music, and German Americans established a multitude of music halls, opera societies, and choral festivals. In 1890, 89 of the 94 performers with the New York Philharmonic Orchestra were German born. One well-known German American visual artist was landscape painter Albert Bierstadt (1830–1902), a member of the Hudson River School of painters. An important architect was Ludwig Mies van der Rohe. Cartoonist Thomas Nast created the political symbols of the Republican elephant and Democratic donkey in the late 1870s, and Charles Schulz created the much-loved *Peanuts* comic strip.

A few of the better-known German American writers are H. L. Mencken, Theodore Dreiser, John Steinbeck, Kurt Vonnegut, and Louise Erdrich (who is also part Chippewa). Well-known German American figures in the world of film include directors Ernst Lubitsch and Billy Wilder; producer Florenz Ziegfeld of the 1920s' Ziegfeld Follies; playwright and lyricist Kurt Weill; and actors Marlene Dietrich, Grace Kelly, Lotte Lenya, and Rod Steiger. Four very well-known German Americans engaged in a different form of theater—Alfred, Otto,

Charles, and John Ringling—created the Ringling Brothers' Circus, and later bought out their competitor, Barnum and Bailey, to become the largest circus enterprise in the US. The Ringling Brothers' Barnum and Bailey Circus was owned and run by members of the Ringling family until it was sold in 1967, retaining the Ringling name.

German Americans have made countless contributions as well to the worlds of science and industry. Among the most famous are physicists Albert Einstein, J. Robert Oppenheimer, and Wernher Von Braun; anthropologist Franz Boas; millionaire John Jacob Astor; piano manufacturer Henry Engelhard (Steinweg) Steinway; automobile manufacturers Henry and Clement Studebaker; Levi Strauss, inventor of denim blue jeans; presidential advisor and US secretary of state, Henry Kissinger; and US presidents Herbert Hoover and Dwight D. Eisenhower.

Babe Ruth and Lou Gehrig are two of the many successful German American baseball players. Swimmer Johnny Weissmuller gained fame playing the character "Tarzan" in several movies in the 1940s, and Gertrude Ederle became the first woman to swim the English Channel in 1926.

Radical pro-Aryan (neo-Nazi) groups represent only a tiny fraction of German Americans in the US but create problems for all German Americans as they fuel lingering fears that "all Germans are Nazis." Other German American organizations do whatever they can to offset the negative impression given by neo-Nazi activists. German American Day was officially proclaimed by President Ronald Reagan in 1987 to be forever after celebrated on 6 October, the date on which Germantown, Pennsylvania, was founded in 1683. Oktoberfests and other cultural festivals help promote understanding of German American heritage and traditions among German and non-German Americans alike. As German Americans now make up almost one-fourth of the total US population, anti-German discrimination is mostly a thing of the past.

BIBLIOGRAPHY

Cook, Bernard A., and Rosemary Petralle Cook. *German Americans*. Vero Beach, FL: Rourke Corporation, 1991.

Galicich, Anne. *The German Americans*. New York: Chelsea House, 1996.

Schouweiler, Thomas. *Germans in America*. Minneapolis: Lerner Publications, 1994.

Tolzmann, Don Heinrich. "The German-American Legacy." *German Life* 1, no. 1 (31 July 1994): 46.

US Bureau of the Census. *Detailed Ancestry Groups for States*. 1990 Census of Population Supplementary Reports, CP-S-1-2. Washington, DC, October 1992.

———. *The Foreign-Born Population in the United States*. 1990 CP-3-1. Washington, DC, July 1993.

—by D. K. Daeg de Mott

GREEK AMERICANS

For more information on Greek history and culture, *see* **Vol. 4: Greeks**.

OVERVIEW

Few Greeks immigrated to the US before the late 1800s, except a small number who fled during the Greek uprising against the Ottoman Empire in the 1820s. Greek war orphans from that uprising were also adopted by Americans. However, most Greek Americans today are descended from immigrants who came to the US during the Great Migration of about 1880–1920. The majority of Greek immigrants were young men from the southern peninusula of Greece, known as the Peloponnesus region, who hoped to work hard in the US, save up a sizeable amount of money, and then return to Greece. By 1925, one out of every four Greek men between the ages of 15 and 45 had gone to the US. About 40% who immigrated between 1908 and 1931 did return to Greece, but the rest stayed in America. A few returned to Greece to marry and then brought their wives back to the US.

These first Greek immigrants were farmers who suffered from poverty because of disruptions in the Greek economy and a population explosion resulting from improvements in sanitation and medicine. Most were uneducated and illiterate and had few job skills to offer in the industrialized work world of the US. They took whatever jobs they could find, usually for very low wages. Many were exploited by *padroni* (contractors who brought primarily Italian immigrants to the US) but even most of those treated like virtual slaves managed to survive and tuck away bits of money to build up their savings slowly.

Most Greek immigrants eventually opened their own businesses. They tended to specialize in shoeshine stands, florist shops, grocery stores, confectionaries, fruit stands, and restaurants, particularly diners. Many of these businesses still exist today, as a high percentage of Greek Americans continue to own their own businesses.

The Immigration Act of 1924 restricted the numbers of immigrants allowed into the US from each country, slowing Greek immigration significantly. World War II (1939–45) and the Greek Civil War (1947–49) further reduced Greek immigration until about 1950. In return for its allies' support, the US passed the Refugee Relief Act to allow refugees from countries devastated by World War II to immigrate to America. Many Greeks took advantage of this opportunity, and the number of Greek immigrants rose dramatically. Another wave of Greek immigration began in the late 1960s when an oppressive regime took over the Greek government and many Greeks decided to flee. Immigration reforms in the US made entering the US much easier by removing many of the previous restrictions. Most of the Greek immigrants to the US since World War II have come to stay, and many are women and professionals.

Greek Americans suffered discrimination at first, which could at times turn violent. But for the most part, Greek Americans had an easier time becoming assimilated because so much of American culture is based on ancient Greek ideals. Although the values of modern Greeks differ greatly from those of ancient Greece, the values of democracy, hard work, and independence have remained constant. Among the educated elite of

America, a number of Hellenic societies extolled the virtues of Greece and welcomed Greek immigrants to the shores of the US. Despite some initial difficulties, therefore, Greek Americans have found themselves largely compatible with US society.

The total Greek American population today is uncertain, with estimates ranging anywhere from 500,000 to 3,000,000. Some 1,112,570 persons reported themselves to be of Greek or Greek Cypriot (from the island of Cyprus) ancestry on the 1990 US Census. Whatever their actual numbers, it is certain that Greek Americans comprise the largest Greek community outside of Greece.

Although Greek Americans are spread across the US, over one-third (37%) live in the northeast. Massachusetts and New Hampshire have the highest percentage of Greek Americans in their total state populations. The top five states with the largest numbers of Greek Americans are (in descending order) New York, California, Illinois, Massachusetts, and Florida. Greek Americans tend to cluster in cities; about 160,000 live in New York City, 88,000 in Chicago, and 76,000 in the Boston area. Only a few of the original "Greektowns" still exist, including Astoria in the Queens borough of New York City, and the Greektown in Detroit. Formerly, Greektowns were located in Lowell, Massachusetts; Salt Lake City, Utah; Tarpon Springs, Florida (where Greek Americans ran a profitable sponge-diving business); St. Louis, Missouri; Chicago, Illinois; and New York City; as well as others on Long Island and across New York State.

The Greek and English languages differ from each other significantly in both spoken and written forms. Most early Greek Americans were illiterate in Greek, however, so the written differences between the languages did not pose a problem for them, since they could not read or write Greek anyway. Many recent Greek immigrants to the US are well educated and already have some English proficiency when they arrive. Therefore, English language ability has not presented a serious obstacle to Greek Americans for the most part. First-generation Greek Americans worked hard to acquire English language skills, and subsequent generations grew up speaking English as their native language. Most second- and third-generation Greek Americans, in fact, never learned Greek.

Many Greek Americans anglicized or shortened their names, particularly those with long surnames, such as Michael Anagnostopoulos (1837–1906), a Latin and Greek teacher at Perkins Institute for the Blind in Boston, who came to be known simply as Anagnos. (Anagnos was one of Helen Keller's teachers.) Traditionally, Greek children are named after their grandparents, and a large number of Greek Americans continue this tradition.

Greek American community life centers around the church, which serves cultural and social, as well as religious, purposes. One of the first things early Greek American communities did was to raise money to build a church. Greek Americans are almost exclusively Eastern (or Greek) Orthodox. They follow Eastern Orthodox birth and death rituals, such as bringing a baby to church 40 days after birth to be blessed and having the child christened within a year after that. When a Greek American dies, a wake is held, with the funeral the following day.

Easter is the most important holiday for Eastern Orthodox Greek Americans. (So that Easter will always come after the Jewish Passover, the Eastern Orthodox Church sometimes cele-brates it one week later than the Western Christian Church. It always occurs sometime in early spring.) Good Friday and Great Saturday services build up to the joyous celebration of Easter Sunday. Christmas (25 December) and Epiphany (6 January) are also important, as is Holy Apostles' Day (29 June), which honors saints Peter and Paul (believed to be the "fathers" of the Christian Church).

Greek Americans also celebrate Greek Independence Day on 25 March, with parades in traditional costumes, speeches, and folk dances. Another secular holiday celebrated by Greek Americans is "No" Day on 28 October, which commemorates the day when the Greek government refused to give in to the Fascists during World War II (1939–45).

To provide a sense of community and mutual support, early Greek Americans formed cultural associations. More than 60 of these associations exist in the US today. Greek cultural associations have helped many Greek Americans adapt to life in America and become successful in US society. Greek Americans are now among the wealthiest of all ethnic groups in the US. Few Greek Americans live below the poverty line. With each succeeding generation, more Greek Americans pursue higher education, are able to enter more skilled professions, and earn higher wages. Therefore, the average income of Greek Americans continues to go up.

Greek Americans take marriage and family very seriously. Although recently on the rise, the divorce rate among Greek Americans is still quite low compared with that of other ethnic groups. First- and second-generation Greek Americans usually marry other Greek Americans, but later generations have begun to marry outside their ethnic boundaries to an increasing degree. Traditional Greek families are quite close and often live in extended family groups. Today's Greek American families are becoming less closely bonded and are more likely to live in nuclear family units. Elderly Greek Americans are also more likely these days to be admitted to a nursing home rather than be cared for at home by family members.

Greek food has become quite popular among the general population of the US. Gyro sandwiches, pita bread, feta cheese, and baklava are enjoyed by Greek and non-Greek Americans alike. Many American cooks are learning the art of baking with phyllo dough (paper-thin sheets of pastry dough). Greek restaurants and diners serve traditional Greek foods (which emphasize lamb and goat meats) with the addition of beef, which is more plentiful in the US and more familiar to American palates than goat meat.

Food is important to Greek Americans and symbolizes friendship, love, and human connection. It is considered an insult to the host if a guest does not eat. The refusal to accept someone's offer of food is seen as a rejection of that person's friendship.

Traditional Greek customs and culture are taught at Greek afternoon and day schools to American-born Greek American children. Although there are currently some 400 afternoon schools with a total of 27,000 students, and 24 day schools (mostly kindergarten–eighth grade) with a total of 6,500 students, attendance is declining rapidly. Thoroughly Americanized third- and fourth-generation Greek American children resent spending their afternoons learning a language and traditions that seem irrelevant to them, when their friends are busy playing or enjoying extracurricular activities.

Early Greek American college students formed intellectual societies, such as the Plato Society founded in Boston in the early 1900s. The first university club in the US was Helicon, established at Harvard in 1911 by Greek American students. These students were members of an elite minority, however. Most Greek Americans were not well educated and did not encourage their children to pursue secondary or higher education. Although attendance rates for Greek Americans at all levels of education are improving, Greek Americans are still among the least formally educated of all ethnic groups in the US.

Greek architecture, with its massive simplicity and soaring columns, has greatly influenced American building construction. The wings of the US Capitol building in Washington, D.C., were designed in the Greek Revival style by Thomas Walter in 1865. Greek American artist Constantino Brumidi (1805–1880) then painted Greek-style frescoes on the ceilings and walls of the Capitol building.

Many other Greek Americans have contributed to American culture, including opera diva Maria Callas (1923–1977); writer Nicholas Gage; Academy Award-winning director Elia Kazan; actor/director John Cassavetes (b.1929); and actors Telly Savalas (1926–1994), best known as TV detective "Kojak"; and Olympia Dukakis, the cousin of Massachusetts governor and one-time US presidential candidate Michael Dukakis (b.1933).

The world of US politics has attracted a number of other Greek Americans in recent decades. Spiro T. Agnew (b.1918) served as US vice-president until forced to resign on 10 October 1973 because of his involvement in criminal activities. Paul Tsongas (1941–1996) became the youngest-ever member of the US Senate in 1978 at age 37, and Olympia Bouchles Snow (b.1947) became the youngest-ever woman to be elected US Representative, in 1978 at age 31. Snow was also the first-ever Greek American woman in the US House of Representatives.

Greek Americans who have made significant contributions to the worlds of science and industry include Dr. George Nicholas Papanicolaou (1908–1962), inventor of the Pap smear used to detect cervical and uterine cancers and Spyros P. Skouras, Hollywood movie mogul. Skouras began a chain of movie theaters, initiated "Cinemascope" technology, and eventually became the president of 20th Century-Fox Film Corporation. He was the first to allow African Americans into theaters in Missouri, and he always deleted racial or ethnic slurs from any film he financed. Skouras discovered and/or promoted a number of successful movie stars, including Marilyn Monroe, Elizabeth Taylor, Gregory Peck, and Henry Fonda.

Ancient Greece was the site of the first Olympic Games, and Greek Americans continue to excel in sports. Successful Greek American athletes include Gus Triandos, Milt Pappas, Bill George, and Alex Karras (who moved on to become a broadcaster and television actor).

Dancing is a favorite pastime for Greek Americans. Although in Greece girls are not allowed to lead or to perform the more difficult, fast folk dances, Greek American girls can both lead and perform any Greek folk dance, fast or slow. Folk dances are performed at cultural festivals as well as at outdoor parties called *glendi*. Traditional Greek foods and music are also enjoyed at *glendi*.

Early Greek Americans spent much of their leisure time in coffeehouses, which were given names like Acropolis or Parthenon. These coffeehouses sometimes had live entertainment and almost always offered different forms of gambling. The gambling got so out of hand in Chicago in the early 20th century that the mayor closed down the coffeehouses. From then on, Greek American coffeehouses had to be much more circumspect about their activities.

Conflicts in the Greek American community between earlier and more recent immigrants (typical of any immigrant group) came to a head in 1967 when the US government backed a military takeover in Greece and supported the resulting oppressive dictatorship for seven more years. The US government also supported Turkey's invasion of Cyprus in 1974. Those Greek Americans who had lived in the US for generations and considered themselves more American than Greek did not question US policy. More recent immigrants, however, who had only lately arrived from Greece, opposed US support of the military dictatorship and Turkish invasion of Cyprus. Either they themselves, or their family and friends, had direct experience of the oppressions in Greece and Cyprus that were being carried out with US support.

Political shifts in Greece since then have perpetuated the discord among Greek Americans. Conflicts between those who emphasize the "Greek" and those who emphasize "American" in the Greek American community continue to create tension and disharmony today.

BIBLIOGRAPHY

Jones, Jayne Clark. *The Greeks in America*. Minneapolis: Lerner Publications, 1990.

Monos, Dimitris. *The Greek Americans*. New York: Chelsea House, 1996.

Phillips, David, and Steven Ferry. *Greek Americans*. Tarrytown, NY: Benchmark Books/Marshall Cavendish, 1996.

US Bureau of the Census. *Detailed Ancestry Groups for States*. 1990 Census of Population Supplementary Reports, CP-S-1-2. Washington, DC, October 1992.

———. *The Foreign-Born Population in the United States*. 1990 CP-3-1. Washington, DC, July 1993.

—by D. K. Daeg de Mott

GRENADIANS

PRONUNCIATION: Gre-NAY-dee-uns
LOCATION: Grenada
POPULATION: 100,000
LANGUAGE: English; French-African-English dialect
RELIGION: Roman Catholicism; Protestantism; Hinduism;
　Christian-African sects

¹ INTRODUCTION

Grenada (pronounced Gre-NAY-duh), located in the Windward Islands, is known for the beauty of its lush, fertile land, and for the spices it produces. The nutmeg grown here (one-third of the world's supply in the 1980s), as well as cloves, mace, and other flavorings, have given the island its nickname, "the Isle of Spice." Grenada was first sighted by Christopher Columbus on his third voyage in 1498, although he never landed there. The Caribs who inhabited the island drove off all would-be settlers, both English and French, for over 150 years. In 1650 a French party headed by Marie Bonnard du Parquet, the governor of neighboring Martinique, succeeded in acquiring the island from the Caribs in exchange for knives, trinkets, and brandy. Having gained a foothold, they soon proceeded to exterminate the native population. Forty of the last Caribs left on the island leaped to their death in a mass suicide at La Morne des Sauteurs ("Leapers' Hill"). The island remained in French hands until it was ceded to the British at the close of the Seven Years War in 1763. After 20 years of alternating French and British rule, Grenada became a British possession under the Treaty of Versailles in 1783.

During the 18th century the British brought in African slaves to work on the island's sugar and tobacco plantations. When these slaves were freed through a proclamation by the British government in 1834, the sugar industry declined, despite the arrival of East Indian indentured laborers to replace them. By the beginning of the 20th century, cocoa and nutmeg had replaced sugar as the island's main sources of income. The new century brought with it a growing desire for greater political autonomy among the people of Grenada, which had been officially declared a British colony in 1877. These nationalistic feelings supported the rise to power of Grenada's first national leader, Eric Gairy, who in 1951 was elected to head an autonomous government under British rule. Remaining at the center of the political stage for over 20 years, Gairy became the nation's first prime minister after independence was granted by Great Britain in 1974.

In 1979 the increasingly autocratic and eccentric leader was overthrown in a coup d'état—the first to occur in an English speaking Caribbean nation. The new prime minister, Maurice Bishop, formed a Marxist government that established close ties with Cuba and other communist countries, from whom they received aid and technical assistance. However, the government's political alignment caused fears among tourists and the international business community, and the country's economy suffered. In October 1983 a faction of the revolutionary government ousted Bishop, who was killed along with several of his associates. A week later, US troops, together with forces from other Caribbean nations, subdued the military council that

had seized power, imprisoning its leaders and removing the Cuban military presence from the island.

After a brief period of interim rule, a democratically elected government headed by veteran politician Herbert Blaize came to power, following elections in 1984. Since the 1983 invasion, Grenada has moved closer politically to the United States, which provided the nation with both disaster relief and a substantial package of long-term economic aid and technical assistance. The international airport at Point Salines, begun under the Bishop government, was completed with US aid, and much of the country's infrastructure was repaired and modernized.

² LOCATION AND HOMELAND

Grenada is the most southerly of the Windward Islands. In addition to its main island, the country consists of two dependencies in the Grenadines—Petit Martinique and Carriacou—and a number of smaller islets. Grenada is one of the smallest independent nations in the Western Hemisphere; its three main islands have a total area of 344 sq km (133 sq mi), a little less than twice the size of Washington, DC.

The island of Grenada itself is green and hilly. A central mountain range runs lengthwise through the island, dividing it in half. The interior also contains rain forests, waterfalls, crater lakes, and many rivers and streams. The coastal land includes swamps and woodlands, as well as fertile plains where fruits, vegetables, and the spices for which the island is famous are grown. Carriacou, the largest of all the Grenadines, has a small central mountain range, rolling hills, and sandy beaches. Petit Martinique is distinguished by one central hill that is 152 m (500 ft) high.

Grenada's total population is estimated at 100,000 people, of which about 93,000 live on the main island, with between 6,000 and 7,000 on Carriacou and under 1,000 on Petit Martinique. The population is predominantly rural, with about 33% living in urban areas. About 85% of Grenada's population is of African descent, while 11% have mixed Black and White ancestry. The rest of the population is divided between Asians (mostly East Indians) and Whites.

³ LANGUAGE

English is the official language of Grenada, but many Grenadians speak a patois, or dialect, that combines English words and grammatical structures with elements of French and African words and rhythms. Many place names are French, such as Grand Anse Bay, Morne Rouge, Sans Souci, and L'Anse aux Épines.

⁴ FOLKLORE

Animals from the jungles of Africa play a prominent role in the *anancy* tales that are popular in Grenada. In these stories, beasts often frighten or trick their enemies, sometimes by taking on the shapes of human beings, and sometimes through other strategems. One example is the story "King Cat," in which rats are invited to a party to celebrate the feigned death of a famous rat-catching cat, who suddenly pounces on them and eats them all except for a pregnant female who lives on to perpetuate the "rat race."

While belief in the supernatural creatures of African legend is less prevalent in Grenada today than in the past, they live on in the region's Carnival figures and still appear as characters in

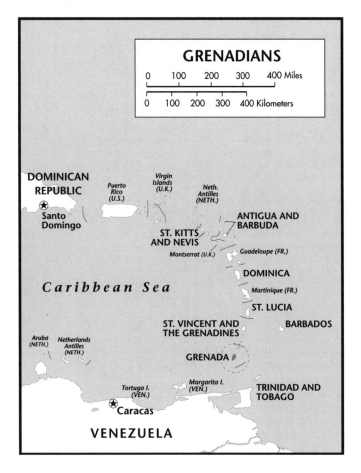

GRENADIANS

| 0 | 100 | 200 | 300 | 400 Miles |

| 0 | 100 | 200 | 300 | 400 Kilometers |

DOMINICAN REPUBLIC

☆ Santo Domingo

Puerto Rico (U.S.)

Virgin Islands (U.K.)

Neth. Antilles (NETH.)

ANTIGUA AND BARBUDA

ST. KITTS AND NEVIS

Montserrat (U.K.)

Guadeloupe (FR.)

Caribbean   Sea

DOMINICA

Martinique (FR.)

ST. LUCIA

ST. VINCENT AND THE GRENADINES

BARBADOS

Aruba (NETH.)

Netherlands Antilles (NETH.)

GRENADA

Tortuga I. (VEN.)

Margarita I. (VEN.)

TRINIDAD AND TOBAGO

☆ Caracas

VENEZUELA

bedtime stories. The name of one such creature—the zombie, or walking dead—has become a commonly used word in the United States, although removed from its original context. In African lore, zombies were dead people brought back to life to do the bidding of Voodoo priests.

Popular folk remedies include a tea made from lime bush leaves that is taken for an upset stomach, and a preparation made of mango leaves that is used for rheumatism. Compresses made from the leaves of certain plants may be applied to the forehead to treat fevers.

5 RELIGION

About 65% of Grenadians are Roman Catholic. Most of the rest belong to Protestant denominations including Anglican (20%), Methodist, Seventh-Day Adventist, and Baptist. Most of Grenada's small East Indian population is Hindu. Shango, a traditional African religion, is still practiced, generally in combination with Christian beliefs. African religious practices are especially prominent on Carriacou, and the mingling of Christian and African traditions can be seen in the island's boat-christening ceremonies, which combine holy water, sacrificial goats, and African-derived Big Drum music.

6 MAJOR HOLIDAYS

Grenada's public holidays are New Year's Day (1 January); Independence Day (7 February); Good Friday and Easter Monday; Labor Day (1 May); Whit Monday (May or June); Corpus

Christi (June); the August holidays (the first Monday and Tuesday of August); Carnival (in mid-August); Thanksgiving (25 October); and Christmas (25 and 26 December).

The country's most important festival is Carnival, celebrated in August instead of during the traditional pre-Lenten season in order to avoid conflicts with the Grenadian independence day, which occurs in February. The opening rounds of calypso and steel band competitions and other preliminary events begin at the end of July. Carnival itself begins with a Sunday night celebration leading into the Jouvert (*jour ouvert*) festivities at dawn on Monday, which feature *Djab Djab Molassi,* who represent devils (*Djab Djab* is derived from *diable,* the French word for "devil"). These revelers streak their faces and bodies with grease or molasses, which they delight in smearing on bystanders.

The main events in the two-day Carnival festival include a pageant by costumed masqueraders, steel band and calypso competitions, and a parade of bands through the streets of St. George's to the market square. Another popular Grenadian Carnival character, called Short Knee, reflects the tumultuous history of the Carnival tradition on the island. The character's costume of knee-length, colorful, baggy trousers was created in the 19th century after the government outlawed the loose, flowing "Pierrot" costumes under which weapons could be hidden.

Another traditional festival is Fisherman's Birthday, celebrated on the feast day of Saints Peter and Paul at the end of June. It is marked by a ritual blessing of nets and boats followed by boat races, all accompanied by food and dancing. The major celebration of this festival takes place at Gouyave.

7 RITES OF PASSAGE

Major life transitions, such as birth, marriage, and death, are marked by religious ceremonies appropriate to each Grenadian's particular faith community.

8 INTERPERSONAL RELATIONS

Grenada's history of British colonization is reflected in many of its customs, such as driving on the left side of the road and the occasional "tea party" which is usually a social fundraising event for a needy cause.

9 LIVING CONDITIONS

While poverty exists on Grenada, few of its people go hungry, thanks to its fertile farmlands. Most Grenadians own land on which they can grow crops to feed their families, selling the remainder at the market. Housing ranges from wooden shacks with tin or corrugated iron roofs among the poorer villagers to the attractive, brightly painted bungalows of those who are better-off financially. Signs of urban poverty common to other developing countries, such as shantytowns, are rarely seen.

Average life expectancy in Grenada is 70 years, and infant mortality is 28 deaths per 1,000 births. In 1990 there was 1 physician for every 1,617 people. There is no railroad on Grenada, and its residents depend on 1,000 km (620 mi) of narrow, winding mountain roads for transportation. In the mid-1980s many of these roads were in poor condition, but major repairs have since been made. The main roads have been resurfaced, and others have been modified for easier access. Still, however, only 600 kilometers of roadway on the island are paved. Most Grenadians do not own cars, and the majority depend on bus transportation.

The opening of the Point Salines International Airport in 1984 was a milestone in Grenadian history, making it possible for major airlines to establish direct service to the island. Begun with Cuban aid under the Marxist regime that was in power at the time of the 1983 invasion, it was completed with U.S. assistance. The capital city of St. George's is Grenada's major port.

10 FAMILY LIFE

Many Grenadians live in extended-family households, which may include up to three generations of family members. Grandparents commonly assist with child care, although day-care facilities are available for working mothers. Elderly family members, when not actually part of the household, usually live only a short distance from their children, to whom they turn when they are in need of care themselves.

Within the past generation, the size of Grenadian families has declined dramatically. Formerly, it was common for a family to have as many as 10 children. However, with greater use of birth control and more women working outside the home, the average number of children dropped to 4 or 5 in the 1980s, and the country actually had a negative population growth rate (-0.2%) between 1985 and 1992, although this was partly due to emigration.

11 CLOTHING

Grenadians wear modern Western-style clothing. Women often wear straw or cloth hats for protection from the sun.

12 FOOD

Grenadian cooks may choose from among a rich and abundant variety of fruits, vegetables, and spices. Items commonly found at the market include yams, avocados, callaloo greens (similar to spinach), oranges, papayas (called "paw-paws"), plantains (which resemble bananas), mangoes, and coconuts. Many fruits are available year-round. The cuisine of Grenada reflects a variety of influences: Amerindian, African, French, British, and East Indian.

About 20 different kinds of fish are caught off the coasts, and both fish and chicken dishes are served at many meals. Popular Caribbean staples eaten on Grenada include pigeon peas and rice, and "callaloo," made from callaloo greens, okra, salted pork, crab, and fresh fish. The local dish most closely identified with Grenada is "oildown," a mixture of salted pork and breadfruit steamed in coconut milk. Another favorite is "turtle toes," a combination of ground lobster, conch, and other seafood shaped into balls and deep fried.

Popular beverages include locally brewed Carib Lager beer; rum punch spiced with lime juice, syrup, and grated nutmeg; "mauby," made from the bark of the maubi tree and downed as a soft drink; and cocoa tea (cocoa beans and spices steeped in hot milk).

13 EDUCATION

The adult literacy rate in Grenada is over 90%, and all children are required to attend school for 12 years. The average primary school has 1 teacher for every 28 pupils, a figure that compares favorably with those in other developing nations. Post-second-

Grenadian women selling their wares to tourists on the beach in St. George. (Susan D. Rock)

ary education is offered at the T. A. Marryshow Community College and University Center (a branch of the University of the West Indies) and more recently at the St. George's University which is offering baccalaureate degree programs at its school of arts and sciences.

14 CULTURAL HERITAGE

Grenadian authors first came to public attention in the 1920s and 1930s. One of the nation's best-known contemporary writers is Wilfred Redhead, author of one-act plays and short stories. The visual arts reflect a high degree of African influence, and Grenada's artists are mostly self-taught. Canute Caliste, who lives on Carriacou, is one of the most prominent. His paintings depict aspects of traditional life on the island, including Carnival bands, boat-launchings, dance festivals, and Big Drum performances. Many of his works include handprinted texts.

Another well-known artist is Elinus Cato, whose brightly painted renderings of town and rural life in Grenada have been exhibited in London and Washington, DC. One of his paintings, *People at Work,* was presented to Queen Elizabeth II when she toured Grenada in 1985. The wooden frame for Cato's painting was crafted by renowned Grenadian woodcarver Stanley Coutain, one of the country's leading sculptors. Other recognized masters at transforming the island's mahogany, teak, and cedar into works of art include Alexander Alexis and John Pivott.

15 WORK

Between 30% and 40% of Grenadians are employed in government or other service sector jobs, and about the same percentage earn a living through some type of agricultural employment, often in the food processing industry. Typical food processing jobs include peeling nutmeg shells and sorting the seeds, and washing bananas and other produce in large vats. The remainder of jobs in Grenada are mostly in construction and manufacturing. The country has a standard eight-hour work day. Grenada had a high rate of unemployment in the 1990s; in 1994 it was reported at 25% of the work force.

16 SPORTS

Cricket is Grenada's most popular sport, and there is a large stadium at Queen's Park, outside the capital city of St. George's. However, Grenadians will start a game on any flat area that is available, and they even play cricket at the beach. Soccer is another favorite sport.

17 ENTERTAINMENT AND RECREATION

Calypso and steel drum music are both popular forms of entertainment in Grenada. The nation's television station, a division of Grenada Broadcasting Corporation (GBC), airs local news, sports, and local entertainment (including coverage of Carnival), as well as programs from the United States. There are also a number of privately owned and operated radio and televisions stations on the island.

18 FOLK ART, CRAFTS, AND HOBBIES

While calypso music is popular in Grenada, as it is throughout the Caribbean, the truly indigenous music of the Windward Islands, to which Grenada belongs, is Big Drum music. Derived from the African call-and-response tradition, it consists of song, dance, and drumming. Although its roots are similar to those of calypso and reggae, it retains a more authentic African character. The Big Drum is actually a set of three drums, originally carved from trees and later made of rum kegs. The skin of male goats is used for the two side drums and the skin of a female goat for the middle one. The middle drum, which has pins threaded across its surface, produces the most complex rhythms.

The singers are usually women, and the lead singer is called a "chantwell." The songs—in either English or French patois (dialect)—resemble those of other Caribbean traditions, such as calypso, in their reliance on satire and social commentary. The dancing is performed inside a ring of people by dancers wearing full skirts and headdresses and who interact with the musicians. On Carriacou, Big Drum music is performed at religious ceremonies including weddings and burial rites.

Woven handicrafts include hats, purses, baskets, placemats, and other items made from straw, bamboo, and wicker. Salad bowls, kitchen utensils, furniture, and other items are fashioned from mahogany and red cedar, and jewelry is made from black coral and turtle shells.

19 SOCIAL PROBLEMS

Poverty in Grenada increased in the 1980s due to the worldwide recession. Unemployment is still high (25% of the work force), and there was an increase in labor disputes in 1995.

20 BIBLIOGRAPHY

Brizan, George I. *Grenada, Island of Conflict: From Amerindians to People's Revolution, 1498–1979.* London: Zed Books, 1984.

Cameron, Sarah, and Ben Box, ed. *Caribbean Islands Handbook.* Chicago: Passport Books, 1995.

Eisenberg, Joyce. *Grenada.* New York: Chelsea House, 1988.

Ferguson, James. *Grenada: Revolution in Reverse.* London: Latin America Bureau, 1990.

Gall, Timothy, and Susan Gall, ed. *Worldmark Encyclopedia of the Nations.* 8th ed. Detroit: Gale Research, 1995.

"Grenadians." *Encyclopedia of World Cultures.* Boston: G. K. Hall, 1992.

Schwab, David, ed. *Insight Guides. Caribbean: The Lesser Antilles.* Boston: Houghton Mifflin, 1996.

Sinclair, Norma. *Grenada: Isle of Spice.* New York: Macmillan, 1987.

Thorndike, Tony. *Grenada: Politics, Economy, and Society.* Boulder, CO: Lynne Rienner, 1985.

United States. Central Intelligence Agency. *World Fact Book.* Washington, DC: Government Printing Office, 1994.

Walton, Chelle Koster. *Caribbean Ways: A Cultural Guide.* Westwood, MA: Riverdale, 1993.

—by R. Wieder, reviewed by D. G. Antoine

GUAJIROS

LOCATION: Venezuela and Colombia (Guajira peninsula, which borders the Caribbean to the north and east, and Venezuela and the Gulf of Maracaibo to the west)
LANGUAGE: Guajiro
RELIGION: Mixture of Roman Catholicism and indigenous religious traditions

¹ INTRODUCTION

The Guajiro Indians are a distinctive and individualistic tribe from northeastern Colombia who have been seminomadic for hundreds of years. Their existence pre-dates the arrival of the Spanish conquerors, although their precise origins and migrations prior to the arrival of the Spanish are uncertain. The conqueror Rodrigo de Bastidas surveyed the coastal areas of the Guajira peninsula along the Caribbean as early as 1500–1501. The Guajiro tribe is divided into clans that are made up of several family groups, with leaders who are recognized as princes.

² LOCATION AND HOMELAND

The Guajiros live in the dry lands and coastal areas of the Guajira peninsula, which borders the Caribbean to the north and east, and Venezuela and the Gulf of Maracaibo to the west. Traditionally the Guajiros have ignored the border that divides Venezuela and Colombia, roaming freely in and out of both countries. Their nomadic habits were recognized and respected by both countries, which accorded them the privilege of citizenship and did not demand from them the formalities that normally have to be observed when crossing from one country to another.

This reluctance to recognize national borders persists to this day, since currently members of the same extended families and clans may live either in remote desert areas or in cities such as Riohacha, the capital of the Guajira, or in a neighborhood of the Venezuelan city of Maracaibo where some have migrated to find work, or in smaller settlements such as Puerto López at the mouth of the oil-rich Gulf of Maracaibo. Many move from one location to another in indefinite patterns that do not conform easily to modern diplomatic requirements.

³ LANGUAGE

Although many Guajiros have had continuous contact with the Spanish language for many years, they continue to speak their own language and often have three names each: a Guajiro name, a Catholic name given to them at birth, and another Spanish name that they usually use when in contact with White people. The Guajiro name is often kept secret, since it is used only by close members of the family on the mother's side.

Despite the difficulty of discovering the Guajiro names, the Colombian writer Eduardo Zalamea Borda, who wrote a novel about the Guajira region, records the names of three girls: Anashka, Ingua, and Pankai. He also records the name of a young boy: Nipaj. The language sounds more guttural than Spanish, and the story of Guajiro lives, their work, their loves and sorrows, and the landscape of sand and boat and sea is often recorded in poetic songs which, according to Zalamea Borda, are often quite melancholy. For example, in a song that refers to a boat and an anchor, the following line is repeated over and over again in a lengthy, sad tone, like the repetitive whistle of a bird:

Eeeeeeeeee guarapáin tanai, eeeeeeeee guarapáin tanai.

Then this sad lament changes into a joyful song.

⁴ FOLKLORE

Although the Guajiro Indians were gradually converted to Catholicism, in particular through the efforts of Capuchin monks who learned the Guajiro language and established some of the first primary schools in the Guajira, beliefs and practices from earlier times persist, in particular because clan identities still form part of the Guajiro identity.

Each clan has a symbol, usually drawn from the animal world, which stands for certain virtues and characteristics with which the clan identifies. This symbol is usually understood by outsiders as a totem. What this means is the power, the aspirations, and the virtues that the clan regards as valuable are expressed by their choice of symbol. Sometimes this symbol or totemic sign is tattooed on the arm.

⁵ RELIGION

Religious life for the Guajiros is a mix of the Catholic beliefs brought to them by the Spaniards who conquered the New World, and the older belief system that includes a different view of the afterlife. The cape at the head of the Guajira peninsula, called the Cabo de la Vela (the Cape of the Sail) is called Jepira by the Guajiros. It is regarded as a sacred place because they believe that Guajiros who have passed away still wander there.

The Wayúu clan records its origin with this poetic myth: "We were born of the Wind of the Northeast and the Goddess of the Rains." Winter itself is thought of as the brother of the Goddess of the Rains and represents the Guajiro Indians as a whole. Whereas in other cultures with different climates winter might represent hardship, in an arid area such as the Guajira, whatever brings water or rain also brings fertility and abundance.

⁶ MAJOR HOLIDAYS

Guajiros who have migrated to towns have become more involved in the celebrations and religious festivals of Catholicism. Even comparatively small towns such as Puerto López have developed a mixed population, including traders of Arab origin who migrated to the Americas in search of a better life, black people whose ancestors came to these shores originally as slaves, white people of Spanish origin, and people who are a mix of all of these. As Guajiros intermingle during religious feast days, they partake of the music, dance, and customs that evolve out of this rich and colorful brew.

The Guajiros also continue to mark special events in their lives according to their own traditions, particularly the Guajiro ceremonial dance known as the *Chichimaya*. This dance is a fertility dance and often takes place when a young girl reaches puberty and is considered able to marry.

The Festival of Uribia in the Guajira intermingles the dances, songs, and music of African, Spanish colonial, and Guajiro Indian origins, such as the *vallenato* music of the neighboring Magdalena region, with its mix of ballad-like

GUAJIRO

| 0 | 250 | 500 | 750 Miles |
| 0 | 250 | 500 | 750 Kilometers |

Caribbean Sea

daring the girl to catch him. The girl has to dance and chase him, trying to step on his feet so that he will lose his balance and fall.

Traditionally, when a Guajiro dies he or she is buried wrapped in a hammock, and at a later date the bones are placed in a clay urn and buried in a tomb near others belonging to the same clan.

⁸INTERPERSONAL RELATIONS

Greetings can be very friendly and enthusiastic. If someone has arrived, pleasure is expressed, and, in a simple shelter with a roof made of dry branches but open on two sides, the welcoming hosts will hang up some hammocks so that the visitor will be able to spend some time with them and spend the night there if necessary. Then the hosts will ask the visitor, "What news do you bring, *waré?*" The *waré,* or friend, is expected to relate news about relatives and friends.

⁹LIVING CONDITIONS

The health of the Guajiros depends to a great extent on where they live. The people as a whole are in a state of transition. Some have migrated to towns. In larger cities such as Maracaibo in Venezuela there is a Guajiro quarter. In other towns they are less settled but might stay for a shorter time to visit friends or relatives or to work for a short time. Even those who do not live permanently in towns increasingly seek the services of town doctors at times.

Guajiros who have not migrated to various towns in Colombia and Venezuela still live in simple circular huts. Traditional house-building is undertaken communally, and the whole family lives under one roof, often in hamlets with others of their clan. This simplicity is well-suited to a seminomadic life because as goatherders they often move about with their flocks, seeking higher ground among the low-lying hill ranges on the Guajira peninsula where they can feed their animals. They sometimes keep pigs and hens.

In remote areas, paths are very basic and sometimes pack animals such as donkeys are used, although Guajiros also use trucks or catch rides with traders or visitors. Guajiros are fine weavers and make excellent hammocks that can be hung in the huts to provide simple sleeping quarters. Hammocks are easily carried from place to place.

¹⁰FAMILY LIFE

The role of the woman is very important among the Guajiros. The society is matrilineal, which means that the identity of the clan is passed on from the mother to her children. The mother's relatives are very important, particularly the maternal uncle and the maternal aunt, who are important figures of authority for the children.

If a boy wishes to marry, his family has to offer a generous bride-price, which may include as many as 30 or more goats. In an area where many forms of agriculture are difficult, the Guajiros regard goats as hardy and extremely valuable assets. The Guajiros also value gold jewelry such as necklaces and bracelets, and these are usually included as offerings in exchange for a bride.

Guajiros usually look for wives from a different clan. If a wife is unfaithful, the husband can return her to her family and her family has to return the gifts received. If a husband has

songs and African drums, as well as the Guajiro *maraca* or rattle, the Guajiro drum, and the Guajiro flute known as the *maasi*.

⁷RITES OF PASSAGE

Many Guajiro infants are not only baptized into the Catholic Church but also have a Guajiro naming ceremony that is conducted in a private manner, usually among the Guajiros themselves. The Guajiro name is always associated with a special family intimacy. Clan identity comes to the infant not through its father, but through its mother. Similarly, the Guajiro name is uttered usually only by close family members on the mother's side. Maternal uncles have a special authority and importance.

When Guajiros become teenagers, they are separated for a time because girls have to remain secluded and cared for by their maternal aunts when they reach puberty. This seclusion, it is thought, helps girls to prepare for married life. Their female relatives instruct and prepare them. For months the girls have to drink specially brewed herbal teas that help them, it is believed, get rid of their childish attitudes and become more mature. They also improve their knowledge of various crafts such as weaving during this time. This time of seclusion is regarded as a rebirth and the girls are each given a new name. They are then ready to go out into the world again, to meet the boys among whom they will eventually find a husband.

At this stage the girls have a coming-out party with the *Chichimaya,* the Guajiro ritual fertility dance. During the *Chichimaya* ceremonial dance, which takes place at dusk, a boy will take his hat off and wave it, dancing backwards in a circle,

been unfaithful, he has to pay with a gift that equals the original bride-price.

When a woman is expecting a child, her husband is expected to protect her in specific ways. For instance, he has to ride before her to search out dangerous snakes that might harm her or the unborn child.

11 CLOTHING

Traditional clothes are striking and distinctive, particularly for women, who wear long, flowing, flowery dresses down to the ankles. They are loose-fitting and therefore cool in a hot climate, and they also protect the woman from the sun. The men are often lean and tall, with strong limbs. Their traditional loincloths are adorned sometimes with bright tassels and pompoms. They also wear pompoms on their sandals as a sign that may indicate their rank as a prince. When they go to towns, they wear simple cotton shirts and trousers, as do other town-dwellers in hot climates in South America.

12 FOOD

Corn and food products made from corn meal are part of the basic diet, but protein is also obtained from fish caught in the coastal waters of the peninsula. Turtles sometimes provide a source of necessary protein in the diet and are considered a delicacy. On festive occasions, meat (usually goat meat) is grilled on simple, open charcoal fires. Some Guajiros also keep pigs and hens, which provide valuable supplements to the basic diet.

13 EDUCATION

The first educational efforts to provide formal schooling for the Guajiros were begun by missionaries. Initially the rate of literacy was very low, but in the last few decades the picture has been changing rapidly as more Guajiros have migrated to towns. In the long run, this will have an important effect on the youngsters as schools in towns become more accessible. Part of the difficulty for the Guajiros is that the lifestyle of some is still quite nomadic, and for others the wives and children are left behind in more remote areas while the men go out in search of seasonal or occasional work. This pattern affects the schooling of many young people.

Many young Guajiros do not progress beyond primary school; others may have just a few years in primary school without completing it; and some, whose lifestyle has changed rapidly due to a move into towns, are able to complete high school.

While parents who remain in remote hamlets feel it is more important for young people to survive in that environment by learning to herd, hunt, or fish, to build simple shelters, and to weave, in towns these expectations change as parents try to help their children adapt to new environments.

14 CULTURAL HERITAGE

By a mixture of independence on the one hand and accommodation on the other, the Guajiros have preserved important elements of their own culture while absorbing belief systems and attitudes from the surrounding Latino culture. Their own music can be plaintive and melancholy. The ritual dance of the *Chichimaya* is a ceremonial dance that has been preserved, and their instruments, such as flutes, rattles, and drums, are still in use.

Their myths, which often deal with their origins, are preserved in storytelling and song.

15 WORK

For centuries the Guajiros have dived for pearls around the Cabo de la Vela. They also worked in the salt-pans that traditionally belonged to them, many of which were subsequently taken over by the Colombian government, which then hired the Guajiros as paid labor. The Guajiros did not like the long, regimented working hours, since they were used to working in a freer pattern, and just enough for their basic needs. Often they would co-opt relatives to make up the full quota of hours. These attitudes still persist among those whose basic needs remain simple and who have not migrated.

Some Guajiros have found work in coal mines, since Colombia has rich coal deposits in the region, and others work in the oil-rich area of Maracaibo in Venezuela.

16 SPORTS

Loren McIntyre, who traveled for 17 years around Latin America and spent some time in the 1960s in the Guajira, records that the Capuchin monks who founded a school for Guajiro orphans tried to teach them basketball unsuccessfully. Apparently the monks thought they were "too individualistic" to develop the team mentality necessary for the game. This anecdote reveals that what the dominant Latino culture thought of as sport was not interesting enough for the Guajiros.

Children who are adapting to town life are also beginning to enjoy Western-style sports. In the traditional way of life, spectator sports do not exist as such, but sporting elements are included in dances and rituals during festivals, or in aspects of daily working life.

17 ENTERTAINMENT AND RECREATION

Town-dwellers have access to local radio and television, and to movie theaters. But the aspect of popular culture that people living along the Caribbean most enjoy is the carnival, and Guajiros enjoy fiestas and carnivals as much as everyone else. The best-known fiesta in the Guajira is the yearly event in Uribia. The Guajiros come in all their finery, the women wearing their jewelry and colorful flowered dresses, their faces dramatically made up with ceremonial paint. They mingle with other peoples who live along the coast and who come to Uribia to listen to the music, enjoy the dancing, and admire the ceremonial elegance of the Guajiros.

18 FOLK ART, CRAFTS, AND HOBBIES

Weaving and jewelry-making, and crafting musical instruments such as flutes and drums, form part of Guajiro life. Their hammocks are well-known and are now sold in coastal towns. The women make their own dresses, and the specific cut and colorful choice of flowery prints is much admired. Dugout canoes, and the basic fishing crafts such as the weaving of nets and the fashioning of rods and fishing spears, are all part of the Guajiro skills.

Generally, whoever was particularly good at a skill was accorded specific recognition and, if customs allowed it, the skill became an aspect of the person's work with and for the community, rather than a separate hobby.

[19] SOCIAL PROBLEMS

In the early 1990s, constitutional reform in Colombia meant that representatives of the indigenous peoples of Colombia entered Congress for the first time. The various groups initially had to organize themselves and to communicate across their own barriers before they could demand and obtain this type of representation. This is an important step forward, but it is still too early to tell what effect this will have on the Guajiros and their problems, which have to do with changing lifestyles and growing differences between those who live in towns and experience specific types of urban poverty such as overcrowding, poor sanitation, etc., and those who suffer from rural poverty with lack of access to health care and education.

[20] BIBLIOGRAPHY

de Friedemann, Nina S. *Fiestas*. Hogta: Villegas Editores, 1995.

Los Pueblos Nómadas, National Geographical Society Spanish Edition. Mexico: Ediciones Diana, S. A., 1978.

Zalamea Borda, Eduardo. *Cuatro arìos a bordo de mi mismo*. Bogota: Compañia Gran Colombiana de Ediciones S. A., 1959.

—by P. Pitchon, reviewed by T. Morin

GUARANÍS

LOCATION: Paraguay; Brazil
LANGUAGE: Guaraní
RELIGION: Traditional indigenous religions

[1] INTRODUCTION

The Guaranís were once one of the most influential Amerindian peoples in the southern part of South America. Eventually they established their settlements in the tropical forests of Paraguay and southern Brazil, and also extended their settlements into northern Argentina. Before the Spanish conquest, during the 15th century, the Guaranís warred with Amerindians as far as the southern limits of the vast Inca Empire, bringing back gold, which they wore as ornaments. In the 16th century the Spanish conquerors found Guaraní settlements over a very wide area, including the islands of the Plata River, parts of the Paraná River delta, along the Uruguayan coast, and along the Paraguay River. Large concentrations of Guaranís lived in the Province of Guairá in Paraguay, where some of them still live today.

When the Spanish first arrived, many Guaranís were friendly and assisted the Spanish in waging war against other Amerindian groups and in establishing new settlements. Many Spanish men, attracted by the beauty of the Guaraní women, married them, and in this way the Guaranís entered into a direct relation with newly found Spanish relatives whom they supported in these early encounters. This was the beginning of the long process of intermarriage that produced the Paraguayans of today. In the countryside, the descendants of Spaniards and Guaranís are still called simply Guaranís, and the language is spoken by many, not just in rural areas but also in towns, including the Paraguayan capital, Asunción.

Other Guaraní groups turned against the Spanish and waged war against them, trying to protect their freedom and their own way of life. This process continued into the 19th century. Some Guaraní groups fell under the control of the Spanish in the cruel *encomienda* system, where they worked for landowners and others and paid a tribute (effectively a type of tax) to them. It was a harsh, exploitative system.

Other Guaranís entered into a complex relationship with the Jesuits, who became very powerful in this part of South America, establishing many missions where Guaranís settled, sometimes with inducements and promises of an easier life, sometimes with threats of punishment. The early Jesuit missions educated the Guaranís, Christianized them, taught them music, and persuaded them to adapt to a different, if dependent, way of life in the missions where they grew crops and kept cattle. Not only were the missions self-sufficient in food, but eventually the mission Guaranís were taught to use modern weapons and became, in effect, a powerful armed branch of the Jesuits, who as a result encountered the opposition of other powerful interest groups such as wealthy landowners. The Spanish Crown ordered the expulsion of the Jesuits from South America in 1767. Guaranís at the missions were dispersed and many returned to their old way of life in the forests. Those who remained had to fight raids on the missions by colonists who stole land from the Guaranís and destroyed both cattle and plantations.

This aspect of the Guaraní story forms the main part of the film *The Mission,* starring Jeremy Irons. He plays the part of a Spanish priest who agonizes over the choice between becoming a man of action and fighting the harsher aspects of the Spanish colonial regime, or remaining a pacifist priest.

In 1848 the Paraguayan dictator Carlos Antonio López decreed that the remaining Guaranís still living in missions should live in ordinary villages like everyone else.

The Guaranís also participated, as Paraguayan citizens, in the war against Brazil, Uruguay, and Argentina (1864–70) and in the devastating War of the Chaco against Bolivia (1932–35), in which so many Paraguayan men lost their lives.

² LOCATION AND HOMELAND

Today the Guaranís who have retained their traditional way of life live in scattered settlements in Paraguay and in southern Brazil. Over the centuries, they migrated over vast areas, sometimes undertaking long journeys that led them to settle in widely diverse regions: forests and coastal areas, near sierras, and in river deltas. It is thought that the Brazilian settlements date from the 19th century. They also made their way into northern Argentina, particularly the province of Misiones.

³ LANGUAGE

The Guaraní language is still widely spoken in Paraguay, a legacy of the influence this distinctive Amerindian people once wielded. However, the wide usage of the language is complemented by two other Guaraní languages which are both secret and sacred. In effect, the Guaranís have a "secular," a "secret," and a "sacred" language. The sacred language is used exclusively by male and female elders of the tribe, who receive divine messages and transmit them to the rest of the tribe. The secret language is a priestly language used only by initiates and shamans and is called *Ñe'e pará,* meaning "the words of our fathers." Guaranís often have a Spanish name for everyday use, as well as a secret Guaraní name. It is the task of the tribal leader to find the origin of the child's soul and bestow a sacred name.

⁴ FOLKLORE

Guaraní folklore is very rich, and many myths hint at their origin in a very poetic way. Among the *mbyás,* a group of Guaranís who have preserved much of their original literature, the Creator, called by them Ñande Ru, gave birth to his son, Pa'í Reté Kuaray, whose body was like the sun, and he is the father of the Guaraní race. Pa'í taught his people not only sacred dances and songs, but also agricultural skills and ethics. He is the destroyer of evil beings and created the honey bee as a sweet offering to humankind. He entrusted to four gods the care of his creation. After the Creator Ñande Ru created the first earth, it was destroyed by a great flood through the will of the gods. Then the Creator asked the son of Jakaira, the God of Spring, to create another earth. Since then, the four gods send the souls of boys to earth, and the wives of the gods send the souls of girls to earth.

The Guaranís are a very religious, even mystical, people, and during a long history of suffering they have had messianic, heroic figures who have led them in a quest for a better life and a search for Paradise, which they call the Land Without Evil.

Sometimes these quests have taken physical form in long treks or river journeys.

A famous Guaraní hero is the chief Aropoty Yu. The Paraguayan president sent a military expedition in 1844 against the Guaranís, and in 1876 it was still the case that no one could enter Guaraní territory without the consent of Aropoty Yu.

⁵ RELIGION

Not all Guaranís profess identical beliefs. Among the three major groups that remain today, known as the Chiripás, the Mbayás, and the Pai-Kaiovás, there are some interesting differences. Generally, they believe that every person has an earthly soul and a divine one. Dreams come from the divine soul and are the source of inspiration for the shamans, who mediate between the divine and earthly realms and who also have the task of identifying evildoers and protecting the tribe as well as curing illness. Some Guaranís believe in reincarnation; others, who have had more Christian influences, believe that evildoers go to a land of darkness, whereas good people go to the Land Without Evil.

Shamans often isolate themselves for periods of time in jungles or forests and live austerely, with a basic vegetarian diet. Among the Guaranís, it is thought that every man and woman eventually receives a protective chant from a dead relative, which is divinely inspired. It is then taught to the rest of the community. Powerful shamans sometimes receive many chants or songs. They are called to their vocation in this manner.

The Guaraní also believe that all living things, including plants, animals, and water, have protective spirits, and that malevolent spirits also exist.

6 MAJOR HOLIDAYS

The Guaranís do not make clear-cut divisions between secular and religious occasions. Most feasts and celebrations have a religious character, and even harvest festivals include sacred rituals.

7 RITES OF PASSAGE

It is thought that the moment of conception of a child is revealed to the parents in dreams. The Guaranís who believe in reincarnation think that a person who has died can reveal that he or she will reincarnate in a particular body. A pregnant woman follows strict dietary rules, eating some foods and avoiding others.

After a child is born, both the father and the mother are in a critical state known as *aku*. The father participates sympathetically in the birth pains of the mother, expressing his suffering, and after the child is born the father retires to his hammock for a time, avoiding all magic rites that might be considered harmful to the child, because it is his duty to protect the child. He has to maintain a strict diet and avoid hunting. The mother of the child avoids all heavy work for a time. Among some Guaranís, the shaman has to determine from what part of the sky the child's soul originated, and give the child a special name.

When a boy becomes an adolescent he undergoes initiation rites in seclusion with a group, under the direction of the shaman. His lower lip is perforated with a piece of wood. He follows a strict diet based on corn for several days. Afterwards he can use adult words and adult ways of addressing people. During the initiation rites, the boy is instructed in appropriate behavior, which includes guidance on working hard, refraining from harming others, being moderate in his habits, not drinking excessively, and never beating his wife.

When a girl reaches adolescence she is secluded for a time under the care of female relatives. Her mother gives her guidance on her future marriage.

Guaranís are allowed informal marriages which are, in effect, a trial period. The young man takes the girl to his parents' house to live there for a time, without formal marriage ceremonies. If he wishes to marry her, he approaches his future father-in-law for permission. The father of the girl is mainly an intermediary, but it is the mother who can object if she feels the match is unsuitable. When a couple forms a family, they are expected to raise their children with kindness and tolerance, and not to hit the children.

Burial rites still include aspects that are closely guarded secrets. Traditionally the Guaraní were buried in large pottery jars which were then covered with a bowl. The funeral urns were then buried. Today they are buried in a folded position directly in the ground, or they are laid out in a hollowed-out tree trunk with their possessions. Some are buried under the ground inside the hut itself, which is then immediately abandoned. It is thought by some Guaranís that the earthly soul wanders, whereas the divine soul goes either to the land of darkness or to the Land Without Evil. Many Paraguayan Guaranís bury their dead in the bush. Then the dead person's house is burned. The mention of his or her name becomes taboo.

8 INTERPERSONAL RELATIONS

Traditional greetings to visitors obliged the female hosts to wail and mourn, reciting the admirable deeds of the visitor's dead relatives. The guest had to cover his or her face with the hands and show appropriate expressions of sorrow, such as crying. Some of these traditional greetings have fallen into disuse.

There are particular celebrations among some groups, particularly the Chiripás, that offer young people a way of getting to know each other and that constitute dating rituals. These celebrations are known as *kotyú*. These are ritual dances that allude to important myths but at the same time allow young men to dance with young women and to express their love. During the kotyú dances, both formal and friendly or even romantic greetings are exchanged. León Cadogan and Alfredo López Austin, who made a special study of Guaraní songs and literature, report that an official who came to investigate the condition of a particular Guaraní group was greeted in this way during the dance:

> An inhabitant from faraway lands do I see. Oh bird!
> In truth, I see, oh bird, an inhabitant
> from faraway lands!

This was a greeting to girls during a kotyú described by Cadogan and López Austin:

> Let us, my sisters, give a brotherly greeting,
> Oh spotless maidens,
> around the Great House
> near the Golden Grasses.

9 LIVING CONDITIONS

War and conquest decimated the Guaranís, and the process of intermarriage over centuries also created the modern Paraguayan nation. Even after the end of the Spanish colonial period, smallpox proved a deadly disease that wiped out many communities. The various transition periods from one type of lifestyle to another, with painful phases of adaptation, have never been particularly orderly but rather cruel and often sudden; therefore, many hardships have affected the health of the Guaranís. In general, those living in traditional ways in remote forest or jungle areas have knowledge of medicinal plants that are effective in a wide range of conditions, such as certain infections, stomach conditions, and snakebites.

The more traditional groups continue to live a sustainable lifestyle that satisfies their simple and basic needs such as food and shelter. Some live mainly apart from a cash economy and without surpluses. In some cases there is an active trade in basic implements for hunting, fishing, or cooking. This has led to the disappearance of clay pots, which are now replaced by aluminum ones that have been exchanged for other items. Fishing hooks, which the Guaranís used to make for themselves out of wood, have been replaced by metal ones.

The traditional extended family unit, which was part of a clan of as many as 50 or 60 families, required the construction of large houses with screened-off sections inside the house and a large communal area. During the Spanish colonial period, disapproval of this method of living on the part of state and religious authorities gradually compelled the Guaranís to abandon this mode of living, and single family huts with thatched roofs began to replace the traditional spacious houses.

The Guaranís in Paraguay live along streams and use bamboo rafts or occasionally canoes for transport. In some jungle areas they can trek for long distances on foot, especially during hunting expeditions. The Guaranís in parts of Brazil use dugout canoes for transport.

10 FAMILY LIFE

The traditional extended family unit demanded a cooperative style of living under the authority of the head of the clan. Generally, Guaranís lived in small groups of large rectangular houses built around a square plaza or courtyard. Today in many areas these houses have been replaced by small individual family units. Even traditional hammocks have been replaced by sleeping mats or platform beds, which are probably less comfortable and practical. Although the Guaranís have never recognized a central authority, the disappearance of their traditional large clan houses in most areas has also undermined the family structure with its shared tasks and support systems.

Some marriage customs are changing, with young people having more say in the choice of marriage partners. In earlier times, child betrothals were sometimes practiced. Chiefs also had several wives in earlier times, although this is no longer the case.

Some Guaranís keep dogs whom they prize as hunting companions, particularly in jungle areas where the jaguar is still hunted. They keep chickens and other farm animals in some areas.

11 CLOTHING

Guaranís who live on protected reservations in parts of northern Argentina and Paraguay have adopted the clothing of the rural Mestizo peasant farmers, with plain shirts and trousers, and a cloak or poncho. In remote areas of Brazil, some of the Guaranís still wear traditional ornaments and very little else. Originally they wore no clothing but used strands of women's hair around their legs in bands as protective ornaments; the lower lip was pierced. In some cases, a type of loincloth was worn by men. In remote areas, the women still wear black body paint and the men wear black and red body paint. Ear ornaments of shell or gold are still worn by some Guaranís.

12 FOOD

The whole community participates in clearing land to grow crops in communities that still live in the traditional style. When the soil is exhausted, the community moves on. While this traditional method is still in use in some areas, in other places the Guaranís have become more settled. The staple foods are cassava and corn. Sweet potatoes and beans, pumpkins, and tropical fruits such as bananas and papayas are also grown. Peanuts provide protein, and sugarcane is a delicacy. In the forests, wild honey is sometimes collected.

Chipas are corn-flour cakes, and the Guaranís also wrap corn dough in leaves and cook the parcels under ashes—this is called *auimi atucupé.* Cassava is often roasted or boiled.

13 EDUCATION

The Jesuits provided the first schools for the Guaranís. After the demise of the Jesuit missions, many Guaranís became *mon-*

teses, taking refuge in remote areas and reverting to earlier lifestyles. Others went to work as salaried peasants on plantations; some went into the towns to find work and continued the process of assimilation. Those that remain today in remote areas, such as some of the Brazilian Guaranís, do not wish to adapt to the prevailing Western lifestyle, nor to provide their children with the schooling which will eventually mean the end of their independent existence.

14 CULTURAL HERITAGE

Much of the music, dancing, songs, and poems of the Guaranís, as well as some of their prayers, legends, and myths, are the means by which they have managed to preserve important aspects of their culture. Some of their songs and poems have made their way into the popular culture of the Paraguayans. Some groups, such as the Mbayás, have preserved many of their legends and stories. All of these, for the Guaranís who still live a more traditional life, form part of an integral whole and are woven into their daily life and activities. Traditional instruments include drums, rattles, and flutes. Sometimes important ethical and social instructions are given in the form of short plays which are performed in front of children in a village.

15 WORK

Guaranís farm, hunt, and fish. Some Guaranís are also beekeepers. In areas where there is still game, they hunt the tapir, the anteater, and the jaguar, as well as the agouti. They do not hunt birds with blowpipes and darts, as do many other tribes who live in the tropical rainforests. Instead, they capture parrots by lassoing them with a small noose attached to the end of a pole.

The Guaranís are able fishers and still shoot fish with bows and arrows in some areas. They also use traps in the form of baskets or nets made of fiber. Fish provides an important source of protein in their diet.

16 SPORTS

Sports really begin as the games that children play. Guaraní children especially enjoy wrestling and racing. They also play variations of tug-of-war. Some studies report that the ancient Itatín group of Guaranís played games with rubber balls. Adults still play a game with a shuttlecock made out of corn. The aim is to throw it at each other and try to keep it in the air as long as possible.

17 ENTERTAINMENT AND RECREATION

Guaranís have always enjoyed celebrations and feasting on those happy occasions, such as the return from a successful hunt, that call for them. Usually they will celebrate with generous quantities of a fermented drink called *chicha,* often made from corn. A good harvest and a good fishing expedition are also occasions for celebration.

18 FOLK ART, CRAFTS, AND HOBBIES

Baskets are woven from pindo palm fibers, and some are made out of twilled fabrics made of *tacuarembó.* Much of the fine pottery that archaeologists have found in various ancient Guaraní settlements is no longer made by the Guaranís. Some of the Paraguayan Guaranís make skin bags from leather. Some still make their own bows and arrows and carve dugout canoes from a single trunk of wood. They also spin cotton using a vertical loom with a circular warp. The cloth is usually white, with brown and black stripes. They also make their own flutes, sometimes from bamboo. They make beads and thread them into necklaces.

19 SOCIAL PROBLEMS

The social problems of the Guaranís differ, depending on whether they live on the few remaining reservations or *reducciones* in Paraguay and northern Argentina, or whether they live in the tropical forests of the Brazilian-Paraguayan border areas. In the latter case, they resent the incursions of the Europeans and cling to their traditional way of life. To maintain their simple, sustainable lifestyle, they need to live in small, scattered settlements, often ranging over a wide area to make use of the slash-and burn agricultural methods that require them to move on when the soil has been exhausted, to find good hunting grounds, and to move on after burials. This lifestyle clashes with the needs of ranchers and poor farmers hungry for land, and with prospectors who want to try their luck in areas that have not previously been settled by non-Indians.

On the reservations, the problems relate to economic limitations and poor prospects for sustaining cultural and economic independence.

20 BIBLIOGRAPHY

Cadogan, León, and Alfredo López Austin. *La Literatura de los Guaraníes.* Mexico: Editorial Joaquín Mortiz, 1970.
Steward, Julian Haynes, ed. *A Handbook of South American Indians.* New York: Cooper Square, 1963.
Various bulletins, Survival International, London.

—by P. Pitchon, reviewed by T. Morin

GUATEMALANS

LOCATION: Guatemala
POPULATION: 10 million
LANGUAGE: Spanish; various Mayan languages; Carib
RELIGION: Roman Catholicism with ancient Mayan beliefs; Protestantism

1 INTRODUCTION

More than 1,000 years before the coming of the Spanish, the Mayas established a number of city-states in what is now Guatemala. The largest of these, Tikal, covered 26 sq km (10 sq mi) and included some 200 major stone structures, including high-rise temples and palaces. By AD 1000, however, the Mayan cities had been abandoned and it is said the majority of the indigenous population had moved to the highlands. Soon after Spanish troops conquered Mexico in 1521, they moved south and subdued the native inhabitants. For the next three centuries the captaincy-general of Guatemala was the center of government for most of Central America. The captaincy-general won its independence from Spain in 1821. Guatemala seceded from the resulting federation of the United Provinces of Central America in 1839.

José Rafael Carrera, a Conservative, ruled Guatemala from 1838 to 1871. Justo Rufino Barrios, a Liberal, ruled from 1873 to 1885. Under Barrios and later, many Indian communities lost their lands, which were developed into coffee and banana plantations. In 1954 the government, considered pro-Communist by the United States, was overthrown with help from the Central Intelligence Agency (CIA). Leftist guerilla groups organized to oppose the right-wing military-dominated and US-backed governments that subsequently ruled the country. Between 1960 and 1996, some 100,000 people lost their lives as a consequence of the fighting between the army and the guerrillas. Many other Guatemalans fled to Mexico and the United States.

2 LOCATION AND HOMELAND

Guatemala is slightly larger than the US state of Tennessee. It is bounded by Mexico on the north and west, by the Pacific Ocean on the south, and by Belize, Honduras, and El Salvador on the east. Eastern Guatemala also has a small Caribbean Sea coastline. The southern half of the country is mountainous, except along the Pacific coast. Some 33 mountains are volcanic, and the area is also subject to earthquakes. The northern third of the country consists of lowland rain forest.

Guatemala had a population of about 10 million people in 1994, making it the most populous country in Central America. They were divided about evenly between Indians and *ladinos,* a term applied to those who have adopted the Spanish language, dress, and lifestyle, regardless of race. Ladinos may be of pure Indian ancestry but are more often *Mestizos,* people of mixed Indian and European descent. About 1% of the population are of purely European ancestry. Blacks, along the Caribbean coast, make up perhaps another 1% of the population.

3 LANGUAGE

Spanish is the official language of Guatemala. Guatemalan Spanish is carefully enunciated and formal, even old-fashioned at times, with an emphasis on politeness and respect. Some words are of Indian origin. Many Indians speak Spanish poorly or not at all. Indian men are more likely to know Spanish than are women, and younger people more often speak Spanish than do older ones. There are 21 Mayan languages spoken in Guatemala, the principal ones being Quiché, Cakchiquel, Kekchí, and Mam. Carib is spoken along the Caribbean coast by the Garifunas, or Black Caribs, the descendants of fugitive slaves and Carib Indians.

⁴ FOLKLORE

Guatemala's folklore is based on Indian cultural beliefs as well as old traditions brought by the Spanish conquerors. According to Quiché legend, for example, the first four humans were made of corn paste into which the Heart of Heaven breathed life. To assure good growing weather before spring planting, the seed is blessed at a special planting. The night before the planting, the men burn incense in the fields and sprinkle the ground with a brew made from fermented sugarcane, while the women pray at home before lighted candles. In the morning the women go to the fields with food for the sowers and place their candles at points representing the four winds.

The shaman (Mayan Priest) is a man or woman credited with being able to mediate with the unknown forces that govern human destiny, to predict the future, and to cast spells. He or she is also a healer *(curandero)* who practices herbal medicine.

The Indians of Central America believe that every person has an animal counterpart called the *nagual* who shares his or her destiny. Tecún Umán, a heroic Quiché warrior who, according to legend, was slain by Pedro de Alvarado, the Spanish leader, had for his nagual the colorful quetzal, Guatemala's increasingly rare national bird.

Particular places serve as shrines for particular gods. The Indians of Alta Verapaz, for example, are careful when approaching a hot spring to leave kindling beside it for the god who boils the water. In return, it is hoped, the god will not cause fever by heating the Indian's blood.

⁵ RELIGION

Some 67% to 80% of all Guatemalans are Roman Catholic. Within this faith, however, the Indians have preserved ancient Mayan beliefs. Their gods, who govern aspects of life like weather and crops, are worshipped under the guise of saints; Jesus and Mary, for example, are identified with the Sun God and Moon Goddess, and the cross with the Four Winds of Heaven. *Cofradías* (brotherhoods), rather than Catholic priests, are in charge of the religious life of an Indian community. Fiestas are the major form of public worship and sometimes conform to the 260-day Mayan religious calendar. Worship is orthodox among ladinos, but routine church attendance is often not possible because of a shortage of priests. Most priests in Guatemala are foreigners.

Perhaps 25% to 33% of the population are Protestant. Protestant missionaries, generally with ties to organizations in the United States, have been very active in Guatemala since the 1880s. Both mainline denominations and evangelical or fundamentalist groups are represented. Protestants are critical of folk Christianity and especially deplore the drunkenness that accompanies fiestas.

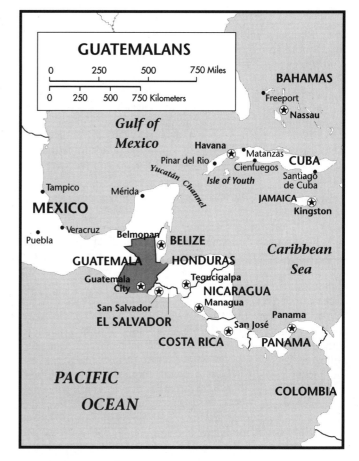

⁶ MAJOR HOLIDAYS

Pilgrims from all over Central America come to Esquipulas on 15 January to worship at the shrine of the Black Christ, a sculpted balsam-wood image 1.5 m (5 ft) high, whose dark color resembled the complexion of the Indians before smoke generated by candles and incense turned it black. A temple, completed in 1758, houses the effigy, which is girdled in white satin embroidered with gold and laden with jewels. Also important is the pilgrimage on 2 February to the village church in Chiantla, famous for its silver image of the Virgin Mary.

For size and scope, Antigua's Holy Week (late March or early April) pageantry is unrivaled in Latin America. Events reach a climax with a Passion procession on the morning of Good Friday. A bright carpet of flowers and dyed sawdust lines the route. Chichicastenango celebrates 21 December, the day of St. Thomas, with a week-long fiesta marked by ritual dances of the Quiché and the *Palo Volador,* in which costumed men dangle by ropes from a 18-m-high (60-ft-high) maypole.

The Garifuna of the Caribbean celebrate their arrival in Guatemala with Yuriman, a simulation of the first farm plantings, in Lívingston each 13–15 May. This festival is accompanied by singing, dancing, and hand-clapping. Like the other nations of Central America (except Panama), Guatemala celebrates 15 September as Independence Day to commemorate the region's declaration of independence from Spain in 1821.

7 RITES OF PASSAGE

In Guatemala's villages, both a midwife and a *brujo* attend a child's birth, the latter to pray for long life and good health and protection against the evil eye, which can be cast on children by a stranger or a blue-eyed person. A breech delivery or one with an umbilical cord around the neck is considered a sign of good fortune. Baptism is the only Church sacrament in which Indians normally partake. An attendant godmother and godfather are essential to the ceremony. Indian babies are carried on their mother's back and breast-fed whenever hungry. Children wear clothing identical to their parents and are put to work at an early age.

In conservative ladino society, group boy-girl activities begin at about age 14, but real dating does not begin until later. A girl's 15th birthday indicates that she has come of age and calls for a special celebration. A boy's coming of age is recognized when he turns 18. A young man still asks a girl's father for her hand in marriage. Engagements of several years are common.

Among Indians, although actual arranged marriages with no say by the prospective partners are rare, a youth's father may seek out a *tertulero,* or matchmaker, to find him a suitable bride—a girl under 16. Once an arrangement is reached, the young man provides a dowry. There is a betrothal feast and there may be a marriage ceremony performed by a village priest if available, followed by a feast.

At Indian funerals the Mayan Priest spins the coffin at the grave to fool the devil and point the deceased's spirit toward heaven. Yellow is the color of mourning, so yellow blossoms are hung in the form of a cross on the grave, with accompanying candles burning. Food is placed at the head of the grave for the spirit of the departed. Indians toll church bells for the dead to acquire merit with the gods.

8 INTERPERSONAL RELATIONS

In Hispanic countries, when people stop to greet each other there will probably be some physical contact as well as words exchanged. Both acquaintances and friends generally shake hands when meeting and parting. Men may pat each other on the back, and women often embrace and kiss each other on one or both cheeks. Men and women will generally do so only if they are relatives. When talking or simply standing or sitting in a public place, people tend to come closer to one another than in the United States. When talking, people may gesture more than in the United States and even touch the other person on the arm or shoulder for emphasis. Family and friends will drop in on each other, especially on Sundays and holidays. These are brief, informal stops.

9 LIVING CONDITIONS

In 1990 it was estimated that the poorer half of the population was receiving only 60% of its daily minimum caloric requirements. The mortality rate for children up to age five is 68 deaths per 1,000 children. Gastrointestinal and respiratory ailments take a heavy toll because of poor sanitation as well as poor nutrition. In rural areas, few people have access to drinkable water.

Because of rural overpopulation, the urban areas have swelled with migrants, many of them in illegal squatter settlements. Peasants mostly live in two-room, dirt-floor adobe structures or ones that use poles for walls. The roofs are made of palm leaves, straw, or tiles. Their small farm plots may be several hours' walk away.

Guatemala's road network is not extensive and, especially in mountainous areas, the roads are seldom paved. Most people rely on secondhand buses—formerly US school buses—for more than purely local transportation. Automobiles range from old, patched-up Japanese models to the luxury cars of the elite.

10 FAMILY LIFE

Guatemala's families are close-knit and generally the only dependable source of help in a society where church and state have a limited impact on daily life. Among ladinos, the nuclear family of father, mother, and children is most common, but a moderately prosperous household often includes other relatives and servants or orphaned children. The extended family forms the basis of the Indian community. Indians rarely take mates outside their own linguistic group and village. Recently married couples typically live with the husband's parents.

Despite Guatemala's rapid population growth and the resulting division of land into ever-smaller plots, children are greatly desired, especially among Indians. During the late 1980s, the average number of births per woman completing her childbearing years was almost six. Ideally, a ladino woman does not work outside the home, but economic necessity has forced many to do so. Indian women tend gardens and household animals. Many earn cash by handicrafts or, in the city, domestic work.

11 CLOTHING

The clothing of many ladinos is similar to that of modern Westerners, but almost every Indian community has its own style of dress. Indeed, an individual's village can be identified by the design of the cloth. It is estimated that there are at least 325 major patterns in the traditional dress that is still everyday garb—particularly among women—in Indian villages. These are handwoven articles made on pre-Spanish looms or foot-powered treadle looms introduced by the Spanish.

However, traditional clothing is worn more frequently by women than men, and more often by poorer Guatemalans in general. Western-style dress is more frequent among people with a higher standing in their communities. Lately, second-hand clothing from the United States, sold at bargain prices, has become popular. It is not uncommon to see traditional garments worn together with a college tee-shirt.

The typical dress of Indian women usually includes a *huipil,* which is a smock-style blouse; a skirt with a belt; a *tzute* (scarf or headdress); and a *rebozo* (shawl). Men may wear brightly colored trousers and a shirt with a belt or sash, a tunic or vest, a jacket, a straw hat, a shoulder bag called a *morral,* and sandals (Indian women normally go barefoot). Most Indian men, however, now wear manufactured clothing largely indistinguishable from their ladino counterparts.

12 FOOD

Guatemalan food is generally simple and not highly spiced. Corn tortillas, rice, beans, tamales, and plantains are the staples. Tortillas and black beans are served at every meal. A classic method of preparing meats is to cook them in water before adding sauce or seasonings. An essential seasoning of Mayan

Despite Guatemala's rapid population growth and the resulting division of land into ever-smaller plots, children are greatly desired. During the late 1980s, the average number of births per woman completing her childbearing years was almost six. (Cory Langely)

foods is squash seeds toasted and ground to a powder. Coffee is lighter and more watery than the brew Americans and Europeans are used to drinking.

¹³ EDUCATION

Education is free and compulsory between the ages of 7 and 13, but enforcement is lax in rural areas, and one out of every five children of those ages was not enrolled in school in 1991. Many do not complete the primary-school cycle because they must work to help their families. The adult literacy rate was only 55% in 1990. Indians are at a particular disadvantage since Spanish is not their mother tongue.

Six years of secondary school can lead either to university education or specialized training. There are six universities. Chief of these is the State University of San Carlos, in Guatemala City. The constitution guarantees it autonomy and not less than 5% of the national budget. The university, which charges no tuition, has more than 50,000 students, many of whom must work part-time while pursuing their studies. Most of the private universities are in Guatemala City, including the Francisco Marroquín University. The private Universidad Rural is based in Chimaltenango.

¹⁴ CULTURAL HERITAGE

Native music developed from a blend of Spanish and Indian influences. But Guatemala is better known for its traditional dances, which are often a kind of musical drama that recalls a historical event with the use of costumes and masks. These are performed at fiestas in honor of the local saint. The Deer Dance symbolizes the struggle between humans and animals. The Dance of the Conquest recalls the victory of the Spanish over the Indians.

Tikal and other monumental sites are testimony to the architectural accomplishments of the Maya. The Spanish influence can be found in colonial-era churches, sculptures, and paintings. Guatemala's best-known 20th-century painter is Carlos Mérida.

The Maya had the most advanced system of writing in the Americas among indigenous peoples. A Spanish priest, Francisco Ximénez, translated the rarest and most sacred book of the Quiché, the *Popol Vuh,* in 1680. This work is a treasure-trove of Mayan beliefs and practices. Because of the heavy hand of the Inquisition, the first history of Guatemala, written by Antonio de Remesal and published in 1619, was ordered "thrown to the stables." Even *Don Quixote* had to be smuggled into the colony. Rafael Landival, a Jesuit, wrote the poem *Rusticatio Mexicana* while in exile in Italy. This was the outstanding Guatemalan work of the colonial era. Famous authors of the 19th century include Jose Batres y Montúfar and José Milla y Vidaurre. Enrique Gómez Carillo (1873–1927) was a novelist and poet. The novelist and poet Miguel Ángel Asturias received the Nobel Prize for literature in 1967.

¹⁵ WORK

Ladinos tend to become shopkeepers, government employees, or laborers in private industries. The *fincas,* or large plantations, employ both ladinos and Indians for seasonal labor during the harvest. The sizable part of the population outside the modern economy continues to till small plots for subsistence, supplemented by income from handicrafts and seasonal plantation work. Many migrants to the cities, unable to find employment, take to street vending. It was estimated in 1992 that 46% of the labor force was unemployed or underemployed. The minimum wage was under $3 a day in 1994.

¹⁶ SPORTS

Soccer is a national passion, played even in the most traditional and remote Indian villages. Guatemala City has the largest soccer stadium in Central America.

¹⁷ ENTERTAINMENT AND RECREATION

Fiestas continue to provide popular entertainment and to reflect much of the creative life of the people. They all include music and dance, eating and drinking, and fireworks. Cinemas, found only in the major cities, mostly play US films dubbed or subtitled in Spanish. Television fare includes dubbed US programs and variety shows and *telenovelas* (soap operas) imported from Mexico and Venezuela.

Guatemala is the heartland of marimba music. Almost every town has a marimba orchestra, which includes the accompaniment of a brass band, and no wedding is complete without marimba music. The repertoire includes many Mexican numbers. Indians employ other instruments for their rites, including the pre-Conquest drum and flute.

18 FOLK ART, CRAFTS, AND HOBBIES

Guatemala's handspun and woven textiles are among the finest in the world. Made by highland Indians, they display brilliant colors and intricate designs, both in the form of raw cloth and finished garments. Cotton, wool, and silk are the traditional fibers for clothing, although acrylics have been introduced. Blankets and rugs are also made from these fibers, while hats, mats, hammocks, and baskets are made with different types of cane and reed as well as fibers from the maguey cactus. Ceramics are produced both by pre-Conquest methods, molding clay by hand and using natural clays and dyes, and with the potter's wheel and glazes and enamels introduced from Spain. Jade jewelry dates from ancient times. Woodcrafted products include traditional masks, carved squash gourds, and colonial-style doors and furniture.

19 SOCIAL PROBLEMS

About 2% of the population owns some 70% of the cultivable land. About 65% of the original forest cover has been destroyed, and about 30% of the land is eroded or seriously degraded. Only 33% of the population has regular access to health services. Domestic violence occurs but receives little attention. The labor code makes legal strikes difficult, and women, usually found in low-wage jobs, are paid significantly less than are men.

20 BIBLIOGRAPHY

Asturias, Miguel Ángel. *Leyendas de Guatemala.* Buenos Aires: Editorial Losada, 1957.

Gall, Timothy, and Susan Gall, ed. *Worldmark Encyclopedia of the Nations.* 8th ed. Detroit: Gale Research, 1995.

Glassman, Paul. *Guatemala Guide.* Moscow, VT: Passport Press, 1978.

Osborne, Lilly de Jongh. *Indian Crafts of Guatemala and El Salvador.* Norman, OK: University of Oklahoma Press, 1965.

Wright, Ronald. *Time Among the Maya.* New York: Weidenfeld & Nicolson, 1989.

—by R. Halasz, reviewed by A. Duarte

GUYANANS

LOCATION: Guyana
POPULATION: 800,000
LANGUAGE: English (official); Creole patois; Hindi; Urdu
RELIGION: Hinduism; Christianity; Islam; native animism

1 INTRODUCTION

Guyana borders the Caribbean Sea to the north, Brazil to the south, Venezuela to the east and Suriname to the west. Its name is derived from the Amerindian word *guiana,* "land of waters." During the 16th and 17th centuries, the great European colonial powers fought to claim the land for their sugarcane plantations, and the country changed hands with bewildering frequency, mostly as a result of wars between the British and the French. Britain shipped in slaves from West Africa to work in the sugarcane fields. Slavery was abolished in 1804. Today, Guyana exports sugar, rice, rum, timber, diamonds, bauxite, shrimp, and molasses.

Guyana became independent from Britain in 1966. Politically, Guyana has moved on a steady course toward socialism from the time of independence. Both the government and the opposition party are Marxist-Leninist, although since the death of the first prime minister, Forbes Burnham, in 1985, ties with the West have been strengthened. Politics are essentially divided along racial lines, and for 28 years, beginning in 1964, Guyana was ruled by one party, the People's National Congress, representing predominantly Afro-Guyanese interests. In 1992, however, a new election saw the return of Dr. Cheddi Jagan of the People's Progressive Party, which represents the predominantly Hindu population.

2 LOCATION AND HOMELAND

The Cooperative Republic of Guyana is an independent republic and member of the British Commonwealth located in the northeast corner of South America.

It comprises an area of 214,970 sq km (83,000 sq mi) and its coastline is about 430 km (270 mi) long. Inland there are many uninhabited areas, and most of the country's population of about 800,000 people live on the narrow coastal strip along the Atlantic coast, much of which has been reclaimed from the sea by a series of canals and some 140 miles of dikes. The capital and chief port is Georgetown. Inland is a huge plateau which forms most of the country's center, crisscrossed with the numerous rapids of Guyana's rivers.

Guyana's population originally came from various parts of the British Empire, although a small number of aboriginal Indians still live seminomadic lives, scattered throughout the inland forest regions. The Afro-Guyanese, descendants of the African slaves shipped in to work on the sugarcane plantations, form one-third of the population. The Asian Indians, who came mostly as indentured labor to replace the Africans when slavery was abolished, form the largest racial group, making up about half of the population, while Portuguese, Chinese, and Amerindians make up the remaining one-sixth of the population.

3 LANGUAGE

The official and principal language of Guyana is English. Guyana is the only South American country to have English as its official language. But a Creole patois is spoken in the country. Hindi and Urdu are also heard among older Asian Indians.

4 FOLKLORE

Much of Guyanan folklore springs from religious and racial backgrounds of its diverse population. Hindus identify with their cultural heroes such as Rama, Krishna, and Mahavira. In fact, many of them give their children names based on characters from the great epic stories of India.

Many Creole folk tales are based on the Afro-centered traditions that emphasize the organic unity between animals—including humans—and nature, and also the unity between the living and the dead.

5 RELIGION

The major religions of Guyana are Hinduism and Christianity (chiefly Anglican and Roman Catholic). There is also a sizable minority of Muslims. About 54% of the population are Hindu, 27% are Christian, and 15% are Muslim. Many Asian Indians accept baptism and membership in Christian churches without abandoning their participation in Hindu rituals. Animistic religion is still practiced by the Amerindian peoples.

Some adherents of Christian groups also practice traditional African beliefs such as *winti,* (meaning literally "wind"). This is a traditional polytheistic and largely secret religion of West African origin. It recognizes a multitude of gods and ghosts, each having their own myths, rites, offerings, taboos, and magical forces. The phenomenon of *obia* (a healer god) can be used to bring illness and other calamities onto the practitioner's enemies.

Hundreds of people turn up for the seven-day festival of Ramayana Yajma when the Brahmins read and explain the *Ramayana.* The *Ramayana* is an ancient epic poem that recounts the dramatic and difficult life of Rama, the royal heir, who is exiled from the court of Ayodha and exiled to the forest for 14 years because some of his royal relatives conspire against him. The sorrows of separation, the necessary courage required to confront tragic events in life, and the way a human being can create meaning and purpose in life are all important themes in the *Ramayana.* Christians as well as Hindus from all over the country participate in Ramayana Yajma, and throughout the week they are fed a variety of Indian dishes, with vegetables forming the main part of the meals provided.

6 MAJOR HOLIDAYS

Much recreational activity is based upon the festivities that accompany Hindu, Muslim, and Christian holidays, such as Christmas, the end of Ramadan, and (in early March) Phagwah, the Hindu New Year, a joyous celebration that celebrates the triumph of good over evil and is noted for the energetic throwing of perfume and water. Easter Monday is also a traditional day for flying kites. Republic Day, on 23 February, is the day the president reports to the nation and is a day for much street marching.

7 RITES OF PASSAGE

Baptism is common, even among Asian Indians who attend Christian churches while maintaining their participation in Hindu rituals. In their homes, Hindus celebrate domestic reli-

gious ceremonies such as Pujas for special occasions like birthdays or anniversaries.

Many Afro-Guyanese couples do not regularize their unions with a license or church ceremony.

8 INTERPERSONAL RELATIONS

Anyone visiting a friend or acquaintance at their home address is expected to call upon everyone else that they know within that neighborhood. Not to do so is considered extremely rude. Open hospitality is a great feature of Guyanese life and no visit can be completed without the offer of a meal or refreshment.

The familiar Hindu caste system, which is a highly localized phenomenon in the villages of India, no longer exists in Guyana. When the low castes and the twice-born Brahmins were thrown together on board ship to travel from India to the Caribbean during the 19th century, the caste system soon became irrelevant. Today there is just one caste for all in Guyana, although the Brahmins do retain their special religious role in interpreting the sacred knowledge of the holy rituals and Sanskrit texts.

9 LIVING CONDITIONS

Out of a population of 800,000 people, some 170,000 live in Georgetown, the capital. Many houses in the center of Georgetown are made of wood. Most people live in small villages and towns along the coast. The houses are built of wood with tin roofs and are constructed on stilts 2.5 m to 3 m (8–10 ft) off the ground to avoid flooding from the sea.

Guyana's gross national product, estimated to be only about $600 per capita in the mid-1990s, makes it one of the world's poorest countries. Food shortages have created widespread malnutrition, and diseases formerly under control such as beri-beri and malaria have reappeared as sanitation problems increase. The economy was shattered by the depressed world demand for bauxite and sugar, which has led to a near break-down in essential public services such as electricity. The country is, however, nearly self-sufficient in food.

There is a limited road and highway system, much of which is only partly paved and partly made of baked clay. In fact, there are only a few hundred kilometers or miles of paved roads, mostly in the coastal region.

10 FAMILY LIFE

Ethnic identity continues to be important within daily life. The mother- and grandmother-dominated family that is common among the Afro-Guyanese differs from the father-oriented Asian Indian family. Bearing children out of wedlock among Africans is not stigmatized, although in recent years many have begun adopting middle-class values by "doing the right thing" and getting married.

The African community is made up of a variety of households ranging from a nuclear monogamous family consisting of a couple and their children to a kind of extended family that includes grandparents, their children, their grandchildren, and other relations.

The Asian Indian traditionally has a different kind of extended family, but the European nuclear pattern is becoming the norm. Upon marriage, the son is expected to take his bride and live for some time with his parents. This is because it is the duty of the parents to guide the children through the early days of marriage. Then, by the sixth or seventh year, the son will have set up his own household with his wife and children.

11 CLOTHING

A skirt and blouse is the popular form of clothing for women, but the sari is being increasingly worn by Hindu women. Hindu men wear a type of shirt called a *kurta* and one-piece trousers called *dhoti* (see **Hindus of Guyana**).

12 FOOD

A tasty Amerindian dish is the pepper pot, a spicy stew which is a characteristic Guyanese dish. The main ingredient is cassava. Farina, a coarse gravel-like flour derived from cassava boiled with local sun-dried beef, is known as *tasso* and is an edible and tasty fare for the Rupununi ranchers, who live in the savannas of the interior.

Dal, of Asian Indian origin, is also a very widespread and popular dish, and not just among the Hindus. It is a dish of lentils, often flavored with a mixture of spices (cinnamon, pepper, and garlic) cooked in oil.

13 EDUCATION

Children receive free, compulsory education. The government assumed full control of education in 1976 and took over Church-run and private primary schools.

The principal university is the University of Georgetown at Turkeyeen, in the eastern part of the capital.

The literacy rate is quite high and is estimated at 98% among men and 95% among women. Despite this, due to economic decline, physical facilities have deteriorated in schools; books and supplies are limited; and many educated Guyanese live abroad, particularly in London and New York.

14 CULTURAL HERITAGE

Post-independent Guyana still bears the imprint of its colonial heritage and, despite government exhortation to the contrary, the people continue to be taught to respect and covet European values. Amerindian culture, which remains uninfluenced by national politics, is recognized as an important element in the cultural life of the country. Amerindian artifacts are featured in museum displays, and their culture inspires local music and painting. Major Amerindian groups include the Caribs, the Arawaks, and the Warraus of the northwest coast. The Makusis are the best-known group of savanna-dwellers, whereas other groups are forest-dwellers.

One of the most mysterious aspects of Guyana's cultural heritage are the hieroglyphics known as the *timchri* scattered on rocks in Guyana's interior, which have not been deciphered and which point to more advanced civilizations.

Noteworthy writers are Wilson Harris, A. J. Seymour, and Walter Rodney. The best-known work of literature is E. R. Braithwaite's novel, *To Sir With Love,* about a black teacher in an all-White London secondary school, which became a famous film.

15 WORK

The country has a three-sector economy: private, public, and cooperative. The government controls over 80% of the economy. The state-controlled sugar enterprise, Guysuco, employs more Guyanese than any other industry. Domestic economy reflects ethnic divisions. Asian Indians and their families control most small businesses such as small farms and shops, while Africans dominate the government sector. But there are an increasing number of Hindus entering the legal and medical professions.

Wages are very low and many people depend on overseas remittances from relatives abroad to survive. Many people also work at more than one job. The unemployment rate is 13.5%.

16 SPORTS

The Guyanese share a passion for cricket that is prevalent throughout the English-speaking Caribbean. The game is one of the few unifying factors in the country. It has been said, however, that cricket in Guyana is totally unlike the game as it is played in England. In Guyana it is closer to the passionate atmosphere of a bullfight in Spain, galvanizing the people's national self-esteem.

The sport plays a special role in the historical, social, and cultural development of the country. By playing host in Georgetown to International Test Cricket Matches against other countries within the British Commonwealth, the people of Guyana have the opportunity to demonstrate their abilities on the international scene and to make a symbolic gesture against their oppressive colonial legacy. There are a number of heroes who have played for the West Indies team including Clive Lloyd, who captained the side for a number of years, Rohan Kanhai, and Neville Kalicharan.

¹⁷ ENTERTAINMENT AND RECREATION

Popular culture is as mixed as the various ethnic groups who live in Guyana. Georgetown offers a wide mix of museums and art galleries, and for the young people there are discos. A favorite kind of music among both Hindu and Afro-Guyanese is something called "chutney," a hot, spicy mixture of traditional Hindu music and rock music.

The cinema still plays a large part in the lives of older people, and the imported films from India reconnect the Hindus with their cultural roots. In the villages outside Georgetown, street cricket is played with a sponge ball, and the pitch is a coconut mat laid out in a field. Card games are also a passion with older people during the quiet times between sowing and harvesting.

¹⁸ FOLK ART, CRAFTS, AND HOBBIES

Many of the folk arts and crafts are entwined with the various Guyanese religions, such as kite-flying and bird-song competitions on Easter Sunday and Monday.

¹⁹ SOCIAL PROBLEMS

Race has been a divisive issue, with the Asian Indians accusing the Africans of racism and repression during the 28 years of rule by the People's National Congress party, during which they claimed that Hindu villages were attacked and plundered by security forces. The Africans dominate the Guyana Defence Force and the police. Street crime and violence are particularly notorious in Georgetown. Community police have now been introduced by the government into the city to try to retake control of the streets.

The new administration has also announced its intention of introducing structural changes with a "human face," and aims to alleviate poverty through a basic-needs strategy. It also intends to increase foreign and local investment, production, and exports. Cheddi Jagan has promised a "lean and clean" government and is determined to end racial discrimination.

²⁰ BIBLIOGRAPHY

Dabydeen, Dr. D. *Across the Dark Water.* London: MacMillan, 1995.

————.*India in the Caribbean.* London: Hansib, 1988.

Daly, Vere T. *A Short History of the Guyanese People.* London: Macmillan Education, 1975.

Frances, J., and I. Frances. *Guyana: Politics and Economics and Society Beyond the Burnham Era.* London: Pinter, n.d.

South America On a Shoestring. Australia: Lonely Planet Publications, 1983.

—by P. Pitchon

HAITIAN AMERICANS

For more information on Haitian history and culture, *see* **Vol. 2: Haitians**.

OVERVIEW

There have been two major stages of Haitian immigration to America, the first in the late 18th and early 19th centuries, and the second in the late 20th century. Both stages were prompted by economic and political unrest in Haiti. The slave rebellion in 1791 in what was then the French colony of St. Domingue drove the first wave of refugees to the American coast, especially to the New Orleans area of Louisiana. After several more years of political upheaval, bloodshed, and general instability, the black general Dessalines declared himself the leader of the independent republic of Haiti and began slaughtering all remaining whites. Those whites who were able to escape, along with many free blacks and mulattoes, as well as some black slaves, fled to America.

The second stage of Haitian immigration to America occurred more recently, beginning in the late 1950s. This time Haitians were fleeing the brutal dictatorship of François "Papa Doc" Duvalier and his son, Jean-Claude "Baby Doc" Duvalier, who succeeded him. At first, those who left Haiti were mostly well-educated professionals who could afford airfare and were considered "desirable" enough for the US to allow them to immigrate. As a result, Haiti suffered a severe "brain drain," adding to its internal troubles. Conditions worsened in Haiti, and by the 1970s life had become intolerable for many Haitians of all social and economic classes.

Lacking the financial resources to pay for airfare, and lacking the skills necessary to be considered "desirable" by the US, most Haitian refugees from the 1970s until today have been forced to take desperate measures to leave Haiti and enter the US. Thousands have piled onto small boats in the past three decades, risking their lives and sacrificing all of their possessions for a chance at a better life in the US. The first Haitian "boat people" arrived in Florida in 1972. Despite efforts by the US Immigration and Naturalization Service (INS) and the US Coast Guard, boat people continue to arrive today.

Some owners and captains of small boats in Haiti have made tremendous profits smuggling refugees across the hundreds of miles of water between Haiti and Florida, or across the much shorter distance to Guantanamo Bay, Cuba. (Cuba does not welcome Haitian immigrants, so it is only a stopping place on the journey to freedom.) Haitian individuals and families sell all they have to raise the money for passage on a boat. The boats are small and overcrowded, conditions are miserable, and the risks are great. Boats capsize, or captains force the passengers overboard to avoid arrest as smugglers. Perhaps hundreds of Haitians have drowned within sight of the US shore. In 1981, a boat carrying more than 60 Haitian passengers, two of them women with nearly full-term pregnancies, capsized only 50 yards off the coast of Florida. Some managed to swim to shore, but 33 drowned, including the two pregnant women (leading the medical authority to list the number of dead at 35). This was only one tragedy among many that have taken the lives of Haitian refugees.

In 1981, US President Ronald Reagan ordered a number of measures to stop the flow of Haitian refugees into America, but Haitians have continued to risk their lives to gain entrance into what they believe to be the "Promised Land." Unfortunately, the US has failed to live up to that designation in the case of Haitian immigrants. The Immigration and Nationality (McCarran–Walter) Act of 1952 severely curtailed legal immigration from West Indian nations. Although US immigration reform in 1965 removed some of the restrictions, it is still difficult for the majority of Haitians to achieve legal immigration status in the US. Nor are they officially considered "refugees."

The nonrefugee status of Haitians is extremely controversial, provoking accusations of racism on the part of the U.S. Immigration and Naturalization Service (INS). Cubans, who are mostly white and are fleeing a left-wing dictatorship, are welcomed as refugees and even assisted by the US government in their efforts to immigrate to the US. Haitians, who are black and are fleeing a right-wing dictatorship, are not. In any case, lacking legal or refugee status, Haitians must enter the US "illegally," subjecting them to various forms of harassment and shutting them out of employment, housing, and other opportunities.

Many incoming Haitians, particularly "boat people," are arrested upon entering the US and placed in city and county jails, federal prisons, or detention camps, such as the Krome Center in south Florida. They may be held there for a period of months or even years. Some sign papers that say they agree to return voluntarily to Haiti, after which they are promptly flown back to that country from which they sacrificed everything to escape. Others are forcibly deported. A number manage to evade the INS and live as fugitives in their new home. The lucky ones are granted legal immigrant status, often through sponsorship by church agencies or other social justice organizations.

The most recent wave of Haitian immigration to the US was prompted by the violent takeover in 1991 of the first democratically elected government in Haiti. Jean-Bertrand Aristide became the first democratically elected president of Haiti in 1990, only to be overthrown eight months later by former Duvalier supporters. Coup leaders then set up a military dictatorship that ruled by force. Masses of Haitians swarmed to the sea to escape the regime. The US placed embargoes on Haiti to pressure the military to surrender its control, creating even more hardship for the Haitian people. Starvation and malnutrition became rampant in Haiti. Finally, when the US threatened a military invasion in 1994, the Haitian military dictatorship stepped down and Aristide was returned peacefully to the presidency. When his term ended in1996, he was succeeded by René Préval.

Conditions in Haiti remain extremely difficult, however. Haiti is the poorest nation in the western hemisphere and is one of the poorest in the entire world. Economic development is proceeding very slowly, and political stability has yet to be established securely. Despite their lack of welcome in the US, Haitian refugees continue to make their way to America, hoping for a better life, even if it is as an illegal alien.

Although Louisiana was the preferred destination for Haitian immigrants of the 18th and 19th centuries, only 633 Louisiana residents claimed Haitian ancestry in the 1990 US Census. The largest Haitian populations today are in New York (107,207) and Florida (105,495). The Miami, Florida, area has one of the greatest concentrations of Haitians in the US. Haitian immigrants have even created a "Little Haiti" section of Miami. According to the US Census, the total Haitian American population in 1990 was 289,521, most of them (225,393) foreign-born. Because so many Haitian immigrants are considered "illegal aliens" and are either in detention centers or in hiding, however, US Census figures are undoubtedly quite low. It is impossible to know for certain just how many Haitian Americans live in the US today.

Haitians, both those who immigrated to America and those who stayed in Haiti, had a tremendous influence on American culture in the 1800s. Those who came to the US brought with them their French and Creole culture. The population of New Orleans increased from 4,446 in 1791 to 8,056 by 1797, mostly through the influx of Haitian refugees. Because they generally had more education and training than the colonists already there, the Haitians rose quickly to the upper ranks of society and shaped that society in significant ways.

The majority of Haitian refugees in the 19th century were Catholic. This is one reason they chose to settle primarily in Louisiana. As a sometime-French, sometime-Spanish colony, the dominant religion was Catholicism, as opposed to the fiercely Protestant character of the English colonies. Haitian Creole Catholics, and later Cajun Catholics, created a French Catholic flavor to Louisiana, especially New Orleans. The festival of Mardi Gras ("Fat Tuesday"), a Cajun-Creole celebration preceding the beginning of Lent, is still a major annual event, drawing visitors from all over the world to New Orleans every February.

Many Haitian refugees today practice Vodou (also known as Voodoo), a blend of African folk religion brought to Haiti by the original African slaves, and the Catholicism of the slave owners. Vodou is predominantly concerned with appeasing the many spirits that rule nature. Ancestor worship is also of central importance. "Voodoo" has been inaccurately popularized in American culture as black magic, where pins are stuck into dolls and people are cursed or turned into zombies. In fact, Vodou practitioners use herbal remedies and a form of psychology interpreted as exorcism to bring people back into balance.

Early Haitian immigrants had many other effects on Louisianan society and culture. Louisiana is the only state in the US today that continues to base its legal system on the Code Napoléon (a code of laws written by Napoleon Bonaparte); other states use English Common Law. Music, food, and architecture all show strong Haitian influences in Louisiana and other places in the South where Haitians settled (such as Charleston, South Carolina). These influences have since spread throughout general American culture. For example, the basic structure of blues singing—an introductory couplet that is repeated, with the theme then developed around the couplet—is based on Haitian folk music. Certain drums and rhythms, as well as the banjo, were introduced into American music by the Haitians. Creole cooking has become quite popular in mainstream American society. "Shotgun" houses (one room wide and several rooms deep with doors at both ends) were introduced by black artisans from Haiti in the 19th century and are identical to houses still found in Haiti today.

Perhaps most importantly, the successful slave revolt in Haiti seriously influenced both white and black Americans. White Americans became extremely fearful of a similar revolt occurring in the US and strove to prevent their black slaves from gaining enough education or organization to consider rebellion. Many white Americans were also afraid that emancipating slaves in the US would lead to a black insurrection (once free, they would take over). Black Americans saw the Haitian revolt as proof that blacks were indeed capable of self-rule. As the first independent black nation in the western hemisphere, Haiti became a symbol of pride for blacks in America.

Haitian refugees of the 18th and 19th centuries adapted quickly to mainstream American society with relatively few difficulties. This has not been the case for 20th century Haitian refugees. Classified as "illegal" by the INS, held in prisons and detention camps or forced to live as fugitives, and suffering from physical and mental health problems resulting from malnutrition, overcrowded conditions, and trauma, most recent Haitian refugees have found it difficult to survive—let alone thrive—in America. Those who are granted "legal" immigrant status often lack the language and job skills to succeed in the industrialized US. A sizeable number end up working as migrant farm workers (as do many "illegal" Haitian immigrants), a scant improvement over their former lives in Haiti.

Today's Haitian refugees also suffer a unique problem among US immigrants. Because 5% of Acquired Immune Deficiency Syndrome (AIDS) cases reported in 1981–1983 were Haitian immigrants who were not homosexual or intravenous drug users, the Center for Disease Control classified Haitians, as an entire ethnic population, a "high risk group." This classification was very controversial because little research was done into why Haitian immigrants contract the disease before they were labeled "high risk" just for being Haitian. The stigma of AIDS has fallen upon all Haitian refugees, causing them to be rejected for housing, employment, and legal immigration opportunities. Subsequent AIDS research has led to modifications in classifications from "high risk *groups*" to "high risk *behaviors*," officially removing Haitians from the list. However, once applied, the social stigma is not so easily removed. Between racism and the fear of AIDS, Haitian Americans have a difficult life ahead of them in the US.

BIBLIOGRAPHY

Hunt, Alfred N. *Haiti's Influence on Antebellum America: Slumbering Volcano in the Caribbean.* Baton Rouge: Louisiana State University Press, 1988.

Miller, Jake C. *The Plight of Haitian Refugees.* New York: Praeger Publishers, 1984.

"Protests Erupt Across Haiti as Leaders Push Austerity." *New York Times.* (17 January 1997).

Tekavec, Valerie. *Teenage Refugees from Haiti Speak Out.* New York: The Rosen Publishing Group, 1995.

US Bureau of the Census. *Detailed Ancestry Groups for States.* 1990 Census of Population Supplementary Reports, CP-S-1-2. Washington, DC, October 1992.

———. *The Foreign-Born Population in the United States.* 1990 CP-3-1. Washington, DC, July 1993.

—by D. K. Daeg de Mott

HAITIANS

LOCATION: Haiti
POPULATION: 6,589,000
LANGUAGE: Haitian Creole; French
RELIGION: Vodou; Roman Catholicism; Protestantism

[1] INTRODUCTION

To a large extent, Haitian history has been shaped by foreign powers: first Spain, then France, and finally the United States. A rich, lush land with a strategic location, Haiti has often been viewed as a valuable piece of real estate.

When Columbus landed on the island of Hispaniola on 6 December 1492, he was greeted by the Taino/Arawak Indians. However, the Spanish conquerors exploited the indigenous population, and by 1550 the Taino/Arawak population had been almost entirely wiped out in violent uprisings or from inhumane forced labor and exposure to imported European diseases. In their quest for gold and other mineral riches, the Spanish resorted to bringing West Africans by force to the New World to work as slaves. The Spanish stayed on the island because it was strategically important as the gateway to the Caribbean, from where many riches were shipped to Europe.

Tortuga Island, off the northwest coast of Hispaniola, was the first French foothold. Reportedly expelled by the Spanish from the nearby island of St. Christopher (St. Kitts), the first French residents of Tortuga, joined by runaway slaves from Hispaniola, survived by curing meats, tanning hides, and pirating Spanish ships. They became known as *buccaneers*, from the Arawak word for smoking meats.

After a French settlement was commissioned on Tortuga in 1659, settlers started encroaching on the northwest part of Hispaniola. In 1670, the French made Cap Français (present-day Cap-Haïtien) their first major settlement on Hispaniola, taking advantage of its distance from the Spanish capital of Santo Domingo. The western part of the island was commonly referred to as Saint-Domingue, which became its official name after Spain relinquished the area to France in 1697 following the signing of the Treaty of Ryswick. Relying on slavery, the French turned Saint-Domingue into one of its richest colonies. Coffee, sugar, cotton, and indigo from Haiti accounted for approximately 67% of France's commercial interests abroad and about 40% of its foreign trade. Because of the high death rate among male slaves, France continually brought new slaves from Africa; the number of enslaved Africans shipped to Haiti by the French totaled over 500,000.

In the mid-1700s, the number of runaway slaves, known as *maroons,* grew. From the safety of the mountains and forests, guerrilla bands of maroons attacked the French colonists. The colonial authorities, often with what was probably the forced help of the mulattos (a Spanish term for persons of mixed African-European heritage), were able to repel the attacks. However, when the Colonial Assembly refused to give mulattos the right to vote, even though they owned land and paid taxes, the mulattos also began to revolt.

But it was the slave rebellion of 1791 that set the colony on the path to independence. The mulattos fought against the French colonists who supported the monarchy, but not against those of the new French Republic, who wanted to give mulattos the right to vote. The slave forces were also split; some fought against the colonists, while others fought both the colonists and the mulattos. Competing for power over the area, Spain and Britain intervened and by 1794 they had almost gained control when tropical disease began to take its toll on their troops. Toussaint L'Ouverture, who had been one of the leaders of the slave rebellion in 1791, then made a crucial decision: he pledged his support to France. Although promising freedom, Spain had shown no signs of moving in that direction, while Britain had actually reinstituted slavery in areas under its control. The French Republicans seemed the best choice for freedom. Thus in 1796, when L'Ouverture rescued the French commander from mulattos seeking to depose him, L'Ouverture was rewarded by being named Lieutenant Governor of Saint-Domingue.

By 1800 L'Ouverture was in command of all Hispaniola. He abolished slavery, but in order to ensure stability and economic survival, he reinstated the plantation system, using enforced contract labor, and became a military dictator. However, he had never formally declared independence from France. In 1802, Napoleon sent forces to depose L'Ouverture, and again the French attempted to use the mulattos to attain victory. Forced into surrender, L'Ouverture was assured by the French that he could retire quietly. But a short time later, he was arrested and exiled to France, where he died in prison. After this deception, the remaining Haitian forces rallied against the French. The French military was fighting the British in Europe as well as the Haitians, and in 1803 Napoleon sold Louisiana to the US to help finance his campaigns. On 1 January 1804, Haiti declared independence, becoming the second independent nation (after the United States) in the Americas and the first free black republic in the world.

Jean-Jacques Dessalines, a former slave who had commanded the black and mulatto forces at the close of the revolution, became the leader of the new nation. Knowing only military organization, he used the military to govern, beginning what became an established tradition of military rule. The newly independent Haiti was not formally recognized by the European powers. The United States, itself a slaveholding power, withheld recognition until 1862, after the slaveholding south had seceded from the Union, sending Frederick Douglass as its consul to Haiti. In 1838, Haiti received its long-awaited recognition from France, after final payment of its "independence debt" (begun in 1825) totaling 150 million French francs, its entire annual budget at the time. After the revolution, the collaboration of Blacks and Mulattos, which had won Haiti independence, turned to conflict. The Black generals of the slave armies were also now competing for power and wealth. Thus, the early regimes of Haiti, whether led by mulattos or blacks, were dictatorial, keeping access to education, wealth, and power to themselves.

From its beginning as an independent nation, Haiti developed two distinct societies. The minority elite lived in towns and controlled the government, military, and trade; they imitated a European lifestyle, using the French language for government, commercial affairs, and education. The peasants, however, lived in the *peyi andeyo,* or "the country outside." The majority peasant population remained outside the formal political, educational, and economic structure.

In 1915, Haitian political instability, American trade and investments, growing US concern over German interests and

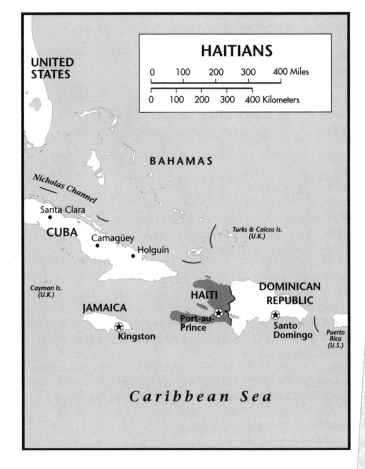

influence in Haiti, and Haiti's strategic importance to the United States led to a US invasion and occupation that would last almost 20 years. US intervention in smaller, neighboring nations (such as Colombia, Cuba, Honduras, and Nicaragua) to protect US interests and promote regional stability was quite common during that period. Under the American occupation, Haitian figureheads were installed, but the United States had veto power over all government decisions, and the Marine Corps served as administrators in the provinces. The United States declared martial law, rewrote the Haitian constitution, took control of Haiti's finances, and passed legislation permitting foreigners to own land in Haiti for the first time since 1804. It also established the Haitian National Guard (*Garde d'Haiti*) as Haiti's first professional military force, which would later be used to create a repressive military regime. The occupation imposed stability and order. Infrastructure and health conditions improved; roads, schools, and hospitals were built using forced corvée labor. Guerilla bands, led by Charlemagne Peralte, reacted against the occupation. Peralte was captured and assassinated by the US Marines in 1919. When the United States withdrew from Haiti in 1934, the level of poverty and illiteracy remained unchanged. The United States left behind a legacy of anti-American feeling and a well-trained national military force. In the absence of any effective political or social institutions, the military remained the only cohesive institution in the country, apart from the Roman Catholic Church.

After a particularly chaotic period, during which attempts at democracy were made but ultimately failed, François "Papa Doc" Duvalier, a doctor who had served as a rural administrator, was elected president in 1957 in military dominated elections. Perceived as an honest and humanitarian public-health expert, as well as a proponent of black power, Duvalier initially enjoyed the support of both the Haitian army and the United States. However, Duvalier soon set out to build a family dictatorship by changing the constitution to solidify his power. Knowing that an independent military was a threat to his presidency, he created the elite Presidential Guard. To maintain power outside the capital, he created a rural militia, commonly known as the *tonton makout,* whose mysterious and brutal tactics terrified the population. Using corruption and intimidation, he created a new elite of his own; in 1964, Duvalier declared himself President-for-Life. Duvalier's regime was marked by terror, corruption, and extremes of wealth and poverty. During the 1960s, US aid and support for Duvalier continued because of the regime's anticommunist stand and Haiti's strategic location near communist-led Cuba.

Naming his 19-year-old son, Jean-Claude, as his successor, "Papa Doc" died in 1971. Although "Baby Doc" was not as brutal as his father nor as politically astute, he continued policies of arbitrary imprisonment and torture of perceived opponents. Corruption and poverty also continued, as did US aid and support, much of which was siphoned off to Duvalier and his cronies. But it was opposition from young Haitians, as well as priests and nuns angered by the poverty and suffering, that eventually led to Duvalier's downfall. In 1983 Pope John Paul II visited the country and, appalled at the conditions there, declared that, "Things must change here." Under the institutional umbrella of the Catholic Church and galvanized by declarations in support of human rights by the Haitian Bishop's Conference, radio stations around the country broadcast uncensored news to the population, especially the sermons and speeches of a young Salesian priest in the slums of Port-au-Prince named Jean-Bertrand Aristide. Encouraged by a grassroots church movement (*Ti Kominite Legliz* or TKL), antigovernment protests swept through Haiti in 1985. Alarmed as people took to the streets, the United States withdrew its aid and support and arranged for Duvalier to step down. After hastily naming a National Council of Government made up of former military supporters, Jean-Claude fled in 1986 to exile in France.

Conditions for the masses did not improve. On election day in November 1987, scores of Haitians were killed at polling stations by soldiers and former *tonton makout* around the country. But the opposition movement could not be quashed and during a string of revolving dictatorships the voice of Father Aristide continued to echo the frustrations of the population. Aristide preached about the need for a *lavalas,* a flood to cleanse the country of corruption and make it clean and new. In 1990 at the urging of friends and supporters, Aristide declared himself a candidate for president to counter the political machinations of the neo-Duvalierist sector. In the country's first free and democratic elections, on 16 December 1990, he was elected president with 67.5% of the popular vote. But the underlying structure of the society and its long tradition of violence, control, and retribution had not changed. There continued to be strong and sometimes violent opposition to Aristide and his followers by those allied to the *ancien régime*. Aristide

pledged to clean up the corrupt and repressive apparatus of the past. Under a unique six-month mandate granted him under the 1987 constitution, allowing him full power to carry out any reforms deemed necessary, Aristide retired eight members of the high command of the *Forces Armées d'Haïti* (FAdH) and removed corrupt members of the judiciary. The military and the wealthy, however, continued to wield power, and in September 1991 the army staged a coup d'état, forcing Aristide into exile.

After Aristide's departure, some 50,000 Haitians fled the island nation by sea, only to be forcibly returned to the country and later to refugee camps at the US naval base at Guantanamo Bay in Cuba by the US Coast Guard. The repression unleashed by the military and their paramilitary allies known as *attachés* resulted in the deaths of some 4,000 citizens and the internal migration of over 300,000 people between urban and rural milieux. In 1993 General Raoul Cédras had agreed to step down in preparation for Aristide's return, under an agreement established at Governors Island, New York, but this was not honored. The United States, in concert with other countries, then applied pressure in the form of a trade embargo mandated by the United Nations, in order to pressure the coup regime to relinquish power. In 1994, after threats of a US invasion, a US negotiating team persuaded the military leadership to step aside so that the democratically elected Aristide could return to his rightful position. To ensure stability, UN troops led by the United States were sent to Haiti as a peacekeeping force. The military leaders went into exile, and on 15 October 1994, Aristide returned to power to begin the long, arduous task of rebuilding Haiti. In the 1995 legislative and municipal elections, the *Lavalas* movement overwhelmingly won the majority in Parliament and mayorships across the country. Presidential elections were held in December 1995, and former Prime Minister René G. Préval of the *Lavalas* coalition won resoundingly. The first peaceful transfer of power between two civilian presidents took place on 7 February 1996.

² LOCATION AND HOMELAND

The name "Haiti" comes from the Taino/Arawak word *ayiti* or *hayti,* which means "mountainous" or "high land." The Haitian homeland is the Republic of Haiti, which occupies the western third of the island of Hispaniola (known in Spanish as *La Isla Española*) in the Caribbean Sea. Hispaniola is located approximately 1,100 km (700 mi) southeast of Florida, between the islands of Cuba, Jamaica, and Puerto Rico. The Republic of Haiti has an area of 27,750 sq km (10,714 sq mi) including the islands of La Tortue, La Gonâve, Les Cayemites, La Navase, La Grande Caye, and Ile de Vâche. Haiti's total size makes it slightly larger in area than the US state of Maryland. The coastline is irregular, and there are two mountain ranges that stretch across the southern peninsula and one that runs along the northern peninsula. Mountains cover fully two-thirds of the interior, and the fertile plains that lie between them are used for agriculture.

Haiti's climate is generally tropical, both hot and humid. There are two rainy seasons: April through June, and August through mid-November. Annual rainfall averages 140–200 cm (56–80 in), with very uneven distribution. Rainfall is heaviest in the southern peninsula and parts of the northern mountains, while the western coast is relatively dry. Temperatures in the summer vary from 29–35°C (85–95°F) in the coastal lowlands to 18–21°C (65–70°F) in the interior highlands.

Haiti was once covered with virgin forests, but much of the natural vegetation has been destroyed by agriculture, grazing, and the exploitation of timber. Indeed, Haiti is in an alarming state of environmental devastation due to deforestation and soil erosion. Only 11% of the land is arable, and that figure is declining at a rapid rate. Haiti is in the process of becoming a desert. Viewed from the air, the state of Haiti's environment presents a harsh contrast to the Dominican Republic.

For the moment, however, pines, ferns, orchids, and other tropical trees and flowers can still be found. But the deterioration of natural vegetation has affected wildlife, which has lost its habitat. Once-common wild boars, guinea fowls, and wild ducks are now scarce, though caimans, flamingos, egrets, and small tropical birds can still be seen.

The population of Haiti was estimated at 6,589,000 in 1995. The last census was held in 1982 and counted 5,053,792 residents. Over 67% of the Haitians in the Republic of Haiti live in rural areas. Port-au-Prince, the capital, has a population of well over 1 million people, more than eight times the population of Cap-Haïtien, the second major city. Other major towns are Gonaïves, Les Cayes, and Jacmel. Almost all Haitians are descendants of the 500,000 enslaved West Africans who won their freedom from France in 1804. Haiti became the first modern independent republic where ethnic Africans made up the majority, which accounts for about 93% of today's population. About 5% have a mixed African-European heritage (traditionally the ruling class), and less than 1% have a solely European ancestry (mostly British and French). An even smaller minority have a Middle Eastern, North American, or Latin American ancestry.

There are over 800,000 Haitians living in the United States, with about 75% residing in either New York or Florida. The Haitian communities in the United States, particularly in South Florida, Boston, and the New York metropolitan area, have successfully established themselves as socially, economically, and culturally vibrant communities. Miami's Little Haiti is now an established community that has become a transitional place where recent arrivals and poorer Haitians settle temporarily until they become economically self-sufficient.

³ LANGUAGE

The two main languages of Haiti are Haitian Creole and French. Traditionally, the two languages served different functions, with Haitian Creole the informal everyday language of all the people, regardless of social class, and French the language of formal situations: schools, newspapers, the law and the courts, and official documents and decrees. All Haitians speak Haitian Creole, and about 85% of the population speaks Haitian Creole only. Since the vast majority of Haitians only speak Haitian Creole, there have been efforts to increase its usage. In 1979, a law was passed that permitted Haitian Creole to be the language of instruction, and the Constitution of 1983 gave Haitian Creole the status of a national language. However, it was only in 1987 that the Constitution granted official status to Haitian Creole. An official orthography was only developed in 1986, since Creole reflects Haiti's dominant oral culture. Only about 20% of the population speaks French, and only about 10% of the population can be considered bilingual in French and Haitian Creole. Fluency in French carries a high status in Haiti. Those who cannot read, write, and speak French often have limited opportunities in business and government.

Creole-speaking Haitians argue that the powerful French-speaking minority uses French language requirements just to maintain its authority. Most Haitians who have lived in the United States also speak English.

The Haitian Creole language evolved from a mixture of African dialect, indigenous Taino/Arawak, the Norman French of pirates, and colonial French. Haitian Creole grammar (or syntax) has strong characteristics of African languages, while its vocabulary is mostly of French origin, with contributions from Spanish, African languages, and, much later, English. Contemporary Haitian Creole incorporates words of diverse linguistic origins, including: Caribbean, with *kannari* (earthen jar) and *sanba* (poet, musician); African, with *houngan* (Vodou priest) and *zonbi* (ghost); Spanish, with *ablado* (talker) and *sapat* (sandal); and English, with *bokit* (bucket). As for the words derived from French, it is important to note that they have been modified in pronunciation or meaning. As an example, the following are borrowed French words with their corresponding meanings in Haitian Creole: *kriye* (to scream or shout), to weep; *bonbon* (candy), sweets; *boutik* (small, exclusive store), a family-operated store; *kabare* (nightclub), cafeteria tray. There are also some Haitian Creole words that have retained the 18th century French pronunciation.

The Haitian Creole language is called *Kreyòl* by native speakers. Some scholars have begun using the term *Ayisyen* (Haitian) as a symbol of national identity and to distinguish it from the generic term "creole," which refers to a number of languages. A creole language is a natural language that arises when peoples with different languages live and work among each other, similar to a pidgin language. Pidgin utilizes a simplified base language for the purposes of trade, with generous contributions from other languages, used to fulfill special, but temporary, communication needs. Pidgins have been used by sailors, traders, and pirates. They are native to no one; in other words, no one speaks a pidgin as a first language. Since a pidgin is used only as a necessity, it is restricted in form and usage. However, when a pidgin becomes the native language of an individual (and subsequently, many individuals who form a speech community), a creole language is born. A creole language is not just a simplified form of a given language, but a full-fledged language that is capable of serving all the intellectual, psychological, and social needs of its speakers. Some examples of Haitian Creole proverbs are:

Yon sel dwèt pa manje kalalou. (You cannot eat okra with one finger—we must all cooperate.)

Chay sòti sout tet, tonbe sou zepol. (The load goes from the head to the shoulder—Problems go from bad to worse.)

Gras a diri, ti wòch goute gres. (Thanks to the rice, the pebble tastes of grease—good things rub off.)

Bon kòk chante nan tout poulaye. (A good rooster sings to all his chickens—a good person is sought after by everyone.)

⁴ FOLKLORE

Haitian culture reflects a profound reverence for one's ancestors, a phenomenon that informs a particular cohesiveness within nuclear families and which extends to the larger family or race. Respect for the ancestors *(zansèt yo)* is reflected in the official observance of 2 January as Heroes or Ancestors' Day, a national holiday one day after the celebration of Independence Day (1 January).

Folk tales are popular in Haiti, especially the antics of Bouki and Ti Malis, who may also be found in the folklore of certain regions in West Africa. Stories are introduced by an invitation to hear a story. The person wishing to tell the story shouts out: *"Krik!"* If people want to hear the tale, and they nearly always do, they answer in chorus: *"Krak!"* The most popular folk tales concern the smart but mischievous Ti Malis and his very slow-witted friend Bouki. Here is one example:

Ti Malise paid Bouki a visit one day. To his amazement, when he got to Bouki's *lakou* (yard), there was Bouki playing dominoes with his dog! "What a brilliant dog you have!" exclaimed Ti Malis. "He can play dominoes." "Ha!" said Bouki, "he's not as smart as you think. I've just won three out of five games !"

Perhaps the most popular form of humor and amusement are riddles. There is a definite form for the riddles. The person "throwing" the riddle or *tire pwen* says: *"Tim-tim,"* and those who want to hear it reply: *"Bwa sèch."* Then the riddle is given. If they get it, they announce it. If they give up, they say *"Bwa sèch,"* which means they eat dry wood, the penalty for not getting the riddle. The riddles themselves are very difficult. They require a transition from the literal problem to quite fanciful and figurative answers. Here are several popular riddles:

1. They serve it food, it stands on four feet, but it cannot eat.
2. I enter white, I come out mulatto.
3. Three very large men are standing under a single little umbrella, but not one of them gets wet. Why?
4. When I sit, I am taller than when I stand.
5. How many coconuts can you put into an empty sack?

1. A table.
2. Bread.
3. It is not raining.
4. A dog.
5. Only one. After that the sack is not empty.

5 RELIGION

Religion is an integral part of Haitian life and culture. Vodou (a mixture of African animism and Christianity, also known as Voodoo) and Roman Catholicism are the two main religions. Over 90% of Haitians participate in the Vodou religion. Because Vodou is nonexclusive, 80% of Haitians are also Roman Catholic, and Protestants of various denominations account for the other 20%, many of whom do not generally participate in Vodou. All three religious sectors are organized at the national level and are officially recognized. The Haitian government does not impose any restrictions on missionary activities, religious instruction, or religious publishing. Various Protestant denominations and foreign missionary groups openly proselytize in Haiti.

Popular misconceptions about Vodou have created negative stereotypes concerning its practices and its adherents. Depicted in books and movies as a cult of sorcerers who practice "black magic," Vodou is in fact a religion based on ancestral spirits, tribal deities, and universal archetypes such as the goddess of the sea, all of whom generally help and protect. Although lacking a fixed theology and an organized hierarchy, this religion has its own rituals, ceremonies, and altars that practitioners do not find to be at odds with Roman Catholicism. Vodou keeps alive old African beliefs while borrowing freely from Christianity. In fact, many Roman Catholic symbols and prayers have blended with Vodou rituals and traditions to make for a unique syncretic and typically Haitian religion. For example, pictures of Catholic saints are painted on the walls of temples to represent the Vodou spirits; at funerals, it is not uncommon for Vodou ceremonies and rituals to be performed for family members first, followed by a more public traditional Roman Catholic ceremony presided over by a priest.

Vodou is derived from a synthesis of African religious beliefs. The word *Vodou* comes from the Fon language of Benin (formerly Dahomey) in West Africa and means "spirit." When Africans of various tribes were brought to Haiti as slaves, they brought with them their beliefs in spirits who acted as intermediaries with a single God Almighty; some of these spirits were ancestors of the living, while others represented human emotions and forces of nature. In time, a system of beliefs and spirits unique to the slaves of Haiti was formed. These spirits, or *lwa,* are inherited or bought by families and can be called upon for help; they can be paid to bring good fortune, to protect, or to attack enemies. Payment is usually in the form of food, drink, or other gifts offered during rituals. Vodouists attribute the good as well as the bad to the spirits. The Roman Catholic clergy, although opposed to Vodou, have a more benign view of it than do Protestants.

6 MAJOR HOLIDAYS

Commemorative Haitian holidays include Independence Day (1 January) and the Anniversary of Jean-Jacques Dessaline's Death (17 October). Dessalines was a former slave who led the slave armies to victory in 1803 and became the leader of Haiti after the revolution. The Anniversary of the Battle of Vertières is on 18 November, which pays homage to the final battle fought in 1803 during the struggle for independence. The landing of Columbus on Hispaniola in 1492 is commemorated on 5 December. Other holidays include Ancestors' Day (2 January), Carnival (all three days before Ash Wednesday), Pan American Day (14 April), Labor Day (1 May), Flag Day (18 May), and New Year's Eve (31 December).

Haitians observe many traditional Roman Catholic holidays, including Good Friday and Easter Sunday (movable, usually in late March or early April), Feast of the Assumption (15 August), All Saints Day (1 November), All Souls Day (2 November), Immaculate Conception (8 December), Christmas Eve (24 December), and Christmas Day (25 December).

7 RITES OF PASSAGE

Major life transitions, such as birth, marriage, and death, are marked by religious ceremonies, often including both Voudou and Christian rites.

Two Haitians working at a pottery wheel. Haitian handicrafts often make use of mahogany, sisal, and straw. Haitians are particularly skilled in woodcarving, weaving, and embroidery. (United Nations)

8 INTERPERSONAL RELATIONS

Many Haitian values are traditional and conservative. Haitians value community cooperation and usually have close extended-family ties. Many are religious and have a strong work ethic as well as a deep respect for authority and societal laws. Education is particularly important, since it is a means of social mobility.

Haiti's unusual history has created a unique culture that is different from the Spanish Caribbean cultures and is dualistic in nature: European vs. African, French vs. Creole, mulatto elites vs. the black masses, urban vs. rural, Christianity vs. Vodou, etc. For Haitians, the color of one's skin, the languages one uses, and the work that one does are all connected and have always been important aspects of interpersonal relations.

Manners are also important in Haitian society. Greetings are exchanged whenever boarding public transportation, walking into a doctor's office, entering a store, etc. When greeting friends, men generally shake hands, women will exchange two kisses, as will men with female friends. Children are taught early on to respect their elders and to greet formally visitors to their home.

It is not unusual for men to refer to each other by their last name, and many individuals are referred to by nicknames. For example, the firstborn male in a family is often given the nick-name *Fanfan*. A woman named Dominique may be called *Dodo* by her friends and family.

9 LIVING CONDITIONS

The poverty in Haiti is reflected in the health statistics of its population. The infant mortality rate is the highest in the Americas, and life expectancy, at approximately 56 years, is the lowest in the Caribbean. Since Haiti has the second-lowest per capita caloric intake in the world, malnutrition is widespread, especially among the young and the poor. More than 67% of the population lives in rural areas, although this pattern has been changing in recent years.

The population is afflicted by a number of infectious diseases, including tuberculosis, parasitic infections, and malaria, since a majority of the people live in malarial areas. Poor sanitation contributes to these illnesses. In 1984, less than 20% of the population had toilets, and only 25% of the rural population had access to potable water. In 1982, the US Center for Disease Control mistakenly classified Haitians as a high-risk group for AIDS, in part because early studies wrongly suggested that the disease originated in Haiti. Although the high-risk classification was finally dropped in 1991, some Haitians in the US are still scorned simply for being Haitian.

Another factor contributing to poor health conditions is the lack of medical services. Political repression caused many doctors to emigrate, and the few remaining ones tended to locate in the capital, where they catered to those who could afford their services, although this pattern has also changed in recent years. There are still more Haitian doctors in the city of Montreal, Canada, though, than there are in Port-au-Prince. Religious and social service agencies have established clinics, but the number of people who require services cannot be accommodated. Rural areas are especially lacking in health services because of poor infrastructure. Given the lack of modern, professional health services, it is not surprising that many of the people rely on traditional herbal remedies and religious healers to diagnose and treat illnesses.

10 FAMILY LIFE

Haitians place great importance on family life. In rural areas, the extended family has traditionally been the social unit. However, deteriorating economic conditions, which brought many peasants to the cities in search of work, have caused a shift in society: the nuclear family has replaced the extended family in certain urban areas. But family ties remain close, and family members tend to be supportive of one another; intergenerational conflicts are rare but increasing because of urbanization and efforts to identify with the world at large.

Men and women play complementary roles, generally sharing household and financial responsibilities. Women assist in farmwork, performing such tasks as weeding and harvesting. At home, women are generally responsible for child care and the daily household tasks, while men do heavy chores, such as gathering firewood.

Officially, there is no discrimination against women in Haiti. Women have recently held prominent positions in both the public and private sectors, and a Ministry for Women's Affairs was established in 1995. For some Haitians, however, women's roles are limited by tradition. Peasant women remain largely in the traditional occupations of farming, marketing, and housework. In general, Haitian women have been more active in the labor force than women in other Latin American countries, perhaps because the rewards for their labor are greater. In the coffee industry, marketers (persons who transport coffee beans to local and urban markets to sell) are almost exclusively female and are known as "Madam Saras." Income earned from agricultural production belongs to both husband and wife, but income earned from nonfarm business activities does not have to be shared with the husband, and, as a result, many women are economically independent.

The most common form of marriage among poorer Haitians is known as *plasaj*, a kind of common-law marriage. Although the Haitian government does not recognize plasaj as legitimate, this relationship is considered normal and proper among the poor. Although wealthy Haitians may openly disapprove of the practice, many affluent Haitian men have children by mistresses and provide financial support for their second "family." Thus, plasaj, in one form or another, is practiced by 85% of the Haitian population. A man or woman may have a number of plasaj relationships in a lifetime. Children born from one *plasaj* relationship regard offspring from another plasaj as brothers and sisters and often live in the same household without conflict. If parents separate, a child may take either the father's or mother's last name.

Haitians value both their family reputation and their children, and they take pains to ensure that all children receive

Haitians at the inauguration of President Aristide in 1990. (PhotoEdit)

equal inheritances. Children are considered a gift from God and are treated accordingly. Children also provide security in old age.

11 CLOTHING

The Haitian mode of dress tends to be informal, conservative, and well-groomed. Comfortable, lightweight Western-style clothes are typically worn, made especially of cotton and linen fabrics. School children all wear uniforms. Men often wear a loose-fitting shirt called a *guayabera,* similar to those of other countries in the region and Latin America. While the wearing of pants by women is no longer inappropriate, most women, especially in rural areas, continue to wear skirts or dresses.

Traditional clothing tends toward a hand- embroidered denim shirt for men, in cotton, linen, or denim; and for women, an embroidered short-sleeved blouse, a colorful skirt, and a scarf wrapping the hair.

12 FOOD

To supplement food and grain imports, Haitians grow corn, rice, beans, bananas, mangoes, avocados, and various other tropical fruits and vegetables. A typical meal will generally include one or two varieties of rice, usually prepared with either red or black beans. It will almost always feature plantain, which can be prepared in a number of ways, usually parboiled then cut into slices which are pressed flat and deep- fried.

Chicken is very common for those who can afford it; this, too, is generally deep-fried. Other typical meats include goat, beef, and pork. The latter is often fried and barbecued *(grio)* and is very popular. Seafoods are especially favored including barbecued lobster, shrimp, and many varieties of fish.

Vegetable dishes include green beans, potatoes, squash, okra, cabbage, eggplant, and salads with generous slices of avocado. Most Haitians prefer a spicy sauce, resembling American cole slaw, which is fiery hot. Only a dash of *piklès* is needed to enhance a dish! Desserts include cake or tarts, often with pineapple garnish.

13 EDUCATION

Haiti's first schools were established shortly after the Constitution of 1805, which mandated free and compulsory primary education. While education has been promoted in principle, a comprehensive and accessible school system never developed. Today, the majority of Haitians receive no formal education, and only a small minority are educated beyond primary school.

In 1978 primary schools, both urban and rural, were merged under the auspices of the National Department of Education (DEN). The education system was then restructured: 10 years of basic education, consisting of three cycles (4-3-3 years), are followed by 3 years of secondary education. Curriculum and materials were also changed. One major change was the use of Haitian Creole as the language of instruction in the first four grades. Other instructional innovations were grouping children by ability and an emphasis on discovery learning rather than on memorization. By 1981, primary school enrollment in urban areas had more than doubled from 1970 figures. School nutrition programs and support from private development agencies contributed to the increased enrollment, but rural enrollments continued to be low. Moreover, dropout rates remained high: 50% in urban areas, and as high as 80% in rural areas. Despite the reforms, obtaining an education in Haiti remains an elusive goal for most. Though education is highly valued, the majority of Haitians do not have access to it. Even though education is technically free in Haiti, it remains beyond the means of most Haitians, who cannot afford the supplemental fees, school supplies, and uniforms required.

The Haitian curriculum requires learning many subjects in detail. Rote learning and memorization are still the norm. Grading and testing are very strict and formal in Haiti; it is much more difficult to attain a grade of B (or its equivalent) in Haiti than it is in the United States. Therefore, Haitian students tend to attach great importance to grades and tests, even quizzes. In Haiti the teacher addresses all students by their last names and has total authority over the class. A student speaks only when asked a question. As a sign of respect, Haitian students do not look their teachers in the eye, but keep their heads down in deference. There are no parent-teacher organizations in Haiti and parents are not routinely asked or encouraged to participate in school matters and decisions. In Haiti, if a parent is called to school, it generally means that the child has committed a great transgression.

Despite recent developments, major obstacles remain in helping the masses in Haiti achieve literacy. To that end, a literacy program was given ministerial status in 1995 in order to develop a nationwide institution to further the teaching of Haitian Creole. Although many sectors of the population do not see the value of becoming literate in Haitian Creole, this attitude is changing as Haitian Creole's usage in the media, in government, and in literature has increased. Even so, among the poor, who tend to view education as a means of escaping poverty rather than as a means for learning, French continues to be prized. While the reforms had sought to make Haitian Creole the language of all primary grades, the government was forced under pressure to limit its use to the first four grades only. Instruction in the secondary level remains almost exclusively in French.

14 CULTURAL HERITAGE

Haiti's uniqueness is reflected in the originality of its paintings, music, and literature. Artists and musicians, drawing from the rich folk life and vitality of the people, have created internationally recognized works and sounds. Haitian paintings have long been recognized around the world; works by better-known Haitian artists have been exhibited in galleries and museums in the United States and France. Handicrafts such as woodcarvings and tapestries employ a similar style. Haitian music, like Haiti itself, is an original blend, containing elements of African drum rhythms and European dance music.

Haitian *kompa* and more recent *rasin* (Vodou-influenced) musical styles are the most popular genres in Haiti today. Every year Haitian bands compete for the best song during the Carnival season, and recent entries reflect other influences of the Caribbean region through the utilization of reggae, dance hall, and rap styles.

Haiti has also produced writers, poets, and essayists of international standing. Attempts to write Haitian Creole date back to the 18th century, but because of its low status in Haiti, until recently there was little interest in writing in anything but French. Haitian literature has been written almost exclusively in French; however, with the recognition of Creole as an official language, novels, poems, and plays are being written increasingly in Creole. In 1975, the first novel to be written entirely in Haitian Creole was published—*Dezafi* by Franketienne poetically depicts Haitian life.

15 WORK

Although in decline since the 1950s, about 67% of the labor force in Haiti still works in agriculture. Deforestation, land erosion, and a declining economy have prompted many farm workers to migrate to the cities or abroad. The main cash crops are coffee and sugarcane. A large number of Haitians work in the Dominican Republic as *braceros,* under grueling conditions. *Bracero* is a Spanish term for a migrant farm worker, someone temporarily hired, usually for a harvest. In the Dominican Republic, Haitian braceros are used to harvest sugarcane, which is still cut by hand with a machete. Although secretly crossing the border is officially illegal, the Haitian government does not strictly enforce the immigration law.

There are estimates that over 100,000 children in Haiti are held in forced domestic labor, which is called *restevek* in Haitian Creole. Young children from rural families are "adopted" and "educated" by more affluent city dwellers to serve as unpaid domestic labor. The children often work long hours, receive little food, and some are known to be beaten or sexually abused.

16 SPORTS

Soccer is the national sport. During the quadrennial World Cup competition, virtually the entire country roots for the national team of Brazil. In rural areas cockfighting is also popular, but only as an informal sport on the weekends. For men, a typical social game is dominoes or cards. For the more affluent, tennis is becoming an increasingly popular sport.

Children may often be seen playing hide-and-seek, hopscotch (marelle), round dances, and marbles. Organized sports in school or local leagues include basketball for girls and soccer for boys.

17 ENTERTAINMENT AND RECREATION

The expressiveness of the Haitian people is evident in their rich oral tradition, which includes storytelling, proverbs, riddles, songs, and games. Storytelling in Haiti is a performance art. The storyteller uses a different voice for each character in the story and may sing songs as part of the narrative.

18 FOLK ART, CRAFTS, AND HOBBIES

Haitian handicrafts often make use of mahogany, sisal, and straw. Haitian craftspeople are particularly skilled in woodcarving, weaving, and embroidery. Wooden sculptures, intricate plaques, and furniture (especially chairs with caned backs and seats) are popular handicrafts, as are embroidered dresses, skirts, blouses, costumes, and men's shirts. Wrought iron items are also a part of Haitian folk art, including candle holders, coffee tables, lamps, and animal figures.

Every year before Christmas, artisans fashion often elaborate works of art known as fanal out of white cardboard and tissue paper within which lighted candles are (carefully!) placed.

19 SOCIAL PROBLEMS

Haiti is the poorest nation in the Western Hemisphere and among the 25 poorest in the world. The elite, a very small percentage of the population, earn over 60% of the national income, while unemployment ranges from 30% to 70%. The penetration of transnational companies into the Haitian economy has contributed to the influx of peasants into Port-au-Prince. These changing demographics have caused both urban problems and social changes. While peasants have traditionally depended on the extended family and cooperative labor to survive, urban slum dwelling has weakened this aspect of the social fabric.

Another problem is Haiti's extreme state of deforestation. With wood fuels accounting for 75% of the country's energy consumption, deforestation of the once green, tree-covered land is now critical. The most direct effect of the destruction of trees has been soil erosion, which has made most of the land unsuitable for farming. The fluctuation of prices for agricultural products in the world market has also contributed to the decline in agriculture. The fall in coffee prices and the fluctuation in sugar prices have had a major impact on agricultural production and planning.

Negative stereotypes and cultural misunderstandings about Haiti are still prevalent, and many Haitian American youngsters lack a sense of ethnic pride because of the negative publicity related to the political turmoil that hinders Haiti's chances to progress socially and economically. As a result of problems such as prejudice and difficulty in English, younger Haitians sometimes present themselves at various times as African Americans, Caribbean Americans, West Indians, or Haitian Americans, depending on the current sociopolitical climate in both Haiti and the United States.

20 BIBLIOGRAPHY

Portions of this article were excerpted from The Haitians: Their History and Culture. Washington, DC: Center for Applied Linguistics, 1994.

Abbott, Elizabeth. Haïti: The Duvaliers and Their Legacy. New York: Touchstone, Simon and Schuster, 1991.

Civan, Michele Burtoff. The Haitians: Their History and Culture. Washington, DC: Center for Applied Linguistics, 1994.

Laguerre, Michel. The Military and Society in Haïti. Knoxville: University of Tennessee Press, 1993.

Leyburn, James G. The Haitian People. New Haven, CT: Yale University Press, 1966.

Nicholls, David. Haiti in Caribbean Context: Ethnicity, Economy, and Revolt. New York: St. Martin's Press, 1985.

Ott, Thomas O. The Haitian Revolution, 1789–1804. Knoxville: University of Tennessee Press, 1973.

Perusse, Roland. Historical Dictionary of Haiti. Metuchen, NJ: Scarecrow Press, 1977.

Savain, Roger E. Haitian-Kreol in Ten Steps: Dis Pa Nan Kreyòl Ayisyen-an. Rochester, VT: Schenkman Books, 1993.

—by D. K. Daeg de Mott

HAWAIIANS

PRONUNCIATION: ha-WHY-uhns
LOCATION: United States (Hawaiian Islands)
POPULATION: 1,000,000
LANGUAGE: English
RELIGION: Christianity (Roman Catholic); Buddhism
RELATED ARTICLES: Vol. 3: Polynesians; Micronesians; Melanesians

¹ INTRODUCTION

The Hawaiian Islands are located about 2,000 miles southwest of San Francisco in the Pacific Ocean. They are part of the larger Polynesian island chain. This island group, known collectively as Hawaii, became the 50th state of the United States in 1959. The first Europeans to visit the islands were probably Captain James Cook, a British naval officer, and his crews aboard two ships, the *Resolution* and the *Discovery*, which visited the islands in 1778. Within 40 years, the native population was substantially reduced by the unfamiliar disease strains that the British brought with them to the islands. Eventually, European and American fur traders and whalers began using the conveniently situated islands as a provisions station, and missionaries also arrived to win converts to Christianity. Foreigners were granted the right to purchase property in 1840, and by the mid-19th century the United States had begun large-scale sugar farming, eventually bringing in thousands of European and Asian contract workers, thus forever changing the ethnic makeup of the islands. In 1893, a group of American businessmen, with military aid, overthrew the reigning monarch, Queen Liliuokalani. In 1898 the Hawaiian Islands were annexed and made a territory of the United States.

In the 20th century, Hawaii became a center of American military power in the Pacific. America's involvement in World War II began when a surprise Japanese air attack destroyed United States military installations in and around Pearl Harbor, an inlet near Honolulu, Hawaii's capital, on 7 December 1941. Since Hawaii achieved statehood in 1959, defense has continued to play an important role in its economy, as has tourism. Descendants of the Asians who came to the islands as plantation workers have, on the whole, fared better than the native population, wielding both economic and political power while the native Hawaiians became increasingly alienated and impoverished. Since the mid-1970s, activists have worked to promote the ethnic, cultural, and economic interests of native Hawaiians, in a movement analogous to that of the Native Americans on the US mainland.

² LOCATION AND HOMELAND

The state of Hawaii is made up of about 130 islands, both large and small. Only seven of the islands are regularly inhabited. Most of the islands were created by volcanic action. The highest point in Hawaii is Mauna Kea, an apparently extinct volcano on the island of Hawaii, which rises to a height of 4,205 m (13,796 ft).

Of the seven main islands, Hawaii is the largest. It was formed by five volcanoes, two of which–Kilauea and Mauna Loa–are still active. The island of Maui is made up of two volcanic complexes joined by a low-lying strip of land. Both of

Maui's volcanoes are dormant today, and one of them, Haleakala, has one of the world's largest extinct volcanic craters. Lanai is a hilly island that rises to a height of 1,027 m (3,369 ft) atop a long-extinct volcano. The island of Molokai is made up of three distinct regions, each formed by a separate volcano. Oahu, the most-populated island, is made up of two rugged mountain ranges, the Waianae Mountains in the west and the Koolau Range in the east. Pearl Harbor, one of the best natural harbors of the Pacific Ocean, is located on Oahu's south coast. Diamond Head and Punchbowl, remnants of extinct volcanoes, are famous landmarks found not far from the city of Honolulu. The island of Kauai is characterized by high precipitation and an abundance of lush vegetation. Kauai has many streams, some of which have worn deep canyons into the rock. Niihau is a private island. Its owners encourage the preservation of traditional Hawaiian culture and discourage outsiders from visiting the island.

Polynesians, who were the original inhabitants of the Hawaiian Islands, inhabit the entire chain of Pacific islands that stretches from Hawaii to New Zealand, to Easter Island, Tahiti, Samoa, and other widely scattered island groups. Today they are estimated to total about 1 million people. Modern Hawaii's population is made up of several ethnic groups. About 33% of the people are White, and more than 60% are of Asian descent, of which the most well-represented nationalities are Japanese, Filipino, Hawaiian (descendants of the Polynesians who originally settled the Hawaiian Islands), and Chinese. Most of the population of modern-day Hawaii is urban. Hawaii's largest cities are Hilo, which is located on the island of Hawaii, and Honolulu, Kailua, Aiea, Kaneohe, Pearl City, and Waipahu, all on the island of Oahu.

³ LANGUAGE

The official language of the Hawaiian Islands today is English, which is spoken at home by about 75% of the population. Few people speak the original Polynesian-based Hawaiian language, which may not survive past the beginning of the 21st century as a spoken language. Most of the native population speaks pidgin, a local creole that incorporates English, Hawaiian, and other Asian and Pacific languages. Spoken with a rising inflection, pidgin, which is especially popular among young people, has a distinctive vocabulary and syntax of its own. Other languages spoken in Hawaii include Japanese, Chinese, and Tagalog.

COMMON HAWAIIAN TERMS:
aloha: a common greeting, used for both hello and good-bye. Also means affection, romantic love, or good wishes
hula: a popular native Hawaiian dance
kahuna: priest or shaman
kane: man (also husband or boyfriend)
lanai: porch
keiki: child, children
lei: garland of flowers or vines
luau: traditional Hawaiian feast
malihini: newcomer or "tenderfoot"
mauna: mountain

COMMON PIDGIN TERMS:
bimbye: eventually ("by and by")
brah: brother (equivalent of "bro" in the US)

Polynesian religion, which declined in the 19th century with the arrival of Christian missionaries on the islands, was animistic, based on a belief in numerous gods and spirits. Chiefs were believed to be descended from the gods and to have sacred powers called *mana,* and there were many taboos *(kapu)* placed on women. One can still see evidence of pre-Christian religion throughout Hawaii in open-air temples called *heiau.*

6 MAJOR HOLIDAYS

Hawaiians celebrate all major Christian holidays as well as all national holidays celebrated in the United States. They also celebrate special festivals of their own, including Lei Day (1 May) and Aloha Week in late September, which is observed throughout the islands with luau (feasts), pageants, balls, and other festivities. Others festivals are unique to a particular island or locality.

7 RITES OF PASSAGE

Rituals marking major life events such as birth, marriage, and death are generally observed within the Christian religious tradition. Among the native Hawaiian population, the ceremony celebrating a birth was traditionally the most important rite of passage.

In ancient times, the bodies of the dead were placed in burial caves, and special care was taken to avoid having the enemies of deceased persons find and dishonor their remains after death.

8 INTERPERSONAL RELATIONS

Sharing possessions and giving gifts have traditionally been central to the Hawaiian way of life. If someone was in need, people always gave generously, safe in the knowledge that others would be there to help them in return. This generous attitude survives in the famous "spirit of aloha," a term that refers to the friendliness, generosity, and openness to strangers for which the Hawaiians are known. "Aloha" is also the universal greeting for "hello" and "goodbye." A popular slang greeting, equivalent to "What's happening?" in the US, is the pidgin phrase "Howzit brah?"

The traditional garland known as a *lei* is presented to people on any happy occasion but especially upon arriving in or leaving Hawaii. A widespread practice in the workplace is the observance of the Hawaiian equivalent of the US "casual day"—"Aloha Friday," marked by playful behavior and the wearing of bright colors and flowers.

9 LIVING CONDITIONS

The traditional mode of transportation for Hawaiians was the outrigger canoe. Villagers used them for fishing and for traveling short distances. To make longer voyages, they used canoes equipped with sails. Today, airplanes and ships are Hawaii's chief means of transport for all kinds of commerce. There are public bus systems on Oahu and Hawaii islands, and the state has a few miles of operating railroad track. Principal ports are Honolulu, Kahului, Hilo, Kawaihae, and Nawiliwili. Hawaii's busiest airport is Honolulu International.

Traditional Hawaiian houses have a wooden frame, with walls and roof made of thatch. They can be round, oval, square, or oblong in shape. Most houses in Hawaii today are built in the Western style out of wood, brick, or concrete block. In the cities, many people live in high-rise apartments or condominiums.

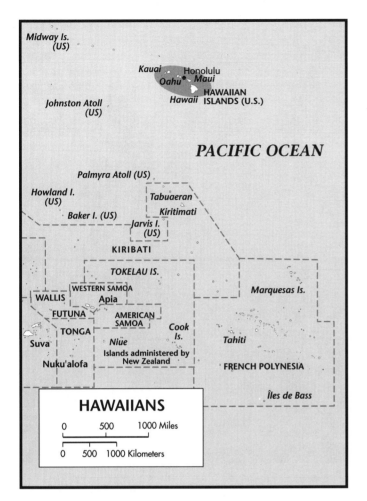

cockaroach: to steal, equivalent to "rip off"

da'kine: all-purpose expression, similar to "whatever" or "you know"

hu hu: angry

ono: number one; i.e., the best

pau hana: quitting time (end of the work day)

4 FOLKLORE

Like all Polynesian peoples, the original Hawaiians believed that their ancestors came from a mythical homeland near Tahiti, called Hawaiki. The original inhabitants of Hawaii offered human sacrifices to the active volcano, Pele, in an attempt to pacify the deity of the mountain, thus preventing violent and disastrous eruptions. Polynesian mythology in general is a complex mix of stories about the creation of the earth and the relationships between the gods and people.

Traditionally, taboos called *kapu* (from which the word "taboo" is derived) were widely observed by the Hawaiian people. Typical kapu included a prohibition on letting one's shadow fall on the body of a king and a ban on men and women eating together.

5 RELIGION

Most Hawaiians are Christian, with a majority of those being Roman Catholic. Buddhists and followers of the Shinto religion are the largest religious minorities in the state. The traditional

Hula contest in Princeville, Kauai, Hawaii. Many Hawaiians are concerned with preserving traditional ways. The women's dances, such as the hula, involved graceful head and body movements that illustrated the songs. The men's dances, which were vigorous and energetic, included slapping the body, stamping the feet, and twirling wooden clubs or spears in the air in mock battles. (Corel Corporation)

10 FAMILY LIFE

Traditional Hawaiian life centered around the extended family. Families were large, and the extended family often lived under the same roof. All family members were expected to work together for the welfare of the *ainga,* or the whole family group. A child had many "mothers" and "fathers," and was never lonely. It was a common practice for grandmothers to adopt and raise children as their own. The children in traditional Hawaiian households were usually spoiled through overindulgence.

Marriages were traditionally arranged without consulting the couple. In most cases, such marriages were intended to strengthen ties between families or political bonds between tribes and clans. Land was usually owned by clans or extended families and worked by individuals. Ownership changed mainly by inheritance or warfare. The roles of both women and men were clearly defined from an early age, and children learned by observing their elders. The burden of providing for and protecting the family fell to the males, while females did the household chores and reared the children.

11 CLOTHING

Modern Hawaiians wear Western-style clothing, but traditional garb can still be seen and, in fact, is often worn for the benefit of the tourists who flock to Hawaii each year. For men it includes a cloth skirt called a *lava-lava,* or *sulu.* Some women wear long, loose-fitting cotton garments called *muumuus.* Skirts are made of tapa cloth, made by stripping the inner bark from paper mulberry trees, soaking it, and then beating it with wooden clubs. Both men and women sometimes wear the familiar grass skirts which are identified with Hawaii in popular imagination.

The early Hawaiians often decorated their bodies with tattoos, a custom which has recently seen a resurgence of popularity among young people, not just in Hawaii, but all over the United States.

12 FOOD

Traditionally, the people of the Hawaiian Islands have depended largely on fish and native plants for food. Hawaiians catch crabs, lobsters, shrimp, and turtles in shallow water. Farther out to sea they catch bonito and tuna. On many islands they eat the fruit of breadfruit and pandanus trees and the meat of coconuts from the coconut palm. Traditional garden crops include sweet potatoes, taro (a plant with a starchy root), bananas, corn, pineapples, rice, and tomatoes. Some farmers also raise chickens and pigs.

A traditional way of preparing food is to cook it in a ground oven, a shallow pit lined with heated stones. The food is placed on the stones and covered with layers of leaves. The pit is then filled with earth to hold in the heat.

13 EDUCATION

The first formal schools in the Hawaiian Islands were established by Protestant missionaries from the United States in the early 19th century. In 1840, the Hawaiian king Kamehameha III established a public school system in the kingdom of Hawaii. Today the state school system is highly centralized, with one school board overseeing all public schools in the state. Elementary and secondary school enrollments have remained relatively stable, although a slight decline was evident in the 1980s. Hawaii's institutions of higher education include Chaminade University of Honolulu, Hawaii Loa College, Hawaii Pacific University, and the University of Hawaii system, which includes several community colleges located throughout the islands.

14 CULTURAL HERITAGE

The return of a loved one, the birth of a child, or the appointment of a new chief were always occasions for celebration in traditional Hawaiian culture. New songs were composed spontaneously to record the event, and dances were enacted to capture the spirit of the gathering. Most dances were performed either sitting or standing. The men's dances, which were vigorous and energetic, included slapping the body, stamping the feet, and twirling wooden clubs or spears in the air in mock battles. The women's dances, such as the hula, involved graceful head and body movements that illustrated the songs. Costumes varied according to the type of dance being performed, but were most often made of leaves and sweet-smelling flowers. Feathers, fine mats, grass skirts, and headdresses were worn for some dances. Traditional Hawaiian musical instruments included bamboo flutes, shell trumpets, panpipes, and slit drums.

15 WORK

The people of Hawaii work at jobs that are similar to those of people in the mainland United States. In the cities they might be lawyers, doctors, or office workers. They may work in factories processing canned pineapples and pineapple juice; manufacturing stone, clay, metal or glass products; and making clothing. Some are engaged in shipbuilding.

Hawaiian farm workers specialize in sugarcane and pineapple production. Other crops include coffee, ornamental flowers and shrubs, papayas, bananas, avocados, taro, grain sorghum, macadamia nuts, alfalfa, beans, potatoes, and cabbage. Livestock farms produce beef cattle, milk and other dairy goods, hogs, chickens, and chicken eggs.

The tourist industry, which has grown rapidly in recent decades, is the leading source of employment for the people of Hawaii. Each year several million tourists visit the state.

16 SPORTS

Hawaiians enjoy all the spectator sports that are popular elsewhere in the United States, such as basketball, football, and baseball. They enjoy watching and participating in golf, hiking, cycling, and polo.

In Hawaii, however, water sports are the most popular. Hawaii is considered one of the best places in the world for surfing. Other popular water sports enjoyed by Hawaiians are sport fishing, boat racing, swimming, windsurfing, body-surfing, snorkeling, and scuba diving.

17 ENTERTAINMENT AND RECREATION

Hawaiians tend to head for the outdoors when they're in the mood for recreation. They enjoy water sports like surfing, scuba diving, snorkeling, and deep sea fishing, and they also like to camp out and hike through Hawaii's spectacular landscape.

Traditionally, islanders enjoyed gathering to celebrate occasions like births and marriages with feasting, dancing, and singing. No such celebration would be complete without *kava,* a drink made from the roots of the native kava plant. For young boys, favorite pastimes were wrestling, dart-throwing, spinning tops, playing marbles, and flying kites. Girls might practice juggling, play cat's cradle, or participate in a game of hopscotch.

18 FOLK ART, CRAFTS, AND HOBBIES

Many Hawaiian islanders are skilled artists and craftsworkers. One important traditional craft is basketweaving. Using the leaves and fibers of native plants, such as palm and pandanus trees, craftspeople weave baskets, mats, and wall hangings, which they decorate with colorful designs. Others specialize in using native woods to carve masks, cooking utensils, and other objects. On a smaller scale, some Hawaiian artisans are skilled at making pottery.

19 SOCIAL PROBLEMS

Although the Hawaiian people as a group have been thoroughly assimilated into the dominant culture of the United States, there are still many among them who are concerned with preserving traditional ways. The influx of new residents in the last decades of the 20th century has caused problems of overcrowding and pollution.

20 BIBLIOGRAPHY

Adler, Peter S. *Beyond Paradise: Encounters in Hawaii Where the Tour Bus Never Runs.* Woodbridge, CT: Oxbow Press, 1993.

Bayer, Wolfgang. *Hawaii, Paradise Lost?* [videorecording]. New York: Phoenix/BFA Films and Video.

Feeney, Stephanie. *Hawaii is a Rainbow.* Honolulu: University of Hawaii Press, 1985.

Gall, Susan, and Irene Natividad, ed. *The Asian American Almanac.* Detroit: Gale Research, 1995.

Linnekin, Jocelyn. "Hawaiians." *Encyclopedia of World Cultures.* Boston: G. K. Hall, 1992.

———. *Children of the Land: Exchange and Status in a Hawaiian Community.* New Brunswick, NJ: Rutgers University Press, 1985.

HINDUS OF GUYANA

LOCATION: Guyana (Atlantic coast area)
POPULATION: About 302,000
LANGUAGE: English; Hindu; Urdu
RELIGION: Hinduism
RELATED ARTICLES: Guyanans

¹ INTRODUCTION

When slavery was abolished in Guyana in the early 19th century, the freed African slaves abandoned the sugar plantations and became peasants or town dwellers. So the plantation owners turned to India to recruit their workers. Over the next 80 years, beginning in about 1838, thousands of Asian Indians from all parts of the Indian subcontinent crossed the *kala-pani,* the Black Waters, as indentured laborers. Many of them were lower-caste Indians, sometimes existing in a state of virtual slavery in their own country, and they were glad to flee their landlords and creditors for the prospect of a new beginning in a new land. But the journey was a dangerous one. Out of 324 persons who embarked on a ship at Calcutta in 1858, as many as 120 died as a result of the conditions on board. Life was not much better when they arrived, for in the early years, they were seen as the "new slaves" and were treated as such until new regulations were brought in to improve their treatment by the owners. By 1917, when immigration ended, a total of 239,000 Asian Indians had left their homes to travel to Guyana. Many of them stayed, being offered land close to the plantations in exchange for giving up their rights to return to India. The former Black African slaves resented the fact that the "dal coolies" appeared to be favored over them by the plantation owners, and this became the basis for a racial resentment between the two groups that continues today.

Politics in Guyana have always been defined along racial lines. During the 1950s and 1960s, the history of the colony was stormy. The first elected government was formed by the People's Progressive Party, representing the Hindu community, and it was led by Cheddi Jagan who is credited as spearheading the movement in the Caribbean towards independence. His policies, however, appeared to be so pro-Communist that the British government suspended the constitution and even sent troops to Guyana. The party was again elected into power in 1963, but rioting broke out between the Asian Indians and the Black Africans, which led to bloodshed. The British decided to introduce proportional representation and the African-dominated People's National Congress (PNC), itself a socialist party, swept into power on a coalition ticket. Its leader, Forbes Burnham, declared the country an independent republic in 1970. For the next two decades, Guyana became virtually a one-party state, and it was not until 1992 that the PNC reign ended and Cheddi Jagan's party took office once more.

² LOCATION AND HOMELAND

Hindus make up almost 40% (or about 302,000 people) of Guyana's 756,000 people of various races, including Africans, Portuguese, Chinese, and Amerindians. The Hindus live on a narrow coastal strip along the Atlantic coast, only 16 km (10 mi) across at its widest point, on land that has been reclaimed from the sea by a series of canals and some 225 km (140 mi) of dikes. Although many live in the capital, Georgetown, and other urban areas, a large number of Hindu families still live in the farming villages they created in the early days when they were first given land by the plantation owners.

³ LANGUAGE

Although the official and principal language of Guyana is English—the only Latin country to have English as its language—Hindu and Urdu are also heard among the older Asian Indians.

⁴ FOLKLORE

Much of Guyanan Hindus' folklore springs from their religious and racial background. The majority of Hindus came from the Gangetic Plain, which produced the great religious heroes of India such as Rama, Krishna, and Mahavira. It was this area that was the scene of the great Asian Indian epics such as the *Ramayana* and the *Mahabharata.*

⁵ RELIGION

All the major Hindu festivals are celebrated by Guyanan Hindus throughout the year. At the end of October is the religious festival of lights, Divali, which celebrates the return of Lord Rama after 14 years in exile. There are also Bhagwats, remarkable socioreligious activities centered on the reading of a sacred text by the Brahmins—usually the *Shrima Bhaga Vata Purama.* These events span 7, 9, or 14 days and involve a variety of rites and massive communal meals with hundreds of participants. The Hindus are often joined by Christians and Muslims who travel from all over the country to take part.

Religious activities also include Pujas, which mark special occasions like birthdays or anniversaries, and a *pundit* is hired to perform the necessary Sanskrit rites over a weekend. No fish or meat must be eaten in the house before a religious function takes place. Even the refrigerator must be emptied for the occasion.

⁶ MAJOR HOLIDAYS

A great part of Guyanan Hindus' recreational activity reflects their tolerant acceptance of other religions and is based upon the festivities that accompany Hindu, Muslim, and Christian holidays, such as Christmas, the end of Ramadan, and (in early March) Phagwah, the Hindu New Year, a joyous celebration that celebrates the triumph of good over evil and is noted for the energetic throwing of perfume and water. Easter Monday is also a traditional day for flying kites. Republic Day, on 23 February, is the day the president reports to the nation and is a day for much street marching.

⁷ RITES OF PASSAGE

Baptism is common among the Hindus, who attend Christian churches while maintaining their participation in their own religious rituals. Many of the names that they confer on their children reflect the epic heroes of their culture, such as Rama, Krishna, etc.

⁸ INTERPERSONAL RELATIONS

The familiar Hindu caste system is a highly localized phenomenon in the villages of India. Therefore, when low-caste Hindus and twice-born Brahmins were thrown together on board ships to become *jahagis* (shipmates) on the sailing boats from India to Guyana in the 19th century, that system soon became irrelevant. Today there is more or less only one common caste for all Hindus in Guyana, although Brahmins do retain their special religious role in interpreting the sacred knowledge of the rituals and Sanskrit texts.

Anyone visiting a friend or acquaintance at their home address is expected to call upon everyone else that they know within that neighborhood. Not to do so is considered extremely rude. Open hospitality is a great feature of Hindu life in Guyana, and no visit can be completed without the offer of a meal or refreshment.

9 LIVING CONDITIONS

Standards of health care declined after Guyanan independence, when many doctors and trained medical personnel emigrated. Years of economic austerity programs led to reduced supplies of medicine and equipment. Food shortages led to widespread malnutrition, particularly during the 1980s.

Some 170,000 Guyanans, out of a population of 800,000, live in Georgetown, the capital. Many of the houses in the center of the city are made of wood. Many Guyanan Hindus live in small villages and towns along the coast. The houses are built of wood with tin roofs and are constructed on stilts 2.5 m to 3 m (8–10 ft) off the ground to avoid flooding from the sea.

During the 1970s and 1980s, the government under Burnham was determined to undermine the rural opposition of the Asian Indian small farmers and so developed a series of farming cooperative policies. As a result, rice production was cut by half, after the farmers lost their subsidies. Guyana is one of the poorest countries in the world and relies heavily on its self-sufficiency in food. Resulting food shortages led to increased malnutrition and the return of diseases that were formerly under control, such as beriberi and malaria. The economy was also badly hit by the depressed world demand for bauxite and sugar. This has led to a near breakdown in essential public services such as electricity.

10 FAMILY LIFE

Ethnic identity continues to be important within daily life. The mother- and grandmother-dominated family among Afro-Guyanese differs from the father-oriented Asian Indian family. The extended family is still typical among Hindus, although the European nuclear pattern is becoming popular. Upon marriage, the son is expected to take his bride and live for some time with his parents. This is because it is the duty of the parents to guide the children through the early days of marriage. Then, by the sixth or seventh year the son will have set up his own household with his wife and children.

Because the caste system has virtually disappeared in Guyana, few fathers of high status would pass up the opportunity for their child to marry into a wealthy, established family because of considerations of caste. The arranged marriage is also not as widespread as it once was, and in urban areas it is almost non-existent.

11 CLOTHING

A skirt and blouse is the popular form of clothing for women, but the sari is being increasingly worn by Hindu women. For Hindu men it is the *kurta* (shirt) or the *dhoti* (one-piece trousers).

12 FOOD

Asian Indian food is very popular throughout Guyana. Curry and dal have become part of everyday life for the whole population. Dal is often flavored by the addition of spices cooked in oil. Hindus in the country serve the food on lotus or banana leaves.

Vegetables, such as pumpkin and eggplant, make up the main part of the diet, although fish is often eaten. Fish are often caught in the ditches and dikes by women using seine nets.

13 EDUCATION

Children receive free, compulsory education. The government assumed full control of education in 1976 and took over Church-run and private primary schools. Due to economic decline, physical facilities have deteriorated in schools; books and supplies are limited; and there are few qualified teachers. During the time of the People's National Congress (PNC) government, education became highly politicized, and teachers were expected to teach loyalty to both the PNC and to socialist objectives.

The principal university is the University of Georgetown at Turkeyeen, in the eastern part of the capital, but many Hindus seek training and higher education abroad.

14 CULTURAL HERITAGE

Post-independent Guyana still bears the imprint of its colonial heritage, and many people still look towards European values. But Hindus keep a strong link with their ancient roots and for many, the cinema provides that link, showing the great epics such as the story of Lord Rama's long 14-year exile. For them it bears many echoes of their own past, reflecting their exile from India.

Young Hindus, too, are rediscovering their culture, through the religious fables as well as through the traditional music played at weddings and festivals.

One of the best known Hindu writers is Dr. David Dabydeen, whose works cover his experiences both in Guyana and Britain. His latest novel is *The Counting House*. Another popular author is Rooplall Monar.

15 WORK

The domestic economy of Guyana reflects the ethnic divisions of the country. Hindu families control most small businesses, such as small farms and shops. In fact, the Hindus are the mainstay of the plantation agriculture of rice and sugar. Meanwhile, the Africans dominate the government sector and security forces. An increasing number of Hindus are entering the legal and medical professions.

Wages for most people, however, are low, and many Hindus depend on overseas remittances from relatives abroad to survive. Most people work at more than one job. Those with farms will often take on part-time unskilled and semiskilled jobs between sowing and harvest times.

Many Hindus, including skilled and professional people, emigrated annually in large numbers to flee what they felt to be political persecution under the previous African-dominated government. They have settled in North America, Canada, Britain, and the Caribbean Islands. This emigration has been a great drain on Guyana's human resources. At the same time, others have sought part time work in western Suriname.

16 SPORTS

Hindus share the Guyanese passion for cricket—a passion that is prevalent throughout the English-speaking Caribbean. The game is one of the few unifying factors in the country, overcoming racial divisions. It has been said, however, that cricket in Guyana is totally unlike the game as it is played in England. In Guyana it has more of the passionate atmosphere of a bullfight in Spain, galvanizing the people's national self-esteem. The sport plays a special role in the historical, social, and cultural development of the country. By playing host in Georgetown to International Test Cricket Matches against other countries within the British Commonwealth, the people of Guyana have the opportunity to demonstrate their abilities on the international scene, and to make a symbolic gesture against their oppressive colonial legacy. The Hindus did not come into the game at Test Match level until the 1950s. There are a number of great Hindu players, however, who have been selected for the West Indies team, including Rohan Kanhai and Neville Kalicharan.

In the villages outside Georgetown, street cricket is played with a sponge ball, and the pitch is a coconut mat laid out on the ground. Even during the rainy seasons, young players can be seen standing thigh-deep in water around a mat laid on the only piece of high, dry ground in a field.

17 ENTERTAINMENT AND RECREATION

Popular culture is as mixed as the various ethnic groups who live in Guyana. Georgetown offers a wide mix of museums and art galleries, and for the young people there are discos. A favorite kind of music among both Hindu and Afro-Guyanese is something called "chutney," a hot, spicy mixture of traditional Hindu music and rock music.

The cinema still plays a large part in the lives of older people, and the favorite films among Hindus are those that are imported from India, depicting the great epics such as the story of Lord Rama.

The young are also turning more and more to the traditional Asian Indian songs and dances in their search for their artistic roots.

18 FOLK ART, CRAFTS, AND HOBBIES

Many of the Guyanan Hindu folk arts and crafts are entwined with the Hindu fables and festivals.

19 SOCIAL PROBLEMS

Race has been a divisive issue in Guyana, with the Hindus accusing the Africans of racism and repression during the 28 years of rule by the People's National Congress party, during which they claimed that Hindu villages were attacked and plundered by security forces. The Africans dominate the Guyana Defence Force and the police. Street crime and violence are particularly notorious in Georgetown. Community police have now been introduced by the government into the city to try to retake control of the streets.

The new government has also announced its intention of introducing structural changes "with a human face" and aims to alleviate poverty through a basic-needs strategy. It also intends to increase foreign and local investment, production, and exports. Cheddi Jagan has promised a "lean and clean" government and is determined to end racial discrimination.

20 BIBLIOGRAPHY

Dabydeen, Dr. David, and Dr. Brinlsey Samaroo, ed. *Across the Dark Waters: Ethnicity and Indian Identity in the Caribbean.* London: MacMillan Caribbean, 1996.

———. *India in the Caribbean.* Special commemorative edition. London: Hansib, 1987.

Daly, Vere T. *A Short History of the Guyanese People.* London: Macmillan Education, 1975.

Frances, J., and I. Frances. *Guyana: Politics and Economics and Society Beyond the Burnham Era.* London: Pinter, n.d.

—by P. Pitchon

HMONG AMERICANS

For more information on Hmong history and culture, *see* **Vol. 3: Hmong**.

OVERVIEW

Hmong Americans first came to the US in 1975 after the take-over of Vietnam and Laos by leftist regimes. Although many sources claim that the US Central Intelligence Agency (CIA) promised to resettle the Hmong if they were defeated, only 1,000 Hmong were evacuated in the first year after defeat. Many Hmong were forced to flee across the borders of Vietnam and Laos into Thailand. There they lived in overcrowded refugee camps for months or even years.

In December 1975, US Congress finally agreed to start resettling Hmong refugees and brought 3,466 Hmong to the US. The following year, 10,200 refugees from Laos, some of them Hmong, were admitted to the US. Hmong immigration continued over the next several years, and by 1990 the Hmong population in the US had reached almost 100,000. Most had arrived during the early 1980s. Hmong Americans are generally very young; about one-third of the 1990 population were born in America.

When the Hmong first arrived in the US, resettlement agencies scattered members of the 12 traditional Hmong clans across the country. As soon as they were able, the Hmong made their way in small family groups to areas where they could reassemble their clan communities. The majority of Hmong Americans now live in California, with sizeable populations also in Minnesota and Wisconsin. Most live in farming towns and small cities.

Hmong Americans belong mainly to two Hmong tribes: White Hmong and Blue (or Green) Hmong. Each tribe speaks a different dialect of the Hmong language. Hmong is a monosyllabic, tonal language, meaning that most words have only one syllable, and the meaning of a word changes depending on which of eight tones (high, low, ascending, descending, etc.) is used to pronounce it. Because the Hmong language is so different from English, Hmong Americans are faced with a serious challenge in developing English-language proficiency.

Hmong legends and folklore have been passed down orally for many generations. Some tales have moral lessons; others convey mythical understandings of the world. Hmong Americans became interested in preserving these stories in written form, and a large bilingual collection, *Myths, Legends, and Folktales from the Hmong of Laos* (edited by Charles Johnson) was published by Macalester College in St. Paul, Minnesota, in 1985.

Most Hmong Americans continue to follow their traditional religious ways. Traditional Hmong religion is pantheistic, recognizing the presence of divine spirit in all things. Spirit cults, shamanism, and ancestor worship are the three major components of traditional Hmong religious life. Some Hmong Americans follow the *Chao Fa* religion of Laos, begun in the 1960s by Hmong prophet Yang Chong Leu (or Shang Lue Yang) who preached a return to traditional Hmong ways. Yang Chong Leu also promoted a traditional system of writing known as *Pahawh Hmong*, still used by *Chao Fa* followers today.

A number of Hmong converted to Christianity in Laos, and even more have converted since their arrival in the US. Religious conversion has caused a great deal of division in the Hmong community, since religion is seen as an integral part of Hmong life, and Christianity is opposed to traditional Hmong beliefs and practices in many ways.

Rites of passage are particular areas of conflict. For example, whereas Christianity rejects the concept of reincarnation, traditional Hmong religion holds that when a man dies, he is reincarnated as a woman, and when a woman dies, she is reincarnated as a man. Therefore, traditional birth and death rituals involve preparations and protections for the soul that is about to enter the body of the newborn or leave the body of the deceased. The Christian Church finds these rituals unnecessary and even offensive and strongly discourages their practice.

Marriage customs have also undergone significant changes in the face of conflicting religious teachings and even societal law codes. Traditionally, a Hmong man may kidnap a young woman and force himself on her sexually, thereby establishing her as a recognized marriage partner. In the US, this is considered rape and is punishable by law (some young Hmong American women have pressed charges against men who carried out this custom). Polygyny (marriage with more than one woman at a time) is accepted and even common in traditional Hmong society but is illegal in the US.

The most important traditional holiday celebrated by Hmong Americans is *noj peb caug*, the New Year Festival. In America, the festival begins sometime around the new moon in December (in Laos, the timing is much more specific) and lasts for a few days. It is the only holiday celebrated by the entire Hmong American community. For Hmong Americans, *noj peb caug* serves as an opportunity to reaffirm their Hmong identity, and so their New Year festivals generally include cultural fairs, dances, and exhibitions designed to teach young Hmong Americans about their ancestral traditions.

Traditional Hmong customs teach that while it is impolite to ask a stranger's name directly, it is polite, and common, to ask someone where he or she lives. It is also considered well mannered to try to keep visitors from leaving, encouraging them to stay and chat for a while longer. Hmong Americans generally hold to these traditional customs and are usually very friendly. They are also quite open to other ethnic groups, welcoming opportunities to teach others about Hmong culture.

Coming from a rural agricultural background, Hmong Americans have had a difficult time adapting to life in the industrialized US. Language barriers and lack of appropriate education and job skills prevent many Hmong Americans from finding adequate employment. In 1990, about two out of every three Hmong Americans lived below the poverty level. Three out of four received public assistance in order to survive. Poverty and unemployment lead to malnutrition, lower immunities, depression, and other stress-related diseases.

Although Hmong Americans are generally very healthy, there was almost an epidemic among Hmong American men in the late 1970s and 1980s of Sudden Unexpected Nocturnal Death Syndrome, in which death occurs suddenly and mysteriously during sleep. Western medical researchers have linked the syndrome to breathing difficulties, but many Hmong Americans believe it is caused by an evil spirit that sits on the victims' chests while they sleep. It is often difficult for Western doctors to work effectively with Hmong American patients because Western and Hmong concepts of disease and healing are so different.

Traditional Hmong healing is based on the shamanistic view of the world that divides the universe into the spirit world and material world. Illness is believed to be caused most often by the loss of one's spirit, when the soul wanders from the body to escape emotional and physical stresses. Hmong shamans perform rituals to call the soul back to the body. There are also Hmong healers who have the *neng*, a healing spirit in their bodies. The *neng* and accompanying healing skills are inherited from another clan member. These healers can not only call back lost souls but also fight off evil spirits that may have brought on an illness.

The Hmong also have a great depth of knowledge about the healing properties of herbs, and most Hmong American households have a small medicinal herb garden. Herbal healers are nearly always women. Massage may be combined with herbal treatments for some ailments, such as stomach ache.

Hmong American families tend to be quite large. According to the 1990 US Census, Hmong American families had an average of 6.38 persons, as compared to 3.06 persons in the average European American family. Hmong Americans are also very young, with over 60% below the age of 18 in 1990.

Since Hmong families are very "child-centered," children are treasured. This does not mean they are indulged, however. Hmong parents are quite strict with their children, exercising a great deal of control over their lives. American values stress personal freedom and a greater degree of independence for young people. Therefore, Hmong American children often come into conflict with their more traditional parents over issues of discipline and freedom of choice. Many Hmong American and other Southeast Asian youth feel moved to escape these conflicts by running away from home, creating a growing population of teenaged runaways.

Extended families were the traditional basis of Hmong households, but building codes in the US prevent large numbers of people from living together under the same roof. So Hmong Americans have had to split up into smaller nuclear-family units. The traditional clans are also losing importance, although clan leaders are still well respected.

Most foreign-born Hmong American adults have had little formal schooling. More than half of those over the age of 25 have less than a fifth grade education. Only about 30% are high school graduates. Young Hmong Americans, however, have shown great aptitude for Western education and have high rates of secondary and post-secondary school attendance. Almost one-third (32%) of Hmong Americans between the ages of 18 and 24 were in college in 1990.

Among older, uneducated Hmong Americans, however, prospects are bleak and unemployment is high. Over 18% of Hmong Americans in the labor force in 1990 were unemployed. Of those who have managed to find employment, most (almost 80%) work at blue-collar jobs.

One source of income for Hmong Americans is the sale of traditional crafts, particularly *paj ntaub* (or *pa ndau*). Done exclusively by Hmong women, *paj ntaub* is a form of needlework that combines embroidery and appliqué to create intricate, colorful geometric designs. These elaborate designs are done entirely by hand without any measuring tools. A wide market has developed in the US and other Western countries for *paj ntaub* items.

Hmong Americans are very concerned with the problems of adapting to life in American society. Hmong organizations have sprung up in Hmong American communities to address these problems and help local Hmong Americans develop the skills they need to succeed. The Hmong National Development is the largest such organization and acts as an advocate to obtain funding for the local organizations. Although Hmong Americans have much to overcome, they are eager to make life work in their new home and to become integral members of American society while remaining true to their Hmong identity.

BIBLIOGRAPHY

Bankston, Carl L., III. "Who Are the Hmong Americans?" In *The Asian American Almanac*, Susan Gall, ed. Detroit: Gale Research, 1995.

Chan, Sucheng, ed. *Hmong Means Free: Life in Laos and America.* Philadelphia: Temple University Press, 1994.

Donnelly, Nancy D. *Changing Lives of Refugee Hmong Women.* Seattle: University of Washington Press, 1994.

Johnson, Charles, ed. *Myths, Legends, and Folktales from the Hmong of Laos.* St. Paul, Minn.: Macalester College, 1985.

Qunicy, Keith. *Hmong, History of a People.* 2nd ed. Cheney, Wash.: Eastern Washington University Press, 1995.

—by D. K. Daeg de Mott

HONDURANS

LOCATION: Honduras
POPULATION: 5 million
LANGUAGE: Spanish; English; local dialects
RELIGION: Roman Catholicism (95%); Protestantism (Methodist, Church of God, Seventh-Day Adventist, and Assembly of God churches); native religions combined with Christianity

¹ INTRODUCTION

Honduras is the second-largest country in Central America but has traditionally been the poorest, although the civil war in Nicaragua during the 1980s dropped that country into last place. The magnificent Mayan ruins at Copán are the remains of a city-state that flourished between the 4th and 9th centuries AD. Christopher Columbus landed in Honduras on his last voyage, in 1502, and the Spanish conquest began in 1524. Because of disease, mistreatment, and the export of slave laborers to other countries, the native population under Spanish control dropped to an estimated 8,000 in 1541. Once all the gold and silver to be had was exploited, Honduras became a poor and neglected land. Harassed by English pirates, the Caribbean coast was effectively out of Spain's control.

Central America freed itself from Spanish rule in 1821, but Honduras did not become independent until 1838. The country fell under the grip of dictators and has experienced some 300 internal rebellions, civil wars, and changes of government since then. Economically, the first shipment of bananas to the United States in 1899 started a new pattern of trade. Coffee and cotton also later became significant export crops. A number of civilians have been elected president since the 1950s, but several of them have been overthrown by the military.

² LOCATION AND HOMELAND

Honduras has a long Caribbean Sea coastline to the north and a small Pacific Ocean coastline on the south, along the Gulf of Fonseca. Guatemala is its neighbor to the west, El Salvador to the south and west, and Nicaragua to the south and east. The Bay Islands lie in the Caribbean. Excluding the coastal areas, Honduras is a mountainous country, with scattered but numerous valleys where forests give way to agriculture and livestock-raising. The nation's largest port and its largest industrial city lie in the Caribbean lowlands. Rainfall is plentiful in Honduras, and there are many rivers.

With just over 5 million people, most of them in the highlands, Honduras is not a crowded country. About 90% of all Hondurans are mestizo, of mixed European and Amerindian ancestry. Of the remainder, about 7% are Indian, 2% are black, and 1% are white.

³ LANGUAGE

Spanish is the national and official language, but English is often understood along the Caribbean coast, and Bay Islanders speak English as their native tongue. Black Caribs (Garifuna), descendants of freed black slaves and Carib Indians, speak a language related to Carib. Miskito, who are of mixed Indian, African, and European descent and live along the Caribbean coast, speak an Indian tongue with contributions from West African and European languages.

⁴ FOLKLORE

Among the folkloric beliefs found throughout Central America is the identification of a human being with a spirit (*nagual*), usually an animal, so closely connected that both are believed to share the same soul. If one dies, so will the other. Similarly, a witch or other evildoer is considered able to assume an animal form. These beliefs are of Indian origin and, since Honduras does not have a large Indian population, are not as strongly held as in Guatemala, for example.

Folk stories tell of a variety of spirits, many of whom live in wells or caves. El Duende is an imp with a big sombrero and a taste for pretty young girls, whom he courts by wearing red trousers and blue jackets and by tossing pebbles at them. *Curanderos* are faith healers who can cure nervous ailments and can dispel the *vista fuerte,* or evil eye, which is often held responsible for children's illnesses. The god of the Lenca, the largest Indian group in Honduras, was Icelaca, who appears as a many-eyed, two-faced stone idol. *La compostura,* a Lenca rite dedicated to the land, consists of offerings to an altar in the shape of a wooden frame on which pine boughs are placed in the form of a cross. Plants on display symbolize the spirits to whom the rite is dedicated.

Lempira was a 16th-century Indian chieftain who fought the Spanish; he is much admired in national mythology, and the national currency is named for him. A hymn to Lempira has, as its chorus, the words: "Hondurans! With epic lyre/and brightly clad/we intone a hymn to Lempira/to the patriot of heroic valor."

⁵ RELIGION

Nearly 95% of the population is Roman Catholic. Protestants account for about 3% and are growing rapidly because of active proselytizing by evangelical groups such as the Methodists, Church of God, Seventh-Day Adventists, and Assemblies of God.

Although nominally Catholic, many Hondurans have incorporated pre-Conquest Indian traditions into their religious practices. The *rogacíon* is a special Mass or procession asking for rain. Each community has its own patron saint. The *guanacasco* is a celebration of the patron saint visited by saints from neighboring communities. Copal (a tree resin) is burned for incense, an ancient Mayan custom, and there are offerings to the sun. Pilgrimages to saints' shrines are common. Most houses will have an image or picture of a saint displayed on a wall.

Black Caribs, although chiefly Methodist, retain many African elements in their religious practices. *Digui* is a rite for the dead. Although most Miskito now belong to the Moravian Church, they formerly worshipped Wan-Aisa as their Supreme God. Yu Lapta was the Sun God, Kati the Moon Goddess, and Alwani was the Thunder God.

⁶ MAJOR HOLIDAYS

As in other Latin American countries, Christmas (25 December) and Holy Week (late March or early April), culminating in Easter Sunday, are the chief religious holidays. A Christmas

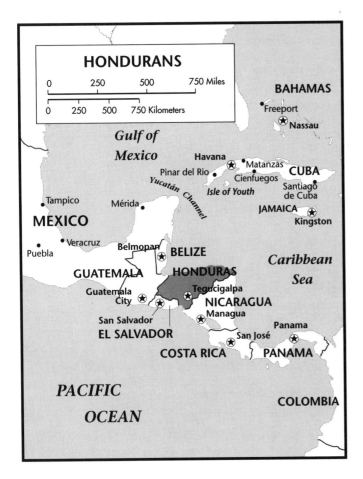

HONDURANS

0   250   500   750 Miles

0   250   500   750 Kilometers

tradition is the *posada,* a celebration held nightly beginning on 16 December.

Just over the border in Guatemala, Esquipulas is the home of a dark-skinned wooden sculpture of Jesus that draws pilgrims from Honduras and other Central American countries to a celebration that begins on 15 January of each year. The feast day of the Virgin of Suyapa, Honduras' patron saint, is on 2 February. A tiny wooden image to which miraculous powers have been attributed since the 18th century is on display at the basilica in Suyapa, a village near Tegucigalpa, the capital. Another manifestation of the Virgin is celebrated on 8 December (the day of the commemoration of the dogma of the Immaculate Conception) at Juticalpa, with a procession bearing her image as the climax. Between 25 December and 6 January, Garifuna men celebrate Yancunú with dancing, singing, and the wearing of masks to bring prosperity in the new year.

Of the secular (nonreligious) holidays, the most important are Independence Day on 15 September, and the birthday of Francisco Morazán on 3 October. Morazán was the last president of the United Provinces of Central America, a federation that only lasted from 1823 to 1842.

7 RITES OF PASSAGE

Baptism of infants is standard and is usually followed by a celebration. Among the upper and middle classes, dating is restricted. A prospective suitor is carefully checked out, and engagements of several years are common. Perhaps half of all Honduran couples, however, live together without a marriage

license or a religious ceremony. A novena is commonly held after death, usually at home. A second novena may be held six months later.

8 INTERPERSONAL RELATIONS

Honduran customs are more conservative and traditional than those of the United States. A great emphasis is normally placed on courtesy and proper dress among the upper and middle classes. On the other hand, friends are more demonstrative than in the United States. Men often embrace on meeting and departing. Women often embrace and kiss one or both cheeks, or at least touch cheeks.

Since most people are named for a saint, they celebrate their saint's day as well as (or in place of) their own birthday. Friends and relatives are invited to the home.

There has been less class conflict in Honduras than in the other Hispanic Central American countries. This is because the country has a relatively large number of peasants tilling their own plots rather than working as laborers for large estates, and because the ruling elite has been willing to form alliances with others. However, social tensions have increased as landowners have accumulated more land in recent decades for cattle grazing.

9 LIVING CONDITIONS

At least two-thirds of the Honduran people live below the poverty line. About one-third have no access to health care, and about one-fifth of all young children are malnourished. At least 0.5 million more housing units are needed in Honduras. The typical dwelling is a two-room adobe bungalow with a tiled roof. Poor peasants, however, live in one-room huts made of bamboo, sugarcane, and corn stalks, with dirt floors. Most of them till small, marginal plots or work for wages on larger farms. Migrants from the country to the city generally live in crowded slums.

The upper and middle classes generally have domestic servants and live in houses with thick adobe, brick, or concrete walls. Many have grillwork over the windows and as part of the structure of balconies on the upper floors. Homes usually have no front yard but rather an enclosed patio.

10 FAMILY LIFE

Family solidarity is of basic importance and depends on mutual assistance from all its members. Families are usually large, since Honduran women give birth to an average of about five children each, and grandparents, plus aunts and uncles and their children, may also live under the same roof. Whether they live together or apart, the various branches of a family share and cooperate, finding work for unemployed members, extending loans, or taking in needy kin. As in other Latin American countries, *compadres* (godparents) also provide support to hard-pressed family members.

11 CLOTHING

Most people dress casually, with the men wearing loose trousers and shirts and the women wearing one-piece calico or cotton dresses or loose blouses and skirts. Open sandals are a common form of footwear. The poor generally are clad in secondhand rather than store-bought clothes. Colonial costumes are worn only on special occasions like fiestas. On these occa-

Hondurans' diet is supplemented by starches like cassava and plantains. (Cory Langley)

sions, the women may wear silk dresses or cotton dresses embroidered with silk, using old Mayan patterns and designs.

The Tolupanes Indians are the only group in Honduras whose dress is distinctive. The *balandrán* is a one-piece, sleeveless male article of clothing. Women wear brightly colored dresses and silver necklaces with brightly painted beads made of dried seeds and thorns.

12 FOOD

Tortillas, made of cornmeal rolled into thin pancakes, are the staple of the diet, supplemented by beans, the chief source of protein. The poor generally eat tortillas and beans at every meal. These are supplemented by starches like cassava and plantains. Rice, meat, eggs, and fish are served less often. Although pigs and chickens are raised widely in the countryside, their meat is reserved for special occasions. Green vegetables are not common in the average diet either.

Mondongo, a richly flavored tripe soup, is a popular Honduran dish. Other specialties include carrots stuffed with cheese, creamed beets and plantains, and corn dumplings in honey. The Caribbean diet is more exotic. The Black Caribs eat cassava in the form of big tortillas, and a mash made of ground plantains and bananas. *Baili* is a flour tortilla dipped in coconut soup with crab. *Tapado* is a soup made from coconut milk to which clams, crab, shrimp, fish heads, and plantains are added. The *mondongo hondureño* recipe includes cleaned beef tripe

(innards), pig's feet, a number of vegetables, bread crumbs, and a tomato sauce with spices and corn oil added.

Chicha is a homemade drink made of fermented corn. The Black Caribs make a drink out of fermented corn and sugarcane.

13 EDUCATION

At least 25% of Hondurans cannot read or write. Education is free and compulsory between the ages of 7 through 14, and more than 80% of all children of primary-school age are in school, but fewer than half enrolled in public schools complete the primary level. The middle and upper classes generally send their children to private schools, often church-run. The chief institution of higher learning, the National Autonomous University of Honduras, is located in Tegucigalpa, the capital, and has branches in San Pedro Sula and La Ceiba. There are three private universities.

14 CULTURAL HERITAGE

José Cecilio del Valle wrote the declaration of independence for the Central American federation, which failed to survive. Father José Trinidad Reyes founded what became the National University in 1847. Juan Ramón Molina was an important 19th-century poet. Rafael Heliodoro Valle, a poet and historian, was the most respected literary figure of the 20th century. Other 20th-century Honduran writers include the novelist Argentina Díaz Lozanto and the poet Clementina Suarez.

José Miguel Gómez was an 18th-century painter. Among 20th-century painters are Arturo López Rodezno and Carlos Garay. The primitive landscape paintings of José Antonio Velásquez are much admired.

Drums and the flute were the musical instruments of the Indians before the Spanish conquest. The main instrument now is the marimba, which is similar to the xylophone and is backed by other band instruments.

15 WORK

More than half the labor force is not formally employed; it includes subsistence farmers, small shopkeepers, and self-employed craftspeople. Women often seek jobs as domestic servants or, in urban areas, act as street vendors. Men supplement their income from tilling their small plots by working on plantations for part of the year. The small middle class consists of professionals, merchants, farmers, business employees, and civil servants. The minimum wage was as low as $1.60 per day for farm workers in the mid-1990s.

16 SPORTS

As elsewhere in Central America, *fútbol* (soccer) is the most popular sport. The so-called Soccer War of 1969 followed matches between the national teams of Honduras and El Salvador; more than 1,000 Hondurans were killed in the four-day struggle. Honduras also has bullfights, and at fiestas such traditional forms of sport as greased-pole climbing and the *carrera de cintas,* a horseback-riding race in which the rider must run a stick through small rings at full gallop, are common.

17 ENTERTAINMENT AND RECREATION

There are more than 20 folk dances, based on combinations of Spanish, Indian, and African influences. The Garifuna hold two fertility dances—*Sanvey* and *Vanaroga*—with different songs by men and women. The Miskito generally form a circle when making music and sing and dance in turn to the accompaniment of drums and other instruments. Social dances are also held. Salsa, merengue, and Mexican *ranchero* music are popular. Fireworks are part of every celebration. Television is still generally restricted to the cities but radio reaches every part of the country.

18 FOLK ART, CRAFTS, AND HOBBIES

Artisans carve objects ranging from wall hangings to furniture from mahogany and other tropical hardwoods. Baskets, mats, and hammocks are woven from plant fibers such as henequen. Ceramics include porcelain objects in the form of animals, especially roosters. The Lenca are noted for their pottery; La Campa and Ojajana also produce distinctive pottery. Other handicrafts include embroidery and leather goods such as belts and handbags.

19 SOCIAL PROBLEMS

Nearly two-thirds of the Honduran people live in poverty. Tuberculosis and gastroenteritis are serious health problems, as are influenza, malaria, typhoid, and pneumonia. Most of the people do not have access to running water and sanitation facilities. Unemployment and underemployment are high, and the country is dependent on income from only two commodities, bananas and coffee. The crime rate has surged in the 1990s, and there is widespread domestic violence against women.

20 BIBLIOGRAPHY

Adams, Richard N. *Cultural Surveys of Panama, Nicaragua, Guatemala, El Salvador, and Honduras.* Detroit: B. Ethridge Books, 1976.

Alvarado, Elvia. *Don't Be Afraid, Gringo: A Honduran Woman Speaks from the Heart.* San Francisco: Institute for Food and Development Policy, 1987.

Euraque, Darío A. *Reinterpreting the Banana Republic: Region and State in Honduras, 1870–1972.* Chapel Hill: University of North Carolina Press, 1996.

Merrill, Tim L., ed. *Honduras: A Country Study.* 3rd ed. Washington, D.C.: Headquarters, Dept. of the Army: For Sale by Supt. of Docs., U.S. G.P.O., 1995.

Meyer, Harvey Kessler. *Historical Dictionary of Honduras.* Metuchen, N.J.: Scarecrow, 1994.

Smith, Katie. *The Human Farm: A Tale of Changing Lives and Changing Lands.* West Hartford, Conn.: Kimarian Press, 1994.

Stonich, Susan C. *"I Am Destroying the Land!": The Political Ecology of Poverty and Environmental Destruction in Honduras.* Boulder, Colo.: Westview, 1993.

—by H. Halasz, reviewed by F. Colecchia

HOPI

LOCATION: United States (Arizona)
POPULATION: 10,000
LANGUAGE: English; Hopi
RELIGION: Traditional Hopi
RELATED ARTICLES: Vol. 2: Native North Americans

1 INTRODUCTION

The Hopi are a Pueblo people, most likely descending from the Hisatsinom (Hopi for "people of long ago") who lived among the cliffs of what is now the Southwest desert as much as 2,000 years ago. A prolonged drought from AD 1275–1300 apparently forced the Hisatsinom to relocate. They split into several different bands who settled in different areas of the region and have since developed into the various Pueblo peoples. The Hopi chose the westernmost area, in northeastern Arizona, and built their homes on the tops of almost inaccessible mesas. This inaccessibility kept them largely protected from the invasions by Spanish and then European American conquerors. Therefore, the Hopi have been able to maintain their traditional ways of life and beliefs almost uninterrupted up through the present day.

This is not to say that the Hopi have suffered no effects from the European invasions of their lands. Between 1519 and 1650, ten previously flourishing Hopi villages were wiped out by disease and bloodshed brought to their lands by the Spanish from Mexico. Conflicts between the Spanish and Pueblo peoples continued throughout the 17th century. The Spanish conquered all the Pueblos by the mid-17th century and built Catholic churches in every village. They forced the Pueblo people to convert to Christianity, using extreme torture as a persuasive tactic. At the Hopi village of Oraibi in 1655, Spanish Friar Salvador de Guerra caught a Hopi in what he called "an act of idolatry" (in other words, following his own Hopi Way). De Guerra whipped the Hopi in front of the whole village until the Hopi was covered in blood. Then de Guerra poured burning turpentine over him. By these methods, Spanish made nominal Christians of the Hopis and other Pueblo peoples and drove Native religious practices underground.

On 10 August 1680, the Pueblos revolted and drove out the Spanish. This was the first time the Pueblo peoples had acted together. Once the Spanish were gone, the Pueblos returned to their independent ways. Therefore, when the Spanish returned in 1692, they met no unified resistance and reconquered the Pueblos fairly easily. The Hopi lived in such a remote area that they remained mostly untouched by this second Spanish conquest. Other Pueblo peoples fled to the Hopi lands and took refuge there. The Hopi moved all their villages to the very tops of the mesas after the 1680 revolt and so were virtually impregnable. In 1700 the Hopi made it very clear to the Spanish that they were not interested in Christianity when they destroyed the mission church in the village of Awatovi (killing the priests and other Spanish in residence, throwing their bodies over the edge of the mesa). No other Christian missions were established in Hopi territory until the 1890s.

In modern times the Hopi have had to fight European American industry and expansion. On 15 May 1971, the Hopi filed suit to stop the Peabody Coal Company from strip mining for coal on 100 square miles of the Hopi reservation. The Hopi consider Black Mesa to be sacred land, and strip mining would be a sacrilegious invasion of that holy place. Ten years later, in 1981, the Hopi sued to stop construction of a ski resort in the San Francisco mountains, another sacred place. The Hopi lost this suit.

The Hopi have only acted as a "tribe" since 1936, when the European American writer Oliver La Farge wrote the Hopi constitution. Before that time, the Hopi were simply people who followed the Hopi Way. The name "Hopi" is a shortened form of *Hopisinom*, which translates as "people of humility, respectful of their environment and earth stewards." Today, Hopi translate their name as "one who follows the path," or "one who walks in the right direction." As the late Hopi elder Percy Lomaquahu of Hotevilla explained it:

> *Hopi* means "good in every respect." Humbleness means peace, honesty—all mean Hopi. True, honest, perfect words—that's what we call Hopi words. In all the languages, not just in Hopi. We strive to be Hopi. We call ourselves Hopi because maybe one or two of us will become Hopi. Each person must look into their heart and make changes so that you may become Hopi when you reach your destination.
>
> (In Stephen Trimble, *The People*... Santa Fe: School of American Research, 1993, p. 58.)

2 LOCATION AND HOMELAND

The Hopi currently live in 12 villages located along the southern rim of Black Mesa in northeastern Arizona. Theirs is the driest of any of the Pueblo lands. Over the centuries, the Hopi have developed a reputation as the most skilled dry-farmers in the world. Ecologists have called them "environmental wizards." The village of Old Oraibi has been inhabited since at least AD 1150, rivaling Acoma as the longest continuously inhabited village in the US. Old Oraibi was for centuries the "capital" of Hopiland. Today it is a village of just over 100 people, but still highly respected by the Hopis of the third Mesa.

Black Mesa is divided by washes into three separate mesas, named in order of approach from the east: First Mesa, Second Mesa, and Third Mesa. Hopiland (or the Hopi reservation) is entirely surrounded by the much larger Navajo reservation. Hopiland encompasses 1.6 million acres over 3,862 square miles. While there are over 10,000 members of the Hopi tribe in the US, only 7,061 of them live on the reservation (according to the 1990 US Census). Modern Hopi communities are located at the bases of the three mesas. The ancient villages remain on the mesa summits. The area receives about ten inches of rain per year.

3 LANGUAGE

The Hopi language is a member of the Uto-Aztecan family of Native North American languages. It is related to the languages of the Ute and Paiute peoples. It is not related to any of the other Pueblo languages. Each of the three mesas in Hopiland has its own dialect of the Hopi language. The first Hopi dictionary is currently being compiled in the Third Mesa dialect. Because the Hopi have lived in an inaccessible region, protected from most of the invasions by Spanish and European American peoples, the language has remained alive into the present day. It is also required that a young Hopi speak the Hopi language in order to be initiated into adulthood.

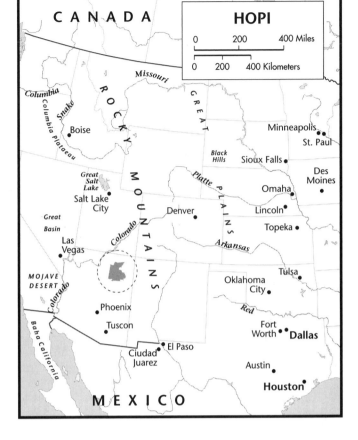

The dictionary currently in process is the first attempt to create a standard written system for the Hopi language. Hopi has never before been a written language, so the oral tradition has grown strong and rich. It has become so poetic and dramatic that it is difficult to write down. Any written material in Hopi will necessarily have lost something in the translation. The dictionary compilers hope that by making a standard written system available, the Hopi people will begin to develop a literature that is their own. It will take some time, however, to adapt the language to written forms.

Ritual forms of the Hopi language are used by an exclusive group of priests and priestesses who keep this ritual language secret. This form of the Hopi language remains unknown to those outside the group.

4 FOLKLORE

All Hopi stories begin with a formal opening: *Aliksa'i*. There is no exact English translation, but it means something like "Attention!" or "Let's take up the story where we left it." Because time for the Hopi is cyclical rather than linear, the Hopi care more about *where* a story happened than *when*.

The Hopi have an emergence-type creation story. The First Way of Life, or First World (Tokpela, meaning "Endless Space") was an infinite void until the Creator created finite forms, including human beings. For a time, all lived peacefully there, until some humans lost sight of the true way and fell into decadence. The Creator allowed those humans who still had sight of the truth (and those who were willing to follow them) to emerge into the Second Way of Life, or Second World (Tokpa, "Dark Midnight") before he destroyed the First Way of Life with fire. The same course of events took place in the Second Way of Life, which the Creator then destroyed with ice after allowing the people to emerge into the Third Way of Life, or Third World (Kuskurza, an ancient name with no modern translation). When the same corruption began to occur in the Third World, representatives from all forms of life held a council and decided the Third World had become out of balance and it was time to migrate to the Fourth Way of Life, (Tivongyapavi, "The Earth Center"). The Creator allowed the peoples to choose a food before destroying the Third World with water. The Hopi chose a short blue ear of corn. Blue corn requires more work to grow, so the Hopi chose a life of hardship and humility. But blue corn is also heartier, so they also chose a life of strength and health. Blue corn symbolism runs throughout Hopi life. Blue corn is sometimes equated with the Hopi Way: planting, tending, and harvesting, it follows the path of the ancestors and fulfills the contract made with Ma'asau, keeper of the Fourth World who allowed the people to emerge into this Fourth World if they agreed to act as its caretakers. It allows the Hopi to reexperience the creation of the world. The Hopi must perform certain rituals and follow religious rules set out for them by Ma'asau if they are to keep this Fourth World in balance. Since the time of contact with Europeans, the Hopi feel this world has lost its balance. They call it koyanisquatsi, "life out of balance." Because of this, they must perform their rituals and follow the Hopi Way even more diligently to regain and maintain this world's balance.

5 RELIGION

The Hopi believe themselves to be the caretakers of the earth, of this Fourth Way of Life (Tivongyapavi, "The Earth Center"). They perform certain rituals and follow a set of religious rules in order to keep this world in balance. These rules and rituals are called "the Hopi Way." Hopi ceremonies focus on creating community harmony, bringing rain for the crops, and honoring katsinas and Hopi ancestors. Katsinas (often called kachinas by European Americans) are spirits who live in the San Francisco mountains near Hopiland. The Hopi do not worship katsinas; rather, the katsinas act as intermediaries between the forces of nature and human beings. The katsinas visit Hopi villages for six months every year, arriving in December for the solstice ceremony (Powamuy) and leaving after the Home Dance (Niman) in July to return to the San Francisco peaks. Throughout the months between December and July, the katsinas dance frequently, bestowing gifts on the people. In Hopi villages katsinas, represented by katsina societies, dance in the village plaza for all to see. Other Pueblo peoples allow only the initiated to see the katsinas dance.

The plaza of each village is the "heart-place," the center of the world for those villagers. It is the place where all four directions come together, where all the balanced forces of the world meet: north-south-east-west, the Sun above and Earth below, winter-summer, male buildings and female space, etc. A half-buried rock surrounded by offerings of corn meal and feathers marks the exact center of each village. The sacred place for the Hopi and other Pueblo peoples is the kiva, an underground chamber entered and exited by a ladder through a hole in the roof. Religious rites and other activities are held in the kiva. The traditional religious leader of the Hopi is called the kikmongwi and is often a member of the Bear Clan, the first clan to arrive in Hopiland, according to Hopi legend.

All Hopi are initiated into katsina societies at about age 9–11. As adults, Hopi may be initiated into priesthood societies (called wuutsim) priestess societies, or Snake societies. Young children are given katsina dolls as teaching tools to learn about the katsinas. Until they are initiated into the katsina society, children are not permitted to learn about esoteric matters.

Another character in the Hopi Way is the sacred clown. Clown dancers break all the social and religious rules, performing acts that the people are forbidden to perform. By showing life as it should not be but often is, clowns allow the Hopi to laugh at themselves and to see how they need to improve their behavior.

During the 1880s, the US government divided up the Native North American reservations between religious groups. The Hopi were assigned to the Mennonites (and Baptists). The Reverend H. R. Voth arrived in 1893 and tried to destroy the Hopi Way and replace it with Mennonite Christianity. The Hopi despised him; modern Hopi still remember Voth and what he attempted to do.

6 MAJOR HOLIDAYS

There are no holidays in the Hopi calendar.

7 RITES OF PASSAGE

When a child is born, a perfectly formed ear of white corn, representing its spiritual mother, is placed next to the newborn child and left there for 20 days. During this time, the child is also kept in darkness because it still belongs to the spirit world. On the 20th day, the mother passes the ear of corn over the child four times and names her or him. All the aunts who wish to be the child's godmother do the same. Then the mother and her mother (the child's grandmother) take the child outside toward the east before sunrise. When the sun comes up over the horizon and shines on the child, the child becomes fully human, belonging completely to the earthly realm from then on until death. The child is called by all of the names given to it by its aunts for the first few years of its life. Eventually, whichever name seems to stick becomes the child's name.

The corn ritual is repeated at the time of the child's initiation into the katsina society at age 9–11, and again at her or his initiation into Priest, Priestess, Snake, or other societies at adulthood. Boys grow their hair long when they are initiated into adulthood. Boys' initiation rites include a ceremonial hunt using the ancient Hopi "throwing stick," modeled after the sparrow hawk's wing. Sparrow hawks hunt by diving down onto their prey (such as a rabbit) and stunning it by hitting it on the back of the head with their wings. They then kill the prey with their talons.

8 INTERPERSONAL RELATIONS

The Hopi Way teaches that all of creation is interdependent with every living being enmeshed in an intricate web of relationships with all other beings. This means that interpersonal relationships must be approached with care and respect to maintain harmony. The Hopi live very closely together in their small, isolated villages and so have learned to deal with each other delicately. They are known as a simple agricultural people.

9 LIVING CONDITIONS

Many Hopi still live in traditional pueblos in either the ancient villages at the tops of the mesas or in the more modern communities at the mesas' bases. The Hopi build their pueblos of stone, rather than adobe as do the rest of the Pueblo peoples. Each pueblo begins as a single room with rooms of other families directly attached. As a family grows and new families are created through marriage and child-bearing, the pueblo grows upward as new rooms are added above. Some pueblos may reach four or five stories high. Traditional pueblos had no door or windows. They were entered and exited by a ladder through a hole in the roof. Modern pueblos have both doors and windows (though not all windows are covered with glass or screens). Many modern pueblos have modern conveniences, including running water and electricity. Some Hopi today live in housing provided by the federal government. About 20% of the housing in Hopiland was built before 1940. More than half was built before 1970. At least 75% of Hopi homes have running water from a public water system. About 8% have wells, and the other 17% haul their water from other sources.

The Hopi are a very adaptable people, managing to maintain their traditional ways while adopting worthwhile elements from neighboring cultures. In Hopiland, traditional healing arts are used in conjunction with modern Western medicine. Those diseases that cannot be cured with traditional medicine are treated with Western medicine, and vice versa.

10 FAMILY LIFE

Clans are vitally important to the Hopi. Clan membership is inherited through the mother. Women own the houses, food, seed for next year's planting, springs and cisterns, and the small gardens near the house (which they tend). Men do the herding, hunting, and larger-scale farming away from the house. Men also gather and haul fuel, do the spinning and weaving, and make moccasins. Women tend to exercise their responsibility at home rather than in public life. Recently, however, more Hopi women are claiming authority outside the home, serving on tribal councils, etc.

In general, Hopi do not discipline their children physically. Instead, they use lectures and teasing to teach children the Hopi Way.

11 CLOTHING

Hopi today wear Western-style clothing except for ceremonial purposes. Traditionally, unmarried Hopi girls wore their hair in a style unique to the Hopi, protruding from both sides of the head in the shape of a squash blossom.

12 FOOD

Corn is the center of Hopi life. They care for it as they do their children—diligently and tenderly. Many of their religious ceremonies focus on bringing rain so that the corn will grow. In the dry desert where the Hopi live, planting corn, melons, squash, beans, and other crops shows faith in life.

The Hopi adopted wheat, melons, apples, peaches, pears, tomatoes, and chiles from the Spanish and Mexicans. They gathered piñon nuts and acorns, wild roots, grasses, and seeds to supplement their diet, especially when the rains did not come and the planted crops failed. They also kept flocks of tame turkeys for meat. All of these foods still figure largely in the Hopi diet.

On most ceremonial occasions and at other special events, the Hopi serve *piki* bread, a paper-thin bread made from blue corn meal. The thin batter is spread on a hot polished stone, then peeled off when it is cooked. Several layers of cooked bread are rolled together while still warm. These layered rolls become crisp when cool.

13 EDUCATION

The Hopi are very concerned with education. They realize that Western education is necessary for survival in today's world, while a traditional education in the Hopi Way is as vital for the world's survival as ever. Therefore, they want their children to have both Hopi and Western educations. From 1887 to 1911, Hopi children were forcibly taken to boarding schools by the US government to be trained in European American ways. Though Hopi students are no longer forced to attend boarding schools, many still do because of a lack of adequate schools at home. Most Hopi children today attend local public schools, which have a majority of Native North Americans enrolled. These schools receive much less funding than schools with a majority of European American students. For example, from 1976 to 1979, the Cibola County school board spent $38 per student at the Laguna-Acoma High School (which has a majority of Native North American students), and $802 per student at Grants High School (with a European American student majority). Justifications for this difference put forth by European Americans, such as the argument that Native North Americans do not pay taxes on tribal lands, simply do not hold up to examination (Native North Americans pay heavy taxes on other things, such as mining revenues, etc.).

In 1986, after years of campaigning and preparation, Hopi High School opened on the Hopi reservation. It is a federally funded Bureau of Indian Affairs (BIA) school and its school board is made up entirely of local Hopi. The school's aims are to give children the opportunity to be more involved in cultural activities at home and to give parents the opportunity to guide their children in day-to-day matters. Students are allowed to be absent on Friday, the day of preparation for ceremonial dances, whenever their village is holding a dance that weekend. The school board hopes eventually to establish a regular four-day school week, so that all students (and faculty) will have Fridays off as a matter of course.

Hopi students have a difficult time in Western educational settings because the Hopi Way is based on cooperation, not competition. Western education values competition, and most grading systems are based on it. So Hopi students are not prepared to be competitive in class, and many fail because of it. In 1990, for those Hopi over the age of 25, 37% had no high school diploma (17% had less than a ninth-grade education). Only about 3% had finished college to receive a Bachelor of Arts, and less than 2% had graduate degrees.

14 CULTURAL HERITAGE

According to the Hopi Way, everything in life is approached as an art. Cooking, farming, raising children, singing, dancing, praying, weaving, making pottery and jewelry—all are forms of art. Traditional Hopi crafts are pottery, weaving, basketry, and carving katsina dolls. Recently, the Hopi have also taken up painting (although the inside walls of kivas have always been decorated with paintings) and silverwork, particularly silver overlay. In ancient times Hopi men wove, Hopi women who lived on First Mesa made pottery, while women on the Second and Third Mesas made baskets (Second Mesa women made coiled baskets, and Third Mesa women made wicker baskets). These trends are still true today, although exceptions do exist. In the late 19th century a Hopi woman named Nampeyo revived the ancient art of pottery after seeing pottery artifacts dug out of the ground during an archaeological excavation. Hopi pottery is made by coiling the clay, then smoothing the surfaces with a polishing stone. The same designs are used today to decorate the pottery as were used by the ancient Hopi.

The Hopi art form best known, perhaps, to non-Hopi is the carving of katsina dolls. The dolls, called *tihu* in Hopi, are given to Hopi children as teaching tools to learn about the katsinas and the Hopi Way. Some Hopis object to the sale of katsina dolls. However, certain Hopi artists have developed their carving skills into a fine art and can sell their dolls to top galleries for thousands of dollars. Traditional katsina dolls are carved out of cottonwood root. Modern dolls for sale may be made of wood or other materials.

A group of five Hopi painters who were trained in Western art schools formed Artist Hopid in 1973 to try to bridge Western and Hopi cultures through art. Hopi photographer and filmmaker Victor Masayesva, Jr., has made two films about the Hopi: *Itam Hakim, Hopiit* (1984) blends narration in English and Hopi with other sounds and images to tell a mythic version of Hopi history, and *Pott Starr* (1990) mixes animation with real-life action to poke fun at commercial tourism in Hopiland and non-Native fascination with Hopi artifacts.

Since there has never been a standard written Hopi language, there is no literary heritage among the Hopi. The oral tradition is very well developed, however. Hopi oral literature is richly poetic and dramatic, defying translation into English or onto paper.

15 WORK

The Hopi are shrewd businesspeople and have always been highly adaptable. There are many skilled laborers among the Hopi who are able to find work in non-Native businesses off the reservation. Yet, the unemployment rate in Hopiland was 26.8% in 1990. The crafting of traditional Hopi arts for sale to tourists, galleries, and collectors provides more income than any other source on the reservation.

16 SPORTS

Hopi play many of the same sports enjoyed by all North Americans.

17 ENTERTAINMENT AND RECREATION

Each Hopi village sponsors religious dance ceremonies during the months of August through mid-October. These dances cele-brate the harvest and give young Hopi a chance to mingle. These dances are open to men and young unmarried women with no children. Young children of both sexes may also attend. The most popular dance is the Butterfly Dance for which men wear embroidered kilts and velvet shirts with ribbons.

18 FOLK ART, CRAFTS, AND HOBBIES

All Hopi crafts are approached as forms of art. Hopi artisans have developed their skills to the level of fine art and can sell some of their pieces for thousands of dollars to top galleries and collectors.

19 SOCIAL PROBLEMS

The Hopi are a peaceful, cooperative people who have learned to live closely together in a respectful way that maintains social harmony. The most serious conflicts among the Hopi themselves arise from the disagreement between Americanized Hopi who campaign for Western "progress," and traditionalists who wish to stay closer to the ancient Hopi Way. The Hopi tribal council was created, at the initiation of the US government's Bureau of Indian Affairs (BIA), by a handful of Americanized Hopi in 1935. The council represents only a minority of Hopi, and many traditionalists actively oppose it. The village of Shongopavi even sued the council in tribal court over proposed development projects.

Conflicts with non-Hopi center on land-use issues. Since 1974 the Hopi and Navajo have been embroiled in a conflict over what was known as the Joint Use Area—a region they have shared since the late 19th century. In 1974, the US Congress passed a bill that partitioned the area between the Hopi and Navajo, requiring about 100 Hopi and thousands of Navajo to relocate. Many of these people had been living peacefully together on that land for generations. After years of wrangling with each other, the Hopi and Navajo are beginning to realize that it is not they but the Peabody Coal mining company that wants this land partitioned (the coal company wants access to the coal located there). So the Hopi and Navajo are now joining together to solve the question of land use in this area, leaving the federal government and mineral companies out of the negotiations.

The Peabody Coal Company is the subject of another Hopi conflict. When Peabody signed the first land-use lease in 1966 to strip mine for coal on Black Mesa, the Hopi tribal council agreed to this lease without consulting the rest of the Hopi. Nearly all Hopi except those on the council oppose strip mining, particularly in the sacred lands of Black Mesa. The coal mine also uses a great deal of already scarce water to transport mined coal down pipelines. This puts tremendous strain on the desert environment—the water table has dropped 70 feet since the mine went into operation. Water is precious to the Hopi; they will not survive if the water table drops much lower.

20 BIBLIOGRAPHY

Champagne, Duane, ed. *The Native North American Almanac.* Detroit: Gale Research, 1994.

Dutton, Bertha P. *American Indians of the Southwest.* Albuquerque: University of New Mexico Press, 1983.

Eagle/Walking Turtle. *Indian America: A Traveler's Companion,* 4th ed. Santa Fe: John Muir Publications, 1995.

Gattuso, John, ed. *Insight Guides: Native America*. Boston: APA/Houghton Mifflin, 1993.

Reddy, Marlita A., ed. *Statistical Record of Native North Americans*, 2nd ed. Detroit: Gale Research, 1995.

Trimble, Stephen. *The People: Indians of the American Southwest*. Santa Fe: School of American Research Press; Seattle: Distributed by University of Washington Press, 1993.

Waldman, Carl. *Encyclopedia of Native American Tribes*. Facts On File, 1988.

—by D. K. Daeg de Mott, reviewed by Y. Hoosava

HUNGARIAN AMERICANS

For more information on Hungarian history and culture, *see* **Vol. 4: Hungarians**.

OVERVIEW

Hungarians have been immigrating to America since the 16th century, but mass migration did not begin until 1880. A small wave did arrive in 1849–1851, consisting of about 4,000 dissidents who had led a successful revolution in Hungary in 1848 but were then defeated by Austria in 1849. Although the total Hungarian American population was just over 4,000 by the time of the American Civil War, some 800 Hungarian Americans served in the Union Army and a much smaller number in the Confederate Army. Of the 800 Union soldiers, almost 100 became high-ranking officers. A few of the Confederate soldiers also became officers. Hungarian Americans thereby had the highest percentage of their total population serving as soldiers and officers in the Civil War services of any ethnic group in America at that time.

The largest wave of Hungarian immigration to America began in 1880 and lasted until 1914. Between 1880 and 1899, about 430,000 Hungarians entered the US. The number jumped to 1,260,000 for the years of 1899–1914, with the peak year in 1907 when 185,000 Hungarians immigrated to the US. Most of the immigrants in this wave were young peasant men who hoped to earn enough money in the US to return to Hungary and set themselves up in better circumstances there. Perhaps 20% of the immigrants actually did return to Hungary. The rest settled permanently in the US.

Although the majority of the immigrants had been farmers in Hungary, few took up farming in America. Their goal was to earn money quickly, and the best place to do that was in the industrial centers of the Northeast and Midwest. They took low-paying, menial jobs that no one else wanted. Many of the jobs were dangerous, such as mining or working in iron and steel mills. Serious injuries and deaths were common. Because most of the immigrants were hoping to return to Hungary in the near future, they saved as much of their earnings, and spent as little of them, as possible.

Despite their concentration in selected US cities, Hungarian Americans did not create "Little Hungarys" during this first major wave of immigration. The young men were not interested in settling down, so they did not buy houses or establish neighborhoods. Instead, they moved from job to job, boarding house to boarding house, waiting for the day when they could return to Hungary. They did organize a number of insurance, or "sick-benefit," societies to help care for each other. Other cultural, social, religious, and political Hungarian American societies sprang up in the late 1800s, but they remained fragmented, local efforts until 1906 when the American Hungarian Federation (AHF) was founded. A national organization, the AHF still exists today.

With the beginning of World War I in Europe in 1914, Hungarian immigration to the US halted. As Hungary and the US were on opposing sides of the war, Hungarian Americans found themselves in a difficult position, caught between their ties to

A Hungarian American debutante ball. (Andrea Henderson)

Hungary and loyalty to their new home. At first, they continued to show allegiance to Hungary, but as this brought them increasing harassment, they began to hide their true feelings. Once the US officially entered the war in 1917, Hungarian Americans felt it necessary to make a show of allegiance to America. Though most Hungarian Americans still sympathized with Hungary, they began to celebrate American holidays and hold "loyalty parades" in order to escape persecution.

At the end of World War I, Hungary was divided into a number of smaller states, ruled by foreign powers. Hungarian Americans who had intended to return to Hungary once they had saved enough money suddenly found themselves without a homeland. Many had not yet become American citizens because of their intention to return to Hungary, but the Hungary they had known no longer existed. Accordingly, the attitude among Hungarian Americans shifted from one of temporary residency in the US to one of permanent residency. The emphasis in their identity changed from "Hungarian" to "American." They moved out of the miserable boarding houses and bought homes. "Little Hungarys" developed on the outskirts of cities. Immigrants who had clung to their Hungarian ways now began to be assimilated into mainstream American culture in language, dress, and other customs.

Hungarian immigration to the US resumed at the end of World War I, but the new immigrants were quite different from those who came before. Instead of peasant farmers, most were well-educated professionals who had been displaced by the

postwar economic upheaval or who disagreed with the increasing German Nazi influence in Hungary. There were a number of leftists, as well as Jews. These new immigrants were not interested in joining the peasant-based Hungarian American community and had little to do with them. Hungarian Americans became polarized between the old immigrants and the new. There was also a sizeable population of second-generation Hungarian Americans developing who felt confined by their parents' "Hungarianness" and wanted to break out of the insular Hungarian American community. By the start of World War II, the Hungarian American community had become quite divided within itself.

World War II was a time of great ambivalence for many Hungarian Americans. Most believed that the Axis powers should be defeated, but they also felt attached to Hungary and could not bring themselves to stand fully against their former homeland. They tried to excuse Hungary's role in the Axis forces by describing Hungary as an "unwilling satellite" of Germany. However, their loyalty to the US effort was genuine this time, and Hungarian Americans freely contributed to the Allied war effort.

The Displaced Persons Acts of 1948 and 1950, passed by the US Congress at the end of World War II to assist refugees, allowed a new wave of Hungarians to immigrate to the US. Three distinct groups of Hungarians have immigrated to America since World War II. The first, referred to as the "45-ers" and "47-ers," or "DPs (Displaced Persons)," consisted of right wing intellectuals, high-ranking Hungarian military officers, and members of the Hungarian elite escaping the new Communist regime. Then, from 1947 to the mid-1950s, middle-class Hungarians began to flee Stalinist oppression in Hungary. Lastly, between 1956 and 1960, a wave of young people came to America seeking better educational and economic opportunities.

Hungarian immigration to America continues today, though in relatively small numbers. Illegal immigration to the US from Hungary has been a reality since the 19th century, increasing each time the US or Hungary placed restrictions on immigration and emigration. Hungarian immigrants are also sometimes classified as other nationalities, due to the multiethnic nature of the Hungarian population and the political division of Hungary into smaller states. Therefore, it is impossible to know the exact number of Hungarian immigrants to the US. In the 1990 US Census, a total of 1,582,302 persons claimed Hungarian ancestry. Of these, 110,337 (7%) were foreign-born.

Although Hungarian Americans now live throughout the US, their population is still concentrated in the Northeast (36%) and Midwest (32%). The top five states in terms of numbers of Hungarian Americans are Ohio (218,145), New York (186,898), California (159,121), Pennsylvania (152,863), and New Jersey (141,627). Other states with sizeable Hungarian American populations include Michigan (109,178), Florida (99,822), Illinois (68,439), Connecticut (49,508), and Indiana (40,828).

The majority of Hungarian Americans are Catholic, but there are also significant numbers of Protestants (particularly Calvinist and Lutheran), Greek Orthodox, and Jews. The first Hungarian worship service in the US was held in 1852 in New York City. It was an ecumenical service for any and all Hungarian Americans, including Catholics, Protestants, Orthodox, and Jews. This ecumenical spirit is still evident in certain Hungarian American churches, while others, such as the Calvinists, have become fractured even among themselves.

Hungarian Americans have made countless contributions to all areas of American life. Noted Hungarian Americans in the arts include classical composer Béla Bartók; symphony conductors Eugene Ormandy, George Széll, Fritz Reiner, Sir Georg Solti, and Antal Doráti; and actor Béla Lugosi. The Hollywood film industry was essentially founded by two Hungarian Americans, Adolph Zukor and William Fox, who felt the New York City film world was too restrictive and moved instead to the southern California desert. Among the many motion picture companies Zukor and Fox started are Paramount Pictures and Twentieth-Century Fox.

The "Manhattan Project," in which the first atomic bomb was developed, consisted of "three Hungarians and one Italian," in the words of Laure Fermi, wife of the one Italian, Enrico Fermi. The three Hungarians (or Hungarian Americans) were physicists Leo Szilárd, Eugene Wigner, and Edward Teller.

Hungarian Americans today remain divided according to generation and time of immigration. Older Hungarian Americans from the first major wave, and some of their children, continue to hold fast to an outdated, idealized image of Hungary. The Hungarian Scouts in Exile organization promotes a similarly idealized Hungarian nationalism among younger generations. Founded in 1945 in Germany, the Hungarian Scouts in Exile first functioned in refugee camps in Central Europe to maintain a sense of Hungarian identity and pride among young refugees. Around 1950, as Hungarian refugees immigrated to the US, the organization's center moved along with them to Garfield, New Jersey. In 1980, there were some 6,000 Hungarian Scouts in 79 troops located in about a dozen countries on five continents. Around one-third of those scouts and troops were in the US.

Hungarian Americans who immigrated between World Wars I and II, and those who immigrated immediately following World War II, were radicals and professionals who were forced to flee Hungary because of political and economic upheavals, the increasing influence of Nazi Germany, and the eventual Communist takeover. They therefore have quite a different picture of Hungary than do the older, first-wave immigrants. More recent immigrants have lived in Communist-dominated Hungary and so have a vision of their former homeland that differs from both first- and second-wave Hungarian Americans. The Hungarian American community is therefore quite divided in regards to their view of and relation to Hungary. This division creates a certain amount of tension in the community and also prevents Hungarian Americans from becoming a unified force in US politics.

BIBLIOGRAPHY

Vardy, Steven Bela. *The Hungarian-Americans*. Boston: Twayne Publishers, 1985.

US Bureau of the Census. *Detailed Ancestry Groups for States*. 1990 Census of Population Supplementary Reports, CP-S-1-2. Washington, DC, October 1992.

———. *The Foreign-Born Population in the United States*. 1990 CP-3-1. Washington, DC, July 1993.

—by D. K. Daeg de Mott

INUIT

ALTERNATE NAMES: Eskimo
LOCATION: United States (Alaska); Canada (Greenland);
Aleutian Islands; Russia (Siberia)
POPULATION: 90,000
LANGUAGE: Inuit
RELIGION: Traditional animism; Christianity
RELATED ARTICLES: Vol. 2: Native North Americans

¹ INTRODUCTION

The Inuit, or Eskimo, are an aboriginal people who make their home in the Arctic and sub-Arctic regions of Siberia and North America.

The word "Eskimo" is not an Eskimo word. It was bestowed upon these hardy, resourceful hunters by their neighbors, the Algonquin Indians of eastern Canada, and means "eaters of raw meat." Early European explorers of the area began using the name, and it is now in general use. Recently, it has begun to be replaced by the Eskimo's own name for themselves, "Inuit," which means, "real people."

The Inuit are descendents of the Thule, whale hunters who migrated from Alaska to Greenland and the arctic regions of Canada around 1000 AD The people and their culture spread rapidly throughout the area, which accounts for the cultural uniformity of today's Inuit. The first Europeans to enter these arctic regions were probably Norseman, who are thought to have arrived in Greenland at around the same time as the Inuit. Major changes in Inuit life and culture occurred during the Little Ice Age (1600–1850), when the climate in their homelands became even colder, changing their subsistence methods. European whalers who arrived in the latter part of the 19th century had a strong impact on the Inuit. The Westerners introduced Christianity; they also brought with them infectious diseases that substantially reduced the Inuit population in some areas. When the whaling industry collapsed early in the 20th century, many Inuit turned to trapping.

Wherever they live, the Inuit are today much involved in the modern world. Not only have they wholeheartedly adopted much of its technology, but also they use imported food, clothing, and housing styles. Their educational, recreational, economic, religious, and governmental institutions have also been heavily influenced by mainstream culture. Significant changes have begun to occur in all areas of their way of life as a result of sustained contact with the outside world.

² LOCATION AND HOMELAND

The Inuit live primarily along the far northern seacoasts of Russia, the US, Canada, and Greenland. All told, there are more than 100,000 Inuit, most of whom live south of the Arctic Circle. The majority, about 46,000, live in Greenland, with approximately 30,000 on the Aleutian Islands and in Alaska, 25,000 in Canada, and 1,500 in Siberia. The Inuit homeland is one of the regions of the world least amenable to human habitation. Most of the land is flat and barren tundra where only the top few inches of the frozen earth thaw out during the summer months. For this reason, the Inuit have always turned their eyes to the sea as the source of their subsistence. Although some settled along rivers and fish from the banks, and others followed caribou herds in their seasonal inland migrations, the majority of Inuit have always lived near the sea, hunting aquatic mammals such as seals, walrus, and whales.

Traditionally, some Inuit groups tended to settle permanently, while others were primarily nomadic. Settlement patterns differed according to geographic location, time of year, and the means of subsistence available in a given area. In Greenland and in Alaska, permanent settlements were the norm. Similarly, the Inuit of Siberia grouped themselves into established villages. In the central areas there were no such settled communities, although individual groups often returned to a favorite fishing or hunting site year after year. But despite these differences, all Inuit groups followed an annual cycle of banding into large groups during the winter and breaking up into smaller hunting bands during the summer months.

³ LANGUAGE

The Inuit language is divided into two major dialect groups: *Inupik* and *Yupik*. Inupik speakers are in the majority and reside in an area stretching from Greenland to western Alaska, while speakers of Yupik inhabit the region comprised of southwestern Alaska and Siberia.

⁴ FOLKLORE

The Inuit have traditionally used spells and amulets for luck. Mythological figures include the Mother of the Sea, believed to control the sea mammals, and the Moon Man, thought to enforce observance of taboos by appearing to the offending party in a dream or in the guise of a polar bear. According to a traditional folktale told by the Tikigaq Inuit of north Alaska, the raven (a traditional trickster figure in Inuit folklore) was originally white but turned black in the course of a deal by which it and the loon agreed to tattoo each other but ended up in a soot-flinging match that turned the loon gray and the raven black.

⁵ RELIGION

Missionaries introduced various forms of Christianity, including Russian Orthodoxy, Catholicism, Anglicanism, and Lutheranism; these have largely replaced traditional Inuit religious practices, although many of the traditional animistic beliefs still linger.

As with most hunting cultures, many traditional Inuit customs and taboos were intended to mollify the souls of hunted animals, such as polar bears, whales, walrus, and seals. In western Alaska and other regions, the souls of seals and whales, both living and dead, were honored in complicated annual ceremonies of thanksgiving.

⁶ MAJOR HOLIDAYS

Today the Inuit observe the holidays of the Christian calendar. Whenever a new totem pole was raised, a feast called a potlatch was held. There would be singing and dancing and varied contests of strength for entertainment. The Inuit who held the potlatch would often give away his most valuable possessions at the ceremony, including his dugout canoe, sculptures of carved ivory, and jewelry.

7 RITES OF PASSAGE

Traditionally, a modest feast was held when an Inuit boy killed his first seal or caribou. Women were married when they reached puberty, and men when they could provide for a family. The Inuit traditionally believed in an afterlife thought to take place in one of two positive realms, one in the sea and one in the sky. Because a person's name was believed to have special powers, after people died their names were given to infants born subsequently, who were thereby believed to inherit the personal qualities of the deceased.

8 INTERPERSONAL RELATIONS

Unlike many aboriginal cultures, traditional Inuit society was not based on the tribal unit. Instead, the basic social unit was the extended family, consisting of a man and wife and their unmarried children, along with their married sons and their nuclear families. In the normal course of events, several such family units join forces to hunt and provide one another with mutual protection and support. Such a group of families was named by adding the suffix *miut*, or "people of," to the name of the geographic region they inhabited.

The leader of the group was typically the oldest male who was still physically able to participate in the hunt. Such a group leader was called upon to resolve quarrels within the group or among his own group and others. In cases where the group leader was unable to settle the issue, the hostile parties might wrestle or engage in public contests in which they hurled jokes and insults back and forth until one was declared the winner. Non-related men often formed close relationships based on mutual support, trade, sharing of domestic arrangements, and protection when traveling through other, possibly hostile, regions.

9 LIVING CONDITIONS

The Inuit had several different forms of traditional housing. In Greenland, they often lived in permanent stone houses. Along the shores of Siberia, they lived in villages made up of houses built from driftwood and earth. Summer housing for many Inuit was a skin tent, while in the winter the igloo, or house made of snow, was common. In Alaskan Inuit society, each village traditionally included a special house called a *kashgee*. This building, while serving as a dwelling place for one man and his family, was also used by the entire village as a ceremonial center and gathering place for the men of the group. In the *kashgee*, the men and boys of the village did their chores and often ate and slept together. Today many Inuit live in single-story wooden prefabricated houses with a combined kitchen and living room area and one or two bedrooms. Most are heated with oil-burning stoves. However, as the Inuit are spread across such a vast area, their housing styles vary.

With the widespread introduction of Western-style foods rich in carbohydrates and sugar over the past 25 years, the Inuit have begun to develop health problems that were unknown to them before, such as tooth decay. Alcoholism poses another major threat to the health of the Inuit, threatening not only the present population but also future generations through Fetal Alcohol Syndrome and other conditions that arise during the prenatal period.

There are two kinds of boats traditionally used by Inuit hunters. The umiak is a large open boat made by covering a wooden frame with walrus hide or some other appropriate material. Especially popular with the Inuit of northern Alaska, it has been used to transport people and goods, and as a vessel from which to hunt large sea mammals such as whales. The other kind of boat favored by Inuit hunters is the kayak. This one-man hunting vessel is entirely covered with seal or caribou skin. The hunter, dressed in waterproof clothing made from the intestines of seals or walrus, sits in a small cockpit and propels himself forward with a double bladed paddle. Alone in his kayak, an Inuit hunter is able to glide silently through the waters and amid the ice floes to close in on his prey. Today it is common for the Inuit to use boats with inboard or outboard motors.

For land transportation, the Inuit dogsled is capable of traveling on land and frozen sea alike. A typical dogsled, drawn by anywhere from 2 to 14 huskies, is usually made of wood but may also be fashioned from pieces of dried salmon. In recent years, dogsleds have been replaced by snowmobiles as the main mode of transportation for many Inuit.

10 FAMILY LIFE

Given the cooperative effort required by a people who depended on hunting for subsistence, family ties—both nuclear and extended—were traditionally paramount among the Inuit, and having a large family was considered desirable. Although stability was valued in marriages, divorce was easily obtainable.

Women often assumed a secondary role in Inuit society. At mealtime, an Inuit women was required to serve her husband and any visitors before she herself was permitted to eat. Sometimes men cemented their ties with each other by temporarily exchanging wives. But at the same time, a common Inuit saying extolled women in this way: "A hunter is what his wife makes him." The women were the ones who gathered firewood, tended the lamps, butchered the animals, and raised the children. They were able to erect the tents in summer and the igloos in winter and drive the dog teams if need be. They contributed to the subsistence requirements of the group by fishing and trapping small animals and birds, and joining in the pursuit of larger, more dangerous game was not unusual for an Inuit woman. Inuit hunters spent many hours waiting at breathing holes, drifting in their kayaks, or tramping through blizzards, so the greatest skill an Inuit woman could possess is that of being able to make good protective clothing. Inuit women learned which skins were suited for each type of clothing, how to cure the skins, and how to sew firm, watertight seams with bone and ivory needles and thread made of dried sinew.

11 CLOTHING

Traditional Inuit clothing was perhaps the most important single factor in ensuring survival in the harsh Arctic environment. The Inuit did not weave fabric. Rather, they made all their clothing from various animal skins and hides. While Inuit clothing was often attractive and decorative, its ability to keep the wearer alive at sub-zero temperatures was of prime importance. The best way to keep warm is to trap a layer of warm air between the body and the outside cold. To do this, Inuit wore layers of loose clothes. If the clothes were tight, the wearers would sweat and the damp clothes would freeze as soon as they were taken off. In winter the Inuit wore two layers of caribou skin clothing. The outer layer had the fur facing out, while the fur of the inner layer faced in. The outer garment, a hooded jacket called a parka, was loose enough for the wearer to pull his or her arms inside and hug them against the body for extra warmth. Sometimes snow goggles made of ivory or wood with small slits to see through were worn to keep out the snow glare.

Today a variety of shops sell modern Western-style clothing to the Inuit. Like their counterparts in cultures throughout the world, young people favor jeans, sneakers, and brightly colored sportswear. However, both old and young still rely on traditional Inuit gear when confronting the elements on any extended outdoor venture or journey.

12 FOOD

Traditionally, Inuit dietary staples were seal, whale, caribou, walrus, polar bear, arctic hare, fish, birds, and berries. Seals were hunted all year round, and the Inuit found a use for almost every part of the animal. With the exception of the bitter gall bladder, all the meat was eaten, usually boiled or raw. Raw blubber was often enjoyed mixed in with meat or berries, while blood soup and dried intestines were favored as snacks. Because they ate raw food, and every part of the animal, the Inuit did not lack vitamins, even though they had almost no vegetables to eat. With the introduction of modern Western-style food, including convenience foods, over the past two to three decades, the Inuit diet has changed, and not for the better. The consumption of foods rich in sugar and carbohydrates has resulted in tooth decay and other diet-related medical problems.

13 EDUCATION

Modern Inuit schools are similar to other schools around the world as far as what the children learn, but the setting could not be more unique. Most Inuit children ski or ride snowmobiles to get to and from school. Because the weather is so cold, they usually receive a good hot breakfast as soon as they arrive in the morning. A typical breakfast might be pancakes or French toast served with milk, juice, and sausages. While Inuit children are taught math, history, spelling, reading, and the use of computers, Inuit teachers are also concerned that the students learn something about their culture and old traditions, including dancing, which was forbidden by the early missionaries because they thought it sinful.

14 CULTURAL HERITAGE

Considering that the Inuit inhabit an area covering more than 5,000 miles of the immense Arctic wilderness, Inuit culture displays an amazing coherence and unity. From Siberia to Greenland, Inuit economic, social, and religious systems are much the same. Only in kinship systems is there any significant variation, with those groups living in western regions differing the most from the Inuit as a whole.

In addition to the prints and carvings for which the Inuit have become famous, dancing, singing, poetry, and storytelling play an important role in their native culture.

15 WORK

Traditional Eskimo subsistence patterns were closely geared to the annual cycle of changing seasons, the most important feature of which was the appearance and disappearance of solid ice on the sea. During summer, when the sea was free of ice, small groups of families traveled to their camps by open boat. There they stayed, hunting the northward-migrating caribou herds by killing them at river crossings or by driving them into large corral-like structures. Spawning fish were netted or speared. With the onset of autumn, the Inuit returned to their settled communities and villages to prepare for winter. The long winter was a time for hunting seal and other aquatic mammals and for trapping birds.

Today most Inuit live a settled existence in centralized villages and towns, participating in the cash economy through wage employment or receiving some form of social assistance. Major employers include the government, the resource extraction industries, and the arts and crafts industry. However, many Inuit are still involved in subsistence hunting and fishing at some level.

16 SPORTS

The Inuit, although mostly concerned with meeting survival needs, do find time to engage in sports. They enjoy games that display physical prowess, such as weightlifting, wrestling, and jumping contests. In addition, they also play a ball game similar in many ways to American football, and ice hockey is popular as well.

17 ENTERTAINMENT AND RECREATION

When the Inuit come together for traditional gatherings, drumming and dancing provide the chief form of entertainment. Quiet evenings at home are spent carving ivory, antler, bone, and soapstone, or playing string games like cat's cradle. Another traditional Inuit game is similar to dice, played on a board and using little models of people and animals instead of dice. The Inuit also enjoy typical modern forms of recreation such as watching television and videos.

18 FOLK ART, CRAFTS, AND HOBBIES

Traditional Inuit arts and crafts are mainly those that involve etching decorations on ivory harpoon heads, needlecases, and other tools. Over the past decades, the Inuit have became famous for their soapstone, bone, and ivory carvings, as well as prints and pictures. Another artistic tradition is the creation of elaborate wooden masks.

19 SOCIAL PROBLEMS

Social problems include unemployment, underemployment, alcoholism, drug abuse, and a high suicide rate.

See also Aleut; Dogsled; Tundra; Indians of North America, Art of; Native American Culture.

20 BIBLIOGRAPHY

Chance, Norman A. *The Iñupiat and Arctic Alaska.* Fort Worth, Tex.: Holt, Rinehart and Winston, 1990.

Condon, Richard. *Inuit Youth: Growth and Change in the Canadian Arctic.* New Brunswick, N.J.: Rutgers University Press, 1987.

Hahn, Elizabeth. *The Inuit.*: Rourke Publications, 1990.

Houston, James A. *Confessions of an Igloo-Dweller.* Boston: Houghton Mifflin, 1995.

Hughes, Jill. *Eskimos.*: Gloucester Press, 1978.

Marquis, Arnold. *A Guide to America's Indians.* University of Oklahoma Press, 1974.

Morrison, David A. *Inuit: Glimpses of an Arctic Past.* Quebec: Canadian Museum of Civilization, 1995.

Osborn, Kevin. *The Peoples of the Arctic.:* Chelsea House, 1990.

Philip, Neil. *Songs Are Thoughts: Poems of the Inuit.* New York: Orchard Books, 1995.

Seidelman, Harold. *The Inuit Imagination: Arctic Myth and Sculpture.* New York: Thames and Hudson, 1994.

IRISH AMERICANS

For more information on Irish history and culture, *see* **Vol. 4: Irish**.

OVERVIEW

Irish emigration to America began in colonial times but reached its peak in the Great Famine years of the 1800s. Early Irish immigrants were mostly Scotch-Irish from Ulster, or Northern Ireland (*see* Scottish And Scotch-Irish Americans). Irish Catholics did not begin to immigrate in large numbers until about 1800, and then they came en masse. In 1790, the US Census counted 44,000 Irish Americans, most of whom were Scotch-Irish. By 1800, the Irish population of America had swelled to 150,000. Most of the newcomers were Irish Catholics fleeing British oppression and the resulting famines.

The Irish constituted the first major Catholic presence in the predominantly Protestant US and as such met with virulent discrimination. The majority of the immigrants were illiterate farmers with few, if any, other job skills. However, they had been so disillusioned with farming in Ireland that they preferred to starve in the cities of America rather than return to growing crops. Irish immigrants congregated in the large industrial centers of the Northeast, Middle Atlantic, and Midwest regions of America, living in overcrowded slum housing and working whatever jobs they could find.

The worst famines in Ireland, caused by a grossly unjust economic system imposed on Ireland by Britain, combined with a potato blight, occurred in 1800, 1807, 1816, 1839, 1845–1848, 1863, and 1879. Between 1800 and 1830, 300,000 Irish immigrated to the US. In 1846–1851, more than one million Irish fled to America. Another 873,000 immigrated in the decades of 1860–1880. Many settled in Philadelphia, Pennsylvania. By 1880, the Irish Catholic population in Philadelphia had reached 6,000, the highest of any community in North America. Other cities, such as New York, Boston, and Chicago, also had large Irish American populations.

Irish immigration to the US continued, with some one million more immigrants arriving between 1880 and 1900. Ireland lost more of its population to the US than any other country. In 1860, there were only five Irish persons left in Ireland for every Irish person in America (compared to 33 Germans in Germany for every German American, and 42 British in Britain for every British American). In the early 1900s, however, Irish immigration to America slowed considerably, and once Irish independence was declared in 1921, immigration virtually ceased. Small numbers of Irish have continued to come to the US since that time, but the mass migration was over.

The Irish were victims of discrimination and violence in the US not only because of their religion but also because of their willingness to work for extremely low wages. Other Americans felt threatened by this huge influx of unskilled laborers whom they perceived to be glutting the job market. Stereotypes of "Paddy" and "Bridget" (common Irish names) as drunken, disorderly, ignorant brutes took shape in American culture. Signs indicating that "No Irish need apply" began going up everywhere. The already dismal conditions of poverty suffered by Irish Americans in the 1800s worsened as they were shut out of jobs, housing, and society. The Irish, however, were accustomed to difficulty and discrimination back in Ireland, and they persevered.

When the US embarked in the mid- and late-1800s on extensive construction operations of canals, railroads, and bridges and expanded its mining industry, Irish Americans were ready to fill the vast need for workers. These jobs, though dangerous and underpaid, were a ticket out of the city slums. The Chesapeake and Ohio Canal and the Erie Canal were both essentially built by Irish Americans. They also laid much of the railroad track across the US. Without the labor of Irish Americans, US development would have occurred much more slowly. Their hard work and enormous contributions to American expansion began to earn Irish Americans some measure of respect among their fellow Americans.

Participation in the armed services also helped improve the image of Irish Americans in the US. Irish American naval captain Oliver Hazard Perry became a hero in the War of 1812, uttering the famous words, "We have met the enemy and they are ours," after defeating a British fleet on Lake Erie. Irish Americans fought on both sides of the American Civil War (1861–65), but most—some 200,000—fought for the Union.

During the Mexican-American War of 1846–1848, a number of Irish Americans defected to the Mexican side. The rate of desertion was very high for the US Army during this war because at least half of the soldiers were recent immigrants (particularly Irish and German), and many of the American-born officers treated them quite badly. When the Mexican army learned that the Irish were Catholic, as were the Mexicans, they tried to lure them to Mexico with offers of land and religious fellowship. Some 250 Irish American soldiers deserted the US Army and joined up with the Mexicans. Led by Captain John Riley, they formed the San Patricio (St. Patrick) Battalion along with about 200 other deserters, many of them German Americans. The San Patricio Battalion fought bravely for the Mexican side, but Mexico was finally defeated, and the deserters were brought to justice. Of those who had survived the fighting, 50 were executed for treason, 5 were pardoned, and another 15 (including Captain Riley) were branded and flogged, then released. Riley and others formed two infantry units that continued to serve the Mexican army for a number of years before disbanding. Some of the Irish American soldiers then returned to the US, but others remained in Mexico, Riley among them. Intermarriage with Mexicans led to the creation of a small Mexican-Irish community. One of its best-known members is actor Anthony Quinn.

Irish Americans themselves unfortunately contributed to their bad image in 1863 when Congress passed the first national draft for military service. Outraged by this invasion of their freedom, Irish Americans in New York City took out their frustrations on the African American community there, which at that time was quite small. With 200,000 Irish Americans against 10,000 African Americans, the African Americans never had a chance. After four days of rioting and violence, 1,200 people (mostly African American) were dead or seriously injured, and the Irish Americans had burned Manhattan's Colored Orphan Asylum to the ground.

Conditions in Irish American slums had become intolerable in the mid-1800s, with epidemics of typhoid (1837), typhus (1842), and cholera (1849) sweeping the population, and chronic outbreaks of tuberculosis and pneumonia claiming even more lives. In 1857, some 85% of the people admitted to

New York City's hospital were Irish immigrants. Infant and child mortality were so high among Irish Americans that immigrant children were expected to live no more than 14 years on the average after arrival in the US. Many Irish Americans turned to alcohol to numb the pain of their squalid lives. Often times, Irish American women and children became prostitutes, and women, children, and men took up other criminal activities to survive.

When gold was discovered in California in 1849, thousands of Irish Americans joined the rush west. A few struck it rich. The rest continued to languish in poverty, either returning to the East and Midwest or settling in the cities of the West. Things were beginning to change, however, for the Irish Americans. New waves of immigrants, this time from Eastern Europe, began to arrive. Dark-haired, dark-eyed, and speaking completely foreign languages (Western European languages are at least related to English), these new immigrants made Irish Americans seem much more "American" in contrast. Irish Americans began to be welcomed somewhat more into mainstream society. The Irish American community was also beginning to make itself known in politics.

The Irish American political machine was based on the units of family, block, and neighborhood. Each neighborhood had a block captain, a ward captain, and a precinct captain. Irish Catholic parishes also provided a political base, with most parishioners following the lead of the priest or local bishop. Irish Americans, therefore, could deliver significant blocs of votes. Years of fighting the British for their rights in Ireland had taught the Irish how to work the political system for their benefit. By the mid-1800s, Irish Americans had taken over the Democratic party and city hall in several major cities and were becoming a voice to be reckoned with in American politics.

New York City's Tammany Hall was one of the most significant political arenas for Irish Americans in the 1800s. William Marcy "Boss" Tweed, an Irish American, became its leader and ruled New York City, and exercised a great deal of influence in state and federal politics as well, from his political throne. Tweed and other Irish American politicians used their positions to promote the welfare of other Irish Americans, providing employment (particularly in blue-collar jobs such as police officers, fire fighters, etc.), food, and services to Irish American citizens and their neighborhoods. Corruption was rampant in American politics at that time, and the Irish American political machine was not immune. Boss Tweed himself was imprisoned in 1873 for illegal activities. But Irish American politicians were no more dishonest than any other, either. Irish Americans made politics work for them, and they improved their situation in America dramatically with their successful political maneuvering. The high point in Irish American Catholic politics occurred in 1960 when Irish American John Fitzgerald Kennedy was elected president of the US, the first Catholic president in US history.

Another important arena for Irish Americans was the labor movement of the 1870s–1930s. Many Irish Americans led the way as workers organized for better working conditions and higher wages. By 1900, over 50 of the 110 unions in the American Federation of Labor (AFL) had Irish American presidents. Mary Harris "Mother" Jones, a powerful leader of the labor movement, was Irish American. Irish Americans continue to be a major force in American labor unions today. In 1955, Irish American George Meany became head of the largest union

thrive in parishes across the US. Irish and non-Irish Americans, Catholics and non-Catholics alike send their children to parochial schools for the solid and affordable education they offer.

Individual Irish Americans who have made significant contributions to American culture are far too numerous to recount. A few of the best-known are composers George M. Cohan and Victor Herbert, singer Bing Crosby, and dancers Gene Kelly and Donald O'Connor. The composer of the song "Dixie," which became the "national anthem" of the South, was Irish American Daniel D. Emmett. Irish American actors include Spencer Tracy, James Cagney, Grace Kelly, Errol Flynn, Buster Keaton, Helen Hayes, Gregory Peck, Walter Brennan, Jackie Gleason, Jack Lemmon, Peter O'Toole, Pierce Brosnan, Brian Dennehy, Patrick Duffy, Mia Farrow, Jack Nicholson, Carroll O'Connor, Ryan O'Neal, and actor/director Robert Redford. Director John Ford is also Irish American. Walt Disney was originally Irish Canadian, before moving to the US.

The best-known Irish American artist by far is Georgia O'Keeffe. Irish American architect Louis H. Sullivan developed the skyscraper design, and Matthew Brady was a well-known photographer. The only American playwright ever awarded the Nobel Prize is Eugene O'Neill, an Irish American. Other Irish American writers include John O'Hara, Flannery O'Connor, F. Scott Fitzgerald, Mary Higgins Clark, Tom Clancy, Kate Chopin (born Katherine O'Flaherty), Margaret Mitchell, William Kennedy, Mary Gordon, Mary McCarthy, Andrew Greeley, J. P. Donleavy, journalist Jimmy Breslin, and poets Galway Kinnell, Frank O'Hara, Robert Creeley, and James Whitcomb Riley.

Irish American leaders in science, industry, and politics include the Kennedy family (John Fitzgerald, Robert; Edward, or Ted; and Joseph Kennedy III, elected to the US Senate in Massachusetts in 1986); former Chicago mayor Richard Daley (who served from 1955 to 1976) and his son, Richard M. Daley, also elected mayor of Chicago (in 1989); one-time New York State governor Alfred E. Smith, who became the first Irish American Catholic to run for US president in 1928; Sandra Day O'Connor, the first woman to be appointed justice of the Supreme Court (in 1981); astronaut Kathryn Sullivan, the first woman to walk in space (in 1984); and Christa Corrigan McAuliffe, who was to be the first teacher in space in the ill-fated *Challenger* shuttle that exploded shortly after take-off in 1986. Henry Ford, builder of the first inexpensive automobile, the Model T, was Irish American, as was James Tobin, winner of the Nobel Prize for Economics in 1981.

Though John F. Kennedy is the only Irish American Catholic elected to the US presidency so far, several other Irish Americans, all Protestant, have also served as US president: Andrew Jackson, James Polk, James Buchanan, Chester A. Arthur, William McKinley, Woodrow Wilson, Richard M. Nixon, and Ronald Reagan. Two notorious Irish Americans were outlaw Billy the Kid (born Henry McCarty), and Senator Joseph R. McCarthy, instigator of the American anti-Communist hysteria of the 1950s, which came to be known as "McCarthyism."

Sports, especially boxing, provided a way out of the slums for young Irish American men in the late 1800s and early 1900s. Irish American boxer Paddy Ryan held the title of world heavyweight champion in the 1880s. Ryan was defeated by Irish American John L. Sullivan in 1892, and Sullivan was subsequently defeated by Irish American "Gentleman Jim" Corbett in 1897. Jack Dempsey and Gene Tunney were successful Irish

Girl waiting for Saint Patrick's Day parade in Massachusetts. (Susan D. Rock)

organization in the US, when the AFL merged with the Congress of Industrial Organizations (CIO) to form the AFL-CIO.

Today's Irish American population, according to the 1990 US Census, is 38,735,539, plus 4,009 who listed themselves as "Northern Irish," and another 29,652 who claimed "Celtic" ancestry. Irish Americans currently make up the second-largest ethnic group in the US, behind German Americans. Although early Irish immigrants settled mostly in the Northeast, Middle Atlantic, and Midwest areas of the US, today's Irish Americans are spread fairly evenly throughout the entire country. The top five states in terms of numbers of Irish Americans are California (3,425,089 Irish, plus 5,958 Northern Irish and Celtic), New York (2,800,128, plus 2,331), Texas (2,368,863, plus 2,353), Pennsylvania (2,255,867, plus 1,171), and Florida (1,898,822, plus 1,457).

The most obvious contribution Irish Americans have made to American culture is the observance of St. Patrick's Day on 17 March. Nearly every community in the US holds a St. Patrick's Day parade, and many Americans, whether Irish or not, wear green on that day. Shamrocks and leprechauns are familiar to all Americans, and several Irish tunes have become American standards ("When Irish Eyes Are Smiling," "Danny Boy," etc.). Irish Americans dominated the American Catholic Church into the 20th century, and Irish Catholicism still tends to define the Catholic Church in America. Many Irish Americans are also Protestant. The parochial school system started in the 1830s–1840s by Irish American Catholics continues to

American boxers in the early 1900s. Baseball has been another favored sport among Irish Americans. The best-known Irish American baseball player today is pitcher Nolan Ryan.

For the most part, Irish Americans today have become part of established mainstream US culture and suffer little discrimination. Most are second- or third-generation Americans, at least; only a small fraction of 1% of the Irish American population today is foreign born. There has been an influx recently, however, of illegal immigrants from Ireland. Escaping a severe job shortage in Ireland, they sidestep immigration quotas by acquiring visitor visas and then staying beyond the expiration of the visa. Because it is fairly easy for them to blend in with mainstream America, few are caught. In 1985, for example, only eight illegal Irish immigrants were deported, as compared to 3,034 Salvadorans and 11,368 Mexicans. Racism most likely plays a part in the disparity as well.

A small group of Irish Americans today face a unique problem. Born to unwed Irish mothers in the 1950s and 1960s, some 400 infants (or more) were sent from Ireland to the US for adoption. Viewed as shameful, these births were hidden and records were falsified to protect the women involved, and their families. Those adoptees are now reaching the age where they want to know about their birth parents. Agencies in Ireland remain largely uncooperative, however, and the falsification of many records makes the search that much more difficult. Adopted Irish American women and men struggle to find out where, and to whom, they were born in Ireland. Others who have not been told they were adopted may not even know they are Irish.

BIBLIOGRAPHY

Day, Mark R. "A Few Good Men." *Irish Voice* 10, no. 12 (19 March 1996): S10.

Gonzales, Juan L., Jr. *Racial and Ethnic Groups in America*, 2nd ed. Dubuque, IA: Kendall/Hunt Publishing, 1993.

Griffin, William D. *The Book of Irish Americans*. New York: Times Books, 1990.

McCarthy, Joseph. "Escaping Hunger, Immigrants Came for a New Life: Irish Search for the American Dream." *an Scathan* 1, no. 3 (31 May 1995): 16.

Mullins, Emer. "The Hidden Children." *Irish Voice* 10, no. 11 (12 March 1996): 22.

US Bureau of the Census. *Detailed Ancestry Groups for States*. 1990 Census of Population Supplementary Reports, CP-S-1-2. Washington, DC, October 1992.

Watts, J. F. *The Irish Americans*. New York: Chelsea House, 1988.

—by D. K. Daeg de Mott

IROQUOIS

LOCATION: United States (New York, Wisconsin); Canada (Quebec, Ontario)
POPULATION: 60,000 (US and Canada)
LANGUAGE: English; various Iroquois dialects
RELIGION: Traditional tribal religions
RELATED ARTICLES: Vol. 2: Native North Americans

¹ INTRODUCTION

The Iroquoian peoples are a group of tribes from the Great Lakes area who speak dialects of the Iroquoian family of Native North American languages and have similar lifestyles. For our purposes, we will only consider those tribes who are members of the Six Nations of the Iroquois Confederacy (or League of the Iroquois): the Mohawk, Oneida, Onondaga, Seneca, Cayuga, and Tuscarora. (Other Iroquoian peoples include the Huron, Erie, and Wyandotte.)

"Iroquois" is the name adopted by the French for the people they encountered in the Great Lakes region. The name was given them either by the Ojibwa (or Chippewa), in which case it means "poisonous snakes," or by the Algonquin, meaning "bad or terrifying man." Both the Ojibwa and Algonquin were enemies of the Iroquois. The Iroquois call themselves *Houdenosaunee*, "People of the Longhouse." The Iroquois are most likely descended from the Owasco peoples, who lived in the Great Lakes area as long as 1,000 years ago. The Owasco were settled agriculturalists who supplemented their diet through hunting and fishing. The Iroquois continued in that tradition well into the 19th century, and even today the basic structure of their life remains the same, though on a much more limited scale.

The Mohawk, Oneida, Onondaga, Seneca, and Cayuga were constantly at war with one another over hunting and fishing grounds, honor and revenge, and, later, trapping grounds for the fur trade, in the early part of their history. Eventually, two men joined together to create the Iroquois Confederacy. An Onondaga named Hiawatha (not the same Hiawatha as in Henry Wadsworth Longfellow's poem) began preaching peace among the Iroquois nations but found little support and even active resistance. According to legend, all three of his daughters died of illness or injuries thought to be caused by the evil wishes of his opponents, particularly an Onondaga chief named Thadodaho who was very powerful and very antagonistic. In despair, Hiawatha left the Onondagas and wandered to the outskirts of a Mohawk village. There he met Deganawida, who was either a Mohawk or a Huron, and the two of them discovered a great sympathy toward each other. Together they convinced the Mohawk to be the first nation to join the Iroquois Confederacy. Soon the Oneida agreed to join as well. Hiawatha and Deganawida knew the Confederacy would not succeed without the support of Thadodaho, so they set about persuading him to join. Finally, Thadodaho agreed and the Onondaga became the third nation in the Confederacy. The Seneca and Cayuga then followed. The Mohawk, as the most eastern tribe, became the Keepers of the Eastern Door; the Seneca, as the westernmost tribe, were designated the Keepers of the Western Door, and the Onondaga, in the center, became the Keepers of the Council Fire. Every year, the 50 sachems (peace chiefs) who made up the Great Council of the Confederacy met at the Onondaga council house to discuss and vote on matters of the Confederacy. Sachems were always men, but they were chosen by the clan matrons, the elder women who headed each clan. Sachems served for life, or until their clan matron decided to remove them from office. Although the five nations each had a different number of sachems on the council, each nation had only one vote. So the sachems of each nation had to decide together how to use their one vote. In this way, each of the five nations had equal power in the Confederacy.

The first European known to have made contact with the Iroquois was the French explorer Jacques Cartier, who encountered the Iroquois in 1534. The Iroquois had already begun receiving European goods, such as metal knives and hatchets, guns, glass beads, and wool cloth, in trade with more eastern tribes. By the 17th century, the Iroquois were trading directly with the French, who were most interested in furs, particularly beaver pelts. The fur trade created tremendous hostilities between the Iroquois Confederacy tribes and their neighbors, especially the Huron. Competition was fierce for the best trapping grounds, and the French fueled the hostilities so that they could maintain control of the fur trade. In 1609 Samuel de Champlain, the governor of New France (now Canada), helped several neighboring, hostile tribes attack the Mohawk. At least 50 Mohawk were killed in the attack. Later, in 1649 the Iroquois invaded Huron territory in the search for more furs (as over-hunting had depleted the number of beaver and other fur-bearing animals in their home territory). The Iroquois decimated the Huron, killing most of them and forcing the others to relocate farther from Iroquois lands.

The Iroquois themselves had their population decimated during the 1600s by diseases introduced by Europeans for which the Iroquois had no immunities or known treatments. Epidemics of measles, influenza, smallpox, tuberculosis, and gastroenteritis (a stomach disorder) wiped out thousands of Iroquois and other Native North Americans. At the height of their power, the Iroquois Confederacy had boasted 10,000 or more members. By the end of the 18th century, their numbers had been reduced by more than half to about 4,000. At the turn of the 20th century (1910), their population had not yet fully recovered, reaching only a little over 7,000.

In 1722–23, the Tuscarora, an Iroquoian tribe from North Carolina, joined the Confederacy. They had been forced by European violence and abuses to move north, and they were surprised and delighted to find people speaking a very similar language, with a very similar lifestyle, living in New York. The Tuscarora settled down there, with the Oneida, and were soon accepted into the Confederacy.

The now Six Nations of the Iroquois Confederacy were split by the American Revolution (1775–83), when the Seneca, Cayuga, Onondaga, and Mohawk were persuaded by Mohawk Joseph Brant (1742–1807) to become British allies, while the Oneida and Tuscarora chose to side with the American colonists. The Iroquois had remained neutral throughout the European struggles for control of the "New World" in the 17th and early 18th centuries. The Onondaga leader Teganissorens had convinced the Iroquois in 1700 not to become involved in the French and British wars, or the British and Dutch battles. Even when many of their Native North American neighbors chose sides in the French and Indian War (1761–63), the Six Nations refused to help either the French or the British. But this resolve

fell apart during the long and disruptive American Revolution, and the Confederacy fell apart as well. When the American colonists finally won the war, many of the four Iroquois nations who had sided with the British relocated to Canada where the atmosphere was friendlier. Of those who stayed, the new US government sent the Cayugas and Mohawks to a reservation (called a "reserve" in Canada) in Ontario, Canada, and forced most of the Oneidas to relocate to a reservation near Green Bay, Wisconsin. Some Iroquois were allowed to remain on their original homelands in what had become New York State, but European American settlement had greatly reduced their territories. Further European American expansion continued to squeeze out the Iroquois until finally the US government (and Canada) confined the Iroquois to small reservations. The Six Nations of the Iroquois Confederacy were now reduced to small subsistence farmers, dependent on the US and Canadian governments for their survival.

Because the Iroquois live in both Canada and the US but think of themselves as one people, in 1974 they were given the right by a treaty to cross the border between the two countries without restriction. In 1924 the US Congress passed a law rescinding this right, and the Iroquois were forced to fight in the courts to regain their rights. Clinton Rickard of the Tuscarora Nation founded the Indian Defense League in 1927 to help in the fight. This was the first advocacy organization for Native North Americans. In 1928 the Iroquois won back their right to cross the European-imposed borderline that passes through their lands. This victory is celebrated each year in July by a "Border Crossing" festival. Conflicts continue to arise, however, between the Iroquois Nations and the US and Canadian nations over these rights. Legal battles also continue over land claims and water rights and over the right of the Iroquois people to possess their own history. Recently, the Iroquois finally succeeded in having some wampum belts (belts of strung beads that tell the stories of Iroquois history) returned to them that had been on display for decades at the New York State Museum.

² LOCATION AND HOMELAND

The Iroquois live mainly on seven reservations in the Finger Lakes and Great Lakes region of New York State and on five reserves (as they are called in Canada) in Quebec and Ontario, Canada. Some Oneida also live on a small reservation near Green Bay, Wisconsin. The largest reservation, or reserve, is the Six Nations Grand River Reserve in Ontario, Canada. Most of the Iroquois on the Grand River Reserve are Mohawk or Cayuga. The reservations and reserves are all located (except for the Oneida reservation in Wisconsin) on the original homelands of the Iroquois, though with only a fraction of the territory. The terrain of these lands is hilly and wooded, covered with deciduous and evergreen forests. The climate is temperate with four distinct seasons. Fertile soil, sufficient rainfall (and snowfall), and an adequate growing season combine to make this area very good for farming. The Iroquois have been settled agriculturalists throughout their history. An abundance of wild game and fish provided large amounts of easily obtained protein for their diet as well. The Iroquois, therefore, were a healthy people who were able to sustain themselves in large, permanent settlements. This allowed them to develop a highly organized social and governmental structure known as the Iroquois Confederacy or League of the Iroquois. Some see great similarities in the government and constitution of the new United States of America and the structure of the Iroquois Confederacy.

Not all Iroquois live on the reservations or reserves. Many have left to find work in cities. The largest groups of off-reservation Iroquois are in the cities of Buffalo, Rochester, Niagara Falls, and Brooklyn, New York.

The total population of Iroquois today is over 60,000 (according to the US Census of 1990 and Canadian Census of 1991). The Mohawk are the most numerous of the Iroquois nations, followed by the Oneida and Seneca. The Cayuga, Onondaga, and Tuscarora nations are much smaller.

IROQUOIS NATION	US/CANADIAN
Mohawk	17,106/9,305
Oneida	11,307
Seneca	9,133
Tuscarora	3,245
Onondaga	1,729
Cayuga	1,111

There were also 1,225 US Census respondents who listed themselves as Seneca-Cayuga, and another 5,158 who just put "Iroquois."

3 LANGUAGE

All Iroquois speak dialects of the Iroquoian family of Native North American languages. There was no written language for most of their history (now it is written with the Roman alphabet), but the Iroquois did use wampum belts—belts of strung beads in various designs—to tell the stories of their history. These wampum belts were a form of recorded information. The Europeans sometimes used wampum belts as money in trade, but the Iroquois never did.

An Iroquois mother chooses her baby's name from a list of those names owned by her clan, choosing one that no other living person is using at that time.

4 FOLKLORE

The Iroquois have a combination earth-diver and culture-hero (or, in this case, two-hero) creation story. Before the earth or anything on it existed, the Sky People lived in Sky World, high in the heavens. They were ruled by Sky Chief and his wife, Sky Woman. When Sky Woman became pregnant, Firedragon—a notorious troublemaker—told Sky Chief that the child was not Sky Chief's. Sky Chief became enraged and tore the Tree of Life, which grew in the center of Sky World, from the ground. Sky Woman bent over to look through the hole it left in the ground. In some versions of the story, she simply fell through the hole. In other versions, Sky Chief pushed her. In any event Sky Woman fell out of Sky World towards the deep waters below. The birds and animals below managed to save her by first having the birds break her fall and support her on their wings, then sending various animals down into the waters to try to find some earth. All failed until Muskrat dove down very deep and came up with a bit of mud in his paw. The animals placed the mud on Turtle's back and the birds set Sky Woman down on top of it. This bit of mud on Turtle's back became the Earth.

Sky Woman eventually gave birth to twin boys, Good Twin and Bad Twin. Good Twin was born first, in the usual way, but

Bad Twin was so impatient he pushed his way out of his mother's body through her armpit and she died. The plants that later became the Iroquois' staple foods sprang up from Sky Woman's grave. Good Twin and Bad Twin became enemies and fought a series of terrible battles, creating the things of this world as they went. Good Twin ultimately won and then created human beings to enjoy this world.

The Iroquois traditionally told stories around the fire during the long winter months when there was little else to do. These stories were told both for entertainment and to educate the young about Iroquois history and traditions.

5 RELIGION

There is a special longhouse in each village that serves as a cultural center for members of the Iroquois community where they can learn about practicing the traditional way of life. In the past, the longhouse was a dwelling and also a spiritual center for the Iroquois. To say someone is "longhouse" today means that they follow the traditional Iroquois way of life.

European missionaries of many denominations established missions among the Iroquois in the 1600s and attempted to convert them to Christianity. Many Iroquois have since become Christian or have combined Christianity with their traditional beliefs. Today, some Iroquois remain purely traditional, but the majority are Christian.

One Mohawk who took strongly to Christianity was Kateri Tekawitha (1656–80). She converted to Christianity in 1670 and became a Catholic nun. Called a saint while still alive by those who knew her, Kateri became a candidate for sainthood in the Roman Catholic Church in 1884 and was declared "venerable" in 1943, then "blessed" in 1980. The campaign to have her declared a full saint continues.

Handsome Lake (?–1815) was a Seneca visionary who started a new religion in the early time called *Gaiwiio*, or "Good Word." Followers of *Gaiwiio* today refer to it as the New Religion.

6 MAJOR HOLIDAYS

The Iroquois celebrate seasonal changes and events relating to the production of food. There were traditionally six to eight festivals each year, including planting, ripening, and harvest times, maple sugar season and berry-picking seasons, and the New Year at midwinter. The most important was the New Year festival. One custom at the New Year festival was dream guessing. People would tell the community, through song, dance, or silent gestures, about a powerful dream they had had, and the members of the community would try to guess the dream. Then the community would come up with a way to make that dream come true. For example, if a woman dreamed of having a plot of land in which to plant corn, the community would give her that land. If someone dreamed of being angry with and doing violence to another member of the community, the people would find a way to work out the conflict through nonviolent means. This custom allowed the Iroquois to resolve any tensions and fulfill unexpressed desires in their community.

A very significant ceremony developed after the founding of the Iroquois Confederacy. When a chief dies, a Condolence ceremony is held where the founding of the Confederacy is commemorated and the Condolence committee talks about the deceased chief and other leaders of the past. The Condolence ceremony helps comfort the mourners of the deceased chief and welcomes the new chief who has been chosen by the clan matron. Deer antlers are placed on the new chief's head.

A modern holiday among the Iroquois is Border Crossing Day, held on the third Saturday of July, which celebrates the birthday of Clinton Rickard, founder of the Indian Defense League of America in 1927. Rickard and the Indian Defense League helped win back the Iroquois' right to cross the US-Canadian border without restriction.

7 RITES OF PASSAGE

Traditionally, babies were given a taste of animal oil right after birth to clean out their system and feed the guardian spirit which lived in their soul from birth until death. When a boy was born, he was then dipped in a stream to make him strong and courageous. The names given Iroquois infants were confirmed by the community at the next major festival.

Most boys upon reaching puberty would go on a Vision Quest. This entailed going alone into the woods without food and waiting for days, or even weeks, for that boy's personal guardian spirit to appear (in the form of an animal or bird). The guardian spirit would give the boy instructions for his adult life, and a special song to sing for courage and protection in times of danger.

At the time of a girl's first menstrual period, she would cook and eat her food alone from special pots. She would continue to do this at each menstrual period thereafter until menopause.

8 INTERPERSONAL RELATIONS

The Iroquois traditionally put a high value on self-reliance, endurance, and courage in both men and women. Gentle and considerate towards their own people, they could be cruel to their enemies. The Iroquois code of honor required revenge for injury or insult. Murder was avenged by murder.

9 LIVING CONDITIONS

Before they were confined to reservations, the Iroquois lived in large villages surrounded by wooden palisades (a fence of tall pointed stakes used for defense) with watchtowers along the top. The villages had to be moved every 10–20 years because the soil would become depleted and the available wood for building and fuel would be used up. They tried to make the new site as close as possible to the previous one.

Villages were made up of as many as 30 longhouses, each of which housed up to 100 or more people. A longhouse was so called because it was rectangular: 130 or more feet (40 or more meters) in length and about 30–33 feet in width. Each longhouse had a center aisle where the cooking fires burned and separate rooms along both sides divided by hide or bark partitions. Each family had one room. Inside the family's room was a sleeping and sitting platform with the belongings stored underneath and shelves above to store food. Bearskins were used as bedcovers.

The Iroquois made elmbark canoes. These canoes were not as fast on the water nor as maneuverable as birchbark canoes, but they were sturdier and could even be used as ladders to climb over the walls of enemy camps.

Today, the Iroquois live on reservations (called "reserves" in Canada) in modern housing and use cars and buses for everyday transportation. Health problems typical to all Native North Americans affect the Iroquois: diabetes, alcoholism, depression.

10 FAMILY LIFE

The Iroquois are matrilineal and matrilocal (lineage is inherited through the mother, and newly married couples live near the bride's family). The extended family is very important to the Iroquois. The main unit of society in traditional times was the *ohwachira,* a group of relatives who trace their ancestry back to one woman. The eldest living woman was usually the head of the *ohwachira.* Two or more *ohwachiras* make up a clan. The Mohawk and Oneida had three clans: Turtle, Bear, and Wolf. The other Iroquois nations had these three clans and more, such as Beaver, Deer, and Hawk. Children in a matrilineal, matrilocal society are raised by their mother and her sisters and brothers, not by their father. Men helped raise their sisters' children, not their own.

Adoption of children and adults was common among the Iroquois. Enemy captives were sometimes adopted into a clan to keep it strong. Most captives were glad to be adopted because they could not return to their homes, having lost respect among the members of their former community by allowing themselves to be captured.

Women were expected to give birth quietly and with courage. To cry or scream during labor, no matter how painful it was, was very bad form. Babies spent most of the first year of their life strapped to a cradleboard, a flat board with a footrest at the bottom and a wooden hoop to protect the baby's head at the top. Cradleboards could be carried on the mother's back, or propped against a tree or house while the mother was working. Cattail fluff was used for diapers.

Once the Iroquois were confined to reservations, family life began to change. Nuclear family units began to live in separate houses, rather than together with their cousins, etc., in a longhouse. With the extended family no longer on the premises to help with childrearing, and European-dominated education which taught that the patrilineal European culture was superior to matrilineal Native North American culture, men became the heads of families rather than women. Traditionalists among the Iroquois continue to struggle to maintain the old ways with matrilineal extended families and a strong clan system. But swimming against the tide of modern Western European culture is difficult.

11 CLOTHING

Modern Iroquois wear Western-style clothing for everyday purposes. For ceremonies and festivals and to make a statement at activist demonstrations, they will wear traditional clothing.

Traditionally, Iroquois clothing was made from animal skins and furs. The men brought home the skins and the women prepared them by removing the hair and flesh with a stone scraper, soaking the hide in boiled deer brains to soften it, then drying and smoking it to make it durable. The leather was then stitched together with sinew. The fur was left on beaver, bobcat, and squirrel skins for warmth and decoration.

Both men and women wore a soft deerskin loincloth in the summer and leather moccasins. Both sexes were generally bare from the waist up in warm weather. In cooler weather, men wore kilts and women wore longer skirts. Both wore leggings and close-fitting, hip-length shirts with sleeves. In the bitter cold of winter, they wore cloaks or robes made of bear, deer, buffalo, or beaverskins, with the fur left on. Clothing was often embroidered with dyed moosehair and porcupine quills.

Adults painted their bodies with figurative or geometrical designs, using paint made from natural materials such as red and yellow ochre, bloodroot, and charcoal, mixed with sunflower seed oil. They wore fur and feather caps and collars and jewelry made of feathers, animal teeth, bone, and shell beads. Women wore their hair in a single braid down the back. Men's hairstyles varied. Warriors preferred the "scalplock" (today often called a "Mohawk"), where the head was shaved bald except for a strip of hair down the center.

After the Europeans arrived, the Iroquois began to wear woolen clothes and to decorate their clothing with glass beads, both obtained in trade with Europeans or other tribes who had traded with the Europeans.

12 FOOD

The Iroquois have been farmers since the beginning of their history. Women traditionally did all the planting, tending, and harvesting of crops, while the men supplemented the diet by hunting and fishing. The only crop grown by men was tobacco, used in religious ceremonies. The women also gathered wild plums, grapes, cherries, berries, crabapples, and nuts (chestnuts, black walnuts, and hickory nuts). In the late winter and early spring, maple sap was collected and boiled down into syrup and sugar. This was the only sweetener available to early Iroquois. Corn, squash, and beans were the staple foods, referred to as "the Three Sisters," daughters of Mother Earth. Corn was called "our life," and squash was "supporter of life." Dried corn was often boiled with wood ashes to add nutrition and help loosen the hulls. Once the hulls were removed, the remaining corn, called *hominy*, was washed and boiled until tender. The Iroquois usually only ate one large meal a day, at midmorning (what would now be called "brunch"), though food was available throughout the day.

John Bartram visited the Iroquois in 1743 and later described a feast they served him, consisting of a corn and fish soup, boiled squash and squash blossoms, and corn dumplings with beans. A modern version of Iroquois corn and fish soup can be made as follows:

Iroquois Soup

4 large mushrooms, sliced
1 medium onion, peeled and thinly sliced
2 (10½ oz.) cans beef consommé
Dash black pepper
¼ teaspoon salt
2 tablespoons yellow corn meal
1 (12 oz.) package frozen haddock fillets
2 tablespoons minced parsley
1 (10 oz.) package frozen baby lima beans
1 clove garlic, crushed
⅓ cup dry sherry (optional)
½ teaspoon basil

Heat corn meal, consommé, mushrooms, garlic, parsley, and seasonings in a large saucepan. Once the liquid boils, reduce heat and simmer for 10 minutes without covering. Add remaining ingredients (optional). If haddock is added, break into bite-size pieces as the soup continues to simmer, and stir occasionally. Simmer about 20 more minutes and serve hot. Makes 4-6 servings.

(Adapted from Kimball and Anderson, *The Art of American Indian Cooking.* Garden City, New York: Doubleday & Co., 1965, p. 169.)

13 EDUCATION

Traditionally, Iroquois children learned the skills they needed to survive in their world by watching and participating in life with their parents, relatives, and other adults. The Iroquois were first introduced to Western European education by French priests at Quebec in 1608. The priests first tried going to the Native North American villages and learning the Native language so that they could then teach the Natives French culture and Christianity. The Natives simply ignored them. So the priests then tried taking young Native North Americans back to France to educate them there. The idea was that when these young European-educated Natives returned to their villages in North America, they would act as role models for the rest of their community. Instead, the young people found it impossible to adapt to such a foreign life in Europe, and when they returned they no longer fit in with their traditional society because they had not learned the skills necessary to survive there. So they became marginalized in both cultures and often turned to alcohol for comfort, becoming depressed alcoholics rather than role models.

The French priests decided then to send Native North American children to Roman Catholic boarding schools, but most of the children ran away from the schools, and their parents did not encourage them to return. Finally, the French set up reserves (known as "reservations" in the US), each with a school, Christian church, and missionary hospital, then forced the Native North Americans to relocate there. The French hoped that the Natives would become acculturated to European ways by living on these reserves. Instead, the reserves became institutions of segregation, separating Native North Americans from the rest of European society (and vice versa). The Native peoples became even more resistant to adopting European ways as a result of their enforced segregation.

The Iroquois were never inclined to adopt Christianity or European ways, at least not in large numbers. A few Iroquois did become Christian, and surface accoutrements such as Western-style clothing, etc., have become standard. Educationally, the Iroquois have done fairly well in recent decades at making the European-dominated system work for them. Lloyd Elm (1934–), an Onondaga educator and administrator, served as the education programs specialist in the Office of Indian Education at the US Department of Education in Washington, D.C., from 1976–1981. Prior to that, he served on the board of directors for the National Education Association (1973–1974), and he now serves on the New York State Board of Regents (which oversees all education in New York).

Of Iroquois 25 years old and older in 1990, only 10.4% have less than a ninth grade education. Almost 72% (71.2% of men, 72.5% of women) are at least high school graduates, and over 41% have some college. Only a fourth of those actually finish college—11.3% (11.2% of men, 11.5% of women) have a Bachelor of Arts degree or higher.

School enrollment is fairly high for primary and middle school students, but falls off somewhat in secondary school and falls drastically in college.

AGE	PERCENT ENROLLED IN SCHOOL IN 1990
3–4	29.9
5–14	94.5
15–17	89.9
18–19	59.0
20–24	28.1

14 CULTURAL HERITAGE

Traditional Iroquois musical instruments are water-drums (drums filled with water to produce a certain pitch), rattles, and the human voice. A modern Iroquois musician is John Kim Bell (1953–), a Mohawk who became the first Native North American symphony conductor when he was hired by the Toronto Symphony in 1980. Bell also produced and co-wrote the orchestral score for the first Native North American ballet, entitled "In the Land of the Spirits." He founded the Canadian Native Arts Foundation in 1988 to provide scholarships to young Native North Americans who wish to pursue training in the arts. Bell was named to the Order of Canada, a medal given by the governor general of Canada in recognition of outstanding merit and achievement.

The Iroquois language never had its own written form, so the oral tradition became strong and rich. Today, Iroquois write both in English and in the Iroquois language written down with the Roman alphabet. Modern Iroquois writers include Beth Brant (1941–), a Mohawk poet and prose author; and E. Pauline Johnson (1861–1913), an early Mohawk poet and performer. Johnson was also one of the first Native North American women to publish short fiction.

The Mohawk actor Jay Silverheels (1912–80) was best known for his portrayal of Tonto, the Lone Ranger's sidekick in the popular 1950s series. (Silverheels was actually the second actor to play Tonto in the series.) He did a great deal of other work in film and was a tireless activist in the areas of alcohol abuse and the elderly. In the 1960s, he founded the Indian Actors Workshop in Hollywood, and in 1979, the year before he died, he became the first Native North American to be awarded a star on Hollywood's Walk of Fame.

Other modern Iroquois in show business include Gary Dale Farmer (1953–), a Cayuga actor, producer, and activist; Graham Greene (1950–), an Oneida actor perhaps best known for his portrayal of Kicking Bird in the 1991 film *Dances with Wolves*, and for his occasional role as Leonard in the television series *Northern Exposure*; and Joanne Shenandoah, an Oneida actress, singer, and songwriter who founded Round Dance Productions, a nonprofit organization dedicated to preserving Native North American culture.

15 WORK

In this modern industrial age, Iroquois (especially Mohawk) men have become famous as high steel construction workers. The work requires the same agility, coordination, and courage as traditional Iroquois occupations, such as hunting and warfare. Iroquois construction workers have traveled all over the US and Canada to build bridges and skyscrapers. The work is very dangerous, and it pays well. Unfortunately, it often separates the men from their families and creates a great deal of stress for everyone—for the men, isolated in large cities, or traveling long distances from home, for weeks or months on end; and for their wives, parents, children, and other loved ones waiting at home, and worrying about their safety.

Many other Iroquois work off-reservation in factories or other industries. Others are professionals, such as teachers, nurses, social workers, doctors, and lawyers. Individual Iroquois have become known for their work as anthropologists, educators, historians, scholars, environmentalists, engineers, journalists, and activists. One well-known 19th-century Seneca, Ely S. Parker (1828–95), became the first Native North American Commissioner of Indian Affairs. Appointed to the post by US president Ulysses S. Grant, a longtime friend of Parker's, he served from 1868 to 1871.

16 SPORTS

The Iroquois invented the game the French named *lacrosse*. It is now Canada's national sport. The Iroquois believe that their ancestors gave them the game to develop their endurance and make them great warriors. Boys began learning to play at a very early age. Many Iroquois today still start lacrosse lessons as small children. Lacrosse is played in much the same way as it was centuries ago. Two teams compete to try to move a small ball (traditionally made of wood or deerhide) down the field toward the other team's goal, and finally into the goal. They carry and throw the ball with long wooden sticks that have a basket at the top, woven from leather thongs. Traditionally, at major festivals each team could have hundreds of men on it and the game could last for hours. Traditional lacrosse was much more violent than today's game. Injuries, often serious ones, were commonplace.

In earlier times children and adults also enjoyed playing a game called "snowsnake," in which a long stick carved and painted to resemble a snake was thrown along an icy path in the snow. The object was to throw it farther than anyone else. Bets were often made on this game. Women played "shinny," a sport resembling today's field hockey.

17 ENTERTAINMENT AND RECREATION

Entertainment and recreation for the Iroquois is similar to that for the general American population.

18 FOLK ART, CRAFTS, AND HOBBIES

Iroquois today are known for their soapstone, wood, bone, and antler carvings and sculptures. They also make baskets, lacrosse sticks, and do leather, feather, and bead work.

19 SOCIAL PROBLEMS

The same problems afflicting other Native North Americans today, such as alcoholism, depression, and suicide, also afflict the Iroquois. They also struggle with the same conflict between traditionalists and progressives. This conflict has become particularly fierce at the Akwesasne Mohawk reservation which straddles the US–Canada border. Violence erupting between traditional and progressive factions has led to many arrests and even a few killings in recent years. In some places this conflict becomes tangled (or is one and the same) with the conflict between traditionally religious and Christian Iroquois.

The loss of land has been a serious problem for the Iroquois, as with other Native North American peoples. In the 1950s the

Senecas lost more than 9,000 acres, forcing 130 families to leave their homes, when the US Army Corps of Engineers built the Kinzua Dam near Warren, Pennsylvania. Damming the Allegheny River caused waters to flood over Seneca lands. In 1960 the Tuscaroras near Niagara Falls lost a significant amount of land to a public reservoir (an artificial pond or lake, used to store water for public consumption) built by the US government. The Iroquois are currently engaged in many legal battles to regain ancestral lands that were stolen from them during the past two or three centuries by European Americans and Canadians.

[20] BIBLIOGRAPHY

Champagne, Duane, ed. *The Native North American Almanac.* Detroit: Gale Research, 1994.

Kimball, Yeffe, and Jean Anderson. *The Art of American Indian Cooking.* Garden City, New York: Doubleday & Co., 1965.

Reddy, Marlita A., ed. *Statistical Record of Native North Americans*, 2nd ed. Detroit: Gale Research, 1995.

Ridington, Jillian and Robin. *People of the Longhouse: How the Iroquoian Tribes Lived.* Buffalo, New York: Firefly Books, 1995.

Sherrow, Victoria. *The Iroquois Indians.* New York: Chelsea House, 1992.

Sneve, Virginia Driving Hawk. *The Iroquois.* New York: Holiday House, 1995.

Waldman, Carl. *Encyclopedia of Native American Tribes.* New York: Facts on File, 1988.

—by D. K. Daeg de Mott

ITALIAN AMERICANS

For more information on Italian history and culture, *see* **Vol. 4 Italians**.

OVERVIEW

Italian Americans are the fifth largest ethnic group in the US, after German, British, African, and Irish Americans. It is estimated that one out of every 20 Americans is of Italian descent. The first Italians to come to America emigrated from northern Italy in the late 18th and early 19th centuries. Few in number, they blended in with American society, making their homes mostly in the familiar terrain of California wine country. These first Italian Americans tended to be well-educated professionals and craftspersons

Beginning around 1880, however, a massive migration began from southern Italy to the US. These immigrants were uneducated, poor farmers or landless peasants who had suffered for many years from poor soil, drought, unemployment, and political corruption and oppression. Between the years of 1860 and 1920, some five million southern Italians moved to the US. Most were young men hoping to find good-paying jobs, save up a significant amount of money, and then return to Italy and their families. Perhaps 1.5 million of them actually did move back to Italy. The rest stayed in America.

The southern Italian immigrants tended to settle in New York City or neighboring areas because they did not have the money to travel very far after disembarking from the ship at Ellis Island. Because Italians preferred to live among their friends and neighbors, subsequent immigrants settled near those who had come before. Small enclaves of Italian Americans from the same region of Italy developed into "Little Italys," some of which still exist today.

Little Italys began as slums. Poor Italian immigrants moved into tenement housing recently vacated by earlier groups of immigrants such as Germans, Jews, or Irish, who had moved up to better housing. However, most Italian Americans chose to stay and improve their housing in Little Italy rather than move out when their financial situations improved.

Like most early immigrants, Italian Americans suffered from prejudice and discrimination, both from other Americans as well as within their own ranks. Northern and southern Italians have a history of mutual dislike, and Italian Americans continued to carry those bad feelings for one another. Other Americans were more accepting of northern Italians because they are generally fair haired and were seen as more "Germanic" and refined. Southern Italians, on the other hand, were seen as dark, brutish, ignorant peasants who would never fit in with sophisticated American society.

In the 1920s, American labor forces began to organize for better wages and working conditions. Because Italian Americans, poor and desperate for work, were willing to take any job for any wage, they were seen as a threat to other American workers. The press began depicting Italian Americans as criminals, suggesting that they were all connected with the Mafia. In fact, very few Italian Americans had any links with the Mafia or other organized crime. But the stereotype of the Italian American gangster had taken hold and has yet to be dislodged.

The trial of Nicola Sacco and Bartolomeo Vanzetti, Italian Americans from Boston who were leaders in the socialist movement, grew out of anti-Italian sentiment and added more fuel to the fire. Arrested in connection with a robbery and killing, they were convicted despite a lack of evidence. After seven years of appeals, they were executed in 1927. Italian American witnesses for the defense were discounted because, according to popular belief at the time, Italians could not be trusted.

The Great Depression of the 1930s worsened the Italian Americans' situation. Not only were jobs hard to find, but also other Americans used the Italian Americans as scapegoats, accusing them of taking jobs away from "real Americans." Violence against Italian Americans, though not a new phenomenon (lynchings and murders had occurred as early as the mid-1880s), increased. Wages fell, and more and more Italian American men found themselves unemployed.

Italian American women's horizons suddenly expanded, on the other hand. Although men were traditionally the sole bread-winners of Italian families, the Depression forced Italian American men to allow their wives and daughters to work outside the home to supplement the family income. This brought Italian American women into contact with more people of all backgrounds, gave them confidence in themselves as independent persons, and caused them to begin to question their husbands' or fathers' authority. The dynamics began to change in Italian American families, and World War II (1939–45) cemented those changes.

Italian American men and women contributed greatly to the American war effort in both World Wars I and II. Although Italian Americans made up only 4% of the US population at the start of World War I, they constituted 12% of US military troops. In World War II, over 500,000 Italian Americans served in the US military. Like other American women, Italian American women went to work on the homefront to support their families and their country, while the men were away at war. By the time the men returned, traditional Italian divisions of labor were gone for good in America.

In the booming postwar economy of the 1950s, Italian Americans finally improved their circumstances. They found good-paying jobs or started their own businesses. Many either moved to better neighborhoods or improved their homes in Little Italys. Young Italian Americans were able to afford higher education and so could advance to managerial or professional positions. By the 1980s, Italian Americans' average family income was about $2,000 higher than that for all US families.

Italian immigration to the US continues today, though at a much slower pace than during the Great Migration of 1880–1920. Due to global developments and improvements in worldwide communications, today's Italian immigrants are generally more knowledgeable and sophisticated than those who came before. The total Italian American (including Sicilian) population in 1990 was 14,714,939, according to the US Census. Of those, only 4% (580,592) were foreign born. Over half of all Italian Americans live in the Northeast, with almost 20% in New York State alone. (More than 17% of the population of New York City is of Italian descent.) New Jersey and California each host 10% of the Italian American population, with another 9% in Pennsylvania and 6% in Massachusetts.

Sicilians have chosen a slightly different settlement pattern than other Italian Americans. The largest Sicilian American population (17%) is in California, with a sizeable number (12%) in New York State. The rest of the Sicilian American population is spread across the US, with noticeable numbers in Ohio, Florida, Illinois, Michigan, and New Jersey.

Most Italian immigrants speak regional dialects of the Italian language. Many early immigrants were illiterate in "official" Italian. Once they arrived in the US, they began to blend their various dialects with elements of official Italian and English, creating a common language known as Italglish. English words such as "picnic," "sandwich," and "son of a gun" were Italianized to become *pichnicco*, *sanguiccio*, and *sonamagogna*. Subsequent generations of Italian Americans were able to choose between the regional dialect of their parents and grandparents, official Italian, English, and Italglish. With each succeeding generation, however, fluency in all but English has diminished.

Italian Americans often anglicize their names to hide their ethnicity and/or ease their acceptance into American society. In earlier times, immigration officials also misspelled Italian names on entrance visas, anglicizing them either intentionally or accidentally. In this way, Rossi became Ross, Gilberti changed to Gilbert, and Bernardo was henceforth Bernard. Well-known Italian Americans who have anglicized their names include Anne Bancroft (Anna Marie Italiano), Tony Bennett (Anthony Benedetto), Dean Martin (Dino Crocetti), and Madonna (Madonna Louise Veronica Ciccone).

Italian Americans adhere to a unique brand of Roman Catholicism. Their faith is filled with festivity, magic, and independent spirit. Although fervent believers, they also staunchly support their right to question the Pope's teachings. Many use contraceptives and promote a woman's right to have an abortion.

The first Catholics to immigrate in large numbers to the US were Irish Catholics. Due to generations of persecution, their faith had become secretive and somber. When the Italian Catholics arrived in America with their parades, bright colors, huge feasts, and parties on any and every occasion, the Irish Catholics were shocked and offended. They refused to allow Italian Catholics to worship in their churches. Finally, the Church in Rome decided to establish separate Italian Catholic parishes in the US. These parishes each have a patron saint, whose feast day is jubilantly celebrated with a *festa*. Italian Americans hold *festas* for a multitude of occasions, and though the specifics vary, each contains dancing, singing, feasting, and a procession through the streets. One of the largest *festas* is that of San Gennaro in New York City.

Weddings are the most highly celebrated rite of passage among Italian Americans, and Christmas and Easter are the most important holidays. Some Italian Americans honor the feast day of St. Lucy (*Santa Lucia*) on 13 December, and most mark the feast day of St. John the Baptist on 24 June. All Souls Day on 1 November is another popular Italian American religious holiday, along with All Souls Eve (31 October), better known as Halloween.

Italian Americans began celebrating Columbus Day on 12 October 1866 in New York City. The tradition grew, and in 1909 Columbus Day became a legal US holiday. Although Columbus Day has come under question in recent years by other ethnic groups in the US, Italian Americans still cling to the holiday as an expression of their cultural heritage.

Italian Americans are very expressive people, communicating as much through gestures as with words. Some common Italian American gestures include slowly raising the chin,

ITALIAN AMERICANS

0   200   200   400 Miles

0   200   200   400 Kilometers

which means "I don't know," or "I'm not going to tell you"; thumbing the nose, an insulting gesture indicating that the other person is a fool; flicking the teeth to express anger; flicking the chin to express indifference; and lifting one eyebrow to say "It's time to talk."

The family is extremely important to Italian Americans. Family loyalty comes above all else. Younger generations of Italian Americans are less likely to live in neighborhoods surrounded by their extended family, so the nuclear family has become more central in recent years. The elderly are still cared for within the family whenever possible, however, in contrast to other Americans who are much more likely to admit their elderly parents and grandparents to nursing homes.

Food is nearly as important as family to Italian Americans. Most mainstream "Italian" restaurants serve an Americanized version of southern Italian cuisine, which centers on pasta (spaghetti, lasagne, ravioli, etc.). Northern Italian cuisine, revolving around polenta (made from cornmeal) and risotto (a rice dish), is less well-known in the US but has been gaining in popularity in recent years. Bread is the staple food for all Italian Americans. Some traditional households use up to 25 pounds of flour per week for the family's homemade bread supply. Homemade pasta can require another 10 pounds of flour each week.

Mealtimes are family times, and as recently as the 1970s, a high school in Cleveland, Ohio, reported problems in keeping its Italian American students in school during lunch hour. Despite regulations to the contrary, the students would leave school to have lunch at home with their families. Dinner times

in the evening are also not to be missed, except in the case of emergency. Wine is always present at evening meals. Italian Americans consider wine a food, not a liquor. Drunkenness is considered disgraceful, however, as expressed in the Sicilian rhyme: *La biviri non misurata / Fa l'uomo asinata* ("Drunkenness makes an ass of a man").

The majority of first-generation Italian Americans were uneducated laborers who believed that hard work was the path to wisdom. They did not, therefore, encourage their children to attend school. The dropout rate among second-generation Italian Americans was high. Gradually, however, succeeding generations of Italian Americans became more interested in education and began attending and finishing school in greater numbers. Today, for example, nearly one-third of the students in the City University System of New York are of Italian descent.

Perhaps the greatest artistic contribution Italian Americans have made to American culture is the love of opera. In 1932, Italian immigrant Lorenzo Da Ponte founded the Italian Opera House in New York City, the first opera house in the US. Italian American Gian-Carlo Menotti composed *The Saint of Bleeker Street*, which debuted on 27 December 1954 in New York City. It was the first opera composed by an Italian American, concerning Italian Americans, and performed by Italian Americans, and it won a Pulitzer prize.

Other Italian American musicians include Enrico Caruso, Frank Sinatra, and Bruce Springsteen (who is half-Italian American, half-Dutch American), along with singer-actors

Annette Funicello, Jimmy Durante, and Madonna. Al Pacino and Sylvester Stallone are well-known Italian American actors, and Penny Marshall (Marsharelli) and Francis Ford Coppola are successful Italian American film directors. An Italian American artist whose creations are very well known is Joe Barbera, of the Hanna-Barbera animation team (creators of Yogi Bear, Tom and Jerry, the Jetsons, and the Smurfs).

Italian Americans hold fast to the traditional Italian work ethic and so have risen to the top of many fields in American society. Physicist Enrico Fermi ushered in the atomic age; Fiorello La Guardia became the first Italian American mayor of New York City in 1933; Geraldine Ferraro won the nomination for Democratic vice presidential candidate in 1984, the first woman ever to do so; and Mario Cuomo served as the governor of New York State from 1986 to 1994. The first Italian American millionaire was sand-and-gravel magnate Generoso Pope, whose son, Generoso Pope, Jr., publishes the *National Enquirer*. Lee Iacocca served as president of both the Ford Motor Company and Chrysler Corporation. Ernest and Julio Gallo, who entered the wine business in 1933, soon dominated the industry. Other successful Italian American businesses include Planters Peanuts, the Bank of America, Mr. Coffee, Chun King, and Celeste Italian Foods Company.

Italian Americans have also been very successful in sports. Charles Atlas (born Angelo Siciliano) was a world-famous bodybuilder whose correspondence course attracted the likes of Italian American baseball player Joe DiMaggio and Mahatma Gandhi. Other well-known Italian American athletes include boxer Rocky Marciano, baseball great Lawrence Peter "Yogi" Berra, football coach Vince Lombardi, quarterback Joe Montana, hockey player Phil Esposito, and gymnast Mary Lou Retton.

Older Italian Americans continue to enjoy the traditional games of *bocce* (lawn bowling) and *morra* (a guessing game where two people each extend some fingers of one hand at the same time and loudly guess what the total number of fingers will be). Most younger Italian Americans, however, have turned to more Americanized pastimes.

For the most part, Italian Americans have adapted to life in the US and are well accepted in American society today. The difficulties of their early years in America have largely been put behind them.

BIBLIOGRAPHY

Bernardo, Stephanie. *The Ethnic Almanac.* Garden City, NY: Dolphin Books/Doubleday & Company, 1981.

Gonzales, Juan L., Jr. *Racial and Ethnic Groups in America*, 2nd ed. Dubuque, IA: Kendall/Hunt Publishing Co., 1993.

Malpezzi, Frances M., and William M. Clements. *Italian-American Folklore.* Little Rock, AR: August House, 1992.

Mindel, Charles H., Robert W. Habenstein, and Roosevelt Wright, Jr., ed. *Ethnic Families in America: Patterns and Variations*, 3rd ed. New York: Elsevier Science Publishing Company, 1988.

US Bureau of the Census. *Detailed Ancestry Groups for States.* 1990 Census of Population Supplementary Reports, CP-S-1-2. Washington, DC, October 1992.

———. *The Foreign-Born Population in the United States.* 1990 CP-3-1. Washington, DC, July 1993.

Washburne, Carolyn Kott. *Italian Americans.* New York: Marshall Cavendish, 1995.

JAMAICANS

LOCATION: Jamaica

POPULATION: 2.5 million

LANGUAGE: English; Patois (Creole dialect with West African, Spanish, and French elements

RELIGION: Christianity; (Anglicanism, Protestantism, and Roman Catholicism); Rastafarianism

1 INTRODUCTION

The official motto of Jamaica is, "Out of Many People, One People." The motto expresses the fact that Jamaicans include people of African, European, Arabic (Lebanese descendants known as "Syrians"), Chinese, and East Indian heritage. These cultures come together to form one people, one spirit. In fact, if Jamaicans had a second official motto it would almost certainly have to be, "No problem, Mon." This phrase and others like, "No pressure, no problem," are typical responses when asked to do something, and often serve as stand-ins for "You're welcome." Decorating tee-shirts and other souvenirs, these phrases capture the care-free, happy-go-lucky spirit of Jamaicans.

Columbus discovered Jamaica in 1494. In the early 1500s, African slaves were brought in to work the sugarcane fields, replacing the native Arawaks who had perished. The island remained under Spanish rule until 1655, when it was captured by the British. During the five-year struggle between the Spanish and the British, a number of runaway slaves (later known as the Maroons), took shelter in the pits that make up the Cockpit Country area of the island. The Maroons maintained an autonomous existence for more than half a century. Abolition came in 1833, and the decline of the plantations followed. The former slaves became peasant farmers.

In 1938, Norman Washington Manley, a well-known lawyer, founded the People's National Party (PNP), espousing a moderate form of socialism. He served as chief minister of Jamaica (1955–59) and prime minister (1959–62). His tenure served to set the stage for Jamaican independence.

In 1958, Jamaica formed the West Indies Federation with nine other British possessions, but it withdrew three years later, which led to the collapse of the federation. Jamaica's withdrawal was led by Sir Alexander Bustamante, a cousin of Manley's. Bustamante was a labor leader. He founded the Bustamante Industrial Trade Union, Jamaica's largest union. Subsequently he formed the moderate Jamaica Labour Party to counteract the more radical PNP. He was chief minister from 1953 to 1955 and became prime minister in 1962 when Jamaica gained full independence. Bustamante, who initiated extensive public works programs and land reform, remained in office until 1967.

In 1972, Michael Manley, son of Norman Manley and leader of the PNP, became prime minister. Manley instituted many socialist changes. Manley's policies created a large trade deficit which brought Jamaica to near bankruptcy by 1980. New elections were held, with conservative Labor Party leader Edward P. G. Seaga rising to power. Seaga won reelection in 1983 but was defeated by Manley in 1989. Manley, who now adopted free-market economic policies, resigned in 1992 due to failing health. He was succeeded as party head and prime minister by

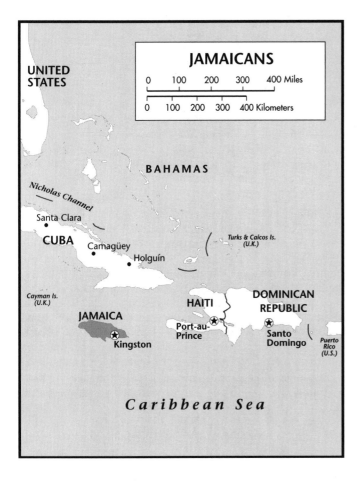

JAMAICANS

Percival J. Patterson. Patterson led the PNP to a landslide victory in 1993.

2 LOCATION AND HOMELAND

Jamaica's population of more than 2.5 million is equally divided between urban and rural dwellers, and grows at a rate just short of 1% each year. Jamaicans are mostly descendants of African Blacks, with minor representations from East Indian, Chinese, and European ancestries.

Located south of Cuba and west of Hispaniola, Jamaica is the third-largest island in the Caribbean Sea. The capital is Kingston, with a population of more than 645,000 people. Most of the soil of the island contains a high percentage of limestone, which makes cultivation difficult. The weather is almost always pleasant, with a mean annual temperature of 27°C (80°F) on the coast. Tourists flock to Jamaica for its beautiful beaches. The towns of Montego Bay, Ocho Rios, and Negril offer some of the most popular resorts. The island is susceptible to hurricanes, however, and suffered considerable damage during Hurricane Gilbert in 1988 when nearly 25% of the population was left homeless and property damage was in excess of $300 million.

Another popular attraction for tourists are the island's more than 800 caves. Many were home to the earliest inhabitants. Others are said to be the home of "duppies," the word Jamaicans use for ghosts.

3 LANGUAGE

Jamaicans speak English, but with a distinct flavor. Elements of Elizabethan English can be heard among Jamaicans engaged in casual conversation. A jug, for example, is referred to as a "goblet." The "th" is substituted with a "d," such that "that" becomes "dat," for example.

While the official language is English, most Jamaicans who live in the rural areas speak a Creole dialect. Patois, as it is called, is influenced mostly by West African languages, but also contains elements of Spanish and French. Perhaps the most famous of the patois words is *I-rie* (meaning "fabulous"), which comes from the language of Rastafarians (a religious sect). Rastafarians place great emphasis on the individual—the singular being "I" and the plural being "I and I." Other words, such as *putta-putta* ("mud") come from Africa.

4 FOLKLORE

Central to Jamaican folklore are the tales of Anansi (or Anancy) the Spider. The tales, brought to the island by the first slaves, tell of the mythical Anansi, a spider (sometimes taking the form of a man) who uses his wits to outsmart his foes. While declining in popularity, Anansi is still the subject of many bedtime stories.

5 RELIGION

Religion is an important part of life for Jamaicans. More than 80% are Christian. Jamaicans' major religions include Anglicanism, Protestantism, and Roman Catholicism.

Nearly 100,000 call themselves Rastafarians. Rastafarians are members of a Jamaican messianic movement dating back to the 1930s. Jamaican Marcus Garvey founded the Universal Negro Improvement Association. His goal was self-reliance for Africans at home and abroad. His "back-to-Africa" theme inspired and influenced many worldwide and is credited as the inspiration behind the independence movements in Ghana, Kenya, and Nigeria, as well as the Civil Rights movement in the US. Today, Garvey is a national hero.

According to Rastafarian belief, the only true God is the late Ethiopian emperor Haile Selassie (originally known as Ras Tafari), and Ethiopia is the true Zion. Rastafarians claim that White Christians have perverted the scriptures to conceal the fact that Adam and Jesus were Black. Rastafarians place great emphasis on spirituality and meditation Their rituals include the use of *ganja* (marijuana) and chanting. The ganja is smoked in a pipe called a "chalice," usually made from goat horn or bamboo. Rastafarians are known for wearing their hair in dreadlocks, sporting beards (a sign of a pact with God), and carrying Bibles.

6 MAJOR HOLIDAYS

Jamaicans celebrate their independence on 6 August. For several weeks beforehand, they stage a huge celebration called "Festival!" During this period artists of all types perform, many as part of competitions. School children get involved in the festivities, fostering their sense of national pride and traditions.

Jonkanoo (John Canoe) is a dancing procession around the time of Christmas. The origins of this celebration are unclear, but many believe its origins to be in East Africa. Celebrants wearing extravagant costumes dance to the music of drums and cane flutes.

Most other holidays and celebrations center around religious themes and include Ash Wednesday, Good Friday, Easter Monday, and Christmas.

⁷ RITES OF PASSAGE

Christian sacraments and traditions define the rites of passage for most Jamaicans and are celebrated in similar fashion to that in the US.

⁸ INTERPERSONAL RELATIONS

Jamaicans tend to be casual, open, and friendly in their relationships. When parting, a typical response is "Peradventure I will see you tomorrow."

⁹ LIVING CONDITIONS

Living conditions vary from luxurious for the affluent to rudimentary for those of lesser economic means. Health care is generally considered good, and the average life expectancy is comparable to that in the US, with women living 76 years and men 72 years, on average. For all Jamaicans, however, dealing with breakdowns of electricity, mail, water, and telephone services is not uncommon.

¹⁰ FAMILY LIFE

Women's liberation has been slow to come to Jamaica. While women are often held in high regard, men are seen as the heads of households. Great importance is placed on a man's virility and a woman's fertility. Men and women tend to marry or start living together at an early age, and a couple that does not have children soon thereafter is deemed unusual.

¹¹ CLOTHING

Everyday wear for Jamaicans is cool and comfortable. Rastafarians have made the colors of the Ethiopian flag—red, green, and gold—popular in clothing. Churchgoers tend to dress very formally on Sundays.

¹² FOOD

Nyam is the patois word meaning "to eat." Jamaicans eat foods that are rich in spices, most commonly pimento, ginger, nutmeg, and pepper. Cassava (Yuca) is a tuber that is widely popular on the island. Bammy is a bread-like snack made from cassava. Ackee and saltfish is a popular Jamaican snack or breakfast dish. Ackee, the national fruit of Jamaica, if not properly prepared, can be poisonous.

For dinner, Jamaicans will typically eat peas and rice accompanied by either jerk chicken or pork. "Jerk" refers to the method of smoking the meat over a pimento wood fire. Below is a simple but spicy recipe.

Curry Chicken

1–3 pounds chicken
2 tablespoon curry powder
lemon juice
3–4 tablespoons cooking oil
onion, thyme, garlic, pepper, salt to taste

Cut chicken into small pieces, and let sit in lemon juice for at least one hour. Remove chicken and season it. Marinate for several minutes. Heat 3–4 tablespoons of cooking oil

Young Jamaican girl holding baby girl. While women are often held in high regard, men are seen as the heads of households. (United Nations)

in a skillet. Add chicken and let cook until done. Serve over white rice or rice and peas.

¹³ EDUCATION

Some 98% of all adult Jamaicans are literate. The law requires children to attend school from age 7 to 15. There is one university, the University of the West Indies, near Kingston. The Institute of Jamaica, also in Kingston, has a library and museum of Jamaican history, art, and natural history.

¹⁴ CULTURAL HERITAGE

Jamaica's musical heritage includes Mento, which is a form of music and dance with roots in African music, and Ska, a soft-style rhythm-and-blues beat. Reggae, however, has almost become synonymous with Jamaica, and Bob Marley synonymous with reggae. Bob Marley spread reggae worldwide. In 1964, Marley formed his group, the Wailers. Their first hit was "Simmer Down." Three years later, Marley converted to the Rastafarian religion. Rastafarian themes dominated his work. Marley became a songwriter for Johnny Nash in 1972. His first international hit was "Stir It Up." In 1973 Bob Marley and the Wailers had their American debut album, *Catch a Fire,* and its follow up, *Burnin'* (which contained the subsequent hits, "Get Up, Stand Up" and "I Shot the Sheriff"—popularized by Eric Clapton). Later albums included *Natty Dread, Rastaman Vibra-*

Nearly 100,000 Jamaicans call themselves Rastafarians. Rastafarians are members of a Jamaican messianic movement dating back to the 1930s. (Jamaica Tourist Board)

tion, and *Uprising.* Marley, who died of cancer in 1981 at the age of 36, was awarded the Jamaican Order of Merit. His work influenced countless reggae and pop artists, including Ziggy Marley (Bob's son), who revitalized reggae in the late 1980s and 1990s.

Dance-hall music (also known as "DJ music") is an offshoot of reggae which has recently risen in popularity with Jamaicans. The music is loud and dancers wear elaborate and colorful outfits. Also popular is "So-Ca," a combination of soul and calypso.

Paintings and sculptures are abundant in Jamaica. One of the most famous painters is John Dunkley, whose work has a primitive quality. Edna Manley (wife of Norman and mother of Michael) is renowned for her sculptures. Also renowned for sculpting is Mallica "Kapo" Reynolds, whose work is on display at the National Gallery in Kingston. In literature, Jamaican-born poet, critic, and educator Louis Aston Marantz Simpson is recognized for his elegant verse. His work, *At the End of the Open Road,* won the 1964 Pulitzer Prize for poetry.

15 WORK

Approximately 25% of the Jamaican work force is devoted to agriculture. Sugar, tropical fruits, coffee, cacao, and spices are grown in quantity for export through the ports of Kingston and Montego Bay. Another 25% is in finance, real estate, and services. Manufacture and trade each account for a little more than 10%. The remainder work in public administration and defense—public utilities, transportation, and communication, construction, and other sectors. Jamaica has recently developed a profitable mining industry. Jamaica is among the world's leading producers of bauxite and alumina, which are exported to Canada, Norway, and the United States for refining into aluminum.

The lack of indigenous energy sources has slowed Jamaica's industrial development. In 1990, Jamaica struggled under a foreign debt of about $4 billion, one of the largest in the world in proportion to population.

Some Jamaicans make a living as "higglers." These are people who buy inexpensive goods overseas and then sell them for a substantial profit on the sidewalks of Jamaica.

16 SPORTS

Sports for Jamaicans can be summed up as follows: cricket, cricket, and more cricket. Vaguely resembling baseball, cricket dates back to 16th-century England. A match can go on for days. George Headley was a legendary Jamaican cricket player of the 1930s. Children and adults alike play and watch the sport throughout the island.

Jamaicans have also excelled in track and field, boxing, and basketball. Jamaicans also enjoy all types of water sports.

17 ENTERTAINMENT AND RECREATION

While the general attitude of Jamaicans is one that is typically laid-back and casual, Jamaicans are passionate about enjoying life. Jamaicans are not ones to sit and watch television (there are only two stations on the island). Entertainment and recreation often take the form of listening to live music (usually reggae), gathering with friends, participating in sports, or enjoying a day of food and fun at the beach.

18 FOLK ART, CRAFTS, AND HOBBIES

Along the tourist areas, Jamaican artisans display their crafts, which include *bankras* (baskets) and *yabbas* (clay bowls).

19 SOCIAL PROBLEMS

Jamaicans have had their share of racial tension and class struggles that disrupt an otherwise unified, peaceful existence. Considered sacred by some, *ganja* (marijuana) is illegal, but the government's actions against its cultivation and use are often seen as superficial.

20 BIBLIOGRAPHY

Black, Clinton V. *History of Jamaica.* London: Collins, 1976.

Cassidy, Frederic G., and R. B. LePage. *Dictionary of Jamaican English.* 2nd ed. Cambridge: Cambridge University Press, 1980.

Jekyl, Walter. *Jamaica Song and Story.* New York: Dover, 1966.

Looney, Robert. *The Jamaican Economy in the 1980s: Economic Decline and Structural Adjustment.* Boulder, CO: Westview Press, 1987.

Senior, Olive. *A–Z of Jamaican Heritage*. Kingston: Heineman Educational Books, 1983.

Tanna, Laura. *Jamaican Folk Tales and Oral Histories*. Kingston: Institute of Jamaica Publications, 1985.

—by L. Gonzales, reviewed by T. Morin

JAPANESE AMERICANS

For more information on Japanese history and culture, *see* **Vol. 3: Japanese**.

OVERVIEW

The first Japanese arrived in America by accident in the early 1800s, swept off in their fishing boats by powerful currents and shipwrecked. Rescued at sea by US ships, they were brought to America, where they usually remained because it was illegal at that time to leave or enter Japan. In 1868, a group of about 150 contract laborers secretly left Japan and came to work on the sugar plantations in Hawaii. After suffering mistreatment and harsh working conditions, they were called back to Japan. About one-third returned, while the others chose to stay on in Hawaii.

In 1885, Japan decided to open its borders in a limited way and allowed a restricted number of emigrants to leave for Hawaii. Most of those who chose to go to Hawaii intended to work hard, save a large sum of money, and return to Japan. A few did, but most ended up staying in Hawaii. Both Japan and Hawaii encouraged the emigration of women to promote a stable home life among Japanese laborers and discourage prostitution, gambling, and other vices to which single young men might succumb. Many Japanese women came to Hawaii and the US west coast as "picture brides." In a system similar to the traditional arranged marriages of Japan, a man and a woman would exchange photos and letters until the woman could travel across the sea to join her husband.

Despite Japanese and Hawaiian efforts, however, some hundreds or even thousands of young Japanese women were brought to Hawaii and the US as prostitutes. Most were either sold into prostitution by their destitute families, kidnapped, or tricked into joining the recruiters. Life was hard for these young women, and they saw little of the profits from their labors.

Other Japanese women came to Hawaii and the US, not as picture brides or prostitutes to serve the male contract laborers, but as contract laborers themselves. Thousands of Japanese women worked as cooks, seamstresses, and field laborers alongside the men. Although they did equal work, they received only $6 per month in wages, as compared to the men's wages of $10 per month.

Groups of Japanese Americans began to establish farming colonies in the early 1900s. Although the first experiment, the Wakamatsu Tea and Silk Colony established in 1869 near Sacramento, California, had failed, later attempts were more successful. Between 1904 and 1919, five farming colonies, each called Yamato Colony, were established in the San Joaquin Valley of California, near Boca Raton, Florida, and near Brownsville, Texas. The Texas colony did not last much longer than the original Wakamatsu failure, and the Florida colony eventually dwindled away (though it struggled along for almost three decades). The three California colonies, however, are still in operation today.

In 1908, as a compromise between Japanese-US relations and anti-Asian racial tensions in California, Japan and the US signed the "Gentleman's Agreement," discontinuing all Japanese emigration to the US except for "former residents, parents,

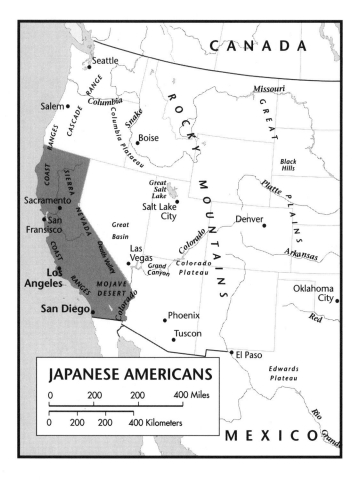

JAPANESE AMERICANS

wives or children of residents" in return for the integration of Japanese American students into American public schools. But fear of the so-called "Yellow Peril" led to further discriminatory acts, such as alien land laws (stating that no one who was ineligible for US citizenship, which included all Asians, could own land); the "Ladies' Agreement" of 1921, barring any more picture brides from entering the US, and, finally, the Asian Exclusion Act of 1924, which prohibited the immigration of anyone ineligible for citizenship, effectively ending Japanese immigration.

In 1929, Japanese Americans created the Japanese American Citizens League (JACL) to fight for their rights and promote a Japanese American identity for all Japanese Americans. The JACL still exists today as the largest Asian American civil rights organization.

Relations between the US and Japan worsened throughout the 1930s. Then, on 7 December 1941, Japanese forces attacked Pearl Harbor in Hawaii, at that time a US Territory (it would become the 50th US state in 1959). The US government immediately seized over 1,000 Japanese American community leaders in Hawaii and on the US west coast and imprisoned them. Two months later, on 10 February 1942, US President Franklin Roosevelt signed Executive Order 9066, which ordered all Japanese Americans to be evacuated from their homes and sent to detention camps. They were also presented with loyalty questionnaires to fill out and sign. At the time, the US government believed this was necessary to prevent those Japanese Americans still loyal to Japan from sabotaging US

military efforts, carrying out espionage for the Japanese government, or staging internal attacks. However, no other immigrant group was detained or had their loyalty questioned during the whole of World War II (1939–45), including German and Italian Americans. Executive Order 9066 was clearly racially motivated, and it would take decades for the US government to redress this grievous wrong.

Most Japanese Americans had been forced to sell their homes and businesses at a moment's notice when informed that they were to be evacuated. After suffering for almost three years in the dreadful living conditions of the internment camps, they were released to a life with no home, no property, and no financial resources. Many were afraid to return to the "Japantowns" of the West Coast because anti-Asian sentiment was still running high there. Consequently, the Japanese American community became much more widely dispersed, scattering across the US.

Japanese Americans also tried to hide their cultural differences, blending in with mainstream American society as much as possible. A great deal of traditional Japanese culture was discarded by Japanese Americans in those first years after World War II, and more has been lost in succeeding generations. The movement for redress (compensation for wrongs done to Japanese Americans), which began in earnest in the 1970s, did lead many young Japanese Americans to examine their history and begin to reclaim their identity as Japanese Americans. Once redress was achieved ($20,000 per internee living when the bill went into effect in 1988, or his or her heirs), however, the rallying point for Japanese Americans as a culture group was gone and interest in a separate Japanese American identity waned once again.

The children and grandchildren of Japanese American internees were encouraged to adopt mainstream American values, traditions, and attitudes. Most grew up speaking only English, learning and experiencing very little of traditional Japanese culture. Because they no longer lived in Japanese American enclaves but were rather dispersed throughout American communities, they made many non-Japanese American friends. This led to a rise in interracial marriages to the point that today there are very few Japanese American children of pure Japanese descent. The Japanese American community may eventually disappear simply through racial blending.

According to the US Census, there were approximately 1,005,000 Japanese Americans living in the US in 1990. Over two-thirds (about 70%) are American-born, almost twice as many as in any other Asian American group. Although Japanese immigration continues into the US, most Japanese Americans are descended from Japanese who arrived before 1924. Some 200,000 Japanese settled in Hawaii and 180,000 on the US mainland between 1885 and 1924.

Most Japanese Americans (72%) still live in the West, with about 67% concentrated in the Pacific region. California has the highest population of Japanese Americans (353,000). Although Hawaii has fewer Japanese Americans (262,000) than California, they comprise a higher percentage of the total population. In 1990, over one-fourth (26.6%) of all Japanese Americans lived in Honolulu alone. At one time, Japanese Americans were in the majority in Hawaii, but today they make up less than 50% of the population. The next highest Japanese American populations are in the states of Washington (43,000), New York (40,000), and Illinois (27,000).

Japanese Americans distinguish themselves by generation. *Issei* are first generation Japanese Americans who were born in Japan. Their children, second generation Japanese Americans, are called *Nisei*. The children of *Nisei* and grandchildren of *Issei* are known as *Sansei*, or third generation Japanese Americans. *Yonsei* are fourth generation Japanese Americans, children of *Sansei*. Many Japanese Americans today are either *Sansei* or *Yonsei*. They have lived in the US longer than some European Americans and consider themselves more American than Japanese. Most do not speak Japanese or follow traditional Japanese customs.

The Japanese are very tolerant, and Japanese Americans likewise follow a variety of religious faiths. In their efforts to assimilate with mainstream American culture, many have become Christian, though they may still visit Buddhist temples on traditional Buddhist holidays. Certain Shinto customs also survive, such as visiting shrines at New Year's and praying to Shinto gods for luck.

Major rites of passage, such as weddings and funerals, may be celebrated in traditional Buddhist or Shinto fashion. Some families take their children to the Buddhist temple for the Infant's First Service, or *Hatsu Mairi,* in May, where the children are formally introduced to the community for the first time. Adult Japanese Americans who choose to pursue Buddhism seriously are given a Buddhist name in the Three Treasures, or *Ti Sarana,* ceremony held every March and September.

Most Japanese Americans continue to celebrate certain traditional Japanese holidays. Although different communities celebrate a variety of holidays, nearly all Japanese Americans recognize New Year's (*Shogatsu*), the Doll Festival (*Hina Matsuri*), Children's Day (*Tango no Sekku*), the Weaving Loom or Star Festival (*Tanabata*), and the Bon Dance (*Bon Odori*). Japanese Americans often add typical American holiday foods, such as ham or turkey, to their traditional Japanese feasts, and girls may display American rather than Japanese dolls on *Hina Matsuri*.

Tanabata had been celebrated in a rather reduced form in the US, consisting of small gatherings of people reading poetry. Recently, however, Japanese Americans are returning to more elaborate displays of traditional *Tanabata* decorations. *Bon Odori* has become the occasion for huge parades with professional dancers in San Francisco and Los Angeles.

Although Japanese Americans have for the most part become thoroughly Americanized, certain traditional customs remain, such as gift giving. Younger generations, however, are beginning to lose touch with the importance of these rituals, much to the chagrin of their parents and grandparents. One traditional Japanese value to which even younger Japanese Americans still adhere is the strong bond between mother and child. Studies show that Japanese American children are held more by their mothers and spend less time alone than other children in the US. Japanese American children are taught to respect their elders, and they grow up with feelings of gratitude and obligation toward their parents that last throughout their lifetime.

Many Japanese Americans continue to eat traditional Japanese foods, such as *sushi*, *sashimi*, *maki*, and *tempura*. Japanese foods have also become popular among the general US population. In May 1964, Hiroaki "Rocky" Aoki (1938–) opened the first Benihana restaurant, in New York City. Though some critics consider the food more American than Japanese, it is prepared in a flamboyant "Japanese" manner by Japanese American chefs wielding large knives at lightning speeds right at the customers' table. Benihana restaurants are now located in cities throughout the world.

Japanese Americans have contributed more than just food to American society. The arts of haiku poetry, origami (paperfolding), ikebana (flower arranging), and Kabuki theater are practiced and enjoyed by many Americans. Actors such as George Takei (*Star Trek*) and Pat Morita (*Happy Days* and the *Karate Kid* films) are well known to most Americans, and musicians including Yoko Ono, Toshiko Akiyoshi, and the jazz band Hiroshima have added elements of their Japanese heritage to the world of American music.

A number of Japanese American writers have found success, including Ronald Takaki, Bill Hosokawa, Jun Atsushi Iwamatsu, Lydia Minatoya, David Mura, Phillip Kan Gotanda, Kyoko Mori, and others. Successful Japanese American artists and architects include Eiko Ishioka, Gyo Obata, and Minoru Yamasaki.

Although the first Japanese immigrants to Hawaii and the US came as contract laborers, they were carefully selected by the Japanese government from the ranks of the well educated to serve as ambassadors of a sort. Most Japanese Americans descend from these hard-working, highly skilled immigrants and carry on their drive to succeed. The unemployment rate among Japanese Americans is a very low 2.1%, and only slightly over 3% live below the poverty line, as compared to almost 10% of the overall American population.

Some Japanese Americans who have risen to the top in their fields are Nobel Prize winners Leo Esaki and Tetsuo Akutso; research scientist Douglas Ishii; Ellison Onizuka, the first Asian American astronaut (who was tragically killed aboard the space shuttle *Challenger* in 1986); US Senators Samuel Ichiye Hayakawa and Daniel Inouye; US representatives Bob Matsui, Patsy Takemoto Mink, and Norman Mineta; Superior Court Judge Lance Ito (who was named to preside over the O. J. Simpson trial in 1994); George Aratani, founder of the Mikasa Corporation (one of the largest privately owned international firms); lawyer and director of the US Office for Civil Rights, Dennis Hayashi; and CBS news correspondent James Hattori.

Japanese Americans have also been very successful in sports. Kristi Yamaguchi won the gold medal for figure skating in the 1992 Winter Olympics and has also won gold and silver medals at World Championship competitions. Several Japanese American baseball players have made the major leagues, and Japanese American athletes have risen to the top in many other sports as well, including gymnastics, boxing, golf, track and field, tennis, volleyball, hockey, football, and basketball. Japanese Americans are also responsible for bringing karate, judo, aikido, and ninjutsu (whose practitioners are called *ninjas*) to the US.

Japanese Americans still suffer the wounds and scars of internment during World War II, and anti-Asian discrimination continues to afflict their lives. Studies have shown that Japanese American men are paid only 88% of what European American men earn for the same work, and few Japanese Americans are promoted to top management positions. With Japan rising rapidly in the world market economy, many American workers feel threatened and project their frustrations onto Japanese Americans. Chinese American Vincent Chin was mistaken for a Japanese by European American auto workers in Detroit in 1982. The auto workers called Chin a "Jap," blamed him for the loss of their jobs, and beat him to death on the street. This sort of racial prejudice prevents Japanese Americans from taking their full and rightful place in American society.

BIBLIOGRAPHY

Bernardo, Stephanie. *The Ethnic Almanac*. Garden City, NY: Dolphin Books/Doubleday & Co., 1981.

Gall, Susan, and Irene Natividad, ed. *The Asian American Almanac*. Detroit: Gale Research, 1995.

Gonzales, Juan L., Jr. *Racial and Ethnic Groups in America*, 2nd ed. Dubuque, IA: Kendall/Hunt Publishing Company, 1993.

Lee, Lauren. *Japanese Americans*. Tarrytown, NY: Benchmark Books/Marshall Cavendish, 1996.

Niiya, Brian, and Sandra Yamate. "Who Are the Japanese Americans?" In *The Asian American Almanac*, Susan Gall and Irene Natividad, ed. Detroit: Gale Research, 1995.

US Bureau of the Census. *Detailed Ancestry Groups for States*. 1990 Census of Population Supplementary Reports, CP-S-1-2. Washington, DC, October 1992.

———. *The Foreign-Born Population in the United States*. 1990 CP-3-1. Washington, DC, July 1993.

—by D. K. Daeg de Mott

JEWISH AMERICANS

See also the article entitled **Traditional Orthodox Jews** in Volume 3.

OVERVIEW

The United States is home to 5.8 million Jews, the largest Jewish population found in any single country and nearly half the world's 14 million Jews. (The next largest concentration of Jews—4.2 million—is found in Israel, the historical homeland of the Jewish people and a modern independent nation since 1948.) The significance of Jewish American contributions to American politics, business, science, and culture far outweighs the demographic importance of this group that represents under 3% of the population. The sonnet of welcome ("The New Colossus") inscribed in 1896 on a bronze plaque at the base of the Statue of Liberty was written by Emma Lazarus, a Jewish American. Its promise ("Give me your tired, your poor, Your huddled masses, yearning to breathe free,") has rung true for generations of Jews fleeing poverty and religious persecution in Europe. In turn, they and their descendants have enriched the lives of many in their adopted country through their love of learning, their humor, their artistic gifts, their commitment to social and political causes, and their energy and ambition, fueled by the determination to provide better lives for their families.

The Jews are neither a race nor a nationality, and religious belief by itself does not provide a satisfactory definition, as there are Jewish atheists and agnostics who reject the traditions of religious observance but still claim Judaism as their cultural and historical heritage. In practical terms, a Jew is someone who is either born to Jewish parents—according to the Orthodox view, it is the mother who must be Jewish—or who converts to Judaism. Historically, the Jews are a Semitic people who trace their ancestry to the Middle East some 4,000 years ago, when the patriarch Abraham founded a monotheistic religion based on the belief in one God who is the creator and ruler of the universe. Abraham's descendants, known as the Hebrews, lived for over 2,000 years in Canaan (later known as Palestine and today the state of Israel). After a period of enslavement in Egypt, they were led to freedom in about 1225 BC by Moses, who is said to have received the Old Testament of the Bible—including the Ten Commandments—from God on Mount Sinai during that time. Except for a brief period of Babylonian captivity, the Jews remained in Palestine until the Romans destroyed their Temple in 70 AD and officially banned their religion in 135 AD, inaugurating the long period known as the Jewish diaspora, or dispersion.

Scattered throughout North Africa and Europe, the Jews remained a minority in every country in which they settled. Rather than a homeland, the unifying force behind their survival as a people became their heritage of religious scholarship, observance, and customs. Under Muslim rule during the Middle Ages, the Jews of Spain and Portugal, known as Sephardim (or Sephardic Jews), enjoyed an unusual period of enlightened tolerance, when they made significant contributions to literature and learning before being expelled in 1492 at the hands of the Spanish Inquisition.

In the northern parts of Europe, Ashkenazic Jews, long persecuted as "Christ killers," were expelled from England, France, and Germany during the 13th and 14th centuries. The majority migrated eastward to Poland, which was home to the world's largest Jewish population by the 19th century. After the Protestant Reformation, Western Europe became more hospitable to the Jews, many of whom were able to attain wealth and status through trade and banking. In late-18th and early 19th-century Germany, the democratic ideals fostered by the French Revolution led to a period of Jewish economic and cultural advancement known as the Jewish Enlightenment, or *Haskalah.* However, by mid-century, political unrest began to threaten Western and then Eastern Europe's Jewish communities, inaugurating a period of emigration, much of it to the United States.

The first wave of Jewish immigration to the New World had begun in 1654, when a party of 23 Sephardic Jews from Brazil arrived in the community that was known as New Amsterdam under Dutch rule and later as New York. In the following decades, Jewish immigrants from England, Holland, Germany, and southern Europe settled in coastal cities along the eastern seaboard, from Rhode Island to Georgia. Their numbers had risen to over 2,000 by the time of the American Revolution, and 6,000 by 1826.

The second wave of Jewish immigration began in the mid 19th century as a result of the social turmoil that had accompanied the failed European revolutionary movements of the 1840s. Immigrants from Germany, as well as from other German-speaking areas of central Europe, increased the size of America's Jewish population to 50,000 by 1850 and 150,000 only a decade later, pushing westward to settle in cities such as Chicago, Cleveland, Detroit, and St. Louis and, ultimately, communities on the west coast, including Portland and San Francisco. By the end of the 19th century, the main impetus for Jewish immigration had shifted to Eastern Europe. Following the massacre of Russia's Czar Alexander II in 1881, a resurgence of anti-Semitism culminated in a wave of brutal massacres known as pogroms. The pogroms, in combination with harsh economic conditions, led to a mass exodus of Eastern European Jews. In the years between 1880 and 1924, one-third of Eastern European Jewry emigrated, with the overwhelming majority bound for the United States. The U.S. Jewish population grew from about 250,000 in 1881 to 4.5 million by the late 1920s to become the largest Jewish community in the world. During these years, Jews accounted for about 8% of all immigrants to America.

The new Eastern European immigrants settled primarily in major cities including New York, Chicago, Philadelphia, and Boston. Many were employed in the garment industry and other types of manual labor. After 1924, Jewish immigration to America—like that of Asians and other non-Western European groups—decreased sharply due to restrictive immigration legislation. Immigration quotas prevailed even during the era of the Nazi holocaust in Europe; only 150,000 Jews managed to enter the United States between 1935 and 1941, after which point it became virtually impossible for Jews to leave Europe. Levels of Jewish immigration increased in the years immediately following World War II, as Holocaust survivors began arriving in the United States. In the decades after the war, about a half-million Jews emigrated to America from Europe and Russia, even though, for the first time in 2,000 years, the Jews once again had a country of their own—Israel, which achieved statehood in 1948. In the 1980s, policy changes in the former Soviet Union allowed large numbers of Soviet Jews to emigrate both to the United States and Israel.

Historically, the greatest number of Jews have settled in the northeastern states, although, mirroring a larger population trend, the number of Jews in southern and western states is increasing. In 1992, the three states with the largest Jewish populations were New York (1.85 million), California (920,000), and Florida (600,000). The metropolitan areas with the largest Jewish populations were New York City (1.45 million), Los Angeles (490,000), Chicago (261,000), Philadelphia (250,000), Boston (228,000), the San Francisco Bay area (210,000), Miami (189,000), and Washington, D.C. (165,000).

Given the high value that Jews have historically placed on literacy and education, early waves of Jewish immigrants tended to become rapidly acculturated into their new country. As 19th century German-speaking immigrants established themselves and attained material prosperity, they gained widespread acceptance within American society and, in turn, were eager to adopt the language and customs of their adopted land. However, the Eastern European Jews who followed them were assimilated more slowly into the mainstream culture. Their previous lives in the Jewish ghettos and *shtetls* (small towns) of Poland and Russia had, to a great extent, isolated them from Western secular ways. Once in America, most crowded together in closely knit communities, clinging to their customs and traditions and continuing (at least at home) to speak Yiddish, the hybrid of medieval German and Hebrew that had been the common language of Jews throughout Europe since the Middle Ages.

Perceived as different in a way that their predecessors had not been, these new immigrants also fell prey to a wave of anti-immigrant sentiment that affected attitudes toward newly arrived non-Jewish immigrants from southern Europe, Asia, and elsewhere. Ironically, the restrictive quotas that grew from the perceived foreignness of Jewish immigrants from Eastern Europe, helped those already here to assimilate more rapidly into the mainstream. With fewer new immigrants to swell its ranks, the Yiddish-speaking working class declined, and American Jews became an increasingly middle-class, educated, and assimilated population. Anti-Semitic feeling in the United States, which had peaked in the 1930s with the broadcasts of the Roman Catholic priest Charles Coughlin, waned after World War II when the full extent of the Nazi atrocities became known. Restrictive quotas, which had been adopted in higher education and hiring, were gradually abandoned, and Jews attained full participation in business, academia, and the professions.

Since about the middle of the 20th century, a modern secular lifestyle has been the norm for the vast majority of Jews in America, as elsewhere in the world. About 70% of American Jews identify themselves as either Conservative or Reform, including many who do not attend services regularly, while another 10% are Orthodox (a category that includes both modern Orthodox Jews, who practice strict religious observance while participating in mainstream American culture, and a small minority of ultra-Orthodox hasidim who rigorously reject most aspects of modern secular life). The American Jewish community also includes secular Jews who do not practice any religious observance but identify themselves as Jewish on the basis of heritage and culture.

In spite of the great variety—in religious observance, in lifestyle, in occupation, in political affiliation—that characterizes Jewish life in America, one cultural tradition that still unifies many Jews and brings them close to their heritage is observance of the Jewish holidays. The most important holidays are Rosh Hashanah (the Jewish New Year) and Yom Kippur (the Day of Atonement), which mark the beginning and end of a 10-day period that occurs in September–October (the Jewish holidays are based on a traditional lunar calendar). Observant Jews attend services and, on Yom Kippur, undertake a 25-hour fast, a solemn period of contemplation and prayer.

Chanukah, observed in December, is, in religious terms, a minor holiday, but it is still one of the best-known and most widely observed. In Jewish homes, candles—one for each night—are lit in an eight-branched candelabra called a menorah to commemorate the burning of an oil lamp for eight days when the Jews recaptured their temple from the Syrians in 164 AD. Children traditionally receive gifts and chocolate Chanukah *gelt* (coins) and play with a top called a *dreydl*. Another important period of observance for Jewish families is Passover, which commemorates the biblical exodus of the Jews from Egypt. The holiday begins with a festive meal, called a *seder*, at which the story of the Exodus is recounted and the guests sample a collection of symbolic foods, each of which has a special significance in relation to the Jews' enslavement in Egypt and their subsequent liberation. The most famous of these is the matzoh, a square of unleavened bread, which is eaten instead of bread and other bakery products throughout the eight-day Passover period. Other Jewish holidays are also associated with special foods, such as the potato pancakes (*latkes*) traditionally served on Chanukah, or the triangular pastries (*hamentashen*) baked on Purim. In addition, many types of "Jewish food"—such as bagels with lox, chicken soup for a cold, deli sandwiches, and kosher dill pickles—not only serve as a unifying tradition shared by observant and non-observant Jews alike but have been assimilated into the larger mainstream culture. As proclaimed by a 1960s poster that depicted a Native American eating a corned beef sandwich: "You don't have to be Jewish to love Levy's rye bread."

BIBLIOGRAPHY

Cohn-Sherbok, Dan. *Atlas of Jewish History.* London: Routledge, 1994.

Howe, Irving. *World of Our Fathers.* New York: Simon & Schuster, 1976.

Kamp, Jim. "Jewish Americans." *Gale Encyclopedia of Multicultural America.* Detroit: Gale Research, 1995.

Moore, Deborah Dash. *To the Golden Cities: Pursuing the American Jewish Dream to Miami and L.A.* New York: Free Press, 1994.

Muggamin, Howard. *The Jewish Americans.* New York: Chelsea House, 1996.

Sachar, Howard M. *A History of the Jews in America.* New York: Knopf, 1992.

Wigoder, Geoffrey. *New Standard Jewish Encyclopedia.* New York: Facts on File, 1992.

—by R. Wieder

JIVARO

PRONUNCIATION: Hee-va-ro
LOCATION: Ecuador; Peru (Eastern slopes of the Andes mountains)
POPULATION: 10,000–30,000
LANGUAGE: Jivaro; Quechua
RELIGION: Traditional mystical and spiritual beliefs

¹ INTRODUCTION

The Jivaro are an Andean tribe often considered to be the most warlike people of South America. Their history as violent warriors goes back to the days of the expansion of the Inca empire when the Jivaro fought to remain free of Inca control. They also battled the Spanish during the conquest, and it is alleged that they massacred nearly 50,000 Spaniards in 1599. In the centuries following the conquest, the Jivaro continued to fight assimilation into modern society and they have resisted successive waves of missionaries. Famed for their practice of shrinking human heads, the Jivaro in recent times have become largely peaceful and are no longer completely isolated from modern society.

² LOCATION AND HOMELAND

The Jivaro live on the eastern slopes of the Andes, where mountain ranges meet the Amazon headwaters. This tropical forest region is characterized by frequent and heavy rainfall, and dense tropical vegetation. The Jivaro are mainly concentrated in Ecuador, although many closely related tribes such as the Aguaruna are found in Peru. Current estimates place the population at approximately 10,000–30,000 people.

³ LANGUAGE

The Jivaro lend their name to a linguistic family. There are a variety of Jivaroan dialects and languages spoken by related groups in the region. Many Jivaro now also speak the Quechua language which is common throughout the Andes.

⁴ FOLKLORE

The Jivaro have a rich mythology. A variety of ancient myths, for example, have been passed down through the generations to explain the origins of the Jivaro peoples. In one story of Jivaro creation, the Andean foothills were subject to a severe flood, killing all but two brothers. Upon the brothers' return to their shelter after the waters had receded, they found dishes of food laid out for them by two parrots. One of the brothers caught one of the gift-bearing parrots and married her. This marriage produced three girls and three boys, whose descendants became the Jivaro people. Jivaro myths such as this one, it is believed, are an amalgamation of traditional Jivaro mythology and more modern beliefs introduced in the past decades by missionaries.

The boa constrictor holds a unique place in Jivaro mythology. The largest snake in the Amazon basin is respected and feared not merely because of its strength, but because it is believed to possess strong supernatural powers.

⁵ RELIGION

The Jivaro belong to a spiritual and mystical world. The Jivaro hold a deep-rooted belief that spiritual forces all around them are responsible for real-world occurrences. They ascribe spiritual significance to animals, plants, and objects. Many daily customs and behaviors are guided by their desire to attain spiritual power or avoid evil spirits. Fearful of witchcraft, the Jivaro often attribute sickness or death to the power of their enemies to cast curses.

There are a great many deities or gods that the Jivaro revere. Primary among these is Nungui or Earth Mother who is believed to have the power to make plants grow. Residing deep underground, she emerges at night to dance in the garden. Women sing to Nungui to ask her to protect the garden, and they carefully weed the garden daily to appease her. Equally important is the quest for an *arutam* soul, which offers protection from injury, disease, or death. This spiritual power is temporary, however, but it can eventually be replaced by killing an enemy. The pursuit of protection by arutam power provides the belief system underlying the pervasive violence in Jivaro society.

⁶ MAJOR HOLIDAYS

Jivaro holidays consist of the various rituals and celebrations that mark major life transitions or events.

⁷ RITES OF PASSAGE

Jivaro rites of passage and celebrations are reflections of their spiritual beliefs. All personal milestones and important events are celebrated with spiritual significance. The most important moment in a young male Jivaro's life is when he is encouraged to gain his *arutam* or protective spirit. Parents fear that without this protective spirit, Jivaro youths will be unlikely to survive into adulthood. At or before puberty, young male Jivaro are led deep into the forest where they consume a hallucinogenic drug called *maikoa* and then await a vision of the *arutam* soul that will protect them from danger. They may remain there for days, fasting and bathing in a waterfall, while they await the sacred vision. If the vision does not come, they return home, then set off again to the forest to make a second attempt. Once this power is received, the boy is allowed to participate in many adult activities, such as hunting. Full adult status, however, is not given until the boy successfully hunts down a sloth and learns the head-shrinking techniques.

⁸ INTERPERSONAL RELATIONS

Despite their warlike reputation, the Jivaro are in fact a very sociable people. When visiting a neighbor or relative's house, guests can expect a hospitable welcome. Beer made from manioc (cassava) root will be offered, and the family meal will be shared. Often, if the distances traveled are great, the guests will be invited to stay for a few days. Banana leaves laid on the dirt floor serve as beds for the visitors.

These visits also provide an opportunity for men to seek new wives. In contrast to Western cultures, it is the men that are fussy about their appearance. A man may spend considerable time before a visit or party painting his face and putting decorative adornments on his clothes and in his hair. On special occasions, complex geometric designs are painted on the nose and cheekbones. Toucan feathers adorn the hair, and ear sticks are

placed through holes in the ear. When trying to attract a young woman, the suitor concocts a homemade mixture of plants, herbs, and oils which acts like a perfume.

Gift-giving is also important among the Jivaro. A common gift for the potential bride are the fangs of a boa constrictor which are purported to bring good luck. If these gestures of affection are reciprocated, the man may begin negotiations with the woman's father to marry her. Romantic love and mutual attraction are paramount in the selection of a spouse. In addition, women seek good hunters and warriors as husbands, while men desire good gardeners and potters. The husband is obligated to pay a bride-price or perform services to the wife's father.

⁹ LIVING CONDITIONS

Jivaro families live in large, one-room shelters, with no internal walls or rooms for privacy. These shelters called *jivaria* generally house large nuclear families averaging 8 to 10 people. Jivaria shelters are built by the male head of the household with help from his male relatives. The houses must be strong enough to withstand both heavy rainfall and enemy attack. The men scour the forest for palm leaves to build a thatched roof to repel the frequent rainfall. The Jivaro seek to build large shelters, up to 24 m (80 ft) in length, which enable them to entertain visitors comfortably. Although they like to dance, it is their custom only to dance indoors, thereby requiring a large floor area.

Although there are no private rooms, the house is divided into two areas, one for men and one for women. There are even separate doors for use by men and women. They have very basic furniture, low-lying beds made of bamboo (with no mattresses), and shelves to store basic pottery.

One unusual characteristic of the Jivaro is the complete lack of any political organization. There are no tribal leaders or community organizations. The sole unit of organization is the family group. The Jivaro population is widely dispersed, with an average of 1.5 km to 8 km (1–5 mi) between houses. Families live in a house for no more than 10 years, as the nearby supply of firewood and small game becomes depleted. Families will then move a few kilometers or miles away to an area richer in resources.

10 FAMILY LIFE

The roles of males and females in Jivaro society are clearly prescribed. These distinct roles are tied to religious beliefs. The division of labor is partly the result of the belief that most inanimate and living objects have either male or female souls. Manioc (cassava), for example, is thought to be female, so all tasks related to the planting, reaping, and processing of manioc is left for females. Planting and reaping corn, which has a male soul, is left to the males.

Jivaro are polygynous, that is, men may have more than one wife. An average Jivaro family will consist of a man with three wives and multiple children. This practice may have developed in response to the decline in the male population as a result of intertribal warfare. Women greatly outnumber men in many villages. Upon the death of the husband, the widow usually becomes the wife of the deceased husband's brother.

Most Jivaro families are not complete without one or two dogs. They are kept, not as pets, but as an essential aid to hunting and for protection from enemies. The essential roles dogs perform give them a privileged position in Jivaro households. They receive generous attention and care. In addition, monkeys or birds are sometimes kept as pets.

11 CLOTHING

Daily dress among the Jivaro is simple. Both men and women wear garb made of plain brown cloth, occasionally painted with vertical stripes. These homewoven clothes are durable and rugged and can last for many years. The women drape the cloth over one shoulder, sometimes belting it at the waist with bark string or a piece of woven cotton. Men wrap the cloth around the waist so that it reaches down below the knees. A common feature of male attire is the *etsemat,* a woven band decorated with feathers that is worn around the head.

Ceremonial dress is more elaborate. Men paint their faces with black and red dyes. An ornament made of bird bones is wrapped around the shoulders, signifying the possession of an *arutam* soul and the spiritual power it provides. More recently, however, the Jivaro are acquiring Western clothing. Often, there is now a preference for using these manufactured clothes for special occasions such a visits to neighboring families.

12 FOOD

The Jivaro have a fairly varied diet of meat and vegetables which they obtain from many sources. The primary element of their diet are the staple vegetables grown in their gardens. These tubers (root plants such as potatoes) and vegetables are supplemented by foraging for wild plantains and other edible plants. The protein in the diet is obtained by raising chickens and hunting wild game. Animals such as wild hogs, peccaries, and monkeys are hunted with great skill with blowguns and curare darts. Spearing fish in the rivers provides another form of protein. As with many other Amazon peoples, the most popular drink among the Jivaro is beer made from fermented manioc (cassava) root.

13 EDUCATION

Most Jivaro children receive no formal education. Rather than learning the modern skills of reading and writing, Jivaro children are taught the skills needed for survival in the jungle. They are, for example, taught how to swim at a very young age. They learn these basic skills from their parents and elder siblings. Due to the widely dispersed population, most children have little contact with playmates other than their siblings.

In less remote Jivaro settlements, some formal schooling may be offered by missionaries.

14 CULTURAL HERITAGE

Songs and music are closely integrated into Jivaro daily life. Songs exist to accompany many daily occurrences and special occasions. Jivaro men sing special songs while weaving, as do women while gardening. At parties or ceremonial events, flutes and drums made with monkey skins are used to accompany the singing.

15 WORK

Much of the workday is dedicated to ensuring a constant supply of food. The Jivaro are primarily subsistence agriculturalists and grow a fairly diverse range of staple crops, such as manioc (cassava) root, sweet potatoes, sugarcane, peanuts, and plantains. The women spend a large proportion of the day dealing with the laborious task of keeping the large garden free from weeds. Women are also responsible for producing the pottery needed for storing food and drinks. Young girls tend to the house and are responsible for such tasks as sweeping the floors with banana leaves.

The men have more varied duties, such as clearing the forest, collecting firewood, and hunting. They also have developed the skill for crafting blowguns and spears, which are essential for game hunting. The process of making a blowgun can take as long as a couple of weeks from start to finish. Wood from a chonta palm tree is split open, tied together, and hollowed out with a mixture of sand and water. The final touch is the addition of a mouthpiece made of bone. Darts are made quickly, by sharpening palm leaves. Curare is placed on the tip of the dart, which can be propelled nearly 30 m (100 ft) to reach monkeys in trees or large birds. Longer blowguns, sometimes up to 4.5 m (15 ft) in length, allow for greater accuracy but are difficult to carry long distances while tracking prey. Most blowguns are therefore between 2 m and 2.5 m (6–8 ft).

The Jivaro are no longer completely isolated from modern society. They frequently trade skins and featherworked handicrafts to obtain goods from the commercial sector. In addition, some Jivaro work as laborers to obtain cash to purchase modern goods. Particularly valued are machetes, axes, and guns, as they are useful tools for life in the forest.

[16] SPORTS

The Jivaro do not participate in sports.

[17] ENTERTAINMENT AND RECREATION

The Jivaro are a festive people, and parties lasting throughout the night or even over several days are common. Evenings spent dancing and drinking manioc (cassava) beer with neighbors is the main form of entertainment. After a few hours spent drinking and talking, the party livens up as the drums are brought out. Dancing and singing ensue, usually until dawn. For the Jivaro, these parties provide a rare occasion for social interaction and communication in a society where there is limited contact with others outside the family on a daily basis.

[18] FOLK ART, CRAFTS, AND HOBBIES

The Jivaro are skilled craftspeople. The women learn to make pottery from a very young age. The art of weaving is one reserved exclusively for men. They spin, weave, and dye cotton wool with natural dyes extracted from tropical plants. Elaborate feather headdresses and artifacts are also widely sought for their artistic beauty. These skills are still taught to successive generations, but the growing availability of Western goods has tended to diminish the quality of traditional goods.

[19] SOCIAL PROBLEMS

Modern society continues to challenge traditional culture.

[20] BIBLIOGRAPHY

Furneaux, Rupert. *Primitive Peoples.* London: David and Charles, 1975.

Harner, Michael J. *The Jivaro: People of the Sacred Waterfalls.* New York: Doubleday Anchor, 1973.

Weyer, Edward. *Primitive Peoples Today.* New York: Doubleday and Company, 1961.

—by C. Sahley

KAYAPOS

LOCATION: Brazil (Amazon jungle)
POPULATION: A few thousand
LANGUAGE: Kayapo
RELIGION: Traditional indigenous beliefs

[1] INTRODUCTION

The Kayapo Indians are one of the main Amerindian groups that remain in the Amazon jungle in Brazil. There are several theories about the origins of the various South American Indian groups, and it is thought that they may have migrated thousands of years ago from Central Asia, crossing into North America and making their way southwards. There are others who believe that this may be true for some but not all Amerindian groups. The Kayapos resisted assimilation and were known traditionally as fierce warriors, raiding enemy tribes and sometimes fighting among themselves.

Their first steady contact with Europeans did not occur until the 20th century, in the 1950s. Since then, due to contact with squatters, loggers, miners, and eventually Brazilian government officials, the Kayapos evolved some new customs and have had to struggle to maintain their way of life. Logging and mining, particularly for gold, as well as some agricultural activities and cattle-ranching in cleared-out sections of the jungle have posed threats to the Kayapos' traditional way of life. Increasing destruction of the rain forest, as well as river pollution caused by chemicals used in gold-mining activities, threatens the delicate balance between humans, plants, and animals successfully maintained for thousands of years by Amazon Indians such as the Kayapos.

[2] LOCATION AND HOMELAND

When the Portuguese conquerors first arrived in Brazil, there were about 5 million Amerindians, but today there are only about 200,000, of which a few thousand are Kayapos, living along the Xingu River in the eastern part of the Amazon rain forest, in several scattered villages. Their lands consist of tropical rain forest and savanna. The Amazon basin, which includes the Amazon River and its tributaries such as the Xingu, is sometimes referred to as Amazonia and includes parts of Venezuela, Colombia, Ecuador, and Peru. In Brazil it covers about 7.8 million sq km (3 million sq mi).

[3] LANGUAGE

The great diversity of Amerindian languages is partly due to the lifestyle of peoples sometimes living at considerable distances from each other, in this way developing distinct mythologies, religious customs, and languages. Even quite small groups such as the Kayapos are divided into smaller tribes with their own chiefs, although they all speak the Kayapo language. Thanks to some work by anthropologists and travelers (including several visits to the Kayapos by the pop star Sting, who made their struggles known to a wider world), we know the names of several Kayapo chiefs. One of these is Raoni, who left his Amazon homeland for a time and traveled widely with Sting. Another Kayapo who traveled with him was the panther-hunter N'goire. Sting also met a powerful medicine-man called Tacuma.

4 FOLKLORE

There is an interesting legend among the Kayapos who live along a lagoon. They say that if one rises at dawn and looks across the lagoon, one can see the ghost of a White man on horseback galloping along the shore. The strange thing about the description of this ghostly rider is that he is said to wear a full suit of armor, rather like a European knight, or perhaps a Portuguese conqueror.

The Kayapos believe their ancestors learned how to live communally from social insects such as bees. This is why mothers and children paint each other's bodies with patterns that look like animal markings, including those of bees.

The flamboyant Kayapo headdress with feathers radiating outward represents the universe. Its shaft is a symbol for the cotton rope by which the first Kayapo, it is said, descended from the sky. Kayapo fields and villages are built in a circle to reflect the Kayapo belief in a round universe.

5 RELIGION

As opposed to the beliefs that some missionaries have brought to the Amazon, including the idea that after death people either descend into Hell or rise up to Heaven, the Kayapos believe that at death a person goes to the village of the dead, where people sleep during the day and hunt at night. There, old people become younger and children become older. In that village in the afterlife, Kayapos believe they have their own traditional assembly building. Kayapo women, it is thought, are permitted only short visits to deliver food to their male relatives.

6 MAJOR HOLIDAYS

Special days for the Kayapos revolve around the seasons, which in the Amazon are the dry season and the rainy season. Kayapo holidays are also linked to their ceremonies, such as the initiation rites held when a boy reaches puberty or when he receives, as a small boy, his special ancestral name. The important dry-season celebration called *Bemp* (after a local fish) also includes marriage rites as well as initiation and naming ceremonies. Kayapos do not divide their time into secular and religious occasions: all events are linked in unifying ways, and the religious, natural, social, and festive elements are interconnected.

7 RITES OF PASSAGE

When children are born, the marriage ties between a husband and wife are formalized. A man may have two or three wives. Young children receive special ancestral names in ceremonies that are regarded as an important means of helping the child develop social ties and his or her identity as a Kayapo. The naming ceremonies are held in each dry or rainy season, along with other rites which include special dances or ceremonies related to the crops the Kayapos grow.

8 INTERPERSONAL RELATIONS

The Kayapos have a traditionally hospitable way of greeting visitors to their homes. Food will be prepared by the women, and a bed made of bamboo will be laid out for a guest. On occasions body paint will be worn (usually geometric designs in black or red paint), and adornments such as shell earrings or brightly colored feathers are worn to decorate the head.

Ceremonial life is very important and continues year-round. Kayapos are often in the midst of a ceremony or making preparations for the next one.

9 LIVING CONDITIONS

The Kayapos live in thatched-roof huts which have an open plan without room divisions inside. The thatch for the roofs is made of palm leaves. The huts are quite roomy and large enough for an entire family. Instead of using mattresses, the bedding usually consists of hammocks, which are much cooler and more comfortable in a jungle environment.

Health protection in the jungle areas where the Kayapos live is achieved through the use of roots and herbs that have medicinal qualities, some of which have been known to the Kayapos for a long time. The Kayapos also have their medicine-men, whom White people sometimes call "witch-doctors."

For transport the Kayapos use canoes to travel long distances in the Amazon. They can also trek for days or weeks at a time. In recent years, road tracks and an airstrip have been built leading out of the Xingu River reservation where they live.

10 FAMILY LIFE

Teenage women of the village are prime candidates for marriage. They usually select partners suggested by their families. Only after the birth of a child is the marriage formalized. Traditional birth control has been discouraged in recent years in order to increase the tribe's numbers.

The Kayapos live in villages in large family groups. The women harvest the family's garden for vegetables. They also prepare body paint with the help of their children. Color dyes are created from mixed fruits and charcoal. There will usually be between two and three wives to every husband, and they will usually have several children each. The men hunt and fish.

11 CLOTHING

Traditionally men cover their lower abdomen with sheaths. The most striking ornamental addition to their attire is a light wooden lip disk which is about 6 cm (2.4 in) in diameter and which stretches their lower lip out to produce the Kayapos' extraordinary and very distinctive appearance. The usage of the lip disk is dying out among the younger men, who find it uncomfortable. More-modern, younger men often wear Western-style shorts. This is due to increasing contact with more-Westernized Brazilians who have come to the Amazon to clear the forest in logging activities or for farming, as well as gold-mining.

A Kayapo chief wears many hats, and also ceremonial feathers as part of his headdress. A headdress made out of bright golden-yellow feathers can look like the rays of the sun: a brilliant crown circling the head. Particular family links are indicated by the use of matching parrot feathers. The feathers signify initiation into adulthood. Other ornaments include beads, cotton bands, or shells, which women also wear.

Girls and boys wear colored cloth bands of various colors such as blue, yellow, or orange, which are tied and sometimes knotted below the waist. Sometimes these colored bands of cloth are also worn crisscrossed across the chest. They also wear ornaments such as beaded necklaces made up of many strands, and wristbands, as well as armbands worn high up towards the shoulder. Occasionally boys also wear knee bands just below the knee. Young Kayapos are usually barefoot, but with greater contact with White settlers some Kayapo chiefs occasionally wear Western-style thonged rubber sandals.

Body paint is an important addition for men and women as well as for children, but it is not a casual form of make-up, and the specific markings and occasions for wearing it are linked to particular rituals and activities.

12 FOOD

Fish is a main source of protein in the Kayapos' diet. Wild fruits and Brazil nuts are eaten. Vegetables are harvested, and animals such as the coati, the monkey, and the turtle are hunted. Some of these animals are eaten more often during festivals. Kayapos are skilled hunters who use blowguns and darts dipped in a type of poison called curare, which instantly paralyzes an animal.

Due to greater contact with White society, Kayapos are changing their diet and can now purchase rice, beans, cookies, sugar, and milk from village stores which have cropped up in various parts of the Amazon to supply loggers, miners, and farmers. Supplies are usually flown in to frontier towns which are not far from the Xingu Reservation where the Kayapos live.

13 EDUCATION

Most Kayapos have continued to teach their young people the skills necessary to survive in the jungle environment, especially hunting and fishing, as well as the art of trekking, and the making of canoes and the skill to use them. Growing vegetables, beading, and body paint preparations, as well as cooking, are skills Kayapo girls are expected to know. In some cases missionaries arriving in the Xingu River area have attempted to offer a more Western-style education, including reading and writing, but many Kayapos have been extremely wary of accepting this type of schooling out of fear that their children will be lost to them and will forget traditional skills.

More recently at a meeting post in a protected area of the Xingu Reservation known as Leonardo (named after a famous Brazilian anthropologist, Leonardo Villas-Boas, who together with his brother tried to help many Amazon Indians), a school has been set up to teach children from various tribes. They learn reading, writing, and arithmetic and receive information about the ways of White people.

14 CULTURAL HERITAGE

Completing a full cycle of festivals is essential to Kayapo culture. Singing, chanting, and dancing are an important part of Kayapo life. The men and women also sing as they go out on a hunt or work the land. They use a type of rattle or *maraca* and sticks to beat rhythms.

15 WORK

Gold-mining, an activity in which many Kayapos were pressured into taking part when the gold rush began in the Amazon in recent years, is hard and often dangerous work. The mercury used in mining pollutes the rivers. The Kayapos are organized into family groups with chiefs who have come together to defend their interests and to find ways of confronting the problems posed not only by mining, but also by the arrival of people who do not appreciate the delicate ecological balance of the Amazon region, which the Kayapos and other tribes have helped maintain during hundreds or perhaps even thousands of years.

The Kayapo chiefs arrive at decisions through a process of consensus and are helping to direct their people in a variety of activities which include harvesting nuts, fruits, and vegetables, as well as the construction of modern housing units for recently arrived settlers. This newer source of work means that the Kayapos no longer restrict themselves just to traditional hunting and fishing, and because they now earn some money for their work they can purchase goods they did not have before.

Some Kayapos have begun to have more contact with White people, but the modern way of life still can seem very bizarre to them. The English pop star Sting, and the French photographer and filmmaker Jean-Pierre Dutilleux, who made so many people aware of threats to the Amazon ecology and the difficulties of the Amerindians in that area, recount in their lively and sympathetic book, *Jungle Stories: The Fight for the Amazon,* that when Raoni, a Kayapo chief, first left his Amazon homeland to visit a Brazilian city during his long struggles to protect his people's way of life, he was amazed at the level of fear and anxiety in the city. He was also appalled to see people who had no food to eat forcing themselves to ask for money while others simply passed them by and ignored them. He concluded that money is bad and worried about the Kayapos being drawn into a cash economy.

16 SPORTS

Traditionally the Kayapos did not develop sporting skills separately from skills that were useful for work. Hunting, fishing, and trekking, for example, have now become sporting activities in White society, but in Kayapo society they are vital to the survival of the people, even though aspects of these activities are also enjoyed in their own right by the Kayapos. Some may obtain great pleasure from teaching the younger members of the tribe the early steps necessary to master these skills, while acquiring prowess in any or all of them is a source of pride.

One activity that Kayapo children enjoy is swimming along the shores of the beautiful and clear waters of the Xingu River, which at least until recently was completely unpolluted from its headwaters right up to the area where it joins the Amazon River. Some villagers who have had more contact with White people have learned to play soccer.

17 ENTERTAINMENT AND RECREATION

Storytelling is a significant aspect of Kayapo life and a means of transmitting Kayapo legends and history, as well as a way of preserving the identity of a people. It is also a form of entertainment. Mostly, however, it forms part of the rituals that give structure and meaning to the life of the Kayapos, interwoven with dance rituals and ceremonies that follow a definite cycle, linked to nature and to the changing seasons, throughout the year.

18 FOLK ART, CRAFTS, AND HOBBIES

Kayapos make beautiful beaded necklaces. Some of them are a brilliant blue or yellow. They also make bracelets and earrings using shells or stones, and headdresses made from the brightly colored feathers of various Amazon birds. The Kayapos are skilled in preparing and applying intricate designs as body paint. They weave sturdy and flexible hammocks and make their own canoes, as well as fishing and hunting implements such as spears, clubs, blow guns, arrows, and darts.

[19] SOCIAL PROBLEMS

Many activities in the Amazon threaten a way of life the Kayapos want to preserve. Poverty together with a population explosion and an unequal system of land ownership in countries such as Brazil have driven many people into the Amazon region in search of land. People use slash-and-burn agricultural methods which are unsuitable when the population density rises, because the forest cannot recover. Although the Kayapos and other Amerindian peoples of the Amazon have practiced this method of agriculture successfully for thousands of years, their numbers have been sufficiently small to allow them to move on to other areas of the rain forest, allowing regrowth of the forest to occur in the patches of fallow land. Now deforestation of the Amazon is occurring at a rapid rate, and some of this destruction is accelerated by the activities of cattle-ranchers who have also come into the Amazon. Beef is supplied in this way largely to fast-food chains in the United States. Land that is overgrazed by cattle quickly becomes completely barren.

Commercial loggers have also contributed to the destruction of the Amazon jungle by providing tropical hardwood for construction in Japan, Western Europe, and the United States. It is also used in paper products. But the level of demand is unsustainable: to keep logging at a level that would not permanently destroy large areas of the jungle, demand would have to drop sharply and protective regulations would have to be enforced. Recently efforts have been made to slow some demand and to find alternatives to tropical hardwoods in construction. The destruction of so many trees contributes to carbon dioxide pollution in the atmosphere and, therefore, to global warming.

A third threat to the sustainable way of life of the Kayapos and other tribes of the Amazon is mining. Parts of the Amazon are rich in iron ore and gold. The smelting furnaces need charcoal, and much of it is taken from irreplaceable virgin forest. The gold rush in the Amazon has created many problems for the Kayapos: frontier mining towns exist close to areas where the Kayapos and other tribes live; Amerindian groups have been affected by diseases to which they had never been exposed before; and mercury used in extracting gold from the mud of the rivers is a pollutant, resulting in mercury poisoning which affects Amerindian communities that live downstream from these mining activities. It is estimated that in 1988, 12% of the mercury released into the atmosphere was due to Amazon gold-mining.

Some Amerindian groups, including the Kayapos, have been attacked and murdered in the search for land. Others have had their land forcibly taken away, and they have had to work for very low wages in miserable conditions in some of the frontier towns. On occasion the Kayapos have attacked those they see as intruders. The delicate balance between plants, animals, and humans has already been severely upset, and the way of life of the Kayapos has been disrupted in areas they used to inhabit. The Kayapos and other Amerindians want to ensure that the Xingu area remains protected, with the support of world opinion and the Brazilian government, and does not become the target of activities that would permanently destroy their beautiful jungle habitat.

[20] BIBLIOGRAPHY

National Geographic Index. Washington, D.C.: National Geographic Society, January–June 1984.

Sting, and Jean-Pierre Dutilleux. *Jungle Stories: The Fight for the Amazon*. Paris and London: Barrie and Jenkins, 1989.

—by P. Pitchon

KITTITIANS AND NEVISIANS

PRONUNCIATION: Ki-TEE-shuns and ne-VEE-juns
LOCATION: St. Kitts and Nevis
POPULATION: About 41,000–45,000
LANGUAGE: English; English-based Creole dialect with West African and French elements
RELIGION: Anglicanism; other Protestant sects; Roman Catholicism

1 INTRODUCTION

The nation of St. Kitts and Nevis (pronounced NEE-vis) consists of two Caribbean islands separated by a narrow strait of water. (Its official name was formerly St. Christopher and Nevis.) St. Kitts, sometimes called "the mother colony of the West Indies," was the first British colony in the region. The islands have been linked administratively since colonial times, when they formed a three-member entity together with the island of Anguilla. The people of the two islands are called Kittitians (ki-TEE-shuns) and Nevisians (ne-VEE-shuns).

Columbus sighted St. Kitts and Nevis in 1493, calling Nevis *Nuestra Señora de las Nieves* ("Our Lady of the Snows") because of the white clouds encircling its highest peak, and naming St. Christopher after the patron saint of travelers (and his own patron saint as well). Like most other islands in the Caribbean, St. Kitts and Nevis received little attention from the Spanish, and European colonization did not begin until the first British colony in the West Indies was established on St. Kitts in 1623. Five years later, the British officially settled Nevis, where Captain John Smith and his men had stopped for several days in 1607 on their way to what would become the colony of Virginia.

The French soon followed the British, and the two nations competed for control of the islands. First, however, they joined forces to exterminate the native Carib population, 2,000 of whom were slaughtered on St. Kitts in a massacre at Bloody Point in 1626, after which their presence on the island was effectively over. The contest for European control of the islands continued until both were ceded to the British under the Treaty of Paris in 1783. Two famous 18th-century figures associated with the island of Nevis were US statesman Alexander Hamilton, who was born there, and British war hero Lord Horatio Nelson, who spent time there as a colonial administrator and married a woman born on the island.

Under the British, sugarcane plantations flourished on both islands, supported by the labor of slaves from West Africa. Typically, an aspiring plantation owner would purchase 20 slaves to clear his land, plant a variety of crops, and build their own huts. When the plantation had expanded sufficiently in terms of both land and numbers of slaves, all of the land would be turned over to sugar production. After 1834, when the British empire abolished slavery, the sugar industry declined in spite of the introduction of indentured servants from East India and other countries. The increasing production of sugar from beets contributed to this trend.

By the beginning of the 20th century, the United States and Europe were producing almost all their own sugar, and the economies of St. Kitts and Nevis were floundering. In the 1930s the British-appointed Moyne Commission investigated conditions in the region, but most of its recommendations were delayed by the onset of World War II. Both St. Kitts and Nevis sent soldiers to fight alongside the British and, in addition, raised funds for the purchase of two Spitfires for Britain's Royal Air Force.

After several different administrative arrangements in the course of the 19th century, St. Kitts, Nevis, and Anguilla were united within a larger Leeward Islands Federation in 1882. From 1958 to 1962, the islands joined the short-lived Federation of the West Indies and in 1967 accepted associated statehood from Britain. Eventually Anguilla withdrew from the federation, and St. Kitts and Nevis achieved full independence on 19 September 1983. Nevis has its own legislative assembly and retains a constitutional right to secede from St. Kitts if the move is supported by a two-thirds majority in a public referendum.

2 LOCATION AND HOMELAND

St. Kitts and Nevis belong to the Leeward Islands, in the Lesser Antilles. Separated from each other by a 3-km (2-mi) strait called The Narrows, they are 300 km (186 mi) southeast of Puerto Rico and 113 km (70 mi) south of Anguilla, with which they were formerly united politically. The country has a total land area of 269 sq km (104 sq mi), about 1.5 times the size of Washington, DC. The oval island of St. Kitts, with its elongated southeast peninsula, and the small, rounded island of Nevis have often been compared to a cricket bat and ball, a reference to the island's national sport. Covering 168 sq km (65 sq mi), St. Kitts is the larger of the two islands and home to the capital city of Basseterre. It has a central mountain range with the country's highest elevation, Mt. Liamuiga, a dormant volcano that rises to 1,157 m (3,792 ft) above sea level. Rain forests are found on the higher mountains, while the fertile but drier lowlands along the coast mostly support sugarcane plantations. Erosion is a problem in certain areas due to faulty agricultural practices, including overgrazing, lack of crop rotation, and inadequate intercropping. Basseterre, the nation's capital city and chief port, is located on the southwestern coast of St. Kitts.

The southeast peninsula of St. Kitts is mostly scrub-covered and contains a large salt pond at its southern end. The former isolation of this area from the rest of the island was significantly reduced by the opening of the Dr. Kennedy Simmonds Highway in 1990. The nearly circular island of Nevis has as its most outstanding feature Nevis Peak, rising to 985 m (3,232 ft) at its center. Like St. Kitts, it has forested mountains in its interior and low-lying areas along the coast. Its soil is less fertile than that of St. Kitts and more badly damaged by erosion. Charlestown is Nevis's only town.

Population estimates for St. Kitts and Nevis range from 41,000 to 45,000, of which 9,000 to 10,000 inhabitants are estimated to live on Nevis and the rest on St. Kitts. The country experienced negative population growth between 1985 and 1993 due to emigration. About 95% of the population is of African descent. The remainder have mixed-race, East Indian, or European ancestry.

3 LANGUAGE

The official language of St. Kitts and Nevis is English, which is spoken in its standard form with correct grammar in formal sit-

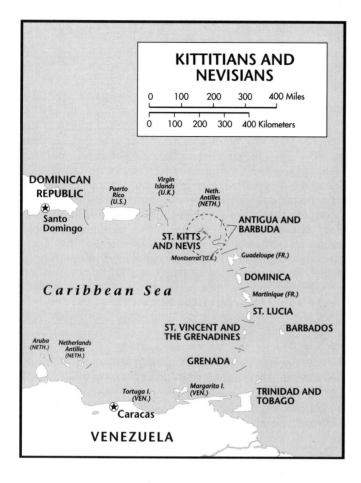

KITTITIANS AND NEVISIANS

0   100   200   300   400 Miles

0   100   200   300   400 Kilometers

uations and with people one does not know well. Informally, however, most residents speak a local English-based Creole dialect with elements from West African languages and French. In common with other West Indian Creole languages, it interchanges subject and object pronouns and expresses past actions with present-tense verbs ("I tell she" for "I told her"). Also, the African-influenced "de" is used in place of "the."

4 FOLKLORE

Like other West Indians, Kittitians and Nevisians tend toward the superstitious, and some still fear the African-influenced black magic called *obeah* that is common to the Caribbean region.

5 RELIGION

Between 33% and 50% of the country's population is Anglican. Other Protestant groups include Methodists, Moravians, Baptists, Seventh-Day Adventists, the Church of God, and the Pilgrim Holiness Church. There is a Roman Catholic minority of about 10%, and the Baha'i religion is also represented.

6 MAJOR HOLIDAYS

Public holidays in St. Kitts and Nevis include New Year's Day (1 January), Good Friday, Labor Day (1 May), Whit Monday, Bank Holiday (first Monday in August), Independence Day (19 September), Prince of Wales's Birthday (14 November), Christmas (25 December), and Boxing Day (26 December). St.

Kitts's annual Carnival celebration is held the last week of the year—from 25 December through 2 January—with the masquerades, calypso and steel band music, and street dancing common to Carnival festivities in the Caribbean. Nevis's Carnival, called Culturama, is held in late July and early August and includes arts and crafts and talent shows in addition to the usual features.

7 RITES OF PASSAGE

Major life transitions, such as birth, marriage, and death, are marked by religious celebrations appropriate to each Kittitian's and Nevisian's faith community.

8 INTERPERSONAL RELATIONS

There is a local handshake called a "bump," which consists of two people clenching their hands into fists and bumping them gently together. "Liming," a term used throughout the Caribbean to denote relaxing and "hanging out," is an especially popular pursuit in St. Kitts and Nevis, which is known for its easygoing lifestyle.

9 LIVING CONDITIONS

Until the 1970s, the typical islander's house was wooden with a corrugated metal roof, often painted red. The houses themselves were often painted in pastel colors. Today, most houses are built from concrete blocks and wood; roofs are still corrugated metal. It is becoming more common for islanders to own the land on which they live, and houses are no longer built on piles of stones in case they had to be moved.

St. Kitts and Nevis has a healthy climate with virtually no tropical disease. However, until the 1990s, high rates of malnutrition and infant mortality posed problems; in recent years, there has been a significant reduction in infant mortality rates. Sanitation conditions in the country are good, and the Pan American Health Organization reported that almost the entire population had access to safe water by 1983. There are three hospitals on St. Kitts and one on Nevis, and there is about 1 physician for every 1,000 people. The average life expectancy in 1993 was 68 years.

The country has a good road network with main roads circling each island. However, drainage ditches called "ghauts" pose an ongoing challenge to motorists, and "watch de ghaut" is a common expression on the islands. There is a state-run motorboat service between St. Kitts and Nevis. The capital city of Basseterre has a deep-water port that can accommodate cargo vessels and cruise ships. St. Kitts has an international airport, while Nevis's airstrip handles only small charter planes.

10 FAMILY LIFE

Family loyalty is strong, and it is not uncommon to find extended households including members of two or three generations.

11 CLOTHING

People on St. Kitts and Nevis take great pride in their appearance, wearing modern Western-style clothing that is generally spotless and in excellent condition. Even for casual wear, women wear mostly skirts or dresses and also avoid wearing pants in the workplace. Men wear jeans or casual slacks, and male business attire generally includes a shirt and tie or at least a button-down shirt, called a shirt jack. Fashion-consciousness on the islands is especially in evidence on weekends, which are considered occasions for dressing up rather than down. School children wear uniforms.

12 FOOD

Dietary staples include yams, plantains, rice and peas, saltfish, stuffed crab back, and a variety of soups, including pumpkin, bean, pepperpot, and fish soups and conch chowder. Lime juice is a common seasoning, and hot pepper sauce made from Scotch Bonnet peppers is a specialty on Nevis. Carib beer is a favorite beverage, and sweet cassava bread—derived from the African *bammie*—is a popular dessert.

Cassava Bread

½ pound cassava, finely grated
3 to 4 ounces grated coconut
½ cup brown sugar
1 teaspoon salt

Salt the grated cassava, wrap in a cloth, and twist to wring out the liquid. In a heavy baking pan, spread out half the cassava and top with brown sugar and grated coconut. Cover with the remaining cassava. Using both hands, push down on the mixture. Preheat oven to 350°F and bake 20 minutes.

13 EDUCATION

Education was formerly provided by the islands' churches, whose generous funding and strict attendance requirements created high standards of schooling that were perpetuated by the government when it took over the educational system. Today the adult literacy rate on St. Kitts and Nevis is 98%, among the highest in the Western Hemisphere. Primary education in St. Kitts and Nevis (ages 5 to 14) is free and compulsory. There are over 30 primary schools and 8 secondary schools.

There is no university on either island, but post-secondary education is offered at a teachers' training college, a technical college, a nursing school, and a one-year academic program whose completion allows enrollment as a second-year student at the University of the West Indies. The government of St. Kitts and Nevis has focused increasingly on vocational education to reduce the country's high unemployment rate and produce more effective and motivated workers.

14 CULTURAL HERITAGE

The first annual St. Kitts Music Festival was held in July 1996. Featuring a variety of music, from reggae to gospel, it was attended by an estimated 15,000 people. On Nevis, the Drama and Cultural Society sponsors an annual play and other cultural events. Nevis's best-known artist is Dame Eva Wilkin—now well over 80 years of age—who portrays the island's people and way of life in pastels and watercolors.

15 WORK

Over 33% of the labor force is engaged in agriculture, and the country's main employer is the sugar industry. It is not unusual for islanders to have more than one source of income, including fishing, selling produce grown on small garden plots, and doing seasonal or part-time work in the sugarcane fields or the tourist industry. Wages in the sugar industry are very low, and sugar producers have had to import labor from neighboring St. Vincent and Guyana because of the difficulty of finding enough local workers, in spite of unemployment rates estimated at between 20% and 25%. Working in the sugarcane fields under a tropical sun is also notoriously grueling. The junglelike clumps of sugarcane, growing 3 m (10 ft) tall, may be infested with insects or rats. Laborers cut into the cane at its base using an implement called a machete. Then they must trim the tops, divide the stalks into smaller lengths, stack them, and clear the debris.

In the 1970s and 1980s, nearly 20% of the population emigrated every year—mostly to the United States, Canada, or Great Britain—in search of better employment opportunities. (The money sent home by emigrants has been a major source of income on the islands, and some experts speculate that it has surpassed the sum earned at home in wages and salaries.) One factor cited in connection with the country's high rate of unemployment is that much of the labor force lacks the employment skills to make the transition from agricultural work to better-paying jobs in the service sector.

16 SPORTS

Cricket is the national sport of St. Kitts and Nevis, and the whole country virtually shuts down for a major match, especially one between teams from the Windward and Leeward Islands. St. Kitts and Nevis has produced such world-class players as Elquemedo Willet, Derrick Parry, and Luther Kelly. The second-most-popular sports are horse-racing on Nevis, and footbal (soccer) of St. Kitts. Horse races are held on holidays including New Year's Day and Labor Day, and even on the religious holidays of Easter Monday and Whit Monday. They are also part of the festivities during such special events as the country's annual Culturama.

17 ENTERTAINMENT AND RECREATION

Music is central to entertainment on St. Kitts and Nevis, and favorite bands become a focal point of conversation for days before and after an appearance on one of the islands. Steel drum, dance-hall, string band, and reggae music are all popular.

18 FOLK ART, CRAFTS, AND HOBBIES

St. Kitts's well-known folk dance troupe, Masquerades, performs a variety of traditional dances from the French-derived *kwadril* to African war dances. The islands' crafts include batiked clothing and wall hangings made from the sea island cotton that has traditionally been Nevis's principal export. Nevisian craftspeople are also known for their fine pottery.

19 SOCIAL PROBLEMS

The country's continued reliance on the sugar industry has made its economy vulnerable to the ups and downs of that volatile commodity, upon which both the agricultural and manufacturing sectors rely for a large percentage of their earnings.

20 BIBLIOGRAPHY

Cameron, Sarah, and Ben Box, ed. *Caribbean Islands Handbook.* Chicago: Passport Books, 1995.
Gall, Timothy, and Susan Gall, ed. *Worldmark Encyclopedia of the Nations.* 8th ed. Detroit: Gale Research, 1995.

Haggerty, Richard A., and John F. Hornbeck. "St. Christopher and Nevis." In *Islands of the Commonwealth Caribbean: A Regional Study,* edited by Sandra W. Meditz and Dennis M. Hanratty. Washington, DC: US Government, 1989.

Harms, Mike. "Nurturing Conservation Naturally in the Twin Isles." *Americas* (March–April 1993): 22.

"Kittsians and Nevisians." In *Encyclopedia of World Cultures* (*Middle America and the Caribbean*). Boston: G. K. Hall, 1992.

Luntta, Karl. *Caribbean Handbook.* Chico, CA: Moon Publications, 1995.

Maxson, Michael. Interview by the editors, 22 July 1996.

Simmonds, Keith C. "Political and Economic Factors Influencing the St. Kitts-Nevis Polity: An Historical Perspective." *Phylon* 48, No. 4 (Winter 1987): 277–86.

Walton, Chelle Koster. *Caribbean Ways: A Cultural Guide.* Westwood, MA: Riverdale, 1993.

Yeadon, David. "St. Kitts-Nevis." In *Insight Guides. Caribbean: The Lesser Antilles,* edited by David Schwab. Boston: Houghton Mifflin, 1996.

—by R. Wieder, reviewed by A. K. Jules

KOREAN AMERICANS

For more information on Korean history and culture, *see* **Vol. 3: Korean Chinese; South Koreans**.

OVERVIEW

The first Koreans arrived in the US in the early 1900s. A total of 7,226 Korean exiles and laborers immigrated to the US between January 1903 and July 1907. The exiles were leaders of a failed coup attempt, including So Chae-pil (1866–1951), who later changed his name to Philip Jaisohn and became the first Korean American medical doctor; Ahn Chang-ho (1878–1938); Park Yong-man (1881–1928); and Syngman Rhee (1875–1965). These four became leaders of the Korean American community and helped create a Korean national independence movement in the US.

Most of the early immigrants from Korea, however, were agricultural laborers. They were recruited to work on the sugar cane plantations of Hawaii after Congress passed the Chinese Exclusion Acts in the late 1800s, barring any more Chinese workers from entering the US. Many of these Korean laborers soon left the plantations and began small businesses of their own. About 2,000 moved to California and started up small farms or retail stores there.

The first wave of Korean immigration included over 1,200 women and children, so there was a sizeable number of families among the early Korean American population. However, single men still outnumbered single women by a significant margin, leaving many unattached men with no prospects for marriage or family. Between 1910 and 1924, some 1,100 Korean "picture brides" arrived in the US to marry Korean workers. The brides and grooms had been introduced to each other through letters and photos (some of which grossly misrepresented the truth). The women were often better educated than the men. By establishing families and adding their well-educated wisdom to the mix, these women helped stabilize and energize the Korean American community.

Korean Americans suffered from the discrimination leveled at all Asian Americans in the early to mid-20th century. Antimiscegenation laws prevented them from marrying European Americans, and the Alien Land Law of 1913 barred them from owning land. European Americans refused to admit them to schools, give them jobs, or allow them to live in certain neighborhoods. Many Korean and other Asian Americans were injured and even killed by racially motivated violence.

Despite sometimes brutal prejudice, however, Korean Americans continued to survive as a community in the US. They also continued to pour their energies into the Korean nationalist movement until Korea won its independence from Japan in 1945. Syngman Rhee then returned to Korea and was elected president of the Republic of Korea (South Korea) in 1948.

The second wave of Korean immigration to the US occurred after the Korean War in the early 1950s. US military personnel brought back Korean women they had married while stationed in Korea, and many US families adopted Korean war orphans. Between 1951 and 1964, some 6,500 Korean women ("war brides") and 6,300 adopted Korean children entered the US. Korean students also began to come in greater numbers to study at American universities, and Korean doctors arrived to further their medical training.

The latest wave of Korean immigration to the US began after Congress passed the Immigration and Naturalization Act of 1965, which allowed entire families to immigrate at once, and granted Korean students and professionals the right to apply for US citizenship. These new citizens, along with the Korean wives of US military personnel (who automatically became US citizens upon their marriage), then applied for permanent residency status for their parents, siblings, spouses, and children. Most of the US immigrants from Korea since 1970 have been close relatives of already established Korean American citizens or permanent residents.

The 1990 US Census estimated the Korean American population at 750,000, but many think it may actually be as high as one million or more. Korean Americans live in communities across the US, with the majority in California. The states of New York, Illinois, New Jersey, Texas, Maryland, Virginia, and Washington also have significant Korean American communities. Although "Koreatowns" developed in Los Angeles and other large cities, for the most part Korean Americans have not settled in ethnic enclaves but rather are scattered throughout US cities, towns, and villages. In fact, Korean Americans are the most widely dispersed of any Asian American population.

Many Korean Americans, even those who have lived in the US for more than one or two generations, continue to speak Korean at home and with other Korean Americans. The same language is spoken throughout North and South Korea (although accents differ from region to region), making it possible for all Korean-speaking Korean Americans to understand one another. A very simple phonetic alphabet was created in the 15th century to replace an extremely complicated set of ideographs. The new alphabet allowed nearly all Korean speakers to become literate. Koreans today continue to have one of the highest literacy rates in the world, at over 95%.

Korean names are usually made up of three syllables: the first is the family name, the second is the generational name, and the last is the personal name (sometimes the order of the generational and personal names is reversed). Because family names customarily come *last* in the US, Korean Americans are often addressed incorrectly. Even when they reverse the traditional order of their names to conform to American conventions, they are often met with confusion because their family names resemble common American personal names (such as "Kim" and "Lee," two of the most common Korean family names).

For centuries, Koreans followed the teachings of Confucius. Although mainly Buddhist today, South Korea remains one of the most Confucian of all Asian countries. Many Korean Americans have become Christian (particularly Protestant), yet they are still strongly influenced by traditional Confucian beliefs. Korean Confucianism emphasizes family responsibility and interdependence, along with respect for one's elders. It also places a high value on hierarchies of authority, which is expressed in the structures of most Korean American organizations and businesses.

About 75% of Korean American families are affiliated with a Christian church, and some 65% attend services regularly. Churches serve many purposes, both sacred and secular, in Korean American communities. For example, information regarding housing and employment opportunities is shared;

Korean American boy at Korean Day Parade in New York City. (Richard B. Levine. Levine & Roberts Stock Photography)

English language classes are offered to foreign-born Korean Americans, and Korean language classes are available for those born in America, and social events provide a chance for widely dispersed Korean Americans to come together as a community. In the first half of the 20th century, churches became the headquarters for the Korean national independence movement. Perhaps most importantly, churches have served as a replacement for the traditional extended family that was often lost in the move from Korea to the US.

Since Congress passed the Immigration and Naturalization Act of 1965, which allowed more Korean family members and entire family groups to enter the US, the extended family has been able to regain some of its traditional strength as the center of society among Korean Americans. Extended family groups, which include families of friends, can once again provide Korean Americans with the physical, emotional, and financial support they need in their new home.

Many Korean Americans continue to eat traditional foods at home. Traditional Korean food is also available at Korean restaurants in some cities, but Korean food has yet to become as popular or widely available as Chinese food in the US.

About one-third of all Korean Americans who are employed own their own businesses. In 1990, Korean Americans had the highest business ownership rate of all ethnic groups in the US. Language and cultural barriers make it difficult for foreign-born Korean Americans to find jobs with other employers, so it is often easier for them to start their own businesses. Korean Americans also like the independence and control of running one's own business.

When Jewish, Italian, and Irish business owners in the inner cities began selling their shops to move to the suburbs during the 1970s and 1980s, Korean Americans took advantage of the opportunities and bought many of the businesses. Racial tensions, crime, and inner-city poverty have made life difficult, however, for the new Korean American owners. Particularly devastating were the Los Angeles riots that erupted on 29 April 1992 and lasted for four days. In the violence and confusion, about 2,300 Korean American businesses were looted or burned. Korean American business owners suffered some $500 million in damage (half of the total estimated damage losses in Los Angeles County). Recovery has been slow in the Korean American community; by February 1993, only 28% of the damaged or destroyed businesses had been reopened.

As a result of the Los Angeles riots, Korean Americans lost faith in American society, and they are now struggling to rebuild their trust in their neighbors. Fortunately, Korean Americans have their extended families, churches, and community organizations to turn to for support. They can also turn to a centuries-old Korean organization called the *kye*, a rotating credit system that also provides emotional support and friendship to its members. A *kye* consists of 12–20 members who each contribute an agreed-upon amount (anywhere from less than $100 to several thousand dollars) to the pot each month. Every month, a different member is given the collective pot, until each member has had a turn. Then the *kye* disbands. *Kyes* have provided the means for many Korean Americans to open businesses, finance higher education, and survive sudden unexpected crises. Since the Los Angeles riots, they have offered a place of financial and emotional security to battered Korean American shop owners.

When Koreans began entering the US in family groups after 1965, the Korean American population came to be divided along generational lines: the *il-se*, or first generation of adult immigrants; the *il-jom-o-se*, or one-point-five (1.5) generation, consisting of the *il-se*'s foreign-born children, and the *i-se*, or second generation, made up of those born subsequently in the US. Generation gaps exist between each of these groups, with the *il-se* embedded in traditional Korean ways, the *i-se* growing up thoroughly American, and the *il-jom-o-se* stumbling between the two worlds. Conflicts and misunderstandings continually arise among members of the various generations, creating a great deal of tension in families as well as in the larger Korean American community.

BIBLIOGRAPHY

Barringer, Herbert R. *Koreans in the United States: A Fact Book.* Honolulu, Hawaii: Center for Korean Studies, University of Hawaii, 1989.

Hyun, Peter. *In the New World: The Making of a Korean American.* Honolulu: University of Hawaii Press, 1995.

Kim, Nan. "Who Are the Korean Americans?" In *The Asian American Almanac,* Susan Gall, ed. Detroit: Gale Research, 1995.

Mangiafico, Luciano. *Contemporary American Immigrants: Patterns of Filipino, Korean, and Chinese Settlement in the United States.* New York: Praeger, 1988.

Melendy, Howard Brett. *Asians in America: Filipinos, Koreans, and East Indians.* New York: Hippocrene, 1981.

Min, Pyong Gap. *Caught in the Middle: Korean Merchants in America's Multiethnic Cities.* Berkeley: University of California Press, 1996.

Pang, Keum Young Ching. *Korean Elderly Women in America: Everyday Life, Health, and Illness.* New York: AMS Press, 1991.

Park, Andrew Sung. *Racial Conflict and Healing: An Asian-American Theological Perspective.* New York: Orbis Books, 1996.

—by D. K. Daeg de Mott

LAOTIAN AMERICANS

For more information on Laotian history and culture, *see* **Vol. 3: Lao**.

OVERVIEW

Prior to 1975, only a very few Laotians migrated to the US. After Vietnam and Laos fell to Communist forces in 1975, however, thousands of Laotians fled their wartorn homeland and applied for entry to the US. With the Indochina Migration and Refugee Assistance Act of 1975, the US gave Laotians refugee status and helped them relocate to America. At first, most of the refugees were government administrators, shopkeepers, and royal army soldiers. Later immigrants tended to be less educated, including farmers and small villagers. Only about 800 Laotian refugees immigrated to the US in 1975, but the following year brought 10,200. The highest numbers of Laotian refugees entered the US in the years between 1979-1981, totalling about 105,000. Since then, Laotian refugee resettlement has continued, though at a much slower pace.

The total Laotian American population in the US in 1990, according to the US Census, was about 150,000. The majority of Laotian Americans live in California, primarily in Fresno, San Diego, Sacramento, and Stockton. Other US states with significant Laotian American populations are Texas, Minnesota, and Washington. Although few Laotians in Laos live in cities, Laotian Americans are largely urban dwellers. Over 95% of foreign-born Laotian Americans lived in urban areas in 1990. Lacking language and industrial job skills, Laotian Americans tend to settle in large cities where they can find work that requires neither.

On average, Laotian Americans are younger than the US population as a whole. This is true for recent refugee populations in general, as only the young are willing and able to leave their homelands for such a risky journey. Laotian Americans also tend to have large families, adding to the youthfulness of their overall population.

The Laotian language is tonal, which means that the meaning of a word depends on the tone in which it is spoken (for example, high, low, rising, etc.). Laotian is written with a phonetic alphabet based on an ancient writing system from India. Laotian is therefore quite different from English in both its spoken and written forms, making English language proficiency quite difficult for Laotian Americans to achieve.

Laotian folklore is often in the form of poetry and is sung to the accompaniment of a hand-held bamboo pipe organ called a *khene*. Many of these poetic tales are told through theater or opera productions, known as *maw lam*. Among the most popular Laotian folktales are those involving Xieng Mieng, a trickster figure. Others are taken from Buddhist writings. Laotian Americans continue to tell these stories at community gatherings, through *maw lam* productions.

Laotian Americans also continue to teach their children Laotian proverbs, which are filled with age-old wisdom, such as "Water a stump and you'll get nothing"; "Speech is silver, silence is gold"; and "It's easy to find friends who will eat with you, but hard to find one who will die with you."

Though some Laotian Americans have converted to Protestant Christianity, most are Buddhists of the Southern School, also known as Theravada Buddhism. Theravada Buddhists emphasize the importance of becoming a monk and achieving *Nirvana* (eternal bliss) by one's own efforts, rather than relying on the help of *Bodhisattvas*, enlightened beings, as is encouraged by the Northern School (or Mahayana Buddhism). Reincarnation and the concept of *Karma* are central to Buddhist beliefs. Laotians also retain a belief in spirits from their ancient, pre-Buddhist days.

Most Laotian Americans, when possible, continue to perform traditional Laotian ceremonies and rites of passage. The lack of available Laotian monks and temples in the US can make this difficult, however. Two Buddhist holidays celebrated by all Buddhist Laotian Americans are *Pha Vet*, held in the fourth lunar month to commemorate the life of the Buddha and *Boon Bang Fay*, or "rocket festival," held in the sixth lunar month. *Boon Bang Fay* festivities include setting off fireworks.

Laotian American communities are very tightly knit, and everyone knows how and what everyone else is doing. Members of the community treat each other with great familiarity, addressing one another respectfully by first name, rather than last. For example, Khamsang Phoumvihane would be addressed as "Mr. Khamsang" rather than "Mr. Phoumvihane."

As recent immigrants, most Laotian Americans lack the necessary English language and relevant job skills to be successful in the American work world. Therefore, there is a high rate of unemployment and a corresponding rate of poverty among Laotian Americans. About one out of every three Laotian Americans lived below the poverty line in 1990. Public assistance eases the situation somewhat, but living conditions remain harsh for the majority of Laotian Americans. Compared to the life-threatening conditions they left in Laos, however, even poverty in America is seen as a great improvement by most Laotian Americans.

Laotian Americans suffer the physical and mental health problems common to recent refugees, including culture shock, post-traumatic stress disorder, insomnia, and other stress-related illnesses. Although traditional Laotian healing methods involve the use of massage and herbal medicines and rituals to address the spiritual causes of illness, Laotian Americans are more likely to turn to mainstream Western medicine to treat their ailments.

In Laos, men deal with the public world, and women manage the household. For Laotian Americans, however, the need to support the family financially under difficult circumstances has led many women to find employment outside the home. Because the women are now working at outside employment, Laotian American men have taken to sharing the household responsibilities as well. Positions of leadership in Laotian American community organizations are still usually held by men, but women are beginning to take a more active public role in the community at large.

Laotian Americans tend to live in nuclear family units, located close by members of their extended family. Families are important, both for social and emotional support as well as financial support. Divorce is rare among Laotian Americans, and families are large (5.01 members on average in 1990, as compared to 3.06 members in the average European American family). Dating is new to foreign-born Laotian Americans; in Laos, young people simply get to know one another through the regular course of daily village life. Foreign-born Laotian American parents, therefore, have difficulties accepting and guiding their children through the dating process.

On special occasions or at cultural celebrations, some Laotian American women wear traditional dress, consisting of a brocade skirt (*sinh*) held in place by a belt of shiny metal buckles or rings, and a shawl draped over the left shoulder and under the right arm. Laotian American men rarely wear their traditional dress, which includes baggy pants called *sampot*.

Many Laotian Americans still eat traditional Laotian foods at home. Most meals include rice or rice noodles, and all the food is spicy. Thai restaurants serve Laotian dishes in the US, and areas with large Laotian American communities have Lao markets where traditional ingredients may be purchased.

Older, foreign-born Laotian Americans tend to lack formal schooling. About one-third (34%) of those over the age of 25 have less than a fifth-grade education. Only 40% have a high school diploma, and a mere 5% have a college degree. Young Laotian Americans are generally succeeding quite well in school, although the drop-out rate is still rather high: 12.2% of Laotian Americans between the ages of 16 and 19 in 1990 were not attending school, nor had they graduated (compared to 9.8% of European Americans in the same age group). Few Laotian Americans continue on to college, perhaps because their families cannot afford it.

Language barriers are also a problem: in 1990, over two-thirds (68%) of Laotian Americans over the age of five did not speak English very well. Although many English language training programs are in place for both children and adults, the English language is significantly different from Laotian in both its spoken and written forms, making the learning process quite slow.

Most Laotian Americans who manage to find employment (the unemployment rate in 1990 among Laotian Americans was 9.3%) work at jobs involving unskilled manual labor. As many as 44% of employed Laotian Americans in 1990 were classified as "operators, fabricators, and laborers."

Laotian Americans face problems common to recent refugee populations. The trauma of the desperate conditions in their former homeland that forced them to leave is still very present and immediate in their minds and hearts. Plus, the conditions in their former homeland usually have not changed a great deal, so there is fear and concern for loved ones who remained behind, with whom regular communication is often difficult or impossible. Post-traumatic stress disorders and culture shock set in shortly after they arrived in the new land that is to become their home but is as yet alien to them. Laotian Americans tend to follow the usual pattern for refugees: Their first year in the US is filled with relief at finally finding safety; the second year brings shock and feelings of helplessness as the strangeness of their new home begins to overwhelm the sense of relief, and by the third and fourth year, they are starting to adjust to their new circumstances and begin to feel at home in the US.

The first waves of Laotian immigrants are now largely adjusted to life in America, although language and cultural barriers still cause a certain degree of difficulty. More recent immigrants are still going through the adjustment period, but they now have a community of longer-standing Laotian Americans to turn to for guidance and support. American-born Laotian Americans find themselves in the troubling position of second-generation immigrants who straddle two worlds: that of their Laotian-born parents, and that of their native American society. Laotian Americans have not been in the US long enough to have produced a significant population of third generation immigrants.

BIBLIOGRAPHY

Bankston, Carl L., III. "Who Are the Laotian Americans?" In *The Asian American Almanac*, Susan Gall, ed. Detroit: Gale Research, 1995.

Haines, David W. *Refugees and Immigrants: Cambodians, Laotians, and Vietnamese in America.* Totowa, N.J.: Rowman & Littlefield, 1989.

—by D. K. Daeg de Mott

LEBANESE AMERICANS

For more information on Lebanese history and culture, see *see* **Vol. 3: Lebanese**.

OVERVIEW

A few Lebanese pioneers immigrated to America in the mid-1800s, but the first real wave of Lebanese immigration did not begin until the late 1870s. Overcrowding and a shortage of tillable land in what was then called Mount Lebanon led to poverty for many of its citizens. The only other economic opportunities available in Mount Lebanon at that time were in the small silk industry, which was failing due to competition from Japan and China, and in wine production, which was severely curtailed by a grapevine disease in the 1870s.

First-wave Lebanese immigrants to the US were mostly young men hoping to earn enough money in America to return to Lebanon and establish themselves in better circumstances there. The majority were Christian because they had been exposed to Western culture through Christian missionaries and schools and felt an affinity with the Christian West. Muslims, on the other hand, were drawn to Muslim countries in West Africa. There were no mosques in America in the 19th century.

Although the great majority of early Lebanese immigrants to the US had been farmers in Lebanon, very few took up farming in America. Young single men looking for fast cash were not interested in settling down to a long-term project like developing a farm. Neither were they interested in the industrial jobs that many other immigrants turned to, such as mining or working in steel mills or factories. Instead, they became traders, peddling their wares from door to door, at first on foot until they could afford a horse and cart. Over 90% of early Lebanese immigrants traded for at least a short time after arriving in the US.

Huge Lebanese American trading networks soon developed. Central suppliers established themselves in various areas of the country, such as Fort Wayne, Indiana. Wholesalers in New York City would purchase large shipments of goods from Lebanon then send them on to the central suppliers. The suppliers would then distribute the goods to individual peddlers to be sold door-to-door. Wholesalers and suppliers sometimes helped Lebanese immigrants pay for their passage to America and find housing once they arrived. The wholesalers and suppliers were generally honest in their dealings with new immigrants, and the immigrants were grateful for the ready employment the traders offered in return.

At first, most of the goods sold through the Lebanese American trading network were religious or handcrafted items from the Holy Land, which were very popular in America in the late 19th and early 20th centuries. Later, Lebanese American peddlers expanded their wares to include typical household items, such as pots and pans, shoelaces, kitchen knives, etc. These types of supplies were particularly welcome in rural areas where they could otherwise be obtained only by traveling a long distance to the nearest town. Some peddlers became so successful that they eventually settled down and set up permanent shops.

Lebanese immigration to America increased steadily until it became a flood in 1908, when Ottoman rulers in Lebanon became exceptionally oppressive, and the military draft was expanded to include Christians. In 1900, some 2,900 Lebanese immigrated to the US. By 1910, the number had jumped to 6,300. As Lebanon became embroiled in the international conflicts leading to World War I (1914–18), more Lebanese fled to America. Over 9,000 Lebanese came to the US in both 1913 and 1914.

Once war was declared in 1914, borders were essentially closed and Lebanese immigration to the US virtually ceased. At the end of the war in 1918, however, Lebanese immediately began leaving again for America. By 1922, the number of Lebanese immigrants to the US had reached 5,100, but this second wave of Lebanese immigration was short-lived. Swarms of immigrants from all over the world, combined with dwindling opportunities as America reached its western shore, led the US to place stringent restrictions on immigration in 1924, reducing the flow of Lebanese (and others) to a mere trickle. For the next two decades, few Lebanese entered the US. Those that did were mostly family members of Lebanese already living in America.

The end of World War II (1939–45) brought a third wave of Lebanese immigration to the US which lasted from about 1950 to the mid-1970s. These third-wave immigrants were quite different from their predecessors, however. Rather than young men looking for quick cash, third-wave Lebanese immigrants tended to be students and young professionals seeking educational and professional advancement.

The most recent wave of Lebanese immigration to the US began in 1975 when Lebanon exploded in civil war. Many of these latest immigrants are well-educated professionals with the financial resources to leave their homes. They wish to escape the wartorn environment in Lebanon, both for their own welfare and their children's. Lebanese Americans continue to send money and other goods to support family and friends who remain in Lebanon, as did the very first Lebanese immigrants to the US. Today, Lebanese Americans are beginning to band together to add their political support as well.

According to the US Census, 394,180 Americans claimed Lebanese ancestry in 1990. From the beginning, Lebanese immigrants settled all across the US. By 1919, a Lebanese American family could be found in almost every town with a population of more than 5,000. Today, Lebanese Americans remain dispersed throughout the country. The top five states in terms of numbers of Lebanese Americans are California (49,776), Michigan (39,673), New York (31,089), Massachusetts (29,700), and Ohio (27,226). Other states with sizeable Lebanese American populations include Florida (24,322), Texas (21,934), and Pennsylvania (19,234).

In order to blend in with mainstream American society, many Lebanese Americans anglicized their names. Some translated the meaning of their names into English: Haddad became Smith; Ashshi became Cook; Yusuf became Joseph. Others simply found English names with similar sounds: Sawaya became Sawyer; Tuma became Thomas; and Jirjus became George. More recent Lebanese immigrants to America tend to keep their Arabic names, now that mainstream US society is more open to multiculturalism.

Muslim Lebanese Americans have always been more likely than Christian Lebanese Americans to retain their Arabic names. Muslims are also more likely to live together in tightly knit communities centered around a mosque. When Henry Ford announced liberal hiring policies and good wages at his automobile manufacturing plant in Detroit, Michigan, in the 1920s, many Muslim Lebanese immigrants took jobs in the Ford plant and settled in Detroit and nearby Dearborn, Michigan. Both communities continue to thrive today.

Besides Christians and Muslims, there is also a small group of Druze Lebanese Americans. Lebanese Druze began immigrating to the US in the 1830s, and a school for Druze girls was opened in America in 1834. As early as 1907, a group of Druze Lebanese Americans had ventured all the way across America to form a society in Seattle, Washington.

The family is the central unit of traditional Lebanese society and it remains central to Lebanese Americans. In 1987, there were about 2,500 members of the Rashid family in America, and some 600–700 attended the US Rashid family reunion which has been held annually since 1972. The American Rashids have also developed a scholarship fund to help members of the Rashid family who remain in Lebanon.

Socializing and visiting with family and friends is also central to Lebanese, both in Lebanon and America. Lebanese American social clubs exist in almost every state in the US. They host cultural events and festivals where Lebanese Americans can gather and eat, dance, and enjoy one another's company. Young Lebanese Americans sometimes use these events as opportunities to meet potential marriage partners. Another common Lebanese American social event is the *mahrajan,* a picnic festival with food, music, and dancing. The first American *mahrajan* was held in 1930 in Bridgeport, Connecticut. Today they are held frequently all over the country.

Food is another central element in Lebanese and Lebanese American society. Lebanese cuisine is rich and varied, and some of its most common dishes, such as *felafel, kibbe,* and *tabbouleh,* have become favorites among the general American public today. Both Lebanese and non-Lebanese Americans enjoy eating at Lebanese restaurants, which can be found in many US cities.

Lebanese Americans have made many other contributions to American culture besides food. Two Lebanese American men began clothing companies in Texas in the 1920s that have since become international businesses. Mansour Farah founded the Farah men's clothier company in 1920, and J. M. Haggar founded the Haggar men's clothiers in 1926. The Haggar company is now said to be the world's largest manufacturer of men's pants. Another highly successful Lebanese American entrepreneur is Ameen Haddad, known as the "potato king" among US potato growers and wholesalers.

Lebanese Americans who have made contributions to American arts include opera singer Rosalind Elias and popular singer Paul Anka; radio and television personality Casey Kasem; actors Danny Thomas, Marlo Thomas, Jamie Farr, and Victor Tayback; woodworker Sam Maloof, whose handcrafted furniture is displayed in national museums and the White House; writer William Blatty, author of *The Exorcist;* and poet Kahlil Gibran.

Many Lebanese Americans have been elected to public office, and others have served in high-ranking public positions. Donna Shalala served as assistant secretary for policy development and research at the US Department of Housing and Urban Development from 1977–1980. Shalala then became president of Hunter College in New York City, transforming it from a struggling inner-city college to a well-respected institution. In 1987, Shalala was appointed chancellor of the University of Wisconsin in Madison. She also served as Secretary of Health and Human Services in President Bill Clinton's administration.

Philip Habib was an important US diplomat during years of crisis in the Middle East, and United Press International (UPI) reporter Helen Thomas has been a White House correspondent for many years. Consumer activist Ralph Nader ran unsuccessfully for US president in 1996, and Nader's sister, Laura Nader, is a professor of anthropology at the University of California, Berkeley. Lois DeBakey, a professor of scientific communication at Baylor College of Medicine, also has a famous brother, Dr. Michael DeBakey, who pioneered open-heart surgery.

Noted Lebanese American figures in sports include tennis player Eddie Dibs, football coach Abe Gibron, and football players Gill George and Doug Flutie (winner of the Heisman Trophy in 1984).

Christian Lebanese Americans have had very few problems since the beginning of their sojourn in the US. Hard-working and friendly, they fit in well with mainstream American society. Muslim Lebanese Americans have met with more discrimination due to their obviously different religious and cultural customs, including traditional Arab dress. Muslim Lebanese Americans are also much more likely to live in insular communities, socializing only with other Muslim Lebanese Americans. Their social isolation increases other Americans' distrust of them. As tensions and conflicts erupted in the Middle East in the 1970s, anti-Arab sentiment grew in the US, and Muslim Lebanese Americans came under greater attack. The rise of Muslim fundamentalism and associated violence in various parts of the world also contributes to non-Muslim Americans' fear of and prejudice against Muslim Lebanese Americans.

Christian Lebanese Americans have historically differentiated themselves from the rest of the Arabs, claiming closer ties with the West because of their religious affiliation. They have therefore escaped most overt discrimination in the US. Some Christian Lebanese Americans, however, have begun to support the new pan-Arab movement in the Middle East and identify themselves increasingly as Arab. With their new Arab identity, they may find themselves the object of anti-Arab discrimination and violence to which they were previously immune.

BIBLIOGRAPHY

Harik, Elsa Marston. *The Lebanese in America.* Minneapolis: Lerner Publications, 1987.

US Bureau of the Census. *Detailed Ancestry Groups for States.* 1990 Census of Population Supplementary Reports, CP-S-1-2. Washington, DC, October 1992.

—by D. K. Daeg de Mott

MATSIGENKA

LOCATION: Peru
LANGUAGE: Matsigenka, a dialect of Arawak; Spanish
RELIGION: Traditional native beliefs

1 INTRODUCTION

The Matsigenka live in southeastern Peru. They have inhabited their present territory since long before the Spanish conquest, where they have sought to live peaceably and to be left alone, being less fierce and more likely to avoid violence than the Arawakan and Panoan groups that surround them. They managed to avoid the influence of the Inca culture and the Spanish conquest, thanks to the uninhabited cloud forest that separates the highlands and the high forest.

Having said that, evidence of contacts between the forest people and those in the highlands pre-dates the Inca Empire. The Matsigenka and their neighbors traded with the highlanders, exchanging cacao, bird feathers, palm wood, cotton, and herbal medicines for stone and metal tools and bits of silver which they used in jewelry. That trade, however, took a different turn in the early 20th century, when the rubber boom and slave trade translated into Matsigenka strongmen trading their own people into slavery in exchange for shotguns and steel tools. The practice continued even after the rubber boom collapsed, as colonists still wanted laborers and household servants.

Despite some degree of dependence on Western culture (medicine, clothing, and tools), the Matsigenka retain most of their own traditions. They reckon time by moons, 12 to a year, by moon quarters, and by the blooming of certain flowers. They measure short objects by spans and half-spans, and long objects with poles, but have no weights. Travel is estimated by sun positions. They regard the Milky Way as a river where animals bathe to gain eternal youth.

2 LOCATION AND HOMELAND

The Matsigenka inhabit the tropical rain forest of the upper Amazon of southeastern Peru. Rain is almost a constant occurrence in this region: the wet season extends from October to March, and then from April until September there is a less wet, but still rainy, season. The landscape is full of mountains, steep inclines with rushing mountain rivers, and hazardous trails, which makes traveling difficult. Copious rainfall on a mountainous terrain causes natural disasters. The Matsigenka are therefore fearful of floods and earthquakes. With the 1947 earthquake, many families disappeared. The condition of the soil—black and rich—and the availability of animals for hunting were very favorable until some 40 years ago. The use of firearms and the intensive agricultural activity by colonizers and Amerindians have reduced considerably the numbers of game animals and the fertility of the land. The Matsigenka traditionally live in small, semipermanent settlement clusters situated, when possible, near a source of water and often on hilltops and ridges, in the past for fear of slave raids and in the present day to avoid competition over resources and the danger of floods. A house up on a hill also allows them to enjoy the breeze and to escape mosquitoes.

3 LANGUAGE

Matsigenka means "people." The Matsigenka language is one of the Arawakan dialects. Arawak is one of the largest and most important linguistic families in South America, both in extent and in number of component languages and dialects. As with any other vernacular, the Matsigenka language gives us an idea of how the Matsigenka perceive the world. The animal kingdom, for example, is divided into five categories: *íbira,* for domestic animals; *yaágágání,* for edible animals and birds; *átsigantatsíri,* for animals that bite; *ógantéri,* for animals that sting; and the last one is divided in two—*sima,* big fish; and *síbaí,* small fish.

Up to 50% of Matsigenka men are bilingual in Matsigenka and Ashaninka. Being able to speak the Ashaninka language facilitates trade. Most men also speak basic Spanish, and an increasing number of children are fluent Spanish-speakers after the first school years. In contrast, most women are monolingual, with only an estimated 30% knowing how to count in Spanish.

4 FOLKLORE

The Matsigenka believe they were originally made out of pieces of wood—palo de balsa—by a powerful creator spirit, Makineri, who cut sturdy saplings into lengths and brought them to life by singing and breathing on them. Makineri was one of many spirits or beings called Tasorinchi, who were created from nothing and were very powerful. They changed many Matsigenka into animals. One of the female Tasorinchi is the "mother of fishes." A male Tasorinchi one tried to drown the Matsigenka by causing a flood. He was then nailed to the trees, where he still lives, and when he struggles to free himself he causes earthquakes. Several Tasorinchi finally became armadillos.

Another myth tells about the Inkakuma spirits, who were mining and dug through the underworld. The Chonchóite, a legendary cannibalistic tribe, emerged from the hole which was eventually plugged and those remaining below became the Kamagárini or demons. One of those demons from the underworld created the Kugapakuri, a tribe of bow hunters; and the Viracocha, the people of the Puna.

The Matsigenka also believe that formerly people lacked teeth and ate only potter's clay. Kashiri, the Moon, brought manioc (cassava) roots to a menstruating girl and taught her to eat them.

The deep sections of the rivers are the home of a great manfish, Quíatsi, who hunts careless swimmers, takes them to the bottom, and weds them to his daughters. He is not considered a bad spirit. Mountain caves are homes of malignant spirits, and roaring winds are feared because they are believed to bring illness and death. The swallows that make their nests in the Matsigenka houses, on the other hand, bring good luck; and a kite (a type of bird), the *yasíbántí,* is protected since it takes the souls of the dead to other levels of existence.

5 RELIGION

Good and evil were the two forces involved in the creation of the world. The Creator made the world by mounding up mud into land. The Evil Contender created the bad things in the world, like stinging flies. These two figures are no longer active, but good and bad spirits are still present. Many things have spirits, and animals have spirit rulers—so if one of them is killed, their spirits should be appeased. Some animals are in fact descendants of humans that committed a crime, like theft or incest. Women have to beware of the various demons that haunt the forests and can impregnate them with a demon child.

It is possible for a human soul to fly to the land of the Unseen Ones by ingesting an alkaloid hallucinogen called *kamarampi,* "death medicine." The Unseen Ones can perform cures, see the future, and instruct. After death, the soul begins a voyage towards a better layer of the cosmos. There are 10 levels of existence. The gods inhabit the top 5. The earth is the eighth level. After death, the soul can choose to remain on the seventh level, above the ground, where people live just as they do on earth but do not suffer or die and can still enjoy earthly pleasures. The higher levels can be reached, providing the soul is not caught and thrown back down by dangerous spirits that inhabit the sixth level, running the risk of falling to the deepest level where all is suffering, perpetual fire, darkness, and hunger. But the soul can be rescued by the Quíbintí, which inhabit the ninth level below the ground, where there is life and happiness. If the soul manages to reach the highest levels, it will be happy forever.

6 MAJOR HOLIDAYS

There is only one major religious holiday but it is celebrated every month: the Moon Festival. The Matsigenka have kept through the centuries the tradition of dedicating one day and night to honor the moon. During the last century, the festival took place from Saturday evening through Sunday. But in the last years, this tradition has not been practiced with the same frequency. During the festival, the Matsigenka wear their best clothes, dance, and drink mildly fermented *masato*. In a big clearing, men in couples march together in a circle playing their *soncari*—pan pipes. Meanwhile, the women, holding hands, form a long line and move as they sing a melody different from the one the men are playing. The words of the song are in an archaic dialect and many young girls do not understand it. When the men finish a certain tune, they stop, look at the women, bow, go back one or two steps, bow again, and then start their music once more. The music and dancing continue through the night, with only a few short breaks to rest, drink masato, and take some coca.

In the last few years, and due to the opening of schools for the Amerindians, the Matsigenka have joined the Peruvians in the celebration of national holidays. For Independence Day—independence from Spanish rule—Matsigenka children march, holding paper lanterns in the shape of stars, houses, airplanes, etc. When available, they like to march to the beat of drums, playing trumpets.

7 RITES OF PASSAGE

Ceremonies are rare among the Matsigenka. Their parties are more about dancing, singing, getting drunk, and joking, rather than invoking spiritual forces. Being a very individualistic people, the curing and spiritual encounters are conducted by individuals in the privacy of their homes.

There are no ceremonies for birth or naming the child. Some baptize their children with a Spanish name; otherwise, the children get a Spanish name from their teacher when they go to school. Puberty rites have disappeared. Girls used to have their hair cut and were isolated for one or two months, during which time they spun cotton.

Marriage does not happen until the accepted groom builds a house and plants a garden near his in-laws' dwelling. The ceremony is attended only by the bride's parents. The father orders his daughter to roast yucca for his new son-in-law. The bride offers some yucca to the groom, and from then on they are considered husband and wife. Both of them have the right to throw the other one out if they get bored with each other.

An extreme lack of death ritual was previously found among the Matsigenka, who not only threw their dead unceremoniously into the river but similarly disposed of hopelessly ill people. They traditionally only buried those who were killed in warfare. To prevent the soul of a person who had died through attack by an evil spirit to linger in sorrow near his or her home, the house was burned down. The remainder of the family moved away so the soul would have no reason to stay and would begin its journey to the higher level of the cosmos.

Nowadays, when a person dies, the family weeps quietly so as not to attract evil spirits. For the first two weeks after a death, the family can only eat green plantains and rice. Afterwards, the closest relative bathes in a special brew and the nuclear family cuts their hair to avoid causing the deaths of other people. The body is washed and dressed in a *cushma* (the standard Matsigenka dress) specially dyed with achiote, and is buried with its personal possessions. It is believed that the soul of a dead person is evil, so the survivors try to forget the dead person to prevent the soul from coming back.

8 INTERPERSONAL RELATIONS

Though each Matsigenka household is virtually self-sufficient, game and fish are shared generously among people of the hamlet. Hamlet-dwellers exchange visits at dusk and on weekends. When a visitor arrives, the host asks, "Néga pijáque?"—"Where are you going?"—and the guest replies, "Naniáquemíni"—"I am visiting you." This is the same greeting used in casual encounters. The host always serves boiled yucca and *masato* (a type of drink), sometimes accompanied by other seasonal foods. At times, the guest brings food.

Gossip and shaming, together with early socialization, are quite effective methods for teaching people to control aggressive impulses. If an individual does commit a crime, such as homicide or incest, he or she is punished by being ostracized or expelled from the community. Verbal fights with limited physical contact occur occasionally within the household and hamlet, usually after drinking at a beer feast. Conflicts with outside groups in the late 20th century are at a minimum. The Matsigenka are courteous towards strangers, but they are generally not too friendly as they fear exploitation. Friends share the meat from the hunts and some of the foods they collect, like palm nuts. They do not, however, buy each other presents.

There is virtually a lack of political organization as it is known by Western society among the Matsigenka. Leaders are elected by tacit agreement, rather than through elections. The basic rule is household autonomy, and the Matsigenka are notorious for leaving an area if their autonomy is compromised. There are no chiefs or councils to set policy, but recently they did form a multicommunity union and elected a council head, mainly to deal with the alien industries moving into their territories. They respect a person's word of honor, so agreements do not require written contracts. They do not have written laws either. Traditions of this kind have made encounters with the Whites and Mestizos difficult.

⁹LIVING CONDITIONS

Matsigenka houses are constructed entirely from local materials. They are built with heavy hardwood posts tied with bark, have palm-wood walls, and are covered with a thatched palm-leaf roof. Houses were traditionally low, oval-shaped structures. Today many have raised palm-wood floors and are larger and rectangular in shape. Inside there is always a fire burning. The Matsigenka prefer to build their homes next to a river or stream. Around the house, there is usually a clearing which helps keep snakes and rats out of the house. They usually plant flowers, and sometimes they place their kitchen in the garden. The clearings are an informal demarcation of ownership, although land is not owned as such. Men announce in advance their intentions to clear gardens in specific locations. Abandoned gardens revert to the public domain.

Some of the plants grown in the kitchen gardens are ingredients for the large number of herbal remedies known to the Matsigenka. It is believed that illnesses are caused by evil spirits—there are no physical causes: the symptoms that follow a snakebite are not caused by the snake's venom but by the spirit that inhabits the snake. A suggestion of nutritional deficiencies is beriberi, which the Matsigenka attribute to eating papaya after sungaro fish, roast crayfish, or hips juice. To cure coughs and rheumatism, they rub the body with the sap of a tree called cobe, which is like menthol. For the shooting pains caused by the bite of a *manií* ant, the remedy is to drink and bathe in an infusion made with a bulb called *manlíbenqui*. They chew coca to counteract fatigue. Despite their impressive knowledge of natural medicine, there is a growing dependence among Matsigenka on Western medicine due to social changes and foreign diseases.

Most of the Matsigenka region is reachable by road. There are bus services, and trucks travel along the highways. Within the region, the Matsigenka often walk, and the traditional carrying devices were tumplines, infant-bearing bands, and small bags. Early explorers observed that Matsigenka men and women could carry up to 34 kg for 24 km (75 lbs for 15 mi) a day.

¹⁰FAMILY LIFE

Traditionally, marriages are arranged at an early age and often with members of the families that share the hamlet. As a result, many Matsigenka are related in some way to everyone else in the vicinity. But this convenient arrangement often fails, and the unmarried ones have to visit other settlements to procure a mate. There are a small number of cases of polygyny, and in such cases, each wife has her own living space within the house. Women provide most of the child care and prepare nearly all of the food. Men participate in the preparation of food for storage, like smoked meat and fish. Infants are fed on demand, pampered, and enjoyed. After the age of 1 year and until the age of 5 years, discipline is by verbal reprimand, rarely accompanied by corporal punishment. Starting at age 5, children begin to acquire adult skills by going with the parent of their sex to work. From then on, scolding is common, but the process is gentle and gradual. Young ones learn the values and customs of the group by oral instruction and imitation. Norms are taught mainly through legends.

According to early explorers, a Matsigenka man could exchange wives with a friend or lend his wife to a visitor. The women practiced abortion and gave birth in the woods, immediately after which the mother returned to routine life. Nowadays they give birth in a special hut built by the husband, aided by an older relative. The husband should be present to cut the umbilical cord with a piece of bamboo; otherwise, the mother's teeth will wear away.

¹¹CLOTHING

The standard dress of the Matsigenka is the *cushma,* with a neck opening that runs from front to back for men in the shape of a V and from side to side for women, in a straight line. It takes a woman about three months, working during her free time, to make a cushma. Made of wild cotton and colored with vegetable dyes, it is ornamented with feathers, beads, etc. The most commonly used dye comes from the bark of a tree called *tsótoroqui.* To extract the dye, the bark is boiled in water. The cloth is then submerged into the resulting liqueur and dried under the sun. The process is repeated three or four times to get the desired color: from lilac to a reddish brown. Whatever the tone, it gets darker all the time as it is exposed to the sun, and it does not run or fade when washed. The cushma has vertical stripes for a man and horizontal for a woman. The designs of the stripes differ between communities so they can easily identify visitors.

For dress occasions, some Matsigenka nowadays wear European clothes. Since cushmas do not have pockets, the Matsigenka men use bags to carry things like matches, a knife, wax, cotton thread, a little bag with coca leaves, and a whistle to call birds. The women carry their things in baskets. As ornaments they wear cotton wrist and ankle bands, various seed necklaces, and gold-colored earrings. As men used to place pins through their noses, some of them have a perforation there. The men make crowns in the shape of topless hats decorated with feathers. Both sexes paint their bodies with achiote, both as decoration and as protection against sunburn and insects. The Matsigenka were known to paint even their animals.

¹²FOOD

Like many other Amerindians in the region, the staple food of the Matsigenka is yucca or manioc (cassava). The long tubers are peeled and then boiled or toasted to make their bread, which is a large flat pancake, and also *masato,* a thirst-quenching drink. Some kinds of yucca have a poisonous juice inside them, and after grating the tuber it must be squeezed out in a *tipiti.* Boiled yucca is also eaten accompanied by soups made with meat, fish, snails, plantains, pumpkins, nuts, fruits, maize, chili, larvae, or eggs.

The importance of the yucca is highlighted by a wonderful story that tells how the Matsigenka came to have it: it was a gift from the Moon, Kashiri. Long ago, the Moon came down in the form of a handsome man wearing a yellow feather crown. He met a girl, married her, and gave manioc, maize (corn), plantains, and other foods to her parents. He also taught them how to grow and prepare yucca the right way. The girl bore four boys, all Suns: the Sun, Venus, the Sun of the Underworld, and the Sun of the Firmament, which gives light to the stars. Then Kashiri went back to heaven. Since then, Kashiri watches over all his daughters—the yucca—and the plants complain to him if people tread on them or do not prepare them the right way.

Early explorers talk about the ways the Matsigenka cooked meat, using a pyramidal or rectangular *babracot;* the smoke helped preserve it for a few days. Rock salt from Cerro de la Sal and pepper were used as condiments. Today their favorite way of preparing big meals for a party is the *pachamanca:* the uncooked food is placed in a hole in the ground that contains hot stones, covered with leaves and earth, and left to cook slowly. They eat their meals with wooden spoons or monkey skulls, and the women eat separately from the men. They also use plates and spoons made of pumpkins, and they have their meals sitting on the floor on mats. Sometimes they drink coffee, but they prefer tea and other warm drinks made with cacao seeds, lemons, maize, and sugarcane.

13 EDUCATION

Education in some ways has been the reason for a change in the traditional living conditions of the Matsigenka, who have been drawn out of their isolation into school communities with airstrips. Matsigenka school communities, with family households of an average of 6 people each, range in size from 100 to 250 individuals. The change started in the 1950s, when the Peruvian government opened monolingual (Spanish) schools in the region. A few years later, a group of Matsigenka became schoolteachers, trained by a Protestant group in Pucallpa at the Summer Institute of Linguistics. The schoolteachers often serve as a link with the commercial world as well. In some communities, the children study in bilingual schools where the text books are in Spanish and Ashaninka. The schools, with only one exception, offer only primary education. Children who finish when they are 13 years old have only one option if they want to go on to secondary education.

School terms are nine months long, from April to December. From 8:00 am until 2:00 pm, five days a week, the students study language, history, social and natural sciences, math, hygiene, sports, music, and religion. Their main problem is learning Spanish. Most of them do not speak it at home, and because their parents do not know it well, they cannot really help the children with lectures and math. Sometimes, Matsigenka children have to repeat a grade a few times before they learn enough Spanish to go on to the next one. There is also the problem of shortage of books and other materials and teachers. Nevertheless, the Matsigenka students learn how to read and write and recently have been finishing school in less time. According to observers, they particularly enjoy extracurricular activities, like playing in the school band.

14 CULTURAL HERITAGE

The Matsigenka like to sing and are good at it. Their songs are hypnotic repetitions and counterpoint, performed in groups of up to four people and accompanied by musical instruments. A traditional instrument is a two-headed, monkey-skin drum. They also play flutes and panpipes. When the singing and the music are mixed with manioc (cassava) beer, the rhythm accelerates into a rapid 4/4 time and the Matsigenka start dancing. While men dart and whirl around the clearing, women dance by walking behind the men, holding hands and singing.

15 WORK

Farming is done in the traditional slash-and-burn method. After the morning bath in the river (from which they bring back water) and breakfast, the men go to the fields carrying a pumpkin container filled with masato (a thirst-quenching drink). They work from dawn until 4:30 pm without lunch and have breaks every two hours. Some days the men go hunting or fishing. Each Matsigenka family has its own clearing, which is made anew every two to three years. Men help one another prepare these clearings, but subsequently each woman cultivates and harvests her own plot. Women clean the house each morning and evening, light the fire, cook and take care of the children. They also make clothes and pots, gather firewood, and help the men with their work.

To supplement their diets, the Matsigenka fish, hunt, and collect nuts, wild fruits, and mushrooms. To fish, the Matsigenka use a drug called *cadge,* bone hooks, grill nets, hand nets, large nets with sinkers, fish pots, spears, and arrows. They also use a weir and dam to drain a section of the river. Men do all the hunting, using bows and arrows and traps. The arrows have cemented, spiraled feathers, and their points are never poisoned. Some Matsigenka have shotguns which make hunting easier, and they end up with enough catch to share with local households and thus offset resentment. To catch birds, the Matsigenka smear a glue on tree limbs. Early explorers observed that the Matsigenka were the only group in the Peruvian montana to keep ducks, along with chickens, which were common elsewhere. To make fire, they used the drill method, with cotton, raw copal, or resin as tinder.

Money has only recently been introduced into the local economy. In communities with schools, they are encouraged to develop commercial crops such as coffee, cacao, peanuts, and beans for sale. The Matsigenka manufacture nearly everything they use, except machetes, axes, aluminum pots, and factory-made cloth. They also trade with their neighbors. A handmade *cushma,* (traditional dress) for example, can be exchanged for a machete, an axe, two cans of gunpowder, or one parrot.

16 SPORTS

Explorers say that archery was the game of Matsigenka boys, while the girls tossed balls made of bladders. For some festivals, the Matsigenka organize archery tournaments, gymnastic events, blindfolded cassava-peeling competitions, and poetry contests. Recently men and women have begun to practice organized sports. Soccer is the most popular. Basketball and volleyball are also played. But the practice of sports in front of crowds or as a commercial activity is not part of their culture. The Matsigenka are good swimmers. They learn to swim at an early age, following the example of older boys who often choose the deeper sections of the rivers and know how to move in torrential waters.

17 ENTERTAINMENT AND RECREATION

The Matsigenka value their free time and find many ways to enjoy it. Conversation is one of their favorite pastimes, whether serious, humorous, or simple gossip. They play word games, laugh at each other's misfortunes, and make fun of different accents or dialects. They discuss sex openly and often exaggerate its practice when telling legends. Children have few inhibitions: they speak their mind and defend their opinions with passion.

Games are another form of entertainment. Two games introduced by Quechua colonizers are very popular. One is called "Pull the Duck." A duck is hanged from a tree with a rope that can be pulled, and the participants try to get the duck down from the tree. The winner keeps the duck. In the second game, they hang a bag of sweets and treats from a tree and dance around it, periodically hitting the bag of sweets with an axe until it falls, and they then fight to get the treats. Recently, card games have been introduced. The Matsigenka play cards, betting small sums of money. For their own pleasure, some men play their flutes and drums. The Matsigenka also have a lot of fun teasing their domestic animals: they really enjoy pulling their dogs' whiskers.

Matsigenka smoke tobacco in pipes or take it as snuff through V-tubes. They also chew it with the ashes. To get drunk, they drink *chicha,* made with yucca, maize, sweet potatoes, bananas, and other produce.

18 FOLK ART, CRAFTS, AND HOBBIES

The Matsigenka make their own pots. They use the clay found in riverbanks and mix it with cotton fiber. When the pot has dried thoroughly, it is put in the fire for an hour, and as soon as it is taken out they fill it up with yucca water to make it waterproof. Decoration is rare in pottery and other objects and simple tools which are made of wood. But they do make children's toys of wood, and necklaces of animal teeth and carved bones. Women spin cotton and weave cloth, make mats for sleeping and sitting, and make the plaited sifters and strainers used in food preparation. Men are responsible for house-building, making bows and arrows, and making the fiber twine for netting.

19 SOCIAL PROBLEMS

In recent times, malnutrition has made the Matsigenka population more susceptible to parasites and epidemics. Cultural changes have affected the Matsigenka's psychological well-being, resulting in a number of suicides and an increase in alcohol consumption, which is helped by the availability of bottled and canned alcoholic drinks. Some communities are so isolated that medical help cannot always reach them. Formal education suffers shortages of teachers and materials. The teachers do not stay very long, as they are often not from the region and find the conditions difficult.

20 BIBLIOGRAPHY

Bennett, Ross S., ed. *Lost Empires, Living Tribes.* Washington, D.C.: National Geographic Book Service, 1982.

Brill, E. J. *Continuity & Identity in Native America.* New York: E. J. Brill, 1988.

Shaver, Harold. *Los Nomatsiguega de la Selva Central.* N.p., 1990.

Steward, Julian Haynes, ed. *Handbook of South American Indians.* New York: Cooper Square, 1963.

Welch, Thomas. *The Indians of South America.* Washington, D.C.: Columbus Memorial Library Organization of American States, 1987.

—by D. Ventura-Alcalay

MAYA

LOCATION: Southeastern Mexico; Guatemala; Belize; Honduras; El Salvador
POPULATION: About 8–10 million
LANGUAGE: Spanish; English; various Mayan dialects
RELIGION: "Folk Catholicism"; evangelical Christianity

1 INTRODUCTION

Today's Maya are descended from one of the great civilizations of the Americas. They live in the same regions of Mexico, Guatemala, Belize, El Salvador, and Honduras as their ancestors and retain many of their ancient traditions. Mayan history reaches back some 4,000 years to what is called the Preclassic period, when civilization first began in Mesoamerica. However, it was during what came to be known as the Classic period—from roughly AD 250 to 900—that Mayan culture reached its peak and the Maya achieved their celebrated advances in architecture, mathematics, agriculture, astronomy, art, and other areas.

They built spectacular temples and palaces, developed several calendars—including one reaching back to 13 August, 3114 BC—and evolved a numerical system capable of recording a number that today would be expressed as 142 followed by 36 zeros. They developed a complex system of writing and, beginning in 50 BC, were the first people in the Western hemisphere to keep written historical records. Around AD 900 the construction of buildings and stelae—stone slabs inscribed with names and dates—ceased abruptly, and the advanced lowland civilization of the Maya collapsed, creating a mystery that has fascinated scholars for many years. Possible causes that have been proposed include warfare, drought, famine, and disease.

The Spanish campaign to subdue the Maya and conquer their lands began around 1520 and ended nearly 200 years later when Tayasal, the last remaining Mayan region (in present-day Guatemala), fell to the conquistadors in 1697. The Spanish seized Mayan lands and enslaved their populations, sending many to labor in the mines of northern Mexico. In addition, thousands of Maya died of diseases spread by the Europeans, especially smallpox. During the first half of the 19th century, the Central American lands won their independence from Spain, but the lives of the Maya did not improve. They labored on vast tobacco, sugarcane, and henequen plantations, in virtual slavery enforced by their continuing debt to the landowners. In the Yucatan, many joined in a protracted rebellion called the Caste War that lasted from 1847 to 1901.

After the revolution of 1910, the Maya in Mexico gained increased legal rights and better educational and job opportunities. However, a steep drop in world prices for henequen—the "green gold" from which twine was made—turned the Yucatan from one of Mexico's richest regions to one of its poorest. In Guatemala, the disenfranchisement and poverty of the Maya—comprising roughly half the population—continued unchanged into the 20th century. Since the 1970s, political violence has forced many Maya to flee to Mexico, where they remain as refugees. In Chiapas, Maya of the Tzeltal and Tzotzil tribes took part in the Zapatista uprising of January 1994.

²LOCATION AND HOMELAND

The modern Maya live in southeastern Mexico and northern Central America, including Guatemala, Belize, Honduras, and El Salvador. Altogether, their homelands cover an area of approximately 323,750 sq km (125,000 sq mi) with a varied terrain that encompasses both northern lowlands and southern highlands. Volcanic mountains dominate the highlands, which are home to the rare quetzal bird of the tropical rain forest. The fertile soil of the highland valleys supports the largest segment of the Maya population. While many Maya have settled in cities—particularly Merida and Cancún—and adopted an urban lifestyle, most remain rural dwellers.

Reliable figures for the total number of Maya are unavailable. Estimates range upward from 4 million. The true figure is probably between 8 and 10 million, including about half of Guatemala's total population of 10 million, close to 2 million Maya in the Mexican Yucatan, and additional numbers in Mexico's Chiapas state, as well as Belize, Honduras, and El Salvador. Among the larger individual groups are about 750,000 Quiché (K'iche') in the midwestern highlands of Guatemala; 445,000 or more Cakchiquel in several Guatemalan departments (provinces); and over 500,000 Mam in southwestern Guatemala and southeastern Chiapas.

³LANGUAGE

Most Maya today speak Spanish, the official language of the countries where they reside (except for Belize, where the official language is English, but much of the population speaks either Spanish or an English-based Creole that contains elements of Spanish and African languages). The two Mayan languages of the Classic period, Yucatecan and Cholan, have subdivided into about 30 separate languages, some of which are not mutually intelligible. The most widely spoken are Mam, Quiché, Kekchí, and Cakchiquel. Advocates of Mayan cultural autonomy protest against the relegation of their indigenous languages to limited use, often in remote rural areas, while Spanish remains the language of government, education, the church, and the media. The following example is drawn from a creation myth in the *Popol Vuh,* the Mayan holy book:

Keje k'ut xax k'o wi ri kaj nay puch, u K'ux Kaj.
Are ub'i ri k'ab'awil, chuch'axik.

(And of course there is the sky, and there is also the Heart of Sky. This is the name of the god, as it is spoken.)

⁴FOLKLORE

The greatest body of Mayan tradition is contained in the *Popol Vuh,* an ancient text first transcribed into Latin and later translated into Spanish that preserves both sacred and secular lore. According to its creation myth, the gods made three different attempts at creating human beings before they had a version they were satisfied with. The first beings, which were made of mud, were destroyed because they had no brains. The next ones were made of wood and proved deficient because they were without emotions and thus could not properly praise their makers. Finally the correct material—maize—was found, and perfect beings were fashioned. Ultimately deciding to protect them by limiting the extent of their knowledge, the gods decided to damage their eyes so they could not see too much, and the resulting beings were the first Maya.

⁵RELIGION

The traditional religions of the Maya, in which astrology and ancestor worship both played a role, were based on a cosmology that embraced the world, the heavens, and an unseen underworld called Xibalba. When Spanish missionaries introduced Catholicism to their regions, the Maya tended to graft it onto their existing religion, creating a unique brand of "folk Catholicism." Their traditional gods that belonged to the natural world, such as corn, rain, and the sun, became associated with Christian saints, and various rituals and festivals were transmuted into forms approved by the church.

Since the 1960s, evangelical Christianity, mostly promoted by churches in the southern United States, has been adopted by large segments of the Mayan population. Entire towns have embraced conservative forms of Protestantism, which have not proven as amenable as Catholicism to the retention of customs related to traditional folk religions, such as the use of alcohol in association with religious rituals or the retention of the sacred brotherhoods—known as *cofradias* in Guatemala and as *cargos* in Chiapas—which traditionally oversee village festivals and other aspects of civic life.

⁶MAJOR HOLIDAYS

Most holidays currently observed by the Maya are the holy days of the Christian calendar, although many of their observances retain a shamanistic character resulting from the grafting of a Christian framework onto the ancient nature worship of their ancestors. The most important celebrations are generally Holy Week (the week leading up to Easter in late March or early April) and Christmas (25 December). The Maya living in the Chamula region of Chiapas are known for their five-day Carnival celebration, called Crazy February, whose Christian significance (the period preceding Lent) merges with the older observance of the five "Lost Days" at the end of the Maya solar calendar. Religious societies called *cargos* sponsor the festivities, which include ceremonial dances, feasting, processions, and ritual reenactments of both religious and historic events, including a mock "manure war."

⁷RITES OF PASSAGE

Major life transitions (such as birth, puberty, and death) are marked by religious ceremonies, many of which combine Christian and ancestral traditions.

⁸INTERPERSONAL RELATIONS

The religious societies known as *cargos* in Chiapas and *cofradias* in Guatemala have been an important vehicle of social cohesion among the Maya. Charged since colonial times with organizing Catholic religious festivals, they provided the means for the Maya to conform nominally to the customs of their colonizers while privately preserving their own religion, traditions, and worldview. Mayan villages today have both civil and religious *cargos,* whose officials may ascend through a hierarchy of positions to ultimately become respected village elders, or *principales.*

⁹LIVING CONDITIONS

Housing varies among the different regions and groups of Maya. The Mam, who live in southwestern Guatemala and southeastern Chiapas, live in houses with adobe walls; small, shuttered windows; roofs of tile or corrugated metal; and a floor of hard-packed dirt. The K'iche' in the Guatemalan highlands build rectangular houses with double-pitched tile roofs and walls of adobe, thatch supported by boards or poles, or other materials. Increasing numbers live in more modern homes built from brick or lumber with tin roofs.

The health of the Tzotzil and Tzeltal Maya of Chiapas has been compromised by their inadequate diet, which consists of fewer than 500 calories a day—one-fifth of the minimum standard set by the United Nations. Life expectancy is only 44 years, and the infant mortality rate is 150 deaths per 1,000 live births. Another factor endangering both infant and adult health is the prevalence of adolescent pregnancies. Maya folk medicine includes the ministrations of ritual healers called *curanderos* and female herbalists who may double as midwives. Common cures include prayers, offerings, herbal remedies, and sweat-baths.

The main means of transport for most Maya is the bus. Buses in Maya areas may be crowded as early as 4:00 or 5:00 AM, often with people traveling from remote villages to the larger market towns. By late afternoon and evening there are fewer travelers on the road. In the Yucatan, human travelers share narrow country roads with a variety of wildlife ranging from lizards to swarms of butterflies, and speed bumps abound on roads in the vicinity of virtually every village. Trains in the Maya regions—like those in many parts of Central and South America—are generally slow, old, and unreliable. In some areas, boats are used for public transportation.

10 FAMILY LIFE

Both nuclear and extended families are found among the Maya. Couples generally marry in their late teens or early 20s. Traditionally, all marriages were arranged, but since the 1950s it has become increasingly common among some groups for young people to choose their own mates. In arranged marriages, contact may be initiated by the couple, followed by negotiation between the two families. Gifts are generally exchanged, and in some cases the bride's parents receive a payment to compensate them for having raised her. Couples often have both civil and religious ceremonies, and they may live with the groom's parents until their first child is born.

Family structure may alternate between nuclear and extended, with the addition of newly married couples who will eventually leave to establish their own homes, or elderly parents who come to live with the family when it becomes hard for them to manage on their own.

11 CLOTHING

The Maya wear both modern Western-style clothing and traditional garb (although the latter is more commonly worn by women). Men generally wear trousers and sport shirts or *guayaberas,* dress shirts with decorative tucks worn outside the belt in place of a jacket. Women wear either traditional woven and embroidered clothing, or stylish dresses and skirt-and-blouse outfits. Traditional women's attire includes the *huipil,* a long, sleeveless tunic; the *quechquémitl,* a shoulder cape; and the *enredo,* a wrap-around skirt. Maya garments are commonly decorated with elaborate and colorful embroidery. The designs, which include humans, animals, and plants, often have some religious significance, and every Maya group and village has its own distinctive patterns of decoration. The decorative designs

for huipiles are often said to appear to women in their dreams. Men often wear the traditional tunics over store-bought shirts. *Fajas* are sashes that hold garments in place and also serve as pockets.

12 FOOD

The Maya generally eat three meals a day: breakfast *(el desayuno),* lunch *(la comida),* and supper *(la cena).* Corn, the most important food of their ancestors, remains the central ingredient in their diet today. Throughout the region, women make daily trips to the village grinder with their corn kernels, returning with dough, or *masa,* from which to make tortillas, the most important food staple, or tamales, which are also popular. After corn, beans *(frijoles)* are the most basic staple, served boiled, fried, or refried. Soups—many of them actually thick stews— form a large part of the Mayan diet. One of the most popular is lime soup *(sopa de lima),* made from chicken, limes, and a variety of spices.

Poultry forms the basis of many meals—either turkey, which is native to the region, or chicken, which was introduced by the Spanish. Plentiful seafood caught on the coasts of the Caribbean and Gulf of Mexico is also an important dietary staple. The Yucatan is known for its *ceviche,* a cold dish made with fish prepared with an acidic marinade (usually lime juice), served with onions, chiles, and cilantro. Popular desserts include flan (a custard introduced by the Spanish) and *Torta del Cielo* (Heavenly Cake), a cake made with rum, almonds, and 10 eggs that is served at weddings and other special occasions.

One of the best-known foods of the Maya is Cochinita Pibil, a pork dish that dates back to pre-Columbian times, when it was made from wild boar cooked in a coal-filled pit. Domesticated pigs, introduced by the Spanish, have replaced the boar, but the dish is prepared with the same seasonings as it was in the past.

Cochinita Pibil

10 whole black peppercorns
⅓ cup lime juice
¼ teaspoon cumin seeds
2 pounds lean pork, cut in 2-inch cubes
5 cloves garlic
Banana leaves or aluminum foil
3 Tablespoons *achiote* paste
3 fresh *xcatic* or other spicy chilies
1 teaspoon dried oregano
Sliced purple raw onions
2 bay leaves
String

The cumin seeds and black peppercorns should be ground to a fine consistency, combined with the garlic, and pureed in a food processor or blender. Mix the spice puree with the lime juice, *achiote* paste, bay leaves, and oregano. Cover the pork with this mixture and marinate for at least 3 hours, or overnight. Place banana leaves on the bottom of a roasting pan, and put the pork, with the marinade, on top of the leaves. Add topping of onions and chiles. After folding the leaves over the meat, tie with the string. Preheat oven to 325°F and bake in covered pan for 1½ hours. Serve with beans, salsa, and heated corn tortillas.

Serve with warmed corn tortillas, beans, and salsa.

13 EDUCATION

The Maya are educated at either public or Catholic schools. In Guatemala, a half-dozen Catholic-run boarding schools are the main source of education for those wishing to progress beyond the basic education available in the villages. Maya concerned with preserving their culture argue that the formal education traditionally available to them has attempted to assimilate them into mainstream Western culture by causing them to lose touch with their own. The Guatemalan Academy of Maya Languages (Academia de Lenguas Mayas) is at the center of a movement to preserve the languages of the Guatemalan Maya by codifying their grammars and alphabets.

14 CULTURAL HERITAGE

The Maya have preserved many aspects of their ancient culture, including their traditional clothing, folklore, agricultural techniques, family structure, language, and dance. Many elements of their ancient religions have also survived for centuries under the guise of Catholic religious observances, although these are now threatened by the growing prevalence of Protestant evangelical sects.

15 WORK

In rural areas, the Maya farm their maize fields, or *milpas*, much as their ancestors did thousands of years ago. Forested sites are turned into new fields by felling the trees and burning the brush (today known as "slash-and-burn" agriculture). Maize kernels are then planted into holes made with digging sticks. Where the ancient Maya used stone tools for clearing and hardened the end of the digging stick with fire, today's farmer uses a steel machete and metal-tipped stick. Because this type of agriculture rapidly depletes the soil, fields must be left fallow for periods ranging from 7 to as many as 20 years. Besides farming, Maya also work as laborers and artisans or own small shops. In urban areas, they work in jobs involving textiles or computers, for example.

16 SPORTS

The ancient Maya played hip-ball, a game that involved keeping a hard rubber ball aloft with any part of the body other than the hands, head, or feet. In some regions, the ball had to be hit through a set of stone rings. Soccer and bullfights are two popular sports in the regions inhabited by the Maya of today.

17 ENTERTAINMENT AND RECREATION

Sunday afternoons after church are the most popular time for recreation. Most businesses are closed, and many people stroll the village streets or relax in local parks. Popular forms of musical entertainment include marimba teams and mariachi bands.

18 FOLK ART, CRAFTS, AND HOBBIES

Maya women are famous for their weaving, often using locally handspun yarn and natural vegetable dyes. Using the pre-Columbian back-strap loom of their ancestors, they produce striped and plain white cloth for shawls, shirts, and children's clothes, some with designs that are over 1,200 years old. Colorful hammocks are woven from fine cotton string. Other craft items include both glazed and unglazed pottery, ceremonial wooden masks, and goods woven from palm, straw, reeds, and sisal.

For centuries, traditional Maya dances have been preserved by the religious men's fraternities called *cofradias*. These dances were performed for both ceremonial and entertainment purposes. The *Pop Wuj* dance depicts the four stages of humankind's development: the Man of Mud, who is destroyed because he does not recognize the gods; the Man of Wood, who is too rigid and ultimately burns; the Monkey Man, who is too silly; and the Human Being, who respects and prays to the gods. The K'iche' Maya of Chichicastenango have a dance that centers around Sijolaj, a harvest king whom the Spaniards identified with St. Thomas.

19 SOCIAL PROBLEMS

The Maya of Yucatan, like many other Mexicans, suffer from overpopulation, unemployment, and periods of political unrest. In Guatemala, Mayan farmers have been crowded onto mountainous areas with poor land, and laborers are forced to work for extremely low wages. The most serious problem for the Maya in that country has been over two decades of violent political repression by the military and right- and left-wing death squads. Thousands have been murdered or "disappeared," and many have fled the country for Mexico or the United States.

20 BIBLIOGRAPHY

Barker, Ann. "Indians and Conquerors." *America* (2 March 1996): 4.

Brosnahan, Tom. *Guatemala, Belize and Yucatan: La Ruta Maya.* Hawthorn, Australia: Lonely Planet Publications, 1994.

Canby, Peter. *The Heart of the Sky: Travels Among the Maya.* New York: HarperCollins, 1992.

Gerlach, Nancy, and Jeffrey Gerlach. *Foods of the Maya: A Taste of the Yucatan.* Freedom, CA: The Crossing Press, 1994.

Hanvik, Jan Michael. "Mayan Culture is Rescued through Dance." *Dance Magazine* (Nov 1994): 40.

Mallan, Chicki. *Belize Handbook.* Chico, CA: Moon Publications, 1995.

Olson, James S. *The Indians of Central and South America: An Ethnohistorical Dictionary.* New York: Greenwood Press, 1991.

Saravia, Albertina, trans. *Popol Wuh: Ancient Stories of the Quiche Indians of Guatemala.* Guatemala City: Editorial Piedra Santa, 1987.

Sexton, James D. *Campesino: The Diary of a Guatemalan Indian.* Tempe, AZ: University of Arizona Press, 1985.

Stuart, George E. "Maya Heartland under Siege." *National Geographic* (Nov 1992): 94–107.

Trout, Lawana Hooper. *The Maya.* New York: Chelsea House, 1991.

Watanabe, John M. "Mam." In *Encyclopedia of World Cultures.* Boston: G. K. Hall, 1992.

———. *Maya Saints and Souls in a Changing World.* Austin, TX: University of Texas Press, 1992.

—by R. Wieder, reviewed by T. Morin

MENNONITES OF PARAGUAY

LOCATION: Paraguay
POPULATION: 15,000
LANGUAGE: Plattdeutsch (Low German dialect); Hochdeutsch (High German); Spanish
RELIGION: Mennonite

¹ INTRODUCTION

The name "Mennonite" derives from Menno Simons, a Roman Catholic priest who led the Anabaptists in the Netherlands and North Germany in the 1530s. The Anabaptists later split into other groups, including the Amish, and the first Mennonites belonged to a church organized in Zurich, Switzerland.

During the 16th century in Holland and Switzerland, Mennonites ran into serious conflict with both the Catholic and Protestant authorities over their religious beliefs. They believe that baptism and church membership should be given out solely to those who have voluntarily given up sin—only those who proved their goodness could be baptized, which is how they came to be called Anabaptists. Persecution scattered the Swiss Mennonites throughout Europe, for as pacifists they believed in the separation of Church and State. What made matters worse was their rejection of compulsory military service, and they were forced to flee to Germany, Russia, and Canada.

In the early 1920s a group of conservative Mennonites in Canada, part of the 1874 migration from Europe, began to look for other places to settle because they felt the Canadian government was beginning to make too many demands on their freedom. These included restrictions on the school system, increasing pressure to serve in the military or support the military effort, and demands that English become the first language in the schools.

Paraguay was attractive to the Mennonites due to the offer of large tracts of nearly uninhabited land, on which they could continue their traditional agricultural way of life, and the government's willingness to grant them political autonomy under a "Privilegium." Under this they were to be responsible for their own schools (with German language instruction) and community law enforcement. They were also to have freedom from taxation, religious liberty, and even exemption from military service. Today, they are in charge of making their own regulations regarding ownership, transfer, and use of land; the building and maintenance of villages, roads, pastures, public buildings like schools, fire houses, governmental institutions, and jails; and the collection of taxes, as well as the training of teachers, the running of their own postal service, and the development of agricultural techniques. The only rights the Paraguayan government retained for itself were the rights to levy and collect taxes, to apprehend and adjudicate criminals, and the right of eminent domain.

The first group of Mennonites arrived in Paraguay in 1927. They were the Sommerfelder, the Summerfield Mennonites from the Canadian prairies. These Sommerfelder formed the Menno colony, the first of three distinct but territorially overlapping Mennonite groups. They originally acquired a tract of land, more than 130,000 hectares (320,000 acres) in the Chaco

to the west of Puerto Casado. The Chaco War between Paraguay and Bolivia severely threatened this first settlement. Although the Mennonite immigrants obtained major concessions under the Privilegium, they soon discovered that they had been given land in the middle of an area under violent dispute. From the beginning of the 20th century, Paraguay and Bolivia had been preparing for armed conflict by building fortifications throughout this part of the Chaco. In 1932 the situation developed into open warfare, and the Mennonite settlements found themselves at the center of ground fighting and air attacks between the two sides. Nomadic Amerindians were often targets for both Bolivians and Paraguayans. While some found refuge with the Mennonites, others were so hostile to the arrival of the settlers that they violently resisted any approach from them. Even as late as the 1940s, Ayoreo hunter-gatherers attacked and killed members of a Mennonite family in the northwest Chaco.

Only a few years after the founding of the Menno colony, Mennonite refugees from the Soviet Union established Fernheim, with its main town at Filadelfia. Neuland was founded in 1947 by Ukrainian-German Mennonites, many of whom had been forcibly conscripted into the German army during World War II and had managed to stay in the West after being released from prisoner-of-war camps. Neuland's largest settlement is Neu-Halbstadt. Of the original 641 family units, 253 were without fathers due to casualties on the Russian Front while serving in German uniform.

Because of their isolation, the Mennonites saw Paraguayans only infrequently, but they regularly came into contact, and sometimes conflict, with Chaco Indians.

² LOCATION AND HOMELAND

The Gran Chaco covers more than 60% of the total area of Paraguay and yet contains only 4% of its population. Great distances separate its small settlements. The paved Ruta 9, known as the Ruta Trans-Chaco, runs 450 km (280 mi) to the town of Filadelfia, the administrative and business center of the area colonized by the European Mennonite immigrants. Beyond Filadelfia, the pavement ends but the highway carries on to the Bolivian border at Eugenio Garay, another 300 km (190 mi) northwest.

The Paraguayan Chaco is the northernmost segment of an enormous plain, which lifts gradually from the southeast to the southwest. Within it are three distinct areas that emerge gradually from east to west. West of the Rio Paraguay, the Low Chaco landscape is a huge savanna of caranday palms, with scattered islands of thorny scrub. The main industry here is ranching. The climate becomes drier the further northwest the Ruta Trans-Chaco runs, and it is within this inhospitable environment that the Mennonite colonists have created successful agricultural communities in the Middle Chaco.

There are about 15,000 Mennonites and a roughly larger number of Amerindians in the region. Through the years, church membership has been 41% of the total population, while about 14.5% of people in the colonies never join the church. Menno's percentage of nonchurch members is only 2.2% because both men and women must belong before the church will perform a marriage ceremony.

³LANGUAGE

The Mennonites prefer to speak Plattdeutsch, a Low German dialect, among themselves at home and in church, but they also speak and understand Hochdeutsch, High German, which is the language used in schools. Most people speak Spanish, and quite a few have a passable grasp of English. Chaco Indians often speak German as well as Spanish, although most prefer their native languages.

⁴FOLKLORE

The Mennonites' faith is based on the Christian Bible, especially the New Testament. Their creed is the Sermon on the Mount (Matthew 5–7) which they believe forbids them from going to war, swearing oaths, or holding offices that require the use of force. The Mennonites believe in adult rather than infant baptism, and as pacifists, they also believe in the separation of Church and State and reject compulsory military service.

⁵RELIGION

Mennonites are Trinitarian, believing in the Father, Son, and Holy Spirit. They believe that Christ is the head of the Church, and only those who submit to Christ can be true members of the Church body. Their religion is based on the philosophy that religion is holy, that its spirit and way of life are different from the world about it and should be maintained as such. They maintain that they should adhere to a pure belief system and a holy life that has to be preserved in its entirety and passed on to the next generation.

⁶MAJOR HOLIDAYS

The important Christian festivals such as Christmas, Easter, and Pentecost are used to reaffirm the traditional beliefs and intensify the religious commitment of Church members.

⁷RITES OF PASSAGE

Mennonites are not baptized as infants, but undergo this religious rite at the age of 18 or whenever the person publicly renounces sin. Communion is also celebrated, but unlike the Catholic practice of celebrating with the bread and wine as the actual body and blood of Christ, Mennonites participate in this ritual as a means of committing themselves, like Jesus, to a life of complete and utter obedience to God.

⁸INTERPERSONAL RELATIONS

Mennonite thought has been characterized by a separation between religion and the world. As a result of severe persecution in the 16th century, Anabaptism was forced to develop a strategy of withdrawal from the outside world in its attempt to survive, and this has become central to Mennonite theology.

Consequently, a strong sense of identity and loyalty has been created within Mennonite society which is maintained and reinforced, first, by cutting themselves off from the outside world, and then by practicing a religious group discipline among themselves. It is this voluntary isolation that has led to the philosophy of encouraging the virtues of hard work, piety, and mutual cooperation.

Some members of the Mennonite community still practice foot-washing, a ritual based on the act of Jesus washing his disciples' feet.

⁹LIVING CONDITIONS

Traditionally, work on the farm is done by hand or by draft animals, but the building of the Trans-Chaco road has brought about a gradual modernization. It has opened up communication with the outside world and increased the opportunities for marketing agricultural produce. A number of long-term credits have also been obtained, the first of which was a $1 million loan from the US. This has allowed the colonies to restructure agriculture and dairy production. Farms have gradually been mechanized. Food production and consumption has improved and, with it, the general level of health in the colony.

The town of Filadelfia has grown considerably. It has been the administrative center of the Fernheim Colony since 1931 and has 1,700 Mennonites out of a total population of 3,300 in the colony. An additional 200 non-Mennonites and more than 1,000 Amerindians also live there. One of the main reasons for Filadelfia's rapid growth is the fact that it is the location of all necessary services, schools, hospitals, cooperative stores, and industry. Many private enterprises are also located within the town, and it has a major airport.

Houses throughout the colonies are built in the simple Dutch or Midwestern American styles.

The administration of the Mennonite society is organized on a colony basis, consisting of a number of villages that originally settled in a region, which in turn is governed by an administrative head, the Oberschulze, with several assistants. The individual family heads who own the land are the backbone of the system, being eligible to take part in all decision-making. The villages meet periodically and decide on all matters not taken care of at the colony level. A committee also looks after various matters such as the promotion of agriculture and economic development, and funds are maintained to take care of widows, orphans, and the poor. The statutes and regulations agreed upon in the village system and at the colony level are enforced by the Mennonite authorities through fines, penalties, and ultimately jail if a person does not conform. Sentences can include hard labor and flogging. Lawbreakers can also be handed over to the Paraguayan authorities in rare cases.

Landowners are the source of juridical power, since only landowners have the authority to vote in colony meetings. Each village, normally made up of 20 to 40 families, constitutes a political unit with an administrator, an assistant, and a clerk as the official group. There are also "tenth men" who assist the village unit. All the village decision-making and authority is vested in this group. Each village, for example, has its law enforcement officer, who is even authorized to arrest people for speeding through the village.

The Colony Authority, which oversees all the villages, holds yearly meetings at which all major decisions are made, such as election of officers, punishment of offenders, levying of taxes and dues, building of secondary schools, laying out new lands for cultivation, refusing a family permission to emigrate (if, for example, it has large debts), and deciding who can own land. It also organizes the levying of taxes to support the school system, the hospital system, and payment of doctors (each colony has a modern, well-equipped hospital and medical staff); the maintenance of roads and public fences; and the provision for power, burial grounds, and health and retirement insurance. Even the maintenance of colony ranches, public pastures, airports, the mail system, and telephone systems are under the control of the Colony Authority.

[10] FAMILY LIFE

Traditionally men have the authority in the family and women are expected to carry out the housekeeping functions and help with raising farm produce. Divorce, once unheard of, does take place, although it is still a relatively rare event.

[11] CLOTHING

Those in rural areas dress more simply than do urban dwellers. Men wear hats and blue or green overalls, and the women wear head coverings and plain, knee-length dresses of one simple color. On important religious occasions, such as Good Friday services, the women will wear plain black dresses and carry black caps in a box. The caps will only be taken out and tied under their shawls once they reach church.

[12] FOOD

The Paraguayan Mennonite communities enjoy large meals, with many traditional German and Russian dishes such as sauerkraut and borscht. They also make a Mennonite cheese, which has become well known throughout Latin America.

[13] EDUCATION

The education system is organized and operated solely by the Mennonites. The system is directed by the administrator of the Colony Authority, two teachers, and two ministers, but an administrator for the school system is also employed. Families contribute to the cost of educating their own children, but the villages assist those with more than three children.

Each village is responsible for the building of the schoolhouse, the hiring of the teacher, and the general operation of the school. The three high schools are directed by the boards, responsible to the authority.

[14] CULTURAL HERITAGE

Through a traditional program of education—Sunday schools, Bible schools, preaching, and home training—the young people are introduced into the Mennonite Christian tradition. Bible study conferences are sponsored at Easter, Christmas, and other occasions to reinforce the Mennonite faith and theology.

[15] WORK

Mennonites are not afraid of settling in the most inhospitable areas and are hard-working farmers. In the Bolivian wilderness (known as the Oriente) north and east of Santa Cruz, for example, they cleared the forest, built their houses, and sowed their crops. Each community trades their farm produce, dairy products, and crops such as cotton, sorgum, and wheat with neighboring towns. It is a Mennonite tradition to cooperate with one another at sowing and harvest times, as well as when building new barns.

[16] SPORTS

Mennonites enjoy games of all sorts but avoid any professional sport. They enjoy competing in friendly contests among each other, but they do not believe in the notion of towns or villages competing against one another. Sport is seen as a physical pastime, meant to be enjoyed for itself, as well as a means of learning to cooperate with others as part of a team.

[17] ENTERTAINMENT AND RECREATION

Mennonites are against music, dancing, and any form of boisterous party. They prefer to live a simple, puritanical lifestyle. Social gatherings are the main form of recreation, such as men getting together to raise a new barn or gather in the harvest, and women preparing and serving meals for friends and neighbors. While Sunday is a day of rest, it is also a day of worship, although simple board games of skill are a favorite family pastime.

[18] FOLK ART, CRAFTS, AND HOBBIES

All Mennonite crafts and hobbies have a practical purpose, from the handcrafted tools and implements made by the men, to the large quilts handmade and stitched together by the women.

[19] SOCIAL PROBLEMS

With the arrival of increasing numbers of Paraguayans settling in the Chaco, the Mennonite communities have come under pressure from the authorities, and there is a growing worry that the government may not honor its Privilegium. More and more Mennonites are investing their money abroad, or looking to emigrate. The election of a Mennonite governor for the department of Boqueron, however, is a sign that Mennonites are deciding to become more involved with Paraguayan affairs.

Meanwhile, the modern world has caught up with Filadelfia, and the arrival of motorbikes and videos is seen as a threat to Mennonite values. At the same time, beer and tobacco, once forbidden in the settlements, are being openly sold, although they are only being bought and consumed by non-Mennonites.

In some areas of South America, the unique Mennonite lifestyle is attracting tourists, but the Mennonites do not like photographs to be taken of them and try to avoid tourists.

[20] BIBLIOGRAPHY

Bernhardson, Wayne. *Argentina, Uruguay and Paraguay: A Lonely Planet Travel Survival Kit.* 2nd ed. Australia: Lonely Planet Publications, 1996.

The Mennonite Encyclopaedia. Vol. 5. Scottdale, PA: Herald Press, 1990.

The Mennonite Quarterly Review 45, no. 4 (October 1971).

The Mennonite Quarterly Review 47, no. 4 (October 1973).

—by P. Pitchon, reviewed by R. Caballero

MEXICAN AMERICANS

For more information on Mexican history and culture, *see* **Vol. 2: Mexicans**.

OVERVIEW

In 1845, the independent republic of Texas became a US state. The Mexicans living there suddenly found themselves living in America. They were not offered US citizenship, however, so they were not officially considered Mexican Americans. The first official Mexican Americans entered the union when Mexico ceded the northern part of its territory to the US at the end of the Mexican-American War (1846–1848). The Mexican inhabitants of that land were given the choice of either becoming US citizens or relocating south to Mexican territory. About 80% (or 80,000) of them chose to stay and become US citizens, comprising the first large group of official Mexican Americans.

Although this new US territory had recently been part of Mexico, and the Mexican Americans residing there were living on land that had been in their families for generations, the new European American settlers assumed authority and relegated the Mexican Americans to second-class status. English was declared the official language; Mexican Americans were only given low-paid, menial work; stores, saloons, and schools were segregated, and landlords and employers put up signs saying, "No Mexicans need apply." Some towns outlawed Mexican *fiestas* (celebrations). Perhaps worst of all, the US broke its promise to the Mexican Americans that they would retain all rights to their lands and instead awarded numerous land claims to European Americans through the courts.

Mexican Americans therefore became impoverished, lower-class citizens in what had once been their own country. A Mexican American middle class did develop along the Rio Grande, which was used as a major trade route between Mexico and the US. Mexican Americans were able to fill the need for trade brokers who were fluent in Spanish and understood Mexican culture. Elsewhere, however, Mexican Americans fell into landless poverty and were forced to work as itinerant laborers.

In the late 1800s, political and economic instability in Mexico prompted thousands of Mexicans to move across the border into the US in search of better opportunities. The Mexican American population rose from 75,000 in 1890 to 562,000 in 1900. The majority were poor and illiterate. They became unskilled laborers, working mostly on farms, in mines, or for the railroad. When the US government restricted Asian immigration, positions that the Chinese had formerly filled in railroad construction became available, and Mexicans leapt at the opportunity. Eventually, some 70% of track-layers and 90% of maintenance crews on US railroads were Mexican. The US mining industry, particularly in Colorado, Arizona, and California, was built largely on the backs of Mexican immigrants, and much of US agriculture for the past 100 years or more has been accomplished through the contributions of Mexican migrant workers.

The largest wave of Mexican immigration to the US, termed the "Great Migration," occurred in the 1920s, partly as a result of the bloody Mexican Revolution (1910–1924). As many as 600,000 Mexicans legally crossed the border between 1920 and 1929. They were given permanent visas, allowing them to do contract work in agriculture but not to become US citizens. Thousands of Mexicans also entered the US illegally in the early 1900s. US employers contributed to this illegal immigration by hiring smugglers, called *coyotes*, to bring the undocumented migrants across the border. The undocumented workers were easily exploited because they had no recourse. Employers could turn them in to immigration officials at any time. Some employers made a practice of hiring undocumented migrants, then turning the workers in to the Immigration and Naturalization Service (INS) as soon as the job was done but before they had paid the workers their wages.

With the onset of World War I (1914–18), US president Woodrow Wilson removed the restrictions on Mexican workers that had formerly limited them to agricultural labor. American men were going off to fight in the war, and workers were needed to fill their places. Because they could now work in other industries, many Mexican contract workers moved north to cities such as Chicago, Detroit, Cleveland, and Pittsburgh where industrial jobs were plentiful. Mexican workers flooded across the border to take advantage of these new opportunities. By 1929, the Mexican American population had reached approximately one million, not counting undocumented migrants.

The boom was short lived, however. In October 1929, the US stock market crashed, and America entered the Great Depression. Job opportunities suddenly became scarce as the economy fell apart. Some 85,000 Mexican workers returned almost immediately to Mexico. Others were driven back across the border by frustrated European Americans who felt that the Mexicans were taking away their jobs. Anti-Mexican sentiment became especially violent in Southern California, and about 75,000 Mexican residents of that state decided to move back to Mexico. Many Mexicans who stayed in the US were forced to go on welfare. European Americans saw them as a burden on an already overburdened economy and insisted that they be forced to leave.

The US and Mexico decided to institute a cooperative repatriation program, where Mexican Americans would be resettled in Mexico. Some 500,000 Mexican Americans were removed to Mexico through this program before Mexico called it off because its economy could not support any more people either. Los Angeles established its own repatriation program in 1931–1934, deporting over 13,000 Mexican Americans, including a number of US-born children.

When the US became involved in World War II (1939–45), American men again left their jobs to fight in the war, and the US again requested Mexican workers to fill their places. These workers, called *braceros* (hired hands), were given only temporary visas. The *braceros* unfortunately displaced Mexican American workers already in the US because they were willing and able to work for less pay than the established Mexican Americans. The *bracero* program actually had little to do with wartime labor shortage. Instead, it was a way for US agriculture to take advantage of the economic difficulties in Mexico, evidenced by the fact that the program was originally intended to last only from 1942-1947, but it continued (in somewhat less official form) until 1964. The original program peaked in 1944 with 62,170 *braceros* brought into the US. The peak year from 1947–1964 was 1956, when some 500,000 *braceros* were employed. Overall, about five million Mexicans came to the US between 1942 and 1964 as seasonal workers.

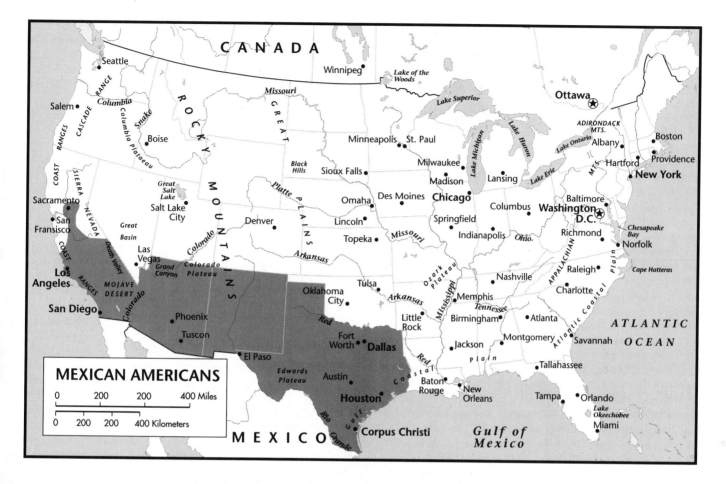

The US also hoped that the *bracero* program would discourage illegal immigration across the border by providing a legal way for Mexicans to work in the US. However, since the program placed restrictions on where *braceros* could work and specified what they would be paid, it actually encouraged undocumented migration. Undocumented migrants could work wherever they could find a job, and employers could pay them less than the *braceros*, so both sides profited from illegal immigration. The fact that the *bracero* program increased, rather than decreased, undocumented migration is shown clearly in INS records. In 1942, the first year of the program, 8,000 undocumented Mexican migrants were deported. By 1951, some 500,000 were arrested and deported.

The INS responded to this increased flow of undocumented migrants by instituting Operation Wetback in 1954. Undocumented Mexican migrants were called wetbacks (or *mojados*), a derogatory term, because they often swam across the Rio Grande to get into the US. Through Operation Wetback, the INS deported 3,800,000 or more undocumented migrants in five years. Economic and political difficulties in Mexico, combined with economic opportunities in the US, however, have continued to encourage the flow of undocumented migrants from Mexico to the US since then. Most undocumented migrants today work at unskilled jobs in restaurants, hotels and motels, hospitals and nursing homes, small manufacturing shops, on assembly lines, in sweatshops with the garment industry, in gardening and landscaping businesses, and in light construction.

Not all Mexican Americans are undocumented migrants. Many entered the US legally and have become US citizens. Others are descendants of the original Mexican Americans who became US citizens in 1848. Second-, third-, and later-generation Mexican Americans have family histories in the US that go back much further than some European Americans' histories. Mexican Americans were one of the most decorated ethnic groups in World War II, earning 39 Congressional Medals of Honor. Some 350,000–500,000 Mexican Americans fought in the US Armed Services during that war. Many of the Mexican American soldiers used the GI Bill after the war to pursue higher education and vocational training, allowing them to move into skilled labor and professional positions.

Mexican Americans have also been at the forefront of the US labor movement since its inception in the 1880s. The best-known Mexican American labor organizer is César Chávez, founder of the National Farm Workers Association in 1962, which later became the United Farm Workers Union. In the 1950s, a rise in ethnic pride began among Mexican Americans, led by people like Reies López "Pete" Tijerina and Rodolfo "Corky" Gonzáles. Called the Chicano Movement (or *El Movimento*), it came to involve legitimate political organization as well as more radical protests, particularly around the issue of the theft of lands by European Americans that originally belonged to Mexican families.

Mexican Americans are the fastest growing ethnic group in the US today. They are also the largest Hispanic group in the US. The estimated Mexican American population in 1993 was

14 million, the largest Mexican population outside of Mexico. About two to four million are undocumented migrants. Almost 80% of Mexican Americans live in either California (6,119,000, or 48.4%) or Texas (3,891,000, or 30.9%). In 1993, 20% of California's population was Mexican American, while Mexican Americans made up 23% of the population of Texas. Mexican Americans have a high birth rate, compared to other US ethnic groups, so their population is increasing more rapidly than the population of other groups. It is projected that by the year 2000, the Mexican American population will have grown to 17 million, and Mexican Americans will make up 30% of California's total population.

Los Angeles has the largest Mexican population outside of Mexico, with an estimated 2.8 million Mexican Americans living in the Los Angeles area in 1992. San Antonio, Texas, has the second largest Mexican American population (448,000), followed by Houston (373,000), and El Paso (282,000). Several other cities in California, Texas, New Mexico, and Arizona have Mexican American populations of over 100,000 or 200,000.

Many Mexican Americans speak only Spanish at home and with their Mexican American families and friends. Foreign-born Mexican Americans experience difficulties in the English-dominated US, even though many cities with large Hispanic populations are de facto bilingual, with signs and other public information printed in both Spanish and English. Non-Hispanic Americans who feel threatened by the growing Hispanic American population have initiated an "English Only" movement in recent years in response to the bilingual movement promoted by the Hispanic community (see **Cuban Americans**).

Mexican Americans are nearly all Catholic, though their brand of Catholicism is somewhat different from European Catholicism. Many elements of Mexican folk religion have been retained, creating a colorful blend of Christianity and magic. Mexican Americans continue to celebrate the countless *fiestas* of their traditional Mexican Catholicism, as well as the conventional Christian holidays of Christmas and Easter, etc.

Mexican Americans also celebrate a number of secular holidays. Diez y Seis ("Sixteen") celebrates the El Grito de Dolores speech delivered by Father Miguel Hidalgo on 16 September 1810, which marked the beginning of Mexico's struggle for independence from Spain. Benito Juarez's defeat of French forces at the city of Pueblo on 5 May 1862 is commemorated each year on Cinco de Mayo ("Fifth of May"). Both of these events are marked with parades, floats, traditional dress and music, and other festivities.

One Mexican American holiday tradition that has become popular in mainstream American culture is the *piñata*, a hollow pottery or plaster jar (usually shaped like an animal) that is filled with candy, fruit, and gifts and hung from the ceiling. Blindfolded children then swing a stick in the air (one at a time), trying to break the *piñata*. Once it is broken, all the children scramble to grab as much of the fallen contents as possible.

Other Mexican American contributions to mainstream American culture include zoot suits (baggy pants, long loose jackets, and wide-brimmed hats made popular by Mexican American youths in the late-1930s and 1940s), and foods such as tacos, burritos, enchiladas, tortilla chips and salsa, and guacamole. Mariachi music played by strolling Mexican American musicians can be heard all across the US, as can Tex-Mex music (or *musica nortena*)—a blend of Mexican and German polka music. Individual Mexican American musicians include singers Vikki Carr (born Florencia Bisenta de Casillas Martínez Cardona) and Joan Baez. Two well-known Mexican American actors are Ricardo Montalban and Anthony Rudolph Oaxaca Quinn, who is also part Irish.

Mexican Americans have also begun to make their mark in the worlds of US politics and science. Joseph Montoya became the first Mexican American elected to the US Senate in 1964. The first Mexican American governors to serve since the early 1900s (Ezequiel C. de Vaca and Octaviano Larrazolo were governors of New Mexico) were elected in 1974 in New Mexico (Jerry Apodaca) and Arizona (Raúl Castro). Henry Cisneros became the first Mexican American mayor of a major US city when he was elected by the citizens of San Antonio, Texas, in 1981. In 1993, Cisneros was named HUD secretary by President Clinton. Educator Lupe Anguiano developed the Bilingual Education Act while serving in the Department of Health, Education, and Welfare, and Federico Peña was appointed US Secretary of Transportation in 1993 by President Bill Clinton. In the sciences, Mexican American astronaut Ellen Ochoa earned the honor of being the first Hispanic woman in space in 1993.

Mexican Americans also shine in sports. Tennis great Richard "Pancho" Gonzáles won the US Open in both 1948 and 1949, and also won the Wimbledon doubles crown (with Frank Parker) in 1949. Gonzáles was very popular with the American and international public. Golfers Lee Trevino and Nancy López are also highly successful and highly popular Mexican American sports figures. National Basketball Association (NBA) referee Tommy Nuñez is the only Hispanic referee in any American major league sport.

Although individual Mexican Americans have become successful in the US, Mexican Americans as a group continue to struggle against racial and ethnic discrimination that confines them to the lower classes of society. Mexican Americans have been stereotyped by European Americans since the beginning of their history together as poor, uneducated, cowardly criminals. Some European American teachers believe, because of these stereotypes, that their Mexican American students will not succeed, so the teachers do not direct much of their energy or attention to those students and, consequently, the students fail. This self-fulfilling prophecy promotes a high dropout rate among Mexican American students, which perpetuates their status as poor and uneducated, confirming the stereotypes. It is a vicious cycle that many Mexican as well as other Americans are trying to break.

Despite their best efforts, however, the majority of Mexican Americans continue to be trapped in a cycle of poverty that prevents them from improving their situation in America. Mexican Americans are severely underrepresented in the professions and politics. In California, for example, where 21% of the total population is Mexican American, only 7 of the 120 members (6%) of the State Legislature were Mexican American in 1993. Only 4–7% of teachers, administrators, and counselors in California were Mexican American, while 80–90% of the student population was Mexican American in some districts. At the federal level, only 9 of the 535 members of US Congress were Latino in 1993. To be represented according to their proportion of the population, Latinos (of whom the largest percentage are Mexican American) would need 44 members in Congress. Until inequities in education and employment are resolved,

Mexican Americans will not be able to obtain the skills and resources necessary to rise to more appropriate levels in American society.

BIBLIOGRAPHY

Catalano, Julie. *The Mexican Americans*. New York: Chelsea House, 1988.

Gonzales, Juan L., Jr. *Racial and Ethnic Groups in America*, 2nd ed. Dubuque, IA: Kendall/Hunt Publishing, 1993.

Jensen, Jeffry. *Hispanic Americans Struggle for Equality*. Vero Beach, FL: Rourke Corporation, 1992.

Marvis, Barbara J. *Contemporary American Success Stories: Famous People of Hispanic Heritage*, vols. I, II, and III. N.p.: Mitchell Lane, 1996.

—by D. K. Daeg de Mott

MEXICANS

LOCATION: Mexico
POPULATION: 95 million
LANGUAGE: Spanish; over 30 Amerindian languages
RELIGION: Roman Catholicism (with Amerindian elements); various Protestant sects

[1] INTRODUCTION

Mexico was the home of several native American civilizations before the arrival of the Spanish in 1519. The Maya, Olmecs, Toltecs, and Aztecs built cities and pyramids. Under Spanish rule these peoples were converted to Christianity, and European customs were added to the indigenous way of life.

Mexico won its independence from Spain in 1821 but lost the northern half of its territory to the United States in 1818. The dictatorship of Porfirio Díaz was overthrown in a revolution that adopted a new, progressive constitution in 1917. A political party founded in 1929 and known since 1945 as the Institutional Revolutionary Party (PRI) has remained in power continuously since then. Although Mexico has greatly advanced economically in the second half of the 20th century, severe recessions followed the fall of the value of its currency in 1982 and 1994.

Some 75 to 90% of Mexico's 95 million people are of mixed European (usually Spanish) and Amerindian descent. The Indian past is officially honored and Spanish colonialism is often deplored. Cuahtémoc, the last Aztec emperor, led the resistance against the Spanish and is a national hero. In practice, however, persons of pure European blood rank highest in social standing and, similarly, Indians are usually on the bottom of the social ladder.

[2] LOCATION AND HOMELAND

Mexico lies between the Pacific Ocean and the Gulf of Mexico and Caribbean Sea, south of the United States and west of Guatemala and Belize. Most of the country is a highland plateau with little rainfall for most of the year. The plateau is enclosed by two mountain chains running the length of the country, the Sierra Madre Oriental to the east and Sierra Madre Occidental to the west. The summit of the highest peak, Orizaba, reaches 5,639 meters (18,502 feet) above sea level. There is tropical rain forest in parts of the South and the Gulf coast. Mexico reaches its narrowest point at the Isthmus of Tehuantepec, then widens to the east, where it includes the Yucatán Peninsula.

[3] LANGUAGE

The official language is Spanish, and Mexico is the world's largest Spanish-speaking nation. Although almost all Mexicans speak at least some Spanish, about 7 or 8% of the people also speak an Indian language as their native tongue. Of the more than 30 Indian language groups, the largest is Náhuatl; others include Mayan, Zapotec, Otomí, and Mixtec.

[4] FOLKLORE

Mexican folk customs derive from beliefs and practices dating back well before the European discovery of America. One of these is herbal medicine. Particularly in Indian communities,

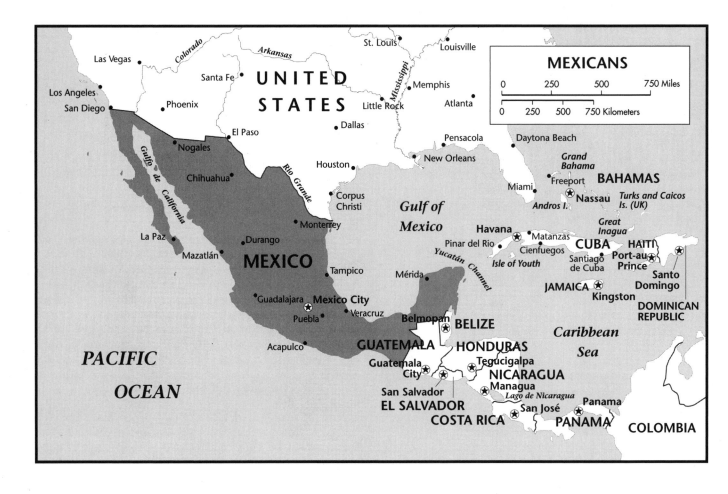

curanderos function as healers and diviners who communicate with nature gods and spirits. Among them are persons seen as sorcerers or witches and credited with similar powers, including the ability to cast or dispel the evil eye (superstition derived from Spain) and to perform certain magic rites to help a person win or retain a loved one.

A wealth of major feasts *(fiestas),* although commemorating Christian saints, also parallel the worship of Indian gods dating back to the pre-European past. The saints are credited with the supernatural powers traditionally attributed to the gods. In Indian communities, *confradías* (brotherhoods) are charged with organizing and financing the annual cycle of fiestas. These events break the monotony of daily life with their bright costumes and ornaments and their traditional dances and music. Traditional masks represent animals, spirits, and religious or mythical figures. Alcohol, and sometimes hallucinogenic drugs, play a role in these observances, as they do in healing and divining.

5 RELIGION

Between 90 and 95% of the Mexican people are Roman Catholics. However, just as early Christianity retained many beliefs and customs of pagan Greece and Rome, Mexican Catholicism includes folklore and practices of the pre-European period. The Virgin of Guadalupe, identified with the Virgin Mary, is credited by the church with miraculously appearing to an Indian soon after the Spanish conquest (and close to the shrine of an

Aztec earth goddess). The Virgin of Guadalupe was proclaimed patron saint of Mexico in 1737. Similarly, many other Christian saints are identified with gods and goddesses of the Indian past.

About 5% of the population is Protestant. Evangelical Christian groups, including Baptists, Mormons, Jehovah's Witnesses, and Seventh-Day Adventists, generally financed and staffed by Americans, have had particular success in southeastern Mexico, especially among Indian communities.

6 MAJOR HOLIDAYS

Holy Week, commemorating the events leading up to and including the crucifixion and resurrection of Jesus, is of overriding importance. It was once commemorated in many outdoor processions and Passion plays, only a few of which remain. United States influence has brought with it Christmas trees (sometimes even in churches), Santa Claus, and gift giving on Christmas Day. This has overshadowed the traditional Hispanic observance of Epiphany, or Twelfth Night, commemorating the journey of the Magi (the Three Kings). Preceding Christmas are the colorful *posadas,* nightly celebrations that begin December 16.

November 2, the Day of the Dead, is a holiday on which people visit the graves of their loved ones and leave behind fruits and flowers. At the evening meal a table is traditionally set with food and drink for the departed. Also typically Mexican is the annual commemoration, on December 12, of the appearance of the Virgin of Guadalupe in 1531. The Basilica of

Guadalupe, in Mexico City, attracts many pilgrims on that day, some, if able, climb its steps on their knees, and Indian groups play music and perform dances outside the cathedral.

Among secular (nonreligious) holidays, the most important is the celebration of national independence on 16 September. The president of Mexico heralds this event on the evening before with the *grito* (cry or shout) given by Father Miguel Hidalgo, the priest who, in the name of the Mexican people, proclaimed independence from Spain in 1810. The birthday of Benito Juárez, March 21, is another national holiday. A Zapotec Indian, Juárez was president of Mexico from 1861 to 1872.

7 RITES OF PASSAGE

Purification by water goes back to the Indian past, so infant baptism is practiced even in Indian communities where the other sacraments are not observed. Most Mexican children also are confirmed. In small towns among well-off families, young couples are still chaperoned on dates, and a suitor must court his future in-laws as well as his intended bride. In Indian communities, marriages may still be arranged and sealed with an exchange of gifts.

Most Mexicans marry young. Because of the separation of church and state, only civil marriages are legally valid, but more than 70% of all couples also marry in church. Many poor couples live together however, without benefit of clergy or legal license.

The dead are not customarily embalmed, and burial takes place 24 hours after death. Wakes are held, with the relatives and friends bringing food, drink, and other gifts to the bereaved.

8 INTERPERSONAL RELATIONS

Politeness and ceremoniousness are more important in Mexican life than in American. Even brief exchanges and questions call for an introductory *buenos días* (good day) or *buenas tardes* (good afternoon). Indirectness of speech is often employed so as not to lay or accept blame or give offense. Government employees, including policemen, are poorly paid, and sometimes will accept or even solicit the *mordida* ("bite" or bribe) as payment for minor infractions or to speedup or dispose of cumbersome paperwork.

Male friends are demonstrative; often they will embrace heartily on meeting and stroll arm in arm. *Machismo* is a male worldview that entails the practice of defending one's honor against any possible challenge to one's masculinity. Carried to violent extremes, this often results in the abuse of women.

In contrast with Americans, Mexicans set little store on punctuality. In fact, arriving on time when invited to dinner or a party is considered rude. Nor is it considered unusual for invited guests not to arrive at all and offer no explanation later. *Mañana*, although literally "tomorrow", may refer to any indefinite future time. Business hours often fluctuate. Public offices, churches, and museums may close for two hours in the early afternoon, when the temperature is highest, the traditional *siesta* time.

9 LIVING CONDITIONS

Most peasants and many workers in Mexico do not earn even the meager legal minimum wage and are unable to feed or house their families decently. Open drains and contaminated

The more traditional forms of women's dress include a wraparound skirt, sometimes flounced and embroidered. (Andrea Henderson)

drinking water are common and a menace to health. Although there is a national health service, more than a third of the population does not receive medical attention. Government subsidies hold down the price of corn tortillas, beans, and cooking oil, but many Mexicans—perhaps as many as two-thirds—eat less than the minimum of 2,000 calories per day required for basic good health. Even so, life expectancy has risen to nearly 70 years, compared to only 37 in 1930.

The right to a "dignified home" is in the constitution, but about two-thirds of the people are poorly housed. The poorest peasants and urban dwellers build their own adobe huts or wooden shanties. Only half of all dwellings have piped water and flush toilets, although almost 90% have electric lighting. Improvised settlements cover the fringes of the Mexico City metropolitan area and other cities. Air pollution is also a problem in Mexico City and other urban centers.

The middle class, estimated at one-sixth to one-third of the population, does not have to deal with as many problems of day-to-day living. A cheap and plentiful supply of domestic workers is available to help take care of homes and children.

10 FAMILY LIFE

"Family values" are alive and well in Mexico, where widespread poverty forces households to stay together for economic as well as social reasons. The household in many cases includes grandparents, aunts, and uncles as well as parents and children. Married children and their spouses also remain part of this unit until they can afford to set up their own households. Well-to-do fathers may build houses for their married children on the parents property. Family groups may gather together for birthdays, saints' days, and other holidays. On Sundays they often go on excursions together. Whether they live under the same roof or not, Mexicans maintain strong bonds with their relatives in order to help each other in various ways, including helping unemployed relations find work. The large number of family businesses are especially important to this form of assistance.

Family solidarity extends even beyond blood ties. *Compadrazgo,* or godparenthood plays a very important part in Mexican life. One study of a Mexico City shantytown found 18 different occasions for involving godparents in celebrations, including not only the Catholic sacraments but even the graduation of a family member from school or the first cutting of a child's hair. In return for his or her aid, a godparent expects loyalty, trust, affection, and respect from the child and parents.

Among middle-class and well-to-do Mexicans, servants also form part of the family unit. Even *arrimados* (renters or "permanent guests") may belong.

11 CLOTHING

The more traditional forms of women's dress include a wraparound skirt, sometimes flounced and embroidered; the *huipil,* a sleeveless garment with holes for the head and arms; and the *quechquemitl,* an upper outer garment with an opening for the head only. The rebozo is a shawl used for carrying babies. Among Indian women these are everyday articles of clothing, elaborately colored and patterned and distinctive for every ethnic group, or even for each village. Upper-class Mexican women may sometimes wear a traditional Spanish costume topped with a fringed and embroidered silk shawl and a tortoiseshell or ivory comb. The *china poblana* costume consists of a richly embroidered white blouse and black shawl, a flounced and spangled red-and-green skirt, high-heeled colored slippers, bracelets, earrings, strings of beads, and ribbons or flowers in the hair.

The peasant's traditional pajamalike trousers and tunic of unbleached cotton, serape (functioning as both a blanket and a cloak), sandals, and wide sombrero have given way to jeans, shirt, shoes or boots, and a straw cowboy-type hat. Sweaters or a leather jacket now ward off the chill. Indian men seldom wear traditional dress except on special occasions. Mariachi musicians can be seen in the traditional Spanish horseman's *charro* costume. This includes a dark suit of suede or velvet, braided in gold or silver embroidery, a flowing red silk necktie, a bright serape, boots and spurs, and an embroidered felt sombrero.

12 FOOD

The staple of Mexican food is corn, supplemented by beans, squash, and chilies, or chili peppers. Cornmeal is patted into a thin pancake called a tortilla, which encloses any of a great variety of fillings to form a soft sandwichlike taco. (The crisp-fried US taco is known as a *tostado*). Fried in chili sauce, the taco becomes an enchilada. The tamale is cornmeal dough wrapped around a filling of meat and chilies, then wrapped in paper, corn husks, or banana leaves for cooking. Tacos made with a tortilla of wheat flour are called burritos. Mole is a rich chili sauce that sometimes contains chocolate, which is native to Mexico. *Mole poblano,* traditionally the national dish, consists of turkey (a native bird) topped with a spicy mole.

13 EDUCATION

Six years of education are free and compulsory for children from ages six through fourteen. However, many of them—and a majority in rural areas—do not complete the required six years. About one out of 10 Mexicans cannot read or write, and about one in five is illiterate for practical purposes. School attendance is lowest among Indians, peasants, urban slum dwellers, and migrants. In poor areas, children are often too undernourished to study.

Secondary-school enrollment has increased greatly in recent years, so that about four out of every five elementary-school graduates now enter high school. Some receive vocational training, while others continue on to the nation's 260 institutions of higher learning. The most important of these is the National Autonomous University of Mexico, in Mexico City. The number of university students has passed one million, but the dropout rate is very high.

Because of inadequate funding, public schooling is often deficient in quality. Private schools at every level, often run by the Catholic Church, now educate most children and youths from middle-class, as well as well-to-do, families.

14 CULTURAL HERITAGE

Mexico's rich cultural life draws on both its Spanish and its Indian heritage. This is most evident in the visual arts. Pre-Conquest temple and palace wall paintings were recalled in the 20th-century murals of Diego Rivera, José Clemente Orozco, David Siquieros, and Juan O'Gorman, which were crowded with stylized figures and themes. Oil paintings by Rivera, his wife Frida Kahlo, Rufino Tamayo, and others are admired for their vibrant color. In architecture, Mexican stone carvers carried on a pre-Conquest tradition in the elaborate 18th-century decorative style known as *churrigueresque.* O'Gorman and Luis Barragán deftly combined pre-Conquest, colonial, and folk forms and traditional building materials with modern structural design in their architecture.

Traditional Indian music is chiefly limited to festive rituals and dances, with drums and flutes as the main instruments. Stringed instruments, including the most popular one in Mexico—the guitar—came from Spain. In mariachi music, these instruments are combines with trumpets. The marimba (similar to the xylophone) dominates in southern Mexico. Traditional song forms are the *corrido,* derived from old Spanish ballads; the *canción,* romantic and sentimental; and the *ranchera,* a Mexican style of country-and-western music. Composer Carlos Chávez drew on such forms in his music.

The Ballet Folklórico mounts productions of traditional dance which incorporate both Indian and Spanish motifs. Best-known of these is the *jarabe tapatío* ("Mexican hat dance"), performed in *charro* and *china poblana* costume. Dating back to pre-Conquest times are the *conchero* dances, which honor the four winds, and the *pascolas,* or deer dances.

The love poetry of Sor Juana Inés de la Cruz is still read, and the plays of Juan Ruiz de Alarcón are still performed. Noted Mexican writers of the 20th century include the poet and essayist Octavio Paz and the novelists Mariano Azuela, Carlos Fuentes, and Juan Rulfo.

Weaver in Mexico City, Mexico. Weaving in cotton and other plant fibers on hand looms is thousands of years old; wool was added after the Spanish conquest. (Corel Corporation)

15 WORK

Mexico's formally employed workers are protected by legislation guaranteeing minimum wages, hours of work, legal holidays, paid vacations, collective bargaining, and the right to strike. The minimum wage, however, was under $3 a day in 1995. Perhaps half of the nation's labor force works outside the formal economy entirely and consists mainly of subsistence farmers and small-scale artisans and merchants. Their hours are long, and the income is generally meager. With half its population under 30 years of age, Mexico is scrambling to find enough jobs for the young people who enter the labor force each year. Migration to the United States helps to relieve the unemployment problem. In the mid 1990s an estimated one to two million undocumented Mexicans were living in the United States.

16 SPORTS

Fútbol (soccer) is by far the most popular sport in Mexico. The top professional teams, including Guadalajara and the Américas team of Mexico City, draw as many as 100,000 spectators to their matches. There is a professional baseball league, and some Mexican players, such as Fernando Valenzuela and Vinnie Castilla, have made it to the major leagues. US television has raised the profile of both basketball and American football in Mexico. Other sports include golf, tennis, swim-

ning), and jai alai. Bullfighting is popular, with about 35 arenas in Mexico. Also popular is the *jaripeo* or rodeo.

17 ENTERTAINMENT AND RECREATION

Television now dominates popular culture, with *telenovelas* (soap operas) and variety shows especially popular. Overwhelmed by American imports, Mexico's film industry has declined greatly since its heyday in the 1930s and 1940s. Older song forms have been giving way to rock 'n' roll, international-style pop, and even Spanish-language rap. Because so many Mexicans have had little schooling, comic books and magazine-style *fotonovelas* are more common reading material than newspapers and books.

18 FOLK ART, CRAFTS, AND HOBBIES

The most important form of folk painting is the *retablo,* a devotional depiction, on canvas, of a miraculous event. It is offered to a saint in gratitude for favors conferred and hung in a church. Other works of art include murals and yarn and bark paintings. Folk sculptures, continuing a pre-Columbian tradition, include masks, papier-mâché skeletons and other grotesque figures, and candle-bearing trees of life made of clay.

The variety of Mexican handicrafts is almost endless. Silver objects include bracelets, rings, necklaces, and earrings. *Milagros,* charms offered to saints in church, may be made of silver, copper, or tin. Objects are also carved in onyx, jade, and other types of stone. There are many regional styles of pottery. The making of hand-blown glass, tile making, leather work, and lacquering are other crafts. Weaving in cotton and other plant fibers on hand looms is thousands of years old; wool was added after the Spanish conquest. Embroidery employs floral, bird, and animal imagery. Toys of all kinds are produced.

The piñata, usually made of papier-mâché or lightweight cardboard, is gaily decorated in many fantastic forms and holds candy. Blindfolded children break it open with a stick at birthday and other celebrations.

19 SOCIAL PROBLEMS

Many Mexicans are poorly fed and housed and do not receive adequate health care. An estimated 200,000 to 400,000 are infected with the AIDS virus. Alcoholism is also a serious health problem. About 30% of the population is not served by a sewage system. Air pollution is a health hazard in Mexico City and other urban centers. Human rights violations include appalling prison conditions, electoral fraud, repression of the labor movement, and the abuse of indigenous and rural peoples.

20 BIBLIOGRAPHY

Bean, Frank D. and et al, ed. *At the Crossroads: Mexican Migration and U.S. Policy.* Lanham, Md.: Rowman & Littlefield, 1997.

Bernard, H. Russell. *Native Ethnography: A Mexican Indian Describes His Culture, Jesus Salinas Pedraza.* Newbury Park, Calif.: Sage Publications, 1989.

Diaz-Guerrero, Rogelio. *Psychology of the Mexican: Culture and Personality.* Austin: University of Texas Press, 1975.

Frye, David. *Indians Into Mexicans: History and Identity in a Mexican Town.* Austin: University of Texas Press, 1996.

Lomnitz, Larissa Adler and Marisol Perez-Lizaur. *A Mexican Elite Family, 1820–1980: Kinship, Class, and Culture.* Translated by Cinna Lomnitz. Princeton, N.J.: Princeton University Press, 1987.

Meyer, Michael C. *The Course of Mexican History.* 5th ed. New York: Oxford University Press, 1995.

Monto, Alexander. *The Roots of Mexican Labor Migration.* Westport, Conn.: Praeger, 1994.

Riding, Allen. *Distant Neighbors.* New York: Knopf, 1984.

Toor, Frances. *A Treasury of Mexican Folkways.* New York: Crown, 1947.

—by R. Halasz, reviewed by G. T. Walker

MISKITO

ALTERNATE NAMES: Mosquito
LOCATION: Nicaragua; Honduras
POPULATION: About 200,000
LANGUAGE: Dialects of Miskito; English; Spanish
RELIGION: Moravian church (majority); Catholicism; fundamentalist Protestantism; Christianity mingled with folk beliefs

1 INTRODUCTION

The Miskito (also spelled "Mosquito") are an indigenous people living in the Caribbean coastal lowlands of Nicaragua and Honduras. They came to international attention in the early 1980s as a result of their resistance activities against Nicaragua's Sandinista government. They are the largest native group in the region (often referred to as the Nicaraguan Atlantic Coast or the Miskito Coast) and have lobbied prominently for the cultural, territorial, economic, and political rights of the region's indigenous peoples.

Although considered a native people, the Miskito as a distinct group actually came into existence as a result of European colonization of the Caribbean region. Their forebears, unaffected by Spanish settlement of western Nicaragua and Honduras in the 16th century, later began welcoming escaped African slaves fleeing British possessions in the region. The mixed-race people that resulted from intermarriage between the slaves and the local population became the Miskitos. Introduced to guns and ammunition by English traders and settlers in the area—it is commonly thought that "Miskito" comes from "musket"—they expanded their territory northward, southward, and westward from its original location at the mouth of the Rio Coco.

Those of the region's native groups that were not assimilated into the Miskito were pushed into the interior and became known as the Sumu. The Miskito became the most important non-White population on the coast, living in peace with the British and serving as an intermediary between them and the Sumu. From the mid-17th century to the late 19th century, the Miskito prospered, thanks to their trade with the British and the abundant natural resources of their territory, which at one time extended as far as the present-day nations of Belize and Panama.

In the late 19th century, an ethnic shift occurred in the region when banana growers began bringing in Black English-speaking laborers from the West Indies to work on their plantations. They and their descendants, who became known as Creoles, took the place of the Miskito as the area's dominant non-White group, settling mainly in the newly established port towns while the Miskito remained in rural villages, retaining their traditional language and way of life. Since Nicaraguan and Honduran independence from Britain in the 19th century, the United States played a greater role in the region, especially in the area of banana production, and its corporate interests, especially the United Fruit Company—now United Brands—remained influential well into the 20th century.

When the Sandinista government that came to power in 1979 moved to consolidate its control over the Miskito and bring them into line with its political and economic policies, it met with widespread resistance. In response, the government forced thousands of Miskito out of their homes, sending them to relocation camps. Activists who joined the resistance were imprisoned, tortured, and killed, and thousands "disappeared." Entire villages were looted and destroyed. Altogether, some 20,000 people were sent to relocation camps. Another 40,000 fled, becoming refugees. In spite of the magnitude of their persecution, they insisted on resisting independently, refusing US pressure to join the Contras and other opposition groups. Their plight drew international attention, and they eventually won significant government concessions. By 1984, the government agreed to grant them limited political autonomy.

President Violeta Barrios de Chamorro, whose 1990 election ended Sandinista rule, established a new ministry to serve as a liaison with the Miskito and the neighboring peoples of the Atlantic coast—the Nicaraguan Institute for the Development of the Atlantic Region (INDERA). The example provided by the Miskito of Nicaragua has inspired demands for autonomy by both the Honduran Miskito and other indigenous peoples in Nicaragua. The call for indigenous autonomy has also spread to many other countries in Latin America.

2 LOCATION AND HOMELAND

The Miskito live along the Caribbean coasts of Nicaragua and Honduras. Their lands have a total area of 37,000 sq km (14,300 sq mi)—equal in size to Taiwan or the Netherlands—and extend 900 km (560 mi) along the Caribbean and 400 km (250 mi) inland up the Rio Coco River. This area is extremely diverse geographically, with a large inland savanna, a tropical forest to the west, coastal lowlands, and the most extensive continental shelf in the Caribbean. Its varied lands include mangrove forests, estuaries, coral reefs, seagrass pastures, and the greatest concentration of coastal lagoons in Central America. Its major rivers include the Patuca, Coco (also known as the Wangki), Prinsapolka, Awaltara (Rio Grande), and Kuringwas.

In 1991, a conservation organization called Mikupia—an acronym that also means "Miskito heart"—was formed to protect the abundant resources of the region, with support from the World Wildlife Federation and the Boston-based human rights group, Cultural Survival. In the same year, President Violeta Barrios de Chamorro created the 1.3 million-hectare (3.2 million-acre) Miskito Cays Protected Area, the largest coastal protected area in Latin America.

The Miskito, like the other indigenous groups and the Creoles living on the Miskito Coast—a population collectively called *costeños*—consider themselves separate from the other inhabitants of Nicaragua and Honduras, whom they call "the Spanish." Altogether, the Miskito are thought to number as many as 200,000, around 150,000 in Nicaragua—where they are the largest indigenous group—and 50,000 in Honduras. Most of the Miskito population is centered in the northeastern-most part of Nicaragua, along the riverbanks and in mining areas in the interior, including Siuna, Rosita, and Bonanza.

Before the persecution by the Sandinistas in the 1980s, there were over 260 Miskito communities with 500 to 1,000 people each. Sixty-five of the 100 communities near the Rio Coco River, the most densely populated area, were destroyed by the Sandinistas. Many Miskito migrated to Honduras in the 1980s to avoid political persecution by the Sandinista government. Major settlements in Honduras are located near the Laguna de Caratasca and the banks of the Rio Patuca.

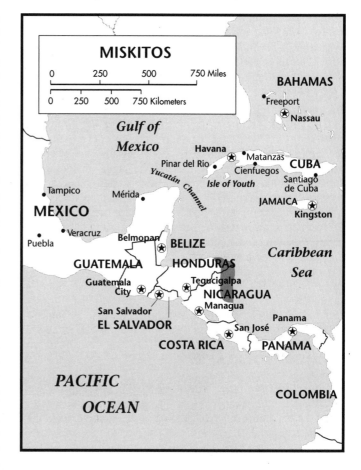

3 LANGUAGE

Besides their native language (Miskito), the Miskito speak Spanish and English and are also familiar with the English-based dialect spoken by the local Creole population. Due to their historically positive attitude toward Britain and the United States—in contrast to their enmity toward the Spanish—they are more likely to speak English than Spanish at home (in addition to Miskito).

Miskito belongs to the Misumalpan family of languages. There are three distinguishable dialects, belonging to the Miskito of eastern Nicaragua, those living along the Rio Coco, and those of eastern Honduras. The dialects, characterized by differences in vocabulary and pronunciation, are all mutually intelligible. Miskito has been influenced by the grammar and vocabulary of West African languages, as well as Spanish, English, and German.

In areas where Miskito is spoken, it has been adopted as the language of the Moravian church, in both spoken and written forms. (The Bible, hymn books, and other religious texts have been translated into Miskito). It has been given official status as an indigenous language in the Nicaraguan Constitution, and the Nicaraguan government has also recognized, by decree, the Miskito's right to be educated in their native language.

4 FOLKLORE

During the colonial era, the British nominally considered the Miskito society a "kingdom." Although its accepted leaders, or "kings," had little real power, legend has transformed them into an important cultural symbol, and they are now a popular subject for local theatrical presentations.

The Miskito believe it is possible to predict a person's death by dreams and other omens.

5 RELIGION

The dominant religion of the Miskito is the Moravian church, which gained a foothold as early as the 17th century through its missionaries and had most of the population converted by the beginning of the 20th century. (Its adherents also include other non-Hispanic populations of eastern Nicaragua, including the Sumu and Rama and the Creoles.) Moravian pastors are important figures in Miskito communities. Their congregations generally provide them with food, an obligation which may take the form of actually planting the pastor's rice and beans themselves. Catholic and fundamentalist Protestant churches have also gained some converts among the Miskito. The traditional folk religion of the Miskito included beliefs in spirits *(lasas)*, omens, and in the powers of natural phenomena such as the moon. Its rituals, including funerals, involved dancing and drinking. When Christianity was introduced, some elements of folk religion were mingled with Christian beliefs and practices.

6 MAJOR HOLIDAYS

The Miskito observe the major holidays of the Christian calendar. Christmas (25 December) is an important holiday and is observed mainly in church. Christmas and New Year's (1 January) are especially festive because there is no plantation work at that time of year.

7 RITES OF PASSAGE

Major life transitions (such as birth, marriage, and death) are marked by religious ceremonies, usually following Christian traditions.

8 INTERPERSONAL RELATIONS

Villagers tend to magnify their personal quarrels, and feuds between different villages are common.

9 LIVING CONDITIONS

Miskito homes are built of split bamboo or lumber with roofs of thatch or corrugated metal. Some houses—usually wooden—consist of two structures, one that serves as a kitchen and the other as sleeping quarters, while bamboo homes are more likely to be composed of a single structure. Houses typically have a porch with a bench and a chair or hammock, and an open front yard which is used for both leisure and various types of work. The Miskito spend most of their time out of doors, and their houses are designed basically as places to cook, eat, sleep, store things, and take shelter from the elements when necessary.

Western medicine coexists side by side with folk medicine among the Miskito, and a patient may receive conventional medical treatment and a "bush remedy" for the same ailment, as well as prayers by the local lay pastor. There are two types of folk practitioner: the *curandero* (herbalist) and the *sukya* (shaman). They use many similar treatment methods, but the curandero makes diagnoses based on the patient's dreams, while the sukya relies on chanting. Folk beliefs attribute illnesses to God, evil spirits, or the weather.

In addition to its distinctive culture, language, and way of life, the Miskito region is isolated from other areas of Nicaragua and Honduras by dense tropical rain forest and rugged mountains that make for difficult travel conditions. There is no comprehensive road network. Only a narrow dirt road connects Miskito lands to those outside them, and even this road is only open seasonally and takes two to three days to negotiate in a specially equipped four-wheel-drive vehicle. Many areas can be reached only on foot or by boat or airplane. There are port facilities at Puerto Lempira and Bilwi.

10 FAMILY LIFE

Young people engage in flirting activities to attract a potential mate, although parental consent must be obtained for marriage. Premarital sex, although common, is officially frowned upon. A couple may have both a civil and a church ceremony, although church weddings are often prohibitively expensive, and civil marriage is accepted in the eyes of the community. Fidelity is expected of both partners once they are married. Family life revolves around having children, who represent the union of the husband's and wife's families. The two families do not consider themselves related to each other until children have been born. In addition, children are their parents' only secure source of support in old age. When a woman remains childless, her husband is likely to father children by other women, and there is a good chance that their marriage will dissolve.

It is a common practice for children to have a godparent, or *libra* (often a female relative), who promises to be responsible for them in the event that the mother dies. Multiple family members, such as grandparents, older siblings, and unmarried aunts, help care for a child. It is considered acceptable for parents to have a child raised by someone else if they cannot afford to do it themselves.

11 CLOTHING

Modern Western-style clothing, either store-bought or sewn from manufactured cloth, has replaced the traditional dress of the Miskito, which was made of locally woven cotton or barkcloth and included loincloths for the men and cotton waist wraps for the women.

12 FOOD

The Miskito eat two main meals, a morning meal eaten shortly before dawn and a late-afternoon meal eaten after workers return from their labor on the plantations. A light snack may be eaten at noontime. Although the Miskito eat the universal Latin American staple of rice and beans, they regard these foods primarily as cash crops and maintain a disdainful attitude toward them, referring to them as either "English food" or "Spanish food" in contrast to their traditional native foods, which include wild game, bananas, and plantains. Manioc (cassava) and other tubers, eaten boiled or baked, are another dietary staple, as are green bananas.

Rice is ground and prepared as a gruel or in small cakes. Coconut milk is heavily used as a flavoring and a thickener for soups and sauces. Meat and fish are eaten sparingly. Maize is not an important part of the diet and is used mostly to make beverages, such as *atol,* made from mashed green corn. A typical Miskito dish is a stew called "rundown," consisting of green bananas, plantains, manioc or other root crops, fish, and coconut milk. Fermented fruits and vegetables are also popular and may be wrapped in leaves and buried until they have soured. Popular beverages include coffee and *wabul,* a beverage made from mashed boiled bananas or plantains and water.

13 EDUCATION

Although Honduras and Nicaragua, where most Miskito live, both have free, compulsory primary education, the educational systems of both countries are inadequate, with low enrollment and graduation rates and high adult illiteracy. Estimates of the adult illiteracy rate in Honduras range from 27% to over 40% and as high as 80% in rural areas (where most Miskito live). Schools are understaffed and undersupplied, with as many as 80 pupils per classroom.

While the Sandinista government effected some improvements in Nicaragua's poor educational record under the earlier Somoza regime, these mostly occurred in the early 1980s before the Contra war drained the country's resources in the latter half of the decade. A 1980 literacy campaign reportedly reduced adult illiteracy to around 23%. During the same period, the government recognized the right of native groups to be educated in their own languages and instituted the first bilingual programs for the Miskito in 1984. By the end of the decade, however, illiteracy had risen to pre-1980 levels and many primary- and secondary-level students were still not enrolled in school. However, rural access to education did improve during the Sandinista era.

14 CULTURAL HERITAGE

Together with their common history and territory, the Miskito have a common culture that, together with their language, has been passed down from generation to generation. In the centuries since the first European contact, some of the Miskito's indigenous art forms—like their religion—have mingled with aspects of European culture. Thus the traditional dance called the *aobaia* is now commonly performed at Christmastime.

The Miskito have a large collection of love songs, of which the following is an example:

Lalma tininska mairin	Wandering lady hummingbird
Naiwa mamunisna	today I sing your praises.
Naha paiaska kra wina	With this blowing breeze
Yang mai lukisna	I am thinking of you.
Prais mai alkra.	Precious thoughts sent to you.

15 WORK

The Miskito have traditionally engaged in hunting, fishing, and subsistence farming, raising beans, rice, yams, bananas, corn, cotton, and sugarcane. Other sources of cash are fur-trapping and extracting the sap from wild rubber trees. Miskito also work as hired laborers for fruit and logging companies, and as gold miners. Increasing numbers are becoming migrant workers and sending cash remittances home to their families.

16 SPORTS

Informal games of baseball are often organized on Sunday afternoons after church.

17 ENTERTAINMENT AND RECREATION

Kihrbaia, or strolling, is a favorite pastime, especially on Sundays. During their leisure time, villagers also enjoy relaxing at home or visiting with relatives. Church activities are an important diversion for women and young girls, who look forward with great anticipation to church conferences held in neighboring villages. For the most part, they are closely tied to their homes and immediate villages while men, who often travel about seeking work, are typically more mobile.

18 FOLK ART, CRAFTS, AND HOBBIES

The Miskito weave baskets and fashion gourds and calabashes into both functional and decorative objects. They still make bark-cloth, which was used for clothing before their adoption of Western-style garments. It is now made into bed coverings. Other handmade items include carved and woven household utensils and furniture and dugout canoes.

19 SOCIAL PROBLEMS

The Miskito generally fare worse than the mixed-race (mestizo) or black (Creole) populations in terms of income, education, and job opportunities. The Sandinista Revolution of the 1980s severely disrupted the lives of the Miskito population, threatening their subsistence and personal safety, leading to large-scale relocations, and creating refugee conditions for many. In the early 1990s, many Miskito were forced to migrate to other regions in search of work, separating from their families for extended periods of time.

Drug traffickers from Colombia have started using the Miskito Coast as a transshipment route and fueling stop, but cocaine consumption by the Miskito has not become a significant local problem. In fact, the Miskito have attempted to resist the intrusion of drug traffickers into their regions.

20 BIBLIOGRAPHY

Hale, Charles R. *Resistance and Contradiction: The Miskitu Indians and the Nicaraguan State 1894–1987.* Stanford, CA: Stanford University Press, 1994.

Helms, Mary W. *Asang: Adaptations to Culture Contact in a Miskito Community.* Gainesville, FL: University Presses of Florida, 1971.

———. "Miskito." In *Encyclopedia of World Cultures.* Boston: G. K. Hall, 1992.

Jukofsky, Diane. "Heart of the Miskito." In *The Law of the Mother: Protecting Indigenous Peoples in Protected Lands,* edited by Elizabeth Kemf. San Francisco: Sierra Club Books, 1993.

Merrill, Tim L. *Honduras: A Country Study.* Washington, DC: US Government Printing Office, 1995.

Nietschmann, Bernard. *Between Land and Water.* New York: Seminar Press, 1973.

———. "The Miskito Nation and the Geopolitics of Self-Determination." In *The Ethnic Dimension in International Relations,* edited by Bernard Schechterman and Martin Slann. Westport, CT: Praeger, 1993.

Noveck, Daniel. "Class, Culture, and the Miskito Indians: A Historical Perspective." *Dialectical Anthropology* 13, no. 1 (1988): 17–29.

Olson, James S. *The Indians of Central and South America: An*

Ethnohistorical Dictionary. New York: Greenwood Press, 1991.

Whisnant, David E. *Rascally Signs in Sacred Places: The Politics of Culture in Nicaragua.* Chapel Hill, NC: University of North Carolina Press, 1995.

Whitten, Norman E., Jr. "Ethnogenesis." In *Encyclopedia of Cultural Anthropology,* edited by David Levinson and Melvin Ember. New York: Holt and Co., 1996.

—by R. Wieder, reviewed by T. Morin

MORMONS

ALTERNATE NAMES: Latter-day Saints
LOCATION: United States and worldwide (more than 50% live in the US, particularly Utah)
POPULATION: 9 million
LANGUAGE: English; language of the country in which they live
RELIGION: Mormonism (Church of Jesus Christ of Latter-day Saints)

[1] INTRODUCTION

Mormons are people who belong to the Christian sect known as the Church of Jesus Christ of Latter-day Saints. They are also referred to as Latter-day Saints. The special way of life practiced by Mormons is called Mormonism.

The Mormon Church was founded by Joseph Smith in Fayette, New York, in 1830. Smith attracted a small group of followers and settled first in Kirtland, Ohio, and then in Jackson County, Missouri. The people with whom the early Mormons came into contact considered their way of life peculiar and undesirable, and as a result the Mormons suffered much persecution. Forced to move again and again, they relocated from their first settlements in Kirtland and Jackson County to northern Missouri, and then to Nauvoo, Illinois. In Nauvoo, the early Mormon church prospered for a while, but hard times soon befell it. The Mormons' neighbors in Nauvoo resented the way they kept to themselves, and did not share in community life, and some became enraged when rumors began to spread that the Mormons practiced polygamy, a lifestyle in which one man has several wives.

Because of the resentment growing in the community at large, Joseph Smith was imprisoned in Carthage, Illinois, in 1844. While Smith was in prison, an armed mob stormed the jail and assassinated him. Brigham Young, who was at that time the head of the church's Council of the Twelve Apostles, replaced Smith as the leader of the Church. In 1846, he organized and directed the mass migration from Nauvoo across the Midwestern plains and the Rocky Mountains to the Great Salt Basin of Utah.

In Utah, the Church continued to grow, but when its leaders acknowledged that polygamy was in fact a Mormon belief, the United States government stepped in to put a stop to the unacceptable practice. In 1862 and 1882 Congress passed antibigamy laws, and in 1879 the Supreme Court ruled that religious freedom could not be claimed as grounds for the practice of polygamy. In 1890 the Mormons officially ended the practice of plural marriage.

Almost 15,000 Mormons served in the US armed forces in World War I. During the 1818-1845 tenure of Mormon president Heber Grant, the number of districts in the Mormon church grew from 83 to 149. The church expanded its missionary efforts in the 1950s and 1960s and began constructing religious centers (temples) in Europe. In 1978, Mormon church authorities announced that they had been instructed by divine revelation to strike down the church's policy of excluding black men from the priesthood.

2 LOCATION AND HOMELAND

About half the world's Mormons live in the United States, mostly in the western part of the country, with the greatest number in Utah, which is their spiritual capital (seven of every ten residents of Utah are Mormons). Today Mormons can also be found in virtually every part of the world, including Europe, South America, Asia, Africa, and Oceania. In 1995, the Church of Jesus Christ of Latter-day Saints estimated its worldwide membership to be over 9 million individuals, double the number of members in 1975.

When the wandering Mormons finally found a home in Utah, Salt Lake City became the center of the Mormon Church. The headquarters of the Church are located in Salt Lake City, as well as the extensive genealogical records which are closely associated with aspects of Mormon religious beliefs. Some of these genealogical records are housed in vaults carved into the sides of the mountains located just outside the city. The reason Mormons place such a high value on genealogy is their belief that they must pray for the souls of family members who died before having had a chance to become members of the Church, in order that these relatives' souls may enter heaven. The extensive genealogical records are kept so that all ancestors of Mormon families will be known and their souls will be saved by the prayers of the living. Mormons are constantly updating these records, which include information not only on Mormons and their families, but on many non-Mormons as well.

3 LANGUAGE

Mormons speak the language of the country in which they live. Since most Mormons live in the United States and other English-speaking countries, the language spoken by most Mormons is English.

4 FOLKLORE

The Mormons have no mythic or heroic figures in the usual sense, although they revere their early leaders, Joseph Smith (the founder of Mormonism) and Brigham Young. Some early Mormon beliefs incorporated elements of European and frontier folklore, infusing them with religious content. Faith healing and speaking in tongues both play a role in the Mormon belief system.

5 RELIGION

Mormonism began when its founder, Joseph Smith, reported having visions of God and other heavenly beings in which he was told that he would be the instrument for renewing and restoring the Christian religion. According to Smith's account, one of the heavenly messengers, an angel named Moroni, directed him to some thin metal plates, gold in appearance and inscribed in a hieroglyphic language, that were hidden under a rock. Smith's translation of the plates, the Book of Mormon, describes the history, wars, and religious beliefs of a group of people who migrated from Jerusalem to America in ancient times.

Mormon religious practices are based on the Bible, the Book of Mormon, and two other books of revelations that were believed to have been divinely revealed to Joseph Smith, *Doctrine and Covenants* and *The Pearl of Great Price*. Although Mormons share most of the beliefs of traditional Christianity, there are also some important differences. Mormons believe

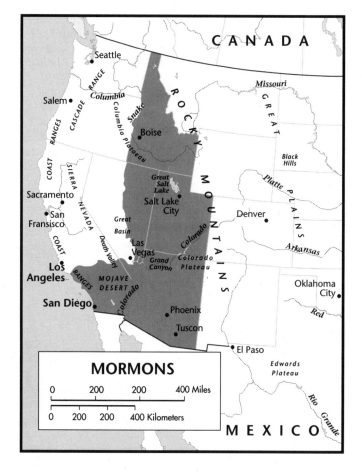

that God reveals his true word to individuals who seek it for their own benefit, to leaders of local Mormon churches, and to the President-Prophet of the Church.

The weekly schedule of the average Mormon church includes several opportunities for the faithful to worship together: there are separate meetings for men, women, children, and young people; and there are two meetings, Sunday School and Sacrament, at which the entire congregation comes together.

At age 19, all Mormon men and some women are expected to devote two years to doing missionary work. During that time, as they call on people at their homes to tell them about the advantages of the Mormon Church and distribute the Book of Mormon, they must support themselves with money they have saved or earned previously; many receive financial assistance from their parents. During this period they keep to a strict "early-to-bed, early-to-rise" schedule, working six days a week with one half-day off for tending to personal business. They are not allowed to attend "X"- or "R"-rated movies, go on dates, go to parties, watch television, or take part in contact sports. They are authorized to baptize whatever converts they make.

6 MAJOR HOLIDAYS

Mormons celebrate the major Christian holidays as well as the national holidays of the countries in which they live.

7 RITES OF PASSAGE

Baptism and marriage are important ceremonies in the Mormon Church. Any person eight years of age or older who wishes to join the Mormon Church may be baptized according to Mormon practices. Mormons also practice "vicarious baptism," or baptism of the dead, as a means of sanctifying the souls of those who have gone before. In vicarious baptism, members of the Church undergo baptismal rites on behalf of their ancestors who died before the doctrines of the Church were revealed to Joseph Smith.

Mormons also have a coming-of-age rite called an "endowment", about which outsiders know little because its content is kept secret. At one time it included an oath to avenge the Church's martyred prophets. Women commonly undergo the endowment ritual before a temple marriage.

Members of the Church of Jesus Christ of Latter-day Saints believe that human beings descend from a pure spiritual state to a condition of mortality at the time of their birth, spend their appointed number of days on the earthly plane, and then, at death, progress to an afterlife where resurrected individuals receive their true reward.

8 INTERPERSONAL RELATIONS

Members of the Mormon church address each other as "Brother" and "Sister."

One of the most important relationships within the church is that of "home-teaching families," a Church-wide support system. Every Mormon family is assigned a member of the local church, who is responsible for visiting the family every month to check on them. Church members and their home-teaching families also contact each other in times of crisis.

Charitable work on behalf of the Church and the poor is a hallmark of Mormon religious belief and practice. All members of the Church of Jesus Christ of Latter-day Saints make generous donations to support Church activities and ongoing building projects, and also to work on welfare farms and a wide variety of other projects whose goal is to produce food and other things that can be of use to those in need.

9 LIVING CONDITIONS

The teachings of the Church of Jesus Christ of Latter-day Saints emphasize hard work, nutritious food, exercise, and a family-centered home life. Statistics seem to show that this emphasis tends to lead to longer lives and a lower rate of cancer than are common among non-Mormons. Mormons live in a variety of ordinary dwellings, and they use the same forms of transportation that are available to non-Mormons.

In 1842, twelve years after the founding of the Church of Jesus Christ of Latter-day Saints, the Mormon Relief Society came into being. The original purpose of the Relief Society was to provide care and assistance to all needy or suffering people who came its way. In the time since it was founded, the Relief Society has branched out into other areas of social work.

Salt Lake City is the home of Welfare Square, an enormous facility whose purpose is to provide various sorts of aid and relief to the poor and the needy. Welfare Square is staffed completely by volunteer workers. It features a large building housing a supermarket well stocked with fresh produce, meat, and dairy products. The building also houses a clothing store and a shoe store. Except for the food, most of what is available at Welfare Square shops is second hand merchandise that has been donated. The Mormons take great care to make sure that the items they sell are packaged attractively so that it will not be demeaning for people to shop there. At Welfare Square one also often finds volunteer craftspeople, such as rug weavers, at work. The stores at Welfare Square provide all the necessities for a needy family's comfort while at the same time providing jobs and volunteer work for those who have a desire to give.

10 FAMILY LIFE

Marriage for Mormons is not just for life, but for all eternity, a belief that contributes to the strength of the Mormon family unit. (Eternal unity is said to be provided for by a special church ceremony known as a "sealing"). The state of Utah, in which Mormons predominate, has one of the nation's highest birth rates and lowest divorce rates. Every Mormon family has its beginnings in a temple marriage, which binds husband and wife together both in this life and in the next. One night a week, usually Monday evening, is set aside strictly for every Mormon family to spend together in fellowship, praying, playing, and working.

The Mormon woman is very supportive of her husband. She serves a vital role as the mother and helpmate in the family and is secure in the knowledge that her husband and children are working with her toward the same goals. The Church's strong opposition to the Equal Rights Amendment in the recent past was based on its belief that granting equal social and political rights to women would result in the disruption of traditional patterns of family life.

One of the most important missions of the Mormon Relief Society is to instruct female Church members in the area of home skills and proper behavior. At the Relief Society, women are taught new ways to make their homes attractive, pleasant, and wholesome places in which to raise families. Nutrition and health are part of the program, as well as awareness of different lifestyles and cultures.

11 CLOTHING

The Church of Jesus Christ of Latter-day Saints places no restrictions on the type of clothing that members may wear, but most Mormons wear plain, simple clothing of the sort worn by much of the community at large.

12 FOOD

Mormon families are instructed to avoid coffee, tea, cola, and other beverages containing caffeine, as well as alcohol and tobacco. Mormons are also asked to fast one Sunday each month and donate the grocery money saved by fasting to charity.

One long-standing Mormon Relief Society project is a food-storage program. Following the dictates of this program, all Mormons are instructed to maintain a year's supply of food for emergencies. As a result of this policy, Mormons have often been accused of hoarding food. Such accusations are totally unfounded, however. The food-storage program is simply intended to maintain the Mormon community in a state of preparedness in the event of a natural disaster or some other sort of emergency.

13 EDUCATION

The Mormons believe strongly in the value of education. The state of Utah has the nation's highest literacy rate (about 95%) and was among the top five states in spending on education during the first half of the 1990s, spending roughly 40% of the

Latter Day Saints Temple for the Mormans located in Salt Lake City, Utah. (Tom Till. Utah Travel Council)

state budget on schooling. Nine out of ten people in Utah finish high school. (Mormon young people take classes in religion all the way through high school.) The Mormon Church also founded and runs Brigham Young University in Provo, Utah. Founded in 1875, it was named for the charismatic leader who became the second head of the Mormons, succeeding Joseph Smith.

The Mormon Church today has one of the largest and most successful Boy Scout programs, with one of the highest levels of participation, anywhere in the world. The stated aims of the Boy Scouts organization—character development, citizenship training, and personal fitness—are also those of the Church, and Scouting thus comes naturally to its members.

In church, Mormon children are encouraged to speak before the entire congregation at a very early age. This gives Mormon young people the confidence to know that whatever they have to share is always appreciated.

14 CULTURAL HERITAGE

The Mormons have always valued the arts; their cargo on the great trek westward included pianos and other musical instruments. The song "Come, Come Ye Saints" was written during this historic journey. The original Mormon pilgrims sang to God for help, for guidance, for relaxation, and for encouragement from the time they started their wagon trains across the country until they reached their new home in the west. Founded in 1847, the Mormon Tabernacle Choir, which carries on this tradition, is one of the most famous choral groups in the world. The Choir includes about 375 members from all ethnic and economic backgrounds.

During the tenure of Mormon leader Brigham Young, a theater was built in Salt Lake City. The Utah Arts Council is the oldest state agency for the arts in the United States.

15 WORK

Members of the Church of Jesus Christ of Latter-day Saints are free to work at all occupations and are active in all walks of life, especially industry, trade, and the professions. Mormons also hold prominent positions in the federal government and the military.

16 SPORTS

Members of the Church of Jesus Christ of Latter-day Saints enjoy all the wholesome sports that non-Mormons do.

17 ENTERTAINMENT AND RECREATION

Members of the Church of Jesus Christ of Latter-day Saints enjoy the same forms of recreation and entertainment as non-Mormons, although their stricter way of life prevents them from participating in any activities they consider to be unwholesome. While vacationing, Mormon families often attend pageants presented at historic Mormon sites, including Nauvoo, Illinois, and Palmyra, New York.

18 FOLK ART, CRAFTS, AND HOBBIES

Antique Mormon furniture featuring stylized designs painted on wood by hand has become a collector's item whose value rises about 10% every year. The Folk Arts Program of the Utah Arts Council supports both visual and performing arts that reflect traditional and ethnic cultures.

19 SOCIAL PROBLEMS

Mormon tradition has come into conflict with feminism, and women speaking out against their traditional restriction to child rearing and homemaking have been excommunicated by the Mormon Church. Tension has also arisen between the strict, fundamentalist beliefs of new converts to Mormonism and the more moderate views generally held by members of multigenerational Mormon families.

see also Smith, Joseph; Young, Brigham; Utah War

20 BIBLIOGRAPHY

Green, Doyle L., and Randall L. Green. *Meet the Mormons: A*

Pictorial Introduction to the Church of Jesus Christ of Latter-day Saints and Its People. Salt Lake City, Ut.: Deseret Books, 1974.

Grolier's Multimedia Encyclopedia: Grolier, 1995.

Hughes, Dean, and Tom Hughes. *Great Stories from Mormon History.* Salt Lake City, UT: Deseret Books, 1994.

Shipps, Jan. *Mormonism, the Story of a New Religious Tradition.* Urbana, IL.: University of Illinois Press, 1985.

Stegner, Wallace. *Mormon Country.* New York: Duell, Cloan & Pearce, 1942.

——. *A Gathering of Zion:.* McGraw-Hill, 1964.

Warner, James A. and Styne M. Slade. *The Mormon Way:* Prentice-Hall, 1976.

Williams, Jean Kinney. *The Mormons, The American Religious Experience.* New York: Franklin Watts, 1996.

NATIVE NORTH AMERICANS

ALTERNATE NAMES: Indians
LOCATION: United States; Canada
POPULATION: 1,959,234 (US); 1,016,335 (Canada)
LANGUAGE: See individual tribes.
RELIGION: See individual tribes.
RELATED ARTICLES: Vol. 2: Choctaw; Comanches; Creeks; Dakota and Lakota; Hopi; Inuit; Iroquois; Navajos; Ojibwa; Paiutes; Seminoles and Miccosukees; and Tlingit

1 INTRODUCTION

Archaeologists generally agree that the first peoples to inhabit the North American continent crossed over from Asia to what is now Alaska on the Bering Land Bridge sometime between 12,000 and 25,000 years ago. When the glaciers melted at the end of the Ice Age, the water levels rose in the Earth's oceans and covered the land bridge, preventing any further migrations. The people who had already crossed over began to spread across the North American continent. According to the terrain and climate of the regions in which they eventually settled, they became either farmers or hunter-gatherers (or sometimes both). Farming tribes tended to form large permanent communities, while those who lived by hunting and gathering traveled in smaller, nomadic bands. By the time the first Europeans arrived (Nordic explorers reached Greenland in ad 985), a huge diversity of well-developed cultures had existed in North America for thousands of years. Over 500 years later, when Columbus "discovered" America, these cultures were centuries more sophisticated. Native North Americans, the First Peoples, were not primitive or backwards or wild savages, as the Europeans often described them. Rather, they were highly skilled providers and preparers of food, clothing, and shelter; fine artists; deeply religious peoples with complex belief systems; and self-governed, independent societies, some with complex governmental structures. From the time Columbus set foot on the Americas, through the next four hundred years, Europeans decimated Native North American cultures and populations, killing perhaps as many as 60 million Native peoples. Some were slaughtered in wars as the Europeans pushed them off their homelands to make room for European expansion. Many others died from European diseases for which they had no immunity or known treatments. Native North American populations did not begin to recover from this holocaust until about 1900.

The first "reservation" for Native North Americans was created in 1638 by the Puritans in what is now Connecticut, for the Quinnipiac Nation. The Quinnipiacs were given a mere 1,200 acres on which to live. They were subject to English rule and were required to convert to Christianity. Through the 17th century, European settlers pushed Native North Americans further and further west in what would become the US. Those who remained in the east, and those in Canada, were squeezed onto smaller and smaller territories. British-ruled Canada began establishing what they called "reserves" for Native North Americans during the 18th century. In Canada, reserves were set aside on the Natives' homelands, rather than forcing them to relocate, sometimes far from their homes, as did the US government when it began confining Natives to reservations.

Reservations and reserves were not the only changes forced upon the Native North Americans by the Europeans. Christian missionaries, beginning in the 17th century with French Jesuits in the northeast and Spanish Franciscans in the southwest, built mission churches and schools near Native communities and worked to "educate" the Natives in European ways and religion. Missionary methods ranged from supportive and helpful to violent and destructive. Jesuit priests in eastern Canada kidnapped young Natives and took them back to France to try to acculturate them there. Many of the young people died in these experiments; others became marginalized in both societies and sunk into alcoholic depressions. In the southwestern US, the Spanish brutalized the Pueblo peoples in their efforts to convert them to Christianity. After the Pueblo peoples staged a successful revolt in 1680, the Spanish agreed to a compromise: the Pueblo peoples would allow them to build their missions in the pueblos, but they must allow the Pueblo peoples to practice their native religion unhindered.

The 17th century also saw the beginning of the decimation of Native populations by European diseases, and the blurring of blood lines through intermarriage between Native North Americans and European traders. (In Canada, an entirely new population known as Métis, or mixed-bloods, was created in the 18th century from the marriage of European traders with Native women. They are now a recognized racial group in Canada.) Suddenly, tribal peoples who had existed in relative stability for millennia found themselves threatened with extinction. During the following centuries, Native North Americans struggled to survive, with varying degrees of success. Some European contributions were welcomed, such as the horse, adopted by Great Plains tribes in the US and Canada during the 18th century, and wheat, which quickly became a staple food of agricultural Native North Americans. For the most part, however, the Europeans brought only destruction to the Native North American peoples.

During the 18th century, Native North Americans stepped lively among frequently shifting allegiances with European powers as the French, Spanish, and British vied for control of the New World. The Native peoples were interested in protecting their lands and their access to food. Whichever European power seemed most likely to allow them to do that became their ally of the moment. In the end, no European nation protected the Natives' interests, despite all the assistance the Natives had given them. In 1763, the British drew the first of a series of boundary lines between land available for European settlement and Native land, or "Indian Territory." This first line ran down the crest of the Appalachian Mountains. Many European settlers ignored this boundary and moved west of the line into the lands supposedly reserved for Native North Americans. Eventually, the line was redrawn further west, and again settlers ignored it. For the next one hundred years, Indian Territory was redefined further and further west, first by the British and then by the US government, forcing Eastern tribes to relocate to unfamiliar terrain occupied by other Native North American nations. The lands allegedly reserved for Native North Americans were becoming crowded, and historically antagonistic tribes were forced to live in close proximity to each other.

In Canada, no imaginary lines were drawn between the European East and Native West, and Native peoples were allowed to stay in their original homelands. However, the lands set aside for them in these regions were small, and less valuable than those claimed by the Europeans. The first organized Native resistance to the Europeans in Canada was Pontiac's War against the British in 1763–66. Pontiac was an Ottawa chief who, with his warriors, successfully captured every British fort west of Niagara Falls except for Fort Detroit and Fort Pitt (today's Pittsburgh). Fort Detroit was under siege for five months before the British finally managed to turn the tables on Chief Pontiac and ultimately win the war.

Differences in culture, language, and worldview made peaceful resolutions to the conflicts between Europeans and Native North Americans almost impossible. Treaties were made, both in the US and Canada, but misunderstandings by both sides and deliberate breaches of promise by the Europeans prevented the treaties from having any lasting positive effects. The Micmac tribe in what is now the Canadian province of New Brunswick signed the first treaty with Europeans in 1725. Canadian Natives signed a total of 11 more treaties between 1871 and 1923 with the British and then Canadian governments. The first treaty between Native North Americans and the US government was signed on 17 September 1778 at Fort Pitt. A total of 389 more treaties were made or remade in the US before Congress passed a law in 1871 forbidding the signing of any more treaties with Native North Americans. The US government broke most of the promises it made to the Native North Americans in those 390 treaties.

The US government not only defied most of its treaties with Native North Americans but also betrayed a promise made to them in its own Articles of Confederation. The Ordinance of 1787, contained in the Articles of Confederation, stated that "land and property shall never be taken from [Native North Americans] without their consent; and in their property, rights and liberty, they shall never be invaded or disturbed, unless in just and lawful wars authorized by Congress." During the 19th century, in blatant disregard of this Ordinance, European American settlers invaded, destroyed, and seized most of the Native North Americans' remaining lands in the US, all with the full support of the US government. In the July-August 1845 issue of the *United States Magazine and Democratic Review*, editor John L. O'Sullivan coined the phrase "manifest destiny" to justify this genocide of the Native Nations. He saw it as "the fulfillment of our manifest destiny to overspread the continent allotted by Providence for the free development of our multiplying millions." Manifest Destiny became the rallying cry for the Mexican War of 1846-48 and was used to justify the annexation of Texas in 1845; the claim to Oregon country disputed with Britain, and the planned seizure of Cuba from Spain, in the 1850s; the Alaska Purchase of 1867; and even annexations of territories outside of the continental US, such as Hawaii and Guam, in the late 1800s.

In Canada, the aim of the government towards the Native Nations was complete assimilation. Rather than drive them out or slaughter them, the Canadians attempted to assimilate the Native North Americans into European Canadian culture. In 1857, the Imperial (British) Government passed the Gradual Civilization Act, which declared Native North Americans in Canada to be noncitizens and created a process by which they could attain citizenship. The government expected all Natives to become Canadian citizens—but in so doing, the Native peoples would renounce all legal distinctions as Native North

Americans, essentially giving up their identities. It is not surprising that few chose to do so. Between 1857 and 1920, only 250 Native North Americans opted to become Canadian citizens.

To encourage assimilation, Canada created boarding schools for Native North American children where they would be taught European languages, values, and customs. These schools, both government-run and missionary schools, were purposely built far from the children's homes to break all contact between the children and their families. The children were placed in European homes for the duration of their education, sometimes not seeing their true families for years on end. Although Native parents resisted sending their children to these schools, government officials insisted that they comply, often kidnapping the children and threatening the parents with cuts in food rations or worse. Boarding schools were also set up in the US by missionaries and by the government, and the scenario was much the same there as in Canada. Students in both Canadian and US boarding schools were subject to physical and sexual abuse; they were punished severely for speaking their native languages or practicing native religions; and their homes, families, and cultures were denigrated. The damaging effects of these schools are still felt by Native North Americans today. Needless to say, this attempt at assimilation was not very successful.

In the US, the Indian Removal Act passed by Congress in 1830 legalized the forcible relocation of many Native North Americans to reservations in the West. The Trail of Tears over which the Cherokees and other southeastern tribes were marched during the winter of 1838 from their homelands to what was then Indian Territory (now Oklahoma), and the Long Walk of the Navajos in 1864 to a concentration camp in New Mexico called Bosque Redondo, are still remembered by Native North Americans everywhere. Some 4,000–8,000 Cherokees (one out of every four) died on the Trail of Tears. Hundreds of Navajos died on the Long Walk, and many more died soon after arriving at Bosque Redondo. The situation worsened for Native North Americans in the US in 1831 when the US Supreme Court reversed the previous US policy and declared Native North American tribes as domestic dependent nations, rather than independent foreign nations. Native North Americans, therefore, no longer had the rights granted to sovereign nations, nor were they given rights as US citizens. Native North Americans in the US effectively had no rights whatsoever.

The Gold Rush which began in the late 1840s in California and soon spread throughout the West (in both the US and Canada) brought swarms of European prospectors and settlers into Native territory. European settlers squeezed out the Native North Americans and upset the fragile balance of nature on the prairies and plains. By 1879, the buffalo herds had disappeared from Canadian prairies, and many Canadian Natives were forced to follow the few remaining buffalo into the US. Native peoples in the US were already struggling to survive on the dwindling supply of buffalo and other game. In an effort to starve the Natives into submission, the US government sponsored massive buffalo hunts, where gunmen rode through Native lands and shot as many buffalo as possible, leaving them to rot on the ground. In California, European Americans killed as many as 84,000 Native North Americans between 1850 and 1880 to rid themselves of competition for gold, land, and other resources.

Finally, by the end of the 19th century, Native North Americans in the US and Canada surrendered to the superior firepower and sheer numbers of the Europeans and resigned themselves to life on reservations and reserves. Both governments outlawed many Native religious practices and continued to whittle away at Native lands through various acts of legislation. The General Allotment Act, passed by the US Congress in 1887, divided up reservation lands between individual Natives—160 acres per person. Whatever lands were left over were sold to European Americans. The 160-acre parcels allotted to Native North Americans were not contiguous but rather were laid out in a checkerboard pattern, making large-scale collective farming or ranching impossible. With this one Act, the US government succeeded in trapping Native North Americans in poverty for generations.

The 20th century has seen some improvements and some setbacks for Native North Americans. The US granted citizenship to all Native North Americans within its boundaries on 2 June 1924, though some individual states did not declare them citizens for years to follow. Canada gave its Native peoples the national franchise in 1960, but separate provinces were slower to give them the provincial franchise. The Indian New Deal of the 1930s in the US made reforms in Native North American land controls, improved conditions on reservations, and lifted restrictions on Native religious practices. Twenty years later, however, the Termination policy of 1954–62 eliminated federal recognition of many Native North American tribes in the US, leaving those peoples with no federal protections or services. The US also embarked on a Relocation Program in the early 1950s to encourage Native North Americans to move off the reservations to urban centers. The government hoped that by living and working in cities, away from their tribal lands, Native North Americans would become more integrated into European American society. In fact, the many Natives who did choose to move to urban centers instead found themselves unqualified and unprepared to succeed in the European American work world. Most of them simply traded poverty on the reservation for poverty in the city. Although Canada had no organized program to encourage Natives to relocate to cities, many did so because there was simply not enough room, nor enough resources or employment opportunities, on their reserves for everyone to survive. They found no more success in Canada's cities than did Native North Americans in the US.

Inspired by the Civil Rights Movement of the 1960s in the US, Native North Americans in both the US and Canada began to band together in pan-tribal organizations to fight for their rights. In the US, the National Indian Youth Council, a radical activist organization, was formed in 1961. The American Indian Movement (AIM) was founded in the US in July 1968 by Dennis Banks and Russell Means. AIM's original goals were to improve the conditions of urban Native North Americans and to prevent harassment of urban Natives by local police. Since then, their activities have expanded to cover a spectrum of Native North American concerns on the national level. The first truly national Canadian Native North American organization was the National Indian Council, formed in 1961. Various other tribal and pan-tribal organizations have since come into being to promote the preservation of Native North American culture; to lobby, demonstrate, and fight for Native North American rights in Canada and the US; and to improve conditions for Natives in both countries. Due to the efforts of these groups, governmental attitudes and approaches are beginning to change. In the 1970s, the Canadian government began funding Native North American organizations, rather than trying to suppress them as it had done in the past. It also adopted a policy of multiculturalism, as opposed to its former policy of assimilation. In both the US and Canada, many Native North American tribes have submitted land claims and brought suit against the government for restitution for broken treaties. The first major land claims case won by Native North Americans was in 1970 when US president Richard Nixon agreed to return 48,000 acres of land (including the sacred Blue Lake) to Taos Pueblo in New Mexico. It was another 12 years before the first Canadian Native land claims case was settled, for the Micmac tribe in Nova Scotia.

Much confusion and disagreement remains, however, on the relation of Native North Americans to the government that rules their lands and lives. Canadian Natives continue to wrestle with the Canadian government over what the Natives believe is their inherent right to self-rule. US Natives struggle to define themselves in the murky area of sovereign dependence. Conditions are still harsh for the majority of Native North Americans, whether they live on reservations, reserves, or in cities. Unemployment, alcoholism, suicide, and cultural dislocation continue to plague these descendants of once-great nations. Racist perceptions of "redskins" and caricatured depictions of Indians persist in the European-dominated cultures of Canada and the US. Dartmouth College in 1969, and Stanford University in 1972, stopped the use of Native North American symbols and mascots for their sports teams, but more than two decades later, other teams like the Cleveland Indians and Atlanta Braves in professional baseball continue to promote racist ideas of Native North Americans with their Chief Wahoo grinning-Indian mascot (Cleveland) and tomahawk chant (Atlanta).

On a potentially positive note, the late 20th century has seen a surge in European Americans' and Canadians' interest in Native North American spirituality and worldview. If this interest leads to increased respect for Native North Americans, it should create significant improvements in their lives. If the Europeans, however, use this as yet another opportunity to steal from the Natives, co-opting their spiritual traditions and Europeanizing them, Native North Americans will once again have one less thing to call their own.

2 LOCATION AND HOMELAND

Native North American tribes are usually grouped into major culture areas based on the geographic area of their traditional homelands. Those culture areas are generally designated as Northeastern (including the Great Lakes region, or Woodlands); Southeastern; Southwestern; Great or Northern Plains; Northwest Coast; Plateau, Great Basin, and Rocky Mountains; California; Alaska; and the Northwest Territory and Arctic Circle. Due to the forced relocation of many tribes in the US during the 19th century to so-called "Indian Territory" in what is now the state of Oklahoma, a new division known as Oklahoman Indians has been added to the list. (Oklahoman Indians identify themselves as such.) These culture areas, except for Oklahoma, are useful for historical discussions of Native North Americans, but today's tribal groupings are based more on differences in political and economic relations with the US and Canadian governments than on geographic regions. In Canada,

Native North Americans are divided into Inuit (a separate culture group living in the subarctic regions), Métis (mixed-bloods who have developed a distinct cultural identity), and North American Indians (all other Canadian Natives), as well as "status" and "nonstatus" Indians (referring to whether or not they are recognized as Native North Americans by the government). In the US, most Native North Americans are now referred to simply by tribe. (There is a great deal of controversy over how to refer to Native North Americans in general: some say Native Americans, some say American Indians, while others use terms such as First Peoples or First Nations. In an attempt to find a middle ground, and with no intention of disrespect to those who prefer other designations, we have chosen to use Native North Americans as the general descriptive term.)

Historically, the terrain and environment of a tribe's homeland determined its way of life. Northeastern tribes lived in temperate woodlands where game animals abounded. They built semipermanent villages made up of wood lodges, cultivated some food, and hunted, fished, and gathered the rest. Southeastern tribes, on the other hand, lived in hotter climates with very fertile ground and a long growing season, so they became settled agriculturalists with large, well-organized communities. Plains tribes relied on the buffalo and wild grasses for their livelihood, while Southwestern tribes eked out a living on carefully tended corn and built apartment-style complexes of adobe. Within each of these culture areas, however, individual tribes had quite different religious beliefs, languages, social customs, and interpersonal relations. It is quite inaccurate to think of Plains tribes, or Southwestern tribes, as single, unified groups with one common lifeway. It is grossly inaccurate to think of Native North Americans as a singly defined unit. However, for the purposes of this article, we will attempt to offer some general statements about Native North Americans as a collection of distinct peoples.

According to the 1990 Census, the total population of Native North Americans in the US was 1,959,234. The Canadian Census of 1991 counted a total of 1,016,335 Native North Americans, including about 500,000 North American Indians; 480,000 Métis and nonstatus Indians; and approximately 35,000 Inuit. Historians and archaeologists guess that the Native North American population was in the tens of millions when Europeans first arrived on the continent. By 1900, the Native population in the US had reached an all-time low of 237,196. The Canadian Native population bottomed out in 1911 at less than 110,000. Since then, Native North American populations in both countries have increased significantly, though they are still far from their original numbers. Native North Americans currently make up about 0.8% of the total US population, and 3.4% of the total Canadian population.

There are 510 federally recognized Native North American tribes in the US, over 200 Alaska Native villages and communities, and some 50 recognized "First Nations" in Canada. A total of about 56.2 million acres in the US have been divided into 278 Native North American reservations, mostly in the Great Plains region and the West. A few are located in the eastern US. In the US, Native North Americans make up less than 50% of the population on many reservations due to land allotment, leasing arrangements, and the opening of reservation lands to non-Natives. While reservations in Arizona, New Mexico, and the Dakotas still have over 90% Native populations, those in California, the Great Lakes states, and Washington have less than 30%. The state of Oklahoma has the largest concentration of Native North Americans in the US (252,420), followed by California (242,164), Arizona (203,527), and New Mexico (134,355). The Cherokee Nation of Oklahoma, according to the 1990 US Census, is the largest Native North American tribe in the US, followed closely by the Navajo, who themselves claim to be the largest tribe. In Canada, the Cree far outdistance the next largest tribe, the Ojibwa. The provinces of Ontario and British Columbia have the greatest concentrations of Native North Americans.

Many Native North Americans have left the reservations and reserves to live in cities. In Canada, anywhere from 60-80% of the Native population lives off-reserve in urban centers such as Winnepeg, Montreal, Vancouver, Edmonton, and Toronto. Some 62% of US Natives are urban dwellers. In the US, the cities of Los Angeles, Oklahoma City, Phoenix, and Tulsa have the largest Native North American populations.

The relatively recent Native North American population increase from the lows of the early 20th century have created a youth-dominated population: 32% of Native North Americans are under 15 years old, while only 5% are over 64 years old. The decimation of tribal populations in the 19th century, plus the crowding together of many different tribes on common reservations in the US, has led to a great deal of intermarrying and blurring of once pure tribal lineages. Many Native North Americans have also married and borne children with European Americans, resulting in a large percentage of mixed-bloods. In Canada, the Métis have developed a distinct cultural identity and are now recognized as such by the Canadian government. Because Native North Americans are eligible for government services and benefits, many with small percentages of Native North American blood register on tribal rolls. Some have such minute traces of Native blood that other Native North Americans refer to them as "no-bloods."

³ LANGUAGE

Linguists guess that there may have originally been as many as 300 separate and distinct Native North American languages before Europeans arrived on the continent. Since that time, many Native languages have become extinct because of European decimation of tribal populations; the assimilation of Native peoples into European-dominated English-speaking society; education (forced and voluntary) of young Native North Americans in English, Spanish, or French; and the loss of faith in elders and traditional tribal culture by young Native North Americans who then reject their native cultures and tongues. Over 100 Native North American languages still exist today, though some are spoken by only a few people. In recent years, there has been a resurgence of interest in traditional Native ways, including languages, by Native North Americans themselves and by the US and Canadian governments. On 30 October 1990, the US Congress passed the Native American Languages Act to preserve, protect, and promote the practice and development of Native North American languages. This Act reversed the 19th century campaign by the US government to eradicate those same languages that it is now trying to protect. Canada's new policy of multiculturalism supports Native languages and traditions, in contrast to its former policy of assimilation which tried to erase them.

The most widely spoken Native North American language today is Navajo, with over 100,000 speakers. Cree, spoken by at least 70,000 people in Canada, runs a close second. Navajo is a member of the Athabaskan language family; Cree is an Algonquian language. Linguists group languages with common roots into families, such as the Romance (Italian, Spanish, French) and Germanic (German, English, Dutch) families in Europe. Native North American languages comprise some 57 families, including Athabaskan, Algonquian (or Algonkian), Caddoan, Chumashan, Eskimo, Iroquoian, Kiowa-Tanoan, Muskogean, Pomoan, Siouan, Uto-Aztecan, Yuman, and others. There are also many "isolates," languages not related to any others, among the huge diversity of Native North American languages. Some examples of isolates are Aleut, Cayuse, Haida, Hopi, Tlingit, Washo, and Zuñi. A number of languages have yet to be classified, such as Kutenai, Salishan, and Wakashan. The greatest linguistic variety exists in the relatively small area of California, which boasts 20 of the 57 Native North American language families. There is more linguistic variety in California than in all of Europe.

The only Native North American language written with its own symbol system is Cherokee. In 1823, a Cherokee named Sequoyah invented a writing system for his language using symbols to represent syllables (such as "ma," "no," "gu"). He borrowed some symbols from English, which he had seen but did not know how to read or speak, so the English letters do not correspond to the English sounds. For example, *D* represents the sound "a," and *T* represents "i." Other Native North American languages have since been written with adapted Roman or Russian (for the Aleut language in Alaska) alphabets. But for millennia, Native North American languages were purely oral. A form of sign language did develop among the Plains tribes so that they could communicate across language barriers. Many Europeans learned this system of gestures as well. Trade languages, with elements of two or more tribal (and even European) languages, developed between neighboring tribes, such as Chinook Jargon in the Pacific Northwest. A very special language was consciously created during World War II by a group of Navajo who devised a code based on the Navajo language, in such a way that even a native Navajo speaker would need the key to understand it. The US used this code for military operations in the Pacific, and the Japanese were never able to break it. The Navajo Code Talkers, as they came to be known, were greatly honored for their invaluable service to the US.

The English language has borrowed many words from Native North Americans since the arrival of English speakers on the continent. The oldest known borrowed word is *raccoon*. Others include *caribou*, *opossum*, *moose*, *skunk*, *woodchuck*, *chipmunk*, *hickory*, *squash*, *pecan*, *succotash*, *moccasin*, and *toboggan*. Many North American place names are Native North American words, such as *Massachusetts*, *Connecticut*, *Manhattan*, *Illinois*, *Michigan*, *Wisconsin*, *Chicago*, *Mississippi* (which means "big-water"), *Niagara*, *Ottawa*, *Ohio*, *Kentucky*, *Tennessee*, *Iowa*, *Missouri*, *Arkansas*, *Kansas*, *Nebraska*, *Minnesota*, *Manitoba*, *Dakota*, *Alabama*, *Appalachia*, *Oklahoma*, *Arizona*, *Utah*, *Seattle*, *Saskatchewan*, *Alaska*, and *Yosemite*.

⁴ FOLKLORE

Separating folklore from religion in Native North American cultures is impossible because all stories are religious teaching stories. Religion is an integral part of daily life for Native North Americans, and the lessons for living that life in a sacred way are passed down from generation to generation through rituals,

Shoshone dancer in Wyoming. Most Native North American tribes continue to hold ceremonial dances. (Pete Saloutos. Wyoming Division of Tourism)

songs and dances, and stories. In the following articles on Native North Americans, therefore, this section will discuss specific stories and characters in those stories, while section #5, "Religion: origin and traditional beliefs," will talk about sacred ceremonies and rituals and the general spiritual worldview of Native North Americans.

Each native North American tribe has its own creation myth, but many of these myths share common themes. There are three basic types of creation stories among Native North American tribes:

1) Earth-diver stories, where an animal or bird dives into the depths of the watery chaos to bring up a bit of mud which becomes the Earth;

2) Culture-hero stories, where great beings create the world and the people in it and teach those people how to live (or sometimes Two-Creator stories, where two great beings create the world through their efforts to compete with each other); and

3) Emergence stories, where the people emerge from a lower world (or worlds) up onto this one.

Trickster tales are also universal among Native North Americans. Trickster figures are usually animals, birds, or insects who teach humans the limits of time and space, and the consequences of disrespectful or unbalanced behavior, by their own follies, errors, and tricks. They sometimes help humans by restoring balance to the world. Native North Americans believe

that the world is made up of paired opposites, such as light-dark, night-day, male-female, sun-moon, etc. Tension between these opposing elements creates movement. Trickster figures keep the world moving by keeping the tension alive between paired opposites, often by turning them on their heads. Common trickster figures (according to region) are: Raven (Northwest), Hare or Raccoon (Great Lakes), Coyote (Southwest and Great Basin), Iktomi the Spider (Plains), Rabbit (Southeast), and Jay or Wolverine (Canada).

5 RELIGION

Modern Native North American religious movements and sacred ways tend to be pan-tribal (crossing tribal boundaries, rather than specific to one or another tribe). Though sacred ways are continually changing, adapting to the realities of life in a changing world, to new experiences and new wisdom, certain core beliefs remain fundamentally unchanged because the basic realities of life remain the same. The four traditional enemies are still poverty, sickness, fatigue, and old age. The sacred boundaries of tribal worlds are still the same and can still be mapped. The seasons continue in the same cycles, and the sun, moon, and stars continue in the same paths. People are still born, and they still die. Native North American sacred ways are involved with survival; the sacred ways are an integral part of life and cannot be separated from daily living. There is no word for "religion" in any Native North American language because it is not seen as a separate enterprise. The disintegration of tribal culture and severe disruption of traditional daily life in the last two centuries, therefore, caused many Native North Americans to lose their understanding of and sense of communion with their traditional sacred ways. In recent years, however, there has been a resurgence of interest in traditional Native North American spirituality, both among Native North Americans themselves and among European Americans and Canadians.

Most Native North Americans share six concepts of the sacred:

1. Unseen powers, sometimes called The Great Mystery, exist;

2. All things in the universe are interdependent and we must, therefore, respect all life and maintain balance and harmony or else destruction will result;

3. Worship strengthens the bonds between the individual, community, and great powers;

4. Sacred traditions and teachers of those traditions teach morals and ethics for everyday life;

5. Trained sacred practitioners (called medicine men and women, shamans, priests and priestesses, etc.) are responsible for special, sometimes secret, knowledge that they preserve in their memories and pass on from generation to generation; and

6. Humor is a necessary part of the sacred because it keeps us in perspective and eases our journey through the difficulties of life.

Sacred rites among different tribes range from complex ritual dances and worship activities to a pervasive sense of sacred living with almost no ceremonial rites. Visions and dreams are considered by all Native North Americans to be powerful experiences worthy of serious attention. Native North Americans do not believe in a separate divine being who rules the universe, like the Judaeo-Christian God. Rather, they believe that all of life and creation is sacred.

In the Native North American worldview, all elements of the universe are paired, and those pairs balance each other, such as male-female, north-south, east-west, up-down, night-day, sun-moon, moist-dry, dark-light, life-death. Each element in the pair is part of the other and necessary to the other: without night, there would be no day but simply a constant, unchanging, undefined sunlight. Because of this belief in balanced opposites, the concepts of good and evil are not nearly as important to Native North Americans as the idea of balanced or imbalanced, or harmony versus disharmony. The sacred is based on relationships that must be kept in balance. The sacred teachings give knowledge about those relationships, how to keep them in balance, and what tragedies will result if they are not kept in balance. This knowledge is taught through stories, ritual experiences, lectures, dances and songs, and the interpretation of visions and dreams.

Prayers are offered before and after many actions, such as waking, going to sleep, hunting, killing, planting, and harvesting. Three standard elements of Native North American prayer rituals are:

1. Purification—sweat baths, smudging with smoke, bathing, etc.;

2. Blessing—a call to the great powers, prayers for the self and others; and

3. Sacrifice—offering something of oneself to the great powers to reestablish one's connection with all else.

Offerings, such as tobacco, feathers, corn meal, or pollen, also often accompany prayers.

Peyotism has a long history with Native North Americans. The use of peyote, an herb of the cactus species that grows along the Rio Grande in Texas and Mexico, was traditionally used by the ancient Aztecs of Mexico. In the early 18th century, the Mescalero Apaches began to use it in their healing ceremonies. Gradually, the use of peyote spread through the tribes of the Southwest and into the Great Plains. By the late 19th century, peyotism had become a pan-tribal religion, eventually incorporated as the Native American Church. Sometimes blending aspects of Christianity (such as belief in the Trinity) with traditional Native North American sacred ways, the Native American Church promotes four basic teachings:

1. Love for one's fellow beings;

2. Responsibility for one's family;

3. Self-reliance; and

4. Refraining from the use of alcohol.

Peyotism has enabled Native North Americans both to assimilate some elements of the dominant European Christian culture as well as to maintain a separate cultural identity and connection with traditional sacred ways. The discouragement of the use of alcohol and encouragement of responsibility and self-reliance have also helped Native North Americans to overcome the despair and accompanying social disintegration that has

resulted from centuries of poverty, discrimination, and cultural dislocation.

⁶ MAJOR HOLIDAYS

As hunter-gatherers and agriculturalists, people who live close to the earth, Native North Americans traditionally celebrated holidays based on the Earth's rhythms. Solstices, equinoxes, planting and harvesting times, the first fish caught each year, and other seasonal events constituted Native North Americans' sacred calendar. Today, many Native North Americans have become Christian and celebrate Christian holidays. Those who are US citizens also celebrate major US holidays such as the Fourth of July (Independence Day). Canadian Native North Americans celebrate Canada Day on 1 July.

However, most tribes continue to hold ceremonial dances and religious rites on their traditional, Earth-based holidays as well. These sacred ceremonies were outlawed for a time by the US and Canadian governments during the late 19th and early 20th centuries. But Native North Americans continued to celebrate them secretly and the ceremonies survived to take on new life in the return to traditional ways that has taken hold in Native North American communities in recent decades.

⁷ RITES OF PASSAGE

Common rites of passage among Native North American tribes are birth, naming, renaming, puberty, marriage, and death. Native North American initiation (or rite of passage) ceremonies mark a point of physical or emotional growth in a person and open that person's eyes to the Great Mysteries to which he or she is now exposed. The ceremonies also teach the person about the new responsibilities involved in being exposed to these powers. Birth rites are centered around rituals to ensure the child's safety into old age. Puberty ceremonies teach the young boy or girl about adult responsibilities and expectations. New names are often given at each passage from one stage of life to the next, or after a dramatic event in a person's life. Though naming customs differ among Native North American tribes, names are always believed to have great importance. In some tribes, a person may have acquired several names by the end of her or his life.

Death is not feared by Native North Americans because it is considered to be one more step on the path of life. Native North American burial rites involve preparations for the deceased's continuing journey after death. For example, in many Native North American tribes, the dead are buried sitting up, facing west (the direction of the life beyond this one), with things they will need as they travel the next part of the path, such as blankets and food. An inevitable part of the life cycle, death is deeply respected as a time of great transition.

⁸ INTERPERSONAL RELATIONS

Most Native North American societies are organized around some sort of extended family unit. In matriarchal tribes, the eldest woman is head of the group and carries a great deal of weight in the larger community as well. Patriarchal tribes look to the eldest man for leadership. Traditionally, most Native North American cultures practiced a similar division of labor in which women were responsible for domestic affairs and men took care of hunting, raiding or warring, and public affairs (such as intertribal business or meetings with Europeans). This

American Indian Exposition in Anadarko, Oklahoma. Native North Americans of today wear Western-style clothing for everyday purposes. Only for ceremonies and powwows do they dress in their traditional ways. (Fred Marvel. Oklahoma Tourism).

division of labor made perfect sense in that women were frequently pregnant and/or nursing an infant and were not able during those times to perform heavy manual labor or venture too far from home. They also needed to be protected in the interest of the survival of the tribe or clan. Biologically speaking, women were more valuable because they could give birth only to one child every two years or so, whereas men could father many children in that same period of time. Therefore, fewer men than women were needed to perpetuate the group.

[9] LIVING CONDITIONS

Whether on reservations or in cities, the great majority of Native North Americans suffer substandard living conditions. In the US, more than one out of every four Native North Americans (or 28%) live below the poverty level, as opposed to one out of eight (12%) of the total US population. Native North Americans are the most disadvantaged group in Canada. Reservations and reserves were established on the poorest land and forced to hold many more people than the land could support. Farming has always been difficult, even at subsistence level, and there are few other sources of income. Many reserves and reservations are located in remote areas, often inaccessible by road, and work opportunities are scarce. Unemployment is extremely high (up to 90% on some Canadian reserves during the winter months), and income levels are extremely low.

Access to modern Western health care is limited by poverty, isolation and lack of transportation, and misunderstandings of government policies and benefits. Entire tribes of Native North Americans were wiped out by epidemics during the 18th - early 20th centuries. Certain communicable diseases, such as tuberculosis, diphtheria, and trachoma, were not brought under control on reservations or reserves until the mid-20th century. Canadian Natives receive free health care, and more than half of all US Native North Americans receive health care from the federal Indian Health Service (IHS), a government-supported health care system like no other in the US. But urban (or other off-reservation) Natives in the US are not covered by the IHS, so they have extremely limited access to health care. Native North Americans in Canada are often too far removed from health centers to take advantage of their services.

The cultural destruction of Native North American tribes over the past three centuries has led to tremendous stress, depression, and the adoption of unhealthy habits and lifestyles (cigarette smoking, junk-food diets, alcohol dependence) by Native North Americans. Hypertension (high blood pressure), strokes, diabetes, cancer, and coronary heart disease are now prevalent among Native North Americans due to these changes in lifestyle. Mental disorders, alcoholism, and suicide have also become serious problems. As compared to the total US population, Native North American death rates from the following disorders are as follows:

alcoholism:	438% greater
tuberculosis:	400% greater
diabetes mellitus:	155% greater
accidents:	131% greater
homicide:	57% greater
pneumonia/flu:	32% greater
suicide:	27% greater

Death rates are similar for Native North Americans in Canada. One study determined that Canadian Natives may have the highest suicide rate of any racial group in the world.

Sexually transmitted diseases are now widespread among Native North Americans, and AIDS is becoming a concern. Toxic waste dumps are often located near reservations and reserves and create further health problems for Native North Americans through contamination of their soil, water, and air. Life expectancy for Native North Americans is at least ten years less, and the infant mortality rate almost twice as high, than for all other races living in the US and Canada.

Federal housing programs provide low-cost housing for Native North Americans on reservations and reserves, but many Native North Americans still do not have adequate housing. Run-down trailers and shacks are not uncommon. Those living in remote areas usually have no electricity, indoor plumbing, running water, or any heat beyond a small cooking stove. Water is either hauled from wells or dipped from streams and brooks that are often polluted.

Native North Americans living in urban areas are usually marginalized as well. Lacking the skills and cultural background to succeed in the Western work world, most urban Natives find themselves unable to get steady, full-time jobs. Instead, they work at occasional odd jobs and struggle to make rent payments on the worst slum housing. Many eventually return to the reservations and reserves, poorer than when they left.

10 FAMILY LIFE

The family relationship is the center and core of Native North American tribes. Extended families figure prominently in all Native North American cultures; clans are common. Many Native North American cultures are matrilineal (and often matrilocal, meaning a newly married couple lives with or near the bride's mother). In a matrilineal society, lineage is inherited through the mother, not the father. A child is born into the mother's clan or kinship group. Therefore, there is no such thing as an illegitimate child because it is always known who a child's mother is (while the identity of a child's father can be unknown). When a child inherits its mother's name or lineage, it is assured of a recognized place in society.

Children are highly valued members of nearly all Native North American societies from the moment of their birth (or even before). Family size tends to be large, particularly since the decimation of Native populations during the 18th and 19th centuries. In order to rebuild clans and tribes, Native North Americans encourage high birth rates. Children are rarely punished physically. Rather, they are scolded in a firm but gentle voice, or are teased into behaving well.

Women are usually responsible for domestic affairs, while men take care of public affairs and any work that requires traveling a distance from home (such as hunting, trapping, raiding, and warfare). In matrilineal societies, women rank as the highest elders with the most authority. Clan mothers, or the eldest women of each kinship group, often choose the men who will be chiefs in public leadership and can remove those chiefs if they feel the men are not leading their people well. In patrilineal societies, women are still highly valued for their reproductive role and their many other contributions to the survival of the group.

11 CLOTHING

Native North Americans of today wear Western-style clothing for everyday purposes. Only for ceremonies and powwows do they dress in their traditional ways. Traditional clothing varies from tribe to tribe, depending on what natural materials were available in their traditional homelands and the climate of the region, as well as by particular tribal custom. Eagle feathers have always been highly valued by many Native North Americans. Eagles are considered powerful beings, and their feathers are believed to possess some of that power. Nowadays, Native North Americans must get permission from the US government to use the feathers of a protected species.

12 FOOD

Thousands of years before Columbus arrived in the New World, Native North Americans of the Hopi and Zuñi tribes were cultivating vegetables and corn. Corn is a very sophisticated agricultural product. First, it had to be created by crossing two types of wild grasses, neither of which was very productive on its own. Because it is a hybrid, corn cannot reseed itself simply by dropping its kernels on the ground. The kernels must be planted and tended carefully in order for them to grow. Native North Americans consider corn to have great spiritual power. Cornmeal and corn pollen are used in many religious ceremonies.

Pacific Northwest tribes had such an abundance of wild fruits and vegetables and fish available to them that they did not need to farm at all. They could gather enough food during the three months of summer to last them the rest of the year. The Plains tribes' primary source of food was the buffalo, along with wild rice in the northern Plains. Alaska and northern Canada Natives have long relied on seal and whale meat and blubber for the bulk of their diet. Most Northeastern and Southeastern Native tribes were farmers like the Southwestern tribes.

When Europeans first began to settle on the eastern shores of the continent, Native North Americans saved them from starvation by showing them what wild foods were edible and how to cultivate other foods unknown to Europeans, such as corn, pumpkins, and squash. Modern-day foods that originated with Native North Americans include corn, pumpkins, squash, lobster, sweet and "Irish" potatoes, tomatoes, peppers, peanuts, avocados, pineapples, certain kinds of beans, maple syrup and sugar, sunflower seeds, and turkey. We can also thank Native North Americans for barbecue, spoon bread, cranberry sauce, mincemeat pie, chili, guacamole, and many other dishes too numerous to mention.

13 EDUCATION

Traditional Native North American education does not separate secular and sacred knowledge because religion and everyday life are completely intertwined. Therefore, Native wisdom involves "seeking life," or knowing what is necessary for survival. Survival requires balance and harmony with all things. The way to wisdom is to sit still, wait, and listen. Native North Americans teach their children to let the Great Mysteries be revealed to them. The children are taught not to ask questions but to listen and wait and the answer will come. Asking questions means a person is not listening well enough or learning anything. A person who asks questions is considered stupid in Native North American society. In a technological society, such as the modern Western society of European-dominated US and Canada, one needs to ask questions because human-made things have origins and definite causes and effects. In an Earth-based society, on the other hand, such as that of traditional Native North Americans, life is based on mysteries that can only be revealed by listening in stillness. Traditional Native North American wisdom is taught mostly through stories, lectures, songs, dances, rituals and ceremonies, vision quests, survival training, and silence.

Western education was introduced to Native North Americans in the 17th century by early Roman Catholic missionary priests. Education was in French, Spanish, or English (depending on the country of origin of the priests). The priests' goal was to "civilize the savages," so they taught the Natives European manners, attitudes, culture, and languages, as well as Christianity. By the 19th century, the US and Canadian federal governments had become involved in Native North American education. In order to assimilate Natives into European culture, the government set up boarding schools and forcibly removed Native children from their homes and placed them in these schools. During vacations, the children were boarded with European American and Canadian families. Any Native parents who resisted having their children taken to these schools were punished by having their rations withheld. Conditions were generally terrible at the boarding schools. Poor health care and nutrition, combined with substandard living conditions, caused widespread illness among the students. Low teacher salaries also attracted unqualified teachers (who could not get better paying jobs), and they were given improper curricula with which to work. Vocational training programs did not fit the marketplace, so Native students graduated with no marketable skills. Students were required to speak English (or French, or Spanish), and any caught speaking in their native tongues were severely punished. Other physical and even sexual abuses have since been revealed. In June 1991, the Department of Indian Affairs (DIA) in Canada publicly acknowledged responsibility for the abuses inflicted on Native North American students at Canadian boarding schools. The DIA promised to fund programs to help abuse victims heal their wounds—physical, psychological, emotional, spiritual, and social—and to treat other damaging effects, such as the breakdown of families, alcoholism, the perpetration of abuse on others by abuse victims, and suicide. The Reverend Douglas Crosby, president of the Oblate Conference of Canada (the largest Roman Catholic missionary order in Canada) also asked forgiveness for abuses inflicted at Catholic missionary schools upon Native North Americans.

The Choctaw and Cherokee tribes of the southeastern US had both developed extensive school systems of their own which taught both Native and Western subjects by the 19th century. The Creeks, Chicksaws, and Seminoles also had schools, and together these Southeastern Natives came to be known to European Americans as the "Five Civilized Tribes." In the

early 1900s, however, the US government closed down the Native-run schools and took control of their education. It was not until the late 1960s that Native North Americans once again became responsible for the formal education of their own children. Ramah High School, on the Navajo reservation in New Mexico, opened in 1968 to become the first Native-controlled high school since the closing of the Five Civilized Tribes' school systems. In Canada, the Cree band (or tribe) of northeastern Alberta took over the Blue Quills school in 1970, becoming the first Canadian band to control its own education. The Canadian government officially gave Native North Americans more control over their education in 1973.

The first tribally controlled college was Navajo Community College, established in 1966. Saskatchewan Indian Federated College became the first Canadian college run by Native North Americans, in May 1976. The US Bureau of Indian Affairs (BIA) provides grants today for 22 tribally controlled community colleges in the US, with a total student body of about 7,000 students. The BIA estimated that over 70,000 US Native North American students attended colleges and universities in 1991, and over 400 were pursuing graduate or law degrees.

Currently, only 7% of Native North American primary and secondary students in the US attend BIA-funded schools. Some 5% attend private or parochial schools, while most (88%) attend public schools. School attendance among Canadian Native North Americans has always been low, due both to traumas experienced at boarding schools and to the remoteness of many reserves. Attendance rates have been improving in recent years, however.

Native children educated in traditional ways encounter great difficulties when entering the Western education system. Traditionally taught not to ask questions, Native students are often considered "slow" or "stupid" by Western teachers and peers. Cultural contexts are often so different that Native students cannot fully understand what they are being taught. Native North American students are among the lowest in achievement and highest in dropout rates. More than 25% of Canadian Natives older than the age of 15 have less than a 9th grade education. At least 34% have some high school but no diploma. A mere 8% of all Native North Americans in Canada over 15 years old have completed high school (only 5% among the Inuit). The percentages in the US are somewhat better, with 55% of US Native North Americans graduating from high school, but this is still well below the national average of 66.5% for the total US population.

The figures for college graduation are even more disparate: 16.2% of the total US population graduates from college, while only 7% of Native North Americans do. In Canada, 4% of Native North Americans have achieved a university degree. Only a handful—1%—of Inuits have finished college.

14 CULTURAL HERITAGE

Native North American music and dance is centered on religious ceremonies. These ceremonies were outlawed in the US and Canada during the late 19th and early 20th centuries, so much of the heritage was lost. The renaissance of Native North American culture in the late 20th century is helping to preserve what is left of traditional music and dance.

The voice has always been the most important musical instrument for Native North Americans. Rattles and/or drums often accompany the voice. A percussion instrument unique to

Native North Americans is the water drum: a small container of wood, pottery, or metal is partially filled with water to create a certain tone. The container is covered with dampened hide stretched tightly, and it is beaten with a hard stick. Some Native North American tribes have used flutes for centuries. Recently, the flute has become popular pan-tribally. The Apache fiddle and musical bows in various tribes also have a long history, while modern fiddles and guitars have been adopted by many tribes in recent years.

Native North American dances express spiritual truths or tell religious stories through movement. Dancers stay close to the earth; there are usually no large leaps into the air. Most dances are performed by groups moving in unison. A few solo dances have always existed in certain tribes, and others have developed as show dances in the latter half of the 20th century (such as the hoop dance, where a solo performer dances with a number of hoops, forming them into intricate designs, usually collecting money contributions on a blanket nearby).

Lacking written language, Native North American cultures developed a highly sophisticated oral tradition. Storytelling is one of the most prized skills a Native North American can possess. Telling an entire story or story cycle can take two to three days. All Native North American stories are coded to contain many teaching elements and symbols that become more clearly understood as the listener matures and hears the story repeatedly. Another form of oral literature is oratory, or speech-making. One of the best-known Native North American orators was Chief Seattle (c.1786–1866) of the Suquamish tribe in the Pacific Northwest.

The first novel ever written by a Native North American was *Life and Adventures of Joaquin Murieta*, by John Rollin Ridge (1827-67), a Cherokee. *Black Elk Speaks*, by Nicholas Black Elk, as told to John G. Neihardt, sparked a new blaze of Native North American writing when it was republished in 1959. It is the autobiography of Nick Black Elk, an Oglala Sioux medicine man. It is considered to rank among the most important holy books of the world. In 1969, N. Scott Momaday, a Kiowa, became the first Native North American to be awarded the Pulitzer Prize, for his novel *House Made of Dawn* (published in 1968). There is a growing list of successful Native North American writers today, including Vine Deloria, Jr., Dee Brown, James Welch, Duane Niatum, Geary Hobson, Leslie Silko, Simon Ortiz, Louise Erdrich (whose first novel, *Love Medicine*, published in 1984, became a best-seller), Paula Gunn Allen, Linda Hogan, Beth Brant, Gerald Vizenor, and poets Wendy Rose, Joy Harjo, and Ray A. Young Bear.

Artistically, Native North Americans do not impose form on an object but rather attempt to uncover the form that is already there. This is true for music as well as the visual arts. Musical instruments are used to reproduce the natural musical patterns that exist in wind and moving water, for example. Traditional patterns and designs for visual art works are also based on the rhythms and lines of natural formations.

Native North American visual arts have a history that goes back perhaps 25,000 years. Many of the patterns and designs seen today have been in use since ancient times. Each tribe has its own particular style and set of patterns and designs that distinguish its art from that of other tribes. Native North American visual arts include rock engravings and paintings; ivory, bone, and soapstone carvings; pottery; jewelry and metalwork; beading and quillwork; weaving; and basketry. Ceremonial cos-

tumes are another expression of visual art. Today, Native North American visual arts fall into four categories: 1) sacred drums and ceremonial costumes and objects; 2) tourist or popular art forms for sale to non-Natives; 3) contemporary art—carvings, prints, and crafts—for sale in small galleries; and 4) mainstream or high art that is created by Native North Americans trained in Western art schools and which is shown in major urban galleries and art institutions. There are many highly skilled Native North Americans working in each of these four categories.

Perhaps the first widely known Native North American in the performing arts was William Penn Adair "Will" Rogers (1879–1935), a cowboy, writer, actor, entertainer, and humorist of mixed-blood Cherokee descent who became very popular during the 1930s. Jay Silverheels (1912–80), a Mohawk actor, gained fame in the 1950s as "Tonto" in the *Lone Ranger* television series in the US. Since the 1970s, Native North Americans have been paving the way for greater recognition and participation in the theater arts, including stage, film, and television. The American Indian Theatre Ensemble (later renamed the Native American Theatre Ensemble) was founded in New York City in the 1970s. It was the first professional acting company of Native North American performing artists. In 1983, the American Indian Registry for the Performing Arts was established for the advocacy and promotion of Native North American actors, directors, producers, and technical workers in film and on television. The Native American Public Broadcasting Consortium was also founded in the early 1980s to support Native North American work in television, video, and film.

Other well-known Native North American artists and entertainers include Navajo artist R. C. Gorman (1932–); Oneida actor Graham Greene (1950–), best known for his work in the 1991 film *Dances with Wolves* and the 1990s television series *Northern Exposure*; Navajo-Ute musician R. Carlos Nakai (1946–); Cree folk musician Buffy Sainte-Marie (1942–); and Osage prima ballerina Maria Tallchief (1925–).

15 WORK

Native North Americans have the highest unemployment rate of all races in the US and Canada. Unemployment soars as high as 90% during the winter months on some Canadian reserves. The average unemployment rate for Native North Americans in Canada was 26% in 1991, more than twice the national average. Native North Americans in the US suffer similar unemployment percentages. Of those who are employed, less than two-thirds work more than six months per year. The average yearly income for those with income was around $13,000 in 1990–91, well below the national averages for the US and Canada.

The General Allotment Act of 1887 (also known as the Dawes Act) prevented Native North American business development on US reservations by dividing the lands up into small, nonadjoining plots that were barely large enough to support subsistence farming. Farming and ranching for profit were impossible, and Native North Americans were not given the education or vocational training necessary to begin other types of businesses. Canadian reserves were also much too small, and located in areas too poor in resources, to support large-scale operations. When educational opportunities improved for Native North Americans so that they could gain the necessary skills to compete in the business world, most of the choicest niches for profitable enterprise had already been filled by European Americans and Canadians.

However, Natives in both the US and Canada have managed to create business opportunities for themselves, including small retail operations, construction companies, hotels, tourist facilities, gas stations, commercial fishing, logging and other work in the forestry industry, Native arts and crafts production, and gambling establishments.

One of the most successful businesses owned and run by Native North Americans is the Blackfeet Writing Company in Montana which makes pens and pencils. In the US, gambling establishments, such as bingo halls and casinos, have become a leading source of income on many reservations since the Federal Indian Gambling Regulatory Act of 1988 made it legal for any federally recognized tribe to engage in gambling activities for profit. At least half of all US tribes have bingo halls, and there are about 40 Native-run casinos in about a dozen US states. The Florida Seminole tribe was the first to adopt reservation gambling as a source of income, in 1979. The total income from gambling on reservations was estimated to be around $5.5 billion in the early 1990s. Gambling revenues are sometimes the only real source of income for smaller, poorer tribes.

Western-educated Native North Americans sometimes succeed in the European American work world, but the work schedule often conflicts with traditional life. Native North American culture is not based on the eight-hour workday or Monday-Friday workweek. Traditional Native religious ceremonies usually do not coincide with US or Canadian official holidays, so it is often difficult for Native North American workers to get the necessary time off. Most jobs are off the reservation or reserve as well, forcing Native workers either to commute long distances daily or to live away from their families, returning only on weekends and/or vacations. This creates a great deal of stress for all concerned.

Because Native North American women have traditionally been responsible for taking care of the home and young children, fewer work at jobs outside the home than do women of European or African descent in the US and Canada. This means that Native households are less likely to have two incomes on which to draw. (Women tend to be the ones to make traditional arts and crafts for sale, however, so in this way they help support their families financially.) To survive, many Native North Americans resort to leasing their land to non-Natives, but the income they receive from these leasing arrangements is usually six to nine times lower than market value. Most Native North Americans, therefore, are relegated to work as small ranchers, laborers on commercial (non-Native) farms, and low-level workers in other non-Native businesses.

16 SPORTS

The best-known Native North American sport, named *lacrosse* by the French, was invented by the Iroquois centuries ago. It is now Canada's national sport. The Iroquois believe that their ancestors gave them the game to develop their endurance and make them great warriors. Traditionally, boys began learning to play at a very early age. Many Iroquois (boys and girls) today still start lacrosse lessons as small children. Most traditional Native North American sports were used to develop the skills needed for survival.

Two modern world–class Native North American athletes are James Francis "Jim" Thorpe (1888–1953), of the Sac and Fox tribe, and Billy Mills (1938), an Oglala Sioux. Jim Thorpe won gold medals in the pentathlon and decathlon at the 1912 Olympic Games. Seven months later, he was stripped of the medals because it had been discovered that he had previously played semi-professional baseball for $15 per week. The rules at that time stated that any athlete who had received pay for athletic performance was officially considered a professional and was therefore ineligible to participate in amateur competitions such as the Olympics. Seventy years later, the medals were restored to Thorpe posthumously during the 1984 Olympics, after a grass-roots campaign led to the discovery that complaints must be made within thirty days of competition. It had been seven months before complaints were lodged against Thorpe. Thorpe also held world records in track-and-field and was a college All-American in lacrosse, basketball, and football. After the 1912 Olympics, Thorpe played professional baseball from 1913–19, with a career batting average of .252. He then played professional football and became the first president of the American Professional Football Association. In 1950, the Associated Press declared Thorpe the greatest athlete of the first half of the 20th century. He was also named to both college and professional halls of fame.

Billy Mills won the 10,000-meter run at the 1964 Olympic Games, and set a world record for the event. He was the first American ever to win a distance race at the Olympics. Completely unknown to the world, he was never expected to win and had to give the official his name when he crossed the finish line in first place. Mills later set another record for the six-mile run. Today he is a successful businessperson and Native North American activist.

17 ENTERTAINMENT AND RECREATION

Traditional Native North American games are a form of education, either to teach spiritual truths or survival skills (such as dexterity and coordination). Almost all traditional games have music and sometimes dance elements. The most popular are handgames or stickgames where one team sings while hiding an object and the other team then tries to guess where it is (sometimes while singing also). The songs are usually simple with repeated phrases, though they sometimes have complicated rhythms and multipart singing. Many Native North American games involve gambling. Gambling has always been a favorite form of entertainment among Native North Americans, and now they are turning that pursuit to profit with bingo halls and casinos on their reservations, catering to Natives and non-Natives alike.

The Inuit peoples of the arctic and subarctic regions of Siberia and North America created a special game to develop manual dexterity. It has come to be known as "cat's cradle." In this game, a piece of string (or sinew) is tied into a continuous loop and then held with the fingers of both hands. By turning the fingers and hands in certain ways, the string is woven into different patterns, some of which can be quite elaborate. When one player has made a pattern, another player reaches in and takes the string onto her or his own hands in such a way as to create another pattern. Sometimes two players can create one pattern together by contributing one or two hands each. The Inuit have played cat's cradle for centuries.

A uniquely Native North American form of entertainment and recreation, called the *powwow,* has developed in the last 100 years. Powwows are gatherings in which Native North Americans from many tribes come together to sing, dance, gamble, and visit with friends and family. The main focus is on dancing, usually with a dance contest (with money as prizes). A few Native North Americans make their living by traveling from one powwow to the next, competing in the dance contests and collecting prize money. Only the best dancers can make enough money to support themselves this way. The dances are traditional ones, formerly used for religious ceremonies, and the costumes are often extravagant expressions of traditional ceremonial garb.

Pau wau was originally the Algonquin word for "medicine man" or "medicine woman" (or spiritual leader). Europeans who saw these *pau waus* dance thought the word referred to the entire ritual, and eventually the word *powwow* came to be applied to tribal gatherings featuring costumed dance. The modern powwow began among the Plains tribes and eventually spread throughout the US and Canada. Up until the 1970s, powwows only took place on reservations and reserves. Now some are held in convention centers and gymnasiums, or other large gathering places, in cities. There are more than 1,000 powwows each year, and an estimated 90% of Native North Americans attend at least one. Alcohol is banned at most powwows as a way to promote healthful recreation. The majority of powwows are open to non-Natives, though they must be respectful of Native customs and may be asked to leave at any time if they are not. Powwows serve as cultural revivals, as well as entertainment, for Native North Americans. Important persons and personal events are also honored at powwows, such as athletic achievements, scholarships, retirements, and deaths.

¹⁸ FOLK ART, CRAFTS, AND HOBBIES

Native North American art is a continuation of traditional forms and methods that have been in existence for centuries. It is therefore impossible to distinguish "folk art" from so-called "fine art" or "high art" (see #14, "Cultural heritage" above). The increased interest in Native North American arts and crafts in recent decades has led to a booming business in counterfeit imitations made by non-Natives but sold as authentic Native North American art. The Indian Arts and Crafts Act of 1990 gave the Indian Arts and Crafts Board (established in 1935) more power to prosecute counterfeiters and thereby protect themselves from this kind of theft.

¹⁹ SOCIAL PROBLEMS

The social problems of Native North Americans have been discussed throughout this article. The forced removal of Native North Americans from their tribal lands by invading European Americans and Canadians, and the resulting disruption of their traditional ways, culture, and heritage, have led to high rates of alcoholism and suicide among Natives. Drug abuse is also on the rise. Poor lands and lack of economic opportunities on reservations and reserves create oppressive poverty and unemployment. Deep-seated racism and widespread discrimination in the larger European-dominated societies of the US and Canada keep Native North Americans under the heel of that oppression. Though Native North American populations are increasing, the vast majority of those numbers are made up of "mixed-bloods," children of intertribal or interracial couples.

Traditional lineages and tribal lifeways are becoming lost in the blur of racial and tribal blending. Finally, the generations of life on reserves and reservations, at the mercy of government handouts, has cultivated a mind-set of dependency on the part of modern Native North Americans. Attempts by Native activists to reclaim control of their economic and political lives are often met with fear and doubt on the part of older Natives. And the US and Canadian governments are not quite ready to give up their hold on Native North American reins. So the political and economic tug-of-war continues between tribal and federal governments over lands, services, jurisdictions, and racial equality.

²⁰ BIBLIOGRAPHY

Beck, Peggy V., Anna Lee Walters, and Nia Francisco. *The Sacred: Ways of Knowledge, Sources of Life.* Tsaile, Arizona: Navajo Community College Press, 1992.

Brown, Dee. *Bury My Heart at Wounded Knee: An Indian History of the American West.* New York: Holt, Rinehart & Winston, 1970.

Champagne, Duane, ed. *The Native North American Almanac.* Detroit: Gale Research, 1994.

Dimensions: Profile of Ethnic Groups. Ottawa: Minister of Supply and Services Canada, 1989.

The Encyclopedia Americana, International Edition. Danbury, Connecticut: Grolier, 1996.

Kimball, Yeffe, and Jean Anderson. *The Art of American Indian Cooking.* Garden City, New Jersey: Doubleday & Company, 1965.

Parfit, Michael. "Powwow: A Gathering of the Tribes." *National Geographic,* vol 185, no. 6. Washington, DC: National Geographic Society, June 1994, pp. 88–113.

Reddy, Marlita A., ed. *Statistical Record of Native North Americans.* Detroit: Gale Research, 1995.

—by D. K. Daeg de Mott, reviewed by M. Brokenleg

NAVAJOS

ALTERNATE NAMES: Diné
LOCATION: United States (Arizona; New Mexico; Colorado, Utah)
POPULATION: 200,000
LANGUAGE: English; Navajo
RELIGION: Native American Church; Christianity
RELATED ARTICLES: Vol. 2: Native North Americans

¹INTRODUCTION

The Navajos are descended from a band of Athabascans who split off from the rest of the Athabascans in Canada sometime around AD 850 and migrated southward. About 200 years later, they settled in what is now north-central New Mexico among Pueblo peoples who had lived there since AD 400. Though the Navajos were originally hunter-gatherers, they were very adaptable people who adopted some of their Pueblo neighbors' ways. Pueblo Indians were farmers, and the Navajos learned from them how to cultivate corn and other crops. They made the shift from hunter-gatherers to agriculturalists so successfully that they came to be known as the Navajo—a name that most likely comes from the Tewa word *návahu'u*, or "the arroyo (riverbed) with the cultivated fields." The Navajo call themselves *Diné*, or "the People." The first recorded mention of the Navajos is from an account written in 1626 by Fray Zárata Salmerón. By the 1630s the Navajo had definitely become a large and powerful tribe, spreading across northern New Mexico into eastern Arizona. At this time they still hunted and gathered some of their food, and they supplemented their supplies by raiding other villages. But they had also begun to live in semi-permanent homes and grow crops, such as corn, beans, and squash. The preferred type of dwelling was the hogan, a dome-shaped structure (usually round, but sometimes hexagonal or octagonal) built of logs covered with mud, or sometimes rocks, with a central air vent in the roof. After the Spanish arrived in the 16th and 17th centuries, the Navajo adopted the use of horses and began to raise livestock such as sheep, goats, and cattle. The traits the Navajo borrowed from both the Pueblo Indians and the Spanish eventually distinguished them from their Apache relatives (also descended from the same Canadian Athabascans).

Conflicts between the Navajos and first the Spanish, then European Americans, escalated during the 19th century. Raids by the Navajo on Spanish settlers, and then European American travelers and settlers, continued despite peace-keeping efforts by the Spanish, however, and the US Army finally decided to do something about the "Navajo problem." US Army General James Carleton began a campaign to round up all the Navajos and incarcerate them in a concentration camp called Bosque Redondo in New Mexico. Carleton enlisted Christopher "Kit" Carson to help. Together they burned Navajo villages, destroyed their crops (including extensive peach orchards in the Canyon de Chelly), and drove all Navajos who refused to surrender into the mountains to freeze and starve. Eventually, all the Navajos who had not been killed, or had not died of starvation and exposure, surrendered to Carleton and Carson and allowed themselves to be marched to the camp. The route was 370 miles, or 470 by an alternate route, and the Navajos cov-

ered it entirely on foot. It is remembered as the "Long Walk of the Navajos." Hundreds died en route, and hundreds more died from the horrible conditions at the camp once they arrived. A few escaped to try to survive in the inaccessible canyons of the area. Conditions at Bosque Redondo were so bad that even European Americans complained about the mistreatment of the Native North Americans there. The US Army decided to relieve General Carleton of his duty in 1866, and the Bureau of Indian Affairs took over management of the Navajos and others at Bosque Redondo. Shortly thereafter, the US government established a reservation for the Navajos on their former homelands, though the reservation covered only a small portion of their original territory.

Some 25 Navajos volunteered to serve in the US military during World War I in 1917–18. By the time of World War II (1939–45) Native North Americans were draftable US citizens. As a result, at least 3,600 Navajos served in that war. The most famous and honored of those World War II Navajo servicemen were the Navajo Code Talkers, a group of 420 Navajo men who devised a code based on the Navajo language that was used for military purposes in the Pacific campaign. The Japanese never broke the code. In 1938 the Navajo Tribal Council had been formed to represent the interests of all Navajos. In 1969 the Navajo Tribal Council passed a resolution to call their land "the Navajo Nation." The Navajo Nation is currently the largest reservation-based Native North American tribe in the US. The government of the Navajo Tribal Council was reorganized after the conviction of Chairman Peter MacDonald on 41 counts of corruption in 1989. Executive, judicial, and legislative branches have been established with a system of checks and balances, and Peterson Zah was elected "president," not chairman, in 1990.

²LOCATION AND HOMELAND

The Navajo reservation is located in the Four Corners area of the US (where Arizona, New Mexico, Colorado, and Utah have a common corner). Most of the reservation lies in Arizona, with the eastern border extending into New Mexico and a small southern portion in Utah. The total area of the reservation is approximately 25,000 sq mi, comprising some 17 million acres. The entire area is an almost level plateau with an average elevation of 5,500 feet. Mountains in some places rise to over 10,000 feet, and deep canyons cut through the plateau. The region is desert or semi-desert with very little rainfall. It is difficult to farm without irrigation. Winters are quite cold, and summers are hot. Navajos also live on other small reservations, such as Ramah in New Mexico (about 540 square miles, supporting a population of more than 2,000 Navajos), the Alamo (or Puertocito) Navajos in New Mexico (with a population of more than 1,200), and the Cañoncito Navajos, also in New Mexico, with a population of a fewer than 1,200. Over 25,000 Navajos also live in the "checkerboard area," which covers the range east of the main Navajo reservation to the Jicarilla Apache reservation in New Mexico. This region is called the "checkerboard area" because lands were allotted in such a way that each alternate square mile belongs to Native North Americans, and the others belong to European Americans.

The total population of Navajos in 1990 was over 200,000. The number of Navajos living on reservations in that year was 143,405—the largest reservation-based Native North American population in the US. The main Navajo reservation is by far the

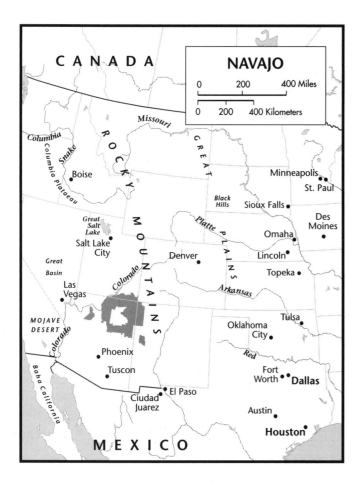

through the east and emerge into the second or Blue World. The Blue World was populated by blue-feathered birds and other animals and beings who did not get along. First Man and First Woman eventually moved to the third or Yellow World where they lived with Coyote (the Navajo trickster figure), Bluebird, and other beings. When Coyote stole the Water Baby, Water Monster flooded the Yellow World. First Man quickly ordered everyone to climb into a reed that gave them entrance into the fourth world. In the fourth world the people discovered that Coyote had stolen the Water Baby. When Coyote took Water Baby back to its mother, the waters receded immediately. However, the beings already living in the fourth world required the entering third-world beings to pass certain tests in order to live there. Locust, the being chosen to take the tests, passed them all, and the people entered safely into the fourth world.

Later, First Man and First Woman formed the four sacred mountains with dirt they had brought from the first (Black) world. Their daughter, White Shell Woman, later gave birth to twin sons. The Twins became the settlers of the Navajo lands and established the plant crops and animals given to them by their father, the Sun. The Twins are regarded as sacred.

Changing Woman is the mother of the four main Navajo clans. She took the people of the clans to the San Francisco Peaks, where the spiritual beings gave the Navajo people their language and also taught them how to use it in prayers and songs. Another important figure is Spider Woman, who taught the Twins how to overcome adversity.

Between ad 700 and 1400, the majority of Navajos gradually followed the San Juan River and migrated to the southwestern US.

5 RELIGION

According to the Navajo, the universe has two classes of people: human beings and Holy People (supernatural beings). The universe functions according to a fixed set of rules, and these rules must be learned and followed to insure safety. *Hózhó* is the Navajo concept of beauty, harmony, balance, health, goodness, etc. Ceremonies are performed to maintain or restore *hózhó*. There are six main groups of ceremonies: Blessing Way (to gain the good will of the Holy People and bring good fortune); War (no longer practiced); Game Way (hunting rituals— no longer practiced); Holy Way (to attract good); Evil Way, or Ghost Way (to exorcise evil), and Life Way (to cure bodily injuries). Each group of ceremonies contains a number of specific ceremonies. For example, the Holy Way group includes Beauty Way (if snakes have been offended), Shooting Way (if thunder and lightning must be appeased), and Mountain Top Way (for conflict with bears). Each ceremony has its own set of chants, and every chant has its own particular sandpainting. Two important ceremonies for the Navajos are the *nidáá'* (called the "squaw dance" by European Americans), a three-day ceremony held in the summer, and healing ceremony held in the summer, and the *yé'ii bicheii* (or Nigh Way), a nine-day healing ceremony held in the winter.

There are about 1,200 different designs for traditional sandpaintings for use in specific ceremonies to treat specific illnesses. Details of each of these designs is handed down by memory from one healer to the next. Each chant also has its own songs, prayers, and herbal medicines. Blessing Way songs are sung in approval of a new headman, for an impending birth,

largest Native North American reservation in the US: it contains a total of 17 million acres.

The Cañoncito Navajos descend from those who favored peace with the European Americans and even worked as scouts for the US Army in campaigns against their own people. Because of this, they came to be known to other Navajos as "Enemy Diné." That negative name was dropped some time ago.

3 LANGUAGE

The Navajo language is part of the Athabascan family of Native North American languages. At least 125,000 Navajos were still fluent in their native tongue in 1987. The Navajo language is one of the few Native North American languages that has been fully recorded. Current education policies among the Navajo aim at restoring the language to its first-tongue status among Navajos. All Navajo-run education is done in both English and Navajo.

Though all Native North American cultures were (and still are, to a large extent) oral cultures, transmitting all information through songs, stories, and chants, the Navajos developed especially long chants compared to other Native North Americans.

4 FOLKLORE

The Navajos tell of their creation with an emergence-type story. First Man and First Woman lived in the first or Black World. When the insect beings who also lived there began to quarrel, First Man and First Woman were forced to leave that world

for men leaving for or returning from military service, marriages, and girls' puberty ceremonies.

Navajos believe that diseases and accidents result from an attack by the Holy People in return for some transgression or offense by the victim. The curing ceremony mends the wrong done. If the person is not cured after the ceremony, this means that the actual wrong that person committed has not yet been uncovered, and the search must continue. The cost of ceremonies is borne by the patient or her or his family. The Blessing Way is the backbone of the Navajo ceremonial system. It is performed frequently throughout the year. Other ceremonies are more specific, or more extensive, and are therefore only performed on occasion or at certain times of the year.

Peyotism took hold among the Navajos around the 1930s. Peyote, first described as a "narcotic cactus," was used as a sacrament and for religious purposes, but its use was prohibited on the Navajo reservation. In 1955 its use was approved by the Tribal Council. About 25,000 Navajos now belong to the Native American Church (incorporated as the peyote religion), and as many as 12,000 more probably attend services without being registered on the rolls. Many Navajos are also at least nominally Christian, though even Christian Navajos usually continue to practice their native religion. One of the keys to understanding the Navajo religion is recognizing that they focus on living well in the world rather than focusing on an afterlife, and they seek to live in harmony with nature.

6 MAJOR HOLIDAYS

As US citizens, Navajos celebrate the Fourth of July, or Independence Day, and Christian Navajos celebrate Christian holidays.

7 RITES OF PASSAGE

The most important rite of passage still celebrated among the Navajo is the *kinaaldá*—the girls' puberty rite. The ceremonies last for more than four days and involve foot races and other rituals related to the ceremony.

8 INTERPERSONAL RELATIONS

Navajos communicate by listening quietly to one another. They speak slowly and thoughtfully, as if they are "weaving" their words. They also make decisions slowly, talking and thinking things over for a long time. Traditionally, Navajos preferred to reach consensus rather than letting majority rule. Today, their government is based on majority rule.

Sharing and reciprocity are central to Navajo interpersonal relations. If a favor is done, a favor can be expected in return, If an injury is done, an injury can be expected in return, unless some kind of compensation is provided. In other words, "an eye for an eye, and a tooth for a tooth," in both good and bad ways. Navajos are very generous as well and share what they have with those in need. However, in response to the modern world around them, Navajos are becoming more aggressive.

9 LIVING CONDITIONS

Some Navajos still live in traditional hogans (round, or sometimes hexagonal or octagonal dwellings built of logs and mud, or rocks, with a central air vent in the roof). Most today, however, live either in modernized hogans or Western-style homes or trailers. Almost all homes, whether modern or traditional,

are still built facing east, an ancient Navajo custom. The Western-style housing provided by the government at low cost on the Navajo reservations does not always fit well with the Navajo lifestyle. In addition, the cheap, lightweight construction often cannot stand up to rough use. Also, maintenance is neglected and funds for upkeep are often difficult to obtain. Most Navajo homes are still without telephones, and those in more remote or isolated areas of the reservations have no running water or electricity. Some families must haul water many miles to use for bathing and cooking. Water conservation is of utmost importance.

Navajos have many health problems stemming from poverty, lack of access to modern health care, the effects of coal and uranium mining (such as very high cancer rates), and pollution in the water, soil, and air. In 1979, near Gallup, New Mexico, gallons of radioactive water accidentally spilled into the Puerco River from the United Nuclear Corporation's uranium mill, making the water undrinkable. It remains undrinkable today both from the uranium spill and other sources of pollution. The Navajo health care system incorporates both Western and traditional Navajo healing methods. New Indian Health Service hospitals provide a room in which traditional Navajo healers may conduct curing ceremonies. Navajo health was greatly improved by Annie Wauneka, who headed a crusade against tuberculosis in the mid-20th century. The number of Navajos with the disease was reduced by almost half between the years of 1953 and 1960. Wauneka received the Presidential Medal of Freedom in 1963 for her work.

A road-improvement campaign on Navajo reservations in recent years has led to many miles of paved roads and even more graveled ones (as opposed to the dirt tracks common and sufficient before the increased use of automobiles).

10 FAMILY LIFE

The family and clan are central to Navajo life. It is believed that every full-blooded Navajo is generally related to no fewer than 12 clans. Clan relationships can be quite complex. Matrilineal and matrilocal, Navajos trace their descent through their mothers, and newly married couples live near the wife's mother. The home, crops, and livestock are owned and cared for by women, while the men represent their families in public and at ceremonials. Extended families are very important to Navajos, with Grandmother holding a place of great respect.

11 CLOTHING

Navajo men today wear Western-style clothing for everyday use: denim jeans, colorful shirts, cowboy boots, and Stetson hats, if they can afford them. Older women tend to wear more traditional dress, dating back to the 1860s: long, full, colorful skirts with velveteen blouses. For very special occasions, some women wear a *biil* (blanket dress), worn with buckskin leggings. Some Navajos still wear leather moccasins for everyday purposes. Navajos are known for their silver and turquoise jewelry.

12 FOOD

Although many Navajo children are fond of hamburgers, pizza, fried chicken, French fries, and soft drinks, mutton stew and fry bread are definitely the two favorite foods for all Navajos. No Navajo gathering is complete without one or more booths making and/or selling mutton stew and fry bread. Navajos who live off-reservation (at school or at work in the city) miss mutton and fry bread more than any other foods. Navajo fry bread is fairly simple to make; the recipe follows:

Navajo Fry Bread

4 cups flour (the modern standard is Bluebird brand milled wheat flour, though any brand will do—white flour makes lighter, fluffier breads)

½ teaspoon salt

2 teaspoons baking powder

1 cup powdered milk

Warm water

Vegetable oil for frying

Sift dry ingredients (flour, salt, baking powder, and powdered milk) together into a large bowl. Stir in water a little at a time until dough is soft. Knead dough with hands until smooth. Cover bowl with cloth and let dough "rest" for about 2 hours Pat or roll 2" balls of dough into circles about 8 inches in diameter and ¼ inch thick. Make a small hole in the center of each circle of dough with your finger. Pour vegetable oil in frying pan or electric skillet to a depth of about ½ inch. Heat oil to 400° (or until a small pinch of dough browns quickly but does not burn). Slide a circle of dough into hot oil—dough will puff up as it cooks. Turn bread over when top is golden brown and fry for one or two more minutes. Repeat with remaining breads. Serve hot, with honey or cinnamon-sugar, or just plain. Serves about 6 people.

(Recipe courtesy of the Navajo Nation Division of Education.)

13 EDUCATION

Navajos today place a great emphasis on education. The Navajo Nation has set up a multimillion-dollar scholarship fund to help worthy Navajo students attend the college or university of their choice. In 1987, more than 4,000 Navajos were students in higher education. The first college ever founded and run by Native North Americans was the Navajo Community College (NCC), opened on the Navajo Reservation in January 1969, near Tsaile, Arizona. Students at NCC are taught to be bilingual, with classes in both Navajo and English. Navajo culture and language is also taught at NCC.

Plans for Ramah Navajo High School began in 1970, the first Native North American-controlled high school since the closing of the Five Civilized Tribes' school systems by the US government in the early 1900s. The educational goals of Ramah High School are to make students bilingual in Navajo and English; to develop their self-esteem as Navajos; to teach them to be analytical and critical of all things, including Navajo history and culture; and to give them the skills they need to be successful in today's world. Ramah children are "children of the Navajo Nation." In 1991, about 70% of Navajo children attended public schools. One recent study found that of Navajos 25 years old and older about 50% had graduated from high school, 25% had some college, only 4.5% had completed college to receive a Bachelor of Arts or higher degree, and 28% had less than a ninth grade education.

The federal Comprehensive Employment Training Act (CETA) has provided Navajo workers with jobs and job training since the 1970s.

14 CULTURAL HERITAGE

Navajo culture is orally transmitted, since for most of Navajo history there was no written language (today, Navajo is written with an adapted Roman alphabet). Because religion cannot be separated from the rest of Navajo life, all music and oral literature was traditionally associated with religious rites, ceremonies, and teaching stories. Today, Navajos are writing works of literature, such as poet Rex Lee Jim, who has published two books of poetry in Navajo (1990 and 1996) and is working on the libretto for the first Navajo-language opera. Rex hopes to found a Navajo School for the Performing Arts on the Navajo Reservation.

Navajo rugs and silver and turquoise jewelry have transcended the level of craft to become fine arts. Rug weaving, done on an upright loom adapted long ago from the neighboring Pueblo tribes, is traditionally a woman's art, with patterns passed down from mother to daughter. Intricately patterned rugs are woven without a printed design to follow. The designs are instead kept entirely in the woman's memory. Silver and turquoise jewelry is crafted by both men and women. Navajo jewelry has come to be highly prized by investors and collectors worldwide.

Sandpaintings began as a religious tradition and have recently become a sought-after art form. Sandpaintings made for show and/or sale are altered enough in design so as not to offend the Holy People. Traditionally made for use in curing ceremonies, sandpaintings have specific designs for treating specific illnesses. In all, there were about 1,200 individual designs that healers had to memorize. Today those 1,200 designs have been supplemented by the secular patterns used for nonreligious sandpaintings. A traditional sandpainting may range in size from 1 to 12 feet in diameter (if circular, or the equivalent if square or rectangular), but most are about 6 feet by 6 feet. They are done with sand colored with natural dyes on a tan sand base. Designs are made up of angular figures made of straight lines and zigzags, representing Navajo spirits, scenery, animals, corn, sun, sky, and rainbows. A sandpainting often takes hours to complete. When finished, in a healing ceremony the ill person sits in the center of the painting and the healer transfers the orderly goodness of the painting into the patient, and transfers the illness from the patient into the painting. The sandpainting is then erased at the end of the ceremony.

15 WORK

Most Navajos are small farmers and herders. Some Navajos serve in the US armed forces. Others work for the Bureau of Indian Affairs (BIA), state, or Navajo tribe. Some find seasonal off-reservation employment. The timber industry and Navajo Tribal Utility generating plant provide some revenue and employment for the Navajo Nation, but unemployment on the reservation remains high. Silversmithing, performed by both men and women, was a traditional source of income, but today crafts are only a minor source. Women have been the most dependable source of income for generations through their weaving of Navajo rugs for sale. The Navajo Nation also leases land to oil and gas companies for drilling, and to mining companies for the extraction of vanadium, uranium, coal, sand, and gravel. But the Navajos get very little return from these operations. The Fort Defiance industrial park financed and built by Navajos and now leased to General Dynamics provides a somewhat better return, but poverty, unemployment, and underemployment are still serious problems for the Navajo Nation. The overall Navajo unemployment rate in 1991 was 34%. Many well-educated Navajos must leave home to find work in cities.

16 SPORTS

Rodeo is very popular among the Navajos. Navajo Community College (NCC) even has a rodeo coach on staff. Winning top honors at the National Intercollegiate Rodeo Association Finals is considered a high achievement and gives the student hero status at NCC.

17 ENTERTAINMENT AND RECREATION

The Navajo Nation Fair, held in Window Rock, Arizona, for nine days each year in September, is the largest such fair in the US. The smaller Northern Navajo Fair is held in Shiprock, New Mexico, usually the first weekend in October. Both fairs feature competitions in traditional song and dance.

18 FOLK ART, CRAFTS, AND HOBBIES

Rug weaving and jewelry making are crafts that have risen to the status of fine arts, along with the making of sandpaintings. The traditional crafts of basketry and pottery are currently being revived. Pottery and basketry are considered women's crafts.

19 SOCIAL PROBLEMS

Like most Native North Americans today, Navajos suffer from widespread alcoholism and drug abuse. Perpetual conflicts exist between more "traditional" Navajos, who want to continue living in traditional ways, and the more "progressive" Navajos, usually the younger generations, who want to modernize life on the reservation. Navajos have a high rate of suicide, even among Native North Americans (all of whom have higher suicide rates than all other races in the US and Canada). Child abuse is also becoming rampant among Navajos.

The Navajo homelands, or *Dinétah*, are being destroyed by environmental damage from oil drilling, mining operations, and overgrazing. Efforts to restore the lands to health are insufficient and not very successful so far. Since 1974, the Navajos have been embroiled in a conflict over what was known as the Joint Use Area—a region shared with Hopi Indians since the late 19th century. In 1874, the US Congress passed a bill that partitioned the area between the Hopis and Navajos, requiring about 100 Hopis and thousands of Navajos to relocate. Many of these people had been living on that land for generations. After years of wrangling with each other, the Hopis and Navajos are beginning to realize that it is not they but the Peabody Coal mining company that wants this land partitioned (the coal company wants access to the coal located there). Efforts are ongoing to resolve the land use conflict.

20 BIBLIOGRAPHY

Dutton, Bertha P. *American Indians of the Southwest*. Albuquerque: University of New Mexico Press, 1983.

Eagle/Walking Turtle. *Indian America: A Traveler's Companion*, 4th ed. Santa Fe: John Muir Publications, 1995.

Gattuso, John, ed. *Insight Guides: Native American*. Boston: APA/Houghton Mifflin, 1993.

Lester, Richard. "What Should You Know About Teaching on the Navajo Reservation?" *Orientation Handbook*, revised edition. Window Rock, AZ: Navajo Nation Division of Education, n.d.

Navajo Division of Education, Office of Diné Culture, Language and Community Services. "Diné Oral Tradition." Curriculum Framework. Photocopy. n. d.

Reddy, Marlita A., ed. *Statistical Record of Native North Americans*. 2nd ed. Detroit: Gale Research, 1995.

Trimble, Stephen. *The People: Indians of the American Southwest*. Santa Fe: School of American Research, 1993.

Waldman, Carl. *Encyclopedia of Native American Tribes*. New York: Facts On File, 1988.

—by D. K. Daeg de Mott, reviewed by E. Tso

NICARAGUANS

ALTERNATE NAMES: Nicas
LOCATION: Nicaragua
POPULATION: 4.4 million
LANGUAGE: Spanish; English; indigenous dialects
RELIGION: Roman Catholicism; Protestantism (Moravian church)

1 INTRODUCTION

Spanish forces subdued the Indian peoples occupying what is now Nicaragua in the 1520s. During the colonial period, Nicaragua was weak and neglected, subject to destructive earthquakes, and plagued by raids from English, Dutch, and French buccaneers. The Caribbean coast was effectively under British control from 1687 until 1894. Nicaragua was one of the five provinces of Central America that declared independence from Spain in 1821. In 1838 it declared its independence from the federation that followed. William Walker, an American adventurer, exploited internal rivalries to briefly install himself as president during the 1850s. A half-century of peace and relative prosperity, during which many coffee and banana plantations were established, followed Walker's execution in neighboring Honduras.

US Marines landed in Nicaragua in 1909 and were kept there almost continuously from 1912 to 1933 to support conservative governments. They fought a guerrilla uprising led by Augusto Cesar Sandino, who was assassinated in 1934, and helped Anastasio Somoza García attain power. The Somoza family ruled Nicaragua with an iron hand until overthrown by the Sandinista National Liberation Front (FSLN) in 1979, after fighting in which an estimated 30,000 to 50,000 people died. Alarmed by the Sandinistas' warm ties with the Soviet Union and Cuba and the insurgents in El Salvador, the United States imposed a trade embargo and sent money and arms to resistance groups known collectively as the Contras. Some 30,000 people died in the decade-long struggle. A 1989 cease-fire was followed by elections in which the Sandinistas were defeated and surrendered political power to the UNO opposition coalition led by Violeta Barrios de Chamorro. Although they continued to control the police and armed forces for a while afterward, under President Chamorro the Nicaraguan Army became more professional and subject to civilian authority.

2 LOCATION AND HOMELAND

Nicaragua is the largest country in Central America, about the size of New York state. It is bounded on the north by Honduras, on the south by Costa Rica, on the east by the Caribbean Sea, and on the west by the Pacific Ocean. The central highlands, including a belt of mountains, 25 of them volcanic, separate the Pacific lowlands from the more extensive Caribbean lowlands (the Miskito Coast), which occupy the eastern half of the country. Lake Nicaragua in the southwest is the largest lake in Central America and has the unusual distinction of being the only lake inhabited by freshwater sharks.

More than 50% of Nicaragua's population of nearly 4.4 million people in 1996 lived in the Pacific lowlands and about 33% lived in the central highlands; fewer than 10% lived in the hot and swampy Caribbean lowlands. Some 69% of the people are Mestizo, of mixed ethnic Spanish and indigenous Indian descent. About 17% are of European descent, about 9% are Black, and 5% are native Indian.

3 LANGUAGE

Spanish is the official and predominant language spoken in Nicaragua. Speech tends to be "aspirated," especially in words ending with the letter "s." As in some other Spanish American countries, *vos* tends to replace *tú* as the singular familiar pronoun, with corresponding changes in verb conjugations. Nicas, as the people call themselves, are known for the quantity and variety of irreverent and off-color jokes in their everyday speech.

English is the predominant language in the Caribbean half of the country, as well as in the capital city, and is the native tongue of the Creoles, Blacks who came from Jamaica and other British West Indies islands as laborers on banana plantations. The Miskito, Nicaragua's main indigenous group, also live in this region. Of mixed Indian, African, and European ancestry, they speak an Indian language related to the Chibcha of South America.

As in many Latin American nations, people have two family names: the mother's family name, which acts as a surname, followed by the father's family name. For example, Mario Garcia Sanchez would be addressed as Señor Garcia.

4 FOLKLORE

Spanish folk practices survived in Nicaragua in combination with Indian folklore, which attributed the very creation of the world to magic. A lively traffic in witchcraft developed from these roots. Love potions, for example, can always find customers. Folk medicine relies both on knowledge of plants native to Nicaragua and on superstitions that derive from the Indian and Spanish past. The *cuadro,* or picture of a saint found in most households, is often credited with magical powers derived from native cult idols. Feasts for local patron saints are often held at the times of planting and harvesting and reflect folk beliefs that divine intervention will result in bountiful crops.

In the Indian mythology found in Nicaragua at the time of the Spanish conquest, the Corn Goddess Cinteotl was an aspect of the Mother Goddess Chicomecoatl. A feast called Xóchitl was held annually in honor of Cinteotl. Soups and fermented drinks derived from corn preserve some of the ritual significance once attributed to that most basic, and hence sacred, grain.

Nicaraguan folk literature abounds in tall tales and fantastic heroes like Pedro Urdemales. In fables, Uncle Coyote is constantly outwitted by the jokester and trickster Uncle Rabbit.

5 RELIGION

Approximately 90% of the Nicaraguan people are Roman Catholic. City dwellers and those from the middle and upper classes are most likely to attend Mass and receive the sacraments. The lower classes tend to be less religious. There is a shortage of priests, and the Church's ability to reach people in rural areas is limited. During the civil war, the bishops were hostile to the ruling Sandinistas, but some priests and nuns have been activists who employ Marxist terminology in what has been described as "liberation theology."

The 10% of the population that are Protestant chiefly live in the Caribbean part of the nation. The Moravian Church is dominant in this region; almost all Miskito and many Creoles are Moravian. Pentecostal churches have made important gains among Nicaragua's poor. The Assemblies of God is the largest of the Pentecostal denominations.

6 MAJOR HOLIDAYS

La Purísima is the most important holiday in Nicaragua. This is a week-long celebration of the Feast of the Immaculate Conception, 8 December on the Church calendar. Elaborate altars to the Virgin Mary are erected or decorated in homes and workplaces, and people, especially children, go from altar to altar singing songs and reciting prayers.

The *posadas* are nine consecutive nights, ending on Christmas Eve (24 December), dedicated to nightly caroling processions commemorating the Holy Family's wanderings in search of shelter in Bethlehem. Holy Week (Easter, in late March or early April) processions are most impressive in Leon and Granada. Managua holds a fiesta in honor of St. Dominic, the city's patron saint, between 1 and 10 August. Masaya has a notable feast to St. Jerome on 30 September, complete with Indian dancers in costume, and a pilgrimage on 16 March in which the Virgin of Masaya and the Christ of Miracles of Nindirí is taken down to Lake Masaya, whose waters are blessed.

An important secular holiday is Independence Day, 15 September, which commemorates the 1821 Central American declaration of independence from Spain. Liberation Day, 19 July, marks the 1979 overthrow of the Somoza regime.

7 RITES OF PASSAGE

The baptism ceremony for the newly born is important. Godparents are responsible for the ceremony and the festivities that follow, and they are expected to concern themselves with the welfare of the child and to provide aid in times of hardship. A child receiving First Communion, usually at the age of nine, is given many gifts. A girl's 15th birthday is often celebrated as denoting that she has come of age. Among the middle and upper classes, dating does not begin until later. Among adults, birthdays have little importance, but the person's saint's day may be marked. Death may be accompanied by a novena for the deceased as well as by the funeral ceremony.

8 INTERPERSONAL RELATIONS

The Hispanic style of greeting is generally more demonstrative than in the United States, and among Hispanic Nicaraguans it tends to be more gregarious and demonstrative than most. Friends almost always shake hands when greeting and parting and often embrace. Women often kiss on one or both cheeks as well as embracing. People often stand closer to one another in conversation than is customary in the United States. A common casual greeting, especially among teenagers, is *"Hola!"* ("Hi").

Visitors may drop in on friends without previous arrangement. Calling cards are often exchanged in social situations as well as in business relations. People of some social standing are greeted with respectful titles such as *Señor, Señora,* and *Señorita* (Mr., Mrs., and Miss, respectively). Older people are often addressed by the respectful titles of *don* or *doña*. Titles reflecting professional attainment are also in common use.

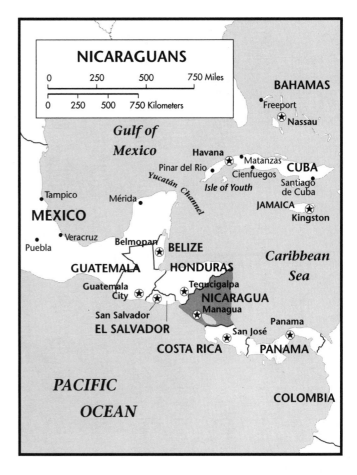

The concept of honor is important in Nicaragua and is upheld vigorously. Personal criticism is considered to be in poor taste. Urban residents are more cosmopolitan, adopting "modern" values, but people in rural areas tend to be more traditional. The concept of *machismo,* in which men are seen as more important than women, is still common in rural areas.

9 LIVING CONDITIONS

The civil war of the 1980s left a bitter legacy as Nicaragua plunged to last place among Central American countries in national income. Indeed, the standard of living fell to that of 1960 or even before. In the mid-1990s, some 75% of Nicaraguans were living below the poverty line.

The Sandinista regime substantially increased spending on health care, broadening and equalizing access to services. There was a substantial drop in infant mortality and the transmission of communicable diseases. However, the system was increasingly strained by shortages of funds and the need to treat war victims. Because health care was subsidized under the Spanish, the economy suffered great damage. In the mid-1990s, most people had no choice but to rely on public facilities that were inadequately staffed, underequipped, and often mismanaged. Most people were malnourished, taking in well below the minimum recommended allowances of calories and protein.

Most people are also poorly sheltered. The national housing deficit, according to a 1990 estimate, was 420,600 units. In rural areas, the most basic dwelling is a dirt-floor straw or palm-frond hut supported by poles and sticks. Its counterpart in

Beans, which provide the main source of protein, and corn tortillas are the basics of the Nicaraguan diet. (AP/Wide World Photos)

towns and cities is a low adobe structure with a tile roof. Squatter settlements are found on the outskirts of the cities. The more substantial homes of the middle and upper classes, of Spanish or Mediterranean style, are nevertheless sparing in ornament, their restraint perhaps reflecting the national vulnerability to earthquakes.

10 FAMILY LIFE

Nicaraguans turn to the family for support because community and church ties tend to be weak. Individuals are judged on the basis of their families and careers are advanced through family ties. The nuclear family of father, mother, and children is fundamental, but the household may be augmented by a grandparent, aunt or uncle, or orphaned children. Newly married couples may take up residence with one or the other set of parents. Godparents, although unrelated by blood or marriage, are also important to the family structure.

Except for the middle and upper classes, marriage is not often formalized, although both civil and church ceremonies have the force of law, and common-law unions were given legal status in the 1980s. The birth rate is high, with the average woman giving birth to nearly six children during her childbearing years. Abortion is illegal except to save the woman's life, but it is not uncommon. Women have major representation in the government, unions, and social organizations, but not in business. Many are heads of households and, in addition to

their domestic duties, have joined the labor force in small-scale commerce, personal services, low-wage sectors such as the garment industry, and, to an increasing degree, in harvesting plantation crops.

11 CLOTHING

Typically women wear simple cotton dresses, while many men wear work shirts, jeans, sneakers or sandals, and straw hats. Even businessmen will often wear sport shirts, or doff their jackets in hot weather in favor of the *guayabera*—a long cotton shirt.

Traditional dress for women varies. In Masaya it consists of a long, loose cotton skirt and short-sleeved cotton blouse, in red, blue, green, or yellow. The fringes of the skirt and blouse and the waistline are embroidered. A shawl is thrown over the shoulder, and a necklace and earrings are worn, with flowers in the hair. For men the native costume is blue cotton trousers, a long-sleeved collarless white cotton shirt, a sheathed machete strapped to the waist, a high-peaked straw hat, and sandals. (Women go barefoot.) More elaborate costumes are worn only for folk dances.

12 FOOD

Beans, which provide the main source of protein, and corn tortillas are the basics of the Nicaraguan diet. Nicaraguans like *gallo pinto*—small red beans with rice—for breakfast. The *nacatamal,* wrapped in a banana-like leaf rather than a corn husk, is the local form of the tamale. In addition to cornmeal, it may contain rice, tomatoes, potatoes, chili, cassava root, and a small piece of meat. The Christmas Eve meal consists of nacatamales with a filling of turkey, chicken, or pork, and raisins, almonds, olives, and chili, served with *sopa borracha* ("drunken soup")—slices of caramel or rice-flour cake covered with a rum-flavored syrup. Another distinctive dish is *vaho,* slowly steaming salted meat and various vegetables piled in layers over banana-like leaves and then covered while heating. Charcoal-grilled steak in a peppery marinade is another favorite. *Tiste* is a beverage made from ground tortillas and cacao beans, with fruit and sugar added. A snack food, the *tajada,* is a deep-fried plantain chip.

Meals usually last longer than they do in the United States, complemented with pleasant conversation. The main meal is eaten at midday, often followed by a siesta, or afternoon rest. The siesta allows people to rest or even sleep during the hottest time of the day, when work is difficult.

Glorious Bananas

2 ripe plantains (very soft)
2 cups (16 ounces) milk
cooking oil
4 Tablespoons grated cheese
¼ cup (2 ounces) sugar
½ teaspoon vanilla extract
1 Tablespoon cornstarch
1 Tablespoon butter
½ teaspoon powdered cinnamon

Slice the plantains and brown them in the cooking oil in a frying pan.

In a bowl, mix the sugar, cornstarch, and cinnamon; add the milk and mix well.

A group of Batahola women sewing in the barrio. About 80% of Nicaraguans work with their hands. (Rita Velazquez)

Add the grated cheese and vanilla.

Use half the butter (½ tablespoon) to grease a Pyrex pan. Pour half the milk mixture into the greased pan, then place the fried plantains on top. Cover with rest of the milk mixture and dot with the remaining butter.

Bake at 350°F for 30 minutes, or until the milk is set.

Note: Do not use small yellow bananas, but plantains, a sort that is used for cooking. They are called *platanos verdes* when green and *platanos maduros* when ripe, but they always need to be cooked.

[Recipe courtesy of Embassy of Nicaragua.]

13 EDUCATION

By making spending on education a priority, the Sandinista government lowered the rate of illiteracy from 52% to 23% of the adult population. School is mandatory and free between the ages of 6 and 13. In the mid-1990s, nearly 80% of primary-school-age children were in school; however, only 39% of females and 44% of males were attending secondary school. Nicaragua's two principal universities are Central American University and the National University of Nicaragua. There are four others.

14 CULTURAL HERITAGE

Native to Central America is the marimba, a kind of xylophone which, however, may have come from Africa. The *son nica* is a driving rhythm overlaid with instrumentals. In Masaya, the traditional capital of the country, the marimba is sometimes accompanied by the oboe, "asses jaw," and a single-string bow with gourd resonator. In the east the music is typically Afro-Caribbean, with banjos, accordions, guitars, and drums.

Traditional dance is sponsored and patronized in Nicaragua more than anywhere else in Central America. There are many dance groups. Dances include *Las Negras, Los Diablitos, El Torovenado, Las Inditas,* and *El Toro Huaco,* all with masked characters, some of them pink and large-nosed to burlesque the Spanish. In *La Gigantora,* a giant woman is paired with a midget. In the *pale volador,* participants unwind from a rope wound around a high pole, swinging to the accompaniment of native Indian percussive instruments. The Caribbean coast also has a maypole dance.

An important specimen of folk drama as well as dance is *El Güegüense,* a farce going back to the 16th or 17th century that combines dance and pointed social satire. As in the nation's fables, the hero is a trickster who uses his wits to frustrate the powerful, in this case the wielders of royal authority.

Foremost of Nicaragua's writers was the poet Rubén Darío (1867–1916), whose innovative verse had a profound effect on

Spanish literature. He is known as the "prince of Spanish-American literature." Other important writers have included the poets Azarias Pallais, Alfonso Cortés, Sálomon de la Selva, and Ernesto Cardenal, and the poet and dramatist Santiago Argüello.

15 WORK

Reflecting the dismal state of the economy, unemployment and underemployment were estimated at 60% of the work force in the mid-1990s, but reliable statistics are hard to come by because many people eke out a living as street vendors or are engaged in other aspects of the informal economy. Social class is based on whether or not one works with the hands, and on that basis 80% of the people are lower class (those who do work with their hands). Nearly 50% of the work force lives by farming, mostly with hand tools and oxen-drawn plows on small subsistence plots. Farm hands are even worse off, employed mostly by large estates only at planting time and harvest season. Most industrial workers are employed in food-processing plants.

16 SPORTS

In other Central American countries soccer reigns supreme, but in Nicaragua (and Panama) baseball is the most popular sport. Nicaraguans were playing in organized leagues in the 1890s, and by the early 1960s even the isolated Miskito were playing regularly. The nation's most famous player is major-league star pitcher Dennis Martínez. Also popular, besides soccer, are boxing, basketball, volleyball, and water sports. Children's games abound; one authority has put their number at no less than 134.

17 ENTERTAINMENT AND RECREATION

Fiestas are an important part of public life and include such diversions as cockfighting, bull-riding, and bull-baiting. Dancing in clubs is popular; Lobo Jack's, in Managua, is the largest disco in Central America. Most films are in English, with Spanish subtitles. In 1993 eight towns had television stations, and there were about 210,000 television sets in use.

Even though the family is the most important unit of society, youth clubs for socializing are becoming more popular.

18 FOLK ART, CRAFTS, AND HOBBIES

Locally made earthenware is decorated much as it was before the Spanish conquest. Other handicraft items include hammocks, baskets, mats, embroidery, leatherwork, coral jewelry, and carved and painted gourds and dolls. Masaya's Artisans Market has the nation's most extensive selection.

19 SOCIAL PROBLEMS

In spite of the fact that the civil war had ended, at least 270 people died in political violence between 1990 and 1994, with police, army, and Sandinistas killing demobilized Contras, and northern Contra bands committing similar acts, often because of land disputes.

Previously undeveloped tracts of rain forest are being cut down at an alarming pace to grow crops and gather fuel wood. Health care is suffering from shortages of food, medicine, and basic medical supplies. Malnutrition and tropical diseases, such as yellow fever and malaria, are serious problems.

20 BIBLIOGRAPHY

Cuadra, Pablo Antonio. *El Nicaragüense*. San José, Costa Rica: Asociación Libro Libre, 1987.

Glassman, Paul. *Nicaragua Guide*. Champlain, New York: Travel Line, 1996.

Merrill, Tim, ed. *Nicaragua: A Country Study*. 3rd ed. Washington, DC: US Government Printing Office, 1994.

Peña Hernández, Enrique. *Folklore de Nicaragua*. Masaya: Editorial Unión, 1968.

—by R. Halasz, reviewed by M. Sobalvarro

NORWEGIAN AMERICANS

For more information on Norwegian history and culture, *see* **Vol. 4: Norwegians**.

OVERVIEW

Legendary Norwegian explorer Leif Ericson (or Leiv Eiriksson) is said to have discovered North America sometime around the year AD 1000, according to Viking sagas. This has yet to be established for certain, but Norwegian Americans look to Ericson as the first example of Norwegian contributions to American history. Since Norwegians began immigrating to the US in significant numbers in the early 1800s, they have made a great many contributions to the culture and history of America.

In the 1800s, the population in Norway expanded beyond available economic opportunities, and many decided to look elsewhere. Members of religious sects other than the state-approved Lutheran Church also chose to go in search of more religious freedom. Norway at that time was fairly isolated from the rest of the world, and little was known there about the young United States. In 1825, however, a group of 52 Quakers and Haugeans (a Lutheran reformist sect) pooled their resources and outfitted a small sloop called *Restauration* to take them to America. They came to be known as the "Sloopers." A baby was born en route, bringing their number to 53. When they arrived in the US, the Sloopers first settled in New York State, near Lake Ontario. The land was difficult to farm there, though, so they eventually moved west, in 1834–35, to Illinois where land was cheaper and easier to till. There they began the Fox River settlement, which became the base camp for future Norwegian immigrants to the US.

The second group of Norwegian immigrants came to America in 1836, settling in Fox River and Chicago. Norwegian immigrants came yearly after that, settling first in Illinois, then spreading north and west to Wisconsin (Muskego became a major settlement in the 1840s), Minnesota, Iowa, North and South Dakota, and eventually to the Pacific Northwest. A few settled in Texas, and some stayed in New York State, near where they first landed, rather than traveling on west. Most Norwegians felt a deep dislike of slavery, which deterred them from settling in the South. Some of those in Texas did own slaves, but for the most part, Norwegian Americans opposed slavery and fought on the side of the Union Army in the American Civil War (1861–65).

In 1862, the Sioux in Minnesota rose up against the European Americans who were invading their lands and pushing them west into alien territory. Many Norwegian Americans were killed or wounded in the Sioux uprising, slowing Norwegian immigration temporarily. The land was too good to resist, however, and soon the Europeans forced the Sioux off the land, confining them on small reservations, driving them out completely, or killing them. Minnesota was added to the "White Man's land," and it became a heavily Norwegian American state.

Norwegian immigration to the US peaked between 1866 and 1914. Over 600,000 Norwegians came to America during these years; only Ireland lost more of its people to the US. In contrast with earlier Norwegian immigrants, who came to America with the intention of settling permanently in their new home, many of the immigrants of the peak years were single young men hoping to earn enough money to return to Norway in better circumstances. As many as 25% did actually return. The rest stayed in America. The Great Depression of the 1930s convinced another 32,000 Norwegian Americans to move back to Norway, but other Norwegian immigrants continued to come to the US, though their numbers have declined steadily since 1914.

Norway is divided into *bygds*, or districts, each of which has developed its own culture with distinctive clothing, customs, folk songs and dances, stories, and language dialect. Immigrants to America tended to settle among others from the same *bygd*, creating small cultural enclaves. In 1902, as Americanization began to take its toll, Norwegian Americans who wanted to maintain their ethnic identity began to form *bygdelags*, or district societies. Within 20 years, 50 *bygdelags* had been established, with a total of more than 75,000 people involved. Many urbanized Norwegian Americans chose not to participate in the societies because they did not want to perpetuate the image of Norwegian "peasant farmers" held by other non-Norwegian Americans. Instead, they wished to be assimilated into American culture and become indistinguishable from mainstream society. The *bygdelags*, therefore, caused some tension in the Norwegian American community.

Most Norwegian Americans were rural in the early days of immigration. They came from peasant farming families in Norway and clung to what they knew, recreating their old environment in their new home. Most Norwegian Americans have continued to resist urbanization, right up through today. Many of the old family farms are still run by descendants of the original settlers. Of the 3,869,395 Norwegian Americans in 1990, according to the US Census, 85% continue to live in the early areas of settlement—the Midwest (52%) and Pacific Northwest (33%). Minnesota has the highest number of Norwegian Americans (757,212), followed by Wisconsin (416,271), California (411,282), Washington State (333,521), North Dakota (189,106), Illinois (167,003), Iowa (152,084), Oregon (124,216), South Dakota (106,361), and Texas (94,096). There are also significant populations of Norwegian Americans in Florida (90,375), New York (90,158), Montana (86,460), and Michigan (72,261).

North Dakota is by far the most "Norwegian" state in the US, with Norwegian Americans making up 29% of the total state population. Minnesota is a distant second with 17%, and South Dakota comes in third with 15%. Although Wisconsin has the second largest number of Norwegian Americans, they make up only 8% of the total state population, making it the fifth most Norwegian state in the US, behind Montana, which is 11% Norwegian American.

Because Norwegian and English are both in the Germanic family of languages, Norwegian immigrants to the US find English relatively easy to learn. Early immigrants incorporated many English words into their Norwegian dialects so that later immigrants, even those who spoke the same original dialect, often could not understand them. Because Norwegian Americans tended to live in isolated farming communities, surrounded by other Norwegian speakers, they retained their native ethnic language longer than many other US immigrants.

Even third generation Norwegian Americans are often fluent in Norwegian. However, Norwegian Americans are still subject to Americanization, and fluency in Norwegian is eventually lost.

Many Norwegian Americans were outraged when the Norwegian Lutheran Church in America (NLCA) decided to hold its services in English rather than Norwegian. The NLCA was formed in 1917 when the three major Norwegian Lutheran synods at that time— Norwegian Synod, the Haugean Synod, and the United Norwegian Lutheran Church—merged. The merged church recognized the Americanization of later generations of Norwegian Americans and chose to minister to their needs. In 1946, the NLCA further enraged conservative Norwegian Americans by dropping "Norwegian" from their name, becoming the Lutheran Church in America (LCA). The LCA absorbed German and Danish Lutherans in 1960 and recently united with the American Lutheran Church to become the Evangelical Lutheran Church in America (ELCA). Two Norwegian speaking congregations still exist, both named "Minnekirken," in Chicago and Minneapolis.

Not all Norwegian Americans are Lutheran. There are also handfuls of Quakers (who were among the first group of immigrants in 1825), Baptists, Presbyterians, Methodists, Mormons, and others. Some Norwegian Americans today belong to no church.

For a time in the 19th and early 20th centuries, Norwegian Americans celebrated *syttende mai*, or 17 May, commemorating the signing of the Norwegian constitution in 1814. Huge centennial celebrations were held in 1914, but then the hyperpatriotic hysteria of the World War I years in the US suppressed any ethnic festivities. The multicultural movement that began in the 1960s, however, allowed *syttende mai* to reemerge for its sesquicentennial in 1964. Today, many Norwegian American communities hold parades and other cultural festivities on 17 May each year. Two of the traditional Norwegian foods served at these feasts and on other special occasions are *lutefisk*, made from specially prepared cod, and *lefse*, a flatbread usually made from potatoes and rolled out paper-thin with a grooved rolling pin that gives it a grid-like texture.

Despite their relative isolation in early years, Norwegian Americans have contributed a great deal to American culture. Three top-notch Norwegian American colleges are located in Minnesota: St. Olaf College (Northfield), founded in 1874; Concordia College (Moorhead), established in 1891; and Augsburg College (Minneapolis), which in 1922 grew out of Augsburg Seminary, founded in 1896. The St. Olaf Choir has achieved international renown since its beginnings in the early 1900s. Founding director F. Melius Christiansen wanted to develop *a cappella* (without accompaniment) singing and created the first chorus of its kind in the US.

Music has always been of great importance to Norwegians and Norwegian Americans. Early Norwegian Americans began many choral societies, some of which still exist today. Norwegian folk dances are still performed by Norwegian American dance groups around the country. Individual Norwegian Americans who have achieved success in the world of music are conductor Ole Windingstad and opera singer Rise Stevens.

The first Norwegian American writer to become well-known in the US was Ole E. Rolvaag, who wrote in Norwegian in the 1920s. His first book published in the US was an English translation (by Lincoln Colcord) of two earlier works that had been published in Norway. The English version was called *Giants in the Earth*, published in 1927. It was selected by the Book of the Month Club and sold almost 80,000 copies by the end of the year. Modern Norwegian American writers include Wallace Stegner, who won the Pulitzer Prize in 1972 for *Angle of Repose*, and poet Robert Bly, now considered the "father of the men's movement" since the publication of his nonfiction book, *Iron John: A Book About Men* in 1990.

Norwegian Americans have also been successful in the worlds of theater, film, and television. Well-known Norwegian American actors include James Arness, James Cagney, and Celeste Holm. Figure skater Sonia Henie also became a popular film star in the 1940s after retiring from a gold-medal Olympic career. Henie skated her way to fame in musical extravaganzas on ice, both live and in Hollywood movies. Sonia Henie is responsible for bringing figure skating to the public, transforming it from an unknown sport to a popular pastime.

Norwegian Americans are also responsible for bringing skiing to America. All forms of skiing were relatively unknown in the US in the 1800s. When Norwegian immigrants came to America, however, they brought with them their love of skiing, both as a sport and as a mode of transportation during the long, snowy winters. Cross-country skiing and ski-jumping were particular Norwegian American specialties. Telemarking (named after a district of Norway), involving a particular way of turning, later became popular.

Two other famous Norwegian American sports figures are football place-kicker Jan Stenerud, who introduced the soccer-style kick now used by most place-kickers, and Knute Rockne, revolutionary football coach at Notre Dame from 1918 to 1931.

Norwegian American figures abound in the worlds of science, industry, and politics. Building on Norwegian Americans' long history as farmers, agriculturalist Norman Borlaug worked with peoples all over the world to develop more productive strains of wheat. Borlaug was awarded the Nobel Peace Prize in 1970 for his work. Earl Bakken invented implantable pacemakers, Dr. Ernest O. Lawrence invented both the cyclotron and color television tube, Dr. Conrad Elvehjem discovered vitamin B6 (niacin), and Dr. Ludwig Hektoen was the first to match blood types of recipients and donors.

Economist Thorstein Veblen coined the phrase "conspicuous consumption" in his landmark book, *The Theory of the Leisure Class*, published in 1899. Veblen is often called the "spiritual father of the New Deal." The Library of Congress cataloging system was created by Norwegian American James Christian Meinich Hanson. Two well-known Norwegian American journalists are Eric Sevareid, a World War II war correspondent for CBS who then became a news commentator at CBS until his retirement, and Eric Utne, publisher of the alternative journal, *Utne Reader*, founded in 1984.

Seattle, Washington, has the highest concentration of Norwegian American businesses anywhere in the US. Over 30 Norwegian American companies are located there. Perhaps the best-known Norwegian American business entrepreneur is Conrad Hilton, the "Hotel King." The international chain of Hilton hotels is now managed by Conrad's son, Barron Hilton.

Norwegian Americans have been represented in federal politics since 1883, when Knute Nelson of Minnesota was elected to the US House of Representatives. Nelson later served on the US Senate from 1895 to 1923. US congressman Andrew Volstead introduced the Prohibition Act in 1919, also known as the

Volstead Act. The consumption of alcohol was traditionally acceptable in Norwegian culture, but it became a problem in the US and many concerned Norwegian Americans joined the temperance movement.

In 1954, Coya Gjesdal Knutson became the first woman from Minnesota to be elected to US Congress, and she then became the first woman ever appointed to the House Committee on Agriculture. Norwegian Americans Hubert H. Humphrey and Walter F. Mondale both served as US vice-president and ran unsuccessful campaigns for president. Earl Warren, half-Norwegian American and half-Swedish American, served as Chief Justice of the Supreme Court from 1953 to 1969, establishing himself as a powerful liberal voice when he ruled against the racial segregation of schools.

Norwegian immigration to the US declined yearly after World War II, coming to nearly a complete stop by the 1980s. Few new immigrants arrive, and previous immigrants have become almost thoroughly Americanized. "Norwegian" identity among Norwegian Americans is now mostly symbolic, remembered in certain foods and customs that are enjoyed on special occasions, and in folk song and dance traditions carried on by cultural associations and small performance groups. Although the economic decline among American farmers has hit the Norwegian American community particularly hard, as such a high percentage of them are farmers, for the most part Norwegian Americans have few problems unique to their community. They adapted quickly and well to their new home and are now an established part of mainstream American culture.

BIBLIOGRAPHY

Hillbrand, Percie V. *The Norwegians in America*. Minneapolis: Lerner Publications, 1991.

Lovoll, Odd S. *The Promise of America: A History of the Norwegian-American People*. Minneapolis: University of Minnesota Press, 1984.

Ojakangas, Beatrice. *Scandinavian Cooking*. Tucson: HPBooks/Fisher Publishing, 1983.

US Bureau of the Census. *Detailed Ancestry Groups for States*. 1990 Census of Population Supplementary Reports, CP-S-1-2. Washington, DC, October 1992.

—by D. K. Daeg de Mott

OJIBWA

ALTERNATE NAMES: Chippewa; Ojibway; Anishinabe
LOCATION: United States; Canada (Great Lakes area, especially around Lake Superior)
POPULATION: Over 70,000
LANGUAGE: English; Ojibwa
RELIGION: Traditional Ojibwa, based on spirits; Christianity
RELATED ARTICLES: Vol. 2: Native North Americans

[1] INTRODUCTION

The Ojibwa, or Chippewa, are descended from the ancient Anishinabe, a name which means "original people." Their neighbors called them "Ojibwe," which is probably a mispronunciation of *kamaziniibiiegaewad*, "picture-makers" (for pictographs they made). Others believe the name refers to the unusual puckered seams on their moccasins. Europeans further distorted their name to become "Chippewa." Today both "Chippewa" and "Ojibwa" (or "Ojibway") are used to designate these people. Many Ojibwa still prefer to call themselves Anishinabe.

The Ojibwa migrated from the northern Atlantic coast, around the mouth of the St. Lawrence River, to the eastern shores of Lake Superior (which they called Kitchigamiing) between ad 1000 and 1400. The Ottawas (who also sometimes refer to themselves today as Anishinabe) and Potawatomis migrated with the Ojibwa. Together they were known as the Three Fires Council. The Three Fires peoples split up when they reached the shores of Lake Huron. The Ottawas settled along the northern shores of Lake Huron; the Potawatomis settled in what is now Michigan; and the Ojibwa continued northwest to Lake Superior. The final Ojibwa homeland became all the lands surrounding Lake Superior (stretching west into what is now Minnesota and the Dakotas, south into Wisconsin and Michigan, and north into Canada).

The Ojibwa became arch enemies of the neighboring Iroquois Confederacy nations because of conflicts over land and competition for the fur trade. The Ojibwa began trading furs for European goods (such as knives, hatchets, fish-hooks, and needles) in the early 1600s, first with friendly eastern Native North American tribes who had already obtained goods from the Europeans and then with the Europeans themselves as the Europeans moved west. The Ojibwa's first contact with Europeans was probably at a Feast of the Dead at a Huron camp in September 1641. Several Ojibwa and a number of French missionaries were guests at the feast. A few weeks later, Father Charles Raymbault and Father Isaac Jogues arrived in Pawatigoong ("the place at the falls"), one of the Ojibwa's main villages, which the French named Sault Sainte Marie (Saint Mary's Rapids). The French called the Ojibwa "Saulters" (People of the Rapids). Other French missionaries soon followed, but the Ojibwa were not very interested in Christianity. They just wanted European trade goods.

In 1659, two French traders, Pierre Esprit Radisson and Medard Chouart des Groseilliers, were guided by the Ojibwa from Quebec down the St. Lawrence River through the Great Lakes to Lake Superior. They visited many Ojibwa camps during the winter and traded goods for furs. When they returned to Quebec with loads of furs in their boats, other traders decided to follow suit. The Ojibwa village at Chequamegon Bay soon became a trading center for French and Native North American peoples. Many of these French traders married Ojibwa women and lived part-time in Ojibwa villages. They adopted Ojibwa clothing and learned the Ojibwa language and Ojibwa customs and skills. These traders came to be known as *voyageurs* because of the long journeys they made along the fur-trade routes. They were also called *coureurs de bois*, or "runners of the woods."

The Ojibwa soon became dependent on European goods and lost their traditional skills, such as making knives and needles from bone (rather than the steel ones provided by the Europeans). The formerly semi-nomadic Ojibwa now settled in permanent villages near trading posts. They hunted for profit, not just survival, and animals that had been their main source of food became scarce because the Ojibwa (and other Native North Americans) now killed more than they could eat for the furs and hides, thus upsetting the balance of nature.

Warfare, between European powers who wanted to control the trade routes, and between Native North Americans over the use of hunting grounds, increased. Native North American use of guns obtained in trade from Europeans (instead of traditional bows and arrows) increased the death toll in warfare. Europeans also brought diseases for which Native North Americans had no immunities or treatments. Between war and disease, Native North American populations, including the Ojibwa, were decimated.

By the late 1600s, the Ojibwa had spread throughout the Great Lakes area, as far east as the modern-day Toronto area. (They fought with the Iroquois for control of this territory and eventually drove the Iroquois to the south.) Other Ojibwa bands moved south into Wisconsin and drove out the Fox tribe to gain control of those lands. Some Ojibwa moved west into eastern Minnesota and fought Sioux tribes for lands there.

The British had begun their own fur trade in North America by the mid-1600s, and the French made a treaty with the Native North Americans around Lake Superior, including the Ojibwa, to trade only with the French. In the late 1600s, however, the French decided the fur market was glutted and stopped buying furs from the Native North Americans for a time. The Ojibwa had become dependent on the fur trade by this time and had no other way to support themselves. When the French reopened trade in 1718, they found the Ojibwa nearly starving.

In 1736, the Sioux attacked French trading posts and became enemies of the Ojibwa, who were allies of the French. The Sioux then launched a series of quick raids on the Ojibwa, which the Ojibwa usually won because they had more European weapons and were better woodsmen than the Sioux. The Ojibwa eventually drove the Sioux entirely out of Wisconsin and northeastern Minnesota.

The French and Indian War between the French and British began in 1761, while the Ojibwa were warring with the Sioux. The Ojibwa sided mostly with the French. Britain won the war in 1763 and took control of the Great Lakes fur trade. The balance of power in the Great Lakes area shifted. To make matters worse for the Ojibwa, where the French had only been interested in furs, the British wanted furs *and* control of the land.

From the mid-1760s to 1770s, the Ojibwa traded peacefully with the British. The Ojibwa tried to stay neutral during the American Revolution (1775–83) so as not to offend either side and be on good terms with whoever won (avoiding a repeat of

their difficult situation at the end of the French and Indian War). When the American colonists won, the fur trade came under the control of the newly established United States of America. The new Americans solidified their control by defeating the British in the War of 1812.

The Ojibwa found that American goods were often inferior to European goods, and American settlers were greedy for land. Some Ojibwa moved to Canada to resume trade with the British. In the 1820s and 1830s, the US fur trade was run mostly by the American Fur Company, owned by John Jacob Astor. Astor wanted to maintain Native North American culture and lands to keep the fur trade going. Settlers, loggers, and miners, however, wanted the Ojibwa's land, so they put pressure on them to move west of the Mississippi River. The Ojibwa were eventually forced to move to reservations established on their homelands in the US and Canada. Nearly all Ojibwa were living on reservations by 1854.

There was not enough land on the reservations to support the Ojibwa's traditional life of hunting, fishing, and gathering food. The US government expected them to become farmers, but the land was not good enough (and the growing season was too short) to grow enough food to sustain everyone throughout the year. The General Allotment Act of 1887, which divided up reservation lands into individually owned 160-acre plots, made the situation even worse. In that northern climate, 160 acres was not enough land on which to grow food for an entire household. The Ojibwa of Red Lake Reservation managed to prevent the government from dividing up their land; it is still owned communally by the tribe.

On the reservations, the Ojibwa were given government housing and Western clothing to wear. Their children were forced to attend European American schools, many of them boarding schools far from home, where their traditional culture was denigrated and denied in an attempt to "civilize" them. There was little opportunity for employment on reservations, and the US government built dams that destroyed thousands of acres of wild rice, the Ojibwa's staple food. The Ojibwa fell into poverty and despair.

The Battle of Leech Lake was triggered in 1898 when an Ojibwa leader named Bugonegijig ("Hole-in-the-Day") escaped from custody and refused to cooperate with European American law officers. Bugonegijig had been arrested on a trumped-up liquor charge (common treatment at the time because law officers were paid for every arrest they made) and then released for lack of witnesses. He refused to cooperate when subpoenaed as a witness in another case and was arrested again, released, and arrested again. This time he escaped, and the US War Department sent about 500 troops into the Leech Lake Reservation. During their lunch break, one of the soldiers' guns accidentally went off. Ojibwa who were hiding in the woods nearby thought the soldiers were shooting at them and fired on the troops in return. The commanding army officer and five soldiers were killed. The government then sent over 1,000 more troops to Leech Lake in preparation for a major battle. Fortunately, both sides agreed to a peaceful settlement before any more fighting occurred. The Ojibwa expressed deep regret for the deaths of the soldiers, and no one else was killed. Several Ojibwa were fined and sent to jail for periods of up to 10 months.

Poverty continued to be a painful reality for the Ojibwa into the 1930s. President Franklin Roosevelt included programs in his New Deal to improve the situation of Native North Americans throughout the US. World War II (1941–45) provided some war-related jobs for Ojibwa, and several hundred served in the US armed forces. After World War II, many Ojibwas left their reservations to live in cities and try to find work there. Some did, but unfortunately many merely found a new sort of poverty because they lacked the skills and cultural background to succeed in the European-dominated urban world.

Despite their many difficulties since the Europeans arrived on the continent, the Ojibwa still live on their ancestral tribal lands and have survived as a tribe and a distinct people. Modern battles are fought in court for land-use, water-use, and other rights. In 1983, two Ojibwa spearfishers were arrested for fishing in waters outside their reservation in northern Wisconsin. A federal court (in what came to be known as the Voigt Decision) upheld the Ojibwa's right to fish in traditional ways on any ancestral tribal lands, whether those lands are currently included in an Ojibwa reservation. The Voigt Decision also gave tribal councils responsibility for regulating Native North American fishing in terms of health, safety, and conservation. In light of this decision, 13 Ojibwa reservations in Michigan, Wisconsin, and Minnesota joined together to form the Great Lakes Indian Fish and Wildlife Commission.

Controversy still rages over fishing rights in off-reservation waters. Extremist European American opposition organizations, supported by white supremacist groups, bombed a boat landing, capsized Ojibwa boats, physically attacked Ojibwa fishers, and verbally abused Ojibwa women in 1989 and 1990.

2 LOCATION AND HOMELAND

The Ojibwa live in the Great Lakes area of the US and Canada, mostly around Lake Superior. The climate of the northern Great Lakes region is subarctic: long, cold, snowy winters, and short summers. One of most important early Ojibwa villages on the shore of Lake Superior was Bowating, now called Sault Sainte Marie. The population of Bowating at the beginning of the 17th century was probably between 250 and 500. There are between 70,and 104,000 Ojibwa in the US today, living mostly on reservations in Michigan, Wisconsin, and Minnesota. A similar number live in Canada, mostly on reservations in Manitoba and Ontario. Many Ojibwas left the reservations in both the US and Canada after World War II (1941–45) and moved to cities to try to find work. Today Toronto, Ontario; Grand Rapids, Michigan; Minneapolis, Minnesota; and Winnipeg, Manitoba all have sizable Ojibwa populations.

The Ojibwa describe months and seasons with "moons." Spring begins with Crust on the Snow Moon (March), and sap begins running in the sugar maple trees. During this "moon," the Ojibwa traditionally moved from their winter hunting grounds to the maple groves. Maple sugaring continues through Moon of Boiling Sap (April). Flowering Moon (May) traditionally signaled the time to move to summer camps. Summer lasts through Strawberry Moon (June), Midsummer Moon (July), and Blueberry Moon (August). Fall begins with Wild Rice Moon (September), when the Ojibwa traditionally moved to the shores of lakes where wild rice grew. Falling Leaves Moon (October) is the time for Ojibwas to prepare for winter. They had traditionally headed for winter hunting grounds by time of Freezing Moon (November). Winter lasts through Spirit Moon (December), Great Spirit Moon (January), and Sucker Fish Moon (February). Then the cycle of the year is completed when the Crust on the Snow Moon appears once again in the sky and the sap begins to run again in the trees.

3 LANGUAGE

The Ojibwa language belongs to the Algonquian family of Native North American languages. In contrast to most Native North American peoples, the Ojibwa did have a system of writing. The ancient Anishinabe and their Ojibwa descendants painted pictographs (pictures used to record information) on birch bark.

Anishinabe and Ojibwa pictographs are considered to be the best example of written records left by any Native North American group north of Mexico.

In the native Ojibwa language, days are counted in terms of "sleeps"; the word "night" is not used by some Ojibwa. *Niizho-tibikut* means "two sleeps."

Children were named at birth after a dream or vision. Friends and relatives rarely addressed children by their birth names, however. Instead, the Ojibwa generally addressed each other by their relationship to the other (such as "daughter," "grandfather," "sister," etc.). Ojibwa children were also given a secret name that only their parents knew. This was done to prevent anyone from casting a spell on them, because spells only work if the spellcaster has a person's true name.

4 FOLKLORE

According to the Ojibwa, Kitchi Manido (Great Spirit) created the universe. First he made the four basic elements: rock, fire, wind, and water; then he made the sun, stars, earth, and everything on it (including humans) from those elements. Kitchi Manido then organized the universe by the Four Directions: Waubanoong (east), Shawanoong (south), Nangabianoong (west), and Keewatinoong (north). Two more sacred directions were also included: Sky above and Earth below. After a while, there was a great flood on the Earth and the seas covered the land. Various animals dove down under the waters to find land but were not successful. Finally, Muskrat dove deep and after a long while came up nearly dead with a bit of mud in his paw, from which Earth was re-created.

Kitchi Manido gave everything in creation a spirit and a purpose in the Circle of Life. He also created Winebozho (First Man), also called Nanabush, born of an Earth Mother and Father Sun. Winebozho is a trickster figure and acts as an intermediary between humans and the spirit world. The Anishinabe were born of Winebozho. The Ojibwa have many Winebozho stories, including teaching stories, stories of how different elements of Ojibwa life were created, and others.

5 RELIGION

As is true for all Native North American peoples, religion is an integral part of the Ojibwa's daily life. The Ojibwa believe that all creation is interconnected and that all things in creation are equally important. Everything in nature is occupied by a *manido*, or spirit. There are lesser and greater spirits, some of whom are evil, though most are good. The one Great Spirit is called Kitchi Manido. Ojibwa must please the spirits to have good health and success. Bad luck, illness, and injury result from angering the spirits. The best way to please the spirits is with a tobacco offering, which is an offering of thanksgiving. Each time an animal is killed, thanks are offered. Before harvesting wild rice or peeling the bark from birch trees, an offering is made. Ojibwa give thanks for all gifts from Kitchi Manido and the spirits of creation.

All Ojibwa ceremonies begin by smoking the Pipe of Peace.

Many Ojibwa converted to Christianity during the 19th and 20th centuries. Others are nominal Christians yet continue to follow traditional religious ways. Some never gave up their ancestral beliefs, and still others are returning to those beliefs and traditions as they strive to reclaim their Native North American identity in this last decade of the 20th century.

6 MAJOR HOLIDAYS

The Ojibwa hold seasonal celebrations, such as the Harvest Feast in autumn after the wild rice harvest. The Feast of the Dead is held each autumn in remembrance of all those who died during the previous year. Among traditional Ojibwa, each family who has suffered the death of one of their members during the past year holds a banquet for the entire village. The food is not necessarily placed on the table, but in an open area outside. A place is set for the deceased, whose spirit remains with the family.

7 RITES OF PASSAGE

Traditionally, when a boy killed his first large animal in a hunt, his family held a celebration because he was learning to provide for his family. Boys were not considered true hunters until they had killed a bear and one other large animal (such as a moose or deer).

At puberty, boys go on Vision Quest: they spend several days alone in the woods without food and wait for their guardian spirit to appear and give them instructions for their adult life. When they return from their Vision Quest, they are treated as men.

The Ojibwa believe that girls are given a gift from the Creator at the time of their first menstruation that is not given to men. To receive this gift, girls are kept isolated in a special shelter away from the village for the duration of their first menstruation. During their seclusion, the girls fast and see only their mothers and grandmothers. When they return to the village, they are henceforth treated as women.

A ceremony is held to initiate a *Mide* apprentice into the *Midewiwin* society (see #9, "Living conditions"). The most important part of the ceremony is the ritual "death" and "rebirth" of the initiate: he or she is "shot" with a sacred shell, or *megis*, then "revived" with the breath of life from the presiding *Mide* leader.

When an Ojibway dies, his or her body is placed on a platform for four days, the time it is believed to take for the person's spirit to journey into the next world. The body is then wrapped in birch bark and buried with the feet pointing southward (the direction of the next world). Food and tools for the journey to the next world are buried with the deceased. Small buildings are sometimes constructed over the grave to shelter the spirit.

8 INTERPERSONAL RELATIONS

The Ojibwa tribe was originally made up of many small, autonomous bands, each with its own leader. That sense of autonomy and division into separate bands is still evident among Ojibwa

of different reservations today. Ojibwa tribal chiefs were devoted to keeping the peace throughout their history.

9 LIVING CONDITIONS

The Ojibwa traditionally lived in wigwams, dome-shaped structures built from saplings cut (by men) and placed in the ground in an oval measuring about 14 by 20 feet. The tops were then tied together to form the dome. Several lighter-weight poles were then tied horizontally to the first poles around the circle to complete the frame. Woven grass mats and strips of birchbark were laid over the frame by the women. Heavy poles were sometimes laid over the mats and bark to hold them in place. A fire burned continually in a central firepit inside the wigwam, the smoke escaping through a hole in the center of the roof. The floor was covered with mats woven by the women from bulrushes, and the door was covered with a piece of animal hide. Low benches and mats were placed around the inside edges of the wigwam for sleeping and sitting, and baskets held the family's belongings. The Ojibwa used deer or bearskin blankets as bedcovers. Each wigwam housed an extended family of parents, grandparents, and children.

A wigwam could be built in less than a day. When the Ojibwa moved to another campground, they would simply roll up the bark and hide covering of the wigwam and take it with them, leaving the pole frame behind. Or they might make the poles into a *travois*, a sort of sled, and pack their belongings on it. They either pulled the *travois* by hand or harnessed it to dogs.

Traditional healing is done by medicine men and women, called *Mide*. Most are a combination of priest and doctor. Mide have a special relationship with the spirit world and also have a wide knowledge of the medicinal uses of plants. They combine herbal medicine with spiritual ceremonies involving song, dance, and prayer. Many Mide become members of the Midewiwin society after a long apprenticeship. There are four degrees of Mide instruction today; in earlier times, there were as many as eight. Most of the ancient birchbark scrolls with Mide songs and history are gone, however, and much of the knowledge of herbal medicine is lost as well.

The Ojibwa became masters of the birchbark canoe. Each canoe weighed between 65 and 125 pounds (29–45 kg). Working together, men and women spent about two weeks building one. Every family had several canoes. In the winter, Ojibwa used (and still use today) snowshoes to travel about in the deep, soft snows. They also used flat, lightweight wooden sleds called *nabagidabanaakoog* (mispronounced as "toboggans" by Europeans).

10 FAMILY LIFE

Ojibwa men traditionally did the hunting, while the women cooked the food, prepared the animal skins, and sewed clothing from them.

Babies are strapped to a cradleboard for most of the first year of their life. A cradleboard is a flat board with a footrest at the bottom and a hoop to protect the baby's head at the top. The baby is placed on a cushion of moss and feathers, then covered with a piece of animal hide or fur. A leather strap is wrapped around the baby and cradleboard to hold the baby in place. The cradleboard can be strapped to the mother's back for carrying or propped against the wigwam (or house) or a tree when the mother is working.

Each Ojibwa household is made up of an extended family: parents, grandparents, and children. The clan system is very strong; clans are patrilineal (inherited through the father) and exogamous (one cannot marry a member of one's own clan). The major Ojibwa clans in earlier days were Crane, Fish, Loon, Bear, Martin, Deer, and Bird. More clans have since been added. Each clan traditionally had certain responsibilities to the community; for example, Fish clan members were responsible for settling disputes between other clans.

Elders are very important in Ojibwa society. They advise adults on the wisest course of action and teach children the ways of the Ojibwa.

11 CLOTHING

Ojibwa today wear Western-style clothing for everyday purposes. At ceremonial dances, they will dress in the traditional way.

Traditional Ojibwa clothing is made from animal skins, mostly deerskin. Men and boys wear a breechcloth—a strip of hide passed between the legs and over a belt to hang down in the front and back. Thigh-high leggings are attached to the belt with a leather thong. In cold weather, fur or animal skin is wrapped around the shoulders.

Women and girls wear a dress made from two pieces of deerskin sewn together at the shoulders and down the sides. They usually wear knee-high leggings tied at the knees with a leather band.

Children's clothes have a similar design to adults' but are made from smaller skins or furs, such as beaver, fawn, squirrel, or rabbit.

All Ojibwas wear leather moccasins with soft soles, traditionally so they could walk quietly in the woods. Men and women both oil and braid their hair. Sometimes they stick feathers and porcupine quills in their hair for decoration. Both men and women also paint their faces; wear earrings, necklaces, and bracelets; and decorate their clothing with quills, feathers, and beadwork. (Beads were first made from shells; stones; animal teeth, claws, and hooves; nuts; berries; and seeds. Later, the Europeans traded glass beads for furs. Because glass beads were smaller, more durable, and easier to work with, designs became more intricate. Ojibwa women expanded from simple geometric patterns to elaborate floral motifs.) Traditional dyes are made from roots, nuts, bark, and berries.

The snowshoes worn in winter were traditionally made from a piece of flexible ash wood fastened in a bow shape with strips of hide from a deer or moose, then strung with rawhide.

12 FOOD

The main traditional foods of the Ojibwa were berries, nuts, leeks, corn, squash, wild potatoes, wild rice, maple sugar, large and small game, and fish. Many of these foods still figure largely in the modern Ojibwa diet.

Wild rice is a type of grass native to North America that grows in very watery areas. It is called *manomin*, or "good berry," by the Ojibwa and was their staple food. It is harvested in the fall by work teams of two people in a canoe. One poles the canoe through the waters; one bends the tops of the grass stalks over the canoe with a stick and knocks the grains off into the bottom of the canoe with another stick. Grains that fall in the water seed next year's crop. The rice is then dried in a large pot over a fire (stirred constantly to prevent burning). After it is

dry, it is threshed (the husk is removed from the kernel) by putting the rice in a sack and beating the sack with a club. Threshing can also be done by putting the rice in a hole in the ground lined with hide and dancing on it. Finally, the rice is winnowed (the kernels sifted from the loosened husks) by putting it on a bark tray and gently shaking the tray so that the husks blow away in the wind, leaving only the edible kernels behind. Today Wabigoon in northwestern Ontario has a wild rice processing plant.

Ojibwa Wild Rice

1 cup wild rice, washed in cold water
¼ teaspoon pepper
2½ cups water
2 tablespoon minced chives
1½ teaspoon salt
Bacon drippings plus enough melted butter or margarine to equal 1/3 cup
4 strips bacon cut into narrow strips
6 eggs

Place the wild rice, water, and 1 teaspoon of the salt in a saucepan and bring to a boil over medium heat. Reduce the heat as low as possible and simmer, uncovered, until all the water is absorbed. Brown the bacon in a large, heavy skillet. Remove bacon from skillet, and drain on paper towels. Save the bacon drippings from the skillet. Beat the eggs with ½ teaspoon of the salt, and the pepper, until light. Pour the beaten eggs into the skillet in which you browned the bacon, and brown the eggs lightly. Turn them over gently, and brown on the other side. When the eggs are firm, cut them into narrow strips. Lightly toss the bacon, egg strips, chives, bacon drippings (plus melted butter or margarine) with the rice. Serve hot. Makes 4 servings.

(Adapted from Yeffe Kimball and Jean Anderson, *The Art of American Indian Cooking*. Garden City, New York: Doubleday & Co., 1965, p. 107.)

13 EDUCATION

Although traditional Ojibwa education has always been important, the Ojibwa are very concerned with Western education today. They want to give their children the skills they need to succeed in the modern Western world and also teach them the traditional ways so that they maintain their Ojibwa culture and identity. Though dropout rates among Ojibwa students fell significantly in the 1970s, over 10% still do not make it through high school. Attendance rates for students under the age of 25 in 1990 were as follows:

AGE	PERCENTAGE IN SCHOOL
3-4	28.6
5-14	93.4
15-17	89.9
18-19	53.3
20-24	19.6

Of a sample of Ojibwas 25 years old and older in 1990, 9.8% had less than a ninth grade education; 69.7% had at least a high school diploma (68.6% of men, 70.6% of women); 37.8% had some college; and 8.2% had a Bachelor of Arts degree or higher (8.5% of men, 8.0% of women).

Museums in Ojibwa communities (run by the Ojibwa themselves) help teach their own people and others about Ojibwa history and traditions.

14 CULTURAL HERITAGE

The Ojibwa were known in earlier days as a people who loved to sing. This is still true of traditional Ojibwa today. The Ojibwa have many sacred songs and dances, accompanied by drums and rattles. The flute is the only solo instrument used by the Ojibwa. Young men used to play the flute when they were courting a young woman to let her know they were nearby so that she would come to hear his music.

The Ojibwa of Lac Courte Oreilles run a public radio station that offers both music and information of interest to Ojibwa.

Modern Ojibwa writers who have found success among their own people and the wider world are Gerald Vizenor (1934), John Rodgers, and Maude Kegg. Kegg recorded Ojibwa legends in both English and the Ojibwa language and received the National Heritage Award in 1990 from the National Foundation for the Arts for her work.

15 WORK

Traditionally, Ojibwa men hunted and fished throughout the year, but particularly in the winter when other food was scarce. Women also fished, but mostly they were responsible for gathering and cooking food, preparing animal skins for use as blankets and clothes, sewing the clothes, weaving mats and baskets, and caring for young children. In the summer, all Ojibwa worked in the fields growing what crops they could in the subarctic climate. Autumn was harvest time, both for the field crops and for the wild rice that grew in the watery areas throughout Ojibwa territory.

The children's job was to keep birds and other marauders away from the field crops as they ripened. Girls would stand on tall platforms in the fields and flap blankets in the air and shake gourd rattles to scare away the birds. Boys would play noisy games between the cornstalks to scare away other animals. The girls were also responsible for keeping waterfowl and other birds from eating the wild rice before the people could harvest it. They would paddle their canoes through the marshes, singing and talking loudly and slapping their paddles on the water.

Today the Ojibwa operate many businesses in their communities, including boat marinas, campgrounds, bingo halls, and hotels. They also continue to hunt, fish, and harvest wild rice.

16 SPORTS

Ojibwa men have played lacrosse for centuries. The games could take all day to finish, and they often got quite rough. Women played a game like field hockey called "shinny," in which they used a curved stick to move a ball made of animal hide over the other team's goal. They also played a version of lacrosse called "double-ball," played with two balls tied together.

Ojibwa children played many games, especially in the winter when there was little else for them to do. One of their favorite winter games was "snow snake." Boys would throw a stick about 6 feet (2 meters) long with a knob at one end, representing a snake (the knob was the snake's head), along a frozen path in the snow to see who could throw it the farthest. The sticks were oiled, polished, and decorated by the players to resemble snakes.

Canoe-racing has long been a favorite sport for Ojibwa of all ages.

17 ENTERTAINMENT AND RECREATION

The Ojibwa have always enjoyed games of skill and chance. They have turned their love of gambling into a profit-making venture today, with highly successful bingo halls located on their reservations. The Ojibwa also love to tell jokes and poke fun at each other and at outsiders.

Powwows have become a place for Ojibwa both to have fun and to promote their traditional Native North American identity. Nearly every Ojibwa community holds at least one powwow a year.

18 FOLK ART, CRAFTS, AND HOBBIES

Two traditional arts that can still be found among the Ojibwa today are basket-weaving and beadwork. Both are considered women's arts.

19 SOCIAL PROBLEMS

Ojibway today suffer from the same cultural conflicts as other Native North Americans trying to survive in the European-dominated society while maintaining their traditional ways. On the White Earth Reservation in Minnesota, the conflict between "full-bloods" (those with pure Ojibwa lineage) and "mixed-bloods" (those whose lineage is Ojibwa mixed with other tribes and races) has been particularly fierce and longstanding. The full-bloods generally want to preserve tradition at the expense of economic development, while the mixed-bloods promote economic development at the expense of tradition.

Conflicts with European Americans over land- and water-use rights rage on, both in courtrooms and on the lands and waters themselves (see also Ojibwa "Introduction" section).

20 BIBLIOGRAPHY

Greene, Jacqueline Dembar. *The Chippewa*. New York: Franklin Watts, 1993.

Kimball, Yeffe, and Jean Anderson. *The Art of American Indian Cooking*. Garden City, New York: Doubleday & Co., 1965.

Lucas, Eileen. *The Ojibwas: People of the Northern Forests*. Brookfield, Connecticut: Millbrook Press, 1994.

Reddy, Marlita A., ed. *Statistical Record of Native North Americans*. Detroit: Gale Research, 1995.

Tanner, Helen Hornbeck. *Indians of North America: The Ojibwa*. New York: Chelsea House Publishers, 1992.

—by D. K. Daeg de Mott, reviewed by D. Kavanaugh

PÁEZ

PRONUNCIATION: Pâ´-es
ALTERNATE NAMES: Nasa (people)
LOCATION: Colombia
POPULATION: 68,487 (1980)
LANGUAGE: Páez
RELIGION: Roman Catholicism; evangelical Protestantism

¹ INTRODUCTION

The Páez Indians of Colombia, unlike their ferocious neighbors, the Pijao Indians, resisted the Spanish conquerors who arrived in the 16th century and have survived until now. One of the first to explore southwestern Colombia, where the Páez live, was Sebastián de Belalcázar, who undertook an expedition from Quito, in Ecuador, into what is today Colombia. He found many tribes there, among them the Pasto Indians in the Nariño region, who were docile and easily conquered, whereas the Pijao fought many bloody battles with the Spaniards and were eventually exterminated entirely. The Páez of the Cauca region resisted, and although decimated and impoverished, their rugged mountain retreats saved them from both complete assimilation and complete extermination.

² LOCATION AND HOMELAND

The Páez Indians have lived for centuries in southwestern Colombia, amid the rugged mountain ranges, along both eastern and western slopes in the state of Cauca and high plateaus of the central range (Cordillera Central) of the Andes Mountains, and north of the headwaters of the Magdalena River. Ethnologists think that the Páez originally migrated in an east–west direction to the territory where their descendants still live, and that by the time of the Spanish conquest they had been settled in this mountainous region of forests, crags, and rivers for about 300 years.

The eastern region is generally referred to as Tierradentro and today is, in effect, an extended reservation with widely scattered settlements, of which the main centers are Inzá and Belalcázar. These are modest settlements which are also missionary centers and include churches and church schools. At the beginning of the 20th century, some Catholic missions were founded by the Lazarist Brothers.

³ LANGUAGE

The Páez language is related to the language spoken by the Chibcha Indians who settled in the valleys and plateaus of the eastern range of the Andes, around the region of Santa Fé de Bogotá, which is the capital of Colombia today. Although the Chibcha language and many other related languages in the region are now extinct, the Páez still speak their own language today.

One of the Páez names still in use is Calambás, which is a family name of a famous Páez hero and chieftain and is still used by his descendants today.

The Spaniards found that the Páez had not only male chiefs, but also female chiefs. A famous female chief was Taravira; her brothers were chiefs, and among them was Avirama. Another chief was called Esmisa, and his father was called Suin. Some of these names are still in use today, alongside Spanish names that some of the Páez also use.

⁴ FOLKLORE

An important part of Páez folklore relates to a hero called Juan Tama, also called the Son of the Star. The legend says that one day when the Morning Star was shining, a group of Indians found a child in a gorge, which was later named the Gorge of the Star. This baby was Juan Tama, who was nursed by several women and grew up to be very strong. Eventually he married the female chief of the Huila region, Doña Maria Mendiguagua, and became chief of all the Indians. He became their teacher and showed them how to guard their land and advised them not to mix with White people.

Juan Tama appointed Calambás, a chief from Pitayó, as his administrator. Calambás proved rebellious and Juan Tama defeated him, but later Juan Tama forgave him because Calambás was so brave. Juan Tama accorded Calambás the right to rule over the Páez Indians of Vitoncó. Juan Tama, knowing that his death was near, went into the lake on the Páramo (the high, cold plateau) of Moras, where he disappeared into the water.

The name Calambás still exists today among those who claim descent from the rebel chief, and even the modern councils that exist today in the Tierradentro region appoint certain people who descend from early Páez chiefs. Lineages are still very important among the Páez.

⁵ RELIGION

Jesuits were originally given responsibility for converting the numerous tribes of southwestern Colombia. They established some mission centers but were stubbornly resisted by the Páez. After centuries of comparatively meager results, from the missionaries' point of view, the task was taken up by the Lazarists. These missionaries began to work among the Páez in 1905. They learned the Páez language and still maintain missions among them. The result today is a rather unique blend of Páez religious customs and beliefs and important aspects of Catholicism. Currently, the Páez still retain their own shamans. Some Páez Indians have also become Catholic priests.

Since the 1930s there have been organized groups of evangelical Protestants among the Páez. There is a New Testament published in the Páez language.

⁶ MAJOR HOLIDAYS

The Páez celebrate several religious Catholic holidays, including Christmas and Holy Week, and they have set their own stamp on them. They have their own music and include some of their own rites. Interestingly, they do not allow the presence of a priest during some of their own celebrations, although they also attend and participate in aspects of church worship in the missionary centers.

⁷ RITES OF PASSAGE

When a woman is going to give birth, she retires to her own special hut, set apart from the family hut, where she gives birth either alone or with the help of a female relative. From very early childhood, both girls and boys learn the skills appropriate for their future responsibilities by observing and imitating their parents.

Adults form their own households and live in family units distanced from other family homes, in high places among the sierras which are often lonely and of difficult access. The Páez are very independent and often dislike living in villages; they prefer to live among their own families, separated from others, and only come together on special occasions, to discuss matters related to the well-being of the tribe as a whole or to their relations with the state authorities, or during major celebrations. However, they take part in local markets held once a week where they buy, sell, or exchange produce and acquire other basic necessities.

Some of the Páez in recent years have moved into villages or small towns. Some travelers to the Páez territory have occasionally reported interesting burial practices. The presence of funeral urns and elaborately decorated burial caves found by archaeologists in the area suggests that in earlier times people were cremated and important personages were accorded splendid funerals. Since then, burial customs have changed and are even now still undergoing a slow process of adaptation and change. José Péres de Barradas, who traveled to Tierradentro in the 1940s, quotes a Dr. Burg who witnessed burial rites for a young girl:

In the Indian cemetery, the men dug a hole in the ground. Meanwhile, the women were in the house with relatives and godparents. The dead girl was lying on the ground, on some cowhides, lightly covered by a *ruana* (a type of cloak or poncho widely used in Colombia by Indians and non-Indians alike). The body faced east, so that the soul would see its way to heaven more easily. By her feet were laurel-wax candles, and by her head, another three candles and a bamboo cross. To her right were her necklaces, and at her feet, all her goods, including her clothing and girdles or sashes, and some fruit including plantains, as well as some *chicha* to drink. Children played by the girl's side, and they were not afraid if they fell on top of her.

The girl's father prepared a bamboo barrow and the women arranged some white clothing for the girl. They combed the dead girl with great care, and because the hair was quite stiff it produced laughter among everyone, even the father. Once she was dressed and placed in the barrow, the father and godfather of the girl took her to the cemetery, followed by rest of the men and women.

The father placed the girl in the ground, lit candles and placed food and *chicha* (a drink made from fermented corn) at her feet, then covered her. During this time, the mourners prayed aloud. The father threw four clumps of earth with his left hand over his daughter and took his leave of her, wishing her a good journey. Then the men, and afterwards the women, did the same. It is believed that at this point the soul begins its journey to heaven. The women continued covering the buried girl with the earth, and the men completed the task, stamping on it with their feet.

Before returning to the family home, the men and women bathed fully dressed in a stream to wash out the spirit of death, and then took part in a funerary banquet.

For nine days they left a cross and flowers, between two candles, where the head of the dead girl had lain. It is customary to leave a gourd filled with water in those places which were once familiar to the person, so that the wandering soul will not suffer thirst.

After one or two months, there is a new purification of the house by the shaman, who sweeps it clean with two pigs' feet and then ensures that this special broom is buried. Afterwards he chews special leaves and spits at the four walls. Then everything is ready. The shaman breaks off a piece of meat and gives it to a dog to eat. Then he does the same with a corn tortilla. If the animal is fine, this is a signal that all may eat, and this is the second funeral banquet.

This account vividly illustrates the mixture of Christian and Amerindian elements in the Páez culture.

8 INTERPERSONAL RELATIONS

The Páez are a reserved people, and there are quite formal greetings required in varying circumstances. A boy has to approach his godparent in a respectful manner when greeting him. A visitor or guest is given a formal "gift of affection," a custom which some think dates back to Spanish colonial times and was incorporated into the customs of the Páez. It usually takes the form of a food offering, such as a chicken or an egg, and includes some vegetables and coffee beans.

The Páez do not engage in Western-style dating as such, but their traditions include trial marriages of about a year for young people who intend to undertake formal marriage and the founding of a family. This year is called the *amaño* or adaptation period. During this time, the young man observes the qualities of the young woman, and she also observes him. If either partner proves unsuitable, the trial marriage can be ended.

9 LIVING CONDITIONS

The Páez are not affected by malaria or other tropical diseases, as the Andean highlands provide a generally healthy climate, and the abundant streams and rivers provide plentiful access to clean water. There is a rainy season which can sometimes be severe and can affect the general state of health of the people. The cold, damp weather often leads to bronchial problems and tuberculosis. Babies and small children occasionally suffer from gastrointestinal problems.

At various times, the Páez were affected by a shortage of salt, which was difficult to obtain, but this is no longer the case. The Páez, although they now have access to some health centers, still depend in many cases on their shamans, who are also medicine-men, to cure them of illnesses.

The lifestyle is simple, even spartan. The Páez today are basically relatively poor farming communities who make do with the basic necessities required for survival. Water is generally carried to homes from springs, water holes, or streams. Occasionally a small cement tank is built near a house or settlement to which water is piped from a spring.

Traditional houses are rectangular and are constructed using basic and locally available materials. They have thatched roofs and walls of cane and sticks, although they have also adapted the more solid *bahareque* style which includes reinforcing the walls with rocks and mud amid double rows of sticks. This is attributed to Spanish influence.

Paéz girls in Colombia. (AP/Wide World Photos)

As they deteriorate, the traditional houses are giving way to those with walls made of adobe blocks or bricks and with roofs of corrugated zinc or cement. Houses are generally divided into two rooms, one for sleeping and storage, and the other, the kitchen, for eating and sitting around the fire to converse and keep warm. There are no windows in mud-walled houses. More modern houses have one or two window spaces that are covered with wooden shutters during bad weather and at night. Floors are of hard-packed earth or, occasionally, of cement or wooden planks. Instead of roof gutters, a shallow ditch surrounds the house to prevent rainwater from entering.

Furnishings are sparse—wooden beds covered by a cowhide, sheepskin, or straw mat, with woolen blankets for covers; a few plain wooden chairs with the back and seat of wood or cowhide; low wooden, carved stools; and perhaps a small table. In addition, a very small rustic temporary shelter with a roof but no walls is set up in the fields where some family members stay to protect their crops at harvest time. Most homes do not have access to electricity, although it is available to some degree in municipal centers and is in the planning stages to become more widely available.

The system of house-building is cooperative: relatives and neighbors come together to help an individual family who is building a house. This system, prevalent among many communities in the Andes, is known as the *minga*. Although the main centers such as Inzá and Belalcázar are communal

focal points, as are other communally built pueblos or villages, the majority of the Páez do not actually live there. They use these places as meeting points to buy and sell goods in the markets and to exchange news or to discuss communal matters, after which they withdraw to their own family homes, separated from others.

When the Páez have to travel outside the reservation on communal business or, in some cases, for the purposes of trade, they will use buses. Locally, some pack animals such as mules or horses are used, and on many occasions the Páez travel on foot.

10 FAMILY LIFE

The Spanish chroniclers who gave us the earliest descriptions of the Páez and other groups reported that there were not only male but also female chiefs, indicating that in some communities the women not only occupied important leadership positions, but that the communities were also matrilineal. The chroniclers also reported that in southwestern Colombia many women went to war alongside the men.

Today the Páez family unit places definite and, in some cases, nearly absolute authority in the hands of the father, whose wishes and commands must be obeyed by his wife and children. Families often include more children than the typical Western household of parents with two or three children; this is also true of many Colombian households generally. Small children are shown affection and given much freedom in how they behave, until the age of six or seven when they are expected to act with more restraint.

Marriage customs blend both Spanish and Páez cultures. Usually either the boy or his parents select a prospective bride and visit her family home in the company of the boy's godparents or *compadres* and ask for her hand in marriage. If the girl's parents consent, the father is first offered a half-bottle of *aguardiente* (a drink made from fermented sugarcane), and subsequently the mother is offered another half-bottle. The boy and his family then take the girl to his home to begin the year of trial marriage. If all goes well, the couple are then usually married in the Catholic Church, and the wedding feast, which includes a hearty banquet and music (usually flutes and drums), lasts for several days.

The Páez keep a variety of pets and farm animals, including dogs, hens, ducks, and turkeys, as well as pigs, and some horses, cows, and sheep.

11 CLOTHING

The cool weather of the Andes mountains has produced some practical and warm clothing, especially the *ruana,* a type of woolen cloak or poncho worn, with local variants, in many areas of the highlands. Wool is sheared and processed by the women, then it is spun into thread for weaving ponchos and skirts on hand looms braced against the outside wall of the house. While walking along the trails or resting from other work, it is common for women to spin wool or cotton yarn, holding the loose ball of wool or cotton in one hand and the simple spindle in the other, or to weave carrying bags by threading long string through loops in the bag. Women are seldom idle. Currently, many women buy ready-made clothing or make blouses or skirts if a treadle sewing machine is available. Some men learn to sew trousers.

A woman's traditional dress consists of two pieces: a heavy woolen skirt pleated at the back and held up by a woven sash, and a blouse which is a single rectangular piece of wool cloth fastened at one shoulder. The wool was traditionally woven on a simple loom made of two upright and two horizontal poles. The process—from shearing sheep, cleaning and carding the wool, and spinning the thread, through the weaving—took much time. Now it is more common for women to wear a cotton blouse and a skirt that falls below the knees. They wear necklaces of 8–10 strands of tiny, hard, white beads.

Young girls wear a simple one-piece dress; young boys wear a long shirt and when away from home, short pants. Mature men and women wear a plastic, straw, or felt hat (even inside the house). Younger people are less apt to do so now, though baseball caps are popular.

Because of the cold, everyone usually carries or wears a poncho. Ready-made sweaters and jackets are now common as well. Women wear tennis shoes, plastic sandals, or low shoes. Men often wear rubber or plastic boots. Children often go barefoot until they go to school.

12 FOOD

The basic diet of the Páez includes potatoes and corn as well as other vegetables that grow in the Andes, including *arracacha* and cassava, beans, and fruits. For special occasions, rich stews with vegetables and potatoes as well as chickens or roasted meats are cooked. Food is cooked either over a wood fire in the center of the kitchen floor, with pots balanced on three stones, or on a dried mud or brick stove on a raised platform by a wall, with a trough for the firewood and several holes in the top large enough to support a cooking pot. The food for large gatherings is cooked in heavy, shallow metal pots large enough to hold food for up to 100 people. While cooking, the food is stirred with large wooden spoons that have bowls about 10 cm to 15 cm (4–6 in) long and 2.5 cm (1 in) deep, and handles 50 cm to 75 cm (20–30 in) long. Plates, bowls, and cups are usually made of enamelware and food is eaten with enamelware or wooden spoons.

A traditional Páez breakfast is hearty and provides the main meal of the day until dinnertime. It is called *mute* (pronounced "moo-the") and is really a soup of boiled cabbage, corn, potatoes, and squash. During the day, the Páez drink fruit juices in their natural state or fermented as *guarapo*.

Because there are times of scarcity, the Páez learn early to endure hunger while working hard on difficult terrain in their fields, which are cultivated without machinery.

13 EDUCATION

Traditionally, the Páez have resisted education for girls in the mission schools (formerly it was thought that they did not need education for their duties at home), but in the last few decades a process is slowly going forward in the villages where schooling, at least at the primary level, is offered to both girls and boys. Under pressure from the Páez communities themselves, more schools are now bilingual, whereas the custom had been for teachers to teach only in Spanish, and children were not allowed to use their own language in class or at play. The result was that few learned to read with understanding. Bilingual education is being encouraged now by some communities and churches. Previously this has meant merely having a bilingual teacher's aide help monolingual Páez-speaking children, but now, along with Spanish, there is more interest in teaching children to read in their mother tongue.

Children attend "primary" school from first through third grades, sometimes through sixth grade. Young people who aspire to a "secondary" education may go to a regional center or larger non-Páez town where they rent lodging, usually with family acquaintances or relatives. Some have earned diplomas through a high-school-by-radio program where the material is dictated over the radio and exams can be taken in a regional area or the state capital. Either way, a high school education is not altogether free, and if parents cannot afford to pay, the student usually finds work to cover expenses while studying. When farm activities require their help, children often skip school.

14 CULTURAL HERITAGE

The Páez have musical instruments which include short and long flutes (*chirimías*) as well as drums made from hollowed-out tree trunks and animal skins, and they play their music during all special occasions as well as during religious celebrations. Many Páez Indians play the flute. Their music can be melancholy, with something of their reserve and love of solitude in it. Their strong attachment to their music has meant that even in the churches of their villages it prevails, since the Páez never accepted the traditional Gregorian music of the Catholic Church.

Some of their music today has incorporated popular elements of Colombian folk tunes prevalent in the Andes, which are a blend of Amerindian and Spanish courtly music, such as the *bambuco*. This music has a gentleness and a sweetness which does not reflect the earlier, warlike reputation of the Páez feared by the early Spanish conquerors and settlers. Guitars are now very popular with young men.

Dances have been an important form of expression for the Páez, and early reports of the Páez include descriptions of a wide range of dances which formed part of all major ceremonies, including the dance known as the *Itsa kó,* which celebrated a girl's coming of age. Earlier songs also celebrated the feats and deeds of warriors, but they have not survived.

15 WORK

The Páez today are mainly farming communities. The land is owned communally by the different communities, and the Indian council or *cabildo* assigns some land for each individual's use. Some tasks must be undertaken communally, and free work days must also be given by each Páez farmer for collective planting as well as for road- or bridge-building and work in the villages.

Since travel in this rocky and mountainous terrain, full of rivers and torrents as well as canyons, is often difficult, the Páez were traditionally proficient bridge-builders, using local materials to allow for passage on foot. The bridges were flexible and made of cane and vines, and some of these traditional bridges are still constructed and regularly repaired today. As the traditional bridges fall into disrepair, new ones are being constructed with steel and cement to accommodate motor vehicles. There are also some unusual bridges covered with thatched roofs, built out of strong logs with supporting stones and sticks, and with floors of wooden boards. They are practical and sturdy and can support the passage of loaded pack animals such as mules, which are often used in the highlands because they are so sure-footed.

Weaving is exclusively done by women, and the husband must obtain the wife's permission to sell any goods she has made. Men and women cultivate plots together.

Many families have their own press for rendering sugarcane stalks into liquid form by pressing them between heavy wooden cylinders that are anchored close together in a straight line. The outside wheels go clockwise while the center one moves counterclockwise. Fastened to the press is a long pole which is tied at one end to a horse or mule who moves in a circle, forcing out the liquid. This is collected below the press. The juice is cooked in large cauldrons over an open wood fire outdoors. After the hot liquid is run through a sieve, it is poured into molds and allowed to harden into blocks of brown sugar. Some of the fresh-squeezed cane juice may be poured into a hollowed-out section of a wooden tree trunk set horizontally on the floor, where it is left to ferment somewhat before being drunk.

16 SPORTS

Although some ball games were introduced at the mission schools for the Páez, traditionally sports did not play a significant role in their lives. They mainly practiced a sport that was a type of wargame. There were two teams, each led by a chief. The teams attacked each other with bows and arrows, and even if there were deaths, apparently they were accepted stoically and not resented. This wargame was performed as a rite to honor the dead after a community feast and is not practiced today. Some young people today are not even familiar with this piece of their history.

Soccer is a very popular sport among young men, and teams compete on Sunday afternoons.

17 ENTERTAINMENT AND RECREATION

Aside from important religious or communal celebrations or major family events such as weddings, the Páez sometimes make a special occasion out of market days. Many villages hold particular markets days, and after the buying and selling has taken place, the Páez enjoy drinking and chatting with their friends and *compadres*.

Priests who visit some communal pueblos on the eve of a particular feast day are greeted with much fanfare, even with fireworks and rockets, as well as a *chirimía* orchestra of flutes and drums. The community leads the priest to the church and takes generous food offerings there. The church is then decorated with candles and flowers. After Vespers, a celebration continues outside by the church door, and the people play music and dance all night. Some travelers who have witnessed these evening festivities have commented on the decorum and reserved behavior of the Páez, even on these occasions, describing a dignified style of dancing where they never touch each other and dance in a very orderly fashion.

Children play and entertain toddlers with whatever they find at hand—sticks, string, or discarded household items. Little girls roll a corn cob in an old cloth then tie it on their backs in the way their mothers carry babies and toddlers. Small transistor radios, cassette players, or "boom boxes" are carried everywhere for pleasure and as status symbols.

18 FOLK ART, CRAFTS, AND HOBBIES

Páez crafts formerly included pottery, weaving, and basketmaking. Weaving is becoming a lost art. Older women continue to weave long colorful sashes with geometric designs and stylized figures of birds, animals, or persons with red wool yarn on a white cotton background. They find that their daughters do not want to learn to do this any more. The belts are used as sashes for their skirts and for tying babies and small children in a cloth on their backs when they are walking or rocking the baby to sleep. Young children, both boys and girls, often carry the babies and entertain them while their mothers are occupied with their work.

The Páez also make jewelry such as beaded necklaces. There is gold in this area, and metalwork is a traditional craft in southwestern Colombia. Earlier jewelry included nose-rings and breastplates, but today inexpensive earrings are popular among Páez women, as well as barrettes to hold their long hair in place.

19 SOCIAL PROBLEMS

Colombia's social and political problems have affected the Páez communities. Guerrillas have waged war for many years in Colombia, and the Páez have sometimes suffered at their hands. In addition, there have been incursions by drug barons and actions by some police forces. In December of 1991 a group of Páez Indians, including women and children, were massacred as they sat down to their evening meal. It is thought that the killers were either working for a local landowner trying to drive the Indians out of the region, or were working on behalf of drug dealers or even the police.

The required one-year military service for 18-year-old males in the country is waived for the indigenous people, although a few Páez young men choose to enter the military to experience life in the world outside their communities.

Although the Páez have lived in this area for centuries, and additionally have had land grants dating back to colonial times, the struggle for land has always existed, and at various times local landowners have tried to drive them out. A Páez Indian who became a Catholic priest, called Father Alvaro Ulcué, who played a role in defending Indian rights, was murdered on his way to a baptism in 1984. Other human rights activists who have acted on behalf of the Páez have also been killed.

Today the Páez are active in the council of Indian communities of the Cauca region, and the Amerindian groups in Colombia have congressional representation, but the struggle for a decent life with a sufficient degree of autonomy continues.

²⁰ BIBLIOGRAPHY

Pérez de Barradas, José. *Colombia de Norte a Sur.* Madrid: Edición del Ministerio de Relaciones Exteriores, Relaciones Culturales, 1943.

Personal communication and bulletins, 1986–96, Survival International, London.

Steward, Julian Haynes, ed. *A Handbook of South American Indians.* New York: Cooper Square, 1963.

—by P. Pitchon, reviewed by F. Gerdel

PAIUTES

ALTERNATE NAMES: Snakes (Northern Paiutes)
LOCATION:, United States (Northern Paiutes: Oregon; Southern Paiutes: along the Colorado River; Nevada; California; Utah)
POPULATION: 11,000
LANGUAGE: English; various dialects of Paiute
RELIGION: Elements of Christianity and Mormonism; traditional Paiute
RELATED ARTICLES: Vol. 2: Native North Americans

¹ INTRODUCTION

Paiutes are often thought of as one group of people, but this is incorrect. Just as the other Tribal groups or Nations, the Paiutes are as diverse as the environment they occupy. The Northern Paiutes mainly occupy the Great Basin Region of the United States. The Great Basin includes the western states of Oregon, Nevada, Idaho, and parts of Utah. The Southern Paiutes occupy the southern portions of Nevada, California, and Utah. Linguistically speaking, the Paiutes belong to the Uto-Aztecan language family, which includes the Shoshone, Hopi, and other Tribal groups in Northern Mexico. Broken down further, the Paiutes are of the Shoshonean Family Stock, specifically, the Numic branch. Aside of the language similarities, there are major differences in cultural material (which depends on the type of environment), religious practices, subsistence patterns, and social practices.

The main sub-groups of Paiutes within the states of Oregon, Idaho, Nevada, Utah, and Southern California are:

GROUP	STATE	ENVIRONMENT
N. Paiute	Coleville, California	Mountains
N. Paiute	Fallon, Nevada/Stillwater	Desert and marsh area
N. Paiute	Fort McDermitt, Nevada	Desert and mountains
N. Paiute	Honey Lake, California	Lake
S. Paiute	Las Vegas, Nevada	Desert
S. Paiute	Lovelock, Nevada	Desert
S. Paiute	Moapa, Nevada	Desert
N. Paiute	Pyramid Lake, Nevada	Desert lake
N. Paiute	Susanville, California	Mountains
N. Paiute	Walker River, Nevada	Desert lake
N. Paiute	Warm Springs, Oregon	Mountains
N. Paiute	Winnemucca/Summit Lake, Nevada	Desert/lake/mountains

Because of the desert environment, the Great Basin Paiutes were broken down into smaller groups or "bands." Bands usually consisted of family units that would include the nuclear family (father, mother, child[ren]) and could include what is considered the extended family—grandparents, uncles, aunts, and cousins. These bands subsisted on the land in a purposeful, non-wasteful, seasonal pattern. The land sustained food items, cultural materials, and shelter. Because the bands had cyclical hunting, fishing, water spots (for drinking and personal hygiene), and gathering food crops such as pinenuts and chokecherries, they did not stay in areas long enough to exhaust their supplies totally. In times of hardship (and as prevention), bands often had "caches" (stores of food, usually hidden in caves).

Each group or band had regular routes to hunt, fish, and gather. Depending on the environment, Northern and Southern bands of Paiutes hunted the following: small game animals—jack rabbit, cottontails, beaver, badgers, and groundhog; fowl—mallard duck, geese, quail, mudhens and sagehens; and large game hunted—deer, big horn sheep, antelope, and even bear at times. Many bands have traditional fishing areas that are even their traditional homeland or base area. Pyramid Lake had a multitude of people fishing for cutthroat trout, rainbow trout, perch, and *Kui-ui* (cui-ui is a prehistoric sucker fish found only at Pyramid Lake). Vegetation gathered were seeds such as pinenuts, sunflower, cattails; and berries that included buck and chokecherries.

Encroachment on traditional Northern Paiute lands began with the fur trappers in the early 1800s. Beaver was plentiful in the river areas, and the trappers followed the rivers to cash in on the pelts. Organized groups were sent into the Nevada rivers; the first recorded trapper was Jedediah Smith in 1827. Later, in 1828, the Hudson Bay Company dispatched Peter Skene Ogden. Ogden ran across a group of Indians believed to be Northern Paiutes in southern Oregon. He tried to capture some, and they told him about the Humbolt River, which was plentiful in beaver.

The first groups of fur trappers did not really have any skirmishes with the Paiutes. The general impression of the bands by the whites was that they were poor and living a scarce existence. Many of the trappers found the indigenous people to be quite peaceful. But that soon ended with a group headed by Joseph Walker. Walker held contempt for the Native people. As his first party crossed into Northern Paiute territory in 1833, the group of forty-three, which had a large herd of cattle, traveled through the Humbolt Sink area. As Walker ran across Indians between 1833–43, he began systematically killing the Native People as he traveled through Nevada. In the end, his group was responsible for killing approximately 100 Indians. As a response to this reign of terror, the indigenous people began distrusting all white people who had crossed their lands and began taking action before the whites could. Many Indians stole livestock from the "trespassers." They felt this was justified, as the whites did not respect the land, nor did they know the weather patterns of the area. The Donner Party incident (a group of settlers trapped in the mountains during the winter resorted to cannibalism to stay alive) led the Native People to believe the whites were strange and cannibals. The Donner Party and the Mexican War helped stop some travel across Nevada up until 1847. Unfortunately, the gold rush of 1848 caused many Native People to be displaced from their homelands, as well as to deviate from their subsistence patterns. Virginia City hosted a small discovery of gold; the major mineral found was silver. The Virginia City range was traditionally a pinenut gathering area; thus, many Indian people had to adopt non-Native foods in order to live. As a result of the shift in subsistence patterns, Native People had to obtain jobs in order to survive. Many were employed as ranch hands, laundry and cleaning helpers, and the like.

The Paiutes probably spread from what is now southern California into the western part of their new territory—eventually stretching from southern Nevada and California to north-central Arizona and southern Utah—sometime around ad 1000. At some point they split into two bands, one going north and the other remaining in the south. The Northern Paiutes, also known

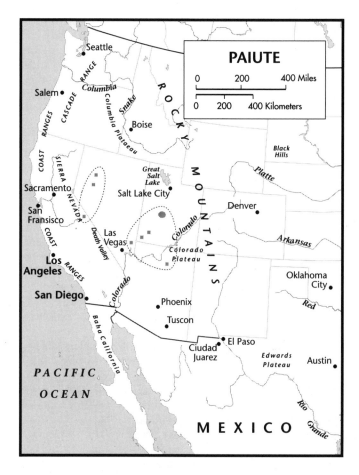

as the Snake Indians or Paviotso, were a more militant people than their southern relatives. After the Northern Paiute or Snake War (1866-68), fought between the Northern Paiutes and the US Army, the Northern Paiutes were imprisoned at various forts and reservations and were eventually forcibly resettled on those reservations.

The first contact the Southern Paiutes had with Europeans was with Spanish explorers in the early 1600s. The Spanish lumped the Southern Paiutes together with the related Ute tribe and called them *Yutas*. (The name of the state of Utah is derived from this word.) The Utes called the Paiutes *Payuch*, and the Paiutes called themselves *Payuts*. The Utes and Paiutes speak dialects of the same language and had very similar lifestyles until the Utes acquired horses from the Spanish and adopted the ways of the Great Plains tribes as horse-mounted buffalo hunters. The Paiutes were less inclined to interact with Europeans and so did not acquire as many horses nor learn to use them as extensively as the Utes did. The Utes, Shoshone, and Northern and Southern Paiutes were probably all one people at first, who then split up and developed into distinct tribes. The respective dialects of their original unified language remain similar enough that they can understand one another even today.

The Southern Paiutes supported the Pueblos in their revolt against the Spanish in 1680. Although they had long been enemies with the Hopi in their struggle for territory, the Southern Paiutes had even less regard for the Spanish and sided with the Hopi in their continued efforts to resist Spanish conquest in the years after the Pueblo Revolt. Because of this, the Spanish left the Southern Paiutes alone for the next 100 years or so. The

Utes, however, had established good relations with the Spanish and frequently raided Southern Paiute camps for goods and slaves to sell to the Spanish. Many Southern Paiute women and children ended up in Spanish hands through Ute slave raids. The Mexicans continued the slave trade after becoming independent of Spain in 1821. At the height of the slave trade in the 1850s, Native North American slaves brought $100 to $400 each.

Paiute lands were never colonized, but many trade and travel routes were opened up across their territory. For the most part, the Southern Paiutes tried to stay out of the way of Europeans and European Americans, and their traditional way of life was not greatly impacted until the 1850–60s. When European Americans first began traveling across Paiute territory in the 1830s and '40s, they described the Southern Paiutes they encountered as completely uncivilized savages—"lizard eaters" and "diggers" (referring to the Paiute method of digging roots for food). Some European Americans even saw them as less than human, portraying the Paiutes as animals in their accounts of their travels. This image of the Southern Paiutes was to remain with them (as much as a century or more) seriously affecting their relations with European America.

The Southern Paiutes were mostly a shy people, avoiding contact with strangers as much as possible. This became difficult as more and more strangers began to pass through their lands. When gold was discovered in California in 1848, swarms of European Americans crossed Paiute territory in pursuit of riches. These gold rushers often shot at the Paiutes and stole food from their fields. The Southern Paiutes rarely fought back and never initiated any attacks on European Americans. They would occasionally take European Americans' cattle that they believed were trespassing on their lands.

In 1847, another group of European Americans arrived in Paiute territory, this time to settle there. Brigham Young led the Mormons (Church of Jesus Christ of Latter Day Saints) to Great Salt Lake in present-day Utah to establish a community of believers. By 1849, the Mormons were expanding into Southern Paiute lands. The Southern Paiutes took the Mormons' trespassing cattle as well, but they also hesitantly welcomed the Mormons' protection from gold rushers and slave raiders. The Mormons believed in establishing friendly relations with the Native North Americans they met, and they were grateful for the Southern Paiutes' help in setting up their colonies. The Southern Paiutes helped the Mormons build houses, prepare fields for farming, and even washed their clothes. Unfortunately, the Mormons also brought disease to the Southern Paiutes, diseases for which the Paiutes had no immunities or known treatments. Epidemics of cholera, scarlet fever, whooping cough, measles, mumps, tuberculosis, and diphtheria killed hundreds of Southern Paiutes who were infected either by direct contact or through the water supply. By the mid-1870s, the Southern Paiutes had probably lost three-fourths (75%) of their population.

During the late 1850-60s, the Paiutes showed European Americans many mines in their territory that they had been working to a small extent for much of their history. The European Americans subsequently took over the mines and forced the Paiutes off their lands. The Paiutes became ghettoized serfs, treated basically as slaves by the European Americans. By the 1870s, the Mormons no longer needed the Paiutes' help, so the Paiutes' last refuge was gone and they became landless and destitute. The US government set up a small reservation for the Paiutes on worthless land in the late 1870s, but only a few Southern Paiutes moved there. Other small reservations were established for different Paiute bands during the late 19th and early 20th centuries, but for the most part, the Paiutes were neglected and shunted around by the government and European American settlers through the first half of the 20th century. In 1957, the US government "terminated" the Utah Paiutes under the Termination policy (which means the government rescinded the Paiutes' recognition as Native North Americans eligible for government services), even though the Utah Paiutes did not meet the government's own standards for tribes eligible for termination. The Southern Paiutes were already impoverished and without the resources to improve their conditions. Once terminated and ineligible for government aid, they suffered severe hardships for many years. Some relief came when the Paiutes won a court case filed through the Indian Claims Commission for over $7 million in payment for lands taken unjustly. Finally, in 1980 the Southern Paiutes were restored to recognition as a Native North American tribe by the US government and once again became eligible for government services and relief programs. Their living conditions are slowly improving.

2 LOCATION AND HOMELAND

There are approximately nine Northern Paiute Bands/Tribes located within the northwest portion of Nevada. The Fort McDermitt Reservation is located near the Oregon-Nevada border and was developed into a reservation in 1889 by Executive Order. Prior to the opening of the reservation, the former military post consisted of 3,945.6 acres, which was originally opened to the general public for settlement. The Pyramid Lake Reservation was also established by Executive Order on 23 March 1874. The Act of 18 May 1916 established the Yerington Reservation. And a year later, 9,456 acres of land was purchased to begin the Yerington Colony (colonies are "Indian lands" within a city). The Reno-Sparks Colony began when twenty acres of land was purchased in 1917 from two individuals. The Reno-Sparks Colony is unique, as its membership consists of Washo, Shoshone, and Paiute people. Reno was a central place for many people to live, but the whites viewed the people as homeless people, as they camped along the riverbanks. The Lovelock Colony existed early, but the Tribal Government was not established until it adopted the Indian Reorganization Act Constitution and By-laws on 14 March 1968.

The Southern Paiutes today live in several communities along the Colorado River. The western communities include the Las Vegas, Pahrump, and Moapa bands of Nevada, and the Chemehuevi band of California. This western territory is made up of mountain ranges and basin area with scrubby creosote bushes, mesquite, and piñon pines. Bighorn sheep, antelope, rabbits, lizards, and desert tortoises are among the common wildlife found there. The eastern communities, including the five bands of the Paiute Indian Tribe of Utah, the Kaibab Tribe, and the San Juan Paiute Tribe, live in a region of high plateaus and deep canyons. At high elevations, fir, spruce, and aspen trees grow. Low elevations are covered with ponderosa pines, piñon pines, juniper, sage, and grasslands. Agave and small cacti grow in the canyon bottoms, and the streams and rivers that cut through the region create narrow green oases with an abundance of wildlife.

Paiute populations were decimated by European diseases beginning in the 1840–50s. Not until the 1930–50s did the Paiutes begin to have more births than deaths in a year. After 1950, their population began to increase slowly. According to the 1990 US Census, today's Paiute population is around 11,000.

³ LANGUAGE

The Northern and Southern Paiutes speak dialects of the Uto-Aztecan family of Native North American languages. Though their dialects are distinct in the Northern and Southern regions, the Northern Paiutes (Pyramid Lake, Fallon, Walker River, Lovelock, Reno-Sparks [which have many members directly from Pyramid Lake], etc.) can understand each other fairly well. However, the Southern Paiutes and Northern Paiutes have some translation difficulties, as many of the groups have adopted other native terminology of their particular outer perimeter or territory.

Because of legislature to terminate Indian Tribes and establishment of government boarding schools, many of the Northern and Southern Paiutes do not have their languages intact, particularly those who live near cities or metropolitan areas.

Through bilingual education programs and special grants, many of the tribes have taken advantage of funds in order to revitalize their language. Fort McDermitt has taken an aggressive measure to ensure the longevity and viability of tribal language. Videotapes have been developed in fluent Paiute (the McDermitt dialect) in order to preserve and teach. Traditional and contemporary activities are recorded and documented for today's and future generation(s). To count from one to ten, the Northern Paiutes say:

NORTHERN PAIUTE TERM	ENGLISH TRANSLATION
simi'yu	One
waha'yu	Two
paha'yu	Three
watsikwi'yu	Four
manigi'yu	Five
naapahi'yu	Six
natakwatsikwi'yu	Seven
simidadu'upi	Eight
simidadu'upi (Pyramid Lake)	Nine
siukadu'upi	Nine
siimano'yu	Ten

To count from one to ten in Southern Paiute, say: *soo'ee, wai, pai, wachuhng'wee, munuh'kee* ("all," meaning all five fingers of one hand), *navai', navaik'uvawt* ("over six"), *wa'ong' wachuhng'wee* ("two fours"), *soowaw' toaho' mawsoo' weinee* ("nearly all the fingers"), *toaho mawsoo' weinee* ("all the fingers").

All Paiutes speak dialects of the Numic branch of the Uto-Aztecan family of Native North American languages. Though their dialects are distinct, they are able to understand one another fairly well. English has become the common language of today's Paiutes, but many still speak their native tongue. Some phrases in Southern Paiute are:

uhdu' vuhts	That's the way it is
mai'nuhgwaik	That's what I said
ai'u whaihump	It's all right
mud'u awvawn' kawduh'vungwu	Don't sit on that one
ai'nekai	Be quiet
kunchuh'eets pono'ai	armpit odor

Northern and Southern Paiutes were often named after physical or behavioral characteristics in early childhood. These names generally remain for one's entire life. They are not embarrassed by these names as they understand the naming conventions, and they fit with the Paiute sense of humor. Some Paiutes are given new names later in life for a significant achievement or action, but even great chiefs and well-respected elders often still go by their childhood names. Examples of Southern Paiute names are Quee tus (Burning Fire), La wa wi (Chipmunk), Mai-mi eno (Waving Hands), and Sang a nim (Wind Blows The Sand).

⁴ FOLKLORE

Traditionally, much of the Northern and Southern Paiute storytelling happened in the winter months when the pace of life slowed, and there was not so much work to be done. Some stories could only be told during the winter because at other times of the year, bears and rattlesnakes were awake and might hear the story and come and bite the storyteller.

Stories were not solely for entertainment purposes; they also served to teach morality. In Northern and Southern Paiutes, Coyote (*Itsa*) was constantly getting into predicaments. He always thought of himself as an extremely handsome individual, yet when he saw himself in reflections, he was scared at the hideous creature that looked at him. He was lazy and always tried to get out of work. He also tried to marry his own daughters. He is cited as the one that *Numanah*, "Creator of All Things" entrusted to deliver people to a designated location. (The People or *Numa*, were to be transported in a pine-pitched covered water jug, and *Itsa* was given strict instructions *not* to open the plug. But he did and tried to place the plug back on. Most of the people got out [in California] and by the time *Itsa* reached Nevada, only a few chubby Indians who weren't able to get out actually made it. That's why Nevada doesn't have a lot of Indian people!)

⁵ RELIGION

The Northern and Southern Paiutes believe there is one most powerful spirit, known to the Northern Paiutes as *Numanah* ("Creator of all Things"); the Southern Paiutes call this spirit *Thuwipu Unipugant* ("One Who Made The Earth"). The sun is the most visible representation of Thuwipu Unipugant. The Paiutes traditionally prayed to the sun every morning, and sometimes at noon and at sunset. Ceremonies to honor the spirits of the world were conducted by a *puagant* (One Who Has Sacred Power). *Puagants* had specific animal spirits as helpers, and often kept a live representative as an assistant.

Northern Paiutes had men and women shaman or curers. For example, the people of the Pyramid Lake area were a matrilineal society. Each gender had specific roles to follow, but both could hold curing or doctoring positions. This was contingent on the powers or gifts that the person had. Some individuals had spirit beings called "water babies" assisting them. The doctor or medicine person would go to Pyramid Lake to pray and these special beings would take them under water to learn doctoring techniques. It is believed that the beings took the medicine people/shamans to the surrounding lakes—Winnemucca (now dried-up due to the Derby Dam, part of the Newlands Reclamation Project in the 1930s) and Walker River. Regular people, if they saw these beings, were believed to die later, as these beings' powers were too great. It is believed that these beings were made from a union of a mermaid (the Northern Paiutes traveled to coastal areas) and a *Numa* (Indian) man. The water babies are their children.

The Ghost Dance Religion was first started in 1869 by a Paiute mystic named Wodziwob, although it failed to take hold among the population. In 1888–90, another Paiute, Wovoka (known as Jack Wilson to European Americans; c.1856–1932), revived the Ghost Dance Religion, preaching that all deceased Native North Americans would return to life, and the balance of power would once again shift from European Americans to Native North Americans. The Ghost Dance was performed to call back the deceased to life. The Ghost Dance Religion incorporated elements of traditional Paiute religion, such as the Round Dance. This time, the Ghost Dance Religion spread rapidly among western Native North American tribes, especially in the Great Plains. The US government and European American citizens felt threatened by Ghost Dance teachings, however, and sought to suppress the religion (even though the religion taught that this shift in power was inevitable and did not preach any form of violence to initiate the shift). Tensions built up until 1890, when the US Army massacred hundreds of Sioux at Wounded Knee Creek in South Dakota (*see* **Dakota and Lakota**). The Ghost Dance Religion declined rapidly after that, although it is occasionally revived by isolated groups even today.

Christian and Mormon religious elements has been adopted over the last century by the Paiutes. Since the 1960s, most San Juan Paiutes have become members of the Full Gospel church, a Pentecostal Protestant denomination. Although members of the Full Gospel Church, however, they continue to combine traditional Paiute beliefs with their new Christian faith.

Revitalization of Native American beliefs or concepts have been readily adopted by tribes whose religious infrastructure has been dismantled. Ceremonies such as the Sun Dance of the Plains Tribes have been accepted into both Northern and Southern Paiutes belief systems. Many believe this was a result of a cultural exchange when the Sioux of South Dakota adopted the Ghost Dance of 1888–90 (Wovoka, from Mason Valley, Nevada). Other adaptations have also been indicative of cultural beliefs. For example, the people of Pyramid Lake used the sweatlodge as a method of personal hygiene and cleansing. It has now been modified to incorporate religious ceremonies, such as prayers and songs to bring in spirits or communicate with the Creator.

⁶ MAJOR HOLIDAYS

Tribal holidays are designated by the Tribal Councils. The National Indian Day holiday is usually held on the last Friday in September to promote Tribal Pride and individual awareness of the tribe's cultural background.

⁷ RITES OF PASSAGE

The three most important times in a Paiute's life were traditionally considered to be puberty, the birth of a first child, and death. A four-day ceremony marked a girl's first menstruation. Her relatives built her a special house away from the rest of the camp and painted the girl's face, hair, and scalp with white clay or red ochre. Every morning, the girl ran to the east before the sun rose (sometimes she also ran to the west at sunset). She followed certain taboos concerning food (she could eat no meat or salt), drink, and touching herself, and was given hard labor to do, such as gathering wood. Every night the girl slept on a "hot bed" made by digging a shallow pit and filling it with warm coals, then covering the coals with earth. At the end of the four days, the girl—now a woman—was fed a small animal's liver wrapped in medicinal plants. Her relatives washed her hair and singed the ends of it, and burnt her old clothes. This puberty ceremony had two purposes: to help the girl grow up strong and healthy with the power gained through the spiritual rituals; and to teach her that she is no longer a child but now has adult responsibilities.

Boys marked puberty with hunting taboos that they then followed until they reached marriageable age (in their mid- to late-teens). Neither the boy nor his mother, father, or any girl or woman who was fertile could eat any game he killed. He gave any meat he brought home from the hunt to the old people in the community. Once he reached marriageable age, his elder relatives washed and singed his hair, painted his head with red ochre, and lifted the hunting taboos.

At the birth of their first child, both husband and wife followed taboos concerning food, drink, and touching themselves that were similar to those placed on girls at their first menstruation. The husband also ran to the east each morning before the sun rose.

When a death happened in the family, the Northern Paiutes typically burned the *kah-nee* (house), until they occupied government housing. Then the Northern Paiutes adapted and began changing around the room, which included new paint, so that the spirit of the person who died would move on to the next world. It is believed that personal items are to be buried with the individual, including food, water and tools for the journey. The Northern Paiutes didn't believe in Hell; however, if a person was bad in life, he or she would have an uneasy afterlife.

Among Southern Paiutes a corpse's face was painted with red ochre, or the body was wrapped in buckskin and then buried or cremated. The body was often buried in the house where the person died. The house was then sometimes burned. Whether or not the deceased was buried there, the house where he or she died was always abandoned. The deceased's belongings were burned and her or his horses and dogs killed. Sometimes a child or other relative of the deceased was also killed to keep the deceased company in the next world. Mourners singed their hair and did not eat meat or salt for four days after the funeral.

In the late 19th century, the Paiutes adopted the Cry Ceremony from their Mojave neighbors. At first it was conducted separately from the traditional Paiute funeral rites, but it eventually became a regular part of the funeral ceremony. In the Cry Ceremony, singers chant songs from evening until dawn for one or more nights to help guide the spirit of the deceased to his or her dwelling place in the next world. Each song is part of one of several song cycles, such as the Salt song cycle or the Bird song cycle. Between times of singing, friends and relatives give speeches about the deceased. Paiutes today still perform the Cry Ceremony.

8 INTERPERSONAL RELATIONS

Prior to the arrival of the whites, the Northern Paiutes grouped in bands. These bands were family units that consisted of a father, mother, their offspring, a sister to the mother (which also could be the man's second wife), aunts, uncles, and grandparents. The bands were relatively small in order to sustain life in a harsh desert environment. A Head man or Head woman led the groups to carry out specific tasks. For example, a rabbit Head person would lead the rabbit drive. This person would have special skills in capturing/hunting the rabbits. They might conduct special prayers prior to the activity and request special blessings from the *Numanah*, "Creator of All Things." Other individuals had special talents/skills in seasonal gathering and other tasks.

Early Southern Paiute communities were led by chiefs called *niavis*. The *niavi* was always male and was usually succeeded by a male family member (often a son). Women had other leadership positions in the community and took part in all community meetings. The community council was made up of all adults, male and female, and made all the decisions concerning community affairs. The *niavi* could make suggestions, but he could not make a decision on behalf of the larger community. He must instead always carry out what the council decided. One of the *niavi*'s most important functions was to give a speech every morning in which he informed the community of the plans for that day and encouraged the people to live in harmony with one another.

Today, the Northern and Southern Paiutes have elected Tribal Representatives who makeup the Tribal Councils. These individuals are elected by the Tribal membership and serve one- to four-year terms. Within Nevada, each of the twelve Tribal groups in the state belong to the Inter-Tribal Council of Nevada, Inc. (ITCN). ITCN was first incorporated in 1963, and the intent of the Inter-Tribal Council was to act as a political vehicle or voice for the Nevada Tribes. Each Tribal Chairperson is a member of the Executive Board, with an annual paid membership of $250. The Executive Board oversees programs such as the Head Start Program (pre-school education designed to target high-risk families); Women's, Infants, and Children (WIC); Job Training Partnership Act (JTPA); Elders Program (Title X); and the Child Care Development Block Grant (CDBG), to name a few. These programs are intended to help build stronger Native American families and raise the living standards of Indian people as a whole.

9 LIVING CONDITIONS

In the winter, the Paiutes traditionally lived in cone-shaped houses made from a frame of poles joined at the tops, covered with juniper bark, rushes, or the like. By the mid-19th century, they sometimes used animal skins or canvas for the covering. In the summer, they made open-sided rectangular houses with roofs of brush held up by poles. Sometimes they simply made a wall of brush for shelter, or even just lived beneath one or more trees. Winter or summer, in whatever type of shelter, the doorway always faced east, toward the sunrise.

During the 19th and 20th centuries, the Paiutes became extremely marginalized and impoverished. Forced onto inadequate reservations, neglected, and eventually "terminated," they had insufficient resources to continue in their traditional ways and little or no access to modern goods and services. In 1968, the average income for the year for a Paiute household was $2,746. New government programs instituted in recent years have improved conditions on Paiute reservations somewhat. New government housing has been built and an effort has been made to create more job opportunities. The Kaibab Paiute tribe now runs its own police department, senior citizen program, and health and education programs. They also have their own social worker, a member of the tribe, who helps them to take advantage of available social services.

10 FAMILY LIFE

Extended families are extremely important to the Paiutes. They maintain close ties with even the most distant relatives. Marriage to anyone even remotely related is discouraged, so Paiutes often have to look to other communities to find marriage partners. Dances and festivals where many communities gather have long been used as places to meet potential spouses.

The Paiutes traditionally had no marriage ceremony. Couples simply set up housekeeping together. Divorce was just as simple: the household was dissolved and the couple went their separate ways. Marriages were often arranged by older relatives (who knew the extensive family tree and could therefore determine who was and was not related to the prospective bride or groom). Marriages were usually monogamous, but on occasion two siblings would share a spouse. Widows and widowers were encouraged to marry a relative of the deceased.

Households were very fluid, and still are. Family members move around easily between homes, children often going to live with aunts, uncles, or grandparents, etc. This is common and accepted. Many mothers also still use traditional cradleboards (a cushioned board to which a baby is strapped for the first year or so of its life).

11 CLOTHING

Today, Native Americans wear contemporary clothing styles. Prior to the settling of the West, the Northern and Southern Paiutes wore clothing that was culturally indicative of their environment. The Northern Paiutes sometimes wore buckskin clothing, but not to the extent of the well-known Plains style. Deer required major skill to obtain on foot and without guns. The Northern Paiutes utilized rabbit skins in the winter for coats and blankets, while sagebrush bark was processed and used for footwear and other articles of clothing such as skirts for year-round wear. Willow basket hats served to protect the head from the sun.

After contact with white people, the clothing changed from natural materials to man-made materials such as the denim pants, long sleeved shirts, and hats for the men, while the women adopted the calico style dresses with aprons of the 1800s. The women exchanged the woven hats for scarves or handkerchieves that were worn over the head and tied under the chin. The women usually cut their bangs straight across.

In the summer, both men and women of the Southern Paiutes wore just a breechcloth (a piece of material passed between the legs and through a belt around the waist to hang over in front and back) made of cliffrose bark or antelope or buckskin with woven yucca sandals or leather moccasins. In winter, a blanket of rabbit fur was added over the shoulders. They either stuffed their moccasins with cliffrose bark or wore socks made of badger skin with the fur turned to the inside.

12 FOOD

Traditionally, Northern Paiutes maintained their subsistence patterns by hunting and gathering. An effort was made to change the "roaming" patterns of the Great Basin Natives by settling them on reservations. Farming was introduced, but for the most part it failed as the Nevada environment is arid and water is a scarce commodity. Native People, such as the Northern Paiutes of Pyramid Lake, became involved in long, drawn-out court battles over water rights. The Newlands Reclamation Act of 1915 caused the Truckee River to be diverted at the Carson River point and from the Derby Dam (a 1930s project). The ramifications included the drying up of Pyramid Lake's sister lake, Winnemucca Lake. This had an impact on the migratory flyway patterns of geese and ducks, in addition to killing a multitude of animal life and even threatening the prehistoric sucker fish to extinction. The *Kui-ui* or cui-ui is found only at Pyramid Lake. Many other fish such as the trout suffered, too.

Traditionally, the people of the Great Basin within Nevada are named after the food that is indicative or prevalent in their area. Examples are the *Kui-ui ticutta*, which translates to "Cui-ui eaters" (Pyramid Lake Paiutes); *Toi Ticutta*, "Cattail Eaters," (Fallon area people); and *Agai Ticutta*, "Trout Eaters," (Walker River Paiutes).

Adoption of non-Indian food became a necessity as the lands were being taken over by white settlers. The Native People began to adopt other foods readily and one in particular has been associated with American Indians—the "frybread" or "fried bread." The Northern Paiutes have incorporated the frybread into their regular dietary patterns. It is generally eaten by itself, with beans, or even in the form of an "Indian taco." This somewhat resembles a Mexican tostada, although the tortilla is substituted for the frybread. Another deviation of the frybread is the "greasebread" ("flat bread" or "Indian bread"). Both breads are made of baking powder, salt, white flour and water. It resembles a biscuit type dough, when made; the frybread is fried in 1 to 2 inches of lard or oil, and the greasebread is fried in very little oil or lard. The frybread is 6 to 9 inches in diameter (it resembles a disc), and the greasebread is flattened to resemble an elongated biscuit.

Southern Paiutes traditionally farmed as their means of supporting themselves. They adopted Pueblo-style farming methods that were diffused from Mexico. Traditionally, they grew corn, squash, melons, beans, sunflowers, and two important herbs: amaranth and chenopodium. By the late 18th or early 19th century, they had acquired wheat from the Mojaves (who had obtained it from the Spanish) and added that to their list of crops. They also gathered wild foods such as seeds, berries, agave, and piñon nuts (piñon nut porridge was one of their staple foods) and hunted wild game to supplement their diet. The Paiutes cooked small game animals whole under the coals of the fire and ate the entire animal. Even the bones were crushed and eaten.

13 EDUCATION

The Paiutes received very sporadic formal education through the early 20th century. Some government-operated day schools were established and then closed. Stewart Indian School (formally Carson Indian School) was established in 1890 and remained open until 1980. This boarding school was originally designed to "de-Indianize" the Indian, by offering vocational-type training; the students (primarily the Washo, Paiute, and Shoshone) were often kidnaped from their families and forbidden to speak their native tongue. The children ranged from kindergarten age to tenth grade. By World War II, Stewart began accepting other Tribal groups. These included the Navajo, Apache, Hopi, Walapai, and Yavapai, to name a few. Although the school primarily remained vocational, in the 1960s a move was made to provide the students with more academics. Sports was a big plus for many of the students, and they readily excelled in boxing, track and field, football (in the early days up until the early 1970s) and basketball. Many delighted the crowds with the type of ball playing that was considered to be "rez ball."

Paiute children were sent to boarding schools for a time, but these were largely unsuccessful. Today, most Paiute children attend public schools. These schools are located a long distance from the Paiute reservations, and the children must spend hours each day on the bus. At the schools, Paiute students are in the minority and suffer from discrimination and harassment. The dropout rate for Paiutes is fairly high.

14 CULTURAL HERITAGE

The Northern and Southern Paiutes within the Great Basin are renowned for their basketmaking skills. Northern Paiute baskets were made from willows. Designs were made from the outer fiber of the willow plant. Southern Paiutes utilized the husks of Devil's Claw seed pods to make designs. Willows were gathered in the early spring and stockpiled for later use. The basketmakers were very selective in willow gathering. They selected straight willows that weren't budding with leaves. The process of preparing willows included soaking them in water to make them more pliable. The bark or outer membrane of the willow was then stripped. The core of the willow was then cleaned out by splitting the willow three ways: one piece was held in the mouth and the other two sections held by the right and left hand. The split was done in one continuous movement.

Because of the arid climate of the Great Basin desert area, Nevada basketry and as other pre-historic artifacts have often been preserved in mint condition. Northern and Southern basket collections can be found in the Smithsonian Institution in Washington, D.C.; University of California at Davis; California's Sacrament Museum of History, as well as the University of Nevada, Reno's Anthropology Collection and the Lost City Museum in Overton, Nevada.

Although the Northern and Southern Paiutes did not have much in the way of material, they utilized the resources available to them in the most advantageous ways. Pine nuts were often "baked" while shaking and tossing the nuts with hot stones in winnowing trays. Water was transported in pine-pitch covered water jugs. Conical shaped baskets were used to store and carry food. Babies were carried in the *hoop* (Northern Paiute) cradleboards. In the West, whites today use one derogatory term for cradleboard; it is mistakenly called a "papoose." This term is very degrading and inappropriate, since the Native People have a name for the baby's basket.

The first autobiography by a Native North American woman ever published was *Life Among the Paiutes*, by Sarah Winnemucca Hopkins (1844-91), published in 1883–84. Sarah Winnemucca, a Northern Paiute, is a controversial figure in Native American history. Many Indian people view her as a traitor and cite her personally for the forced march to the Fort Malheur

Reservation. Sarah was born at Pyramid Lake, and her family was well known within Indian country and among the whites. She acted as an interpreter at Fort McDermitt, and she allegedly informed the US Army of the whereabouts of a so-called renegade group of Indians. Sarah Winnemucca, however, has been credited for starting a day school at the Lovelock Colony, and for being an early leader in Indian education, and for advocating against the wrongdoing of Indian Agents. Her cousin, Young Winnemucca (also referred as Numaga) was the reluctant war leader in the Battle of Pyramid Lake of 1860.

15 WORK

Traditionally, Paiutes were small farmers and hunter-gatherers. Both men and women helped with the farming; women did most of the gathering, and men did most of the hunting. Women made baskets and leather goods, first for everyday use, then for sale to traders and, later, tourists.

Today, unemployment and underemployment are serious problems for the Paiutes. The biggest source of income is from basketweaving. The San Juan Paiute women began making Navajo wedding baskets for Navajo ceremonies in the late 19th century. The Navajo either traded or paid for the baskets, but the prices were not high. In the mid-20th century a Navajo paid $25–60 for a wedding basket. In 1985 the Paiutes held their first basketry exhibition at the Wheelwright Museum of the American Indian in Santa Fe, New Mexico. It was very successful and led to more sales and exhibitions. The Paiutes set up a basketry cooperative to help promote their art form. Today, Paiute basketweavers are able to be much more creative and ask much higher prices for their baskets.

16 SPORTS

Young Paiutes today enjoy modern Western sports, such as basketball and softball. Traditionally, the Paiutes played a game they called *kwepu'kok*, or "shinny," which was like field hockey.

17 ENTERTAINMENT AND RECREATION

Traditionally, winter was a time for relaxation for the Paiutes. There was less work to be done, and days and nights were spent telling stories and playing games (mostly gambling games). Three favorite traditional Paiute games were *naiung'wee* ("hand game"), *too'dookweep* ("stick dice"), and *tawsu-hng'uhmp* ("rabbit-head game"). In the hand game, two teams sat facing each other and took turns hiding bone or wood cylinders, called "bones," one striped and one plain. Each team would sing songs to give its side luck while the other team tried to guess in whose hands the striped and plain "bones" were hidden. Teams bet valuable goods, such as buckskin, jewelry, and horses on the outcome of the game.

The stick dice game was played with dice made from flat-sided sticks, colored on one side. The sticks were tossed in the air, and the particular combination in which they landed determined the number of points won. This game was also the occasion of high-stakes gambling.

Paiutes also bet on the rabbit-head game, in which a rabbit's skull was attached by a string about 8 to 12 inches long to a pointed bone (called a *tawsuhng'uhmp*). The player held the bone pin in his or her hand and tossed the skull into the air, attempting to catch it on the pin. If the pin went through the nose, ear, or eye holes in the skull, the player won 2 points. Catching it through the tooth sockets earned the player 5 points, and the small hole below the ear gained the player 10 points. A player continued tossing and catching the skull until she or he missed.

18 FOLK ART, CRAFTS, AND HOBBIES

Besides basketry, Paiutes are known for their porcupine quill-work on buckskin. They traditionally used roots for dyes to color the quills.

19 SOCIAL PROBLEMS

The Paiutes suffer from centuries of poverty, discrimination, and neglect. They are still viewed by European Americans in terms of old negative stereotypes first promoted in the 19th century, such as "lizard eaters" and "diggers." At best, Paiutes are patronized by well-meaning European Americans. At worst, they are subject to harassment and racist mistreatment.

In the European-dominated world, Paiutes are faced with prejudice and cultural insensitivity at the hands of non-Native teachers, classmates, workmates, and employers. It is not uncommon for Paiute students in biology classes to have to handle bones known to have been taken from Paiute burials. On the reservation, Paiutes struggle to maintain their traditional identity and Paiute ways under very limiting circumstances. Just recently reinstated by the US government in 1980 as a recognized Native North American tribe (after being "terminated" in 1957), the Paiutes have a long way to go to make up for years of deprivation and marginalization.

20 BIBLIOGRAPHY

Brown, Dee. *Bury My Heart at Wounded Knee: An Indian History of the American West.* New York: Holt, Rinehart & Winston, 1970.

Canfield, Gae Whitney. *Sarah Winnemucca of the Northern Paiutes.* Norman, OK: University of Oklahoma Press, 1983.

Champagne, Duane, ed. *The Native North American Almanac.* Detroit: Gale Research, 1994.

D'Azevedo, Warren, et al. *Handbook of the North American Indians. Volume 11. Great Basin.* Washington, DC: Smithsonian Institution, 1986.

Eagle/Walking Turtle. *Indian America: A Traveler's Companion,* 4th ed. Santa Fe: John Muir Publications, 1995.

Franklin, Robert J., and Pamela A. Bunte. *The Paiute.* New York: Chelsea House, 1990.

Gattuso, John, ed. *Insight Guides: Native America.* Boston: APA/Houghton Mifflin, 1993.

Inter-Tribal Council of Nevada, Inc. *Numa: A Northern Paiute History.* Salt Lake City: University of Utah Printing Service, 1976.

Knack, Martha C., and Omer C. Stewart. *As Long as the River Shall Run. An Ethnohistory of Pyramid Lake Indian Reservation.* Berkeley and Los Angeles: University of California Press, 1984.

Martineau, LaVan. *Southern Paiutes. Legends, Lore, Language, and Lineage.* Las Vegas, NV: KC Publications, 1992.

Reddy, Marlita A., ed. *Statistical Record of Native North Americans,* 2nd ed. Detroit: Gale Research, 1995.

Scott, Lalla. *Karnee. A Paiute Narrative.* Reno, NV: University of Nevada Press, 1966.

Shaw Harner, Nellie. *Indians of Coo-yu-ee Pah. (Pyramid Lake) The History of the Pyramid Lake Indians in Nevada.* Sparks, NV: Western Printing & Publishing Co., 1974.

Stone, Helen. *Coyote Tales and Other Paiute Stories You Have Never Heard Before.* Reno, NV: Great Basin Press, 1991.

Waldman, Carl. *Encyclopedia of Native American Tribes.* New York: Facts On File, 1988.

—by D. K. Daeg de Mott,
reviewed by H. I. Brady of the Northern Paiutes

PANAMANIANS

LOCATION: Panama
POPULATION: 2.6 million
LANGUAGE: Spanish; English; native Indian languages
RELIGION: Roman Catholicism; Protestantism; Islam; small numbers of Jews, Hindus, and Baha'is

¹INTRODUCTION

Panama first made an impact on world history when a Spanish expedition led by Vasco Nuñez de Balboa crossed the isthmus in 1513 and discovered the Pacific Ocean. Geography made it a strategic link for the Spanish empire, especially for the transshipment of gold and silver from Peru. English buccaneers, notably Sir Francis Drake and Henry Morgan, burned and looted its ports and towns. Panama declared its independence from Spain in 1821 and became part of Colombia.

The discovery of gold in California in 1848 brought hundreds of thousands of fortune seekers from Europe and the east coast of the United States to Panama, since the isthmus crossing was for them the fastest route to the gold fields. A rail line was constructed to speed them on their way. In the 1880s the French tried, but failed, to build a canal across the isthmus. When Colombia balked at allowing the United States to take over the project, Panama declared its independence, with US backing, in 1903. The United States was granted "in perpetuity" an 8-km (5-mi) strip on either side of the canal, which was completed in 1914.

Before long, Panamanians were demanding a revision of the treaty that, in effect, cut their nation in two. A settlement was not reached, however, until 1977, when the United States agreed to return the Canal Zone to Panama in 1979 and to return the canal itself to Panama at the beginning of the year 2000. Relations plummeted again in 1988, when Panama's strongman, General Manuel Antonio Noriega, was indicted in US courts for drug trafficking. In December 1989, 23,000 US troops landed in Panama City, seizing Noriega and installing a new government. At least 4,000 people died in the assault, mostly civilians, and damage was estimated at $2 billion.

²LOCATION AND HOMELAND

Panama, which is a little smaller than the US state of South Carolina, occupies the narrowest part of the American mainland separating the Atlantic and Pacific oceans. It is bounded on the west by Costa Rica, on the east by Colombia, on the north by the Caribbean Sea—an inlet of the Atlantic—and on the south by the Pacific. Heavily forested mountain ranges form the spine of the country, with the highest peak reaching 3,475 km (11,401 ft) above sea level. The Panama Canal runs through a gap in these mountains. There are also more than 1,600 islands off the shores of the mainland. The climate is tropical except at mountain elevations, and rainfall is heavy.

Panama had a population of about 2.6 million in the mid-1990s. In keeping with its position at the crossroads of the world, Panama has a varied racial composition. More than two-thirds of its people are Mestizo, which in Panama includes descent from Africans as well as Indians and Europeans. A smaller number are White or Black, the latter being descendants of migrants from the British West Indies who helped construct the railway and canal and who worked on banana plantations. The Indian population is about 150,000, with the Guaymí, Cuna, and Chocó the chief peoples. There are also significant numbers of Chinese—mostly descendants of railway workers—and of immigrants from the Indian subcontinent and Arab countries.

³ LANGUAGE

Spanish is the official and almost universally spoken language. Panamanian Spanish is spoken very rapidly in a distinctive accent and includes a lot of slang and many distinctive words. English is the first language of some of the Blacks who are descended from West Indians and is widely spoken and understood in the commercial sector, which includes international banking and trade. It is also the compulsory second language in schools. The Indian groups still speak their own languages, as do immigrants from many parts of the world.

⁴ FOLKLORE

Many peasants believe that on All Souls' Day (2 November), those who died during the previous year are summoned before God and the devil for judgment, with their good and bad deeds weighed on a scale. There are two types of *curanderos* (folk healers): herbal-medicine practitioners, who also may cure by praying and making the sign of the cross over the patient; and *hechiceros* (sorcerers), who traffic in secret potions. The witch (*bruja*) is a malevolent old woman possessed by the devil. Witches can transform themselves into animals, especially deer, but only some can fly. To avoid harm from witches, one should turn a piece of clothing inside out. Also to be feared are black dogs and black cats and the *chivato*, a malignant animal spirit.

There are numerous other spirits, including *duendos* (fairies). A red shirt on a newborn wards off evil, as does a necklace of the teeth of jaguars or crocodiles, and the infant is bathed in water in which certain leaves and plants have been steeped. Panamanian folklore is perhaps best expressed in the nation's many festivals, during which folk dramas and dances are performed.

⁵ RELIGION

More than 80% of the people are Roman Catholic; Protestants and Muslims account for about another 5% each. The constitution specifies that the Catholic faith shall be taught in public schools, but it is not a compulsory subject. To be completely integrated into the mainstream of Panama society, however, requires at least a nominal adherence to the faith. As elsewhere in Latin America, women are the mainstay of the Church. There were fewer than 300 Catholic priests in Panama in the mid-1980s. In addition to churches and mosques, Panama City has a Jewish synagogue and Hindu and Baha'i temples.

⁶ MAJOR HOLIDAYS

Carnival is celebrated on the four days before Ash Wednesday (in February), especially in Panama City, where the festivities include music, dancing, costumes, and a big Mardi Gras parade. It comes to an end at dawn on Ash Wednesday with a mock ceremony called the "Burial of the Sardine." Las Tablas also has an outstanding Carnival celebration. Holy Week (late March or early April) also is marked by costumed dances and

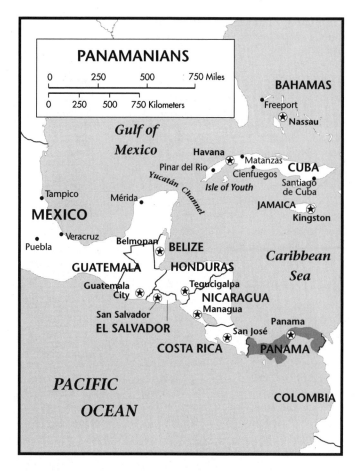

drama, and by Good Friday processions. Dramatizations of the Passion are held in Rio de Jesús and Pesé. Los Santos holds a traditional Corpus Christi festival.

Portobelo's Festival of the Black Christ, on 21 October, draws purple-clad pilgrims to a life-size statue, housed in a colonial-era church, that is said to have miraculous powers and is paraded through the streets on that day. Similar is the pilgrimage to Atalaya on the first Sunday of Lent to the shrine of Jesus of Nazareth. Each town has a yearly fiesta in honor of its patron saint, culminating in a procession in which the saint's image is carried through the streets.

The chief secular holidays are 3 and 28 November, which commemorate Panama's independence from Colombia and Spain, respectively. Mother's Day, which falls on the day of the Immaculate Conception (8 December) in the Church calendar, is also a national holiday, reverently observed.

⁷ RITES OF PASSAGE

The one indispensable sacrament for Panama's Catholics is baptism. Even peasants in remote areas will make the trek to the nearest church, although they may have to wait for the annual fiesta, when a priest will be present. It is believed that fairies, witches, or the devil can carry away a child who is not baptized. First Communion is generally observed only by the middle and upper classes. A country boy receives his first machete at the age of seven or eight as an early portent of *machismo*, the spirit of male assertiveness common to Hispanic America. Most boys are put to work early, doing farm chores when not attending school. In the cities, boys can earn money shining shoes or selling papers. Girls help their mothers in the home.

The street is the playground for lower-class urban youth, who also may join a *padilla* (gang). Girls are more closely supervised. A girl's 15th birthday is an important event and in well-off families is marked by a debut with a reception and dance. Middle- and upper-class girls enjoy more freedom than in most other Latin American countries. Nevertheless, dating and courtship are closely linked, and a girl is expected not to date more than one boy at a time.

Every effort is made to bury the dead in consecrated ground. The *velorio,* or wake, is an all-night affair in the home, with the deceased, in his or her best dress, on display. This is followed by a novena that may be repeated the next month and the next year. A Mass may be held if a church is near.

8 INTERPERSONAL RELATIONS

Like other Hispanic Americans, Panamanians greet friends and relatives more demonstratively than is the custom in the United States. Common among men is the *abrazo* (embrace), particularly if they have not seen each other for some time. Acquaintances will shake hands both on meeting and departing. Women often embrace and kiss on one or both cheeks. People are likely to stand closer to one another in conversation than is common in North America.

9 LIVING CONDITIONS

Panama, Costa Rica, and Belize are more prosperous than the other Central American countries. The average life expectancy of 73 years in Panama is almost as long as in North America. In the early 1990s, 80% of the people had access to health care services, and 83% had access to safe water and adequate sanitation. Rural areas, however, have disproportionately high infant and maternal mortality rates, and 25% of Panama's children under five years of age are considered malnourished.

The basic peasant dwelling is the *rancho* or *quincha,* a hut supported by poles, with walls of palm fronds, cane, clay, or boards. The thatched roof is of palm fronds or grass. The building of such a house is a local event in which neighbors gather to help. Houses in town are often of cement block, with a tile roof. The urban poor usually live in overcrowded, decaying two-story frame houses with tin roofs. Migrants from rural areas often settle in squatter communities on the urban outskirts. Better-class houses generally do not have a front yard but have an enclosed patio in the rear. There are high-rise apartment buildings in Panama City, some of which are condominiums.

10 FAMILY LIFE

The nuclear family of parents and children prevails in Panama, and the average household has five members. Wider kinship relations are essential, however. The extended family provides economic support in a society where the larger community cannot be counted on for help. Married children may visit their parents every day, and grandparents, uncles and aunts, and cousins routinely gather together on Sundays, holidays, and birthdays. Also buttressing the nuclear family are godparents, who are expected to take a lifelong interest in their godchild's

The nuclear family of parents and children prevails in Panama, and the average household has five members. Wider kinship relations are essential, however. The extended family provides economic support in a society where the larger community cannot be counted on for help. (Cory Langley)

welfare as well as to provide gifts on baptism, confirmation, and marriage.

Church and civil marriage are both legal, and a recent marriage code recognizes traditional Indian cultural marriage rites as the equivalent of a civil ceremony. Formal marriage, however, is not the rule outside the middle and upper classes, most new couples merely taking up residence in a new home. One study reported that 72% of Panama's children were born from unstable, short-term unions. There is little social stigma to illegitimacy, and many households are headed by a woman; some are three-generation households headed by a single mother who has a daughter or daughters who are themselves single mothers. In contrast to men, women are expected to be gentle, long-suffering, forgiving and, above all, devoted to their children.

The average Panamanian woman is more likely to practice birth control than are her Central American sisters, giving birth, on average, to three children. Abortion is illegal except to save the life of the mother. Poor women must work outside the home, at least in urban areas. While the constitution mandates equal pay for equal work, wages for women are often lower than those for men for equivalent work, and women hold only 4% of managerial positions. Middle- and upper-class women are under social pressure to attend church services regularly

Peasant clothing has traditionally consisted of simple cotton garments, homemade sandals, and handwoven straw hats. More recently rural folk have begun to adopt urban dress, which is much like the summertime clothing in North America.
(Cory Langley)

and otherwise to take part in the religious life of the community.

¹¹ CLOTHING

Peasant clothing has traditionally consisted of simple cotton garments, homemade sandals, and handwoven straw hats. More recently rural folk have begun to adopt urban dress, which is much like the summertime clothing in North America.

By contrast, there is a wealth of costume displayed at the nation's many fiestas. The spectacular *pollera,* an embroidered two-piece dress with an off-the-shoulder neckline, is the national costume for women and is perhaps the most beautiful traditional apparel in Latin America. Handmade lace joins the flounces on both blouse and skirt in a color that matches the embroidery. Beneath the skirt are several handmade petticoats. Heavy gold chains are worn around the neck, the hair is studded with flowers and glittering gold jewelry, and the feet are encased in satin slippers. The pollera is of Andalusian origin, while the far simpler and more rustic men's *montuno* is of Indian origin. Made of unbleached muslin embroidered in bright colors, the montuno consists of a long shirt with a fringe hanging over short trousers. It is accompanied by sandals and a true Panama hat: braided, not woven.

¹² FOOD

The Panamanian diet differs from that of the other Central American countries (except Belize) because rice is at least as important as corn. A basic breakfast is *guacho,* rice mixed with red beans. However, meat, yams, yucca, and other ingredients can be added for a more filling meal. Cornmeal is used for tortillas, tamales, and empanadas, which are like tamales but are fried, not steamed. *Sancocho* is a traditional dish of meat, potatoes, yuccas and yams, corn, perhaps beans or peas, turnips, onions, carrots, and plantains. It is boiled and flavored with the coriander leaf. *Lechona* (suckling pig) is wedding fare. *Carimañola* is yucca root fried and wrapped around seasoned ground meat. Panama's bountiful seafood catch yields many dishes. Roast iguana, tapir, and monkey are treats in the remote forested areas. *Chicha* is a fruit drink rather than, as elsewhere in Central America, one made from fermented cornmeal. *Seco* is rum prepared from sugarcane.

¹³ EDUCATION

Panama had a literacy rate approaching 90% in 1990. Public education is free between the ages of 6 and 15, and six years of primary school are compulsory. About 90% of all children of primary-school age, and 50% of those of secondary-school age, were in school in 1990. These figures were excellent for Central America. There are three universities. Nearly 75% of the nation's university students are enrolled at the University of Panama. The other institutions of higher education are Technical University and the Church-run University of Santa Maria la Antigua.

¹⁴ CULTURAL HERITAGE

Panama has two traditional song forms, both of Spanish origin: the *copla,* sung by women, and the *mejorana,* sung by men and accompanied by the small native guitar of the same name. The *saloma* is a male song style with yodeling and falsetto. Blacks sing calypso, and the Cuna and Chocó have their own songs to the accompaniment of flutes. Panama has a national symphonic orchestra and a national school of music.

The most popular folk dance, the *tamborito,* is of African origin. Drums furnish the rhythmic background, while female voices sing coplas to the melody. Couples dance one at a time within a circular area. The *cumbia* is a circular dance for any number of couples, set to simple repetitive melodies and accented drumbeats. The *punto,* more graceful and dignified, has precise and formal movements that echo the refinement of 19th-century ballroom dances. As a dance form, the mejorana exists in both rustic and refined versions, with men in one line facing women in the other. A national mejorana festival is held every 24 September in Guararé.

A wealth of costumed folk dramas are performed at festivals. In *Los Montezumas,* the confrontation of the Spanish and Aztecs in Mexico is recounted. *Los Grandiablos,* a dance-drama, portrays Lucifer and his band of devils in battle with the Archangel Michael for the possession of a soul. The Congos, descendants of slaves, perform a dance-drama in a special dialect during their Carnival festivities.

Important Panamanian poets have included Dário Herrera and Ricardo Miró. Leading Panamanian painters have included

Roberto Lewis and Humberto Ivaldi. Among composers have been Narciso Garay, Roque Cordero, and Gonzalo Brenes.

15 WORK

Panama's leading economic sectors are government services, commerce, and agriculture. Many subsistence farmers still clear plots by slashing and burning, then move on when the soil loses its fertility. They are being displaced by cattle ranchers. Other peasants find seasonal work on banana, sugar, and coffee plantations. Most factory jobs are in food processing. Panama has become one of the major international banking centers in the Americas, and the Colón Free Zone is the world's most important duty-free trading zone except for Hong Kong. The official unemployment rate of about 15% appears to be considerably understated.

16 SPORTS

Baseball is Panama's most popular sport. A number of Panamanians have played in the major leagues, and Panama-born Rod Carew is in baseball's Hall of Fame. There have been several Panamanian boxing champions, including Roberto Durán. Swimming, fishing, hunting, and horseback riding are popular. Panama City has horse-racing with parimutuel betting.

Bullfighting in Panama is merely teasing, in which participants annoy the beast while nimbly avoiding danger. It is performed at festivals. Cockfights, accompanied by wagers, are popular throughout the country. Cuna and Guaymí Indians hold pole-tossing contests. Children play a game like marbles with cashew seeds.

17 ENTERTAINMENT AND RECREATION

For rural people, festivals are still the high points of the year. These include agricultural fairs, in which a queen is crowned, judges pick prize-winning animals, and carnival rides draw youngsters. Traditional forms of live entertainment, however, are giving way to the lure of discos, movies, and television. By law, all foreign-language movies must be subtitled in Spanish. There are five television stations. Panama City has lots of nightclubs and more than 20 gambling casinos.

18 FOLK ART, CRAFTS, AND HOBBIES

Handicraft articles include baskets, straw hats, net and saddle bags, hammocks, straw mats, gourds, woodcarvings, and masks. Most pottery is dark red and dull-finished. *Molas* are colorful handstitched appliqué textiles made by Cuna Indian women. Georgina Linares is known for her paintings on leather.

19 SOCIAL PROBLEMS

There is a serious street-crime problem in urban slums. Spousal violence against women is widespread. According to official 1994 statistics, one-fifth of all families do not have enough money for a minimum diet, and a further one-fourth cannot meet their basic needs. The nation's forests are being reduced at an alarming rate, and soil erosion is a serious problem.

20 BIBLIOGRAPHY

Adams, Richard N. *Cultural Surveys of Panama—Nicaragua—Guatemala—El Salvador—Honduras*. Detroit: B. Ethridge, 1976.

Biesanz, Richard, and Mavis Biesanz. *The People of Panama*. New York: Columbia University Press, 1955.

Cheville, Lila R., and Richard A. Cheville. *Festivals and Dances of Panama*. Privately printed in Panama, 1977.

Revilla Argüeso, Ángel. *Cultura hispanoamericana en el istmo de Panamá*. Panama City: Ecu Ediciones, 1987.

—by R. Halasz

PARAGUAYANS

LOCATION: Paraguay
POPULATION: 4.1 million
LANGUAGE: Spanish; Guarani
RELIGION: Roman Catholicism (official)

¹ INTRODUCTION

An isolated, landlocked country, Paraguay has for much of its history deliberately kept itself apart from the rest of Latin America. Tucked away in the south-central part of the continent, it is a sparsely populated country, a hot, subtropical lowland that has been dubbed "the empty quarter" of South America. It also had the unenviable reputation of being the most infamous and long-lasting of all of South America's police states. Gradually, however, since the late 1980s, that has changed as the country has tentatively adopted a more democratic approach. Economic changes are also starting to transform the country, particularly with the development of the world's largest hydroelectric project at Itaipu, situated in eastern Paraguay, along the Brazilian frontier. Otherwise, mineral resources, including petroleum, are almost nonexistent.

When the first Europeans arrived in the 16th century, Guarani-speaking people inhabited most of what is now eastern Paraguay, while west of the Rio Paraguay many other Amerindian tribes, known collectively as "Guaycuru" to the Guarani, lived in the Chaco territories. The Paraguayans threw out their Spanish governor in 1811 and proclaimed independence. But because the colony was regarded as being so isolated and economically unimportant, the Spanish authorities did not bother to do anything about it and left the new country to its own devices.

In 1864 Paraguay launched a disastrous attack against Argentina, Uruguay, and Brazil. Known as the War of the Triple Alliance, the Paraguayan forces were badly defeated, and the country lost 150,000 sq km (58,000 sq mi) of territory. But far worse, it lost much of its population through combat, famine, and disease. One estimate says it lost nearly all its males between the ages of 15 and 70. It was a blow from which the country has never completely recovered.

The Colorado Party has been the dominant political force in Paraguayan political life ever since it won the civil war in 1947. Following that war, the party was able to depend on the president and virtual dictator, General Alfredo Stroessner, and the military in maintaining its privileged status. During the years 1954 to 1989, it was common for any political opposition to be met with torture and assassination. Then, in 1989 the brutal dictatorship was overthrown by General Andres Rodriguez, who was elected to the presidency in an election that saw a wide spectrum of opposition parties gain a larger percentage of congressional seats than ever before. Democratic elections were held in 1991, and General Rodriguez's Colorado Party won a legislative majority. An era of political debate and activity never seen before was opening up for the first time in Paraguay's history.

Paraguay relies on agriculture for much of its export industry, and the most important crops grown are cassava, sugarcane, maize (corn), soybeans, and cotton, as well as cattle products. It remains one of the most industrially undeveloped countries in South America.

² LOCATION AND HOMELAND

Lying within the heart of South America, Paraguay is surrounded by the huge, neighboring countries of Brazil, Argentina, and Bolivia. With an area of 407,000 sq km (157,000 sq mi), it is slightly larger than Germany and almost exactly the size of California. Although half the country is covered by timber, much of it has little commercial value.

Dividing the country into two unequal halves is the Rio Paraguay. This river connects the capital, Asunción, with the Rio Parana and the Atlantic Ocean. The great majority of the population live in the eastern section of this divide, making up about 40% of the whole country.

Contraband has become one of Paraguay's major sources of currency. Electronic goods and agricultural produce find their way through Ciudad del Este to and from Brazil. There is also a substantial trade in stolen cars and illegal drugs, including cocaine.

Paraguay's population of 4.1 million is approximately one-seventh the size of that of the state of California, which has about the same area. Asunción is the largest city, with 500,000 residents, but only 43% of Paraguayans live in urban areas, compared with 80% in Argentina and Uruguay. Most people can claim to be native Paraguayans, and 90% are Mestizo, of mixed Spanish and Guarani blood. Many Paraguayans are peasant farmers, who make a living by selling their small surplus of crops.

The Paraguayan life expectancy of 65 years is lower than that in any other country in South America except Bolivia and Peru.

About 20% of Paraguayans are of European stock, including about 100,000 Germans. In the 1930s, German Mennonites, a pacifist, religious sect similar to the Amish sects of North America, were allowed in by the government to establish agricultural settlements in central Chaco. Despite the harsh, challenging conditions of the region, the Mennonites have been very successful, although there have been problems of continuing friction with a number of local Amerindian tribes. Japanese immigrants have also settled in parts of eastern Paraguay, along with Brazilian agricultural colonists, many of German origin, who have moved across the border in recent years. Paraguay's Amerindians represent 3% of the population, and most of them live in the Chaco region.

³ LANGUAGE

Both Spanish and Guarani are Paraguay's official languages. This is a reflection of its colonial history, for when the Spaniards settled in the country they were overwhelmingly outnumbered by the Guarani native Amerindians. As a result, intermarrying became the norm. Today, more than 75% of Paraguayans are Mestizos, of mixed Spanish-Guarani heritage, many of them preferring to speak Guarani. Spanish, however, is the official language of government and commerce, although even upper-class Paraguayans speak Guarani.

Several other Amerindian languages are spoken in the Chaco and isolated parts of eastern Paraguay, including Lengua, Nivacle, and Ache. Contact with the Mennonites has also meant that for many Amerindians, German has become their second language, rather than Spanish.

PARAGUAYANS

0   250   500   750 Miles

0   250   500   750 Kilometers

commemorated on 1 March, and February sees the celebration of the popular Latin American festival, Carnival.

7 RITES OF PASSAGE

Due to the influence of the Catholic church, baptisms, First Communion and saints' days play an important part in the lives of many families.

8 INTERPERSONAL RELATIONS

A popular social pastime is the drinking of *mate,* Paraguayan tea made from holly leaves. It is regarded as being more significant than a simple drink like tea or coffee and is, in fact, seen as an important ritual to be shared among family, friends, and colleagues. It is the very act of sharing that is regarded by those taking part as being the whole purpose of drinking *mate.* At each sitting, one person is responsible for filling a gourd almost to the top with the tea. Water is heated, but not boiled, in a kettle and poured into the vessel. The liquid is then sipped by each person from a silver tube which has a bulbous filter at its lower end to prevent the leaves from entering the tube.

9 LIVING CONDITIONS

Asunción has preserved much of its 19th-century architecture, with narrow streets full of low buildings. Meanwhile, a steady flood of rural poor has caused large shanty towns to mushroom in open spaces by the river and close to the railway. Some 40% of the population still survive in rural areas, enduring poor sanitation and malnutrition. Paraguay has one of the highest infant mortality rates in South America, and its levels of welfare place it very low by world and South American standards. Paraguay's social welfare system, however, does provide cash and medical care for sickness, maternity, and injury at work, as well as pensions for old age.

Most rural Paraguayans live in one-room houses, called *ranchos.* Most have earthen floors; reed, wood, or brick walls; and a thatched roof, sloped to carry off the heavy rains. A separate or attached shed serves as a kitchen. Few houses have indoor plumbing. Urban dwellers—over 40% of the population— occupy small, pastel-colored houses of brick or stucco, with tiled roofs and iron grillwork covers on the windows. The urban poor live in shacks, although, unlike other large Latin American cities, Asunción does not have sprawling slum areas.

Paraguay's geographical isolation has led to high transport costs, which have driven up the price of its exports in comparison with other Latin American countries.

10 FAMILY LIFE

Population growth is encouraged, although child abandonment and high rates of maternal mortality are problems. There is also a high level of illegitimacy, particularly in rural areas. This is often blamed on the great distances that separate rural dwellings from the nearest towns, as well as the extreme poverty of the peasants who cannot afford the expense of the wedding ceremony. Marriage itself may be performed both as a civil and a religious ceremony.

4 FOLKLORE

The historical merging of Spanish and Guarani blood over the centuries has created a Spanish-Guarani culture, which is reflected in the folklore, arts, and literature of the country.

5 RELIGION

The state religion of Paraguay is Roman Catholicism, although the Church is weaker and less influential than in most other Latin American countries. Two of the reasons for this are Paraguay's traditional isolation from mainstream South America, and the fact that the government has shown less interest in religion as an institution. As a result, a number of irregular religious practices have grown up over the years. In fact, in some rural areas, priests are seen as healers and men of magic, rather than as official representatives of the Church.

At the same time, fundamentalist Protestants have not had as much success in finding converts in Paraguay as they have in other Latin American countries, although the Mennonites have had some influence among Chaco Indians since they arrived in the 1930s.

6 MAJOR HOLIDAYS

Christmas and Easter are major Christian holidays, as well as the Diá de la Virgen, on 8 December, celebrating the Immaculate Conception. The War of the Triple Alliance in the 1860s is

11 CLOTHING

In urban areas, Paraguayans dress as people do in America or Europe. Many rural women wear a shawl, called a *rebozo,* and a simple dress or a skirt and blouse. The men generally wear

Most Paraguayans in rural areas survive on subsistence crops on small landholdings, selling any surplus at local markets. (Anne Kalosh)

loose trousers, called *bomachas,* a shirt or jacket, a neckerchief, and a poncho. Rural people generally go barefoot.

12 FOOD

Paraguayan food is similar to that of Argentina and Uruguay, although there are significant differences. People eat less meat than in either of the other River Plate republics, although *parrillada,* grilled meat, is still a popular item on restaurant menus. At the same time, the influence of Guarani tastes in tropical and subtropical ingredients can often be seen in Paraguayan recipes.

A common part of almost every meal is grain, particularly maize (corn), and tubers such as cassava. *Locro* is a maize stew, while *mazamorra* is a maize mush.

The national dish and dietary staple is *sopa paraguaya,* which is not a soup but rather a cornbread with cheese and onion. Cassava dishes are the mainstay of the rural poor, for the vegetable thrives abundantly on thin to mediocre soils.

13 EDUCATION

Education is only compulsory up to the age of 12. The literacy rate is 81%, making it the lowest of the River Plate republics, although it is higher than all the Andean countries except Ecuador. There is higher education at the Universidad Nacional and the Universidad Catolica in Asunción, both of which also have branches throughout the country.

14 CULTURAL HERITAGE

In general, very little Paraguayan literature is available to English-speaking readers, but novelist and poet Augusto Roa Bastos introduced Paraguay to the international literary stage by winning the Spanish government's Cervantes prize in 1990. Although he was forced to spend much of his life in exile from the Stroessner dictatorship, Roa Bastos uses Paraguayan themes and history, intertwining them with the story of his country's politics.

Works by other important Paraguayan writers, such as novelist Gabriel Cassaccia and poet Evio Romero, are not readily available in English.

15 WORK

Most people in rural areas survive on subsistence crops on small landholdings, selling any surplus at local markets. They then supplement their incomes by laboring on the large *estancias* and plantations.

There are still small, but important, populations of Amerindians in the Chaco and in scattered areas of eastern Paraguay. Until very recently, some of them relied on hunting and gathering for their livelihood. The Nivacle and Lengua are the largest groups, who both number around 10,000 people, and many of them work as laborers on the large agricultural estates.

Many Paraguayans, either for political or economic reasons, live outside the country, mostly in Brazil and Argentina. Between 1950 and 1970, more than 350,000 Paraguayans migrated to Argentina to find work. Although the official minimum wage in Paraguay is approximately us$200 per month, the Ministry of Justice and Labor is unable to enforce its regulations, and it is estimated that about 70% of Paraguayan workers earn less than the minimum wage.

16 SPORTS

Soccer, like elsewhere in this part of Latin America, is the most popular sport, both for watching and playing. Asunción's most popular team, Olimpico, is on a level with the best Argentine and Uruguayan teams.

Paraguayans also enjoy basketball, volleyball, horse-racing, and swimming.

17 ENTERTAINMENT AND RECREATION

Theater is popular in Paraguay, and productions are staged in Guarani as well as Spanish. The visual arts are also very important and popular. Asunción offers many galleries, the most important being the Museo del Barro, which mounts a wide range of modern works. Classical and folk music are performed at venues throughout the capital.

Religious holidays are celebrated with festivals that include music, dancing, and parades, as well as athletic contests.

18 FOLK ART, CRAFTS, AND HOBBIES

Paraguay's most famous traditional craft is the production of multicolored spider-web lace in the Asunción suburb of Itaugua, where the cottage industry is practiced by skilled women from childhood to old age. Paraguayan harps and guitars, as well as filigree gold and silver jewelry and leather goods, are made in the village of Luque, while the Amerindian communities of Chaco produce high-caliber craft items of their own.

¹⁹ SOCIAL PROBLEMS

When Juan Carlos Wasmosy was elected as Paraguay's first civilian president in many years, he was nominated by the then-ruling Colorado Party merely as a figurehead. Since then, however, he has clashed with the still-powerful military establishment, particularly General Lino Oviedo, who led the coup against the previous military dictatorship.

Meanwhile, the military's position is being challenged as it comes under scrutiny for its treatment and abuse of conscripts, from groups like the Movimiento de Objeccion de la Conciencia. At the same time, President Wasmosy is also being investigated for his business dealings, connected with Paraguay's major hydroelectric projects.

So far, Paraguayan industry, which is mainly concerned with the processing of agricultural products, has seen little benefit from the hydroelectric boom. The economic growth of the 1970s has been almost wiped out by the long delays in finishing two major hydroelectric projects. In 1994, the economic growth rate was only 3.6%, while inflation has been running at roughly 45%.

²⁰ BIBLIOGRAPHY

Bernhardson Wayne. *Argentina, Uruguay and Paraguay: A Lonely Planet Travel Survival Kit.* 2nd ed. Lonely Planet Publications, 1996.

Warren, Harris Gaylord. *Paraguay and the Triple Alliance.* Austin: University of Texas, 1978.

———. *Rebirth of the Paraguayan Republic.* Pittsburgh: University of Pittsburgh Press, 1985.

Williams, John Hoyt. *The Rise and Fall of the Paraguayan Republic.* Austin: University of Texas, 1979.

—by P. Pitchon, reviewed by R. Caballero

PEMON

ALTERNATE NAMES: Arecuna, Kamarakoto, Taurepan
LOCATION: Venezuela
POPULATION: Unknown
LANGUAGE: Pemon
RELIGION: Indigenous beliefs mingled with Christian elements

¹ INTRODUCTION

The Pemon-Caribs are known in the literature as Arecuna, Kamarakoto, and Taurepan. They call themselves Pemon and became widely known relatively recently when Capuchin missionaries and Protestant evangelists from Guyana and Brazil came, together with the first gold and diamond mine workers, to their territory in the southeast of Venezuela. There are no historical sources from before 1750, when the area was mentioned in the context of determining borderlines by individuals who never visited the area. The first real incursions date from 1838 and 1843. At the end of the 19th century, English Protestant missionaries started to evangelize among the Pemon, followed later by all kinds of Christian groups, but it was only in 1931 that the first Capuchin mission post in the Pemon area was established, 20 km (12 mi) from the Brazilian border. From 1936 onward, the gold and diamond rush penetrated the area and, during the 1960s, the air connection and overland route were built. But the diamond mining operations have been intermittent. This, together with the poor quality of Pemon agricultural land and grasses for pasturage, and the late opening of the Pemon area, has spared them from major land invasions. Many traditions and much of the original communication—language, smoke signals, and swift-footed walks—have survived.

² LOCATION AND HOMELAND

The expanse of the Pemon's tribal territory covers the coastal area of the Atlantic in Venezuela, the inland mountain savanna area, and the Amazon area. They are the most far-flung of the Central Guiana Highlands peoples. The Guayana region "La Gran Sabana," in the state of Bolivar, is characterized by big table-mountains and an immense savanna. The German writer and explorer, Uwe George, when describing what he saw in this part of the Pemon territory, in a remote corner of southeastern Venezuela near the border with Brazil and Guyana, spoke of the *tepuis,* the Pemon word for enormous sandstone mesas. The tepuis are the remains of mighty sandstone plateaus that once stretched across the entire area. In the course of time the plateaus were largely worn down by erosion, leaving only the tepuis as giant monuments to their existence. There are more than 100 such tepuis, but fewer than half have been extensively explored. Many of them are hidden by dense cloud cover for days at a time, like the surface of Venus. "In some respects," George says, "we know more about that distant planet than we do about the vast and mysterious tepuis of Venezuela." As a result of millions of years of isolation, much of the plant and animal life atop the tepuis is unique. In the area south of the Orinoco River, the countryside is dominated by lowlands; and further south, towards and into the Amazon region, the terrain turns mountainous.

[3] LANGUAGE

Father Cesareo de Armellada was the author of the first grammar and dictionary of the Pemon language (1943), formerly called Taurepan. The world of the Pemon is shown in their very descriptive language. Their word for "sugarcane" is *kaiwara-kún-imá*, which means "pineapple with very long leg." The word for "pineapple" itself, *kaiwara,* means "a sweet with wrinkles." The Pemon word for "dew" is *chirké-yetakú,* which means "star's saliva." *Yetakú* is "saliva" or, more precisely, "juice of the teeth."

There is no word for "year" in the Pemon language, and the day is divided into "dawning," "morning," "noontime," "afternoon," and then just "dark" or "nighttime." Most temporal references only cover "yesterday," "today," "tomorrow," and *pena*, "time past." The Pemon speak their own Carib language among each other, and Spanish or pidgin Spanish with the *criollos* (mixed-blood Venezuelans). In the mission villages and mining areas of the state of Bolivar, more and more youngsters also use Spanish in their own Amerindian society. Most Pemon people have Christian names now. They often have two Amerindian names as well, one of which is a sacred and secret name.

[4] FOLKLORE

The religious notions from the time before contact with the Christian world have been preserved by accounts from anthropologists and folk tales. The Pemon traditionally believed that each person has five souls which look like shadows of a human. The fifth one is the one that talks and leaves the body to travel around when the person is dreaming. This is the only one that goes to the beyond after death, en route to the Milky Way. Before arriving, it meets the Father of the Dogs, and if the person has mistreated his or her dogs, their souls will recognize the person and kill him or her. One of the other four souls inhabits the knee and stays put for a while after death to turn later into a bad spirit. The other three souls turn into birds of prey after death. All animals and plants are believed to have souls. Stones, on the other hand, do not have souls but house bad spirits.

The *Makunaima* is a sequence of creation tales of the Pemon land, crops, techniques, and social practices. It starts with the creation of a wife for the first Pemon—the Sun—by a water nymph. The basic sexual division of labor, and the ideas of proficiency in subsistence tasks as a prerequisite to a successful marriage, are laid out in this story. At the time, the Sun was a person. One day he went to the stream and saw a small woman with long hair. He managed to grasp her hair, but she told him, "Not me! I will send you a woman to be your companion and your wife." Her name was Tuenkaron, and the next day she sent the Sun a White woman. He fed her, and she lit a fire. But when the Sun sent her to the stream, as she came in contact with water, she collapsed into a little heap of clay. The woman was made of white earth. The next day Tuenkaron sent him a black woman. She was able to bring water, but when she tried to light a fire, she melted: the woman was made of wax. The third woman was red, a rock-colored woman. The sun tested her— she did not melt or collapse. She was strong and able to contribute to the running of the household. They had several children, and these are the Pemon.

[5] RELIGION

Though the Pemon have been relatively spared the influence of the modern nation-state, as not enough of anything valuable has been found to attract wholesale colonization, the presence of missions has left its mark. Most of the Amerindian thoughts and consciousness came to be mixed to a lesser or higher degree with Christian elements. *Chichikrai* is the name for Jesus Christ in three syncretistic Christian Amerindian cults: Hallelujah, Chochiman, and San Miguel. These cults have the nature of a spiritual movement. "Hallelujah" as a name suggests Christian influence. However, while to Christians it means "Praise the Lord," to the Amerindian it means "the word of god." This is because, in a vision given by God to a former shaman, who had converted to Christianity and was then betrayed by the missionaries, God taught the shaman the new religion and told him it was called "Hallelujah." Some Hallelujah beliefs are similar to Christian beliefs. They believe in God and Jesus Christ as his son but do not acknowledge the concept of salvation through Jesus Christ's death and resurrection. In spite of the strength of Catholicism, the Pemon believe in Kanaima—the spirit of evil; and social traditions, like cross-cousin marriage, that are opposed by the Church are practiced by many Pemon. Cult saints, like Maria Leonza, a female saint of Amerindian origin whose role is a healing and protecting one, sometimes can hardly be discerned from another local saint, the Virgin of the Valley, who is actually a Maria (Mary, mother of Jesus) in the Catholic sense.

An important attempt to prevent the disappearance of Pemon beliefs and traditions was made in 1985 at the AVEC Congress on Bilingual Education. It was declared that the Amerindians have a natural right to uphold their traditional beliefs, and that Jesus Christ and the New Testament are only additions to that indigenous religion.

6 MAJOR HOLIDAYS

As most Pemon have been evangelized, their major holidays are the same as those celebrated by Catholics. Holy Week and Christmas are duly kept, with open demonstrations of sorrow during the first and joy in the latter. As is common all over Latin America, religious practices are a potpourri of new and old beliefs and, particularly in the case of peoples like the Pemon Indians whose cultural memory has not been lost, the shadows of the past can be traced, even when hidden behind a thick layer of Catholicism.

7 RITES OF PASSAGE

Traditional rites of passage were associated with the life-cycle (birth, puberty, and death), but most are no longer celebrated. Baptism in a Catholic mission is the only important rite of passage nowadays. Often the father will give the child a name in the Pemon language which is secret, and it is forbidden to use the secret name to address any person, male or female. Not so with Spanish names, and the Pemon are eager to baptize their children to give them such names. Women usually do not have last names, and men adopt the ones of their *criollo* (mixed-blood Venezuelan) bosses in the diamond mines. Brothers, therefore, sometimes end up with different last names.

One of the traditional rites of passage ruled eating habits during pregnancy to protect the soul of the child. The parents were forbidden to eat big fish, some species of birds, and many mammals. The big fish, for example, would take the child's soul into the water where it would drown. The parents were allowed, on the other hand, to eat small fish and the dove *wakuwa,* which is the one that brings the soul to the baby.

The rites of puberty also involved forbidden foods for males for a year after the first ceremony in which an alderman lashed the boy's body, made incisions in his body, and applied magical substances to the wounds. Finally, the boy had to endure the challenge of the ants. Girls' hair was cut before their first menstruation, and the edges of their mouths were tattooed in a traditional design. At the first sign of menstruation, the girl would retire to her hammock and was considered impure. Her grandmother would then paint her whole body. At some point during puberty, the girls also had to endure the challenge of the ants, on their hands, arms, face, and feet.

8 INTERPERSONAL RELATIONS

Marriage is the key to the social organization of the Pemon people: it determines the pattern of visits between villages, which is at the heart of their social life. Reciprocal visits for beer parties and meetings with relatives tie neighborhoods and regions together. The prestige of a settlement is often gauged by the quality and quantity of manioc (cassava) beer offered by the hosts. Conversation is animated when the family gathers around the pepper pot, and if guests are present, the men will eat first. Overt conflict, anger, and fighting are strongly reproved by the Pemon. The basic response to conflict is to

withdraw from the conflict situation, often by taking an extended visit to relatives living elsewhere and waiting for things to calm down. Gossip, ridicule, and sometimes ostracism are used as ways of controlling situations. Gossip, however, is a double edged weapon: the Pemon say trouble occurs over false gossip and women. As the Pemon do not approve of anger or displays of hostility, physical punishment of their children is very rare. If an adult strikes a child at all, it is so mildly as to be merely a reminder. Pemon children learn by example and are given free rein.

9 LIVING CONDITIONS

In the old days, when somebody in a Pemon village fell ill, the local shaman or *paisan* ascribed the illness to one of the many mythical spirits. For healing, the shaman uses his *taren* recipes, a mixture of magical and medicinal plants and charms. The *taren* is a magical invocation, a verbal spell which can aid in the birth of a child, counter the bite of various snakes, heal headaches and stomach pain, and so on. The taren can only be taught on a one-to-one basis, and its performance is as private as possible. *Taren esak* are practitioners and may be men or women who do not have to be shamans. The problem is that the traditional taren and *murang* treatments can not heal the Old World diseases easily, to which the Amerindians are still extremely sensitive, as they were in the first centuries of the colonial period when their population was decimated. Today, "medicine-men" as well as dentists have the task to visit the Amerindian villages in their area regularly, but the modern *criollo* (mixed-blood Venezuelan) doctors are too far distant. Still, mission-provided antibiotics and vaccines have reduced Pemon infant mortality rates.

The Pemon's traditional housing consists of huts whose walls are made of clay or bark, with roofs made of palm leaves. Their shape is either oblong or rounded and, more recently, square. Also recent is the introduction of walls within the house. The hammocks are hung from the beams of the roof, and a fire is kept at one or two corners of the house. Arrows, knifes, axes, and fishing rods are piled up in one corner, while baskets, haversacks, and pumpkins hang on the walls. The Pemon, even those who live in the forest, like to build their houses out in the open savanna. They place them near watercourses, and often the settlements are known by the name of the adjacent watercourse. Living on the savanna and cultivating in the forest often means traveling long distances on foot to get to the fields and back.

10 FAMILY LIFE

Marriage is the basis of the principal economic unit: the couple. The relationship between the father-in-law and son-in-law is most important. For the father-in-law, his son-in-law is the substitute for his own son; therefore, after the marriage, the son-in-law will detach himself from his own father and take care of his father-in-law. In the Pemon society there is no wedding ceremony. The groom simply moves his hammock to his father-in-law's house and starts working with him.

The Pemon believe that the man forms the baby in the woman's uterus through repeated copulation. The solid parts of the baby—the bones—come from the father, and the blood comes from the mother. The mother gives birth behind a partition installed in the hut for this purpose, helped by her mother or mother-in-law. During the 10 days after the birth, the parents remain behind a partition with their newborn.

The Pemon love their children, and their attitude towards them is lenient. Grown-ups never impose severe prohibitions, and parents are not constantly reminding their children how they should behave. Children learn by following the parents' example and very seldom require discipline or punishment.

Pemon women can run the household well enough by themselves, and they often do so, as their husbands are absent for long periods on trading trips, working at missions, or in the diamond mines.

11 CLOTHING

Formerly, the Pemon went naked or used only a loincloth. The traditional dress of a Pemon woman used to be an apron made of cotton or beads. The men wore loincloths, which in the 20th century were made of a bright red fabric obtained from the *criollos* (mixed-blood Venezuelans). But influenced by the Capuchin missions, by 1945 the Pemon had started wearing Western cotton clothes: the men tend to wear khaki, while the women make their dresses using cotton fabrics with patterns. At the beginning of the 20th century, the women wore metal earrings, which they bought, known as "butterfly" earrings. It was also common to see facial tattoos and bands of cotton or glass beads around their arms and legs. The mixture of indigenous and outside items is not exclusive: the Pemon might wear Venezuelan *alpargatas* or Western-style shoes, but it does not mean they have abandoned their own sandals, made from parts of the moriche palm stalk.

12 FOOD

Yucca, manioc root, or cassava, as for many other Amerindian groups, is an important ingredient for the Pemon's culinary art. The peeling, washing, and grating of this root is done by women, who then proceed to squeeze out the acid and, with the resulting dough, prepare their flat bread or fermented drinks. One of these beverages, the *cachiri,* is made with bitter yucca paste which is grated and chewed and mixed with a red root—cachiriyek—also grated. The mix is then boiled for a whole day. The resulting brew is mildly intoxicating.

Also part of the Pemon diet are a spinachlike vegetable called *aurosa,* peppers, more than 10 varieties of bananas, potatoes, pineapple, plantain, and sugarcane. Women gather peppers and aurosa daily for the pepper pot, a soup that forms part of every meal. Fishing provides the principal source of animal protein in the Pemon diet. In the past, hunting was not very effective, though men put a lot of time into it. The situation changed, however, with the arrival of firearms in the 1940s. Birds and mammals—such as deer and vampire bats—became an important part of their diet. During the rainy season, the Pemon capture flying ants, and throughout the year, they gather the larvae found in the moriche palm.

13 EDUCATION

One of the Pemon tools for educating their young is oral tradition. Their many stories are used by the elders to teach their sense of morality and concept of the world. "A-pantoní-pe nichii," "May you take advantage of this story," are often the closing words of the narrator.

Since the law of 1979, bilingual education at Amerindian primary schools is compulsory. Most of the main languages in Amerindian territory have at least one schoolbook. Though the teachers' organizations and the government have proved their good will in the recent past, the difficulties are considerable; they include long distances, bureaucracy, and Amerindian teachers sometimes too acculturated to cooperate wholeheartedly or just too poor to travel to the federal bilingual course far away in the middle of the industrialized part of the country. Some Pemon children spend time in mission boarding or day schools, through the primary school years and sometimes beyond.

14 CULTURAL HERITAGE

Music and dance are important components of Pemon activity. The same forms of dances and melodies, with different texts, are performed in medical contexts, shamanistic wars, or hunting preparations. They also accompany various rites of passage, incidental celebrations, and nonpublic healing rituals. *Mari'* or *Mari'k,* for example, is the Pemon word for the dance and music that used to be performed in public by the *paisan* (shaman) and his assistants. In one Mari'k everyone sang and danced, and stamped the *waronka*—a hollow tube of wood or bamboo, or a branch around which strings of rustling and rattling seeds or shells are hung. They also played flutes and a kind of horn made from a long, straight bamboo tube. The Pemon paisan generally restrained himself to a bundle of rustling leaves, the drum *sambura,* or the waronka.

Nowadays there are no paisans left in the Christianized Pemon villages, and some Pemon seem to be ashamed of tokens from the past, like old instruments. Still, on occasions when *cachiri*-drinking makes them receptive to tradition, spontaneously an old dance starts. With sticks and empty cans and tins, they sing songs full of endlessly repeated short phrases, varied by improvisation, jokes, and remnants of the old shaman songs.

15 WORK

Work for the Pemon is part of life, and there is no word for working other than *senneka,* which means "being active" more than "laboring." Only when they started working with the missionaries or miners did they adopt the Spanish word *trabajo* (work) which turned into *trabasoman* to characterize work done in the European fashion. The Pemon's means of subsistence are based in slash-and-burn horticulture, fishing, hunting, and collection of wild fruits and insects. There is now considerable flexibility in the division of work in all areas among the Pemon people. Traditionally, for example, men were responsible for the preparation of the soil, while women were in charge of weeding, harvesting, and transporting the produce.

Processing bitter manioc (cassava) takes a long time and a great deal of effort, but women break the monotony with the aid and companionship of other women. The arrival of metal tools made the preparation of the fields less difficult, so the men have more time for mining diamonds and gold. The task of fishing is usually shared. Catching the small fish found in the savanna is possible with the help of the *inek,* a poisonous plant that asphyxiates the fish and brings them to the surface where they can be easily trapped with nets. The men go up the river and pound the stems of the inek to extract the poison, while the women and children wait down the river to gather the fish with the nets. A Pemon man is a hunter, fisherman, woodsman, clearer of fields, maker of fiber basketry, and house-builder. A Pemon woman is a manioc-processor, weaver and tier of cotton, seamstress, and tier of fish nets. Cooking and procuring water and wood is left to the women. They are also responsible for the care of the children, though men help.

16 SPORTS

Spectator sports were not very common among aboriginal tribes. Most of the talents applauded by indigenous societies were and are part and parcel of Amerindians' day-to-day life— essential survival skills. Fishing, hunting, and merely getting from one place to another demand the ability to run fast, jump high and long, master archery and swimming, etc. But though good hunters might be admired, hunting is still above all a subsistence activity.

Pemon Indians who are in close contact with Whites participate in the national sporting culture.

17 ENTERTAINMENT AND RECREATION

The Pemon culture is very rich in what is known as oral literature: tales and legends that the Amerindians call *pantón*. There is no specific time dedicated to telling stories, but the favorite moment is just before going to sleep. The morning is the time to narrate and interpret dreams, and storytelling might happen again after meals. Stories and legends are considered luxuries of such worth to justify a trip to visit other tribes to procure them. The possessor of stories is called *sak* and, for the Pemon, a guest that tells stories or brings news or new songs is always welcome.

Dancing and beer accompany Pemon ceremonies, which draw large groups for periods of several weeks. Their gatherings are informal: while lines of men and women dance in a circle inside the round house for Hallelujah ceremonies, others slip in and out for conversation or for a gourdfull of manioc (cassava) beer.

18 FOLK ART, CRAFTS, AND HOBBIES

The Pemon value the abilities of their artisans: outstanding persons are recognized for their individual skills. Some women are renowned for the quality of their clay bowls. They are mainly made in the Kamarata and Uriman areas by women who learned the skill from their mothers. As not many females know the skills, and good clay sites are limited, the bowls are dispersed in the trade network. Basketry is another main Pemon art form. Men manufacture all basketry and fiber articles, including eating mats, strainers, baskets, and squeezers used in everyday household production. But everyday basketry is different from the more elaborate forms, which can be used as trade items. As in the case of pottery, only certain men are skilled at making complex patterned baskets. The Pemon also make wooden dugout and bark canoes, paddles, and bows, and weave hammocks and baby carriers.

19 SOCIAL PROBLEMS

The Venezuelan government's presence has increased substantially in the area of Santa Elena along the border with Brazil during the last 25 years. Road penetration of the eastern portion of the Gran Sabana dates from the early 1970s. Land entitlement for the communities has been recognized by experts and international support organizations as the most pressing issue facing the Pemon in the 1990s. Venezuela recognizes land rights for their Amerindian population but in many cases provides only provisional titles which can be easily ignored. Gold, diamonds, and wood are once again attracting outsiders, and their arrival often leads to violation of Amerindian rights. The tourist industry is also threatening the region, as what has been a controlled eco-friendly enterprise could turn into a virtual invasion if plans to build big hotels are approved.

20 BIBLIOGRAPHY

Brill, E. J. *Continuity & Identity in Native America.* New York: E. J. Brill, 1988.

Como son los Indios Pemones de la Gran Sabana. R.P. Cesareo de Armellada, 1946.

Cuentos y no cuentos. Fray Cesareo de Armellada. Instituto Venezolano de Lenguas Indigenas. Caracas, 1988.

Hacia el Indio y su Mundo. Gilberto Antolinez, 1972.

Los Aborigenes de Venezuela. Fundacion La Salle de Ciencias Naturales.

National Geographic, May 1989. "Venezuela's Islands in Time," Uwe George.

Order without Government: The Society of the Pemon Indians of Venezuela. David John Thomas, 1982.

Survival International documents and information, London, 1996

Tauron Panton: Cuentos y Leyendas de los Pemon. Padre Cesareo de Armellada.

—by D. Ventura-Alcalay

PERUVIANS

LOCATION: Peru
POPULATION: 24,523,408
LANGUAGE: Spanish; Quechua
RELIGION: Roman Catholicism, intertwined with native beliefs
RELATED ARTICLES: Quechua, Aymara, Shipibo

¹ INTRODUCTION

Once the seat of the expansive Inca Empire, Peru is a dramatic mix of old and new. After the conquest of the Incas, Peru's capital, Lima, became the center of Spain's colonial power structure in the Americas. Often called the "city of kings" in honor of Charles V, its name is a modification of the river which divides it, the Rimac. In Quechua, Rimac means "river that speaks." This combination of a strong Spanish influence with a rich indigenous heritage has shaped Peru's traditions, politics, and culture.

Peru's political history in the 20th century has been characterized by swings from democracy to military dictatorship. Most recently, a leftist military government, the result of a military coup on 27 August 1976, instituted an economic program that promoted agricultural cooperatives, expropriated foreign companies, and decreed worker participation in modern industry. A return to democracy in 1980 lasted until 1992 when a democratically elected president, Alberto Fujimori, closed down the Congress, implemented martial law, and ruled as a dictator. Fujimori successfully battled two of Peru's greatest ills, inflation and terrorism, and after reopening Congress, was reelected with popular support on 19 April 1995.

² LOCATION AND HOMELAND

Three times the size of California, Peru has an extremely varied geography ranging from tropical rain forest to arid desert. With Ecuador and Bolivia, it is one of the three Andean countries on the Pacific coast of South America. Peru can be conveniently divided into three basic geographical areas. The *sierra,* or Andes mountains, which covers 27% of Peru's land area, is the home not only to domesticated llamas and alpacas, but also to the majority of Peru's population of 24 million people. On the Pacific coast is one of the world's driest deserts. The capital city of Lima is located on the coastal desert, making access to water problematic for its nearly 8 million residents. In sharp contrast, areas of the Amazon rain forest in the north and east of Peru receive a massive 190 to 320 cm (75–125 in) of rain annually. The tropical rain forest covers 67% of Peru's landmass but is rapidly being destroyed by logging companies.

Peru's population of 24,523,408 people can be subdivided into four groups: white, 15%; mestizo or mixed-blood, 37%; indigenous, 45% (*see* **Quechua**); and black and Asian, 3%. The Quechua and the Aymara constitute the two main Amerindian tribes. Many Amerindians are illiterate and speak only their native language and no Spanish. Ethnic identity in Peru, however, tends to be culturally defined. For example, if an Amerindian speaks Spanish and adopts Western dress, he or she may be considered a mestizo or *cholo.* Although the percentage of the population that is indigenous is not declining, Peru's culture is becoming increasingly *mestijado;* that is, a mix of Western and traditional customs.

³ LANGUAGE

The two official languages of Peru are Spanish and Quechua. Quechua, the language of the Incas which is still widely spoken throughout the Andes, was made an official language by the military government of 1968–1975. The dominant language in urban areas, however, is Spanish. Although there are some vernacular differences between the Spanish spoken in Spain and in Peru, the primary difference is the accent.

In Peru, as in other Hispanic countries, names comprise three parts: the given name, the father's surname, and the mother's maiden name. For example: Pedro (given name) Suárez (father's name) Durán (mother's name).

⁴ FOLKLORE

Many of the beliefs and practices that comprise Peruvian folklore are associated with the native faith and customs that prevailed before the arrival of the Spanish conquerors. For example, the Incas believed that they descended from the Sun God, Inti, and that the reigning Inca was an offspring of the Sun. Though they did not practice human sacrifice, many were headhunters. The Incas believed that the possession of another's head increased the owner's spiritual strength. While headhunting no longer exists, a blending of Indian and European beliefs often persists in current festivals and other observances. In Pacaroztambo, 30 November—St. Andrew's Day—signals the close of the planting season. Eight crosses taken from the churches are set up on the mountains that overlook the fields to protect the crops from natural disasters. They remain there until 3 May (Cruz Velakuy), the beginning of the harvest. There is one cross for each of the four *ayllus* (the basic unit of Inca society) of the two *moieties* (the two main divisions of the tribe). The latter take turns preparing the annual celebration.

At San Pedro de Casta, *La fiesta del agua* takes place the first Sunday in October. The gates of the principal river, the Carhuaymac, are opened to fill the irrigation ditches which have been cleaned and repaired. Close to La Toma, the river gate, is a cave in which the God of the Water, Pariapunko, lives. The head of the festival goes into the cave bearing gifts of coca, cigarettes, and *chicha* beer. He begs the god to favor the community with the water it needs.

⁵ RELIGION

Peruvians are fervent Catholics. Catholics comprise 90% of the population. No Peruvian town, no matter how small or remote, is complete without a church. As with many Andean customs, their religious practices carefully intertwine modern and traditional beliefs. The Peruvian version of Catholicism, for example, has incorporated some of the traditional gods and spirits by referring to them as saints or lords. In fact, when the Spanish converted the Amerindians to Christianity, they moved many of the Christian holidays to coincide with existing traditional festivals. In so doing, many traditional festivals continue to be practiced, with minor modifications, within the Christian framework. It is also considered appropriate in Peru for a Christian to make the sign of the cross while walking or driving by a church.

⁶ MAJOR HOLIDAYS

One of the most colorful festivals is the month-long celebration of the Lord of the Earthquakes in October. Peru is subject to

constant tremors and earthquakes, and in the past many of its cities have been severely damaged by them. In October, a weekly procession through the streets of Lima features a painting of Christ that has survived successive quakes, trailed by throngs of followers dressed in purple robes. Strict Catholics will dress in purple on these days, whether they are able to attend the procession or not.

A secular holiday that is of great importance to Peruvians is their Independence Day, *28 de Julio,* or 28 July. This occasion is celebrated with much festivity—dancing, eating, and drinking. On this day, all homes are obligated by law to fly the Peruvian flag. As late as 1966, there were more than 150 holidays including Sundays.

7 RITES OF PASSAGE

Baptism of infants, First Communion, and confirmation of children in church are common. Perhaps half of all couples live together without regularizing their unions with a license or a church ceremony. A birthday may not necessarily be celebrated; the person's namesake saint's day is likely to be observed instead. A novena (nine consecutive days of special prayers) for the dead is usually held in the home of the deceased, with friends invited on the final night. Often a second novena is held later.

8 INTERPERSONAL RELATIONS

It is poor manners to arrive on time if invited to a dinner or a party. Tardiness of an hour or more is expected. If hosts expect

the guests to arrive more promptly, they will ask them to observe *hora inglesa* (English time). When being introduced to a woman at a social occasion, the proper greeting is a kiss on the cheek. Men, when introduced to each other, will shake hands.

At an informal gathering, when a group of friends are drinking together, it is a sign of friendship to share the same glass. When a large bottle of beer or *pisco* (a Peruvian alcoholic beverage) is opened, the bottle and glass are passed around in a circle. One is expected to serve oneself a small serving, drink it quickly, then pass both the bottle and glass to the next person. To ask for a separate glass would give offense.

The "okay" sign (touching your finger to your thumb) is considered a rude gesture in Peru.

9 LIVING CONDITIONS

Approximately one-third of the entire Peruvian population lives in Lima. Of the nearly 8 million residents of Lima, over half live in urban squatter settlements, known as *pueblos jóvenes* (young towns). Migration to Lima from the Andean region drives the development of pueblos jóvenes. Uninhabited land is selected and invaded by a group of settlers overnight. The initial housing is usually made out of light reed matting. More-permanent structures are built gradually, bit by bit as the family can afford to buy bricks and mortar. The vast majority of dwellings in the pueblos jóvenes are still under construction years after the initial incursion into the area.

In addition to poor housing, residents of the pueblos jóvenes suffer from a lack of basic services. While the majority now have electricity in their houses, water is scarce. Most homes have a large water tank behind the house, which the residents fill with water purchased from water trucks. These unsanitary conditions create serious health hazards. Restricted access to safe water puts children and the elderly at high risk for gastrointestinal infections. The largest killer of infants in Peru continues to be one of the most easily treated ailments: diarrhea. In 1991, a cholera epidemic swept the country, killing nearly 3,000 people.

The residents of the modern suburbs of Lima have living standards comparable to those found in the US. Suburban houses range from high-rise apartments to grand colonial houses. In periods of drought, however, even these sectors have their water and electricity rationed by the municipality.

Men have an average life expectancy of 64 years; women, of 68 years.

10 FAMILY LIFE

In countries without a welfare system or social security system, the family bonds together not only as a social unit, but as an economic one as well. The basic household unit includes parents, children, and, in many cases, grandparents or aunts and uncles. In middle-class households, it may also include a live-in servant or nanny to look after young children. This small extended family group shares household chores and tasks, and those who are able generate income for the family. Financial difficulties mean that children live at home until they get married as young adults.

The bonds within families are also supplemented by bonds between families. *Compadrazgo* (Godparenthood) is an important tie between friends and forges bonds of obligation between two families. Godparents are expected not only to

Most Peruvians don Western clothes for both everyday and special occasions. One useful custom that is often retained, however, is the use of a shawl across the shoulders to carry small children. (Sally Keener)

contribute a modest amount of financial support for the Godchild, but to provide emotional support and guidance to the family. These interfamily social arrangements expand a family's support network.

Although *machismo,* an attitude of male superiority and sexism, is widespread, Peruvian women are neither meek nor shy and participate actively in important family decisions. Women play an active role both in family and community life. In the urban squatter settlements, or *pueblos jóvenes,* women often take a leading role in community organizations that lobby the municipality or provide services to the community. They also make significant contributions to family income.

11 CLOTHING

In Andean areas, women wear colorful woven skirts with many layers of petticoats underneath. Solid-colored llama wool sweaters offer protection against the cold Andean night air. Hats are used throughout Peru. Each region has its own style of hat, and it is possible to tell which region an Amerindian is from by his or her hat. Men wear simple trousers and Western-style button-down shirts, and sandals.

As the process of urbanization in Peru has advanced, so has the process of Westernization. Most Peruvians don Western clothes for both everyday and special occasions. Young Peruvians in urban areas prefer jeans, American tennis shoes, and

Western-style skirts over the traditional alpaca and llama wool clothes worn in the Andean regions. Upon arrival in Lima, most migrants abandon the use of their traditional clothes in favor of tee-shirts and skirts. One useful custom that is often retained, however, is the use of a shawl across the shoulders to carry small children.

12 FOOD

Peru has one of the most developed cuisines of Latin America. Many dishes are a delicate combination of indigenous, Spanish, and African ingredients and cooking traditions. Seafood is the dominant ingredient on the coast, yucca and plantains in the jungle, and potatoes in the Andes. In fact, the potato originates in Peru, and there are over 100 varieties still being grown in the Andes.

The national dish of Peru is *ceviche,* a spicy dish of onions and seafood. In ceviche, the fish is cooked not by applying heat but by soaking it for a few hours in lime juice. The acid in the lime juice has the effect of breaking down the protein, thus "cooking" the fish. Sliced onion, hot peppers, and chopped coriander are then added. Ceviche is purported to have beneficial effects on hangovers. It is customary for partygoers to eat ceviche at dawn.

The high cost of living has led many mothers living in low-income neighborhoods to organize and form communal kitchens. These groups, now recognized by the government, receive subsidized food and cook for 100 or so people for a small fee. Most of Lima's shantytowns, or *pueblos jóvenes,* will have communal kitchens, organized and operated by the residents themselves. It has been estimated that 1.5 million people in Lima alone rely on these kitchens for affordable meals.

13 EDUCATION

Children are obligated to attend school. Peruvian children, dressed in solid gray uniforms, attend either the morning session or the afternoon/evening period. The literacy rate in Peru is relatively high, reaching 92% for males and 79% for females.

The relatively small number of universities in Peru means that it can be difficult to gain admission. Only 3% of the population is able to attend university. An informal rite of passage common in Lima is for friends to tackle a successful male entrant—and shave his head!

The Peruvian army, because of its dedication to civic action, has worked to counteract illiteracy, especially prevalent among its Amerindian draftees. Measures are taken to teach inductees to read and write. During the final three months of service, the draftee undergoes special training to provide him with a trade.

14 CULTURAL HERITAGE

The different ethnic groups that have migrated to Peru have left a rich musical heritage. Both *musica criolla* of Spanish influence and Andean folk music are popular. A traditional music, recently becoming popular with young Peruvians, is Afro-Peruvian music. This rhythmic music has its roots in the protest songs of the Black population of Peru. The cultural center of Afro-Peruvian music is the town of Chincha, on the Pacific coast south of Lima. In the 1980s and 1990s, Afro-Peruvian music has witnessed a strong revival and is now popular in the bars and dance halls of Lima. Musical shows for tourists feature the *Alcatraz,* a traditional Afro-Peruvian fire dance. Alc-

The basic household unit includes parents, children, and, in many cases, grandparents or aunts and uncles. (Cory Langley)

atraz dancers tuck a piece of paper into their back pockets or around their waist, leaving a short tail hanging out. A second dancer follows behind with a lit candle trying to set the tail on fire. The first dancer must move his or her hips vigorously to prevent the paper tail from catching fire. Other dances include *el Zapateo,* in which intricate footsteps on hard wood are used as percussion.

Peru also has a strong literary tradition. Available in English translation is José María Arguedas' novel about life in the Andes entitled *Yawar Fiesta,* as well as the writings of poet Cesar Vallejo, whose masterpiece is *Trilce.* One of the most revered contemporary writers in Peru is the novelist Mario Vargas Llosa. Vargas Llosa is known worldwide both for his writings and for his bid for the presidency in 1990. His comic autobiographical narrative, *Aunt Julia and the Script Writer,* was recently made into a Hollywood movie starring Keanu Reeves. Other outstanding writers include the novelist Ciro Alegría, dramatists Salvador Bandy and Gregór Díaz, and poets Cecilia Bustamante and Cesar Moro.

15 WORK

Formal paid employment is difficult to find in Peru. Most families are forced to seek varied and innovative means to generate an income, struggling to earn a living by whatever means possible. Approximately 80% of the population are either subsistence farmers or operate their own tiny enterprise. Both women and children make important contributions to family income, either from small-scale cottage industries in their homes, or as traders outside the home. Common economic activities include part-time tailoring, kerosene sales, food processing, or even charging neighbors for watching one's TV. Children may contribute by selling goods on the street or through activities such as collecting tin cans. Even if the father is working, most families will be involved in a multitude of economic activities. Other economic survival strategies include labor for labor swaps with neighbors, or raising chickens for family consumption.

Outside urban areas, Peruvians are largely subsistence farmers. The dry Andean terrain makes agriculture a challenge. Steep slopes are farmed by a process of terracing, in which multileveled steps are created to provide flat areas for planting. Potatoes and corn, which adapt well to high altitudes, are the primary crops.

16 SPORTS

As in most other Latin American cultures, soccer is the dominant sport in Peru. The love of soccer is one of the few cultural traits that transcends both ethnic and socioeconomic boundaries. Even in densely populated urban shantytowns, large pieces of land are often set aside for a soccer field. Middle class children set up goals and play in the streets.

Lima's two soccer teams, Alianza Lima and Universitaria, have an intense rivalry that has kept *Limeños* (residents of Lima) fascinated for years. This rivalry has a particular poignancy. In 1987 the plane carrying the members of Alianza Lima crashed when landing in Lima, leaving no survivors.

17 ENTERTAINMENT AND RECREATION

Popular culture in Peru is varied. In the evenings, young people flock to both Western-style bars and discos, or to *peñas* where traditional Peruvian folk music is played. In Lima, an old colonial suburb of the city called *Barranco* has become the focus of trendy and artsy activities. A variety of music halls, theaters, book shops, and art galleries attract crowds of middle-class youth.

Also popular in Peru are televised soap operas. Produced largely in Venezuela or Mexico, these evening shows attract a vast following. Soap operas are also produced in magazine format. *Fotonovelas,* as they are called, present soap operas with a series of photos and captions. Fotonovelas are the reading material of choice of many in the *pueblos jóvenes* (urban shantytowns).

18 FOLK ART, CRAFTS, AND HOBBIES

See the article on the **Quechua** in this volume.

19 SOCIAL PROBLEMS

Peru has one of the worst human rights records in the world. The Peruvian government has been battling the Maoist Shining Path guerrillas since the early 1980s. In its battle to eliminate this violent terrorist group, the military has kidnapped and killed many suspected Shining Path sympathizers. Trade union officials, university professors, and students have all been targeted by the government. The military has been successful in weakening the Shining Path movement, but human rights abuses remain a serious problem.

20 BIBLIOGRAPHY

Lobo, Susan. *A House of My Own: Social Organization in the Squatter Settlements of Lima, Peru.* Tucson, AZ: University of Arizona Press, 1982.

Jenkins, Dilwyn. *Peru: The Real Guide.* New York: Prentice Hall, 1985.

MacDonald, Margaret, ed. *Folklore of World Holidays.* Detroit: Gale Research, 1992.

—by C. Sahley, reviewed by F. Colecchia

POLISH AMERICANS

For more information on Polish history and culture, *see* **Vol. 3: Poles**.

OVERVIEW

Polish settlers helped establish the Jamestown colony in Virginia in the early 1600s. Polish adventurers and radicals came across the sea to help the American colonists win the Revolutionary War (1775–83), including heroes Tadeusz Kosciuszko (1746–1817), who later returned to the US to serve as liaison between President Thomas Jefferson and leaders of the French Revolution and Count Kazimierz Pulaski (1747-1779), sometimes called the "father of the American cavalry," who was killed in the battle of Savannah, Georgia. Since then, millions of people from Poland have immigrated to the US.

When Poland was partitioned in the 1770s between Russia, Austria, and Prussia, members of the Polish upper class chose to escape the new oppressive governments. Many came to America. So many came, in fact, that Polish America became known as the "Fourth Province" of Poland, the other three being those areas controlled by Russia, Austria, and Prussia, respectively. (Another term for the Polish community outside of Poland is "Polonia.") A few groups of peasant farmers also came to America, looking for better economic opportunities. They set up Polish farming communities in places like Panna Maria, Texas, the first permanent Polish community in America, founded in 1854.

Polish immigration from the 1770s to about 1870 is sometimes referred to as the "first wave," but more often, the first wave is considered to have begun in 1870 when Polish serfs were given their freedom. The US also began encouraging immigration to help rebuild the country after the devastation of the American Civil War (1861–65). Up to two million Poles immigrated to the US between 1870 and 1914, when the beginning of World War I brought immigration to a halt.

Most Polish immigrants in this first large wave of immigration, also called the "old emigration," were single young men looking for the chance to work at wage-earning jobs, save up their money, and return to Poland. Some 30% actually did return to Poland, but the rest stayed in the US. As uneducated (though generally literate) peasant farmers, they were unskilled and unprepared for the industrialized world of America. They took whatever jobs they could find, working in mines, mills, factories, slaughterhouses, refineries, and foundries. Once established in their new home, many sent for their families or returned to Poland to marry, then brought their wives back to the US with them. Women and children went to work then to support the family.

The second wave, or "new emigration," of Polish Americans came to the US under the Displaced Persons Act of 1948, which allowed Europeans who had been displaced by the destruction of World War II to enter the US as immigrants. These second-wave Polish Americans tended to be well-educated intellectuals, the writers, artists, and scholars who had been targeted by the Nazis for elimination. A number of them were Jewish (*see* **Vol. 2: Jewish Americans**). The new emigration added depth to the already established Polish American community.

In the 1960s and 1970s, "Polack" jokes became popular in the US, portraying Polish and Polish American people as stupid, crude, and lazy. The Polish American community fought back with a campaign showing the great achievements of Polish writers and scholars, etc., but the discrimination continued. Even Ronald Reagan, while running for President in 1980, told "Polack" jokes to a group of reporters. When the Solidarity movement took off in Poland, however, Americans were drawn into sympathy with the revolutionary Poles, and "Polack" jokes died out. First-generation Polish Americans were allowed to vote in the 1990 Polish presidential elections, and they helped bring Lech Walesa, leader of the Solidarity movement, into office.

A third wave of Polish immigration to the US has begun recently, though it is small in number. Like first-wave immigrants, these are mostly young men hoping to find better economic opportunities in America so that they can save up their money and return home to Poland.

Today, some eight million Americans claim Polish ancestry. Early immigrants generally settled in the industrial cities of the Northeast and Midwest, such as Cleveland and Toledo, Ohio; South Bend, Indiana; Wilkes-Barre, Hazleton, and Pittsburgh, Pennsylvania; Milwaukee, Wisconsin; Minneapolis–St. Paul, Minnesota; Omaha, Nebraska; St. Louis, Missouri; Chicago, Illinois; Detroit, Michigan; and Buffalo and New York City, New York. Few of the old purely Polish neighborhoods still exist (excepting Greenpoint, in Brooklyn, New York, which continues to attract new Polish immigrants), but many of the cities of early settlement still host large Polish American populations:

Chicago	800,000
Detroit	515,000
New York	480,000
Philadelphia	290,000
Buffalo	230,000
Pittsburgh	215,000
Milwaukee	200,000
Cleveland	68,000

Los Angeles also has a fair-sized Polish American population today at 170,000.

The Polish American community has been in the US for several generations, and traditional Polish ways are being lost by later generations. Polish language proficiency is limited or nonexistent among third- and subsequent-generation Polish Americans. Some first- and second-generation Polish Americans lament that their children speak Spanish or some other language learned in school better than they speak Polish.

Many Polish Americans chose to shorten or otherwise Americanize their names in order to blend in better with the mainstream society when they first arrived. Immigration officials simplified others' names on their entry papers because they either could not understand the actual name or did not care to write it out. In today's climate of multiculturalism and ethnic pride, some young Polish Americans are reclaiming their true Polish names.

Nearly all Polish Americans are either Catholic or Jewish. When Polish Catholics arrived in America, they found the Roman Catholic churches controlled by Irish Catholics who had arrived earlier. The Irish Catholics did not welcome the

newcomers, and Polish Americans began establishing their own churches whenever and wherever possible. In 1896, a number of Polish Americans decided to separate from the Roman Catholic church entirely and formed the Polish National Catholic Church (PNCC) instead. The PNCC is very similar to the Roman Catholic Church in all but two important ways: PNCC priests are allowed to marry, and church officials are *elected*, rather than appointed.

Polish Americans celebrate the holidays and rites of passage common to their tradition, be it Catholic or Jewish. Many Polish American Catholics continue to hold the traditional Polish Christmas Eve feast called *Wigilia*, and sing *koledy*—Polish Christmas carols. A secular holiday celebrated by all Polish Americans is 3 May, commemorating the Polish Constitution of 1791, the first democratic constitution in all of Europe.

Polish Americans continue to hold to the traditional Polish values of hard work and tenacity, good manners, and generosity. They are also competitive within their personal community, striving to achieve higher status (usually by means of material goods) than those around them. However, Polish Americans are also very loyal to their community, so the competition is good-natured, even joyful. The people of Poland learned to be wary of change after centuries of upheaval and constant shifts in governmental oppressors. Polish Americans carry on that wariness, placing a high value on security, stability, respectability, and order. For this reason, as well as religious convictions, the divorce rate is quite low among Polish Americans as compared to other ethnic groups in the US.

Polish Americans have contributed a great deal to American culture. Kielbasa (Polish sausage), pierogi, Polish dill pickles, sauerkraut, Polish ham, and babka (an egg-dough cake) are all fairly common items in the American diet. Vodka, originated by the Polish, not the Russians, is now the favorite liquor in the US. Polish American writers, musicians, actors and directors, and even fashion designers (Oleg Cassini and Helena Rubinstein) have all made a serious impact on US society.

Writer Czeslaw Milosz won the Nobel Prize for literature in 1980. Other successful Polish American writers include Isaac Bashevis Singer, Jerzy Kosinski, and playwright Janusz Glowacki. The first well-known Polish American film actor was silent-screen star Pola Negri (credited with introducing painted toenails to American women). She was followed by Gloria Swanson, Loretta Swit, Stephanie Powers, and Charles (Buchinsky) Bronson, among others. Producer/director/screenwriter Joseph L. Mankiewicz is another important figure in American film, as are producer Samuel Goldwyn; producer/director Roman Polanski; the founders of Warner Brothers Studio, Harry, Albert, and Jack Warner; and filmmakers Zbigniew Rybczynski and Agnieszka Holland.

Polka music is probably the best-known contribution Polish Americans have made to American culture. Many individual Polish Americans have also made significant contributions to the world of music, including pianists Liberace and Arthur Rubinstein; orchestral conductors Leopold Stokowski and Arthur Rodzinski; singers Bobby Vinton, Pat (Andrzejewski) Benatar, and Huey Lewis; drummer Gene Krupa; and jazz violinist Michal Urbaniak.

In the world of industry, Joseph "Jock" Yablonski was a strong force in the United Mine Workers union. He ran for president of the union in 1969 but lost. While appealing the decision, he was assassinated, along with his wife and daughter. More recently, Martha (Kostyra) Stewart, home economics maven, has become enormously popular. Her books and magazine are highly successful, and she made numerous appearances on morning and afternoon talk shows. In the 1990s she starred in her own television show.

Polish Americans are well represented in the US government. Edmund Muskie served as a US senator for a number of years, then ran unsuccessfully for US vice-president, with presidential candidate Hubert Humphrey in 1968. He later served as the US Secretary of State during Jimmy Carter's presidency. Another Polish American, Zbigniew Brzezinski, also served in Carter's administration, as National Security Advisor. Other Polish American politicians include US Senators Barbara Mikulski and Frank Murkowski, and former Chair of the House Ways and Means Committee, Dan Rostenkowski.

A form of baseball was probably introduced to America by Polish settlers in the Jamestown colony in the early 1600s. Baseball remained Polish Americans' favorite sport for many generations. In the 1870s Oscar Bielaski was the first Polish American to play professional baseball. When the National League was formed in 1876, Bielaski joined the Chicago White Stockings (as they were then named). Men's baseball stars since that time include Stan "the Man" Musial, Carl Yastrzemski, and Dave Dombrowski. Sophie Kurys, Loretta (Jasczak) Jester, Connie Wisniewski, and Jenny Romatowski were among the stars of the short-lived women's professional baseball league.

Two Polish Americans have won the Heisman Trophy for college football: Johnny Lujack and Leon Hart. Ron Jaworski, Bill Romanowski, Alex Wojciechowicz, Bill Osmanski, and Ed Danowski are all successful professional football players. Wayne Gretzky is considered by some to be the best hockey player ever to take the ice. Ed Olczyk is another well-respected hockey player. Janet Lynn found great success on the ice as a figure skater.

Polish American culture is celebrated at several Polish American festivals, usually held in the summer. The parades, feasts, and polka music are enjoyed by Polish and non-Polish Americans alike. Few Americans are aware that October is Polish American Heritage Month. Polish American organizations are trying to increase awareness of Polish American heritage among the general American public as well as among younger generations of Polish Americans, many of whom have lost touch with their traditional culture.

BIBLIOGRAPHY

Dolan, Sean. *The Polish Americans*. New York: Chelsea House, 1997.

Gabor, Al. *Polish Americans*. New York: Marshall Cavendish, 1995.

Lopata, Helena Znaniecka. "The Polish American Family." *Ethnic Families in America: Patterns and Variations*, 3rd ed., Charles H. Mindel, Robert W. Habenstein, and Roosevelt Wright, Jr., ed. New York: Elsevier Science Publishing, 1988.

Obidinski, Eugene. "Proclaiming Polish Praises." *Polish-American Journal* 84, no. 11 (1 November 1995): 3.

Smigielski, John J. "Saving My Roots." *Polish-American Journal* 84, no. 6 (1 June 1995): 3.

Tarapacki, Tom. "Chasing the American Dream." *Polish-American Journal* 85, no. 2 (1 February 1996): 7.

PUERTO RICAN AMERICANS

For more information on Puerto Rican history and culture, *see* **Vol. 2: Puerto Ricans**.

OVERVIEW

A few Puerto Rican political exiles from the unsuccessful attempt to overthrow Spanish rule emigrated to the US in the late 19th century, but large-scale Puerto Rican immigration to the US mainland did not begin until the early 1900s. Puerto Rico became a US territory in 1898 when the US defeated Spain in the Spanish-American War, making it fairly easy (legally speaking) for Puerto Ricans to immigrate to the US. The rate of immigration was slow at first, however, because transportation by ship was too expensive for most Puerto Ricans. By the time of World War I (1914–18), the number of Puerto Ricans arriving on the US mainland had risen sharply, despite the continuing high travel costs. This was due to conditions in both Puerto Rico and the US.

In Puerto Rico, improved health care and public health systems had caused a sudden population boom, resulting in high unemployment, overcrowding, and poverty. In the US, the war economy had created a surfeit of unskilled jobs. Many Puerto Ricans decided that the prospect of employment in the US was worth the cost of transportation. In 1917, citizens of Puerto Rico were granted US citizenship and were therefore exempt from the immigration quotas established in 1924 for other nationalities. Competition for jobs in the US decreased as the flow of other immigrants lessened, and Puerto Ricans rushed to fill the demand for unskilled laborers. Worsening economic conditions in Puerto Rico, combined with a series of natural disasters, drove the number of Puerto Rican immigrants to the US to an all-time high. By 1930, the Puerto Rican American population had reached approximately 53,000.

With the onset of the Great Depression in 1929, economic opportunities in the US decreased rapidly and it was no longer worth the cost for Puerto Ricans to relocate. Immigration consequently slowed considerably during the 1930s. US agriculturalists, however, were looking for cheap farm laborers in the 1930s, and a number of Puerto Ricans began to travel to the US mainland during the off-season of Puerto Rico's sugarcane industry (which was summer and fall harvest season in the US) to become migrant workers along the Atlantic coast. By 1940, Puerto Ricans made up a significant percentage of Atlantic coast migrant workers. The work was exhausting and paid very little, and living conditions were miserable, but many laborers felt it was better than being unemployed in Puerto Rico. After increasing protests by Americans over the terrible treatment of migrant farm workers, the US government passed laws in 1947 to improve their conditions. Although conditions did improve somewhat, the life of migrant farm workers and their families was still harsh (and continues to be so today).

When World War II began in 1939, sea transportation was suspended because of German submarine activity. Puerto Rican immigration to the US therefore ceased until the war ended in 1945. The second wave of Puerto Rican immigration, termed "the great migration" began as soon as the war was over and lasted through the mid–1960s. Air travel had become a very affordable option, and in the booming postwar economy in the US, unskilled jobs were plentiful. Puerto Rican immigration to the US mainland surged, peaking in the 1950s. By 1960, the Puerto Rican American population had risen to almost 900,000. Since the mid–1960s, Puerto Rican immigration has slowed somewhat, but the numbers of new arrivals each year are still significant.

It is difficult to determine the exact Puerto Rican American population because there is a high rate of travel between Puerto Rico and the US mainland. It is impossible to know who is immigrating on a permanent basis, who is coming on a trial basis, and who is just visiting family and friends or traveling on business. There are no official immigration records because Puerto Ricans are US citizens and cross the border freely, and US Census figures are only approximate because not all Puerto Ricans report themselves as "Puerto Rican." Some place themselves in the catch-all categories of "Latin American," or "Hispanic," etc. The *estimated* Puerto Rican American population, therefore, is somewhere around 2,700,000.

About 95% of Puerto Rican Americans are urban, concentrated in the larger cities of New York, New Jersey, Illinois, Florida, California, Pennsylvania, Connecticut, and Massachusetts. Half of all Puerto Rican Americans live in New York City, giving it the highest Puerto Rican American population in the US. In fact, in 1970 New York City's Puerto Rican population was higher than that of San Juan, the capital of Puerto Rico and the country's largest city. By 1980, the numbers had reversed, but New York City continues to have the second highest Puerto Rican population in the world. Many Puerto Rican Americans in New York City call themselves *Nuyoricans*. In the US, Puerto Rican Americans are the second largest Hispanic group, after Mexican Americans. Their population is very young, with 45% under 20 years old.

At the time of the "great migration," many US cities had just begun to implement public housing systems in which people were randomly assigned housing in public housing projects throughout the city. Puerto Ricans, therefore, were scattered across neighborhoods. They were not able to develop the same sort of ethnic communities in which other earlier immigrants had found comfort and support. Despite these public housing systems, however, Puerto Rican Americans did manage to congregate in certain areas, especially in New York City. The stretch along East 116th Street has been called *El Barrio* ("the Neighborhood"), or Spanish Harlem, since the 1930s because of the heavy concentration of Puerto Rican Americans who live there.

In New York City and other places in the US with large Hispanic American populations, signs and other public information are written in both English and Spanish. Puerto Rican Americans still encounter a language barrier, however, because English is the standard language of American business and education. Most Puerto Rican Americans continue to speak Spanish at home and with their friends, making it more difficult for them to become fluent in English. Bilingual education programs have been instituted in some elementary schools to help Puerto Rican and other Hispanic American children succeed, but many still fail. The drop-out rate among Puerto Rican American high school students was as high as 75% in the 1970s and 1980s. Though more Puerto Rican American students are finishing high school today, the percentage of those who drop out is still among the highest of any ethnic group in America.

Puerto Ricans have two surnames: the father's family name, followed by the mother's family name. In Puerto Rico, both names are usually used when addressing someone, but if only one name is used, it is the father's. To avoid confusion in the US, many Puerto Rican Americans drop their mother's family name altogether.

Most Puerto Rican Americans (80%) are Roman Catholic. However, Puerto Rican Catholicism is quite different from mainline American Catholicism. When the Spanish introduced Catholicism to Puerto Rico in the 1500s, the Puerto Ricans simply blended Christian teachings and rituals with their previous beliefs, creating a magical religion of saints and spirits. When Puerto Rican Catholics began to immigrate to the US, they found Irish, Italian, and German Catholic churches that were quite strange to them. They were never allowed to establish their own ethnic parishes (as the Italians and Germans were), so they struggled to maintain their particular brand of religion at home while attending the unfamiliar European churches. Eventually, European Catholics moved on to better neighborhoods, and the parishes became predominantly Puerto Rican American. The language of church services shifted to Spanish, and traditional Puerto Rican rites and festivals began to be celebrated, such as Three Kings Day (or Epiphany) on 6 January, and *Fiesta de San Juan* (The Feast of St. John the Baptist) on 24 June.

The influence of Hispanic Americans on the Roman Catholic Church in America is finally being felt. In 1972, there was only one Hispanic bishop in the US. By 1990, there were 21 Hispanic bishops and 2 Hispanic archbishops. Three Kings Day and the Fiesta de San Juan are celebrated each year in many cities with huge festivals, fairs, processionals, and fireworks. *Bótanicas*, shops that sell charms, incense, herbs, magic potions, candles, and *santos* (homemade statuettes of religious figures), are found in every Puerto Rican American neighborhood.

Not all Puerto Rican Americans are Catholic, however. About 20% are Protestant, with the largest share belonging to the Pentecostal Church and other evangelical denominations. There are also Baptists, Methodists, Lutherans, and Episcopalians. Some Puerto Rican Americans choose to follow various combinations of spiritualism and folk religion, such as *Mesa Blanca, Santería, Brujería,* and *Curandera.* A number of Puerto Rican Americans follow both Christianity and a spiritualist folk religion.

Family is very important to Puerto Ricans, and immigration has always been in whole family groups. Puerto Rican families are typically large, and Puerto Rican Americans in New York City continue to have the largest families of all city residents. A high percentage of Puerto Rican American families are headed by single females (almost 44% in New York City), many of whom are on welfare. Puerto Rican Americans have the highest poverty rate (37% overall; 57% of children under 18) among Hispanic Americans. This is partly due to their young average age, which is a result of the high number of children per family.

Despite their relative poverty and poor performance in school, many individual Puerto Rican Americans have found success in the US. Puerto Rican American contributors to the world of American arts include actors Rita Moreno, Freddie Prinze, Erik Estrada, Liz Torres, Jimmy Smits, Esai Morales,

Roxann Biggs-Dawson, Raul Julia, José Ferrer, and Chita Moreno; television personalities Geraldo Rivera and Vanna White; and film director Leon Ichaso.

Salsa music has become popular with the wider American public. Some individual Puerto Rican American contributors to the world of music are opera singer Justino Díaz; singer-guitarist José Feliciano; pop singers Tony Orlando and Julian; rappers Lisa M and Vico-C; the teen singing group Menudo; bandleader and percussionist Tito Puente; violinist José Figueroa; jazz trombonist Juan Tizol; and jazz flutist Dave Valentin.

Well-known Puerto Rican American visual artists include Dennis Mario Rivera, Roberto Lebrón, Ramón Carrasquillo, Rafael Ferrer, and Wilfred Labrosa. Ballet artists Brunhilda Ruiz, Tina Ramirez, and Edward Villella are all Puerto Rican American. Many Puerto Rican American writers have found success, including René Marqués, Piri Thomas, Jesús Colón, Miguel Algarín, J. L. Torres, Ed Vega, Judith Ortíz-Cofer, Nicholasa Mohr, Pablo Guzmán, and David Hernández.

Though voter registration and turnout among Puerto Rican Americans is consistently low, preventing them from becoming a significant voice in the political scene, Puerto Rican Americans have managed to make a mark in US politics. Herman Badillo became the first Puerto Rican American in the US Congress when he was elected to the House of Representatives from New York City in 1970 and Dr. Antonia Novello was appointed US surgeon general by President George Bush in 1990.

Sports is perhaps where Puerto Rican Americans have become best known among the wider American public. Golfer Juan A. "Chi Chi" Rodriguez and horse jockey Angel Cordero are famous in their arenas. Boxers Sixto Escobar and Carlos Ortiz, tennis player GiGi Fernández, and Olympic swimmer Chayenne Vasallo have also been highly successful. The sport with the most Puerto Rican American success stories, however, is baseball. Roberto Clemente, Orlando Manuel Cepeda, Ruben Sierra, Sandy Alomar, Sr., Sandy Alomar, Jr., Roberto Alomar, Joey Cora, Carlos Baerga, Juan Gonzalez, Bernie Williams, José Santiago, Edgar Martinez, Carlos Delgado, and José Valentin are all stars of the game.

One of the biggest contributions that Puerto Rican Americans could make to American culture is a new attitude towards race. In Puerto Rico, centuries of interracial marriage have led to a kaleidoscope of skin colors and facial features. Social structure in Puerto Rico is therefore not based as strictly on race as it is in the US. "Black" and "White" as rigid categories do not exist in Puerto Rico. Perhaps as Puerto Rican Americans become a larger part of American society, those categories will be erased in the US as well.

BIBLIOGRAPHY

Aliotta, Jerome J. *The Puerto Ricans*. New York: Chelsea House, 1996.

Jensen, Jeffrey. *Hispanic Americans Struggle for Equality.* Vero Beach, FL: Rourke Corporation, 1992.

Press, Petra. *Puerto Ricans*. Tarrytown, NY: Benchmark Books, 1996.

PUERTO RICANS

LOCATION: Puerto Rico
POPULATION: 3.8 million in Puerto Rico; 2.7 million on US mainland
LANGUAGE: Spanish; English
RELIGION: Christian (mostly Roman Catholic); Santeria

¹ INTRODUCTION

Known as "the isle of enchantment," Puerto Rico is a densely-populated island in the Caribbean. Currently a commonwealth of the United States, "Bori(n)quen," as the native Arawark (Taino) Indians called it (and locals still affectionately refer to it), was discovered and claimed for Spain by Columbus during his second voyage in 1493. Columbus renamed the island San Juan Bautista (St. John the Baptist), from which the island's capital, San Juan, takes its name. "Puerto Rico," the name given to it by Ponce de Leon (a 16th century settler and seeker of the Fountain of Youth), means "rich port."

The Spanish brought African slaves to the island starting in 1518, just a few years after they had introduced sugarcane. By the end of 16th century, most of the native population had disappeared. The Spanish fought off a number of attacks from the British, the French, and the Dutch, but they never had to contend with a war of independence as they did in other colonies. Following the Spanish-American War, Spain ceded Puerto Rico to the US in 1898. Under the Jones Act of 1917, all Puerto Ricans were made citizens of the United States. In 1948, Puerto Ricans for the first time elected their own governor, Luis Munoz Marin. Munoz Marin introduced "Operation Bootstrap," a plan to improve the island's economy by attracting industry through tax incentives and low labor costs. In 1952 the island became a commonwealth of the United States. As a commonwealth, Puerto Rico's residents have the same rights, privileges, and obligations as other US citizens but pay no federal income tax and lack voting representation in Congress and the right to participate in presidential elections.

In 1993, residents voted to remain a commonwealth (48.6% of the vote) versus becoming the 51st state to join the union (46.3%) or obtaining full independence (4.4%).

Today, more than 3.8 million Puerto Ricans inhabit the island. Another 2.7 million Puerto Ricans live on the US mainland, many in New York City. Puerto Ricans in New York City often refer to themselves as "Nuyoricans."

² LOCATION AND HOMELAND

Approximately 1,609 km (1,000 mi) east-southeast of Miami, Florida, Puerto Rico (160 km or 100 mi long and 51 km or 32 mi wide) offers beaches, mountains, and urban areas. It is in the urban areas where most of its nearly 4 million inhabitants are found. The capital, San Juan, is home to nearly 0.5 million residents. The next-largest municipality, Bayamon, boasts about half as many dwellers. In addition to the main island, Puerto Rico also consists of several smaller islands, including Culebra, Mona, and Vieques.

Puerto Rico enjoys a subtropical marine climate with an annual mean temperature of 24°C (75°F). Puerto Rico is a popular beach resort and is one of the world's busiest cruise ship ports. Unfortunately, the island is often in the path of hurricanes. In 1989, Hurricane Hugo brought much damage.

Unique to the island is the Coqui, a tiny frog that sings "co-kee." Its likeness, however, is sure to be found the world over on tee-shirts, hats, and other souvenirs.

³LANGUAGE

Puerto Ricans speak both Spanish and English, but predominantly Spanish. In 1991, Governor Rafael Hernandez Colon signed a law making Spanish the only official language. Two years later, his successor, Pedro Rossello, restored English as an official language. The Spanish spoken in Puerto Rico (or any other former Spanish colony) is as different from the Spanish spoken in Spain as American English is different from the English spoken in England—that is to say, different, but still the same language.

"Spanglish," a mix of English and Spanish, can sometimes be heard on the island but is most often spoken in Puerto Rican communities on the US mainland.

In Puerto Rico names are traditionally composed of three parts: first (given) name, father's surname, and mother's maiden name; for example, Juan Gomez Lopez.

⁴FOLKLORE

Puerto Rican folklore, with origins in Taino, Spanish, and African traditions, deals mostly with stories of demons who roam the island after dark, seeking food or people, or protecting gold stashed by pirates. Other tales give an account of hurricanes and the damage they cause.

The legend of "El Chupacabras" (The Goat Sucker) spread throughout Puerto Rico in the early 1990s. "Chupa" is said to be a panther-like creature that stands on its hind legs and hops around like a kangaroo. It has claws on its appendages and plumage down its back. Some believe that the creature, which leaves behind bloodless animal carcasses with surgically precise incisions, may be a space alien. Others believe it is the work of satanic cults.

⁵RELIGION

Most Puerto Ricans are Christian, mainly Roman Catholic. Santeria, the religion introduced by the African slaves, is also prevalent.

⁶MAJOR HOLIDAYS

While every town has its own feast honoring a patron saint, the main festivities occur on San Juan Bautista Day. At midnight celebrants dip their fully clothed bodies in water in order to bring themselves good luck.

Puerto Ricans also celebrate American holidays such as the Fourth of July and Memorial Day. Christmas celebrations take place on 25 December (as is done on the mainland) and on 6 January, Three Kings Day (as is traditional). During the Christmas season, Puerto Ricans carry out what is called an *asalto* ("assault"). Celebrants go from house to house, singing songs called *aquinaldos*. Members of each household then join in and move to the next house.

⁷RITES OF PASSAGE

The rites of passage in Puerto Rico are mainly those of the Catholic Church. Soon after a child is born it is baptized, and

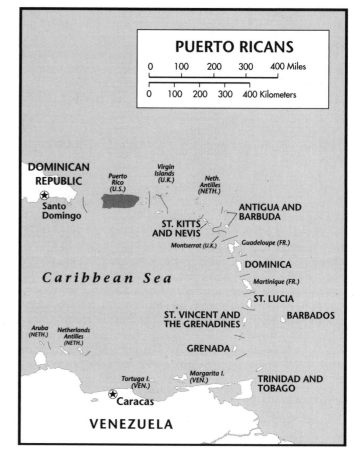

great emphasis is often placed on the *padrinos* (godparents). First Holy Communion is cause for great celebration. Death is mourned in much the same way as on the US mainland.

⁸INTERPERSONAL RELATIONS

Puerto Ricans, like many other peoples of the Caribbean, are characterized as being warm, open, and friendly—they will give you the shirt off their back.

⁹LIVING CONDITIONS

Puerto Ricans enjoy a standard of living that is among the highest in the Caribbean. Health care on the island has continued to improve since the 1940s. The majority of Puerto Ricans have cars. Puerto Rico ranks sixth among all nations in cars per person. While per capita income for Puerto Ricans is higher than that of other Caribbean nations, it is much lower than that of any of the 50 US states.

¹⁰FAMILY LIFE

The extended-family setting prevails over that of the nuclear family. The role of Puerto Rican women is similar to that of women on the US mainland, minus 10 years of progress in the feminist movement.

¹¹CLOTHING

The *guayabera,* an embroidered man's shirt, is considered a traditional, elegant article of clothing and is still worn today in both formal and informal settings. For everyday purposes, however, people tend to wear casual attire.

12 FOOD

"Fondas," small, cafeteria-like restaurants on the island, are popular eateries for locals and tourists alike looking for generous portions at reasonable prices. *Arroz con gandules* (rice with pigeon peas) is a typical Puerto Rican dish. *Pasteles* are tamales made from plantains and stuffed with meat. In large cities, like San Juan, one can find most of the same fast-food chains found on the US mainland.

Like many other Latin Americans, Puerto Ricans typically have a simple breakfast; the most common breakfast is *cafe con leche* (coffee—usually espresso—with milk). If one happens to visit a family at dinnertime, they are likely to insist that the visitor stay and eat. To refuse may be considered impolite.

Puerto Rico is known for its rum. The Bacardi family, which moved the center of its production from Cuba to Puerto Rico in the 1930s, is the world's largest producer of rum.

Like many of the Caribbean people, Puerto Ricans are known for their sweet tooth. Most desserts employ ingredients that are grown right on the island. Below is a simple recipe for something called *Polvo de Amor* ("love powder").

Love Powder

1 coconut
1 pound of sugar

Open the coconut and extract the milk. Grate the meat. Mix with sugar and cook in a kettle. Stir for 5 minutes on a high flame. Reduce heat and stir for an additional 10 minutes. Serve crisp and golden brown.

13 EDUCATION

Some 90% of the island's population is literate. The government spends more money on education than on any other sector. The University of Puerto Rico provides higher education at several campuses throughout the island.

14 CULTURAL HERITAGE

Puerto Rican culture has strong roots in Spanish and African traditions. Nowhere are those traditions more visible than in its popular music. Like other Spanish-speaking nations, salsa is the music of choice for Puerto Ricans. It blends elements of Spanish music with African rhythms.

The *Decima* (literally, "tenth") is a poetic form of traditional Puerto Rican music in which the *Jibaro* (peasant farmer) expresses his hopes, dreams, and letdowns. The decima is usually improvised.

In the world of classical music, Puerto Rico boasts cellist Pablo Casals. Born in Spain in 1876 of a Puerto Rican mother, Casals is recognized the world over as one of the finest classical musicians of all time. He founded the Puerto Rican Symphony Orchestra, the Conservatory of Music, and the Festival Casals, a series of classical music concerts held in mid-June. Casals, who passed away at the age of 97 in 1973, is considered a national hero.

Other notable Puerto Rican "exports" in the arts include Raul Julia, Tito Puente, Jose Ferrer, Rita Moreno, Chita Rivera, and Jose Feliciano. Feliciano and his music embody the Puerto Rican spirit and its American influences. A true crossover artist, Feliciano is as acclaimed for his English-language recordings as for those in Spanish. One of his better-known works, "Feliz Navidad," is a bilingual piece which has become a holiday classic.

Of all the Puerto Rican painters, none has gained greater acclaim than Jose Campeche. Campeche lived during the late 18th century and spent all of his life in San Juan. He was the son of a freed slave and an immigrant from the Canary Islands. The artist is renowned for his masterful religious works. Francisco Oller, born in 1833, demonstrated a European influence in his works. Oller applied the impressionist style to scenes depicting plantations, palm trees, and other local sights.

In literature, poet Francisco de Ayerra y Santa Maria and Latin scholar Alonso Ramirez stand out as notable contributors from the time of the conquistadors. The 19th century brought noted poets such as Lola Rodrigues de Tio, Jose Gautier Benitez, and Jose Gualberto Padilla ("El Caribe"). That same era featured distinguished writers such as Salvador Brau, Eugenio Maria Hostos, and Alejandro Tapia y Rivera. The 20th century has been marked by works that deal with Puerto Rico's relationship with the United States. Poets and writers include Jose de Diego, Evaristo Ribera Chevremont, Antonio Pedreira, Enrique A. Laguerre, Pedro Juan Soto, and Rene Marques.

15 WORK

Puerto Rico is strong in commerce, finance, tourism, and communications. The labor force of more than 1 million is divided almost equally among services, government, commerce, and manufacturing. Puerto Rico is the world's largest producer of pharmaceuticals. The island's gross national product (GNP) is by far the largest in the Caribbean, and one of the largest in Latin America. The "siesta" is becoming a thing of the past, as more and more businesses adopt a "nine-to-five" mentality.

16 SPORTS

As in other Spanish-speaking Caribbean islands, baseball reigns supreme above all other sports in Puerto Rico—both as a participatory and as a spectator sport. Professional baseball is played by teams in the Caribbean League. Often players from the US major leagues will also play in the Caribbean League. Roberto Clemente, who played in the major leagues with the Pittsburgh Pirates in the 1960s and 1970s, is arguably one of the finest athletes Puerto Rico has ever produced, and one of the best players of the game. Tragically, Clemente died at the height of his career in an airplane accident while performing charity work.

Other notable Puerto Rican athletes include jockey Angel Cordero, tennis player "Gigi" Fernandez, and golfer "Chi Chi" Rodriguez.

17 ENTERTAINMENT AND RECREATION

Like others in the Caribbean, Puerto Ricans cherish baseball, basketball, and a good game of dominoes. Highly controversial, cockfighting remains of great interest. To pass the time, people read, listen to one or more of the over 100 radio stations, or watch any of a half-dozen TV stations. On weekends, high school and college students frequent dance clubs and bars.

[18] FOLK ART, CRAFTS, AND HOBBIES

Carved religious figures called *santos* (saints) have been produced for more than 400 years on the island of Puerto Rico. *Mundillos* (tattered fabrics) is a lace craft that is equally old and equally popular. Musical artisans in Puerto Rico make *cuatros* (four-stringed guitars). Other craftspeople make *caretas,* festive masks (made of papier-mâché) in the shape of animal or devil heads, used during the Lenten season.

[19] SOCIAL PROBLEMS

Puerto Rico is not immune to the problems of racial and sexual discrimination that plague the world. Large, densely populated cities like San Juan suffer the same social and criminal problems as do other large, densely populated cities on the mainland—AIDS, drugs, theft, unemployment, and violent crimes. The annual murder rate on the island is approaching 900. In response, many of the wealthier neighborhoods have barricaded themselves with electronic gates.

[20] BIBLIOGRAPHY

Carrion, Arturo Morales, ed. *Puerto Rico: A Political and Cultural History.* New York: W. W. Norton, 1983.

Gordon, Raoul. *Puerto Rican Culture: An Introduction.* New York: Gordon Books, 1982.

Luxner, Larry, and Ani Luxner. *Insight Pocket Guide: Puerto Rico.* Hong Kong: APA Publications, 1994.

Wagenheim, Kal, and Olga Jimenez de Wagenheim, ed. *The Puerto Ricans: A Documentary History.* Princeton: Markus Weiner Publishing, 1993.

—by L. Gonzalez, reviewed by T. Morin

QUECHUA

LOCATION: Peru; Ecuador; Bolivia (Central Andes regions)
POPULATION: About 7.5 million
LANGUAGE: Quechua
RELIGION: Combination of pre-Columbian and Roman Catholic elements

[1] INTRODUCTION

The Quechua Indians of the central Andes are the direct descendants of the Incas. The Inca Empire, which existed for a century before the arrival of the Spanish, was a highly developed civilization. The Inca Empire stretched from parts of present-day Colombia in the north, southward into Chile. The Incas had an impressive governing structure. The government imposed tribute and taxes on the population which were exacted in the form of labor and in crops. Vast warehouses were used to store food which was then distributed in times of famine. The Incas also had an immense army, used to continuously expand the empire and conquer new peoples.

The Spanish conquistadors arrived in South America in the early 1500s. When they arrived, the Inca king had already succumbed to the many European diseases that preceded the conquistadors. The Incas were in a state of civil war when Spanish forces arrived. After the Spanish captured the new Inca king, Atahualpa, the Incas suffered a swift defeat.

Peru attained independence from the Spanish in 1821. Modern-day Peru has struggled to modernize, plagued by problems of hyperinflation, poor governments, and terrorism. Most Quechua still live in the Andean highlands, relying on subsistence agriculture and pastoralism as did their Inca ancestors.

[2] LOCATION AND HOMELAND

Quechua Indians still live in the areas once governed by the Inca Empire in Peru, Ecuador, and Bolivia. At least one-third of Peru's 23 million inhabitants are Quechua Indians, still living as subsistence farmers throughout the Andes. The geographical conditions between regions differ dramatically. In mountain valleys there is rich soil and access to water that is suitable for farming. Most Quechua, however, live on the stark, steep slopes of the central Andes. Here the soil is poor, the wind strong, and the weather cold.

Migration and urbanization in the past few decades have drawn many Quechua to Lima, the capital city of Peru, where there is now a large indigenous and Mestizo (mixed-race) population.

[3] LANGUAGE

The Quechua language is known by its speaker as *Runa Simi,* or the language of the people. Today the term *quechua* refers more to the language than to a concrete ethnic group. In this sense, the Quechua extend throughout all the territory where Quechua is spoken, including a number of ethnic groups that speak Quechua and whose original language has disappeared. In the colonial chronicles, the term is used to refer to an ethnic group, whose original homeland is hard to determine. They seem to have inhabited the region of northwest Peru and to have expanded southward to the Andean region of Ecuador until they reached Peru. The diffusion of the Quechua language stems from Inca politics, continued throughout the colonial period, that gave Quechua a superior status to the other languages spoken in the Andes.

The Quechua language was the administrative language of the Inca state. Today it is spoken by nearly 8 million people in Peru alone, 1–2 million in Ecuador, and 1 million in Bolivia. Quechua words that have been assimilated into the English language include *puma, condor, llama,* and *coca.* Unlike most other native South American languages, Quechua is an official language of Peru, accorded the same status as Spanish. Although it is unusual, senators and congresspersons can give speeches in the Peruvian Congress in Quechua. The present Bolivian vice-president, Hugo Cárdenas, gave his acceptance speech in Spanish, Quechua, and Aymara.

4 FOLKLORE

The myth of Incarrí perhaps reveals the most about the feelings of the vanquished Inca. After the conquest of Peru in 1532, the Inca rulers retreated from Cuzco to Vilcabamba, where they resisted the Spanish invasion for nearly 50 years. In 1579 the last rebel Inca, Tupac Amaru, was captured and beheaded by the Spanish. The Spaniards stuck his head on a pike and placed it in the plaza of Cuzco as a warning to the rebels. The head disappeared, and they say that it is buried. The myth tells that it is slowly growing its body back and when the body is complete, the Incas will return to rule their land.

Many of the ancient Quechua myths are still preserved in their oral tradition. Most of them narrate the origin of different ethnic groups, or of mountains, rivers, and lakes.

5 RELIGION

Quechua religion combines both pre-Columbian and Catholic elements. The most significant pre-Columbian influence that endures is the belief in supernatural forces that govern everyday events, such as weather and illness. The continued belief in supernatural powers controlling rain, harvests, earthquakes, and the like serves a utilitarian purpose to the agricultural Quechua. By making offerings to the powers that control natural forces, the Quechua feel that they can influence events and not merely be helpless in the face of bad weather or disease. When drinking alcohol, for example, it is customary to first offer a drink to Mother Earth, Pachamama. The first sip of beer or wine is spilled on the ground, out of respect for Pachamama.

This religious Andean world is populated by gods who have human attributes, like love and hate—sometimes they love each other and other times they hate and fight each other. For this reason, the Andean religion has two dimensions in the lives of the people: first, in human terms to promote social cohesion; and second, in transcendental terms to relate gods and humans.

Despite the continued importance of pre-Columbian rituals, the Quechua have adopted the Catholic calendar of festivals. This calendar has been integrated into the pre-Columbian agricultural timetable. The festival of Carnival, for example, marks both the beginning of Lent and the planting season. Catholic symbols, as well, have dual meanings. The cross, introduced by the Catholic Church, not only symbolizes Christianity and Christ but is used to symbolize the *Womanize* (mountain deities) in some rituals, and fertility in other rites. The Quechua, therefore, have not merely adopted Christianity but have incorporated it into their indigenous beliefs.

6 MAJOR HOLIDAYS

While the Quechua celebrate important Catholic holidays such as Christmas and Easter, they have not abandoned their ancient holidays. In the ancient Inca capital of Cuzco, the Inca Sun Festival is still celebrated. The Inti Raymi festival, as it is called, draws thousands of tourists from all over the world to witness its spectacular festivities. Donning replicas of Inca tunics, rather than contemporary Andean garb, Quechua Indians reenact the Inca sun-worshiping ceremony. The Inti Raymi festival, which celebrates the June solstice, reflects the Inca's vast knowledge of astronomy. On this occasion, there is much eating, drinking, and dancing. True to Inca traditions, a llama is also sacrificed on this day.

7 RITES OF PASSAGE

Major life transitions, such as birth, puberty, and death, are marked by rituals and celebrations that combine Catholic and indigenous traditions.

8 INTERPERSONAL RELATIONS

Courtship and marriage involve a lengthy series of rituals and stages. Most unmarried youths meet (and flirt) during one of the community's many festivals. When a young couple decides that they are ready to consider marriage, the family of the bride is visited by the family of the prospective groom. The groom himself stays home while his parents and godparents discuss the wedding and negotiate what each family will donate to the newlyweds. The engagement is made official at a later date when the bride and groom exchange rosaries. At the wedding, there is a public procession as the bride leaves her home to join her husband's *ayllu* or community. Various other rituals, including fertility rites, follow the wedding.

⁹ LIVING CONDITIONS

The dominant building material throughout most of the Andes is adobe. Adobe has the advantages of being highly durable, free, and widely available. Adobe can be made almost year-round with the rich Andean soil. Roofs are now more often made of tiles, rather than of the traditional thatched material used in the past. House-building is a communal affair, based on the ancient Inca system of labor exchange known as *mita*. Neighbors will be offered *chicha* beer, cigarettes, and food in return for their help in the construction of a new home. In exchange, those who participated in the house-building are owed labor which they can claim at any time.

Although the Peruvian government has made efforts to decentralize its health care services, the quality of health care in rural communities is still extremely poor. Most remote communities have no access to medical care, and even those villages that do have a public health center receive little more than basic first aid. Given the cold, damp conditions, respiratory illnesses are the major cause of illness and death among the Quechua. Although vaccination rates are gradually increasing, infectious diseases such as measles and whooping cough are still frequent causes of death. Given the absence of good medical care provided by the state, most Quechua first turn to a *curandero* (literally, "curer") who provides herbal medicines and treatment.

¹⁰ FAMILY LIFE

Children in Quechua society play many important roles. From a very young age they participate in economic activities and in performing key household tasks. Children are highly valued by the Quechua, and childless couples are sometimes considered to be social outcasts. As in most other subsistence economies, children are essential as they are expected to provide long-term economic security to their parents as they age. However, limited access to birth control makes it difficult to limit family size. While an optimum family size is considered by many Quechua to be 3 or 4 children, many families have up to 10 or more children. Generally, male children are more highly valued than females, as their economic potential is seen to be greater.

It is difficult to generalize about the role of women in Quechua society. Women clearly play a subordinate role compared to men in the community political structure. Women are less likely to receive a formal education, do not hold significant positions of power within the community, and are excluded from many potentially profitable economic activities. A clear sexual division of labor exists with regard to both agricultural and household tasks. Women's role in the family, however, is more ambiguous. Women do have a say in family matters, such as decisions about finances or issues surrounding the upbringing of the children. However, there is little evidence to suggest that they are free from subordination in family life as well.

¹¹ CLOTHING

Traditional Andean clothing reflects strong Spanish influences. In 1572, the Spanish prohibited the Quechua from wearing native Inca tunics and wrap-around dresses. Andean peoples then adopted the clothing still in use today. Quechua women wear skirts and blouses, with colorful woven shawls around their shoulders. Men wear trousers, shirts, and woven ponchos. Sandals are the preferred footwear for both men and women.

The style and color of clothing worn by Quechua Indians does vary dramatically from region to region. The Otavalo of Ecuador, an important subgroup of the Quechua, have a very distinctive dress. They wear white trousers and shirts, covered by a solid black poncho. Otavalo men are also famed for their long black braids.

¹² FOOD

The potato was first domesticated in Peru approximately 4,500 years ago. The potato and quinoa grain remain as two of the main staples of the Quechua diet. Common dishes include meat or potato stews, spiced with hot peppers, coriander, or peanuts. For community feasts, a *pachamanca,* or underground oven, is occasionally used. Taking up to four days to prepare, a hole is dug in the ground, lined with bricks or rocks, then layered with hot coals. Potatoes, meat, beans, and corn are placed in the ground, covered, and left to cook slowly. The pachamanca is particularly common in the central Andes of Peru.

Also considered a delicacy is guinea pig. The preferred dish for festivals, guinea pigs are often raised in the house and provide a productive use for kitchen scraps and discarded food. The use of guinea pigs as an important source of protein predates the Incas.

¹³ EDUCATION

Formal education in Peru is required until the age of 16. In rural areas, however, the percentage of students who finish their schooling is much lower than in urban areas. This is, in part, because children play a valuable role in household and agricultural tasks and their labor cannot be spared. The schooling received is generally very poor. Teaching methods are based on rote memorization rather than teaching children problem-solving skills. Personal initiative is rarely encouraged, and teachers generally have low expectations of what their students can achieve. A further problem emerges for Quechua children, as Spanish is the primary language taught at schools.

¹⁴ CULTURAL HERITAGE

The characteristic music of the central Andes is called *huayno*. The mountain origins of huaynos are reflected in their lyrics that recount daily life in mountain villages and proclaim Andean nationalism. Traditional instruments still widely used for this lively form of music include drums, flutes, and the *charrango,* a mandolin-style guitar made from an armadillo shell. Many huayno singers have been given recording contracts and are increasingly popular in urban areas.

Quechua folk music also includes beautiful, haunting pan-pipe music. One of these songs, *El Condor Pasa,* was recorded by Simon and Garfunkel in the 1960s and was a hit record.

As the Incas did not write, there is not a tradition of Quechua literature. In 20th-century Peru, however, there has emerged a tradition of *indigenista* writers that focus on the life of the indigenous peoples of the Andes. Jose Maria Arguedas, Cesar Vallejo, and Ciro Alegría have written influential books that portray the oppression of the Quechua throughout the centuries and chronicle their hard life in the Andes. These authors have contributed to a growing Andean nationalism and pride.

15 WORK

Most Quechua rely on subsistence farming for their livelihood. Corn, potatoes, and grains are crops that have adapted to the high-altitude environment. Land is still farmed using the Inca method of terracing on steep slopes. This labor-intensive approach to agriculture absorbs a tremendous amount of time, leaving little time to dedicate to other economic activities.

Trade is highly developed between different villages and regions. In addition to agricultural products, many communities produce pottery, textiles, belts, hats, and other handicrafts for cash sales. In most communities, there is a weekly market day, which plays an important role in the economic and social fabric of the village. Most farmers bring their surplus goods, produce, or livestock to sell at the market. The vast majority of petty vendors throughout the Andes are women.

16 SPORTS

The Quechua, as part of a Mestizo society, participate in many of the manifestations of Western culture. Although there are no definite Quechua sports, the Quechua participate in a variety of Western sports, such as soccer.

17 ENTERTAINMENT AND RECREATION

Socializing is the primary form of recreation in Quechua society. The Quechua celebrate a great many religious festivals, national holidays, and birthdays. Parties and festivals are events that are eagerly anticipated and require many weeks of planning. Many festivals, in fact, involve up to eight days of drinking, feasting, and dancing.

18 FOLK ART, CRAFTS, AND HOBBIES

The most significant handicraft produced by the Quechua are textiles. Women throughout the Andes can be seen spinning wool almost all day, even while they are sitting at the market or waiting for a bus. Both llama and sheep wool are used. The "belt loom" still in use by the Quechua dates back to pre-Columbian eras. The Quechua are skilled weavers, and their products are increasingly in demand for the tourist and export markets.

19 SOCIAL PROBLEMS

Male drunkenness is a serious social problem throughout the central Andes. Drinking alcoholic beverages is not only an accepted behavior at the Quechua's many festivals and parties, it is also an expected behavior. Alongside feasting and dancing, becoming drunk is a core part of most social occasions. Unfortunately, this behavior often spills over into daily life. Excessive male drinking is common, and this has a negative impact on both family relations and family finances. Spousal abuse is a common result of alcoholism.

20 BIBLIOGRAPHY

Doughty, Paul. *Hueylas: An Andean District in Search of Progress.* Ithaca, NY: Cornell University Press, 1968.

Isbell, Billie Jean. *To Defend Ourselves: Ecology and Ritual in an Andean Village.* Prospect Heights, IL: Waveland Press, 1978.

Kennet, Frances. *Ethnic Dress: A Comprehensive Guide to the Folk Costume of the World.* New York: Facts on File, 1995.

Moss, Joyce, and George Wilson. *Peoples of the World: Latin Americans.* London and Detroit: Gale Research, 1989.

Rycroft, W. Stanley. *Indians of the High Andes.* New York: Committee and Cooperation in Latin America, 1946.

—by C. Sahley, reviewed by V. Salles-Reese

RUSSIAN AMERICANS

For more information on Russian history and culture, *see* **Vol. 4: Russians**.

OVERVIEW

The term "Russian Americans" is somewhat confusing because it can be used to refer either to ethnic Russian immigrants or to immigrants from any of the former soviets of the Soviet Union (including Ukraine, Latvia, Lithuania, etc.). In this article, Russian Americans will be used to refer only to ethnic Russian immigrants. Russian Jewish immigrants will be mentioned in this article, but they are discussed in more detail in the article on Jewish Americans.

Most Russian American scholars and ethnic Russian Americans count three major waves of immigration to the US: The first wave happened just after the Russian Revolution of 1917–21, stretching from the 1920s into the 1930s; the second wave occurred after World War II, from 1945 until the early 1950s; and the third wave began in the 1970s and continues today. A sizeable number of immigrants came to the US from Russia before 1920, but they were of varied ethnic origins and so are discounted by most ethnic Russian Americans.

The very first Russians to set foot on the North American continent were fur traders from Siberia who traveled across the Bering Strait in the 1700s in search of game. They settled in Alaska and maintained a Russian colony there for a time. During the 18th and early 19th centuries, Russians from the middle class fled Russia to escape the oppressive government of that time, many emigrating to the US. In 1861 Russian peasants (or serfs) were given their freedom, and a host of them emigrated to America. Between 1861 and 1914, 9 out of 10 Russian immigrants to the US were peasants. Most were single young men, hoping to find employment and a better life in America. A few young women also came to the US to escape arranged marriages in their homeland. During this same time, a number of German–Russian Mennonites, Molokans (another religious sect), and Jews fled religious persecution in Russia and settled in America.

The "first" wave of Russian American immigration (according to scholars and ethnic Russian Americans) consisted largely of members of the Russian middle class and aristocracy who suddenly found their homeland inhospitable after the Communist Revolution of 1917. About 40,000 Russians came to the US in the first few years after the Revolution. When Stalin took over the Soviet government in 1930, he introduced strict regulations forbidding emigration. For the next 14 years, only 14,060 Russians managed to escape the Soviet Union and come to America.

Most of these "first"-wave Russian Americans were well-educated, skilled laborers or professionals. They had a much easier time acclimating to life in the industrialized US than did the peasants of earlier immigrations. However, first-wave Russian Americans met with a sudden surge of hostility from non-Russian Americans who suspected them of being Communists (called "Reds"). The "Red Scare" of 1919–20 drove many Russian Americans to hide their ethnicity. Some 3,000 Russian Americans were arrested and jailed as suspected Communists and, although most were soon released, a number were deported to the Soviet Union. In actuality, very few Russian Americans were Communist sympathizers. Most had in fact *fled* the Communist government.

The pressure to assimilate caused much of Russian culture and heritage to be lost by Russian American immigrants. Many Americanized their names, stopped speaking Russian, and adopted American customs. The same was true of the "second" wave of Russian American immigrants, who entered the US under the Displaced Persons Act of 1948. Europeans displaced by the destruction of World War II were allowed to immigrate to the US. Those Russians who immigrated encountered a second surge of anti-Communism in America, led by Senator Joseph McCarthy. Russian Americans again felt driven to hide their ethnicity and become "American" as soon as possible.

No one was allowed legally to leave the Soviet Union again until the 1960s and 1970s, when Russian Jews were permitted to emigrate to Israel. Some then moved to the US shortly after arriving in Israel. A handful of elite Russians, such as artists, scientists, and athletes, defected (illegally renounced their Soviet citizenship and requested residency in the US) while visiting America on Soviet-sponsored tours or exchanges. Stalin's own daughter, Svetlana Alliluyeva, defected to the US. Other defectors include ballet artists Rudolf Nureyev, Natalia Makarova, and Valery Jalina Banov; poet Joseph Brodsky; cellist and conductor Mstislav Rostropovich; and scientists Valery Chalidze and Chores Medvedev. However, the number of Russian immigrants, legal or illegal, was very small during these decades.

The "third" wave of Russian immigration to the US, beginning with Russian Jews in the early 1970s, picked up speed with the collapse of the Soviet Union in 1991. Since then, almost one million Russians have immigrated to the US. A majority of them are still Russian Jews, most of whom settle in New York City, but a number of other ethnic Russians are also making the trip across the globe in search of a better life.

The 1990 US Census counted 2,952,987 "Russian" Americans, but this includes many who are not ethnic Russians. The population of ethnic Russian Americans is estimated at about 750,000. Some 11% of the total census population of "Russian" Americans are foreign-born. The five US states with the highest numbers of "Russian" Americans, in descending order, are New York (596,875), California (447,752), Florida (232,298), New Jersey (229,449), and Pennsylvania (215,841).

The very first Russians in America, the Siberian fur traders, settled in Alaska. Russian immigrants who came between 1870 and 1920 tended to settle in large cities of the Northeast and Midwest, including New York City, Philadelphia, Chicago, Buffalo, and Detroit. Some Russians who fled to China after the Revolution in 1917 later fled persecutions in China, ending up in California. Some settled in the San Francisco area and others in Los Angeles. German–Russian Mennonites established farms in the Midwest, particularly in the states of Kansas, Nebraska, the Dakotas, and Minnesota. A religious sect known as the Molokans escaped persecution in Russia and moved to Los Angeles. Today, there are about 20,000 Molokans in California and a few thousand more in Oregon.

Most of the Russian immigrants who have arrived since the 1960s and '70s have settled in and around New York City. Brooklyn Beach in Brooklyn, New York, is one of the few Russian neighborhoods left in America. About 15,000–25,000 Russian-speakers live there. Some 110,000 Russian Americans

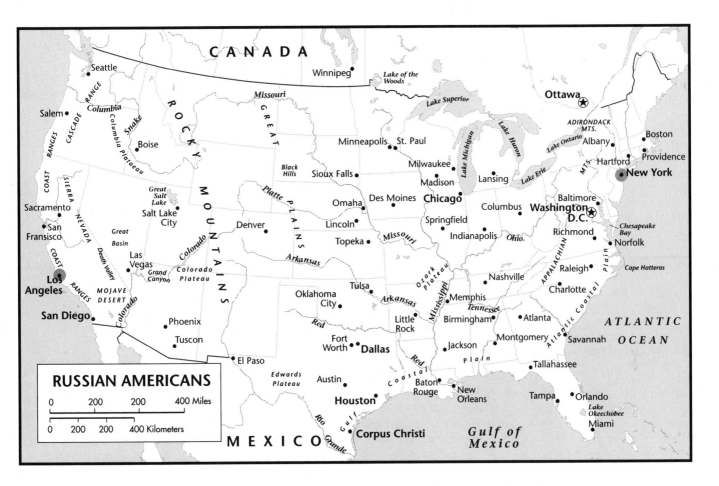

RUSSIAN AMERICANS

0   200   200   400 Miles

0   200   200   400 Kilometers

lived in San Francisco in 1990, the largest collection of Russian Americans in a single neighborhood in the US. Other small Russian American neighborhoods exist, but there are no real "Russiantowns" to speak of today, excepting Brooklyn Beach and the San Francisco Russian American community.

First-generation Russian Americans strive to learn English as quickly as possible in order to blend in with their American environment and enable themselves to get better jobs. Their children grow up speaking both English and Russian, but when they establish homes of their own, they speak only English. Therefore, by the third generation, most Russian Americans no longer speak Russian. The Orthodox Church in North America (OCNA), which began in Alaska in 1792, now uses English in its liturgy. Most Russian Americans, if they are not Jewish, belong to the OCNA. The more conservative Russian Orthodox Church in Exile (ROCE), which started in the former Yugoslavia in 1922 and spread to the US after World War II, uses only Russian in its liturgy. Traditionalists believe that the Russian language is the only thing that gives Russians their true identity and to lose it is to lose one's heritage.

The OCNA has about one million members. The much smaller ROCE has only 100,000 members. About half of the Russian American population is Jewish; a minority are Mennonite or belong to other Protestant denominations. A very small group of Russian Americans belong to the Old Believers sect of the Russian Orthodox Church, following the teachings of the Church prior to changes that were made in 1654. These Old Believers live in intentionally isolated communities in Alaska

and Oregon, speak only Russian, wear 17th-century clothing, and keep themselves separate from the rest of society.

Russian Americans celebrate the rites of passage and holidays common to their particular religious tradition, be it Jewish, Orthodox, Protestant, or Mennonite. They have also adopted traditional American holidays such as Thanksgiving and the Fourth of July. Most were not supporters of the Soviet government and so do not celebrate any Soviet holidays.

Russians love to party, however, so they find many occasions to celebrate together. Russian Americans are no less festive. Births, weddings, holy days, graduations, the purchase of a new home, new jobs, even funerals are all reasons to gather together and eat, drink, and be merry. Hospitality and generosity are highly valued by Russian Americans, and old-time traditions such as welcoming guests with a loaf of bread are still honored.

Russian families are traditionally very close and, though Americanizing influences have lessened the bonds somewhat, most Russian Americans are still closely tied to their families, particularly first- and second-generation immigrants. Elderly relatives are cared for at home, and women give birth at home. Young women often live with their parents until they marry, and sons tend to settle near their parents after marriage. Later-generation Russian Americans are more Americanized with a greater focus on individual nuclear family units.

Food is an important part of Russian Americans' ethnic identity, and many of their traditional foods have become common among the general American population. Mennonite farmers introduced hard wheat to American farmers, and it is now grown on many farms across the US. Chicken Kiev (batter-fried chicken breasts stuffed with butter and herbs), beef stroganoff (thinly sliced beef in sour cream sauce), and borscht (beet soup) are well-known to most Americans. Bagels, pumpernickel bread, sour cream, vodka, and lemon in tea are even better-known Russian additions to the American menu.

Russian Americans have made tremendous contributions to the cultural life of America as well. Russian folk music, played on the balalaika (a triangular guitar with a flat back, usually with three strings), and Russian folk dances are very popular with the general American population. Classical music and dance abound with Russian Americans, including composers Igor Stravinsky and Sergei Rachmaninoff; conductors Serge Koussevitsky, Mstislav Rostropovich, and Nicholas Sokomoff; violinists Isaac Stern, Yehudi Menuhin, and Mischa Elman; pianist Vladimir Horowitz; and ballet artists Michael Fokin, George Balanchine, Natalia Makarova, Valery Banov, Alexandra Danilova, Rudolf Nureyev, and Mikhail Barishnikov. Popular music composers Irving Berlin, Efram Zimbalist, Louis Gruenberg, and Dmitri Tiomkin also contributed greatly to American culture.

Russian American visual artists include Vitaly Komar and Alexander Melamid, who work together, and Louise Nevelson (Berliawsky). There are many highly successful Russian American writers, including Isaac Asimov, Aleksandr Solzhenitsyn, Joseph Brodsky, Ayn Rand, Saul Bellow, Vladimir Nabokov, and Irina Ratushinskaya. Director Konstantin Stanislavsky (founder of The Actors' Studio in New York City) made a tremendous impact on American theater and film, and actors Natalie Wood and Yaakov Smirnoff (a comedian) found success in film and television.

In the worlds of science and industry, Russian Americans have made countless contributions. Some noted examples are David Dubinsky, founder of the International Ladies Garment Workers' Union in 1900 (it has 175,000 members today); Vladimir Zwerykin, inventor of the tube that made television possible, and inventor of the electron microscope; Solman Waksman, who discovered the bacterium that causes tuberculosis; and George Gamow, who played a critical role in the development of nuclear fission technology.

For the most part, Russian Americans have successfully adapted to American life, suffering little overt discrimination excepting the two "Red Scare" eras. Perhaps the greatest problem Russian Americans face at this juncture is the rapid loss of their traditional culture. Americanization is quickly turning Russian Americans into merely "Americans," with little of their Russian heritage remaining. Some see this as a good thing; others grieve the loss.

BIBLIOGRAPHY

Ferry, Steven. *Russian Americans*. Tarrytown, NY: Benchmark Books/Marshall Cavendish, 1996.

Magosci, Paul R. *The Russian Americans*. New York: Chelsea House, 1996.

Salz, Marianna. "New Americans: A Tale of Three Cultures; Yours, Mine and Ours." *Jewish Exponent* 199, no. 3 (18 January 1996): 16.

US Bureau of the Census. *Detailed Ancestry Groups for States*. 1990 Census of Population Supplementary Reports, CP-S-1-2. Washington, DC, October 1992.

————. *The Foreign-Born Population in the United States*. 1990 CP-3-1. Washington, DC, July 1993.

ST. LUCIANS

PRONUNCIATION: (saint) LOO-shahns
LOCATION: St. Lucia
POPULATION: 140,000–151,000
LANGUAGE: English; French-based dialect with West African, English, and Spanish influences
RELIGION: Roman Catholicism; small groups of Anglicans, Methodists, Baptists, and Seventh-Day Adventists; Hinduism; Islam

¹ INTRODUCTION

St. Lucia (pronounced LOO-shah) is a nation in the Windward Islands with a distinctive mix of cultures. Its mostly Black population is descended from West African slaves who worked for both French and British plantation owners. Although the British, its final colonizers, ruled the island for 165 years without interruption, the island's previous history produced a culture that is pervasively French in many ways.

Although it was formerly thought that Christopher Columbus sighted St. Lucia on 13 December (St. Lucy's Day) in 1502, historians now believe that there is no real evidence for such a sighting. However, it was apparently seen and named by some explorer within the same time period because it appears under its present name on a 1520 Vatican map. In the 17th century, the English made two unsuccessful attempts to settle on the island. Following an agreement with the native Carib population in 1660, the French established a presence on the island. However, their claims were disputed by the British, and St. Lucia alternated between French and British control 14 times until 1814, when it became a British Crown Colony under the Treaty of Paris.

Although political control ultimately went to the British, the cultural influence of the French has persisted to the present day, reflected in the dominance of Catholicism among the population, the islanders' French-based patois (dialect), and such customs as its Flower Festivals. Sugarcane continued its previous dominance over the economy for some time, although the plantation owners were forced to modify their operations when the British abolished slavery in 1834. One consequence was the *meytage* system of sharecropping, devised to induce former slaves to continue working the land. Later in the 19th century, St. Lucia became a major shipping center for coal.

In the 20th century, the island reduced its dependence on sugar, whose volatile market made for an unstable economy, and expanded its production of bananas. Today, St. Lucia produces the largest banana crop in the Windward Islands. Throughout the century, the island gradually moved toward self-government, beginning with the establishment of a constitution in 1924. Universal adult suffrage was granted in 1951, and in 1958 St. Lucia joined the short-lived West Indies Federation. In 1967 full internal autonomy was achieved, and on 22 February 1979, St. Lucia became an independent state within the British Commonwealth.

On 10 September 1994, the island was struck by Tropical Storm Debbie, which inflicted greater damage than that caused by Hurricane Allen in 1980. Some 61 cm (24 in) of rain fell within seven hours, killing 4 people and injuring 24. The capital city of Roseau was flooded, a laboratory building located there was swept out to sea, and over two-thirds of the nation's banana crop was destroyed.

2 LOCATION AND HOMELAND

The second-largest of the Windward Islands, St. Lucia has an area of approximately 620 sq km (239 sq mi), between three and four times the size of Washington, DC. St. Lucia's geographical position between the former French colony of Martinique to the north and the former British colony of St. Vincent to the south parallels its dual historical exposure to the cultures of France and England.

The island is volcanically formed, and like neighboring St. Vincent, Martinique, and Dominica, it has a mountainous interior with lush rain forests. Its highest point, Mt. Gimie, in the southern half of the island, rises to 951 m (3,118 ft) above sea level, and the twin peaks of Gros Piton and Petit Piton on the southwest coast are prominent as well. Fertile plains that support the country's banana plantations are located at the base of the central mountains, and numerous rivers flow from the interior to the Caribbean.

St. Lucia's population is variously estimated at between 140,000 and around 151,000 people, almost evenly divided between urban and rural areas. The capital city of Castries had just under 52,000 people in 1991, and its current population is estimated at between 57,000 and 60,000. About 90% of the people on St. Lucia are of African or mixed descent. The remainder are European or East Indian. Overcrowding on the island due to high fertility rates has resulted in migration to neighboring Caribbean countries such as Trinidad and Guyana, or to the United States, Canada, and Britain.

3 LANGUAGE

Although the official language of St. Lucia is English, a majority of its people speak a patois (dialect) based on French and influenced by the grammar of West African languages, with a largely French vocabulary that includes words from English and Spanish. This language—which historically had no written form—was developed by French plantation owners and their African slaves before the British took final possession of the island in the 19th century and set about making English the national tongue. Today, English—in its most proper British style—is the language of the schools, government, and media, but patois prevails at home, on the streets, and at informal occasions. More than half of St. Lucia's residents are more comfortable with patois than English, and as many as 20%—especially elderly rural dwellers—speak little English or none at all. Some court cases are even tried in patois.

In recent years, greater recognition has been accorded to patois as a symbol of St. Lucian cultural identity. Cultural groups on the island even offer instruction in it. A written form has been developed for teaching purposes, and patois primers are available, including *Mwen Vin Wakonte Sa Ba'w* ("I am going to explain it to you") and *Se'kon Sa I Fèt* ("Know how it is done"). The Folk Research Centre in Castries has published a patois handbook and dictionary and a collection of folk tales and common expressions called *Annou Di-Y an Kweyol*. The name of St. Lucia in patois is "Sent Lisi."

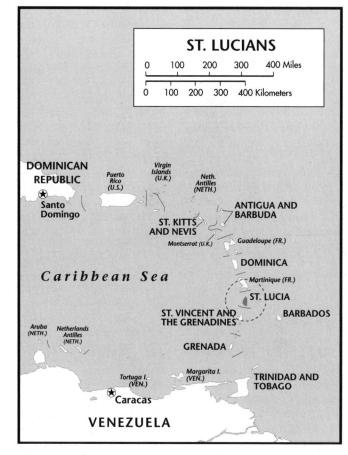

4 FOLKLORE

The African-derived quasi-religious belief system called *obeah* is practiced in St. Lucia, although it has been outlawed since the 1950s. Many of its practices are meant to ward off harm at the hands of various spirits, devils, and human beings. It is thought to be capable of healing the sick, harming one's enemies, and accomplishing more mundane goals such as "fixing" a court case. Its features include the preparation of herbal potions.

5 RELIGION

St. Lucia's French heritage is reflected in the fact that about 80% of the island's population is Roman Catholic, with smaller groups belonging to the Anglican, Methodist, Baptist, and Seventh-Day Adventist churches. The island's East Indians are either Hindu or Muslim. The Catholic population celebrates saints' days.

6 MAJOR HOLIDAYS

St. Lucia's public holidays include New Year's Day (1 January), Independence Day (22 February), Good Friday, Easter Monday, Labor Day (1 May), Queen's Official Birthday (5 June), Corpus Christi (6 June), August Bank Holiday (first Monday in August), Thanksgiving Day (first Monday in October), St. Lucia Day (13 December), Christmas (25 December), and Boxing Day (26 December). The annual Carnival celebration, a focus of many of the island's cultural activities, is held in Castries right before Shrove Tuesday and Ash Wednesday. The finals of the calypso competition and the naming of the Carnival King and Queen are held over the weekend, followed by the spirited street revels of J'Ouvert, which begin at 4:00 AM on Monday morning. The more orderly costumed bands parade on Monday and Tuesday.

A tradition unique to St. Lucia are its two competing flower festivals—held on the feast days of two saints—which grew out of the historical rivalry between France and Britain for control of the island. La Rose, the Feast of St. Rose of Lima, is held on August 30. Its counterpart, La Marguerite (the Feast of St. Margaret Mary Alacoque) occurs on October 17. Each festival, planned and staged by a special society, includes costumed parades and a "royal court" of kings and queens. Special songs called *belairs* are composed for the festivals by society members, and the evening of each festival is spent feasting and dancing traditional dances.

The National Day, St. Lucia Day on 13 December, is an important occasion. St. Lucia (St. Lucy), who is associated with light, is the island's patron saint—its motto is "the land, the people, the light." St. Lucia Day is marked by nationwide cultural and sporting events.

[7] RITES OF PASSAGE

Major life transitions are marked by religious ceremonies appropriate to each St. Lucian's particular faith community. For instance, Catholics hold funeral wakes on the first and eighth nights after a person's death. Mourners gather at the house of the deceased, providing coffee, sugar, and rum, and music is performed. The music played inside the house (generally hymns and gospel) is for the dead, while that played outside (drumming or unaccompanied songs) is meant to comfort the mourners.

[8] INTERPERSONAL RELATIONS

The distinction between English and patois has traditionally been linked to social standing. While English was historically the language of culture and education, patois implied a lack of status and sophistication, and it was once common for St. Lucians to hide their knowledge of it. Parents who harbored ambitions for their children would insist that they speak English, even at home. The 20% of the population who do not speak English are still excluded from full participation in the island's social, economic, and political life. However, the government has initiated outreach measures designed to bring that group fully into the mainstream. At the same time, there has been a revival of respect for patois as a symbol of cultural pride among St. Lucians.

Social relations in St. Lucia are strongly influenced by the overwhelmingly Roman Catholic religious affiliation of the island's inhabitants.

[9] LIVING CONDITIONS

Health conditions on St. Lucia improved substantially in the 1980s, with a decrease in infant mortality and an increase in average life expectancy, which stood at 72 years in the early 1990s. Free services provided by the health care system include both curative and preventive care, the latter including immunization, family planning, and nutrition programs. There are approximately 3,400 persons per physician, and most (70%) of

the country's urban dwellers had access to safe drinking water as of 1990. There are two major hospitals located near Castries and Vieux Fort. Other service providers include a network of clinics.

A 760-km (470-mi) road network links the island's villages, towns, and major residential areas, with the major cross-island route running from Castries in the northwest to Vieux Fort in the south. Local mass transit is provided by vans and minibuses, which are known as "transports." Rural dwellers often reach the nearest town or main road by footpath. Castries and Vieux Fort are the country's most important ports, with ferry links from Vieux Fort to St. Vincent and the Grenadines. Hewanorra International Airport accommodates jet aircraft, while the smaller Vigie Airport is used for flights to neighboring islands in the Caribbean.

An existing housing shortage due to overcrowding on the island—especially in urban areas—was worsened by damage from Tropical Storm Debbie in 1994.

[10] FAMILY LIFE

Couples in St. Lucia, as in other parts of the West Indies, are united in three basic types of relationships: legal marriage, unmarried cohabitation, and "visiting unions," where the man and woman live apart and the woman raises the children. Visiting unions are more likely to occur in early adulthood, while married relationships are more common later in life. The traditional nuclear family is mostly found among the upper classes, with female-headed families the norm at other levels of society. Many households are largely composed of different generations of women, and women have the major decision-making responsibilities. Children acquire a strong sense of responsibility toward their families from an early age and are expected to care for their parents as they age.

In rural areas, men and women do the same types of farm work, but women also take care of the majority of domestic chores and assume primary responsibility for child-rearing.

[11] CLOTHING

St. Lucians wear modern Western-style clothing. Some older women may still be seen in the traditional national costume consisting of a madras head-tie and a skirt with lace petticoats draped at the sides. Costumes are also worn at the Flower Festivals and the Carnival celebration.

[12] FOOD

Like its language, St. Lucia's cuisine combines the island's French and African heritages. It is based on the local produce and seafood catch, liberally spiced and prepared in clay pots heated by coals. The waters surrounding the island contain crab, tuna, dolphin fish, conch, flying fish, and snapper, while its tropical climate yields breadfruit, dasheen, green-skinned pumpkin and yam, avocado, coconut, guava, mango, and papaya. (Produce is generally available year-round). Favorite Caribbean dishes enjoyed on St. Lucia include fish soup, callaloo, and plantains prepared in many different ways. *Pouile Dudon* is a French-derived sweet-and-spicy chicken meal. The national dish is saltfish and green figs (a type of banana also known as "bluggoe").

Saltfish and Green Figs

¼ pound salted codfish
2 tablespoons vegetable oil
water
3 medium-sized green figs (unripe bananas)
1 small onion, finely chopped

Place the salted codfish into a bowl, breaking it into large chunks. Add water to cover and let soak for 12 hours, adding fresh water at least twice.

Cut the bananas into 2.5-cm (1-in) pieces and boil in about 2 cups of water, simmering about 15 minutes.

Boil the salted fish in 3 cups of water for 15 minutes, or until tender. Drain thoroughly, remove any remaining skin or bones, and shred or flake.

In a large skillet, sauté the fish together with the onion for about 5 minutes. Stir in the drained bananas and cook for 2 more minutes.

Optional: garnish with tomato or avocado slices, or celery sticks.

13 EDUCATION

Education on St. Lucia is free and compulsory between the ages of 5 and 15. The literacy rate of the adult population has been estimated at about 80%, a figure related to the fact that some 20% of the populace speaks only the French-based Lucian dialect, or patois. There are 83 primary schools and 13 secondary schools. In the 1980s only 6 of the nation's secondary schools offered schooling beyond the junior secondary level (equivalent to junior high school), sending many young people into the work force without having received a full education. Higher education is offered at Sir Arthur Lewis Community College and a branch of the University of the West Indies.

14 CULTURAL HERITAGE

Nobel-prize-winning poet and playwright Derek Wolcott was born in St. Lucia in 1930. Although he has long divided his time between Boston and Trinidad, where he founded a theater workshop, he has established an international writers' retreat called the Rat Island Foundation off the coast of his native land. Wolcott's works represent a fusion of the English language and literary tradition with Caribbean culture and folklore. Other St. Lucian writers include Walcott's twin brother, Roderick Walcott, novelist Garth St. Omer, and poet and short-story writer John Robert Lee.

In addition to Wolcott, St. Lucia has produced another Nobel- prize winner: economist Sir Arthur Lewis. The country's visual artists include Dunstan St. Omer, known for his religious paintings, and Llewellyn Xavier, the St. Lucia-born creator of Mail Art who has become involved in environmental conservation on the island in recent years. Modern dance has thrived on St. Lucia, and two of its best-known performers are Michael Francis and Carlton Ishmael.

In addition to the calypso and reggae music that are universally popular in the Caribbean, two other musical styles—zouk and cadance—are heard on French-influenced islands like St. Lucia. The St. Lucia International Jazz Festival has been held annually since 1992, with the dual goals of bringing top international performers to the island and encouraging local musicians. Festival participants have included such acclaimed artists as Herbie Hancock, Nancy Wilson, and Ramsey Lewis. The 1993 festival was attended by 6,000 people.

15 WORK

The cooperative labor ethos of St. Lucians extends from the family to the neighborhood *cou-de-main* tradition, where villagers organize themselves into work parties to help their neighbors with such tasks as building a new house or organizing a major family event such as a wedding. The majority of the work force is engaged in agriculture, with light manufacturing and a growing tourist industry employing most of the rest.

16 SPORTS

As is the case in other British-influenced Caribbean islands, cricket is very popular on St. Lucia, whose team competes regularly against the British team (which itself has a number of West Indian players).

17 ENTERTAINMENT AND RECREATION

Dancing is extremely popular on St. Lucia, and dances are held regularly, even in the smallest towns. In the 1980s, up to one-third of a popular radio news program broadcast in patois was devoted to dance announcements. Other favorite forms of recreation include beach parties, full-moon parties, and simply gathering with friends at night to discuss the day's events. Popular music on the island includes the Caribbean calypso and reggae styles as well as the French-influenced zouk and beguine. As on other islands in the West Indies, the rum shop is the traditional male after-hours gathering place.

18 FOLK ART, CRAFTS, AND HOBBIES

St. Lucia has a rich and varied folk music tradition, which can be heard on a CD collection compiled by the island's Folk Research Centre and recorded at the Smithsonian Institution in Washington, DC *(Musical Traditions of St. Lucia)*. The island's traditional music includes work songs that originated during the days of slavery, as well as beach party and game songs, "play-song-dance" music, and Carnival music. Some of St. Lucia's folk instruments, including the violin, guitar, and mandolin, are of European origin. Instruments of African origin include the *bélè* (or *ka*) drum; a long, hollow tube called the *baha;* a rattle called the *chakchak,* the *zo* (bones); and the *gwaj* (scraper). Various types of banjos and a four-stringed instrument called the *cuatro* are also native to the island.

The music itself shows both French and African influences. The former are evident in the St. Lucian *kwadril,* derived from a French dance form, and the latter can be seen in the *koutoumba,* derived from African call-and-response forms. St. Lucian gospel songs are called *sankeys* (in honor of American singer and songwriter Ira D. Sankey). Each year the calypso tunes currently popular on the island appear in a recorded collection called *Lucian Kaiso.* The St. Lucian kwadril, like the French version, consists of five distinct parts with complicated steps that must be carefully learned and memorized. The kwadril has enjoyed a revival since the mid-1980s, when it was recognized as a unique cultural expression rather than simply a vestige of European colonialism.

Traditional crafts on St. Lucia include pottery, woodcarving, and weaving. The Craft Centre at Choiseul was established by the St. Lucian government to preserve the island's folk art heritage and help support its craftspeople.

[19] SOCIAL PROBLEMS

In recent years, low banana prices have affected St. Lucia's economy, and the situation has been exacerbated by farmers' strikes and the damage wrought by Tropical Storm Debbie in 1994. In that year, the St. Lucia Banana Growers' Association was forced into receivership and confronted a heavy debt load. Prime Minister John Compton estimated that it would take two years and cost US$30 million to repair the damage from the storm. It was feared that up to one-fifth of the island's fertile farm lands might have been permanently ruined for crop production.

[20] BIBLIOGRAPHY

Cameron, Sarah, and Ben Box, ed. *Caribbean Islands Handbook.* Chicago: Passport Books, 1995.

Frank, David B. "Political, Religious, and Economic Factors Affecting Language Choice in St. Lucia." *International Journal of the Sociology of Language* 102 (1993): 39–56.

Gall, Timothy, and Susan Gall, ed. *Worldmark Encyclopedia of the Nations.* 8th ed. Detroit: Gale Research, 1995.

Guilbault, Jocelyne. "Musical Traditions of St. Lucia, West Indies." Washington, D.C.: Smithsonian Institution, 1993.

Hornbeck, John F. "St. Lucia." In *Islands of the Commonwealth Caribbean: A Regional Study,* edited by Sandra W. Meditz and Dennis M. Hanratty. Washington, DC: US Government, 1989.

Jones, Rose. "St. Lucians." In *Encyclopedia of World Cultures.* Boston: G. K. Hall, 1992.

Lannert, John, and Gary Steckles. "Jazz Mainstream Discovers Local Wonders of St. Lucia." *Billboard* (4 September 1993).

Luntta, Karl. *Caribbean Handbook.* Chico, CA: Moon Publications, 1995.

Nash, Jonell. "Eat in St. Lucia." *Essence.* (April 1991): 70.

Schwab, David, ed. *Insight Guides. Caribbean: The Lesser Antilles.* Boston: Houghton Mifflin, 1996.

Walton, Chelle Koster. *Caribbean Ways: A Cultural Guide.* Westwood, MA: Riverdale, 1993.

Walcott, Derek. *Another Life.* New York: Farrar Straus & Giroux, 1973.

———. *The Antilles: Fragments of Epic Memory. The Nobel Lecture.* New York: Farrar Straus & Giroux, 1993.

———. "The Commonwealth: Pedestal or Pyre?" *New Statesman & Society* (21 July 1995): 30.

———. *Omeros.* New York: Farrar Straus & Giroux, 1993.

—by R. Wieder

ST. VINCENTIANS

LOCATION: St. Vincent and the Grenadines
POPULATION: About 107,000
LANGUAGE: English; local dialect with French, West African, Spanish, and English elements
RELIGION: Protestant sects (80–90%): Anglicans, Methodist, and Seventh-Day Adventists; Roman Catholicism; Hinduism; Islam

[1] INTRODUCTION

In spite of its small size, St. Vincent and the Grenadines has a tumultuous early history. Control of its constituent islands was vigorously contested by both Amerindian and European groups for nearly 300 years, and its heritage includes the unique mingling of Africans and Amerindians that produced the group known as the Black Caribs. The Amerindian population on the island of St. Vincent guarded their homeland so vigorously that it became the last major Caribbean island to be colonized.

Christopher Columbus's sighting of the island in 1498 is thought to have taken place on 22 January, the feast day of the saint for which it is named. Aggressively defended by its native Carib population, St. Vincent remained impervious to European settlement attempts until the 18th century. However, when a passing Dutch ship carrying settlers and slaves was shipwrecked off the coast of Bequia in 1675, the Caribs welcomed the Africans who were the sole survivors of the disaster. They were allowed to settle on the island and mix with its population. The resulting people, whose numbers were swelled by escaped slaves from the neighboring islands of Barbados and St. Lucia, became known as the Black Caribs. Ensuing tensions between this group and the "pure" or Yellow Caribs on the island led to hostilities and territorial division by 1700.

In the 18th century, the French, the British, and the Caribs fought for control of the island, which was ultimately ceded to Britain by the Treaty of Paris in 1763. However, the French retained control of some of the Grenadines for a number of years, establishing a strong cultural influence in the area. On St. Vincent, sugarcane plantations flourished under the British in the first part of the 19th century. East Indian and Portuguese indentured laborers were brought to the island to make up for the labor shortage that followed the abolition of slavery by Great Britain in 1834.

In the mid-1800s, sugar prices fell and the islands sank into an economic depression that lasted for decades. The century ended with two natural disasters, a hurricane in 1898 and the most destructive eruption to date of La Soufrière, St. Vincent's active volcano. Clouds and gases from the eruption were recorded as far away as Barbados, and nearly 2,000 people lost their lives. (La Soufrière's most recent major eruption in 1979 forced over 16,000 people to evacuate their homes and blanketed much of the island with ash, resulting in extensive crop damage. However, no lives were lost.)

Long administered as a British crown colony, St. Vincent and the Grenadines moved gradually toward full independence following the breakup of the West Indies Federation (of which it had been a member) in 1962. Internal self-government was granted in 1969 and full independence came on 27 October 1979. The period of independent statehood has been marked by secessionist tendencies in the Grenadines, including a rebellion on Union Island immediately following independence and protests in the early 1980s. The eruption of La Soufrière in 1979 was followed a year later by Hurrican Allen, which caused extensive crop damage. In 1987, Hurricane Emily destroyed an estimated 70% of the nation's banana crop.

² LOCATION AND HOMELAND

St. Vincent and the Grenadines is located among the Windward Islands in the southern portion of the Lesser Antilles. St. Vincent is 32 km (20 mi) south of St. Lucia, while the Grenadines stretch southward toward Grenada. Thirty-two of the Grenadines are part of St. Vincent and the Grenadines, while the rest belong to Grenada. Barbados lies 161 km (100 mi) to the east. St. Vincent itself has a total area of 345 sq km (133 sq mi), while the land area of the Grenadines totals 44 sq km (17 sq mi), bringing the country's total area to 389 sq km (150 sq mi).

St. Vincent is a volcanic island whose highest point—at 1,234 m (4,048 ft)—is La Soufrière, an active volcano whose last major eruption, in 1979, caused serious crop and property damage but no loss of life, thanks to modern warning systems. (A previous eruption in 1902 killed close to 2,000 people.) La Soufrière is the northern end of a mountain range that runs southward to Mt. St. Andrew, bisecting most of the island. The mountains are heavily forested, with numerous streams fed by heavy rainfall.

Of the Grenadines associated with St. Vincent, the largest are Bequia (pronounced Beck-way), Canouan, Mayreau, Mustique, Isle D'Quatre, and Union Island. Bequia,14.5 km (9 mi) south of St. Vincent, is the largest of the Grenadines. It is also the last Caribbean island on which whaling is still practiced (with the approval of the International Whaling Commission, which has granted the island a special Aboriginal Whaling Status). The home of the country's prime minister, Sir James Mitchell, the island has only had electricity since the 1960s and was only reachable by sea until the construction of an airport in 1992.

Farm animals outnumber the human population on Mayreau, which had its first—and only—telephone installed in 1990. Union Island (with an area of 8 sq km or 3 sq mi), the country's southern port of entry, was also the site of a secessionist revolt by about 50 young men a few days after St. Vincent and the Grenadines was declared an independent nation in 1979. Perhaps the best-known of the Grenadines is Mustique, a tiny semiprivately owned island with homes belonging to such well-known public figures as Mick Jagger and England's Princess Margaret, as well as other wealthy but lesser-known owners.

St. Vincent and the Grenadines has an estimated population of 107,000 people, of whom some 99,000 live on St. Vincent and about 8,000 on the Grenadines. About 25% of the country's population live in the capital of Kingstown or in one of its suburbs. Kingstown itself has an estimated population of 15,000–16,000 people, and the surrounding area has another 10,000 people. The ethnic composition of the population is estimated as 65% Black, 20% of mixed Black and White ancestry, 5.5% East Indian, 3.5% White, and 2% descended from the island's native Carib population, with the remainder being immigrants from North America, Latin America, and Asia. There is a Carib reservation at Sandy Bay in the northern part of St. Vincent.

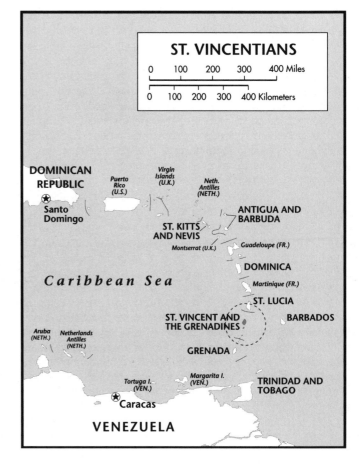

³ LANGUAGE

English is the official language of St. Vincent and the Grenadines, but most people on the islands speak a local dialect, or Creole, that contains elements of both French and West African grammar and a vocabulary that is mostly French with some African, Spanish, and English words. It includes one of the most characteristic features of West Indian Creole languages, the use of object pronouns in the subject position, as in "Me going down town." There are many French place names in St. Vincent and the Grenadines, including Sans Souci, Petit Vincent, and Mayreau, as well as Carib names, which include Bequia (one of the Grenadines) and the Commantawana Bay on St. Vincent.

St. Vincentians have historically prided themselves on their ability to speak standard English correctly, while devaluing the use of the Creole that is for most the language of everyday life. In recent years, however, Creole has enjoyed an enhanced reputation as its use has become associated with cultural and national pride, especially among young people. Skits, speeches, and other activities in Creole have become popular in the schools, long the bastion of proper English.

⁴ FOLKLORE

The folklore of St. Vincent and the Grenadines reflects its combined English, African, and French heritage, as well as Creole and West Indian influences. Like other West Africans, Vincentians tend toward the superstitious, and some still fear the African-influenced black magic called obeah that is common in the Caribbean region. The nation's best-known folk tradition is its annual summer carnival celebration.

5 RELIGION

Between 80% and 90% of the population are Protestant, with Anglicans representing the greatest share, and other sects including Methodists and Seventh-Day Adventists. Catholics account for about 10% of the population, and a small minority are Hindu or Muslim, from the East Indian community.

6 MAJOR HOLIDAYS

Public holidays in St. Vincent and the Grenadines include New Year's Day (1 January), St. Vincent and the Grenadines Day (22 January), Good Friday, Easter Monday, Labor Day (1 May), Whit Monday, Carnival Tuesday (9 July), CARICOM Day (11 July), Emancipation Day (1 August), Independence Day (27 October), Christmas (25 December), and Boxing Day (26 December). The nation's Carnival celebration ("Vincy Mas") is held in late June and early July and features costumed parades, calypso and steel drum bands, and "jump-up" (street dancing). The final two days are J'Ouvert (a Monday when revelers stream into the streets at dawn), and Mardi Gras, and there are boisterous street parties on both days. Preliminary rounds in preparation for the Carnival calypso competitions can be heard throughout the island in the two months preceding the festivities.

Union Island holds sporting and cultural events, including a calypso competition, at Eastertime, and a Big Drum festival in May.

7 RITES OF PASSAGE

Major life transitions, such as birth, marriage, and death, are marked by religious ceremonies appropriate to each St. Vincentian's faith community.

8 INTERPERSONAL RELATIONS

"What di' man say?" is a typical greeting. Popular slang among young people on the islands includes "Irie" (an all-purpose phrase that is something like "stay cool" or "see you later") and "Sic too bad" (similar to "awesome").

9 LIVING CONDITIONS

St. Vincentians generally own their own homes, growing produce for their own consumption and selling the surplus at the market. Women are more likely to own homes through inheritance, while men typically build their own; it is not uncommon for a family to live in a house owned by the wife. Besides inheritance, another way that a woman commonly acquires a home is by having a son or daughter build it for her. A typical rural dwelling is a single-story wooden house with a tin roof, often painted red.

According to recent estimates, there is 1 physician per 3,800 people. Common health problems include parasitic diseases and circulatory disorders. Gastrointestinal diseases are also prevalent, although less so than before. Average life expectancy was 71 years as of 1992. Medical care is provided at the Central General Hospital in Kingstown, as well as at 35 clinics and dispensaries in various other locations.

Parts of St. Vincent are accessible only by foot or boat. The country's road area is divided nearly equally between all-weather and rough roads. Local transportation is provided by open-air buses and small minibus-taxis sporting colorful hand-painted names such as "Mad Dog II," "Stragglin' Man," and "Say Wha Yo Like." The E. T. Joshua Airport is located on the island's southern tip, near Kingstown, and there are smaller airports or airstrips on Bequia, Union, Canouan, and Mustique islands.

10 FAMILY LIFE

Three types of family arrangement common throughout the much of the West Indies are found on St. Vincent and the Grenadines: legal marriage, unmarried cohabitation, and "visiting unions," where the man and woman live apart and the woman raises the children. Visiting unions are more likely to occur in early adulthood, while married relationships are more common later in life. Even in visiting unions (also referred to as "friending"), strong links are maintained between father and child, and there is equal recognition of kinship through legal and nonlegal unions.

Infants are highly valued and receive a large amount of attention and physical affection from all members of the household. Fathers, sons, grandparents, and daughters with no children of their own may actually provide the greatest amount of attention if the mother is too busy taking care of the family's washing and cooking, as well as raising its produce and, in many cases, serving as the household's water carrier.

Men are responsible only for those children they have actually fathered, whether through a present or previous relationship. Thus they retain obligations toward children living in different households. This means that the mother occupies a central position in the household as the only person with obligations toward all its members, including the children from both her present and previous relationships, as well as her husband and any grandparents, aunts, or uncles who may live with the family.

Although women accounted for 38% of the nation's work force in the 1980s, traditional gender roles and expectations kept most women from receiving an education equal to that of men.

11 CLOTHING

People on St. Vincent and the Grenadines wear modern Western-style clothing. They favor light and brightly colored clothes and are interested in the latest fashions. Some young people enjoy dressing in attention-getting items such as bright orange jeans, the latest in expensive footwear, or shirts with popular designer names. Children wear uniforms to school.

12 FOOD

Staple foods include rice, sweet potatoes, and fruits, especially those of the banana family, which includes plantains and bluggoe ("green figs"), in addition to ordinary bananas. Another widely eaten food, breadfruit, is associated with a famous historical incident, the mutiny on board the *Bounty* by the crew of Captain William Bligh in 1789. Bligh's men mutinied on a voyage to gather breadfruit and other items to be shipped to Jamaica and St. Vincent. Although he and 19 loyal sailors were cast adrift and compelled to sail 6,667 km (3,600 mi) in an open boat before reaching dry land, Bligh undertook a second voyage in 1793, gathering the breadfruit that ultimately found its way to St. Vincent and the rest of the Caribbean. Today, St. Vincent's local rum is called Captain Bligh in honor of the tenacious seaman, and its national dish is jackfish and breadfruit. Arrowroot, a major cash crop, is used in desserts, including arrowroot sponge and arrowroot custard. Popular fare includes dishes containing spicy Scotch Bonnet peppers.

13 EDUCATION

Primary education is free but not compulsory, and there are both government-operated secondary schools, which are free, and government-assisted private schools, which charge tuition. In 1994/95, 76% of all children at the primary level were attending school, while only 24% of older students were enrolled in secondary school. At the post-secondary level, St. Vincent has a technical college and a teacher training college affiliated with the University of the West Indies. Most students seeking a higher education must leave the country, attending college at other campuses of the University of the West Indies or in the United States, Canada, or Great Britain. The adult literacy rate of St. Vincent and the Grenadines is estimated at 85%.

14 CULTURAL HERITAGE

The Big Drum music of the Windward Islands, to which St. Vincent and the Grenadines belongs, reflects the islands' African cultural roots, combining the African call-and-response tradition with features of calypso and reggae, but retaining an authentic African flavor. The Big Drum is actually a set of three drums, originally carved from trees and later made of rum kegs. The singers are usually women, and the lead singer is called a "chantwell." The songs—in either English or patois (dialect)—resemble those of other Caribbean traditions, such as calypso, in their reliance on satire and social commentary. Dances are performed inside a ring of people by dancers wearing full skirts and headdresses who interact with the musicians.

15 WORK

Many St. Vincentians practice agriculture or fishing, either at a subsistence level or for profit. Those who farm small plots bring their surplus fruits, vegetables, chickens, or fish to sell at the modern market in Kingstown on Saturdays. Bananas are St. Vincent's main commercial crop. Most banana growers cultivate only 0.8 to 2 hectares (2–5 acres) of land. Translucent blue plastic bags cover the "hands" (bunches of bananas) to protect them from the full heat of the sun, retain moisture, and prevent bruising. The sensitive bananas must be harvested at exactly the right time, and radio broadcasts keep farmers advised of the best harvesting time. The growers are paid for their harvest at the stations where bananas are boxed. Hundreds of thousands of dollars are counted into small envelopes every week and distributed to as many as 3,000 waiting St. Vincentians with receipts in their hands.

On the Grenadines, most men are fishermen or boat-builders. The island of Bequia has a tradition of whaling, a skill the islanders have been practicing since the 19th century. The International Whaling Commission has granted the Bequians Aboriginal Whaling Status, a classification reserved for people who hunt whales for local consumption rather than commercial use and who have a whaling tradition that is closely linked to their familial, cultural, and community ties. No more than three whales are caught in any one year. The whales are subdued with harpoons, which today are often shot from a whale gun rather than thrown by hand. They are then towed to the island of Petit Nevis to be processed and sold. A successful catch is considered an important event on Bequia, and much of the island's population flocks to Petit Nevis to see the whale.

St. Vincent and the Grenadines has a high rate of unemployment, estimated at about 25% in the early 1990s.

16 SPORTS

Cricket, the most popular sport, is played throughout the islands on any piece of flat ground and even on the beach. Other sports include soccer (called "football"), netball, volleyball, and basketball.

17 ENTERTAINMENT AND RECREATION

Nighttime gatherings outdoors are a favorite form of recreation and may include singing, dancing, and the universally popular pastime of gossiping. With the recent growth of tourism on the islands, it has become common for locals to gather at hotel and restaurant entertainment facilities to eat, drink, dance, and socialize. Men on St. Vincent and the Grenadines, like those elsewhere in the Caribbean, are inveterate players of dominoes.

18 FOLK ART, CRAFTS, AND HOBBIES

Folk music is played on the four-stringed quatro, as well as the guitar, fiddle, drums, and a variety of percussion instruments. Bequia is known for its skilled model-boat-builders, who fashion small-scale versions of yachts, whaleboats, and other vessels that are faithful in every detail. Even the island's children make model boats—out of coconut shells with brightly colored sails.

19 SOCIAL PROBLEMS

The low percentage of young people who complete their secondary education has created a shortage of skilled workers on the islands, exacerbated by the fact that the better-educated segments of the population often emigrate and live abroad until retirement.

There is a high level of concern about drug-related crime on the islands.

20 BIBLIOGRAPHY

Cameron, Sarah, and Ben Box, ed. *Caribbean Islands Handbook.* Chicago: Passport Books, 1995.

Cosover, Mary Jo. "St. Vincent and the Grenadines," In *Islands of the Commonwealth Caribbean: A Regional Study,* edited by Sandra W. Meditz and Dennis M. Hanratty. Washington, D.C.: U.S. Government, 1989.

Defreitas, Michael. "St. Vincent: Modern Outlook, Antique Style." *Americas* (English Edition) 42, no. 2 (Mar–Apr 1990): 44.

Gall, Timothy, and Susan Gall, ed. *Worldmark Encyclopedia of the Nations.* 8th ed. Detroit: Gale Research, 1995.

Iaconetti, Joan. "Anchoring Progress in Tradition." *Americas* (English Edition) 46, no. 6 (Nov–Dec 1994): 6.

Luntta, Karl. *Caribbean Handbook.* Chico, CA: Moon Publications, 1995.

Potter, Robert B. *St. Vincent and the Grenadines.* Santa Barbara, CA: Clio, 1992.

Schwab, David, ed. *Insight Guides. Caribbean: The Lesser Antilles.* Boston: Houghton Mifflin, 1996.

Walton, Chelle Koster. *Caribbean Ways: A Cultural Guide.* Westwood, MA: Riverdale, 1993.

Young, Virginia Heyer. *Becoming West Indian: Culture, Self, and Nation in St. Vincent.* Washington, DC: Smithsonian Institution Press, 1993.

—by R. Wieder

SALVADORANS

LOCATION: El Salvador; United States
POPULATION: About 5 million
LANGUAGE: Spanish
RELIGION: Roman Catholicism; Protestantism

¹INTRODUCTION

El Salvador is the smallest and most densely populated country in Central America. When the Spanish arrived in 1524, it was occupied by the Pilpil Indians, who spoke a language similar to that of the Aztecs. Atlactal, their leader, initially defeated the forces led by Pedro de Alvarado, and Atonatl, an archer, wounded Alvarado. Both are remembered as heroes, but the whole area fell under Spanish control by 1540. The Indians were put to work on plantations that produced tropical products like cacao and indigo.

El Salvador declared its independence from Spain in 1821 and belonged to a Central American federation from 1823 to 1841. For the next century, the government was dominated by the coffee-growing industry. When, during the Depression, coffee prices dropped and wages were cut, peasants rose in revolt in 1932. The military crushed the revolt and then massacred about 15,000 to 30,000 people, mainly Indians. Military rulers governed the country until 1980.

During the 1980s, armed left- and right-wing groups fought for power. About 70,000 people were killed in the struggle. Many were victims of right-wing death squads, including Archbishop Oscar Romero, the country's highest-ranking Roman Catholic prelate, who was killed while saying Mass. About one-fourth of the 5 million or so people in El Salvador became refugees or displaced persons during the war, and more than0.5 million left the country. A peace agreement was reached in 1992, and a Conservative was elected president in 1994.

²LOCATION AND HOMELAND

El Salvador is slightly smaller than the US state of Massachusetts. It is bounded on the north and east by Honduras, on the north and west by Guatemala, and on the south by the Pacific Ocean. The Gulf of Fonseca to the east separates it from Nicaragua. Two east–west mountain ranges cross El Salvador: the Sierra Madre along the border with Honduras, and a southern range that includes more than 20 volcanoes. The country also lies in an earthquake zone.

The climate is tropical, with the rainy season extending from May to October. Most of the people live in the fertile central zone or in the metropolitan area of San Salvador, the capital. About 90% of the people are Mestizo, of mixed European and Indian ancestry. Of the remainder, almost all are Indians. Whites account for only about 1% of the population. Of the more than 1 million people displaced by the civil war, about 500,000 settled in other parts of El Salvador, 250,000 emigrated to Mexico, and 150,000 moved to the United States. By 1990 there were believed to be 1 million Salvadorans in the US.

³LANGUAGE

Spanish is the official and universally spoken language. Very few people still speak an Indian language.

4 FOLKLORE

According to the Pilpil creation myth, Teotl rubbed two branches together to produce the sparks that became the stars. Teopantlí, the reformer who rules the universe, then appeared in the heavens. A handful of fire that condensed down below into a ball of light became Tónal, the sun. Metzti, the moon, was created by a tear from Teopantlí. Metzti projected her light onto the earth, creating mountains, canyons, and wild beasts.

Ten-year-old Cipitín, a kind of Cupid, is the god of young love in national folklore. Always elusive, he hides behind the foliage. From high in the treetops he shakes flowers off the branches so they will fall on girls passing below. He has a sweetheart, Tenáncin, who lives with him in a cavern inside a volcano.

Folk medicine is not as prominent in El Salvador as it is in Mexico and Guatemala, where Indian heritage remains stronger. Witchcraft is sometimes blamed for illnesses and love problems. *Ojo* (eye) is the name given to infant illnesses attributed to the infant being seen by a strong person, who does not necessarily intend any ill will.

5 RELIGION

More than 90% of all Salvadorans are Roman Catholic. In the late 1960s, activist clergy began condemning the army's violence and human-rights abuses. Priests went into the countryside to educate peasants and organize them into cooperatives and unions. Dozens were killed by right-wing groups, and others joined the guerrillas. The Church continued to operate social programs in the 1990s, but most were less political than before.

About 3% of the population are Protestant. A number of groups, including the Baptists, Mormons, and Seventh-Day Adventists, have been active in missionary work developed and financed in the United States. Evangelists preach a message of personal salvation through belief in Jesus rather than through social action.

6 MAJOR HOLIDAYS

Many Salvadorans journey over the border to Esquipulas, Guatemala, each January to honor the "Black Christ," a mahogany image of Jesus placed in a basilica built to house it in 1758. San Vincente also holds elaborate festivities for this occasion, with processions on 14 and 30 January. Indian men perform a dance in the local church to an accompaniment of fife and drums.

On 20 January, Villa Delgado holds a fiesta for St. Sebastian, including a bullfight farce set to fife and drums. The Day of the Cross is held on 3 May nationwide. Homeowners set up a cross in the patio or garden, decorated with fruits and flowers. A folk belief is that if no cross is erected, the devil will come and dance until midnight. Between 1 and 6 August, San Salvador holds a fiesta commemorating the Transfiguration of Christ with sports events, games, and parties. A float stops across from the cathedral, and from there a figure representing Jesus makes his way underground into the church, where he reappears in white robes. Pilgrims flock to San Antonio del Monte for a fiesta held between 22 and 26 August; an image of the saint in the local church is credited with miraculous powers. Christmas is celebrated with nightly *posada* processions from 16 December to Christmas Eve (24 December). In Izalco, the period between Christmas and the Feast of the Epiphany(6 Jan-

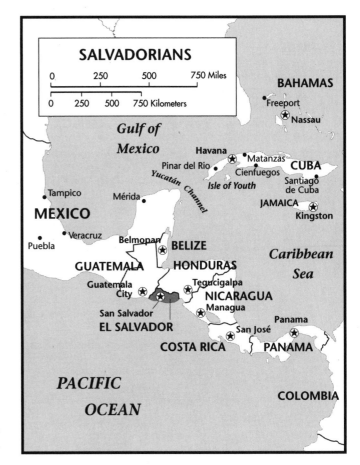

uary) is celebrated with nightly processions and *Jeu Jeu,* an Indian rain dance. Izalco and Texistepeque have notable Holy Week (late March or early April) celebrations.

Among secular (nonreligious) holidays, 5 November commemorates the day in 1811 on which Father José Matías Delgado gave the first call for independence in all of Central America. Independence Day is 15 September.

7 RITES OF PASSAGE

Baptism of infants and confirmation of children in church are common. Perhaps half of all couples, however, live together without regularizing their unions with a license or a church ceremony. A birthday may not necessarily be celebrated; the person's namesake saint's day is likely to be observed instead. A novena for the dead is usually held in the home of the deceased, with friends invited on the final night. Often a second novena is held later.

8 INTERPERSONAL RELATIONS

El Salvador shares the customs of other Latin American countries. A greater degree of formality is expected in relations with strangers than in the United States, but punctuality is rarely esteemed. People generally stand closer to one another and gesture more than in the United States when conversing. Unconventional behavior, including inappropriate dress, is frowned upon in this tradition-conscious society.

Wedding dinner in Segundo Montes, El Salvador. Perhaps half of all Salvadoran couples, however, live together without regularizing their unions with a license or a church ceremony. (David Johnson)

⁹ LIVING CONDITIONS

A sharp contrast between great wealth and extreme poverty has characterized Salvadoran society since colonial times. About 2% of the people own 60% of the nation's productive land and account for about 33% of the national income. The elite generally live in San Salvador, in houses typically surrounded by walls many meters high and topped with barbed wire. They travel periodically to their country estates and send their children to private schools. The middle class, about 8% of the population, includes professionals, government employees, teachers, and small business owners. Many army officers come from such a background. The vast majority of people are laborers or peasants who own or rent small plots of land.

In the early 1980s, the poor were taking in fewer calories than anywhere else in the Western Hemisphere. Their diet consists mainly of corn, beans, rice, and sorghum, with only about1 kg (2 lbs) of meat a month for a family of six. Malnutrition is particularly common among children. The rural population rarely has access to sewage systems, and surface water is seriously polluted. In the countryside, peasants live in one-room, earthen-floor, thatched-roof huts made of adobe or wood frames with mud or rubble fill. The poorest such homes are made of poles and straw. In the cities, a poor family may occupy a single room of a compound or establish a shanty in a squatter community on the edge of town.

¹⁰ FAMILY LIFE

A provision in El Salvador's civil code requires a man to protect his wife and a wife to be obedient to her husband. Often, however, there is no man around, although Salvadoran women give birth to an average of more than five children. Many marriages have fallen apart as spouses travel in search of work, often outside the country. The dislocations caused by the civil war of the 1980s have had the same effect. About 60% of all births are out of wedlock. The institution of *compadrazgo* (godparenthood) provides aid to the family from outsiders but is not as common as it is in Mexico.

The constitution includes a provision guaranteeing equality for women, but girls are generally expected to be passive and submissive, while boys are taught to be the opposite. There is a history of sexual abuse in the countryside. However, the nation has more women professionals than ever before, including nearly 30% of its doctors and lawyers.

¹¹ CLOTHING

Because the 1932 massacres targeted people of Indian appearance, native El Salvadorans exchanged their dress for European clothes. Few Indians retain traditional dress today, which for men usually meant white cotton trousers and shirt, sandals, and a large palm-leaf hat with a high crown. Women wore a *huipil* (blouse) with short puffed sleeves; a tightly wrapped skirt called a *refajo;* and a large, bright cotton cloth on the head. Fes-

In Salvadoran families, there is often no man around as spouses travel in search of work, often outside the country. (PhotoEdit)

tive dress for women now consists of a cotton skirt above a petticoat, trimmed with a few ruffles around the bottom and reaching to the ankles, and a blouse trimmed with lace and embroidery around the sleeves and neck.

12 FOOD

The staple of the Salvadoran diet is corn. The *pupusa* is (like a tortilla) a cornmeal pancake, often fried. It is folded over and filled with soft, white cheese or some other stuffing such as chopped meat or fried pork rinds *(chicharrón)* or simply *frijoles* (red or black beans). *Gallo de chicha* is chicken marinated in a fermented cornmeal brew mixed with brown sugar. The *quesadilla* is a sweetish bread or cake served as a flat, thin square. El Salvador's markets abound with fruits, some of them unfamiliar to Americans.

13 EDUCATION

In 1990, 73% of Salvadorans over the age of 15 were literate. About 70% of all children of primary-school age were enrolled, but only 15% of children old enough for secondary schooling were enrolled there. Although public education is free, many parents are unable to afford the school materials their children need to attend. Thousands of schools closed during the civil war, when spending on education per pupil dropped by 67%. Half the work force has had no more than three years of schooling. The National University, which is in San Salvador, allows many poorly qualified students to attend but graduates few. The University of Central America, also in San Salvador, is a private institution run by Jesuits.

14 CULTURAL HERITAGE

Juan José Bernal, a priest, wrote poetry during the colonial period. Francisco Galindo was a 19th-century poet and dramatist. Salvador Salazar Arrué, writing under the pen name Salarué, was a prominent short-story writer. Claudia Lars was an outstanding poet. Manlio Argueta and Claribel Alegría are novelists and poets. Roque Dalton was a left-wing poet killed by his own guerrilla comrades. Other 20th-century writers include Francisco Gavidia, cofounder of the national theater; Alberto Masferrer, essayist and poet; and Juan Ramón Uriarte, essayist and educator.

Among artists, Juan Francisco Cisneros was a 19th-century painter. Arrué was known for his tapestries as well as his writings. José Mejía Vides created paintings and woodcuts.

The marimba, an instrument that resembles the xylophone, is popular throughout Central America. Before the arrival of the Spanish, music was based on a five-tone scale, and the marimba was a keyboard composed of long gourds. Drums and flutes—also traditional Indian instruments—accompany over 30 types of dance performed as a ritual on the local saint's day. *La historia* is a dance that dramatizes the conflict between the Moors and Christians in Spain. A *gracejo* (jester) dressed in rags interrupts the narrative with bawdy exclamations. *Turco del monto* is a mountain-pig dance performed at several local festivals. Masks made of cloth, coconut fiber, wood, or gourds may be worn in Indian dances.

15 WORK

The minimum wage in 1995 was only $2 per day in agriculture and $3.50 a day in industry and commerce. Half the work force was believed to be unemployed or underemployed. About 70% were unskilled laborers, and about 33% were engaged in agriculture. The average Salvadoran earned about $1,400 a year, but peasants averaged less than half that much. By 1995 Salvadorans working in the United States were sending home nearly $1 billion a year to their relatives, a greater inflow of cash than from all Salvadoran exports combined.

16 SPORTS

Fútbol (soccer) is the national passion. The so-called 1969 Soccer War with Honduras followed two matches by the national teams of both countries and resulted in as many as 3,000 deaths, mainly civilians. Basketball is also popular. Other sports include horseback riding, bicycling, motorcycling, swimming, baseball, tennis, golf, and sports fishing.

17 ENTERTAINMENT AND RECREATION

Popular music is dominated by the Mexican music industry. Nightlife is found in San Salvador, in the form of clubs, discos, and marimba street bands. The fiestas offer popular entertainment on a large scale and are accompanied by games like greased-pole climbing and the *carrera de cintas,* in which contestants on horseback must put a stick through a ribboned loop while riding at full gallop.

¹⁸ FOLK ART, CRAFTS, AND HOBBIES

Weaving of textiles on pre-Conquest hand looms may still be done in Izalco, where belts are made, and Panchimalco, where women have a long history of weaving skirts, headcloths, and carrying cloths. Cotton is dyed, but not silk or wool. Foot-pedaled looms, introduced by the Spanish, are still used to produce hammocks and bedspreads in San Sebastián. Hats are woven from palm fibers, while hammocks, saddle and net bags, and *petates* (large woven mats) are made from henequen fiber. Baskets are made from palm leaves, rushes, reeds, or wicker. Wicker furniture is made in Nahuizalco.

Molded both by hand and the potter's wheel, ceramic pieces are decorated with a red clay dissolved in water and applied with a corn husk. Izalco is the traditional center for gourds, made into bowls, jugs, and cups and often decorated and finished. Also handmade in El Salvador are dolls of wood or dried corn husks, tiny clay figurines for nativity scenes, wooden stirrups and small lacquered boxes, powder puffs made from goose feathers, and silk shawls.

¹⁹ SOCIAL PROBLEMS

In the mid 1990s, about 270,000 children were working up to 12 hours a day, and 90% of the Indian population lived in extreme poverty. El Salvador has the second-highest rate of deforestation in the world. Erosion depletes 20% of the topsoil each year, and 90% of the rivers are polluted. About 50% of the population, mostly in the countryside, do not have access to uncontaminated water. San Salvador is dirty, overcrowded, and crime-ridden.

²⁰ BIBLIOGRAPHY

Adams, Richard N. *Cultural Surveys of Panama, Nicaragua, Guatemala, El Salvador, and Honduras.* Detroit: B. Ethridge Books, 1976.

Brauer, Jeff, Julian Smith, and Veronica Wiles. *On Your Own in El Salvador.* Charlottesville, VA: On Your Own Publications, 1995.

Osborne, Lilly de Jongh. *Four Keys to El Salvador.* New York: Funk and Wagnalls, 1956.

—by R. Halasz, reviewed by F. Colecchia

SCOTTISH AND SCOTCH-IRISH AMERICANS

OVERVIEW

Though their numbers have never been large, Scottish and Scotch-Irish Americans have contributed the qualities of pragmatism, utilitarianism, individualism, and self-reliance to the general "American" character. Throughout their early history, Scottish and Scotch-Irish Americans tended to be people of the frontier. They were used to dealing with difficult conditions in their homelands of Scotland and Northern Ireland, and they preferred to be far away from interfering neighbors and governments. Much of the early American frontier was settled by the Scots.

Scottish immigrants to America include three distinct groups: Highlanders, Lowlanders, and Scotch-Irish (or Ulster Scots). Highlanders came from the north of Scotland, where the land is rugged and the people fierce. The clannish Highlanders wore kilts and spoke Gaelic. Lowlanders came from southern Scotland, which had been much more influenced by English language and culture. The Scotch-Irish were originally from the lowlands but had been sent to Northern Ireland (Ulster) by English rulers who hoped to establish a Protestant stronghold in that Catholic land. The Ulster Scots kept to themselves, mingling very little with their Catholic neighbors and preserving their Scottish identity.

The first Scottish immigrants to America were prisoners of war, sent to the colonies by English ruler Oliver Cromwell after he defeated Scotland in 1650. The Scottish prisoners of war served out their sentences by laboring in the English colonies of North America. Scots were legally barred from emigrating to America until England and Scotland were united in 1707. After the union, Scots were given the same freedoms as English citizens. In the early 18th century, a number of Scots were sent to America as political prisoners of England, much like the earlier prisoners of war. Another large group of nonvoluntary immigrants were Scottish soldiers who had been brought to America to fight in the Seven Years' War (1754–1761). At the end of the war, the soldiers were discharged and the majority elected to remain in America. Of the 12,000 Scottish soldiers discharged, only 76 returned to Scotland.

Voluntary Scottish emigration to America began after the union of England and Scotland in 1707. Conditions were already difficult for Scottish farmers with a cold, rainy climate, short growing season, and rocky ground. When the English began encouraging Scottish landlords to raise rents, seize grazing grounds, and evict tenants in order to squash Scottish uprisings, many Scots decided to look elsewhere for better opportunities. Wealthy landowners in America advertised for "indentured servants," emigrants who would work for a period of years in exchange for passage to America, and a number of Scots hired on. Others sold their farms and livestock to pay for their passage.

Whole communities packed up and moved to America, setting up Scottish towns in the English colonies. In 1738, 83 families from a neighborhood in Argyllshire, Scotland, immigrated to the Lake George area of New York. Others settled throughout the 13 colonies, although North Carolina was a favorite destination, particularly for Highlanders. Pennsylvania was also popular, especially with the Scotch-Irish.

The Scotch-Irish began to leave Ireland en masse in the early 18th century, seeking self-government and religious freedom. They had become quite disillusioned with the English government, which was high-handed and oppressive. They were also tired of being persecuted by the Catholics for being Protestant, and by the Anglicans (the official church of England, also Protestant) for being Presbyterian. Pennsylvania encouraged religious freedom for all, and in the early 18th century it was still largely unsettled frontier, so it was very attractive to the Scotch-Irish. By 1749, about 25% of the total population of Pennsylvania was Scotch-Irish. Many of their descendants still live in towns such as Gettysburg, Chambersburg, Carlisle, and York.

Scotch-Irish Americans, with their anti-English stance, were quite ready to join the rebel cause in the American Revolution. Scottish Americans from the Highlands and Lowlands, however, tended to side with the British crown. Fearing that the Scots would side with the rebels, the English prohibited Scottish emigration to America beginning in 1775. The damage was already done, however, and the Scotch-Irish (and some Scottish) Americans contributed significantly to the downfall of the British. Scottish and Scotch-Irish American Revolutionary War leaders include Patrick Henry; John Stark and Henry Knox, who led the rebel troops at the Battle of Bunker Hill (1775); naval commander John Paul Jones, and General "Mad" Anthony Wayne. After the Revolution, many Scottish emigrants chose to go to British-friendly Canada, rather than to the US, for the next several years.

Scots also played a great part in the opening of the American frontier. Scottish and Scotch-Irish Americans tended to be the first to clear an area, then they would sell it to other settlers who would improve it while the Scots moved on. The Scots were such fierce fighters and defenders of their territory that eventually the American government had to step in to protect friendly Native North American peoples from Scottish American attacks. Some of the best-known frontiersmen were of Scottish descent, including Daniel Boone, Christopher "Kit" Carson, and Davy Crockett. Somewhat later, Scottish American Sam Houston led the Texans to independence and became the first president of the Republic of Texas.

Other Scottish American contributions to America in the 19th century include the Whiskey Rebellion of 1792–94, and the Ku Klux Klan. Scotch-Irish farmers in the Pittsburgh area of Pennsylvania distilled whiskey from their surplus corn, both for their own consumption and for sale. They refused to pay required local and federal taxes, however. The federal government finally sent in troops to force payment. The farmers almost set fire to Pittsburgh in retaliation but were discouraged from doing so at the last minute by members of the clergy. The Ku Klux Klan, a secret society advocating white supremacy, was founded in the South after the Civil War (1861–65) by a group of Scotch-Irish Americans.

After its post-Revolutionary War decline, Scottish immigration to the US picked up again in the 19th century and continued at a fairly steady pace into the early 20th century. Perhaps the largest wave occurred after World War I (1914–18), when Britain descended into an economic depression with high

Two Scottish American men in kilts. (Alex McNeill)

unemployment. Over 300,000 Scots emigrated to the US between 1921 and 1930 in search of better opportunities. When the Great Depression hit America in 1929–30, however, conditions became just as bad there as in Scotland, and Scottish immigration to the US virtually ceased. Since then, negligible numbers of Scots have moved to America.

In the 1990 US Census, 5,393,581 Americans claimed Scottish ancestry, and 5,617,773 reported their ancestry as Scotch-Irish. Scottish and Scotch-Irish Americans are now spread throughout the United States with no significant concentrations anywhere. The top five states with the highest number of Scottish Americans are California (646,674), Florida (316,732), Texas (306,854), New York (266,312), and Michigan (252,104). For Scotch-Irish Americans, the top five states are California (546,496), Texas (495,886), North Carolina (343,345), Florida (320,217), and Pennsylvania (270,299).

Although Scottish Highlanders spoke Gaelic when they first arrived in America, they quickly shifted to English to avoid harassment, and fluency in Gaelic was rapidly lost. Subsequent generations of Scottish Americans learned English as their first language. Some learned no Gaelic at all. Today, few Scottish or Scotch-Irish Americans speak Gaelic.

In 1560, John Knox, a Catholic priest in Scotland, broke away from the Roman Catholic Church and formed a Protestant denomination that he called the Church of Scotland. Scottish immigrants brought their religion to America, where it came to be known as the Presbyterian Church. The Scots, particularly the Scotch-Irish, were fiercely religious and loyal to the Presbyterian Church. Though they were persecuted in many of the Anglican-dominated English colonies in early America, they held fast to their Presbyterian faith. In 1860, the Reformed Presbyterian Church, made up mostly of Scotch-Irish Americans, declared that it would not serve Holy Communion to slaveholders. It was the first church in America to take a stand against slavery.

Scottish and Scotch-Irish Americans have made significant contributions to all areas of American life. "Scotch broth," a soup made from lamb, barley, and vegetables, is well loved in America, as is Scotch whiskey. Plaid woolen clothing and tweed (a woolen cloth) are both worn by many Americans. Bagpipe music is familiar to all, and Scottish folksingers, such as Jean Redpath, have a wide following in the US. Many colleges and universities were founded by Scottish and Scotch-Irish Americans, including the Universities of Virginia, North Carolina, Pittsburgh, and Pennsylvania; Allegheny College, Grove City, Waynesboro, and others in Pennsylvania; and perhaps best known of all, Princeton University, founded in 1746 as a Presbyterian seminary in New Jersey.

Writers from Washington Irving, Edgar Allan Poe, and Herman Melville to F. Scott Fitzgerald, Henry and William James, John Kenneth Galbraith, James Reston, Norman Maclean, and poet Richard Hugo all claim Scottish or Scotch-Irish ancestry. The New York Library was begun with the collections of Scottish American James Lenox in the 1800s. The first newspaper printed in America was the *Boston Newsletter*, published by Scottish American John Campbell. Hugely successful newspaper publisher Horace Greeley was a Scottish American.

One of the earliest American-born actors of note was Edwin Forrest, a Scottish American. Modern dancer Isadora Duncan; artists Gilbert Stuart, George Innes, and Thomas Hart Benton, and composers Edward MacDowell and Stephen Foster were also of Scottish descent. A Scottish American who made many educational and artistic programs possible was steel magnate and philanthropist Andrew Carnegie. It is estimated that Carnegie gave over $350 million in his lifetime to found schools, libraries, concert halls, museums, etc., and to fund art, research, and other projects. The Carnegie Foundation has continued his philanthropic work since his death.

The worlds of American science and industry owe a great deal to Scottish Americans. Alexander Graham Bell invented the telephone; Samuel F. B. Morse invented the telegraph; Peter Cooper built the first American locomotive; Robert Fulton developed the first steamboat; and Cyrus McCormick invented the wheat harvester. Naturalist John Muir helped found the US national park system, Asa Gray was a well-known botanist; and William Maclure is sometimes called the "father of American geology."

Politics has always been a favorite pastime of the Scots as has going to battle. Many Scottish and Scotch-Irish Americans have played a part in both arenas in the US, beginning with seven of the signers of the Declaration of Independence, including the first to sign, John Hancock. Scottish and Scotch-Irish American Revolutionary War leaders have already been

mentioned. In later US military engagements, Scottish and Scotch-Irish American leaders include Captain Oliver Hazard Perry (War of 1812); Union generals George B. McClellan and Ulysses S. Grant, and Confederate generals Thomas "Stonewall" Jackson, J. E. B. Stuart, and Robert E. Lee (Civil War); and General Douglas MacArthur (World War II). Commodore Matthew C. Perry established the first trade relations with Japan in modern times.

In politics, Scottish and Scotch-American figures abound, such as Andrew Mellon, US Secretary of the Treasury from 1921 to 1931; Alexander Hamilton (who is also part-French); Philip Murray, who served as the president of the Congress of Industrial Organizations (CIO); and Adlai Stevenson and George McGovern, both of whom ran unsuccessfully for US President. Scottish and Scotch-Irish Americans who ran successfully for US President include James Monroe, Andrew Jackson, James K. Polk, James Buchanan, Andrew Johnson, Ulysses S. Grant, Chester A. Arthur, Grover Cleveland, Benjamin Harrison, William McKinley, Theodore Roosevelt, Woodrow Wilson, Harry S. Truman, Dwight D. Eisenhower, Lyndon Baines Johnson, and Richard M. Nixon.

The greatest contribution Scots have made to American sports is the game of golf, which was invented in Scotland and brought to America by Scottish and Scotch-Irish immigrants. Scots also brought the sport of curling, known better to Canadians than Americans, though there are American teams. An individual sports figure of Scottish descent is baseball great Grover Cleveland Alexander.

Scottish and Scotch-Irish Americans today make up only a little over 4% of the total US population, yet they have shaped American culture significantly since colonial days. For many generations, Scottish and Scotch-Irish Americans simply blended in with the rest of the population, becoming a fairly inconspicuous part of the general "American" backdrop. In recent years, however, there has been a resurgence of interest in Scottish and Scotch-Irish heritage among members of those groups in the US. Highland Games (Scottish festivals that involve piping, dancing, track events, and sheepherding contests) have become popular again, and Scottish American societies are popping up throughout the country. Although clans quickly lost importance in early America, "clan" gatherings are once again being organized in the US as glorified family reunions. Most Scottish and Scotch-Irish Americans are several generations removed from Scotland and Northern Ireland, so their ethnic identity is largely symbolic, yet nonetheless fiercely defended today.

BIBLIOGRAPHY

Henderson, Nancy Wallace. *The Scots Helped Build America*. New York: Julian Messner, 1969.

Hunter, James. *A Dance Called America: The Scottish Highlands, the United States, and Canada*. Edinburgh/London: Mainstream Publishing, 1994.

Jackson, Carlton. *A Social History of the Scotch-Irish*. Lanham, MD: Madison Books, 1993.

Johnson, James E. *The Scots and Scotch-Irish in America*. Minneapolis: Lerner Publications, 1966.

US Bureau of the Census. *Detailed Ancestry Groups for States*. 1990 Census of Population Supplementary Reports, CP-S-1-2. Washington, DC, October 1992.

SEMINOLES AND MICCOSUKEES

LOCATION: United States (Florida)
POPULATION: 2,500 Seminoles; 500 Miccosukees
LANGUAGE: Mikasuki (Hitchiti); Muskogee; Creek; English
RELIGION: Traditional religion; Christianity
RELATED ARTICLES: Vol. 2: Native North Americans

¹ INTRODUCTION

Groups of tribal peoples who lived in southern Alabama and Georgia were called "Creeks" by the British. Around 1740 some of these people moved south to Spanish-held Florida. There in the northern part of the state, they established permanent settlements. These Creek people, once they moved to Florida were called "Seminoles." The derivative of this name has been attributed both to the Creek *simanoli* which means "runaway" and to the Spanish *cimmaron* or "wild," like an animal. The first Seminole settlers in Florida, were Oconee Creeks who spoke the language known by linguists as Hitchiti or Mikasuki (the people themselves call the language "i.laponki."; they call themselves "i.laponathi."). Other bands of Seminoles came into Florida: Yuchi, Ochise, Tallahassee.

When the Creeks lost the Red Stick War against the Americans at Horseshoe Bend in 1813–14, there was a great influx of Red Stick Creek refugees who joined the Seminoles in Florida.

From the earliest Spanish records of exploration it is known that southeastern Indians kept slaves as part of their economic system. Slaves were taken as part of the spoils of war. When the British arrived, they wanted the Indians' slaves to work on their plantations in the Carolinas and the West Indies. The Indians began to trade their slaves to the British for trade goods. It was a lucrative market. Soon they were making raids on other groups of Indians for that specific purpose, often wiping out entire Indian towns. The over-slaving of Native American populations in the southeast was one of the reasons that trade in African slavery escalated.

By the late 18th century, African slaves began to escape from the plantations in the American South. They fled to Spanish Florida where the Seminoles had settled. The Africans were welcomed by the Seminoles, who could no longer make slave raids due to European influences and had an economic need for slave workers. Slavery among the Seminoles was not harsh as it had been in the plantation system. The slaves were required to work and give tribute to their masters, but they were treated with respect.

The white masters wanted the runaway slaves back. There was something else that the Seminoles had that the southern plantation owners wanted. Cattle. By the early 19th-century, the Seminoles had massed sizable herds of cattle, based on feral cattle which strayed from the large Spanish haciendas. The Seminole settlements were situated on prime grazing lands near Tallahassee and Mikasuki and south on the Alachua (or Payne's) Prairie near present day Gainesville. Their herds multiplied.

Cattle and slave raids by Georgians and Seminoles over the Georgia/Florida border and into Alachua created the catalyst for war. It was, in fact, Seminole cattle and runaway slaves that provided the impetus for the First Seminole War in Florida in 1818. The War was little more than a series of raids to destroy the Seminole settlements and capture cattle and slaves. But politically it was very important. The unauthorized raid was made into Spanish Florida under the command of Andrew Jackson, who also captured the Spanish capital at Pensacola. Jackson was reprimanded by Washington for his rash actions attacking another country, but he had succeeded in demonstrating the weakness of Spain's hold on Florida. Ultimately, in 1821, Florida was ceded to the United States and Jackson, the greatest enemy of the Seminoles, was appointed Territorial Governor. The Treaty of Ft. Moultrie Creek in 1923 placed the Seminoles on a reservation in the middle of the state. They were not able to have contact with the coasts.

In 1830, under President Jackson, Congress passed the Indian Removal Act. This Act specified that all Indian tribes east of the Mississippi would be removed to the Indian Territory west of the Mississippi. This was considered to be for their own good as settlement was encroaching on them. This forced migration is the famous Trail of Tears. In Florida, the Treaty of Payne's Landing was made by the government in 1832. This treaty specified that seven Seminole chiefs would inspect the Indian Territory prior to their leaving Florida and give their consent to emigrate. When the delegation returned to Florida, however, they said that they had been forced into signing the treaty and that it was therefore not valid. The removal date was January 1, 1836. The Seminoles did not want to emigrate and began their patriotic resistance, the Second Seminole War, 1835 to 1842. Best known leaders from this war are Osceola, Alligator, Jumper, Micanopy, Coacoochee, and Sam Jones (Abiaki). Osceola was martyred by the whites, as he was captured in a truce situation and then died in prison. Many other Seminoles were captured and emigrated by ship from Florida to New Orleans. From there they journeyed overland to Indian Territory. From a pre-First Seminole War population of 6,000, only 300–400 remained in southern Florida.

The Third Seminole War was fought 1855–1858. By this time, settlers were moving south into the state. The state's cattle interests were politically important. The Seminoles again had accumulated cattle and were considered to be in the way of progress. Leader Billy Bowlegs was taken on a trip to Washington, Boston, and New York to show him the powerful United States and to persuade him to acquiesce to leave for Indian Territory. He would not. This war was fought mainly in the lower Florida Everglades.

The Third Seminole War ended, like the Second Seminole War, with the United States troops' withdrawal, not with a formal "peace treaty." Thus today's Florida Seminole Tribe and the Miccosukee Tribe of Indians of Florida consider themselves "unconquered," a fact that every tribal child knows.

² LOCATION AND HOMELAND

About 200 Seminoles were left in Florida after the Third Seminole War. Today, these people constitute nearly 2,500 persons. Reservations were established for them relatively near their post-war centers of population. The reservations are located in Brighton, Big Cypress, Tampa, Ft. Pierce, Immokalee, Ft. Lauderdale, Ft. Myers, West Palm Beach, and Naples. The Seminole Tribal Headquarters is on the Hollywood Reservation in the city of Hollywood, Florida. This location was the site of the old Florida Seminole Agency in the 1920s. In the 1950s, the

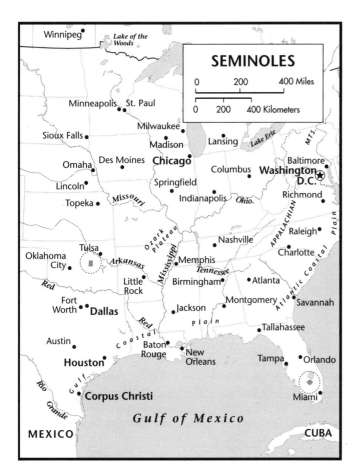

century, these people founded a tourism economy that eventually spread to the whole population, creating the popular alligator wrestling show and an important crafts market. Tourism promoted the wearing of Seminole traditional patchwork clothing, their foremost art form. Cultural tourism continues to be very important to both tribes today, as the tribes explore European tourist markets.

3 LANGUAGE

The Seminoles speak languages from the Muskhogean family of Native American languages. There are two unintelligible languages spoken within the Seminole Tribe. All of the Miccosukee Tribe of Indians of Florida and two-thirds of the Seminole Tribe of Florida speak Mikasuki (also called Hitchiti). Those people, however, call their language i.laponki. and themselves i.laponathi. The remaining one-third of the members of the Seminole Tribe of Florida speak Muskogee or Creek. Since today all tribal leaders and most of the population speak English, there is no problem with communication affecting tribal unity.

Many of Florida's place names are derived from Seminole words. For example, Tallahassee (the state's capital) comes from the Muskogee word for "old town," and Okeechobee means "big water" in Mikasuki.

4 FOLKLORE

The Seminoles' creation myth involves the Creator instilling powers to the clan animals, the Panther, and all other animals. When the earth was made, he put the animals in a large shell. When the time was right, the shell would open and they would come out. A tree root cracked the shell. The Wind helped make the crack large enough for the Panther to come out first as the Creator had wished. After the Wind, the Bird came out next, then the Bear, Deer, Snake, Frog and Otter. These are the original Seminole clans. The Creator gave them all duties. The Panther, for instance, has the power to heal, so only people of the Panther clan are to make official medicine.

The Seminole clans are Panther, Bird, Otter, Wind, Bear, Deer, Frog and Snake. Big Towns was created long ago when two sisters of Spanish descent were adopted into the tribe.

The Green Corn Dance is a special ceremony for the Seminoles. It is attended by traditional people. Few Christians attend. It marks the ripening of the corn in late May or early June and is a new year's celebration. The four-day ceremony is a rite of purification, of starting anew. Rites of passage are conducted. Court is held and punishments are meted out. Fires are extinguished, the men take sweat baths and drink medicine, a tea made from native holly. The Black Drink causes them to vomit, cleansing their body. There is a day of fasting and one of feasting. There is dancing and stickball playing, men against women.

At the Corn Dance grounds a medicine man builds a fire out of four logs pointing in the four directions. An ear of ripe corn is placed on top of each log, and dried kindling is laid in the center of the logs. While praying to the Breathmaker (fisaki omici), the bundle carrier (the highest-ranking medicine man) creates a spark and lights the fire. From that fire, the symbol of the Breath Maker, all the other fires in the village are lit. When traveling, a Seminole woman always takes some ashes from her last fire with her. In that way, the corn dance fire is always with her family.

newly chartered Seminole Tribe and the Bureau of Indian Affairs were housed in a single building. Recently, the Seminole Tribe of Florida has opened a four-story, modern office building. Tribal members live in subdivisions of modern houses on most reservations. At Brighton and Big Cypress some houses are scattered throughout the hammocks, where they have been built on the families' traditional camp sites. The Miccosukee Tribe (about 500 persons) is headquartered on the Tamiami Trail, 40 miles west of Miami and a large reservation is in the Big Cypress.

After the Third Seminole War, the Florida Seminoles resumed their hunting and trade economy, selling furs, hides, and bird plumes to trading posts located on the rivers which flowed out of the Everglades basin. Their travel was primarily by dugout sailing canoes made of cypress wood. Carts pulled by yokes of oxen were also used by those living in the Big Cypress and around Lake Okeechobee. The Everglades, rivers, coastal ridges, and beaches teemed with wildlife. Gathering activities provided vegetables, the starch "coontie," and medicinal plants.

The Oklahoma Seminoles were placed on a reservation in an environment very different from Florida. They were wards of the government and were no longer able to subsist off the land.

The Florida Seminoles retained their freedom and wanted no contact with the government. Early in the 20th century, the hide market declined and programs to drain the Everglades for farming began. The Seminoles living around the city of Miami found a new economy in tourism. Over the decades of the 20th-

The four directions (north, south, east, and west) and the number four are very important to the Seminoles and play a major part in their traditions and lives. The four medicine colors are white, black, yellow and red.

The Bundlecarrier (the head religious leader), the medicine men and women, elders, and some of the tribal leadership are involved daily in traditional practices and are anxious to support and promote such awareness to the tribe at large.

5 RELIGION

Since the Seminoles began converting in the latter 1930s, Christian Seminole churches have scheduled revivals at the time of the Corn Dance. Attendance at the native gathering was chastised. In turn, the traditional people did not want the Christians to attend. These chasms have aided in curtailing many traditional ways.

6 MAJOR HOLIDAYS

The Green Corn Dance, which marks the beginning of the new year, is the most significant holiday for Traditional Seminoles and Miccosukees. Some families have a major get-together for the celebration of Thanksgiving. This holiday is at the same time of year as the Seminoles' former Hunting Dance, which has become obsolete. Thanksgiving continues the tradition of a fall get-together.

Both Tribes hold Christmas parties. This is especially true for the affluent Seminole Tribe of Florida, who host a huge party at the Broward Convention Center with a leading country and western singer for entertainment.

7 RITES OF PASSAGE

Traditionally, babies received a name four days after they were born. Modern legal requirements, however, have made the Seminoles conform to name-giving at birth. For the past 40 years or so, especially with many families receiving Christianity, children have been given first and last names at birth. When a baby is four months old, traditional families cut its hair and nails, which are hidden to keep bad luck from the child.

Young boys attend a "Boy's School" at the age of 12 to learn traditional ways in preparation for receiving their man's name at the next Green Corn Dance. They fast, take medicine, and attend school taught by a high-ranking medicine man or bundle carrier. At the four-day Corn Dance, little children are given their second names, marriages and divorces are ratified, widows and widowers are reinstated into the community. Young people, such as the graduates of the Boy's School, receive their adult names which are given by the medicine man. The names are usually those of deceased elders, who in turn had been given names of their deceased elders. These names are seldom used in public, but are used in the families by traditional speakers.

A death in the village was once a very serious stigma. The spirits of the dead were feared, as they might not wish to leave and might try to take one of the living with them. Very important rites followed a death of a clan member. If a person died in a village, the entire village had to be moved. As a result, if a person was known to be deathly ill, a structure was made outside the village area where they would be cared for till death. For the same reason, the birthing house was also placed outside the village.

Marriage in 1900 took place in early to late teens. Divorces were simple in this matrilineal society (where the woman was in charge of the family). The wife or her relatives would place the husband's belongings outside the camp. Today, Seminole couples may or may not choose to marry, and teen pregnancies may or may not result in marriage. With the mother's clan being the most important thing to be passed on to a baby, the father is not as important an entity as he is in many other cultures.

8 INTERPERSONAL RELATIONS

Prior to the First Seminole War (1818) the Seminoles lived in large villages with huge fields, herds of cattle, droves of hogs, and horses. Each village had a *mico* (chief) and a council of warriors and elders. They elected war chiefs whenever one was necessary. There were medicine men. Because the Seminole make no distinction between the body, soul, and spirit, the medicine man worked to heal all three. He was highly respected in the society. This continues to be true today. Even some Christian burials have the medicine man (or medicine he has prepared) in attendance to assure this rite of passage.

It was common practice for Seminole men to practice polygyny (having two or more wives) in the 19th century. Women were the heads of the family and were responsible for large villages of their clan members. Polygyny was practiced with the consent of the first wife. Most often her sister was taken as the second wife. Doubtless this situation eased some of the burdens of the first wife's position. Polygyny was practiced by some in the Seminole communities well into the 20th century.

9 LIVING CONDITIONS

The Seminoles are very adaptable people. They have had to alter their housing and general way of life due to forced relocations. When they settled in northern Florida, their permanent villages were large and made up of many families, all with their own compounds—settlements called Tallahassee, Miccosukee, and Cuscowilla. Each family had two houses, a storehouse and a two-story cooking and sleeping house. The houses were built of logs.

After the Second Seminole War (1835–1842), the Seminole population was further south. They then utilized an open-sided house, thatched with palmetto fronds, with a dwelling platform three feet off the ground called a *chickee*. It appears most probable that the chickee was borrowed from the earlier Indians who lived in south Florida, the Calusa, as they had long utilized this type of structure. Chickees can last years in a sunny location. (Many families build the traditional chickee in their yard as an outside work area or as a garage for their car.) This type of home was well adapted to the Everglades where the climate is hot and humid with periods of heavy rain. They slept on blankets and bedding purchased at the trading post. They made cheesecloth mosquito nets. At night these were unrolled from the ceiling from which they were suspended and were tucked in around their beds. Furniture consisted of work platforms and tables in various locations around the camp. The chickee platforms provided seating during the day when the bedding had been put away.

The Seminoles again grouped in settlements, usually on large islands just within the Everglades interior, until 1900–1920s when subsistence became difficult and whites encroached. The large settlements then broke up, and the families formed nuclear or extended family camps: a man, wife, children, her mother and father, and perhaps an unmarried brother or uncle. They moved to smaller islands deeper in the Everglades. These camps consisted of several chickees for sleeping and working and a central cooking chickee.

In the latter 1930s some Seminole children began to ask to be sent to school. Because there were no schools for Indian children in Florida, they were sent to Indian boarding schools such as the one at Cherokee, North Carolina. When these children returned to Florida, they had become accustomed to flush toilets, hot and cold running water, and showers. They had none of these in their chickees on the reservations where by the 1940s many of them were living. This was the impetus for standard housing. The first houses were small, wood frame houses that were donated to the Seminoles' cause and moved from the towns of Ft. Lauderdale and Pompano Beach to the reservation at Dania. The local women's clubs, chapters of the Daughters of the American Revolution, and the Friends of the Seminoles contributed time and ingenuity to see this project through. They also set up a revolving fund to loan money to Seminole families so that they could finance and build their first concrete block houses or refurbish the donated houses. Seminoles could not borrow money from a bank as they did not own their own property. It was a new experience for the Seminole women to use electric stoves rather than their open cooking fires. Various architectural designs for reservation housing were attempted over the years to make housing comfortable in the hot climate, but none were better than the chickee. There are modern subdivisions on the reservations today, and many families have air conditioning.

10 FAMILY LIFE

Traditional Seminole society is matrilineal. This means that kinship is carried through the mother. Her children inherit her clan and pass it on to their children. Anyone of that clan (on any reservation in Florida, whether Seminole or Miccosukee tribal members) is considered a "relative." One must never marry a clan member, since it would be considered incest. Thus, one must always know one's clan members. The traditional ways taught that a father has little to do with the upbringing of his own children. Instead, he had obligations to his sister's children, who were his own clan members. Thus, it was a child's maternal aunts and uncles who educated and disciplined. In the traditional camp, the extended family would have included aunts, uncles, maternal grandparents, and cousins, with the eldest woman as the head of the family. Matrilocal refers to residence. Seminole society has not been matrilocal since the 1960s when subdivision housing became available. Traditionally, married couples would reside with the wife's mother. Today, most communities are not organized around the clan system. Clan is still very important to the Seminole community, however, influencing tribal politics and many other relationships.

11 CLOTHING

As soon as European trade goods became available from colonists, the Indians of the southeast began to obtain them. These goods included items of wearing apparel. The Creeks had most of their trade relationship with the British who had the finest trade goods. Fine paisley shawls, cotton goods, and wools in blue and red became highly prized and can be seen in engrav-

ings of southeastern Indians from the 18th century. From the first writings we find that Seminole clothing was of British cotton. A man's outfit consisted of a knee-length shirt with an open ruffled coat over it, woolen leggings, and one-piece leather moccasins. A turban made of a shawl blanket, trade silver, finger-woven yarn, and bead garters (perhaps a sash with long tassels), and a woolen shot bag woven with beaded designs completed his dress attire. Women wore a short, ruffled blouse and a long skirt. They, too, wore silver trade bracelets and earrings and long strands of necklace beads that were popular everyday attire well into the mid-20th century.

Women and young girls of the 19th and early 20th century were accustomed to wearing as many necklace beads as they could from chest to chin. It was a mark of wealth and popularity. Bead necklaces and bracelets were also birth gifts. Necklace beads were standard suitor and engagement gifts. Women were buried with all of their possessions, including necklace beads.

Seminole women acquired the hand-cranked sewing machine in the latter 1800s. In time, the machine technology changed their hand-sewn garments (described above) that had changed little since the 19th century. The man's main garment, the shirt, began to change around 1900. It became banded with inserted and appliquéd ornamentation forming horizontal stripes. A belt was inserted at the waist. The ruffled coat, however, retained its traditional design even till today. Leggings by this time were of smoked, tanned deer hide. Plaid wool shawls formed their turbans. Moccasins remained the same. The old-style yarn garters and belts were owned by only a few elders, as were the beaded bags. When those men died, the only examples of this work were to be seen in museum collections.

Women continued to wear the blouse and skirt, but by the 1920s the blouse ruffle had become longer, eventually forming a separate ornamental cape over a plain bodice.

Machine-sewn patchwork as it exists today is the Seminole and Miccosukee's premier art form and cultural identifier. It began being made around 1917 by the i.laponathi. This was also the time when these Mikasuki-speaking Seminoles began to reside in the tourist attractions in Miami. Leisure time and the tourist market cannot be overlooked for the blossoming and great evolution of this art form. Until the 1950s, traditional clothing was all that was worn by Seminole and Miccosukee women. The popular Seminole jacket evolved from the aforementioned man's shirt. Today, elders continue to wear their traditional dress, while most people have some patchwork clothing to wear for special occasions.

Seminole and Miccosukee youth dress in clothing bearing popular name brands and rarely wear Seminole attire. Clothing contests at annual festivals such as Seminole Fair promote 19th-century and modern patchwork clothing and offer cash prizes as incentives. Today, machine-sewn patchwork continues its evolution in intricate creations that command high prices.

Seminole men of the 18th and early 19th century wore their hair in bangs in front, shaved on the sides, with two long queues braided down the crown to the back of the head. Women wore their hair in bangs with their long tresses gathered up in a knot on top of the head. The men began to cut their hair in a "bowl-cut" in the last two decades of the 19th century. The women's hairstyles began to change around the 1920s. The bun was loosened and worn under a hairnet held in place with hair pins. The hair then began to be pulled forward and rolled, forming a crown around the face. By the 1940s this style became highly accented by the addition of a "hairboard," a crescent-shaped piece of cardboard over which the hair was fanned, held in place with a hairnet and pinned down. Styles of Seminole women's hair can be seen in the dolls they made over the decades of the 20th century. Many dolls sold today continue to show the popular Seminole "hairboard" of the 1940s.

12 FOOD

The cook fire is one of the most important of all Seminole traditions. It was the hub of the camp. Children were taught to respect the fire, which was a focal point of the clan in each camp. Traditionally, Seminoles from different clans were not supposed to eat from foods prepared from the same fire. In a large gathering, separate cooking fires were made.

The Seminoles did not eat three prescribed meals as many Europeans do. Thus, food was kept hot and ready at all times. The staple was (and continues to be in many families) a type of soup called *sofki* (Creek) or *o'they* (Mikasuki). Sofki is a cooking term for any food put in water and cooked down so that it can be consumed as a liquid. While corn and grits are the common ingredients for sofki today, meats and even fruits such as guavas were traditionally made into sofki. Sofki was kept on the fire so that anyone who wanted food could stir the kettle with the large sofki spoon and sip about two cups of liquid from it at a time.

The entire family might sit on the eating platform together for an evening or special meal. However, when guests were present, the women and children waited to eat. There were many traditional customs concerning the serving of refreshments and food to guests.

Pumpkin bread

2 cups self-rising flour
½ to 1 cup of sugar (to taste)
Enough canned pumpkin to make a soft dough
Oil for frying

Blend ingredients lightly. Turn onto a floured surface. Knead. Pull off a large piece of dough and knead it with your fingers to form a cake 4 inches in diameter and ¼ to ½ inch wide. Fry in 1 to 2 inches of oil. Turn over when one side gets lightly browned. Lay on paper towels to soak up grease.

13 EDUCATION

In the latter 1930s there were no public schools open to Seminoles Indians in Florida, so the first Seminole students who requested a formal education attended Indian Boarding School at Cherokee, North Carolina. These students became the first Seminole high school graduates. These early graduates held a number of the first official tribal positions after 1957 when the Seminole Tribe of Florida was formally organized.

Both tribes comply with state regulations concerning mandatory public school education. The Seminole Tribe and the Bureau of Indian Affairs operate Ah-Fach-Kee School on the isolated Big Cypress Reservation. Originally kindergarten through eighth grade, the school has recently added a high school program. The BIA provided the first educational endeavors on the Brighton Reservation (1938) and in Big Cypress (1943) and instituted the first Head Start programs.

Since 1972, the Seminole Tribe has been contracting for the Tribe's educational services. The Tribe's Ah-Fach-Kee School on the Big Cypress Reservation offers programs in Seminole history, culture, and language as part of the curriculum. Other students on that isolated reservation and on the Brighton Reservation are bused to schools in distant towns. Children living on reservations which are near cities attend county public schools. The Tribe has an active high school equivalency program. Annually, more tribal members are seeking higher education and obtaining degrees.

The Miccosukee Tribe has been operating its own bi-lingual elementary school since the early 1960s.

14 CULTURAL HERITAGE

Traditional songs are in the form of lullabies, songs which are sung in the telling of stories, and medicine songs used when preparing medicine or doctoring. Other songs are sung for specific dances during the Green Corn Dance.

Of the modern-day music, the Seminoles and Miccosukees tend towards country and western music. The Seminole Tribe hosts bluegrass festivals and hires top country stars to perform at the annual Tribal Christmas party. Miccosukee brothers, Lee and Stephen Tiger, formed a rock band, Tiger Tiger, in the 1970s. Seminole Tribal Chairman, James E. Billie is an accomplished singer and songwriter. His songs concern Native Americans, Seminoles, and the Everglades. By far the popular favorite with young and old is "Big Alligator!"

Traditional dancing takes place ceremonially at the Green Corn Dance. The dancers form a single line (some dances use couples) following a dance boss. The dance boss follows the lead of the medicine man who keeps time with a rattle while singing. The men in the line repeat his phrases. These dances are representational of an animal: Catfish, Lightning Bug, Black Bird, etc. Some of these dances can often be seen in performance at Seminole Fair in February.

Three publications have been written by members of the Seminole Tribe. Former chairwoman Betty Nae Jumper published *...And With the Wagon Came God* (1985), discussing early Christian contact with the Seminoles. Also from Jumper, *Legends of the Seminoles* (1994) is a collection of folktales with color illustrations. Moses Jumper, Sr. has published a book of poetry.

15 WORK

Following the Seminole Wars of the l9th century, the Seminoles resumed their trade in Everglades products—furs, hides, bird plumage, beeswax, honey, etc. They sold to trading posts set up by settlers on the rivers flowing out of the Everglades. This market began to decline early in the 20th century. They then developed a relationship with tourism through non-Indian operated tourist attractions, specifically in Miami and Silver Springs. By the 1930s this was the major economy. Families lived "on exhibition" during the months of the tourist season made and sold crafts to the tourists.

This economy continues to be lucrative for Seminole families. Today, "cultural tourism" is an industry that is being heavily promoted by both the Seminole and Miccosukee Tribes. The two major Seminole attractions are Kissimmee Billie Swamp Safari and the Ah-Tha-Thi-Ki Museum in Big Cypress. The museum also has branch facilities in Hollywood and Tampa. Okalee Indian Village is operated by the tribe in

Hollywood. The Miccosukee Culture Center is operated by that tribe on the Tamiami Trail 40 miles west of Miami.

For decades, the Seminole Tribe struggled to create a notable cattle industry. They have succeeded and are known throughout the country as producers of fine calves. In the 1970s the Tribe pioneered the concept of tax-free cigarette shops on sovereign reservation land. High-stakes bingo followed. These enterprises have made the long impoverished Seminole Tribe wealthy. Much of the proceeds goes into better education and health care for tribal members. Importantly, with this new financial independence, the tribe has been able to take charge of its business interests. They are able to support political candidates who can offer them assistance and can hire lobbyists to protect their prized reservation lands from harm. Yet, the tribe does not view these lucrative enterprises as permanent situations. They know that a high court ruling could take them away. They would then fall back on revenues from cattle production (19th largest in the nation), citrus (the world's number one producer of lemons), and tourism. Tribal members receive monthly dividends from gaming revenues.

16 SPORTS

Before the Second Seminole War (1835), "stick ball," a game similar to lacrosse, was played by southeastern Indians as a man's war game, town against town. Deaths were not uncommon. The post-war version of this game is played ceremonially at the annual Green Corn Dance, men against women. The men use two stick ball racquets, the women use only their hands. The object was to throw the ball and hit the ball pole above a mark and score.

Alligator wrestling for the enjoyment of spectators was created in the tourist attractions by a non-Indian, early in the 20th century and soon became popular with young Seminole men. For many decades, alligator wrestling has been a very respected occupation within the Seminole and Miccosukee tribal communities. It is considered a cultural activity. Alligator wrestling is performed at most tribal festivals and attractions and continues to be a crowd thriller.

The Seminole Tribe's Recreation Department is very active in sponsoring team sports. There are full facility gyms on all major reservations. Members of the Seminole Tribe also belong to bowling, basketball and softball leagues. The Tribe sponsors national and circuit rodeos during the year and sends tribal members to compete in such competitions as the Indian National Finals Rodeo.

17 ENTERTAINMENT AND RECREATION

Like most families in the United States, the Seminoles and Miccosukees have the advantages of cable TV, computers, the Internet. There is a great difference in the generational mindset.

18 FOLK ART, CRAFTS, AND HOBBIES

Many Seminole women (and a few men) make machine-sewn patchwork. Since the early 1900s, this form of artistic expression has identified these Native Americans. Patchwork was originally made in simple and large designs. Over the decades it was refined and is today made extremely complex. This colorful art form is used as decorative ornamentation in the women's traditional skirts and men's jackets. It is accented by rows of tiny rickrack to enhance the designs.

The oldest commercial craft is doll making. The women make dolls out of the fiber of the palmetto (also used in basketmaking). Dolls are dressed in traditional Seminole garb. Seminole and Miccosukee men carve souvenirs, miniature canoes, and Everglades animals, as well as popular tomahawks and lances for the tourist trade. The commercial sale of crafts has been a major household industry for most of the 20th century. Many Seminole and Miccosukee families sell crafts (they also buy from other Seminole and Miccosukee craftsmen and women) at seasonal and weekend fairs.

19 SOCIAL PROBLEMS

Generation gaps are problematical, but they are typical to all cultures. However, the Seminoles have had to learn elements of someone else's culture. Problems arise in learning how to deal with situations outside one's cultural upbringing. As an example, the traditional decisionmaking process should result in a total consensus of agreement, not just a majority. Christianity and other European-influenced ideals first replaced the traditional Seminole ideology at the tribal decisionmaking level.

Aggression is not a traditional attribute of Seminole culture; in fact, people who showed aggressive or ambitious tendencies would have been considered atypical and "crazy" to a traditional Seminole or Miccosukee. In the old days, such a person could have been ordered killed for "deviant" behavior. Today, tribal leaders must be able to function aggressively in order to uphold and protect tribal rights.

All tribal members are in some way participants in the nontraditional system today. Yet, traditional cultural patterns often remain. For instance, a parent may not demand that children study their lessons, or may not encourage them to excel in school, as involvement in others' affairs and the stimulation of ambition is not traditional behavior.

Thus, there are inherent social conflicts continuing to plague tribal members as they move into the 21st century. However, both the Seminole and Miccosukee Tribes enter the 21st century fortified by new economic landfalls such as gaming, that provide these formally impoverished tribes with the means to continue in their upwardly mobile swing, paying for those services which will aid them in their future endeavors. In looking back over their tumultuous history, they celebrate the fact that they have survived and are prospering!

20 BIBLIOGRAPHY

Blackard, David M. *Patchwork and Palmettos: Seminole-Miccosukee Folk Art Since 1820*. Ft. Lauderdale: The Ft. Lauderdale Historical Society, 1990.

Cline, Howard F. *Notes on Colonial Indians and Communities in Florida 1700-1821*. New York: Garland, 1974.

Covington, James W. *The Seminoles of Florida*. Gainesville, FL: University Presses of Florida, 1993.

Greenlee, Robert F. "Folktales of the Florida Seminole." *American Anthropologist* 46:317-28.

Kersey, Harry A. *"Pelts, Plumes, and Hides: White Traders among the Seminole Indians 1870-1930."* Gainesville, FL: University Presses of Florida, 1975.

MacCauley, Clay. "The Seminole Indians of Florida." In Fifth Annual Report of the Bureau of American Ethnology, pp. 469531. Washington, DC: Government Printing Office, 1883-84, 1887.

Mahon, John K. *History of the Second Seminole War, 1935-*

1842. Gainesville, FL: University Presses of Florida, 1967.

Spoehr, Alexander. "The Florida Seminole Camp." Anthropological Series, Field Museum of Natural History 33:1-27, 1941.

Sturtevant, William C. "Creek Into Seminole." In *North American Indian in Historical Perspective,* ed. Eleanore B. Leacock and Nancy O. Lurie, ed. pp. 92-128. New York: Random House, 1971.

———. "The Mikasuki Seminole: Medical Beliefs and Practices." Ph.D. Dissertation, Yale University. Ann Arbor: University Microfilms, 1954.

West, Patsy. "I.laponathi.: The Florida Seminoles in the 1930s" *Native Peoples* 9:3 26-33 (Spring 1996).

———. "The Miami Indian Tourist Attractions: A History and Analysis of a Transitional Mikasuki Seminole Environment." *Florida Anthropologist* 34:200-24, 1981.

———. "Seminole Indian Settlements of Pine Island, Broward County Florida" *The Florida Anthropologist* 42 (1) 43-56, 1989.

—by P. West

SUMU

LOCATION: Nicaragua; Honduras (Eastern coasts)
POPULATION: 13,000–16,000
LANGUAGE: Sumu; Spanish
RELIGION: Protestantism (Moravian church); Catholicism

¹ INTRODUCTION

The Sumu are an indigenous group living on the eastern coasts of Nicaragua and Honduras, in the area commonly known as the Atlantic or Miskito (also spelled Mosquito) Coast, which they share with their traditional adversaries, the Miskito. The Sumu are the second-most-populous native group in the region, after the Miskito. Historically, the Sumu were composed of at least 10 subgroups, and their territory stretched from the Rio Patuca in present-day Honduras to the Rio Escondido in Nicaragua.

In the 17th century, the Miskito—a mixed-race people resulting from intermarriage between escaped African slaves and other segments of the local population—were introduced to guns and ammunition by English traders and settlers in the area, who wanted help in their colonial rivalry with the Spanish. The Miskito used their newfound fire power to enhance their own position as well, expanding their territory northward, southward, and westward from its original location at the mouth of the Rio Coco. They demanded tribute from the Sumu or captured them, enslaving them or incorporating them into the Miskito population.

The beleaguered Sumu ultimately retreated into the interior of the region, living by the headwaters of the coastal rivers. The Miskito became the most important non-White population on the coast, living in peace with the British and serving as an intermediary between them and the Sumu, whose numbers declined sharply as a result of Spanish, British, and Miskito aggression and the spread of European diseases. From the mid-17th century to the late 19th century, the Miskito prospered, thanks to their trade with the British and the abundant natural resources of their territory, which at one time extended as far as the present-day nations of Belize and Panama. Moravian missionaries arrived in the region in the 1849. After converting large numbers of Miskito, they began directing their efforts at the Sumu at the beginning of the 20th century.

In the late 19th century, an ethnic shift occurred in the region when banana growers began bringing in Black English-speaking laborers from the West Indies to work on their plantations. They and their descendants, who became known as Creoles, took the place of the Miskito as the area's dominant non-White group, relegating both the Miskito and the Sumu to a lower social status. The Creoles settled mainly in the newly established port towns while the indigenous groups remained in rural villages, retaining their traditional languages and way of life. With Nicaraguan and Honduran independence from Britain in the 19th century, the United States began to play a greater role in the region, especially in the area of banana production, and its corporate interests, particularly the United Fruit Company—now United Brands—remained influential well into the 20th century.

When the Sandinista government came to power in 1979 and moved to consolidate its control over the native peoples of the

Atlantic coast, they met with widespread resistance from the Miskito, who formed their own Contra force, a supposed alliance between the native groups of the region called *Misura* (a combination of the groups' names: Miskito, Sumu, and Rama). However, most of the Sumu did not want to become involved in the hostilities between the Miskito and the government. They tried to stay out of the conflict, but the Miskito raided their settlements, drafting young men and torturing and murdering those who resisted (or were suspected of resisting). In 1982 the Miskito occupied Musawas, the largest Sumu settlement, conscripting, killing, or evacuating its residents. Throughout northern Nicaragua, innocent civilians were terrorized and murdered. Schools and clinics were destroyed; farms went untended and livestock were killed.

Caught between pressure from Misura and from the Sandinistas themselves, between 2,000 and 3,000 Sumu fled to refugee camps in Honduras, while others hid in the mountains, were forced into military service, or relocated to the coast. Their persecutors even raided the refugee camps to draft Sumu men. By 1985 conditions in the camps had led the Sumu to begin returning to their homes, and by 1987 about half the refugees had returned to Nicaragua, where the worst of the fighting was over. Although Nicaragua nominally granted autonomy to the native groups of the Atlantic coast in 1987, the threat of either Sandinista or Misura violence remained ever-present.

President Violeta Barrios de Chamorro, whose 1990 election ended Sandinista rule, established a new ministry to serve as a liaison with the peoples of the Atlantic coast—the Nicaraguan Institute for the Development of the Atlantic Region (INDERA). The Sumu have drawn international attention due to their political plight, as well as their role in conserving the natural resources of their homeland. Theirs was a small community to begin with, and the continuing violence in their region has threatened them with virtual extinction through the reduction of their birth rate and the destruction of their settlements. As of the late 1980s, many were living in either Honduran refugee camps or resettlement camps in Nicaragua.

2 LOCATION AND HOMELAND

The Sumu live in isolated inland villages along the main rivers of what is known as the Atlantic or Miskito Coast, located in Nicaragua and Honduras. The Miskito Coast is extremely diverse geographically, with a large inland savanna, a tropical rain forest (home to most of the Sumu), coastal lowlands, and the most extensive continental shelf in the Caribbean. Its major rivers include the Patuca, Coco (also known as the Wangki), Prinsapolca, Awaltara (Rio Grande), and Kuringwas. There are three main subgroups among the Sumu, each living in a different region. In Nicaragua, the Sumu live along the Bocay, Umbra, and Waspuk tributaries of the Rio Coco river and near the headwaters of the Prinsapolka and Grande rivers. In Honduras, they live along the Patuca River.

Each of the Sumu subgroups speaks its own variant of a common language. The communities of the Panamaka—who account for 70% of the Sumu—center around the Bocay, Saslaya, and Waspuk rivers and the mining town of Bonanza. The Tawahka, who make up another 20%, live along the Rio Bambana in northern Nicaragua and far up the Rio Patuca in eastern Honduras. The Ulwa, who represent 10% of the Sumu, live along the Prinzapolca and Rio Grande de Matagalpa rivers at around the midpoint of the Nicaraguan coast. During the pro-

tracted warfare of the 1980s, the Sumu suffered persecution at the hands of both the Sandinista government and the Miskito resistance, which destroyed a great number of their settlements. Many Sumu fled to refugee camps in Honduras, but most have been repatriated in the years since 1985 and are attempting to rebuild their shattered communities. Altogether, there are thought to be between 13,000 and 15,000 Sumu in Nicaragua and 1,000 in Honduras.

3 LANGUAGE

Sumu, like the language of the Miskito, is a Misumalpan tongue derived from the Chibchan family. Outside influences have produced loanwords from English, Spanish, and Miskito. There are three distinct Sumu dialects: Tawahka and Panamaka, which are very similar to each other, and Ulwa, which is more divergent. Most Sumu are multilingual, speaking Spanish in school and their native language at home. In addition, many learn to speak Miskito within their communities. Few Sumu know how to write in their own language, but its written form may enjoy a resurgence with the growth of bilingual education that has accompanied the demands of indigenous groups, including the Sumu, for greater cultural autonomy.

4 FOLKLORE

The Sumu traditionally believed in a sun god, called Mapapak, who lived in the heavens. Other forces of nature, including the moon and the wind, were also worshipped. A variety of spirits (*walasa, nawah,* and *dimalah*) were thought to have either harmful or beneficial influences on human beings and were even thought capable of causing death. Much Sumu folklore has been preserved by its shamans, or *sukia,* who also serve as priests, exorcists, herbalists, and spiritual advisors.

5 RELIGION

The Sumu in Nicaragua are mostly adherents of the Moravian Church, a Protestant sect. The Tawahka Sumu in Honduras are mostly Catholic. Although their traditional religion—which involved sun and moon worship and a belief in both benevolent and malevolent spirits—declined with the arrival of Moravian missionaries in the 19th century, some Sumu continue to hold beliefs associated with it. Its holy men, or shamans, were called *sukia.*

6 MAJOR HOLIDAYS

Holiday celebrations combine the major holy days of the Christian calendar, including Christmas (25 December) and Easter (late March or early April), with the traditional Sumu practices of singing, dancing, and drinking.

7 RITES OF PASSAGE

Festivities mark major events in the life-cycle, such as weddings and funerals. Special ceremonies, such as the *asang lawana,* formerly marked rites of passage for both men and women.

8 INTERPERSONAL RELATIONS

The Sumu family traditionally functioned as an independent economic unit. Men felled trees and hunted, while women performed agricultural work and household chores. Although there is still some division of labor according to gender, today both men and women participate in the cash economies of the countries in which they live. The Sumu formerly had a labor-exchange system called *birbiri* for heavy physical work, but today it is more common to exchange commodities for cash.

Elders are honored and respected but have no formal evaluation in social status. Shamans have traditionally exercised some authority within Sumu society.

9 LIVING CONDITIONS

Sumu dwellings are typically wooden or post-and-pole structures, with thatch or tin roofs and floors made of board, split bamboo, or palm branches. They mostly consist of one room—although some have interior divisions—and generally have windows and doors. Instead of having a foundation, houses are usually raised several meters or feet off the ground on posts. Although modern medicine is replacing traditional Sumu folk remedies that use roots, leaves, bark, and seeds, herbal cures are still used for a variety of purposes, including the treatment of poisonous snake bites.

The Sumu generally live in remote areas that make for difficult travel conditions. The home of the Tawahka in Honduras is accessible only by plane and canoe. In Nicaragua, the Rio Bocay and Rio Coco are the only means of transportation to and from Sumu villages, and those making the journey run risks from white water, rocky shoals, and portages. Groups attempting to improve access to these areas have recently had success with dugout canoes modified to accommodate an outboard motor.

10 FAMILY LIFE

Most Sumu live in extended families with two or three generations under one roof. Men formerly had more than one wife, but today monogamy is the rule. Courtship customs include the presentation of gifts—such as food and firewood—by the suitor to the young woman's parents. Once married, the couple generally lives with in-laws until their house is built. At one time, marriage with outsiders was strictly forbidden, but today it is common for the Sumu to marry Blacks, Mestizos, or members of other native groups—even their traditional enemies, the Miskito. In addition to their domestic responsibilities, women take part in farm work, including planting, weeding, and harvesting.

11 CLOTHING

Formerly, Sumu women made loincloths and skirts from pounded tuno tree bark and other clothing from cotton they spun, dyed, and wove by hand. Today, however, the Sumu, like other inhabitants of Nicaragua and Honduras, wear mass-produced Western-style clothing, mostly lightweight cotton.

12 FOOD

Dietary staples for the Sumu include root crops, such as sweet manioc (cassava) and yams; plantains and green bananas, which are boiled, or baked; rice and beans; and fish. Corn is pounded to make tortillas. Ripe plantains and bananas are mashed together with other ingredients, including maize and palm fruits, and mixed with water to produce a fermented beverage called *mishla* or *wasak*. The role that fish and wild game play in the Sumu diet varies depending on their availability. The Sumu also keep chickens, ducks, turkeys, pigs, and cows.

13 EDUCATION

Although Honduras and Nicaragua, where most Sumu live, both have free, compulsory primary education, the educational systems of both countries are inadequate, with low enrollment and graduation rates and high adult illiteracy. Estimates of the adult illiteracy rate in Honduras range from 27% to over 40% and as high as 80% in rural areas (where most Sumu live). Schools are understaffed and undersupplied, with as many as 80 pupils per classroom.

Sumu children receive a practical education that prepares them for daily life by observing and helping their parents, an activity that breaks down along gender lines, establishing sharply differentiated future roles. While boys participate in farming, fishing, and hunting with their fathers, girls help their mothers with domestic chores.

14 CULTURAL HERITAGE

Many of the traditional Sumu flute melodies imitate bird calls, with accompaniment provided by rattles and drums.

15 WORK

The Sumu have traditionally lived by subsistence agriculture, raising root crops, maize, plantains, bananas, and other produce, both for food and cash. They use the same slash-and-burn farming techniques as their ancestors to clear forest land for planting. However, today they mostly fish with hook and line rather than the spears of their ancestors, and hunt wild game with shotguns and .22-caliber rifles, which have replaced bows and arrows and blowguns. Sumu villagers traditionally helped each other with major tasks, such as house-building, through a traditional system of labor exchange called *biribiri* that usually involved kinship networks. Today, however, the exchange of labor has been replaced by payments of produce, supplies, or cash.

In addition to their traditional subsistence activities, the Sumu have been employed by Europeans since the 17th century for a variety of tasks, which have included tapping trees for saps, resins, and gums; catching shrimp, turtles, and lobsters; and panning for gold. Today many own small stores or work as teachers, nurses, boatmen, or ministers.

16 SPORTS

Popular sports in the Nicaraguan and Honduran homelands of the Sumu include baseball, soccer, basketball, and volleyball. Cockfighting is a favorite spectator sport among the Sumu and other groups living along the Mosquito Coast.

17 ENTERTAINMENT AND RECREATION

Holidays and other special occasions are marked with singing, dancing, and drinking alcoholic beverages including *mishla,* a fermented beverage made from fruit and water.

18 FOLK ART, CRAFTS, AND HOBBIES

The traditional crafts of spinning, weaving, and dyeing cotton for clothes and household items such as sheets have been replaced by the production of more decorative items for marketing, such as carved tree gourds, tuno bark tapestries, and *majao* bags. Tuno bark is also used for making blankets and mosquito netting, and twine for weaving bags and hammocks is made from pounded majao bark.

¹⁹SOCIAL PROBLEMS

The Sumu, like the Miskito and other native groups in eastern Nicaragua and Honduras, generally fare worse than the mixed-race (Mestizo) or black (Creole) populations in terms of income, education, and job opportunities. Many hold low-paying, dangerous mining jobs. The Sumu are additionally victimized by the historically disdainful attitude of the Miskito, who refer to them as "slaves" *(Albatuina)* and "flatheads" *(Ialtanta),* ridiculing their language and customs.

In the 1980s, the Sumu suffered mistreatment at the hands of both the Sandinista government and Miskito resistance forces, who drove as many as 3,000 Sumu from their homelands by a campaign of terror that included forced conscription, mass kidnappings, rape, torture, and murder. Repatriation began in the mid-1980s, and the Sumu are now struggling to rebuild their homes and reestablish their culture in the wake of the devastation of the past 15 years. In 1987 the Tawahka Sumu in Honduras formed the Federación Indígena Tawahka de Honduras (FITH) to protect the group's political, economic, territorial, and cultural rights. The comparable group in Nicaragua is Sumu Kalpapakna Wahaini Lani (SUKAWALA), also known as the Sumu Brotherhood.

²⁰BIBLIOGRAPHY

Americas Watch Committee. *The Sumus in Nicaragua and Honduras: An Endangered People.* New York and Washington, DC: Americas Watch, 1987.

Helms, Mary W. *Asang: Adaptations to Culture Contact in a Miskito Community.* Gainesville: University Presses of Florida, 1971.

Herlihy, Peter H. "Securing a Homeland: The Tawahka Sumu of Mosquitia's Rain Forest." In *State of the Peoples: A Global Human Rights Report on Societies in Danger,* edited by Marc S. Miller. Boston: Beacon Press, 1993.

———. "Sumu." In *Encyclopedia of World Cultures.* Boston: G. K. Hall, 1992.

Manuel, Anne. "No Place to Be Neutral: The Plight of the Sumu Indians." *Commonweal* 115 (1988): 107–109.

Merrill, Tim L., ed. *Honduras: A Country Study.* Washington, DC: US Government Printing Office, 1995.

———. *Nicaragua: A Country Study.* Washington, DC: US Government Printing Office, 1994.

New River Bocay Project Web site. httsp://198.82.212.56/pub/compages/bocay/

Nietschmann, Bernard. "The Miskito Nation and the Geopolitics of Self-Determination." In *The Ethnic Dimension in International Relations,* edited by Bernard Schechterman and Martin Slann. Westport, CT: Praeger, 1993.

Olson, James S. *The Indians of Central and South America: An Ethnohistorical Dictionary.* New York: Greenwood Press, 1991.

Parent, Derek A. Rio Platano Biosphere Reserve Web site. http://www.vir.com/~derekp/aboutres.html

—by R. Wieder

SURINAMESE

LOCATION: Suriname
POPULATION: 410,000 in Suriname; 200,000 in Holland (the Netherlands)
LANGUAGE: Dutch (official); English; Spanish; Sranan; Hindi; Sranan Tongo (Taki-Taki)
RELIGION: Christianity; Hinduism; Islam

¹INTRODUCTION

Suriname became a British colony in 1650 and a Dutch colony in 1667. The Dutch made what is known in history as the worst land-swap deal ever—taking Suriname in exchange for Nieuw Amsterdam, or New York, as the new British owners called it!

The Dutch planted sugarcane and coffee, importing West African slaves to work on the plantations. But the brutality of the owners drove many slaves into the interior, where they successfully evaded capture and eventually were granted recognition as free citizens by the frustrated Dutch. Indentured workers were then brought from Java, China, and India to work in the fields, and it is this rich ethnic mixture that influences the modern Surinamese society today.

Suriname's journey from independence in 1975 has been marred by several military coups that led to the brutal repression of opposition and a rebellious uprising by the Maroon communities, evolved from Black African slaves, within the rain forest interior. The National Army carried out raids on their villages, killing and detaining large numbers of them, which resulted in the flight of 10,000 to 20,000 Maroons to French Guiana. It was not until 1987 that a new constitution was created, returning the country to civilian rule. During the military dictatorship, Suriname was cut off from aid by Holland and America, and the loss of $800 million of aid has badly damaged the economy. In 1990 another army coup deposed President Ramsewak Shankar. In 1991 Ronald Venetiaane became president, and in 1992 a peace accord was signed with the two main guerrilla groups, the Surinamese Liberation Army and the Tucayana Amazonas.

Despite setbacks, Suriname now exports alumina, aluminum, bauxite, rice, timber, shrimp, and bananas.

²LOCATION AND HOMELAND

Formerly Dutch Guiana, Suriname is the smallest country in Latin America with the smallest population, estimated in 1990 at 410,000. Located on the north-central coast of South America, it has an area of 163,820 sq km (63,251 sq mi)—but 17,635 sq km (6,809 sq mi) remain as disputed territories with neighboring Guyana and French Guiana. Suriname has a narrow coastal plain near or below sea level, much of it swampy and requiring draining systems and dikes. A central massif of low, forested mountain ranges covers 80% of the entire country.

Suriname has a humid tropical climate throughout the year, tempered along the coast by the northeast trade winds. Rainfall is over 300 cm (118 in) annually in the rain forests, and averages 193 cm (76 in) along the coast. The country is rich in wildlife, including monkeys, anteaters, armadillos, sloths, tapirs, deer, jaguars, pumas, and ocelots. There are also snakes, birds, and a wide variety of insects, and the rivers teem with fish.

The capital is Paramaribo, an Amerindian name. Many place names are taken from the Amerindians, as are the names of rivers, animals, plants, and common tools used by everyone.

The population is principally composed of Asian Indians who make up 33% of the total, and Creoles (mixed African and European stock) who also make up 33%. The remainder include the Javanese and smaller groups of Maroons, Chinese, and South American Indians. It is also a youthful country, with about 75% of its people under 30 years old, and 40% under 15 years of age.

3 LANGUAGE

The official language of Suriname is Dutch, but many people speak English. Other languages are Sranan, a Creole tongue; Hindi, and other Asian Indian, African, and Amerindian languages. Altogether, 22 languages are spoken. The most common language is Sranan Tongo, also called Taki-Taki, which combines elements of English, Dutch, and several African languages. The main working language is Spanish.

4 FOLKLORE

The African slaves who escaped into the wild forest recreated the myths and legends of the West African culture from which they had been torn. They reestablished the tribal hierarchies, customs, and polytheistic beliefs that had governed their lives in Africa. The Maroons of Suriname, as the Black descendants are known, form the largest Maroon population in this part of the hemisphere, and their culture has influenced the thinking of many of the urban Creoles. There are six main Maroon tribes, each with their own chieftain or Granman.

Many Surinamese folk tales are based on Afro-centered traditions and emphasize the persistence of African belief, the organic unity between animals, and between humans and nature generally, as well as the continuing link between the living and the dead.

There is a particular folk tale about a cunning spider who outwits humans and animals. Many of the stories take place in Africa. In Creole folklore, riddles play an important part. The *lai tori* riddles, despite European influence, are overwhelmingly of African origin.

5 RELIGION

The main religion in Suriname is Christianity, followed by Hinduism and Islam. Some Christian groups also practice traditional African beliefs such as Obeah and Winti, which translated literally means "wind." This is a traditionally polytheistic and largely secret religion of West African origin. It recognizes that there are a multitude of gods and ghosts each having their own myths, rites, offerings, taboos, and magical forces. The phenomenon of Obeah is that it is a healer god, who can also be invoked to bring illness and other calamities to one's enemy. The cult of Obeah exists not only in Suriname, but also in neighboring Guyana, formerly a British colony, and in several Caribbean islands such as Jamaica.

6 MAJOR HOLIDAYS

The Muslim holiday Id ul Fitr, or Lebaran or Bodo in Indonesian, celebrates the end of fasting during Ramadan. The Hindu festival of Holi Phagwa varies each year and is a lively event when water, paint, talc, and colored powder are liberally

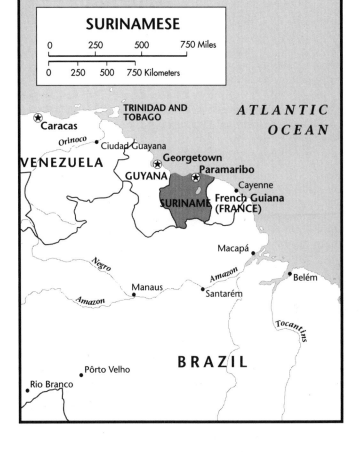

thrown into the streets at passersby. The Maroons celebrate with their "dance feasts" in the interior. These are competitions between men or women and are accompanied by songs and rhythmic clapping and chanting from the audience.

Independence Day, a major national holiday, is on 25 November.

7 RITES OF PASSAGE

Naming ceremonies at birth are important in all the diverse religious cultures in Suriname. Wedding ceremonies are also considered to be major occasions and can be elaborate and colorful, with generous feasting. Circumcision is practiced by Muslims.

Among Hindus, the birth ceremony traditionally takes place before the umbilical cord is cut. This ceremony is called *jatakarma*. The naming ceremony occurs 10 days after the child is born. Among the Christians there are Catholics, Lutherans, and Moravians, who baptize their children according to their own religious traditions, as do those of the Reformed Church.

8 INTERPERSONAL RELATIONS

Generally, status is based not on race or creed but on a person's education, profession, and economic position, as well as on how much political influence that person is able to wield.

The familiar Hindu caste system is a highly localized phenomenon in the villages of India. So when low-caste people and twice-born Brahmins were thrown together on board ship to become *jahagis* (shipmates) on the sailing boats from India to Suriname in the 19th century, that system soon became irrelevant. Today there is more or less only one common caste for all Hindus in Suriname, although Brahmins do retain their special religious role in interpreting the sacred knowledge of the rituals and Sanscrit texts.

Anyone visiting a friend or acquaintance at their home address is expected to call upon everyone else that they know within that neighborhood. Not to do so is considered extremely rude.

⁹ LIVING CONDITIONS

The birth and death rates in Suriname are lower than the average for Latin America as a whole. Life expectancy is 68 years for men and 73 for women, one of the highest in Latin America.

The gross national product (GNP) suffered a sharp decline during the troubles of the 1980s because of political instability caused by military coups. It was the ensuing reign of terror against the Maroon uprising that led to Dutch and American aid being withdrawn. The loss of one-fifth of its GNP caused havoc in the country's economy.

Since then, the GNP has nonetheless become one of the highest in South America. Health is generally good, although many doctors emigrated to the Netherlands after independence. Sanitary conditions and nutrition are generally adequate.

There is a poor transport infrastructure, with only 25% of the roads paved and fewer than 160 km (100 mi) of railways. Navigable rivers and canals are important for freight and passenger transport.

¹⁰ FAMILY LIFE

The Maroon men are close to their children, passing on ritual knowledge to their sons and playing an active role in the raising of the family. Many of the men have more than one wife, though few have more than three wives at a time. Care of the children is entrusted to one parent rather than two, and children spend their first four to six years with the mother. Many are then given to the father of another relative, and there may be further shifts at later ages in order to accommodate the child's developing needs, or changes in the parents' marital status or residence patterns.

¹¹ CLOTHING

Many of the Javanese women in Suriname still wear sarongs as they would in Indonesia, while the Creole women continue to wear the *kotomissie* traditional costume and the *angisa*, the handkerchief.

¹² FOOD

The food of Suriname reflects the ethnic diversity of the country. There are the *warungs*—Javanese food stalls serving *bami goreng* (fried noodles) and *nasi goreng* (fried rice). Creole food uses tubers, such as cassava and sweet potatoes, and plantains with chicken and fish, including shrimp.

Rice is the staple diet for most people. There is also *pom*, which is a purée of the taro root, a relative of cassava, which is tastily spiced and served with *kip* (chicken). *Moksie alesie* is a

Diners at a lodge on Kumalu Island, Suriname. Surinamese cuisine reflects the ethnic diversity of the population, which includes Javanese and Creole influences. (Anne Kalosh)

rice dish with meat, chicken, white beans, tomatoes, peppers, and spices.

¹³ EDUCATION

Education is free and compulsory from the age of 6 years until 12 years. Most students leaving primary education continue on into secondary school, while higher education is provided by the government at the Anton de Kom University. Literacy rates are high, about 95% for both men and women.

¹⁴ CULTURAL HERITAGE

Among the Maroon tribes, children are expected to learn or participate in the world of artistic production, performance, and appreciation from a very early age. Many of the Maroons' huts display the fine woodcarvings for which they are famous and that adorn furniture, tools, and boots. They also carve their drums, which must never be touched by any female. These drums are used to accompany skillful and intense dancing during the dance feasts.

At night in the capital city, Paramaribo, one will hear in the distance the mellow sounds of metallic music. This is the famous traditional "gamelan" music played by the Javanese to accompany their dances.

Hindu weddings and religious plays are elaborately ceremonial and make use of exquisite costumes. The cosmopolitan mix of the country means that everyone, Hindus, Muslims, and Christians, frequently attends these ceremonies.

15 WORK

Much of the farmland has fallen fallow as a result of the civil war between the government and the Maroons during their uprising. Low wages and sharp price increases (tenfold for gasoline) set off a series of strikes in post offices, banks, and offices early in 1993. Many families depend on relatives in the Netherlands who send home money. The Asian Indians are mostly small farmers, while the Creoles are concentrated in retail, politics, and the professions in urban areas. The Javanese work mainly on Dutch-owned plantations.

In 1975 approximately 40,000 Surinamese fled to Amsterdam, expecting racial unrest with independence. That exodus continued throughout the 1980s as nepotism, corruption, and lack of central planning hindered economic development. Today there are some 200,000 Surinamese living in Holland—almost a third of Suriname's population.

The majority of Surinamese work for the government or in the service sector, such as banking, insurance, education, and medical institutions. Others supplement their incomes by working illegally in neighboring Guyana and French Guiana. There are no unemployment benefits or other social provisions, and the unemployed must obtain a "certificate of poverty" to receive free medical care.

16 SPORTS

Soccer is a popular game played in towns and villages everywhere, and a great hero of the game is Ruud Gullit, of Suriname descent, who went on to become the captain of the Dutch national team. Another popular sport is swimming, and the country took great pride when Anthony Nesty won a gold medal for Suriname in the 100-meter butterfly event at the 1988 Olympic Games.

17 ENTERTAINMENT AND RECREATION

A distinctive pastime practiced throughout Suriname are the birdsong competitions held in parks and public plazas on Sundays and holidays. People carrying their songbird (usually a small black tua-tua) in a cage are a frequent sight on the streets of Paramaribo as they set off for a training session or simply to take the bird for a stroll.

Young people enjoy outings, sporting events, and the cinema, as well as dancing.

18 FOLK ART, CRAFTS, AND HOBBIES

The Afro-centered culture of the Maroons makes a distinctive contribution to the arts and crafts of the country's museums and galleries in the form of woodcarvings and sculpture.

The Hindu and Javanese cultures are reflected in their religious festivals, dress, and ceremonies.

19 SOCIAL PROBLEMS

The signing of a peace treaty between the government and the Jungle Commandos, the rebel Maroons, has not ended the violence. Certain parts of the interior are still off-limits to visitors as they are controlled by groups of armed rebels. The violent reprisals inflicted on the Maroon villages during the war drove many refugees across the border into French Guiana where they were put into camps. Since the treaty, the French authorities have been persuading or compelling the refugees to return to Suriname, increasing the tension in some war-devastated areas.

Meanwhile, the government has been forced to take action to try to resolve its continuing economic crisis. Inflation was around 54% by mid-1993 and was heading towards 100%.

20 BIBLIOGRAPHY

British World Data Annual. World Bibliographical Series, Vol.117, Clio Press.

Caribbean Handbook,1994/1995, Cable and Wireless.

Price, Sally, and Richard Price. *Afro-American Arts of the Suriname Rain Forest.* Los Angeles: University of California Press,1980.

—by P. Pitchon

SWEDISH AMERICANS

For more information on Swedish history and culture, *see* **Vol. 4: Swedes**.

OVERVIEW

In the 1600s, Sweden attempted to establish a colony called New Sweden in North America near today's Wilmington, Delaware. It was the first permanent settlement in the Delaware River Valley. New Sweden was never very successful, however, and it was soon abandoned. Some 200 years passed before Swedes began to immigrate to the US on a large scale. Then, they came en masse. Between 1851 and 1929, 1.2 million Swedish immigrants entered the US. Only Ireland and Norway (and perhaps Iceland) lost a higher percentage of their population to America.

Several factors in Sweden encouraged emigration. Political upheavals, a repressive government, religious oppression (it was illegal to belong to any but the official Lutheran Church), a rigid class system, and mandatory military service all drove Swedes to look elsewhere for more freedom. Above and beyond these concerns, however, were economic considerations. Sweden's population, largely rural, had expanded beyond available farm land. Industrialization had not yet taken hold, so there were few jobs to be had off the farm, even in Stockholm. A series of droughts and floods created years of famine, and a soaring inflation rate made what little cash people had worth less and less.

The first wave of Swedish immigration to the US, beginning in 1851, consisted largely of entire farming families. They settled in the Midwest, where the terrain was much like what they had known in Sweden. At that time, the US was expanding westward and promoted settlement by offering acreage at low prices. The Homestead Act of 1862, which offered free land to those willing to farm it for a certain number of years, drew huge numbers of Swedes to the US. The descendants of some of the original Swedish American homesteaders continue to work those farms today.

A second major wave of Swedish immigrants to the US from the late 1870s to early 1890s included many more urban Swedes who settled in cities and industrial areas of New York State and New England. Others joined earlier immigrants in Chicago. Swedish farmers continued to immigrate as well and began spreading westward, all the way to California. A number of Swedish Mormons, who had been converted in Sweden by Mormon missionaries, settled in Utah, the center of the Mormon community. Today, 6% of the Utah population is Swedish American, making it the third most Swedish state in the Union (after Minnesota and Nebraska).

The last major wave of Swedish American immigration began in the early 1900s and lasted until the stock market crash of 1929 (minus the World War I years [1914–18]). With the onset of the Great Depression, economic opportunities were no better in the US than in Sweden, and many of Sweden's repressive government measures had been lifted. There was no longer any compelling reason to leave Sweden, therefore, and emigration virtually ceased. Since 1930, only a very small number of Swedes have immigrated to the US.

In 1990, the total Swedish American population, according to the US Census, was 4,680,863. Over 40% live in the states of California (587,772), Minnesota (536,203), Illinois (374,965), Washington (257,953), and Michigan (194,063). As mentioned above, the top three most Swedish states are Minnesota (12.2% Swedish), Nebraska (6.2%), and Utah (6%). North Dakota (5.6%), South Dakota (4.8%), and Wyoming (4.6%) also have significant Swedish American populations, as do Oregon, Colorado, and Iowa (all 4%).

The rate of intermarriage with people of other ethnic backgrounds has been fairly low for Swedish Americans. In 1980, almost 30% of Swedish Americans claimed pure Swedish ancestry—a very high percentage considering how few new immigrants had arrived since 1930. Due to their relative isolation in Swedish American farming communities, and the low rate of ethnic intermarriage, Swedish Americans retained their ethnic language longer than many other American immigrant groups. However, Americanization eventually took its toll and fluency in Swedish was largely lost.

During the hyperpatriotic hysteria of the World War I years in the US, many Swedish Americans chose to hide their ethnicity and become as "American" as possible. Parents spoke only English with their children at home. They Americanized their names: Svenson became Swanson, Nilsson became Nelson, and Bengtson became Benson. In 1925, the Augustana Synod (the largest Lutheran or any other denomination among Swedish Americans) began conducting its church services in English, much to the chagrin of conservative Swedish Americans. By 1935, all Swedish American Lutheran church services were in English.

The majority of Swedish Americans are Lutheran, though a number are Baptist, Methodist, Congregationalist, and Episcopal. Many Janssonists, a revivalist Lutheran sect, immigrated to the US in the 1800s, along with converted Mormons. The Augustana Synod, a conservative form of Lutheranism, claims the most Swedish American members. The second largest Swedish American denomination is the Swedish Evangelical Mission Covenant of America, formed in 1885 by the merger of the Evangelical Lutheran Mission Synod and the Asgar Synod. In 1960, the Augustana Synod united with the United Lutheran Synod (a German denomination) to form the Lutheran Church of America (LCA). In 1987, the LCA and the American Lutheran Church merged to form the Evangelical Lutheran Church in America.

Many Swedish Americans continue to celebrate the traditional 20 days of Swedish Christmas, beginning on 13 December with St. Lucia's Day. On Christmas Eve, they serve the traditional foods of *lutfisk*, dried cod soaked in lye; and rice porridge. Another traditional Swedish food still enjoyed by Swedish Americans is *limpa*, a type of rye bread.

Swedish Americans have made countless contributions to American culture, beginning with the introduction of the log cabin in pioneer days. Early Swedish immigrants were mostly peasant farmers to whom higher education had been denied in the class-oriented system of Sweden. They were thrilled, therefore, to have access to education in America and took full advantage of it. The Swedish American Lutheran Church founded a number of colleges that continue to offer high-quality education today, including Augustana College and Theological Seminary, founded in 1860 in Rock Island, Illinois; Gustavus Adolphus College (1862, St. Peter, Minnesota);

Bethel Institute (1871, St. Paul, Minnesota); Bethany College (1881, Lindsborg, Kansas); North Park College (1891, Chicago, Illinois); and Upsala College (1893, East Orange, New Jersey).

More than 300 Swedish American writers were publishing their works in the early 20th century, but none achieved national prominence. The best known Swedish American writer is poet and historian Carl Sandburg. In visual arts, sculptor Carl Milles designed a number of public fountains in both Sweden and the US, including the huge *Meeting of the Waters* in St. Louis, Missouri, which celebrates the convergence of the Mississippi and Missouri Rivers. Successful Swedish American actors include Greta Garbo (born Greta Louisa Gustafson), Ingrid Bergman, Ann-Margret (Olsson), and Candice Bergen and her father, ventriloquist Edgar Bergen.

A number of Swedish Americans have also made great contributions in the areas of business, industry, science, and politics. Earl Warren, half-Swedish American and half-Norwegian American, served as Chief Justice of the Supreme Court from 1953 to 1969, establishing himself early as a powerful liberal voice when he ruled against the racial segregation of schools. US Representative John Anderson from Illinois ran unsuccessfully as a third-party candidate in the 1980 US presidential election. Joe (Häglund) Hill gained attention as a labor union activist in the early 1900s. Hill was convicted of murder and executed in 1915, although many believed he had been framed.

Swedish American John Ericsson designed the Union Army ship *Monitor* that defeated the Confederate ship *Merrimack* in 1862 during the American Civil War. Pioneer aviator Charles Lindbergh, even before his child was kidnapped, was perhaps one of the most famous Swedish Americans. Scientist Gustavus August Eisen, who made numerous contributions in botany, zoology, and archaeology, is most remembered for founding the Sequoia National Park in California in 1890. Chester Carlson invented xerography in 1938 and went on to found the Xerox Corporation. Glenn Seaborg discovered plutonium and was awarded the Nobel Prize in Chemistry in 1951. Business entrepreneur Walter Hoving served as chair of the board of Tiffany & Company and as president of the Lord & Taylor clothing company; and Carl A. Swanson & Sons invented TV dinners.

Swedish immigrants adapted quickly and well to life in the US, lending their skills in farming, fishing, logging, mining, and construction to the building of America. Today they are part of mainstream America and suffer few, if any, problems unique to their community.

BIBLIOGRAPHY

McGill, Allyson. *The Swedish Americans*. New York: Chelsea House, 1988.

Moberg, Vilhelm. *The Unknown Swedes: A Book About Swedes and America, Past and Present*. Translated and edited by Roger McKnight. Carbondale, IL: Southern Illinois University Press, 1988.

US Bureau of the Census. *Detailed Ancestry Groups for States*. 1990 Census of Population Supplementary Reports, CP-S-1-2. Washington, DC, October 1992.

—by D. K. Daeg de Mott

TENETEHARA

ALTERNATE NAMES: Guajajara and Tembé
LOCATION: Brazil
LANGUAGE: Tupí-Guaraní

[1] INTRODUCTION

The Tenetehara are also known as Guajajara and Tembé when treated as two independent tribes. They seem to have inhabited the northeastern Brazilian region since pre-Columbian times. The first recorded encounter with the Christian world dates from the beginning of the 17th century, though it is possible they had contact with the Portuguese slave-traders who used to roam the region searching for Amerindians to capture. By the middle of the 17th century, three separate expeditions were organized by Jesuits to find Tenetehara and bring them to their missions. Various mission villages were established with some degree of success: the Colony of Januario, established in 1854, 20 years later had a population of 120 Tenetehara. At the same time, Neo-Brazilians started advancing into Tenetehara territory, a trend that continues until the present day.

Although the first 50 years of contact between the Tenetehara and Europeans were marked by slave raids, massacres, and epidemics, the Tenetehara made adjustments in their culture and society to changing external circumstances and survived. The story of the meeting between the Tenetehara and the Neo-Brazilians has been generally peaceful, except for several sporadic uprisings. The result of the contact between neighbors becomes evident when elements from one culture, such as clothes, tools, and myths, are found integrated into the other.

[2] LOCATION AND HOMELAND

The Tenetehara live in the north of Brazil, in the states of Pará and Maranhao, east of the Amazon River. They live close to rivers, surrounded by trees and palms in the dense tropical forest. The palms, especially the babassú, are quite useful as their leaves and nuts provide shelter and nourishment and the nuts can be sold to outsiders. From December through June, everything is wet: it is the rainy season. Then comes an equally long period that offers completely the opposite: the dry season. In the past, the Tenetehara had sufficient territory to move their settlements when the gardens were used up, every five or six years. Early explorers noticed that Tenetehara villages tended to be large, with each house holding 10 or more related families, under a powerful chief—usually a shaman. There are indications that the villages' average size was approximately 200 people.

[3] LANGUAGE

The Tenetehara are one of the Tupí-Guaraní-speaking people of northeastern Brazil. Their language is considered by grammarians to be unique because of the characteristic way in which the words are formed and put together. Those traits make it difficult for the language to be learned as a second language by adults whose first language is English or Spanish. To say, for example, "The woman ate the mango," the Tenetehara would say, "Eat woman mango"; "John killed Peter" would be "Kill John Peter." That way more-complicated sentences like, "His daughter lit his cigar and took it to him" end up being something like "Lit daughter tobacco taking to."

4 FOLKLORE

In one Tenetehara myth, Maira stole fire from the vultures and hid it in the urucú wood so the Tenetehara could use this wood to make fire. Maira also gave the yucca and maize (corn) to them and then abandoned his wife, who was pregnant with his son, Maira-üra (üra is "son"). While she was searching for her husband, Maira's wife stayed one night in the house of Mukwüra and conceived a second time. She gave birth to twins, and they continued searching for Maira.

The other main Tenetehara hero is Tupan, the creator and protector. He was later identified with the Christian God by the missionaries, who emphasized his influence. Among some groups, Tupan was the "demon of thunder."

The Tenetehara also tell many animal stories. One tells about the difficulties of the Gamba when he tries to arrange a good marriage for his daughter. On one occasion she marries a wood tick, and Gamba tries to imitate his son-in-law by floating to the ground on a leaf from a treetop, only to fall hard to the ground.

5 RELIGION

With the exception of culture heroes, Tenetehara supernatural beings are dangerous: Maranaüwa, the owner of the forest and animals that inhabit it, for instance, punishes Amerindians who needlessly kill some species, like white-lipped peccaries. Zurupari, the forest demon, causes hunters to get lost in the forest and then kills them. Uwan, known also as Upóre and Uzare, is the spirit of the rivers and river animals and plants. He is also malignant and causes illnesses. These spirits, though often known by different names, are also part of Neo-Brazilian folklore.

Apart from the spirits, the Tenetehara also have to deal with ghosts (azang). Ghosts are the souls of people who died in adverse circumstances, such as from sorcery or by slowly wasting away, and also the souls of those that broke incest taboos during their life. They wander through the forests and appear in the shape of animals to hunters. They also haunt cemeteries and abandoned houses, so the Tenetehara avoid such places at night.

Because the supernatural world is so menacing, the Tenetehara need their shamans to protect them. A shaman can invoke the spirit that caused the problem in the first place, be possessed by it, and have its powers to solve the crisis. Each shaman can only call a number of spirits with which he is familiar; therefore, the more spirits he knows how to call, the more powerful he is.

6 MAJOR HOLIDAYS

There are two major holidays celebrated by the Tenetehara: the Honey Festival and the Maize (Corn) Festival. The Honey Festival is held during the last days of the dry season, after months of collecting enough wild honey to last until the end of the next season. During those collecting months, in the evenings, people gather to sing and bless the honey. As soon as the 20 to 30 gourd containers (each holding 1–2 liters or about 1–2 quarts) are filled, the leader sends out invitations to nearby villages. When the time comes, they sing the songs learned from the ani-

mals in mythical times and dance in circles while they drink honey mixed with water. The ceremony lasts as long as there is honey to drink.

Songs and dances are also the basic elements of the Maize Festival. It takes place during the rains of January through March, accompanying the growth of the maize. During the festival, the shamans conjure spirits that will protect the crop.

7 RITES OF PASSAGE

Through pregnancy and even after the birth of a child, a Tenetehara couple must observe a series of restrictions aimed at protecting the child. Most of these restrictions limit the variety of animals they are allowed to eat or hunt; the Tenetehara believe, for example, that killing a jaguar during pregnancy may cause the birth of an insane child. For the first 10 days after birth, the parents can only eat yucca flour, small fish, and roast maize (corn), drinking only water. And they cannot have sexual relationships until the child is "hard," i. e., 6 months old.

Until the evening of the puberty ceremony, children are forbidden to eat some meats, like peccary, guariba monkey, wild goose, and various forest fowls. That night they are given official permission to eat such meats and have their first taste of them, as the men of the village would have been hunting during the previous days for the feast that follows the singing. Because of this, some outsiders called the Tenetehara puberty ceremony the Festival of Roasted Meat. In the past, adolescents of both sexes were isolated for 10 days, after which they would end the isolation by breaking the entrails of an agouti stretched across the door. The boy's penis would have been then checked by the fathers in search for signs of masturbation and, if found, he would have been whipped. The girls were chased by the young men of the village from their doors to the stream or pool where they could have a bath.

Some of this has been lost. The boys are no longer isolated in most cases. The girls do spend some days lying in their hammocks or behind a palm-leaf screen and are still chased. For the ceremony, boys are painted red, and falcon feathers are glued on their chest and arms. The girls are painted black, and sometimes some white falcon feathers are glued to their hair. At dawn the ceremony begins, with songs and dances and shamans calling spirits.

After the puberty ceremony, the girl can consummate the marriage with her husband, who would have been living with her family since their "marriage." There are no special wedding ceremonies: the young man simply moves into his father-in-law's house. If the girl is not married yet, her father will find her a husband after the puberty ceremony. Monogamy is generally the rule.

The Tenetehara bury their dead nowadays in cemeteries outside the villages. The bodies are wrapped in mats made of babassú palm leaves or placed in boxes. It is reported that formerly they used to bury the first dead person in the house, and after the second death the house was destroyed.

8 INTERPERSONAL RELATIONS

Tenetehara culture and society has been modified through centuries of contact with the outside world. The result is a new culture and social system—a combination of aboriginal and borrowed elements. In 1855 a report from the Brazilian authorities described the inhabitants of some Tenetehara villages as "happily endowed for social life." They were perceived as docile and industrious. The president of Maranhao then said that "these Indians like peace and work: they are docile, hospitable, and faithful." But although they were deemed to be "almost white and intelligent," the Tenetehara retained many aspects of their own culture, among them their sense of community. Their villages vary in size according to resources. If tensions arise between extended families, a group breaks off to form a new settlement where they carry out the cooperative economic and ceremonial activities of the society. Gardening and collecting are two of those cooperative activities that involve large extended families. Children often help when collecting babassú nuts. As for the children, they are loved passionately: corporal punishment or abuse of Tenetehara's young is simply not tolerated.

9 LIVING CONDITIONS

A Tenetehara village can be as simple as two rows of houses with a wide street between them. Rows are added as the village grows. In the past, a large ceremonial house could be found situated at the end of the village street. Some of the ceremonial houses were erected just for the Honey Feast, during which the villagers danced inside, and then they were destroyed.

A typical Tenetehara house is rectangular in shape, with the walls and roofs covered with babassú palm leaves. There are no inner walls, even if more than one nuclear family lives in the house. Each family—husband, wife, and their children—has its own fire and hangs its hammocks around it, thus creating their own space within the house. Their belongings are hung on the upright supports against the walls, and sometimes there are shelves near the roof to store maize (corn), yucca, or farming instruments.

The traditional Tenetehara doctor is the shaman. Shamans can cure illness by invoking the powers of the spirits that caused the illness and then removing the cause by sucking or massaging the patient. The cure involves songs and dances, the shaman smokes large cigars, and when he is finally possessed by a spirit or a ghost, he shows by his actions which one it is.

10 FAMILY LIFE

The Tenetehara basic social groupings are extended families and widely extended bilateral kin groups. Families are the organizers of ceremonial and cooperative economic activities. Although there are indications of infanticide—only in the case of twins, as they are believed to be the children of dangerous supernatural beings—and knowledge of some formulas to produce abortion, the Tenetehara generally do not limit family size. During pregnancy, long taboos are imposed on the parents, but despite this discomfort, the Tenetehara like large families. Men are proud to father several children, and women are eager to bear children. According to the American anthropologist Charles Wagley, this desire for large families was one of the reasons for their survival. Many Tenetehara died from new diseases, war, and slavery when contact was first established with Europeans. But new babies were born and replaced their population until they adjusted to the new circumstances.

11 CLOTHING

Covering the body is one of the habits the Tenetehara acquired through contact with other cultures, particularly Christians. Nudity was traditionally the rule. But then they adopted not just clothes from Neo-Brazilians but also the socially attributed values that accompany them: it is prestigious to have new or better clothes than other people. Women always wear skirts now, and men wear pants and shirts.

12 FOOD

The Tenetehara are tropical forest horticulturalists who practice the slash-and-burn system. The staple food of the region is yucca or cassava, which is used to make bread and beverages. Maize (corn) and peanuts were already traditional crops by the time steel instruments were introduced, tools which made it easier to grow new plants such as rice, bananas, and lemons. As their villages have traditionally been situated near rivers and streams, fishing adds protein to their diets. They also hunt tapir, deer, peccary, monkeys, and various forest fowls for their meat and collect forest fruits and nuts. The Tenetehara drink *chicha*, a fermented alcoholic drink made from various plants.

13 EDUCATION

Many Tenetehara are bilingual. They have learned Portuguese, and most of them still speak their own language as well. Being able to communicate clearly with the Brazilians is considered very important, not only to carry out trade, find work, and take part in the national life, but also to defend their rights when needed. As some have lost their own language, there are already projects to forward bilingual education in schools where Amerindian attendance is high. There are some primary schools provided by the government agency FUNAI, but secondary education is more scarce. Many schools are still run and funded by missionaries, as they were in the first stages of colonization. As to the level of education achieved, it is difficult to generalize, but as the Tenetehara are one of the tribes that adapted best to the change of circumstances brought about by European settlers, formal education is not alien and, when possible, is readily attained.

14 CULTURAL HERITAGE

Singing and dancing are not only the Tenetehara's most favorite pastimes, but they also play a central role in their ceremonial rites. The Tenetehara are very fond of music, and some of their songs are considered by many to be the most beautiful of the region. Each ceremony has its own particular songs, and they should not be sung out of season because it would upset the spirits. The songs of the Honey Festival are believed to have been brought to the tribe by a young Tenetehara shaman who visited the Village of the Jaguar during the festival of the animals when each animal sang a song.

To be a shaman, it is essential to have a good voice. At shamanistic sessions, the shaman sings the group of songs attributed to the spirit he is calling until the spirit itself enters his body and sings through him. When possessed, the shaman dances, imitating the animal of the spirit inside him; e.g., a toad spirit will make him hop. Meanwhile, men and women dance, usually stamping their feet on one spot. In some ceremonies, they form lines facing each other and approach and retreat. In the Maize (Corn) Festival dance, they make a large circle and move with a skipping step.

15 WORK

Agriculture is a central activity for the Tenetehara. The produce not only provides food for the families but also can be traded for manufactured articles. The task used to be divided between females and males according to the product. Women planted and harvested cotton and peanuts, while men cultivated yucca, maize (corn), and other plants. Nowadays, men do most of the planting and the women help when required. The land is cleared and the dry vegetation burned to create a garden, which is said to be owned by the head of the family but is cultivated and used by the entire extended family. The gardens are planted throughout December using metal tools, such as steel axes, hoes, and bush knives, obtained through trade with Neo-Brazilians.

As with agriculture, hunting and collecting wild foods have a dual purpose: complementing their own diets, and trade. Babassú nuts and copaiba oil are good products to sell in order to buy clothes, guns, fishhooks, and salt. Hunting is nowadays carried out with shotguns, when available, or with bows and arrows. The skins can be sold to Neo-Brazilians and the meat kept for consumption. The Tenetehara fish with hooks and lines, though poisoning drying pools with timbó is also known.

16 SPORTS

No specifically Tenetehara sports have been noted. However, having been close to European and Brazilian culture, popular sports have become familiar. Boys play tops and marbles in the same manner as the Neo-Brazilian children of the region. Many Brazilian Amerindians are very keen on soccer and play it frequently.

17 ENTERTAINMENT AND RECREATION

Singing and dancing are favorite pastimes among the Tenetehara. New tunes learned from their fellow country people are welcome. But singing their own native songs is a pleasure the Tenetehara often indulge. Many evenings throughout the year, men and women gather for a *zingareté,* which means "to sing much," and enjoy their secular songs just for the fun of it. No native alcoholic beverages are known, but they do buy the usual from Neo-Brazilians. On the other hand, the smoke of native tobacco and hashish has lingered over many a zingareté—and other activities—since long ago.

The Tenetehara also hold parties in which some play bamboo flutes and skin drums, and couples dance to Neo-Brazilian rhythms, like the samba. Sometimes they hire Neo-Brazilian musicians to play their instruments.

18 FOLK ART, CRAFTS, AND HOBBIES

Apart from their leather headbands and wands made of wood with tail feathers of the red macaw, the rest of the Tenetehara crafts are basically necessary utensils made of available raw materials. This does not mean that they do not decorate what they make, for aesthetic reasons or to distinguish one object from the rest. Their baskets, for example, have woven geometric designs. They are made principally with a split flexible creeper, woven also into round sieves—for straining yucca flour—and flexible *tipitis,* which are used to squeeze the poisonous juice from the bitter manioc (cassava). The Tenetehara also weave native cotton to make hammocks.

Gourds are used to make eating utensils. The gourd is boiled and then allowed to dry. Then a single hole is cut to make a jug for drinking water or wild honey, or the gourd is cut in half and the interior mass scraped out to make a bowl. The inside of the bowl is stained black, and the outside is decorated with geometric incisions and black lines.

Pottery has been largely abandoned as the Tenetehara can now buy metal utensils. Pottery used to be simple, decorated only with incised designs. Their bows and arrows are made of pau d'arco wood, with bowstrings of twined tocum fibers. Both bow and arrows are 1 m (3 ft) long and nowadays the arrows have steel points.

19 SOCIAL PROBLEMS

The northeastern tribes of Brazil have seen their land swallowed up by colonizers in recent years. It is history repeating itself, only this time the many colonizers do not come from lands across the ocean but from Brazil itself. Although the Brazilian government has an organization that takes care of the Amerindian population (FUNAI), another body, the INCRA, has opened the region for settlement. Harried and hemmed in by settlers, the Tenetehara, along with other regional tribes, are running the risk of social breakdown once again.

20 BIBLIOGRAPHY

Derbyshire, Desmond C., and Geoffrey K. Pullman, ed. *Handbook of Amazonian Languages.* Berlin, N.Y.: Mouton de Gruyter, 1986.

Haines, Raymond B., and William T. Wickers, ed. *Adaptive Responses of Native Amazonians.* San Diego: Academic Press, 1983.

Hemming, John. *Amazon Frontier: The Defeat of the Brazilian Indians*. London: Macmillan, 1987.

Henley, Paul. *Amazon Indians*. Morristown, N.J.: Silver Burdett, 1980.

Lyon, Patricia J. *Native South Americans, Ethnology of the Least Known Continent*. Prospect Heights, Ill.: Traveland Press, 1985.

Mowat, Linda. *Cassava and Chicha, Bread and Beer for the Amazonian Indians*. Princes Risborough, Aylesbury, Bucks, UK: Shire, 1989.

Stewrad, Julian Haynes, ed. *Handbook of South American Indians*. New York: Cooper Square, 1963.

—by D. Ventura-Alcalay

TLINGIT

LOCATION: United States (Alaska)
POPULATION: 14,000
LANGUAGE: English; Tlingit
RELIGION: Christianity; native Tlingit

¹ INTRODUCTION

Tlingit (meaning "the people") is the name given to a native group of the Northwest Coast whose original homeland was located in the Alaskan panhandle. With the exception of a part of the Prince of Wales Island, the thirteen tribes that make up the Tlingit group occupied the land of the panhandle south of Yakutat Bay. The Tlingit developed as a coastal culture, well adapted to the rugged, heavily forested coastal areas that they inhabited.

Beginning in the 18th century, the Tlingit tribes experienced frequent conflicts with the early Russian fur traders who first entered the area at that time. In 1799, Russian adventurers built a fort on one of the islands that makes up the southeastern archipelago. But three years later, in 1802, they were driven out by Tlingit warriors. Some time later, however, a Russian trader by the name of Aleksandr Andreyevich Baranov was successful in recapturing the fort. Baranov turned the fort into a trading post which, over time, grew into the present-day city of Sitka. By 1867 the United States had won control over Alaska and opened Tlingit lands to settlers and prospectors searching for gold.

In the 20th century, the Tlingit, like other Alaskan natives, have fought for their civil rights and for control over the natural resources of their ancestral lands. In 1971, the Alaska Native Claims Settlement Act transferred about 100 million acres of land back to native Alaskans, including the Tlingit, who were organized into a regional corporation called Sealaska with title to 330,000 acres of land and 660,000 acres of mineral rights. Today Tlingit work in industry, business, government, and the professions. In 1994 the Tlingit gained media attention when two Tlingit youths from Alaska who had attacked a pizza delivery man in Washington state, were turned over to an adhoc tribal court, which imposed a traditional punishment of banishment to an isolated island off the coast of Alaska.

² LOCATION AND HOMELAND

In the 18th century, at the time of the initial European entry into the area, the total number of members of the thirteen Tlingit tribes was estimated to be about 10,000. Over the course of the next one hundred years, their numbers dwindled; at one time only about 4,500 remained. As of the 1990 US census, Tlingit in the United States numbered 13,925. The 1991 Canadian census listed 1,170 Tlingit. Almost all contemporary Tlingit live in the state of Alaska. Many of their original villages on the southeastern Alaska coast between Ketchikan and Yakutat are still populated. This is an area of rugged mountains with snow-capped peaks, offshore islands, and plentiful streams.

³ LANGUAGE

The language of the Tlingit Indians belongs to the Na-Dene linguistic family. Thus, it is more closely related to the languages of other native groups in North America than to those of the peoples of the Arctic. Older Tlingit still speak three different dialects of their language: northern, central, and southern.

⁴FOLKLORE

The most important character in Tlingit mythology is the trickster figure Raven, who is also considered the ancestor of the Tlingit. The power of animal spirits in general and communication between the spirits of animals and humans are also themes in Tlingit myths, as is reincarnation. Traditional beliefs encompassed an afterlife spent in one of two domains, corresponding roughly to the Judeo-Christian Heaven and Hell: *Kiwa-a* was the heaven for the virtuous, while those who had been morally deficient went to a place of torment called *Ketl-kiwa*, or Dog Heaven.

A common Tlingit folk belief was that if a girl going through puberty looked at the sky, she would cause a storm. A special hood with tassels was worn by girls of this age to shroud their eyes.

⁵RELIGION

Like the other native peoples of the Northwest Coast, many Tlingit belong to the Russian Orthodox church, to which their forebears were converted by the Russian missionaries who followed the traders that arrived in the area in the 18th century.

The traditional religion of the Tlingit, like that of most hunting and gathering cultures, was based on animism, the belief that spirits—which the Tlingit called *jek*—inhabit people, animals, and objects in the natural world. They believed that the environment can be influenced in magical ways, either for good or ill, by human intervention, a belief that led to the development of a whole constellation of customs and taboos intended to ensure prosperity and prevent disaster. Many such customs and taboos were designed to placate and mollify the souls of the animals that were the chief prey of the Tlingit. The Tlingit are also thought to have believed in a creator, called *Kah-shu-goon-yah*, who controlled both the heavens and the earth, and whose name—which means "divisible-rich-man"—was always whispered rather than uttered aloud. Each Tlingit clan had a totem animal with which it identified, and erected totem poles as tributes to their totem animals. The Tlingit also paid homage to their ancestors and included them as elements of totem pole designs.

The most important human figure in Tlingit religious belief was the shaman, who served many vital roles within Tlingit society. The Tlingit shaman could be either male or female and functioned as priest, doctor, and counselor to his or her people.

⁶MAJOR HOLIDAYS

Today many Tlingit observe the holidays of the Russian Orthodox calendar. Within traditional Tlingit society, by far the single most important occasion was a gathering called a *potlatch*, a communal ceremony that centered around feasting and gift-giving and that accompanied almost every major event in Tlingit life. A potlatch might be given by a retiring chief in honor of the occasion of his role being taken over by a new leader. Potlatches were held to celebrate birthdays and to legitimize adoptions and marriages. Sometimes a potlatch would be held for no other reason than to demonstrate in no uncertain terms the wealth and status of the host or to make a good impression on guests or visiting dignitaries. At other times, a Tlingit might

host a potlatch as a means of saving face and restoring dignity following an embarrassing public failure or a personal disappointment.

The potlatch, a ritual common to many preliterate cultures, takes many forms, but its purpose and its nature are always the same. It is an ostentatious display of wealth and prestige, which calls for as much showing off as possible, the entire point of the ritual being to waste or destroy publicly as much of the host's wealth as possible. The goal of the potlatch is to demonstrate that the host is so wealthy that even such large-scale waste cannot damage his economic situation. The potlatch simply serves to establish and reinforce his standing within the community. The host of a potlatch might throw precious oil on the fire until the flames leap out to singe the surrounding guests. A wealthy chief might kill a valuable slave with a special club known as a "slave killer" and then fling the slave's scalp to his rival. Many beautiful things were made by Tlingit craftspeople simply in order that a chief or other notable person might give them away or destroy them at a potlatch.

⁷RITES OF PASSAGE

Major life events of the Tlingit were traditionally marked by the potlatch (also called a *koolex*). Such events included the transfer of ancestral names to children; the point at which a daughter became eligible for marriage; a son's coming-of-age (also marked by the erection of a memorial totem-pole and the construction of a new house); a marriage; and funeral rites.

8 INTERPERSONAL RELATIONS

Unlike that of most other American Indian groups, Tlingit society evolved as an aristocracy. At the top of the Tlingit social ladder were the chiefs, who were considered to be of royal blood. Directly beneath the chiefs in rank and privilege were members of the nobility, and beneath them were the working-class (or common) people, the majority of the population. At the bottom of Tlingit society was a slave class made up of members of other tribes who had been captured in war. Tlingit society equated wealth with the right to rule; chieftainship, along with the rights, advantages, and prerogatives that accompany it, was passed on from one generation to the next of the same wealthy family. Tlingit chiefs and nobles controlled all the tribe's wealth, determined the social rank of the members of the tribe, laid claim to the best fishing and hunting areas, and maintained the exclusive right to practice certain highly esteemed crafts.

Even today, class and social status are important in Tlingit villages.

9 LIVING CONDITIONS

The Tlingit have three advocacy organizations that promote their culture, rights, and welfare. The Alaska Native Brotherhood is concerned with cultural preservation; the Tlingit-Haida Association (Haida are a neighboring tribe) address housing and other social welfare issues; and the corporation Sealaska lobbies for economic and political power. Some Tlingit villages have their own city officials, police forces, and school boards.

The Tlingit have access to, and use, modern medical services. Traditionally, they had a system of folk medicine that included principles of hygiene and a knowledge of herbs. When necessary, they consulted with a special healer who had more advanced knowledge of medical practices.

10 FAMILY LIFE

Arranged marriages were formerly the norm, but this practice has diminished during the 20th century. Divorce was rare in traditional Tlingit culture, as it was considered an affront to the clans of both the husband and wife. The Tlingit had an elaborate system of kinship by which their society was divided into two halves, or moieties, called Raven-Crow and Eagle-Wolf. Although the various rules and prohibitions attached to this system are still upheld theoretically, in practice they are often broken, and its terminology has fallen into disuse among the younger Tlingit. A child's lineage is linked to the maternal rather than the paternal side of the family, so maternal relatives traditionally played an important role in a child's upbringing. Traditionally, sons learned how to hunt, fish, and fight from their maternal uncles; daughters learned domestic skills from their maternal grandmother and aunts, who also prepared them for childbearing and taught them the history of their clan. The family elders still hold a high level of respect and influence among the Tlingit, including those who are college educated.

11 CLOTHING

In the summer, Tlingit men traditionally wore no clothes or only a breechcloth made of animal skin. In the winter, they wore shirts with trousers or leggings made from deer, caribou, or other animal skins. These were decorated with fringes at the sides and bottom and with rows of porcupine quills. Women wore cedar-bark skirts and capes in the summer and skirts or tunics of buckskin during the cooler seasons. Both men and women went barefoot much of the time, even in snow during the winter. On especially rough terrain, they wore moccasins, or snow-shoes with webbing or spikes. Women wore their hair loose or in braids, with ornaments of wood or shells and beads, and both men and women wore feathers in their hair. People who became shamans were forbidden to cut or even comb their hair. A fur cap was a common form of winter headgear. Both men and women painted their faces, either the entire face or only the upper or lower part. Black and red were the colors most often used. Often, rings were painted around the eyes. Tattooing was also common. Mourners wore old clothes and cut their hair short.

The Tlingit of today wear modern, Western-style clothing appropriate to their northern climate. Traditional clothing, masks, and headdresses are still worn on ceremonial occasions, and by dancers and other performing groups. Traditional Tlinglit garments are known for their intricate beadwork, typically in white on a red background. Chilkat blankets, with their abstract animal designs, are valued by collectors of folk art.

12 FOOD

The traditional Tlingit diet consisted of fish, meat, and wild plants. Given their resource-rich environment, they rarely experienced times of deprivation. The rivers of their Alaskan homeland abound with salmon, halibut, herring, candlefish, and other fish (which the Tlingit caught with nets and traps, speared shot them with bow and arrow, or sometimes simply stunned with a club. Skimming the open sea in their enormous dugout canoes, they hunted whales, seals, sea lion, and walrus. On land, they hunted deer, mountain goats, bear, and small animals and availed themselves of the bounty of bird's eggs, berries, and edible plants that were theirs for the taking.

Although today's Tlingit eat typical modern-day American fare (including packaged convenience foods), salmon, their traditional staple, still plays a prominent role in their diet, along with other fish, including halibut, herring, and cod, as well as crabs and other shellfish. Salmon is eaten both fresh and dried, and salmon grilled over a smoking fire is especially popular. Oil from the euchalon, or candlefish, is used as a dip with many foods.

13 EDUCATION

Modern Tlingit young people attend public schools, where, much like school-aged children everywhere in the United States, they are taught basic subjects like math, history, spelling, reading, science, social studies, and the use of computers. But Tlingit teachers are also concerned that their students learn something about their culture and old traditions before this knowledge is lost completely. The Tlingit place a high value on education, and many work in business, industry, government, and the professions.

14 CULTURAL HERITAGE

An elaborate woodcarving tradition can be seen in Tlingit homes and on their boats, and Tlingit ceremonial costumes are decorated with individualized crest designs. Characteristics of Tlingit art include stylized conventional forms and the practice of filling in any blank spaces. The most favored colors are red, black, and green. Perhaps the most famous form of Tlingit art is the elaborately patterned Chilkat blanket.

Although the dancing societies that were important to other tribes of the Northwest Coast did not hold a prominent place among the Tlingit, they did have a dance tradition. Special dance aprons that were like miniature Chilkat blankets were worn by shamans, chiefs, and other tribe members. Other elements of the traditional dance costume included belts made from ropes of shredded cedar bark, headbands also made from cedar bark, special collars or bibs, and headdresses with eagle feathers. Shamans in particular were known for their wild dancing, characterized by spirited gesticulation. Today, dancing groups still perform for local ceremonies and for visitors in several Tlingit villages.

[15] WORK

Traditionally, the Tlingit worked at hunting and gathering the food they needed to survive. However, this way of life declined after 1880, and the Tlingit began to participate in the Western cash economy. World War II and the discovery of large oil reserves in Alaska created many opportunities for employment in construction and other jobs for the Tlingit and other native groups in Alaska. Instead of engaging in traditional fishing practices, many of today's Tlingit drive diesel-powered boats with hydraulic hoists and industrial-size nets. Tlingit women often work in fish canneries or produce crafts for sale. Many Tlingit work in urban areas, some of them settling permanently in large towns and cities and working in government, business, and the professions.

[16] SPORTS

Tlingit men enjoy engaging in contests of strength such as wrestling.

[17] ENTERTAINMENT AND RECREATION

Traditional Tlingit feasts and dances usually took place in the winter. The frequent potlatches held in Tlingit villages provided the major source of entertainment. Today the Tlingit enjoy modern types of recreation, such as watching television or renting movies.

[18] FOLK ART, CRAFTS, AND HOBBIES

The Tlingit are expert carvers and use the wood, especially red cedar, that is so plentiful in their native habitat extensively in their arts and crafts, especially for storage boxes, dishes, and ceremonial masks. They make excellent baskets, some of which are so tightly woven as to be waterproof, and also weave fine blankets of dog hair and mountain goat wool. They are experts at finishing their wooden artifacts with inlays of bone, copper, and shells, which are found in abundance everywhere at the water's edge. All Tlingit crafts are highly ornamented with elaborate and beautiful designs. Since the arrival of tourists by steamship, the Tlingit have maintained an active crafts industry.

[19] SOCIAL PROBLEMS

Many Tlingit Indians today live in poverty in substandard housing. They face the imminent destruction of their culture and way of life and experience difficulty in adapting themselves to the ways of the prevalent society. As a result, many suffer from alcoholism, drug abuse, and other forms of social distress.

[20] BIBLIOGRAPHY

Dauenhauer, Nora M., and Richard D. Dauenhauer, eds. *Haa shuka, Our Ancestors: Tlingit Oral Narratives.* Seattle: University of Washington Press, 1987.

Jonaitis, Aldona. *Art of the Northern Tlingit.* Seattle: University of Washington Press, 1986.

Marquis, Arnold. *A Guide to America's Indians.* University of Oklahoma Press, 1974.

Obery, Kalervo. *The Social Economy of the Tlingit Indians.* Seattle: University of Washington Press, 1973.

Osborn, Kevin. *The Peoples of the Arctic.* Chelsea House, 1990.

Pelton, Mary Helen, and Jacqueline DiGennaro. *Images of a People: Tlingit Myths and Legends.* Englewood, Colo.: Libraries Unlimited, 1992.

Straley, John. *The Woman Who Married a Bear.* New York: Soho Press, 1992.

TRINIDADIANS AND TOBAGONIANS

LOCATION: Trinidad and Tobago
POPULATION: 1.3 million
LANGUAGE: English; English-derived Creole with African and other elements; Hindi and Urdu; Spanish
RELIGION: Roman Catholicism; Church of England and Church of Scotland; Methodist, Seventh-Day Adventist, Pentecostal, Baptist, and other churches; Hinduism; Islam; Christian-African sects

¹ INTRODUCTION

The nation of Trinidad and Tobago consists of two Caribbean islands that have been united politically since 1962. (The people of both islands are generally referred to today as "Trinidadians.") The islands were inhabited by the Arawaks, Caribs, and other Amerindian groups when sighted by Christopher Columbus in 1498. The explorer is said to have named Trinidad, where he landed, either for three hills visible in the distance or in honor of the Holy Trinity. (The name "Tobago" is thought to derive from the Carib word for tobacco). It took nearly 100 years for the Spanish to establish their first permanent settlement on Trinidad, and they regularly had to defend the island from attacks by the Dutch, French, and British. Eventually sugar plantations were established and slaves brought in from West Africa to work on them. A British expedition captured Trinidad in 1797, and the island was ceded to the British in 1802. By 1814, Tobago, which had changed hands several times, was also a British possession.

During the 19th century, the ethnic diversity of Trinidad's population expanded as the British brought in indentured servants from India to work on the sugar plantations following the freeing of the island's West African slaves by the British in 1834. A variety of Europeans fleeing religious persecution or seeking employment also settled there, and Chinese laborers arrived toward the end of the century. In 1888 Tobago was joined with Trinidad as a colonial territory under the name Trinidad and Tobago.

Following World War I, the people of Trinidad and Tobago, like those of other colonial territories, sought greater political representation with a view toward eventual independence. Their nationalistic aspirations came to be embodied in one revered leader, Eric Williams, who in 1955 founded the People's National Movement (PNM), which gained legislative control of the territory the following year. After a brief membership in the Federation of the West Indies, Trinidad and Tobago became an independent member of the British Commonwealth in 1962 and a republic in 1976. Throughout these changes, Williams remained the head of the government until his death in 1981.

The worldwide oil crisis of the 1970s gave newfound value to Trinidad and Tobago's offshore oil reserves—first discovered in 1910—and the nation enjoyed a period of great prosperity and development which ended after the Middle Eastern nations began releasing their stockpiled oil at the end of the decade. World oil prices declined, and Trinidad and Tobago suffered an economic recession. In the 1990s, the nation has faced the challenge of stabilizing its economy and reducing its dependence on world oil prices. In 1995, unemployment rates were at their lowest level in 10 years, inflation was down, and economic growth was predicted.

² LOCATION AND HOMELAND

Trinidad and Tobago are the southernmost islands of the West Indies, with Trinidad located only 11 km (7 mi) from Venezuela on the South American continent. With an area of 4,828 sq km (1,864 sq mi), Trinidad is the largest island of the Lesser Antilles. Three mountain ranges stretch across the country from east to west: the Northern Range; the Montserrat Hills, which cut across the island's center; and the Southern Range, which runs along the southern coast. Tiny Tobago, located about 34 km (21 mi) northeast of Trinidad, is only about 42 km (26 mi) long and 11 km (7 mi) wide. It consists of lowlands dominated by a chain of volcanic hills that runs the length of the island.

While the different ethnic groups on Trinidad and Tobago have succeeded in living peacefully together, each has retained its cultural identity, lending richness and diversity to the nation's character and daily life. In 1993, an estimated 43% of Trinidad and Tobago's 1.3 million people were Black, 40% were of East Indian descent, 14% were of mixed descent, and smaller numbers were Chinese and European. The island of Tobago is predominantly Black.

³ LANGUAGE

The languages of Trinidad and Tobago reflect its diverse ethnic heritage. English is the nation's official language, while the common language of the great majority of residents is an English-derived Creole that contains elements of African and other languages. Hindi and Urdu are spoken by segments of the Indian population, and Spanish, the language of the nation's first European conquerors, is spoken in some areas as well.

Creole is a type of hybrid language found throughout the Caribbean area, created by the blending of various European and African languages. The Trinidadian Creole blends English with the syntax and vocabulary of West African languages, including Twi and Yoruba. Plural pronouns differ from those of standard English: the plural form of "you" is *Allyu,* and the French-English *ah wee* means "ours." French expressions such as *il fait chaud* and *il y a* are mirrored in the Trinidadian "it making hot" and "it have," which is used for "there is." French words also show up in the names for vegetation (*pomme* for apple) and mythological figures.

Crops grown by East Indian Trinidadians have come to be called by their Hindi names, such as *beigun* for eggplant. One of Trinidad and Tobago's most popular prepared foods, *roti,* also has a Hindi name, reflecting the culture from which it originates. Amerindian-derived words include the names of foods—cassava, balata, and roocoo—as well as place names, including Tunapuna, Guayaguayare, and Carapichaima. The Creole spoken on Tobago, which differs slightly from that of Trinidad, has similarities to the Creole spoken in Jamaica, another country with a predominantly Black population.

⁴ FOLKLORE

Trinidadian folklore, which is often reflected in Carnival themes and costumes, includes devils in disguise, a wolfman

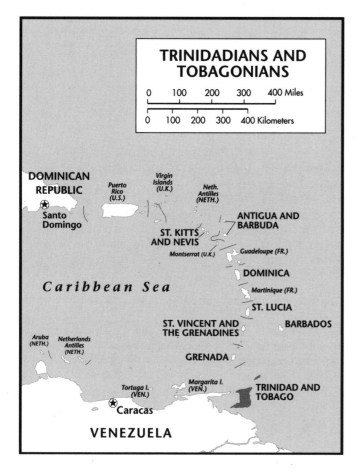

TRINIDADIANS AND TOBAGONIANS

0 100 200 300 400 Miles

0 100 200 300 400 Kilometers

DOMINICAN REPUBLIC
Santo Domingo

Puerto Rico (U.S.)

Virgin Islands (U.K.)

Neth. Antilles (NETH.)

ANTIGUA AND BARBUDA

ST. KITTS AND NEVIS

Montserrat (U.K.)

Guadeloupe (FR.)

DOMINICA

Martinique (FR.)

ST. LUCIA

Caribbean Sea

ST. VINCENT AND THE GRENADINES

BARBADOS

Aruba (NETH.)

Netherlands Antilles (NETH.)

GRENADA

Tortuga I. (VEN.)

Margarita I. (VEN.)

TRINIDAD AND TOBAGO

Caracas

VENEZUELA

named Lagahoo, and a variety of other sinister figures. Folk tales are told about Papa Bois, the ruler of the forest, and his son, Callaloo, whose legendary battle with Mancrab supplied a memorable theme for well-known Carnival designer Peter Minshall. Other folklore figures include Diablesse—a character comparable to Circe in Greek mythology—who attracts men and then turns them into hogs, after which they fall down a precipice. The spirits of unbaptized children, called Douens, have their feet turned backwards and are said to raid people's gardens.

5 RELIGION

About 33% of Trinidad and Tobago's population are Roman Catholic. Besides Catholicism, Trinidadians of African descent belong to the Church of England and the Church of Scotland, as well as the Methodist, Seventh-Day Adventist, Pentecostal, and other religions. The Baptist religion is especially popular on Tobago. Trinidad's Indian community embraces the Hindu and Muslim religions: Hindus account for 25% of Trinidad and Tobago's population, and Muslims for 6%. Some Africans are also turning to Islam, but in their own organizations (through the "Black Muslim" movement) rather than those of their East Indian neighbors.

There are also religious sects that combine Christianity with African religious beliefs and practices. The best known of these is Shango, based on a religion practiced by the Yoruba tribe in Africa, that embraces both Shango, the god of thunder and

lightning, and Christian saints. Through dance and drumming, its priests, called *mogbas,* summon spirits known as *orishas.*

6 MAJOR HOLIDAYS

Due to the nation's religious diversity, Trinidad and Tobago has an abundance of public holidays. In addition to the major Christian holy days, recognition is accorded to the Hindu holidays of Divali (pronounced "Duwali") and Ramleema and the Muslim festival of Hosay, a religious rite that has grown into a four-day festival that includes a potpourri of Trinidadian cultural elements, such as tassa drumming, which is Hindu in origin. Other holidays, such as Emancipation Day (1 August) and Independence Day (31 August) commemorate important dates in the nation's history.

Trinidad and Tobago's most important festival, however, is its Carnival, recognized as one of the world's most extravagant and colorful pre-Lenten celebrations, equaling or topping New Orleans' Mardi Gras and Brazil's Carnival. The festivities are held annually in the final two days preceding Lent. The entire nation participates in this 200-year-old tradition, which is thought to have started with the first influx of French settlers to the islands in 1783. The main activities take place in Port of Spain, although festivities are also held in San Fernando, Scarborough, and other locations. Preparations for Carnival begin months in advance, as the participating groups, called "bands," plan their "mas" (short for "masquerade") costumes. Each band chooses a historical, cultural, fantastic, or folkloric theme—past ones include Bright Africa, Ye Saga of Merrie England, and Callaloo (a folk character as well as the name for a popular Trinidadian food)—and hundreds of coordinated costumes are painstakingly debated, designed, and assembled to be paraded and judged.

Aside from the costumed bands, calypso and steel drum groups provide the other major focus of Carnival, and a series of musical competitions is held in the period leading up to the Carnival itself. On the night of Dimanche Gras, the Sunday before Ash Wednesday, the King and Queen of Carnival are chosen based on their costumes. The Carnival festivities officially begin at dawn on Monday morning, called Jour Ouvert, or Joovay, and include an "anything goes" parade, in which revelers wear a gamut of individually designed satirical and outrageous costumes. Next come massive parades by the organized bands—ranging from 500 to over 2,000 members—accompanied by flatbed trucks full of musicians and huge speakers. The climax of the celebration is the judging of the Carnival's best band, which takes place at the Queens Park Savannah, and awards are also given for the best calypso and steel drum groups.

7 RITES OF PASSAGE

Major life transitions, such as birth, marriage, and death, are marked by religious ceremonies appropriate to each Trinidadian's faith community.

8 INTERPERSONAL RELATIONS

The spirit of Trinidad and Tobago's famous Carnival carries over, in more modest forms, into everyday life on the islands: Trinidadians are known for their penchant for enjoying life, even in the face of adversity. When curfews were imposed during a period of civil unrest in 1970, they held "Curfew fêtes";

Trinidadian steel drum music originated when members of traditional African percussion bands began using discarded oil drums. With their bottoms cut off and their tops hammered into a convex shape marked by a pattern of dents that produce different pitches, these objects turn into musical instruments capable of a surprising range of musical nuance and expression in the hands of expert players. (Susan D. Rock)

when the country's economy fell victim to plummeting oil prices in the 1980s, people threw "Recession fêtes." An important part of the Trinidadian calypso tradition is the refusal to take not only themselves but also others too seriously, and there is a special term—*picong*—for calypso's irreverent satirizing of people and institutions, both great and small.

Another aspect of this casual attitude can be seen in the practice called *liming,* which is the counterpart of "hanging out" in the United States. Trinidadian men have a long tradition of congregating at street corners, on front stoops, or near movie houses, chatting and whiling the time away as they take in the passing scene. Young limers are more apt to pick a single spot from which to survey the action, while for older men liming (or "taking a lime") may involve spending part of a day or evening at a series of places. Although it is frowned upon by some segments of society (signs proclaiming "No Limers" or "No Liming" signs can be seen in public places), this seemingly aimless activity can be an important way of maintaining social visibility while keeping up with what is going on in the community. Long before it was heard in the United States, the phrase "Yo! Wha' appenin" was a common working-class greeting in Port of Spain.

⁹ LIVING CONDITIONS

The traditional Trinidadian house, called an *ajoupa,* was built of thatch and mud. Today, most Trinidadians live in wooden houses with roofs of galvanized metal. There are generally three or four rooms; almost all houses have indoor plumbing, and most have electricity. Several houses often share one yard. There is a serious housing shortage in Trinidad and Tobago, and many city dwellers live in slums and tenement buildings. The government has attempted to meet the needs of low-income families by erecting modern concrete dwellings throughout the country.

Modern medical care has reduced the incidence of traditional diseases such as malaria, tuberculosis, typhoid, and syphilis, and the average life expectancy in Trinidad and Tobago is estimated at 72 years. While roads are adequate in the nation's more densely settled areas, rural roads often consist of single-lane dirt paths, and some areas of Tobago have virtually no usable roads. In the cities, minibuses called maxi-taxis are a popular form of public transportation. In the mid-1980s, there was about one car for every four people in Trinidad and Tobago.

10 FAMILY LIFE

Women wield considerable authority within African families in Trinidad and Tobago, and many are heads of households. Common-law marriages are widespread within the African community. Among the Indian population, large extended-family households are common, and even members of smaller households have a strong sense of obligation toward their relatives outside the nuclear family. Arranged marriages are common, and the man is always considered the head of the household. Marriage is regarded as a lifetime commitment—divorce, and even the remarriage of widows, is frowned upon.

11 CLOTHING

Most Trinidadians wear modern Western-style clothing. The Caribbean "shirt jac," a belted jacket worn with a scarf and no shirt, is popular among men in Port of Spain. Traditional clothing—including men's turbans and women's saris—is worn by some members of the country's Indian population. Every year special clubs spend months preparing extravagant "mas" (short for "masquerade") costumes for Trinidad and Tobago's famous Carnival celebration preceding Ash Wednesday. The brightly colored, eye-catching outfits—coordinated to be worn by hundreds or even thousands of people—may be made of either cotton or such dressy fabrics as velvet, satin, and lamé, as well as beads, feathers, sequins, shells, leaves, and straw. They are often accompanied by a profusion of body paint and glitter.

12 FOOD

The rich and varied cuisine of Trinidad and Tobago combines African, East Indian, Amerindian, Chinese, Middle Eastern, and European influences. Breakfast is usually continental-style, consisting of coffee (or cocoa) and bread, while lunch and dinner (which is eaten at 8:00 or 9:00 PM) are both substantial meals, generally consisting of meat, rice, vegetables, and fruit. The most important meal of the week is Sunday dinner, and many women are at the market by dawn on Sunday morning to buy their provisions.

One of the country's most popular foods is *roti*. Sold at restaurants, bars, and outdoor stands throughout the country, it consists of an Indian flat bread with a variety of fillings—including curried beef, chicken, lamb, and beef, and cooked vegetables—to which curried potatoes and chickpeas are added. The type of bread most commonly used for roti is *dhalpourri,* which consists of two thin layers of dough with ground split peas in between. Another favorite dish is *sans coche,* a stew containing pork, salted beef, pig's tails, onions, chives, and various other spices, served with dumplings. Other popular dishes include *callaloo,* a mixture of okra and puréed dasheen leaves (also called callaloo greens) with either crab or salted pork added for flavor, and *coocoo,* a cake similar to cornbread, made from cornflour and okra.

The national beverage of Trinidad and Tobago is rum, which is consumed liberally, especially during the country's national holidays and numerous festivals. Nonalcoholic drinks include *sorrel,* made from the petals of the sorrel flower; *ginger beer,* which is similar to ginger ale; and *peanut punch,* which is something like a peanut-butter milkshake.

13 EDUCATION

Formal education—which begins at age five—is highly valued in Trinidad and Tobago, and the country has a literacy rate of about 96%. In 1986 about 75% of high-school-age students were enrolled in school. The University of the West Indies has a campus on Trinidad. Other facilities for higher education include government-supported technical colleges, five teachers' colleges, and John F. Kennedy College, a liberal arts college near Port of Spain.

14 CULTURAL HERITAGE

Given the country's small size and the fact that it had no written literary tradition until the 20th century, Trinidad and Tobago has produced an impressive roster of eminent writers, including V. S. Naipaul, who emigrated as a young man but brought his homeland to life for readers around the world in such books as *Miguel Street* and *A House for Mr. Biswas.* Other well-known Trinidad-born writers include Michael Anthony, Samuel Selvon, and Paul Keens-Douglas. Derek Wolcott, the 1992 Nobel laureate in literature, was born in St. Lucia but has spent much of his time in Trinidad, where he founded the Trinidad Theatre workshop in Port of Spain in 1959.

Peter Minshall, a celebrated designer for Carnival masquerade bands and other art forms in Trinidad and Tobago, has also achieved renown in the international art world. Several active theater groups in Trinidad and Tobago mount stage productions regularly; some of the most interesting take place at the Little Carib Theater.

15 WORK

About 34% of the labor force in Trinidad and Tobago is employed in service-related jobs; 17% in trade; 15% in mining and manufacturing; 10% in agriculture, forestry, and fishing; and the remainder in other occupations. Agriculture in Trinidad and Tobago is carried out on both large mechanized farms and on small tracts of land worked by peasant farmers without modern farm machinery. The oil industry, which brought great wealth to the country in the 1970s, employs only about 3% of the work force. The nation has had a high rate of unemployment—sometimes approaching 20%—for decades. In 1994 it was over 19%. Emigration has removed many skilled workers and professionals from the nation's labor force.

16 SPORTS

Sports in Trinidad and Tobago reflect the historical influence of the British. Cricket is so popular that champion player Brian Lara is hailed as a national hero and has even received government recognition for his achievements. Another Trinidadian favorite is the quintessentially British sport of soccer (called "football" in Trinidad and Tobago, as it is in Britain). Most cities, towns, and even villages have their own soccer teams. Horse-racing is very popular as well.

17 ENTERTAINMENT AND RECREATION

Music plays an important role in everyday life in Trinidad and Tobago, and much Trinidadian entertainment includes or revolves around it. The latest calypso songs, with their witty commentaries on public figures and controversial issues, can be heard on radios and sound systems throughout the country. SoCa—primarily recorded music which combines soul ("So-")

and calypso ("-Ca") as well as other styles—has been universally popular since the 1980s. Trinidadians also enjoy watching movies and television, and American soap operas are especially popular. Trinidadians of Indian descent enjoy seeing movies from India, a country noted for its film industry.

One Caribbean leisure-time tradition that is fast disappearing in Trinidad and Tobago is the rum shop, where working-class men have traditionally met after work to drink and socialize. The country's remaining rum shops are few in number but retain their spirit of informality and camaraderie.

¹⁸ FOLK ART, CRAFTS, AND HOBBIES

Two forms of native Trinidadian music—calypso and steel drum music—have become famous throughout the world. Calypso was originally developed by plantation workers as a covert way to poke fun at their owners and overseers and at rival work gangs. This subversive tradition continues today in calypso music that mocks politicians and other local figures and comments satirically on current affairs.

Steel drum music originated when members of traditional African percussion bands began using discarded oil drums. With their bottoms cut off and their tops hammered into a convex shape marked by a pattern of dents that produce different pitches, these objects turn into musical instruments capable of a surprising range of musical nuance and expression in the hands of expert players. The drums (called "pans") are tuned to four musical ranges: bass (also called "boom"), cello pan, guitar pan, and ping-pong.

In addition to steel drums, which are a prime example of Trinidadian crafts, the nation's artisans also produce hand-beaten copper jewelry, woven straw goods, pottery, woodcarvings, boldly printed fabrics, and other handmade goods.

¹⁹ SOCIAL PROBLEMS

As Trinidad and Tobago becomes an increasingly urbanized society, its cities face housing shortages and difficulty in providing essential public services. Immigration of unskilled workers has contributed to the overcrowding of urban areas, while emigration of skilled workers has raised concern about a so-called "brain drain" depriving the country of needed talent. High unemployment has led to social unrest, particularly among the country's youth (43% of persons aged 15 to 19 were unemployed in 1994), and there has been an increase in serious crime, much of it drug- and gang-related.

²⁰ BIBLIOGRAPHY

Brereton, Bridget. *A History of Modern Trinidad.* London: Heinemann, 1981.

Gall, Timothy, and Susan Gall, ed. *Worldmark Encyclopedia of the Nations.* 8th ed. Detroit: Gale Research, 1995.

Lieber, Michael. *Street Life: Afro-American Culture in Urban Trinidad.* Boston: G. K. Hall, 1981.

Meditz, Sandra W., and Dennis M. Hanratty. *Islands of the Caribbean Commonwealth: A Regional Study.* Washington, DC: US Government, 1989.

Naipaul, V. S. *The Middle Passage.* New York: Vintage, 1962.

Saft, Elizabeth. *Insight Guides: Trinidad and Tobago.* Boston: Houghton Mifflin, 1996.

Segal, Daniel A. "Trinidadians and Tobagonians." In *Encyclopedia of World Cultures.* Boston: G. K. Hall, 1992.

Urosevich, Patti. *Trinidad and Tobago.* New York: Chelsea House, 1988.

Yelvington, Kevin, ed. *Trinidad Ethnicity.* London: MacMillan, 1992.

Walton, Chelle Koster. *Caribbean Ways: A Cultural Guide.* Westwood, MA: Riverdale, 1993.

Warner, Keith Q. *Kaiso! A Study of the Calypso as Oral Literature.* Washington, DC: Three Continents Press, 1982.

—by R. Wieder

UKRAINIAN AMERICANS

For more information on Ukrainian history and culture, *see* **Vol. 4: Ukrainians**.

OVERVIEW

Few Ukrainians immigrated to the US before 1865. At that time, however, Ukraine was divided between Russia (eastern Ukraine), Austria (western Ukraine), and Hungary (Transcarpathia). The Austrians were fairly supportive of Ukrainian identity and gave the Ukrainians a certain amount of autonomy. The Russians and Hungarians, on the other hand, were very oppressive, the Hungarians especially so. The first wave of Ukrainian American immigrants came to the US to escape the oppressions of their foreign rulers. Most were poor farmers from Transcarpathia.

Official immigration records list only 67,218 Ukrainians entering the US between 1899 and 1906 and 187,058 between 1907 and 1914. This is certainly a low count, however, because Ukrainians were not listed as such until 1899 (most were called "Ruthenians" instead), and even after 1899, many were mistakenly recorded as Poles, Slovaks, Hungarians, or Russians. It is estimated that there were actually closer to 500,000 Ukrainian Americans living in the US by 1914.

About 85% of these first-wave Ukrainian immigrants settled in Pennsylvania, New York, and New Jersey. As poor farmers, they lacked job skills relevant to the industrialized US, and their lack of English-language skills presented another roadblock to success. Therefore, most worked as low-paid unskilled laborers. A large number took jobs in the coal mines of Pennsylvania because the wages were higher due to the dangerous nature of the work. Many were injured, became sick, or even died in the mines.

The second wave of Ukrainian immigration to the US occurred between 1920 and 1939. The numbers were much lower during this second wave because of new immigration laws in the US that placed quotas on the numbers of immigrants allowed in, and because the newly formed Soviet Union forbade emigration. Only about 40,000 Ukrainians entered the US during this period. Most of these second-wave Ukrainian immigrants settled in cities of the Northeast, Mid-Atlantic, and Midwest, such as New York City, Philadelphia, Pittsburgh, Cleveland, Detroit, and Chicago.

In 1948, the US passed the Displaced Persons Act, allowing people who had been displaced by the destruction of World War II (1939–45) to immigrate to the US. Many Ukrainians took advantage of this opportunity, creating the third wave of Ukrainian American immigration. Some 85,000 Ukrainians entered the US under this Act, most of them to escape Soviet rule. These third-wave immigrants were generally much better educated than previous Ukrainian immigrants to the US. They also were more likely to have lived in cities in the Ukraine, so they had more experience with the industrialized urban world. Third-wave Ukrainian Americans adjusted much more quickly and easily to American life than did first- or second-wave immigrants.

The Ukrainian National Republic declared its independence from the Soviet Union in 1991 and became a recognized nation of the world a few months later. A fourth wave of Ukrainian immigration to the US began at this time, as Ukrainians were once again free to leave *and* needed money to help build up their newly independent country. Most fourth-wave Ukrainian Americans come to the US hoping to earn money to send back to the Ukraine and eventually to return themselves.

As the Soviet Union collapsed, more and more former Soviet citizens emigrated to find a better, more prosperous life elsewhere. Of all former-Soviet emigrés in 1993, 38% were Ukrainians emigrating to the US. Many came under the auspices of the Lautenberg Amendment, passed by US Congress in 1989, which makes it much easier to claim refugee status.

According to the US Census, there were 740,803 Ukrainian Americans in 1990. The majority are American-born and have become very Americanized. The largest concentrations of Ukrainian Americans are in Philadelphia, Pittsburgh, New York City, northern New Jersey, Los Angeles, Detroit, Cleveland, and northern Chicago. Ukrainian American churches and cultural societies offer English-language classes for first-generation immigrants, and Ukrainian language and culture classes for subsequent generations of American-born Ukrainian Americans.

Because Ukrainians lacked a cohesive national identity for so much of their history, their cultural identity became centered on the Ukrainian Church. The Ukrainian Catholic Church follows the Byzantine Rite, rather than the Latin Rite followed by earlier Catholic immigrants to the US. Therefore, Ukrainian Catholics set up their own churches when they came to the US. By 1898, there were 51 Ukrainian Catholic Churches in America.

Around the turn of the century, many Ukrainian Americans began converting to Russian Orthodox because Ukrainian Catholic churches were not available in their communities, and Russian Orthodox was closer to their Byzantine Rite than were Roman Catholic churches. So Ukrainian Catholics in the US petitioned the Pope for a Ukrainian bishop to serve in America. The Pope finally agreed, and in 1907, the first American Ukrainian Catholic bishop was appointed. In 1913, the Catholic Church set up a separate jurisdiction for American Ukrainian Catholics, and by 1914 there were 206 parishes in the US. Today there are about 145,000 Ukrainian Catholics in America.

The Ukrainian Orthodox Church grew more slowly in the US. Orthodox Ukrainian Americans began gathering together for worship in Chicago in the early 1900s. In 1924, an American Ukrainian Orthodox archbishop was appointed, and by 1932 there were 32 parishes in the US. Today there are about 25,000 Ukrainian Orthodox in America.

In 1892, a group of Ukrainian Protestant farmers started a church in Yale, Virginia. Other Ukrainian Protestant farmers settled in North Dakota, and by 1914, North Dakota had more Ukrainian Protestant farming communities than any other state in the US. Ukrainian American Protestants belong to a variety of denominations, such as Presbyterian or Baptist.

Besides traditional religious holidays (Christmas, Easter, etc.) and common American holidays (Thanksgiving, Fourth of July, etc.), Ukrainian Americans also celebrate Ukrainian Independence Day on 22 January, and Taras Shevchenko Day on 14 March.

Ukrainian Americans maintain their ethnic identity through their various churches and through cultural and other ethnic organizations. There are more than 37 of these organizations in the US today, including insurance clubs, credit unions, sports clubs, political associations, and women's leagues. These organizations were originally established to help Ukrainian immigrants adjust to life in the US. They then became concerned with providing opportunities for second- and subsequent-generation Ukrainian Americans to learn about their Ukrainian heritage and maintain their Ukrainian identity. In recent years they have focused on providing for aging Ukrainian Americans and lobbying for government funding and services, etc.

The first Ukrainian American all-day school (kindergarten–eighth grade) was established in Philadelphia, Pennsylvania, by the Ukrainian Catholic Church in 1925. By 1947 there were 18 all-day Ukrainian American schools in the US. Most Ukrainian parishes also had weekday afternoon or Saturday morning classes in Ukrainian language and culture. Some Ukrainian American high schools and junior colleges were established in the 1930s. By 1990 the Ukrainian Catholic Church had 21 all-day schools, 4 high schools, and 2 colleges.

Saturday "heritage schools" are run by the Ukrainian Orthodox Church and the Ukrainian Educational Council of the Ukrainian Congress Committee of America. These schools offer an 11-year study program in Ukrainian language, culture, history, literature, etc. The Ukrainian Research Institute founded in 1968 at Harvard University offers doctoral programs in Ukrainian studies, publishes Ukrainian-studies books, and has a large Ukrainian library.

Ukrainian Americans are proud of their Ukrainian cultural heritage and encourage their children to learn Ukrainian folk dances and folk songs. *Bandura* (the national musical instrument of the Ukraine) schools exist throughout the US. The Ukrainian National Chorus toured the US in 1922–23, with great success and introduced the now-classic Christmas carol, "Carol of the Bells," to American audiences. Shortly after their highly successful tour, the entire Chorus emigrated to the US. Other Ukrainian American musicians include opera stars Paul Plishka and Andrij Dobriansky, both with the Metropolitan Opera Company.

Perhaps the best-known Ukrainian American is actor Jack Palance (born Walter Jack Palahniuk). Anna Sten, John Hodiak, Nick Adams (Nicholas Adamchok), Mike Mazurki, and George Dzundza are among other Ukrainian Americans who have found success in the acting world. Sculptor Alexander Archipenko (1887–1964) and painter Jacques Hnizdovsky are two renowned Ukrainian American visual artists. Ukrainian American literature is still, for the most part, written in Ukrainian by first-generation immigrants and known only to other Ukrainian Americans.

Although early Ukrainian immigrants to the US were generally uneducated farmers who worked as low-paid unskilled laborers in America, subsequent generations (and more recent immigrants) have increased their levels of education and are now well represented in all of the major professions. Many have risen to the top of their respective fields, such as Igor Sikorsky, founder of Sikorsky Aviation Corporation. Ukrainian Americans are also well-represented in government from the local to the federal level. Mary Beck was the first Ukrainian American woman elected to public office and served longer than any other Ukrainian American before or since. Beck served on the Detroit City Council from 1950 to 1970.

Two Ukrainian American soccer teams, the Ukrainian Nationals of Philadelphia and the New York Ukrainians, played in the national championships, both in the 1960s. Many individual Ukrainian Americans have also been successful athletes, including hockey players Bill Moseienko, Terry Sawchuck, Dave Balon, and Walter Tkaczuk; and football players Bronko Nagurski, George Andrie, Bill Malinchak, George Tatasovic, John Machuzak, and Don Chuy. Probably the best-known Ukrainian American athlete, however, is football player and coach Mike Ditka.

Summer camps, called *Taboruvannia*, are very popular with Ukrainian American children. Thousands attend these Ukrainian American camps each summer to learn about their Ukrainian heritage and/or simply enjoy the company of other Ukrainian American youngsters. *Taboruvannia* come in many varieties, including educational/recreational, sports, music, and other types of camps.

Ukrainian American women continue to do traditional embroidery, but perhaps the most loved Ukrainian folk art in America is the painting of Ukrainian Easter eggs, known as *pysanka* (*pysanky*). Classes in traditional egg-painting techniques are offered across the US, and many craft stores now carry the necessary materials.

Problems in the Ukrainian American community stem almost entirely from divisions within the community itself, particularly between fourth-wave immigrants and those who immigrated to America in earlier waves. Fourth-wave Ukrainian Americans tend to see their time in the US as temporary, so they are not interested in becoming involved in the Ukrainian American community to any great extent. Established Ukrainian Americans from earlier waves of immigration resent the new immigrants for their lack of interest. The fourth-wave immigrants also tend to head for California and the Pacific Northwest, where jobs are more plentiful, rather than settling in established Ukrainian American communities.

Religious conflict has also increased because many of the newest Ukrainian immigrants are Protestant or Jewish, rather than Catholic or Orthodox like the majority of earlier immigrants. As the church has always been the center of Ukrainian cultural identity in America, these religious differences make it difficult for new immigrants to fit in with the earlier Ukrainian American cultural establishment.

Perhaps the most heated argument today among Ukrainian Americans is the legitimacy of the newest wave of immigrants. Some Ukrainian Americans feel that no one should leave the new Ukrainian National Republic. Rather, those who are there should stay and support it in its fledgling growth. They also question the "refugee" status of many of the new immigrants because the Ukraine is now an independent republic, no longer subject to any oppressive foreign rule. However, few (if any) Ukrainian Americans have returned to the Ukraine to give *their* support to the new republic, so the new immigrants question established Ukrainian Americans' right to criticize them for leaving.

BIBLIOGRAPHY

Dushnyck, Walter, and Fr. Nicholas L. Chirovsky, ed. *The Ukrainian Heritage in America*. New York: Ukrainian Congress Committee of America, 1991.

Kuropas, Myron B. *Ukrainians in America.* Minneapolis: Lerner Publications, 1996.

———. "Faces and Places: Is Suicidal Nationalism Killing Us?" *The Ukrainian Weekly* 62, no. 27 (3 July 1994): 9 ff.

"A Summertime Appreciation." *The Ukrainian Weekly* 62, no. 30 (24 July 1994): 6.

Woronowycz, Roman. "Diaspora Perplexed: What Do You Do with New Immigrants?" *The Ukrainian Weekly* 63, no. 28 (9 July 1995): 1 ff.

—by D. K. Daeg de Mott

URUGUAYANS

LOCATION: Uruguay
POPULATION: 3,137,668
LANGUAGE: Spanish
RELIGION: Roman Catholicism; some Judaism; Afro-Brazilian churches; evangelical Protestantism

¹ INTRODUCTION

During the expansion of colonial rule in Latin America, Uruguay became the source of conflict between the two leading powers, Spain and Portugal. The Portuguese, based in Brazil, migrated south into Uruguay in 1680 and founded a new colony called Colonia de Sacramento. In response to this challenge, Spain established a fort in nearby Montevideo, the present-day capital of Uruguay. A struggle for control over Uruguay ensued. Uruguay fell under Portuguese control and later became a province of Brazil. Uruguay was only granted full independence in 1828, through an agreement between Argentina and Brazil.

National independence, however, gave rise to internal political struggles. Conflicts between the two major political parties, the Colorados (Reds) and the Blancos (Whites), initiated a violent civil war that lasted from the mid-1830s to 1851. A period of peace and relative prosperity followed. In 1903, President José Batile y Ordonez was elected and launched a successful program of modernization and reform. Following a trend that swept most of South America, however, Uruguay later succumbed to a military dictatorship in 1973. Democracy was restored in 1985. The last national election was held in 1994; the next will be held in November 1999.

² LOCATION AND HOMELAND

Uruguay is located between Brazil and Argentina on the Atlantic coast of South America. Its terrain is characterized by gently rolling hills and natural grasslands. In contrast to the Andean or Amazonian countries, a high proportion of Uruguay's territory is suitable for agriculture. Most of Uruguay's grasslands are currently used for grazing sheep and cattle. In addition, Uruguay produces a wide range of fruits, cereals, and other agricultural products.

Unlike many other Latin American countries, Uruguay does not have a native population. Although there were Amerindian groups that lived in Uruguayan territory at the time of the colonial expansion, they were either displaced or annihilated. As a result, since 1830 the Uruguayans have been ethnically European, descending mainly from Italians or Spaniards. There is also a small population of Afro-Uruguayans (2.5% of the population).

³ LANGUAGE

The official language of Uruguay is Spanish. No Amerindian languages are currently spoken in Uruguay. In regions close to the Brazilian border, however, a Spanish-Portuguese dialect called Portuñol (or Portuniol) is spoken.

4 FOLKLORE

The name given to Uruguay's capital, Montevideo, originates in Ferdinand Magellan's visit to the region in 1520. According to legend, a sailor on board saw land and shouted, *"Monte vide eu"*—"I see a hill." The origin of the city's name is also from a phrase in Spanish found on early maps: *"Monte VI de E.O.,"* or "The sixth hill from east to west."

5 RELIGION

Most Uruguayans are descendants of Italians and Spaniards, and they have inherited the Roman Catholic tradition. Although the Church has historically played an important role in Uruguayan society and culture, it has no official role in politics. A variety of minority religions are practiced in Uruguay in addition to Catholicism. A small Jewish population, for example, exists in Montevideo. Many Afro-Uruguayans who live in the Barrio Sur (South Neighborhood) of Montevideo practice the Afro-Brazilian religion of *Condomble*. A more recent phenomenon is the growth of evangelical Protestantism.

There is a sharp separation between church and state. This has actually led to the renaming of many religious holidays. Many have been given secular (nonreligious) names. Christmas, for instance, is widely referred to as Family Day. Similarly, Easter Week is also known as Criollo Week.

6 MAJOR HOLIDAYS

Perhaps the most celebrated holiday in Uruguay is Carnaval (or Carnival), a week-long celebration that marks the commencement of Lent. During Carnaval, the country virtually comes to a halt, as stores close and people celebrate. Drinking, feasting, and dancing accompany a series of street parades with music and elaborate costumes. Competitions are held for the best musical performance. Water-throwing is a key ritual during Carnaval. Water balloons and buckets of water are used to drench friends and strangers alike!

Many of Uruguay's festivals celebrate its cattle-raising heritage. During Easter Week, a Cowboy Festival (Fiesta Gaucha) is held in Montevideo. Rodeo competitions are the main event. Contestants compete in a variety of events, such as knife-throwing, riding, and lassoing. Grilled beef and folk music accompany these Easter celebrations.

7 RITES OF PASSAGE

Major life transitions, such as birth, puberty, and death, are marked by rituals and celebrations appropriate to each Uruguayan's particular religious tradition.

8 INTERPERSONAL RELATIONS

The most substantial meal of the day in Uruguay is not dinner, but lunch. Many Uruguayan employees are given a two-hour lunch break that enables them to return home for a large, home-cooked meal with their families. Evening meals are traditionally much lighter. When invited to an Uruguayan home, one may be offered *mate,* an herbal tea. Traditionally, *mate* is drunk through a silver straw, called a *bombilla,* from a carved gourd. The gourd and straw are passed around and shared by all present. In most urban homes, however, *mate* is now served in tea cups.

In Uruguay, the Italian influence in both language and culture can be felt. For example, to say goodbye, most Uruguayans

have adopted the Italian *ciao* or *addio* in place of the Spanish *adios*. In addition, it is proper to kiss someone both when saying hello and upon departing.

9 LIVING CONDITIONS

Uruguay does not have the extreme inequality of incomes and standards of living found in other Latin American countries. However, there is a marked difference in patterns of living in urban and rural areas. Nearly half the population lives in the capital, Montevideo. Montevideo is a modern city, with high-rise apartments and office buildings. The city has many restaurants, cinemas, and shopping centers. Many of the poorer residents, however, live in small homes or shacks on the outskirts of the city.

A substantial proportion of the population continue to live in rural areas. For many, cattle- and sheep-ranching is their way of life. Many people are employed by large-scale farms, called *estancias.* Uruguayan cowboys, called *gauchos,* still wear traditional dress as they brand cattle, fix fencing, and round up the herd. Most gauchos live in simple communal housing on the farm where they work. Other households live in adobe homes.

The life expectancy in Uruguay (72 years) is almost equal to that of developed countries. Uruguay's relative prosperity gives most residents access to health care (94%) and clean water (98%). Adequate living conditions mean that the rate of infectious disease is low in comparison to other Latin American countries. Uruguay also has a varied agricultural sector, and

Street scene in the town of Colonia del Sacramento, Uruguay. There is a marked difference in patterns of living in urban and rural areas. Nearly half the population lives in the capital, Montevideo. (Mary A. Dempsey)

locally grown beef and vegetables are affordable for most households.

¹⁰ FAMILY LIFE

The rights of women in Uruguay were historically more advanced than in other Latin American countries. As early as 1907, divorce due to spousal abuse became legally recognized. In addition, women now have the right to a divorce without giving a reason. This privilege is not offered to men. This growing legal protection of women and the secularization of society (i.e., the separation of church and state) enables women to escape traditional female stereotypes. A significant proportion of women in Uruguay work outside the home. Girls in Uruguay are also more likely to complete their schooling than are their counterparts in other Latin American countries.

Marriage in Uruguay can now be formalized through a civil, or nonreligious, ceremony. There is no requirement, as in other Latin American countries, that weddings be performed in a church. Civil weddings also mean that the bride no longer has to vow to obey her husband. Instead, both the man and woman pledge to treat their partner with respect.

Families in Uruguay are relatively small in comparison with other countries in the region. Most urban families have access to birth control and choose to limit the size of their families. In rural areas, however, access to birth control is more restricted and women typically have more children.

¹¹ CLOTHING

The lifestyle of Uruguay's cowboys, or *gauchos,* has not changed dramatically since the 1800s. Gauchos proudly use the distinctive clothing worn by their ancestors. Because they spend most waking hours on horseback, gauchos have adopted the use of very baggy pants called *bombachas.* Wide-brimmed black hats offer protection from the midday sun, while woolen ponchos are used for warmth in the evenings. Leather boots and intricately tooled leather saddles complete the rugged picture.

In contrast, urban Uruguayans wear modern European dress. Today's youths favor jeans and tee-shirts, while suits and ties are appropriate attire for businessmen.

¹² FOOD

Not surprisingly for a cattle-ranching country, beef features predominantly in Uruguayan cuisine. Uruguayans are reputed to be among the largest consumers of beef per capita in the world. *Churrasco,* or grilled steak, can be said to be the national dish. Sometimes the meat is grilled with the skin on, in order to prevent it from drying out. Also very popular are *chivitos:* hot steak sandwiches, topped with bacon, eggs, cheese, lettuce, and tomatoes.

The Uruguayans have also adapted traditional Spanish dishes. A Uruguayan version of *puchero,* Spanish meat stew, is sometimes cooked with blood sausage. Although this dish is considered a delicacy, it has been nicknamed *olla podrida,* or "rotten pot." Uruguay's cuisine also has a significant Italian influence. Pasta and lasagna are Uruguayan favorites.

Puchero
(Uruguayan meat stew)

4 pounds ossobuco (veal shanks), cut into six pieces
1 cup chopped celery
6 carrots, peeled
6 white potatoes, peeled
1 onion
6 zucchini
1 pound green beans
1 bunch parsley
6 ears of sweet corn, peeled
4 teaspoons salt
1 squash (medium size), cut into 6 pieces, unpeeled

Fill a large saucepan with water and bring it to a boil. Add all ingredients to boiling water, putting the meat in first, then carrots, onion, green beans, corn, squash, and celery. Then add potatoes and zucchini. Add parsley and salt to season the stew. Cover and simmer for 30 minutes, or until potatoes are tender. Drain off broth and serve meat and vegetables. To enhance the flavor, the stew may be served with mustard, mayonnaise, tomato, onion, or pepper sauce. If desired, add rice or noodles to remaining broth and serve in soup bowls.

(Recipe courtesy of the Embassy of Uruguay.)

13 EDUCATION

Uruguayans are among the most-educated people in Latin America, with a literacy rate topping 97%. The impressive educational system in Uruguay originates in the government of José Batile y Ordonez. Early in the 1900s, this president introduced sweeping educational reforms and invested in developing Uruguay's educational structures. Children are obligated by law to attend school until the age of 12.

14 CULTURAL HERITAGE

Uruguay has a rich literary tradition, combining both European and indigenous cultural influences. Perhaps the most-celebrated poet was Juan Zorrilla de San Martin. Referred to as the "poet of the Fatherland," he wrote a poem in 1879 about the native Amerindians. The poem "Tabare" has been considered to be among the most powerful in Uruguay's literary history. A more-recent writer of international acclaim is Juan Carlos Onetti, a contemporary novelist.

Uruguay's musical tradition has been shaped by its European history—as in Argentina, the tango is a popular form of dance. One exception to the European influence is *candombe,* an Afro-Brazilian musical and dance form that is also popular in Uruguay.

15 WORK

Uruguay's population works in many different sectors of the economy. Many urban dwellers find work in the industrial sector, including textile plants, breweries, and canning factories. Many industries are closely tied to the processing of agricultural products. For example, the leather industry generates employment. Small firms produce shoes, purses, bags, and other leather items. In addition, wool is an important export.

In addition to industry and manufacturing, Montevideo offers jobs as waiters, taxi drivers, and shopkeepers. Unemployment, however, is a major problem. Many Uruguayans are unable to find paid employment and are forced to develop their own small-scale enterprises. Many of these people turn to street vending, tailoring, or other activities to make a living.

Agriculture is the primary driving force behind the Uruguayan economy. Sheep- and cattle-ranching are the most important agricultural activities. Growing crops such as fruits, wheat, oats, sugar, and corn is less important than raising livestock.

16 SPORTS

Uruguayans love soccer (*futbol)* and enjoy the game both as spectators and participants. They have won the World Cup twice, first in 1930 and later in 1950. In the second World Cup game, Uruguay beat the strong favorite, Brazil. The country responded with such jubilation that the government declared a national holiday! Soccer is also a favorite of youths. Informal neighborhood matches can be seen not only in soccer fields but also on quiet streets throughout the city.

Uruguayans are equally passionate about horses. Rodeos where *gauchos* (cowboys) demonstrate their equestrian skills are always widely attended. Horse-racing is also very popular. Uruguay also shares with Argentina a passion for polo. Regular matches between the two countries are held on the Punte del Este.

17 ENTERTAINMENT AND RECREATION

Many Uruguayan families flock to the beaches on weekends for rest and recreation. Many beautiful beaches provide an opportunity for swimming and sunbathing. Uruguayans are also fond of camping. The coastal forests provide numerous sites for camping and fishing. Weekends are often a time in the cities for visiting friends or having large family lunches. Montevideo also has a varied night life. Restaurants, cinemas, and musical shows are widely attended on weekends.

18 FOLK ART, CRAFTS, AND HOBBIES

Most of Uruguay's crafts involve processing the raw materials produced by the large cattle- and sheep-ranching sector. Uruguayans excel in producing handcrafted leather goods. Belts, hats, boots, and purses of high quality are carefully crafted from home-grown leather.

Many craft items are produced by a well-known handicraft cooperative in Montevideo called *Manos de Uruguay* (Hands of Uruguay). This cooperative includes skilled artisans from all over Uruguay. They spin the wool, dye it, and knit sweaters. Manos de Uruguay produces over 100,000 sweaters each year! In addition to handmade woolen items, they also make ceramic crafts.

19 SOCIAL PROBLEMS

Uruguay's highly urbanized society faces the same problems common to other industrialized countries. Unemployment typically ranges from 10% to 15%, and there is a serious lack of housing. There is, however, no major drug abuse problem.

[20] BIBLIOGRAPHY

Birnbaum's South America 1994. New York: HarperCollins, 1995.

Hudson, Rex, and Sandra W. Meditz. *Uruguay: A Country Study.* Washington, D.C.: Federal Research Division, Library of Congress, 1992.

Land and Peoples: Central and South America. Vol. 6. Danbury, CT: Grolier Incorporated, 1991.

Morrison, Marion. *Let's Visit Uruguay.* London: Burke Publishing Company Limited, 1985.

———. *Uruguay.* Enchantment of the World Series. Chicago: Children's Press, 1992.

Moss, Joyce, and George Wilson. *Peoples of the World: Latin Americans.* Detroit and London: Gale Research, Inc. 1989.

Rojas-Lombardi, Felipe. *The Art of South American Cooking.* New York: HarperCollins, 1991.

—by C. Sahley, reviewed by H. A. Azeves

VAUPÉS

LOCATION: Colombia (along the Vaupés River)
LANGUAGE: A variety of Amerindian or mixed languages and dialects, including Tukano and Lingua Geral; Spanish; Portuguese
RELIGION: Indigenous beliefs

[1] INTRODUCTION

The Vaupés Indians of Colombia comprise several major tribes, including the Caribes, the Cubeos, the Uananas, the Karapanas, the Tucanos, and the Macús. Another tribe, the Arawaks, live further north along the Isana river. All of these groups share certain important features that relate directly to the lifestyle in a region consisting of tropical jungle and areas of savanna, along a major river, the Vaupés, and its tributaries. For example, it is now clear that conservation methods practiced in these areas of northwest Amazonia have been successful for thousands of years. It is also evident to historians and anthropologists that the trade along the rivers of the Vaupés among the varying tribal groups has been going on for a very long time. It is assumed that the origins of the Amerindians of this region lie in Central Asia. All of these groups share certain religious aspects, including shamanic practices, which are also found in Asia.

When Colombia was first colonized by the Spanish, the Vaupés region, due to its large expanses of dense jungle, remained remote and often inaccessible. Nevertheless, missionaries and traders made contact with the various tribes over the centuries, and rubber-tapping in particular brought more commerce to the region.

Eventually, during the 20th century, the regional capital of the Vaupés, called Mitú, became a point of contact between the tribes of the Vaupés and regional government officials and traders. Although many Amerindians of the Vaupés, particularly the Cubeos, have resisted the efforts of White missionaries to Christianize them and to persuade them to adopt Western norms, some groups of Amerindians from many of these tribes have begun a process of cultural adaptation which is painful and, initially, at least, often plunges them into a type of dependence and poverty which is quite different from the rather magnificent self-sufficiency of which some of the Vaupés Indians are still capable.

[2] LOCATION AND HOMELAND

The Vaupés region with its major rivers, such as the Vaupés and its tributaries, the Cuduyarí and the Querarí, forms part of the extensive Amazon basin which continues into Brazil. The Amerindian tribes of the Vaupés relate themselves geographically more to the Vaupés River and its tributaries, rather than to the boundaries of a particular municipality, department, or country. The Vaupés River itself flows on into Brazil, and trade along this river system, which eventually flows into the Amazon River, has existed between the various tribes for centuries.

The Cubeos live between the Vaupés River and its tributary the Cuduyarí; whereas another major tribe, the Tukanos, live in the area between the Tiquié and the Poporí, which are both tributaries of the Vaupés. The Macús are scattered in several areas and also live among some of the other tribes, but some of their settlements lie in the area between the Apoporis and the Poco River, while other Macús live to the east of the Desanas, near the Negro River. The Karapanas and the Uananas live to the north of the Tukanos. In all cases, the Amerindians of the Vaupés divide the rivers and their banks into specific locations, some of which are, in effect, farming, hunting, or fishing areas belonging to particular clans, families, or individuals, whereas certain large rocks and other areas are considered sacred grounds.

3 LANGUAGE

The Vaupés Indians speak a variety of languages and dialects. It is not unusual for a single large home or *maloca,* which houses several nuclear families that together form the extended family unit, to include four or five languages. This is because there are strict rules governing suitable partners for marriage. In a maloca where several brothers live, there may be a number of wives, therefore, who speak other languages. One of the major languages of the Vaupés which, in effect, is understood by many is the Tukano language.

Those who have had contact with missionaries, traders, and government officials also speak some Spanish and Portuguese. There is also a dialect or language that has developed over time, containing a mixture of Spanish, Portuguese, and Amerindian, known as Lingua Geral, which means, in Portuguese, a "general language" that enables different types of people in this region and in the bordering areas between Colombia and Brazil to communicate with each other.

The Vaupés Indians often have a Spanish name, but among many of them, particularly the Cubeos, the name must be given to them by a White person. This confers an immense advantage, in their view, because it may be used without restrictions. Their Amerindian names are never used casually but are instead closely guarded. When they refer to each other publicly, among themselves, they will use a name relating to their position as a relative. For example, among the Cubeos, a woman may refer to her grandchild or to a young person as *Teumi,* which means, "little one" and is used affectionately.

4 FOLKLORE

One of the most important characters of Vaupés folklore, shared by several of the tribes, is Vaí Mahse, the Master of the Animals. His name is pronounced *Vaeeh Mahsuh.* He can appear in a variety of forms, including that of a red dwarf, and he watches over the balance of nature so that humans, as hunters, do not exceed themselves when hunting animals. He also is said to wander over the Milky Way, which is a pathway for him, where he watches over the activities of animals and humans. He is a guardian of all the animals.

A hero shared by several tribes is Kúwai. He is a mythical figure and is regarded as "the one who has the power to transform, to change." Kúwai is not perceived as a god in the strict sense, but rather as a teacher who taught the mysteries of creation, the use and manufacture of tools, and the practical arts such as fishing and farming. He is also seen as the creator of rivers.

Early travelers to the Vaupés region refer to a god called Yuruparí, but several anthropologists think this is a term used by all the Amerindians of the Vaupés region to refer to any sacred or taboo element or thing.

5 RELIGION

In general, most of the Vaupés Indians see the earth as midway between the underworld and the sky, and they generally accept the existence of spirits and ghosts, as well as entities relating to nature. They have a concept of the body as separate from the person's spirit or soul, and there is among some groups a cult of their ancestors, who are not only figures from the past but whose presence can be invoked in the present, through the appropriate rituals, to accompany their descendants. There are a great variety of colorful myths to explain the origins of the various peoples of the region, but their very color and variety, indicative of a rich imagination, can sometimes veil a deeper, metaphysical way of thinking that links the proper conduct of humans and society to a genuinely spiritual purpose in life.

The Tukano peoples of the Vaupés believe there is a balance in nature that must be maintained, and everything humans take from nature must be replaced. Humans themselves have access to two worlds: the outer, or what we might call objective reality; and the inner, psychic, or mental reality. To fulfill the principle of restitution in nature, humans must come to understand that everything that can be perceived through the senses in the physical world also has a fundamental meaning in the mental or psychological world. To know and to understand these significances or meanings is the main aim in life for the Tukanos.

All the Amerindians of the Vaupés have shamans who mediate between this world and the spirit world. The Cubeos have a division between shamans who are essentially healers and the much rarer shaman known as the *yaví,* or "jaguar," who is supremely powerful and who can, it is believed, take the form of a jaguar.

⁶ MAJOR HOLIDAYS

Many of the Vaupés Indians do not observe the major national holidays of Colombia, including Independence Day, or the arrival of Christopher Columbus on American shores, or major Catholic holidays. They still live within their own cultural and religious norms, and their festivals coincide with major life events such as initiation rites, naming rites, or marriage rites. In the capital of the Vaupés region, the town of Mitú, there has been a gradual process of adaptation carried on in part by some Vaupés Indian women who have married townsmen and have begun over the last few decades to participate in the national holidays.

⁷ RITES OF PASSAGE

When a child is born, a Vaupés woman will retire to a special place to give birth, outside the large hut where she lives with her extended family. Quite often she will give birth outdoors, in her own field where she grows manioc (cassava). She will reenter the hut or *maloca* through a special entrance, usually at the back of the house. Among some groups, the baby and the parents will be ritually painted, and this paint will last for a few days.

Childhood is somewhat different for boys and girls. The girls remain close to their mother and learn a wide array of skills that are considered appropriate for women, whereas boys essentially form groups and are allowed to play collectively until they reach adolescence.

Young children are treated with great tolerance and permissiveness, but the upbringing becomes much stricter when they become teenagers. After boys have reached puberty they are eventually initiated in a group, in secret rites well away from the gaze of girls and women. They are assisted by shamans, and they have to take special substances that will give them visions of the spirit world. Afterwards they are entitled to wear special ritual jewelry and ornaments, as well as a headband decorated with feathers. They can also look for a suitable wife.

Among many Vaupés Indians, when a person dies, he or she is wrapped in his or her hammock and buried in his or her canoe. All the Amerindians of this region believe that a person's spirit leaves the body when he or she dies.

⁸ INTERPERSONAL RELATIONS

The Amerindians of the Vaupés region who continue to live in the traditional manner have particular orders and levels of importance governing their relations. The men have a greater status than the women, and young men who have been initiated have a greater standing than younger boys. These societies have been evolving, and chieftains have been replaced in importance by shamans and people with secret or hidden knowledge.

Among the Cubeos, the strongest bonds are between brothers. Their settlements are usually sparsely populated and include extended family units of about 35 or 40 members, including brothers, their wives, and their children. The Tukanos also live in extended family units consisting of up to seven or eight nuclear families (husbands, wives, and children). Strict rules govern marriage. Among the Tukanos, men must choose wives who speak a different language and therefore belong to a different group known as a *phratry* (derived from the Latin word for "brother"). Each phratry is composed of about 20 smaller groups called *sibs*. Each sib shares a common mythical ancestor. Groups defined in this way do not occupy particular areas and so cannot be called tribes.

The notion of a language group as a particular type of phratry also includes mental and psychological elements (the common mythical ancestor that unites each subgroup or sib). This is close to the idea of other types of Amerindian groups organized as clans with particular totems, which are sometimes symbolized by animals and the virtues of the particular animals. These totems or clan symbols form part of the inner landscape of a person and contribute to his or her identity.

The peoples of the Vaupés often gather for drinking parties and social occasions during which fermented drinks called *chicha* and *mihí* are consumed. This is a way of cementing relationships between groups or sibs which make up the larger phratries. Among these groups, those who live "down river" have a higher standing than those who live "up river." This means that the "up river" groups will often prepare the *chicha* for the "down river" groups.

The most important factor governing any occasion is the right inner mood of the person or persons taking part, and this applies both to work-related activities and to social or ceremonial occasions. Among the Tukanos and the Arawaks, the *chicha* is served in an elaborate, formal manner by hosts carrying the chicha-laden gourds, who dance towards the guests in single file in a crouching position. During these social occasions young men and women are provided with an opportunity to dance together. The dances usually begin quite formally, first with only the male dancers, and as the evening progresses the girls gather courage and join them, overcoming their initial shyness.

⁹ LIVING CONDITIONS

Some travelers to the Vaupés have observed that the Amerindians who have managed to preserve their lifestyle and resist the pressures of the missionaries to abandon their spacious, communal longhouses in favor of smaller, rather miserable, single-family huts are in better health than the groups who are in a state of transition, attempting to adapt to White society. This may well be because the Amerindians who continue to live in the traditional manner have not lost their knowledge of medicinal herbs and plants. It is also possible that the stresses of adaptation may contribute to illness. Nevertheless, some groups are not averse to seeking the help of White doctors who live in the town of Mitú, the capital of the Vaupés region.

The attitude to consumption is interesting in the Vaupés, since ritual objects and handicrafts created by the different tribes are highly valued and there has been a form of barter in existence for hundreds and perhaps thousands of years. A good fishing area along the river is an important possession and may be given as a gift even to a child. At the same time, the Vaupés peoples display an amazing detachment, even in relation to highly prized ritual objects which are considered irreplaceable, in the case of children who take these objects without permission or destroy them. There is a calm acceptance and an equanimity which is part of a tolerant attitude to young children.

The traditional longhouses or *malocas* are about 18 m (60 ft) long and almost 12 m (40 ft) wide, built with sloping palm-thatched roofs. Up to seven or eight nuclear families live together, usually brothers, their wives, and children. Inside there are communal spaces, nuclear-family spaces, spaces for young men at the front of the house, and special spaces at the back reserved for women and young children. The front entrance is reserved for males, the back entrance for females. The outer front walls are often painted with geometric motifs related to the views of these cultures about the life-giving forces of the universe.

The attitude that what is consumed must be replaced in some way is essentially a successful attitude of conserving resources in the environment. This makes for a standard of living sufficient for the basic needs of life, without excesses which are seen to be harmful if they create imbalances in nature.

The most important form of transport in the Vaupés is the canoe, although hunters can trek on foot for days in the jungle or the savanna if necessary.

10 FAMILY LIFE

The role of women is significant as bearers of children and cultivators of food. They are also skilled in various handicrafts such as pottery and some types of weaving and are expected to prepare the food. Women usually own their own small fields where they grow manioc (cassava). This field is not simply an economically productive unit, but also a private space. An interesting and important aspect of a woman's life is her role as a trader. She often has less contact with White society than some of the men and has continued to engage in the traditional form of barter in use among the Vaupés for centuries. This is not just a form of trade, but a pattern of social relationships which becomes established through this type of barter and which imposes a series of obligations. Among many groups, people take great care in what they ask for, because merely asking for a particular object imposes an obligation to surrender it. Every object has a history (where it was obtained, from whom, and under what circumstances) that invests the object with less impersonal meanings than those of objects obtained in a Western-style, mass-consumption society where only certain things may keep these associations in the mind of the consumer.

Among the Tukanos, when a man wishes to take a wife, his father and some male relatives have to kidnap the girl and take her to the house where the prospective groom awaits her. Among the Cubeos, it is the groom himself who has to kidnap the girl, take her to his canoe, and then to his home. If the girl is unhappy, she can escape back to her parental home, and her parents will respect her if she wants to stay with them. Even after the marriage rites, this situation may arise, and the family of the girl will never force her to stay with her husband if she is unhappy. The "kidnap" must be understood as a ritual that always precedes marriage.

Some Amerindians of the Vaupés, particularly the Cubeos, have been known to keep dangerous animals as pets, even anaconda snakes!

11 CLOTHING

The Vaupés Indians wear a type of loincloth and some forms of feathered headbands and arm bracelets, as well as body paint. Women who live in the traditional manner also use body paint, but some have adopted skirts or even loose cotton dresses as a result of contacts with White society, including missionaries and traders.

12 FOOD

The staple food of the Vaupés is manioc, also called cassava, which is made into flour and cakes. Wild fruits and nuts are also eaten, and an important source of protein is fish. Sometimes the peccary and the tapir are hunted, as well as some species of monkey.

Some cooking utensils have the advantage not only of being made locally, but also of being multifunctional and graceful: a circular mat woven from the mirití palm serves as a cooking-pot cover and a plate.

Men grow tobacco and some plants that provide the ingredients used in initiation rites, and women grow manioc. Girls and boys help women gather wild fruits and nuts.

13 EDUCATION

Some children in the Vaupés have attended mission schools, and their traditional way of life has been altered in favor of the single-family unit preferred by missionaries. For many others, a traditional Amerindian education includes learning a number of tribal languages, as well as all the survival skills necessary for their traditional lifestyle, including hunting, fishing, farming, weaving, tool-making, and house-building. These are accompanied by instruction in correct understanding of the principles of conservation and a view of nature and the cosmos as an interplay of forces and energies where a balance has to be maintained.

14 CULTURAL HERITAGE

Music can be either sacred or secular. Sacred instruments are prepared and stored with care and used on ceremonial occasions. They include flutes, rattles, and drums. Both singing and dancing are important to the Amerindians of the Vaupés. These activities can occur in a religious and ceremonial context, such as initiation rites or the invocation of ancestor or burial ceremonies, or they can occur in a secular context such as social drinking parties to celebrate the completion of a house. Certain melodies played by young men on reed flutes are courtship songs well known in the area, suggesting unsung words meaning: "If the women from these parts do not want us, we will go somewhere else!"

The literature of the Vaupés Indians is oral, although some petroglyphs (symbolic designs and drawings on large stones along the river suggesting written hieroglyphic messages) have been found. This suggests that these cultures may be very old.

The myths and legends of the Vaupés represent a rich body of oral literature. There are stories of the origin of the world and of the peoples and all the natural elements, as well as of the plants and animals. The Desanas, a branch of the Tukanos, refer not only to the physical sun, but also to the invisible Sun Father who sent Pamurí Mahse, who carried his staff and searched everywhere in the Vaupés for a place to establish humanity. He stood in his canoe and probed the riverbank to find fertile ground. He had to find a place where his staff would cast no shadow. Finally he found this place, and seed fell from his staff into a deep pool in the river, and from this seed the first Desana was born.

15 WORK

Some Vaupés Indians have worked in the past in the rubber-tapping industry, although others who do not participate in the cash economy and live in more remote areas, relying on barter and exchange, have regarded this as a calamity, a type of slave-labor which destroys the culture. Trade among tribes is an important activity, although trade with White people is becoming more common, and some Indian traders have become adept at bargaining. Hunting, fishing, and farming are major activities. The Vaupés Indians make beautiful fish traps along the riverbanks out of delicately woven reeds, and they also use blowpipes and spears for hunting. The fine arrows or darts used in the blowpipes are dipped in a specially prepared *curare* poison that paralyzes the prey.

16 SPORTS

The Vaupés Indians are remarkable boaters. This is due to the large number of rapids along the Vaupés River, which they navigate with marvelous skill in their canoes. While this activity is not, strictly speaking, conceived by them as a sport, much of the thrill and the intense concentration experienced by the sportsperson is present during this activity, even when it is linked to the necessity of travel rather than sport.

17 ENTERTAINMENT AND RECREATION

Children play a game relating to jungle demons and the *tem tem* bird. Girls and boys play the demons who surround a boy who is the tem tem bird and who has to try to break out of the circle. In another game, a girl builds a thatched palm shelter and waits inside for a boy hunter to free her. Some travelers to the area have described a game of catch where the ball is made out of corn.

A main form of recreation, which is enjoyed mainly by young adults but which also includes whole families, is the social drinking party where vast quantities of fermented manioc (cassava) beer or *chicha* is consumed, and people dance and sing all night, or until they drop! This type of reunion occurs between groups organized as *sibs,* a type of kinship that relies on a common mythical ancestor and is a type of clan.

18 FOLK ART, CRAFTS, AND HOBBIES

The arts and crafts of the Vaupés include jewelry-making, particularly delicately beaded necklaces, as well as basket-weaving. The Makú Indians are particularly skilled basket-weavers, and their baskets are deep and pleasingly shaped, as well as lightweight and strong. Makú baskets are an easily traded item along the Vaupés River. Body-painting is practiced by all the Indians of the region, and the attractive geometric motifs are also repeated on the walls of their spacious longhouses. The motifs refer to fertility, creation, and various entities from the spirit world, or animals who have counterparts in the spirit world, such as jaguars. The jaguar is a symbol of power, and very often jaguar spots are painted on people or on particular places as a form of protection.

The Vaupés Indians also make musical instruments such as reed flutes and larger flutes known as *chirimías.* Pottery, made mainly by women, takes a variety of pleasing shapes.

19 SOCIAL PROBLEMS

The social problems of the Vaupés Indians relate mainly to the incursions of missionaries, traders, people involved in the rubber industry, and government officials, as well as, on occasion, curious but unsympathetic travelers who have disturbed the

delicately balanced lifestyle that survived for hundreds or perhaps thousands of years. Missionaries over the years have disapproved of the extended family households and have tried to persuade the Vaupés Indians to live in single-family units. For this they have been heavily criticized by anthropologists who point out that the extended household is a form of social organization which, once it is broken up, impoverishes the families both physically and psychologically because they are deprived of important support systems well-suited to their environment.

20 BIBLIOGRAPHY

Goldman, Irving. *Los Cubeo.* Mexico: Instituto Indigenista Interamericano, 1968.

Hugh-Jones, Stephen. *The Palm and the Pleiades.* Cambridge: Cambridge University Press, 1979.

Reichel-Dolmatoff, Gerardo. *Indios de Colombia.* Bogotá: Villegas Editores, 1991.

———. *The Forest Within.* London and Colombia: Themis Books in association with the COAMA Programme, and the Gaia Foundation, 1996.

—by P. Pitchon

VENEZUELANS

LOCATION: Venezuela
POPULATION: 21 million
LANGUAGE: Spanish; Amerindian languages
RELIGION: Roman Catholicism; some Protestantism, Judaism, and native Amerindian religions

¹ INTRODUCTION

Venezuela was colonized by the Spanish in the 16th century. The Spanish conquerors initially explored the lengthy Caribbean coastline. They fought with a variety of Amerindian tribes and later brought slaves from Africa. Venezuelans today are descended partly or wholly from all three types of people. There are still about 15 groups of Amerindian tribes in Venezuela.

Unlike Peru, Venezuela never became the seal of the Spanish viceroys, but it holds an honored place in Latin American history because its capital, Caracas, is the birthplace of the great Simón Bolívar. He freed Venezuela, along with Colombia, Peru, Ecuador, and Bolivia, from Spanish rule and, thanks to his efforts, Venezuela became an independent nation. The decisive defeat of the Spanish forces took place at Carabobo in 1821, and every Venezuelan attributes the origin of the country as an independent nation to this great battle and to the vision and bravery of Bolívar, known as *El Libertador,* or The Liberator.

Venezuela endured various dictatorships during the 20th century, but there have been free elections and democratically elected presidents since 1958. Thanks to an abundance of oil, Venezuela has made rapid progress, and the wealth generated by oil may have kept it free of the violence generated in some neighboring countries such as Colombia and Peru.

² LOCATION AND HOMELAND

Venezuela is the size of Texas and Oklahoma combined. It shares a border with Colombia to the west, with Brazil to the south, and with Guyana to the east. In the north its Caribbean coastline is around 3,000 km (1,865 mi) long. The central part of Venezuela consists of vast, grassy plains; the south is partly jungle, and a range of the Andes mountains crosses Venezuela from the Colombian border, running in a northeasterly direction. These features contribute to Venezuela's variety, from Andean peaks clad in eternal snow, to rain forests, beaches, and savannas. The greater part of the country has a warm climate.

While most of the population is descended from the Spanish or is of mixed Spanish-Amerindian or Spanish-African blood, there are still over 20 pure Amerindian groups, speaking their own languages and numbering about 200,000 people out of a total population of 21 million people. During the 20th century there has been some Italian, Spanish, and Portuguese immigration, as well as immigration from neighboring Colombia.

³ LANGUAGE

The official language of Venezuela is Spanish. The country offers a variety of accents. There is a difference in the Andean region, where Spanish is spoken more slowly, as compared to the rest of Venezuela where the language is spoken more rapidly, a feature it shares with other Caribbean areas of Latin America.

Each of the surviving Amerindian tribes continues to speak its own language; among these are the Guajiros who live near Maracaibo, the Warao in the Orinico River region, and the Makiratare and Yanomani in the Amazon region in the south.

⁴ FOLKLORE

The folklore in Venezuela has evolved from blending of Spanish, African, and Amerindian customs. Several colorful festivals are the result of this blending of cultures. Carnival, known simply as *Carnaval,* is a nationwide yearly event that lasts for several days and begins just before Ash Wednesday (in February). There is a dramatic Dance of the Devils where people parade and dance in costumes and masks in the streets of San Francisco de Yare on Corpus Christi. Black African music influences the Fiesta de San Juan, held in Miranda state in June.

⁵ RELIGION

Most Venezuelans are Roman Catholic, although there are also some Protestants, and a Jewish community that resides mainly in Caracas. Some Venezuelan Amerindians have also adopted Roman Catholicism, although several tribes, particularly in the Amazon region, continue to practice their own forms of religion, which share some features with other Amerindian groups throughout the Americas, including a deep reverence for nature.

One of Venezuela's important religious events takes place in the town of Guanare. It is an annual feast day honoring the Virgin, known in Venezuela as Nuestra Señora de Comoroto, Venezuela's patron saint. It commemorates the occasion in 1652 when the Virgin is said to have appeared to an Amerindian chief on the shores of the Guanaguare River, encouraging him to accept baptism, and leaving him a tiny image of herself. The chief was frightened and ran away and later died of snakebite. Just before his death, however, he asked to be baptized and advised his tribespeople to undergo the same ritual.

⁶ MAJOR HOLIDAYS

Aside from religious festivals and the national Carnival, the major holiday in Venezuela is Independence Day, celebrated on 19 April. Other public holidays marking important historical events include Simón Bolívar's birthday on 24 July, the victory over the Spanish in the Battle of Carabobo on 5 July, and the discovery of America on 12 October. Labor Day on 1 May is also a public holiday.

⁷ RITES OF PASSAGE

Since most of Venezuela is Roman Catholic, baptism and First Communion of children are important occasions. Most children will also bear the name of a saint, either exclusively or combined with another name, and many celebrate their saint's day as well as their actual birthday. When a person dies, prayers are held during nine days at the person's home, and relatives and close friends are usually in attendance.

⁸ INTERPERSONAL RELATIONS

Venezuelans are considered outgoing and friendly, and their spirit of gaiety is evident in their love of social gatherings and parties. In common with many other Latin Americans, they

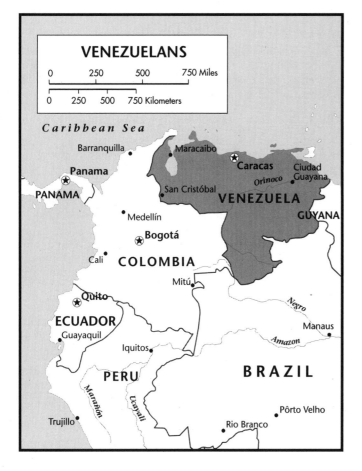

VENEZUELANS

0   250   500   750 Miles

0 250 500 750 Kilometers

Caribbean Sea

and the newer universities have contributed to the creation of a growing middle class, and this is reflected in more building of middle-class homes.

The rapid expansion of urban areas and the drift of people from the countryside to the cities in search of work put pressure on many urban services, including transport. To ease the traffic jams, which were particularly acute in Caracas, the government built a subway system.

10 FAMILY LIFE

Venezuelans value family ties, and the bonds between the extended family—which includes grandparents, aunts, uncles, and cousins—are very important. Occasions for larger family gatherings include major events such as birthdays, baptisms, First Communions, weddings, and major holidays. The extended family is regarded as a close source of support, particularly when there are young children, and also as a source of help in obtaining jobs in a society where personal contacts are important even to secure introductions that may lead to work opportunities. Extended families also gather on weekends or on short holiday visits to sites such as beaches. In smaller towns, the extended family gathers often for family meals and celebrations. The family offers a secure network in the absence of some state services and benefits that are taken for granted in wealthier societies.

Women have made considerable progress in gaining access to what were traditionally male professions, including medicine, dentistry, economics, and the legal profession. In middle-class households, the working woman relies on servants to help in the home; in poorer households, older relatives or older children provide help wherever possible.

11 CLOTHING

In cities, men wear lightweight suits or shirts and trousers that suit Venezuela's climate. Women are generally very fashion-conscious and take considerable care grooming themselves, taking as much care of their hair and nails as of their clothes, which are frequently washed and carefully pressed. A woman is expected always to look her best, and the Venezuelan woman often succeeds, even when wearing informal clothing such as a blouse, simple trousers, and sandals, or a simple shirt and skirt. She will choose accessories and makeup carefully.

12 FOOD

A typical Venezuelan dish, which is in fact a hearty meal derived from the cattle-ranching areas of Los Llanos, consists of shredded beef, called *carne mechada,* served with fried plantains, black beans, cornmeal pancakes called *arepas,* rice, and sometimes white cheese.

Another type of corn pancake, called *cachapa,* is often served for breakfast with jam. A staple, tasty snack is the *empanada,* a fried cornmeal turnover sometimes stuffed with cheese, meat, or chicken.

In many poor households, tropical fruits such as coconuts, mangoes, watermelons, pineapples, and papayas enrich the basic diet of beans, rice, and plantains. In coastal areas the diet includes fish, which is often served fried or in a stew called a *sancocho,* with vegetables.

have a more easygoing attitude to time and are tolerant of late arrivals to meetings. Even business lunches can be lengthy affairs, lasting two or three hours.

Formal greetings include shaking hands, but women usually greet each other with a kiss on the cheek. In some other Latin American countries, the formal *usted* is used when addressing a person who is not well-known to the speaker, and this formality may continue for a long time. But Venezuelans tend to be more informal and they often use the more informal *tu* when addressing each other.

9 LIVING CONDITIONS

Even in the prosperous 1960s and 1970s, when the oil boom changed Caracas from a relatively quiet town to a busy center with shopping malls, numerous highways, many skyscrapers, and expanding residential areas, the contrast between prosperous and poor housing was vivid: lavish hotels and apartments blocks vied with shantytowns which were sometimes only a few streets away on the surrounding hillsides. Some of this housing was so precarious that it would slide down the mountainside in the wake of torrential rains. Although some of this poorer housing included dirt floors and corrugated iron roofs, Venezuelans living in these conditions nevertheless had electricity, refrigerators, and televisions, which was not the case in neighboring, less-prosperous South American countries.

This contrast also existed, but to a lesser extent, in other less-populated towns. Since then, the expansion of education

ist painter Armando Reverón is admired throughout the American continent, and he has been succeeded by others who have become known internationally, such as Hector Poleo, Alejandro Otero, Marisol, and the sculptor Jesús Soto. One of Venezuela's first poets was Andrés Rello, who knew Simón Bolívar. Venezuela's best-known poet is Andrés Eloy Blanco, who died in 1955. One of his poems, "Angelitos Negros," became world-famous when it was made into a popular song and sung by artists everywhere. Here is a translation of a line from that poem, which speaks with longing for the equality of all races:

> Painter, you who paint churches,
> Paint me little Black angels,
> For God loves them too.

Venezuela's most famous novelist is Rómulo Gallegos. In one of his novels, *Doña Bárbara,* he created a strong-willed, unforgettable character of the same name. His novel *Canaima* is a dramatic account of humans' struggle to survive, psychologically and physically, in the jungle. A contemporary of Rómulo Gallegos was Miguel Otero Silva, who died in 1985. His novel, *Casas Muertas,* is widely admired. Another internationally known writer was Mariano Picón-Salas, born in Merida. Also worthy of mention is Arturo Uslar Pietri, who greatly enriched the modern Venezuelan cultural scene as both a novelist and a historian. He also became well-known as a journalist, continuing a Latin American tradition in which literary figures also engage in high-quality journalistic writing.

The *joropo* is Venezuela's national dance, and the music is played with a small harp, rattles, and a four-string guitar called the *cuatro.*

15 WORK

The prosperity of the 1960s and 1970s based on the oil boom was followed by a world drop in oil prices that affected Venezuela as a major oil-producing country. Job opportunities declined for many Venezuelans, and recently a period of difficult adjustment has been a burden to poor people in particular, but has also affected the middle class in Venezuela. Traditionally the poor relied on government subsidies for basic foodstuffs and cheap transport. When these subsidies were lifted and prices rose, the people suffered many economic setbacks.

Farming and cattle-ranching are major sources of work in rural areas. In cities, people work in a wide range of commercial activities or find work in factories. During times of economic hardship, casual labor increases and many have to find a living as street vendors, or in the building trades when work is available.

For university graduates, the prospects vary depending on the choice of career. Mining is an important activity and mining engineers usually find jobs, as do oil engineers. Economists find work in business or banking, and medical and legal careers are still popular. Newer careers include the media, and television is a growth industry in Venezuela.

16 SPORTS

Soccer is a national passion in Venezuela. In coastal areas, water sports such as swimming, boating, and fishing are very popular. Inland, in the grassy plains known as Los Llanos, riding is popular both for work and pleasure, and fine equestrians take part in colorful rodeos known as *toros colcados,* in

Venezuelan woman picking coffee beans. Farming and cattle-ranching are major sources of work in rural areas. In cities, people work in a wide range of commercial activities or find work in factories. (Anne Kalosh)

13 EDUCATION

Formal schooling begins in Venezuela at the age of six and is compulsory for the first six years. The four-year high school leads to a one-year preparation for college, which usually lasts four years but can be longer if the chosen university career is medicine or engineering. Many poorer households cannot afford schooling, and young people who are unable to complete high school often have to go out to work to supplement the family income. They might find work as street vendors or messengers, or in the building trade. In rural areas they will work in the fields.

Greater numbers of Venezuelans are nevertheless finding their way to universities and colleges, a few of which offer completely free tuition. There are about 30 universities, located in several towns. The largest is Universidad Central in Caracas with about 70,000 students, and another well-known university, Universidad de los Andes in the Andean town of Merida, has over 30,000 students.

Women have made great progress in university education, and about half of the student body at university level is now female.

14 CULTURAL HERITAGE

Venezuela has produced fine writers, painters, poets, musicians, and, more recently, playwrights. The work of expression-

which they compete to bring a bull down by grabbing its tail while riding at top speed.

17 ENTERTAINMENT AND RECREATION

Venezuelans enjoy visiting their beautiful national parks, and they are also fond of traveling and taking part in a variety of festivals around the country, which include singing, playing instruments, and dancing. In the major cities there are nightclubs and discos. Venezuelans also enjoy eating out.

Television is popular, and Venezuela produces a variety of soap operas known as *telenovelas*. Going to bullfights is also a popular pastime.

18 FOLK ART, CRAFTS, AND HOBBIES

Anthropologists and local historians have played an important part in helping Venezuelans become acquainted with the arts and crafts of the various Amerindian tribes. Much of their handiwork is now more readily available and includes pottery, baskets, hammocks, and rugs.

19 SOCIAL PROBLEMS

Venezuela has undergone a period of economic and political uncertainty that has affected job opportunities, and there has been an increase in crime in the last few years. Over half the population is under 18 years of age. In this uneasy climate, sections of the military have twice tried to take power by force. Although both these attempts failed, and Venezuela has preserved its status as a democratic country, the social ease and confidence of the more prosperous years have not yet returned.

20 BIBLIOGRAPHY

Arellano Moreno, A. *Caracas, Su Evolución y Su Regimen Legal.* Caracas: Ediciones Edime, 1972.

Dydynski, Drzystof. *Venezuela.* Australia: Lonely Planet Publications, 1994.

Galeano, Eduardo. *Faces and Masks.* London: Mandarin, 1989.

Uslar Pietri, J. *Historia Politica de Venezuela.* Madrid: Ediciones Edime, 1970.

—by P. Pitchon, reviewed by T. Morin

VIETNAMESE AMERICANS

For more information on Vietnamese history and culture, *see* **Vol. 3: Vietnamese.**

OVERVIEW

Before 1970, only 3,788 Vietnamese had immigrated to the US. The first real wave of Vietnamese immigration to the US began on 30 April 1975 when Saigon fell to North Vietnamese communist forces. At least 65,000 South Vietnamese fled the country that same day. By the end of 1975, some 130,000 Vietnamese refugees had entered the US. These early refugees tended to be well educated and wealthy; many were high-ranking military officers and government officials. With their high level of skills and education, they adapted quickly to American life and within 10 years were at an equal economic level with the average American citizen.

Because of its involvement in the Vietnam War, the US government felt a responsibility toward the South Vietnamese refugees. Congress passed the Indochina Refugee Act in 1975, allowing up 200,000 Southeast Asians to enter the US under a special "parole" status. The US government also allocated $405 million in resettlement aid to help South Vietnamese and other Southeast Asian refugees start a new life in America. The refugees were moved to resettlement camps in the US where their papers were processed and they were given English language classes. Private organizations matched each of them with a sponsor somewhere in the US who would then help them resettle in the sponsor's community. Although most of these first refugees could only find low-paying jobs and many ended up on welfare, the US government planned to phase out its aid program by 1977.

However, the situation in Vietnam worsened, and by 1978 thousands more refugees had fled the country. Some 85,000 climbed aboard overcrowded, flimsy boats and attempted to cross the sea to safety. These desperate folk came to be known as the "boat people." US Congress passed the Refugee Act in 1980 to admit more Vietnamese refugees. In this second wave of Vietnamese immigration, 95,000 refugees entered the US in 1980 and 86,000 in 1981. In contrast to the first wave, most of these refugees were poorly educated farmers and fishers who had a much more difficult time adapting to life in the industrialized US.

The Orderly Departure Program was put into effect in 1982 to reduce the number of people risking their lives in boats to escape Vietnam. Under this new program, 66,000 more Vietnamese entered the US between 1983 and 1991. In 1987, Congress passed the Amerasian Homecoming Act to help Amerasian teenagers (the children of Vietnamese women and American military men) and their families immigrate to the US.

The total estimated population of Vietnamese Americans in 1991 was 850,000. About 250,000 were American born. At first, Vietnamese refugees settled near their US sponsors throughout the US. The US government hoped to spread out the impact so that no one community would be overly burdened by a sudden influx of newcomers. Most Vietnamese settled in Cal-

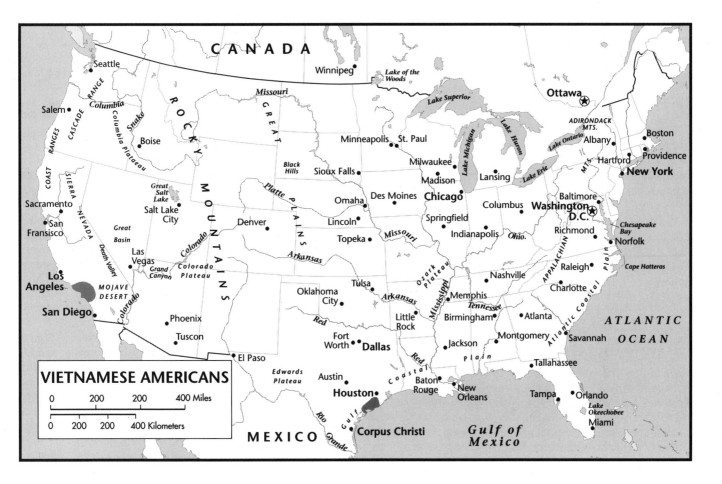

VIETNAMESE AMERICANS

0   200   200   400 Miles

0   200   200   400 Kilometers

ifornia (27,199), with a large number in Texas (9,130) and sizeable groups (3,500–7,000) in Pennsylvania, Florida, Washington, Illinois, New York, and Louisiana.

However, family and kinship groups are very important to traditional Vietnamese, so they began a secondary migration within the US to rejoin their families. They also moved from smaller towns and rural areas to cities where they would have better access to jobs and community and government services. Many also moved to warmer climates. California and Texas now host nearly half of all Vietnamese Americans; the largest Vietnamese American populations are in California. "Little Saigon," south of Los Angeles, is the center of the Vietnamese American community.

Acquiring English language proficiency is no easy task for Vietnamese Americans. The Vietnamese language differs from English in fundamental ways, making the shift from one to the other extremely difficult. American-born Vietnamese Americans, who have grown up speaking English, and those who came to the US as small children, are easily bilingual. Older foreign-born Vietnamese Americans, however, still speak Vietnamese almost exclusively at home and among friends and family and struggle to speak English when necessary in non-Vietnamese society. Vietnamese Americans have not been in the US long enough to have a significant population of third-generation immigrants (children born to American-born Vietnamese) who might begin to lose their fluency in Vietnamese.

Although Roman Catholics make up only 10% of the population of Vietnam, about 29–40% of Vietnamese Americans are Catholic. This is due both to the high percentage of Roman Catholics among the first wave of refugees, and the involvement of Roman Catholic organizations in refugee resettlement in the US. Many Vietnamese refugees, in gratitude to their Roman Catholic US sponsors, at least nominally converted to Roman Catholicism. There are now about 100 Vietnamese American Catholic communities and 22 official parishes, and over 800 Vietnamese American priests and nuns in the US. The largest parish is in New Orleans with some 10,000 parishioners.

Most Vietnamese Americans, however, are Buddhist of the "Northern School," also known as Mahayana Buddhism. In 1991, there were 80 Vietnamese Buddhist temples in the US. Other religions are also represented among Vietnamese Americans, including Confucianism (considered a philosophy rather than a religion by some), Taoism, Cao-Dai (a combination of Eastern belief systems), and Hoa-Hao (a meditative sect originating in the Mekong Delta in 1939). A small minority of Vietnamese Americans are either Muslim or Protestant.

The most important holiday for Vietnamese Americans is Tet, the Vietnamese New Year. Occurring sometime between mid-January and mid-February (based on the Chinese lunar calendar), it is a combination New Year, spring, family, and national festival. Traditionally, Tet lasts for seven days, but most Vietnamese Americans celebrate only the first three. As every Vietnamese has two birthdays, their personal birthday and Tet, Tet also becomes a community-wide birthday party. Other elements of Tet include the payment of debts, forgiveness of past wrongs, and vows of personal improvement.

First-wave Vietnamese Americans, who were generally well educated and had job skills relevant to the industrialized American work world, now enjoy living conditions comparable to or better than the national average. Second-wave refugees, however, have had a more difficult time succeeding in the US. With less formal schooling and few relevant job skills, many second-wave refugees have either been stuck in low-paying blue-collar jobs or remain unemployed. At least half of Vietnamese American families who arrived in the US after 1976 live below the poverty line.

Health problems common to recent refugees, such as post-traumatic stress disorder, insomnia, and lowered immunities, plague the Vietnamese American community. Many Vietnamese Americans were also exposed to tuberculosis either in Vietnam or in refugee camps. Another health-related difficulty is that traditional Vietnamese healing methods, such as rubbing tiger balm into the skin with the rough edge of a coin, leave marks that are sometimes misinterpreted by other Americans as signs of child abuse.

Child abuse is a complex issue concerning Vietnamese Americans. Corporal punishment is an accepted and expected mode of discipline in traditional Vietnamese families. Current American culture, however, regards physical beatings as abuse. Therefore, cross-cultural conflict occurs regularly between Vietnamese American parents and non-Vietnamese American teachers, social workers, neighbors, and others. Even American-born Vietnamese American children are beginning to resist their parents' traditional modes of discipline, threatening to call the police—or actually doing so—when approached with a beating.

Traditionally, the family is the center of Vietnamese culture. Most Vietnamese Americans continue to cling to the family as their source of support in their new home, as well as continuing to support those they left behind, sending an average of $100 per month to family members in Vietnam and sponsoring their relatives to join them in the US whenever possible. Extended families often live together; in 1985, 55% of Vietnamese American households consisted of multiple generations of extended kin.

Vietnamese Americans tend to eat traditional Vietnamese foods at home. A few cities with large Vietnamese American populations now boast Vietnamese restaurants where traditional foods are served. Large amounts of garlic and hot peppers are used in traditional Vietnamese cooking, to the extent that many Vietnamese Americans exude the odor of garlic from their pores. Other Americans who are not used to this amount of garlic may find the odor offensive, and Vietnamese Americans have had to learn to reduce their garlic intake in the interest of wider community relations.

Young Vietnamese Americans, like other Asian American students, tend to be high achievers at school. Despite language and cultural barriers, they work hard and are eager to acquire the skills necessary to succeed in their American homeland. Many adult Vietnamese Americans attend adult education classes for English language and job skills training. Vietnamese Americans often describe themselves with the traditional Vietnamese phrase *tran can cu*, which expresses a combination of hard work, persistence, ambition, and patience. Their short history in the US so far shows this to be an apt description.

Vietnamese Americans have found the most employment success in the area of small business ownership. Most are family run and serve primarily Vietnamese American customers. Typical Vietnamese American businesses include restaurants, specialty grocery stores, laundries and tailor shops, convenience stores, beauty salons, car repair garages, and real estate offices. In 1986, there were at least 1,000 Vietnamese American businesses in Los Angeles alone. The US Census Bureau counted a total of 25,671 Vietnamese American businesses throughout the US in 1987, with combined receipts equalling $1.36 billion.

Vietnamese Americans suffer from the same problem that all new immigrant communities face: the tension between foreign-born elders who continue to hold to traditional values and American-born young people who have been acculturated to American values. In the Vietnamese American community, this breakdown of traditional generational authority and respect has led to a particularly violent situation. Vietnamese American teenagers are bonding together in youth gangs to protect themselves from anti-Asian discrimination and to give each other the support they feel is lacking at home. Most often, gang violence is directed at other Vietnamese Americans. Much of it goes unreported because the victims do not trust the police, fear retaliation on the part of the gangs, and/or do not wish to give the Vietnamese American community a bad name.

There is also some tension between first-wave and second-wave Vietnamese Americans. The more educated and successful first-wave refugees criticize second-wave refugees for their lack of success and dependence on welfare. Second-wave refugees, on the other hand, resent the privilege and snobbery of the first-wave refugees. For the most part, this tension is a continuation of class conflicts in Vietnam between the educated elite (the first wave of refugees) and less educated laborers (the second wave).

BIBLIOGRAPHY

Fjelstad, Karen Elaine. *Tu Phu Cong Dong: Vietnamese Women and Spirit Possession in the San Francisco Bay Area.* N.p., 1995.

Haines, David W. *Refugees as Immigrants: Cambodians, Laotians, and Vietnamese in America.* Totowa, N.J.: Rowman & Littlefield, 1989.

Kibria, Nazli. *Family Tightrope: The Changing Lives of Vietnamese Americans.* Princeton, N.J.: Princeton University Press, 1993.

Nash, Jesse William. *Vietnamese Values: Confucian, Catholic, American.* N.p., 1987.

Rutledge, Paul. *The Vietnamese Experience in America.* Bloomington: Indiana University Press, 1992.

Wieder, Rosalie. "Who Are the Vietnamese Americans?" In *The Asian American Almanac*, Susan Gall and Irene Natividad, ed. Detroit: Gale Research, 1995.

—by D. K. Daeg de Mott

XAVANTE

ALTERNATE NAMES: Crixá, Curixá, Puxití, Tapacuá
LOCATION: Brazil
LANGUAGE: Gê
RELIGION: Indigenous beliefs

¹ INTRODUCTION

In the late 16th century, the Portuguese colonizers named the Amerindians that inhabited the north of the Goiás region. The chosen name was *Xavante,* and the reason for it is unknown. The name the Amerindians used for themselves bears no resemblanceto it: *Auwe,* meaning people. The Xavante were numerous, strong, and rebellious. The Lisbon government only managed to dominate them for the first time in 1784, when they were put into mission villages surrounded by military guards. The Xavante had resisted the invasion of their lands by attacking mining camps and raiding the settlers' cattle and crops. It is perhaps because of this kind of resistance that the colonial governors called the period between 1784 and 1788 the "pacification." Life in mission villages was not kind to the Xavante and, by the time the gold mines were exhausted and many of the settlers left, a group of the surviving Xavante abandoned the missions. They went west, crossed the rivers Araguia and das Montes, and settled in eastern Mato Grosso, in the land of Roncador. From that time until 1946, the Xavante repelled any attempt at contact by White people.

Efforts to "pacify" the Xavante started again during the 1940s, this time by the Brazilian government, with the aim to open their lands to settlement. Contact was established, and the Xavante had made many adjustments during the last decades in order to deal with a wider society. However, they continue to this day to preserve a strong sense of identity. Until 1988 the Xavante, like all Amerindians in Brazil, were legally considered to be minors: they were not allowed to vote or make decisions for themselves. In 1983, Mario Juruna, a Xavante, became the first Amerindian to be elected as a member of the Brazilian Congress. He served until 1986. Brazilian Amerindians are now regarded as full citizens.

² LOCATION AND HOMELAND

The Xavante live in the state of Mato Grosso, which is the size of France, Germany, and Great Britain combined. It is situated in the southwest of Brazil. *Mato Grosso* in Portuguese means "dense forest." Xavante villages used to be found at intervals for the entire length of the Rio das Montes, until the land was sold to private companies during the 1960s. Afterwards, the new settlers pushed the Xavante to the vast wasteland of eastern Mato Grosso, and even drove them to seek the patronage of either the missions or the Indian Protection Service posts, which they had fought so successfully in the past. The forest, now depleted, once supplied rubber and rare timbers; diamonds and silver are still mined. The region is known as the Serra do Roncador or Snoring Mountains, though there is no real sierra (highlands). The hillocks look like mountains, however, because of the flatness of the surrounding countryside. The Xavante land is referred to as "savanna" but is really poor country, not a prairie, and only occasionally productive land. The Xavante prefer it to the tropical jungle because it is open country where hunting, one of their favorite activities, is more thrilling. They also consider the savanna to be more beautiful than the jungle and choose to build their villages out in the open.

Still, there are patches of tropical jungle all over their territory, usually along the water courses. These local jungles, known as "galleries," are appreciated by the Xavante because in them they can find water and wild roots and fruits, which are the basis of their diet, as well as palms and trees that provide leaves and woods used to manufacture various artifacts. The seasons in the region are clearly marked: a very dry season from May to September, when even a shower of rain is most unusual and the lakes turn into an expanse of dried mud, followed by heavy rains in October—by January, hunters and Amerindians get used to walking perpetually in ankle-deep water.

³ LANGUAGE

The Xavante, though dispersed through a vast region, share a common language and culture. They are one of the Gê-speaking tribes of Amazonia. They have also been known by the names Crixá, Curixá, Puxití, and Tapacuá. Understanding their language often leads to a deeper understanding of their culture. *Ro was'té-di,* for example, is what the Xavante call the close country or local jungle. *Ro* means "country" and *was'té* means "bad," making no secret of their dislike of anything that is not open, that is not the savanna, which they call *ro pse-di* or *ro we-de: pse* means "good," and *we* means "pretty" or "beautiful." It is easy to guess, therefore, where they prefer to spend time and live their lives.

Xavante boys are not named at birth. They receive their first name at a ceremony performed by the mother's brother when they are about five or six years old. Although the naming ceremony is quite important, as it establishes their father's brother-in-law's rights over the boy, adult Xavante rarely bother to learn the names of the boys because they will take fresh names when the time comes to enter the "Bachelors' hut" (adolescence). At initiation, boys take a third name, and when they graduate to the status of Mature Men, yet another. Each name cancels out previous ones. Nowadays, not all Xavante pass through so many names by the time they reach maturity. On the other hand, some take even a fifth name: a man may assume further names if he so wishes.

As for girls, the ceremony of bestowal of their names is performed by the whole community, but no rights are asserted. This is because women do not play a part in Xavante politics.

⁴ FOLKLORE

The Xavante tradition is very rich in legends that try to explain natural phenomenons and their history. Many highlight the value of the qualities the Xavante appreciate most: strength and courage. One tells of two young men who had the power of making new varieties of fruits grow, using only their words. But a time came when they started using their powers to frighten their friends. Finally, they were killed, and in the place where their blood was shed, two trees grew. The Xavante use the wood from those trees to make sticks that they place in their ears to protect themselves from dangers like jaguars and bad dreams.

Another legend tells about a hunter who was abandoned by his friends in the jungle because his body was covered with horrible boils. The vultures came and took him to heaven to heal. When the hunter returned to earth, he brought some potatoes, which became part of the Xavante diet.

The Xavante believe that the stars are the eyes of heavenly people who are watching us from up above. It happened that once a young man fell in love with the beauty of a particular star. When he fell asleep, the star came to earth in the shape of a woman and found him. Their love grew, and so did the palm where they were sitting, taking them up to the sky. When the young man came back to earth, he told his family about his affair and then went back to heaven and stayed with his loved one forever.

5 RELIGION

Xavante are more concerned with change or discovery than with the question of creation. "The world was created because in the beginning there was nothing" was an explanation given to an interested academic. "Then Aiwamdzú came out of the earth. He was the creator and he was Xavante." By the time Aiwamdzú appeared, the earth already existed, but it was empty. The east—the beginning of the sky—had not been created yet. The north and the south were created afterwards, as well as the Whites and their towns. More-detailed are origin myths that tell about people becoming human after being like animals. For example, one myth tells how people used to eat only rotten wood because it was soft enough to chew and could be eaten without preparation, something animals do. But then a young girl discovered maize (corn) and a young boy discovered fire, so they could grow proper food and cook it.

The beliefs and ceremonies of the Xavante revolve around their reverence for life and fertility. Thus, the good spirits, the Danimite, protect and create life, while the bad ones, the Tsimihöpari, cause illness and death. During the *Way'a* celebration, the Xavante act out a fight between the good and bad spirits with songs and dances. The good spirits win, and the bad ones are buried in symbolic barrows. Extinction is thereby avoided and the Xavante people will not only live on but will be even stronger. A similar ceremony shows the recovery of an ill Xavante. For a whole night a group of men, some painted black as bad spirits, dance and sing until the good spirits defeat the bad ones, who are once again symbolically buried.

6 MAJOR HOLIDAYS

Xavante holidays are full of joy and happiness. A sensational one is the *buriti* competition, in which their great athletic abilities are put to test and celebrated. Some holidays are aimed at bringing back the good times, known as *Roweda*. Though in many of their holidays the men have a more active role than the women, some do have women as central figures. One of them is the ceremony of the naming of a child, in which many of the staged legends have women as protagonists. They tell about the female contributions to their cultural wealth, such as the time when their ancestors could only eat rotten wood and roots. The women, however, thanks to their immense curiosity, found a parakeet in the jungle that had white maize (corn). They took some of this maize and brought it back to the village and started to cultivate it. To get the quality of maize and the kind of beans that the Xavante prefer, they had to fight bad spirits in their houses and with great courage drive them away. During the naming ceremony, the men imitate the voices of animals, like jaguars, leopards, wolves, and storks.

7 RITES OF PASSAGE

The Xavante are divided into groups according to their ages—Babies; Not-Babies; Children; Boys and Girls; Bachelors; Young Men and Women; Mature Men and Women; and Elders. Each group is formed by those born in the same five-year period. Passing from one group to the next is celebrated with special rites, songs, and dances. When a group reaches adolescence, the boys leave their home and move into the Bachelors' hut. During this transition their ears are pierced and they take long baths in the river, receive presents, and take part in races. Through dramatic representations of legends, they learn the origins and significance of the new role they are about to take up. This is also the occasion to officially introduce brides- and grooms-to-be, to each other and to the rest of the village.

Among the Xavante, coupling is a process strictly regulated by laws. Marital relationships within families are discouraged. The decisions are made mainly by the parents, though they do listen to their children and take their feelings into account.

Like other Gê-speaking groups, the Xavante have an elaborate social organization. A village is divided in two halves called *moieties*. A moiety membership can be based on descent or on such distinctions as whether a person was born during the dry or rainy season. Moieties can carry out a number of reciprocal functions, such as burying each other's dead.

8 INTERPERSONAL RELATIONS

"The Xavante are full of life" is very often the opinion of those who have had the chance to meet them and especially to witness their many festivals. The sight of their bodies artistically painted with bright colors, the joy and energy transmitted through their songs and dances, and the wisdom imparted via representations accompanied by their own timeless rhythms all communicate vitality and an enduring commitment to survival.

The Xavante community sense is evident in the way they organize their economy. They exchange goods and distribute their wealth with one premise in mind: it should be equal both within families and among the members of the tribe. They guarantee their survival as a group with a cyclical system of give and take.

Hierarchy is mostly an organizational tool. When the Xavante hold council discussions, it is up to the chief to begin the deliberations. But that does not mean that he has more power, as all decisions are made by consensus and every man in the council has his say. Whatever is decided is commonly announced by shouting it through the village at dusk and dawn.

9 LIVING CONDITIONS

Since being contacted by outsiders in the middle of the 20th century, the Xavante have gradually ceased to be nomadic. They now live in independent horseshoe-shaped villages on the open savanna. The opening of the horseshoe faces the water. The center is the setting for meetings of the council of aldermen: it is there where important decisions are made. Some Xavante have abandoned this traditional crescent for oblong Brazilian-style houses in rows by the side of the missions, but most favor the original "beehive" houses. Built by women, the round structures are made of sticks and cane and are covered with palm leaves all the way to the floor. Up to three families can share one house. Inside the houses, the light is perpetually dim, and the smoke and odor of cooking lingers while the insects crawl or buzz around.

Before and after the first "pacification" carried out by the Portuguese, the Xavante furiously defended their land and people. After their experience in the missions, around the middle of the 19th century, they remained isolated for some 80 years. The isolation protected them, among other things, from epidemic disease. When contact with outsiders was restored in the 20th century, various studies described the Xavante as powerful, numerous, and muscular, with keen vision, lack of dental decay, slow pulses, and low blood pressure. They were also among the tallest and heaviest of Lowland South American Indians. But contact often led to a demographic crisis, through introduced diseases, and deaths by fighting to resist territorial incursion. Still, the Xavante groups that survived the shock have not only recovered but have increased their numbers. In some cases, the doubling time of population is 15 years or less. The Brazilian government Indian Agency initiated a vaccination program in 1990.

10 FAMILY LIFE

Women are still the queens of Xavante homes. They build the houses, and inside they manage the whole operation: they prepare the food and distribute it. Collecting, the most important economic activity, is primarily a woman's job. Though gathering is not regarded as a prestigious activity, it is an essential contribution to the household and the survival of the group. It also provides one of the few opportunities for women to go out and have a good time together. In the past, women were also responsible for the preparation of the land, as well as the planting and harvesting. Nowadays, due to the increasing importance of agriculture for the society, and a wider variety of crops, men share those tasks.

It is quite common to find Xavante men married to more than one woman. Young men marry 5 to 10 years later than young girls, as the boys are not permitted to marry until they are initiated. At the ceremony, the boys are introduced to their future wives, but the girls are often so young that the couples wait years before they can go to the next step: the wedding hunt. When the time comes, the bride then takes part in the *Adaba* ceremony: she kneels in front of her house until one of her friends approaches and removes all of her necklaces. The groom goes out hunting with a few friends and can only come back when he has caught enough game to impress his father-in-law. If all goes well, he can then visit his bride at night until their first child is born, after which he moves into her family's house.

Frequently a man's brothers marry into the same household with the younger sisters of their older brother's wife. Cases of polygyny also often involve sisters: a young man marries the eldest daughter in a household and then marries her younger sisters as they become of marriageable age. Some monogamous or widowed men marry much younger women. Women, however, if widowed after the age of 30 usually do not remarry.

11 CLOTHING

Like many tribes of the eastern Brazil region, the Xavante originally went virtually naked. In contrast with the lack of clothes, however, there was an abundance of ornaments (such as earplugs), distinctive haircuts, body painting, and tattoos. Men wore penis-sheaths from the moment they entered the Bachelors' hut and were never seen without it again. The sheath is a tiny conical spiral of palmito bark. It is worn over the folds of the foreskin, covering only the tip of the genital organ, and the men would only take it off when urinating or having sex. In fact, were it to fall off when they were running or bathing, it would be the cause for great embarrassment.

Nowadays, though, men usually wear shorts, and most no longer wear their penis-sheaths or their ear-plugs. Women have taken to wearing clothes and even make-up when they can get it. Most Xavante wear boots, and both sexes cut their hair short. In traditional Xavante communities, it is the men who do all the preening, but that has changed since contact with Whites and other tribes.

The Xavante are noted for their beautiful body painting. Urucú scarlet seeds are used to make red paint, and genipa is used for black ink. Red is the Xavante's favorite color. It is thought to be beautiful and have beneficial and creative properties. Furthermore, they believe it makes a person strong. Some of the designs also have special powers: the armbands of the wrestlers are believed to increase strength. Babassú nuts are the Xavante's favorite cosmetic. Men, who are more into taking care of their appearance than women, keep a supply of nuts which they chew carefully to extract the milky juice with which they oil their hair and bodies at least once a day.

12 FOOD

The Xavante have a real passion for meat. Any game is hunted and eaten. Peccary, deer, and anteaters are fairly plentiful. Pigs, wild or domestic, steppe rats, monkeys, and armadillos, as well as most birds, are also part of their diet. The meat is roasted for a long time and protected with a covering of ash and earth so it can be kept for any length of time. Turtles are sought for their meat and their nourishing and fatty eggs.

Preferences aside, the Xavante live primarily on roots, nuts, and fruits. The roots are boiled or roasted and eaten with their skins, unless they are too dirty. Nuts and palmitos are eaten year-round. Palmitos are edible shoots of a palm that grows all over the interior of Brazil and can be found canned in supermarkets around the world. The Xavante collect the shoots and eat the younger ones raw. Older, thicker ones are cooked in an earth oven. Nuts, particularly babassú nuts, are a constant in the Xavante diet. Whenever they are hungry, they help themselves to their supply of nuts. This is the only food they eat without offering some to everyone present. From July until the end of the year, carob fruit is a staple food. Carob, burití (a fruit with a high vitamin-C content), and piquí are the most important fruits in the Xavante diet.

When first encountered, the Xavante mainly grew maize (corn), yucca, two kinds of beans, a few types of pumpkins, and potatoes. Later on, some groups were encouraged by government programs to grow upland rice, keep enough for their own needs, and sell the rest.

To prepare the brew for feasts, the women start the fermentation by chewing some corn or cassava mash and spitting it into a bowl, which is then covered and kept in a dark corner for three days. The result is a mildly alcoholic beverage that, according to some explorers, if drunk in huge quantities can produce a "grand intoxication." The Xavante also eat honey anytime they catch sight of a beehive. As many bees are stingless, the Xavante simply climb the trees, open the hive, and eat the contents, bees and all.

13 EDUCATION

The level of formal education among the Xavante varies according to the geographical situation of their villages. It ranges from groupings where only one or two of the younger men speak some basic Portuguese for the purpose of dealing with the outside world, to villages where most children and young Xavante are literate and some have become teachers in their own hometown.

The very important skills to face life, like learning how to overcome exhaustion, pain, and fear, are taught by the elders through traditional legends. Many bear the message: "Be strong and courageous, and multiply." The education of children is a shared responsibility. In the early years, the mother is the main figure, but as they grow older, the grandparents help with the education of the girls. The boys, on the other hand, are guided by their godfathers, a group of young men about 10 years older.

14 CULTURAL HERITAGE

Music and dance are at the core of the Xavante's ceremonies. Accounts of the Jaguar and girls naming ceremonies tell of groups of men singing from the morning through the day and the following night, of the hiding of gourd flutes for the girls to fetch, and of beating time with rattles made of pig's teeth. In their relentless quest "to make beautiful" the melodies, the Xavante choreograph their dances in a series of highly formalized patterns designed to inspire and delight both the performers and spectators.

15 WORK

The Xavante practice shifting cultivation. Toward the end of the rainy season, a man fells an acre or two of trees and leaves them to dry. Just before the next rainy season begins, he sets them on fire. The ashes add mineral nutrients to the soil. Planting is time-consuming and sometimes even dangerous, for gardens attract snakes and stinging insects. Traditionally, the Xavante planted crops that required virtually no tending, such as maize (corn), beans, and pumpkins. Manioc (cassava) is also an important crop. These shrubs with starchy tuberous roots, even with indifferent cultivation, will yield four or five tons of tubers, which is quite convenient as the Xavante do not like to give much time or thought to their agriculture. Hunting is their passion: Xavante men spend a lot of their time planning communal hunts, discussing the possibility of finding deer or peccary in particular regions, or going out to enjoy the activity for the fun of it. Fishing, which used to be the males' responsibility, is still a very important activity among the Xavante.

The traditional way of hunting is using darts with curare. Curare is a formula whose active ingredient comes from the sap of the vine *Strychnos toxifera,* along with 30 other magical ingredients, like stinging ants and powdered snake fangs. The active ingredient blocks nervous impulses to the muscles so they become flaccid, making the animals easy to retrieve: a monkey would simply fall to the ground. Nowadays, the Xavante hunt with firearms. Meat is regarded as a prime delicacy.

Having said that, wild roots, nuts, and fruits gathered in their wanderings are really the basis of the Xavante's diet, rather than meat. The Xavante collect roots and babassú nuts as part of their day-to-day activities. Fish are also stupefied with poisonous forest vines. Their sap dispersed through the water par-alyzes the breathing apparatus but leaves the meat edible. This method works best in low waters and slow currents, as the poison lingers long enough to take effect.

However, the Xavante traditionally were not particularly interested in fishing. They did not have special arrows for the task and preferred to walk rather than sail, so they had rafts instead of canoes and would cross rivers by swimming. Nevertheless, the introduction of metal hooks and nylon have transformed some sedentary Xavante into passionate fishers: it is a way of feeding the family without wasting time planting.

16 SPORTS

The Xavante are superb runners. As often as once a week, teams of relay runners, each carrying a length of burití palm which weighs around 80 kg (175 lbs), compete in a long race which may begin far out in the plain, ending with a dash into the village. The runners decorate their bodies with red and black vegetable dyes and tie a white cord around their necks with the tufted ends in the front like a bow tie. The winner is the team that can continue the longest, so the one who arrives first does not always win. The Xavante are reputed to be capable of catching game on foot. In some communities, the Xavante have developed a passion for soccer. Everybody plays, young and old, and when all the men get tired of playing, the women take over.

17 ENTERTAINMENT AND RECREATION

Hunting provides not only a means of subsistence but also a source of entertainment. Xavante men spend hours planning treks and telling tales of fights and hunting exploits. Xavante men enjoy all aspects of hunting, especially since it allows them to make a public exhibition of their manliness. It is an expression of virility. Xavante women, for their part, are interested in the end product. They are cold towards an unsuccessful hunter, discuss at great length the prospect of getting meat, and send their children to find out for them when the hunters are expected to return.

Xavante ceremonies have been compared to classical ballet, as the performers try to create a harmonious spectacle where beauty is most important. The Xavante word for "ceremony" is *dasïpse,* which translates as "something that makes oneself good." The performances are carefully prepared, enjoyed by players and spectators, and regarded as a major form of aesthetic expression.

18 FOLK ART, CRAFTS, AND HOBBIES

Among the first Xavante artifacts to become known to the outside world were the *uibro*. Characteristically used by the Young Men's age-grade, the *uibro* are war clubs that symbolize power. They are made from a young tree so that part of the root can be left as a knob at one end. The other end is sharpened to a point, and the club is exposed to the heat of the fire to make it hard. Many uibro were found by the corpses of people they had killed in the days when the Xavante were fighting the Brazilians. Other more polished clubs, decorated with woven bastwork, are carried by Mature Men. With one end pointed and the other broad, they can be used for digging and striking respectively.

One of the most stunning art forms of the Xavante is body painting. The process of making the paint the Xavante use to decorate their bodies is almost as elaborate and interesting as the designs themselves. They use the pasty covering of scarlet seeds, which are boiled to release the pigment. The bright red pigment is then mixed with oil and left until it congeals. The mixture is shaped into a ball and is then ready for use as a dye, insect repellent, or in decoration. To make domestic objects of wood, the Xavante use a chisel and fire. Fire is made by twirling between their palms a thin stick of wood into the surface of a thicker one until sparks are produced that ignite the sawdust. The chisel has been made in the same way for the last 200 years. Using a splinter of stone, they rub a piece of iron until they can cut it. Then it is sharpened with another type of fine stone. Finally, it is attached to the handle, which is made of wood. Other tools are the cutting teeth of the piranha fish and the sharp claw of the great armadillo. Palm leaves and bark from trees are plaited to make most household utensils, such as baskets, mats, and fans. A Xavante man can make a carrying basket out of green palm fronds in a matter of minutes, an ability that proves useful when hunting away from home.

[19] SOCIAL PROBLEMS

Amerindian tribes in Brazil are still burdened by colonization. The groups that survived the European "discovery" of the Americas are being pushed off of their land at the end of the 20th century by private companies. Contact with Whites has also created the need among the Xavante to learn the national language and culture, in order to be able to function in the new imposed way of life. However, education is not attainable by all, a fact that leaves many unable either to continue living in their traditional way or to embrace the new one.

Nevertheless, the Xavante are recognized as one of the most forceful people of the many Brazilian tribes. They frequently send their representative to Brasilia to defend their rights and insist on better treatment. The Xavante Mario Juruna, the first Amerindian to become a deputy in Brazil's parliament, spoke of the dangers and the wishes of his people: "Indian wealth lies in customs and communal traditions and land which is sacred. Indians can and want to choose their own road, and this road is not civilization made by Whites . . . . Indian civilization is more human. We do not want paternalistic protection from Whites. Indians today . . . want political power."

[20] BIBLIOGRAPHY

Bennett, Ross S., ed. *Lost Empires, Living Tribes*. Washington, D.C.: National Geographic Book Service, 1982.

Graham, Laura R. *Performing Dreams: Discourses of Immortality Among Xavante of Central Brazil*. Austin: University of Texas Press, 1995.

Maybury-Lewis, David. *Akwe-Shavante Society*. Oxford: Oxford University Press, 1974.

Steward, Julian Haynes, ed. *Handbook of South American Indian*. New York: Cooper Square, 1963.

—by D. Ventura-Alcalay

GLOSSARY

a capella: singing without musical accompaniment.

aboriginal: the first inhabitants of a country. A species of animals or plants which originated within a given area.

acupuncture: ancient practice of treating disease or relieving pain by inserting needles into pressure points on the body. The Chinese are associated with this medical treatment.

adobe: a clay from which bricks are made for use in making houses.

adult literacy: the capacity of adults to read and write.

agglutinative tongue: a language in which the suffixes and prefixes to words retain a certain independence of one another and of the stem to which they are added. Turkish is an example of an agglutinative tongue.

agrarian economy: an economy where agriculture is the dominant form of economic activity.

active volcano: a large rock mass formed by the expulsion of molten rock, or lava, which periodically erupts.

acute accent: a mark (') used to denote accentual stress of a single sound.

agglutinative tongue: a language in which the suffixes and prefixes to words retain a certain independence of one another and of the stem to which they are added. Turkish is an example of an agglutinative tongue.

agrarian economy: an economy where agriculture is the dominant form of economic activity.

agrarian society: a society where agriculture dominates the day-to-day activities of the population.

All Saints' Day: a Christian holiday on 1 November (a public holiday in many countries). Saints and martyrs who have no special festival are commemorated. In the Middle Ages, it was known as All Hallows' Day; the evening of the previous day, October 31, was called All Hallow Even, from which the secular holiday Halloween is derived.

All Souls' Day: a Christian holiday. This day, 2 November, is dedicated to prayer for the repose of the souls of the dead.

allies: groups or persons who are united in a common purpose. Typically used to describe nations that have joined together to fight a common enemy in war.

Altaic language family: a family of languages spoken by people in portions of northern and eastern Europe, and nearly the whole of northern and central Asia, together with some other regions, and divided into five branches, the Ugrian or Finno-Hungarian, Samoyed, Turkish, Mongolian, and Tungus.

altoplano: refers to the high plains of South American mountain ranges on the Pacific coast.

Amerindian: a contraction of the two words, American Indian. It describes native peoples of North, South, or Central America.

Amerindian language group: the language groups of the American Indians.

Amish: Anabaptist Protestants originally from Germany. Settled in Pennsylvania and the American Midwest.

Anabaptist: Christian sect that was founded in Switzerland during the 16th century. Rejected infant baptism as invalid.

ancestor worship: the worship of one's ancestors.

Anglican: pertaining to or connected with the Church of England.

animism: the belief that natural objects and phenomena have souls or innate spiritual powers.

anthropologist: one who studies the characteristics, customs, and development of mankind.

anti-miscegenation laws: prohibition of marriage or sexual relations between men and women of different races.

anti-Semitism: agitation, persecution, or discrimination (physical, emotional, economic, political, or otherwise) directed against the Jews.

apartheid: the past governmental policy in the Republic of South Africa of separating the races in society.

appliqué: a trimming made from one cloth and sewn onto another cloth.

aquaculture: the culture or "farming" of aquatic plants or animals.

arable land: land which can be cultivated by plowing, as distinguished from grassland, woodland, common pasture, and wasteland.

archipelago: any body of water having many islands, or the islands themselves collectively.

arctic climate: cold, frigid weather similar to that experienced at or near the North Pole.

arid: dry; without moisture; parched with heat.

aristocracy: a small minority that controls the government of a nation, typically on the basis of inherited wealth. Political power is restricted to its members. Also may referred to any privileged elite of a country.

artifacts: objects or tools that date back to an ancient period of human history.

Ash Wednesday: a Christian holiday. The first day of Lent, observed 46 days before Easter, is so called from the practice of placing ashes on the forehead of the worshipper as a sign of penitence. In the Roman Catholic Church, these ashes are obtained from burning palm branches used in the previous year's Palm Sunday observation. (Palm Sunday commemorates the entry of Jesus into Jerusalem a week before Easter Sunday, and it begins Holy Week.) On Ash Wednesday, the ashes are placed on the forehead of the communicant during Mass. The recipient is told, "Remember that you are dust, and unto dust you shall return" or "Turn away from sin and be faithful to the Gospel."

Ashura: a Muslim holiday. This fast day was instituted by Muhammad as the equivalent of the Jewish Yom Kippur but later became voluntary when Ramadan replaced it as a holiday of penance. It also commemorates Noah's leaving the ark on Mt. Ararat after the waters of the Great Flood had subsided. In Iran, the martyrdom of Husayn, grandson of Muhammad, is commemorated with passion plays on this day.

assembly: in government, a body of legislators that meets together regularly.

Assumption: a Christian holiday. This holiday, observed on 15 August in many countries, celebrates the Roman Catholic and Eastern Orthodox dogma that, following Mary's death, her body was taken into heaven and reunited with her soul.

atheist: a person who denies the existence of God, or of a supreme intelligent being.

atherosclerosis: a disease of the arteries. Characterized by blockages that prevent blood flow from the heart to the brain and other parts of the body.

atoll: a coral island, consisting of a strip or ring of coral surrounding a central lagoon. Such islands are common in the Pacific Ocean and are often very picturesque.

aurora borealis: the northern lights, consisting of bands of light across the night sky seen in northern geographical locations.

Australoid: pertains to the type of aborigines of Australia.

Austronesian language: a family of languages which includes Indonesian, Melanesian, Polynesian, and Micronesian subfamilies.

B

babushka: a head scarf worn by women.

Baltic States: the three formerly communist countries of Estonia, Latvia, and Lithuania that border on the Baltic Sea.

Bantu language group: a name applied to the south African family of tongues. The most marked peculiarity of these languages is their prevailing use of prefixes instead of suffixes in derivation and inflection. Some employ clicks and clucks as alphabetic elements.

baptism: any ceremonial bathing intended as a sign of purification, dedication, etc. Baptisms are performed by immersion of the person in water, or by sprinkling the water on the person.

Baptist: a member of a Protestant denomination which practices adult baptism by immersion.

barren land: unproductive land, partly or entirely treeless.

barter: Trade in which merchandise is exchanged directly for other merchandise or services without use of money.

bilingual: able to speak two languages. Also used to describe anything that contains or is expressed in two languages, such as directions written in both English and Spanish.

boat people: a term used to describe individuals (refugees) who attempt to flee their country by boat.

Bolshevik Revolution: pertaining to the Russian revolution of 1917. Russian communists overthrew Tsar Nicholas II and ended the feudal Russian empire.

borscht: cold beet soup, topped with sour cream.

Brahman: a member of the sacred caste among the Hindus. There are many subdivisions of the caste, often remaining in isolation from one another.

bratwurst: seasoned fresh German sausage. Made from pork or veal.

bride price: the price paid to the family of the bride by the young man who seeks to marry her.

bride wealth: the money or property or livestock a bride brings to her marriage. *See* **dowry**.

Buddhism: the religious system common in India and eastern Asia. Founded by and based upon the teachings of Gautama Buddha, Buddhism asserts that suffering is an inescapable part of life. Deliverance can only be achieved through the practice of charity, temperance, justice, honesty, and truth.

bureaucracy: a system of government which is characterized by division into bureaus of administration with their own divisional heads. Also refers to the institutional inflexibility and red tape of such a system.

bush country: a large area of land which is wild with low, bushlike vegetation.

Byzantine Empire: an empire centered in the city of Byzantium, now Istanbul in present-day Turkey.

C

Cajun: name given to Canadians who emigrated to Louisiana from Acadia, the old name for Nova Scotia. Contraction of the name Accadian.

Calvinist: a follower of the theological system of John Calvin.

Candlemas: a Christian holiday. A national holiday on 2 February in Liechtenstein, this observation is now called the Presentation of the Lord, commemorating the presentation of the infant Jesus in the Temple at Jerusalem. Before a 1969 Vatican reform, it commemorated the Purification of Mary 40 days after giving birth to a male child in accordance with a Jewish practice of the time.

capital punishment: the ultimate act of punishment for a crime; the death penalty.

capitalism: an economic system in which goods and services and the means to produce and sell them are privately owned, and prices and wages are determined by market forces.

cash crop: a crop that is grown to be sold, rather than kept for private use.

caste system: one of the artificial divisions or social classes into which the Hindus are rigidly separated according to the religious law of Brahmanism. The privileges and disabilities of a caste are passed on to each succeeding generation.

Caucasian: the "white" race of human beings, as determined by genealogy and physical features.

Caucasoid: belonging to the racial group characterized by light skin pigmentation. Commonly called the "white race," although it can refer to peoples of darker skin color.

celibate: a person who voluntarily abstains from marriage. In some religious practices, the person will often take a vow of abstention from sexual intercourse as well.

censorship: the practice of withholding certain items of news that may cast a country in an unfavorable light or give away secrets to the enemy.

census: an official counting of the inhabitants of a state or country with details of sex and age, family, occupation, possessions, etc.

Central Powers: in World War I, Germany and Austria-Hungary, and their allies, Turkey and Bulgaria.

centrally planned economy: an economic system in which all aspects are supervised and regulated by the government.

cerebrovascular: pertains to the brain and the blood vessels leading to and from the brain.

chancellery: the office of an embassy or consulate.

chaperone: an older married person, usually female, who supervises the activities of young, unmarried couples.

chattel: refers to the movable personal property of an individual or group. It cannot refer to real estate or buildings.

cholera: an acute infectious disease characterized by severe diarrhea, vomiting, and often, death.

Christianity: the religion founded by Jesus Christ.

Christmas: a Christian holiday. The annual commemoration of the nativity of Jesus is held on 25 December. A midnight Mass ushers in this joyous celebration in many Roman Catholic churches. The custom of distributing gifts to children on Christmas Eve derives from a Dutch custom originally observed on the evening before St. Nicholas' Day (6 December). The day after Christmas—often called Boxing Day, for the boxed gifts customarily given—is a public holiday in many countries.

Church of England: the national and established church in England. The Church of England claims continuity with the branch of the Catholic Church which existed in England before the Reformation. Under Henry VIII, the spiritual supremacy and jurisdiction of the Pope were abolished, and the sovereign was declared head of the church.

chaplet: a wreath or garland of flowers placed on a woman's head.

cistern: a natural or artificial receptacle or reservoir for holding water or other fluids.

city-state: an independent state consisting of a city and its surrounding territory.

civil law: the law developed by a nation or state for the conduct of daily life of its own people.

civil rights: the privileges of all individuals to be treated as equals under the laws of their country; specifically, the rights given by certain amendments to the U.S. Constitution.

civil unrest: the feeling of uneasiness due to an unstable political climate or actions taken as a result of it.

civil war: a war between groups of citizens of the same country who have different opinions or agendas. The Civil War of the United States was the conflict between the states of the North and South from 1861 to 1865.

coca: a shrub native to South America, the leaves of which produce alkaloids which are used in the production of cocaine.

cohabitation: living together as husband and wife without being legally married.

cold war: refers to conflict over ideological differences that is carried on by words and diplomatic actions, not by military action. The term is usually used to refer to the tension that existed between the United States and the USSR from the 1950s until the breakup of the USSR in 1991.

collard greens: a hearty, leafy green vegetable. Popular part of southern American and West Indian cuisine.

collective farm: a large farm formed from many small farms and supervised by the government; usually found in communist countries.

collective farming: the system of farming on a collective where all workers share in the income of the farm.

colloquial: belonging to the language of common or familiar conversation, or ordinary, everyday speech; often especially applied to common words and phrases which are not used in formal speech.

colonial period: in the United States, the period of time when the original thirteen colonies were being formed.

colonist: any member of a colony or one who helps settle a new colony.

colony: a group of people who settle in a new area far from their original country, but still under the jurisdiction of that country. Also refers to the newly settled area itself.

commerce: the trading of goods (buying and selling), especially on a large scale, between cities, states, and countries.

commodity: any items, such as goods or services, that are bought or sold, or agricultural products that are traded or marketed.

common law: a legal system based on custom and legal precedent. The basic system of law of the United States.

common law spouse: a husband or wife in a marriage that, although not legally formalized through a religious or state-sanctioned ceremony, is legally acknowledged based on the agreement of the two people to consider themselves married.

communicable disease: referring to infectious or contagious diseases.

communion: 1. The act of partaking of the sacrament of the Eucharist; the celebration of the Lord's Supper. 2. A body of Christians who have one common faith, but not necessarily ecclesiastical union; a religious denomination. 3. Union in religious worship, or in doctrine and discipline.

communism: a form of government whose system requires common ownership of property for the use of all citizens. All profits are to be equally distributed and prices on goods and services are usually set by the state. Also, communism refers directly to the official doctrine of the former USSR.

compulsory education: the mandatory requirement for children to attend school until they have reached a certain age or grade level.

condolence: expression of sympathy.

Condomblé: American name for the Yoruba pantheon of 401 gods and goddesses.

Confucianism: the ethical system taught by the Chinese philosopher Confucius. It was enlarged upon by his contemporary Mencius so that political systems would be tested with the same ethical standards. (*See* **Taoism**)

constitution: the written laws and basic rights of citizens of a country or members of an organized group.

consumer goods: items that are bought to satisfy personal needs or wants of individuals.

Coptic Christians: members of the Coptic Church of Egypt, formerly of Ethiopia.

Corpus Christi: a Christian holiday. This holiday in honor of the Eucharist is observed on the Thursday or Sunday after Trinity Sunday, which is the Sunday after Pentecost. In the Roman Catholic and Eastern Orthodox Churches, the Eucharist is a sacrament in which the consecrated bread and wine become the body and blood of Jesus Christ, a belief stemming from New Testament accounts of the Last Supper.

corrugated steel: galvanized metal with furrows that give added strength. This metal is often used as roofing materials on houses in tropical countries because of its strength.

coup d'état: a sudden, violent overthrow of a government or its leader.

covert action: secret, concealed activities carried out without public knowledge.

cricket (sport): a game played by two teams with a ball and bat, with two wickets being defended by a batsman.

criminal law: the branch of law that deals primarily with crimes and their punishments.

crown colony: a colony established by a commonwealth over which the monarch has some control, as in colonies established by the British Commonwealth.

Crowning of Our Lady of Altagracia: a Christian holiday in honor of Mary, this day is celebrated in the Dominican Republic on 15 August with a pilgrimage to her shrine. (Altagracia Day, 21 January, is also a holiday in the Dominican Republic.)

Crusades: military expeditions by European Christian armies in the 11th, 12th, and 13th centuries to win land controlled by the Muslims in the Middle East.

cuisine: a particular style of preparing food, especially when referring to the cooking of a particular country or ethnic group.

cultivable land: land that can be prepared for the production of crops.

cursive script: a style of writing in which the letters are joined together in a flowing manner.

Cushitic language group: a group of Hamitic languages which are spoken in Ethiopia and other areas of eastern Africa.

cyclone: any atmospheric movement, general or local, in which the wind blows spirally around and in towards a center. In the northern hemisphere, the cyclonic movement is usually counter-clockwise, and in the southern hemisphere, it is clockwise.

Cyrillic alphabet: an alphabet adopted by the Slavic people and invented by Cyril and Methodius in the 9th century as an alphabet that was easier for the copyist to write. The Russian alphabet is a slight modification of it.

D

Day of Our Lady of Mercy (Las Mercedes): a Christian holiday in honor of Mary, this observance on 24 September is a holiday in the Dominican Republic.

Day of Santa Rosa of Lima: a Christian holiday. The feast day in honor of the first native-born saint of the New World, declared patron saint of South America by Pope Clement X in 1671, is 23 August, but in Peru, she is commemorated by a national holiday on 30 August.

Day of St. Peter and St. Paul: a Christian holiday. This observance, on 29 June, commemorates the martyrdom of the two apostles traditionally believed to have been executed in Rome on the same day (c. AD 67) during the persecution of Christians ordered by Emperor Nero.

deforestation: the removal of a forest ecosystem.

deity: a being with the attributes, nature, and essence of a god; a divinity.

delta: triangular-shaped deposits of soil formed at the mouths of large rivers.

democracy: a form of government in which the power lies in the hands of the people, who can govern directly, or indirectly by electing representatives.

demography: that department of anthropology which relates to vital and social statistics and their application to the comparative study of races and nations.

desegregation: the act of removing restrictions on people of a particular race that keep them separate from other groups, socially, economically, and, sometimes, physically.

détente: the official lessening of tension between countries in conflict.

developed countries: countries which have a high standard of living and a well-developed industrial base.

diacritics: as in diacritical marks, a dot, line, or other mark added or put adjacent to a letter or sign in order to give it a different sound or to indicate some particular accent, tone, stress, or emphasis. An example of diacritical marks would be those used in dictionaries to aid in pronunciation of words.

dialect: One of a number of related forms of speech regarded as descending from a common origin. The speech pattern of a locality or social class as distinguished from the generally accepted literary language.

dictatorship: a form of government in which all the power is retained by an absolute leader or tyrant. There are no rights granted to the people to elect their own representatives.

direct descendant: the offspring in an unbroken line of ancestors.

divine origin: having originated directly, or by direct descendant, from a divine being.

dogma: a principle, maxim, or tenet held as being firmly established.

domicile: a place of residence of an individual or family; a place of habitual abode.

dowry: the sum of the property or money that a bride brings to her groom at their marriage.

druid: a member of a Celtic religion practiced in ancient Britain, Ireland, and France.

Druze: a member of a religious sect of Syria, living chiefly in the mountain regions of Lebanon.

ducal: Referring to a duke or a dukedom.

dysentery: painful inflammation of the large intestine.

E

Easter: the chief Christian holiday is Easter, the annual celebration of the resurrection of Jesus Christ. Like Passover, the Jewish feast from which it is derived, the date of observation is linked to the phases of the moon. Since the Christian calendar is a solar one rather than a lunar one, the date of Easter changes from year to year. Easter is celebrated on the first Sunday after the first full moon following the spring equinox; in the Gregorian calendar, it can occur as early as 22 March or as late as 25 April. The Easter date determines the date of many other Roman Catholic holidays, such as Ash Wednesday, Ascension, and Pentecost.

Easter Monday: a Christian holiday. The day after Easter is a public holiday in many countries.

empire: a group of territories ruled by one sovereign, or supreme ruler.

Epiphany of Our Lord: a Christian holiday. Traditionally observed on 6 January but now observable on the Sunday falling between 2 January and 7 January, this feast commemorates the adoration of the Magi, who journeyed to the place of Jesus' birth. In the Orthodox churches, however, it is the feast celebrating Jesus' baptism.

episcopal: belonging to or vested in bishops or prelates; characteristic of or pertaining to a bishop or bishops.

equestrian culture: a culture that depends on horses for its livelihood. Mastery of the horse is an essential part of the culture's identity.

escarpment: a steep cliff formed from a geological fault or erosion.

ethnographic: referring to the division of anthropology which studies primitive cultures.

ethnolinguistic group: a classification of related languages based on common ethnic origin.

exodus: the departure or migration of a large body of people or animals from one country or region to another.

extinction: dying out of a species of animals or a culture of people.

F

fauna: referring to species of animals found in a specific region.

Feast of Our Lady of Angels: a Christian holiday. This feast, on 2 August, is celebrated as a national holiday in Costa Rica in honor of the Virgin Mary. Pilgrimage is made to the basilica in Cartago, which houses a black stone statue of the Virgin.

fetishism: the practice of worshipping a material object which one believes has mysterious powers residing in it or is the representation of a deity to which worship may be paid and from which supernatural aid is expected.

feudal society: In medieval times, an economic and social structure in which persons could hold land given to them by a lord (nobleman) in return for service to that lord.

Finno-Ugric language group: a subfamily of languages spoken in northeastern Europe, including Finnish, Hungarian (Ugric, Magyar), Estonian, Lapp, and others.

flora: referring to native plant life in a specific region.

folk religion: a religion with origins and traditions among the common people of a nation or region; relevant to their particular lifestyle.

folk tale: an oral story that is passed from generation to generation. Folktales are cultural records of the history and progress of different ethnic groups.

free-market economy: an economic system that relies on the market, as opposed to government planners, to set the prices for wages and products.

fundamentalist: a person who holds religious beliefs based on the complete acceptance of the words of the Bible or other holy scripture as the truth. For instance, a fundamentalist would believe the story of creation exactly as it is told in the Bible and would reject the idea of evolution.

G

gastroenteritis: inflammation of the stomach and small intestines.

geometric pattern: a design of circles, triangles, or lines on cloth.

geriatrics: the study and treatment of diseases of old age.

Germanic language group: a large branch of the Indo-European family of languages including German itself, the Scandinavian languages, Dutch, Yiddish, Modern English, Modern Scottish, Afrikaans and others. The group also includes extinct languages such as Gothic, Old High German, Old Saxon, Old English, Middle English and the like.

glottal stop: a sound formed in speech by a brief but complete closure of the glottis, the opening between the vocal cords. It is a typical sound in certain British dialects.

godparent: a male or female adult who is asked by the parents of a newborn child to assume responsibility for the care and rearing of the child in the event of the death of the parents. Godparents sometimes contribute school tuition, gifts on birthdays and holidays, as well as take an active part in the child's life.

Good Friday: a Christian holiday. The day after Holy Thursday, it is devoted to remembrance of the crucifixion of Jesus and is given to penance and prayer.

Greek Catholic: a person who is a member of an Orthodox Eastern Church.

Greek Orthodox: the official church of Greece, a self-governing branch of the Orthodox Eastern Church.

H

haiku: a form of Japanese poetry, consisting of three lines. Each line has a specific measurement of syllables.

Hanukkah: a Jewish holiday. The Festival of Lights, corresponding roughly to the winter solstice, is celebrated over an eight-day period beginning on 25 Kislev, the third month. Also known as the Feast of Dedication and Feast of the Maccabees, Hanukkah commemorates the rededication of the Temple at Jerusalem in 164 BC. According to tradition, the one ritually pure container of olive oil, sufficient to illuminate the Temple for one day, miraculously burned for eight days, until new oil could be prepared. A feature of the Hanukkah celebration is the lighting in each Jewish home of an eight-branched candelabrum, the menorah. This festival, though not a public holiday in Israel, is widely observed with the lighting of giant menorahs in public places.

harem: in a Muslim household, refers to the women (wives, concubines, and servants in ancient times) who live there and also to the area of the home they live in.

harmattan: an intensely dry, dusty wind felt along the coast of Africa between Cape Verde and Cape Lopez. It prevails at intervals during the months of December, January, and February.

Hinduism: the religion professed by a large part of the inhabitants of India. It is a development of the ancient Brahmanism, influenced by Buddhistic and other elements. Its forms are varied and numerous.

Holi: a Hindu holiday. A festival lasting 3 to 10 days, Holi closes the old year with processions and merriment. It terminates on the full moon of Phalguna, the last month, corresponding to February or March.

Holocaust: the mass slaughter of European civilians, the vast majority Jews, by the Nazis during World War II.

Holy (Maundy) Thursday: a Christian holiday. The Thursday preceding Easter commemorates the Last Supper, the betrayal of Jesus by Judas Iscariot, and the arrest and arraignment of Jesus. In Rome, the pope customarily performs a ceremony in remembrance of Jesus' washing of his apostles' feet (John 13:5–20).

Holy Roman Empire: a kingdom consisting of a loose union of German and Italian territories that existed from around the ninth century until 1806.

Holy Saturday: a Christian holiday. This day commemorates the time during which Jesus was buried and, like Good Friday, is given to solemn prayer.

homeland: a region or area set aside to be a state for a people of a particular national, cultural, or racial origin.

homogeneous: of the same kind or nature, often used in reference to a whole.

homophonic: music that has a single part with no harmonies.

Horn of Africa: the Horn of Africa comprises Djibouti, Eritrea, Ethiopia, Somalia, and Sudan.

human rights issues: any matters involving people's basic rights which are in question or thought to be abused.

humanist: a person who centers on human needs and values, and stresses dignity of the individual.

hydrology: the science of dealing with the earth's waters and their distribution above and below ground.

I

Id al-Adha: a Muslim holiday. The Great Festival, or Sacrificial Feast, celebrates the end of the special pilgrimage season, or Hajj, to Mecca and Medina, an obligation for Muslims once in their lifetime if physically and economically feasible. The slaughter of animals pays tribute to Abraham's obedience to God in offering his son to the Lord for sacrifice; a portion of the meat is supposed to be donated to the poor. The feast begins on 10 Dhu'l-Hijja and continues to 13 Dhu'l-Hijja (14 Dhu'l-Hijja in a leap year). In Malaysia and Singapore, this festival is celebrated as Hari Raya Haji; in Indonesia, Lebaran Haji; in Turkey, Kurban Bayrami.

Id al-Fitr: a Muslim holiday. The Little Festival, or Breaking-Fast-Festival, which begins just after Ramadan, on 1 Shawwal, the 10th month, is the occasion for three or four days of feasting. In Malaysia and Singapore, this festival is called Hari Raya Puasa; in Turkey, Seker Bayrami.

Iemanja: Brazilian name for Yoruba river goddess, Yemoja. Represented as a mermaid.

Immaculate Conception: a Christian holiday. This day, 8 December, celebrates the Roman Catholic dogma asserting that Mary's conception, as the future mother of God, was uniquely free from original sin. In Paraguay, it is observed as the Day of Our Lady of Caacupé.

incursion: a sudden or brief invasion or raid.

indigenous: born or originating in a particular place or country; native to a particular region or area.

indigent: person without any means of economic support.

indigo: a blue dye that is extracted from plants.

Indo-Aryan language group: the group that includes the languages of India; within a branch of the Indo-European language family.

Indo-European language family: the large family of languages that includes those of India, much of Europe, and southwestern Asia.

indulgence: a Catholic blessing given for a person's soul after death.

infant mortality: infant deaths.

infant mortality rate: the number of deaths of children less than one year old per 1,000 live births in a given year.

infanticide: the act of murdering a baby.

infidel: one who is without faith, or unbelieving; particularly, one who rejects the distinctive doctrines of a particular religion, while perhaps remaining an adherent to another religion.

inflective: refers to a language in which differences in tone and pitch give meaning to words and indicate grammatical constructions.

interferon: a drug used in the treatment of cancer in Mexico.

Inuit: an indigenous people of northwestern Canada. They are sometimes mistakenly called Eskimos.

Islam: the religious system of Mohammed, practiced by Muslims and based on a belief in Allah as the supreme being and Mohammed as his prophet. The term also refers to those nations in which it is the primary religion.

isthmus: a narrow strip of land with connecting large bodies of water on either side.

J

Jehovah's Witness: a member of a Christian sect that believes that the end of the world is near and that God should establish a theocracy on earth.

Judaism: the religious system of the Jews, based on the Old Testament as revealed to Moses and characterized by a belief in one God and adherence to the laws of scripture and rabbinic traditions.

Judeo-Christian: the dominant traditional religious makeup of the United States and other countries based on the worship of the Old and New Testaments of the Bible.

Juneteenth: an African American holiday that celebrates the freeing of slaves in America. It is thought to coincide with the surrender of the Confederacy to the Union armies.

Junkanoo: a holiday celebrated around December in the Caribbean and South America. It also has been observed in the United States in Alabama. The holiday has West African origins. Also known as John Canoe and Yancanu.

K

kale: Another hearty, green leafy vegetable that is sometimes mixed with spinach and collard greens to vary the flavor of these vegetables.

khan: a title given Genghis Khan and his successors who ruled over Turkey and Mongolia in the Middle Ages.

kielbasa: seasoned Polish sausage. Made from beef or pork.

L

lagoon: a shallow body of water connected to a larger body of water. It is sometimes separated from the larger body by reefs.

lama: a celebrated priest or ecclesiastic belonging to that variety of Buddhism known as Lamaism. The Dalai-Lama and the tesho- or bogdo-lama are regarded as supreme pontiffs.

land reforms: steps taken to create a fair distribution of farm land, especially by governmental action.

latke: potato pancake.

Leeward Islands: northern islands of the Lesser Antilles in the Caribbean that stretch from Puerto Rico southward.

leprosy: an infectious disease of the skin or nerves which can cause ulcers of the skin, loss of feeling, or loss of fingers and toes.

life expectancy: an individual's expected lifespan, calculated as an average.

lingua franca: Originally, a mixed language or jargon of Mediterranean ports, consisting of Italian mixed with Arabic, Turkish, Greek, French, and Spanish. Nowadays, the phrase is used to denote any hybrid tongue used similarly in other parts of the world; an international dialect.

linguist: a person skilled in the use of languages.

linguistic group: a group of related languages.

literacy: the ability to read and write.

lox: kosher smoked salmon.

Lutheran: of or pertaining to Martin Luther (1483–1546), the reformer, to the Evangelical Protestant Church of Germany which bears his name, or to the doctrines taught by Luther or held by the Evangelical Lutheran Church.

M

macron: a horizontal mark placed over a vowel to indicate its pronunciation as long.

maize: another name (Spanish or British) for corn or the color of ripe corn.

Malayo-Polynesian language group: also referred to as the Austronesian language group, which includes the Indonesian, Polynesian, Melanesian, and Micronesian subfamilies.

mangrove: a kind of evergreen shrub growing along tropical coasts.

marimba: a type of xylophone found in Central and South America.

massif: a central mountain-mass or the dominant part of a range of mountains. A part of a range which appears, from the position of the depression by which it is more or less isolated, to form an independent whole.

matriarchy: a society in which women are recognized as the leaders of the family or tribe.

matrifocal: a society in which women are the focus of activity or attention.

matrilineal (descent): descending from, or tracing descent through, the maternal line.

Mayan language family: the languages of the Central American Indians, further divided into two subgroups: the Maya and the Huastek.

Mecca (Mekkah): a city in Saudi Arabia; a destination of pilgrims in the Islamic world.

Mennonite: a member of the Christian denomination which originated in Friesland, Holland in the early part of the 16th century and upholds the doctrine of which Menno Simons (1492–1559) was the chief exponent.

mestizo: the offspring of a person of mixed blood; especially, a person of mixed Spanish and American Indian parentage.

metamorphosis: referring to the shamanic practice of changing from a person to an animal.

Methodist: a member of the Christian denomination founded by John Wesley (1703–1791). The name was first applied to Wesley and his companions on account of their methodical habits in study and in religious life.

millennium: any one-thousand-year period, but also refers to a real or imagined period of peace and happiness.

missionary: a person sent by ecclesiastical authority to work to spread his religious faith in a community where his church has no self-supporting organization.

Mohammed (or Muhammed or Mahomet): an Arabian prophet, known as the "Prophet of Allah" who founded the religion of Islam in 622, and wrote The Koran, the scripture of Islam. Also commonly spelled Muhammed, especially by Islamic people.

Mongol: one of an Asiatic race chiefly resident in Mongolia, a region north of China proper and south of Siberia.

Mongoloid: having physical characteristics like those of the typical Mongols (Chinese, Japanese, Turks, Eskimos, etc.).

monogamy: the practice of marrying one spouse.

monolingual: speaking one language only.

monsoon: a wind occurring in the alternation of the tradewinds in India and the north Indian Ocean. They occur between April and October when the regular northeast tradewinds are reversed and, with occasional interruptions, the wind blows at almost a steady gale from the southwest. In some areas, as in China, the change of the monsoons is followed with storms and much rain.

Moors: one of the Arab tribes that conquered Spain in the 8th century.

Mormon: an adherent of the religious body the Church of Jesus Christ of Latter-day Saints founded in 1830 by Joseph Smith.

Moslem: a follower of Mohammed (spelled Muhammed by many Islamic people), in the religion of Islam.

mosque: a Mohammedan place of worship and the ecclesiastical organization with which it is connected.

mother tongue: a tongue or language to which other languages owe their origin. One's native language.

Motown: nickname for Detroit. A contraction of Motor City Town.

mujahideen or **mujahedeen:** *see* **mujahidin.**

mujahidin: rebel fighters in Islamic countries, especially those supporting the cause of Islam.

mulatto: one who is the offspring of parents of whom one is white and the other is black.

multicultural: awareness of the effect and existence of more than one cultural viewpoint within one's value system and world view.

multilingual: having the ability to speak several languages. Also used to describe anything that contains or is expressed in several languages, such as directions written in English, Spanish, and French.

mummify: ancient method used to preserve the dead. Associated with ancient Egyptian culture.

Muslim: same as Moslem.

Muslim New Year: a Muslim holiday. Although in some countries 1 Muharram, which is the first month of the Islamic year, is observed as a holiday, in other places the new year is observed on Sha'ban, the eighth month of the year. This practice apparently stems from pagan Arab times. Shab-i-Bharat, a national holiday in Bangladesh on this day, is held by many to be the occasion when God ordains all actions in the coming year.

N

native tongue: one's natural language. The language that is indigenous to an area.

Nobel Laureate: a person awarded a prize for lifetime achievement in literature, sciences, economics, or peace. Prize founded by Swedish industrialist Alfred Nobel, inventor of dynamite.

nomad: a wanderer; member of a tribe of people who have no fixed place or abode, but move about from place to place depending on the availability of food sources.

novena: a series of prayers in honor of a saint for a specific reason.

O

obsidian: a black, shiny volcanic rock, resembling glass.

official language: the language in which the business of a country and its government is conducted.

Ottoman Empire: a Turkish empire founded by Osman I in about 1603, that variously controlled large areas of land around the Mediterranean, Black, and Caspian Seas until it was dissolved in 1918.

outback region: the rural interior region of the continent of Australia. It is sparsely populated, mainly by aboriginal peoples.

overgrazing: allowing animals to graze in an area to the point that the ground vegetation is damaged or destroyed.

P

pagan: a person who worships more than one diety. Sometimes refers to non-Christians.

pagoda: in the Far East, a sacred tower, usually pyramidal in outline, richly carved, painted, or otherwise adorned, and of several stories. They can be, but are not always, connected to a temple.

Paleoasiatic languages: languages that date back to a prehistoric or unwritten era in linguistic history.

parochial: an institution supported by a church or parish.

parody: dance or song ridiculing a serious subject in a silly manner. Usually focuses on the person or people who dominate another cultural group.

Parsi: one of the descendants of those Persians who settled in India about the end of the seventh century in order to escape Mohammedan persecution, and who still retain their ancient religion. Also Parsee.

Passover (Pesach): a Jewish holiday. Pesach, lasting seven days in Israel and eight outside it, begins on 15 Nisan, at roughly the spring equinox, and recalls the exodus of the Hebrews from Egypt and their delivery from bondage. The chief festival of Judaism, Pesach begins with a ceremonial family meal, or seder, at which special foods (including unleavened bread, or matzoh) are eaten and the Passover story (Haggadah) is read.

pastoralist: a nomadic people who move with their herds of sheep or cattle, searching for pasture and water.

patois: a dialect peculiar to a district or locality, in use especially among the peasantry or uneducated classes; hence, a rustic, provincial, or barbarous form of speech.

patriarchal system: a social system in which the head of the family or tribe is the father or oldest male. Kinship is determined and traced through the male members of the tribe.

patrilineal (descent): Descending from, or tracing descent through, the paternal line.

patrilocal: a society in which men take the larger role in activities and receive greater attention.

peccary: a pig-like animal native to North and South America and the Caribbean Islands. Noted for its musky smell, sharp tusks, and gray color.

pentatonic: music consisting of a five tone scale.

Pentecost Monday (Whitmonday): a Christian holiday. This public holiday observed in many countries occurs the day after Pentecost (derived from the ancient Greek pentekostos, "fiftieth"), or Whitsunday, which commemorates the descent of the Holy Spirit upon Jesus' apostles on the seventh Sunday after Easter and is derived from the Jewish feast of Shavuot. It was an important occasion for baptism in the early church, and the name "Whitsunday" originated from the white robes worn by the newly baptized.

Pentecostal: having to do with Pentecost, a Christian holiday celebrated the seventh Sunday after Easter, marking the day that the Holy Spirit descended upon the Apostles.

peyote: the tops of the small spineless mescal cactus. Native to the southwestern United States and northern Mexico.

phoneme: slightly different sounds in a language that are heard as the same by a native speaker.

pierogie: a Polish dumpling made from pastry dough. It contains various fillings, such as meat and potatoes.

pilgrimage: a journey to a sacred place in order to perform some religious vow or duty, or to obtain some spiritual or miraculous benefit.

polygamy: the practice of having two or more spouses at the same time.

polygyny: the practice of having two or more wives and/or mistresses.

polyphonic: combining a number of harmonic sounds. Music that has more than one sound.

polytheism: belief and worship of many gods.

post traumatic stress disorder: psychological disorder that accompanies violent or tragic experiences. Known as shell-shock during World War I.

Prayer Day: a Christian holiday. This Danish public holiday is observed on the fourth Friday after Easter.

Presbyterian: of or pertaining to ecclesiastical government by elders or by presbyteries.

Prophet Muhammed: *see* **Mohammed**.

proselytizing: inducing or persuading someone to become the adherent of some religion, doctrine, sect, or party. To convert.

Protestant: a member or an adherent of one of those Christian bodies which descended from the Reformation of the sixteenth century. Originally applied to those who opposed or protested the Roman Catholic Church.

province: an administrative territory of a country.

Purim: a Jewish holiday. This holiday, celebrated on 14 Adar (Adar Sheni in a leap year), commemorates the delivery of the Jews from potential annihilation at the hands of Haman, viceroy of Persia, as described in the Book of Esther, which is read from a scroll (megillah). The day, though not a public holiday in Israel, is widely marked by charity, exchange of edible gifts, and feasting.

R

rabbi: a Jewish religious leader; head of a congregation.

racial integration: to remove all restrictions and barriers preventing complete access to society to persons of all races.

racially homogeneous: composed of persons all of the same race.

rain forest: a tropical vegetation in the equatorial region of the world which consists of a dense growth of a wide variety of broadleaf evergreen trees and vines.

Raksha Bandhan: a Hindu holiday. During this festival, which usually falls in August, bracelets of colored thread and tinsel are tied by women to the wrists of their menfolk, thus binding the men to guard and protect them during the year. It is celebrated on the full moon of Sravana.

Ramadan: a Muslim holiday. The first day of Ramadan (the ninth month) is a public holiday in many countries, although the religious festival does not officially begin until the new moon is sighted from the Naval Observatory in Cairo, Egypt. The entire month commemorates the period in which the Prophet received divine revelation and is observed by a strict fast from sunrise to sundown. This observance is one of Islam's five main duties for believers.

Rastafarian: a member of a Jamaican cult begun in 1930 as a semi-religious, semi-political movement. Rastafarians are usually lower class men who are anti-white and advocate the return of blacks to Africa.

refugee: one who flees to a refuge, shelter or place of safety. One who in times of persecution or political commotion flees to a foreign country for safety.

respiratory: pertaining to the lungs and other breathing passages.

Roman alphabet: the alphabet of the ancient Romans from which the alphabets of most modern western European languages, including English, are derived.

Roman Catholic Church: the designation of the church of which the pope or bishop of Rome is the head, and which holds him, as the successor of St. Peter and heir of his spiritual authority, privileges, and gifts, as its supreme ruler, pastor, and teacher.

Romance language: the group of languages derived from Latin: French, Spanish, Italian, Portuguese and other related languages.

Rosh Hashanah: a Jewish holiday. The Jewish New Year is celebrated on 1 Tishri, the first month. In synagogues, the sounding of the shofar (ram's horn) heralds the new year. Rosh Hashanah begins the observance of the Ten Penitential Days, which culminate in Yom Kippur. Orthodox and Conservative Jews outside Israel celebrate 2 Tishri, the next day, as well.

runic music: music that is ancient, obscure, and mystical.

Russian Orthodox: the arm of the Orthodox Eastern Church which was the official church of czarist Russia.

S

Sacred Heart: a Christian holiday. The Friday of the week after Corpus Christi is a holiday in Colombia. The object of devotion is the divine person of Jesus, whose heart is the symbol of his love for mankind.

Samaritans: a native or an inhabitant of Samaria; specifically, one of a race settled in the cities of Samaria by the king of Assyria after the removal of the Israelites from the country.

samba: a Brazilian dance and musical tradition based on two beats to the measure.

sambo: indicates a person of visible African ancestry. Familiar form of address for an uncle from the Foulah language of West Africa.

Santería: Christian religion with West African origins. It merges Christian saints with Yoruban dieties.

savanna: a treeless or near treeless plain of a tropical or subtropical region dominated by drought-resistant grasses.

schistosomiasis: a tropical disease that is chronic and characterized by disorders of the liver, urinary bladder, lungs, or central nervous system.

sect: a religious denomination or group, often a dissenting one with extreme views.

self-determination: the desire of a culture to control its economic and social development.

Semitic tongue: an important family of languages distinguished by triliteral verbal roots and vowel inflections.

Seventh-day Adventist: one who believes in the second coming of Christ to establish a personal reign upon the earth. They observe the seventh day of the week as the Sabbath and believe in the existence of the spirit of prophecy among them.

shaman: holy man or woman said to have the power to heal diseases. Also thought to have magical powers.

shamanism: a religion centered on a belief in good and evil spirits that can be influenced only by shamans.

Shavuot: a Jewish holiday. This festival, on 6 Sivan, celebrates the presentation of the Ten Commandments to Moses on Mt. Sinai and the offering of the first harvest fruits at the temple in Jerusalem. The precursor of the Christian Pentecost, Shavuot takes place on the 50th day after the first day of Passover.

Shia Muslim: member of one of two great sects of Islam. Shia Muslims believe that Ali and the Imams are the rightful successors of Mohammed (also commonly spelled Muhammed). They also believe that the last recognized Imam will return as a messiah. Also known as Shiites. (*Also see* **Sunni Muslim**.)

Shiites: *see* **Shia Muslim**.

Shintoism: the system of nature- and hero-worship which forms the indigenous religion of Japan.

Shivarati (Mahashivarati): a Hindu holiday. Dedicated to the god Shiva, this holiday is observed on the 13th day of the dark half of Magha, corresponding to January or February.

Shrove Monday and Shrove Tuesday: a Christian holiday. These two days occur just prior to the beginning of Lent (a term which derives from the Middle English lente, "spring"), the Christian season of penitence that ends with Easter Sunday. These are days of Carnival, public holidays of feasting, and merriment in many lands. Shrove Tuesday is also known as Mardi Gras.

shunning: Amish practice of not interacting in any way with a person who has been cast out by the church and the community.

sierra: a chain of hills or mountains.

Sikh: a member of a politico-religious community of India, founded as a sect around 1500 and based on the principles of monotheism and human brotherhood.

Sino-Tibetan language family: the family of languages spoken in Eastern Asia, including China, Thailand, Tibet, and Burma.

slash-and-burn agriculture: a hasty and sometimes temporary way of clearing land to make it available for agriculture by cutting down trees and burning them.

slave trade: the transportation of black Africans beginning in the 1700s to other countries to be sold as slaves-people owned as property and compelled to work for their owners at no pay.

Slavic languages: a major subgroup of the Indo-European language family. It is further subdivided into West Slavic (including Polish, Czech, Slovak and Sorbian), South Slavic (including Bulgarian, Serbo-Croatian, Slovene, and Old Church Slavonic), and East Slavic (including Russian Ukrainian and Byelorussian).

Society of Friends: a religious sect founded about 1650 whose members shun military service and believe in plain dress, behavior and worship. Also referred to as the Quaker religion by those outside it.

Solemnity of Mary, Mother of God: a Christian holiday. Observed on 1 January, this celebration was, before a 1969 Vatican reform, the Feast of the Circumcision of Our Lord Jesus Christ.

sorghum: a type of tropical grass that is grown for grain, syrup, and livestock feed.

St. Agatha's Day: a Christian holiday. Celebrated on 5 February, it is the feast day of the patron saint of San Marino. St. Agatha is also the patron saint of nurses, firefighters, and jewelers.

St. Dévôte Day: a Christian holiday. Observed on 27 January in Monaco in honor of the principality's patron saint, this day celebrates her safe landing after a perilous voyage, thanks to a dove who directed her ship to the Monaco shore.

St. James's Day: a Christian holiday. Observed on 25 July, this day commemorates St. James the Greater, one of Jesus' 12 apostles. St. James is the patron saint of Spain.

St. Joseph's Day: a Christian holiday. The feast day in honor of Mary's husband is observed on 19 March as a public holiday in several countries.

St. Patrick's Day: a Christian holiday. This holiday, observed on 17 March, is celebrated in Ireland to honor its patron saint.

St. Stephen's Day: a Christian holiday. The feast day in honor of the first martyred Christian saint is 26 December, the day after Christmas. St. Stephen is the patron saint of Hungary.

steppe: a level tract of land more or less devoid of trees. It is a name given to certain parts of European and Asiatic Russia, of which the most characteristic feature is the absence of forests.

stigmatize: branding someone as a disgrace because of his or her behavior.

straits: a narrow passage of water connecting two bodies of water.

stroganoff: Russian beef stew. Sauce made from sour cream and wine.

subcontinent: a landmass of great size, but smaller than any of the continents; a large subdivision of a continent.

subsistence farming: farming that provides the minimum food goods necessary for the continuation of the farm family.

Sudanic language group: a related group of languages spoken in various areas of northern Africa, including Yoruba, Mandingo and Tshi.

Sufi: a Mohammedan mystic who believes (a) that God alone exists, and all visible and invisible beings are mere emanations from Him; (b) that, as God is the real author of all the acts of mankind, man is not a free agent, and there can be no real difference between good and evil; (c) that, as the soul existed before the body, and is confined within the latter as in a cage, death should be the chief object of desire, for only then does the soul return to the bosom of the divinity; and (d) that religions are matters of indifference, though some are more advantageous than others, and Sufism is the only true philosophy.

Sukkot: a Jewish holiday. This ancient Jewish harvest festival, which begins on 15 Tishri, recalls the period in which harvesters left their homes to dwell in the fields in sukkot, or booths—small outdoor shelters of boards, leaves, and branches—in order to facilitate gathering the crops before the seasonal rains began. In religious terms, it commemorates the 40 years of wandering in the desert by the ancient Hebrews after their exodus from Egypt. The 8th day of Sukkot (and the 22d day of Tishri) is Shmini Azeret/Simhat Torah, a joyous holiday in which the annual cycle of reading the Torah (the Five Books of Moses) is completed and begun anew. Outside of Israel, Simhat Torah and the beginning of a new reading cycle are celebrated on the next day, 23 Tishri.

sultan: a king of a Muslim state.

Sunni Muslim: Member of one of two major sects of the religion of Islam. Sunni Muslims adhere to strict orthodox traditions and believe that the four caliphs are the rightful successors to Mohammed, founder of Islam. (Mohammed is commonly spelled Muhammed, especially by Islamic people.) (*Also see* **Shia Muslim**.)

surname: a person's last name. Generally different from his or her first name.

T

taboo: a system, practice, or act whereby persons, things, places, actions, or words are placed under ban, curse, or prohibition, or set apart as sacred or privileged in some specific manner.

taiga: a coniferous forest in the far northern areas of Canada, Alaska, and Eurasia.

Taoism: the doctrine of Lao-Tzu, an ancient Chinese philosopher (about 500 BC) as laid down by him in the Tao-te-ching.

Thaipusam: a Hindu holiday. A holiday in Malaysia, Thaipusam honors Subrimaya, son of Shiva and an important deity in southern India. The three-day festival is held in the month of Magha according to when Pusam, a section of the lunar zodiac, is on the ascendant.

Tibeto-Burman language group: a subgroup of the Sino-Tibetan language family which includes Tibetan and Burmese.

Tishah b'Av: a Jewish holiday. This holiday, which takes place on 9 Av, commemorates the destruction of the First Temple by the Babylonians (Chaldeans) in 586 BC and of the Second Temple by the Romans in AD 70. It is observed by fasting.

toboggan: a kind of sled without runners or a steering mechanism.

topography: an accurate drawing representing the surface of a region on maps and charts.

toucan: a brightly colored, fruit-eating bird of tropical America with a distinctive beak.

trachoma: contagious, viral infection of the cornea. Causes scarring in the eye.

tribal society: a society based on tribal consciousness and loyalties.

tribal system: a social community in which people are organized into groups or clans descended from common ancestors and sharing customs and languages.

tsetse fly: any of the several African insects which can transmit a variety of parasitic organisms through its bite. Some of these organisms can prove fatal to both human and animal victims.

tundra: a nearly level treeless area whose climate and vegetation are more characteristically arctic due to its northern position. Although the region attains seasonal temperatures warm enough to allow a thin layer of soil on the surface to unthaw enough to support the growth of various species of plants, the subsoil is permanently frozen.

tutelary: a god or spirit who acts a guardian that watches over a person or group of people.

typhoon: a violent hurricane occurring in the China Sea or Philippine region, principally between the months of July and October.

U

unemployment rate: the overall unemployment rate is the percentage of the work force (both employed and unemployed) who claim to be unemployed. The natural unemployment rate is the lowest level at which unemployment in an economy can be maintained and still reflect a balance of the labor market and the product market.

untouchables: in 19th century India, members of the lowest caste in the caste system, a hereditary social class system. They were considered unworthy to touch members of higher castes.

urban center: a city.

USSR: an abbreviation of Union of Soviet Socialist Republics.

V

veldt: in South Africa, an unforested or thinly forested tract of land or region, a grassland.

Vesak: this last full moon day of Visakha highlights a three-day celebration of the birth, enlightenment, and death of the Buddha. It falls in April or May.

voodoo: a belief system which is based on sorcery and other primitive rites and the power of charms and fetishes, originating in Africa.

W

wadi(s): the channel of a watercourse which is dry except in the rainy season. Also called wady.

Windward Islands: a southern group of islands stretching south to Trinidad. Part of the Lesser Antilles, but does not include Barbados.

Y

Yom Kippur: a Jewish holiday. The Day of Atonement, spent in fasting, penitence, and prayer, is the most solemn day in Judaism. It takes place on 10 Tishri.

yucca: a plant native to Mexico, Central and South America, and the southwestern United States. Can grow to the 12 feet in height.

yurt: a framework tent of stretched felt or skins. Associated with Siberia and Mongolia.

Z

Zoroastrianism: the system of religious doctrine taught by Zoroaster and his followers in the Avesta; the religion prevalent in Persia until its overthrow by the Muslims in the 7th century.

INDEX

The "v" accompanied by a numeral that precedes the colon in these index citations designates the volume number for *Worldmark Encyclopedia of Cultures and Daily Life*. Thus, v1 references are found in the Africa volume; v2 in Americas; v3 in Asia; and v4 in Europe. Page numbers follow the colon.

E

O

P